American Women Writers

Diverse Voices in Prose since 1845

American Women Writers

Diverse Voices in Prose Since 1845

Eileen Barrett
Mary Cullinan

California State University at Hayward

St. Martin's Press New York

Senior editor: Mark Gallaher
Development editor: Edward Mitchell-Hutchinson
Managing editor: Patricia Mansfield-Phelan
Project editor: Suzanne Holt
Production supervisor: Alan Fischer
Text design: Susan Phillips
Cover design: Celine Brandes
Cover art: Tapestry: *Taking the Veil* by Christina Benson Vos

Manufactured in the United States of America.
65432
fedcba

For information, write:
St. Martin's Press, Inc.
175 Fifth Avenue
New York, NY 10010

ISBN: 0-312-04121-7 (paper)
0-312-06556-6 (cloth)

Library of Congress Cataloging-in-Publication Data

Barrett, Eileen.
American women writers : diverse voices in prose since 1845 / Eileen Barrett and Mary Cullinan.
p. cm.
ISBN 0-312-06556-6 (cloth)
0-312-04121-7 (paper)
1. American prose literature—Women authors. 2. American prose literature—19th century. 3. American prose literature—20th century. 4. Women—United States—Literary collections.
I. Cullinan, Mary. II. Title.
PS647.W6B37 1992
818′.08′09287—dc20 90-71610
CIP

Acknowledgments

Maya Angelou, "Preach It" and "A Job on the Streetcars" from *I Know Why the Caged Bird Sings*. Copyright © 1970 by Maya Angelou. Reprinted by permission of Random House, Inc.

Acknowledgments and copyrights are continued at the back of the book on pages 775–776, which constitute an extension of the copyright page.

 The text of this book has been printed on recycled paper.

PREFACE

American Women Writers brings together fifty-seven women writing in the United States, in English, during the nineteenth and twentieth centuries. Informed by feminist scholarship, it demonstrates some of the major contributions women have made to literature. The anthology includes an introduction that creates the critical context for the selections and describes the history of women's prose writing during the past two centuries in this country.

In making the selections, we focused on five goals. First, we want *American Women Writers* to reflect the power and scope of American women's prose. We chose a number of well-known pieces, such as Charlotte Perkins Gilman's "The Yellow Wallpaper" and Alice Walker's "In Search of Our Mothers' Gardens." We also selected what we believe to be some of the best stories and essays by lesser-known writers, such as Alice Cary, Constance Fenimore Woolson, and Agnes Smedley. In fact, Smedley's biographical portraits titled "Cell Mates" appear here for the first time (as far as we know) since their original publication in 1920.

We have also chosen powerful but less well-known stories by acclaimed writers, such as Louisa May Alcott, Kate Chopin, and Flannery O'Connor. Other works—those by Edith Wharton, Zora Neale Hurston, and Gertrude Stein, for instance—illustrate literary styles that helped to shape the course of writing in the United States. And although the majority of our selections are short works, we include three long pieces from different historical periods: Rebecca Harding Davis's *Life in the Iron Mills* depicts oppressive working conditions in the mid-nineteenth century, Willa Cather's "The Old Beauty" describes the life of an elderly woman at the turn of the century, and Maxine Hong Kingston's "At the Western Palace" captures the dilemmas of immigration for contemporary women.

Second, we strive to reflect the cultural diversity of society and literature in the United States. Almost half of the writers presented are African American, Asian American, Native American, or Chicana. Nearly one-third of the pieces selected describe the lives of working people. The stories of Rebecca Harding Davis, Hisaye Yamamoto, and Cynthia Ozick focus on human behavior in times of change and upheaval—the advent of industrialization, the incarceration of Japanese Americans during World War II, and the repercussions of the Holocaust in Europe on life in the United States. Still other works, such as those of Zitkala-Să, Marita Bonner, and Cherríe Moraga, comment on the problems facing Native Americans, African Americans, Chicanas, lesbians, and other groups that traditionally have been silenced in our society.

Third, we want the anthology to help readers understand how these women developed *as writers.* What aspects of their lives inspired them to write? What prompted their choice of topics and themes? What social, educational, and political events influenced them? To help answer some of these questions, we have provided a short biographical sketch about each writer. In addition, we have included selections that suggest how historical and political events affect fiction. Anna Julia Cooper's essay on the higher education of women, for example, not only carries a powerful message and exemplifies vigorous, well-crafted prose, but also sheds light on the educational experience of the writers who were her contemporaries. Writing on women's hunger, Meridel LeSueur reveals her command of journalistic prose. At the same time, she describes some of the obstacles working-class women writing in the 1930s had to overcome. Adrienne Rich's essay on the lesbian experience offers a method for interpreting romantic friendships described by many nineteenth-century writers and for appreciating the fiction of contemporary lesbian writers.

A fourth goal of *American Women Writers* is to help readers see continuity as well as diversity among the works. Thus, though our primary organization is chronological, we have compiled a thematic table of contents suggesting connections and common concerns among the selections. The pieces fall into categories ranging from the fears and fascinations of childhood to the social, artistic, political, and personal concerns of adulthood, to the preoccupations of old age. The nonfiction works we have included address issues of race, class, gender, and sexual orientation.

Finally, we hope readers will enjoy the power and diversity of the voices in this anthology and appreciate the importance of literary traditions that accurately reflect women's lives. To help readers explore further the wealth of writing produced by women, we have provided a bibliography of general works in feminist criticism and a short bibliography for each writer. We hope, too, that by introducing some of these writers into the classroom, *American Women Writers* will further encourage efforts to reprint significant works that have been forgotten or that have never reached the wide audience they deserve.

Eileen Barrett
Mary Cullinan

CONTENTS

American Women Writers

Diverse Voices in Prose since 1845

INTRODUCTION

CRITICAL BACKGROUND: FEMINIST SCHOLARSHIP

The last two decades have been an extraordinary time for feminist literary scholarship. Critics have reinterpreted the work of established women writers and drawn attention to the work of those who are lesser known. They have examined nontraditional genres such as newspaper and magazine articles, speeches, slave narratives, and legends to help create a cultural and literary context for the study of multiethnic literature. In short, the work of critics in feminist and ethnic studies has changed the way we read, analyze, and teach literature.

This kind of scholarly work in literature began in the early 1970s with courses, anthologies, and criticism that analyzed the images of women in literature. Examining works from the established literary tradition of the United States, feminist scholars analyzed how mostly white male writers, from Nathaniel Hawthorne to Norman Mailer, represented women in their fiction. In the tradition of Virginia Woolf's *A Room of One's Own,* for example, Mary Ellmann used wit and verve to examine the stereotypical images of women in her text *Thinking about Women.* Kate Millett, on the other hand, employed a polemical style in *Sexual Politics* to argue that representations of women in literature reflected prevailing cultural misogyny and the desire to reinforce gender divisions.

With these early arguments laying the groundwork, feminist criticism quickly expanded to study the representation of women by women writers. The earliest critics who took this approach read the works of white women writers included in the literary tradition. Nina Auerbach, for example, analyzed Louisa May Alcott's *Little Women* in the context of other male and female writers who described communities of women. Sandra Gilbert and Susan Gubar, at the same time, studied the poetry of Emily Dickinson in the context of the anxiety Dickinson and major nineteenth-century British writers felt as literary women treading on the territory of men.

In the mid-1970s, feminist scholars also studied the work of lesser-known women writers. Nina Baym, for example, in *Woman's Fiction,* turned her attention to that group of prolific and popular novelists publishing in the nineteenth century whom Hawthorne had dubbed a "damned mob of scribbling women." Other feminist critics of nineteenth-century American literature showed how different critical categories had been applied to male and female writers who were using similar settings and techniques. Whereas male writers such as William Dean Howells and Henry James were praised as literary realists, female writers such as Mary Wilkins Freeman, Sarah Orne Jewett, Kate Chopin, and Ellen Glasgow frequently were trivialized as "local colorists."

Throughout their reading of texts, these critics raised broader questions about how gender shapes art and its appreciation. Annette Kolodny in *The Lay of the Land,* to cite one example, analyzed works by men from the seventeenth through the twentieth centuries and found recurrent images of conquest and rape. Judith Fetterley in *The Resisting Reader* discussed the different ways men and women read the works of such male writers as Washington Irving, Ernest Hemingway, F. Scott Fitzgerald, and Norman Mailer. Whereas literature pretends to speak universal truths about human experience, she argued, the classics of American literature consistently describe an exclusively male experience. Thus, the female reader is "co-opted into participation in an experience from which she is explicitly excluded."

Fetterley's work helped lead the way toward critical examination of the relationship between gender and reading. If a reader is more likely to enjoy literature that uses language, imagery, and themes reflecting that reader's experience, these critics asked, what part has the gender of the critic played in the selection of what is great literature?

These questions inevitably pointed to the problems concerning the literary canon itself. Baym noted in *Woman's Fiction* that the traditional criteria for what constituted great literature suggested a bias toward things male, "in favor, say, of whaling ships rather than sewing circles as a symbol of the human community." At the same time, Lillian Robinson questioned the creation of an alternate canon of women's literature that focused on white, heterosexual, middle-class writers and themes. Arguing that canonizing forgotten works is not the solution, she concluded that we must examine the assumptions and biases underlying the criteria used to canonize all literature. This examination of critical practice flourished throughout the 1980s as critics challenged Eurocentric assumptions and gender biases and called for the study of literature to reflect the diversity of culture.

In the early 1980s, Gloria Hull, Patricia Bell Scott, and Barbara Smith were among the first Black feminist critics to address the erasure of African American women from history and literature. In their anthology *All the Women Are White, All the Blacks Are Men, But Some of Us Are Brave,* they pointed out that women's studies typically focuses on the experience of white women, while Black scholars examine the lives of Black men. For these authors, naming a discipline "Black women's studies" directly defies, in their words, "what passes for culture and thought on the North American continent."

Lillian Faderman found a comparable erasure of lesbian identity throughout literature. In *Surpassing the Love of Men,* she traced how literature reflects and reinforces changing social attitudes toward lesbianism and feminism. For example, Faderman described how during the early–twentieth-century sexual reform movement, scientists developed theories that stigmatized lesbian sexuality as deviant. As a result, although images of romantic friendships between women had been acceptable in nineteenth-century literature, writing about love between women ceased to be an option for any would-be popular writer from around the turn of the century until the feminist movement of the 1970s.

Elaine H. Kim addressed a similar problem in *Asian American Literature: An Introduction to the Writings and Their Social Context.* Traditional historians of the United States, she pointed out, have distorted and erased the experience of Asian Americans. Thus, Asian American writers confront a major obstacle: the misconceptions of their white readers. Writers such as Maxine Hong Kingston, to use Kim's example, find themselves taking pains in their work to fill in cultural and historical background for their uninformed readers. The challenge becomes, as Kim wrote, how to preserve artistic and cultural integrity in light of such ignorance.

In *Studies in American Indian Literature: Critical Essays and Course Designs,* Paula Gunn Allen and her contributors demonstrated how tribal peoples' fundamental views of life differ dramatically from those of people from a Judeo-Christian background. Indeed, the form and content of Native American literature reflect these differences. Similarly, the critics included in María Herrera-Sobek's *Beyond Stereotypes: The Critical Analysis of Chicana Literature* challenged racist imagery, in particular the prevalent portrait of Chicanas as "whore-virgin-mother." These critics discovered in the writing of Chicanas a search for an identity that could free them from these imposed images.

Thanks to the efforts of these scholars to gain critical acceptance for neglected writers, the 1980s also saw the republication of many women's works that had been lost for decades. The poetry and prose of the nineteenth-century African American writers Frances Watkins Harper and Anna Julia Cooper now are available in paperback. In recent years, feminist journals have published stories and poems by Chinese American and Mexican American turn-of-the-century writers who were precursors of the current Asian American and Chicana literary movements. Fiction focusing on working-class women has been republished: Agnes Smedley's *Daughter of Earth* and Rebecca Harding Davis's *Life in the Iron Mills,* both out of print for over fifty years, are now available. A major writer of the Harlem Renaissance whose work was unavailable fifteen years ago, Zora Neale Hurston, is now one of the most frequently taught writers in twentieth-century literature courses.

The rediscovery of these writers through feminist scholarship reminds us that women have long been writing on subjects of social and political significance. The publication of the Schomburg Library's collection of nineteenth-century Black women writers, for example, has enhanced the connection between nineteenth- and twentieth-century African American writers. Now we can read the feminist essays of Anna Julia Cooper along with those of Audre Lorde, the fiction of Harriet Wilson along with that of Toni Cade Bambara. The republication of work by Sarah Winnemucca Hopkins, a nineteenth-century Paiute, and by Helen Hunt Jackson, a nineteenth-century white woman who described the genocidal treatment of Native Americans, demonstrates that writers from different backgrounds can share common themes. Through these and other projects, feminist scholarship has discovered literary traditions of prose writing by women. It also has revealed how easily these traditions can be lost to history.

HISTORICAL BACKGROUND

In the first half of the nineteenth century, publishing and writing in the United States changed drastically. A rapid rise in population created a huge, literate audience eager to buy magazines, newspapers, and books. As the demand for written materials increased, publishers were more willing to pay writers reasonable sums for their work.

In a society in which "respectable" women were supposed to stay at home, writing enabled women to support a family without seeming to venture into male-dominated jobs. Ironically, while writing appeared to keep women safely at home, it also enabled their voices to be heard far beyond the realms of their immediate families. Margaret Fuller, for example, edited *The Dial,* the influential publication of the transcendentalist movement, and became a reviewer, columnist, and foreign correspondent for Horace Greeley's *New York Tribune.* Writing to a large audience, she argued for women's right to education and meaningful employment.

In the decades before the Civil War, a number of women were active in the temperance and antislavery movements as well as in the emerging struggle for women's rights. Elizabeth Cady Stanton, for instance, helped to organize the Seneca Falls Women's Rights Convention in 1848. With Susan B. Anthony, Stanton became a major voice for women's suffrage, property rights, liberalized divorce laws, and other feminist issues.

Although these white, often wealthy women argued for the abolition of slavery, they frequently failed to comprehend or address the problems facing African American and Native American women. Some African American women managed to publish accounts of their experiences in slavery and of the racism they encountered in the North both before and after slavery was abolished. Some white northerners were not pleased to see their imperfections revealed in such books as Harriet Wilson's *Our Nig* and Harriet Jacobs's *Incidents in the Life of a Slave Girl.* Even in this century, although slave narratives written by men were reissued and studied, works by women remained out of circulation and their authorship was questioned. Only in recent years, as research confirms the authenticity of these narratives, have they become available to a wide audience.

Despite efforts to silence or belittle them, the strong voices of African American women such as Sojourner Truth, Frances Harper, and Anna Julia Cooper managed to be heard. Freed from slavery in 1827, Sojourner Truth spent much of her life lecturing for the abolition of slavery, for women's rights, and for the rights of African Americans once they had been freed. Frances

Harper also traveled extensively, advocating educational reforms, the abolition of slavery, and criminal prosecution of those accused of lynching. As an educator, speaker, and author, Anna Julia Cooper became one of the most articulate spokespeople for African American women at the turn of the century.

Native Americans, too, encountered obstacles to being heard in the nineteenth century. Speaking a variety of languages and coming from primarily oral traditions, most American Indians were unable to write of the genocide undertaken by whites against other people. A Paiute, Sarah Winnemucca Hopkins, became one of the first Native Americans to overcome such obstacles and describe both the culture of her tribespeople and the wrongs committed against them.

Despite the works by women of color, mainstream literary life in this period continued to revolve around male writers living in eastern cities. In the mid-nineteenth century, Boston was the center for established writers such as Ralph Waldo Emerson, Nathaniel Hawthorne, James Russell Lowell, and Oliver Wendell Holmes. Yet in Boston as well as New York, the literary establishment helped to spawn a medium that enabled women from different geographic regions, social classes, and ethnic backgrounds to publish their writing: the literary magazine.

Before books and circulating libraries were widely available, most people encountered fiction and poetry in magazines. The *Atlantic Monthly, Scribner's Monthly,* and *Harper's Monthly* published important literary works, such as Henry James's *The American* and *The Portrait of a Lady.* As the "quality" literary periodicals flourished, they were followed by less-expensive and more-popular magazines such as *Ladies' Home Journal* and *McClure's,* all eager to publish fiction and poetry. Knowing that many of their readers were women, publishers sought women writers and even editors. As editor of the *Atlantic,* William Dean Howells became a major arbiter of literary taste, as did the publishers James and Annie Fields. All three helped to publish and nurture talented women writers from a variety of backgrounds.

While featuring the work of women writers, the periodicals that flourished in the second half of the nineteenth century—and continued to prosper well into the twentieth century—served as a stage for a new genre in literature: regional, realistic fiction. The growing country was becoming aware of its regional differences, its individual dialects, and its cultural idiosyncrasies. Yet, while people in the United States were proud of these differences, they realized that industrialization was obliterating the unique features of isolated rural communities. A number of writers captured these rapidly disappearing regional landscapes for enthusiastic readers.

Much of the realistic fiction written by women focuses on details of domestic life in rural areas: it has introduced the small dramas of villages such as Alice Cary's rural Clovernook and Alice Brown's Tiverton. While these women wrote for an audience demanding stories that capture bittersweet memories of a passing way of life, notes of anger and protest simmer beneath the surface of these tales. The characters revel in their sudden widowhood or choose a single life over marriage, young girls glimpse the power that men will have over them, wives assert themselves over demanding husbands, old women fight the patriarchal systems of town and church. These writers planted seeds of discontent and even revolution in their nostalgic evocations of rural life.

Although many of the characters in these tales are women restricted by their economic dependence on fathers and husbands, the authors themselves often experienced a new type of freedom. A number of these women, including Sarah Orne Jewett, Alice Cary, and Alice Brown, never married, and supported themselves successfully through their writing. The freedom of economic success, however, was sometimes accompanied by questions of artistic integrity. Knowing what audiences wanted, the periodical writers did not experiment with style and form as much as they might have—nor did they overtly challenge the social order that supported them. Writers such as Rebecca Harding Davis and Mary Wilkins Freeman, despite (or because of) their marriages, faced severe financial problems that compelled them to write predictable, marketable pieces.

It is tempting to view the turn of the century as a major marker for changes in the American woman writer's situation. Women ventured more openly into the workplace. Immigrant and ethnic voices began to be heard in literary and political forums. Middle- and working-class writers from the South and West began to overshadow the New England writers. Such changes, however, came slowly. Some of them came about early in the nineteenth century; some are still taking place today.

The new century did usher in some changes for the American writer. To satisfy readers eager for stories that revealed the variety of cultures, dialects, and customs in the United States, editors began publishing works by new immigrants and ethnic minorities. Stories and essays by Sui Sin Far, one of the first Asian women to write about Chinese Americans, were published in magazines such as *The Century* and *Good Housekeeping* in the 1910s. Anzia Yezierska, born in Poland, achieved popularity with fictional accounts about Eastern European Jewish immigrants in New York City. Zitkala-Ša published her Indian tales in the *Atlantic* during the first decade of the twentieth century. Although not a Native American, Mary Hunter Austin revealed the importance of Native American dance and poetic traditions through her popular stories and essays.

The first years of the twentieth century saw changes, too, in the characters and themes appearing in women's writing. Authors such as Charlotte Perkins Gilman and Ellen Glasgow frequently depicted white middle-class female characters who, while not always able to have careers, yearn to break out of their restricted lives. Some seek sexual freedom; others, like Gilman's narrator in "The Yellow Wallpaper," reveal what happens when men attempt to paralyze a woman's body and mind. Although Glasgow sometimes made fun of intellectual, "rebellious" women, she also advocated women's economic and spiritual independence from men.

The 1920s symbolize for many in the United States the decade of the liberated woman. During World War I, greater numbers of women entered the workforce in jobs traditionally held by men, and in 1920 women's potential for political power increased when they gained the right to vote. These professional and political opportunities benefited women writers, who became increasingly independent economically. Moreover, their work became more experimental and more concerned with political and social issues. Lesbian writers such as Gertrude Stein found intellectual and personal freedom living as expatriates in Paris. New York City, a center for literary and artistic experimentation, attracted writers as different as Zora Neale Hurston and Susan Glaspell.

With its proximity to the New York publishing industry and to white patrons who could finance Black art, Harlem became the cultural capital of Black America. The Harlem Renaissance was a channeling of political and social energy into poetry, music, fiction, and art. During the 1920s, Black writers were published in greater numbers than in any other single decade until the 1960s. Unlike most of the nineteenth-century African American writers, who wrote principally for white middle-class readers, the writers of the Harlem Renaissance wrote for a diverse white and Black audience. The African American journals *Crisis* and *Opportunity* became important outlets for the prose and poetry of women writers such as Zora Neale Hurston and Marita Bonner. A central figure during the final years of the Renaissance, Hurston had an extraordinary skill for capturing the rich, imaginative, lyrical language of her people. Trained as an anthropologist, she used African American cultural traditions to create a literature that has profoundly affected the work of Alice Walker, Toni Cade Bambara, and other contemporary Black writers.

Despite the importance of their work during this period, women writers were obscured again by the work of their male colleagues. Eugene O'Neill became a major American playwright whose association with the Provincetown Players was studied extensively; Susan Glaspell's plays went out of print, and her association with the same Provincetown Players was almost forgotten. Whereas the writings of Langston Hughes and Claude McKay continued to receive limited critical attention, the writings of Hurston and Bonner were generally ignored.

The end of the 1920s brought far-reaching changes to the United States and the rest of the world. The spread of an unprecedented economic depression and the rise of fascism in the 1930s and the 1940s created demands for social change from a broad spectrum of writers. With the horrors of military oppression abroad and breadlines and hunger marches at home, Communist party reforms appealed to both intellectuals and working-class people. Even writers without marked leftist leanings wrote powerful social protest.

Once again, the writers most remembered for this era—John Steinbeck, John Dos Passos, and Richard Wright, for instance—are male. Nonetheless, the grim times engendered eloquent women writers such as Agnes Smedley, Meridel LeSueur, Ann Petry, Tillie Olsen, and Kay Boyle. Smedley spent years in China reporting on the revolutionary movement and its implications for women, and she described women's prison conditions in the United States. LeSueur recounted the sufferings of working-class women in the radical journals of the time. Petry's novel *The Street* depicted the hardships suffered during the depression by poor Black women. Born into a socialist family, Olsen worked as an organizer for the Communist party and wrote for publications such as the (then-leftist) *New Republic* that advocated reform. Boyle drew upon her experiences in Europe to convey the horrifying rise of Nazism to American readers.

The efforts of these women to combat the traditional silencing of women writers were thwarted by the post–World War II McCarthy era, in which socially conscious writers were branded as Communist and un-American. Smedley, Olsen, LeSueur, and Boyle were arrested and fired from their jobs, and their writing was suppressed. Neither Boyle nor Olsen published again until the 1960s; Smedley's and LeSueur's work was reprinted only in the 1970s.

Less-overtly political regional writing appeared in new forms in these postwar years. The white southern experience proved to be a wellspring of inspiration for Carson McCullers, Flannery O'Connor, Eudora Welty, and Katherine Anne Porter. These writers provided a female counterpoint to William Faulkner's version of Southern Gothic. Shirley Jackson and Jean Stafford, westerners who settled in New England, redefined in often startling ways the rural virtue and naiveté fostered by earlier regionalists. The New York writers Hortense Calisher, Grace Paley, and Cynthia Ozick examine throughout their work the experience of Jews in the post-Holocaust United States.

The vocal protest movements that began in the 1960s have influenced writers to the present day. Many contemporary writers have protested economic exploitation and discrimination based on class, race, gender, and sexual preference. A new generation of talented African American, Asian American, Chicana, and Native American women have given new voice to themes developed by their foremothers. Writers such as Paule Marshall and Maya Angelou use traditional storytelling, autobiography, journalism, and feminist criticism to underscore what it means to be Black and female in modern America. Hisaye Yamamoto, Maxine Hong Kingston, and Amy Tan use autobiography and fiction to dramatize the mesh of Asian and American cultures. Born of Spanish-speaking families in the United States, Estela Portillo Trambley, Helena Maria Viramontes, and Cherríe Moraga fuse the literary traditions and genres of several cultures to explore issues of race and ethnicity. Leslie Marmon Silko and Louise Erdrich exemplify the articulate Native American women writers concerned with the unique culture and history of their people. Lesbian writers of all cultural backgrounds—Adrienne Rich, Audre Lorde, and Cherríe Moraga, for example—have created an extensive body of literature describing their version of the American experience.

Looking back over nearly two hundred years of writing, one sees startling changes in the way women have viewed themselves and their society. Equally startling, though, are the repetitions of themes through the decades: the voices of protest, both muted and dissonant; the concerns with personal freedom; the insights into female consciousness; the celebration of women's roles as mothers, daughters, wives, lovers, workers, and artists. These themes echo through the pages of *American Women Writers.*

SOJOURNER TRUTH
(1797?–1883)

When Sojourner Truth commanded the podium at the 1851 Woman's Rights Convention in Akron, Ohio, and delivered her "A'n't I a Woman?" speech, she earned renown as one of the country's most brilliant speakers and first Black feminists. She spoke for thousands of women like herself who had suffered the atrocities of slavery. Her voice and actions continue to inspire contemporary activists and writers to confront similar injustices with courage, wisdom, and moral conviction.

Truth was born Isabella Baumfree, a slave on a New York estate owned by a Dutch family. When her mother's slave master died, Truth and her younger brother stood for sale on the auction block. At nine years of age, she was sold for $100 to John Neely. From Neely she was purchased by a fisherman named Schryver, for whom she did arduous manual labor. Eighteen months later, John J. Dumont bought her; by the time she reached thirteen, she had been sold three times.

Emancipated by New York State law in 1827, Truth worked as a domestic in New York City and gained a reputation as a gifted preacher. In 1843 she traveled throughout New England and New York, lecturing for the end of slavery and women's rights.

As a free woman, she choose the name "Sojourner" to represent her journey for freedom, and "Truth" to reflect the message she would tell the people. With wit and verbal skill, and a resonant voice marked with a Dutch accent, she disarmed many opponents. In 1864 The National Freedman's Relief Association appointed Truth counselor to the freedpersons of Arlington Heights, Virginia. A frequent rider of Washington's streetcars, she successfully protested seating discrimination, and Congress banned segregated cars in the District of Columbia. When conductors failed to enforce the law, Truth took them to court and won. In this manner, she became a model for freedom riders of the twentieth-century civil rights movement.

Her compassion for destitute freed slaves in the North led her to petition Congress for public land. She envisioned a western state where African Americans could stake claims and farm rather than remain dependent on government assistance. She gave her first lecture on this subject in 1870; she traveled widely in search of support throughout 1872. An illness in 1875 prevented her from presenting her petitions to Congress. Her dreams for a Black state ended with her death in Battle Creek, Michigan, in 1883.

Truth neither read nor wrote English. The speeches she gave were recorded and transcribed by others. The selections we have included were published first in The History of Woman Suffrage (1886), *edited by Susan B. Anthony, Elizabeth*

Cady Stanton, and Matilda Joslyn Gage. Frances D. Gage recorded Truth's "A'n't I a Woman?" speech at the Akron Convention (May 28–29, 1851). Truth's May 9, 1867, address to the American Equal Rights Association was recorded by Anthony and her co-editors.

■ A'N'T I A WOMAN?

Wall, chilern, whar dar is so much racket dar must be somethin' out o' kilter. I tink dat 'twixt de niggers of de Souf and de womin at de Norf, all talkin' 'bout rights, de white men will be in a fix pretty soon. But what's all dis here talkin' 'bout?

Dat man ober dar say dat womin needs to be helped into carriages, and lifted ober ditches, and to hab de best place everywhar. Nobody eber helps me into carriages, or ober mud-puddles, or gibs me any best place! And a'n't I a woman? Look at me! Look at my arm! I have ploughed, and planted, and gathered into barns, and no man could head me! And a'n't I a woman? I could work as much and eat as much as a man—when I could get it—and bear de lash as well! And a'n't I a woman? I have borne thirteen chilern, and seen 'em mos' all sold off to slavery, and when I cried out with my mother's grief, none but Jesus heard me! And a'n't I a woman?

Den dey talks 'bout dis ting in de head; what dis dey call it? ("Intellect," whispered someone near.) Dat's it, honey. What's dat got to do wid womin's rights or nigger's rights? If my cup won't hold but a pint, and yourn holds a quart, wouldn't ye be mean not to let me have my little half-measure full?

Den dat little man in black dar, he say women can't have as much rights as men, 'cause Christ wan't a woman! Whar did your Christ come from? Whar did your Christ come from? From God and a woman! Man had nothin' to do wid Him.

If de fust woman God ever made was strong enough to turn de world upside down all alone, dese women togedder ought to be able to turn it back, and get it right side up again! And now dey is asking to do it, de men better let 'em. 'Bleeged to ye for hearin' on me, and now ole Sojourner han't got nothin' more to say.

1851/1886

ADDRESS TO THE FIRST ANNUAL MEETING OF THE AMERICAN EQUAL RIGHTS ASSOCIATION

My friends, I am rejoiced that you are glad, but I don't know how you will feel when I get through. I come from another field—the country of the slave. They have got their liberty—so much good luck to have slavery partly destroyed; not entirely. I want it root and branch destroyed. Then we will all be free indeed. I feel that if I have to answer for the deeds done in my body just as much as a man, I have a right to have just as much as a man. There is a great stir about colored men getting their rights, but not a word about the colored women; and if colored men get their rights, and not colored women theirs, you see the colored men will be masters over the women, and it will be just as bad as it was before. So I am for keeping the thing going while things are stirring; because if we wait till it is still, it will take a great while to get it going again. White women are a great deal smarter, and know more than colored women, while colored women do not know scarcely anything. They go out washing, which is about as high as a colored woman gets, and their men go about idle, strutting up and down; and when the women come home, they ask for their money and take it all, and then scold because there is no food. I want you to consider on that, chil'n. I call you chil'n; you are somebody's chil'n, and I am old enough to be mother of all that is here. I want women to have their rights. In the courts women have no right, no voice; nobody speaks for them. I wish woman to have her voice there among the pettifoggers. If it is not a fit place for women, it is unfit for men to be there.

I am above eighty years old; it is about time for me to be going. I have been forty years a slave and forty years free, and would be here forty years more to have equal rights for all. I suppose I am kept here because something remains for me to do; I suppose I am yet to help to break the chain. I have done a great deal of work; as much as a man, but did not get so much pay. I used to work in the field and bind grain, keeping up with the cradler; but men doing no more, got twice as much pay; so with the German women. They work in the field and do as much work, but do not get the pay. We do as much, we eat as much, we want as much. I suppose I am about the only colored woman that goes about to speak for the rights of the colored women. I want to keep the thing stirring, now that the ice is cracked. What we want is a little money. You men know that you get as much again as women when you write, or for what you do. When we get our rights we shall not have to come to you for money, for then we shall have money enough in our own pockets; and may be you will ask us for money. But help us now until we get it. It is a good consolation to know that when we have got this battle once fought we shall not be coming to you any more. You have been having our rights so long, that you think, like a slave-holder, that you own us. I know that it is hard for one who has held the reins for so long to give up; it cuts like a knife. It will feel all the better when it closes up again. I have been in Washington about three years, seeing about these colored people. Now colored men have the right to vote. There ought to be equal rights now more than ever, since colored people have got their freedom. I am going to talk several times while I am here; so now I will do a little singing. I have not heard any singing since I came here.

We are going home. There, children, in heaven we shall rest from all our labors; first do all we have to do here. There I am determined to go, not to stop short of that beautiful place, and I do not mean to stop till I get there, and meet you there, too.

1867/1886

MARGARET FULLER
(1810–1850)

Margaret Fuller's writing perhaps speaks less powerfully to present-day readers than does her example as a successful intellectual and activist in the American women's movement. Refusing to accept a passive role, Fuller found that her formidable intelligence and manner threatened even those men who purported to be her friends. Fictional versions of Fuller appear frequently in the novels and stories of her time: Nathaniel Hawthorne used her partly as a model for the powerful figure of Zenobia in The Blithedale Romance, *and Henry James may have created the feminists of* The Bostonians *in her image. Her impact on most men was summed up by Ralph Waldo Emerson: "Men thought she carried too many guns."*

Educated by her father, Fuller learned to read Latin by the time she was seven. After two years in school, she returned home to study French, Greek, German, Italian, "metaphysics," and history. In 1835, she began teaching at Bronson Alcott's school in Boston, and then taught at Greene Street School in Providence, Rhode Island. Emerson and others urged her to become editor of the transcendentalist magazine The Dial *in 1840. She also worked as a correspondent for Horace Greeley's* New York Tribune. *From 1839 to 1845, Fuller helped to support herself by conducting weekly "Conversations" for women in Boston—meetings at which literary and philosophical topics were discussed. Fuller intended these Conversations to be conducive to women's self-development, a partial compensation for the advanced education they were routinely denied. Although the Conversations were too expensive to be easily available to anyone outside the upper class, Fuller also worked with less-privileged women. She frequently visited women prisoners in Sing Sing, and she planned the first halfway house for women convicts.*

When living in Europe, Fuller became one of the first war correspondents, covering the revolutions of 1848 for the Tribune. *She had an affair with and married an impoverished Italian nobleman, Giovanni Angelo Ossoli, who was fighting for the Roman Republic. With the defeat of the Republic, she set sail with him and their son for the United States; all three were drowned in a shipwreck within sight of Long Island.*

Margaret Fuller admired women who were political and social rebels: George Sand, Mme. de Staël, and Mary Wollstonecraft—all Europeans. Fuller was the first American woman to establish an intellectual renown and a radical reputation akin to that of those women.

In Woman in the Nineteenth Century, *her best-known work, Fuller argues that women need to seek economic as well as social equality. Women, Fuller insisted, must learn to be self-reliant and should not expect help from even the most liberal of men. Not one man in a hundred million, she wrote, could rise above the basic belief that women are made for men. She insisted that women should be free to choose any vocation they wished: "If you ask me what offices they may fill—I reply—any. I do not care what case you put; let them be sea-captains, if you will."*

■ *from* WOMAN IN THE NINETEENTH CENTURY

EDUCATION OF WOMEN

Another sign of the times is furnished by the triumphs of Female Authorship. These have been great, and are constantly increasing. Women have taken possession of so many provinces for which men had pronounced them unfit, that, though these still declare there are some inaccessible to them, it is difficult to say just *where* they must stop.

The shining names of famous women have cast light upon the path of the sex, and many obstructions have been removed. When a Montague could learn better than her brother, and use her lore afterwards to such purpose as an observer, it seemed amiss to hinder women from preparing themselves to see, or from seeing all they could, when prepared. Since Somerville has achieved so much, will any young girl be prevented from seeking a knowledge of the physical sciences, if she wishes it? De Staël's name was not so clear of offence; she could not forget the Woman in the thought; while she was instructing you as a mind, she wished to be admired as a Woman; sentimental tears often dimmed the eagle glance. Her intellect, too, with all its splendor, trained in a drawing-room, fed on flattery, was tainted and flawed; yet its beams make the obscurest school-house in New England warmer and lighter to the little rugged girls who are gathered together on its wooden bench. They may never through life hear her name, but she is not the less their benefactress.

The influence has been such, that the aim certainly is, now, in arranging school instruction for girls, to give them as fair a field as boys. As yet, indeed, these arrangements are made with little judgment or reflection; just as the tutors of Lady Jane Grey, and other distinguished women of her time, taught them Latin and Greek, because they knew nothing else themselves, so now the improvement in the education of girls is to be made by giving them young men as teachers, who only teach what has been taught themselves at college, while methods and topics need revision for these new subjects, which could better be made by those who had experienced the same wants. Women are, often, at the head of these institutions; but they have, as yet, seldom been thinking women, capable of organizing a new whole for the wants of the time, and choosing persons to officiate in the departments. And when some portion of instruction of a good sort is got from the school, the far greater proportion which is infused from the general atmosphere of society contradicts its purport. Yet books and a little elementary instruction are not furnished in vain. Women are better aware how great and rich the universe is, not so easily blinded by narrowness or partial views of a home circle. "Her mother did so before her" is no longer a sufficient excuse. Indeed, it was never received as an excuse to mitigate the severity of censure, but was adduced as a reason, rather, why there should be no effort made for reformation.

Whether much or little has been done, or will be done,—whether women will add to the talent of narration the power of systematizing,—whether they will carve marble, as well as draw and paint,—is not important. But that it should be acknowledged that they have intellect which needs developing—that they should not be considered complete, if beings of affection and habit alone—is important.

Yet even this acknowledgment, rather conquered by Woman than proffered by Man, has been sullied by the usual selfishness. Too much is said of women being better educated, that they may become better companions and mothers *for men.* They should be fit for such companionship, and we have mentioned, with satisfaction, instances where it has been established. Earth knows no fairer, holier relation than that of a mother. It is one which, rightly understood, must both promote and require the highest attainments. But a being of infinite scope must not be treated with an exclusive view to any one relation. Give the soul free course, let the organization, both of body and mind, be freely developed, and the being will be fit for any and every relation to which it may be called. The intellect, no more than the sense of hearing, is to be cultivated not merely that Woman may be a more valuable companion to Man, but because the Power who gave a power, by its mere existence signifies that it must be brought out toward perfection.

In this regard of self-dependence, and a greater simplicity and fullness of being, we must hail as a preliminary the increase of the class contemptuously designated as "old maids."

We cannot wonder at the aversion with which old bachelors and old maids have been regarded. Marriage is the natural means of forming a sphere, of taking root in the earth; it requires more strength to do this without such an opening; very many have failed, and their imperfections have been in every one's way. They have been more partial, more harsh, more officious and impertinent, than those compelled by severer friction to render themselves endurable. Those who have a more full experience of the instincts have a distrust as to whether the unmarried can be thoroughly human and humane, such as is hinted in the saying, "Old maids' and bachelors' children are well cared for," which derides at once their ignorance and their presumption.

Yet the business of society has become so complex, that it could now scarcely be carried on without the presence of these despised auxiliaries; and detachments from the army of aunts and uncles are wanted to stop gaps in every hedge. They rove about, mental and moral Ishmaelites, pitching their tents amid the fixed and ornamented homes of men.

In a striking variety of forms, genius of late, both at home and abroad, has paid its tribute to the character of the Aunt and the Uncle, recognizing in these personages the spiritual parents, who have supplied defects in the treatment of the busy or careless actual parents.

They also gain a wider, if not so deep experience. Those who are not intimately and permanently linked with others, are thrown upon themselves; and, if they do not there find peace and incessant life, there is none to flatter them that they are not very poor, and very mean.

A position which so constantly admonishes, may be of inestimable benefit. The person may gain, undistracted by other relationships, a closer communion with the one. Such a use is made of it by saints and sibyls. Or she may be one of the lay sisters of charity, a canoness, bound by an inward vow,—or the useful drudge of all men, the Martha, much sought, little prized,—or the intellectual interpreter of the varied life she sees; the Urania of a half-formed world's twilight.

Or she may combine all these. Not "needing to care that she may please a husband," a frail and limited being, her thoughts may turn to the centre, and she may, by steadfast contemplation entering into the secret of truth and love, use it for the good of all men, instead of a chosen few, and interpret through it all the forms of life. It is possible, perhaps, to be at once a priestly servant and a loving muse.

Saints and geniuses have often chosen a lonely position, in the faith that if, undisturbed by the pressure of near ties, they would give themselves up to the inspiring spirit, it would enable them to understand and reproduce life better than actual experience could.

How many "old maids" take this high stand we cannot say: it is an unhappy fact that too many who have come before the eye are gossips rather, and not always good-natured gossips. But if these abuse, and none make the best of their vocation, yet it has not failed to produce some good results. It has been seen by others, if not by themselves, that beings, likely to be left alone, need to be fortified and furnished within themselves; and education and thought have tended more and more to regard these beings as related to absolute Being, as well as to others. It has been seen that, as the breaking of no bond ought to destroy a man, so ought the missing of none to hinder him from growing. And thus a circumstance of the time, which springs rather from its luxury than its purity, has helped to place women on the true platform.

Perhaps the next generation, looking deeper into this matter, will find that contempt is put upon old maids, or old women, at all, merely because they do not use the elixir which would keep them always young. Under its influence, a gem brightens yearly which is only seen to more advantage through the fissures Time makes in the casket. No one thinks of Michael Angelo's Persican Sibyl, or St. Theresa, or Tasso's Leonora, or the Greek Electra, as an old maid, more than of Michael Angelo or Canova as old bachelors, though all had reached the period in life's course appointed to take that degree.

1845

HARRIET JACOBS
(1813?–1897)

In Incidents in the Life of a Slave Girl, *Harriet Jacobs, using the pseudonym Linda Brent, narrates the story of her life to an audience of mostly white northern women. Her purpose throughout her writing is clear: she hopes to persuade her audience to abolish slavery. Thus, Jacobs's personal story is inseparable from the political purpose of telling that story.*

Harriet Jacobs was born a slave in Edenton, North Carolina, around 1813. Her first mistress, Margaret Horniblow, taught her to read and write. Upon Horniblow's death, the eleven-year-old Jacobs became the legal property of a three-year-old named Mary Norcom. When James Norcom, the father of Jacobs's young mistress, became her master, Jacobs's life of sexual abuse began.

To avoid becoming James Norcom's sexual slave, Jacobs became the mistress of another white man, with whom she had two children. Nonetheless, Norcom's relentless pursuit forced Jacobs to hide for years in her grandmother's house. In 1842, after nearly seven years, she escaped to the North, where she found work as a nursemaid and where, after great travail, both of her children joined her. Through her activities in the antislavery movement, Jacobs met Amy Post, an active feminist, who encouraged her to publish her story.

"Slavery is terrible for men; but it is far more terrible for women," Jacobs wrote in her narrative, breaking the silence surrounding sexual slavery and making an irrefutable connection between racial and sexual oppression. With this assertion, Jacobs expanded the genre of the slave narrative, which Frederick Douglass had so effectively employed, to include the experience of women.

In 1852, Jacobs's abolitionist friends bought her freedom for $300. The irony of that purchase did not escape this ex–slave woman, who explained in Incidents: *"So I was* sold *at last! A human being* sold *in the free city of New York! The bill of sale is on record, and future generations will learn from it that women were articles of traffic in New York, late in the nineteenth century of the Christian religion."*

For many years Harriet Jacobs's Incidents in the Life of a Slave Girl *was considered spurious. Recent scholarship by Jean Yellin has identified the places and people whose names Jacobs altered in her narrative, proving the authenticity of this story. For example, Yellin discovered that Dr. Flint, Linda's slave master in the narrative, was Dr. James Norcom, and that Mrs. Bruce, the northern employer who purchased Linda's freedom, was Cornelia Grinnell Willis.*

Included here are four chapters from the narrative. "The Trials of Girlhood" chronicles the early stages of Dr. Flint's sexual abuse of Linda Brent. "The

Loophole of Retreat" describes the years Linda hid in her grandmother's attic. In "Incidents in Philadelphia," Linda and another escaped slave arrive in a free state only to discover a northern brand of racism. "Prejudice against Color" depicts the northern racism Linda experienced when employed as a nurse for the Bruce family.

■ *from* INCIDENTS IN THE LIFE OF A SLAVE GIRL

CHAPTER V: THE TRIALS OF GIRLHOOD

During the first years of my service in Dr. Flint's family, I was accustomed to share some indulgences with the children of my mistress. Though this seemed to me no more than right, I was grateful for it, and tried to merit the kindness by the faithful discharge of my duties. But I now entered on my fifteenth year—a sad epoch in the life of a slave girl. My master began to whisper foul words in my ear. Young as I was, I could not remain ignorant of their import. I tried to treat them with indifference or contempt. The master's age, my extreme youth, and the fear that his conduct would be reported to my grandmother, made him bear this treatment for many months. He was a crafty man, and resorted to many means to accomplish his purposes. Sometimes he had stormy, terrific ways, that made his victims tremble; sometimes he assumed a gentleness that he thought must surely subdue. Of the two, I preferred his stormy moods, although they left me trembling. He tried his utmost to corrupt the pure principles my grandmother had instilled. He peopled my young mind with unclean images, such as only a vile monster could think of. I turned from him with disgust and hatred. But he was my master. I was compelled to live under the same roof with him—where I saw a man forty years my senior daily violating the most sacred commandments of nature. He told me I was his property; that I must be subject to his will in all things. My soul revolted against the mean tyranny. But where could I turn for protection? No matter whether the slave girl be as black as ebony or as fair as her mistress. In either case, there is no shadow of law to protect her from insult, from violence, or even from death; all these are inflicted by fiends who bear the shape of men. The mistress, who ought to protect the helpless victim, has no other feelings towards her but those of jealousy and rage. The degradation, the wrongs, the vices, that grow out of slavery, are more than I can describe. They are greater than you would willingly believe. Surely, if you credited one half the truths that are told you concerning the helpless millions suffering in this cruel bondage, you at the north would not help to tighten the yoke. You surely would refuse to do for the master, on your own soil, the mean and cruel work which trained bloodhounds and the lowest class of whites do for him at the south.

Every where the years bring to all enough of sin and sorrow; but in slavery the very dawn of life is darkened by these shadows. Even the little child, who is accustomed to wait on her mistress and her children, will learn, before she is twelve years old, why it is that her mistress hates such and such a one among the slaves. Perhaps the child's own mother is among those hated ones. She listens to violent outbreaks of jealous passion, and cannot help understanding what is the cause. She will become prematurely knowing in evil things. Soon she will learn to tremble when she hears her master's footfall. She will be compelled to realize that she is no longer a child. If God has bestowed beauty upon her, it will prove her greatest curse. That which commands admiration in the white woman only hastens the degradation of the female slave. I know that some are too much brutalized by slavery to feel the humiliation of their position; but many slaves feel it most acutely, and shrink from the memory of it. I cannot tell how much I suffered in the presence of these wrongs, nor how I am still pained by the retrospect. My master met me at every turn, reminding me that I belonged to him, and swearing by heaven and earth that he would compel me to submit to him. If I went out for a breath of fresh air, after a day of unwearied toil, his footsteps dogged me. If I knelt by my mother's grave, his dark shadow fell on me even there. The light heart which nature had given me became heavy with sad forebodings. The other slaves in my master's house noticed the change. Many of them pitied me; but none dared to ask the cause. They had no need to inquire. They knew too well the guilty practices under that roof; and they were aware that to speak of them was an offence that never went unpunished.

I longed for some one to confide in. I would have given the world to have laid my head on my grandmother's faithful bosom, and told her all my troubles. But Dr. Flint swore he would kill me, if I was not as silent as the grave. Then, although my grandmother was all in all to me, I feared her as well as loved her. I had been accustomed to look up to her with a respect bordering upon awe. I was very young, and felt shamefaced about telling her such impure things, especially as I knew her to be very strict on such subjects. Moreover, she was a woman of a high spirit. She was usually very quiet in her demeanor; but if her indignation was once roused, it was not very easily quelled. I had been told that she once chased a white gentleman with a loaded pistol, because he insulted one of her daughters. I dreaded the consequences of a violent outbreak; and both pride and fear kept me silent. But though I did not confide in my grandmother, and even evaded her vigilant watchfulness and inquiry, her presence in the neighborhood was some protection to me. Though she had been a slave, Dr. Flint was afraid of her. He dreaded her scorching rebukes. Moreover, she was known and patronized by many people; and he did not wish to have his villainy made public. It was lucky for me that I did not live on a distant plantation, but in a town not so large that the inhabitants were ignorant of each other's affairs. Bad as are the laws and customs in a slaveholding community, the doctor, as a professional man, deemed it prudent to keep up some outward show of decency.

O, what days and nights of fear and sorrow that man caused me! Reader, it is not to awaken sympathy for myself that I am telling you truthfully what I suffered in slavery. I do it to kindle a flame of compassion in your hearts for my sisters who are still in bondage, suffering as I once suffered.

I once saw two beautiful children playing together. One was a fair white child; the other was her slave, and also her sister. When I saw them embracing each other, and heard their joyous laughter, I turned sadly away from the lovely sight. I foresaw the inevitable blight that would fall on the little slave's heart. I knew how soon her laughter would be changed to sighs. The fair child grew up to be a still fairer woman. From childhood to womanhood her pathway was blooming with flowers, and overarched by a sunny sky. Scarcely one day of her life had been clouded when the sun rose on her happy bridal morning.

How had those years dealt with her slave sister, the little playmate of her childhood? She, also, was very beautiful; but the flowers and sunshine of love were not for her. She drank the cup of sin, and shame, and misery, whereof her persecuted race are compelled to drink.

In view of these things, why are ye silent, ye free men and women of the north? Why do your tongues falter in maintenance of the right? Would that I had more ability! But my heart is so full, and my pen is so weak! There are noble men and women who plead for us, striving to help those who cannot help themselves. God bless them! God give them strength and courage to go on! God bless those, every where, who are laboring to advance the cause of humanity!

CHAPTER XXI: THE LOOPHOLE OF RETREAT

A small shed had been added to my grandmother's house years ago. Some boards were laid across the joists at the top, and between these boards and the roof was a very small garret, never occupied by any thing but rats and mice. It was a pent roof, covered with nothing but shingles, according to the southern custom for such buildings. The garret was only nine feet long and seven wide. The highest part was three feet high, and sloped down abruptly to the loose board floor. There was no admission for either light or air. My uncle Phillip, who was a carpenter, had very skilfully made a concealed trap-door, which communicated with the storeroom. He had been doing this while I was waiting in the swamp. The storeroom opened upon a piazza. To this hole I was conveyed as soon as I entered the house. The air was stifling; the darkness total. A bed had been spread on the floor. I could sleep quite comfortably on one side; but the slope was so sudden that I could not turn on the other without hitting the roof. The rats and mice ran over my bed; but I was weary, and I slept such sleep as the wretched may, when a tempest has passed over them. Morning came. I knew it only by the noises I heard; for in my small den day and night were all the same. I suffered for air even more than for light. But I was not comfortless. I heard the voices of my children. There was joy and there was sadness in the sound. It made my tears flow. How I longed to speak to them! I was eager to look on their faces; but there was no hole, no crack, through which I could peep. This continued darkness was oppressive. It seemed horrible to sit or lie in a cramped position day after day, without one gleam of light. Yet I would have chosen this, rather than my lot as a slave, though white people considered it an easy one; and it was so compared with the fate of others. I was never cruelly over-worked; I was never lacerated with the whip from head to foot; I was never so beaten and bruised that I could not turn from one side to the other; I never had my heel-strings cut to prevent my running away; I was never chained to a log and forced to drag it about, while I toiled in the fields from morning till night; I was never branded with hot iron, or torn by bloodhounds. On the contrary, I had always been kindly treated, and tenderly cared for, until I came into the hands of Dr. Flint. I had never wished for freedom till then. But though my life in slavery was comparatively devoid of hardships, God pity the woman who is compelled to lead such a life!

My food was passed up to me through the trap-door my uncle had contrived; and my grandmother, my uncle Phillip, and aunt Nancy would seize such opportunities as they could, to mount up there and chat with me at the opening. But of course this was not safe in the daytime. It must all be done in darkness. It was impossible for me to move in an erect position, but I crawled about my den for exercise. One day I hit my head against something, and found it was a gimlet. My uncle had left it sticking there when he made the trap-door. I was as rejoiced as Robinson Crusoe could have been at finding such a treasure. It put a lucky thought into my head. I said to myself, "Now I will have some light. Now I will see my children." I did not dare to begin my work during the daytime, for fear of attracting attention. But I groped round; and having found the side next the street, where I could frequently see my children, I stuck the gimlet in and waited for evening. I bored three rows of holes, one above another; then I bored out the interstices between. I thus succeeded in making one hole about an inch long and an inch broad. I sat by it till late into the night, to enjoy the little whiff of air that floated in. In the morning I watched for my children. The first person I saw in the street was Dr. Flint. I had a shuddering, superstitious feeling that it was a bad omen. Several familiar faces passed by. At last I heard the merry laugh of children, and presently two sweet little faces were looking up at me, as though they knew I was there, and were conscious of the joy they imparted. How I longed to *tell* them I was there!

My condition was now a little improved. But for weeks I was tormented by hundreds of little red insects, fine as a needle's point, that pierced through my skin, and produced an intolerable burning. The good grandmother gave me herb teas and cooling medicines, and finally I got rid of them. The heat of my den was intense, for nothing but thin shingles protected me from the scorching summer's sun. But I had my consolations. Through my peeping-hole I could watch the children, and when they were near enough, I could hear their talk. Aunt Nancy brought me all the news she could hear at Dr. Flint's. From her I learned that the doctor had written to New York to a colored woman, who had been born and raised in our neighborhood, and had breathed his contaminating atmosphere. He offered her a reward if she could find out any thing about me. I know not what was the nature of her reply; but he soon after started for New York in haste, saying to his family that he had business of importance to transact. I peeped at him as he passed on his way to the steamboat. It was a satisfaction to have miles of land and water between us, even for a little while; and it was a still greater satisfaction to know that he believed me to be in the Free States. My little den seemed less dreary than it had done. He returned, as he did from his former journey to New York, without obtaining any satisfactory information. When he passed our house next morning, Benny was standing at the gate. He had heard them say that he had gone to find me, and he called out, "Dr. Flint, did you bring my mother home? I want to see her." The doctor stamped his foot at him in a rage, and exclaimed, "Get out of the way, you little damned rascal! If you don't, I'll cut off your head."

Benny ran terrified into the house, saying, "You can't put me in jail again. I don't belong to you now." It was well that the wind carried the words away from the doctor's ear. I told my grandmother of it, when we had our next conference at the trap-door; and begged of her not to allow the children to be impertinent to the irascible old man.

Autumn came, with a pleasant abatement of heat. My eyes had become accustomed to the dim light, and by holding my book or work in a certain position near the aperture I contrived to read and sew. That was a great relief to the tedious monotony of my life. But when winter came, the cold penetrated through the thin shingle roof, and I was dreadfully chilled. The winters there are not so long, or so severe, as in northern latitudes; but the houses are not built to shelter from cold, and my little den was peculiarly comfortless. The kind grandmother brought me bed-clothes and warm drinks. Often I was obliged to lie in bed all day to keep comfortable; but with all my precautions, my shoulders and feet were frostbitten. O, those long, gloomy days, with no object for my eye to rest upon, and no thoughts to occupy my mind, except the dreary past and the uncertain future! I was thankful when there came a day sufficiently mild for me to wrap myself up and sit at the loophole to watch the passers by. Southerners have the habit of stopping and talking in the streets, and I heard many conversations not intended to meet my ears. I heard slave-hunters planning how to catch some poor fugitive. Several times I heard allusions to Dr. Flint, myself, and the history of my children, who, perhaps, were playing near the gate. One would say, "I wouldn't move my little finger to catch her, as old Flint's property." Another would say, "I'll catch *any* nigger for the reward. A man ought to have what belongs to him, if he *is* a damned brute." The opinion was often expressed that I was in the Free States. Very rarely did any one suggest that I might be in the vicinity. Had the least suspicion rested on my grandmother's house, it would have been burned to the ground. But it was the last place they thought of. Yet there was no place, where slavery existed, that could have afforded me so good a place of concealment.

Dr. Flint and his family repeatedly tried to coax and bribe my children to tell something they had heard said about me. One day the doctor took them into a shop, and offered them some bright little silver pieces and gay handkerchiefs if they would tell where their mother was. Ellen shrank away from him, and would not speak; but Benny spoke up, and said, "Dr. Flint, I don't know where my mother is. I guess she's in New York; and when you go there again, I wish you'd ask her to come home, for I want to see her; but if you put her in jail, or tell her you'll cut her head off, I'll tell her to go right back."

CHAPTER XXXI: INCIDENTS IN PHILADELPHIA

I had heard that the poor slave had many friends at the north. I trusted we should find some of them. Meantime, we would take it for granted that all were friends, till they proved to the contrary. I sought out the kind captain, thanked him for his attentions, and told him I should never cease to be grateful for the service he had rendered us. I gave him a message to the friends I had left at home, and he promised to deliver it. We were placed in a row-boat, and in about fifteen minutes were landed on a wood wharf in Philadelphia. As I stood looking round, the friendly captain touched me on the shoulder, and said, "There is a respectable-looking colored man behind you. I will speak to him about the New York trains, and tell him you wish to go directly on." I thanked him, and asked him to direct me to some shops where I could buy gloves and veils. He did so, and said he would talk with the colored man till I returned. I made what haste I could. Constant exercise on board the vessel, and frequent rubbing with salt water, had nearly restored the use of my limbs. The noise of the great city confused me, but I found the shops, and bought some double veils and gloves for Fanny and myself. The shopman told me they were so many levies. I had never heard the word before, but I did not tell him so. I thought if he knew I was a stranger he might ask me where I came from. I gave him a gold piece, and when he returned the change, I counted it, and found out how much a levy was. I made my way back to the wharf, where the captain introduced me to the colored man, as the Rev. Jeremiah Durham, minister of Bethel church. He took me by the hand, as if I had been an old friend. He told us we were too late for the morning cars to New York, and must wait until the evening, or the next morning. He invited me to go home with him, assuring me that his wife would give me a cordial welcome; and for my friend he would provide a home with one of his neighbors. I thanked him for so much kindness to strangers, and told him if I must be detained, I should like to hunt up some people who formerly went from our part of the country. Mr. Durham insisted that I should dine with him, and then he would assist me in finding my friends. The sailors came to bid us good by. I shook their hardy hands, with tears in my eyes. They had all been kind to us, and they had rendered us a greater service than they could possibly conceive of.

I had never seen so large a city, or been in contact with so many people in the streets. It seemed as if those who passed looked at us with an expression of curiosity. My face was so blistered and peeled, by sitting on deck, in wind and sunshine, that I thought they could not easily decide to what nation I belonged.

Mrs. Durham met me with a kindly welcome, without asking any questions. I was tired, and her friendly manner was a sweet refreshment. God bless her! I was sure that she had comforted other weary hearts, before I received her sympathy. She was surrounded by her husband and children, in a home made sacred by protecting laws. I thought of my own children, and sighed.

After dinner Mr. Durham went with me in quest of the friends I had spoken of. They went from my native town, and I anticipated much pleasure in looking on familiar faces. They were not at home, and we retraced our steps through streets delightfully clean. On the way, Mr. Durham observed that I had spoken to him of a daughter I expected to meet; that he was surprised, for I looked so young he had taken me for a single woman. He was approaching a subject on which I was extremely sensitive. He would ask about my husband next, I thought, and if I answered him truly, what would he think of me? I told him I had two children, one in New York and the other at the south. He asked some further questions, and I frankly told him some of the most important events of my life. It was painful for me to do it; but I would not deceive him. If he was desirous of being my friend, I thought he ought to know how far I was worthy of it. "Excuse me, if I have tried your feelings," said he. "I did not question you from idle curiosity. I wanted to understand your situation, in order to know whether I could be of any service to you, or your little girl. Your straight-forward answers do you credit; but don't answer every body so openly. It might give some heartless people a pretext for treating you with contempt."

That word *contempt* burned me like coals of fire. I replied, "God alone knows how I have suffered; and He, I trust, will forgive me. If I am permitted to have my children, I intend to be a good mother, and to live in such a manner that people cannot treat me with contempt."

"I respect your sentiments," said he. "Place your trust in God, and be governed by good principles, and you will not fail to find friends."

When we reached home, I went to my room, glad to shut out the world for a while. The words he had spoken made an indelible impression upon me. They brought up great shadows from the mournful past. In the midst of my meditations I was startled by a knock at the door. Mrs. Durham entered, her face all beaming with kindness, to say that there was an anti-slavery friend down stairs, who would like to see me. I overcame my dread of encountering strangers, and went with her. Many questions were asked concerning my experiences, and my escape from slavery; but I observed how careful they all were not to say any thing that might wound my feelings. How gratifying this was, can be fully understood only by those who have been accustomed to be treated as if they were not included within the pale of human beings. The anti-slavery friend had come to inquire into my plans, and to offer assistance, if needed. Fanny was comfortably established, for the present, with a friend of Mr. Durham. The Anti-Slavery Society agreed to pay her expenses to New York. The same was offered to me, but I declined to accept it; telling them that my grandmother had given me sufficient to pay my expenses to the end of my journey. We were urged to remain in Philadelphia a few days, until some suitable escort could be found for us. I gladly accepted the proposition, for I had a dread of meeting slaveholders, and some dread also of railroads. I had never entered a railroad car in my life, and it seemed to me quite an important event.

That night I sought my pillow with feelings I had never carried to it before. I verily believed myself to be a free woman. I was wakeful for a long time, and I had no sooner fallen asleep, than I was roused by fire-bells. I jumped up, and hurried on my clothes. Where I came from, every body hastened to dress themselves on such occasions. The white people thought a great fire might be used as a good opportunity for insurrection, and that it was best to be in readiness; and the colored people were ordered out to labor in extinguishing the flames. There was but one engine in our town, and colored women and children were often required to drag it to the river's edge and fill it. Mrs. Durham's daughter slept in the same room with me, and seeing that she slept through all the din, I thought it was my duty to wake her. "What's the matter?" said she, rubbing her eyes.

"They're screaming fire in the streets, and the bells are ringing," I replied.

"What of that?" said she, drowsily. "We are used to it. We never get up, without the fire is very near. What good would it do?"

I was quite surprised that it was not necessary for us to go and help fill the engine. I was an ignorant child, just beginning to learn how things went on in great cities.

At daylight, I heard women crying fresh fish, berries, radishes, and various other things. All this was new to me. I dressed myself at an early hour, and sat at the window to watch that unknown tide of life. Philadelphia seemed to me a wonderfully great place. At the breakfast table, my idea of going out to drag the engine was laughed over, and I joined in the mirth.

I went to see Fanny, and found her so well contented among her new friends that she was in no haste to leave. I was also very happy with my kind hostess. She had had advantages for education, and was vastly my superior. Every day, almost every hour, I was adding to my little stock of knowledge. She took me out to see the city as much as she deemed prudent. One day she took me to an artist's room, and showed me the portraits of some of her children. I had never seen any paintings of colored people before, and they seemed to me beautiful.

At the end of five days, one of Mrs. Durham's friends offered to accompany us to New York the following morning. As I held the hand of my good hostess in a parting clasp, I longed to know whether her husband had repeated to her what I had told him. I supposed he had, but she never made any allusion to it. I presume it was the delicate silence of womanly sympathy.

When Mr. Durham handed us our tickets, he said, "I am afraid you will have a disagreeable ride; but I could not procure tickets for the first class cars."

Supposing I had not given him enough money, I offered more. "O, no," said he, "they could not be had for any money. They don't allow colored people to go in the first-class cars."

This was the first chill to my enthusiasm about the Free States. Colored people were allowed to ride in a filthy box, behind white people, at the south, but there they were not required to pay for the privilege. It made me sad to find how the north aped the customs of slavery.

We were stowed away in a large, rough car, with windows on each side, too high for us to look out without standing up. It was crowded with people, apparently of all nations. There were plenty of beds and cradles, containing screaming and kicking babies. Every other man had a cigar or pipe in his mouth, and jugs of whiskey were handed round freely. The fumes of the whiskey and the dense tobacco smoke were sickening to my senses, and my mind was equally nauseated by the coarse jokes and ribald songs around me. It was a very disagreeable ride. Since that time there has been some improvement in these matters.

CHAPTER XXXV: PREJUDICE AGAINST COLOR

It was a relief to my mind to see preparations for leaving the city. We went to Albany in the steamboat Knickerbocker. When the gong sounded for tea, Mrs. Bruce said, "Linda, it is late, and you and baby had better come to the table with me." I replied, "I know it is time baby had her supper, but I had rather not go with you, if you please. I am afraid of being insulted." "O no, not if you are with *me*," she said. I saw several white nurses go with their ladies, and I ventured to do the same. We were at the extreme end of the table. I was no sooner seated, than a gruff voice said, "Get up! You know you are not allowed to sit here." I looked up, and, to my astonishment and indignation, saw that the speaker was a colored man. If his office required him to enforce the by-laws of the boat, he might, at least, have done it politely. I replied, "I shall not get up, unless the captain comes and takes me up." No cup of tea was offered me, but Mrs. Bruce handed me hers and called for another. I looked to see whether the other nurses were treated in a similar manner. They were all properly waited on.

Next morning, when we stopped at Troy for breakfast, every body was making a rush for the table. Mrs. Bruce said, "Take my arm, Linda, and we'll go in together." The landlord heard her, and said, "Madam, will you allow your nurse and baby to take breakfast with my family?" I knew this was to be attributed to my complexion; but he spoke courteously, and therefore I did not mind it.

At Saratoga we found the United States Hotel crowded, and Mr. Bruce took one of the cottages belonging to the hotel. I had thought, with gladness, of going to the quiet of the country, where I should meet few people, but here I found myself in the midst of a swarm of Southerners. I looked round me with fear and trembling, dreading to see some one who would recognize me. I was rejoiced to find that we were to stay but a short time.

We soon returned to New York, to make arrangements for spending the remainder of the summer at Rockaway. While the laundress was putting the clothes in order, I took an opportunity to go over to Brooklyn to see Ellen. I met her going to a grocery store, and the first words she said, were, "O, mother, don't go to Mrs. Hobbs's. Her brother, Mr. Thorne, has come from the south, and may be he'll tell where you are." I accepted the warning. I told her I was going away with Mrs. Bruce the next day, and would try to see her when I came back.

Being in servitude to the Anglo-Saxon race, I was not put into a "Jim Crow car," on our way to Rockaway, neither was I invited to ride through the streets on the top of trunks in a truck; but every where I found the same manifestations of that cruel prejudice, which so discourages the feelings, and represses the energies of the colored people. We reached Rockaway before dark, and put up at the Pavilion—a large hotel, beautifully situated by the sea-side—a great resort of the fashionable world. Thirty or forty nurses were there, of a great variety of nations. Some of the ladies had colored waiting-maids and coachmen, but I was the only nurse tinged with the blood of Africa. When the tea bell rang, I took little Mary and followed the other nurses. Supper was served in a long hall. A young man, who had the ordering of things, took the circuit of the table two or three times, and finally pointed me to a seat at the lower end of it. As there was but one chair, I sat down and took the child in my lap. Whereupon the young man came to me and said, in the blandest manner possible, "Will you please to seat the little girl in the chair, and stand behind it and feed her? After they have done, you will be shown to the kitchen, where you will have a good supper."

This was the climax! I found it hard to preserve my self-control, when I looked round, and saw women who were nurses, as I was, and only one shade lighter in complexion, eyeing me with a defiant look, as if my presence were a contamination. However, I said nothing. I quietly took the child in my arms, went to our room, and refused to go to the table again. Mr. Bruce ordered meals to be sent to the room for little Mary and I. This answered for a few days; but the waiters of the establishment were white, and they soon began to complain, saying they were not hired to wait on negroes. The landlord requested Mr. Bruce to send me down to my meals, because his servants rebelled against bringing them up, and the colored servants of other boarders were dissatisfied because all were not treated alike.

My answer was that the colored servants ought to be dissatisfied with *themselves,* for not having too much self-respect to submit to such treatment; that there was no difference in the price of board for colored and white servants, and there was no justification for difference of treatment. I staid a month after this, and finding I was resolved to stand up for my rights, they concluded to treat me well. Let every colored man and woman do this, and eventually we shall cease to be trampled under foot by our oppressors.

1861

ELIZABETH CADY STANTON (1815–1902)

In March 1851, Elizabeth Cady Stanton met Susan B. Anthony; during the next fifty years, these two women forged both an enduring friendship and a political alliance that profoundly changed the status of women in the United States. Stanton's gift for speaking and writing, combined with Anthony's gift for political organizing, helped make the second half of the nineteenth century a model period of feminist activism.

Born the seventh of eleven children in Johnstown, New York, forty miles northwest of Albany, Elizabeth Cady grew up in comfortable surroundings. Her father was a wealthy landowner, lawyer, and state supreme court judge; her mother was an outspoken member of the community. As a girl, Cady read voraciously, choosing freely from the family library. With her brothers, she studied Greek, mathematics, philosophy, and law.

Following her father's cases, Cady learned about politics. When at the age of eleven she discovered the inequity of property laws for women, she planned to cut the offending document out of her father's law book. Realizing the futility of her deed taught her an important lesson: one must take political action to change laws. Years later, in 1848, Cady successfully lobbied for the New York Married Women's Property Act, the country's first such law.

In 1840, she married Henry Stanton, a prominent abolitionist who introduced her to such luminaries as Theodore Weld, Angelina Grimké Weld, and Sarah Grimké. The Stantons spent their honeymoon at the first World Anti-Slavery Convention in London, where Stanton sided with Lucretia Mott (and against her own husband) in favor of admitting female delegates. Together the two women planned a convention for women's rights.

In 1848, Stanton, Mott, and other feminists organized the Seneca Falls Women's Rights Convention. In 1860 Stanton lectured in favor of liberalized divorce laws; in 1866 she ran as an independent candidate for Congress from New York City. She fought to have the Fourteenth Amendment cover suffrage for women. In language unfortunately tinged with racism, she opposed the Fifteenth Amendment, which granted suffrage to Black men but not to women. In May 1869, Stanton and Anthony organized the National Woman Suffrage Association for ratification of a woman's suffrage amendment. Throughout the 1870s she was a regular lecturer.

In the 1850s and 1860s, Stanton contributed to the movement through her writing, beginning with a column in Amelia Bloomer's Lily. *From 1853 until 1856 she wrote monthly articles for* Una, *a women's rights paper, on child care, education, and dress reform. With Anthony in 1868, Stanton founded and edited* The Revolution, *a magazine whose motto read: "Men, their rights and nothing more; women, their rights and nothing less."*

In the 1880s, Stanton, Susan Anthony, and Matilda Joslyn Gage collaborated on the monumental History of Woman Suffrage, *a six-volume work completed after the deaths of its authors. Stanton and Anthony worked together almost daily, composing what Stanton described as "the united product of two brains."* The Woman's Bible, *Stanton's feminist critique of the Judeo-Christian tradition, became a controversial best-seller when it appeared in 1895. Stanton dedicated her 1898 autobiography,* Eighty Years and More, *to Susan B. Anthony, "my steadfast friend for half a century."*

The speeches included here, edited by Ellen Carol DuBois, mark the beginning and the culmination of Stanton's feminist philosophy. The first was the opening address to the Seneca Falls convention in 1848. The second, "The Solitude of Self," synthesized Stanton's feminist worldview and her insistence on independence. She delivered it in 1892 in Washington, D.C., as president of the National American Woman's Suffrage Association.

ADDRESS DELIVERED AT SENECA FALLS

I should feel exceedingly diffident to appear before you at this time, having never before spoken in public, were I not nerved by a sense of right and duty, did I not feel the time had fully come for the question of woman's wrongs to be laid before the public, did I not believe that woman herself must do this work; for woman alone can understand the height, the depth, the length, and the breadth of her own degradation. Man cannot speak for her, because he has been educated to believe that she differs from him so materially, that he cannot judge of her thoughts, feelings, and opinions by his own. Moral beings can only judge of others by themselves. The moment they assume a different nature for any of their own kind, they utterly fail. . . .

Among the many important questions which have been brought before the public, there is none that more vitally affects the whole human family than that which is technically called Woman's Rights. Every allusion to the degraded and inferior position occupied by women all over the world has been met by scorn and abuse. From the man of highest mental cultivation to the most degraded wretch who staggers in the streets do we meet ridicule, and coarse jests, freely bestowed upon those who dare assert that woman stands by the side of man, his equal, placed here by her God, to enjoy with him the beautiful earth, which is her home as it is his, having the same sense of right and wrong, and looking to the same Being for guidance and support. So long has man exercised tyranny over her, injurious to himself and benumbing to her faculties, that few can nerve themselves to meet the storm; and so long has the chain been about her that she knows not there is a remedy. . . .

As the nations of the earth emerge from a state of barbarism, the sphere of woman gradually becomes wider, but not even under what is thought to be the full blaze of the sun of civilization, is it what God designed it to be. In every country and clime does man assume the responsibility of marking out the path for her to tread. In every country does he regard her as a being inferior to himself, and one whom he is to guide and control. From the Arabian Kerek, whose wife is obliged to steal from her husband to supply the necessities of life; from the Mahometan who forbids pigs, dogs, women and other impure animals, to enter a Mosque, and does not allow a fool, madman or woman to proclaim the hour of prayer; from the German who complacently smokes his meerschaum, while his wife, yoked with the ox, draws the plough through its furrow; from the delectable carpet-knight, who thinks an inferior style of conversation adapted to woman; to the legislator, who considers her incapable of saying what laws shall govern her, is the same feeling manifested. . . .

Let us consider . . . man's superiority, intellectually, morally, physically.

Man's intellectual superiority cannot be a question until woman has had a fair trial. When we shall have had our freedom to find out our own sphere, when we shall have had our colleges, our professions, our trades, for a century, a comparison then may be justly instituted. When woman, instead of being taxed to endow colleges where she is forbidden to enter—instead of forming sewing societies to educate "poor, but pious," young men, shall first educate herself, when she shall be just to herself before she is generous to others; improving the talents God has given her, and leaving her neighbor to do the same for himself, we shall not hear so much about this boasted superiority. . . .

In consideration of man's claim to moral superiority, glance now at our theological seminaries, our divinity students, the long line of descendants from our Apostolic fathers, the immaculate priesthood, and what do we find there? Perfect moral rectitude in every relation of life, a devoted spirit of self-sacrifice, a perfect union of thought, opinion and feeling among those who profess to worship the one God, and whose laws they feel themselves called upon to declare to a fallen race? Far from it. . . . Is the moral and religious life of this class what we might expect from minds said to be fixed on such mighty themes? By no means. . . . The lamentable want of principle among our lawyers, generally, is too well known to need comment. The everlasting backbiting and bickering of our physicians is proverbial. The disgraceful riots at our polls, where man, in performing the highest duty of citizenship, ought surely to be sober-minded, the perfect rowdyism that now characterizes the debates in our national Congress,—all these are great facts which rise up against man's claim for moral superiority. In my opinion, he is infinitely woman's inferior in every moral quality, not by nature, but made so by a false education. In carrying out his own selfishness, man has greatly improved woman's moral nature, but by an almost total shipwreck of his own. Woman has now the noble virtues of the martyr. She is early schooled to self-denial and suffering. But man is not so wholly buried in selfishness that he does not sometimes get a glimpse of the narrowness of his soul, as compared with woman. Then he says, by way of an excuse for his degradation, "God made woman more self-denying than man. It is her nature. It does not cost her as much to give up her wishes, her will, her life, even, as it does him. He is naturally selfish. God made him so."

No, I think not. . . . God's commands rest upon man as well as woman. It is as much his duty to be kind, self-denying and full of good works, as it is hers. As much his duty to absent himself from scenes of violence as it is hers. A place or position that would require the sacrifice of the delicacy and refinement of woman's nature is unfit for man, for these virtues should be as carefully guarded in him as in her. The false ideas that prevail with regard to the purity necessary to constitute the perfect character in woman, and that requisite for man, has done an infinite deal of mischief in the world. I would not have woman less pure, but I would have man more so. I would have the same code of morals for both. . . .

Let us now consider man's claim to physical superiority. Methinks I hear some say, surely, you will not contend for equality here. Yes, we must not give an inch, lest you take an ell. We cannot accord to man even this much, and he has no right to claim it until the fact has been fully demonstrated. . . . We cannot say what the woman might be physically, if the girl were allowed all the freedom of the boy in romping, climbing, swimming, playing whoop and ball. Among some of the Tartar tribes of the present day, women manage a horse, hurl a javelin, hunt wild animals, and fight an enemy as well as a man. The Indian women endure fatigues and carry burdens that some of our fair-faced, soft-handed, moustached young gentlemen would consider quite impossible for them to sustain. The Croatian and Wallachian women perform all the agricultural operations in addition to their domestic labors, and it is no uncommon sight in our cities, to see the German immigrant with his hands in his pockets, walking complacently by the side of his wife, whilst she bears the weight of some huge package or piece of furniture upon her head. Physically, as well as intellectually, it is use that produces growth and development.

But there is a class of objectors who say they do not claim superiority, they merely assert a difference. But you will find by following them up closely, that they soon run this difference into the old groove of superiority. . . .

We have met here to-day to discuss our rights and wrongs, civil and political, and not, as some have supposed, to go into the detail of social life alone. We do not propose to petition the legislature to make our husbands just, generous and courteous, to seat every man at the head of a cradle, and to clothe every woman in male attire. None of these points, however important they may be considered by leading men, will be touched in this Convention. . . .

We are assembled to protest against a form of government, existing without the consent of the governed—to declare our right to be free as man is free, to be represented in the government which we are taxed to support, to have such disgraceful laws as give man the power to chastise and imprison his wife, to take the wages which she earns, the property which she inherits, and, in case of separation, the children of her love; laws which make her the mere dependent on his bounty. It is to protest against such unjust laws as these that we are assembled today, and to have them, if possible, forever erased from our statute-books, deeming them a shame and a disgrace to a Christian republic in the nineteenth century. . . .

And, strange as it may seem to many, we now demand our right to vote according to the declaration of the government under which we live. . . . We have no objection to discuss the question of equality, for we feel that the weight of argument lies wholly with us, but we wish the question of equality kept distinct from the question of rights, for the proof of the one does not determine the truth of the other. All white men in this country have the same rights, however they may differ in mind, body or estate. The right is ours. The question now is, how shall we get possession of what rightfully belongs to us? We should not feel so sorely grieved if no man who had not attained the full stature of a Webster, Clay, Van Buren, or Gerrit Smith could claim the right of the elective franchise. But to have drunkards, idiots, horse-racing, rumselling rowdies, ignorant foreigners, and silly boys fully recognized, while we ourselves are thrust out from all the rights that belong to citizens, it is too grossly insulting to the dignity of woman to be longer quietly submitted to. The right is ours. Have it we must. Use it we will. The pens, the tongues, the fortunes, the indomitable wills of many women are already pledged to secure this right. The great truth, that no just government can be formed without the consent of the governed, we shall echo and re-echo in the ears of the unjust judge, until by continual coming we shall weary him. . . .

But what would woman gain by voting? Men must know the advantages of voting, for they all seem very tenacious about the right. Think you, if woman had a vote in this government, that all those laws affecting her interests would so entirely violate every principle of right and justice? Had woman a vote to give, might not the office-holders and seekers propose some change in her condition? Might not Woman's Rights become as great a question as free soil?

"But you are already represented by your fathers, husbands, brothers and sons?" Let your statute books answer the question. We have had enough of such representation. In nothing is woman's true happiness consulted. Men like to call her an angel—to feed her on what they think sweet food—nourishing her vanity; to make her believe that her organization is so much finer than theirs, that she is not fitted to struggle with the tempests of public life, but needs their care and protection!! Care and protection—such as the wolf gives the lamb—such as the eagle the hare he carries to his eyrie!! Most cunningly he entraps her, and then takes from her all those rights which are dearer to her than life itself—rights which have been baptized in blood—and the maintenance of which is even now rocking to their foundations the kingdoms of the Old World.

The most discouraging, the most lamentable aspect our cause wears is the indifference, indeed, the contempt, with which women themselves regard the movement. Where the subject is introduced, among those even who claim to be intelligent and educated, it is met by the scornful curl of the lip, and by expression of ridicule and disgust. But we shall hope better things of them when they are enlightened in regard to their present position. When women know the laws and constitutions under which they live, they will not publish their degradation by declaring themselves satisfied, nor their ignorance, by declaring they have all the rights they want. . . .

Let woman live as she should. Let her feel her accountability to her Maker. Let her know that her spirit is fitted for as high a sphere as man's, and that her soul requires food as pure and exalted as his. Let her live *first* for God, and she will not make imperfect man an object of reverence and awe. Teach her her responsibility as a being of conscience and reason, that all earthly support is weak and unstable, that her only safe dependence is the arm of omnipotence, and that true happiness springs from duty accomplished. Thus will she learn the lesson of individual responsibility for time and eternity. That neither father, husband, brother, or son, however willing they may be, can discharge her high duties of life, or stand in her stead when called into the presence of the great Searcher of Hearts at the last day. . . .

Let me here notice one of the greatest humbugs of the day, which has long found for itself the most valuable tool in woman—"The Education Society." The idea to me, is simply absurd, for women, in their present degradation and ignorance, to form sewing societies for the education of young men for the ministry. An order of beings above themselves, claiming to be gifted with superior powers, having all the avenues to learning, wealth and distinction thrown freely open to them, who, if they had but the energy to avail themselves of all these advantages, could easily secure an education for themselves, while woman herself, poor, friendless, robbed of all her rights, oppressed on all sides, civilly, religiously and socially, must needs go ignorant herself. Now, is not the idea preposterous, for such a being to educate a great, strong, lazy man, by working day and night with her needle, stitch, stitch, and the poor widow always throws in her mite, being taught to believe that all she gives for the decoration of churches and their black-coated gentry, is given unto the Lord. I think a man, who, under such conditions, has the moral hardihood to take an education at the hands of woman, and at such an expense to her, should, as soon as he graduates, with all his honors thick upon him, take the first ship for Turkey, and there pass his days in earnest efforts to rouse the inmates of the harems to a true sense of their degradation, and not, as is his custom, immediately enter our pulpits to tell us of his superiority to us, "weaker vessels,"—his prerogative to command, ours to obey, his duty to preach, ours to keep silence. . . . The last time when an appeal of this kind was made to me, I told the young girl that I would send her to school a year, if she would go, but I would never again give one red cent to the Education Society. And I do hope that every Christian woman, who has the least regard for her sex, will make the same resolve. We have worked long enough for man, and at a most unjust and unwarrantable sacrifice of self, yet he gives no evidence of gratitude, but has, thus far, treated his benefactors with scorn, ridicule and neglect. . . .

One common objection to this movement is, that if the principles of freedom and equality which we advocate were put into practice, it would destroy all harmony in the domestic circle. Here let me ask, how many truly harmonious households have we now? . . . The only happy households we now see are those in which husband and wife share equally in counsel and government. There can be no true dignity or independence where there is subordination to the absolute will of another, no happiness without freedom. Let us then have no fears that the movement will disturb what is seldom found, a truly united and happy family. . . .

There seems now to be a kind of moral stagnation in our midst. Philanthropists have done their utmost to rouse the nation to a sense of its sins. . . . Our churches are multiplying on all sides, our missionary societies, Sunday schools, and prayer meetings and innumerable charitable and reform organizations are all in operation, but still the tide of vice is swelling, and threatens the destruction of everything, and the battlements of righteousness are weak against the raging elements of sin and death. Verily, the world waits the coming of some new element, some purifying power, some spirit of mercy and love. The voice of woman has been silenced in the state, the church, and the home, but man cannot fulfill his destiny alone, he cannot redeem his race unaided. There are deep and tender chords of sympathy and love in the heart of the down-fallen and oppressed that woman can touch more skillfully than man. The world has never yet seen a truly great and virtuous nation, because in the degradation of woman the very fountains of life are poisoned at their source. It is vain to look for silver and gold from mines of copper and lead. It is the wise mother that has the wise son. So long as your women are slaves you may throw your colleges and churches to the winds. . . . Truly are the sins of the fathers visited upon the children to the third and fourth generation. God, in his wisdom, has so linked the whole human family together that any violence done at one end of the chain is felt throughout its length, and here, too, is the law of restoration, as in woman all have fallen, so in her elevation shall the race be recreated.

. . . We do not expect our path will be strewn with the flowers of popular applause, but over the thorns of bigotry and prejudice will be our way, and on our banners will beat the dark storm-clouds of opposition from those who have entrenched themselves behind the stormy bulwarks of custom and authority, and who have fortified their position by every means, holy and unholy. But we will steadfastly abide the result. Unmoved we will bear it aloft. Undaunted we will unfurl it to the gale, for we know that the storm cannot rend from it a shred, that the electric flash will but more clearly show to us the glorious words inscribed upon it, "Equality of Rights."

1848

THE SOLITUDE OF SELF

The point I wish plainly to bring before you on this occasion is the individuality of each human soul; our Protestant idea, the right of individual conscience and judgment; our republican idea, individual citizenship. In discussing the rights of woman, we are to consider, first, what belongs to her as an individual, in a world of her own, the arbiter of her own destiny, an imaginary Robinson Crusoe, with her woman, Friday, on a solitary island. Her rights under such circumstances are to use all her faculties for her own safety and happiness.

Secondly, if we consider her as a citizen, as a member of a great nation, she must have the same rights as all other members, according to the fundamental principles of our Government.

Thirdly, viewed as a woman, an equal factor in civilization, her rights and duties are still the same—individual happiness and development.

Fourthly, it is only the incidental relations of life, such as mother, wife, sister, daughter, which may involve some special duties and training. . . .

The strongest reason for giving woman all the opportunities for higher education, for the full development of her faculties, her forces of mind and body; for giving her the most enlarged freedom of thought and action; a complete emancipation from all forms of bondage, of custom, dependence, superstition; from all the crippling influences of fear—is the solitude and personal responsibility of her own individual life. The strongest reason why we ask for woman a voice in the government under which she lives; in the religion she is asked to believe; equality in social life, where she is the chief factor; a place in the trades and professions, where she may earn her bread, is because of her birthright to self-sovereignty; because, as an individual, she must rely on herself. No matter how much women prefer to lean, to be protected and supported, nor how much men desire to have them do so, they must make the voyage of life alone, and for safety in an emergency, they must know something of the laws of navigation. To guide our own craft, we must be captain, pilot, engineer; with chart and compass to stand at the wheel; to watch the winds and waves, and know when to take in the sail, and to read the signs in the firmament over all. It matters not whether the solitary voyager is man or woman; nature, having endowed them equally, leaves them to their own skill and judgment in the hour of danger, and, if not equal to the occasion, alike they perish.

To appreciate the importance of fitting every human soul for independent action, think for a moment of the immeasurable solitude of self. We come into the world alone, unlike all who have gone before us, we leave it alone, under circumstances peculiar to ourselves. No mortal ever has been, no mortal ever will be like the soul just launched on the sea of life. There can never again be just such a combination of prenatal influences; never again just such environments as make up the infancy, youth and manhood of this one. Nature never repeats herself, and the possibilities of one human soul will never be found in another. No one has ever found two blades of ribbon grass alike, and no one will ever find two human beings alike. Seeing, then, what must be the infinite diversity in human character, we can in a measure appreciate the loss to a nation when any large class of the people is uneducated and unrepresented in the government.

We ask for the complete development of every individual, first, for his own benefit and happiness. In fitting out an army, we give each soldier his own knapsack, arms, powder, his blanket, cup, knife, fork and spoon. We provide alike for all their individual necessities; then each man bears his own burden.

Again, we ask complete individual development for the general good; for the consensus of the competent on the whole round of human interests, on all questions of national life; and here each man must bear his share of the general burden. It is sad to see how soon friendless children are left to bear their own burdens, before they can analyze their feelings; before they can even tell their joys and sorrows, they are thrown on their own resources. The great lesson that nature seems to teach us at all ages is self-dependence, self-protection, self-support. . . .

In youth our most bitter disappointments, our brightest hopes and ambitions, are known only to ourselves. Even our friendship and love we never fully share with another; there is something of every passion, in every situation, we conceal. Even so in our triumphs and our defeats. . . .

We ask no sympathy from others in the anxiety and agony of a broken friendship or shattered love. When death sunders our nearest ties, alone we sit in the shadow of our affliction. Alike amid the greatest triumphs and darkest tragedies of life, we walk alone. On the divine heights of human attainment, eulogized and worshipped as a hero or saint, we stand alone. In ignorance, poverty and vice, as a pauper or criminal, alone we starve or steal; alone we suffer the sneers and rebuffs of our fellows; alone we are hunted and hounded through dark courts and alleys, in by-ways and high-ways; alone we stand in the judgment seat; alone in the prison cell we lament our crimes and misfortunes; alone we expiate them on the gallows. In hours like these we realize the awful solitude of individual life, its pains, its penalties, its responsibilities; hours in which the youngest and most helpless are thrown on their own resources for guidance and consolation. Seeing, then, that life must ever be a march and a battle, that each soldier must be equipped for his own protection, it is the height of cruelty to rob the individual of a single natural right.

To throw obstacles in the way of a complete education is like putting out the eyes; to deny the rights of property is like cutting off the hands. To refuse political equality is to rob the ostracized of all self-respect; of credit in the market place, of recompense in the world of work, of a voice in choosing those who make and administer the law, a choice in the jury before whom they are tried, and in the judge who decides their punishment. [Think of] . . . woman's position! Robbed of her natural rights, handicapped by law and custom at every turn, yet compelled to fight her own battles, and in the emergencies of life to fall back on herself for protection. . . .

The young wife and mother, at the head of some establishment, with a kind husband to shield her from the adverse winds of life, with wealth, fortune and position, has a certain harbor of safety, secure against the ordinary ills of life. But to manage a household, have a desirable influence in society, keep her friends and the affections of her husband, train her children and servants well, she must have rare common sense, wisdom, diplomacy, and a knowledge of human nature. To do all this, she needs the cardinal virtues and the strong points of character that the most successful statesman possesses. An uneducated woman trained to dependence, with no resources in herself, must make a failure of any position in life. But society says women do not need a knowledge of the world, the liberal training that experience in public life must give, all the advantages of collegiate education; but when for the lack of all this, the woman's happiness is wrecked, alone she bears her humiliation; and the solitude of the weak and the ignorant is indeed pitiable. In the wild chase for the prizes of life, they are ground to powder.

In age, when the pleasures of youth are passed, children grown up, married and gone, the hurry and bustle of life in a measure over, when the hands are weary of active service, when the old arm chair and the fireside are the chosen resorts, then men and women alike must fall back on their own resources. If they cannot find companionship in books, if they have no interest in the vital questions of the hour, no interest in watching the consummation of reforms with which they might have been identified, they soon pass into their dotage. The more fully the faculties of the mind are developed and kept in use, the longer the period of vigor and active interest in all around us continues. If, from a life-long participation in public affairs, a woman feels responsible for the laws regulating our system of education, the discipline of our jails and prisons, the sanitary condition of our private homes, public buildings and thoroughfares, an interest in commerce, finance, our foreign relations, in any or all these questions, her solitude will at least be respectable, and she will not be driven to gossip or scandal for entertainment.

The chief reason for opening to every soul the doors to the whole round of human duties and pleasures is the individual development thus attained, the resources thus provided under all circumstances to mitigate the solitude that at times must come to everyone.

. . . Inasmuch, then, as woman shares equally the joys and sorrows of time and eternity, is it not the height of presumption in man to propose to represent her at the ballot box and the throne of grace, to do her voting in the state, her praying in the church, and to assume the position of high priest at the family altar?

Nothing strengthens the judgment and quickens the conscience like individual responsibility. Nothing adds such dignity to character as the recognition of one's self-sovereignty; the right to an equal place, everywhere conceded—a place earned by personal merit, not an artificial attainment by inheritance, wealth, family and position. Conceding, then, that the responsibilities of life rest equally on man and woman, that their destiny is the same, they need the same preparation for time and eternity. The talk of sheltering woman from the fierce storms of life is the sheerest mockery, for they beat on her from every point of the compass, just as they do on man, and with more fatal results, for he has been trained to protect himself, to resist, and to conquer. Such are the facts in human experience, the responsibilities of individual sovereignty. Rich and poor, intelligent and ignorant, wise and foolish, virtuous and vicious, man and woman; it is ever the same, each soul must depend wholly on itself.

Whatever the theories may be of woman's dependence on man, in the supreme moments of her life, he cannot bear her burdens. Alone she goes to the gates of death to give life to every man that is born into the world; no one can share her fears, no one can mitigate her pangs; and if her sorrow is greater than she can bear, alone she passes beyond the gates into the vast unknown.

From the mountain-tops of Judea long ago, a heavenly voice bade his disciples, "Bear ye one another's burdens"; but humanity has not yet risen to that point of self-sacrifice, and if ever so willing, how few the burdens are that one soul can bear for another! . . .

So it ever must be in the conflicting scenes of life, in the long, weary march, each one walks alone. We may have many friends, love, kindness, sympathy and charity, to smooth our pathway in everyday life, but in the tragedies and triumphs of human experience, each mortal stands alone.

But when all artificial trammels are removed, and women are recognized as individuals, responsible for their own environments, thoroughly educated for all positions in life they may be called to fill; with all the resources in themselves that liberal thought and broad culture can give; guided by their own conscience and judgment, trained to self-protection, by a healthy development of the muscular system, and skill in the use of weapons and defence; and stimulated to self-support by a knowledge of the business world and the pleasure that pecuniary independence must ever give; when women are trained in this way, they will in a measure be fitted for those hours of solitude that come alike to all, whether prepared or otherwise. As in our extremity we must depend on ourselves, the dictates of wisdom point to complete individual development.

In talking of education, how shallow the argument that each class must be educated for the special work it proposes to do, and that all those faculties not needed in this special work must lie dormant and utterly wither for want of use, when, perhaps, these will be the very faculties needed in life's greatest emergencies! Some say, "Where is the use of drilling girls in the languages, the sciences, in law, medicine, theology. As wives, mothers, housekeepers, cooks, they need a different curriculum from boys who are to fill all positions. The chief cooks in our great hotels and ocean steamers are men. In our large cities, men run the bakeries; they make our bread, cake and pies. They manage the laundries; they are now considered our best milliners and dressmakers. Because some men fill these departments of usefulness, shall we regulate the curriculum in Harvard and Yale to their present necessities? If not, why this talk in our best colleges of a curriculum for girls who are crowding into the trades and professions, teachers in all our public schools, rapidly filling many lucrative and honorable positions in life?"

. . . Women are already the equals of men in the whole realm of thought, in art, science, literature and government. . . . The poetry and novels of the century are theirs, and they have touched the keynote of reform, in religion, politics and social life. They fill the editor's and professor's chair, plead at the bar of justice, walk the wards of the hospital, speak from the pulpit and the platform. Such is the type of womanhood that an enlightened public sentiment welcomes to-day, and such the triumph of the facts of life over the false theories of the past.

Is it, then, consistent to hold the developed woman of this day within the same narrow political limits as the dame with the spinning wheel and knitting needle occupied in the past? No, no! Machinery has taken the labors of woman as well as man on its tireless shoulders; the loom and the spinning wheel are but dreams of the past; the pen, the brush, the easel, the chisel, have taken their places, while the hopes and ambitions of women are essentially changed.

We see reason sufficient in the outer conditions of human beings for individual liberty and development, but when we consider the self-dependence of every human soul, we see the need of courage, judgment and the exercise of every faculty of mind and body, strengthened and developed by use, in woman as well as man.

Whatever may be said of man's protecting power in ordinary conditions, amid all the terrible disasters by land and sea, in the supreme moments of danger, alone woman must ever meet the horrors of the situation. The Angel of Death even makes no royal pathway for her. Man's love and sympathy enter only into the sunshine of our lives. In that solemn solitude of self, that links us with the immeasurable and the eternal, each soul lives alone forever. A recent writer says: "I remember once, in crossing the Atlantic, to have gone upon the deck of the ship at midnight, when a dense black cloud enveloped the sky, and the great deep was roaring madly under the lashes of demoniac winds. My feeling was not of danger or fear (which is a base surrender of the immortal soul) but of utter desolation and loneliness; a little speck of life shut in by a tremendous darkness. . . ."

And yet, there is a solitude which each and every one of us has always carried with him, more inaccessible than the ice-cold mountains, more profound than the midnight sea; the solitude of self. Our inner being which we call ourself, no eye nor touch of man or angel has ever pierced. It is more hidden than the caves of the gnome; the sacred adytum of the oracle; the hidden chamber of Eleusinian mystery, for to it only omniscience is permitted to enter.

Such is individual life. Who, I ask you, can take, dare take on himself the rights, the duties, the responsibilities of another human soul?

1892

ALICE CARY (1820–1871)

Alice Cary was well known in the nineteenth century for her poetry and her fiction. Both she and her sister, Phoebe, published poetry while still in their teens, their work appearing primarily in magazines and newspapers of their home city, Cincinnati. Alice Cary's early verses were praised by Edgar Allan Poe and John Greenleaf Whittier, who wrote a poem about her titled "The Singer." Horace Greeley, a lifelong friend, included her in his volume Eminent Women of the Age, *published in 1869.*

Like "Having Our Way," a number of Alice Cary's stories portray sisters, and many combine real events with dreamlike sequences that explore the psyches of her characters. Her stories often focus on women trapped in bad marriages or disappointed by the limitations of their lives. Cary's characters live hard, often cheerless lives.

Born near the village of Mount Healthy, Ohio, Cary used this rural area as the basis for the town of Clovernook, the recurring setting for her fiction. She began publishing fiction in Cincinnati publications and then, in 1850, moved with her sister to New York, where they supported themselves by writing. In the 1850s and 1860s, Alice and Phoebe Cary's Sunday evening literary salons attracted writers and artists as well as abolitionists and feminists. Alice Cary served as president of the first woman's club in America, later called Sororsis, which was formed to provide support for women interested in the arts and literature. Turning down offers of marriage, Cary lived with her sister until Phoebe's death.

Clovernook; or, Recollections of Our Neighborhood in the West, *the first of Alice Cary's short-story collections, established her as a fiction writer. She went on to write three novels, further books of sketches, and short stories, as well as volumes of poetry. Throughout the 1850s, Cary wrote a weekly poem for the* New York Ledger, *to which she also contributed short stories and satirical pieces. In the last two decades of her life, Cary was published in a wide range of periodicals, including the* Overland Monthly, *edited by Bret Harte.*

In her preface to Clovernook; or, Recollections of Our Neighborhood in the West, *Cary discusses briefly her role as a writer; she explains she is writing in part to capture the essence of a community before it changed. In her own way, she is a historian: "In the interior of my state," she writes, "which was a wilderness when first my father went to it, and is now crowned with a dense and prosperous population, there is surely as much in the simple manners, and in the little histories every day revealed, to interest us in humanity." Claiming to be more a witness than an artist, she also hopes to reveal the nature of rural, agrarian life to her readers in cities. As readers, we can see that she is doing far more than recording a regional history: she is also exploring the consciousness of female characters, many of whom are unloved, neglected, haunted by loneliness or death.*

"Having Our Way," published in Clovernook Children *in 1854, reveals this dark side of Cary's realism. For Cary, even childhood is fraught with dangers. The sequence of disappointments the sisters experience is a sad coming-of-age for them, while the figure of Peter foreshadows the more ominous males encountered by Cary's adult women characters.*

■ HAVING OUR WAY

The harvesters were busy with mowing; it was a bright, sunshiny day, but whether June or July, I don't remember; the roses were all gone from the bushes, I know, and the little brown bird, that had her nest in the sweet-brier, was teaching her young ones to fly. Rosalie, my older sister, whose eyes and hair were blacker than a crow's, had climbed on a chair, against the window by the brier-bush, and was watching the old bird as she fluttered in and out of the bush, twittering and chirping, as if she said to the young ones, "Come, you can fly as well as I can!"

All at once Rosalie clapped her hands, and called me to see; one of the little birds had made its way through the bush, and was fluttering right against the window. I ran, but had only caught an imperfect view of it, when the gray cat, that had been watching under the bush, leaped nimbly up, and the little bird was gone.

The old bird flew in and out from her nest, and hopped to the ground, and then to the fence, and then up in the tree, making a noise as if she were crying—for it was unlike any singing she had ever done before.

As fast as we could we ran out of the house, and, lying flat on the ground, lifted up the long limbs of the bush, and looked under. We were too late; there stood the cat, twisting her tail, and beating the ground with it, as she held down the bird with one paw—its little wings outspread and quite still. Rosalie cried, and she well might cry, for it was piteous to see the little dead bird, and to hear the moaning of the mother.

We brought crumbs and scattered them on the ground, but she would not pick them as she had done many a time before. Poor thing! in her anguish she seemed to quite forget that there were living birds in the nest that she must care for still. I think it was to divert our attention, and to pacify us, that our mother called to us that she wished a coffee-pot of water carried to the meadow. Wiping our eyes, we tied on our sunbonnets, and were soon on the way, the water standing in bright drops on the coffee-pot's lid and sides.

It was a deep, narrow path in which we walked, one right behind the other, and saying nothing, for we were both thinking very sadly of the dead bird. Another time we would have walked on the short, cool grass, that, sprinkled with yellow dandelions, grew along each side of the hot, dusty path; but now we were not thinking of our own comfort at all.

The hay-makers saw us as soon as we reached the fence, and, placing the coffee-pot in the shade of a large stump, to keep the water cool, we sat down in the edge of the meadow, and waited for their approach. We could hear the strokes, and see the grass falling very fast before their scythes, which never once did they stop to whet, but bending low, and step by step, they came nearer and nearer. On reaching the place, one of them said that we were little women, I remember; and another told Rosalie that at home he had a little girl with eyes and hair as black as hers; and another—a brawny-armed man, with drops of sweat among his gray whiskers, who drank the most, and seemed to enjoy it the most—said, as he drew a long breath, and turned the coffee-pot bottom side up, that he could tell us where we could fill it with berries, and that we deserved so much for our pains.

We forgot the gray cat and the poor bird, and were in a moment tripping lightly over the green swaths, smelling sweet in the sunshine. Peter, whom I have mentioned before, was loading the hay that was made, and already there was such a great heap of it in the rack, that the horses drawing the wagon were almost hidden by it. Very smooth and even he laid it, all around, for Peter had skill in some things, if not in others. He told us that there were bushels and bushels of berries on the vines, and that we would have no difficulty in filling the coffee-pot by the time he should get a full load on, and that then we might ride home on the top, which pleased us very much; but as we hurried toward the meadowside next the woods, where the blackberry-vines were, he called after us, saying we must be very careful, for he expected likely enough there were a hundred snakes there—thus making us as uncomfortable as possible. It was always the way with Peter, if he made us happy in one way, he made us unhappy in another. At first we were afraid, and kept along the edges of the "patch," as we called it. There were not so many berries as Peter had said, but there were a good many, and we picked industriously, and at last had partly filled the pot, and were about to start toward home, for our fingers were full of little thorns that made them ache, and our faces were scratched badly, when Peter, who had taken one load of hay into the barn and was come for another, leaving his team, came to assist us. In a few minutes he had trodden paths for us in deep among the briers, where the berries were large and ripe, so that we forgot the thorns and the scratches, and picked with new energy and far more success.

We had the coffee-pot filled so that we could not shut the lid down, in a little while, and were making our way out of the briers, talking of what nice pies we should have the next day, when Peter called to us, "Look here!" and, turning toward him, we saw that he was running toward us, with a great black snake dangling from his pitchfork. We were terribly frightened, as may be supposed, and, as we ran, spilled the berries so carefully gathered. He called us to stop, saying the snake was dead. It was long before we could be persuaded to do so; but at length he threw it across the fence, and seemed so heartily sorry for what he had done, that we tried to still the beating of our hearts, and gather up the berries from the ground. He aided us with right good will, and gathered other berries from the vines, until we had quite as many as at first. He then coaxed us to go close to the snake, then hanging limberly over the fence. We were afraid to go very near, though it was dead, and not quite dead either, for its slim, bluish tail moved, though its small head was mashed flat, and its white belly spotted with blood. Then Peter took it in his hands, and put it around his neck, to show us that he was not afraid, and that it could not hurt us. Afterward he lifted us up to the top of the load of hay, and told us, if we would not tell about his scaring us, he would take us to town the next morning, and that we might sell our berries for money enough to buy us each a new dress, perhaps. Of course, we were delighted, and promised Peter that we would not tell, but that he must ask if we might go. He knew that it had not been right to frighten us, and though we assured him we would not say anything about it, he kept repeating over and over, "Now you won't—now you mustn't say a word about it—if you do, I will not take you to town."

There was no need of his fear; we could not have been hired for a thousand dollars to tell it, for that would have been a small thing compared to going to market with Peter, and buying dresses with the money we had earned ourselves. We were little girls, I don't know precisely how old, but somewhere about ten years, I should think, and Rosalie twelve; I had been to town once, and she never. In her fancy, she pictured it like places we read of in Fairy-land; and, indeed, it was a scene of wonderful beauty, even to me. I supposed that the people who lived there were a great deal happier than we, having almost everything they wanted. Once my mother had taken me there with her, and bought me some cakes, and showed me the outside of the Museum, and a great big building, with a fine yard, and trees about it, where she said children lived whose fathers and mothers were dead. I thought they must be happy, whether they had anybody to love them or not; I have learned better since.

Peter was very eloquent in our behalf, and I need not say that we pleaded our own cases very earnestly. Peter would take good care of us, we knew; and, besides, we could take care of ourselves; and we were sure we wanted to see something, some time in our lives; then we could sell our berries, and get something, and we could see the town, and go to Aunt Wilton's; and we finished every sentence with, "Come, mother, let us go!" Peter said we would be just as safe as we would be in our beds; that he would engage to bring us home well and hearty; that it would afford us more pleasure, maybe, than it would to go to London, when we were big—which was very true. So, at last, quite against her judgment I think, she said, if we would promise to be right good girls, we might go, but that Peter must not set out until daylight.

Perhaps there were never two happier children in the world than we were that night; we were helping mother, and helping Peter, and helping everybody—now gathering plantain leaves to lay over the basket of butter that was to be done up in white cloths and hung down in the well until morning; now assisting Peter to put the tar on the wheels of the little market wagon; now combing our hair, though we were yet to sleep a night, and knew it would be of no use; and now examining our nice shoes and dresses, to see that all was right. Our berries we spread out in two large, flat milk-pans, and set out in the dew, to keep as nice and fresh as possible. Afterward we went with Peter to the orchard, and when he shook down the yellow apples from what we called the early tree, we gathered them in baskets, until we had two or three bushels of them. Nine o'clock had never come so soon, but when the preparations were done, the time passed very slowly, and it seemed to us that the morning would be long in coming. When Peter got the cup of hot water, and the razor,—for he shaved his face every week when he went to market, though he had no beard,—we told him to hurry, as if that would make it time to go any sooner.

We went to bed at last, having all our things hung over chairs, ready to put on in the morning; and, guessing at the amount of money we should get for the berries, and planning what we should do with it, we fell asleep.

"Come, girls, are you going to town?" said our mother, coming close to the bed with a lighted candle in her hand. "Yes!" we said, and were both wide awake and dressing ourselves in a minute. We could hear the rattling of the harness, and the treading of the horses, and knew that Peter was "hitching up," and trembled lest he should go and leave us; but he did not, and we were soon sitting, side by side, on the straw that filled the wagonbed, with baskets of apples, butter, blackberries and all.

There were no signs of daylight yet, for Peter had started sooner than he said, and a smart sough of wind put the candle out just as our mother said good-by, but not until I had seen how thoughtful and uneasy she looked about us. We passed several market wagons on the way, but none passed us, for Peter was a fast driver, and, indeed, would have been quite ashamed to have anybody's horses surpass his. We had gone down a long hill, over which was a very bad road, with only a narrow strip of the woods cut away, where Peter told us a man had been seen walking without any head, and then we came into a flat open valley, where there was a creek, with a covered bridge over it, before we saw the white daylight sprinkled along the eastern hills. Then the houses began to be closer together, and finer than they were where we lived, and Rosalie and I wished each one we passed was our home. I remember the blue gate-posts before one house, the winding walk that went up to another, and the white porch, full of pots and flowers, that fronted another. Peter told us who lived in those places, and that the owners were very rich, describing their wealth as greater than it really was, I suspect, as if in some way it were an honor to him to know anything of men possessing an extraordinary amount of money.

The sun was not yet risen when we rode into town, crossed two or three canal bridges, passed along a common, and through several streets, into a wide one, where the market was held. The market-house itself was a long low building, roofed over, but open at the sides, and furnished with continuous rows of stalls, for meat and vegetables. On each side of this, and close against the sidewalk, stood the wagons of the country people, from one end of which the horses were eating oats and corn, with their harnesses on, while at the other stood men, women and children, selling eggs, and butter, and apples, and cheese and berries, and home-made yarn and stockings, and many other things, which I need not mention.

Peter soon backed his wagon into a little space between two others, and, unharnessing the horses, gave them their bait of corn and of fresh clover.

Rosalie and I took the leaves from the top of the basket of berries, and, placing them in full view, waited for somebody to buy. We supposed they would all be taken in a minute, and that we could get for them almost any price we chose to ask, for Peter had told us so. But, on the contrary, one after another went past, and scarcely looked at our berries when we said they were fifteen cents a quart. All about us there were berries that looked fresher and nicer than ours, and those who had them, sold them too. At first we cared very little for this, so many things did we see to amuse us; for the street was thronged with people of all colors, and ages, and conditions. At last a fat gentleman, who wore a white waistcoat and a gold chain and spectacles, and who had a negro man behind him carrying a great willow basket, and two square tin pails, with lids, stopped, and, smiling, said, "How do you do, my little friends?" And then he asked us if we had ever been to town before, and said he supposed we intended to buy everybody out! No, we said, we only expected to get new dresses. "Ah!" he replied, "then you mean to put the rest of your money in the bank." We didn't know of any banks but the clay ones at home, and we knew we were not going to bury our money there; so we said, "No, sir!" and that was all. "Well, then," said he, "if you don't want to buy out the town, nor put your money in the bank, why do you ask a thousand dollars for a quart of your berries?" Of course, we told him we did not ask a thousand dollars a quart, but only fifteen cents. "Well, my little girls, I'll tell you what I'll do," and, taking out a purse of red netted silk, through which gold and silver shone temptingly, he selected two ten-cent pieces, and, offering one to each of us, said he would give us so much for all the berries we had. We hesitated, and the black man said, "If massa guv you dat, you better 'cept, case dere de wust berries any whars bout."

"They are just like all country folks," said the man in the white waistcoat, who kept eating our berries all the while he stood by us; "they want to get three times as much as a thing is worth; the berries grow while they are asleep, and they ask as much as if they had worked a year to make them"; and so he went along, seeming vexed, and saying, at the last, "My little ladies, your berries taste too much of the silver I'm afraid."

When he was gone, we said we didn't like him as well as we did the man who had told us where to find the berries, though he wore a tow string, instead of a gold chain, to his watch.

Peter had sold all he had to sell long ago, and had left us to dispose of our berries, while he went to buy sugar, and coffee, and tea, and other things to take home, and when he returned, he was to go with us to buy the new dresses.

The sun broke through the mist that obscured it at first, and shone out hot; the horses switched the flies, and drooped their heads, slavering at the mouth, and turning their ears back as though they were tired and mad; and from the loss of sleep, and having had no breakfast, and the jolting ride, we were tired, and began to be discouraged too. The people had mostly bought their marketing and gone home, and though we only asked ten cents a quart for our berries, nobody offered to buy them.

Almost directly facing the wagon there stood a little frame house, painted white, and having green blinds; and fronting it was a yard, not much larger than the coverlet on our bed at home, and here grew a cedar-tree; and the paved walk, leading from the front door to the gate, topped with green, divided and ran on either side of the tree, which kept it from running straight. It was a brick walk, washed red and clean; but, though it looked so nice, an old lady came out and began sweeping it. We thought what a beautiful place it was, and how well we should like to live there, where we could see all the people that came to market; and that little yard and one cedar-tree seemed to us better than all our fields and thick woods at home.

Particularly, we noticed the lady who was sweeping, so tidy and motherly and kind she looked. She was short and thick, and wore a plain cap of thin muslin over her gray hair, and a dress of drab-colored stuff, and a white neckerchief, crossed and pinned smoothly over her bosom.

When she had brushed the walk quite down to the gate, she shook the dust from the broom and looked into the street for a minute. Presently she went back into the house, and directly came out again with a little tin basin in her hand, as if it might be for our berries; and, sure enough, that it was.

When I told her how much we asked for them, she replied, "Thee asks too much, and unless thee sell as others sell, thee will have to take thy berries home." She then offered us a twenty-five cent piece for all we had, and, seeing the people were mostly gone out of the market, we poured them into her basin and took the money. We were disappointed, at first, for we knew that was not enough to buy even one dress; but after a time we began to think what we could buy, and so we climbed out of the wagon and walked along the street.

We had not gone far when we saw an old woman standing by a table, on which were gingercakes and a keg of beer, and tumblers to drink it from. We thought she must be a very nice person, for she asked all the country people to have some of her cakes and beer, which many of them did. We looked wistfully, I dare say, as we saw the beer foaming up in the tumblers, and the hungry men breaking open the round, yellow cakes. "Come, dears, won't you have some too?" she said, filling two tumblers, and reaching them toward us. "What good folks there are in town!" we thought, and, thanking her, we drank the beer, and were turning away, when all at once she seized us each by the arm, saying, "What do you mean, you little wretches! would you steal my beer?"

We fancied ourselves thrust into a dark jail, and starving to death, for we were almost frightened out of our senses, and, laying on the table all the money we had, we ran back to the market wagon as fast as we could, glad to escape with our lives.

The horses were harnessed, and Peter was waiting for us to go and buy the new dresses; but we could buy no new dresses, nor anything else, for the woman had kept all our money; and so we learned that people may offer us beer, or anything else, and expect to be paid for it after all.

Peter had just taken up the reins to start home, saying, we were little fools to give her all the money, when Aunt Wilton came along, carrying a basket not larger than my two hands. She said we must go home with her, but it seemed to me she didn't want us to go all the time. When she went on, Peter said we must go and get some breakfast, or we would be sick, and if she didn't want us, why, he didn't care.

So, feeling uncomfortable, and the more for what he had said, we went to breakfast with Aunt Wilton. About the visit, and whom we met there, and the end of it, I will tell you in another story.

But you will see, from what I have written, that it would have been better if we had taken our mother's advice, and staid at home.

1854

FRANCES ELLEN WATKINS HARPER (1825–1911)

Frances Watkins Harper was a writer, lecturer, and spokesperson in the forefront of the nineteenth-century Black and women's movements. She was a poet of remarkable skill and achievement as well as the author of a novel and a number of short stories.

Frances Ellen Watkins was born free in the slaveholding state of Maryland. Orphaned at age three and raised by an aunt, she attended a Baltimore school for free Blacks, founded and run by her uncle, William J. Watkins. The training she received for teaching included the study of classics, rhetoric, and the Bible. When Frances turned thirteen, she took a position as a live-in maid for a white Baltimore family, the Armstrongs. Mr. Armstrong owned a bookstore, and Watkins was allowed access to the enormous family library. After completing her formal education, she became the first female faculty member of Union Seminary, an African Methodist Episcopal school in Columbus, Ohio.

By 1854, Frances Watkins was involved with the abolitionist movement in New England. While living in New Bedford, Massachusetts, she gave antislavery lectures, and between 1854 and 1864 she became a traveling representative of the State Antislavery Society of Maine. At age thirty-five, she married Fenton Harper in Cincinnati. The couple and their daughter, Mary, lived on a farm in Columbus, Ohio, until Fenton died in 1863. During the 1860s and 1870s, Frances Harper supported herself and her daughter by lecturing and selling her poems.

In 1869, Harper argued at the American Equal Rights Association meeting in favor of the Fifteenth Amendment, which granted suffrage to Black men while denying it to women. In response to Elizabeth Cady Stanton, who did not want "ignorant negroes and foreigners" making laws, Harper sided with Frederick Douglass, arguing that it was more realistic and expedient to push for one issue at a time. This position never lessened her feminism. In an 1878 essay titled "Coloured Women of America" she asserted that "the women as a class are quite equal to the men in energy and executive ability."

Throughout her life, Harper worked actively for social change. She toured the South during Reconstruction. Between 1872 and 1900, in Philadelphia, she organized Sunday schools, worked for Black education, headed temperance work for Blacks in the National Woman's Christian Temperance Union, and founded the National Association of Colored Women. In her late sixties she condemned the government's unwillingness to stop the lynching of Blacks.

Literature was both an art form and a means of social protest for Harper, whose writing appeared in almost every Black independent publication of the period.

Her first volume of poetry, Forest Leaves, *appeared in 1846. Nine years later she published* Poems on Miscellaneous Subjects, *with an introduction by William Lloyd Garrison. Her "The Two Offers" (1859) is believed to be the first short story by an African American writer. During her career, she produced eleven books of poetry and prose in an effort to achieve her ambition to "make the songs for the people."*

In her only novel, Iola Leroy, or Shadows Uplifted *(1892), Harper uses a popular genre of the period, the romance, to chronicle Iola Leroy's affirmation of her racial heritage. Born to a slaveholding father and a mulatto mother, Iola is raised ignorant of her racial identity. Indeed, while receiving her education in the North, she defends slavery to her abolitionist friends. Upon her father's death, however, she is sold for $2000 as part of his property. The novel describes Iola's release from slavery, her work as a nurse with the Union Army, and her growing commitment to her race. The two chapters we have included, "Diverging Paths" and "Dawning Affections," focus on Iola's choice between two marriage proposals.*

■ *from* IOLA LEROY

CHAPTER XXVII: DIVERGING PATHS

On the eve of his departure from the city of P———, Dr. Gresham called on Iola, and found her alone. They talked awhile of reminiscences of the war and hospital life, when Dr. Gresham, approaching Iola, said:—

"Miss Leroy, I am glad the great object of your life is accomplished, and that you have found all your relatives. Years have passed since we parted, years in which I have vainly tried to get a trace of you and have been baffled, but I have found you at last!" Clasping her hand in his, he continued, "I would it were so that I should never lose you again! Iola, will you not grant me the privilege of holding this hand as mine all through the future of our lives? Your search for your mother is ended. She is well cared for. Are you not free at last to share with me my Northern home, free to be mine as nothing else on earth is mine." Dr. Gresham looked eagerly on Iola's face, and tried to read its varying expression. "Iola, I learned to love you in the hospital. I have tried to forget you, but it has been all in vain. Your image is just as deeply engraven on my heart as it was the day we parted."

"Doctor," she replied, sadly, but firmly, as she withdrew her hand from his, "I feel now as I felt then, that there is an insurmountable barrier between us."

"What is it, Iola?" asked Dr. Gresham, anxiously.

"It is the public opinion which assigns me a place with the colored people."

"But what right has public opinion to interfere with our marriage relations? Why should we yield to its behests?"

"Because it is stronger than we are, and we cannot run counter to it without suffering its penalties."

"And what are they, Iola? Shadows that you merely dread?"

"No! no! the penalties of social ostracism North and South, except here and there some grand and noble exceptions. I do not think that you fully realize how much prejudice against colored people permeates society, lowers the tone of our religion, and reacts upon the life of the nation. After freedom came, mamma was living in the city of A———, and wanted to unite with a Christian church there. She made application for membership. She passed her examination as a candidate, and was received as a church member. When she was about to make her first communion, she unintentionally took her seat at the head of the column. The elder who was administering the communion gave her the bread in the order in which she sat, but before he gave her the wine some one touched him on the shoulder and whispered a word in his ear. He then passed mamma by, gave the cup to others, and then returned to her. From that rite connected with the holiest memories of earth, my poor mother returned humiliated and depressed."

"What a shame!" exclaimed Dr. Gresham, indignantly.

"I have seen," continued Iola, "the same spirit manifested in the North. Mamma once attempted to do missionary work in this city. One day she found an outcast colored girl, whom she wished to rescue. She took her to an asylum for fallen women and made an application for her, but was refused. Colored girls were not received there. Soon after mamma found among the colored people an outcast white girl. Mamma's sympathies, unfettered by class distinction, were aroused in her behalf, and, in company with two white ladies, she went with the girl to that same refuge. For her the door was freely opened and admittance readily granted. It was as if two women were sinking in the quicksands, and on the solid land stood other women with life-lines in their hands, seeing the deadly sands slowly creeping up around the hapless victims. To one they readily threw the lines of deliverance, but for the other there was not one strand of salvation. Sometime since, to the same asylum, came a poor fallen girl who had escaped from the clutches of a wicked woman. For her the door would have been opened, had not the vile woman from whom she was escaping followed her to that place of refuge and revealed the fact that she belonged to the colored race. That fact was enough to close the door upon her, and to send her back to sin and to suffer, and perhaps to die as a wretched outcast. And yet in this city where a number of charities are advertised, I do not think there is one of them which, in appealing to the public, talks more religion than the managers of this asylum. This prejudice against the colored race environs our lives and mocks our aspirations."

"Iola, I see no use in your persisting that you are colored when your eyes are as blue and complexion as white as mine."

"Doctor, were I your wife, are there not people who would caress me as a white woman who would shrink from me in scorn if they knew I had one drop of negro blood in my veins? When mistaken for a white woman I should hear things alleged against the race at which my blood would boil. No, Doctor, I am not willing to live under a shadow of concealment which I thoroughly hate as if the blood in my veins were an undetected crime of my soul."

"Iola, dear, surely you paint the picture too darkly."

"Doctor, I have painted it with my heart's blood. It is easier to outgrow the dishonor of crime than the disabilities of color. You have created in this country an aristocracy of color wide enough to include the South with its treason and Utah with its abominations, but too narrow to include the best and bravest colored man who bared his breast to the bullets of the enemy during your fratricidal strife. Is not the most arrant Rebel to-day more acceptable to you than the most faithful colored man?"

"No! no!" exclaimed Dr. Gresham, vehemently. "You are wrong. I belong to the Grand Army of the Republic. We have no separate State Posts for the colored people, and, were such a thing proposed, the majority of our members, I believe, would be against it. In Congress colored men have the same seats as white men, and the color line is slowly fading out in our public institutions."

"But how is it in the Church?" asked Iola.

"The Church is naturally conservative. It preserves old truths, even if it is somewhat slow in embracing new ideas. It has its social as well as its spiritual side. Society is woman's realm. The majority of church members are women, who are said to be the aristocratic element of our country. I fear that one of the last strongholds of this racial prejudice will be found beneath the shadow of some of our churches. I think, on account of this social question, that large bodies of Christian temperance women and other reformers, in trying to reach the colored people even for their own good, will be quicker to form separate associations than our National Grand Army, whose ranks are open to black and white, liberals and conservatives, saints and agnostics. But, Iola, we have drifted far away from the question. No one has a right to interfere with our marriage if we do not infringe on the rights of others."

"Doctor," she replied, gently, "I feel that our paths must diverge. My life-work is planned. I intend spending my future among the colored people of the South."

"My dear friend," he replied, anxiously, "I am afraid that you are destined to sad disappointment. When the novelty wears off you will be disillusioned, and, I fear, when the time comes that you can no longer serve them they will forget your services and remember only your failings."

"But, Doctor, they need me; and I am sure when I taught among them they were very grateful for my services."

"I think," he replied, "these people are more thankful than grateful."

"I do not think so; and if I did it would not hinder me from doing all in my power to help them. I do not expect all the finest traits of character to spring from the hot-beds of slavery and caste. What matters it if they do forget the singer, so they don't forget the song? No, Doctor, I don't think that I could best serve my race by forsaking them and marrying you."

"Iola," he exclaimed, passionately, "if you love your race, as you call it, work for it, live for it, suffer for it, and, if need be, die for it; but don't marry for it. Your education has unfitted you for social life among them."

"It was," replied Iola, "through their unrequited toil that I was educated, while they were compelled to live in ignorance. I am indebted to them for the power I have to serve them. I wish other Southern women felt as I do. I think they could do so much to help the colored people at their doors if they would look at their opportunities in the light of the face of Jesus Christ. Nor am I wholly unselfish in allying myself with the colored people. All the rest of my family have done so. My dear grandmother is one of the excellent of the earth, and we all love her too much to ignore our relationship with her. I did not choose my lot in life, and the simplest thing I can do is to accept the situation and do the best I can."

"And is this your settled purpose?" he asked, sadly.

"It is, Doctor," she replied, tenderly but firmly. "I see no other. I must serve the race which needs me most."

"Perhaps you are right," he replied; "but I cannot help feeling sad that our paths, which met so pleasantly, should diverge so painfully. And yet, not only the freedmen, but the whole country, need such helpful, self-sacrificing teachers as you will prove; and if earnest prayers and holy wishes can brighten your path, your lines will fall in the pleasantest places."

As he rose to go, sympathy, love, and admiration were blended in the parting look he gave her; but he felt it was useless to attempt to divert her from her purpose. He knew that for the true reconstruction of the country something more was needed than bayonets and bullets, or the schemes of selfish politicians or plotting demagogues. He knew that the South needed the surrender of the best brain and heart of the country to build, above the wastes of war, more stately temples of thought and action.

CHAPTER XXXI: DAWNING AFFECTIONS

"Doctor," said Iola, as they walked home from the *conversazione,* "I wish I could do something more for our people than I am doing. I taught in the South till failing health compelled me to change my employment. But, now that I am well and strong, I would like to do something of lasting service for the race."

"Why not," asked Dr. Latimer, "write a good, strong book which would be helpful to them? I think there is an amount of dormant talent among us, and a large field from which to gather materials for such a book."

"I would do it, willingly, if I could; but one needs both leisure and money to make a successful book. There is material among us for the broadest comedies and the deepest tragedies, but, besides money and leisure, it needs patience, perseverance, courage, and the hand of an artist to weave it into the literature of the country."

"Miss Leroy, you have a large and rich experience; you possess a vivid imagination and glowing fancy. Write, out of the fullness of your heart, a book to inspire men and women with a deeper sense of justice and humanity."

"Doctor," replied Iola, "I would do it if I could, not for the money it might bring, but for the good it might do. But who believes any good can come out of the black Nazareth?"

"Miss Leroy, out of the race must come its own thinkers and writers. Authors belonging to the white race have written good racial books, for which I am deeply grateful, but it seems to be almost impossible for a white man to put himself completely in our place. No man can feel the iron which enters another man's soul."

"Well, Doctor, when I write a book I shall take you for the hero of my story."

"Why, what have I done," asked Dr. Latimer, in a surprised tone, "that you should impale me on your pen?"

"You have done nobly," answered Iola, "in refusing your grandmother's offer."

"I only did my duty," he modestly replied.

"But," said Iola, "when others are trying to slip out from the race and pass into the white basis, I cannot help admiring one who acts as if he felt that the weaker the race is the closer he would cling to it."

"My mother," replied Dr. Latimer, "faithful and true, belongs to that race. Where else should I be? But I know a young lady who could have cast her lot with the favored race, yet chose to take her place with the freed people, as their teacher, friend, and adviser. This young lady was alone in the world. She had been fearfully wronged, and to her stricken heart came a brilliant offer of love, home, and social position. But she bound her heart to the mast of duty, closed her ears to the syren song, and could not be lured from her purpose."

A startled look stole over Iola's face, and, lifting her eyes to his, she faltered:—

"Do you know her?"

"Yes, I know her and admire her; and she ought to be made the subject of a soul-inspiring story. Do you know of whom I speak?"

"How should I, Doctor? I am sure you have not made me your confidante," she responded, demurely; then she quickly turned and tripped up the steps of her home, which she had just reached.

After this conversation Dr. Latimer became a frequent visitor at Iola's home, and a firm friend of her brother. Harry was at that age when, for the young and inexperienced, vice puts on her fairest guise and most seductive smiles. Dr. Latimer's wider knowledge and larger experience made his friendship for Harry very valuable, and the service he rendered him made him a favorite and ever-welcome guest in the family.

"Are you all alone," asked Robert, one night, as he entered the cosy little parlor where Iola sat reading. "Where are the rest of the folks?"

"Mamma and grandma have gone to bed," answered Iola. "Harry and

Lucille are at the concert. They are passionately fond of music, and find facilities here that they do not have in the South. They wouldn't go to hear a seraph where they must take a negro seat. I was too tired to go. Besides, 'two's company and three's a crowd,' " she added, significantly.

"I reckon you struck the nail on the head that time," said Robert, laughing. "But you have not been alone all the time. Just as I reached the corner I saw Dr. Latimer leaving the door. I see he still continues his visits. Who is his patient now?"

"Oh, Uncle Robert," said Iola, smiling and flushing, "he is out with Harry and Lucille part of the time, and drops in now and then to see us all."

"Well," said Robert, "I suppose the case is now an affair of the heart. But I cannot blame him for it," he added, looking fondly on the beautiful face of his niece, which sorrow had touched only to chisel into more loveliness. "How do you like him?"

"I must have within me," answered Iola, with unaffected truthfulness, "a large amount of hero worship. The characters of the Old Testament I most admire are Moses and Nehemiah. They were willing to put aside their own advantages for their race and country. Dr. Latimer comes up to my ideal of a high, heroic manhood."

"I think," answered Robert, smiling archly, "he would be delighted to hear your opinion of him."

"I tell him," continued Iola, "that he belongs to the days of chivalry. But he smiles and says, 'he only belongs to the days of hard-pan service.' "

"Some one," said Robert, "was saying to-day that he stood in his own light when he refused his grandmother's offer to receive him as her son."

"I think," said Iola, "it was the grandest hour of his life when he made that decision. I have admired him ever since I heard his story."

"But, Iola, think of the advantages he set aside. It was no sacrifice for me to remain colored, with my lack of education and race sympathies, but Dr. Latimer had doors open to him as a white man which are forever closed to a colored man. To be born white in this country is to be born to an inheritance of privileges, to hold in your hands the keys that open before you the doors of every occupation, advantage, opportunity, and achievement."

"I know that, uncle," answered Iola; "but even these advantages are too dearly bought if they mean loss of honor, true manliness, and self respect. He could not have retained these had he ignored his mother and lived under a veil of concealment, constantly haunted by a dread of detection. The gain would not have been worth the cost. It were better that he should walk the ruggedest paths of life a true man than tread the softest carpets a moral cripple."

"I am afraid," said Robert, laying his hand caressingly upon her head, "that we are destined to lose the light of our home."

"Oh, uncle, how you talk! I never dreamed of what you are thinking," answered Iola, half reproachfully.

"And how," asked Robert, "do you know what I am thinking about?"

"My dear uncle, I'm not blind."

"Neither am I," replied Robert, significantly, as he left the room.

Iola's admiration for Dr. Latimer was not a one-sided affair. Day after day she was filling a larger place in his heart. The touch of her hand thrilled him with emotion. Her lightest words were an entrancing melody to his ear. Her noblest sentiments found a response in his heart. In their desire to help the race their hearts beat in loving unison. One grand and noble purpose was giving tone and color to their lives and strengthening the bonds of affection between them.

1892

HARRIET E. WILSON
(1828?–1870?)

Our Nig: Or, Sketches from the Life of a Free Black, In a Two-Story White House, North, Showing That Slavery's Shadows Fall Even There, *written by "*Our Nig,*" was printed in Boston in 1859. The author, Harriet E. Wilson, explains in her preface that she did not write the book as a literary work; she wrote it simply because, "deserted by kindred, disabled by failing health," she hoped to support herself and her child. She frankly asks her "colored brethren" for help, "hoping they will not condemn this attempt of their sister to be erudite, but rally around me a faithful band of supporters and defenders." The book, a seemingly autobiographical fiction focusing on the mistreatment of a Black indentured servant by a white northern woman, was one of the first novels written by a Black writer in the United States.*

Information about the author of Our Nig *is scanty. Henry Louis Gates, Jr., with the help of Davis Ames Curtis, director of research for the Yale Black Periodical Fiction project, and a host of research assistants, searched birth records, tax records, church records, city directories, and other such sources through scores of cities in New Hampshire and Massachusetts to track down information about a Harriet E. Wilson. This detective work, combined with a close examination of details in the text of* Our Nig, *enabled Gates and Curtis to put together a few details about Wilson's life. However, they admit that even these scraps of information could pertain to another woman by the same name.*

One poignant document that may provide insight into Wilson's life is an obituary, dated 1860, for George Mason Wilson, aged seven years and eight months, the son of Thomas and Harriet E. Wilson. If George Mason Wilson was indeed the son of the author, her efforts to maintain his "feeble life" by writing a book proved futile. Other pieces of information indicate that before her marriage, the author was probably an indentured servant for a white family in New Hampshire; then, upon meeting George Mason, she moved to Massachusetts and worked in the straw hat industry. Her husband deserted her periodically and finally disappeared after their child was born. As her health deteriorated, according to a letter of endorsement appended to Our Nig, *she was taken in by a kind family. Little else may be known concerning the life of Harriet Wilson.*

The book itself is a remarkable work. Its form and its epigraphs, such as the citation from Byron in the chapter selected here, show that the writer had read both English and American literature—poetry and prose as well as popular novels. Although her writing is clearly influenced by the style of sentimental novels, Wilson chose highly controversial, even taboo, topics for her book—interracial marriage and the racism of white northerners. Even her title is startling, as Gates points out in his introduction: "That Harriet Wilson, moreover, dared to entitle her text with the most feared and hated epithet by which the very humanity of black people had been demeaned adds to the list of ironies in her endeavor."

Our Nig *tells the story of Frado, the daughter of a white woman and a Black man, who has been abandoned by her impoverished mother and taken in as a servant by the Bellmont family. "A Friend for Nig," the fourth chapter of the book, captures the pain and bewilderment of Frado's childhood. This chapter also shows Wilson's efforts to balance her portrait of the cruel Mrs. Bellmont with more kindly portraits of other white characters.*

from OUR NIG

CHAPTER IV: A FRIEND FOR NIG

Hours of my youth! when nurtured in my breast,
To love a stranger, friendship made me blest;—
Friendship, the dear peculiar bond of youth,
When every artless bosom throbs with truth;
Untaught by worldly wisdom how to feign;
And check each impulse with prudential reign;
When all we feel our honest souls disclose—
In love to friends, in open hate to foes;
No varnished tales the lips of youth repeat,
No dear-bought knowledge purchased by deceit.

BYRON

With what differing emotions have the denizens of earth awaited the approach of to-day. Some sufferer has counted the vibrations of the pendulum impatient for its dawn, who, now that it has arrived, is anxious for its close. The votary of pleasure, conscious of yesterday's void, wishes for power to arrest time's haste till a few more hours of mirth shall be enjoyed. The unfortunate are yet gazing in vain for golden-edged clouds they fancied would appear in their horizon. The good man feels that he has accomplished too little for the Master, and sighs that another day must so soon close. Innocent childhood, weary of its stay, longs for another morrow; busy manhood cries, hold! hold! and pursues it to another's dawn. All are dissatisfied. All crave some good not yet possessed, which time is expected to bring with all its morrows.

Was it strange that, to a disconsolate child, three years should seem a long, long time? During school time she had rest from Mrs. Bellmont's tyranny. She was now nine years old; time, her mistress said, such privileges should cease.

She could now read and spell, and knew the elementary steps in grammar, arithmetic, and writing. Her education completed, as *she* said, Mrs. Bellmont felt that her time and person belonged solely to her. She was under her in every sense of the word. What an opportunity to indulge her vixen nature! No matter what occurred to ruffle her, or from what source provocation came, real or fancied, a few blows on Nig seemed to relieve her of a portion of ill-will.

These were days when Fido was the entire confidant of Frado. She told him her griefs as though he were human; and he sat so still, and listened so attentively, she really believed he knew her sorrows. All the leisure moments she could gain were used in teaching him some feat of dog-agility, so that Jack pronounced him very knowing, and was truly gratified to know he had furnished her with a gift answering his intentions.

Fido was the constant attendant of Frado, when sent from the house on errands, going and returning with the cows, out in the fields, to the village. If ever she forgot her hardships it was in his company.

Spring was now retiring. James, one of the absent sons, was expected home on a visit. He had never seen the last acquisition to the family. Jack had written faithfully of all the merits of his colored *protegé,* and hinted plainly that mother did not always treat her just right. Many were the preparations to make the visit pleasant, and as the day approached when he was to arrive, great exertions were made to cook the favorite viands, to prepare the choicest table-fare.

The morning of the arrival day was a busy one. Frado knew not who would be of so much importance; her feet were speeding hither and thither so unsparingly. Mrs. Bellmont seemed a trifle fatigued, and her shoes which had, early in the morning, a methodic squeak, altered to an irregular, peevish snap.

"Get some little wood to make the fire burn," said Mrs. Bellmont, in a sharp tone. Frado obeyed, bringing the smallest she could find.

Mrs. Bellmont approached her, and, giving her a box on her ear, reiterated the command.

The first the child brought was the smallest to be found; of course, the second must be a trifle larger. She well knew it was, as she threw it into a box on the hearth. To Mrs. Bellmont it was a greater affront, as well as larger wood, so she "taught her" with the raw-hide, and sent her the third time for "little wood."

Nig, weeping, knew not what to do. She had carried the smallest; none left would suit her mistress; of course further punishment awaited her; so she gathered up whatever came first, and threw it down on the hearth. As she expected, Mrs. Bellmont, enraged, approached her, and kicked her so forcibly as to throw her upon the floor. Before she could rise, another foiled the attempt, and then followed kick after kick in quick succession and power, till she reached the door. Mr. Bellmont and Aunt Abby, hearing the noise, rushed in, just in time to see the last of the performance. Nig jumped up, and rushed from the house, out of sight.

Aunt Abby returned to her apartment, followed by John, who was muttering to himself.

"What were you saying?" asked Aunt Abby.

"I said I hoped the child never would come into the house again."

"What would become of her? You cannot mean *that*," continued his sister.

"I do mean it. The child does as much work as a woman ought to; and just see how she is kicked about!"

"Why do you have it so, John?" asked his sister.

"How am I to help it? Women rule the earth, and all in it."

"I think I should rule my own house, John,"—

"And live in hell meantime," add Mr. Bellmont.

John now sauntered out to the barn to await the quieting of the storm.

Aunt Abby had a glimpse of Nig as she passed out of the yard; but to arrest her, or show her that *she* would shelter her, in Mrs. Bellmont's presence, would only bring reserved wrath on her defenceless head. Her sister-in-law had great prejudices against her. One cause of the alienation was that she did not give her right in the homestead to John, and leave it forever; another was that she was a professor of religion, (so was Mrs. Bellmont;) but Nab, as she called her, did not live according to her profession; another, that she *would* sometimes give Nig cake and pie, which she was never allowed to have at home. Mary had often noticed and spoken of her inconsistencies.

The dinner hour passed. Frado had not appeared. Mrs. B. made no inquiry or search. Aunt Abby looked long, and found her concealed in an outbuilding. "Come into the house with me," implored Aunt Abby.

"I ain't going in any more," sobbed the child.

"What will you do?" asked Aunt Abby.

"I've got to stay out here and die. I ha'n't got no mother, no home. I wish I was dead."

"Poor thing," muttered Aunt Abby; and slyly providing her with some dinner, left her to her grief.

Jane went to confer with her Aunt about the affair; and learned from her the retreat. She would gladly have concealed her in her own chamber, and ministered to her wants; but she was dependent on Mary and her mother for care, and any displeasure caused by attention to Nig, was seriously felt.

Toward night the coach brought James. A time of general greeting, inquiries for absent members of the family, a visit to Aunt Abby's room, undoing a few delicacies for Jane, brought them to the tea hour.

"Where's Frado?" asked Mr. Bellmont, observing she was not in her usual place, behind her mistress' chair.

"I don't know, and I don't care. If she makes her appearance again, I'll take the skin from her body," replied his wife.

James, a fine looking young man, with a pleasant countenance, placid, and yet decidedly serious, yet not stern, looked up confounded. He was no stranger to his mother's nature; but years of absence had erased the occurrences once so familiar, and he asked, "Is this that pretty little Nig, Jack writes to me about, that you are so severe upon, mother?"

"I'll not leave much of her beauty to be seen, if she comes in sight; and now, John," said Mrs. B., turning to her husband, "you need not think you are going to learn her to treat me in this way; just see how saucy she was this morning. She shall learn her place."

Mr. Bellmont raised his calm, determined eye full upon her, and said, in a decisive manner: "You shall not strike, or scald, or skin her, as you call it, if she comes back again. Remember!" and he brought his hand down upon the table. "I have searched an hour for her now, and she is not to be found on the premises. Do *you* know where she is? Is she *your* prisoner?"

"No! I have just told you I did not know where she was. Nab has her hid somewhere, I suppose. Oh, dear! I did not think it would come to this; that my own husband would treat me so." Then came fast flowing tears, which no one but Mary seemed to notice. Jane crept into Aunt Abby's room; Mr. Bellmont and James went out of doors, and Mary remained to condole with her parent.

"Do you know where Frado is?" asked Jane of her aunt.

"No," she replied. "I have hunted everywhere. She has left her first hiding-place. I cannot think what has become of her. There comes Jack and Fido; perhaps he knows;" and she walked to a window near, where James and his father were conversing together.

The two brothers exchanged a hearty greeting, and then Mr. Bellmont told Jack to eat his supper; afterward he wished to send him away. He immediately went in. Accustomed to all the phases of indoor storms, from a whine to thunder and lightning, he saw at a glance marks of disturbance. He had been absent through the day, with the hired men.

"What's the fuss?" asked he, rushing into Aunt Abby's.

"Eat your supper," said Jane; "go home, Jack."

Back again through the dining-room, and out to his father.

"What's the fuss?" again inquired he of his father.

"Eat your supper, Jack, and see if you can find Frado. She's not been seen since morning, and then she was kicked out of the house."

"I shan't eat my supper till I find her," said Jack, indignantly. "Come, James, and see the little creature mother treats so."

They started, calling, searching, coaxing, all their way along. No Frado. They returned to the house to consult. James and Jack declared they would not sleep till she was found.

Mrs. Bellmont attempted to dissuade them from the search. "It was a shame a little *nigger* should make so much trouble."

Just then Fido came running up, and Jack exclaimed, "Fido knows where she is, I'll bet."

"So I believe," said his father; "but we shall not be wiser unless we can outwit him. He will not do what his mistress forbids him."

"I know how to fix him," said Jack. Taking a plate from the table, which was still waiting, he called, "Fido! Fido! Frado wants some supper. Come!" Jack started, the dog followed, and soon capered on before, far, far into the fields, over walls and through fences, into a piece of swampy land. Jack followed close, and soon appeared to James, who was quite in the rear, coaxing and forcing Frado along with him.

A frail child, driven from shelter by the cruelty of his mother, was an object of interest to James. They persuaded her to go home with them, warmed her by the kitchen fire, gave her a good supper, and took her with them into the sitting-room.

"Take that nigger out of my sight," was Mrs. Bellmont's command, before they could be seated.

James led her into Aunt Abby's, where he knew they were welcome. They chatted awhile until Frado seemed cheerful; then James led her to her room, and waited until she retired.

"Are you glad I've come home?" asked James.

"Yes; if you won't let me be whipped tomorrow."

"You won't be whipped. You must try to be a good girl," counselled James.

"If I do, I get whipped;" sobbed the child. "They won't believe what I say. Oh, I wish I had my mother back; then I should not be kicked and whipped so. Who made me so?"

"God;" answered James.

"Did God make you?"

"Yes."

"Who made Aunt Abby?"

"God."

"Who made your mother?"

"God."

"Did the same God that made her make me?"

"Yes."

"Well, then, I don't like him."

"Why not?"

"Because he made her white, and me black. Why didn't he make us *both* white?"

"I don't know; try to go to sleep, and you will feel better in the morning," was all the reply he could make to her knotty queries. It was a long time before she fell asleep; and a number of days before James felt in a mood to visit and entertain old associates and friends.

1859

REBECCA HARDING DAVIS
(1831–1910)

The writing career of Rebecca Harding Davis exemplifies a dilemma for many nineteenth- and twentieth-century writers: the desire to write literature versus the need to support oneself. In many ways, Davis's life dictated the choice for her.

Davis grew up in Wheeling, Virginia, a mill town on the Ohio River. She was the eldest of five children; her father was a successful businessman. From the front porch of her family's comfortable home, Davis watched the ironworkers trudge to the mill each day.

Educated at home by her mother, Davis read the works of John Bunyan, Sir Walter Scott, and Maria Edgeworth. Reading Hawthorne's Moral Tales *encouraged her to believe that someone from a town like hers could write fiction. At age fourteen, she attended Washington Female Seminary in Pennsylvania. During her years at school, Davis was introduced to the antislavery movement by Francis Julius LeMoyne, the 1840 abolitionist candidate for vice-president. After graduating in 1848 as class valedictorian, she returned to Wheeling, where she lived for the next thirteen years.*

Life in the Iron Mills, *a novella based on the lives of the mill workers she watched daily, was published in April 1861 in the most prestigious magazine of the period, the* Atlantic Monthly. *The publication led to a lasting friendship between Davis and the magazine editors, James and Annie Fields. The success of this work was followed by the serial publication in the* Atlantic *of* Margret Howth: A Story of Today, *and her Civil War novel,* David Gaunt.

While visiting the Fields in Boston, Davis met Louisa May Alcott, Ralph Waldo Emerson, Oliver Wendell Holmes, Nathaniel Hawthorne, and other admirers of her writing. At the same time that she published in the prestigious Atlantic Monthly, *however, she wrote potboilers such as "The Murder in the Glenn Ross" and a serialized novel,* The Second Life. *The considerations were practical:* Peterson's Magazine *paid at least twice as much as the* Atlantic.

Although in her later years Davis produced little work of the quality of her early fiction, she consistently wrote about important social and political issues. In Waiting for the Verdict, *for example, she described post–Civil War racism. The main character of* Dallas Galbraith *is a thirteen-year-old who works in a coal mine, and the subject of* Put Out of the Way *is the mistreatment of the insane. Davis, then, was a social historian. Moreover, as Tillie Olsen has noted, "even in her most slipshod novels . . . a breathing character, a stunning insight, a scene as transcendent as any written in her century, also confirms for us what a great writer was lost in her." For years after her death, Davis was known primarily as the mother of journalist Richard Harding Davis.*

Thanks to the efforts of scholars and writers such as Olsen, Life in the Iron Mills, *the story included here, can be read and appreciated by a new generation of readers. This novella describes the atrocious working conditions and the hardships of daily life in the nineteenth-century iron mills. At the same time, it conveys the creative human spirit, the irrepressible life of the workers surviving in the midst of adversity.*

■ LIFE IN THE IRON MILLS

Is this the end?
O Life, as futile, then, as frail!
What hope of answer of redress?

A cloudy day: do you know what that is in a town of iron-works? The sky sank down before dawn, muddy, flat, immovable. The air is thick, clammy with the breath of crowded human beings. It stifles me. I open the window, and, looking out, can scarcely see through the rain the grocer's shop opposite, where a crowd of drunken Irishmen are puffing Lynchburg tobacco in their pipes. I can detect the scent through all the foul smells ranging loose in the air.

The idiosyncrasy of this town is smoke. It rolls sullenly in slow folds from the great chimneys of the iron-foundries, and settles down in black, slimy pools on the muddy streets. Smoke on the wharves, smoke on the dingy boats, on the yellow river,—clinging in a coating of greasy soot to the house-front, the two faded poplars, the faces of the passers-by. The long train of mules, dragging masses of pig-iron through the narrow street, have a foul vapor hanging to their reeking sides. Here, inside, is a little broken figure of an angel pointing upward from the mantel-shelf; but even its wings are covered with smoke, clotted and black. Smoke everywhere! A dirty canary chirps desolately in a cage beside me. Its dream of green fields and sunshine is a very old dream,—almost worn out, I think.

From the back-window I can see a narrow brick-yard sloping down to the river-side, strewed with rain-butts and tubs. The river, dull and tawny-colored, (*la belle rivière!*) drags itself sluggishly along, tired of the heavy weight of boats and coal-barges. What wonder? When I was a child, I used to fancy a look of weary, dumb appeal upon the face of the negro-like river slavishly bearing its burden day after day. Something of the same idle notion comes to me to-day, when from the street-window I look on the slow stream of human life creeping past, night and morning, to the great mills. Masses of men, with dull, besotted faces bent to the ground, sharpened here and there by pain or cunning; skin and muscle and flesh begrimed with smoke and ashes; stooping all night over boiling caldrons of metal, laired by day in dens of drunkenness and infamy; breathing from infancy to death an air saturated with fog and grease and soot, vileness for soul and body. What do you make of a case like that, amateur psychologist? You call it an altogether serious thing to be alive: to these men it is a drunken jest, a joke,—horrible to angels perhaps, to them commonplace enough. My fancy about the river was an idle one: it is no type of such a life. What if it be stagnant and slimy here? It knows that beyond there waits for it odorous sunlight,—quaint old gardens, dusky with soft, green foliage of apple-trees, and flushing crimson with roses,—air, and fields, and mountains. The future of the Welsh puddler passing just now is not so pleasant. To be stowed away, after his grimy work is done, in a hole in the muddy graveyard, and after that,—*not* air, nor green fields, nor curious roses.

Can you see how foggy the day is? As I stand here, idly tapping the window-pane, and looking out through the rain at the dirty back-yard and the coal-boats below, fragments of an old story float up before me,—a story of this old house into which I happened to come to-day. You may think it a tiresome story enough, as foggy as the day, sharpened by no sudden flashes of pain or pleasure.—I know: only the outline of a dull life, that long since, with thousands of dull lives like its own, was vainly lived and lost: thousands of them,—massed, vile, slimy lives, like those of the torpid lizards in yonder stagnant water-butt.—Lost? There is a curious point for you to settle, my friend, who study psychology in a lazy, *dilettante* way. Stop a moment. I am going to be honest. This is what I want you to do. I want you to hide your disgust, take no heed to your clean clothes, and come right down with me,—here, into the thickest of the fog and mud and foul effluvia. I want you to hear this story. There is a secret down here, in this nightmare fog, that has lain dumb for centuries: I want to make it a real thing to you. You, Egoist, or Pantheist, or Arminian, busy in making straight paths for your feet on the hills, do not see it clearly,—this terrible question which men here have gone mad and died trying to answer. I dare not put this secret into words. I told you it was dumb. These men, going by with drunken faces and brains full of unawakened power, do not ask it of Society or of God. Their lives ask it; their deaths ask it. There is no reply. I will tell you plainly that I have a great hope; and I bring it to you to be tested. It is this: that this terrible dumb question is its own reply; that it is not the sentence of death we think it, but, from the very extremity of its darkness, the most solemn prophecy which the world has known of the Hope to come. I dare make my meaning no clearer, but will only tell my story. It will, perhaps, seem to you as foul and dark as this thick vapor about us, and as pregnant with death; but if your eyes are free as mine are to look deeper, no perfume-tinted dawn will be so fair with promise of the day that shall surely come.

My story is very simple,—only what I remember of the life of one of these men,—a furnace-tender in one of Kirby & John's rolling-mills,—Hugh Wolfe. You know the mills? They took the great order for the Lower Virginia railroads there last winter; run usually with about a thousand men. I cannot tell why I choose the half-forgotten story of this Wolfe more than that of myriads of these furnace-hands. Perhaps because there is a secret underlying sympathy between that story and this day with its impure fog and thwarted sunshine,—or perhaps simply for the reason that this house is the one where the Wolfes lived. There were the father and son,—both hands, as I said, in one of Kirby & John's mills for making railroad-iron,—and Deborah, their cousin, a picker in some of the cotton-mills. The house was rented then to half a dozen families. The Wolfes had two of the cellar-rooms. The old man, like many of the puddlers and feeders of the mills, was Welsh,—had spent half of his life in the Cornish tin-mines. You may pick the Welsh emigrants, Cornish miners, out of the throng passing the windows, any day. They are a trifle more filthy; their muscles are not so brawny; they stoop more. When they are drunk, they neither yell, nor shout, nor stagger, but skulk along like beaten hounds. A pure, unmixed blood, I fancy: shows itself in the slight angular bodies and sharply-cut facial lines. It is nearly thirty years since the Wolfes lived here. Their lives were like those of their class: incessant labor, sleeping in kennel-like rooms, eating rank pork and molasses, drinking—God and the distillers only know what; with an occasional night in jail, to atone for some drunken excess. Is that all of their lives?—of the portion given to them and these their duplicates swarming the streets to-day?—nothing beneath?—all? So many a political reformer will tell you,—and many a private reformer, too, who has gone among them with a heart tender with Christ's charity, and come out outraged, hardened.

One rainy night, about eleven o'clock, a crowd of half-clothed women stopped outside of the cellar-door. They were going home from the cotton-mill.

"Good-night, Deb," said one, a mulatto, steadying herself against the gas-post. She needed the post to steady her. So did more than one of them.

"Dah's a ball to Miss Potts' to-night. Ye'd best come."

"Inteet, Deb, if hur'll come, hur'll hef fun," said a shrill Welsh voice in the crowd.

Two or three dirty hands were thrust out to catch the gown of the woman, who was groping for the latch of the door.

"No."

"No? Where's Kit Small, then?"

"Begorra! on the spools. Alleys behint, though we helped her, we dud. An wid ye! Let Deb alone! It's ondacent frettin' a quite body. Be the powers, an' we'll have a night of it! there'll be lashin's o' drink,—the Vargent be blessed and praised for 't!"

They went on, the mulatto inclining for a moment to show fight, and drag the woman Wolfe off with them; but, being pacified, she staggered away.

Deborah groped her way into the cellar, and, after considerable stumbling, kindled a match, and lighted a tallow dip, that sent a yellow glimmer over the room. It was low, damp,—the earthen floor covered with a green, slimy moss,—a fetid air smothering the breath. Old Wolfe lay asleep on a heap of straw, wrapped in a torn horse-blanket. He was a pale, meek little man, with a white face and red rabbit-eyes. The woman Deborah was like him; only her face was even more ghastly, her lips bluer, her eyes more watery. She wore a faded cotton gown and a slouching bonnet. When she walked, one could see that she was deformed, almost a hunchback. She trod softly, so as not to waken him, and went through into the room beyond. There she found by the half-extinguished fire an iron saucepan filled with cold boiled potatoes, which she put upon a broken chair with a pint-cup of ale. Placing the old candlestick beside this dainty repast, she untied her bonnet, which hung limp and wet over her face, and prepared to eat her supper. It was the first food that had touched her lips since morning. There was enough of it, however: there is not always. She was hungry,—one could see that easily enough,—and not drunk, as most of her companions would have been found at this hour. She did not drink, this woman,—her face told that, too,—nothing stronger than ale. Perhaps the weak, flaccid wretch had some stimulant in her pale life to keep her up,—some love or hope, it might be, or urgent need. When that stimulant was gone, she would take to whiskey. Man cannot live by work alone. While she was skinning the potatoes, and munching them, a noise behind her made her stop.

"Janey!" she called, lifting the candle and peering into the darkness. "Janey, are you there?"

A heap of ragged coats was heaved up, and the face of a young girl emerged, staring sleepily at the woman.

"Deborah," she said, at last, "I'm here the night."

"Yes, child. Hur's welcome," she said, quietly eating on.

The girl's face was haggard and sickly; her eyes were heavy with sleep and hunger: real Milesian eyes they were, dark, delicate blue, glooming out from black shadows with a pitiful fright.

"I was alone," she said, timidly.

"Where's the father?" asked Deborah, holding out a potato, which the girl greedily seized.

"He's beyant,—wid Haley,—in the stone house." (Did you ever hear the word *jail* from an Irish mouth?) "I came here. Hugh told me never to stay me-lone."

"Hugh?"

"Yes."

A vexed frown crossed her face. The girl saw it, and added quickly,—

"I have not seen Hugh the day, Deb. The old man says his watch lasts till the mornin'."

The woman sprang up, and hastily began to arrange some bread and flitch in a tin pail, and to pour her own measure of ale into a bottle. Tying on her bonnet, she blew out the candle.

"Lay ye down, Janey dear," she said, gently, covering her with the old rags. "Hur can eat the potatoes, if hur's hungry."

"Where are ye goin', Deb? The rain's sharp."

"To the mill, with Hugh's supper."

"Let him bide till th' morn. Sit ye down."

"No, no,"—sharply pushing her off. "The boy'll starve."

She hurried from the cellar, while the child wearily coiled herself up for sleep. The rain was falling heavily, as the woman, pail in hand, emerged from the mouth of the alley, and turned down the narrow street, that stretched out, long and black, miles before her. Here and there a flicker of gas lighted an uncertain space of muddy footwalk and gutter; the long rows of houses, except an occasional lager-bier shop, were closed; now and then she met a band of mill-hands skulking to or from their work.

Not many even of the inhabitants of a manufacturing town know the vast machinery of system by which the bodies of workmen are governed, that goes on unceasingly from year to year. The hands of each mill are divided into watches that relieve each other as regularly as the sentinels of an army. By night and day the work goes on, the unsleeping engines groan and shriek, the fiery pools of metal boil and surge. Only for a day in the week, in half-courtesy to public censure, the fires are partially veiled; but as soon as the clock strikes midnight, the great furnaces break forth with renewed fury, the clamor begins with fresh, breathless vigor, the engines sob and shriek like "gods in pain."

As Deborah hurried down through the heavy rain, the noise of these thousand engines sounded through the sleep and shadow of the city like far-off thunder. The mill to which she was going lay on the river, a mile below the city-limits. It was far, and she was weak, aching from standing twelve hours at the spools. Yet it was her almost nightly walk to take this man his supper, though at every square she sat down to rest, and she knew she should receive small word of thanks.

Perhaps, if she had possessed an artist's eye, the picturesque oddity of the scene might have made her step stagger less, and the path seem shorter; but to her the mills were only "summat deilish to look at by night."

The road leading to the mills had been quarried from the solid rock, which rose abrupt and bare on one side of the cinder-covered road, while the river, sluggish and black, crept past on the other. The mills for rolling iron are simply immense tent-like roofs, covering acres of ground, open on every side. Beneath these roofs Deborah looked in on a city of fires, that burned hot and fiercely in the night. Fire in every horrible form: pits of flame waving in the wind; liquid metal-flames writhing in tortuous streams through the sand; wide caldrons filled with boiling fire, over which bent ghastly wretches stirring the strange brewing; and through all, crowds of half-clad men, looking like revengeful ghosts in the red light, hurried, throwing masses of glittering fire. It was like a street in Hell. Even Deborah muttered, as she crept through, "'T looks like t' Devil's place!" It did,—in more ways than one.

She found the man she was looking for, at last, heaping coal on a furnace. He had not time to eat his supper; so she went behind the furnace, and waited. Only a few men were with him, and they noticed her only by a "Hyur comes t' hunchback, Wolfe."

Deborah was stupid with sleep; her back pained her sharply; and her teeth chattered with cold, with the rain that soaked her clothes and dripped from her at every step. She stood, however, patiently holding the pail, and waiting.

"Hout, woman! ye look like a drowned cat. Come near to the fire,"—said one of the men, approaching to scrape away the ashes.

She shook her head. Wolfe had forgotten her. He turned, hearing the man, and came closer.

"I did no' think; gi' me my supper, woman."

She watched him eat with a painful eagerness. With a woman's quick instinct, she saw that he was not hungry,—was eating to please her. Her pale, watery eyes began to gather a strange light.

"Is't good, Hugh? T'ale was a bit sour, I feared."

"No, good enough." He hesitated a moment. "Ye're tired, poor lass! Bide here till I go. Lay down there on that heap of ash, and go to sleep."

He threw her an old coat for a pillow, and turned to his work. The heap was the refuse of the burnt iron, and was not a hard bed; the half-smothered warmth, too, penetrated her limbs, dulling their pain and cold shiver.

Miserable enough she looked, lying there on the ashes like a limp, dirty rag,—yet not an unfitting figure to crown the scene of hopeless discomfort and veiled crime: more fitting, if one looked deeper into the heart of things,—at her thwarted woman's form, her colorless life, her waking stupor that smothered pain and hunger,—even more fit to be a type of her class. Deeper yet if one could look, was there nothing worth reading in this wet, faded thing, half-covered with ashes? no story of a soul filled with groping passionate love, heroic unselfishness, fierce jealousy? of years of weary trying to please the one human being whom she loved, to gain one look of real heart-kindness from him? If anything like this were hidden beneath the pale, bleared eyes, and dull, washed-out-looking face, no one had ever taken the trouble to read its faint signs: not the half-clothed furnace-tender, Wolfe, certainly. Yet he was kind to her: it was his nature to be kind, even to the very rats that swarmed in the cellar; kind to her in just the same way. She knew that. And it might be that very knowledge had given to her face its apathy and vacancy more than her low, torpid life. One sees that dead, vacant look steal sometimes over the rarest, finest of women's faces,—in the very midst, it may be, of their warmest summer's day; and then one can guess at the secret of intolerable solitude that lies hid beneath the delicate laces and brilliant smile. There was no warmth, no brilliancy, no summer for this woman; so the stupor and vacancy had time to gnaw into her face perpetually. She was young, too, though no one guessed it; so the gnawing was the fiercer.

She lay quiet in the dark corner, listening, through the monotonous din and uncertain glare of the works, to the dull plash of the rain in the far distance,—shrinking back whenever the man Wolfe happened to look towards her. She knew, in spite of all his kindness, that there was that in her face and form which made him loathe the sight of her. She felt by instinct, although she could not comprehend it, the finer nature of the man, which made him among his fellow-workmen something unique, set apart. She knew, that, down under all the vileness and coarseness of his life, there was a groping passion for whatever was beautiful and pure,—that his soul sickened with disgust at her deformity, even when his words were kindest. Through this dull consciousness, which never left her, came, like a sting, the recollection of the dark blue eyes and lithe figure of the little Irish girl she had left in the cellar. The recollection struck through even her stupid intellect with a vivid glow of beauty and of grace. Little Janey, timid, helpless, clinging to Hugh as her only friend: that was the sharp thought, the bitter thought, that drove into the glazed eyes a fierce light of pain. You laugh at it? Are pain and jealousy less savage realities down here in this place I am taking you to than in your own house or your own heart,—your heart, which they clutch at sometimes? The note is the same, I fancy, be the octave high or low.

If you could go into this mill where Deborah lay, and drag out from the hearts of these men the terrible tragedy of their lives, taking it as a symptom of the disease of their class, no ghost Horror would terrify you more. A reality of soul-starvation, of living death, that meets you every day under the besotted faces on the street,—I can paint nothing of this, only give you the outside outlines of a night, a crisis in the life of one man: whatever muddy depth of soul-history lies beneath you can read according to the eyes God has given you.

Wolfe, while Deborah watched him as a spaniel its master, bent over the furnace with his iron pole, unconscious of her scrutiny, only stopping to receive orders. Physically, Nature had promised the man but little. He had already lost the strength and instinct vigor of a man, his muscles were thin, his nerves weak, his face (a meek, woman's face) haggard, yellow with consumption. In the mill he was known as one of the girl-men: "Molly Wolfe" was his *sobriquet.* He was never seen in the cockpit, did not own a terrier, drank but seldom; when he did, desperately. He fought sometimes, but was always thrashed, pommelled to a jelly. The man was game enough, when his blood was up: but he was no favorite in the mill; he had the taint of school-learning on him,—not to a dangerous extent, only a quarter or so in the free-school in fact, but enough to ruin him as a good hand in a fight.

For other reasons, too, he was not popular. Not one of themselves, they felt that, though outwardly as filthy and ash-covered; silent, with foreign thoughts and longings breaking out through his quietness in innumerable curious ways: this one, for instance. In the neighboring furnace-buildings lay great heaps of the refuse from the ore after the pig-metal is run. *Korl* we call it here: a light, porous substance, of a delicate, waxen, flesh-colored tinge. Out of the blocks of this korl, Wolfe, in his off-hours from the furnace, had a habit of chipping and moulding figures,—hideous, fantastic enough, but sometimes strangely beautiful: even the mill-men saw that, while they jeered at him. It was a curious fancy in the man, almost a passion. The few hours for rest he spent hewing and hacking with his blunt knife, never speaking, until his watch came again,—working at one figure for months, and, when it was finished, breaking it to pieces perhaps, in a fit of disappointment. A morbid, gloomy man, untaught, unled, left to feed his soul in grossness and crime, and hard, grinding labor.

I want you to come down and look at this Wolfe, standing there among the lowest of his kind, and see him just as he is, that you may judge him justly when you hear the story of this night. I want you to look back, as he does every day, at his birth in vice, his starved infancy; to remember the heavy years he has groped through as boy and man,—the slow, heavy years of constant, hot work. So long ago he began, that he thinks sometimes he has worked there for ages. There is no hope that it will ever end. Think that God put into this man's soul a fierce thirst for beauty,—to know it, to create it; to *be*—something, he knows not what,—other than he is. There are moments when a passing cloud, the sun glinting on the purple thistles, a kindly smile, a child's face, will rouse him to a passion of pain,—when his nature starts up with a mad cry of rage against God, man, whoever it is that has forced this vile, slimy life upon him. With all this groping, this mad desire, a great blind intellect stumbling through wrong, a loving poet's heart, the man was by habit only a coarse, vulgar laborer, familiar with sights and words you would blush to name. Be just: when I tell you about this night, see him as he is. Be just,—not like man's law, which seizes on one isolated fact, but like God's judging angel, whose clear, sad eye saw all the countless cankering days of this man's life, all the countless nights, when, sick with starving, his soul fainted in him, before it judged him for this night, the saddest of all.

I called this night the crisis of his life. If it was, it stole on him unawares. These great turning-days of life cast no shadow before, slip by unconsciously. Only a trifle, a little turn of the rudder, and the ship goes to heaven or hell.

Wolfe, while Deborah watched him, dug into the furnace of melting iron with his pole, dully thinking only how many rails the lump would yield. It was late,—nearly Sunday morning; another hour, and the heavy work would be done,—only the furnaces to replenish and cover for the next day. The workmen were growing more noisy, shouting, as they had to do, to be heard over the deep clamor of the mills. Suddenly they grew less boisterous,—at the far end, entirely silent. Something unusual had happened. After a moment, the silence came nearer; the men stopped their jeers and drunken choruses. Deborah, stupidly lifting up her head, saw the cause of the quiet. A group of five or six men were slowly approaching, stopping to examine each furnace as they came. Visitors often came to see the mills after night: except by growing less noisy, the men took no notice of them. The furnace where Wolfe worked was near the bounds of the works; they halted there hot and tired: a walk over one of these great foundries is no trifling task. The woman, drawing out of sight, turned over to sleep. Wolfe, seeing them stop, suddenly roused from his indifferent stupor, and watched them keenly. He knew some of them: the overseer, Clarke,—a son of Kirby, one of the mill-owners,—and a Doctor May, one of the town-physicians. The other two were strangers. Wolfe came closer. He seized eagerly every chance that brought him into contact with this mysterious class that shone down on him perpetually with the glamour of another order of being. What made the difference between them? That was the mystery of his life. He had a vague notion that perhaps to-night he could find it out. One of the strangers sat down on a pile of bricks, and beckoned young Kirby to his side.

"This *is* hot, with a vengeance. A match, please?"—lighting his cigar. "But the walk is worth the trouble. If it were not that you must have heard it so often, Kirby, I would tell you that your works look like Dante's Inferno."

Kirby laughed.

"Yes. Yonder is Farinata himself in the burning tomb,"—pointing to some figure in the shimmering shadows.

"Judging from some of the faces of your men," said the other, "they bid fair to try the reality of Dante's vision, some day."

Young Kirby looked curiously around, as if seeing the faces of his hands for the first time.

"They're bad enough, that's true. A desperate set, I fancy. Eh, Clarke?"

The overseer did not hear him. He was talking of net profits just then,—giving, in fact, a schedule of the annual business of the firm to a sharp peering little Yankee, who jotted down notes on a paper laid on the crown of his hat: a reporter for one of the city-papers, getting up a series of reviews of the leading manufactories. The other gentlemen had accompanied them merely for amusement. They were silent until the notes were finished, drying their feet at the furnaces, and sheltering their faces from the intolerable heat. At last the overseer concluded with—

"I believe that is a pretty fair estimate, Captain."

"Here, some of you men!" said Kirby, "bring up those boards. We may as well sit down, gentlemen, until the rain is over. It cannot last much longer at this rate."

"Pig-metal,"—mumbled the reporter,—"um!—coal facilities,—um!—hands employed, twelve hundred,—bitumen,—um!—all right, I believe, Mr. Clarke;—sinking-fund,—what did you say was your sinking-fund?"

"Twelve hundred hands?" said the stranger, the young man who had first spoken. "Do you control their votes, Kirby?"

"Control? No." The young man smiled complacently. "But my father brought seven hundred votes to the polls for his candidate last November. No force-work, you understand,—only a speech or two, a hint to form themselves into a society, and a bit of red and blue bunting to make them a flag. The Invincible Roughs,—I believe that is their name. I forget the motto: 'Our country's hope,' I think."

There was a laugh. The young man talking to Kirby sat with an amused light in his cool gray eye, surveying critically the half-clothed figures of the puddlers, and the slow swing of their brawny muscles. He was a stranger in the city,—spending a couple of months in the borders of a Slave State, to study the institutions of the South,—a brother-in-law of Kirby's,—Mitchell. He was an amateur gymnast,—hence his anatomical eye; a patron, in a *blasé* way, of the prize-ring; a man who sucked the essence out of a science or philosophy in an indifferent, gentlemanly way; who took Kant, Novalis, Humboldt, for what they were worth in his own scales; accepting all, despising nothing, in heaven, earth, or hell, but one-idea'd men; with a temper yielding and brilliant as summer water, until his Self was touched, when it was ice, though brilliant still. Such men are not rare in the States.

As he knocked the ashes from his cigar, Wolfe caught with a quick pleasure the contour of the white hand, the blood-glow of a red ring he wore. His voice, too, and that of Kirby's, touched him like music,—low, even, with chording cadences. About this man Mitchell hung the impalpable atmosphere belonging to the thoroughbred gentleman. Wolfe, scraping away the ashes beside him, was conscious of it, did obeisance to it with his artist sense, unconscious that he did so.

The rain did not cease. Clark and the reporter left the mills; the others, comfortably seated near the furnace, lingered, smoking and talking in a desultory way. Greek would not have been more unintelligible to the furnace-tenders, whose presence they soon forgot entirely. Kirby drew out a newspaper from his pocket and read aloud some article, which they discussed eagerly. At every sentence, Wolfe listened more and more like a dumb, hopeless animal, with a duller, more stolid look creeping over his face, glancing now and then at Mitchell, marking acutely every smallest sign of refinement, then back to himself, seeing as in a mirror his filthy body, his more stained soul.

Never! He had no words for such a thought, but he knew now, in all the sharpness of the bitter certainty, that between them there was a great gulf never to be passed. Never!

The bells of the mills rang for midnight. Sunday morning had dawned. Whatever hidden message lay in the tolling bells floated past these men unknown. Yet it was there. Veiled in the solemn music ushering the risen saviour was a key-note to solve the darkest secrets of a world gone wrong,—even this social riddle which the brain of the grimy puddler grappled with madly tonight.

The men began to withdraw the metal from the caldrons. The mills were deserted on Sundays, except by the hands who fed the fires, and those who had no lodgings and slept usually on the ash-heaps. The three strangers sat still during the next hour, watching the men cover the furnaces, laughing now and then at some jest of Kirby's.

"Do you know," said Mitchell, "I like this view of the works better than when the glare was fiercest? These heavy shadows and the amphitheatre of smothered fires are ghostly, unreal. One could fancy these red smouldering lights to be the half-shut eyes of wild beasts, and the spectral figures their victims in the den."

Kirby laughed. "You are fanciful. Come, let us get out of the den. The spectral figures, as you call them, are a little too real for me to fancy a close proximity in the darkness,—unarmed, too."

The others rose, buttoning their over-coats, and lighting cigars.

"Raining, still," said Doctor May, "and hard. Where did we leave the coach, Mitchell?"

"At the other side of the works.—Kirby, what's that?"

Mitchell started back, half-frightened, as, suddenly turning a corner, the white figure of a woman faced him in the darkness,—a woman, white, of giant proportions, crouching on the ground, her arms flung out in some wild gesture of warning.

"Stop! Make that fire burn there!" cried Kirby, stopping short.

The flame burst out, flashing the gaunt figure into bold relief.

Mitchell drew a long breath.

"I thought it was alive," he said, going up curiously.

The others followed.

"Not marble, eh?" asked Kirby, touching it.

One of the lower overseers stopped.

"Korl, Sir."

"Who did it?"

"Can't say. Some of the hands; chipped it out in off-hours."

"Chipped to some purpose, I should say. What a flesh-tint the stuff has! Do you see, Mitchell?"

"I see."

He had stepped aside where the light fell boldest on the figure, looking at it in silence. There was not one line of beauty or grace in it: a nude woman's form, muscular, grown coarse with labor, the powerful limbs instinct with some one poignant longing. One idea: there it was in the tense, rigid muscles, the clutching hands, the wild, eager face, like that of a starving wolf's. Kirby and Doctor May walked around it, critical, curious. Mitchell stood aloof, silent. The figure touched him strangely.

"Not badly done," said Doctor May. "Where did the fellow learn that sweep of the muscles in the arm and hand? Look at them! They are groping,—do you see?—clutching: the peculiar action of a man dying of thirst."

"They have ample facilities for studying anatomy," sneered Kirby, glancing at the half-naked figures.

"Look," continued the Doctor, "at this bony wrist, and the strained sinews of the instep! A working-woman,—the very type of her class."

"God forbid!" muttered Mitchell.

"Why?" demanded May. "What does the fellow intend by the figure? I cannot catch the meaning."

"Ask him," said the other dryly. "There he stands,"—pointing to Wolfe, who stood with a group of men, leaning on his ash-rake.

The Doctor beckoned him with the affable smile which kind-hearted men put on, when talking with these people.

"Mr. Mitchell has picked you out as the man who did this,—I'm sure I don't know why. But what did you mean by it?"

"She be hungry."

Wolfe's eyes answered Mitchell, not the Doctor.

"Oh-h! But what a mistake you have made, my fine fellow! You have given no sign of starvation to the body. It is strong,—terribly strong. It has the mad, half-despairing gesture of drowning."

Wolfe stammered, glanced appealingly at Mitchell, who saw the soul of the thing, he knew. But the cool, probing eyes were turned on himself now,—mocking, cruel, relentless.

"Not hungry for meat," the furnace-tender said at last.

"What then? Whiskey?" jeered Kirby, with a coarse laugh.

Wolfe was silent a moment, thinking.

"I dunno," he said, with a bewildered look. "It mebbe. Summat to make her live, I think,—like you. Whiskey ull do it, in a way."

The young man laughed again. Mitchell flashed a look of disgust somewhere,—not at Wolfe.

"May," he broke out impatiently, "are you blind? Look at that woman's face! It asks questions of God, and says, 'I have a right to know.' Good God, how hungry it is!"

They looked a moment; then May turned to the mill-owner:—

"Have you many such hands as this? What are you going to do with them? Keep them at puddling iron?"

Kirby shrugged his shoulders. Mitchell's look had irritated him.

"*Ce n'est pas mon affaire.* I have no fancy for nursing infant geniuses. I suppose there are some stray gleams of mind and soul among these wretches. The Lord will take care of his own; or else they can work out their own salvation. I have heard you call our American system a ladder which any man can scale. Do you doubt it? Or perhaps you want to banish all social ladders, and put us all on a flat table-land,—eh, May?"

The Doctor looked vexed, puzzled. Some terrible problem lay hid in this woman's face, and troubled these men. Kirby waited for an answer, and, receiving none, went on, warming with his subject.

"I tell you, there's something wrong that no talk of '*Liberté*' or '*Égalité*' will do away. If I had the making of men, these men who do the lowest part of the world's work should be machines,—nothing more,—hands. It would be kindness. God help them! What are taste, reason, to creatures who must live such lives as that?" He pointed to Deborah, sleeping on the ash-heap. "So many nerves to sting them to pain. What if God had put your brain, with all its agony of touch, into your fingers, and bid you work and strike with that?"

"You think you could govern the world better?" laughed the Doctor.

"I do not think at all."

"That is true philosophy. Drift with the stream, because you cannot dive deep enough to find bottom, eh?"

"Exactly," rejoined Kirby. "I do not think. I wash my hands of all social problems,—slavery, caste, white or black. My duty to my operatives has a narrow limit,—the pay-hour on Saturday night. Outside of that, if they cut korl, or cut each other's throats, (the more popular amusement of the two,) I am not responsible."

The Doctor sighed,—a good honest sigh, from the depths of his stomach.

"God help us! Who is responsible?"

"Not I, I tell you," said Kirby, testily. "What has the man who pays them money to do with their souls' concerns, more than the grocer or butcher who takes it?"

"And yet," said Mitchell's cynical voice, "look at her! How hungry she is!"

Kirby tapped his boot with his cane. No one spoke. Only the dumb face of the rough image looking into their faces with the awful question, "What shall we do to be saved?" Only Wolfe's face, with its heavy weight of brain, its weak, uncertain mouth, its desperate eyes, out of which looked the soul of his class,—only Wolfe's face turned towards Kirby's. Mitchell laughed,—a cool, musical laugh.

"Money has spoken!" he said, seating himself lightly on a stone with the air of an amused spectator at a play. "Are you answered?"—turning to Wolfe his clear, magnetic face.

Bright and deep and cold as Arctic air, the soul of the man lay tranquil beneath. He looked at the furnace-tender as he had looked at a rare mosaic in the morning; only the man was the more amusing study of the two.

"Are you answered? Why, May, look at him! '*De profundis clamavi.*' Or, to quote in English, 'Hungry and thirsty, his soul faints in him.' And so Money sends back its answer into the depths through you, Kirby! Very clear the answer, too!—I think I remember reading the same words somewhere:—washing your hands in Eau de Cologne, and saying, 'I am innocent of the blood of this man. See ye to it!'"

Kirby flushed angrily.

"You quote Scripture freely."

"Do I not quote correctly? I think I remember another line, which may amend my meaning: 'Inasmuch as ye did it unto one of the least of these, ye did it unto me.' Deist? Bless you, man, I was raised on the milk of the Word. Now, Doctor, the pocket of the world having uttered its voice, what has the heart to say? You are a philanthropist, in a small way,—*n'est ce pas?* Here, boy, this gentleman can show you how to cut korl better,—or your destiny. Go on, May!"

"I think a mocking devil possesses you to-night," rejoined the Doctor, seriously.

He went to Wolfe and put his hand kindly on his arm. Something of a vague idea possessed the Doctor's brain that much good was to be done here by a friendly word or two: a latent genius to be warmed into life by a waited-for sun-beam. Here it was: he had brought it. So he went on complacently:—

"Do you know, boy, you have it in you to be a great sculptor, a great man?—do you understand?" (talking down to the capacity of his hearer: it is a way people have with children, and men like Wolfe,)—"to live a better, stronger life than I, or Mr. Kirby here? A man may make himself anything he chooses. God has given you stronger powers than many men,—me, for instance."

May stopped, heated, glowing with his own magnanimity. And it was magnanimous. The puddler had drunk in every word, looking through the Doctor's flurry, and generous heat, and self-approval, into his will, with those slow, absorbing eyes of his.

"Make yourself what you will. It is your right."

"I know," quietly. "Will you help me?"

Mitchell laughed again. The Doctor turned now, in a passion,—

"You know, Mitchell, I have not the means. You know, if I had, it is in my heart to take this boy and educate him for"—

"The glory of God, and the glory of John May."

May did not speak for a moment; then, controlled, he said,—

"Why should one be raised, when myriads are left?—I have not the money, boy," to Wolfe, shortly.

"Money?" He said it over slowly, as one repeats the guessed answer to a riddle, doubtfully. "That is it? Money?"

"Yes, money,—that is it," said Mitchell, rising, and drawing his furred coat about him. "You've found the cure for all the world's diseases.—Come, May, find your good-humor, and come home. This damp wind chills my very bones. Come and preach your Saint-Simonian doctrines to-morrow to Kirby's hands. Let them have a clear idea of the rights of the soul, and I'll venture next week they'll strike for higher wages. That will be the end of it."

"Will you send the coach-driver to this side of the mills?" asked Kirby, turning to Wolfe.

He spoke kindly: it was his habit to do so. Deborah, seeing the puddler go, crept after him. The three men waited outside. Doctor May walked up and down, chafed. Suddenly he stopped.

"Go back, Mitchell! You say the pocket and the heart of the world speak without meaning to these people. What has its head to say? Taste, culture, refinement? Go!"

Mitchell was leaning against a brick wall. He turned his head indolently, and looked into the mills. There hung about the place a thick, unclean odor. The slightest motion of his hand marked that he perceived it, and his insufferable disgust. That was all. May said nothing, only quickened his angry tramp.

"Besides," added Mitchell, giving a corollary to his answer, "it would be of no use. I am not one of them."

"You do not mean"—said May, facing him.

"Yes, I mean just that. Reform is born of need, not pity. No vital movement of the people's has worked down, for good or evil; fermented, instead, carried up the heaving, cloggy mass. Think back through history, and you will know it. What will this lowest deep—thieves, Magdalens, negroes—do with the light filtered through ponderous Church creeds, Baconian theories, Goethe schemes? Some day, out of their bitter need will be thrown up their own light-bringer,—their Jean Paul, their Cromwell, their Messiah."

"Bah!" was the Doctor's inward criticism. However, in practice, he adopted the theory; for, when, night and morning, afterwards, he prayed that power might be given these degraded souls to rise, he glowed at heart, recognizing an accomplished duty.

Wolfe and the woman had stood in the shadow of the works as the coach drove off. The Doctor had held out his hand in a frank, generous way, telling him to "take care of himself, and to remember it was his right to rise." Mitchell had simply touched his hat, as to an equal, with a quiet look of thorough recognition. Kirby had thrown Deborah some money, which she found, and clutched eagerly enough. They were gone now, all of them. The man sat down on the cinder-road, looking up into the murky sky.

"'T be late, Hugh. Wunnot hur come?"

He shook his head doggedly, and the woman crouched out of his sight against the wall. Do you remember rare moments when a sudden light flashed over yourself, your world, God? when you stood on a mountain-peak, seeing your life as it might have been, as it is? one quick instant, when custom lost its force and every-day usage? when your friend, wife, brother, stood in a new light? your soul was bared, and the grave,—a foretaste of the nakedness of the Judgment-Day? So it came before him, his life, that night. The slow tides of pain he had borne gathered themselves up and surged against his soul. His squalid daily life, the brutal coarseness eating into his brain, as the ashes into his skin: before, these things had been a dull aching into his consciousness; to-night, they were reality. He gripped the filthy red shirt that clung, stiff with soot, about him, and tore it savagely from his arm. The flesh beneath was muddy with grease and ashes,—and the heart beneath that! And the soul? God knows.

Then flashed before his vivid poetic sense the man who had left him,—the pure face, the delicate, sinewy limbs, in harmony with all he knew of beauty or truth. In his cloudy fancy he had pictured a Something like this. He had found it in this Mitchell, even when he idly scoffed at his pain: a Man all-knowing, all-seeing, crowned by Nature, reigning,—the keen glance of his eye falling like a sceptre on other men. And yet his instinct taught him that he too—He! He looked at himself with sudden loathing, sick, wrung his hands with a cry, and then was silent. With all the phantoms of his heated, ignorant fancy, Wolfe had not been vague in his ambitions. They were practical, slowly built up before him out of his knowledge of what he could do. Through years he had day by day made this hope a real thing to himself,—a clear, projected figure of himself, as he might become.

Able to speak, to know what was best, to raise these men and women working at his side up with him: sometimes he forgot this defined hope in the frantic anguish to escape,—only to escape,—out of the wet, the pain, the ashes, somewhere, anywhere,—only for one moment of free air on a hill-side, to lie down and let his sick soul throb itself out in the sunshine. But to-night he panted for life. The savage strength of his nature was roused; his cry was fierce to God for justice.

"Look at me!" he said to Deborah, with a low, bitter laugh, striking his puny chest savagely. "What am I worth, Deb? Is it my fault that I am no better? My fault? My fault?"

He stopped, stung with a sudden remorse, seeing her hunchback shape writhing with sobs. For Deborah was crying thankless tears, according to the fashion of women.

"God forgi' me, woman! Things go harder wi' you nor me. It's a worse share."

He got up and helped her to rise; and they went doggedly down the muddy street, side by side.

"It's all wrong," he muttered, slowly,—"all wrong! I dunnot understan'. But it'll end some day."

"Come home, Hugh!" she said, coaxingly; for he had stopped, looking around bewildered.

"Home,—and back to the mill!" He went on saying this over to himself, as if he would mutter down every pain in this dull despair.

She followed him through the fog, her blue lips chattering with cold. They reached the cellar at last. Old Wolfe had been drinking since she went out, and had crept nearer the door. The girl Janey slept heavily in the corner. He went up to her, touching softly the worn white arm with his fingers. Some bitterer thought stung him, as he stood there. He wiped the drops from his forehead, and went into the room beyond, livid, trembling. A hope, trifling, perhaps, but very dear, had died just then out of the poor puddler's life, as he looked at the sleeping, innocent girl,—some plan for the future, in which she had borne a part. He gave it up that moment, then and forever. Only a trifle, perhaps, to us: his face grew a shade paler,—that was all. But, somehow, the man's soul, as God and the angels looked down on it, never was the same afterwards.

Deborah followed him into the inner room. She carried a candle, which she placed on the floor, closing the door after her. She had seen the look on his face, as he turned away: her own grew deadly. Yet, as she came up to him her eyes glowed. He was seated on an old chest, quiet, holding his face in his hands.

"Hugh!" she said, softly.

He did not speak.

"Hugh, did hur hear what the man said,—him with the clear voice? Did hur hear? Money, money,—that it wud do all?"

He pushed her away,—gently, but he was worn out; her rasping tone fretted him.

"Hugh!"

The candle flared a pale yellow light over the cobwebbed brick walls, and the woman standing there. He looked at her. She was young, in deadly earnest; her faded eyes, and wet, ragged figure caught from their frantic eagerness a power akin to beauty.

"Hugh, it is true! Money ull do it! Oh, Hugh, boy, listen till me! He said it true! It is money!"

"I know. Go back! I do not want you here."

"Hugh, it is t' last time. I'll never worrit hur again."

There were tears in her voice now, but she choked them back.

"Hear till me only to-night! If one of t' witch people wud come, them we heard of t' home, and gif hur all hur wants, what then? Say, Hugh!"

"What do you mean?"

"I mean money."

Her whisper shrilled through his brain.

"If one of t' witch dwarfs wud come from t' lane moors to-night, and gif hur money, to go out,—*out,* I say,—out, lad, where t' sun shines, and t' heath grows, and t' ladies walk in silken gownds, and God stays all t' time,—where t' man lives that talked to us to-night,—Hugh knows,—Hugh could walk there like a king!"

He thought the woman mad, tried to check her, but she went on, fierce in her eager haste.

"If *I* were t' witch dwarf, if I had t' money, wud hur thank me? Wud hur take me out o' this place wid hur and Janey? I wud not come into the gran' house hur wud build, to vex hur wid t' hunch,—only at night, when t' shadows were dark, stand far off to see hur."

Mad? Yes! Are many of us mad in this way?

"Poor Deb! poor Deb!" he said, soothingly.

"It is here," she said, suddenly jerking into his hand a small roll. "I took it! I did it! Me, me!—not hur! I shall be hanged, I shall be burnt in hell, if anybody knows I took it! Out of his pocket, as he leaned against t' bricks. Hur knows?"

She thrust it into his hand, and then, her errand done, began to gather chips together to make a fire, choking down hysteric sobs.

"Has it come to this?"

That was all he said. The Welsh Wolfe blood was honest. The roll was a small green pocket-book containing one or two gold pieces, and a check for an incredible amount, as it seemed to the poor puddler. He laid it down, hiding his face again in his hands.

"Hugh, don't be angry wud me! It's only poor Deb,—hur knows?"

He took the long skinny fingers kindly in his.

"Angry? God help me, no! Let me sleep. I am tired."

He threw himself heavily down on the wooden bench, stunned with pain and weariness. She brought some old rags to cover him.

It was late on Sunday evening before he awoke. I tell God's truth, when I say he had then no thought of keeping this money. Deborah had hid it in his pocket. He found it there. She watched him eagerly, as he took it out.

"I must gif it to him," he said, reading her face.

"Hur knows," she said with a bitter sigh of disappointment. "But it is hur right to keep it."

His right! The word struck him. Doctor May had used the same. He washed himself, and went out to find this man Mitchell. His right! Why did this chance word cling to him so obstinately? Do you hear the fierce devils whisper in his ear, as he went slowly down the darkening street?

The evening came on, slow and calm. He seated himself at the end of an alley leading into one of the larger streets. His brain was clear to-night, keen, intent, mastering. It would not start back, cowardly, from any hellish temptation, but meet it face to face. Therefore the great temptation of his life came to him veiled by no sophistry, but bold, defiant, owning its own vile name, trusting to one bold blow for victory.

He did not deceive himself. Theft! That was it. At first the word sickened him; then he grappled with it. Sitting there on a broken cart-wheel, the fading day, the noisy groups, the church-bells' tolling passed before him like a panorama, while the sharp struggle went on within. This money! He took it out, and looked at it. If he gave it back, what then? He was going to be cool about it.

People going by to church saw only a sickly mill-boy watching them quietly at the alley's mouth. They did not know that he was mad, or they would not have gone by so quietly: mad with hunger; stretching out his hands to the world, that had given so much to them, for leave to live the life God meant him to live. His soul within him was smothering to death; he wanted so much, thought so much, and *knew*—nothing. There was nothing of which he was certain, except the mill and things there. Of God and heaven he had heard so little, that they were to him what fairy-land is to a child: something real, but not here; very far off. His brain, greedy, dwarfed, full of thwarted energy and unused powers, questioned these men and women going by, coldly, bitterly, that night. Was it not his right to live as they,—a pure life, a good, true-hearted life, full of beauty and kind words? He only wanted to know how to use the strength within him. His heart warmed, as he thought of it. He suffered himself to think of it longer. If he took the money?

Then he saw himself as he might be, strong, helpful, kindly. The night crept on, as this one image slowly evolved itself from the crowd of other thoughts and stood triumphant. He looked at it. As he might be! What wonder, if it blinded him to delirium,—the madness that underlies all revolution, all progress, and all fall?

You laugh at the shallow temptation? You see the error underlying its argument so clearly,—that to him a true life was one of full development rather than self-restraint? that he was deaf to the higher tone in a cry of voluntary suffering for truth's sake than in the fullest flow of spontaneous harmony? I do not plead his cause. I only want to show you the mote in my brother's eye: then you can see clearly to take it out.

The money,—there it lay on his knee, a little blotted slip of paper, nothing in itself; used to raise him out of the pit; something straight from God's hand. A thief! Well, what was it to be a thief? He met the question at last, face to face, wiping the clammy drops of sweat from his forehead. God made this money—the fresh air, too—for his children's use. He never made the difference between poor and rich. The Something who looked down on him that moment through the cool gray sky had a kindly face, he knew,—loved his children alike. Oh, he knew that!

There were times when the soft floods of color in the crimson and purple flames, or the clear depth of amber in the water below the bridge, had somehow given him a glimpse of another world than this,—of an infinite depth of beauty and of quiet somewhere,—somewhere,—a depth of quiet and rest and love. Looking up now, it became strangely real. The sun had sunk quite below the hills, but his last rays struck upward, touching the zenith. The fog had risen, and the town and river were steeped in its thick, gray damp; but overhead, the sun-touched smoke-clouds opened like a cleft ocean,—shifting, rolling seas of crimson mist, waves of billowy silver veined with blood-scarlet, inner depths unfathomable of glancing light. Wolfe's artist-eye grew drunk with color. The gates of that other world! Fading, flashing before him now! What, in that world of Beauty, Content, and Right, were the petty laws, the mine and thine, of mill-owners and mill-hands?

A consciousness of power stirred within him. He stood up. A man,—he thought, stretching out his hands,—free to work, to live, to love! Free! His right! He folded the scrap of paper in his hand. As his nervous fingers took it in, limp and blotted, so his soul took in the mean temptation, lapped it in fancied rights, in dreams of improved existences, drifting and endless as the cloud-seas of color. Clutching it, as if the tightness of his hold would strengthen his sense of possession, he went aimlessly down the street. It was his watch at the mill. He need not go, need never go again, thank God!—shaking off the thought with unspeakable loathing.

Shall I go over the history of the hours of that night? how the man wandered from one to another of his old haunts, with a half-consciousness of bidding them farewell,—lanes and alleys and back-yards where the mill-hands lodged,—noting, with a new eagerness, the filth and drunkenness, the pig-pens, the ash-heaps covered with potato-skins, the bloated, pimpled women at the doors,—with a new disgust, a new sense of sudden triumph, and, under all, a new, vague dread, unknown before, smothered down, kept under, but still there? It left him but once during the night, when, for the second time in his life, he entered a church. It was a sombre Gothic pile, where the stained light lost itself in far-retreating arches; built to meet the requirements and sympathies of a far other class than Wolfe's. Yet it touched, moved him uncontrollably. The distances, the shadows, the still, marble figures, the mass of silent kneeling worshippers, the mysterious music, thrilled, lifted his soul with a wonderful pain. Wolfe forgot himself, forgot the new life he was going to live, the mean terror gnawing underneath. The voice of the speaker strengthened the charm; it was clear, feeling, full, strong. An old man, who had lived much, suffered much; whose brain was keenly alive, dominant; whose heart was summer-warm with charity. He taught it to-night. He held up Humanity in its grand total; showed the great world-cancer to his people. Who could show it better? He was a Christian reformer; he had studied the age thoroughly; his outlook at man had been free, world-wide, over all time. His faith stood sublime upon the Rock of Ages; his fiery zeal guided vast schemes by which the gospel was to be preached to all nations. How did he preach it to-night? In burning, light-laden words he painted the incarnate Life, Love, the universal Man: words that became reality in the lives of these people,—that lived again in beautiful words and actions, trifling, but heroic. Sin, as he defined it, was a real foe to them; their trials, temptations, were his. His words passed far over the furnace-tender's grasp, toned to suit another class of culture; they sounded in his ears a very pleasant song in an unknown tongue. He meant to cure this world-cancer with a steady eye that had never glared with hunger, and a hand that neither poverty nor strychnine-whiskey had taught to shake. In this morbid, distorted heart of the Welsh puddler he had failed.

Wolfe rose at last, and turned from the church down the street. He looked up; the night had come on foggy, damp; the golden mists had vanished, and the sky lay dull and ash-colored. He wandered again aimlessly down the street, idly wondering what had become of the cloud-sea of crimson and scarlet. The trial-day of this man's life was over, and he had lost the victory. What followed was mere drifting circumstance,—a quicker walking over the path,—that was all. Do you want to hear the end of it? You wish me to make a tragic story out of it? Why, in the police-reports of the morning paper you can find a dozen such tragedies: hints of shipwrecks unlike any that ever befell on the high seas; hints that here a power was lost to heaven,—that there a soul went down where no tide can ebb or flow. Commonplace enough the hints are,—jocose sometimes, done up in rhyme.

Doctor May, a month after the night I have told you of, was reading to his wife at breakfast from this fourth column of the morning-paper: an unusual thing,—these police-reports not being, in general, choice reading for ladies; but it was only one item he read.

"Oh, my dear! You remember that man I told you of, that we saw at Kirby's mill?—that was arrested for robbing Mitchell? Here he is; just listen:—'Circuit Court. Judge Day. Hugh Wolfe, operative in Kirby & John's Loudon Mills. Charge, grand larceny. Sentence, nineteen years hard labor in penitentiary.'—Scoundrel! Serves him right! After all our kindness that night! Picking Mitchell's pocket at the very time!"

His wife said something about the ingratitude of that kind of people, and then they began to talk of something else.

Nineteen years! How easy that was to read! What a simple word for Judge Day to utter! Nineteen years! Half a lifetime!

Hugh Wolfe sat on the window-ledge of his cell, looking out. His ankles were ironed. Not usual in such cases; but he had made two desperate efforts to escape. "Well," as Haley, the jailer, said, "small blame to him! Nineteen years' imprisonment was not a pleasant thing to look forward to." Haley was very good-natured about it, though Wolfe had fought him savagely.

"When he was first caught," the jailer said afterwards, in telling the story, "before the trial, the fellow was cut down at once,—laid there on that pallet like a dead man, with his hands over his eyes. Never saw a man so cut down in my life. Time of the trial, too, came the queerest dodge of any customer I ever had. Would choose no lawyer. Judge gave him one, of course. Gibson it was. He tried to prove the fellow crazy; but it wouldn't go. Thing was plain as day-light: money found on him. 'Twas a hard sentence,—all the law allows; but it was for 'xample's sake. These mill-hands are gettin' onbearable. When the sentence was read, he just looked up, and said the money was his by rights, and that all the world had gone wrong. That night, after the trial, a gentleman came to see him here, name of Mitchell,—him as he stole from. Talked to him for an hour. Thought he came for curiosity, like. After he had gone, thought Wolfe was remarkable quiet, and went into his cell. Found him very low; bed all bloody. Doctor said he had been bleeding at the lungs. He was as weak as a cat; yet, if ye'll b'lieve me, he tried to get a-past me and get out. I just carried him like a baby, and threw him on the pallet. Three days after, he tried it again: that time reached the wall. Lord help you! he fought like a tiger,—giv' some terrible blows. Fightin' for life, you see; for he can't live long, shut up in the stone crib down yonder. Got a death-cough now. 'T took two of us to bring him down that day; so I just put the irons on his feet. There he sits, in there. Goin' to-morrow, with a batch more of 'em. That woman, hunchback, tried with him,—you remember?—she's only got three years. 'Complice. But *she's* a woman, you know. He's been quiet ever since I put on irons:

giv' up, I suppose. Looks white, sick-lookin'. It acts different on 'em, bein' sentenced. Most of 'em gets reckless, devilish-like. Some prays awful, and sings them vile songs of the mills, all in a breath. That woman, now, she's desper't'. Been beggin' to see Hugh, as she calls him, for three days. I'm a-goin' to let her in. She don't go with him. Here she is in this next cell. I'm a-goin' now to let her in."

He let her in. Wolfe did not see her. She crept into a corner of the cell, and stood watching him. He was scratching the iron bars of the window with a piece of tin which he had picked up, with an idle, uncertain, vacant stare, just as a child or idiot would do.

"Tryin' to get out, old boy?" laughed Haley. "Them irons will need a crow-bar beside your tin, before you can open 'em."

Wolfe laughed, too, in a senseless way.

"I think I'll get out," he said.

"I believe his brain's touched," said Haley, when he came out.

The puddler scraped away with the tin for half an hour. Still Deborah did not speak. At last she ventured nearer, and touched his arm.

"Blood?" she said, looking at some spots on his coat with a shudder.

He looked up at her. "Why, Deb!" he said, smiling,—such a bright, boyish smile, that it went to poor Deborah's heart directly, and she sobbed and cried out loud.

"Oh, Hugh, lad! Hugh! dunnot look at me, when it wur my fault! To think I brought hur to it! And I loved hur so! Oh, lad, I dud!"

The confession, even in this wretch, came with the woman's blush through the sharp cry.

He did not seem to hear her,—scraping away diligently at the bars with the bit of tin.

Was he going mad? She peered closely into his face. Something she saw there made her draw suddenly back,—something which Haley had not seen, that lay beneath the pinched, vacant look it had caught since the trial, or the curious gray shadow that rested on it. That gray shadow,—yes, she knew what that meant. She had often seen it creeping over women's faces for months, who died at last of slow hunger or consumption. That meant death, distant, lingering: but this—Whatever it was the woman saw, or thought she saw, used as she was to crime and misery, seemed to make her sick with a new horror. Forgetting her fear of him, she caught his shoulders, and looked keenly, steadily, into his eyes.

"Hugh!" she cried, in a desperate whisper,—"oh, boy, not that! for God's sake, not *that!*"

The vacant laugh went off his face, and he answered her in a muttered word or two that drove her away. Yet the words were kindly enough. Sitting there on his pallet, she cried silently a hopeless sort of tears, but did not speak again. The man looked up furtively at her now and then. Whatever his own trouble was, her distress vexed him with a momentary sting.

It was market-day. The narrow window of the jail looked down directly on the carts and wagons drawn up in a long line, where they had unloaded. He could see, too, and hear distinctly the clink of money as it changed hands, the busy crowd of whites and blacks shoving, pushing one another, and the chaffering and swearing at the stalls. Somehow, the sound, more than anything else had done, wakened him up,—made the whole real to him. He was done with the world and the business of it. He let the tin fall, and looked out, pressing his face close to the rusty bars. How they crowded and pushed! And he,—he should never walk that pavement again! There came Neff Sanders, one of the feeders at the mill, with a basket on his arm. Sure enough, Neff was married the other week. He whistled, hoping he would look up; but he did not. He wondered if Neff remembered he was there,—if any of the boys thought of him up there, and thought that he never was to go down that old cinder-road again. Never again! He had not quite understood it before; but now he did. Not for days or years, but never!—that was it.

How clear the light fell on that stall in front of the market! and how like a picture it was, the dark-green heaps of corn, and the crimson beets, and golden melons! There was another with game: how the light flickered on that pheasant's breast, with the purplish blood dripping over the brown feathers! He could see the red shining of the drops, it was so near. In one minute he could be down there. It was just a step. So easy, as it seemed, so natural to go! Yet it could never be—not in all the thousands of years to come—that he should put his foot on that street again! He thought of himself with a sorrowful pity, as of some one else. There was a dog down in the market, walking after his master with such a stately, grave look!—only a dog, yet he could go backwards and forwards just as he pleased: he had good luck! Why, the very vilest cur, yelping there in the gutter, had not lived his life, had been free to act out whatever thought God had put into his brain; while he—No, he would not think of that! He tried to put the thought away, and to listen to a dispute between a countryman and a woman about some meat; but it would come back. He, what had he done to bear this?

Then came the sudden picture of what might have been, and now. He knew what it was to be in the penitentiary,—how it went with men there. He knew how in these long years he should slowly die, but not until soul and body had become corrupt and rotten,—how, when he came out, if he lived to come, even the lowest of the mill-hands would jeer him,—how his hands would be weak, and his brain senseless and stupid. He believed he was almost that now. He put his hand to his head, with a puzzled, weary look. It ached, his head, with thinking. He tried to quiet himself. It was only right, perhaps; he had done wrong. But was there right or wrong for such as he? What was right? And who had ever taught him? He thrust the whole matter away. A dark, cold quiet crept through his brain. It was all wrong; but let it be! It was nothing to him more than the others. Let it be!

The door grated, as Haley opened it.

"Come, my woman! Must lock up for t' night. Come, stir yerself!"

She went up and took Hugh's hand.

"Good-night, Deb," he said, carelessly.

She had not hoped he would say more; but the tired pain on her mouth just then was bitterer than death. She took his passive hand and kissed it.

"Hur'll never see Deb again!" she ventured, her lips growing colder and more bloodless.

What did she say that for? Did he not know it? Yet he would not be impatient with poor old Deb. She had trouble of her own, as well as he.

"No, never again," he said, trying to be cheerful.

She stood just a moment, looking at him. Do you laugh at her, standing there, with her hunchback, her rags, her bleared, withered face, and the great despised love tugging at her heart?

"Come, you!" called Haley, impatiently.

She did not move.

"Hugh!" she whispered.

It was to be her last word. What was it?

"Hugh, boy, not *THAT!*"

He did not answer. She wrung her hands, trying to be silent, looking in his face in an agony of entreaty. He smiled again, kindly.

"It is best, Deb. I cannot bear to be hurted any more."

"Hur knows," she said, humbly.

"Tell my father good-bye; and—and kiss little Janey."

She nodded, saying nothing, looked in his face again, and went out of the door. As she went, she staggered.

"Drinkin' to-day?" broke out Haley, pushing her before him. "Where the Devil did you get it? Here, in with ye!" and he shoved her into her cell, next to Wolfe's, and shut the door.

Along the wall of her cell there was a crack low down by the floor, through which she could see the light from Wolfe's. She had discovered it days before. She hurried in now, and, kneeling down by it, listened, hoping to hear some sound. Nothing but the rasping of the tin on the bars. He was at his old amusement again. Something in the noise jarred on her ear, for she shivered as she heard it. Hugh rasped away at the bars. A dull old bit of tin, not fit to cut korl with.

He looked out of the window again. People were leaving the market now. A tall mulatto girl, following her mistress, her basket on her head, crossed the street just below, and looked up. She was laughing; but, when she caught sight of the haggard face peering out through the bars, suddenly grew grave, and hurried by. A free, firm step, a clear-cut olive face, with a scarlet turban tied on one side, dark, shining eyes, and on the head the basket poised, filled with fruit and flowers, under which the scarlet turban and bright eyes looked out half-shadowed. The picture caught his eye. It was good to see a face like that. He would try to-morrow, and cut one like it. *To-morrow!* He threw down the tin, trembling, and covered his face with his hands. When he looked up again, the daylight was gone.

Deborah, crouching near by on the other side of the wall, heard no noise. He sat on the side of the low pallet, thinking. Whatever was the mystery which the woman had seen on his face, it came out now slowly, in the dark there, and became fixed,—a something never seen on his face before. The evening was darkening fast. The market had been over for an hour; the rumbling of the carts over the pavement grew more infrequent: he listened to each, as it passed, because he thought it was to be for the last time. For the same reason, it was, I suppose, that he strained his eyes to catch a glimpse of each passer-by, wondering who they were, what kind of homes they were going to, if they had children,—listening eagerly to every chance word in the street, as if—(God be merciful to the man! what strange fancy was this?)—as if he never should hear human voices again.

It was quite dark at last. The street was a lonely one. The last passenger, he thought, was gone. No,—there was a quick step: Joe Hill, lighting the lamps. Joe was a good old chap; never passed a fellow without some joke or other. He remembered once seeing the place where he lived with his wife. "Granny Hill" the boys called her. Bedridden she was; but so kind as Joe was to her! kept the room so clean!—and the old woman, when he was there, was laughing at "some of t' lad's foolishness." The step was far down the street; but he could see him place the ladder, run up, and light the gas. A longing seized him to be spoken to once more.

"Joe!" he called, out of the grating. "Good-bye, Joe!"

The old man stopped a moment, listening uncertainly; then hurried on. The prisoner thrust his hand out of the window, and called again, louder; but Joe was too far down the street. It was a little thing; but it hurt him,—this disappointment.

"Good-bye, Joe!" he called, sorrowfully enough.

"Be quiet!" said one of the jailers, passing the door, striking on it with his club.

Oh, that was the last, was it?

There was an inexpressible bitterness on his face, as he lay down on the bed, taking the bit of tin, which he had rasped to a tolerable degree of sharpness, in his hand,—to play with, it may be. He bared his arms, looking intently at their corded veins and sinews. Deborah, listening in the next cell, heard a slight clicking sound, often repeated. She shut her lips tightly, that she might not scream, the cold drops of sweat broke over her, in her dumb agony.

"Hur knows best," she muttered at last, fiercely clutching the boards where she lay.

If she could have seen Wolfe, there was nothing about him to frighten her. He lay quite still, his arms outstretched, looking at the pearly stream of moonlight coming into the window. I think in that one hour that came then he lived back over all the years that had gone before. I think that all the low, vile life, all his wrongs, all his starved hopes, came then, and stung him with a farewell poison that made him sick unto death. He made neither moan nor cry, only turned his worn face now and then to the pure light, that seemed so far off, as one that said, "How long, O Lord? how long?"

The hour was over at last. The moon, passing over her nightly path, slowly came nearer, and threw the light across his bed on his feet. He watched it steadily, as it crept up, inch by inch, slowly. It seemed to him to carry with it a great silence. He had been so hot and tired there always in the mills! The years had been so fierce and cruel! There was coming now quiet and coolness and sleep. His tense limbs relaxed, and settled in a calm languor. The blood ran fainter and slow from his heart. He did not think now with a savage anger of what might be and was not; he was conscious only of deep stillness creeping over him. At first he saw a sea of faces: the mill-men,—women he had known, drunken and bloated,—Janeys timid and pitiful,—poor old Debs: then they floated together like a mist, and faded away, leaving only the clear, pearly moonlight.

Whether, as the pure light crept up the stretched-out figure, it brought with it calm and peace, who shall say? His dumb soul was alone with God in judgment. A Voice may have spoken for it from far-off Calvary, "Father, forgive them, for they know not what they do!" Who dare say? Fainter and fainter the heart rose and fell, slower and slower the moon floated from behind a cloud, until, when at last its full tide of white splendor swept over the cell, it seemed to wrap and fold into a deeper stillness the dead figure that never should move again. Silence deeper than the Night! Nothing that moved, save the black nauseous stream of blood dripping slowly from the pallet to the floor!

There was outcry and crowd enough in the cell the next day. The coroner and his jury, the local editors, Kirby himself, and boys with their hands thrust knowingly into their pockets and heads on one side, jammed into the corners. Coming and going all day. Only one woman. She came late, and outstayed them all. A Quaker, or Friend, as they call themselves. I think this woman was known by that name in heaven. A homely body, coarsely dressed in gray and white. Deborah (for Haley had let her in) took notice of her. She watched them all—sitting on the end of the pallet, holding his head in her arms—with the ferocity of a watch-dog, if any of them touched the body. There was no meekness, or sorrow, in her face; the stuff out of which murderers are made, instead. All the time Haley and the woman were laying straight the limbs and cleaning the cell, Deborah sat still, keenly watching the Quaker's face. Of all the crowd there that day, this woman alone had not spoken to her,—only once or twice had put some cordial to her lips. After they all were gone, the woman, in the same still, gentle way, brought a vase of wood-leaves and berries, and placed it by the pallet, then opened the narrow window. The fresh air blew in, and swept the woody fragrance over the dead face. Deborah looked up with a quick wonder.

"Did hur know my boy wud like it? Did hur know Hugh?"

"I know Hugh now."

The white fingers passed in a slow, pitiful way over the dead, worn face. There was a heavy shadow in the quiet eyes.

"Did hur know where they'll bury Hugh?" said Deborah in a shrill tone, catching her arm.

This had been the question hanging on her lips all day.

"In t' town-yard? Under t' mud and ash? T' lad'll smother, woman! He wur born on t' lane moor, where t' air is frick and strong. Take hur out, for God's sake, take hur out where t' air blows!"

The Quaker hesitated, but only for a moment. She put her strong arm around Deborah and led her to the window.

"Thee sees the hills, friend, over the river? Thee sees how the light lies warm there, and the winds of God blow all the day? I live there,—where the blue smoke is, by the trees. Look at me." She turned Deborah's face to her own, clear and earnest. "Thee will believe me? I will take Hugh and bury him there to-morrow."

Deborah did not doubt her. As the evening wore on, she leaned against the iron bars, looking at the hills that rose far off, through the thick sodden clouds, like a bright, unattainable calm. As she looked, a shadow of their solemn repose fell on her face: its fierce discontent faded into a pitiful, humble quiet. Slow, solemn tears gathered in her eyes: the poor weak eyes turned so hopelessly to the place where Hugh was to rest, the grave heights looking higher and brighter and more solemn than ever before. The Quaker watched her keenly. She came to her at last, and touched her arm.

"When thee comes back," she said, in a low, sorrowful tone, like one who speaks from a strong heart deeply moved with remorse or pity, "thee shall begin thy life again,—there on the hills. I came too late; but not for thee,—by God's help, it may be."

Not too late. Three years after, the Quaker began her work. I end my story here. At evening-time it was light. There is no need to tire you with the long years of sunshine, and fresh air, and slow, patient Christ-love, needed to make healthy and hopeful this impure body and soul. There is a homely pine house, on one of these hills, whose windows overlook broad, wooded slopes and clover-crimsoned meadows,—niched into the very place where the light is warmest, the air freest. It is the Friends' meeting-house. Once a week they sit there, in their grave, earnest way, waiting for the Spirit of Love to speak, opening their simple hearts to receive His words. There is a woman, old, deformed, who takes a humble place among them: waiting like them: in her gray dress, her worn face, pure and meek, turned now and then to the sky. A woman much loved by these silent, restful people; more silent than they, more humble, more loving. Waiting: with her eyes turned to hills higher and purer than these on which she lives,—dim and far off now, but to be reached some day. There may be in her heart some latent hope to meet there the love denied her here,—that she shall find him whom she lost, and that then she will not be all-unworthy. Who blames her? Something is lost in the passage of every soul from one eternity to the other,—something pure and beautiful, which might have been and was not: a hope, a talent, a love, over which the soul mourns, like Esau deprived of his birthright. What blame to the meek Quaker, if she took her lost hope to make the hills of heaven more fair?

Nothing remains to tell that the poor Welsh puddler once lived, but this figure of the mill-woman cut in korl. I have it here in a corner of my library. I keep it hid behind a curtain,—it is such a rough, ungainly thing. Yet there are about it touches, grand sweeps of outline, that show a master's hand. Sometimes,—to-night, for instance,—the curtain is accidentally drawn back, and I see a bare arm stretched out imploringly in the darkness, and an eager, wolfish face watching mine: a wan, woful face, through which the spirit of the dead korl-cutter looks out, with its thwarted life, its mighty hunger, its unfinished work. Its pale, vague lips seem to tremble with a terrible question. "Is this the End?" they say,—"nothing beyond?—no more?" Why, you tell me you have seen that look in the eyes of dumb brutes,—horses dying under the lash. I know.

The deep of the night is passing while I write. The gas-light wakens from the shadows here and there the objects which lie scattered through the room: only faintly, though; for they belong to the open sunlight. As I glance at them, they each recall some task or pleasure of the coming day. A half-moulded child's head; Aphrodite; a bough of forest-leaves; music; work; homely fragments, in which lie the secrets of all eternal truth and beauty. Prophetic all! Only this dumb, woful face seems to belong to and end with the night. I turn to look at it. Has the power of its desperate need commanded the darkness away? While the room is yet steeped in heavy shadow, a cool, gray light suddenly touches its head like a blessing hand, and its groping arm points through the broken cloud to the far East, where, in the flickering, nebulous crimson, God has set the promise of the Dawn.

1861

LOUISA MAY ALCOTT
(1832–1888)

Louisa May Alcott is most famous for her novel Little Women. *Even today young girls respond enthusiastically to the story of the rebellious Jo March and her growth into womanhood. Alcott also wrote novels and short stories for adults and published sentimental tales and gothic thrillers in efforts to support her parents and sisters. Alcott's heroines are unusual for her time in that they frequently have careers outside the home and find satisfaction in their work as well as in their family life.*

Alcott grew up in a New England family interested in educational issues, abolition, and women's rights. Her father, Bronson Alcott, a friend of both Thoreau and Emerson, introduced her to many of the most prominent thinkers of the time. However, when her father left the family impoverished through his efforts to found the forward-thinking Temple School and the utopian community Fruitlands, the Alcott women supported the family. In 1862, Louisa May Alcott went to Washington, D.C., to work as a nurse taking care of soldiers wounded in the Civil War. After returning home with typhoid fever, she wrote Hospital Sketches, *a collection of vignettes drawn from her experiences, which proved popular with the public and began her career as a serious writer. Her first novel,* Moods, *about the problems facing working women, was not a critical success, but in 1869,* Little Women, *her second novel, established her international reputation.*

Little Women *was followed by* Good Wives, An Old-Fashioned Girl, Little Men, Eight Cousins, Rose in Bloom, *and a number of other works for children and adults.* Work, *her most feminist novel, depicts the jobs available to women in the nineteenth century. Alcott also wrote short stories and revised her earlier ones throughout the 1870s and 1880s, publishing them in a series of collected stories titled* Aunt Jo's Scrapbag.

A number of Alcott's novels and stories reflect her interest in social problems, and particularly women's issues. She went to debates on women's suffrage in 1874 and attended the Women's Congress of 1875 in Syracuse. Her thoughts on practical education for girls appear in Eight Cousins. *She also wrote her opinions on women's issues for the* Women's Journal, *which had been founded in Boston in 1870. In 1876, when women were excluded from Centennial celebrations in Concord, Alcott wrote about the women's counterdemonstrations. She also wrote about her experience as the first woman to register to vote in Concord.*

Never healthy after her bout with typhoid fever, Alcott continued writing up until her death. In the last year of her life, she spent considerable time in the rest home run by one of the first women graduates of the Boston medical school, whose fictional counterpart appears in Jo's Boys.

In "How I Went Out to Service," which was published in The Independent *in 1874, Alcott uses autobiographical material to depict the way in which the harsh realities of working as a servant become part of a young woman's growing up. Of course, unlike the characters created by Harriet Wilson and Rebecca Harding Davis, the young woman in Alcott's story is able to quit her job and return to her middle-class home.*

■ HOW I WENT OUT TO SERVICE

When I was eighteen I wanted something to do. I had tried teaching for two years, and hated it; I had tried sewing, and could not earn my bread in that way, at the cost of health; I tried story-writing and got five dollars for stories which now bring a hundred; I had thought seriously of going upon the stage, but certain highly respectable relatives were so shocked at the mere idea that I relinquished my dramatic aspirations.

"What *shall* I do?" was still the question that perplexed me. I was ready to work, eager to be independent, and too proud to endure patronage. But the right task seemed hard to find, and my bottled energies were fermenting in a way that threatened an explosion before long.

My honored mother was a city missionary that winter, and not only served the clamorous poor, but often found it in her power to help decayed gentlefolk by quietly placing them where they could earn their bread without the entire sacrifice of taste and talent which makes poverty so hard for such to bear. Knowing her tact and skill, people often came to her for companions, housekeepers, and that class of the needy who do not make their wants known through an intelligence office.

One day, as I sat dreaming splendid dreams, while I made a series of little petticoats out of the odds and ends sent in for the poor, a tall, ministerial gentleman appeared, in search of a companion for his sister. He possessed an impressive nose, a fine flow of language, and a pair of large hands, encased in black kid gloves. With much waving of these somber members, Mr. R. set forth the delights awaiting the happy soul who should secure this home. He described it as a sort of heaven on earth. "There are books, pictures, flowers, a piano, and the best of society," he said. "This person will be one of the family in all respects, and only required to help about the lighter work, which my sister has done herself hitherto, but is now a martyr to neuralgia and needs a gentle friend to assist her."

My mother, who never lost her faith in human nature, in spite of many impostures, believed every word, and quite beamed with benevolent interest as she listened and tried to recall some needy young woman to whom this charming home would be a blessing. I also innocently thought:

"That sounds inviting. I like housework and can do it well. I should have time to enjoy the books and things I love, and D——— is not far away from home. Suppose I try it."

So, when my mother turned to me, asking if I could suggest any one, I became as red as a poppy and said abruptly:

"Only myself."

"Do you really mean it?" cried my astonished parent.

"I really do if Mr. R. thinks I should suit," was my steady reply, as I partially obscured my crimson countenance behind a little flannel skirt, still redder.

The Reverend Josephus gazed upon me with the benign regard which a bachelor of five and thirty may accord a bashful damsel of eighteen. A smile dawned upon his countenance, "sicklied o'er with the pale cast of thought," or dyspepsia; and he softly folded the black gloves, as if about to bestow a blessing as he replied, with emphasis:

"I am sure you would, and we should think ourselves most fortunate if we could secure your society, and—ahem—services for my poor sister."

"Then I'll try it," responded the impetuous maid.

"We will talk it over a little first, and let you know to-morrow, sir," put in my prudent parent, adding, as Mr. R. arose: "What wages do you pay?"

"My dear madam, in a case like this let me not use such words as those. Anything you may think proper we shall gladly give. The labor is very light, for there are but three of us and our habits are of the simplest sort. I am a frail reed and may break at any moment; so is my sister, and my aged father cannot long remain; therefore, money is little to us, and any one who comes to lend her youth and strength to our feeble household will not be forgotten in the end, I assure you." And, with another pensive smile, a farewell wave of the impressive gloves, the Reverend Josephus bowed like a well-sweep and departed.

"My dear, are you in earnest?" asked my mother.

"Of course, I am. Why not try this experiment? It can but fail, like all the others."

"I have no objection; only I fancied you were rather too proud for this sort of thing."

"I am too proud to be idle and dependent, ma'am. I'll scrub floors and take in washing first. I do housework at home for love; why not do it abroad for money? I like it better than teaching. It is healthier than sewing and surer than writing. So why not try it?"

"It is going out to service, you know, though you are called a companion. How does that suit?"

"I don't care. Every sort of work that is paid for is service; and I don't mind being a companion, if I can do it well. I may find it is my mission to take care of neuralgic old ladies and lackadaisical clergymen. It does not sound exciting, but it's better than nothing," I answered, with a sigh; for it *was* rather a sudden downfall to give up being a Siddons and become a Betcinder.

How my sisters laughed when they heard the new plan! But they soon resigned themselves, sure of fun, for Lu's adventures were the standing joke of the family. Of course, the highly respectable relatives held up their hands in holy horror at the idea of one of the clan degrading herself by going out to service. Teaching a private school was the proper thing for an indigent gentlewoman. Sewing even, if done in the seclusion of home and not mentioned in public, could be tolerated. Story-writing was a genteel accomplishment and reflected credit upon the name. But leaving the paternal roof to wash other people's teacups, nurse other people's ails, and obey other people's orders for hire—this, this was degradation; and headstrong Louisa would disgrace her name forever if she did it.

Opposition only fired the revolutionary blood in my veins, and I crowned my iniquity by the rebellious declaration:

"If doing this work hurts my respectability, I wouldn't give much for it. My aristocratic ancestors don't feed or clothe me and my democratic ideas of honesty and honor won't let me be idle or dependent. You need not know me if you are ashamed of me, and I won't ask you for a penny; so, if I never do succeed in anything, I shall have the immense satisfaction of knowing I am under no obligation to any one."

In spite of the laughter and the lamentation, I got ready my small wardrobe, consisting of two calico dresses and one delaine, made by myself, also several large and uncompromising blue aprons and three tidy little sweeping-caps; for I had some English notions about housework and felt that my muslin hair-protectors would be useful in some of the "light labors" I was to undertake. It is needless to say they were very becoming. Then, firmly embracing my family, I set forth, one cold January day, with my little trunk, a stout heart, and a five-dollar bill for my fortune.

"She will be back in a week," was my sister's prophecy, as she wiped her weeping eye.

"No, she won't, for she has promised to stay the month out and she will keep her word," answered my mother, who always defended the black sheep of her flock.

I heard both speeches, and registered a tremendous vow to keep that promise, if I died in the attempt—little dreaming, poor innocent, what lay before me.

Josephus meantime had written me several remarkable letters, describing the different members of the family I was about to enter. His account was peculiar, but I believed every word of it and my romantic fancy was much excited by the details he gave. The principal ones are as follows, condensed from the voluminous epistles which he evidently enjoyed writing:

"You will find a stately mansion, fast falling to decay, for my father will have nothing repaired, preferring that the old house and its master should crumble away together. I have, however, been permitted to rescue a few rooms from ruin; and here I pass my recluse life, surrounded by the things I love. This will naturally be more attractive to you than the gloomy apartments my father inhabits, and I hope you will here allow me to minister to your young and cheerful nature when your daily cares are over. I need such companionship and shall always welcome you to my abode.

"Eliza, my sister, is a child at forty, for she has lived alone with my father and an old servant all her life. She is a good creature, but not lively, and needs stirring up, as you will soon see. Also I hope by your means to rescue her from the evil influence of Puah, who, in my estimation, is a *wretch.* She has gained entire control over Eliza, and warps her mind with great skill, prejudicing her against *me* and thereby desolating my home. Puah hates *me* and always has. Why I know not, except that I will not yield to her control. She ruled here for years while I was away, and my return upset all her nefarious plans. It will always be my firm opinion that she has tried to *poison me,* and may again. But even this dark suspicion will not deter me from my duty. I cannot send her away, for both my deluded father and my sister have entire faith in her, and I cannot shake it. She is faithful and kind to them, so I submit and remain to guard them, even at the risk of my life.

"I tell you these things because I wish you to know all and be warned, for this old hag has a specious tongue, and I should grieve to see you deceived by her lies. Say nothing, but watch her silently, and help me to thwart her evil plots; but do not trust her, or beware."

Now this was altogether romantic and sensational, and I felt as if about to enter one of those delightfully dangerous houses we read of in novels, where perils, mysteries, and sins freely disport themselves, till the newcomer sets all to rights, after unheard of trials and escapes.

I arrived at twilight, just the proper time for the heroine to appear; and, as no one answered my modest solo on the rusty knocker, I walked in and looked about me. Yes, here was the long, shadowy hall, where the ghosts doubtless walked at midnight. Peering in at an open door on the right, I saw a parlor full of ancient furniture, faded, dusty, and dilapidated. Old portraits stared at me from the walls and a damp chill froze the marrow of my bones in the most approved style.

"The romance opens well," I thought, and, peeping in at an opposite door, beheld a luxurious apartment, full of the warm glow of firelight, the balmy breath of hyacinths and roses, the white glimmer of piano keys, and tempting rows of books along the walls.

The contrast between the two rooms was striking, and, after an admiring survey, I continued my explorations, thinking that I should not mind being "ministered to" in that inviting place when my work was done.

A third door showed me a plain, dull sitting room, with an old man napping in his easy-chair. I heard voices in the kitchen beyond, and, entering there, beheld Puah the fiend. Unfortunately, for the dramatic effect of the tableaux, all I saw was a mild-faced old woman, buttering toast, while she conversed with her familiar, a comfortable gray cat.

The old lady greeted me kindly, but I fancied her faded blue eye had a weird expression and her amiable words were all a snare, though I own I was rather disappointed at the commonplace appearance of this humble Borgia.

She showed me to a tiny room, where I felt more like a young giantess than ever, and was obliged to stow away my possessions as snugly as in a ship's cabin. When I presently descended, armed with a blue apron and "a heart for any fate," I found the old man awake and received from him a welcome full of ancient courtesy and kindliness. Miss Eliza crept in like a timid mouse, looking so afraid of her buxom companion that I forgot my own shyness in trying to relieve hers. She was so enveloped in shawls that all I could discover was that my mistress was a very nervous little woman, with a small button of pale hair on the outside of her head and the vaguest notions of work inside. A few spasmodic remarks and many awkward pauses brought me to teatime, when Josephus appeared, as tall, thin, and cadaverous as ever. After his arrival there was no more silence, for he preached all suppertime something in this agreeable style.

"My young friend, our habits, as you see, are of the simplest. We eat in the kitchen, and all together, in the primitive fashion; for it suits my father and saves labor. I could wish more order and elegance; but *my* wishes are not consulted and I submit. I live above these petty crosses, and, though my health suffers from bad cookery, I do not murmur. Only, I must say, in passing, that if you *will* make your battercakes green with saleratus, Puah, I shall feel it my duty to throw them out of the window. *I* am used to poison; but I cannot see the coals of this blooming girl's stomach destroyed, as mine have been. And, speaking of duties, I may as well mention to you, Louisa (I call you so in a truly fraternal spirit), that I like to find my study in order when I come down in the morning; for I often need a few moments of solitude before I face the daily annoyances of my life. I shall permit *you* to perform this light task, for *you* have some idea of order (I see it in the formation of your brow), and feel sure that *you* will respect the sanctuary of thought. Eliza is so blind she does not see dust, and Puah enjoys devastating the one poor refuge I can call my own this side the grave. We are all waiting for you, sir. My father keeps up the old formalities, you observe; and I endure them, though *my* views are more advanced."

The old gentleman hastily finished his tea and returned thanks, when his son stalked gloomily away, evidently oppressed with the burden of his wrongs, also, as I irreverently fancied, with the seven "green" flapjacks he had devoured during the sermon.

I helped wash up the cups, and during that domestic rite Puah chatted in what I should have considered a cheery, social way had I not been darkly warned against her wiles.

"You needn't mind half Josephus says, my dear. He likes to hear himself talk and always goes on so before folks. I sometimes thinks his books and new ideas have sort of muddled his wits, for he is as full of notions as a paper is of pins; and he gets dreadfully put out if we don't give in to 'em. But, gracious me! they are so redicklus sometimes and so selfish I can't allow him to make a fool of himself or plague Lizy. She don't dare to say her soul is her own; so I have to stand up for her. His pa don't know half his odd doings; for I try to keep the old gentleman comfortable and have to manage 'em all, which is not an easy job I do assure you."

I had a secret conviction that she was right, but did not commit myself in any way, and we joined the social circle in the sitting room. The prospect was not a lively one, for the old gentleman nodded behind his newspaper; Eliza, with her head pinned up in a little blanket, slumbered on the sofa, Puah fell to knitting silently; and the plump cat dozed under the stove. Josephus was visible, artistically posed in the luxurious recesses of his cell, with the light beaming on his thoughtful brow, as he pored over a large volume or mused with upturned eye.

Having nothing else to do, I sat and stared at him, till, emerging from a deep reverie, with an effective start, he became conscious of my existence and beckoned me to approach the "sanctuary of thought" with a dramatic waft of his large hand.

I went, took possession of an easy chair, and prepared myself for elegant conversation. I was disappointed, however; for Josephus showed me a list of his favorite dishes, sole fruit of all that absorbing thought, and, with an earnestness that flushed his saffron countenance, gave me hints as to the proper preparation of these delicacies.

I mildly mentioned that I was not a cook; but was effectually silenced by being reminded that I came to be generally useful, to take his sister's place, and see that the flame of life which burned so feebly in this earthly tabernacle was fed with proper fuel. Mince pies, Welsch rarebits, sausages, and strong coffee did not strike me as strictly spiritual fare; but I listened meekly and privately resolved to shift this awful responsibility to Puah's shoulders.

Detecting me in gape, after an hour of this high converse, he presented me with an overblown rose, which fell to pieces before I got out of the room, pressed my hand, and dismissed me with a fervent "God bless you, child. Don't forget the dropped eggs for breakfast."

I was up betimes next morning and had the study in perfect order before the recluse appeared, enjoying a good prowl among the books as I worked and becoming so absorbed that I forgot the eggs, till a gusty sigh startled me, and I beheld Josephus, in dressing gown and slippers, languidly surveying the scene.

"Nay, do not fly," he said, as I grasped my duster in guilty haste. "It pleases me to see you here and lends a sweet, domestic charm to my solitary room. I like that graceful cap, that housewifely apron, and I beg you to wear them often; for it refreshes my eye to see something tasteful, young, and womanly about me. Eliza makes a bundle of herself and Puah is simply detestable."

He sank languidly into a chair and closed his eyes, as if the mere thought of his enemy was too much for him. I took advantage of this momentary prostration to slip away, convulsed with laughter at the looks and words of this bald-headed sentimentalist.

After breakfast I fell to work with a will, eager to show my powers and glad to put things to rights, for many hard jobs had evidently been waiting for a stronger arm that Puah's and a more methodical head than Eliza's.

Everything was dusty, moldy, shiftless, and neglected, except the domain of Josephus. Up-stairs the paper was dropping from the walls, the ancient furniture was all more or less dilapidated, and every hold and corner was full of relics tucked away by Puah, who was a regular old magpie. Rats and mice reveled in the empty rooms and spiders wove their tapestry undisturbed, for the old man would have nothing altered or repaired and his part of the house was fast going to ruin.

I longed to have a grand "clearing up"; but was forbidden to do more than to keep things in livable order. On the whole, it was fortunate, for I soon found that my hands would be kept busy with the realms of Josephus, whose ethereal being shrank from dust, shivered at a cold breath, and needed much cosseting with dainty food, hot fires, soft beds, and endless service, else, as he expressed it, the frail reed would break.

I regret to say that a time soon came when I felt supremely indifferent as to the breakage, and very skeptical as to the fragility of a reed that ate, slept, dawdled, and scolded so energetically. The rose that fell to pieces so suddenly was a good symbol of the rapid disappearance of all the romantic delusions I had indulged in for a time. A week's acquaintance with the immates of this old house quite settled my opinion, and further developments only confirmed it.

Miss Eliza was a nonentity and made no more impression on me than a fly. The old gentleman passed his days in a placid sort of doze and took no notice of what went on about him. Puah had been a faithful drudge for years, and, instead of being a "wretch," was, as I soon satisfied myself, a motherly old soul, with no malice in her. The secret of Josephus's dislike was that the reverend tyrant ruled the house, and all obeyed him but Puah, who had nursed him as a baby, boxed his ears as a boy, and was not afraid of him even when he became a man and a minister. I soon repented of my first suspicions, and grew fond of her, for without my old gossip I should have fared ill when my day of tribulation came.

At first I innocently accepted the fraternal invitations to visit the study, feeling that when my day's work was done I earned a right to rest and read. But I soon found that this was not the idea. I was not to read; but to be read to. I was not to enjoy the flowers, pictures, fire, and books; but to keep them in order for my lord to enjoy. I was also to be a passive bucket, into which he was to pour all manner of philosophic, metaphysical, and sentimental rubbish. I was to serve his needs, soothe his sufferings, and sympathize with all his sorrows—be a galley slave, in fact.

As soon as I clearly understood this, I tried to put an end to it by shunning the study and never lingering there an instant after my work was done. But it availed little, for Josephus demanded much sympathy and was bound to have it. So he came and read poems while I washed dishes, discussed his pet problems all meal-times, and put reproachful notes under my door, in which were comically mingled complaints of neglect and orders for dinner.

I bore it as long as I could, and then freed my mind in a declaration of independence, delivered in the kitchen, where he found me scrubbing the hearth. It was not an impressive attitude for an orator, nor was the occupation one a girl would choose when receiving calls; but I have always felt grateful for the intense discomfort of that moment, since it gave me the courage to rebel outright. Stranded on a small island of mat, in a sea of soapsuds, I brandished a scrubbing brush, as I indignantly informed him that I came to be a companion to his sister, not to him, and I should keep that post or none. This I followed up by reproaching him with the delusive reports he had given me of the place and its duties, and assuring him that I should not stay long unless matters mended.

"But I offer you lighter tasks, and you refuse them," he began, still hovering in the doorway, whither he had hastily retired when I opened my batteries.

"But I don't like the tasks, and consider them much worse than hard work," was my ungrateful answer, as I sat upon my island, with the softsoap conveniently near.

"Do you mean to say you prefer to scrub the hearth to sitting in my charming room while I read Hegel to you?" he demanded, glaring down upon me.

"Infinitely," I responded promptly, and emphasized my words by beginning to scrub with a zeal that made the bricks white with foam.

"Is it possible!" and, with a groan at my depravity, Josephus retired, full of ungodly wrath.

I remember that I immediately burst into jocund song, so that no doubt might remain in his mind, and continued to warble cheerfully till my task was done. I also remember that I cried heartily [?] when I got to my room, I was so vexed, disappointed, and tired. But my bower was so small I should soon have swamped the furniture if I had indulged copiously in tears; therefore I speedily dried them up, wrote a comic letter home, and waited with interest to see what would happen next.

Far be it from me to accuse one of the nobler sex of spite or the small revenge of underhand annoyances and slights to one who could not escape and would not retaliate; but after that day a curious change came over the spirit of that very unpleasant dream. Gradually all the work of the house had been slipping into my hands; for Eliza was too poorly to help and direct, and Puah too old to do much besides the cooking. About this time I found that even the roughest work was added to my share, for Josephus was unusually feeble and no one was hired to do his chores. Having made up my mind to go when the month was out, I said nothing, but dug paths, brought water from the well, split kindlings, made fires, and sifted ashes, like a true Cinderella.

There never had been any pretense of companionship with Eliza, who spent her days mulling over the fire, and seldom exerted herself except to find odd jobs for me to do—rusty knives to clean, sheets to turn, old stockings to mend, and, when all else failed, some paradise of moths and mice to be cleared up; for the house was full of such "glory holds."

If I remonstrated, Eliza at once dissolved into tears and said she must do as she was told; Puah begged me to hold on till spring, when things would be much better; and pity pleaded for the two poor souls. But I don't think I could have stood it if my promise had not bound me, for when the fiend said "Budge" honor said "Budge not" and I stayed.

But, being a mortal worm, I turned now and then when ireful Josephus trod upon me too hard, especially in the matter of boot-blacking. I really don't know why that is considered such humiliating work for a woman; but so it is, and there I drew the line. I would have cleaned the old man's shoes without a murmur; but he preferred to keep their native rustiness intact. Eliza never went out, and Puah affected carpet-slippers of the Chinese-junk pattern. Josephus, however, plumed himself upon his feet, which, like his nose, were large, and never took his walks abroad without having his boots in a high state of polish. He had brushed them himself at first; but soon after the explosion I discovered a pair of muddy boots in the shed, set suggestively near the blacking-box. I did not take the hint; feeling instinctively that this amiable being was trying how much I would bear for the sake of peace.

The boots remained untouched; and another pair soon came to keep them company, whereat I smiled wickedly as I chopped just kindlings enough for my own use. Day after day the collection grew, and neither party gave in. Boots were succeeded by shoes, then rubbers gave a pleasing variety to the long line, and then I knew the end was near.

"Why are not my boots attended to?" demanded Josephus, one evening, when obliged to go out.

"I'm sure I don't know," was Eliza's helpless answer.

"I told Louizy I guessed you'd want some of 'em before long," observed Puah with an exasperating twinkle in her old eye.

"And what did she say?" asked my lord with an ireful whack of his velvet slippers as he cast them down.

"Oh! she said she was so busy doing your other work you'd have to do that yourself; and I thought she was about right."

"Louizy" heard it all through the slide, and could have embraced the old woman for her words, but kept still till Josephus had resumed his slippers with a growl and retired to the shed, leaving Eliza in tears, Puah chuckling, and the rebellious handmaid exulting in the china-closet.

Alas! for romance and the Christian virtues, several pairs of boots were cleaned that night, and my sinful soul enjoyed the spectacle of the reverend bootblack at his task. I even found my "fancy work," as I called the evening job of paring a bucketful of hard russets with a dull knife, much cheered by the shoe-brush accompaniment played in the shed.

Thunder-clouds rested upon the martyr's brow at breakfast, and I was as much ignored as the cat. And what a relief that was! The piano was locked up, so were the bookcases, the newspapers mysteriously disappeared, and a solemn silence reigned at table, for no one dared to talk when that gifted tongue was mute. Eliza fled from the gathering storm and had a comfortable fit of neuralgia in her own room, where Puah nursed her, leaving me to skirmish with the enemy.

It was not a fair fight, and that experience lessened my respect for mankind immensely. I did my best, however—grubbed about all day and amused my dreary evenings as well as I could; too proud even to borrow a book, lest it should seem like a surrender. What a long month it was, and how eagerly I counted the hours of that last week, for my time was up Saturday and I hoped to be off at once. But when I announced my intention such dismay fell upon Eliza that my heart was touched, and Puah so urgently begged me to stay till they could get some one that I consented to remain a few days longer, and wrote posthaste to my mother, telling her to send a substitute quickly or I should do something desperate.

That blessed woman, little dreaming of all the woes I had endured, advised me to be patient, to do the generous thing, and be sure I should not regret it in the end. I groaned, submitted, and did regret it all the days of my life.

Three mortal weeks I waited; for, though two other victims came, I was implored to set them going, and tried to do it. But both fled after a day or two, condemning the place as a very hard one and calling me a fool to stand it another hour. I entirely agreed with them on both points, and, when I had cleared up after the second incapable lady, I tarried not for the coming of a third, but clutched my property and announced my departure by the next train.

Of course, Eliza wept, Puah moaned, the old man politely regretted, and the younger one washed his hands of the whole affair by shutting himself up in his room and forbidding me to say farewell because "he could not bear it." I laughed, and fancied it done for effect then; but I soon understood it better and did not laugh.

At the last moment, Eliza nervously tucked a sixpenny pocketbook into my hand and shrouded herself in the little blanket with a sob. But Puah kissed me kindly and whispered, with an odd look: "Don't blame us for anything. Some folks is liberal and some ain't." I thanked the poor old soul for her kindness to me and trudged gayly away to the station, whither my property had preceded me on a wheelbarrow, hired at my own expense.

I never shall forget that day. A bleak March afternoon, a sloppy, lonely road, and one hoarse crow stalking about a field, so like Josephus that I could not resist throwing a snowball at him. Behind me stood the dull old house, no longer either mysterious or romantic in my disenchanted eyes; before me rumbled the barrow, bearing my dilapidated wardrobe; and in my pocket reposed what I fondly hoped was, if not a liberal, at least an honest return for seven weeks of the hardest work I ever did.

Unable to resist the desire to see what my earnings were, I opened the purse and beheld *four dollars.*

I have had a good many bitter minutes in my life; but one of the bitterest came to me as I stood there in the windy road, with the sixpenny pocket-book open before me, and looked from my poor chapped, grimy, chill-blained hands to the paltry sum that was considered reward enough for all the hard and humble labor they had done.

A girl's heart is a sensitive thing. And mine had been very full lately; for it had suffered many of the trials that wound deeply yet cannot be told; so I think it as but natural that my first impulse was to go straight back to that sacred study and fling this insulting money at the feet of him who sent it. But I was so boiling over with indignation that I could not trust myself in his presence, lest I should be unable to resist the temptation to shake him, in spite of his cloth.

No, I would go home, show my honorable wounds, tell my pathetic tale, and leave my parents to avenge my wrongs. I did so; but over that harrowing scene I drop a veil, for my feeble pen refuses to depict the emotions of my outraged family. I will merely mention that the four dollars went back and the reverend Josephus never heard the last of it in that neighborhood.

My experiment seemed a dire failure and I mourned it as such for years; but more than once in my life I have been grateful for that serio-comico experience, since it has taught me many lessons. One of the most useful of these has been the power of successfully making a companion, not a servant, of those whose aid I need, and helping to gild their honest wages with the sympathy and justice which can sweeten the humblest and lighten the hardest task.

1874

CONSTANCE FENIMORE WOOLSON (1840–1894)

Considered an important contributor to the development of late-nineteenth-century American fiction, Constance Fenimore Woolson was a well-known writer in her day. She published essays, travel articles, short fiction, and serialized novels in popular magazines. Now that she is being read again with increased interest, much of her fiction that has long been out of print has been reissued.

The grandniece of James Fenimore Cooper, Woolson came from a well-to-do family and was educated in fashionable girls' schools. She read widely in English, French, Italian, and American literature and greatly admired the work of Charlotte Brontë, George Eliot, George Sand, and Ivan Turgenev. Woolson's childhood in Ohio as well as subsequent travels in the post–Civil War South influenced much of her early writing. The last fifteen years of her life were spent in Europe, where, in 1880, she began a close friendship with Henry James. Woolson's and James's literary relationship influenced the work of both writers as they contrasted the nature of American and European societies. Woolson wrote some of the earliest feminist literary criticism, and her letters show her abiding interest in what it means to be a woman writer.

Woolson published four collections of short pieces, most of which had appeared in national publications such as the Atlantic Monthly, Scribner's Monthly, *and* Harper's. Castle Nowhere: Lake-Country Sketches *draws on her recollections of the Great Lakes area, while the pieces in* Rodman the Keeper: Southern Sketches *capture characters and settings of the South during Reconstruction. She was one of the first writers to examine the plight of the South after the war. The second of her five novels,* For the Major, *set in a remote North Carolina village, is a minor classic of American fiction.*

The Front Yard and Other Italian Stories *and* Dorothy and Other Italian Stories, *both published posthumously, introduce international themes comparable to those of Henry James. In these stories, Americans in Europe analyze the effects of European culture on Americans while examining their own feelings about European culture and society. Like James's fiction, Woolson's writing is more analytical than plot-driven; she is interested in motivation more than in action.*

In 'Miss Grief,' *Woolson tells the tale of a penniless female writer whose talent far exceeds that of a successful male writer. Woolson's use of the male writer to narrate the story increases its poignancy: his voice reflects both his sympathy for*

Miss Grief and his appreciation of her talent while also expressing the natural sense of superiority he feels as a man.

■ 'MISS GRIEF'

"A conceited fool" is a not uncommon expression. Now, I know that I am not a fool, but I also know that I am conceited. But, candidly, can it be helped if one happens to be young, well and strong, passably good looking, with some money that one has inherited and more that one has earned—in all, enough to make life comfortable—and if upon this foundation rests also the pleasant superstructure of a literary success? The success is deserved, I think: certainly it was not lightly gained. Yet even with this I fully appreciate its rarity. Thus, I find myself very well entertained in life: I have all I wish in the way of society, and a deep, though of course carefully concealed, satisfaction in my own little fame; which fame I foster by a gentle system of noninterference. I know that I am spoken of as "that quiet young fellow who writes those delightful little studies of society, you know"; and I live up to that definition.

A year ago I was in Rome, and enjoying life particularly. I had a large number of my acquaintances there, both American and English, and no day passed without its invitation. Of course I understood it: it is seldom that you find a literary man who is good tempered, well dressed, sufficiently provided with money, and amiably obedient to all the rules and requirements of "society." "When found, make a note of it"; and the note was generally an invitation.

One evening, upon returning to my lodgings, my man Simpson informed me that a person had called in the afternoon, and upon learning that I was absent had left not a card, but her name—"Miss Grief." The title lingered—Miss Grief! "Grief has not so far visited me here," I said to myself, dismissing Simpson and seeking my little balcony for a final smoke, "and she shall not now. I shall take care to be 'not at home' to her if she continues to call." And then I fell to thinking of Isabel Abercrombie, in whose society I had spent that and many evenings: they were golden thoughts.

The next day there was an excursion; it was late when I reached my rooms, and again Simpson informed me that Miss Grief had called.

"Is she coming continuously?" I said, half to myself.

"Yes, sir: she mentioned that she should call again."

"How does she look?"

"Well, sir, a lady, but not so prosperous as she was, I should say," answered Simpson, discreetly.

"Young?"

"No, sir."

"Alone?"

"A maid with her, sir."

But once outside in my little high-up balcony with my cigar, I again forgot Miss Grief and whatever she might represent. Who would not forget in that moonlight, with Isabel Abercrombie's face to remember?

The stranger came a third time, and I was absent; then she let two days pass, and began again. It grew to be a regular dialogue between Simpson and myself when I came in at night: "Grief today?"

"Yes, sir."

"What time?"

"Four, sir."

"Happy the man," I thought, "who can keep her confined to a particular hour!"

But I should not have treated my visitor so cavalierly if I had not felt sure that she was eccentric and unconventional—qualities extremely tiresome in a woman no longer young or attractive. If she were not eccentric, she would not have persisted in coming to my door day after day in this silent way, without stating her errand, leaving a note, or presenting her credentials in any shape. I made up my mind that she had something to sell—a bit of carving or some intaglio supposed to be antique. It was known that I had a fancy for oddities. I said to myself, "She has read or heard of my 'Old Gold' story, or else 'The Buried God,' and she thinks me an idealizing ignoramus upon whom she can impose. Her sepulchral name is at least not Italian; probably she is a sharp countrywoman of mine, turning, by means of the present aesthetic craze, an honest penny when she can."

She had called seven times during a period of two weeks without seeing me, when one day I happened to be at home in the afternoon, owing to a pouring rain and a fit of doubt concerning Miss Abercrombie. For I had constructed a careful theory of that young lady's characteristics in my own mind, and she had lived up to it delightfully until the previous evening, when with one word she had blown it to atoms and taken flight, leaving me standing, as it were, on a desolate shore, with nothing but a handful of mistaken inductions wherewith to console myself. I do not know a more exasperating frame of mind, at least for a constructor of theories. I could not write, and so I took up a French novel (I model myself a little on Balzac). I had been turning over its pages but a few moments when Simpson knocked, and, entering softly, said, with just a shadow of a smile on his well-trained face, "Miss Grief." I briefly consigned Miss Grief to all the Furies, and then, as he still lingered—perhaps not knowing where they resided—I asked where the visitor was.

"Outside, sir—in the hall. I told her I would see if you were at home."

"She must be unpleasantly wet if she had no carriage."

"No carriage, sir: they always come on foot. I think she *is* a little damp, sir."

"Well, let her in; but I don't want the maid. I may as well see her now, I suppose, and end the affair."

"Yes, sir."

I did not put down my book. My visitor should have a hearing, but not much more: she had sacrificed her womanly claims by her persistent attacks upon my door. Presently Simpson ushered her in. "Miss Grief," he said, and then went out, closing the curtain behind him.

A woman—yes, a lady—but shabby, unattractive, and more than middle-aged.

I rose, bowed slightly, and then dropped into my chair again, still keeping the book in my hand. "Miss Grief?" I said interrogatively as I indicated a seat with my eyebrows.

"Not Grief," she answered—"Crief: my name is Crief."

She sat down, and I saw that she held a small flat box.

"Not carving, then," I thought—"probably old lace, something that belonged to Tullia or Lucrezia Borgia." But, as she did not speak, I found myself obliged to begin: "You have been here, I think, once or twice before?"

"Seven times; this is the eighth."

A silence.

"I am often out; indeed, I may say that I am never in," I remarked carelessly.

"Yes, you have many friends."

"—Who will perhaps buy old lace," I mentally added. But this time I too remained silent; why should I trouble myself to draw her out? She had sought me; let her advance her idea, whatever it was, now that entrance was gained.

But Miss Grief (I preferred to call her so) did not look as though she could advance anything; her black gown, damp with rain, seemed to retreat fearfully to her thin self, while her thin self retreated as far as possible from me, from the chair, from everything. Her eyes were cast down; an old-fashioned lace veil with a heavy border shaded her face. She looked at the floor, and I looked at her.

I grew a little impatient, but I made up my mind that I would continue silent and see how long a time she would consider necessary to give due effect to her little pantomime. Comedy? Or was it tragedy? I suppose full five minutes passed thus in our double silence; and that is a long time when two persons are sitting opposite each other alone in a small still room.

At last my visitor, without raising her eyes, said slowly, "You are very happy, are you not, with youth, health, friends, riches, fame?"

It was a singular beginning. Her voice was clear, low, and very sweet as she thus enumerated my advantages one by one in a list. I was attracted by it, but repelled by her words, which seemed to me flattery both dull and bold.

"Thanks," I said, "for your kindness, but I fear it is undeserved. I seldom discuss myself even when with my friends."

"I am your friend," replied Miss Grief. Then, after a moment, she added slowly, "I have read every word you have written."

I curled the edges of my book indifferently; I am not a fop, I hope, but—others have said the same.

"What is more, I know much of it by heart," continued my visitor. "Wait: I will show you"; and then, without pause, she began to repeat something of mine word for word, just as I had written it. On she went, and I—listened. I intended interrupting her after a moment, but I did not, because she was reciting so well, and also because I felt a desire gaining upon me to see what she would make of a certain conversation which I knew was coming—a conversation between two of my characters which was, to say the least, sphinx-like, and somewhat incandescent as well. What won me a little, too, was the fact that the scene she was reciting (it was hardly more than that, though called a story) was secretly my favorite among all the sketches from my pen which a gracious public has received with favor. I never said so, but it was; and I had always felt a wondering annoyance that the aforesaid public, while kindly praising beyond their worth other attempts of mine, had never noticed the higher purpose of this little shaft, aimed not at the balconies and lighted windows of society, but straight up toward the distant stars. So she went on, and presently reached the conversation: my two people began to talk. She had raised her eyes now, and was looking at me soberly as she gave the words of the woman, quiet, gentle, cold, and the replies of the man, bitter, hot, and scathing. Her very voice changed, and took, though always sweetly, the different tones required, while no point of meaning, however small, no breath of delicate emphasis which I had meant, but which the dull types could not give, escaped an appreciative and full, almost overfull, recognition which startled me. For she had understood me—understood me almost better than I had understood myself. It seemed to me that while I had labored to interpret, partially, a psychological riddle, she, coming after, had comprehended its bearings better than I had, though confining herself strictly to my own words and emphasis. The scene ended (and it ended rather suddenly), she dropped her eyes, and moved her hand nervously to and fro over the box she held; her gloves were old and shabby, her hands small.

I was secretly much surprised by what I had heard, but my ill humor was deep-seated that day, and I still felt sure, besides, that the box contained something which I was expected to buy.

"You recite remarkably well," I said carelessly, "and I am much flattered also by your appreciation of my attempt. But it is not, I presume, to that alone that I owe the pleasure of this visit?"

"Yes," she answered, still looking down, "it is, for if you had not written that scene I should not have sought you. Your other sketches are interiors—exquisitely painted and delicately finished, but of small scope. *This* is a sketch in a few bold, masterly lines—work of entirely different spirit and purpose."

I was nettled by her insight. "You have bestowed so much of your kind attention upon me that I feel your debtor," I said, conventionally. "It may be that there is something I can do for you—connected, possibly, with that little box?"

It was impertinent, but it was true; for she answered, "Yes."

I smiled, but her eyes were cast down and she did not see the smile.

"What I have to show you is a manuscript," she said after a pause which I did not break; "it is a drama. I thought that perhaps you would read it."

"An authoress! This is worse than old lace," I said to myself in dismay.—Then, aloud, "My opinion would be worth nothing, Miss Crief."

"Not in a business way, I know. But it might be—an assistance personally." Her voice had sunk to a whisper; outside, the rain was pouring steadily down. She was a very depressing object to me as she sat there with her box.

"I hardly think I have the time at present—" I began.

She had raised her eyes and was looking at me; then, when I paused, she rose and came suddenly toward my chair. "Yes, you will read it," she said with her hand on my arm—"you will read it. Look at this room; look at yourself; look at all you have. Then look at me, and have pity."

I had risen, for she held my arm, and her damp skirt was brushing my knees.

Her large dark eyes looked intently into mine as she went on: "I have no shame in asking. Why should I have? It is my last endeavor; but a calm and well-considered one. If you refuse I shall go away, knowing that Fate has willed it so. And I shall be content."

"She is mad," I thought. But she did not look so, and she had spoken quietly, even gently. "Sit down," I said, moving away from her. I felt as if I had been magnetized; but it was only the nearness of her eyes to mine, and their intensity. I drew forward a chair, but she remained standing.

"I cannot," she said in the same sweet, gentle tone, "unless you promise."

"Very well, I promise; only sit down."

As I took her arm to lead her to the chair, I perceived that she was trembling, but her face continued unmoved.

"You do not, of course, wish me to look at your manuscript now?" I said, temporizing; "it would be much better to leave it. Give me your address, and I will return it to you with my written opinion; though, I repeat, the latter will be of no use to you. It is the opinion of an editor or publisher that you want."

"It shall be as you please. And I will go in a moment," said Miss Grief, pressing her palms together, as if trying to control the tremor that had seized her slight frame.

She looked so pallid that I thought of offering her a glass of wine; then I remembered that if I did it might be a bait to bring her here again, and this I was desirous to prevent. She rose while the thought was passing through my mind. Her pasteboard box lay on the chair she had first occupied; she took it, wrote an address on the cover, laid it down, and then, bowing with a little air of formality, drew her black shawl round her shoulders and turned toward the door.

I followed, after touching the bell. "You will hear from me by letter," I said.

Simpson opened the door, and I caught a glimpse of the maid, who was waiting in the anteroom. She was an old woman, shorter than her mistress, equally thin, and dressed like her in rusty black. As the door opened she turned toward it a pair of small, dim, blue eyes with a look of furtive suspense. Simpson dropped the curtain, shutting me into the inner room; he had no intention of allowing me to accompany my visitor further. But I had the curiosity to go to a bay window in an angle from whence I could command the street door, and presently I saw them issue forth in the rain and walk away side by side, the mistress, being the taller, holding the umbrella: probably there was not much difference in rank between persons so poor and forlorn as these.

It grew dark. I was invited out for the evening, and I knew that if I should go I should meet Miss Abercrombie. I said to myself that I would not go. I got out my paper for writing, I made my preparations for a quiet evening at home with myself; but it was of no use. It all ended slavishly in my going. At the last allowable moment I presented myself, and—as a punishment for my vacillation, I suppose—I never passed a more disagreeable evening. I drove homeward in a murky temper; it was foggy without, and very foggy within. What Isabel really was, now that she had broken through my elaborately built theories, I was not able to decide. There was, to tell the truth, a certain young Englishman—But that is apart from this story.

I reached home, went up to my rooms, and had a supper. It was to console myself; I am obliged to console myself scientifically once in a while. I was walking up and down afterward, smoking and feeling somewhat better, when my eye fell upon the pasteboard box. I took it up; on the cover was written an address which showed that my visitor must have walked a long distance in order to see me: "A. Crief."—"A Grief," I thought; "and so she is. I positively believe she has brought all this trouble upon me: she has the evil eye." I took out the manuscript and looked at it. It was in the form of a little volume, and clearly written; on the cover was the word "Armor" in German text, and, underneath, a pen-and-ink sketch of a helmet, breastplate, and shield.

"Grief certainly needs armor," I said to myself, sitting down by the table and turning over the pages. "I may as well look over the thing now; I could not be in a worse mood." And then I began to read.

Early the next morning Simpson took a note from me to the given address, returning with the following reply: "No; I prefer to come to you; at four; A. CRIEF." These words, with their three semicolons, were written in pencil upon a piece of coarse printing paper, but the handwriting was as clear and delicate as that of the manuscript in ink.

"What sort of a place was it, Simpson?"

"Very poor, sir, but I did not go all the way up. The elder person came down, sir, took the note, and requested me to wait where I was."

"You had no chance, then, to make inquiries?" I said, knowing full well that he had emptied the entire neighborhood of any information it might possess concerning these two lodgers.

"Well, sir, you know how these foreigners will talk, whether one wants to hear or not. But it seems that these two persons have been there but a few weeks; they live alone, and are uncommonly silent and reserved. The people round there call them something that signifies 'the Madames American, thin and dumb.' "

At four the "Madames American" arrived; it was raining again, and they came on foot under their old umbrella. The maid waited in the anteroom, and Miss Grief was ushered into my bachelor's parlor. I had thought that I should meet her with great deference; but she looked so forlorn that my deference changed to pity. It was the woman that impressed me then, more than the writer—the fragile, nerveless body more than the inspired mind. For it was inspired: I had sat up half the night over her drama, and had felt thrilled through and through more than once by its earnestness, passion, and power.

No one could have been more surprised than I was to find myself thus enthusiastic. I thought I had outgrown that sort of thing. And one would have supposed, too (I myself should have supposed so the day before), that the faults of the drama, which were many and prominent, would have chilled any liking I might have felt, I being a writer myself, and therefore critical; for writers are as apt to make much of the "how," rather than the "what," as painters, who, it is well known, prefer an exquisitely rendered representation of a commonplace theme to an imperfectly executed picture of even the most striking subject. But in this case, on the contrary, the scattered rays of splendor in Miss Grief's drama had made me forget the dark spots, which were numerous and disfiguring; or, rather, the splendor had made me anxious to have the spots removed. And this also was a philanthropic state very unusual with me. Regarding unsuccessful writers, my motto had been "Vae victis!"

My visitor took a seat and folded her hands; I could see, in spite of her quiet manner, that she was in breathless suspense. It seemed so pitiful that she should be trembling there before me—a woman so much older than I was, a woman who possessed the divine spark of genius, which I was by no means sure (in spite of my success) had been granted to me—that I felt as if I ought to go down on my knees before her, and entreat her to take her proper place of supremacy at once. But there! one does not go down on one's knees, combustively, as it were, before a woman over fifty, plain in feature, thin, dejected, and ill dressed. I contented myself with taking her hands (in their miserable old gloves) in mine, while I said cordially. "Miss Crief, your drama seems to me full of original power. It has roused my enthusiasm: I sat up half the night reading it."

The hands I held shook, but something (perhaps a shame for having evaded the knees business) made me tighten my hold and bestow upon her also a reassuring smile. She looked at me for a moment, and then, suddenly and noiselessly, tears rose and rolled down her cheeks. I dropped her hands and retreated. I had not thought her tearful: on the contrary, her voice and face had seemed rigidly controlled. But now here she was bending herself over the side of the chair with her head resting on her arms, not sobbing aloud, but her whole frame shaken by the strength of her emotion. I rushed for a glass of wine; I pressed her to take it. I did not quite know what to do, but, putting myself in her place, I decided to praise the drama; and praise it I did. I do not know when I have used so many adjectives. She raised her head and began to wipe her eyes.

"Do take the wine," I said, interrupting myself in my cataract of language.

"I dare not," she answered; then added humbly, "that is, unless you have a biscuit here or a bit of bread."

I found some biscuit; she ate two, and then slowly drank the wine, while I resumed my verbal Niagara. Under its influence—and that of the wine too, perhaps—she began to show new life. It was not that she looked radiant—she could not—but simply that she looked warm. I now perceived what had been the principal discomfort of her appearance heretofore: it was that she had looked all the time as if suffering from cold.

At last I could think of nothing more to say, and stopped. I really admired the drama, but I thought I had exerted myself sufficiently as an anti-hysteric, and that adjectives enough, for the present at least, had been administered. She had put down her empty wineglass, and was resting her hands on the broad cushioned arm of her chair with, for a thin person, a sort of expanded content.

"You must pardon my tears," she said, smiling; "it was the revulsion of feeling. My life was at a low ebb: if your sentence had been against me, it would have been my end."

"Your end?"

"Yes, the end of my life; I should have destroyed myself."

"Then you would have been a weak as well as wicked woman," I said in a tone of disgust. I do hate sensationalism.

"Oh no, you know nothing about it. I should have destroyed only this poor worn tenement of clay. But I can well understand how *you* would look upon it. Regarding the desirableness of life, the prince and the beggar may have different opinions. We will say no more of it, but talk of the drama instead." As she spoke the word "drama" a triumphant brightness came into her eyes.

I took the manuscript from a drawer and sat down beside her. "I suppose you know that there are faults," I said, expecting ready acquiescence.

"I was not aware that there were any," was her gentle reply.

Here was a beginning! After all my interest in her—and, I may say under the circumstances, my kindness—she received me in this way! However, my belief in her genius was too sincere to be altered by her whimsies; so I persevered. "Let us go over it together," I said. "Shall I read it to you, or will you read it to me?"

"I will not read it, but recite it."

"That will never do; you will recite it so well that we shall see only the good points, and what we have to concern ourselves with now is the bad ones."

"I will recite it," she repeated.

"Now, Miss Crief," I said bluntly, "for what purpose did you come to me? Certainly not merely to recite: I am no stage manager. In plain English, was it not your idea that I might help you in obtaining a publisher?"

"Yes, yes," she answered, looking at me apprehensively, all her old manner returning.

I followed up my advantage, opened the little paper volume and began. I first took the drama line by line, and spoke of the faults of expression and structure; then I turned back and touched upon two or three glaring impossibilities in the plot. "Your absorbed interest in the motive of the whole no doubt made you forget these blemishes," I said apologetically.

But, to my surprise, I found that she did not see the blemishes—that she appreciated nothing I had said, comprehended nothing. Such unaccountable obtuseness puzzled me. I began again, going over the whole with even greater minuteness and care. I worked hard: the perspiration stood in beads upon my forehead as I struggled with her—what shall I call it—obstinacy? But it was not exactly obstinacy. She simply could not see the faults of her own work, any more than a blind man can see the smoke that dims a patch of blue sky. When I had finished my task the second time, she still remained as gently impassive as before. I leaned back in my chair exhausted, and looked at her.

Even then she did not seem to comprehend (whether she agreed with it or not) what I must be thinking. "It is such a heaven to me that you like it!" she murmured dreamily, breaking the silence. Then, with more animation, "And *now* you will let me recite it!"

I was too weary to oppose her; she threw aside her shawl and bonnet, and, standing in the center of the room, began.

And she carried me along with her: all the strong passages were doubly strong when spoken, and the faults, which seemed nothing to her, were made by her earnestness to seem nothing to me, at least for that moment. When it was ended, she stood looking at me with a triumphant smile.

"Yes," I said, "I like it, and you see that I do. But I like it because my taste is peculiar. To me originality and force are everything—perhaps because I have them not to any marked degree myself—but the world at large will not overlook as I do your absolutely barbarous shortcomings on account of them. Will you trust me to go over the drama and correct it at my pleasure?" This was a vast deal for me to offer; I was surprised at myself.

"No," she answered softly, still smiling. "There shall not be so much as a comma altered." Then she sat down and fell into a reverie as though she were alone.

"Have you written anything else?" I said after a while, when I had become tired of the silence.

"Yes."

"Can I see it? Or is it *them?*"

"It is *them.* Yes, you can see all."

"I will call upon you for the purpose."

"No, you must not," she said, coming back to the present nervously. "I prefer to come to you."

At this moment Simpson entered to light the room, and busied himself rather longer than was necessary over the task. When he finally went out, I saw that my visitor's manner had sunk into its former depression: the presence of the servant seemed to have chilled her.

"When did you say I might come?" I repeated, ignoring her refusal.

"I did not say it. It would be impossible."

"Well, then, when will you come here?" There was, I fear, a trace of fatigue in my tone.

"At your good pleasure, sir," she answered humbly.

My chivalry was touched by this: after all, she was a woman. "Come tomorrow," I said. "By the way, come and dine with me then; why not?" I was curious to see what she would reply.

"Why not, indeed? Yes, I will come. I am forty-three: I might have been your mother."

This was not quite true, as I am over thirty: but I look young, while she—Well, I had thought her over fifty. "I can hardly call you 'mother,' but we might compromise upon 'aunt,' " I said, laughing. "Aunt what?"

"My name is Aaronna," she gravely answered. "My father was much disappointed that I was not a boy, and gave me as nearly as possible the name he had prepared—Aaron."

"Then come and dine with me tomorrow, and bring with you the other manuscripts, Aaronna," I said, amused at the quaint sound of the name. On the whole, I did not like "aunt."

"I will come," she answered.

It was twilight and still raining, but she refused all offers of escort or carriage, departing with her maid, as she had come, under the brown umbrella. The next day we had the dinner. Simpson was astonished—and more than astonished, grieved—when I told him that he was to dine with the maid; but he could not complain in words, since my own guest, the mistress, was hardly more attractive. When our preparations were complete, I could not help laughing: the two prim little tables, one in the parlor and one in the anteroom, and Simpson disapprovingly going back and forth between them, were irresistible.

I greeted my guest hilariously when she arrived, and, fortunately, her manner was not quite so depressed as usual: I could never have accorded myself with a tearful mood. I had thought that perhaps she would make, for the occasion, some change in her attire; I have never known a woman who had not some scrap of finery, however small, in reserve for that unexpected occasion of which she is ever dreaming. But no: Miss Grief wore the same black gown, unadorned and unaltered. I was glad that there was no rain that day, so that the skirt did not at least look so damp and rheumatic.

She ate quietly, almost furtively, yet with a good appetite, and she did not refuse the wine. Then, when the meal was over and Simpson had removed the dishes, I asked for the new manuscripts. She gave me an old green copybook filled with short poems, and a prose sketch by itself; I lit a cigar and sat down at my desk to look them over.

"Perhaps you will try a cigarette?" I suggested, more for amusement than anything else, for there was not a shade of Bohemianism about her; her whole appearance was puritanical.

"I have not yet succeeded in learning to smoke."

"You have tried?" I said, turning round.

"Yes: Serena and I tried, but we did not succeed."

"Serena is your maid?"

"She lives with me."

I was seized with inward laughter, and began hastily to look over her manuscripts with my back toward her, so that she might not see it. A vision had risen before me of those two forlorn women, alone in their room with locked doors, patiently trying to acquire the smoker's art.

But my attention was soon absorbed by the papers before me. Such a fantastic collection of words, lines, and epithets I had never before seen, or even in dreams imagined. In truth, they were like the work of dreams: they were *Kubla Khan,* only more so. Here and there was radiance like the flash of a diamond, but each poem, almost each verse and line, was marred by some fault or lack which seemed wilful perversity, like the work of an evil sprite. It was like a case of jeweller's wares set before you, with each ring unfinished, each bracelet too large or too small for its purpose, each breastpin without its fastening, each necklace purposely broken. I turned the pages, marvelling. When about half an hour had passed, and I was leaning back for a moment to light another cigar, I glanced toward my visitor. She was behind me, in an easy chair before my small fire, and she was—fast asleep! In the relaxation of her unconsciousness I was struck anew by the poverty her appearance expressed; her feet were visible, and I saw the miserable worn old shoes which hitherto she had kept concealed.

After looking at her for a moment, I returned to my task and took up the prose story; in prose she must be more reasonable. She was less fantastic perhaps, but hardly more reasonable. The story was that of a profligate and commonplace man forced by two of his friends, in order not to break the heart of a dying girl who loves him, to live up to a high imaginary ideal of himself which her pure but mistaken mind has formed. He has a handsome face and sweet voice, and repeats what they tell him. Her long, slow decline and happy death, and his own inward ennui and profound weariness of the rôle he has to play, made the vivid points of the story. So far, well enough, but here was the trouble: through the whole narrative moved another character, a physician of tender heart and exquisite mercy, who practiced murder as a fine art, and was regarded (by the author) as a second Messiah! This was monstrous. I read it through twice, and threw it down; then, fatigued, I turned round and leaned back, waiting for her to wake. I could see her profile against the dark hue of the easy chair.

Presently she seemed to feel my gaze, for she stirred, then opened her eyes. "I have been asleep," she said, rising hurriedly.

"No harm in that, Aaronna."

But she was deeply embarrassed and troubled, much more so than the occasion required; so much so, indeed, that I turned the conversation back upon the manuscripts as a diversion. "I cannot stand that doctor of yours," I said, indicating the prose story; "no one would. You must cut him out."

Her self-possession returned as if by magic. "Certainly not," she answered haughtily.

"Oh, if you do not care—I had labored under the impression that you were anxious these things should find a purchaser."

"I am, I am," she said, her manner changing to deep humility with wonderful rapidity. With such alternations of feeling as this sweeping over her like great waves, no wonder she was old before her time.

"Then you must take out that doctor."

"I am willing, but do not know how," she answered, pressing her hands together helplessly. "In my mind he belongs to the story so closely that he cannot be separated from it."

Here Simpson entered, bringing a note for me: it was a line from Mrs. Abercrombie inviting me for that evening—an unexpected gathering, and therefore likely to be all the more agreeable. My heart bounded in spite of me; I forgot Miss Grief and her manuscripts for the moment as completely as though they had never existed. But, bodily, being still in the same room with her, her speech brought me back to the present.

"You have had good news?" she said.

"Oh no, nothing especial—merely an invitation."

"But good news also," she repeated. "And now, as for me, I must go."

Not supposing that she would stay much later in any case, I had that morning ordered a carriage to come for her at about that hour. I told her this. She made no reply beyond putting on her bonnet and shawl.

"You will hear from me soon," I said; "I shall do all I can for you."

She had reached the door, but before opening it she stopped, turned and extended her hand. "You are good," she said: "I give you thanks. Do not think me ungrateful or envious. It is only that you are young, and I am so—so old." Then she opened the door and passed through the anteroom without pause, her maid accompanying her and Simpson with gladness lighting the way. They were gone. I dressed hastily and went out—to continue my studies in psychology.

Time passed; I was busy, amused and perhaps a little excited (sometimes psychology is exciting). But, though much occupied with my own affairs, I did not altogether neglect my self-imposed task regarding Miss Grief. I began by sending her prose story to a friend, the editor of a monthly magazine, with a letter making a strong plea for its admittance. It should have a chance first on its own merits. Then I forwarded the drama to a publisher, also an acquaintance, a man with a taste for phantasms and a soul above mere common popularity, as his own coffers knew to their cost. This done, I waited with conscience clear.

Four weeks passed. During this waiting period I heard nothing from Miss Grief. At last one morning came a letter from my editor. "The story has force, but I cannot stand that doctor," he wrote. "Let her cut him out, and I might print it." Just what I myself had said. The package lay there on my table, travel worn and grimed; a returned manuscript is, I think, the most melancholy object on earth. I decided to wait, before writing to Aaronna, until the second letter was received. A week later it came. "Armor" was declined. The publisher has been "impressed" by the power displayed in certain passages, but the "impossibilities of the plot" rendered it "unavailable for publication"—in fact, would "bury it in ridicule" if brought before the public, a public "lamentably" fond of amusement, "seeking it, undaunted, even in the cannon's mouth." I doubt if he knew himself what he meant. But one thing, at any rate, was clear: "Armor" was declined.

Now, I am, as I have remarked before, a little obstinate. I was determined that Miss Grief's work should be received. I would alter and improve it myself, without letting her know: the end justified the means. Surely the sieve of my own good taste, whose mesh had been pronounced so fine and delicate, would serve for two. I began; and utterly failed.

I set to work first upon "Armor." I amended, altered, left out, put in, pieced, condensed, lengthened; I did my best, and all to no avail. I could not succeed in completing anything that satisfied me, or that approached, in truth, Miss Grief's own work just as it stood. I suppose I went over that manuscript twenty times: I covered sheets of paper with my copies. But the obstinate drama refused to be corrected; as it was it must stand or fall.

Wearied and annoyed, I threw it aside and took up the prose story: that would be easier. But, to my surprise, I found that that apparently gentle "doctor" would not out: he was so closely interwoven with every part of the tale that to take him out was like taking out one especial figure in a carpet: that is, impossible, unless you unravel the whole. At last I did unravel the whole, and then the story was no longer good, or Aaronna's: it was weak, and mine. All this took time, for of course I had much to do in connection with my own life and tasks. But, though slowly and at my leisure, I really did try my best as regarded Miss Grief, and without success. I was forced at last to make up my mind that either my own powers were not equal to the task, or else that her perversities were as essential a part of her work as her inspirations, and not to be separated from it. Once during this period I showed two of the short poems to Isabel, withholding of course the writer's name. "They were written by a woman," I explained.

"Her mind must have been disordered, poor thing!" Isabel said in her gentle way when she returned them—"at least, judging by these. They are hopelessly mixed and vague."

Now, they were not vague so much as vast. But I knew that I could not make Isabel comprehend it, and (so complex a creature is man) I do not know that I wanted her to comprehend it. These were the only ones in the whole collection that I would have shown her, and I was rather glad that she did not like even these. Not that poor Aaronna's poems were evil: they were simply unrestrained, large, vast, like the skies or the wind. Isabel was bounded on all sides, like a violet in a garden bed. And I liked her so.

One afternoon, about the time when I was beginning to see that I could not "improve" Miss Grief, I came upon the maid. I was driving, and she had stopped on the crossing to let the carriage pass. I recognized her at a glance (by her general forlornness), and called to the driver to stop. "How is Miss Grief?" I said. "I have been intending to write to her for some time."

"And your note, when it comes," answered the old woman on the crosswalk fiercely, "she shall not see."

"What?"

"I say she shall not see it. Your patronizing face shows that you have no good news, and you shall not rack and stab her any more on *this* earth, please God, while I have authority."

"Who has racked or stabbed her, Serena?"

"Serena, indeed! Rubbish! I'm no Serena: I'm her aunt. And as to who has racked and stabbed her, I say you, *you*—YOU literary men!" She had put her old head inside my carriage, and flung out these words at me in a shrill, menacing tone. "But she shall die in peace in spite of you," she continued. "Vampires! you take her ideas and fatten on them, and leave her to starve. You know you do—*you* who have had her poor manuscripts these months and months!"

"Is she ill?" I asked in real concern, gathering that much at least from the incoherent tirade.

"She is dying," answered the desolate old creature, her voice softening and her dim eyes filling with tears.

"Oh, I trust not. Perhaps something can be done. Can I help you in any way?"

"In all ways if you would," she said, breaking down and beginning to sob weakly, with her head resting on the sill of the carriage window. "Oh, what have we not been through together, we two! Piece by piece I have sold all."

I am goodhearted enough, but I do not like to have old women weeping across my carriage door. I suggested, therefore, that she should come inside and let me take her home. Her shabby old skirt was soon beside me, and, following her directions, the driver turned toward one of the most wretched quarters of the city, the abode of poverty, crowded and unclean. Here, in a large bare chamber up many flights of stairs, I found Miss Grief.

As I entered I was startled: I thought she was dead. There seemed no life present until she opened her eyes, and even then they rested upon us vaguely, as though she did not know who we were. But as I approached a light came into them: she recognized me, and this sudden revivification, this return of the soul to the almost deserted body, was the most wonderful thing I ever saw. "You have good news of the drama?" she whispered as I bent over her: "tell me. I *know* you have good news."

What was I to answer? Pray, what would you have answered, puritan?

"Yes, I have good news, Aaronna," I said. "The drama will appear." (And who knows? Perhaps it will in some other world.)

She smiled, and her now brilliant eyes did not leave my face.

"He knows I'm your aunt: I told him," said the old woman, coming to the bedside.

"Did you?" whispered Miss Grief, still gazing at me with a smile. "Then please, dear Aunt Martha, give me something to eat."

Aunt Martha hurried across the room, and I followed her. "It's the first time she's asked for food in weeks," she said in a husky tone.

She opened a cupboard door vaguely, but I could see nothing within. "What have you for her?" I asked with some impatience, though in a low voice.

"Please God, nothing!" answered the poor old woman, hiding her reply and her tears behind the broad cupboard door. "I was going out to get a little something when I met you."

"Good Heavens! is it money you need? Here, take this and send; or go yourself in the carriage waiting below."

She hurried out breathless, and I went back to the bedside, much disturbed by what I had seen and heard. But Miss Grief's eyes were full of life, and as I sat down beside her she whispered earnestly, "Tell me."

And I did tell her—a romance invented for the occasion. I venture to say that none of my published sketches could compare with it. As for the lie involved, it will stand among my few good deeds, I know, at the judgment bar.

And she was satisfied. "I have never known what it was," she whispered, "to be fully happy until now." She closed her eyes, and when the lids fell I again thought that she had passed away. But no, there was still pulsation in her small, thin wrist. As she perceived my touch she smiled. "Yes, I am happy," she said again, though without audible sound.

The old aunt returned; food was prepared, and she took some. I myself went out after wine that should be rich and pure. She rallied a little, but I did not leave her: her eyes dwelt upon me and compelled me to stay, or rather my conscience compelled me. It was a damp night, and I had a little fire made. The wine, fruit, flowers, and candles I had ordered made the bare place for the time being bright and fragrant. Aunt Martha dozed in her chair from sheer fatigue—she had watched many nights—but Miss Grief was awake, and I sat beside her.

"I make you my executor," she murmured, "as to the drama. But my other manuscripts place, when I am gone, under my head, and let them be buried with me. They are not many—those you have and these. See!"

I followed her gesture, and saw under her pillows the edges of two more copybooks like the one I had. "Do not look at them—my poor dead children!" she said tenderly. "Let them depart with me—unread, as I have been."

Later she whispered, "Did you wonder why I came to you? It was the contrast. You were young—strong—rich—praised—loved—successful: all that I was not. I wanted to look at you—and imagine how it would feel. You had success—but I had the greater power. Tell me, did I not have it?"

"Yes, Aaronna."

"It is all in the past now. But I am satisfied."

After another pause she said with a faint smile, "Do you remember when I fell asleep in your parlor? It was the good and rich food. It was so long since I had had food like that!"

I took her hand and held it, conscience stricken, but now she hardly seemed to perceive my touch. "And the smoking?" she whispered. "Do you remember how you laughed? I saw it. But I had heard that smoking soothed—that one was no longer tired and hungry—with a cigar."

In little whispers of this sort, separated by long rests and pauses, the night passed. Once she asked if her aunt was asleep, and when I answered in the affirmative she said, "Help her to return home—to America: the drama will pay for it. I ought never to have brought her away."

I promised, and she resumed her bright-eyed silence.

I think she did not speak again. Toward morning the change came, and soon after sunrise, with her old aunt kneeling by her side, she passed away.

All was arranged as she had wished. Her manuscripts, covered with violets, formed her pillow. No one followed her to the grave save her aunt and myself; I thought she would prefer it so. Her name was not "Crief," after all, but "Moncrief"; I saw it written out by Aunt Martha for the coffin plate, as follows: "Aaronna Moncrief, aged forty-three years, two months, and eight days."

I never knew more of her history than is written here. If there was more that I might have learned, it remained unlearned, for I did not ask.

And the drama? I keep it here in this locked case. I could have had it published at my own expense; but I think that now she knows its faults herself, perhaps, and would not like it.

I keep it; and, once in a while, I read it over—not as a *memento mori* exactly, but rather as a memento of my own good fortune, for which I should continually give thanks. The want of one grain made all her work void, and that one grain was given to me. She, with the greater power, failed—I, with the less, succeeded. But no praise is due to me for that. When I die "Armor" is to be destroyed unread: not even Isabel is to see it. For women will misunderstand each other; and, dear and precious to me as my sweet wife is, I could not bear that she or anyone should cast so much as a thought of scorn upon the memory of the writer, upon my poor dead, "unavailable," unaccepted "Miss Grief."

1880

SARAH WINNEMUCCA HOPKINS (1844?–1891)

Sarah Winnemucca Hopkins was a translator, activist, lecturer, educator, and writer. Her 1883 autobiography Life among the Piutes *was one of the earliest written by a Native American woman. This work describes the Northern Paiutes during their early period of contact with whites. Throughout, Winnemucca Hopkins records the crimes committed against her people as well as the efforts by some of her tribe to assimilate. On the one hand, she remembers her mother burying her alive to hide her from whites. On the other hand, she recalls her grandfather, who had fought alongside with whites in the Mexican war, defending the traders who killed his son.*

The daughter of Northern Paiutes, Winnemucca was born near Humboldt Lake. When the first whites arrived in the territory, she was a young girl called Thocmetony ("Shell Flower") whose maternal grandfather was the leader of the Paiutes living in what later became northeastern California, southern Oregon, and western Nevada.

The crimes committed against the Paiutes were numerous during Winnemucca's life. For example, although the Paiutes were a nomadic tribe who relied on seasonal fishing and hunting, they were confined to reservations that required skill in farming. Without the necessary knowledge, these people quickly became dependent on the U.S. military and government agencies. In 1867, when the railroad came through, the Paiutes were robbed of the most valuable parts of the Pyramid Lake Reservation.

Beginning in the 1870s, Winnemucca, skilled in languages, became a spokesperson for her people and traveled to Carson City, Nevada, and San Francisco to complain about the government agents. In her autobiography she described her work as an interpreter and displayed her firsthand knowledge of how agents exploited American Indians. Unfortunately, her efforts were often futile; despite her protests, in 1879 her people were forced into Washington State to live on the Yakima Reservation, far away from their ancestral land.

Winnemucca had three short marriages before she married Lieutenant Lewis H. Hopkins of Virginia in 1881. Two years later, she moved east with her husband. While in Boston she made two staunch allies, Elizabeth Palmer Peabody and her sister Mary Mann. With their help Hopkins lectured throughout the Northeast on the conditions on American Indian reservations. An independent woman, Hopkins was a controversial public figure. The press criticized her, for example, after she was arrested for attacking a man who molested her. But whenever stories about her private life were used to discredit her, she responded with feminist insight: "Everyone knows what a woman must suffer who undertakes to act against bad men."

At the urging of Mann and Peabody, she wrote and published Life among the Piutes: Their Wrongs and Claims. *Mann, who edited Hopkins's writing, died in 1887, but Peabody continued to support her projects, especially in education. In the late 1880s Hopkins opened the Peabody School, the first educational institution for Indians run by Indians. She died on October 17, 1891, while visiting her sister in Montana, and was buried at Henry Lake, Montana.*

Like Harriet Jacobs, Hopkins envisioned a primarily white and Christian audience. "Oh, my good Christian people," she pleads in her autobiography, "how long are you going to stand by and see us suffer at your hands?" Her avowed purpose as a writer was "to influence the public mind by the details of the Indian wrongs."

The section we have chosen differs from the rest of Hopkins's autobiography, which chronicles historical events. Instead, "Domestic and Social Moralities" describes the cultural practices of her people and focuses on children. In her depiction of the Spring Festival of Flowers, for example, Hopkins conveys the Paiutes' ritual celebration of nature. Moreover, Hopkins takes the occasion to make several trenchant comparisons between the white culture and that of her people.

from LIFE AMONG THE PIUTES
CHAPTER II: DOMESTIC AND SOCIAL MORALITIES

Our children are very carefully taught to be good. Their parents tell them stories, traditions of old times, even of the first mother of the human race; and love stories, stories of giants, and fables; and when they ask if these last stories are true, they answer, "Oh, it is only coyote," which means that they are make-believe stories. Coyote is the name of a mean, crafty little animal, half wolf, half dog, and stands for everything low. It is the greatest term of reproach one Indian has for another. Indians do not swear,—they have no words for swearing till they learn them of white men. The worst they call each is bad or coyote; but they are very sincere with one another, and if they think each other in the wrong they say so.

We are taught to love everybody. We don't need to be taught to love our fathers and mothers. We love them without being told to. Our tenth cousin is as near to us as our first cousin; and we don't marry into our relations. Our young women are not allowed to talk to any young man that is not their cousin, except at the festive dances, when both are dressed in their best clothes, adorned with beads, feathers or shells, and stand alternately in the ring and take hold of hands. These are very pleasant occasions to all the young people.

Many years ago, when my people were happier than they are now, they used to celebrate the Festival of Flowers in the spring. I have been to three of them only in the course of my life.

Oh, with what eagerness we girls used to watch every spring for the time when we could meet with our hearts' delight, the young men, whom in civilized life you call beaux. We would all go in company to see if the flowers we were named for were yet in bloom, for almost all the girls are named for flowers. We talked about them in our wigwams, as if we were the flowers, saying, "Oh, I saw myself today in full bloom!" We would talk all the evening in this way in our families with such delight, and such beautiful thoughts of the happy day when we should meet with those who admired us and would help us to sing our flower-songs which we made up as we sang. But we were always sorry for those that were not named after some flower, because we knew they could not join in the flower-songs like ourselves, who were named for flowers of all kinds.[1]

At last one evening came a beautiful voice, which made every girl's heart throb with happiness. It was the chief, and every one hushed to hear what he said to-day.

"My dear daughters, we are told that you have seen yourselves in the hills and in the valleys, in full bloom. Five days from to-day your festival day will come. I know every young man's heart stops beating while I am talking. I know how it was with me many years ago. I used to wish the Flower Festival would come every day. Dear young men and young women, you are saying, 'Why put it off five days?' But you all know that is our rule. It gives you time to think, and to show your sweetheart your flower."

All the girls who have flower-names dance along together, and those who have not go together also. Our fathers and mothers and grandfathers and grandmothers make a place for us where we can dance. Each one gathers the flower she is named for, and then all weave them into wreaths and crowns and scarfs, and dress up in them.

Some girls are named for rocks and are called rock-girls, and they find some pretty rocks which they carry; each one such a rock as she is named for, or whatever she is named for. If she cannot, she can take a branch of sage-brush, or a bunch of rye-grass, which have no flower.

They all go marching along, each girl in turn singing of herself; but she is not a girl any more,—she is a flower singing. She sings of herself, and her sweetheart, dancing along by her side, helps her sing the song she makes.

---

[1] Indian children are named from some passing circumstance; as, for instance, one of Mrs. Hopkins' brothers was named Black-eye, because when a very small child, sitting in a sister's lap, who had beautiful black eyes, he said, "What beautiful black eyes you have!" If they observed the flight of a bird, or an animal, in short, anything striking that became associated with them, that would be their appellation.—ED.

I will repeat what we say of ourselves. "I, Sarah Winnemucca, am a shell-flower, such as I wear on my dress. My name is Thocmetony. I am so beautiful! Who will come and dance with me while I am so beautiful? Oh, come and be happy with me! I shall be beautiful while the earth lasts. Somebody will always admire me; and who will come and be happy with me in the Spirit-land? I shall be beautiful forever there. Yes, I shall be more beautiful than my shell-flower, my Thocmetony! Then, come, oh come, and dance and be happy with me!" The young men sing with us as they dance beside us.

Our parents are waiting for us somewhere to welcome us home. And then we praise the sage-brush and the rye grass that have no flower, and the pretty rocks that some are named for; and then we present our beautiful flowers to these companions who could carry none. And so all are happy; and that closes the beautiful day.

My people have been so unhappy for a long time they wish now to *disincrease,* instead of multiply. The mothers are afraid to have more children, for fear they shall have daughters, who are not safe even in their mother's presence.

The grandmothers have the special care of the daughters just before and after they come to womanhood. The girls are not allowed to get married until they have come to womanhood; and that period is recognized as a very sacred thing, and is the subject of a festival, and has peculiar customs. The young woman is set apart under the care of two of her friends, somewhat older, and a little wigwam, called a teepee, just big enough for the three, is made for them, to which they retire. She goes through certain labors which are thought to be strengthening, and these last twenty-five days. Every day, three times a day, she must gather, and pile up as high as she can, five stacks of wood. This makes fifteen stacks a day. At the end of every five days the attendants take her to a river to bathe. She fasts from all flesh-meat during these twenty-five days, and continues to do this for five days in every month all her life. At the end of the twenty-five days she returns to the family lodge, and gives all her clothing to her attendants in payment for their care. Sometimes the wardrobe is quite extensive.

It is thus publicly known that there is another marriageable woman, and any young man interested in her, or wishing to form an alliance, comes forward. But the courting is very different from the courting of the white people. He never speaks to her, or visits the family, but endeavors to attract her attention by showing his horsemanship, etc. As he knows that she sleeps next to her grandmother in the lodge, he enters in full dress after the family has retired for the night, and seats himself at her feet. If she is not awake, her grandmother wakes her. He does not speak to either young woman or grandmother, but when the young woman wishes him to go away, she rises and goes and lies down by the side of her mother. He then leaves as silently as he came in. This goes on sometimes for a year or longer, if the young woman has not made up her mind. She is never forced by her parents to marry against her wishes.

When she knows her own mind, she makes a confidant of her grandmother, and then the young man is summoned by the father of the girl, who asks him in her presence, if he really loves his daughter, and reminds him, if he says he does, of all the duties of a husband. He then asks his daughter the same question, and sets before her minutely all her duties. And these duties are not slight. She is to dress the game, prepare the food, clean the buckskins, make his moccasins, dress his hair, bring all the wood,—in short, do all the household work. She promises to "be himself," and she fulfils her promise. Then he is invited to a feast and all his relatives with him. But after the betrothal, a teepee is erected for the presents that pour in from both sides.

At the wedding feast, all the food is prepared in baskets. The young woman sits by the young man, and hands him the basket of food prepared for him with her own hands. He does not take it with his right hand; but seizes her wrist, and takes it with the left hand. This constitutes the marriage ceremony, and the father pronounces them man and wife. They go to a wigwam of their own, where they live till the first child is born. This event also is celebrated. Both father and mother fast from all flesh, and the father goes through the labor of piling the wood for twenty-five days, and assumes all his wife's household work during that time. If he does not do his part in the care of the child, he is considered an outcast. Every five days his child's basket is changed for a new one, and the five are all carefully put away at the end of the days, the last one containing the navel-string, carefully wrapped up, and all are put up into a tree, and the child put into a new and ornamented basket. All this respect shown to the mother and child makes the parents feel their responsibility, and makes the tie between parents and children very strong. The young mothers often get together and exchange their experiences about the attentions of their husbands; and inquire of each other if the fathers did their duty to their children, and were careful of their wives' health. When they are married they give away all the clothing they have ever worn, and dress themselves anew. The poor people have the same ceremonies, but do not make a feast of it, for want of means.

Our boys are introduced to manhood by their hunting of deer and mountain-sheep. Before they are fifteen or sixteen, they hunt only small game, like rabbits, hares, fowls, etc. They never eat what they kill themselves, but only what their father or elder brothers kill. When a boy becomes strong enough to use larger bows made of sinew, and arrows that are ornamented with eagle-feathers, for the first time, he kills game that is large, a deer or an antelope, or a mountain-sheep. Then he brings home the hide, and his father cuts it into a long coil which is wound into a loop, and the boy takes his quiver and throws it on his back as if he was going on a hunt, and takes his bow and arrows in his hand. Then his father throws the loop over him, and he jumps through it. This he does five times. Now for the first time he eats the flesh of the animal he has killed, and from that time he eats whatever he kills but he has always been faithful to his parents' command not to eat what he has killed before. He can now do whatever he likes, for now he is a man, and no longer considered a boy. If there is a war he can go to it; but the Piutes, and other tribes west of the Rocky Mountains, are not fond of going to war. I never saw a war-dance but once. It is always the whites that begin the wars, for their own selfish purposes. The government does not take care to send the good men; there are a plenty who would take pains to see and understand the chiefs and learn their characters, and their good will to the whites. But the whites have not waited to find out how good the Indians were, and what ideas they had of God, just like those of Jesus, who called him Father, just as my people do, and told men to do to others as they would be done by, just as my people teach their children to do. My people teach their children never to make fun of any one, no matter how they look. If you see your brother or sister doing something wrong, look away, or go away from them. If you make fun of bad persons, you make yourself beneath them. Be kind to all, both poor and rich, and feed all that come to your wigwam, and your name can be spoken of by every one far and near. In this way you will make many friends for yourself. Be kind both to bad and good, for you don't know your own heart. This is the way my people teach their children. It was handed down from father to son for many generations. I never in my life saw our children rude as I have seen white children and grown people in the streets.

The chief's tent is the largest tent, and it is the council-tent, where every one goes who wants advice. In the evenings the head men go there to discuss everything, for the chiefs do not rule like tyrants; they discuss everything with their people, as a father would in his family. Often they sit up all night. They discuss the doings of all, if they need to be advised. If a boy is not doing well they talk that over, and if the women are interested they can share in the talks. If there is not room enough inside, they all go out of doors, and make a great circle. The men are in the inner circle, for there would be too much smoke for the women inside. The men never talk without smoking first. The women sit behind them in another circle, and if the children wish to hear, they can be there too. The women know as much as the men do, and their advice is often asked. We have a republic as well as you. The council-tent is our Congress, and anybody can speak who has anything to say, women and all. They are always interested in what their husbands are doing and thinking about. And they take some part even in the wars. They are always near at hand when fighting is going on, ready to snatch their husbands up and carry them off if wounded or killed. One splendid woman that my brother Lee married after his first wife died, went out into the battle-field after her uncle was killed, and went into the front ranks and cheered the men on. Her uncle's horse was dressed in a splendid robe made of eagles' feathers and she snatched it off and swung it in the face of the enemy, who always carry off everything they find, as much to say, "You can't have that—I have it safe"; and she staid and took her uncle's place, as brave as any of the men. It means something when the women promise their fathers to make their husbands *themselves.* They faithfully keep with them in all the dangers they can share. They not only take care of the children together, but they do everything together; and when they grow blind, which I am sorry to say is very common, for the smoke they live in destroys their eyes at last, they take sweet care of one another. Marriage is a sweet thing when people love each other. If women could go into your Congress I think justice would soon be done to the Indians. I can't tell about all Indians; but I know my own people are kind to everybody that does not do them harm; but they will not be imposed upon, and when people are too bad they rise up and resist them. This seems to me all right. It is different from being revengeful. There is nothing cruel about our people. They never scalped a human being.

The chiefs do not live in idleness. They work with their people, and they are always poor for the following reason. It is the custom with my people to be very hospitable. When people visit them in their tents, they always set before them the best food they have, and if there is not enough for themselves they go without.

The chief's tent is the one always looked for when visitors come, and sometimes many come the same day. But they are all well received. I have often felt sorry for my brother, who is now the chief, when I saw him go without food for this reason. He would say, "We will wait and eat afterwards what is left." Perhaps little would be left, and when the agents did not give supplies and rations, he would have to go hungry.

At the council, one is always appointed to repeat at the time everything that is said on both sides, so that there may be no misunderstanding, and one person at least is present from every lodge, and after it is over, he goes and repeats what is decided upon at the door of the lodge, so all may be understood. For there is never any quarrelling in the tribe, only friendly counsels. The sub-chiefs are appointed by the great chief for special duties. There is no quarrelling about that, for neither sub-chief or great chief has any salary. It is this which makes the tribe so united and attached to each other, and makes it so dreadful to be parted. They would rather all die at once than be parted. They believe that in the Spirit-land those that die still watch over those that are living. When I was a child in California, I heard the Methodist minister say that everybody that did wrong was burned in hell forever. I was so frightened it made me very sick. He said the blessed ones in heaven looked down and saw their friends burning and could not help them. I wanted to be unborn, and cried so that my mother and the others told me it was not so, that it was only here that people did wrong and were in the hell that it made, and that those that were in the Spirit-land saw us here and were sorry for us. But we should go to them when we died, where there was never any wrongdoing, and so no hell. That is our religion.

My people capture antelopes by charming them, but only some of the people are charmers. My father was one of them, and once I went with him on an antelope hunt.

The antelopes move in herds in the winter, and as late in the spring as April. At this time there was said to be a large herd in a certain place, and my father told all his people to come together in ten days to go with him in his hunt. He told them to bring their wives with them, but no small children. When they came, at the end of ten days, he chose two men, who he said were to be his messengers to the antelopes. They were to have two large torches made of sage-brush bark, and after he had found a place for his camp, he marked out a circle around which the wigwams were to be placed, putting his own in the middle of the western side, and leaving an opening directly opposite in the middle of the eastern side, which was towards the antelopes.

The people who were with him in the camp then made another circle to the east of the one where their wigwams were, and made six mounds of sage-brush and stones on the sides of it, with a space of a hundred yards or more from one mound to the next one, but with no fence between the mounds. These mounds were made high, so that they could be seen from far off.

The women and boys and old men who were in the camp, and who were working on the mounds, were told to be very careful not to drop anything and not to stumble over a sage-brush root, or a stone, or anything, and not to have any accident, but to do everything perfectly and to keep thinking about the antelopes all the time, and not to let their thoughts go away to anything else. It took five days to charm the antelopes, and if anybody had an accident he must tell of it.

Every morning early, when the bright morning star could be seen, the people sat around the opening to the circle, with my father sitting in the middle of the opening, and my father lighted his pipe and passed it to his right, and the pipe went round the circle five times. And at night they did the same thing.

After they had smoked the pipe, my father took a kind of drum, which is used in this charming, and made music with it. This is the only kind of musical instrument which my people have, and it is only used for this antelope-charming. It is made of a hide of some large animal, stuffed with grass, so as to make it sound hollow, and then wound around tightly from one end to the other with a cord as large as my finger. One end of this instrument is large, and it tapers down to the other end, which is small, so that it makes a different sound on the different parts. My father took a stick and rubbed this stick from one end of the instrument to the other, making a penetrating, vibrating sound, that could be heard afar off, and he sang, and all his people sang with him.

After that the two men who were messengers went out to see the antelopes. They carried their torches in their right hands, and one of them carried a pipe in his left hand. They started from my father's wigwam and went straight across the camp to the opening; then they crossed, and one went around the second circle to the right and the other went to the left, till they met on the other side of the circle. Then they crossed again, and one went round the herd of antelopes one way and the other went round the other way, but they did not let the antelopes see them. When they met on the other side of the herd of antelopes, they stopped and smoked the pipe, and then they crossed, and each man came back on the track of the other to the camp, and told my father what they saw and what the antelopes were doing.

This was done every day for five days, and after the first day all the men and women and boys followed the messengers, and went around the circle they were to enter. On the fifth day the antelopes were charmed, and the whole herd followed the tracks of my people and entered the circle where the mounds were, coming in at the entrance, bowing and tossing their heads, and looking sleepy and under a powerful spell. They ran round and round inside the circle just as if there was a fence all around it and they could not get out, and they staid there until my people had killed every one. But if anybody had dropped anything, or had stumbled and had not told about it, then when the antelopes came to the place where he had done that, they threw off the spell and rushed wildly out of the circle at that place.

My brother can charm horses in the same way.

The Indian children amuse themselves a great deal by modelling in mud. They make herds of animals, which are modelled exceedingly well, and after setting them up, shoot at them with their little bows and arrows. They also string beads of different colors and show natural good taste.

1883

SARAH ORNE JEWETT
(1849–1909)

Sarah Orne Jewett wrote lyrical stories that captured the changes in the United States during the second half of the nineteenth century. In her stories we see classic American themes—the movement from a rural to an urban society, the migration of workers from farms to towns, the impact of industrialization on craftspeople, the complex relationships between humans and nature. The economy and seeming simplicity of her prose, as well as the emphasis on mood and character rather than plot, have led critics to compare her with Flaubert and other European writers.

Born into a wealthy, well-established family in Maine, Jewett read extensively at home and also attended Miss Rayne's School and Berwick Academy. She began publishing short stories under pseudonyms while in her teens. "Mr. Bruce," her first story to be published in the Atlantic Monthly, *appeared when she was twenty. She quickly joined the thriving literary life of Boston and New York, becoming acquainted with William Dean Howells, James Lowell, John Greenleaf Whittier, Harriet Beecher Stowe, Henry James, and other established writers and editors. Howells encouraged her to publish her first collection of stories,* Deephaven, *which appeared in 1881. These stories brought New England to life in much the same way Mark Twain and Bret Harte had brought the South and the West to life for readers around the world.*

During this time, Jewett also became friends with Annie and James T. Fields, who edited the Atlantic. *After James Fields's death in 1881, Jewett's relationship with Annie Fields became the central one in her life. They traveled to Europe four times, visited the Caribbean, and spent part of each year living together. After Jewett's death, Annie Fields deleted much of the intimate material from Jewett's letters, so we know only a little about their relationship.*

In the thirty years following her first publications, Jewett published nearly 150 stories and sketches in national magazines. A Country Doctor, *a novel with autobiographical elements, appeared in 1884, and the pastoral romance* A Marsh Island *in 1885.* A White Heron and Other Stories *was published in 1886. She wrote dozens of children's stories, three adult novels, and a children's history. Seriously injured in 1902 on her fifty-third birthday in a carriage accident, she ceased writing.*

Jewett was always conscious that she was creating literature, not simply writing publishable material. In a preface to a collection of Jewett's short stories, Willa Cather quotes from one of Jewett's letters: "The thing that teases the mind over and over for years, and at last gets itself put down rightly on paper—whether little or great, it belongs to Literature." Jewett wrote with the eye and ear of an artist, using the brief form of the short story to capture nuances of speech, subtleties of the natural world, and idiosyncrasies of character that had "teased" her mind until she could capture them perfectly.

In "Going to Shrewsbury," Jewett relies heavily on dialogue to capture the tragedy and dignity of the elderly Mrs. Peet. The story reflects Jewett's ability to create memorable settings and characters with spare descriptions and only the simplest of plots.

GOING TO SHREWSBURY

The train stopped at a way station with apparent unwillingness, and there was barely time for one elderly passenger to be hurried on board before a sudden jerk threw her almost off her unsteady old feet and we moved on. At my first glance I saw only a perturbed old countrywoman, laden with a large basket and a heavy bundle tied up in an old-fashioned bundle-handkerchief; then I discovered that she was a friend of mine, Mrs. Peet, who lived on a small farm, several miles from the village. She used to be renowned for good butter and fresh eggs and the earliest cowslip greens; in fact, she always made the most of her farm's slender resources; but it was some time since I had seen her drive by from market in her ancient thorough-braced wagon.

The brakeman followed her into the crowded car, also carrying a number of packages. I leaned forward and asked Mrs. Peet to sit by me; it was a great pleasure to see her again. The brakeman seemed relieved, and smiled as he tried to put part of his burden into the rack overhead; but even the flowered carpet-bag was much too large, and he explained that he would take care of everything at the end of the car. Mrs. Peet was not large herself, but with the big basket, and the bundle-handkerchief, and some possessions of my own we had very little spare room.

"So this 'ere is what you call ridin' in the cars! Well, I do declare!" said my friend, as soon as she had recovered herself a little. She looked pale and as if she had been in tears, but there was the familiar gleam of good humor in her tired old eyes.

"Where in the world are you going, Mrs. Peet?" I asked.

"Can't be you ain't heared about me, dear?" said she. "Well, the world's bigger than I used to think 't was. I've broke up,—'t was the only thing *to* do,—and I'm a-movin' to Shrewsbury."

"To Shrewsbury? Have you sold the farm?" I exclaimed, with sorrow and surprise. Mrs. Peet was too old and too characteristic to be suddenly transplanted from her native soil.

"'T wa'n't mine, the place wa'n't." Her pleasant face hardened slightly.

"He was coaxed an' over-persuaded into signin' off before he was taken away. Is'iah, son of his sister that married old Josh Peet, come it over him about his bein' past work and how he'd do for him like an own son, an' we owed him a little somethin'. I'd paid off everythin' but that, an' was fool enough to leave it till the last, on account o' Is'iah's bein' a relation and not needin' his pay much as some others did. It's hurt me to have the place fall into other hands. Some wanted me to go right to the law; but 't wouldn't be no use. Is'iah's smarter 'n I be about them matters. You see he's got my name on the paper, too; he said 't was somethin' 'bout bein' responsible for the taxes. We was scant o' money, an' I was wore out with watchin' an' being broke o' my rest. After my tryin' hard for risin' forty-five year to provide for bein' past work, here I be, dear, here I be! I used to drive things smart, you remember. But we was fools enough in '72 to put about everythin' we had safe in the bank into the spool factory that come to nothin'. But I tell ya I could ha' kept myself long's I lived, if I could ha' held the place. I'd parted with most o' the woodland, if Is'iah'd coveted it. He was welcome to that 'cept what might keep me in ovenwood. I've always desired to travel an' see somethin' o' the world, but I've got the chance now when I don't value it no great."

"Shrewsbury is a busy, pleasant place," I ventured to say by way of comfort, though my heart was filled with rage at the trickery of Isaiah Peet, who had always looked like a fox and behaved like one.

"Shrewsbury's be'n held up consid'able for me to smile at," said the poor old soul, "but I tell ye, dear, it's hard to go an' live twenty-two miles from where you've always had your home and friends. It may divert me, but it won't be home. You might as well set out one o' my apple-trees on the beach, so 't could see the waves come in,—there wouldn't be no please to it."

"Where are you going to live in Shrewsbury?" I asked presently.

"I don't expect to stop long, dear creatur'. I'm 'most seventy-six year old," and Mrs. Peet turned to look at me with pathetic amusement in her honest wrinkled face. "I said right out to Is'iah, before a roomful o' the neighbors, that I expected it of him to git me home an' bury me when my time come, and do it respectable; but I wanted to airn my livin', if 't was so I could, till then. He'd made sly talk, you see, about me electin' to leave the farm and go 'long some o' my own folks; but"—and she whispered this carefully—"he didn't give me no chance to stay there without hurtin' my pride and dependin' on him. I ain't said that to many folks, but all must have suspected. A good sight on 'em 's had money of Is'iah, though, and they don't like to do nothin' but take his part an' be pretty soft spoken, fear it'll git to his ears. Well, well, dear, we'll let it by bygones, and not think of it no more"; but I saw the great tears roll slowly down her cheeks, and she pulled her bonnet forward impatiently, and looked the other way.

"There looks to be plenty o' good farmin' land in this part o' the country," she said, a minute later. "Where be we now? See them handsome farm buildin's; he must be a well-off man." But I had to tell my companion that we were still within the borders of the old town where we had both been born. Mrs. Peet gave a pleased little laugh, like a girl. "I'm expectin' Shrewsbury to pop up any minute. I'm feared to be kerried right by. I wa'n't never aboard of the cars before, but I've so often thought about 'em I don't know but it seems natural. Ain't it jest like flyin' through the air? I can't catch holt to see nothin'. Land! and here's my old cat goin' too, and never mistrustin'. I ain't told you that I'd fetched her."

"Is she in that basket?" I inquired with interest.

"Yis, dear. Truth was, I calc'lated to have her put out o' the misery o' movin', and spoke to one o' the Barnes boys, an' he promised me all fair; but he wa'n't there in season, an' I kind o' made excuse to myself to fetch her along. She's an old creatur', like me, an' I can make shift to keep her some way or 'nuther; there's probably mice where we're goin', an' she's a proper mouser that can about keep herself if there's any sort o' chance. 'T will be somethin' o' home to see her goin' an' comin', but I expect we're both on us goin' to miss our old haunts. I'd love to know what kind o' mousin' there's goin' to be for me."

"You mustn't worry," I answered, with all the bravery and assurance that I could muster. "Your niece will be thankful to have you with her. Is she one of Mrs. Winn's daughters?"

"Oh, no, they ain't able; it's Sister Wayland's darter Isabella, that married the overseer of the gre't carriage-shop. I ain't seen her since just after she was married; but I turned to her first because I knew she was best able to have me, and then I can see just how the other girls is situated and make me some kind of a plot. I wrote to Isabella, though she *is* ambitious, and said 't was so I'd got to ask to come an' make her a visit, an' she wrote back she would be glad to have me; but she didn't write right off, and her letter was scented up dreadful strong with some sort o' essence, and I don't feel heartened about no great of a welcome. But there, I've got eyes, an' I can see *how* 't is when I get *where* 't is. Sister Winn's gals ain't married, an' they've always boarded an' worked in the shop on trimmin's. Isabella's well off; she had some means from her father's sister. I thought it all over by night an' day, an' I recalled that our folks kept Sister Wayland's folks all one winter, when he'd failed up and got into trouble. I'm reckonin' on sendin' over to-night an' gittin' the Winn gals to come and see me and advise. Perhaps some on 'em may know of somebody that'll take me for what help I can give about house, or some clever folks that have been lookin' for a smart cat, any ways; no, I don't know's I could let her go to strangers.

"There was two or three o' the folks round home that acted real warm-hearted towards me, an' urged me to come an' winter with 'em," continued the exile; "an' this mornin' I wished I'd agreed to, 't was so hard to break away. But now it's done I feel more 'n ever it's best. I couldn't bear to live right in sight o' the old place, and come spring I shouldn't 'prove of nothing Is'iah ondertakes to do with the land. Oh, dear sakes! now it comes hard with me not to have had no child'n. When I was young an' workin' hard and into everything, I felt kind of free an' superior to them that was so blessed, an' their houses cluttered up from mornin' till night, but I tell ye it comes home to me now. I'd be most willin' to own to even Is'iah, mean's he is; but I tell ye I'd took it out of him 'fore he was a grown man, if there'd be'n any virtue in cow-hidin' of him. Folks don't look like wild creatur's for nothin'. Is'iah's got fox blood in him, an' p'r'haps 't is his misfortune. His own mother always favored the looks of an old fox, true's the world; she was a poor tool,—a poor tool! I'd know's we ought to blame him same's we do.

"I've always been a master proud woman, if I was riz among the pastures," Mrs. Peet added, half to herself. There was no use in saying much to her; she was conscious of little beside her own thoughts and the smouldering excitement caused by this great crisis in her simple existence. Yet the atmosphere of her loneliness, uncertainty, and sorrow was so touching that after scolding again at her nephew's treachery, and finding the tears come fast to my eyes as she talked, I looked intently out of the car window, and tried to think what could be done for the poor soul. She was one of the old-time people, and I hated to have her go away; but even if she could keep her home she would soon be too feeble to live there alone, and some definite plan must be made for her comfort. Farms in that neighborhood were not valuable. Perhaps through the agency of the law and quite in secret, Isaiah Peet could be forced to give up his unrighteous claim. Perhaps, too, the Winn girls, who were really no longer young, might have saved something, and would come home again. But it was easy to make such pictures in one's mind, and I must do what I could through other people, for I was just leaving home for a long time. I wondered sadly about Mrs. Peet's future, and the ambitious Isabella, and the favorite Sister Winn's daughters, to whom, with all their kindliness of heart, the care of so old and perhaps so dependent an aunt might seem impossible. The truth about life in Shrewsbury would soon be known; more than half the short journey was already past.

To my great pleasure, my fellow-traveler now began to forget her own troubles in looking about her. She was an alert, quickly interested old soul, and this was a bit of neutral ground between the farm and Shrewsbury, where she was unattached and irresponsible. She had lived through the last tragic moments of her old life, and felt a certain relief, and Shrewsbury might be as far away as the other side of the Rocky Mountains for all the consciousness she had of its real existence. She was simply a traveler for the time being, and began to comment with delicious phrases and shrewd understanding of human nature, on two or three persons near us who attracted her attention.

"Where do you s'pose they be all goin'?" she asked contemptuously. "There ain't none on 'em but what looks kind o' respectable. I'll warrant they've left work to home they'd ought to be doin'. I knowed, if ever I stopped to think, that cars was hived full o' folks, an' wa'n't run to an' fro for nothin'; but these can't be quite up to the average, be they? Some on 'em 's real thrif'less? guess they've be'n shoved out o' the last place, an' goin' to try the next one,—*like me*, I suppose you'll want to say! Jest see that flauntin' old creatur' that looks like a stopped clock. There! everybody can't be o' one goodness, even preachers."

I was glad to have Mrs. Peet amused, and we were as cheerful as we could be for a few minutes. She said earnestly that she hoped to be forgiven for such talk, but there were some kinds of folks in the cars that she never had seen before. But when the conductor came to take her ticket she relapsed into her first state of mind, and was at a loss.

"You'll have to look after me, dear, when we get to Shrewsbury," she said, after we had spent some distracted moments in hunting for the lost ticket, and the cat had almost escaped from the basket, and the bundle-handkerchief had become untied and all its miscellaneous contents scattered about our laps and the floor. It was a touching collection of the last odds and ends of Mrs. Peet's housekeeping: some battered books, and singed holders for flatirons, and the faded little shoulder shawl that I had seen her wear many a day about her bent shoulders. There were her old tin match-box spilling all its matches, and a goose-wing for brushing up ashes, and her much-thumbed Leavitt's Almanac. It was most pathetic to see these poor trifles out of their places. At last the ticket was found in her left-hand woolen glove, where her stiff, work-worn hand had grown used to the feeling of it.

"I shouldn't wonder, now, if I come to like living over to Shrewsbury first-rate," she insisted, turning to me with a hopeful, eager look to see if I differed. "You see 't won't be so tough for me as if I hadn't always felt it lurking within me to go off some day or 'nother an' see how other folks did things. I do' know but what the Winn gals have laid up somethin' sufficient for us to take a house, with the little mite I've got by me. I might keep house for us all, 'stead o' boardin' round in other folks' houses. That I ain't never been demeaned to, but I dare say I should find it pleasant in some ways. Town folks has got the upper hand o' country folks, but with all their work an' pride they can't make a dandelion. I do' know the times when I've set out to wash Monday mornin's, an' tied out the line betwixt the old pucker-pear tree and the corner o' the barn, an' thought, 'Here I be with the same kind o' week's work right over again.' I'd wonder kind o' f'erce if I couldn't git out of it noways; an' now here I be out of it, and an uprooteder creatur' never stood on the airth. Just as I got to feel I had somethin' ahead come that spool-factory business. There! you know he never was a forehanded man; his health was slim, and he got discouraged pretty nigh before ever he begun. I hope he don't know I'm turned out o' the old place. 'Is'iah's well off; he'll do the right thing by ye,' says he. But my! I turned hot all over when I found out what I'd put my name to,— me that had always be'n counted a smart woman! I did understand to read it over, but I couldn't sense it. I've told all the folks so when they laid it off on to me some: but hand-writin' is awful tedious readin' and my head felt that day as if the works was gone."

"I ain't goin' to sag on to nobody," she assured me eagerly, as the train rushed along. "I've got more work in me now than folks expects at my age. I may be consid'able use to Isabella. She's got a family, an' I'll take right holt in the kitchen or with the little gals. She had four on 'em last I heard. Isabella was never one that liked house-work. Little gals! I do' know now but what they must be about grown, time does slip away so. I expect I shall look outlandish to 'em. But there! everybody knows me to home, an' nobody knows me to Shrewsbury; 't won't make a mite o' difference, if I take holt willin'."

I hoped, as I looked at Mrs. Peet, that she would never be persuaded to cast off the gathered brown silk bonnet and the plain shawl that she had worn so many years; but Isabella might think it best to insist upon more modern fashions. Mrs. Peet suggested, as if it were a matter of little consequence, that she had kept it in mind to buy some mourning; but there were other things to be thought of first, and so she had let it go until winter, any way, or until she should be fairly settled in Shrewsbury.

"Are your nieces expecting you by this train?" I was moved to ask, though with all the good soul's ready talk and appealing manner I could hardly believe that she was going to Shrewsbury for more than a visit; it seemed as if she must return to the worn old farmhouse over by the sheep-lands. She answered that one of the Barnes boys had written a letter for her the day before, and there was evidently little uneasiness about her first reception.

We drew near the junction where I must leave her within a mile of the town. The cat was clawing indignantly at the basket, and her mistress grew as impatient of the car. She began to look very old and pale, my poor fellow-traveler, and said that she felt dizzy, going so fast. Presently the friendly red-cheeked young brakeman came along, bringing the carpet bag and other possessions, and insisted upon taking the alarmed cat beside, in spite of an aggressive paw that had worked its way through the wicker prison. Mrs. Peet watched her goods disappear with suspicious eyes, and clutched her bundle-handkerchief as if it might be all that she could save. Then she anxiously got to her feet, much too soon, and when I said good-by to her at the car door she was ready to cry. I pointed to the car which she was to take next on the branch line of railway, and I assured her that it was only a few minutes' ride to Shrewsbury, and that I felt certain she would find somebody waiting. The sight of that worn, thin figure adventuring alone across the platform gave my heart a sharp pang as the train carried me away.

Some of the passengers who sat near asked me about my old friend with great sympathy, after she had gone. There was a look of tragedy about her, and indeed it had been impossible not to get a good deal of her history, as she talked straight on in the same tone, when we stopped at a station, as if the train were going at full speed, and some of her remarks caused pity and amusements by turns. At the last minute she said, with deep self-reproach, "Why, I haven't asked a word about your folks; but you'd ought to excuse such an old stray hen as I be."

In the spring I was driving by on what the old people of my native town call the sheep-lands road, and the sight of Mrs. Peet's former home brought our former journey freshly to my mind. I had last heard from her just after she got to Shrewsbury, when she had sent me a message.

"Have you ever heard how she got on?" I eagerly asked my companion.

"Didn't I tell you that I met her in Shrewsbury High Street one day?" I was answered. "She seemed perfectly delighted with everything. Her nieces have laid up a good bit of money, and are soon to leave the mill, and most thankful to have old Mrs. Peet with them. Somebody told me that they wished to buy the farm here, and come back to live, but she wouldn't hear of it, and thought they would miss too many privileges. She has been going to concerts and lectures this winter, and insists that Isaiah did her a good turn."

We both laughed. My own heart was filled with joy, for the uncertain, lonely face of this homeless old woman had often haunted me. The rain-blackened little house did certainly look dreary, and a whole lifetime of patient toil had left few traces. The pucker-pear tree was in full bloom, however, and gave a welcome gayety to the deserted door-yard.

A little way beyond we met Isaiah Peet, the prosperous money-lender, who had cheated the old woman of her own. I fancied that he looked somewhat ashamed, as he recognized us. To my surprise, he stopped his horse in most social fashion.

"Old Aunt Peet's passed away," he informed me briskly. "She had a shock, and went right off sudden yisterday forenoon. I'm about now tendin' to the funeral 'rangements. She's be'n extry smart, they say, all winter,—out to meetin' last Sabbath; never enjoyed herself so complete as she has this past month. She'd be'n a very hard-workin' woman. Her folks was glad to have her there, and give her every attention. The place here never was good for nothin'. The old gen'leman,—uncle, you know,—he wore hisself out tryin' to make a livin' off from it."

There was an ostentatious sympathy, and half-suppressed excitement from bad news which were quite lost upon us, and we did not linger to hear much more. It seemed to me as if I had known Mrs. Peet better than any one else had known her. I had counted upon seeing her again, and hearing her own account of Shrewsbury life, its pleasures and its limitations. I wondered what had become of the cat and the contents of the faded bundle-handkerchief.

1889

KATE CHOPIN
(1850–1904)

Kate Chopin was a prominent author of novels and short fiction. Much of her writing reflects the years she spent living among white Creoles in Louisiana. Inspired by Guy de Maupassant, whose stories she translated, and Gustave Flaubert, whose Madame Bovary *influenced* The Awakening, *Chopin became a major American realist. Born Katherine O'Flaherty in Missouri in 1850, Chopin was the child of middle-class, slave-owning parents. Her mother was descended from a French Creole family, and her father was an Irish merchant in St. Louis. The death of her half-brother George, who fought and died in the Confederate army, inspired a number of her Civil War stories.*

O'Flaherty received a Catholic education, graduating from the Academy of the Sacred Heart in 1868. She married Oscar Chopin, a Louisiana Creole, in 1870, and with him she moved to New Orleans. When Oscar Chopin's business as a cotton merchant suffered, the family moved to the quiet village of Cloutierville in northwest Louisiana. After her husband's death in 1882, Chopin managed the family business until 1884, when she returned to St. Louis and began writing seriously to support herself and her six children.

Chopin published her first novel, At Fault, *in 1890. The success of this work inspired her to contribute short fiction to such established magazines as* Vogue, *the* Century, *and the* Atlantic Monthly. *A collection of her stories,* Bayou Folk, *was published in 1894.* The Awakening *appeared in 1899, when she was an acclaimed author of three novels and more than one hundred short stories.*

In The Awakening, *Chopin traces Edna Pontellier's growing disillusionment with her role as wife and mother. The novel deals frankly with Edna's sexuality, as it pictures her wavering between her attractions to men other than her husband and her desire for independence. When it was first published, reviewers called it an unhealthy book, arguing that it was unnecessary "for a writer of so great refinement and poetic grace to enter the overworked field of sex fiction." One reviewer deemed it a vulgar story that "could hardly be described in language fit for publication." Chopin wrote little after its publication. The novel went out of print in 1906 and remained so for more than fifty years.*

Thanks in part to the work of contemporary feminist critics, Kate Chopin has assumed her rightful place in the American literature canon. Her stories "Desiree's Baby" and "The Story of an Hour" are frequently anthologized; The Awakening *is now an unquestioned classic.*

"A Respectable Woman," one of the stories we have selected, first appeared

in an 1894 issue of Vogue, *the only magazine willing to publish Chopin's more unconventional tales. Three years later, Chopin included it in the second volume of her collected stories,* A Night in Acadie. *"A Respectable Woman" candidly portrays the heroine's sexual attraction to her husband's best friend. Here, then, Chopin rehearses the subject of her most famous novel.*

In "The Falling in Love of Fedora," Chopin boldly describes a character's attraction to both a man and a woman. First published in 1897 under the pen name "La Tour" in the St. Louis Criterion, *this work was rejected by the editors of the* Atlantic Monthly, *who claimed that it lacked a story. Contemporary readers will appreciate the significant story it does tell of Fedora's confusion about her sexuality.*

A RESPECTABLE WOMAN

Mrs. Baroda was a little provoked to learn that her husband expected his friend, Gouvernail, up to spend a week or two on the plantation.

They had entertained a good deal during the winter; much of the time had also been passed in New Orleans in various forms of mild dissipation. She was looking forward to a period of unbroken rest, now, and undisturbed tête-à-tête with her husband, when he informed her that Gouvernail was coming up to stay a week or two.

This was a man she had heard much of but never seen. He had been her husband's college friend; was now a journalist, and in no sense a society man or "a man about town," which were, perhaps, some of the reasons she had never met him. But she had unconsciously formed an image of him in her mind. She pictured him tall, slim, cynical; with eye-glasses, and his hands in his pockets; and she did not like him. Gouvernail was slim enough, but he wasn't very tall nor very cynical; neither did he wear eye-glasses nor carry his hands in his pockets. And she rather liked him when he first presented himself.

But why she liked him she could not explain satisfactorily to herself when she partly attempted to do so. She could discover in him none of those brilliant and promising traits which Gaston, her husband, had often assured her that he possessed. On the contrary, he sat rather mute and receptive before her chatty eagerness to make him feel at home and in face of Gaston's frank and wordy hospitality. His manner was as courteous toward her as the most exacting woman could require; but he made no direct appeal to her approval or even esteem.

Once settled at the plantation he seemed to like to sit upon the wide portico in the shade of one of the big Corinthian pillars, smoking his cigar lazily and listening attentively to Gaston's experience as a sugar planter.

"This is what I call living," he would utter with deep satisfaction, as the air that swept across the sugar field caressed him with its warm and scented velvety touch. It pleased him also to get on familiar terms with the big dogs that came about him, rubbing themselves sociably against his legs. He did not care to fish, and displayed no eagerness to go out and kill grosbecs when Gaston proposed doing so.

Gouvernail's personality puzzled Mrs. Baroda, but she liked him. Indeed, he was a lovable, inoffensive fellow. After a few days, when she could understand him no better than at first, she gave over being puzzled and remained piqued. In this mood she left her husband and her guest, for the most part, alone together. Then finding that Gouvernail took no manner of exception to her action, she imposed her society upon him, accompanying him in his idle strolls to the mill and walks along the batture. She persistently sought to penetrate the reserve in which he had unconsciously enveloped himself.

"When is he going—your friend?" she one day asked her husband. "For my part, he tires me frightfully."

"Not for a week yet, dear. I can't understand; he gives you no trouble."

"No. I should like him better if he did; if he were more like others, and I had to plan somewhat for his comfort and enjoyment."

Gaston took his wife's pretty face between his hands and looked tenderly and laughingly into her troubled eyes. They were making a bit of toilet sociably together in Mrs. Baroda's dressing-room.

"You are full of surprises, ma belle," he said to her. "Even I can never count upon how you are going to act under given conditions." He kissed her and turned to fasten his cravat before the mirror.

"Here you are," he went on, "taking poor Gouvernail seriously and making a commotion over him, the last thing he would desire or expect."

"Commotion!" she hotly resented. "Nonsense! How can you say such a thing? Commotion, indeed! But, you know, you said he was clever."

"So he is. But the poor fellow is run down by overwork now. That's why I asked him here to take a rest."

"You used to say he was a man of ideas," she retorted, unconciliated. "I expected him to be interesting, at least. I'm going to the city in the morning to have my spring gowns fitted. Let me know when Mr. Gouvernail is gone; I shall be at my Aunt Octavie's."

That night she went and sat alone upon a bench that stood beneath a live oak tree at the edge of the gravel walk.

She had never known her thoughts or her intentions to be so confused. She could gather nothing from them but the feeling of a distinct necessity to quit her home in the morning.

Mrs. Baroda heard footsteps crunching the gravel; but could discern in the darkness only the approaching red point of a lighted cigar. She knew it was Gouvernail, for her husband did not smoke. She hoped to remain unnoticed, but her white gown revealed her to him. He threw away his cigar and seated himself upon the bench beside her; without a suspicion that she might object to his presence.

"Your husband told me to bring this to you, Mrs. Baroda," he said, handing her a filmy, white scarf with which she sometimes enveloped her head and shoulders. She accepted the scarf from him with a murmur of thanks, and let it lie in her lap.

He made some commonplace observation upon the baneful effect of the night air at that season. Then as his gaze reached out into the darkness, he murmured, half to himself:

" 'Night of south winds—night of the large few stars!
Still nodding night—' "

She made no reply to this apostrophe to the night, which indeed, was not addressed to her.

Gouvernail was in no sense a diffident man, for he was not a self-conscious one. His periods of reserve were not constitutional, but the result of moods. Sitting there beside Mrs. Baroda, his silence melted for the time.

He talked freely and intimately in a low, hesitating drawl that was not unpleasant to hear. He talked of the old college days when he and Gaston had been a good deal to each other; of the days of keen and blind ambitions and large intentions. Now there was left with him, at least, a philosophic acquiescence to the existing order—only a desire to be permitted to exist, with now and then a little whiff of genuine life, such as he was breathing now.

Her mind only vaguely grasped what he was saying. Her physical being was for the moment predominant. She was not thinking of his words, only drinking in the tones of his voice. She wanted to reach out her hand in the darkness and touch him with the sensitive tips of her fingers upon the face or the lips. She wanted to draw close to him and whisper against his cheek—she did not care what—as she might have done if she had not been a respectable woman.

The stronger the impulse grew to bring herself near him, the further, in fact, did she draw away from him. As soon as she could do so without an appearance of too great rudeness, she rose and left him there alone.

Before she reached the house, Gouvernail had lighted a fresh cigar and ended his apostrophe to the night.

Mrs. Baroda was greatly tempted that night to tell her husband—who was also her friend—of this folly that had seized her. But she did not yield to the temptation. Beside being a respectable woman she was a very sensible one; and she knew there are some battles in life which a human being must fight alone.

When Gaston arose in the morning, his wife had already departed. She had taken an early morning train to the city. She did not return till Gouvernail was gone from under her roof.

There was some talk of having him back during the summer that followed. That is, Gaston greatly desired it; but this desire yielded to his wife's strenuous opposition.

However, before the year ended, she proposed, wholly from herself, to have Gouvernail visit them again. Her husband was surprised and delighted with the suggestion coming from her.

"I am glad, chère amie, to know that you have finally overcome your dislike for him; truly he did not deserve it."

"Oh," she told him, laughingly, after pressing a long, tender kiss upon his lips, "I have overcome everything! you will see. This time I shall be very nice to him."

1894

THE FALLING IN LOVE OF FEDORA

Fedora had determined upon driving over to the station herself for Miss Malthers.

Though one or two of them looked disappointed—notably her brother—no one opposed her. She said the brute was restive, and shouldn't be trusted to the handling of the young people.

To be sure Fedora was old enough, from the standpoint of her sister Camilla and the rest of them. Yet no one would ever have thought of it but for her own persistent affectation and idiotic assumption of superior years and wisdom. She was thirty.

Fedora had too early in life formed an ideal and treasured it. By this ideal she had measured such male beings as had hitherto challenged her attention, and needless to say she had found them wanting. The young people—her brothers' and sisters' guests, who were constantly coming and going that summer—occupied her to a great extent, but failed to interest her. She concerned herself with their comforts—in the absence of her mother—looked after their health and well-being, contrived for their amusements, in which she never joined. And, as Fedora was tall and slim, and carried her head loftily, and wore eye-glasses and a severe expression, some of them—the silliest—felt as if she were a hundred years old. Young Malthers thought she was about forty.

One day when he stopped before her out in the gravel walk to ask her some question pertaining to the afternoon's sport, Fedora, who was tall, had to look up into his face to answer him. She had known him eight years, since he was a lad of fifteen, and to her he had never been other than the lad of fifteen.

But that afternoon, looking up into his face, the sudden realization came home to her that he was a man—in voice, in attitude, in bearing, in every sense—a man.

In an absorbing glance, and with unaccountable intention, she gathered in every detail of his countenance as though it were a strange, new thing to her, presenting itself to her vision for the first time. The eyes were blue, earnest, and at the moment a little troubled over some trivial affair that he was relating to her. The face was brown from the sun, smooth, with no suggestion of ruddiness, except in the lips, that were strong, firm and clean. She kept thinking of his face, and every trick of it after he passed on.

From that moment he began to exist for her. She looked at him when he was near by, she listened for his voice, and took notice and account of what he said. She sought him out; she selected him when occasion permitted. She wanted him by her, though his nearness troubled her. There was uneasiness, restlessness, expectation when he was not there within sight or sound. There was redoubled uneasiness when he was by—there was inward revolt, astonishment, rapture, self-contumely; a swift, fierce encounter betwixt thought and feeling.

Fedora could hardly explain to her own satisfaction why she wanted to go herself to the station for young Malthers's sister. She felt a desire to see the girl, to be near her; as unaccountable, when she tried to analyze it, as the impulse which drove her, and to which she often yielded, to touch his hat, hanging with others upon the hall pegs, when she passed it by. Once a coat which he had discarded hung there too. She handled it under pretense of putting it in order. There was no one near, and, obeying a sudden impulse, she buried her face for an instant in the rough folds of the coat.

Fedora reached the station a little before train time. It was in a pretty nook, green and fragrant, set down at the foot of a wooded hill. Off in a clearing there was a field of yellow grain, upon which the sinking sunlight fell in slanting, broken beams. Far down the track there were some men at work, and the even ring of their hammers was the only sound that broke upon the stillness. Fedora loved it all—sky and woods and sunlight; sounds and smells. But her bearing—elegant, composed, reserved—betrayed nothing emotional as she tramped the narrow platform, whip in hand, and occasionally offered a condescending word to the mail man or the sleepy agent.

Malthers's sister was the only soul to disembark from the train. Fedora had never seen her before; but if there had been a hundred, she would have known the girl. She was a small thing; but aside from that, there was the coloring; there were the blue, earnest eyes; there, above all, was the firm, full curve of the lips; the same setting of the white, even teeth. There was the subtle play of feature, the elusive trick of expression, which she had thought peculiar and individual in the one, presenting themselves as family traits.

The suggestive resemblance of the girl to her brother was vivid, poignant even to Fedora, realizing, as she did with a pang, that familiarity and custom would soon blur the image.

Miss Malthers was a quiet, reserved creature, with little to say. She had been to college with Camilla, and spoke somewhat of their friendship and former intimacy. She sat lower in the cart than Fedora, who drove, handling whip and rein with accomplished skill.

"You know, dear child," said Fedora, in her usual elderly fashion, "I want you to feel completely at home with us." They were driving through a long, quiet, leafy road, into which the twilight was just beginning to creep. "Come to me freely and without reserve—with all your wants; with any complaints. I feel that I shall be quite fond of you."

She had gathered the reins into one hand, and with the other free arm she encircled Miss Malthers's shoulders.

When the girl looked up into her face, with murmured thanks, Fedora bent down and pressed a long, penetrating kiss upon her mouth.

Malthers's sister appeared astonished, and not too well pleased. Fedora, with seemingly unruffled composure, gathered the reins, and for the rest of the way stared steadily ahead of her between the horses' ears.

1895

MARY WILKINS FREEMAN
(1852–1930)

In her short stories, Mary Wilkins Freeman re-creates the life of close-knit, rural New England communities in the nineteenth century. The village inhabitants are the descendants of Puritans: hardy, stoical, often stern and inflexible. Her women characters, however, often surprise us, striking out as they do against the oppression, frustration, and limitation of their lives.

Freeman is a New England realist in the tradition of Washington Irving, Harriet Beecher Stowe, James Fenimore Cooper, and Sarah Orne Jewett. She captures the rhythms of local dialects, the pace and texture of small-town life, and the deterioration of economic and social conditions as the industrial age replaced the agricultural life of New England. Famous during her lifetime, Freeman was awarded the William Dean Howells Gold Medal for Fiction from the American Academy of Letters. She and Edith Wharton were the first women to be elected members of the National Institute of Arts and Letters.

Freeman attended school in a Vermont town similar to the ones in many of her stories and then briefly attended Mount Holyoke Seminary. She began her writing career by publishing poetry, but after her father's death in 1884, she supported herself and her aunt by publishing short stories in national publications such as Harper's New Monthly *and* Harper's Bazaar. *Many of her best stories were collected in* A Humble Romance and Other Stories *and* A New England Nun and Other Stories. *One of her best-known novels,* Pembroke, *based on an incident from Freeman's family history, appeared in 1894. A prolific writer, Freeman published children's stories, essays, and a play as well as poetry, novels, and short stories. Her marriage in 1902 to Dr. Charles Manning Freeman led to many years of unhappiness, but she continued to publish short stories and novels throughout his numerous bouts with alcoholism.*

In 1908, Freeman took part in a highly publicized transatlantic novel-writing competition in which she represented the United States. The competition pitted her against a well-known English writer, Max Pemberton. In two months, Freeman wrote The Shoulders of Atlas, *winning the contest and a $20,000 prize.*

Also in 1908, Freeman took part in another project that attracted much public attention—a collaborative novel, The Whole Family. *This project, initiated by William Dean Howells, included chapters written by Howells, Alice Brown, Henry James, and other prominent writers. For the opening chapter, Howells created a stereotypical, submissive spinster; in the second chapter, Freeman transformed the spinster into an independent, stylish woman who has remained single by her own choice. Howells was furious when he saw Freeman's chapter and wanted it withdrawn from the project; however, the editor (herself single) insisted on printing it.*

"The Revolt of 'Mother'" reveals Freeman's ability to capture emotion and power in the flat, understated dialect of a New England village. Focusing on a female character who shows a surprising ability to assert herself in her highly structured society, the story depicts a battle between the sexes that is both poignant and comic.

THE REVOLT OF "MOTHER"

"Father!"

"What is it?"

"What are them men diggin' over there in the field for?"

There was a sudden dropping and enlarging of the lower part of the old man's face, as if some heavy weight had settled therein; he shut his mouth tight, and went on harnessing the great bay mare. He hustled the collar on to her neck with a jerk.

"Father!"

The old man slapped the saddle upon the mare's back.

"Look here, father, I want to know what them men are diggin' over in the field for, an' I'm goin' to know."

"I wish you'd go into the house, mother, an 'tend to your own affairs," the old man said then. He ran his words together, and his speech was almost as inarticulate as a growl.

But the woman understood; it was her most native tongue.

"I ain't goin' into the house till you tell me what them men are doin' over there in the field," said she.

Then she stood waiting. She was a small woman, short and straight-waisted like a child in her brown cotton gown. Her forehead was mild and benevolent between the smooth curves of gray hair; there were meek downward lines about her nose and mouth; but her eyes, fixed upon the old man, looked as if the meekness had been the result of her own will, never of the will of another.

They were in the barn, standing before the wide open doors. The spring air, full of the smell of growing grass and unseen blossoms, came in their faces. The deep yard in front was littered with farm wagons and piles of wood; on the edges, close to the fence and the house, the grass was a vivid green, and there were some dandelions.

The old man glanced doggedly at his wife as he tightened the last buckles on the harness. She looked as immovable to him as one of the rocks in his pasture-land, bound to the earth with generations of blackberry vines. He slapped the reins over the horse, and started forth from the barn.

"*Father!*" said she.

The old man pulled up. "What is it?"

"I want to know what them men are diggin' over there in that field for."

"They're diggin' a cellar, I s'pose, if you've got to know."

"A cellar for what?"

"A barn."

"A barn? You ain't goin' to build a barn over there where we was goin' to have a house, father?"

The old man said not another word. He hurried the horse into the farm wagon, and clattered out of the yard, jouncing as sturdily on his seat as a boy.

The woman stood a moment looking after him, then she went out of the barn across a corner of the yard to the house. The house, standing at right angles with the great barn and a long reach of sheds and out-buildings, was infinitesimal compared with them. It was scarcely as commodious for people as the little boxes under the barn eaves were for doves.

A pretty girl's face, pink and delicate as a flower, was looking out of one of the house windows. She was watching three men who were digging over in the field which bounded the yard near the road line. She turned quietly when the woman entered.

"What are they digging for, mother?" said she. "Did he tell you?"

"They're diggin' for—a cellar for a new barn."

"Oh, mother, he ain't going to build another barn?"

"That's what he says."

A boy stood before the kitchen glass combing his hair. He combed slowly and painstakingly, arranging his brown hair in a smooth hillock over his forehead. He did not seem to pay any attention to the conversation.

"Sammy, did you know father was going to build a new barn?" asked the girl.

The boy combed assiduously.

"Sammy!"

He turned, and showed a face like his father's under his smooth crest of hair. "Yes, I s'pose I did," he said, reluctantly.

"How long have you known it?" asked his mother.

" 'Bout three months, I guess."

"Why didn't you tell of it?"

"Didn't think 'twould do no good."

"I don't see what father wants another barn for," said the girl, in her sweet, slow voice. She turned again to the window, and stared out at the digging men in the field. Her tender, sweet face was full of a gentle distress. Her forehead was as bald and innocent as a baby's, with the light hair strained back from it in a row of curl-papers. She was quite large, but her soft curves did not look as if they covered muscles.

Her mother looked sternly at the boy. "Is he goin' to buy more cows?" said she.

The boy did not reply; he was tying his shoes.

"Sammy, I want you to tell me if he's goin' to buy more cows."

"I s'pose he is."

"How many?"

"Four, I guess."

His mother said nothing more. She went into the pantry, and there was a clatter of dishes. The boy got his cap from a nail behind the door, took an old arithmetic from the shelf, and started for school. He was lightly built, but clumsy. He went out of the yard with a curious spring in the hips, that made his loose home-made jacket tilt up in the rear.

The girl went to the sink, and began to wash the dishes that were piled up there. Her mother came promptly out of the pantry, and shoved her aside. "You wipe 'em," said she; "I'll wash. There's a good many this mornin'."

The mother plunged her hands vigorously into the water, the girl wiped the plates slowly and dreamily. "Mother," said she, "don't you think it's too bad father's going to build that new barn, much as we need a decent house to live in?"

Her mother scrubbed a dish fiercely. "You ain't found out yet we're women-folks, Nanny Penn," said she. "You ain't seen enough of men-folks yet to. One of these days you'll find it out, an' then you'll know that we know only what men-folks think we do, so far as any use of it goes, an' how we'd ought to reckon men-folks in with Providence, an' not complain of what they do any more than we do of the weather."

"I don't care; I don't believe George is anything like that, anyhow," said Nanny. Her delicate face flushed pink, her lips pouted softly, as if she were going to cry.

"You wait an' see. I guess George Eastman ain't no better than other men. You hadn't ought to judge father, though. He can't help it, 'cause he don't look at things jest the way we do. An' we've been pretty comfortable here, after all. The roof don't leak—ain't never but once—that's one thing. Father's kept it shingled right up."

"I do wish we had a parlor."

"I guess it won't hurt George Eastman any to come to see you in a nice clean kitchen. I guess a good many girls don't have as good a place as this. Nobody's every heard me complain."

"I ain't complained either, mother."

"Well, I don't think you'd better, a good father an' a good home as you've got. S'pose your father made you go out an' work for your livin'? Lots of girls have to that ain't no stronger an' better able to than you be."

Sarah Penn washed the frying-pan with a conclusive air. She scrubbed the outside of it as faithfully as the inside. She was a masterly keeper of her box of a house. Her one living-room never seemed to have in it any of the dust which the friction of life with inanimate matter produces. She swept, and there seemed to be no dirt to go before the broom; she cleaned, and one could see no difference. She was like an artist so perfect that he has apparently no art. To-day she got out a mixing bowl and a board, and rolled some pies, and there was no more flour upon her than upon her daughter who was doing finer work. Nanny was to be married in the fall, and she was sewing on some white cambric and embroidery. She sewed industriously while her mother cooked, her soft milk-white hands and wrists showed whiter than her delicate work.

"We must have the stove moved out in the shed before long," said Mrs. Penn. "Talk about not havin' things, it's been a real blessin' to be able to put a stove up in that shed in hot weather. Father did one good thing when he fixed that stove-pipe out there."

Sarah Penn's face as she rolled her pies had that expression of meek vigor which might have characterized one of the New Testament saints. She was making mince-pies. Her husband, Adoniram Penn, liked them better than any other kind. She baked twice a week. Adoniram often liked a piece of pie between meals. She hurried this morning. It had been later than usual when she began, and she wanted to have a pie baked for dinner. However deep a resentment she might be forced to hold against her husband, she would never fail in sedulous attention to his wants.

Nobility of character manifests itself at loop-holes when it is not provided with large doors. Sarah Penn's showed itself to-day in flaky dishes of pastry. So she made the pies faithfully, while across the table she could see, when she glanced up from her work, the sight that rankled in her patient and steadfast soul—the digging of the cellar of the new barn in the place where Adoniram forty years ago had promised her their new house should stand.

The pies were done for dinner. Adoniram and Sammy were home a few minutes after twelve o'clock. The dinner was eaten with serious haste. There was never much conversation at the table in the Penn family. Adoniram asked a blessing, and they ate promptly, then rose up and went about their work.

Sammy went back to school, taking soft sly lopes out of the yard like a rabbit. He wanted a game of marbles before school, and feared his father would give him some chores to do. Adoniram hastened to the door and called after him, but he was out of sight.

"I don't see what you let him go for, mother," said he. "I wanted him to help me unload that wood."

Adoniram went to work out in the yard unloading wood from the wagon. Sarah put away the dinner dishes, while Nanny took down her curl-papers and changed her dress. She was going down to the store to buy some more embroidery and thread.

When Nanny was gone, Mrs. Penn went to the door. "Father!" she called.

"Well, what is it?"

"I want to see you jest a minute, father."

"I can't leave this wood nohow. I've got to git it unloaded an' go for a load of gravel afore two o'clock. Sammy had ought to helped me. You hadn't ought to let him go to school so early."

"I want to see you jest a minute."

"I tell ye I can't, nohow, mother."

"Father, you come here." Sarah Penn stood in the door like a queen; she held her head as if it bore a crown; there was that patience which makes authority royal in her voice. Adoniram went.

Mrs. Penn led the way into the kitchen, and pointed to a chair. "Sit down, father," said she; "I've got somethin' I want to say to you."

He sat down heavily; his face was quite stolid, but he looked at her with restive eyes. "Well, what is it, mother?"

"I want to know what you're buildin' that new barn for, father?"

"I ain't got nothin' to say about it."

"It can't be you think you need another barn?"

"I tell ye I ain't got nothin' to say about it, mother; an' I ain't goin' to say nothin'."

"Be you goin' to buy more cows?"

Adoniram did not reply; he shut his mouth tight.

"I know you be, as well as I want to. Now, father, look here"—Sarah Penn had not sat down; she stood before her husband in the humble fashion of a Scripture woman—"I'm goin' to talk real plain to you; I never have sence I married you, but I'm goin' to now. I ain't never complained, an' I ain't goin' to complain now, but I'm goin' to talk plain. You see this room here, father; you look at it well. You see there ain't no carpet on the floor, an' you see the paper is all dirty, an' droppin' off the walls. We ain't had no new paper on it for ten years, an' then I put it on myself, an' it didn't cost but ninepence a roll. You see this room, father; it's all the one I've had to work in an' eat in an' sit in sence we was married. There ain't another woman in the whole town whose husband ain't got half the means you have but what's got better. It's all the room Nanny's got to have her company in; an' there ain't one of her mates but what's got better, an' their fathers not so able as hers is. It's all the room she'll have to be married in. What would you have thought, father, if we had had our weddin' in a room no better than this? I was married in my mother's parlor, with a carpet on the floor, an' stuffed furniture, an' a mahogany card-table. An' this is all the room my daughter will have to be married in. Look here, father!"

Sarah Penn went across the room as though it were a tragic stage. She flung open a door and disclosed a tiny bedroom, only large enough for a bed and bureau, with a path between. "There, father," said she—"there's all the room I've had to sleep in forty year. All my children were born there—the two that died, an' the two that's livin'. I was sick with fever there."

She stepped to another door and opened it. It led into the small, ill-lighted pantry. "Here," said she, "is all the buttery I've got—every place I've got for my dishes, to set away my victuals in, an' to keep my milk-pans in. Father, I've been takin' care of the milk of six cows in this place, an' now you're goin' to build a new barn, an' keep more cows, an' give me more to do in it."

She threw open another door. A narrow crooked flight of stairs wound upward from it. "There, father," said she, "I want you to look at the stairs that go up to them two unfinished chambers that are all the places our son an' daughter have had to sleep in all their lives. There ain't a prettier girl in town nor a more ladylike one than Nanny, an' that's the place she has to sleep in. It ain't so good as your horse's stall; it ain't so warm an' tight."

Sarah Penn went back and stood before her husband. "Now, father," said she, "I want to know if you think you're doin' right an' accordin' to what you profess. Here, when we was married, forty year ago, you promised me faithful that we should have a new house built in that lot over in the field before the year was out. You said you had money enough, an' you wouldn't ask me to live in no such place as this. It is forty year now, an' you've been makin' more money, an' I've been savin' of it for you ever since, an' you ain't built no house yet. You've built sheds an' cow-houses an' one new barn, an' now you're goin' to build another. Father, I want to know if you think it's right. You're lodgin' your dumb beasts better than you are your own flesh an' blood. I want to know if you think it's right."

"I ain't got nothin' to say."

"You can't say nothin' without ownin' it ain't right, father. An' there's another thing—I ain't complained; I've got along forty year, an' I s'pose I should forty more, if it wa'n't for that—if we don't have another house. Nanny she can't live with us after she's married. She'll have to go somewheres else to live away from us, an' it don't seem as if I could have it so, noways, father. She wa'n't ever strong. She's got considerable color, but there wa'n't never any backbone to her. I've always took the heft of everything off her, an' she ain't fit to keep house an' do everything herself. She'll be all worn out inside of a year. Think of her doin' all the washin' an' ironin' an' bakin' with them soft white hands an' arms, an' sweepin'! I can't have it so, noways, father."

Mrs. Penn's face was burning; her mild eyes gleamed. She had pleaded her little cause like a Webster; she had ranged from severity to pathos; but her opponent employed that obstinate silence which makes eloquence futile with mocking echoes. Adoniram arose clumsily.

"Father, ain't you got nothin' to say?" said Mrs. Penn.

"I've got to go off after that load of gravel. I can't stan' here talkin' all day."

"Father, won't you think it over, an' have a house built there instead of a barn?"

"I ain't got nothin' to say."

Adoniram shuffled out. Mrs. Penn went into her bedroom. When she came out, her eyes were red. She had a roll of unbleached cotton cloth. She spread it out on the kitchen table, and began cutting out some shirts for her husband. The men over in the field had a team to help them this afternoon; she could hear their halloos. She had a scanty pattern for the shirts; she had to plan and piece the sleeves.

Nanny came home with her embroidery, and sat down with her needlework. She had taken down her curl-papers, and there was a soft roll of fair hair like an aureole over her forehead; her face was as delicately fine and clear as porcelain. Suddenly she looked up, and the tender red flamed all over her face and neck. "Mother," said she.

"What say?"

"I've been thinking—I don't see how we're goin' to have any—wedding in this room. I'd be ashamed to have his folks come if we didn't have anybody else."

"Mebbe we can have some new paper before then; I can put it on. I guess you won't have no call to be ashamed of your belongin's."

"We might have the wedding in the new barn," said Nanny, with gentle pettishness. "Why, mother, what makes you look so?"

Mrs. Penn had started, and was staring at her with a curious expression. She turned again to her work, and spread out a pattern carefully on the cloth. "Nothin'," said she.

Presently Adoniram clattered out of the yard in his two-wheeled dump cart, standing as proudly upright as a Roman charioteer. Mrs. Penn opened the door and stood there a minute looking out; the halloos of the men sounded louder.

It seemed to her all through the spring months that she heard nothing but the halloos and the noises of saws and hammers. The new barn grew fast. It was a fine edifice for this little village. Men came on pleasant Sundays, in their meeting suits and clean shirt bosoms, and stood around it admiringly. Mrs. Penn did not speak of it, and Adoniram did not mention it to her, although sometimes, upon a return from inspecting it, he bore himself with injured dignity.

"It's a strange thing how your mother feels about the new barn," he said, confidentially, to Sammy one day.

Sammy only grunted after an odd fashion for a boy; he had learned it from his father.

The barn was all completed ready for use by the third week in July. Adoniram had planned to move his stock in on Wednesday; on Tuesday he received a letter which changed his plans. He came in with it early in the morning. "Sammy's been to the post-office," said he, "an' I've got a letter from Hiram." Hiram was Mrs. Penn's brother, who lived in Vermont.

"Well," said Mrs. Penn, "what does he say about the folks?"

"I guess they're all right. He says he thinks if I come up country right off there's a chance to buy jest the kind of a horse I want." He stared reflectively out of the window at the new barn.

Mrs. Penn was making pies. She went on clapping the rolling-pin into the crust, although she was very pale, and her heart beat loudly.

"I dun' know but what I'd better go," said Adoniram. "I hate to go off jest now, right in the midst of hayin', but the ten-acre lot's cut, an' I guess Rufus an' the others can git along without me three or four days. I can't get a horse round here to suit me, nohow, an' I've got to have another for all that wood-haulin' in the fall. I told Hiram to watch out, an' if he got wind of a good horse to let me know. I guess I'd better go."

"I'll get out your clean shirt an' collar," said Mrs. Penn calmly.

She laid out Adoniram's Sunday suit and his clean clothes on the bed in the little bedroom. She got his shaving-water and razor ready. At last she buttoned on his collar and fastened his black cravat.

Adoniram never wore his collar and cravat except on extra occasions. He held his head high, with a rasped dignity. When he was all ready, with his coat and hat brushed, and a lunch of pie and cheese in a paper bag, he hesitated on the threshold of the door. He looked at his wife, and his manner was defiantly apologetic. "*If* them cows come to-day, Sammy can drive 'em into the new barn," said he; "an' when they bring the hay up, they can pitch it in there."

"Well," replied Mrs. Penn.

Adoniram set his shaven face ahead and started. When he had cleared the door-step, he turned and looked back with a kind of nervous solemnity. "I shall be back by Saturday if nothin' happens," said he.

"Do be careful, father," returned his wife.

She stood in the door with Nanny at her elbow and watched him out of sight. Her eyes had a strange, doubtful expression in them; her peaceful forehead was contracted. She went in, and about her baking again. Nanny sat sewing. Her wedding-day was drawing nearer, and she was getting pale and thin with her steady sewing. Her mother kept glancing at her.

"Have you got that pain in your side this mornin'?" she asked.

"A little."

Mrs. Penn's face, as she worked, changed, her perplexed forehead smoothed, her eyes were steady, her lips firmly set. She formed a maxim for herself, although incoherently with her unlettered thoughts. "Unsolicited opportunities are the guide-posts of the Lord to the new roads of life," she repeated in effect, and she made up her mind to her course of action.

"S'posin' I *had* wrote to Hiram," she muttered once, when she was in the pantry—"s'posin' I had wrote, an' asked him if he knew of any horse? But I didn't, an' father's goin' wa'n't none of my doin'. It looks like a providence." Her voice rang out quite loud at last.

"What you talkin' about, mother?" called Nanny.

"Nothin'."

Mrs. Penn hurried her baking; at eleven o'clock it was all done. The load of hay from the west field came slowly down the cart track, and drew up at the new barn. Mrs. Penn ran out. "Stop!" she screamed—"stop!"

The men stopped and looked; Sammy upreared from the top of the load, and stared at his mother.

"Stop!" she cried out again. "Don't you put the hay in that barn; put it in the old one."

"Why, he said to put it in here," returned one of the hay-makers, wonderingly. He was a young man, a neighbor's son, whom Adoniram hired by the year to help on the farm.

"Don't you put the hay in the new barn; there's room enough in the old one, ain't there?" said Mrs. Penn.

"Room enough," returned the hired man, in his thick, rustic tones. "Didn't need the new barn, nohow, far as room's concerned. Well, I s'pose he changed his mind." He took hold of the horses' bridles.

Mrs. Penn went back to the house. Soon the kitchen windows were darkened, and a fragrance like warm honey came into the room.

Nanny laid down her work. "I thought father wanted them to put the hay into the new barn?" she said, wonderingly.

"It's all right," replied her mother.

Sammy slid down from the load of hay, and came in to see if dinner was ready.

"I ain't goin' to get a regular dinner to-day, as long as father's gone," said his mother. "I've let the fire go out. You can have some bread an' milk an' pie. I thought we could get along." She set out some bowls of milk, some bread, and a pie on the kitchen table. "You'd better eat your dinner now," said she. "You might jest as well get through with it. I want you to help me afterward."

Nanny and Sammy stared at each other. There was something strange in their mother's manner. Mrs. Penn did not eat anything herself. She went into the pantry, and they heard her moving dishes while they ate. Presently she came out with a pile of plates. She got the clothes-basket out of the shed, and packed them in it. Nanny and Sammy watched. She brought out cups and saucers, and put them in with the plates.

"What you goin' to do, mother?" inquired Nanny, in a timid voice. A sense of something unusual made her tremble, as if it were a ghost. Sammy rolled his eyes over his pie.

"You'll see what I'm goin' to do," replied Mrs. Penn. "If you're through, Nanny, I want you to go up-stairs an' pack up your things; an' I want you, Sammy, to help me take down the bed in the bedroom."

"Oh, mother, what for?" gasped Nanny.

"You'll see."

During the next few hours a feat was performed by this simple, pious New England mother which was equal in its way to Wolfe's storming of the Heights of Abraham. It took no more genius and audacity of bravery for Wolfe to cheer his wondering soldiers up those steep precipices, under the sleeping eyes of the enemy, than for Sarah Penn, at the head of her children, to move all their little household goods into the new barn while her husband was away.

Nanny and Sammy followed their mother's instructions without a murmur; indeed, they were overawed. There is a certain uncanny and superhuman quality about all such purely original undertakings as their mother's was to them. Nanny went back and forth with her light loads, and Sammy tugged with sober energy.

At five o'clock in the afternoon the little house in which the Penns had lived for forty years had emptied itself into the new barn.

Every builder builds somewhat for unknown purposes, and is in a measure a prophet. The architect of Adoniram Penn's barn, while he designed it for the comfort of four-footed animals, had planned better than he knew for the comfort of humans. Sarah Penn saw at a glance its possibilities. Those great box-stalls, with quilts hung before them, would make better bedrooms than the one she had occupied for forty years, and there was a tight carriage-room. The harness-room, with its chimney and shelves, would make a kitchen of her dreams. The great middle space would make a parlor, by-and-by, fit for a palace. Up stairs there was as much room as down. With partitions and windows, what a house would there be! Sarah looked at the row of stanchions before the allotted space for cows, and reflected that she would have her front entry there.

At six o'clock the stove was up in the harness-room, the kettle was boiling, and the table set for tea. It looked almost as home-like as the abandoned house across the yard had ever done. The young hired man milked, and Sarah directed him calmly to bring the milk to the new barn. He came gaping, dropping little blots of foam from the brimming pails on the grass. Before the next morning he had spread the story of Adoniram Penn's wife moving into the new barn all over the little village. Men assembled in the store and talked it over, women with shawls over their heads scuttled into each other's houses before their work was done. Any deviation from the ordinary course of life in this quiet town was enough to stop all progress in it. Everybody paused to look at the staid, independent figure on the side track. There was a difference of opinion with regard to her. Some held her to be insane; some, of a lawless and rebellious spirit.

Friday the minister went to see her. It was in the forenoon, and she was at the barn door shelling pease for dinner. She looked up and returned his salutation with dignity, then she went on with her work. She did not invite him in. The saintly expression of her face remained fixed, but there was an angry flush over it.

The minister stood awkwardly before her, and talked. She handled the pease as if they were bullets. At last she looked up, and her eyes showed the spirit that her meek front had covered for a lifetime.

"There ain't no use talkin', Mr. Hersey," said she. "I've thought it all over an' over, an' I believe I'm doin' what's right. I've made it the subject of prayer, an' it's betwixt me an' the Lord an' Adoniram. There ain't no call for nobody else to worry about it."

"Well, of course, if you have brought it to the Lord in prayer, and feel satisfied that you are doing right, Mrs. Penn," said the minister, helplessly. His thin gray-bearded face was pathetic. He was a sickly man; his youthful confidence had cooled; he had to scourge himself up to some of his pastoral duties as relentlessly as a Catholic ascetic, and then he was prostrated by the smart.

"I think it's right jest as much as I think it was right for our forefathers to come over from the old country 'cause they didn't have what belonged to 'em," said Mrs. Penn. She arose. The barn threshold might have been Plymouth Rock from her bearing. "I don't doubt you mean well, Mr. Hersey," said she, "but there are things people hadn't ought to interfere with. I've been a member of the church for over forty year. I've got my own mind an' my own feet, an' I'm goin' to think my own thoughts an' go my own ways, an' nobody but the Lord is goin' to dictate to me unless I've a mind to have him. Won't you come in an' set down? How is Mis' Hersey?"

"She is well, I thank you," replied the minister. He added some more perplexed apologetic remarks; then he retreated.

He could expound the intricacies of every character study in the Scriptures, he was competent to grasp the Pilgrim Fathers and all historical innovators, but Sarah Penn was beyond him. He could deal with primal cases, but parallel ones worsted him. But, after all, although it was aside from his province, he wondered more how Adoniram Penn would deal with his wife than how the Lord would. Everybody shared the wonder. When Adoniram's four new cows arrived, Sarah ordered three to be put in the old barn, the other in the house shed where the cooking-stove had stood. That added to the excitement. It was whispered that all four cows were domiciled in the house.

Toward sunset on Saturday, when Adoniram was expected home, there was a knot of men in the road near the new barn. The hired man had milked, but he still hung around the premises. Sarah Penn had supper all ready. There were brown-bread and baked beans and a custard pie; it was the supper that Adoniram loved on a Saturday night. She had on a clean calico, and she bore herself imperturbably. Nanny and Sammy kept close at her heels. Their eyes were large, and Nanny was full of nervous tremors. Still there was to them more pleasant excitement than anything else. An inborn confidence in their mother over their father asserted itself.

Sammy looked out of the harness-room window. "There he is," he announced, in an awed whisper. He and Nanny peeped around the casing. Mrs. Penn kept on about her work. The children watched Adoniram leave the new horse standing in the drive while he went to the house door. It was fastened. Then he went around to the shed. That door was seldom locked, even when the family was away. The thought how her father would be confronted by the cow flashed upon Nanny. There was a hysterical sob in her throat. Adoniram emerged from the shed and stood looking about in a dazed fashion. His lips moved; he was saying something, but they could not hear what it was. The hired man was peeping around a corner of the old barn, but nobody saw him.

Adoniram took the new horse by the bridle and led him across the yard to the new barn. Nanny and Sammy slunk close to their mother. The barn doors rolled back, and there stood Adoniram, with the long mild face of the great Canadian farm horse looking over his shoulder.

Nanny kept behind her mother, but Sammy stepped suddenly forward, and stood in front of her.

Adoniram stared at the group. "What on airth you all down here for?" said he. "What's the matter over to the house?"

"We've come here to live, father," said Sammy. His shrill voice quavered out bravely.

"What"—Adoniram sniffed—"what is it smells like cookin'?" said he. He stepped forward and looked in the open door of the harness-room. Then he turned to his wife. His old bristling face was pale and frightened. "What on airth does this mean, mother?" he gasped.

"You come in here, father," said Sarah. She led the way into the harness-room and shut the door. "Now, father," said she, "you needn't be scared. I ain't crazy. There ain't nothin' to be upset over. But we've come here to live, an' we're goin' to live here. We've got jest as good a right here as new horses an' cows. The house wa'n't fit for us to live in any longer, an' I made up my mind I wa'n't goin' to stay there. I've done my duty by you forty year, an' I'm goin' to do it now; but I'm goin' to live here. You've got to put in some windows and partitions; an' you'll have to buy some furniture."

"Why, mother!" the old man gasped.

"You'd better take your coat off an' get washed—there's the wash-basin—an' then we'll have supper."

"Why, mother!"

Sammy went past the window, leading the new horse to the old barn. The old man saw him, and shook his head speechlessly. He tried to take off his coat, but his arms seemed to lack the power. His wife helped him. She poured some water into the tin basin, and put in a piece of soap. She got the comb and brush, and smoothed his thin gray hair after he had washed. Then she put the beans, hot bread, and tea on the table. Sammy came in, and the family drew up. Adoniram sat looking dazedly at his plate, and they waited.

"Ain't you goin' to ask a blessin', father?" said Sarah.

And the old man bent his head and mumbled.

All through the meal he stopped eating at intervals, and stared furtively at his wife; but he ate well. The home food tasted good to him, and his old frame was too sturdily healthy to be affected by his mind. But after supper he went out, and sat down on the step of the smaller door at the right of the barn, through which he had meant his Jerseys to pass in stately file, but which Sarah designed for her front house door, and he leaned his head on his hands.

After the supper dishes were cleared away and the milk-pans washed,

Sarah went out to him. The twilight was deepening. There was a clear green glow in the sky. Before them stretched the smooth level of field; in the distance was a cluster of hay-stacks like the huts of a village; the air was very cool and calm and sweet. The landscape might have been an ideal one of peace.

Sarah bent over and touched her husband on one of his thin, sinewy shoulders. "Father!"

The old man's shoulders heaved: he was weeping.

"Why, don't do so, father," said Sarah.

"I'll—put up the—partitions, an'—everything you—want, mother."

Sarah put her apron up to her face; she was overcome by her own triumph.

Adoniram was like a fortress whose walls had no active resistance, and went down the instant the right besieging tools were used. "Why, mother," he said, hoarsely, "I hadn't no idee you was so set on't as all this comes to."

1891

ALICE BROWN
(1857–1948)

Alice Brown's short stories focus on the unique sensibility of New England. She used realistic detail and dialect to portray a village society that was rapidly disappearing. Many of her characters are middle-aged or elderly women who come into conflict with their narrow-minded communities when they attempt to break out of the roles assigned them. Brown's stories rarely have dramatic action. Her heroines make quiet decisions in an effort to improve the quality of their lives. The stories are filled with dry humor and astute comments about village life and about the way people interact with each other. Like Sarah Orne Jewett, Brown often combines accurate details with an almost mystical feeling about the natural world.

A New Hampshire native, Brown was graduated from Robinson Seminary in Exeter and taught school for five years before she took a job as a magazine editor. Working on the staff of Christian Register and then The Youth's Companion, Brown made her home in Boston. Here she became friends with William Dean Howells, Annie Fields, Robert Frost, and Thomas Wentworth Higginson. Her close friendship with the poet Louise Imogen Guiney led to their founding of the Women's Rest Tour Association and its magazine, Pilgrim Scrip. Established to encourage and assist women in traveling abroad, the association elected Julia Ward Howe its first president.

Brown began publishing her own writing in the 1890s. She coauthored a study of Robert Louis Stevenson with Guiney and also published collections of poetry and short stories. Her short-story collections Meadow-Grass: Tales of New England Life (1895) and Tiverton Tales (1899) contain many of her most enduring works. Between 1895 and 1920, Brown published nine volumes of short stories, many of which had appeared in prominent magazines such as the Atlantic Monthly, Harper's, Scribner's, and McClure's. She remained a popular literary figure through World War I, serving as president of the Women's Rest Tour Association and, later, the Boston Authors' Club.

Brown published literary criticism, sketches, and biographical pieces, as well as fiction and dramas. In 1914 she won the Winthrop Ames prize of $10,000 for Children of Earth: A Play of New England. Although she continued to publish short stories, novels, and plays through the 1940s, her reputation waned in the 1920s. Only in recent years have critics again come to praise her plain style, acute ear for dialect, and subtle humor.

Brown's best works are the New England short stories. Although she wrote stories in a popular genre that she knew would sell, she also viewed her work as serving a sociological or historical purpose. Knowing that the traditions and speech *of rural New England were rapidly giving way to an industrial society, she saw her work as capturing a fading era.*

In "Heartsease," published first in the Atlantic Monthly *in 1894 and later collected in* Tiverton Tales, *Brown uses a simple situation to address problems of old age. Freed temporarily from the constraints of her well-meaning family, the elderly heroine experiences the joy of independence. Like many of Brown's stories, "Heartsease" explores the psyche of a simple character with shrewd insight as well as humor.*

HEARTSEASE

"For as for heartsease, it groweth in a single night."

"What be you doin' of, Mis' Lamson?" asked Mrs. Pettis, coming in from the kitchen, where she had been holding a long conversation with young Mrs. Lamson on the possibility of doing over sugar-barberry. Mrs. Pettis was a heavy woman, bent almost double with rheumatism, and she carried a baggy umbrella for a cane. She was always sighing over the difficulty of "gittin' round the house," but nevertheless she made more calls than any one else in the neighborhood. "It kind o' limbered her up," she said, "to take a walk after she had been bendin' over the dish-pan."

Mrs. Lamson looked up with an alert, bright glance. She was a little creature, and something still girlish lingered in her straight, slender figure and the poise of her head. "Old Lady Lamson" was over eighty, and she dressed with due deference to custom; but everything about her gained, in the wearing, an air of youth. Her aggressively brown front was rumpled a little, as if it had tried to crimp itself, only to be detected before the operation was well begun, and the purple ribbons of her cap flared rakishly aloft.

"I jest took up a garter," she said, with some apology in her tone. "Kind o' fiddlin' work, ain't it?"

"Last time I was here, you was knittin' mittins," continued Mrs. Pettis, seating herself laboriously on the lounge, and leaning forward upon the umbrella clutched steadily in two fat hands. "You're dretful forehanded. I remember I said so then. 'Samwel 'ain't got a mittin to his name,' I says, 'nor he won't have 'fore November.' "

"Well, I guess David's pretty well on 't for everything now," answered Mrs. Lamson, with some pride. "He's got five pair o' new mittins, an' my little blue chist full o' stockin's. I knit 'em two-an'-two, an' two-an'-one, an' toed some on 'em off with white, an' some with red, so 's to keep 'em in pairs. But

Mary said I better not knit any more, for fear the moths 'd git into 'em, an' so I stopped an' took up this garter. But *'tis* dretful fiddlin' work!"

A brief silence fell upon the two, while the sweet summer scents stole in at the window,—the breath of the cinnamon rose, of growing grass and good brown earth. Mrs. Pettis pondered, looking vacantly before her, and Old Lady Lamson knit hastily on. Her needles clicked together, and she turned her work with a jerk in beginning a row. But neither was oppressed by lack of speech. They understood each other, and no more thought of "making talk" than of pulling up a seed to learn whether it had germinated. It was Mrs. Pettis who, after a natural interval, felt moved to speak.

"Mary's master thoughtful of you, ain't she? 'Tain't many sons' wives would be so tender of anybody, now is it?"

Mrs. Lamson looked up sharply, and then, with the same quick movement, bent her eyes on her work.

"Mary means to do jest what's right," she answered. "If she don't make out, it ain't for lack o' tryin'."

"So I says to Samwel this mornin'. 'Old Lady Lamson 'ain't one thing to concern herself with,' says I, 'but to git dressed an' set by the winder. When dinner-time comes, she's got nothin' to do but hitch up to the table; an' she don't have to touch her hand to a dish.' Now ain't that so, Mis' Lamson?"

"That's so," agreed Mrs. Lamson, with a little sigh, instantly suppressed. "It's different from what I thought to myself 'twould be when Mary come here. ' 'Tain't in natur' she'll have the feelin' for me she would for her own,' I says; but I b'lieve she has, an' more too. When she come for good, I made up my mind I'd put up with everything, an' say 'twas all in the day's work; but law! I never had to. She an' David both act as if I was sugar or salt, I dunno which."

"Don't ye never help 'round, washin'-days?"

"Law, no! Mary won't hear to 't. She'd ruther have the dishes wait till everything's on the line; an' if I stir a step to go into the gardin to pick a mess o' beans or kill a currant worm, she's right arter me. 'Mother, don't you fall!' she says, a dozen times a day. 'I dunno what David 'd do to me, if I let anything happen to you.' An' David, he's ketched it, too. One night, 'long towards Thanksgivin' time, I kicked the soapstone out o' bed, an' he come runnin' up as if he was bewitched. 'Mother,' says he, 'did you fall? You 'ain't had a stroke, have ye?' "

Old Lady Lamson laughed huskily; her black eyes shone, and her cap ribbons nodded and danced, but there was an ironical ring to her merriment.

"Do tell!" responded Mrs. Pettis, in her ruminating voice. "Well, things were different when we was young married folks, an' used to do our own spinnin' an' weavin'."

"I guess so!" Mrs. Lamson dropped her busy hands in her lap, and leaned back a moment, in eager retrospect. "Do you recollect that Friday we spun from four o'clock in the mornin' till six that evenin', because the men-folks had gone in the ma'sh, an' all we had to do was to stop an' feed the critters?

An' Hiram Peasley come along with tinware, an' you says, 'If you're a mind to stop at my house, an' throw a colander an' a long-handled dipper over the fence, under the flowerin'-currant, an' wait till next time for your pay, I'll take 'em,' says you. 'But I ain't goin' to leave off spinnin' for anything less n' Gabriel's trumpet,' says you. I remember your sayin' that, as if 'twas only yisterday; an' arter you said it, you kind o' drawed down your face an' looked scairt. An' I never thought on 't ag'in till next Sabbath evenin', when Jim Bellows rose to speak, an' made some handle about the Day o' Judgment, an' then I tickled right out."

"How you do set by them days!" said Mrs. Pettis, striving to keep a steady face, though her heavy sides were shaking. "I guess you remember 'em better 'n your prayers!"

"Yes, I laughed out loud, an' you passed me a pep'mint over the pew, an' looked as if you was goin' to cry. 'Don't,' says you; an' it sort o' come over me you knew what I was laughin' at. Why, if there ain't John Freeman stoppin' here,—Mary's sister's brother-in-law, you know. Lives down to Bell P'int. Guess he's pullin' up to give the news."

Mrs. Pettis came slowly to her feet, and scanned the farmer, who was hitching his horse to the fence. When he had gone round to the back door, she turned, and grasped her umbrella with a firmer hand.

"Well, I guess 'twon't pay me to set down ag'in," she announced. "I'm goin' to take it easy on the way home. I dunno but I'll let down the bars, an' poke a little ways into the north pastur', an' see if I can't git a mite o' pennyr'yal. I'll be in ag'in to-morrer or next day."

"So do, so do," returned Mrs. Lamson.

" 'Tain't no use to ask you to come down, I s'pose? You don't git out so fur, nowadays."

"No," said the other, still with that latent touch of sarcasm in her voice. "If I should fall, there'd be a great hurrah, boys,—'fire on the mountain, run, boys, run!' "

Mrs. Pettis toiled out into the road; and Old Lady Lamson, laying her knitting on the table, bent forward, not to watch her out of sight, but to make sure whether she really would stop at the north pasture.

"No, she's goin' by," she said aloud, with evident relief. "No, she ain't either. I'll be whipped if she ain't lettin' down the bars! '*Twould* smell kind o' good, I declare!"

She was still peering forward, one slender hand on the window-sill, when Mary, a pretty young woman, with two nervous lines between her eyes, came hurrying in.

"Mother," she began, in that unnatural voice which is supposed to allay excitement in another, "I dunno what I'm goin' to do. Stella's sick."

"You don't say!" said Old Lady Lamson, turning away from the window. "What do they think 'tis?"

"Fever, John says. An' she's so full-blooded it'll be likely to go hard with her. They want me to go right down, an' David's got to carry me. John would, but he's gone to be referee in that land case, an' he won't be back for a day or two. It's a mercy David's just home from town, so he won't have to change his clo'es right through. Now, mother, if you should have little 'Liza Tolman come an' stay with you, do you think anything would happen, s'posin' we left you alone just one night?"

A little flush rose in the old lady's withered cheek. Her eyes gleamed brightly through her glasses.

"Don't worry one mite about me," she replied, in an even voice. "You change your dress, an' git off afore it's dark. I shall be all right."

"David's harnessin' now," said Mary, beginning to untie her apron. "I sent John down to the lower barn to call him. But, mother, if anything should happen to you—"

"Lord-a-massy! nothin' 's goin' to!" the old lady broke forth, in momentary impatience. "Don't stan' here talkin'. You better have your mind on Stella. Fever's a quicker complaint than old age. It al'ays was, an' al'ays will be."

"Oh, I know it! I know it!" cried Mary, starting toward the door. "There ain't a thing for you to do. There's new bread an' preserves on the dairy-wheel, an' you have 'Liza Tolman pick you up some chips, an' build the fire for your tea; an' don't you wash the dishes, mother. Just leave 'em in the sink. An' for mercy sake, take a candle, an' not meddle with kerosene—"

"Come, come, ain't you ready?" came David's voice from the door. "I can't keep the horse stan'in' here till he's all eat up with flies."

Mary fled to her bedroom, unbuttoning her dress as she ran; and David came in, bringing an air of outdoor freshness into the little sitting-room, with his regal height, his broad shoulders, and tanned, fresh face.

"Well, mother," he said, putting a hand of clumsy kindliness on her shoulder, "if anything happens to you while we're gone, I shall wish we'd let the whole caboodle of 'em die in their tracks. Don't s'pose anything will, do ye?"

"Law, no, David!" exclaimed the old lady, looking at him with beaming pride. "You stan' still an' let me pick that mite o' lint off your arm. I shall be tickled to death to git rid on ye."

"Now, mother," counselled Mary, when she came out of the bedroom, hastily tying her bonnet strings, "you watch the school-children, an' ask 'Liza Tolman to stay with you, an' if she can't, to get one of the Daltons; an' tell her we'll give her some Bartlett pears when they're ripe."

"Yes, yes, I hear," answered the old lady, rising, and setting back her chair in its accustomed corner. "Now, do go along, or ye won't be down to Grapevine Run afore five o'clock."

She watched them while they drove out of the yard, shading her eyes with one nervous hand.

"Mother," called Mary, "don't you stan' there in that wind, with nothin' on your head!"

The old lady turned back into the house, and her face was alive with glee.

"Wind!" she ejaculated scornfully, and yet with the tolerance of one too happy for complaint. "Wind! I guess there wouldn't be so much, if some folks would save their breath to cool their porridge!"

She did not go back to the sitting-room and her peaceful knitting. She walked into the pantry, where she gave the shelves a critical survey, and then, returning to the kitchen, looked about her once more.

"If it's one day sence I've been down sullar," she said aloud, "it's two year." She was lighting a candle as she spoke. In another moment, she was taking sprightly steps down the stairs into the darkness below.

"Now, mother, don't you fall!" she chuckled, midway in the descent; and it was undeniable that the voice sounded much like Mary's in her anxious mood. "Now, ain't I a mean creatur' to stan' here laughin' at 'em!" she went on. "Well, if she don't keep things nice! 'Taters all sprouted; an' the preserve cupboard never looked better in my day. Mary's been well brought up,—I'll say that for her."

Old Lady Lamson must have spent at least half an hour in the cellar, for when she ascended it was after four o'clock, and the school-children had passed the house on their way home. She heard their voices under the elms at the turn of the road.

"I ain't to blame if I can't ketch 'em," she remarked calmly, as she blew out her light. "I don't see 's anybody could say I was to blame. An' I couldn't walk up to the Tolmans' to ask 'Liza. I might fall!"

She set about her preparations for supper. It was a favorite maxim in the household that the meal should be eaten early, "to get it out of the way"; and to-night this unaccustomed handmaid had additional reasons for haste. But the new bread and preserves were ignored. She built a rousing fire in the little kitchen stove; she brought out the moulding-board, and with trembling eagerness proceeded to mix cream-of-tartar biscuits. Not Cellini himself nor Jeannie Carlyle had awaited the results of passionate labor with a more strenuous eagerness; and when she drew out the panful of delicately browned biscuits, she set it down on the table, and looked at it in sheer delight.

"I'll be whipped if they ain't as good as if I'd made 'em every night for the last two year!" she cried. "I 'ain't got to git my hand in, an' that's truth an' fact!"

She brought out some "cold b'iled dish," made her strong green tea, and sat down to a banquet such as they taste who have reached the Delectable Mountains. It held within it all the savor of a happy past; it satisfied her hungry soul.

After she had washed the supper dishes and scrupulously swept the hearth, she rested, for a moment's thought, in the old rocking-chair, and then took her way, candle in hand, to the attic. There was no further self-confidence on the stairs; she was too serious, now. Her hours were going fast. The attic, in spite of the open windows, lay hot under summer's touch upon the shingles outside, and odorous of the dried herbs hanging in bunches here and there.

"Wormwood—thoroughwort—spearmint," she mused, as she touched them, one after another, and inhaled their fragrance. " 'Tain't so long ago I was out pickin' herbs an' dryin' 'em. Well, well, well!"

She made her way under the eaves, and pulled out a hair-trunk, studded with brass nails. A rush-bottomed chair stood near-by, and, setting her candle in it, she knelt before the trunk and began lifting out its contents: a brocaded satin waistcoat of a long-past day, a woolen comforter knit in stripes, a man's black broadcloth coat. She smoothed them, as she laid them by, and there was a wondering note in her lowered voice.

"My Lord!" she whispered reverently, as if speaking to One who would hear and understand, "it's over fifty year!"

A pile of yellowed linen lay in the bottom of the trunk, redolent of camphor from contact with its perishable neighbors. She lifted one shirt after another, looking at them in silence. Then she laid back the other clothes, took up her candle and the shirts, and went downstairs again. In hot haste, she rebuilt the kitchen fire, and set two large kettles of water on the stove. She dragged the washing-bench into the back kitchen from its corner in the shed, and on it placed her tubs; and when the water was heated, she put the garments into a tub, and rubbed with the vigor and ease of a woman well accustomed to such work. All the sounds of the night were loud about her, and the song of the whippoorwill came in at the open door. He was very near. His presence should have been a sign of approaching trouble, but Old Lady Lamson did not hear him. Her mind was reading the lettered scroll of a vanished year.

Perhaps the touch of the warm water on her hands recalled her to the present.

"Seems good to feel the suds," she said, happily, holding up one withered hand, and letting the foam drip from her fingers. "I wish't I could dry outdoor! But when mornin' come, they'd be all of a sop."

She washed and rinsed the garments, and, opening a clothes-horse, spread them out to dry. Then she drew a long breath, put out her candle, and wandered to the door. The garden lay before her, unreal in the beauty of moonlight. Every bush seemed an enchanted wood. The old lady went forth, lingering at first, as one too rich for choosing; then with a firmer step. She closed the little gate, and walked out into the country road. She hurried along to the old signboard, and turned aside unerringly into a hollow there, where she stooped and filled her hands with tansy, pulling it up in great bunches, and pressing it eagerly to her face.

"Seventy-four year ago!" she told the unseen listener of the night, with the same wonder in her voice. "Sir laid dead, an' they sent me down here to pick tansy to put round him. Seventy-four year ago!"

Still holding it, she rose, and went through the bars into the dewy lane. Down the wandering path, trodden daily by the cows, she walked, and came out in the broad pasture, irregular with its little hillocks, where, as she had been told from her babyhood, the Indians used to plant their corn. She entered the woods by a cart-path hidden from the moon, and went on with a light step, gathering a bit of green here and there,—now hemlock, now a needle from the sticky pine,—and inhaling its balsam on her hands. A sharp descent, and she had reached the spot where the brook ran fast, and where lay "Peggy's b'ilin' spring," named for a great-aunt she had never seen, but whose gold beads she had inherited, and who had consequently seemed to her a person of opulence and ease.

"I wish't I'd brought a cup," she said. "There ain't no such water within twenty mile."

She crouched beside the little black pool, where the moon glinted in mysterious, wavering symbols to beckon the gaze upward, and, making a cup of her hand, drank eagerly. There was a sound near-by, as if some wood creature were stirring; she thought she heard a fox barking in the distance. Yet she was really conscious only of the wonder of time, the solemn record of the fleeting years.

When she made her way back through the woods, the moon was sinking, and the shadows had grown heavy. As she reached the bars again, on her homeward track, she stopped suddenly, and her face broke into smiling at the pungent fragrance rising from the bruised herbage beneath her feet. She stooped and gathered one telltale, homely weed, mixed as it was with the pasture grass. "Pennyr'yal," she said happily, and felt the richness of being.

When Old Lady Lamson had ironed her shirts and put them away again, all hot and sweet from the fire, it was five o'clock, and the birds had long been trying to drag creation up from sleep, to sing with them the wonders of the dawn. At six, she had her cup of tea, and when, at eight, her son drove into the yard, she came placidly to the side door to meet him, her knitting in her hands.

"Well, if I ain't glad!" called David. "I couldn't git it out o' my mind somethin' 'd happened to you. Stella's goin' to be all right, they think, but nothin' will do but Mary must stay a spell. Do you s'pose you an' I could keep house a week or so, if I do the heft o' the work?"

Old Lady Lamson's eyes took on the look which sometimes caused her son to inquire suspiciously, "Mother, what you laughin' at?"

"I guess we can, if we try hard enough," she said, soberly, rolling up her yarn. "Now you come in, an I'll git you a bite o' somethin' t' eat."

1894

ANNA JULIA COOPER
(1858?–1964)

Anna Julia Cooper's remarkable career and thoughtful, scholarly writing are sources of inspiration even today for educators, feminists, and women of color. Cooper believed that Black women had been mute ever since their arrival in the United States, and she worked throughout her life to be a voice for those women.

Born a slave, Cooper, at age nine, became a "pupil teacher" at St. Augustine's Normal and Collegiate Institute, an Episcopalian school. From St. Augustine's, she went on to a career in education that lasted the rest of her life. She received both B.A. and M.A. degrees from Oberlin College in Ohio, and taught at Oberlin from 1882 until 1884. She also taught French and German at Wilberforce University and returned to St. Augustine's in 1885 to teach Latin, Greek, and mathematics. In 1901 she became the first woman appointed principal of a public school in Washington, D.C. While principal, she fought and won a battle against Congress, which was proposing a "special colored curriculum" for Black youths in public schools that would focus on vocational rather than academic training. She also worked to better the education of adult working people by establishing night classes and other educational opportunities.

From 1906 until 1911, Cooper served as professor of languages, ancient and modern, at Lincoln University in Missouri. In 1925 she received a Ph.D. from the Sorbonne. While in Paris, she published a book, written in French, that focused on the attitude of France toward slavery in the United States.

A feminist as well as a writer and educator, Cooper worked hard to bring about the freedom and equality of women. In 1894 she helped found the Colored Women's League in Washington, D.C., which led to the first Colored Social Settlement House in Washington. The book from which the following selection is taken, A Voice from the South—By a Black Woman from the South, *is a pioneering collection of essays, speeches, and reflections on American womanhood as well as on the particular situation of Black women. Cooper argues energetically against the social forces and structures—including the Church—that have silenced women. With a knowledge of history and literature ranging from ancient Greece to modern times, Cooper attacks the assumptions and prejudices regarding women and African Americans that are ingrained in American society while also stressing the vital roles of women, especially Black women, in American life.*

In "The Higher Education of Women," Cooper calls on Black men and women to give girls a chance to become educated. In logical but passionate prose, she stresses the vital importance of having educated Black women in society. A radical essay when it appeared in 1892, "The Higher Education of Women" confronts issues that are still relevant today.

THE HIGHER EDUCATION OF WOMEN

In the very first year of our century, the year 1801, there appeared in Paris a book by Silvain Marechal, entitled "Shall Woman Learn the Alphabet." The book proposes a law prohibiting the alphabet to women, and quotes authorities weighty and various, to prove that the woman who knows the alphabet has already lost part of her womanliness. The author declares that women can use the alphabet only as Moliere predicted they would, in spelling out the verb *amo;* that they have no occasion to peruse Ovid's *Ars Amoris,* since that is already the ground and limit of their intuitive furnishing; that Madame Guion would have been far more adorable had she remained a beautiful ignoramus as nature made her; that Ruth, Naomi, the Spartan woman, the Amazons, Penelope, Andromache, Lucretia, Joan of Arc, Petrarch's Laura, the daughters of Charlemagne, could not spell their names; while Sappho, Aspasia, Madame de Maintenon, and Madame de Stael could read altogether too well for their good; finally, that if women were once permitted to read Sophocles and work with logarithms, or to nibble at any side of the apple of knowledge, there would be an end forever to their sewing on buttons and embroidering slippers.

Please remember this book was published at the *beginning* of the Nineteenth Century. At the end of its first third, (in the year 1833) one solitary college in America decided to admit women within its sacred precincts, and organized what was called a "Ladies' Course" as well as the regular B.A. or Gentlemen's course.

It was felt to be an experiment—a rather dangerous experiment—and was adopted with fear and trembling by the good fathers, who looked as if they had been caught secretly mixing explosive compounds and were guiltily expecting every moment to see the foundations under them shaken and rent and their fair superstructure shattered into fragments.

But the girls came, and there was no upheaval. They performed their tasks modestly and intelligently. Once in a while one or two were found choosing the gentlemen's course. Still no collapse; and the dear, careful, scrupulous, frightened old professors were just getting their hearts out of their throats and preparing to draw one good free breath, when they found they would have to change the names of those courses; for there were as many ladies in the gentlemen's course as in the ladies', and a distinctively Ladies' Course, inferior in scope and aim to the regular classical course, did not and could not exist.

Other colleges gradually fell into line, and to-day there are one hundred and ninety-eight colleges for women, and two hundred and seven coeducational colleges and universities in the United States alone offering the degree of B.A. to women, and sending out yearly into the arteries of this nation a warm, rich flood of strong, brave, active, energetic, well-equipped, thoughtful women—women quick to see and eager to help the needs of this needy world—women who can think as well as feel, and who feel none the less because they think—women who are none the less tender and true for the parchment scroll they bear in their hands—women who have given a deeper, richer, nobler and grander meaning to the word "womanly" than any one-sided masculine definition could ever have suggested or inspired—women whom the world has long waited for in pain and anguish till there should be at last added to its forces and allowed to permeate its thought the complement of that masculine influence which has dominated it for fourteen centuries.

Since the idea of order and subordination succumbed to barbarian brawn and brutality in the fifth century, the civilized world has been like a child brought up by his father. It has needed the great mother heart to teach it to be pitiful, to love mercy, to succor the weak and care for the lowly.

Whence came this apotheosis of greed and cruelty? Whence this sneaking admiration we all have for bullies and prize-fighters? Whence the self-congratulation of "dominant" races, as if "dominant" meant "righteous" and carried with it a title to inherit the earth? Whence the scorn of so-called weak or unwarlike races and individuals, and the very comfortable assurance that it is their manifest destiny to be wiped out as vermin before this advancing civilization? As if the possession of the Christian graces of meekness, non-resistance and forgiveness, were incompatible with a civilization professedly based on Christianity, the religion of love! Just listen to this little bit of Barbarian brag:

> As for Far Orientals, they are not of those who will survive. Artistic attractive people that they are, their civilization is like their own tree flowers, beautiful blossoms destined never to bear fruit. If these people continue in their old course, their earthly career is closed. Just as surely as morning passes into afternoon, so surely are these races of the Far East, if unchanged, destined to disappear before the advancing nations of the West. Vanish, they will, off the face of the earth, and leave our planet the eventual possession of the dwellers where the day declines. Unless their newly imported ideas really take root, it is from this whole world that Japanese and Koreans, as well as Chinese, will inevitably by excluded. Their Nirvana is already being realized; already, it has wrapped Far Eastern Asia in its winding sheet.—*Soul of the Far East*—*P. Lowell.*

Delightful reflection for "the dwellers where day declines." A spectacle to make the gods laugh, truly, to see the scion of an upstart race by one sweep of his generalizing pen consigning to annihilation one-third the inhabitants of the globe—a people whose civilization was hoary headed before the parent elements that begot his race had advanced beyond nebulosity.

How like Longfellow's Iagoo, we Westerners are, to be sure! In the few hundred years we have had to strut across our allotted territory and bask in the afternoon sun, we imagine we have exhausted the possibilities of humanity. Verily, we are the people, and after us there is none other. Our God is power; strength, our standard of excellence, inherited from barbarian ancestors through a long line of male progenitors, the Law Salic permitting no feminine modifications.

Says one, "The Chinaman is not popular with us, and we do not like the Negro. It is not that the eyes of the one are set bias, and the other is dark-skinned; but the Chinaman, the Negro is weak—*and Anglo Saxons don't like weakness.*"

The world of thought under the predominant man-influence, unmollified and unrestrained by its complementary force, would become like Daniel's fourth beast: "dreadful and terrible, and *strong* exceedingly;" "it had great iron teeth; it devoured and brake in pieces, and stamped the residue with the feet of it;" and the most independent of us find ourselves ready at times to fall down and worship this incarnation of power.

Mrs. Mary A. Livermore, a woman whom I can mention only to admire, came near shaking my faith a few weeks ago in my theory of the thinking woman's mission to put in the tender and sympathetic chord in nature's grand symphony, and counteract, or better, harmonize the diapason of mere strength and might.

She was dwelling on the Anglo-Saxon genius for power and his contempt for weakness, and described a scene in San Francisco which she had witnessed.

The incorrigible animal known as the American small-boy, had pounced upon a simple, unoffending Chinaman, who was taking home his work, and had emptied the beautifully laundried contents of his basket into the ditch. "And," said she, "when that great man stood there and blubbered before that crowd of lawless urchins, to any one of whom he might have taught a lesson with his two fists, *I didn't much care.*"

This is said like a man! It grates harshly. It smacks of the worship of the beast. It is contempt for weakness, and taken out of its setting it seems to contradict my theory. It either shows that one of the highest exponents of the Higher Education can be at times untrue to the instincts I have ascribed to the thinking woman and to the contribution she is to add to the civilized world, or else the influence she wields upon our civilization may be potent without being necessarily and always direct and conscious. The latter is the case. Her voice may strike a false note, but her whole being is musical with the vibrations of human suffering. Her tongue may parrot over the cold conceits that some man has taught her, but her heart is aglow with sympathy and loving kindness, and she cannot be true to her real self without giving out these elements into the forces of the world.

No one is in any danger of imagining Mark Antony "a plain blunt man," nor Cassius a sincere one—whatever the speeches they may make.

As individuals, we are constantly and inevitably, whether we are conscious of it or not, giving out our real selves into our several little worlds, inexorably adding our own true ray to the flood of starlight, quite independently of our professions and our masquerading; and so in the world of thought, the influence of thinking woman far transcends her feeble declamation and may seem at times even opposed to it.

A visitor in Oberlin once said to the lady principal, "Have you no rabble in Oberlin? How is it I see no police here, and yet the streets are as quiet and orderly as if there were an officer of the law standing on every corner."

Mrs. Johnston replied, "Oh, yes; there are vicious persons in Oberlin just as in other towns—*but our girls are our police.*"

With from five to ten hundred pure-minded young women threading the streets of the village every evening unattended, vice must slink away, like frost before the rising sun: and yet I venture to say there was not one in a hundred of those girls who would not have run from a street brawl as she would from a mouse, and who would not have declared she could never stand the sight of blood and pistols.

There is, then, a real and special influence of woman. An influence subtle and often involuntary, an influence so intimately interwoven in, so intricately interpenetrated by the masculine influence of the time that it is often difficult to extricate the delicate meshes and analyze and identify the closely clinging fibers. And yet, without this influence—so long as woman sat with bandaged eyes and manacled hands, fast bound in the clamps of ignorance and inaction, the world of thought moved in its orbit like the revolutions of the moon; with one face (the man's face) always out, so that the spectator could not distinguish whether it was disc or sphere.

Now I claim that it is the prevalence of the Higher Education among women, the making it a common everyday affair for women to reason and think and express their thought, the training and stimulus which enable and encourage women to administer to the world the bread it needs as well as the sugar it cries for; in short it is the transmitting the potential forces of her soul into dynamic factors that has given symmetry and completeness to the world's agencies. So only could it be consummated that Mercy, the lesson she teaches, and Truth, the task man has set himself, should meet together: that righteousness, or *rightness,* man's ideal,—and *peace,* its necessary 'other half,' should kiss each other.

We must thank the general enlightenment and independence of woman (which we may now regard as a *fait accompli*) that both these forces are now at work in the world, and it is fair to demand from them for the twentieth century a higher type of civilization than any attained in the nineteenth. Religion, science, art, economics, have all needed the feminine flavor; and literature, the expression of what is permanent and best in all of these, may be gauged at any time to measure the strength of the feminine ingredient. You will not find theology consigning infants to lakes of unquenchable fire long after women have had a chance to grasp, master, and wield its dogmas. You will not find science annihilating personality from the government of the Universe and making of God an ungovernable, unintelligible, blind, often destructive physical force; you will not find jurisprudence formulating as an axiom the absurdity that man and wife are one, and that one the man—that the married woman may not hold or bequeath her own property save as subject to her husband's direction; you will not find political economists declaring that the only possible adjustment between laborers and capitalists is that of selfishness and rapacity—that each must get all he can and keep all that he gets, while the world cries *laissez faire* and the lawyers explain, "it is the beautiful working of the law of supply and demand;" in fine, you will not find the law of love shut out from the affairs of men after the feminine half of the world's truth is completed.

Nay, put your ear now close to the pulse of the time. What is the keynote of the literature of these days? What is the banner cry of all the activities of the last half decade? What is the dominant seventh which is to add richness and tone to the final cadences of this century and lead by a grand modulation into the triumphant harmonies of the next? Is it not compassion for the poor and unfortunate, and, as Bellamy has expressed it, "indignant outcry against the failure of the social machinery as it is, to ameliorate the miseries of men!" Even Christianity is being brought to the bar of humanity and tried by the standard of its ability to alleviate the world's suffering and lighten and brighten its woe. What else can be the meaning of Matthew Arnold's saddening protest, "We cannot do without Christianity," cried he, "and we cannot endure it as it is."

When went there by an age, when so much time and thought, so much money and labor were given to God's poor and God's invalids, the lowly and unlovely, the sinning as well as the suffering—homes for inebriates and homes for lunatics, shelter for the aged and shelter for babes, hospitals for the sick, props and braces for the falling, reformatory prisons and prison reformatories, all show that a "mothering" influence from some source is leavening the nation.

Now please understand me. I do not ask you to admit that these benefactions and virtues are the exclusive possession of women, or even that women are their chief and only advocates. It may be a man who formulates and makes them vocal. It may be, and often is, a man who weeps over the wrongs and struggles for the amelioration: but that man has imbibed those impulses from a mother rather than from a father and is simply materializing and giving back to the world in tangible form the ideal love and tenderness, devotion and care that have cherished and nourished the helpless period of his own existence.

All I claim is that there is a feminine as well as a masculine side to truth; that these are related not as inferior and superior, not as better and worse, not as weaker and stronger, but as complements—complements in one necessary and symmetric whole. That as the man is more noble in reason, so the woman is more quick in sympathy. That as he is indefatigable in pursuit of abstract truth, so is she in caring for the interests by the way—striving tenderly and lovingly that not one of the least of these "little ones" should perish. That while we not unfrequently see women who reason, we say, with the coolness and precision of a man, and men as considerate of helplessness as a woman, still there is a general consensus of mankind that the one trait is essentially masculine and the other is peculiarly feminine. That both are needed to be worked into the training of children, in order that our boys may supplement their virility by tenderness and sensibility, and our girls may round out their gentleness by strength and self-reliance. That, as both are alike necessary in giving symmetry to the individual, so a nation or a race will degenerate into mere emotionalism on the one hand, or bullyism on the other, if dominated by either exclusively; lastly, and most emphatically, that the feminine factor can have its proper effect only through woman's development and education so that she may fitly and intelligently stamp her force on the forces of her day, and add her modicum to the riches of the world's thought.

For woman's cause is man's: they rise or sink
Together, dwarfed or godlike, bond or free:
For she that out of Lethe scales with man
The shining steps of nature, shares with man
His nights, his days, moves with him to one goal.
If she be small, slight-natured, miserable,
How shall men grow?
. . . Let her make herself her own
To give or keep, to live and learn and be
All that not harms distinctive womanhood.
For woman is not undeveloped man
But diverse; could we make her as the man
Sweet love were slain; his dearest bond is this,
Not like to like, but like in difference.
Yet in the long years liker must they grow;
The man be more of woman, she of man;
He gain in sweetness and in moral height,
Nor lose the wrestling thews that throw the world;
She mental breadth, nor fail in childward care,
Nor lose the childlike in the larger mind;
Till at the last she set herself to man,
Like perfect music unto noble words.

Now you will argue, perhaps, and rightly, that higher education for women is not a modern idea, and that, if that is the means of setting free and invigorating the long desired feminine force in the world, it has already had a trial and should, in the past, have produced some of these glowing effects. Sappho, the bright, sweet singer of Lesbos, "the violet-crowned, pure, sweetly smiling Sappho" as Alcaeus calls her, chanted her lyrics and poured forth her soul nearly six centuries before Christ, in notes as full and free, as passionate and eloquent as did ever Archilochus or Anacreon.

Aspasia, that earliest queen of the drawing-room, a century later ministered to the intellectual entertainment of Socrates and the leading wits and philosophers of her time. Indeed, to her is attributed, by the best critics, the authorship of one of the most noted speeches ever delivered by Pericles.

Later on, during the Renaissance period, women were professors in mathematics, physics, metaphysics, and the classic languages in Bologna, Pavia, Padua, and Brescia. Olympia Fulvia Morata, of Ferrara, a most interesting character, whose magnificent library was destroyed in 1553 in the invasion of Schweinfurt by Albert of Brandenburg, had acquired a most extensive education. It is said that this wonderful girl gave lectures on classical subjects in her sixteenth year, and had even before that written several very remarkable Greek and Latin poems, and what is also to the point, she married a professor at Heidelberg, and became a *help-meet for him.*

It is true then that the higher education for women—in fact, the highest that the world has ever witnessed—belongs to the past; but we must remember that it was possible, down to the middle of our own century, only to a select few; and that the fashions and traditions of the times were before that all against it. There were not only no stimuli to encourage women to make the most of their powers and to welcome their development as a helpful agency in the progress of civilization, but their little aspirations, when they had any, were chilled and snubbed in embryo, and any attempt at thought was received as a monstrous usurpation of man's prerogative.

Lessing declared that "the woman who thinks is like the man who puts on rouge—ridiculous;" and Voltaire in his coarse, flippant way used to say, "Ideas are like beards—women and boys have none." Dr. Maginn remarked, "We like to hear a few words of sense from a woman sometimes, as we do from a parrot—they are so unexpected!" and even the pious Fenelon taught that virgin delicacy is almost as incompatible with learning as with vice.

That the average woman retired before these shafts of wit and ridicule and even gloried in her ignorance is not surprising. The Abbe Choisi, it is said, praised the Duchesse de Fontanges as being pretty as an angel and silly as a goose, and all the young ladies of the court strove to make up in folly what they lacked in charms. The ideal of the day was that "women must be pretty, dress prettily, flirt prettily, and not be too well informed;" that it was the *summum bonum* of her earthly hopes to have, as Thackeray puts it, "all the fellows battling to dance with her;" that she had no God-given destiny, no soul with unquenchable longings and inexhaustible possibilities—no work of her own to do and give to the world—no absolute and inherent value, no duty to self, transcending all pleasure-giving that may be demanded of a mere toy; but that her value was purely a relative one and to be estimated as are the fine arts—by the pleasure they give. "Woman, wine and song," as "the world's best gifts to man," were linked together in praise with as little thought of the first saying, "What doest thou," as that the wine and the song should declare, "We must be about our Father's business."

Men believed, or pretended to believe, that the great law of self development was obligatory on their half of the human family only; that while it was the chief end of man to glorify God and put his five talents to the exchangers, gaining thereby other five, it was, or ought to be, the sole end of woman to glorify man and wrap her one decently away in a napkin, retiring into "Hezekiah Smith's lady during her natural life and Hezekiah Smith's relict on her tombstone;" that higher education was incompatible with the shape of the female cerebrum, and that even if it could be acquired it must inevitably unsex woman, destroying the lisping, clinging, tenderly helpless, and beautifully dependent creatures whom men would so heroically think for and so gallantly fight for, and giving in their stead a formidable race of blue stockings with corkscrew ringlets and other spinster propensities.

But these are eighteenth century ideas.

We have seen how the pendulum has swung across our present century. The men of our time have asked with Emerson, "that woman only show us how she can best be served:" and woman has replied: the chance of the seedling and of the animalcule is all I ask—the chance for growth and self development, the permission to be true to the aspirations of my soul without incurring the blight of your censure and ridicule.

Audetque viris concurrere virgo.

In soul-culture woman at last dares to contend with men, and we may cite Grant Allen (who certainly cannot be suspected of advocating the unsexing of woman) as an example of the broadening effect of this contest on the ideas at least of the men of the day. He says in his *Plain Words on the Woman Question,* recently published:

"The position of woman was not [in the past] a position which could bear the test of nineteenth-century scrutiny. Their education was inadequate, their social status was humiliating, their political power was nil, their practical and personal grievances were innumerable; above all, their relations to the family—to their husbands, their children, their friends, their property—was simply insupportable."

And again: "As a body we 'Advanced men' are, I think, prepared to reconsider, and to reconsider fundamentally, without prejudice or misconception, the entire question of the relation between the sexes. We are ready to make any modifications in those relations which will satisfy the woman's just aspiration for personal independence, for intellectual and moral development, for physical culture, for political activity, and for a voice in the arrangement of her own affairs, both domestic and national."

Now this is magnanimous enough, surely; and quite a step from eighteenth century preaching, is it not? The higher education of Woman has certainly developed the men;—let us see what it has done for the women.

Matthew Arnold during his last visit to America in '82 or '83, lectured before a certain co-educational college in the West. After the lecture he remarked, with some surprise, to a lady professor, that the young women in his audience, he noticed, paid as close attention as the men, *all the way through.* This led, of course, to a spirited discussion of the higher education for women, during which he said to his enthusiastic interlocutor, eyeing her philosophically through his English eyeglass: "But—eh—don't you think it—eh—spoils their *chawnces,* you know!"

Now, as to the result to women, this is the most serious argument ever used against the higher education. If it interferes with marriage, classical training has a grave objection to weigh and answer.

For I agree with Mr. Allen at least on this one point, that there must be marrying and giving in marriage even till the end of time.

I grant you that intellectual development, with the self-reliance and capacity for earning a livelihood which it gives, renders woman less dependent on the marriage relation for physical support (which, by the way, does not always accompany it). Neither is she compelled to look to sexual love as the one sensation capable of giving tone and relish, movement and vim to the life she leads. Her horizon is extended. Her sympathies are broadened and deepened and multiplied. She is in closer touch with nature. Not a bud that opens, not a dew drop, not a ray of light, not a cloud-burst or a thunderbolt, but adds to the expansiveness and zest of her soul. And if the sun of an absorbing passion be gone down, still 'tis night that brings the stars. She has remaining the mellow, less obtrusive, but none the less enchanting and inspiring light of friendship, and into its charmed circle she may gather the best the world has known. She can commune with Socrates about the *daimon* he knew and to which she too can bear witness; she can revel in the majesty of Dante, the sweetness of Virgil, the simplicity of Homer, the strength of Milton. She can listen to the pulsing heart throbs of passionate Sappho's encaged soul, as she beats her bruised wings against her prison bars and struggles to flutter out into Heaven's aether, and the fires of her own soul cry back as she listens. "Yes; Sappho, I know it all; I know it all." Here, at last, can be communion without suspicion; friendship without misunderstanding; love without jealousy.

We must admit then that Byron's picture, whether a thing of beauty or not, has faded from the canvas of to-day.

> "Man's love," he wrote, "is of man's life a thing apart,
> 'Tis woman's whole existence.

Man may range the court, camp, church, the vessel and
the mart,
Sword, gown, gain, glory offer in exchange.
Pride, fame, ambition, to fill up his heart—
And few there are whom these cannot estrange.
Men have all these resources, we *but one—*
To love again and be again undone."

This may have been true when written. *It is not true to-day.* The old, subjective, stagnant, indolent and wretched life for woman has gone. She has as many resources as men, as many activities beckon her on. As large possibilities swell and inspire her heart.

Now, then, does it destroy or diminish her capacity for loving?

Her standards have undoubtedly gone up. The necessity of speculating in "chawnces" has probably shifted. The question is not now with the woman "How shall I so cramp, stunt, simplify and nullify myself as to make me eligible to the honor of being swallowed up into some little man?" but the problem, I trow, now rests with the man as to how he can so develop his God-given powers as to reach the ideal of a generation of women who demand the noblest, grandest and best achievements of which he is capable; and this surely is the only fair and natural adjustment of the chances. Nature never meant that the ideals and standards of the world should be dwarfing and minimizing ones, and the men should thank us for requiring of them the richest fruits which they can grow. If it makes them work, all the better for them.

As to the adaptability of the educated woman to the marriage relation, I shall simply quote from that excellent symposium of learned women that appeared recently under Mrs. Armstrong's signature in answer to the "Plain Words" of Mr. Allen, already referred to. "Admitting no longer any question as to their intellectual equality with the men whom they meet, with the simplicity of conscious strength, they take their place beside the men who challenge them, and fearlessly face the result of their actions. They deny that their education in any way unfits them for the duty of wifehood and maternity or primarily renders these conditions any less attractive to them than to the domestic type of woman. On the contrary, they hold that their knowledge of physiology makes them better mothers and housekeepers; their knowledge of chemistry makes them better cooks; while from their training in other natural sciences and in mathematics, they obtain an accuracy and fair-mindedness which is of great value to them in dealing with their children or employees."

So much for their willingness. Now the apple may be good for food and pleasant to the eyes, and a fruit to be desired to make one wise. Nay, it may even assure you that it has no aversion whatever to being tasted. Still, if you do not like the flavor all these recommendations are nothing. Is the intellectual woman *desirable* in the matrimonial market?

This I cannot answer. I confess my ignorance. I am no judge of such things. I have been told that strong-minded women could be, when they thought it worth their while, quite endurable, and, judging from the number of female names I find in college catalogues among the alumnae with double patronymics, I surmise that quite a number of men are willing to put up with them.

Now I would that my task ended here. Having shown that a great want of the world in the past has been a feminine force; that that force can have its full effect only through the untrammelled development of woman; that such development, while it gives her to the world and to civilization, does not necessarily remove her from the home and fireside; finally, that while past centuries have witnessed sporadic instances of this higher growth, still it was reserved for the latter half of the nineteenth century to render it common and general enough to be effective; I might close with a glowing prediction of what the twentieth century may expect from this heritage of twin forces—the masculine battered and toil-worn as a grim veteran after centuries of warfare, but still strong, active, and vigorous, ready to help with his hard-won experience the young recruit rejoicing in her newly found freedom, who so confidently places her hand in his with mutual pledges to redeem the ages.

> And so the twain upon the skirts of Time,
> Sit side by side, full-summed in all their powers,
> Dispensing harvest, sowing the To-be,
> Self-reverent each and reverencing each.

Fain would I follow them, but duty is nearer home. The high ground of generalities is alluring but my pen is devoted to a special cause: and with a view to further enlightenment on the achievements of the century for THE HIGHER EDUCATION OF COLORED WOMEN, I wrote a few days ago to the colleges which admit women and asked how many colored women had completed the B.A. course in each during its entire history. These are the figures returned: Fisk leads the way with twelve; Oberlin next with five; Wilberforce, four; Ann Arbor and Wellesley three each, Livingstone two, Atlanta one, Howard, as yet, none.

I then asked the principal of the Washington High School how many out of a large number of female graduates from his school had chosen to go forward and take a collegiate course. He replied that but one had ever done so, and she was then in Cornell.

Others ask questions too, sometimes, and I was asked a few years ago by a white friend, "How is it that the men of your race seem to outstrip the women in mental attainment?" "Oh," I said, "so far as it is true, the men, I suppose, from the life they lead, gain more by contact; and so far as it is only apparent, I think the women are more quiet. They don't feel called to mount a barrel and harangue by the hour every time they imagine they have produced an idea."

But I am sure there is another reason which I did not at that time see fit to give. The atmosphere, the standards, the requirements of our little world do not afford any special stimulus to female development.

It seems hardly a gracious thing to say, but it strikes me as true, that while our men seem thoroughly abreast of the times on almost every other subject, when they strike the woman question they drop back into sixteenth century logic. They leave nothing to be desired generally in regard to gallantry and chivalry, but they actually do not seem sometimes to have outgrown that old contemporary of chivalry—the idea that women may stand on pedestals or live in doll houses, (if they happen to have them) but they must not furrow their brows with thought or attempt to help men tug at the great questions of the world. I fear the majority of colored men do not yet think it worth while that women aspire to higher education. Not many will subscribe to the "advanced" ideas of Grant Allen already quoted. The three R's, a little music and a good deal of dancing, a first rate dress-maker and a bottle of magnolia balm, are quite enough generally to render charming any woman possessed of tact and the capacity for worshipping masculinity.

My readers will pardon my illustrating my point and also giving a reason for the fear that is in me, by a little bit of personal experience. When a child I was put into a school near home that professed to be normal and collegiate, i.e. to prepare teachers for colored youth, furnish candidates for the ministry, and offer collegiate training for those who should be ready for it. Well, I found after a while that I had a good deal of time on my hands. I had devoured what was put before me, and, like Oliver Twist, was looking around to ask for more. I constantly felt (as I suppose many an ambitious girl has felt) a thumping from within unanswered by any beckoning from without. Class after class was organized for these ministerial candidates (many of them men who had been preaching before I was born). Into every one of these classes I was expected to go, with the sole intent, I thought at the time, of enabling the dear old principal, as he looked from the vacant countenances of his sleepy old class over to where I sat, to get off his solitary pun—his never-failing pleasantry, especially in hot weather—which was, as he called out "Any one!" to the effect that "*any* one" then meant "*Annie* one."

Finally a Greek class was to be formed. My inspiring preceptor informed me that Greek had never been taught in the school, but that he was going to form a class *for the candidates for the ministry,* and if I liked I might join it. I replied—humbly I hope, as became a female of the human species—that I would like very much to study Greek, and that I was thankful for the opportunity, and so it went on. A boy, however meager his equipment and shallow his pretentions, had only to declare a floating intention to study theology and he could get all the support, encouragement and stimulus he needed, be absolved from work and invested beforehand with all the dignity of his far away office. While a self-supporting girl had to struggle on by teaching in the summer and working after school hours to keep up with her board bills, and actually to fight her way against positive discouragements to the higher education; till one such girl one day flared out and told the principal "the only mission opening before a girl in his school was to marry one of those candidates." He said he didn't know but it was. And when at last that same girl announced her desire and intention to go to college it was received with about the same incredulity and dismay as if a brass button on one of those candidate's coats had propounded a new method for squaring the circle or trisecting the arc.

Now this is not fancy. It is a simple unvarnished photograph, and what I believe was not in those days exceptional in colored schools, and I ask the men and women who are teachers and co-workers for the highest interests of the race, that they give the girls a chance! We might as well expect to grow trees from leaves as hope to build up a civilization or a manhood without taking into consideration our women and the home life made by them, which must be the root and ground of the whole matter. Let us insist then on special encouragement for the education of our women and special care in their training. Let our girls feel that we expect something more of them than that they merely look pretty and appear well in society. Teach them that there is a race with special needs which they and only they can help; that the world needs and is already asking for their trained, efficient forces. Finally, if there is an ambitious girl with pluck and brain to take the higher education, encourage her to make the most of it. Let there be the same flourish of trumpets and clapping of hands as when a boy announces his determination to enter the lists; and then, as you know that she is physically the weaker of the two, don't stand from under and leave her to buffet the waves alone. Let her know that your heart is following her, that your hand, though she sees it not, is ready to support her. To be plain, I mean let money be raised and scholarships be founded in our colleges and universities for self-supporting, worthy young women, to offset and balance the aid that can always be found for boys who will take theology.

The earnest well trained Christian young woman, as a teacher, as a home-maker, as wife, mother, or silent influence even, is as potent a missionary agency among our people as is the theologian; and I claim that at the present stage of our development in the South she is even more important and necessary.

Let us then, here and now, recognize this force and resolve to make the most of it—not the boys less, but the girls more.

1892

CHARLOTTE PERKINS GILMAN (1860–1935)

Charlotte Perkins Gilman, a leading American feminist intellectual at the turn of the century, was the author of six books of essays, nine novels, and close to two hundred short stories. A popular as well as prolific writer, Gilman was in great demand as a lecturer on women's suffrage, trade unions, and socialism. She was an important social theorist whose work was rediscovered in the early 1970s.

Gilman was raised by a single parent in Connecticut. Her father, a member of the famous Beecher family of New England, left her mother when Charlotte and her brother, Thomas, were children. To support her family, Mary Perkins moved into a cooperative household in 1874. The experience had a lasting effect on young Charlotte, who later went on to advocate cooperative living as a means by which women could be freed from the domestic sphere.

In 1898, Charlotte Perkins would set forth these arguments in Women and Economics, *a popular book that went into eleven editions. She argued that the oppression of women was tied to the sexual division of labor, and she advocated socializing and professionalizing domestic tasks to free women from housework. Keeping women in the home, she reasoned, was a waste of a vast source of economic growth: the work women could do in the public sphere would improve the country's economy and be a first step toward true equality between the sexes. In the selection included, from* Women and Economics, *Perkins analyzes the social construction of gender, prefiguring the concerns of many current feminist theorists.*

After her friend and companion, Martha Luther, married in 1881, Perkins hoped to combine her desire to become a writer with family life. She married Walter Stetson, an aspiring artist, in May 1884. But after the birth of her daughter in 1885, Perkins fell into a serious depression. She consulted the internationally famous neurologist Silas Weir Mitchell, a specialist in women's nervous diseases who also attended Edith Wharton and Agnes Smedley. "The Yellow Wallpaper," based on her experience with Mitchell's so-called cure, describes the treatment to which he subjected Perkins and other depressed women.

Fortunately, Perkins recovered from both the depression and Mitchell's treatment. Through her writing, she found a cure for herself and for others. Critics, however, misunderstood her intentions in writing "The Yellow Wallpaper." When it first appeared, they ranked it among the most powerful horror stories ever written, comparing her favorably to Edgar Allan Poe. One Boston physician, in fact, protested that the story could drive anyone mad who read it. But as Perkins explains in her essay "Why I Wrote 'The Yellow Wallpaper,' " the story "was not intended to drive people crazy, but to save people from being driven crazy, and it worked."

Gilman and Stetson separated amicably, and Gilman moved with her daughter and mother to Pasadena, California. In the spring of 1900, she married George Houghton Gilman, with whom she lived until his death in 1934. By this time, she herself had inoperable cancer. She put her estate in order, said good-bye to family and friends, and committed suicide (with chloroform) in 1935.

from WOMEN AND ECONOMICS

CHAPTER III: SEX DISTINCTIONS

In establishing the claim of excessive sex-distinction in the human race, much needs to be said to make clear to the general reader what is meant by the term. To the popular mind, both the coarsely familiar and the over-refined, "sexual" is thought to mean "sensual"; and the charge of excessive sex-distinction seems to be a reproach. This should be at once dismissed, as merely showing ignorance of the terms used. A man does not object to being called "masculine," nor a woman to being called "feminine." Yet whatever is masculine or feminine is sexual. To be distinguished by femininity is to be distinguished by sex. To be over-feminine is to be over-sexed. To manifest in excess any of the distinctions of sex, primary or secondary, is to be over-sexed. Our hypothetical peacock, with his too large and splendid tail, would be over-sexed, and no offence to his moral character!

The primary sex-distinctions in our race as in others consist merely in the essential organs and functions of reproduction. The secondary distinctions, and this is where we are to look for our largest excess—consist in all those differences in organ and function, in look and action, in habit, manner, method, occupation, behavior, which distinguish men from women. In a troop of horses, seen at a distance, the sexes are indistinguishable. In a herd of deer the males are distinguishable because of their antlers. The male lion is distinguished by his mane, the male cat only by a somewhat heavier build. In certain species of insects the male and female differ so widely in appearance that even naturalists have supposed them to belong to separate species. Beyond these distinctions lies that of conduct. Certain psychic attributes are manifested by either sex. The intensity of the maternal passion is a sex-distinction as much as the lion's mane or the stag's horns. The belligerence and dominance of the male is a sex-distinction: the modesty and timidity of the female is a sex-distinction. The tendency to "sit" is a sex-distinction of the hen: the tendency to strut is a sex-distinction of the cock. The tendency to fight is a sex-distinction of males in general: the tendency to protect and provide for, is a sex-distinction of females in general.

With the human race, whose chief activities are social, the initial tendency to sex-distinction is carried out in many varied functions. We have differentiated our industries, our responsibilities, our very virtues, along sex lines. It will therefore be clear that the claim of excessive sex-distinction in humanity, and especially in woman, does not carry with it any specific "moral" reproach, though it does in the larger sense prove a decided evil in its effect on human progress.

In primary distinctions our excess is not so marked as in the farther and subtler development; yet, even here, we have plain proof of it. Sex-energy in its primal manifestation is exhibited in the male of the human species to a degree far greater than is necessary for the processes of reproduction,—enough, indeed, to subvert and injure those processes. The direct injury to reproduction from the excessive indulgence of the male, and the indirect injury through its debilitating effect upon the female, together with the enormous evil to society produced by extra-marital indulgence,—these are facts quite generally known. We have recognized them for centuries, and sought to check the evil action by law, civil, social, moral. But we have treated it always as a field of voluntary action, not as a condition of morbid development. We have held it as right that man should be so, but wrong that man should do so. Nature does not work in that way. What it is right to be, it is right to do. What it is wrong to do, it is wrong to be. This inordinate demand in the human male is an excessive sex-distinction. In this, in a certain over-coarseness and hardness, a too great belligerence and pride, a too great subservience to the power of sex-attraction, we find the main marks of excessive sex-distinction in men. It has been always checked and offset in them by the healthful activities of racial life. Their energies have been called out and their faculties developed along all the lines of human progress. In the growth of industry, commerce, science, manufacture, government, art, religion, the male of our species has become human, far more than male. Strong as this passion is in him, inordinate as is his indulgence, he is a far more normal animal than the female of his species,—far less over-sexed. To him this field of special activity is but part of life,—an incident. The whole world remains besides. To her it is the world. This has been well stated in the familiar epigram of Madame de Staël,—"Love with man is an episode, with woman a history." It is in woman that we find most fully expressed the excessive sex-distinction of the human species,—physical, psychical, social. See first the physical manifestation.

To make clear by an instance the difference between normal and abnormal sex-distinction, look at the relative condition of a wild cow and a "milch cow," such as we have made. The wild cow is a female. She has healthy calves, and milk enough for them; and that is all the femininity she needs. Otherwise than that she is bovine rather than feminine. She is a light, strong, swift, sinewy creature, able to run, jump, and fight, if necessary. We, for economic uses, have artificially developed the cow's capacity for producing milk. She has become a walking milk-machine, bred and tended to that express end, her value measured in quarts. The secretion of milk is a maternal function,—a sex-function. The cow is over-sexed. Turn her loose in natural conditions, and, if she survive the change, she would revert in a very few generations to the plain cow, with her energies used in the general activities of her race, and not all running to milk.

Physically, woman belongs to a tall, vigorous, beautiful animal species, capable of great and varied exertion. In every race and time when she has opportunity for racial activity, she develops accordingly, and is no less a woman for being a healthy human creature. In every race and time where she is denied this opportunity,—and few, indeed, have been her years of freedom,—she has developed in the lines of action to which she was confined; and those were always lines of sex-activity. In consequence the body of woman, speaking in the largest generalization, manifests sex-distinction predominantly.

Woman's femininity—and "the eternal feminine" means simply the eternal sexual—is more apparent in proportion to her humanity than the femininity of other animals in proportion to their caninity or felinity or equinity. "A feminine hand" or "a feminine foot" is distinguishable anywhere. We do not hear of "a feminine paw" or "a feminine hoof." A hand is an organ of prehension, a foot an organ of locomotion: they are not secondary sexual characteristics. The comparative smallness and feebleness of woman is a sex-distinction. We have carried it to such an excess that women are commonly known as "the weaker sex." There is no such glaring difference between male and female in other advanced species. In the long migrations of birds, in the ceaseless motion of the grazing herds that used to swing up and down over the continent each year, in the wild, steep journeys of the breeding salmon, nothing is heard of the weaker sex. And among the higher carnivora, where longer maintenance of the young brings their condition nearer ours, the hunter dreads the attack of the female more than that of the male. The disproportionate weakness is an excessive sex-distinction. Its injurious effect may be broadly shown in the Oriental nations, where the female in curtained harems is confined most exclusively to sex-functions and denied most fully the exercise of race-functions. In such peoples the weakness, the tendency to small bones and adipose tissue of the over-sexed female, is transmitted to the male, with a retarding effect on the development of the race. Conversely, in early Germanic tribes the comparatively free and humanly developed women—tall, strong, and brave—transmitted to their sons a greater proportion of human power and much less of morbid sex-tendency.

The degree of feebleness and clumsiness common to women, the comparative inability to stand, walk, run, jump, climb, and perform other race-functions common to both sexes, is an excessive sex-distinction; and the ensuing transmission of this relative feebleness to their children, boys and girls alike, retards human development. Strong, free, active women, the sturdy, field-working peasant, the burden-bearing savage, are no less good mothers for their human strength. But our civilized "feminine delicacy," which appears somewhat less delicate when recognized as an expression of sexuality in excess,—makes us no better mothers, but worse. The relative weakness of women is a sex-distinction. It is apparent in her to a degree that injures motherhood, that injures wifehood, that injures the individual. The sex-usefulness and the human usefulness of women, their general duty to their kind, are greatly injured by this degree of distinction. In every way the over-sexed condition of the human female reacts unfavorably upon herself, her husband, her children, and the race.

In its psychic manifestation this intense sex-distinction is equally apparent. The primal instinct of sex-attraction has developed under social forces into a conscious passion of enormous power, a deep and lifelong devotion, overwhelming in its force. This is excessive in both sexes, but more so in women than in men,—not so commonly in its simple physical form, but in the unreasoning intensity of emotion that refuses all guidance, and drives those possessed by it to risk every other good for this one end. It is not at first sight easy, and it may seem an irreverent and thankless task, to discriminate here between what is good in the "master passion" and what is evil, and especially to claim for one sex more of this feeling than for the other; but such discrimination can be made.

It is good for the individual and for the race to have developed such a degree of passionate and permanent love as shall best promote the happiness of individuals and the reproduction of species. It is not good for the race or for the individual that this feeling should have become so intense as to override all other human faculties, to make a mock of the accumulated wisdom of the ages, the stored power of the will; to drive the individual—against his own plain conviction—into a union sure to result in evil, or to hold the individual helpless in such an evil union, when made.

Such is the condition of humanity, involving most evil results to its offspring and to its own happiness. And, while in men the immediate dominating force of the passion may be more conspicuous, it is in women that it holds more universal sway. For the man has other powers and faculties in full use, whereby to break loose from the force of this; and the woman, specially modified to sex and denied racial activity, pours her whole life into her love, and, if injured here, she is injured irretrievably. With him it is frequently light and transient, and, when most intense, often most transient. With her it is a deep, all-absorbing force, under the action of which she will renounce all that life offers, take any risk, face any hardships, bear any pain. It is maintained in her in the face of a lifetime of neglect and abuse. The common instance of the police court trials—the woman cruelly abused who will not testify against her husband—shows this. This devotion, carried to such a degree as to lead to the mismating of individuals with its personal and social injury, is an excessive sex-distinction.

But it is in our common social relations that the predominance of sex-distinction in women is made most manifest. The fact that, speaking broadly, woman have, from the very beginning, been spoken of expressively enough as "the sex," demonstrates clearly that this is the main impression which they have made upon observers and recorders. Here one need attempt no farther proof than to turn the mind of the reader to an unbroken record of facts and feelings perfectly patent to every one, but not hitherto looked at as other than perfectly natural and right. So utterly has the status of woman been accepted as a sexual one that it has remained for the woman's movement of the nineteenth century to devote much contention to the claim that women are persons! That women are persons as well as females,—an unheard of proposition!

In a "Handbook of Proverbs of All Nations," a collection comprising many thousands, these facts are to be observed: first, that the proverbs concerning women are an insignificant minority compared to those concerning men; second, that the proverbs concerning women almost invariably apply to them in general,—to the sex. Those concerning men qualify, limit, describe, specialize. It is "a lazy man," "a violent man," "a man in his cups." Qualities and actions are predicated of man individually, and not as a sex, unless he is flatly contrasted with woman, as in "A man of straw is worth a woman of gold," "Men are deeds, women are words," or "Man, woman, and the devil are the three degrees of comparison." But of woman it is always and only "a woman," meaning simply a female, and recognizing no personal distinction: "As much pity to see a woman weep as to see a goose go barefoot." "He that hath an eel by the tail and a woman by her word hath a slippery handle." "A woman, a spaniel, and a walnut-tree,—the more you beat 'em, the better they be." Occasionally a distinction is made between "a fair woman" and "a black woman"; and Solomon's "virtuous woman," who commanded such a high price, is familiar to us all. But in common thought it is simply "a woman" always. The boast of the profligate that he knows "the sex," so recently expressed by a new poet,—"The things you will learn from the Yellow and Brown, they'll 'elp you an' 'eap with the White"; the complaint of the angry rejected that "all women are just alike!"—the consensus of public opinion of all time goes to show that the characteristics common to the sex have predominated over the characteristics distinctive of the individual,—a marked excess in sex-distinction.

From the time our children are born, we use every means known to accentuate sex-distinction in both boy and girl; and the reason that the boy is not so hopelessly marked by it as the girl is that he has the whole field of human expression open to him besides. In our steady insistence on proclaiming sex-distinction we have grown to consider most human attributes as masculine attributes, for the simple reason that they were allowed to men and forbidden to women.

A clear and definite understanding of the difference between race-attributes and sex-attributes should be established. Life consists of action. The action of a living thing is along two main lines,—self-preservation and race-preservation. The processes that keep the individual alive, from the involuntary action of his internal organs to the voluntary action of his external organs,—every act, from breathing to hunting his food, which contributes to the maintenance of the individual life,—these are the processes of self-preservation. Whatever activities tend to keep the race alive, to reproduce the individual, from the involuntary action of the internal organs to the voluntary action of the external organs; every act from the development of germ-cells to the taking care of children, which contributes to the maintenance of the racial life,—these are the processes of race-preservation. In race-preservation, male and female have distinctive organs, distinctive functions, distinctive lines of action. In self-preservation, male and female have the same organs, the same functions, the same lines of action. In the human species our processes of race-preservation have reached a certain degree of elaboration; but our processes of self-preservation have gone farther, much farther.

All the varied activities of economic production and distribution, all our arts and industries, crafts and trades, all our growth in science, discovery, government, religion,—these are along the line of self-preservation: these are, or should be, common to both sexes. To teach, to rule, to make, to decorate, to distribute,—these are not sex-functions: they are race-functions. Yet so inordinate is the sex-distinction of the human race that the whole field of human progress has been considered a masculine prerogative. What could more absolutely prove the excessive sex-distinction of the human race? That this difference should surge over all its natural boundaries and blazon itself across every act of life, so that every step of the human creature is marked "male" or "female,"—surely, this is enough to show our over-sexed condition.

Little by little, very slowly, and with most unjust and cruel opposition, at cost of all life holds most dear, it is being gradually established by many martyrdoms that human work is woman's as well as man's. Harriet Martineau must conceal her writing under her sewing when callers came, because "to sew" was a feminine verb, and "to write" a masculine one. Mary Somerville must struggle to hide her work from even relatives, because mathematics was a "masculine" pursuit. Sex has been made to dominate the whole human world,—all the main avenues of life marked "male," and the female left to be a female, and nothing else.

But while with the male the things he fondly imagined to be "masculine" were merely human, and very good for him, with the female the few things marked "feminine" were feminine, indeed; and her ceaseless reiterance of one short song, however sweet, has given it a conspicuous monotony. In garments whose main purpose is unmistakably to announce her sex; with a tendency to ornament which marks exuberance of sex-energy, with a body so modified to sex as to be grievously deprived of its natural activities; with a manner and behavior wholly attuned to sex-advantage, and frequently most disadvantageous to any human gain; with a field of action most rigidly confined to sex-relations; with her overcharged sensibility, her prominent modesty, her "eternal femininity,"—the female of genus homo is undeniably over-sexed.

This excessive distinction shows itself again in a marked precocity of development. Our little children, our very babies, show signs of it when the young of other creatures are serenely asexual in general appearance and habit. We eagerly note this precocity. We are proud of it. We carefully encourage it by precept and example, taking pains to develope the sex-instinct in little children, and think no harm. One of the first things we force upon the child's dawning consciousness is the fact that he is a boy or that she is a girl, and that, therefore, each must regard everything from a different point of view. They must be dressed differently, not on account of their personal needs, which are exactly similar at this period, but so that neither they, nor any one beholding them, may for a moment forget the distinction of sex.

Our peculiar inversion of the usual habit of species, in which the male carries ornament and the female is dark and plain, is not so much a proof of excess indeed, as a proof of the peculiar reversal of our position in the matter of sex-selection. With the other species the males compete in ornament, and the females select. With us the females compete in ornament, and the males select. If this theory of sex-ornament is disregarded, and we prefer rather to see in masculine decoration merely a form of exuberant sex-energy, expending itself in non-productive excess, then, indeed, the fact that with us the females manifest such a display of gorgeous adornment is another sign of excessive sex-distinction. In either case the forcing upon girl-children of an elaborate ornamentation which interferes with their physical activity and unconscious freedom, and fosters a premature sex-consciousness, is as clear and menacing a proof of our condition as could be mentioned. That the girl-child should be so dressed as to require a difference in care and behavior, resting wholly on the fact that she is a girl,—a fact not otherwise present to her thought at that age,—is a precocious insistence upon sex-distinction, most unwholesome in its results. Boys and girls are expected, also, to behave differently to each other, and to people in general,—a behavior to be briefly described in two words. To the boy we say, "Do"; to the girl, "Don't." The little boy must "take care" of the little girl, even if she is larger than he is. "Why?" he asks. Because he is a boy. Because of sex. Surely, if she is the stronger, she ought to take care of him, especially as the protective instinct is purely feminine in a normal race. It is not long before the boy learns his lesson. He is a boy, going to be a man; and that means all. "I thank the Lord that I was not born a woman," runs the Hebrew prayer. She is a girl, "only a girl," "nothing but a girl," and going to be a woman,—only a woman. Boys are encouraged from the beginning to show the feelings supposed to be proper to their sex. When our infant son bangs about, roars, and smashes things, we say proudly that he is "a regular boy!" When our infant daughter coquettes with visitors, or wails in maternal agony because her brother has broken her doll, whose sawdust remains she nurses with piteous care, we say proudly that "she is a perfect little mother already!" What business has a little girl with the instincts of maternity? No more than the little boy should have with the instincts of paternity. They are sex-instincts, and should not appear till the period of adolescence. The most normal girl is the "tom-boy,"—whose numbers increase among us in these wiser days,—a healthy young creature, who is human through and through, not feminine till it is time to be. The most normal boy has calmness and gentleness as well as vigor and courage. He is a human creature as well as a male creature, and not aggressively masculine till it is time to be. Childhood is not the period for these marked manifestations of sex. That we exhibit them, that we admire and encourage them, shows our over-sexed condition.

1898

THE YELLOW WALLPAPER

It is very seldom that mere ordinary people like John and myself secure ancestral halls for the summer.

A colonial mansion, a hereditary estate, I would say a haunted house and reach the height of romantic felicity—but that would be asking too much of fate!

Still I will proudly declare that there is something queer about it.

Else, why should it be let so cheaply? And why have stood so long untenanted?

John laughs at me, of course, but one expects that.

John is practical in the extreme. He has no patience with faith, an intense horror of superstition, and he scoffs openly at any talk of things not to be felt and seen and put down in figures.

John is a physician, and *perhaps*—(I would not say it to a living soul, of course, but this is dead paper and a great relief to my mind)—*perhaps* that is one reason I do not get well faster.

You see, he does not believe I am sick! And what can one do?

If a physician of high standing, and one's own husband, assures friends and relatives that there is really nothing the matter with one but temporary nervous depression—a slight hysterical tendency—what is one to do?

My brother is also a physician, and also of high standing, and he says the same thing.

So I take phosphates or phosphites—whichever it is—and tonics, and air and exercise, and journeys, and am absolutely forbidden to "work" until I am well again.

Personally, I disagree with their ideas.

Personally, I believe that congenial work, with excitement and change, would do me good.

But what is one to do?

I did write for a while in spite of them; but it *does* exhaust me a good deal—having to be so sly about it, or else meet with heavy opposition.

I sometimes fancy that in my condition, if I had less opposition and more society and stimulus—but John says the very worst thing I can do is to think about my condition, and I confess it always makes me feel bad.

So I will let it alone and talk about the house.

The most beautiful place! It is quite alone, standing well back from the road, quite three miles from the village. It makes me think of English places that you read about, for there are hedges and walls and gates that lock, and lots of separate little houses for the gardeners and people.

There is a *delicious* garden! I never saw such a garden—large and shady, full of box-bordered paths, and lined with long grape-covered arbors with seats under them.

There were greenhouses, but they are all broken now.

There was some legal trouble, I believe, something about the heirs and co-heirs; anyhow, the place has been empty for years.

That spoils my ghostliness, I am afraid, but I don't care—there is something strange about the house—I can feel it.

I even said so to John one moonlight evening, but he said what I felt was a draught, and shut the window.

I get unreasonably angry with John sometimes. I'm sure I never used to be so sensitive. I think it is due to this nervous condition.

But John says if I feel so I shall neglect proper self-control; so I take pains to control myself—before him, at least, and that makes me very tired.

I don't like our room a bit. I wanted one downstairs that opened onto the piazza and had roses all over the window, and such pretty old-fashioned chintz hangings! But John would not hear of it.

He said there was only one window and not room for two beds, and no near room for him if he took another.

He is very careful and loving, and hardly lets me stir without special direction.

I have a schedule prescription for each hour in the day; he takes all care from me, and so I feel basely ungrateful not to value it more.

He said he came here solely on my account, that I was to have perfect rest and all the air I could get. "Your exercise depends on your strength, my dear," said he, "and your food somewhat on your appetite; but air you can absorb all the time." So we took the nursery at the top of the house.

It is a big, airy room, the whole floor nearly, with windows that look all ways, and air and sunshine galore. It was nursery first, and then playroom and gymnasium, I should judge, for the windows are barred for little children, and there are rings and things in the walls.

The paint and paper look as if a boys' school had used it. It is stripped off—the paper—in great patches all around the head of my bed, about as far as I can reach, and in a great place on the other side of the room low down. I never saw a worse paper in my life. One of those sprawling, flamboyant patterns committing every artistic sin.

It is dull enough to confuse the eye in following, pronounced enough constantly to irritate and provoke study, and when you follow the lame uncertain curves for a little distance they suddenly commit suicide—plunge off at outrageous angles, destroy themselves in unheard-of contradictions.

The color is repellent, almost revolting: a smouldering unclean yellow, strangely faded by the slow-turning sunlight. It is a dull yet lurid orange in some places, a sickly sulphur tint in others.

No wonder the children hated it! I should hate it myself if I had to live in this room long.

There comes John, and I must put this away—he hates to have me write a word.

. . .

We have been here two weeks, and I haven't felt like writing before, since that first day.

I am sitting by the window now, up in this atrocious nursery, and there is nothing to hinder my writing as much as I please, save lack of strength.

John is away all day, and even some nights when his cases are serious.

I am glad my case is not serious!

But these nervous troubles are dreadfully depressing.

John does not know how much I really suffer. He knows there is no reason to suffer, and that satisfies him.

Of course it is only nervousness. It does weigh on me so not to do my duty in any way!

I meant to be such a help to John, such a real rest and comfort, and here I am a comparative burden already!

Nobody would believe what an effort it is to do what little I am able—to dress and entertain, and order things.

It is fortunate Mary is so good with the baby. Such a dear baby!

And yet I *cannot* be with him, it makes me so nervous.

I suppose John never was nervous in his life. He laughs at me so about this wallpaper!

At first he meant to repaper the room, but afterward he said that I was letting it get the better of me, and that nothing was worse for a nervous patient than to give way to such fancies.

He said that after the wallpaper was changed it would be the heavy bedstead, and then the barred windows, and then that gate at the head of the stairs, and so on.

"You know the place is doing you good," he said, "and really, dear, I don't care to renovate the house just for a three months' rental."

"Then do let us go downstairs," I said. "There are such pretty rooms there."

Then he took me in his arms and called me a blessed little goose, and said he would go down cellar, if I wished, and have it whitewashed into the bargain.

But he is right enough about the beds and windows and things.

It is as airy and comfortable a room as anyone need wish, and, of course, I would not be so silly as to make him uncomfortable just for a whim.

I'm really getting quite fond of the big room, all but that horrid paper.

Out of one window I can see the garden—those mysterious deep-shaded arbors, the riotous old-fashioned flowers, and bushes and gnarly trees.

Out of another I get a lovely view of the bay and a little private wharf belonging to the estate. There is a beautiful shaded lane that runs down there from the house. I always fancy I see people walking in these numerous paths and arbors, but John has cautioned me not to give way to fancy in the least. He says that with my imaginative power and habit of story-making, a nervous weakness like mine is sure to lead to all manner of excited fancies, and that I ought to use my will and good sense to check the tendency. So I try.

I think sometimes that if I were only well enough to write a little it would relieve the press of ideas and rest me.

But I find I get pretty tired when I try.

It is so discouraging not to have any advice and companionship about my work. When I get really well, John says we will ask Cousin Henry and Julia down for a long visit; but he says he would as soon put fireworks in my pillow-case as to let me have those stimulating people about now.

I wish I could get well faster.

But I must not think about that. This paper looks to me as if it *knew* what a vicious influence it had!

There is a recurrent spot where the pattern lolls like a broken neck and two bulbous eyes stare at you upside down.

I get positively angry with the impertinence of it and the everlastingness. Up and down and sideways they crawl, and those absurd unblinking eyes are everywhere. There is one place where two breadths didn't match, and the eyes go all up and down the line, one a little higher than the other.

I never saw so much expression in an inanimate thing before, and we all know how much expression they have! I used to lie awake as a child and get more entertainment and terror out of blank walls and plain furniture than most children could find in a toy-store.

I remember what a kindly wink the knobs of our big old bureau used to have, and there was one chair that always seemed like a strong friend.

I used to feel that if any of the other things looked too fierce I could always hop into that chair and be safe.

The furniture in this room is no worse than inharmonious, however, for we had to bring it all from downstairs. I suppose when this was used as a playroom they had to take the nursery things out, and no wonder! I never saw such ravages as the children have made here.

The wallpaper, as I said before, is torn off in spots, and it sticketh closer than a brother—they must have had perseverance as well as hatred.

Then the floor is scratched and gouged and splintered, the plaster itself is dug out here and there, and this great heavy bed, which is all we found in the room, looks as if it had been through the wars.

But I don't mind it a bit—only the paper.

There comes John's sister. Such a dear girl as she is, and so careful of me! I must not let her find me writing.

She is a perfect and enthusiastic housekeeper, and hopes for no better profession. I verily believe she thinks it is the writing which made me sick!

But I can write when she is out, and see her a long way off from these windows.

There is one that commands the road, a lovely shaded winding road, and one that just looks off over the country. A lovely country, too, full of great elms and velvet meadows.

This wallpaper has a kind of sub-pattern in a different shade, a particularly irritating one, for you can only see it in certain lights, and not clearly then.

But in the places where it isn't faded and where the sun is just so—I can see a strange, provoking, formless sort of figure that seems to skulk about behind that silly and conspicuous front design.

There's sister on the stairs!

. . .

Well, the Fourth of July is over! The people are all gone, and I am tired out. John thought it might do me good to see a little company, so we just had Mother and Nellie and the children down for a week.

Of course I didn't do a thing. Jennie sees to everything now.

But it tired me all the same.

John says if I don't pick up faster he shall send me to Weir Mitchell in the fall.

But I don't want to go there at all. I had a friend who was in his hands once, and she says he is just like John and my brother, only more so!

Besides, it is such an undertaking to go so far.

I don't feel as if it was worthwhile to turn my hand over for anything, and I'm getting dreadfully fretful and querulous.

I cry at nothing, and cry most of the time.

Of course I don't when John is here, or anybody else, but when I am alone.

And I am alone a good deal just now. John is kept in town very often by serious cases, and Jennie is good and lets me alone when I want her to.

So I walk a little in the garden or down that lovely lane, sit on the porch under the roses, and lie down up here a good deal.

I'm getting really fond of the room in spite of the wallpaper. Perhaps *because* of the wallpaper.

It dwells in my mind so!

I lie here on this great immovable bed—it is nailed down, I believe—and follow that pattern about by the hour. It is as good as gymnastics, I assure you. I start, we'll say, at the bottom, down in the corner over there where it has not been touched, and I determine for the thousandth time that I *will* follow that pointless pattern to some sort of a conclusion.

I know a little of the principle of design, and I know this thing was not arranged on any laws of radiation, or alternation, or repetition, or symmetry, or anything else that I ever heard of.

It is repeated, of course, by the breadths, but not otherwise.

Looked at in one way, each breadth stands alone; the bloated curves and flourishes—a kind of "debased Romanesque" with delirium tremens—go waddling up and down in isolated columns of fatuity.

But, on the other hand, they connect diagonally, and the sprawling outlines run off in great slanting waves of optic horror, like a lot of wallowing sea-weeds in full chase.

The whole thing goes horizontally, too, at least it seems so, and I exhaust myself trying to distinguish the order of its going in that direction.

They have used a horizontal breadth for a frieze, and that adds wonderfully to the confusion.

There is one end of the room where it is almost intact, and there, when the crosslights fade and the low sun shines directly upon it, I can almost fancy radiation after all—the interminable grotesque seems to form around a common center and rush off in headlong plunges of equal distraction.

It makes me tired to follow it. I will take a nap, I guess.

I don't know why I should write this.

I don't want to.

I don't feel able.

And I know John would think it absurd. But I *must* say what I feel and think in some way—it is such a relief!

But the effort is getting to be greater than the relief.

. . .

Half the time now I am awfully lazy, and lie down ever so much. John says I mustn't lose my strength, and has me take cod liver oil and lots of tonics and things, to say nothing of ale and wine and rare meat.

Dear John! He loves me very dearly, and hates to have me sick. I tried to have a real earnest reasonable talk with him the other day, and tell him how I wish he would let me go and make a visit to Cousin Henry and Julia.

But he said I wasn't able to go, nor able to stand it after I got there; and I did not make out a very good case for myself, for I was crying before I had finished.

It is getting to be a great effort for me to think straight. Just this nervous weakness, I suppose.

And dear John gathered me up in his arms, and just carried me upstairs and laid me on the bed, and sat by me and read to me till it tired my head.

He said I was his darling and his comfort and all he had, and that I must take care of myself for his sake, and keep well.

He says no one but myself can help me out of it, that I must use my will and self-control and not let any silly fancies run away with me.

There's one comfort—the baby is well and happy, and does not have to occupy this nursery with the horrid wallpaper.

If we had not used it, that blessed child would have! What a fortunate escape! Why, I wouldn't have a child of mine, an impressionable little thing, live in such a room for worlds.

I never thought of it before, but it is lucky that John kept me here after all; I can stand it so much easier than a baby, you see.

Of course I never mention it to them any more—I am too wise—but I keep watch for it all the same.

There are things in that wallpaper that nobody knows about but me, or ever will.

Behind that outside pattern the dim shapes get clearer every day.

It is always the same shape, only very numerous.

And it is like a woman stooping down and creeping about behind that pattern. I don't like it a bit. I wonder—I begin to think—I wish John would take me away from here!

It is so hard to talk with John about my case, because he is so wise, and because he loves me so.

But I tried it last night.

It was moonlight. The moon shines in all around just as the sun does.

I hate to see it sometimes, it creeps so slowly, and always comes in by one window or another.

John was asleep and I hated to waken him, so I kept still and watched the moonlight on that undulating wallpaper till I felt creepy.

The faint figure behind seemed to shake the pattern, just as if she wanted to get out.

I got up softly and went to feel and see if the paper *did* move, and when I came back John was awake.

"What is it, little girl?" he said. "Don't go walking about like that—you'll get cold."

I thought it was a good time to talk, so I told him that I really was not gaining here, and that I wished he would take me away.

"Why, darling!" said he. "Our lease will be up in three weeks, and I can't see how to leave before.

"The repairs are not done at home, and I cannot possibly leave town just now. Of course, if you were in any danger, I could and would, but you really are better, dear, whether you can see it or not. I am a doctor, dear, and I know. You are gaining flesh and color, your appetite is better, I feel really much easier about you."

"I don't weigh a bit more," said I, "nor as much; and my appetite may be better in the evening when you are here but it is worse in the morning when you are away!"

"Bless her little heart!" said he with a big hug. "She shall be as sick as she pleases! But now let's improve the shining hours by going to sleep, and talk about it in the morning!"

"And you won't go away?" I asked gloomily.

"Why, how can I, dear? It is only three weeks more and then we will take a nice little trip of a few days while Jennie is getting the house ready. Really, dear, you are better!"

"Better in body perhaps—" I began, and stopped short, for he sat up straight and looked at me with such a stern, reproachful look that I could not say another word.

"My darling," said he, "I beg of you, for my sake and for our child's sake, as well as for your own, that you will never for one instant let that idea enter your mind! There is nothing so dangerous, so fascinating, to a temperament like yours. It is a false and foolish fancy. Can you not trust me as a physician when I tell you so?"

So of course I said no more on that score, and we went to sleep before long. He thought I was asleep first, but I wasn't, and lay there for hours trying to decide whether that front pattern and the back pattern really did move together or separately.

On a pattern like this, by daylight, there is a lack of sequence, a defiance of law, that is a constant irritant to a normal mind.

The color is hideous enough, and unreliable enough, and infuriating enough, but the pattern is torturing.

You think you have mastered it, but just as you get well under way in following, it turns a back-somersault and there you are. It slaps you in the face, knocks you down, and tramples upon you. It is like a bad dream.

The outside pattern is a florid arabesque, reminding one of a fungus. If you can imagine a toadstool in joints, an interminable string of toadstools, budding and sprouting in endless convolutions—why, that is something like it.

That is, sometimes!

There is one marked peculiarity about this paper, a thing nobody seems to notice but myself, and that is that it changes as the light changes.

When the sun shoots in through the east window—I always watch for that first long, straight ray—it changes so quickly that I never can quite believe it.

That is why I watch it always,

By moonlight—the moon shines in all night when there is a moon—I wouldn't know it was the same paper.

At night in any kind of light, in twilight, candlelight, lamplight, and worst of all by moonlight, it becomes bars! The outside pattern, I mean, and the woman behind it is as plain as can be.

I didn't realize for a long time what the thing was that showed behind, that dim sub-pattern, but now I am quite sure it is a woman.

By daylight she is subdued, quiet. I fancy it is the pattern that keeps her so still. It is so puzzling. It keeps me quiet by the hour.

I lie down ever so much now. John says it is good for me, and to sleep all I can.

Indeed he started the habit by making me lie down for an hour after each meal.

It is a very bad habit, I am convinced, for you see, I don't sleep.

And that cultivates deceit, for I don't tell them I'm awake—oh, no!

The fact is I am getting a little afraid of John.

He seems very queer sometimes, and even Jennie has an inexplicable look.

It strikes me occasionally, just as a scientific hypothesis, that perhaps it is the paper!

I have watched John when he did not know I was looking, and come into the room suddenly on the most innocent excuses, and I've caught him several times *looking at the paper!* And Jennie too. I caught Jennie with her hand on it once.

She didn't know I was in the room, and when I asked her in a quiet, a very quiet voice, with the most restrained manner possible, what she was doing with the paper, she turned around as if she had been caught stealing, and looked quite angry—asked me why I should frighten her so!

Then she said that the paper stained everything it touched, that she had found yellow smooches on all my clothes and John's and she wished we would be more careful!

Did not that sound innocent? But I know she was studying that pattern, and I am determined that nobody shall find it out but myself!

. . .

Life is very much more exciting now than it used to be. You see, I have something more to expect, to look forward to, to watch. I really do eat better, and am more quiet than I was.

John is so pleased to see me improve! He laughed a little the other day, and said I seemed to be flourishing in spite of my wallpaper.

I turned it off with a laugh. I had no intention of telling him it was *because* of the wallpaper—he would make fun of me. He might even want to take me away.

I don't want to leave now until I have found it out. There is a week more, and I think that will be enough.

I'm feeling so much better!

I don't sleep much at night, for it is so interesting to watch developments; but I sleep a good deal during the daytime.

In the daytime it is tiresome and perplexing.

There are always new shoots on the fungus, and new shades of yellow all over it. I cannot keep count of them, though I have tried conscientiously.

It is the strangest yellow, that wallpaper! It makes me think of all the yellow things I ever saw—not the beautiful ones like buttercups, but old, foul, bad yellow things.

But there is something else about that paper—the smell! I noticed it the moment we came into the room, but with so much air and sun it was not bad. Now we have had a week of fog and rain, and whether the windows are open or not, the smell is here.

It creeps all over the house.

I find it hovering in the dining-room, skulking in the parlor, hiding in the hall, lying in wait for me on the stairs.

It gets into my hair.

Even when I go to ride, if I turn my head suddenly and surprise it—there is that smell!

Such a peculiar odor, too! I have spent hours in trying to analyze it, to find what it smelled like.

It is not bad—at first—and very gentle, but quite the subtlest, most enduring odor I ever met.

In this damp weather it is awful. I wake up in the night and find it hanging over me.

It used to disturb me at first. I thought seriously of burning the house—to reach the smell.

But now I am used to it. The only thing I can think of that it is like is the *color* of the paper! A yellow smell.

There is a very funny mark on this wall, low down, near the mopboard. A streak that runs round the room. It goes behind every piece of furniture, except the bed, a long, straight, even *smooch,* as if it had been rubbed over and over.

I wonder how it was done and who did it, and what they did it for. Round and round and round—round and round and round—it makes me dizzy!

I really have discovered something at last.

Through watching so much at night, when it changes so, I have finally found out.

The front pattern *does* move—and no wonder! The woman behind shakes it!

Sometimes I think there are a great many women behind, and sometimes only one, and she crawls around fast, and her crawling shakes it all over.

Then in the very bright spots she keeps still, and in the very shady spots she just takes hold of the bars and shakes them hard.

And she is all the time trying to climb through. But nobody could climb through that pattern—it strangles so; I think that is why it has so many heads.

They get through, and then the pattern strangles them off and turns them upside down, and makes their eyes white!

If those heads were covered or taken off it would not be half so bad.

. . .

I think that woman gets out in the daytime!

And I'll tell you why—privately—I've seen her!

I can see her out of every one of my windows!

It is the same woman, I know, for she is always creeping, and most women do not creep by daylight.

I see her in that long shaded lane, creeping up and down. I see her in those dark grape arbors, creeping all around the garden.

I see her on that long road under the trees, creeping along, and when a carriage comes she hides under the blackberry vines.

I don't blame her a bit. It must be very humiliating to be caught creeping by daylight!

I always lock the door when I creep by daylight. I can't do it at night, for I know John would suspect something at once.

And John is so queer now that I don't want to irritate him. I wish he would take another room! Besides, I don't want anybody to get that woman out at night but myself.

I often wonder if I could see her out of all the windows at once.

But, turn as fast as I can, I can only see out of one at one time.

And though I always see her, she *may* be able to creep faster than I can turn! I have watched her sometimes away off in the open country, creeping as fast as a cloud shadow in a wind.

If only that top pattern could be gotten off from the under one! I mean to try it, little by little.

I have found out another funny thing, but I shan't tell it this time! It does not do to trust people too much.

There are only two more days to get this paper off, and I believe John is beginning to notice. I don't like the look in his eyes.

And I heard him ask Jennie a lot of professional questions about me. She had a very good report to give.

She said I slept a good deal in the daytime.

John knows I don't sleep very well at night, for all I'm so quiet!

He asked me all sorts of questions, too, and pretended to be very loving and kind.

As if I couldn't see through him!

Still, I don't wonder he acts so, sleeping under this paper for three months.

It only interests me, but I feel sure John and Jennie are affected by it.

. . .

Hurrah! This is the last day, but it is enough. John is to stay in town over night, and won't be out until this evening.

Jennie wanted to sleep with me—the sly thing; but I told her I should undoubtedly rest better for a night all alone.

That was clever, for really I wasn't alone a bit! As soon as it was moonlight and that poor thing began to crawl and shake the pattern, I got up and ran to help her.

I pulled and she shook. I shook and she pulled, and before morning we had peeled off yards of that paper.

A strip about as high as my head and half around the room.

And then when the sun came and that awful pattern began to laugh at me, I declared I would finish it today!

We go away tomorrow, and they are moving all my furniture down again to leave things as they were before.

Jennie looked at the wall in amazement, but I told her merrily that I did it out of pure spite at the vicious thing.

She laughed and said she wouldn't mind doing it herself, but I must not get tired.

How she betrayed herself that time!

But I am here, and no person touches this paper but Me—not *alive!*

She tried to get me out of the room—it was too patent! But I said it was so quiet and empty and clean now that I believed I would lie down again and sleep all I could, and not to wake me even for dinner—I would call when I woke.

So now she is gone, and the servants are gone, and the things are gone, and there is nothing left but that great bedstead nailed down, with the canvas mattress we found on it.

We shall sleep downstairs tonight, and take the boat home tomorrow.

I quite enjoy the room, now it is bare again.

How those children did tear about here!

This bedstead is fairly gnawed!

But I must get to work.

I have locked the door and thrown the key down into the front path.

I don't want to go out, and I don't want to have anybody come in, till John comes.

I want to astonish him.

I've got a rope up here that even Jennie did not find. If that woman does get out, and tries to get away, I can tie her!

But I forgot I could not reach far without anything to stand on!

This bed will *not* move!

I tried to lift and push it until I was lame, and then I got so angry I bit off a little piece at one corner—but it hurt my teeth.

Then I peeled off all the paper I could reach standing on the floor. It sticks horribly and the pattern just enjoys it! All those strangled heads and bulbous eyes and waddling fungus growths just shriek with derision!

I am getting angry enough to do something desperate. To jump out of the window would be admirable exercise, but the bars are too strong even to try.

Besides I wouldn't do it. Of course not. I know well enough that a step like that is improper and might be misconstrued.

I don't like to *look* out of the windows even—there are so many of those creeping women, and they creep so fast.

I wonder if they all come out of that wallpaper as I did?

But I am securely fastened now by my well-hidden rope—you don't get *me* out in the road there!

I suppose I shall have to get back behind the pattern when it comes night, and that is hard!

It is so pleasant to be out in this great room and creep around as I please!

I don't want to go outside. I won't, even if Jennie asks me to.

For outside you have to creep on the ground, and everything is green instead of yellow.

But here I can creep smoothly on the floor, and my shoulder just fits in that long smooch around the wall, so I cannot lose my way.

Why, there's John at the door!

It is no use, young man, you can't open it!

How he does call and pound!

Now he's crying to Jennie for an axe.

It would be a shame to break down that beautiful door!

"John, dear!" said I in the gentlest voice. "The key is down by the front steps, under a plantain leaf!"

That silenced him for a few moments.

Then he said, very quietly indeed, "Open the door, my darling!"

"I can't," said I. "The key is down by the front door under a plantain leaf!" And then I said it again, several times, very gently and slowly, and said it so often that he had to go and see, and he got it of course, and came in. He stopped short by the door.

"What is the matter?" he cried. "For God's sake, what are you doing!"

I kept on creeping just the same, but I looked at him over my shoulder.

"I've got out at last," said I, "in spite of you and Jane. And I've pulled off most of the paper, so you can't put me back!"

Now why should that man have fainted? But he did, and right across my path by the wall, so that I had to creep over him every time!

1892

EDITH WHARTON
(1862–1937)

Edith Wharton, who began writing at sixteen, achieved both popular and critical acclaim during her lifetime. Her novels The House of Mirth, Ethan Frome, The Custom of the Country, *and* The Age of Innocence *secure her position on any list of major American writers. Feminist critics have analyzed her ironic portrayal of upper-class New York society and her descriptions of the repercussions patriarchal society has on even the most privileged women.*

Wharton's works include fourteen novels, seven novellas, and eleven collections of short stories. She published three books of poems, a book on writing, and her autobiography, A Backward Glance, *in addition to numerous critical essays and books on interior decorating and gardening. Wharton's accomplishments were rewarded in her lifetime. In 1921 she received the Pulitzer Prize in fiction for* The Age of Innocence. *She was the first woman to receive an honorary degree from Yale and the first woman gold medalist of the American Society of Arts and Letters.*

Edith Newbold Jones was born on January 24, 1862. Her parents were upper-class New Yorkers who never had to work. Their concession to the economic constraints of the post–Civil War era was to spend six years in Europe. Upon their return, they divided their time between a Newport, Rhode Island, estate and a New York City brownstone.

Edith Jones married Edward Wharton when she was twenty-three. Together they lived on their combined inheritance until their obvious incompatibility led to a divorce in 1913. She and her husband owned a mansion in Newport, two brownstones in New York, and a home in Lenox, Massachusetts, called The Mount. After her divorce, Wharton took up permanent residence in France.

In the last decades of the nineteenth century, Wharton met the writer whose work she most admired, Henry James. By 1902, the year her first novel, The Valley of Decision, *appeared, Wharton and James had embarked on their lifelong friendship. In her autobiography,* A Backward Glance, *Wharton explains that between their first meetings and the publication of her first novel, she had been able to find herself "and was no longer afraid to talk to Henry James of the things we both cared about."*

The House of Mirth, *Wharton's second novel, was a huge success when it appeared in 1905. In this biting indictment of the New York society she knew well, Wharton portrays Lily Bart's destruction by the machinations of the upper-class marriage game. In other works, Wharton conveys her sensitivity to the hidden parts of women's lives in rural New England. In* Summer, *for example, Wharton traces how the tedium of rural life leads the young heroine to an affair. Pregnant and abandoned by her lover, Charity's only recourse is marriage to her adoptive father. Recent criticism points out feminist themes throughout Wharton's work that shatter the picture of her as a demure novelist of manners.*

In her autobiography Wharton wrote that she could not "remember the time when I did not want to 'make' up stories." Her first story, "Mrs. Manstey's View," was published in Scribner's Magazine *when she was nineteen. As a twentieth-century realist, she tried to make each work of fiction, as she puts it in* The Writing of Fiction, *"a shaft driven straight into the heart of experience." In its ironic description of upper-class social mores, "Autres Temps . . ." is just that shaft. It also reflects Wharton's recurring interest in how marriage and divorce affect women's lives.*

AUTRES TEMPS . . .

I.

Mrs. Lidcote, as the huge menacing mass of New York defined itself far off across the waters, shrank back into her corner of the deck and sat listening with a kind of unreasoning terror to the steady onward drive of the screws.

She had set out on the voyage quietly enough,—in what she called her "reasonable" mood,—but the week at sea had given her too much time to think of things and had left her too long alone with the past.

When she was alone, it was always the past that occupied her. She couldn't get away from it, and she didn't any longer care to. During her long years of exile she had made her terms with it, had learned to accept the fact that it would always be there, huge, obstructing, encumbering, bigger and more dominant than anything the future could ever conjure up. And, at any rate, she was sure of it, she understood it, knew how to reckon with it; she had learned to screen and manage and protect it as one does an afflicted member of one's family.

There had never been any danger of her being allowed to forget the past. It looked out at her from the face of every acquaintance, it appeared suddenly in the eyes of strangers when a word enlightened them: "Yes, *the* Mrs. Lidcote, don't you know?" It had sprung at her the first day out, when, across the dining-room, from the captain's table, she had seen Mrs. Lorin Boulger's revolving eye-glass pause and the eye behind it grow as blank as a dropped blind. The next day, of course, the captain had asked: "You know your ambassadress, Mrs. Boulger?" and she had replied that, No, she seldom left

Florence, and hadn't been to Rome for more than a day since the Boulgers had been sent to Italy. She was so used to these phrases that it cost her no effort to repeat them. And the captain had promptly changed the subject.

No, she didn't, as a rule, mind the past, because she was used to it and understood it. It was a great concrete fact in her path that she had to walk around every time she moved in any direction. But now, in the light of the unhappy event that had summoned her from Italy,—the sudden unanticipated news of her daughter's divorce from Horace Pursh and remarriage with Wilbour Barkley—the past, her own poor miserable past, started up at her with eyes of accusation, became, to her disordered fancy, like the afflicted relative suddenly breaking away from nurses and keepers and publicly parading the horror and misery she had, all the long years, so patiently screened and secluded.

Yes, there it had stood before her through the agitated weeks since the news had come—during her interminable journey from India, where Leila's letter had overtaken her, and the feverish halt in her apartment in Florence, where she had had to stop and gather up her possessions for a fresh start—there it had stood grinning at her with a new balefulness which seemed to say: "Oh, but you've got to look at me *now,* because I'm not only your own past but Leila's present."

Certainly it was a master-stroke of those arch-ironists of the shears and spindle to duplicate her own story in her daughter's. Mrs. Lidcote had always somewhat grimly fancied that, having so signally failed to be of use to Leila in other ways, she would at least serve her as a warning. She had even abstained from defending herself, from making the best of her case, had stoically refused to plead extenuating circumstances, lest Leila's impulsive sympathy should lead to deductions that might react disastrously on her own life. And now that very thing had happened, and Mrs. Lidcote could hear the whole of New York saying with one voice: "Yes, Leila's done just what her mother did. With such an example what could you expect?"

Yet if she had been an example, poor woman, she had been an awful one; she had been, she would have supposed, of more use as a deterrent than a hundred blameless mothers as incentives. For how could any one who had seen anything of her life in the last eighteen years have had the courage to repeat so disastrous an experiment?

Well, logic in such cases didn't count, example didn't count, nothing probably counted but having the same impulses in the blood; and that was the dark inheritance she had bestowed upon her daughter. Leila hadn't consciously copied her; she had simply "taken after" her, had been a projection of her own long-past rebellion.

Mrs. Lidcote had deplored, when she started, that the *Utopia* was a slow steamer, and would take eight full days to bring her to her unhappy daughter; but now, as the moment of reunion approached, she would willingly have turned the boat about and fled back to the high seas. It was not only because she felt still so unprepared to face what New York had in store for her, but

because she needed more time to dispose of what the *Utopia* had already given her. The past was bad enough, but the present and future were worse, because they were less comprehensible, and because, as she grew older, surprises and inconsequences troubled her more than the worst certainties.

There was Mrs. Boulger, for instance. In the light, or rather the darkness, of new developments, it might really be that Mrs. Boulger had not meant to cut her, but had simply failed to recognize her. Mrs. Lidcote had arrived at this hypothesis simply by listening to the conversation of the persons sitting next to her on deck—two lively young women with the latest Paris hats on their heads and the latest New York ideas in them. These ladies, as to whom it would have been impossible for a person with Mrs. Lidcote's old-fashioned categories to determine whether they were married or unmarried, "nice" or "horrid," or any one or other of the definite things which young women, in her youth and her society, were conveniently assumed to be, had revealed a familiarity with the world of New York that, again according to Mrs. Lidcote's traditions, should have implied a recognized place in it. But in the present fluid state of manners what did anything imply except what their hats implied—that no one could tell what was coming next?

They seemed, at any rate, to frequent a group of idle and opulent people who executed the same gestures and revolved on the same pivots as Mrs. Lidcote's daughter and her friends: their Coras, Matties and Mabels seemed at any moment likely to reveal familiar patronymics, and once one of the speakers, summing up a discussion of which Mrs. Lidcote had missed the beginning, had affirmed with headlong confidence: "Leila? Oh, *Leila's* all right."

Could it be *her* Leila, the mother had wondered, with a sharp thrill of apprehension? If only they would mention surnames! But their talk leaped elliptically from allusion to allusion, their unfinished sentences dangled over bottomless pits of conjecture, and they gave their bewildered hearer the impression not so much of talking only of their intimates, as of being intimate with every one alive.

Her old friend Franklin Ide could have told her, perhaps; but here was the last day of the voyage, and she hadn't yet found courage to ask him. Great as had been the joy of discovering his name on the passenger-list and seeing his friendly bearded face in the throng against the taffrail at Cherbourg, she had as yet said nothing to him except, when they had met: "Of course I'm going out to Leila."

She had said nothing to Franklin Ide because she had always instinctively shrunk from taking him into her confidence. She was sure he felt sorry for her, sorrier perhaps than any one had ever felt; but he had always paid her the supreme tribute of not showing it. His attitude allowed her to imagine that compassion was not the basis of his feeling for her, and it was part of her joy in his friendship that it was the one relation seemingly unconditioned by her state, the only one in which she could think and feel and behave like any other woman.

Now, however, as the problem of New York loomed nearer, she began to regret that she had not spoken, had not at least questioned him about the hints she had gathered on the way. He did not know the two ladies next to her, he did not even, as it chanced, know Mrs. Lorin Boulger; but he knew New York, and New York was the sphinx whose riddle she must read or perish.

Almost as the thought passed through her mind his stooping shoulders and grizzled head detached themselves against the blaze of light in the west, and he sauntered down the empty deck and dropped into the chair at her side.

"You're expecting the Barkleys to meet you, I suppose?" he asked.

It was the first time she had heard any one pronounce her daughter's new name, and it occurred to her that her friend, who was shy and inarticulate, had been trying to say it all the way over and had at last shot it out at her only because he felt it must be now or never.

"I don't know. I cabled, of course. But I believe she's at—they're at—*his* place somewhere."

"Oh, Barkley's; yes, near Lenox, isn't it? But she's sure to come to town to meet you."

He said it so easily and naturally that her own constraint was relieved, and suddenly, before she knew what she meant to do, she had burst out: "She may dislike the idea of seeing people."

Ide, whose absent short-sighted gaze had been fixed on the slowly gliding water, turned in his seat to stare at his companion.

"Who? Leila?" he said with an incredulous laugh.

Mrs. Lidcote flushed to her faded hair and grew pale again. "It took *me* a long time—to get used to it," she said.

His look grew gently commiserating. "I think you'll find—" he paused for a word—"that things are different now—altogether easier."

"That's what I've been wondering—ever since we started." She was determined now to speak. She moved nearer, so that their arms touched, and she could drop her voice to a murmur. "You see, it all came on me in a flash. My going off to India and Siam on that long trip kept me away from letters for weeks at a time; and she didn't want to tell me beforehand—oh, I understand *that,* poor child! You know how good she's always been to me; how she's tried to spare me. And she knew, of course, what a state of horror I'd be in. She knew I'd rush off to her at once and try to stop it. So she never gave me a hint of anything, and she even managed to muzzle Susy Suffern—you know Susy is the one of the family who keeps me informed about things at home. I don't yet see how she prevented Susy's telling me; but she did. And her first letter, the one I got up at Bangkok, simply said the thing was over—the divorce, I mean—and that the very next day she'd—well, I suppose there was no use waiting; and *he* seems to have behaved as well as possible, to have wanted to marry her as much as—"

"Who? Barkley?" he helped her out. "I should say so! Why what do you suppose—" He interrupted himself. "He'll be devoted to her, I assure you."

"Oh, of course; I'm sure he will. He's written me—really beautifully. But it's a terrible strain on a man's devotion. I'm not sure that Leila realizes—"

Ide sounded again his little reassuring laugh. "I'm not sure that you realize. *They're* all right."

It was the very phrase that the young lady in the next seat had applied to the unknown "Leila," and its recurrence on Ide's lips flushed Mrs. Lidcote with fresh courage.

"I wish I knew just what you mean. The two young women next to me—the ones with the wonderful hats—have been talking in the same way."

"What? About Leila?"

"About *a* Leila; I fancied it might be mine. And about society in general. All their friends seem to be divorced; some of them seem to announce their engagements before they get their decree. One of them—*her* name was Mabel—as far as I could make out, her husband found out that she meant to divorce him by noticing that she wore a new engagement-ring."

"Well, you see Leila did everything 'regularly,' as the French say," Ide rejoined.

"Yes, but are these people in society? The people my neighbours talk about?"

He shrugged his shoulders. "It would take an arbitration commission a good many sittings to define the boundaries of society nowadays. But at any rate they're in New York; and I assure you you're *not;* you're farther and farther from it."

"But I've been back there several times to see Leila." She hesitated and looked away from him. Then she brought out slowly: "And I've never noticed—the least change—in—in my own case—"

"Oh," he sounded deprecatingly, and she trembled with the fear of having gone too far. But the hour was past when such scruples could restrain her. She must know where she was and where Leila was. "Mrs. Boulger still cuts me," she brought out with an embarrassed laugh.

"Are you sure? You've probably cut *her;* if not now, at least in the past. And in a cut if you're not first you're nowhere. That's what keeps up so many quarrels."

The word roused Mrs. Lidcote to a renewed sense of realities. "But the Purshes," she said—"the Purshes are so strong! There are so many of them, and they all back each other up, just as my husband's family did. I know what it means to have a clan against one. They're stronger than any number of separate friends. The Purshes will *never* forgive Leila for leaving Horace. Why, his mother opposed his marrying her because of—of me. She tried to get Leila to promise that she wouldn't see me when they went to Europe on their honeymoon. And now she'll say it was my example."

Her companion, vaguely stroking his beard, mused a moment upon this; then he asked, with seeming irrelevance, "What did Leila say when you wrote that you were coming?"

"She said it wasn't the least necessary, but that I'd better come, because it was the only way to convince me that it wasn't."

"Well, then, that proves she's not afraid of the Purshes."

She breathed a long sigh of remembrance. "Oh, just at first, you know—one never is."

He laid his hand on hers with a gesture of intelligence and pity. "You'll see, you'll see," he said.

A shadow lengthened down the deck before them, and a steward stood there, proffering a Marconigram.

"Oh, now I shall know!" she exclaimed.

She tore the message open, and then let it fall on her knees, dropping her hands on it in silence.

Ide's enquiry roused her: "It's all right?"

"Oh, quite right. Perfectly. She can't come; but she's sending Susy Suffern. She says Susy will explain." After another silence she added, with a sudden gush of bitterness: "As if I needed any explanation!"

She felt Ide's hesitating glance upon her. "She's in the country?"

"Yes. 'Prevented last moment. Longing for you, expecting you. Love from both.' Don't you *see*, the poor darling, that she couldn't face it?"

"No, I don't." He waited. "Do you mean to go to her immediately?"

"It will be too late to catch a train this evening; but I shall take the first to-morrow morning." She considered a moment. "Perhaps it's better. I need a talk with Susy first. She's to meet me at the dock, and I'll take her straight back to the hotel with me."

As she developed this plan, she had the sense that Ide was still thoughtfully, even gravely, considering her. When she ceased, he remained silent a moment; then he said almost ceremoniously: "If your talk with Miss Suffern doesn't last too late, may I come and see you when it's over? I shall be dining at my club, and I'll call you up at about ten, if I may. I'm off to Chicago on business to-morrow morning, and it would be a satisfaction to know, before I start, that your cousin's been able to reassure you, as I know she will."

He spoke with a shy deliberateness that, even to Mrs. Lidcote's troubled perceptions, sounded a long-silenced note of feeling. Perhaps the breaking down of the barrier of reticence between them had released unsuspected emotions in both. The tone of his appeal moved her curiously and loosened the tight strain of her fears.

"Oh, yes, come—do come," she said, rising. The huge threat of New York was imminent now, dwarfing, under long reaches of embattled masonry, the great deck she stood on and all the little specks of life it carried. One of them, drifting nearer, took the shape of her maid, followed by luggage-laden stewards, and signing to her that it was time to go below. As they descended to the main deck, the throng swept her against Mrs. Lorin Boulger's shoulder, and she heard the ambassadress call out to some one, over the vexed sea of hats: "So sorry! I should have been delighted, but I've promised to spend Sunday with some friends at Lenox."

II.

Susy Suffern's explanation did not end till after ten o'clock, and she had just gone when Franklin Ide, who, complying with an old New York tradition, had caused himself to be preceded by a long white box of roses, was shown into Mrs. Lidcote's sitting-room.

He came forward with his shy half-humorous smile and, taking her hand, looked at her for a moment without speaking.

"It's all right," he then pronounced.

Mrs. Lidcote returned his smile. "It's extraordinary. Everything's changed. Even Susy has changed; and you know the extent to which Susy used to represent the old New York. There's no old New York left, it seems. She talked in the most amazing way. She snaps her fingers at the Purshes. She told me—*me,* that every woman had a right to happiness and that self-expression was the highest duty. She accused me of misunderstanding Leila; she said my point of view was conventional! She was bursting with pride at having been in the secret, and wearing a brooch that Wilbour Barkley'd given her!"

Franklin Ide had seated himself in the arm-chair she had pushed forward for him under the electric chandelier. He threw back his head and laughed. "What did I tell you?"

"Yes; but I can't believe that Susy's not mistaken. Poor dear, she has the habit of lost causes; and she may feel that, having stuck to me, she can do no less than stick to Leila."

"But she didn't—did she?—openly defy the world for you? She didn't snap her fingers at the Lidcotes?"

Mrs. Lidcote shook her head, still smiling. "No. It was enough to defy *my* family. It was doubtful at one time if they would tolerate her seeing me, and she almost had to disinfect herself after each visit. I believe that at first my sister-in-law wouldn't let the girls come down when Susy dined with her."

"Well, isn't your cousin's present attitude the best possible proof that times have changed?"

"Yes, yes; I know." She leaned forward from her sofa-corner, fixing her eyes on his thin kindly face, which gleamed on her indistinctly through her tears. "If it's true, it's—it's dazzling. She says Leila's perfectly happy. It's as if an angel had gone about lifting gravestones, and the buried people walked again, and the living didn't shrink from them."

"That's about it," he assented.

She drew a deep breath, and sat looking away from him down the long perspective of lamp-fringed streets over which her windows hung.

"I can understand how happy you must be," he began at length.

She turned to him impetuously. "Yes, yes; I'm happy. But I'm lonely, too—lonelier than ever. I didn't take up much room in the world before; but now—where is there a corner for me? Oh, since I've begun to confess myself, why shouldn't I go on? Telling you this lifts a gravestone from *me!* You see, before this, Leila needed me. She was unhappy, and I knew it, and though we hardly ever talked of it I felt that, in a way, the thought that I'd been through the same thing, and down to the dregs of it, helped her. And her needing me helped *me.* And when the news of her marriage came my first thought was that now she'd need me more than ever, that she'd have no one but me to turn to. Yes, under all my distress there was a fierce joy in that. It was so new and wonderful to feel again that there was one person who wouldn't be able to get on without me! And now what you and Susy tell me seems to have taken my child from me; and just at first that's all I can feel."

"Of course it's all you feel." He looked at her musingly. "Why didn't Leila come to meet you?"

"That was really my fault. You see, I'd cabled that I was not sure of being able to get off on the *Utopia,* and apparently my second cable was delayed, and when she received it she'd already asked some people over Sunday—one or two of her old friends, Susy says. I'm so glad they should have wanted to go to her at once; but naturally I'd rather have been alone with her."

"You still mean to go, then?"

"Oh, I must. Susy wanted to drag me off to Ridgefield with her over Sunday, and Leila sent me word that of course I might go if I wanted to, and that I was not to think of her; but I know how disappointed she would be. Susy said she was afraid I might be upset at her having people to stay, and that, if I minded, she wouldn't urge me to come. But if *they* don't mind, why should I? And of course, if they're willing to go to Leila it must mean—"

"Of course. I'm glad you recognize that," Franklin Ide exclaimed abruptly. He stood up and went over to her, taking her hand with one of his quick gestures. "There's something I want to say to you," he began—

. . .

The next morning, in the train, through all the other contending thoughts in Mrs. Lidcote's mind there ran the warm undercurrent of what Franklin Ide had wanted to say to her.

He had wanted, she knew, to say it once before, when, nearly eight years earlier, the hazard of meeting at the end of a rainy autumn in a deserted Swiss hotel had thrown them for a fortnight into unwonted propinquity. They had walked and talked together, borrowed each other's books and newspapers, spent the long chill evenings over the fire in the dim lamplight of her little pitch-pine sitting-room; and she had been wonderfully comforted by his presence, and hard frozen places in her had melted, and she had known that she would be desperately sorry when he went. And then, just at the end, in his odd indirect way, he had let her see that it rested with her to have him stay. She could still relive the sleepless night she had given to that discovery. It was preposterous, of course, to think of repaying his devotion by accepting such a sacrifice; but how find reasons to convince him? She could not bear to let him think her less touched, less inclined to him than she was: the generosity of his love deserved that she should repay it with the truth. Yet how let him see what she felt, and yet refuse what he offered? How confess to him what had been on her lips when he made the offer: "I've seen what it did to one man; and there must never, never be another"? The tacit ignoring of her past had been the element in which their friendship lived, and she could not suddenly, to him of all men, begin to talk of herself like a guilty woman in a play. Somehow, in the end, she had managed it, had averted a direct explanation, had made him understand that her life was over, that she existed only for her daughter, and that a more definite word from him would have been almost a breach of delicacy. She was so used to behaving as if her life were over! And, at any rate, he had taken her hint, and she had been able to spare her sensitiveness and his. The next year, when he came to Florence to see her, they met again in the old friendly way; and that till now had continued to be the tenor of their intimacy.

And now, suddenly and unexpectedly, he had brought up the question again, directly this time, and in such a form that she could not evade it: putting the renewal of his plea, after so long an interval, on the ground that, on her own showing, her chief argument against it no longer existed.

"You tell me Leila's happy. If she's happy, she doesn't need you—need you, that is, in the same way as before. You wanted, I know, to be always in reach, always free and available if she should suddenly call you to her or take refuge with you. I understood that—I respected it. I didn't urge my case because I saw it was useless. You couldn't, I understood well enough, have felt free to take such happiness as life with me might give you while she was unhappy, and, as you imagined, with no hope of release. Even then I didn't feel as you did about it; I understood better the trend of things here. But ten years ago the change hadn't really come; and I had no way of convincing you that it was coming. Still, I always fancied that Leila might not think her case was closed, and so I chose to think that ours wasn't either. Let me go on thinking so, at any rate, till you've seen her, and confirmed with your own eyes what Susy Suffern tells you."

III.

All through what Susy Suffern told and retold during their four-hours' flight to the hills this plea of Ide's kept coming back to Mrs. Lidcote. She did not yet know what she felt as to its bearing on her own fate, but it was something on which her confused thoughts could stay themselves amid the welter of new impressions, and she was inexpressibly glad that he had said what he had, and said it at that particular moment. It helped her to hold fast to her identity in the rush of strange names and new categories that her cousin's talk poured out on her.

With the progress of the journey Miss Suffern's communications grew more and more amazing. She was like a cicerone preparing the mind of an inexperienced traveller for the marvels about to burst on it.

"You won't know Leila. She's had her pearls reset. Sargent's to paint her. Oh, and I was to tell you that she hopes you won't mind being the least bit squeezed over Sunday. The house was built by Wilbour's father, you know, and it's rather old-fashioned—only ten spare bedrooms. Of course that's small for what they mean to do, and she'll show you the new plans they've had made. Their idea is to keep the present house as a wing. She told me to explain—she's so dreadfully sorry not to be able to give you a sitting-room just at first. They're thinking of Egypt for next winter, unless, of course, Wilbour gets his appointment. Oh, didn't she write you about that? Why, he wants Rome, you know—the second secretaryship. Or, rather, he wanted England; but Leila insisted that if they went abroad she must be near you. And of course what she says is law. Oh, they quite hope they'll get it. You see Horace's uncle is in the Cabinet,—one of the assistant secretaries,—and I believe he has a good deal of pull—"

"Horace's uncle? You mean Wilbour's, I suppose," Mrs. Lidcote interjected, with a gasp of which a fraction was given to Miss Suffern's flippant use of the language.

"Wilbour's? No, I don't. I mean Horace's. There's no bad feeling between them, I assure you. Since Horace's engagement was announced—you didn't know Horace was engaged? Why, he's marrying one of Bishop Thorbury's girls: the red-haired one who wrote the novel that every one's talking about, 'This Flesh of Mine.' They're to be married in the cathedral. Of course Horace *can,* because it was Leila who—but, as I say, there's not the *least* feeling, and Horace wrote himself to his uncle about Wilbour."

Mrs. Lidcote's thoughts fled back to what she had said to Ide the day before on the deck of the *Utopia.* "I didn't take up much room before, but now where is there a corner for me?" Where indeed in this crowded, topsy-turvey world, with its headlong changes and helter-skelter readjustments, its new tolerances and indifferences and accommodations, was there room for a character fashioned by slower, sterner processes and a life broken under their inexorable pressure? And then, in a flash, she viewed the chaos from a new angle, and order seemed to move upon the void. If the old processes were changed, her case was changed with them; she, too, was a part of the general readjustment, a tiny fragment of the new pattern worked out in bolder freer harmonies. Since her daughter had no penalty to pay, was not she herself released by the same stroke? The rich arrears of youth and joy were gone; but was there not time enough left to accumulate new stores of happiness? That, of course, was what Franklin Ide had felt and had meant her to feel. He had seen at once what the change in her daughter's situation would make in her view of her own. It was almost—wondrously enough!—as if Leila's folly had been the means of vindicating hers.

. . .

Everything else for the moment faded for Mrs. Lidcote in the glow of her daughter's embrace. It was unnatural, it was almost terrifying, to find herself standing on a strange threshold, under an unknown roof, in a big hall full of pictures, flowers, firelight, and hurrying servants, and in this spacious unfamiliar confusion to discover Leila, bareheaded, laughing, authoritative, with a strange young man jovially echoing her welcome and transmitting her orders; but once Mrs. Lidcote had her child on her breast, and her child's "It's all right, you old darling!" in her ears, every other feeling was lost in the deep sense of well-being that only Leila's hug could give.

The sense was still with her, warming her veins and pleasantly fluttering her heart, as she went up to her room after luncheon. A little constrained by the presence of visitors, and not altogether sorry to defer for a few hours the "long talk" with her daughter for which she somehow felt herself tremulously unready, she had withdrawn, on the plea of fatigue, to the bright luxurious bedroom into which Leila had again and again apologized for having been obliged to squeeze her. The room was bigger and finer than any in her small apartment in Florence; but it was not the standard of affluence implied in her daughter's tone about it that chiefly struck her, nor yet the finish and complexity of its appointments. It was the look it shared with the rest of the house, and with the perspective of the gardens beneath its windows, of being part of an "establishment"—of something solid, avowed, founded on sacraments and precedents and principles. There was nothing about the place, or about Leila and Wilbour, that suggested either passion or peril: their relation seemed as comfortable as their furniture and as respectable as their balance at the bank.

This was, in the whole confusing experience, the thing that confused Mrs. Lidcote most, that gave her at once the deepest feeling of security for Leila and the strongest sense of apprehension for herself. Yes, there was something oppressive in the completeness and compactness of Leila's well-being. Ide had been right: her daughter did not need her. Leila, with her first embrace, had unconsciously attested the fact in the same phrase as Ide himself and as the two young women with the hats. "It's all right, you old darling!" she had said: and her mother sat alone, trying to fit herself into the new scheme of things which such a certainty betokened.

Her first distinct feeling was one of irrational resentment. If such a change was to come, why had it not come sooner? Here was she, a woman not yet old, who had paid with the best years of her life for the theft of the happiness that her daughter's contemporaries were taking as their due. There was no sense, no sequence, in it. She had had what she wanted, but she had had to pay too much for it. She had had to pay the last bitterest price of learning that love has a price: that it is worth so much and no more. She had known the anguish of watching the man she loved discover this first, and of reading the discovery in his eyes. It was a part of her history that she had not trusted herself to think of for a long time past: she always took a big turn about that haunted corner. But now, at the sight of the young man downstairs, so openly and jovially Leila's, she was overwhelmed at the senseless waste of her own adventure, and wrung with the irony of perceiving that the success or failure of the deepest human experiences may hang on a matter of chronology.

Then gradually the thought of Ide returned to her. "I chose to think that our case wasn't closed," he had said. She had been deeply touched by that. To everyone else her case had been closed so long! *Finis* was scrawled all over her. But here was one man who had believed and waited, and what if what he believed in and waited for were coming true? If Leila's "all right" should really foreshadow hers?

As yet, of course, it was impossible to tell. She had fancied, indeed, when she entered the drawing-room before luncheon, that a too-sudden hush had fallen on the assembled group of Leila's friends, on the slender vociferous young women and the lounging golf-stockinged young men. They had all received her politely, with the kind of petrified politeness that may be either a tribute to age or a protest at laxity; but to them, of course, she must be an old woman because she was Leila's mother, and in a society so dominated by youth the mere presence of maturity was a constraint.

One of the young girls, however, had presently emerged from the group, and, attaching herself to Mrs. Lidcote, had listened to her with a blue gaze of admiration which gave the older woman a sudden happy consciousness of her long-forgotten social graces. It was agreeable to find herself attracting this young Charlotte Wynn, whose mother had been among her closest friends, and in whom something of the soberness and softness of the earlier manners had survived. But the little colloquy, broken up by the announcement of luncheon, could of course result in nothing more definite than this reminiscent emotion.

No, she could not yet tell how her own case was to be fitted into the new order of things; but there were more people—"older people" Leila had put it—arriving by the afternoon train, and that evening at dinner she would doubtless be able to judge. She began to wonder nervously who the new-comers might be. Probably she would be spared the embarrassment of finding old acquaintances among them; but it was odd that her daughter had mentioned no names.

Leila had proposed that, later in the afternoon, Wilbour should take her mother for a drive: she said she wanted them to have a "nice, quiet talk." But Mrs. Lidcote wished her talk with Leila to come first, and had, moreover, at luncheon, caught stray allusions to an impending tennis-match in which her son-in-law was engaged. Her fatigue had been a sufficient pretext for declining the drive, and she had begged Leila to think of her as peacefully resting in her room till such time as they could snatch their quiet moment.

"Before tea, then, you duck!" Leila with a last kiss had decided; and presently Mrs. Lidcote, through her open window, had heard the fresh loud voices of her daughter's visitors chiming across the gardens from the tennis-court.

IV.

Leila had come and gone, and they had had their talk. It had not lasted as long as Mrs. Lidcote wished, for in the middle of it Leila had been summoned to the telephone to receive an important message from town, and had sent word to her mother that she couldn't come back just then, as one of the young ladies had been called away unexpectedly and arrangements had to be made for her departure. But the mother and daughter had had almost an hour together, and Mrs. Lidcote was happy. She had never seen Leila so tender, so solicitous. The only thing that troubled her was the very excess of this solicitude, the exaggerated expression of her daughter's annoyance that their first moments together should have been marred by the presence of strangers.

"Not strangers to me, darling, since they're friends of yours," her mother had assured her.

"Yes; but I know your feeling, you queer wild mother. I know how you've always hated people." (*Hated people!* Had Leila forgotten why?) "And that's why I told Susy that if you preferred to go with her to Ridgefield on Sunday I should perfectly understand, and patiently wait for our good hug. But you didn't really mind them at luncheon, did you, dearest?"

Mrs. Lidcote, at that, had suddenly thrown a startled look at her daughter. "I don't mind things of that kind any longer," she had simply answered.

"But that doesn't console me for having exposed you to the bother of it, for having let you come here when I ought to have *ordered* you off to Ridgefield with Susy. If Susy hadn't been stupid she'd have made you go there with her. I hate to think of you up here all alone."

Again Mrs. Lidcote tried to read something more than a rather obtuse devotion in her daughter's radiant gaze. "I'm glad to have had a rest this afternoon, dear; and later—"

"Oh, yes, later, when all this fuss is over, we'll more than make up for it, sha'n't we, you precious darling?" And at this point Leila had been summoned to the telephone, leaving Mrs. Lidcote to her conjectures.

These were still floating before her in cloudy uncertainty when Miss Suffern tapped at the door.

"You've come to take me down to tea? I'd forgotten how late it was," Mrs. Lidcote exclaimed.

Miss Suffern, a plump peering little woman, with prim hair and a conciliatory smile, nervously adjusted the pendent bugles of her elaborate black dress. Miss Suffern was always in mourning, and always commemorating the demise of distant relatives by wearing the discarded wardrobe of their next of kin. "It isn't *exactly* mourning," she would say; "but it's the only stitch of black poor Julia had—and of course George was only my mother's step-cousin."

As she came forward Mrs. Lidcote found herself humorously wondering whether she were mourning Horace Pursh's divorce in one of his mother's old black satins.

"Oh, *did* you mean to go down for tea?" Susy Suffern peered at her, a little fluttered. "Leila sent me up to keep you company. She thought it would be cozier for you to stay here. She was afraid you were feeling rather tired."

"I was; but I've had the whole afternoon to rest in. And this wonderful sofa to help me."

"Leila told me to tell you that she'd rush up for a minute before dinner, after everybody had arrived; but the train is always dreadfully late. She's in despair at not giving you a sitting-room; she wanted to know if I thought you really minded."

"Of course I don't mind. It's not like Leila to think I should." Mrs. Lidcote drew aside to make way for the housemaid, who appeared in the doorway bearing a table spread with a bewildering variety of tea-cakes.

"Leila saw to it herself," Miss Suffern murmured as the door closed. "Her one idea is that you should feel happy here."

It struck Mrs. Lidcote as one more mark of the subverted state of things that her daughter's solicitude should find expression in the multiplicity of sandwiches and the piping-hotness of muffins; but then everything that had happened since her arrival seemed to increase her confusion.

The note of a motor-horn down the drive gave another turn to her thoughts. "Are those the new arrivals already?" she asked.

"Oh, dear, no; they won't be here till after seven." Miss Suffern craned her head from the window to catch a glimpse of the motor. "It must be Charlotte leaving."

"Was it the little Wynn girl who was called away in a hurry? I hope it's not on account of illness."

"Oh, no; I believe there was some mistake about dates. Her mother telephoned her that she was expected at the Stepleys', at Fishkill, and she had to be rushed over to Albany to catch a train."

Mrs. Lidcote meditated. "I'm sorry. She's a charming young thing. I hoped I should have another talk with her this evening after dinner."

"Yes, it's too bad." Miss Suffern's gaze grew vague. "You *do* look tired, you know," she continued, seating herself at the teatable and preparing to dispense its delicacies. "You must go straight back to your sofa and let me wait on you. The excitement has told on you more than you think, and you mustn't fight against it any longer. Just stay quietly up here and let yourself go. You'll have Leila to yourself on Monday."

Mrs. Lidcote received the tea-cup which her cousin proffered, but showed no other disposition to obey her injunctions. For a moment she stirred her tea in silence; then she asked: "Is it your idea that I should stay quietly up here till Monday?"

Miss Suffern set down her cup with a gesture so sudden that it endangered an adjacent plate of scones. When she had assured herself of the safety of the scones she looked up with a fluttered laugh. "Perhaps, dear, by to-morrow you'll be feeling differently. The air here, you know—"

"Yes, I know." Mrs. Lidcote bent forward to help herself to a scone. "Who's arriving this evening?" she asked.

Miss Suffern frowned and peered. "You know my wretched head for names. Leila told me—but there are so many—"

"So many? She didn't tell me she expected a big party."

"Oh, not big: but rather outside of her little group. And of course, as it's the first time, she's a little excited at having the older set."

"The older set? Our contemporaries, you mean?"

"Why—yes." Miss Suffern paused as if to gather herself up for a leap. "The Ashton Gileses," she brought out.

"The Ashton Gileses? Really? I shall be glad to see Mary Giles again. It must be eighteen years," said Mrs. Lidcote steadily.

"Yes," Miss Suffern gasped, precipitately refilling her cup.

"The Ashton Gileses; and who else?"

"Well, the Sam Fresbies. But the most important person, of course, is Mrs. Lorin Boulger."

"Mrs. Boulger? Leila didn't tell me she was coming."

"Didn't she? I suppose she forgot everything when she saw you. But the party was got up for Mrs. Boulger. You see, it's very important that she should—well, take a fancy to Leila and Wilbour; his being appointed to Rome virtually depends on it. And you know Leila insists on Rome in order to be near you. So she asked Mary Giles, who's intimate with the Boulgers, if the visit couldn't possibly be arranged; and Mary's cable caught Mrs. Boulger at Cherbourg. She's to be only a fortnight in America; and getting her to come directly here was rather a triumph."

"Yes; I see it was," said Mrs. Lidcote.

"You know, she's rather—rather fussy; and Mary was a little doubtful if—"

"If she would, on account of Leila?" Mrs. Lidcote murmured.

"Well, yes. In her official position. But luckily she's a friend of the Barkleys. And finding the Gileses and Fresbies here will make it all right. The times have changed!" Susy Suffern indulgently summed up.

Mrs. Lidcote smiled. "Yes; a few years ago it would have seemed improbable that I should ever again be dining with Mary Giles and Harriet Fresbie and Mrs. Lorin Boulger."

Miss Suffern did not at the moment seem disposed to enlarge upon this theme; and after an interval of silence Mrs. Lidcote suddenly resumed: "Do they know I'm here, by the way?"

The effect of her question was to produce in Miss Suffern an exaggerated access of peering and frowning. She twitched the tea-things about, fingered her bugles, and, looking at the clock, exclaimed amazedly: "Mercy! Is it seven already?"

"Not that it can make any difference, I suppose," Mrs. Lidcote continued. "But did Leila tell them I was coming?"

Miss Suffern looked at her with pain. "Why, you don't suppose, dearest, that Leila would do anything—"

Mrs. Lidcote went on: "For, of course, it's of the first importance, as you say, that Mrs. Lorin Boulger should be favorably impressed, in order that Wilbour may have the best possible chance of getting Rome."

"I *told* Leila you'd feel that, dear. You see, it's actually on *your* account—so that they may get a post near you—that Leila invited Mrs. Boulger."

"Yes, I see that." Mrs. Lidcote, abruptly rising from her seat, turned her eyes to the clock. "But, as you say, it's getting late. Oughtn't we to dress for dinner?"

Miss Suffern, at the suggestion, stood up also, an agitated hand among her bugles. "I do wish I could persuade you to stay up here this evening. I'm sure Leila'd be happier if you would. Really, you're much too tired to come down."

"What nonsense, Susy!" Mrs. Lidcote spoke with sudden sharpness, her hand stretched to the bell. "When do we dine? At half-past eight? Then I must really send you packing. At my age it takes time to dress."

Miss Suffern, thus projected toward the threshold, lingered there to repeat: "Leila'll never forgive herself if you make an effort you're not up to." But Mrs. Lidcote smiled on her without answering, and the icy light-wave propelled her through the door.

V.

Mrs. Lidcote, though she had made the gesture of ringing for her maid, had not done so.

When the door closed, she continued to stand motionless in the middle of her soft, spacious room. The fire which had been kindled at twilight danced on the brightness of silver and mirrors and sober gilding; and the sofa toward which she had been urged by Miss Suffern heaped up its cushions in inviting proximity to a table laden with new books and papers. She could not recall having ever been more luxuriously housed, or having ever had so strange a sense of being out alone, under the night, in a wind-beaten plain. She sat down by the fire and thought.

A knock on the door made her lift her head, and she saw her daughter on the threshold. The intricate ordering of Leila's fair hair and the flying folds of her dressing-gown showed that she had interrupted her dressing to hasten to her mother; but once in the room she paused a moment, smiling uncertainly, as though she had forgotten the object of her haste.

Mrs. Lidcote rose to her feet. "Time to dress, dearest? Don't scold, I sha'n't be late."

"To dress?" Leila stood before her with a puzzled look. "Why, I thought, dear—I mean, I hoped you'd decided just to stay here quietly and rest."

Her mother smiled. "But I've been resting all the afternoon!"

"Yes, but—you know you *do* look tired. And when Susy told me just now that you meant to make the effort—"

"You came to stop me?"

"I came to tell you that you needn't feel in the least obliged—"

"Of course. I understand that."

There was a pause during which Leila, vaguely averting herself from her mother's scrutiny, drifted toward the dressing-table and began to disturb the symmetry of the brushes and bottles laid out on it.

"Do your visitors know that I'm here?" Mrs. Lidcote suddenly went on.

"Do they—Of course—why, naturally," Leila rejoined, absorbed in trying to turn the stopper of a salts-bottle.

"Then won't they think it odd if I don't appear?"

"Oh, not in the least, dearest. I assure you they'll *all* understand." Leila laid down the bottle and turned back to her mother, her face alight with reassurance.

Mrs. Lidcote stood motionless, her head erect, her smiling eyes on her daughter's. "Will they think it odd if I *do?*"

Leila stopped short, her lips half parted to reply. As she paused, the colour stole over her bare neck, swept up to her throat, and burst into flame in her cheeks. Thence it sent its devastating crimson up to her very temples, to the lobes of her ears, to the edges of her eye-lids, beating all over her in fiery waves, as if fanned by some imperceptible wind.

Mrs. Lidcote silently watched the conflagration; then she turned away her eyes with a slight laugh. "I only meant that I was afraid it might upset the arrangement of your dinner-table if I didn't come down. If you can assure me that it won't, I believe I'll take you at your word and go back to this irresistible sofa." She paused, as if waiting for her daughter to speak; then she held out her arms. "Run off and dress, dearest; and don't have me on your mind." She clasped Leila close, pressing a long kiss on the last afterglow of her subsiding blush. "I do feel the least bit overdone, and if it won't inconvenience you to have me drop out of things, I believe I'll basely take to my bed and stay there till your party scatters. And now run off, or you'll be late; and make my excuses to them all."

VI.

The Barkleys' visitors had dispersed, and Mrs. Lidcote, completely restored by her two days' rest, found herself, on the following Monday alone with her children and Miss Suffern.

There was a note of jubilation in the air, for the party had "gone off" so extraordinarily well, and so completely, as it appeared, to the satisfaction of Mrs. Lorin Boulger, that Wilbour's early appointment to Rome was almost to be counted on. So certain did this seem that the prospect of a prompt reunion mitigated the distress with which Leila learned of her mother's decision to return almost immediately to Italy. No one understood this decision; it seemed to Leila absolutely unintelligible that Mrs. Lidcote should not stay on with them till their own fate was fixed, and Wilbour echoed her astonishment.

"Why shouldn't you, as Leila says, wait here till we can all pack up and go together?"

Mrs. Lidcote smiled her gratitude with her refusal. "After all, it's not yet sure that you'll be packing up."

"Oh, you ought to have seen Wilbour with Mrs. Boulger," Leila triumphed.

"No, you ought to have seen Leila with her," Leila's husband exulted.

Miss Suffern enthusiastically appended: "I *do* think inviting Harriet Fresbie was a stroke of genius!"

"Oh, we'll be with you soon," Leila laughed. "So soon that it's really foolish to separate."

But Mrs. Lidcote held out with the quiet firmness which her daughter knew it was useless to oppose. After her long months in India, it was really imperative, she declared, that she should get back to Florence and see what was happening to her little place there; and she had been so comfortable on the *Utopia* that she had a fancy to return by the same ship. There was nothing for it, therefore, but to acquiesce in her decision and keep her with them till the afternoon before the day of the *Utopia's* sailing. This arrangement fitted in with certain projects which, during her two days' seclusion, Mrs. Lidcote had silently matured. It had become to her of the first importance to get away as soon as she could, and the little place in Florence, which held her past in every fold of its curtains and between every page of its books, seemed now to her the one spot where that past would be endurable to look upon.

She was not unhappy during the intervening days. The sight of Leila's well-being, the sense of Leila's tenderness, were, after all, what she had come for; and of these she had had full measure. Leila had never been happier or more tender; and the contemplation of her bliss, and the enjoyment of her affection, were an absorbing occupation for her mother. But they were also a sharp strain on certain overtightened chords, and Mrs. Lidcote, when at last she found herself alone in the New York hotel to which she had returned the night before embarking, had the feeling that she had just escaped with her life from the clutch of a giant hand.

She had refused to let her daughter come to town with her; she had even rejected Susy Suffern's company. She wanted no viaticum but that of her own thoughts; and she let these come to her without shrinking from them as she sat in the same high-hung sitting-room in which, just a week before, she and Franklin Ide had had their memorable talk.

She had promised her friend to let him hear from her, but she had not kept her promise. She knew that he had probably come back from Chicago, and that if he learned of her sudden decision to return to Italy it would be impossible for her not to see him before sailing; and as she wished above all things not to see him she had kept silent, intending to send him a letter from the steamer.

There was no reason why she should wait till then to write it. The actual moment was more favorable, and the task, though not agreeable, would at least bridge over an hour of her lonely evening. She went up to the writing-table, drew out a sheet of paper and began to write his name. And as she did so, the door opened and he came in.

The words she met him with were the last she could have imagined herself saying when they had parted. "How in the world did you know that I was here?"

He caught her meaning in a flash. "You didn't want me to, then?" He stood looking at her. "Suppose I ought to have taken your silence as meaning that. But I happened to meet Mrs. Wynn, who is stopping here, and she asked me to dine with her and Charlotte, and Charlotte's young man. They told me they'd seen you arriving this afternoon, and I couldn't help coming up."

There was a pause between them, which Mrs. Lidcote at last surprisingly broke with the exclamation: "Ah, she *did* recognize me, then!"

"Recognize you?" He stated. "Why—"

"Oh, I saw she did, though she never moved an eyelid. I saw it by Charlotte's blush. The child has the prettiest blush. I saw that her mother wouldn't let her speak to me."

Ide put down his hat with an impatient laugh. "Hasn't Leila cured you of your delusions?"

She looked at him intently. "Then you don't think Margaret Wynn meant to cut me?"

"I think your ideas are absurd."

She paused for a perceptible moment without taking this up; then she said, at a tangent: "I'm sailing tomorrow early. I meant to write to you—there's the letter I'd begun."

Ide followed her gesture, and then turned his eyes back to her face. "You didn't mean to see me, then, or even to let me know that you were going till you'd left?"

"I felt it would be easier to explain to you in a letter—"

"What in God's name is there to explain?" She made no reply, and he pressed on: "It can't be that you're worried about Leila, for Charlotte Wynn told me she'd been there last week, and there was a big party arriving when she left: Fresbies and Gileses, and Mrs. Lorin Boulger—all the board of examiners! If Leila has passed *that*, she's got her degree."

Mrs. Lidcote had dropped down into a corner of the sofa where she had sat during their talk of the week before. "I was stupid," she began abruptly. "I ought to have gone to Ridgefield with Susy. I didn't see till afterward that I was expected to."

"You were expected to?"

"Yes. Oh, it wasn't Leila's fault. She suffered—poor darling; she was distracted. But she'd asked her party before she knew I was arriving."

"Oh, as to that—" Ide drew a deep breath of relief. "I can understand that it must have been a disappointment not to have you to herself just at first. But, after all, you were among old friends or their children: the Gileses and Fresbies—and little Charlotte Wynn." He paused a moment before the last name, and scrutinized her hesitatingly. "Even if they came at the wrong time, you must have been glad to see them all at Leila's."

She gave him back his look with a faint smile. "I didn't see them."

"You didn't see them?"

"No. That is, excepting little Charlotte Wynn. That child is exquisite. We had a talk before luncheon the day I arrived. But when her mother found out that I was staying in the house she telephoned her to leave immediately, and so I didn't see her again."

The colour rushed to Ide's sallow face. "I don't know where you get such ideas!"

She pursued, as if she had not heard him: "Oh, and I saw Mary Giles for a minute too. Susy Suffern brought her up to my room the last evening, after dinner, when all the others were at bridge. She meant it kindly—but it wasn't much use."

"But what were you doing in your room in the evening after dinner?"

"Why, you see, when I found out my mistake in coming,—how embarrassing it was for Leila, I mean—I simply told her I was very tired, and preferred to stay upstairs till the party was over."

Ide, with a groan, struck his hand against the arm of his chair. "I wonder how much of all this you simply imagined!"

"I didn't imagine the fact of Harriet Fresbie's not even asking if she might see me when she knew I was in the house. Nor of Mary Giles's getting Susy, at the eleventh hour, to smuggle her up to my room when the others wouldn't know where she'd gone; nor poor Leila's ghastly fear lest Mrs. Lorin Boulger, for whom the party was given, should guess I was in the house, and prevent her husband's giving Wilbour the second secretaryship because she'd been obliged to spend a night under the same roof with his mother-in-law!"

Ide continued to drum on his chair-arm with exasperated fingers. "You don't *know* that any of the acts you describe are due to the causes you suppose."

Mrs. Lidcote paused before replying, as if honestly trying to measure the weight of this argument. Then she said in a low tone: "I know that Leila was in an agony lest I should come down to dinner the first night. And it was for me she was afraid, not for herself. Leila is never afraid for herself."

"But the conclusions you draw are simply preposterous. There are narrow-minded women everywhere, but the women who were at Leila's knew perfectly well that their going there would give her a sort of social sanction, and if they were willing that she should have it, why on earth should they want to withhold it from you?"

"That's what I told myself a week ago, in this very room after my first talk with Susy Suffern." She lifted a misty smile to his anxious eyes. "That's why I listened to what you said to me the same evening, and why your arguments half convinced me, and made me think that what had been possible for Leila might not be impossible for me. If the new dispensation had come, why not for me as well as for the others? I can't tell you the flight my imagination took!"

Franklin Ide rose from his seat and crossed the room to a chair near her sofa-corner. "All I cared about was that it seemed—for the moment—to be carrying you toward me," he said.

"I cared about that, too. That's why I meant to go away without seeing you." They gave each other grave look for look. "Because, you see, I was mistaken," she went on. "We were both mistaken. You say it's preposterous that the women who didn't object to accepting Leila's hospitality should have objected to meeting me under her roof. And so it is; but I begin to understand why. It's simply that society is much too busy to revise its own judgments. Probably no one in the house with me stopped to consider that my case and Leila's were identical. They only remembered that I'd done something which, at the time I did it, was condemned by society. My case has been passed on and classified: I'm the woman who has been cut for nearly twenty years. The older people have half forgotten why, and the younger ones have never really known: it's simply become a tradition to cut me. And traditions that have lost their meaning are the hardest of all to destroy."

Ide sat motionless while she spoke. As she ended, he stood up with a short laugh and walked across the room to the window. Outside, the immense black prospect of New York, strung with its myriad lines of light, stretched away into the smoky edges of the night. He showed it to her with a gesture.

"What do you suppose such words as you've been using—'society,' 'tradition,' and the rest—mean to all the life out there?"

She came and stood by him in the window. "Less than nothing, of course. But you and I are not out there. We're shut up in a little tight round of habit and association, just as we're shut up in this room. Remember, I thought I'd got out of it once; but what really happened was that the other people went out, and left me in the same little room. The only difference was that I was there alone. Oh, I've made it habitable now, I'm used to it; but I've lost any illusions I may have had as to an angel's opening the door."

Ide again laughed impatiently. "Well, if the door won't open, why not let another prisoner in? At least it would be less of a solitude—"

She turned from the dark window back into the vividly lighted room.

"It would be more of a prison. You forget that I know all about that. We're all imprisoned, of course—all of us middling people, who don't carry our freedom in our brains. But we've accommodated ourselves to our different cells, and if we're moved suddenly into new ones we're likely to find a stone wall where we thought there was thin air, and to knock ourselves senseless against it. I saw a man do that once."

Ide, leaning with folded arms against the window-frame, watched her in silence as she moved restlessly about the room, gathering together some scattered books and tossing a handful of torn letters into the paper-basket. When she ceased, he rejoined: "All you say is based on preconceived theories. Why didn't you put them to the test by coming down to meet your old friends? Don't you see the inference they would naturally draw from your hiding yourself when they arrived? It looked as though you were afraid of them—or as though you hadn't forgiven them. Either way, you put them in the wrong instead of waiting to let them put you in the right. If Leila had buried herself in a desert do you suppose society would have gone to fetch her out? You say you were afraid for Leila and that she was afraid for you. Don't you see what all these complications of feeling mean? Simply that you were too nervous at the moment to let things happen naturally, just as you're too nervous now to judge them rationally." He paused and turned his eyes to her face. "Don't try to just yet. Give yourself a little more time. Give *me* a little more time. I've always known it would take time."

He moved nearer, and she let him have her hand. With the grave kindness of his face so close above her she felt like a child roused out of frightened dreams and finding a light in the room.

"Perhaps you're right—" she heard herself begin; then something within her clutched her back, and her hand fell away from him.

"I know I'm right: trust me," he urged. "We'll talk of this in Florence soon."

She stood before him, feeling with despair his kindness, his patience and his unreality. Everything he said seemed like a painted gauze let down between herself and the real facts of life; and a sudden desire seized her to tear the gauze into shreds.

She drew back and looked at him with a smile of superficial reassurance. "You *are* right—about not talking any longer now. I'm nervous and tired, and it would do no good. I brood over things too much. As you say, I must try not to shrink from people." She turned away and glanced at the clock. "Why, it's only ten! If I send you off I shall begin to brood again; and if you stay we shall go on talking about the same thing. Why shouldn't we go down and see Margaret Wynn for half an hour?"

She spoke lightly and rapidly, her brilliant eyes on his face. As she watched him, she saw it change, as if her smile had thrown a too vivid light upon it.

"Oh, no—not to-night!" he exclaimed.

"Not to-night? Why, what other night have I, when I'm off at dawn? Besides, I want to show you at once that I mean to be more sensible—that I'm not going to be afraid of people any more. And I should really like another glimpse of little Charlotte." He stood before her, his hand in his beard, with the gesture he had in moments of perplexity. "Come!" she ordered him gaily, turning to the door.

He followed her and laid his hand on her arm. "Don't you think—hadn't you better let me go first and see? They told me they'd had a tiring day at the dressmaker's. I daresay they have gone to bed."

"But you said they'd a young man of Charlotte's dining with them. Surely he wouldn't have left by ten? At any rate, I'll go down with you and see. It takes so long if one sends a servant first." She put him gently aside, and then paused as a new thought struck her. "Or wait; my maid's in the next room. I'll tell her to go and ask if Margaret will receive me. Yes, that's much the best way."

She turned back and went toward the door that led to her bedroom; but before she could open it she felt Ide's quick touch again.

"I believe—I remember now—Charlotte's young man was suggesting that they should all go out—to a music-hall or something of the sort. I'm sure—I'm positively sure that you won't find them."

Her hand dropped from the door, his dropped from her arm, and as they drew back and faced each other she saw the blood rise slowly through his sallow skin, redden his neck and ears, encroach upon the edges of his beard, and settle in dull patches under his kind troubled eyes. She had seen the same blush on another face, and the same impulse of compassion she had then felt made her turn her gaze away again.

A knock on the door broke the silence, and a porter put his head into the room.

"It's only just to know how many pieces there'll be to go down to the steamer in the morning."

With the words she felt that the veil of painted gauze was torn in tatters, and that she was moving again among the grim edges of reality.

"Oh, dear," she exclaimed, "I never *can* remember! Wait a minute; I shall have to ask my maid."

She opened her bedroom door and called out: "Annette!"

1911

SUI SIN FAR
(1865–1914)

Essayist, journalist, and short-fiction writer, Sui Sin Far was among a small number of writers of Chinese descent publishing in the United States before World War I. She incorporated ancient Chinese myths and fairy tales into stories that focus on the interactions of Chinese and whites in American cities at the turn of the century. Her first publications appeared during an especially racist period, when Chinese women were barred from entering the United States.

Sui Sin Far was born Edith Eaton in England in 1865. She was the eldest daughter of fourteen surviving children; her father, Edward Eaton, was English, and her mother, Grace Lotus Blossom Trefusius, was Chinese with an English education. Because Edward Eaton's family disapproved of his marriage, the family settled in 1874 in Montreal, where Edward struggled to support the family with his landscape painting. Despite their poverty, the Eaton family produced talented adults: one brother became a prosperous inventor, two sisters became painters, one sister became a lawyer, and Edith and her younger sister Winnifred became successful writers.

An early bout with rheumatic fever left Far ill much of her life. Upon a doctor's advice, she moved west, to San Francisco, in 1898. Two years later, she settled in Seattle, where for ten years she taught English to the Chinese immigrants whose lives she described in essays and stories.

Throughout her life and writing, Far confronted race discrimination against the Chinese. Whereas Winnifred wrote under the more acceptable Japanese-sounding name Onoto Watanna, Far chose to publish under her Chinese name. Indeed, the impetus behind much of her work was to correct misconceptions about Chinese Americans and to celebrate her cultural heritage.

Her first known publication, an article titled "A Trip in a Horse Car," appeared in 1888, and her last essay, called "Chinese Workmen in America," in July 1913. Throughout her career, she published in national magazines such as The Century, New England, Good Housekeeping, *and* The New York Evening Post. *Approximately twenty stories and one collection of stories,* Mrs. Spring Fragrance, *have been discovered in recent years. Scholars also believe that Far completed a novel, unfortunately lost after her death.*

An independent woman who decried sexism as well as racism, Far never married. In fact, she broke an engagement when her white fiancé suggested she disguise her ethnic background. After returning the engagement ring, she wrote in her diary: "Joy, oh, joy! I'm free once more. Never again shall I be untrue to my own heart. Never again will I allow any one to 'hound' or 'sneer' me into matrimony."

The story we have included first appeared in Mrs. Spring Fragrance. *"The Wisdom of the New" captures the clash of Chinese and American cultures that Far frequently described. By employing three points of view—that of the Chinese man, the Chinese woman, and the white woman—Far conveys gender as well as cultural differences.*

THE WISDOM OF THE NEW

I.

Old Li Wang, the peddler, who had lived in the land beyond the sea, was wont to declare: "For every cent that a man makes here, he can make one hundred there."

"Then, why," would ask Sankwei, "do you now have to move from door to door to fill your bowl with rice?"

And the old man would sigh and answer:

"Because where one learns how to make gold, one also learns how to lose it."

"How to lose it!" echoed Wou Sankwei. "Tell me all about it."

So the old man would tell stories about the winning and the losing, and the stories of the losing were even more fascinating than the stories of the winning.

"Yes, that was life," he would conclude. "Life, life."

At such times the boy would gaze across the water with wistful eyes. The land beyond the sea was calling to him.

The place was a sleepy little south coast town where the years slipped by monotonously. The boy was the only son of the man who had been the town magistrate.

Had his father lived, Wou Sankwei would have been sent to complete his schooling in another province. As it was he did nothing but sleep, dream, and occasionally get into mischief. What else was there to do? His mother and sister waited upon him hand and foot. Was he not the son of the house? The family income was small, scarcely sufficient for their needs; but there was no way by which he could add to it, unless, indeed, he disgraced the name of Wou by becoming a common fisherman. The great green waves lifted white arms of foam to him, and the fishes gleaming and lurking in the waters seemed to beseech him to draw them from the deep; but his mother shook her head.

"Should you become a fisherman," said she, "your family would lose face. Remember that your father was a magistrate."

When he was about nineteen there returned to the town one who had been absent for many years. Ching Kee, like old Li Wang, had also lived in the land beyond the sea; but unlike old Li Wang he had accumulated a small fortune.

" 'Tis a hard life over there," said he, "but 'tis worth while. At least one can be a man, and can work at what work comes his way without losing face." Then he laughed at Wou Sankwei's flabby muscles, at his soft, dark eyes, and plump, white hands.

"If you lived in America," said he, "you would learn to be ashamed of such beauty."

Whereupon Wou Sankwei made up his mind that he would go to America, the land beyond the sea. Better any life than that of a woman man.

He talked long and earnestly with his mother. "Give me your blessing," said he. "I will work and save money. What I send home will bring you many a comfort, and when I come back to China, it may be that I shall be able to complete my studies and obtain a degree. If not, my knowledge of the foreign language which I shall acquire, will enable me to take a position which will not disgrace the name of Wou."

His mother listened and thought. She was ambitious for her son whom she loved beyond all things on earth. Moreover, had not Sik Ping, a Canton merchant, who had visited the little town two moons ago, declared to Hum Wah, who traded in palm leaves, that the signs of the times were that the son of a cobbler, returned from America with the foreign language, could easier command a position of consequence than the son of a school-teacher unacquainted with any tongue but that of his motherland?

"Very well, " she acquiesced; "but before you go I must find you a wife. Only your son, my son, can comfort me for your loss."

II.

Wou Sankwei stood behind his desk, busily entering figures in a long yellow book. Now and then he would thrust the hair pencil with which he worked behind his ears and manipulate with deft fingers a Chinese counting machine. Wou Sankwei was the junior partner and bookkeeper of the firm of Leung Tang Wou & Co. of San Francisco. He had been in America seven years and had made good use of his time. Self-improvement had been his object and ambition, even more than the acquirement of a fortune, and who, looking at his fine, intelligent face and listening to his careful English, could say that he had failed?

One of his partners called his name. Some ladies wished to speak to him. Wou Sankwei hastened to the front of the store. One of his callers, a motherly looking woman, was the friend who had taken him under her wing shortly after his arrival in America. She had come to invite him to spend the evening with her and her niece, the young girl who accompanied her.

After his callers had left, Sankwei returned to his desk and worked steadily until the hour for his evening meal, which he took in the Chinese restaurant across the street from the bazaar. He hurried through with this, as before going to his friend's house, he had a somewhat important letter to write and mail. His mother had died a year before, and the uncle, to whom he was writing, had taken his wife and son into his home until such time as his nephew could send for them. Now the time had come.

Wou Sankwei's memory of the woman who was his wife was very faint. How could it be otherwise? She had come to him but three weeks before the sailing of the vessel which had brought him to America, and until then he had not seen her face. But she was his wife and the mother of his son. Ever since he had worked in America he had sent money for her support, and she had proved a good daughter to his mother.

As he sat down to write he decided that he would welcome her with a big dinner to his countrymen.

"Yes," he replied to Mrs. Dean, later on in the evening, "I have sent for my wife."

"I am so glad," said the lady. "Mr. Wou"—turning to her niece—"has not seen his wife for seven years."

"Deary me!" exclaimed the young girl "What a lot of letters you must have written!"

"I have not written her one," returned the young man somewhat stiffly.

Adah Charlton looked up in surprise. "Why—" she began.

"Mr. Wou used to be such a studious boy when I first knew him," interrupted Mrs. Dean, laying her hand affectionately upon the young man's shoulder. "Now, it is all business. But you won't forget the concert on Saturday evening."

"No, I will not forget," answered Wou Sankwei.

"He has never written to his wife," explained Mrs. Dean when she and her niece were alone, "because his wife can neither read nor write."

"Oh, isn't that sad!" murmured Adah Charlton, her own winsome face becoming pensive.

"They don't seem to think so. It is the Chinese custom to educate only boys. At least it has been so in the past. Sankwei himself is unusually bright. Poor boy! He began life here as a laundryman, and you may be sure that it must have been hard on him, for, as the son of a petty Chinese Government official, he had not been accustomed to manual labor. But Chinese character is wonderful; and now after seven years in this country, he enjoys a reputation as a business man amongst his countrymen, and is as up to date as any young American."

"But, Auntie, isn't it dreadful to think that a man should live away from his wife for so many years without any communication between them whatsoever except through others."

"It is dreadful to our minds, but not to theirs. Everything with them is a matter of duty. Sankwei married his wife as a matter of duty. He sends for her as a matter of duty."

"I wonder if it is all duty on her side," mused the girl.

Mrs. Dean smiled. "You are too romantic, Adah," said she. "I hope, however, that when she does come, they will be happy together. I think almost as much of Sankwei as I do of my own boy."

III.

Pau Lin, the wife of Wou Sankwei, sat in a corner of the deck of the big steamer, awaiting the coming of her husband. Beside her, leaning his little queued head against her shoulder, stood her six-year-old son. He had been ailing throughout the voyage, and his small face was pinched with pain. His mother, who had been nursing him every night since the ship had left port, appeared very worn and tired. This, despite the fact that with a feminine desire to make herself fair to see in the eyes of her husband, she had arrayed herself in a heavily embroidered purple costume, whitened her forehead and cheeks with powder, and tinted her lips with carmine.

He came at last, looking over and beyond her. There were two others of her country-women awaiting the men who had sent for them, and each had a child, so that for a moment he seemed somewhat bewildered. Only when the ship's officer pointed out and named her, did he know her as his. Then he came forward, spoke a few words of formal welcome, and, lifting the child in his arms, began questioning her as to its health.

She answered in low monosyllables. At his greeting she had raised her patient eyes to his face—the face of the husband whom she had not seen for seven long years—then the eager look of expectancy which had crossed her own faded away, her eyelids drooped, and her countenance assumed an almost sullen expression.

"Ah, poor Sankwei!" exclaimed Mrs. Dean, who with Adah Charlton stood some little distance apart from the family group.

"Poor wife!" murmured the young girl. She moved forward and would have taken in her own white hands the ringed ones of the Chinese woman, but the young man gently restrained her. "She cannot understand you," said he. As the young girl fell back, he explained to his wife the presence of the stranger women. They were here to bid her welcome; they were kind and good and wished to be her friends as well as his.

Pau Lin looked away. Adah Charlton's bright face, and the tone in her husband's voice when he spoke to the young girl, aroused a suspicion in her mind—a suspicion natural to one who had come from a land where friendship between a man and a woman is almost unknown.

"Poor little thing! How shy she is!" exclaimed Mrs. Dean.

Sankwei was glad that neither she nor the young girl understood the meaning of the averted face.

Thus began Wou Sankwei's life in America as a family man. He soon became accustomed to the change, which was not such a great one after all. Pau Lin was more of an accessory than a part of his life. She interfered not at all in his studies, his business, or his friends, and when not engaged in housework or sewing, spent most of her time in the society of one or the other of the merchants' wives who lived in the flats and apartments around her own. She kept up the Chinese custom of taking her meals after her husband or at a separate table, and observed faithfully the rule laid down for her by her late mother-in-law: to keep a quiet tongue in the presence of her man. Sankwei, on his part, was always kind and indulgent. He bought her silk dresses, hair ornaments, fans, and sweetmeats. He ordered her favorite dishes from the Chinese restaurant. When she wished to go out with her women friends, he hired a carriage, and shortly after her advent erected behind her sleeping room a chapel for the ancestral tablet and gorgeous goddess which she had brought over seas with her.

Upon the child both parents lavished affection. He was a quaint, serious little fellow, small for his age and requiring much care. Although naturally much attached to his mother, he became also very fond of his father who, more like an elder brother than a parent, delighted in playing all kinds of games with him, and whom he followed about like a little dog. Adah Charlton took a great fancy to him and sketched him in many different poses for a book on Chinese children which she was illustrating.

"He will be strong enough to go to school next year," said Sankwei to her one day. "Later on I intend to put him through an American college."

"What does your wife think of a Western training for him?" inquired the young girl.

"I have not consulted her about the matter," he answered. "A woman does not understand such things."

"A woman, Mr. Wou," declared Adah, "understands such things as well as and sometimes better than a man."

"An American woman, maybe," amended Sankwei; "but not a Chinese."

From the first Pau Lin had shown no disposition to become Americanized, and Sankwei himself had not urged it.

"I do appreciate the advantages of becoming westernized," said he to Mrs. Dean, whose influence and interest in his studies in America had helped him to become what he was, "but it is not as if she had come here as I came, in her learning days. The time for learning with her is over."

One evening, upon returning from his store, he found the little Yen sobbing pitifully.

"What!" he teased, "A man—and weeping."

The boy tried to hide his face, and as he did so, the father noticed that his little hand was red and swollen. He strode into the kitchen where Pau Lin was preparing the evening meal.

"The little child who is not strong—is there anything he could do to merit the infliction of pain?" he questioned.

Pau Lin faced her husband. "Yes, I think so," said she.

"What?"

"I forbade him to speak the language of the white women, and he disobeyed me. He had words in that tongue with the white boy from the next street."

Sankwei was astounded.

"We are living in the white man's country," said he. "The child will have to learn the white man's language."

"Not my child," answered Pau Lin.

Sankwei turned away from her. "Come, little one," said he to his son, "we will take supper tonight at the restaurant, and afterwards Yen shall see a show."

Pau Lin laid down the dish of vegetables which she was straining and took from a hook a small wrap which she adjusted around the boy.

"Now go with thy father," said she sternly.

But the boy clung to her—to the hand which had punished him. "I will sup with you," he cried, "I will sup with you."

"Go," repeated his mother, pushing him from her. And as the two passed over the threshold, she called to the father: "Keep the wrap around the child. The night air is chill."

Late that night, while father and son were peacefully sleeping, the wife and mother arose, and lifting gently the unconscious boy, bore him into the next room where she sat down with him in a rocker. Waking, he clasped his arms around her neck. Backwards and forwards she rocked him, passionately caressing the wounded hand and crooning and crying until he fell asleep again.

The first chastisement that the son of Wou Sankwei had received from his mother, was because he had striven to follow in the footsteps of his father and use the language of the stranger.

"You did perfectly right," said old Sien Tau the following morning, as she leaned over her balcony to speak to the wife of Wou Sankwei. "Had I again a son to rear, I should see to it that he followed not after the white people."

Sien Tau's son had married a white woman, and his children passed their grandame on the street without recognition.

"In this country, she is most happy who has no child," said Lae Choo, resting her elbow upon the shoulder of Sien Tau. "A Toy, the young daughter of Lew Wing, is as bold and free in her ways as are the white women, and her name is on all the men's tongues. What prudent man of our race would take her as wife?"

"One needs not to be born here to be made a fool of," joined in Pau Lin, appearing at another balcony door. "Think of Hum Wah. From sunrise till midnight he worked for fourteen years, then a white man came along and persuaded from him every dollar, promising to return double-fold within the moon. Many moons have risen and waned, and Hum Wah still waits on this side of the sea for the white man and his money. Meanwhile, his father and mother, who looked long for his coming, have passed beyond returning."

"The new religion—what trouble it brings!" exclaimed Lae Choo. "My man received word yestereve that the good old mother of Chee Ping—he who was baptized a Christian at the last baptizing in the Mission around the corner—had her head secretly severed from her body by the steadfast people of the village, as soon as the news reached there. 'Twas the first violent death in the records of the place. This happened to the mother of one of the boys attending the Mission corner of my street."

"No doubt, the poor old mother, having lost face, minded not so much the losing of her head," sighed Pau Lin. She gazed below her curiously. The American Chinatown held a strange fascination for the girl from the seacoast village. Streaming along the street was a motley throng made up of all nationalities. The sing-song voices of girls whom respectable merchants' wives shudder to name, were calling to one another from high balconies up shadowy alleys. A fat barber was laughing hilariously at a drunken white man who had fallen into a gutter; a withered old fellow, carrying a bird in a cage, stood at the corner entreating passersby to have a good fortune told; some children were burning punk on the curbstone. There went by a stalwart Chief of the Six Companies engaged in earnest confab with a yellow-robed priest from the joss house. A Chinese dressed in the latest American style and a very blond woman, laughing immoderately, were entering a Chinese restaurant together. Above all the hubbub of voices was heard the clang of electric cars and the jarring of heavy wheels over cobblestones.

Pau Lin raised her head and looked her thoughts at the old woman, Sien Tau.

"Yes," nodded the dame, " 'tis a mad place in which to bring up a child."

Pau Lin went back into the house, gave little Yen his noonday meal, and dressed him with care. His father was to take him out that afternoon. She questioned the boy, as she braided his queue, concerning the white women whom he visited with his father.

It was evening when they returned—Wou Sankwei and his boy. The little fellow ran up to her in high glee. "See, mother," said he, pulling off his cap, "I am like father now. I wear no queue."

The mother looked down upon him—at the little round head from which the queue, which had been her pride, no longer dangled.

"Ah!" she cried. "I am ashamed of you; I am ashamed!"

The boy stared at her, hurt and disappointed.

"Never mind, son," comforted his father. "It is all right."

Pau Lin placed the bowls of seaweed and chickens' liver before them and went back to the kitchen where her own meal was waiting. But she did not eat. She was saying within herself: "It is for the white woman he has done this; it is for the white woman!"

Later, as she laid the queue of her son within the trunk wherein lay that of his father, long since cast aside, she discovered a picture of Mrs. Dean, taken when the American woman had first become the teacher and benefactress of the youthful laundryman. She ran over with it to her husband. "Here," said she; "it is a picture of one of your white friends." Sankwei took it from her almost reverently. "That woman," he explained, "has been to me as a mother."

"And the young woman—the one with eyes the color of blue china—is she also as a mother?" inquired Pau Lin gently.

But for all her gentleness, Wou Sankwei flushed angrily.

"Never speak of her," he cried. "Never speak of her!"

"Ha, ha, ha! Ha, ha, ha!" laughed Pau Lin. It was a soft and not unmelodious laugh, but to Wou Sankwei it sounded almost sacrilegious.

Nevertheless, he soon calmed down. Pau Lin was his wife, and to be kind to her was not only his duty but his nature. So when his little boy climbed into his lap and besought his father to pipe him a tune, he reached for his flute and called to Pau Lin to put aside work for that night. He would play her some Chinese music. And Pau Lin, whose heart and mind, undiverted by change, had been concentrated upon Wou Sankwei ever since the day she had become his wife, smothered, for the time being, the bitterness in her heart, and succumbed to the magic of her husband's playing—a magic which transported her in thought to the old Chinese days, the old Chinese days whose impression and influence ever remain with the exiled sons and daughters of China.

IV.

That a man should take himself two wives, or even three, if he thought proper, seemed natural and right in the eyes of Wou Pau Lin. She herself had come from a home where there were two broods of children and where her mother and her father's other wife had eaten their meals together as sisters. In that home there had not always been peace; but each woman, at least, had the satisfaction of knowing that her man did not regard or treat the other woman as her superior. To each had fallen the common lot—to bear children to the man, and the man was master of all.

But, oh! the humiliation and shame of bearing children to a man who looked up to another woman—and a woman of another race—as a being above the common uses of women. There is a jealousy of the mind more poignant than any mere animal jealousy.

When Wou Sankwei's second child was two weeks old, Adah Charlton and her aunt called to see the little one, and the young girl chatted brightly with the father and played merrily with Yen, who was growing strong and merry. The American women would not, of course, converse with the Chinese; but Adah placed beside her a bunch of beautiful flowers, pressed her hand, and looked down upon her with radiant eyes. Secure in the difference of race, in the love of many friends, and in the happiness of her chosen work, no suspicion whatever crossed her mind that the woman whose husband was her aunt's protégé tasted everything bitter because of her.

After the visitors had gone, Pau Lin, who had been watching her husband's face while the young artist was in the room, said to him:

"She can be happy who takes all and gives nothing."

"Takes all and gives nothing," echoed her husband. "What do you mean?"

"She has taken all your heart," answered Pau Lin, "but she has not given you a son. It is I who have had that task."

"You are my wife," answered Wou Sankwei. "And she—oh! how can you speak of her so? She, who is as a pure water-flower—a lily!"

He went out of the room, carrying with him a little painting of their boy, which Adah Charlton had given to him as she bade him goodbye and which he intended showing with pride to the mother.

It was on the day that the baby died that Pau Lin first saw the little picture. It had fallen out of her husband's coat pocket when he lifted the tiny form in his arms and declared it lifeless. Even in that first moment of loss Pau Lin, stooping to pick up the portrait, had shrunk back in horror, crying: "She would cast a spell! She would cast a spell!"

She set her heel upon the face of the picture and destroyed it beyond restoration.

"You know not what you say and do," sternly rebuked Sankwei. He would have added more, but the mystery of the dead child's look forbade him.

"The loss of a son is as the loss of a limb," said he to his childless partner, as under the red glare of the lanterns they sat discussing the sad event.

"But you are not without consolation," returned Leung Tsao. "Your firstborn grows in strength and beauty."

"True," assented Wou Sankwei, his heavy thoughts becoming lighter.

And Pau Lin, in her curtained balcony overhead, drew closer her child and passionately cried:

"Sooner would I, O heart of my heart, that the light of thine eyes were also quenched, than that thou shouldst be contaminated with the wisdom of the new."

V.

The Chinese women friends of Wou Pau Lin gossiped among themselves, and their gossip reached the ears of the American woman friend of Pau Lin's husband. Since the days of her widowhood Mrs. Dean had devoted herself earnestly and whole-heartedly to the betterment of the condition and the uplifting of the young workingmen of Chinese race who came to America. Their appeal and need, as she had told her niece, was for closer acquaintance with the knowledge of the Western people, and *that* she had undertaken to give them, as far as she was able. The rewards and satisfactions of her work had been rich in some cases. Witness Wou Sankwei.

But the gossip had reached and much perturbed her. What was it that they said Wou Sankwei's wife had declared—that her little son should not go to an American school nor learn the American learning? Such bigotry and narrow-mindedness! How sad to think of! Here was a man who had benefited and profited by living in America, anxious to have his son receive the benefits of a Western education—and here was this man's wife opposing him with her ignorance and hampering him with her unreasonable jealousy.

Yes, she had heard that too. That Wou Sankwei's wife was jealous—jealous—and her husband the most moral of men, the kindest and the most generous.

"Of what is she jealous?" she questioned Adah Charlton. "Other Chinese men's wives, I have known, have had cause to be jealous, for it is true some of them are dreadfully immoral and openly support two or more wives. But not Wou Sankwei. And this little Pau Lin. She has everything that a Chinese woman could wish for."

A sudden flash of intuition came to the girl, rendering her for a moment speechless. When she did find words, she said:

"Everything that a Chinese woman could wish for, you say. Auntie, I do not believe there is any real difference between the feelings of a Chinese wife and an American wife. Sankwei is treating Pau Lin as he would treat her were he living in China. Yet it cannot be the same to her as if she were in their own country, where he would not come in contact with American women. A woman is a woman with intuitions and perceptions, whether Chinese or American, whether educated or uneducated, and Sankwei's wife must have noticed, even on the day of her arrival, her husband's manner towards us, and contrasted it with his manner towards her. I did not realize this before you told me that she was jealous. I only wish I had. Now, for all her ignorance I can see that the poor little thing became more of an American in that one half hour on the steamer than Wou Sankwei, for all your pride in him, has become in seven years."

Mrs. Dean rested her head on her hand. She was evidently much perplexed.

"What you say may be, Adah," she replied after a while; "but even so, it is Sankwei whom I have known so long, who has my sympathies. He has much to put up with. They have drifted seven years of life apart. There is no bond of interest or sympathy between them, save the boy. Yet never the slightest hint of trouble has come to me from his own lips. Before the coming of Pau Lin, he would confide in me every little thing that worried him, as if he were my own son. Now he maintains absolute silence as to his private affairs."

"Chinese principles," observed Adah, resuming her work. "Yes, I admit Sankwei has some puzzles to solve. Naturally, when he tries to live two lives—that of a Chinese and that of an American."

"He is compelled to that," retorted Mrs. Dean. "Is it not what we teach these Chinese boys—to become Americans? And yet, they are Chinese, and must, in a sense, remain so."

Adah did not answer.

Mrs. Dean sighed. "Poor, dear children, both of them," mused she. "I feel very low-spirited over the matter. I suppose you wouldn't care to come down town with me. I should like to have another chat with Mrs. Wing Sing."

"I shall be glad of the change," replied Adah, laying down her brushes.

Rows of lanterns suspended from many balconies shed a mellow, moonshiny radiance. On the walls and doors were splashes of red paper inscribed with hieroglyphics. In the narrow streets, booths decorated with flowers, and banners, and screens painted with immense figures of josses diverted the eye; while bands of musicians in gaudy silks, shrilled and banged, piped and fluted.

Everybody seemed to be out of doors—men, women, and children—and nearly all were in holiday attire. A couple of priests, in vivid scarlet and yellow robes, were kowtowing before an altar covered with rich cloth, embroidered in white and silver. Some Chinese students from the University of California stood looking on with comprehending, half-scornful interest; three girls lavishly dressed in colored silks, with their black hair plastered back from their faces and heavily bejewelled behind, chirped and chattered in a gilded balcony above them like birds in a cage. Little children, their hands full of half-moon-shaped cakes, were pattering about, with eyes, for all the hour, as bright as stars.

Chinatown was celebrating the Harvest Moon Festival, and Adah Charlton was glad that she had an opportunity to see something of the celebration before she returned East. Mrs. Dean, familiar with the Chinese people and the mazes of Chinatown, led her around fearlessly, pointing out this and that object of interest and explaining to her its meaning. Seeing that it was a gala night, she had abandoned her idea of calling upon the Chinese friend.

Just as they turned a corner leading up to the street where Wou Sankwei's place of business and residence was situated, a pair of little hands grasped Mrs. Dean's skirt and a delighted little voice piped: "See me! See me!" It was little Yen, resplendent in mauve-colored pantaloons and embroidered vest and cap. Behind him was a tall man whom both women recognized.

"How do you happen to have Yen with you?" Adah asked.

"His father handed him over to me as a sort of guide, counsellor, and friend. The little fellow is very amusing."

"See over here," interrupted Yen. He hopped over the alley to where the priests stood by the altar. The grown people followed him.

"What is that man chanting?" asked Adah. One of the priests had mounted a table, and with arms outstretched towards the moon sailing high in the heavens, seemed to be making some sort of an invocation.

Her friend listened for some moments before replying:

"It is sort of apotheosis of the moon. I have heard it on a like occasion in Hankow, and the Chinese *bonze* who officiated gave me a translation. I almost know it by heart. May I repeat it to you?"

Mrs. Dean and Yen were examining the screen with the big josses.

"Yes, I should like to hear it," said Adah.

"Then fix your eyes upon Diana."

"Dear and lovely moon, as I watch thee pursuing thy solitary course o'er the silent heavens, heart-easing thoughts steal o'er me and calm my passionate soul. Thou art so sweet, so serious, so serene, that thou causest me to forget the stormy emotions which crash like jarring discords across the harmony of life, and bringest to my memory a voice scarce ever heard amidst the warring of the world—love's low voice.

"Thou art so peaceful and so pure that it seemeth as if naught false or ignoble could dwell beneath thy gentle radiance, and that earnestness—even the earnestness of genius—must glow within the bosom of him on whose head thy beams fall like blessings.

"The magic of thy sympathy disburtheneth me of many sorrows, and thoughts, which, like the songs of the sweetest sylvan singer, are too dear and sacred for the careless ears of day, gush forth with unconscious eloquence when thou art the only listener.

"Dear and lovely moon, there are some who say that those who dwell in the sunlit fields of reason should fear to wander through the moonlit valleys of imagination; but I, who have ever been a pilgrim and a stranger in the realm of the wise, offer to thee the homage of a heart which appreciates that thou graciously shinest—even on the fool."

"Is that really Chinese?" queried Adah.

"No doubt about it—in the main. Of course, I cannot swear to it word for word."

"I should think that there would be some reference to the fruits of the earth—the harvest. I always understood that the Chinese religion was so practical."

"Confucianism is. But the Chinese mind requires two religions. Even the most commonplace Chinese has yearnings for something above everyday life. Therefore, he combines with his Confucianism, Buddhism—or, in this country, Christianity."

"Thank you for the information. It has given me a key to the mind of a certain Chinese in whom Auntie and I are interested."

"And who is this particular Chinese in whom you are interested?"

"The father of the little boy who is with us tonight."

"Wou Sankwei! Why, here he comes with Lee Tong Hay. Are you acquainted with Lee Tong Hay?"

"No, but I believe Aunt is. Plays and sings in vaudeville, doesn't he?"

"Yes: he can turn himself into a German, a Scotchman, an Irishman, or an American, with the greatest ease, and is as natural in each character as he is as a Chinaman. Hello, Lee Tong Hay."

"Hello, Mr. Stimson."

While her friend was talking to the lively young Chinese who had answered his greeting, Adah went over to where Wou Sankwei stood speaking to Mrs. Dean.

"Yen begins school next week," said her aunt, drawing her arm within her own. It was time to go home.

Adah made no reply. She was settling her mind to do something quite out of the ordinary. Her aunt often called her romantic and impractical. Perhaps she was.

VI.

"Auntie went out of town this morning," said Adah Charlton. "I phoned for you to come up, Sankwei, because I wished to have a personal and private talk with you."

"Any trouble, Miss Adah?" inquired the young merchant. "Anything I can do for you?"

Mrs. Dean often called upon him to transact little business matters for her or to consult with him on various phases of her social and family life.

"I don't know what I would do without Sankwei's head to manage for me," she often said to her niece.

"No," replied the girl, "you do too much for us. You always have, ever since I've known you. It's a shame for us to have allowed you."

"What are you talking about, Miss Adah? Since I came to America your aunt has made this house like a home to me, and, of course, I take an interest in it and like to do anything for it that a man can. I am always happy when I come here."

"Yes. I know you are, poor old boy," said Adah to herself.

Aloud she said: "I have something to say to you which I would like you to hear. Will you listen, Sankwei?"

"Of course I will," he answered.

"Well then," went on Adah, "I asked you to come here today because I have heard that there is trouble at your house and that your wife is jealous of you."

"Would you please not talk about that, Miss Adah? It is a matter which you cannot understand."

"You promised to listen and heed. I do understand, even though I cannot speak to your wife nor find out what she feels and thinks. I know you Sankwei, and I can see just how the trouble has arisen. As soon as I heard that your wife was jealous I knew why she was jealous."

"Why?" he queried.

"Because," she answered unflinchingly, "you are thinking far too much of other women."

"Too much of other women?" echoed Sankwei dazedly. "I did not know that."

"No, you didn't. That is why I am telling you. But you are, Sankwei. And you are becoming too Americanized. My aunt encourages you to become so, and she is a good woman, with the best and highest of motives; but we are all liable to make mistakes, and it is a mistake to try and make a Chinese man into an American—if he has a wife who is to remain as she always has been. It would be different if you were not married ad were a man free to advance. But you are not."

"What am I to do then, Miss Adah? You say that I think too much of other women besides her, and that I am too much Americanized. What can I do about it now that it is so?"

"First of all you must think of your wife. She has done for you what no American woman would do—came to you to be your wife, love you and serve you without even knowing you—took you on trust altogether. You must remember that for many years she was chained in a little cottage to care for your ailing and aged mother—a hard task indeed for a young girl. You must remember that you are the only man in the world to her, and that you have always been the only one that she has ever cared for. Think of her during all the years you are here, living a lonely hard-working life—a baby and an old woman her only companions. For this, she had left all her own relations. No American woman would have sacrificed herself so.

"And, now, what has she? Only you and her housework. The white woman reads, plays, paints, attends concerts, entertainments, lectures, absorbs herself in the work she likes, and in the course of her life thinks of and cares for a great many people. She has much to make her happy besides her husband. The Chinese woman has him only."

"And her boy."

"Yes, her boy," repeated Adah Charlton, smiling in spite of herself, but lapsing into seriousness the moment after. "There's another reason for you to drop the American for a time and go back to being a Chinese. For the sake of your darling little boy, you and your wife should live together kindly and cheerfully. That is much more important for his welfare than that he should go to the American school and become Americanized."

"It is my ambition to put him through both American and Chinese schools."

"But what he needs most of all is a loving mother."

"She loves him all right."

"Then why do you not love her as you should? If I were married I would not think my husband loved me very much if he preferred spending his evenings in the society of other women than in mine, and was so much more polite and deferential to other women than he was to me. Can't you understand now why your wife is jealous?"

Wou Sankwei stood up.

"Goodbye," said Adah Charlton, giving him her hand.

"Goodbye," said Wou Sankwei.

Had he been a white man, there is no doubt that Adah Charlton's little lecture would have had a contrary effect from what she meant it to have. At least, the lectured would have been somewhat cynical as to her sincerity. But Wou Sankwei was not a white man. He was a Chinese, and did not see any reason for insincerity in a matter as important as that which Adah Charlton had brought before him. He felt himself exiled from Paradise, yet it did not occur to him to question, as a white man would have done, whether the angel with the flaming sword had authority for her action. Neither did he lay the blame for things gone wrong upon any woman. He simply made up his mind to make the best of what was.

VII.

It had been a peaceful week in the Wou household—the week before little Yen was to enter the American school. So peaceful indeed that Wou Sankwei had begun to think that his wife was reconciled to his wishes with regard to the boy. He whistled softly as he whittled away at a little ship he was making for him. Adah Charlton's suggestions had set coursing a train of thought which he curved around Pau Lin so closely that he had decided that, should she offer any further opposition to the boy's attending the American school, he would not insist upon it. After all, though the American language might be useful during this century, the wheel of the world would turn again, and then it might not be necessary at all. Who could tell? He came very near to expressing himself thus to Pau Lin.

And now it was the evening before the morning that little Yen was to march away to the American school. He had been excited all day over the prospect, and to calm him, his father finally told him to read aloud a little story from the Chinese book which he had given him on his first birthday in America and which he had taught him to read. Obediently the little fellow drew his stool to his mother's side and read in his childish sing-song the story of an irreverent lad who came to great grief because he followed after the funeral of his grandfather and regaled himself on the crisply roasted chickens and loose-skinned oranges which were left on the grave for the feasting of the spirit.

Wou Sankwei laughed heartily over the story. It reminded him of some of his own boyish escapades. But Pau Lin stroked silently the head of the little reader, and seemed lost in reverie.

A whiff of fresh salt air blew in from the Bay. The mother shivered, and Wou Sankwei, looking up from the fastening of the boat's rigging, bade Yen close the door. As the little fellow came back to his mother's side, he stumbled over her knee.

"Oh, poor mother!" he exclaimed with quaint apology. " 'Twas the stupid feet, not Yen."

"So," she replied, curling her arm around his neck, " 'tis always the feet. They are to the spirit as the cocoon to the butterfly. Listen, and I will sing you the song of the Happy Butterfly."

She began singing the old Chinese ditty in a fresh birdlike voice. Wou Sankwei, listening, was glad to hear her. He liked having everyone around him cheerful and happy. That had been the charm of the Dean household.

The ship was finished before the little family retired. Yen examined it, critically at first, then exultingly. Finally, he carried it away and placed it carefully in the closet where he kept his kites, balls, tops, and other treasures. "We will set sail with it tomorrow after school," said he to his father, hugging gratefully that father's arm.

Sankwei rubbed the little round head. The boy and he were great chums.

What was that sound which caused Sankwei to start from his sleep? It was just on the border land of night and day, an unusual time for Pau Lin to be up. Yet, he could hear her voice in Yen's room. He raised himself on his elbow and listened. She was softly singing a nursery song about some little squirrels and a huntsman. Sankwei wondered at her singing in that way at such an hour. From where he lay he could just perceive the child's cot and the silent child figure laying motionless in the dim light. How very motionless! In a moment Sankwei was beside it.

The empty cup with its dark dregs told the tale.

The thing he loved the best in all the world—the darling son who had crept into his heart with his joyousness and beauty—had been taken from him—by her who had given.

Sankwei reeled against the wall. The kneeling figure by the cot arose. The face of her was solemn and tender.

"He is saved," smiled she, "from the Wisdom of the New."

In grief too bitter for words the father bowed his head upon his hands.

"Why! Why!" queried Pau Lin, gazing upon him bewilderedly. "The child is happy. The butterfly mourns not o'er the shed cocoon."

Sankwei put up his shutters and wrote this note to Adah Charlton:

> I have lost my boy through an accident. I am returning to China with my wife whose health requires a change.

1912

MARY HUNTER AUSTIN
(1868–1934)

Mary Hunter Austin left her mark on literature with her nature writing and her tales of Native American culture. She published eight novels and three collections of stories.

Austin was born Mary Hunter in Carlinville, Illinois, on September 9, 1868. Her father, a prominent Carlinville lawyer, introduced her to the romantic poets and the American transcendentalists. Her mother, Susanna Hunter, educated her in politics. As the regional president of the Women's Christian Temperance Union, Susanna invited Frances Willard, a well-known feminist, to speak at the Union's ninth annual convention in Carlinville. Impressed by Willard's analysis of marriage and politics, the fourteen-year-old Mary Hunter became an active member of the Young Adults' Temperance Union. Thus began her lifelong interest in social and political reform.

Mary Hunter majored in science rather than literature at Blackburn College, overcoming her mother's objections by arguing that she could teach herself to write but needed someone else to teach her science. After college Mary, her mother, and her two brothers moved to a homestead in southern California. They settled in the Tejon Valley, an environment inhospitable to farming yet the inspiration for Mary's nature writing. In 1891 she married Stafford Wallace Austin.

Austin published her first story, "The Mother of Felipe," in San Francisco's Overland Monthly *magazine in 1892. In 1903 her highly acclaimed book* The Land of Little Rain *appeared. Her early writings brought her to the attention of William James and Charlotte Perkins Gilman and other members of the San Francisco literary circle. During this period, she separated from her husband and moved to an artists' community in Carmel, California, that included the writers George Sterling and Jack London. Though she enjoyed the company of these writers, she pointed out their sexism. "Like most males," she wrote to London, "you have no capacity for knowing superior women."*

After returning from a two-year European sojourn in 1910, Austin settled for twelve years in New York City. She frequently contributed to The Nation *and the* New Republic *and was prominent in New York literary circles. Disenchanted with the city and longing for a natural environment, she moved to Santa Fe, New Mexico, in 1922. Here she met the young photographer Ansel Adams, with whom she collaborated on* Taos Pueblo *(1930), a combination of her prose and his photographs.*

During the 1920s, Austin became a staunch advocate of Native Americans, in both art and politics. She argued in the Yale Review, *for example, that Native*

American dance drama was an important precursor to modern dance drama. In 1922, she fought to defeat the Bursum bill, which would have taken land away from Pueblo Indians in New Mexico. In The American Rhythm *(1923) she traced the influence of Native American rhythm on the American poetic tradition.*

The stories we have chosen reflect Austin's lifelong love for Native American people and culture and her interest in women's lives. "The Coyote-Spirit and the Weaving Woman" appeared first in Austin's 1910 collection The Basket Woman. *"Papago Wedding," first published in* American Mercury, *won the O. Henry prize for the best short story in 1925.*

THE COYOTE-SPIRIT AND THE WEAVING WOMAN

The Weaving Woman lived under the bank of the stony wash that cut through the country of the mesquite dunes. The Coyote-Spirit, which, you understand, is an Indian whose form has been changed to fit with his evil behavior, ranged from the Black Rock where the wash began to the white sands beyond Pahranagat; and the Goat-Girl kept her flock among the mesquites, or along the windy stretch of sage below the campoodie; but as the Coyote-Spirit never came near the wickiups by day, and the Goat-Girl went home the moment the sun dropped behind Pahranagat, they never met. These three are all that have to do with the story.

The Weaving Woman, whose work was the making of fine baskets of split willow and roots of yucca and brown grass, lived alone, because there was nobody found who wished to live with her, and because it was whispered among the wickiups that she was different from other people. It was reported that she had an infirmity of the eyes which caused her to see everything with rainbow fringes, bigger and brighter and better than it was. All her days were fruitful, a handful of pine nuts as much to make merry over as a feast; every lad who went by a-hunting with his bow at his back looked to be a painted brave, and every old woman digging roots as fine as a medicine man in all his feathers. All the faces at the campoodie, dark as the mingled sand and lava of the Black Rock country, deep lined with work and weather, shone for this singular old woman with the glory of the late evening light on Pahranagat. The door of her wickiup opened toward the campoodie with the smoke going up from cheerful hearths, and from the shadow of the bank where she sat to make baskets she looked down the stony wash where all the trails converged that led every way among the dunes, and saw an enchanted mesa covered with misty bloom and gentle creatures moving on trails that seemed to lead to the places where one had always wished to be.

Since all this was so, it was not surprising that her baskets turned out to be such wonderful affairs, and the tribesmen, though they winked and wagged their heads, were very glad to buy them for a haunch of venison or a bagful of mesquite meal. Sometimes, as they stroked the perfect curves of the bowls or traced out the patterns, they were heard to sigh, thinking how fine life would be if it were so rich and bright as she made it seem, instead of the dull occasion they had found it. There were some who even said it was a pity, since she was so clever at the craft, that the weaver was not more like other people, and no one thought to suggest that in that case her weaving would be no better than theirs. For all this the basket-maker did not care, sitting always happily at her weaving or wandering far into the desert in search of withes and barks and dyes, where the wild things showed her many a wonder hid from those who have not rainbow fringes to their eyes; and because she was not afraid of anything, she went farther and farther into the silent places until in the course of time she met the Coyote-Spirit.

Now a Coyote-Spirit, from having been a man, is continually thinking about men and wishing to be with them, and, being a coyote and of the wolf's breed, no sooner does he have his wish than he thinks of devouring. So as soon as this one had met the Weaving Woman he desired to eat her up, or to work her some evil according to the evil of his nature. He did not see any opportunity to begin at the first meeting, for on account of the infirmity of her eyes the woman did not see him as a coyote, but as a man, and let down her wicker water bottle for him to drink, so kindly that he was quite abashed. She did not seem in the least afraid of him, which is disconcerting even to a real coyote; though if he had been, she need not have been afraid of him in any case. Whatever pestiferous beast the Indian may think the dog of the wilderness, he has no reason to fear him except when by certain signs, as having a larger and leaner body, a sharper muzzle, and more evilly pointed ears, he knows him the soul of a bad-hearted man going about in that guise. There are enough of these Coyote-Spirits ranging in Mesquite Valley and over towards Funeral Mountains and about Pahranagat to give certain learned folk surmise as to whether there may not be a strange breed of wolves in that region; but the Indians know better.

When the Coyote-Spirit who had met the basket woman thought about it afterward, he said to himself that she deserved all the mischance that might come upon her for that meeting. "She knows," he said, "that this is my range, and whoever walks in a Coyote-Spirit's range must expect to take the consequences. She is not at all like the Goat-Girl."

The Coyote-Spirit had often watched the Goat-Girl from the top of Pahranagat, but because she was always in the open where no lurking-places were, and never far from the corn lands where the old men might be working, he had made himself believe he would not like that kind of a girl. Every morning he saw her come out of her leafy hut, loose the goats from the corral, which was all of cactus stems and broad leaves of prickly-pear, and lead them out among the wind-blown hillocks of sand under which the trunks of the mesquite flourished for a hundred years, and out of the tops of which the green twigs bore leaves and fruit; or along the mesa to browse on bitterbrush and the tops of scrubby sage. Sometimes she plaited willows for the coarser kinds of basketwork, or, in hot noonings while the flock dozed, worked herself collars and necklaces of white and red and turquoise-colored beads, and other times sat dreaming on the sand. But whatever she did, she kept far enough from the place of the Coyote-Spirit, who, now that he had met the Weaving Woman, could not keep his mind off her. Her hut was far enough from the campoodie so that every morning he went around by the Black Rock to see if she was still there, and there she sat weaving patterns in her baskets of all that she saw or thought. Now it would be the winding wash and the wattled huts beside it, now the mottled skin of the rattlesnake or the curled plumes of the quail.

At last the Coyote-Spirit grew so bold that when there was no one passing on the trail he would go and walk up and down in front of the wickiup. Then the Weaving Woman would look up from her work and give him the news of the season and the tribesmen in so friendly a fashion that he grew less and less troubled in his mind about working her mischief. He said in his evil heart that since the ways of such as he were known to the Indians,—as indeed they were, with many a charm and spell to keep them safe,—it could be no fault of his if they came to harm through too much familiarity. As for the Weaving Woman, he said, "She sees me as I am, and ought to know better," for he had not heard about the infirmity of her eyes.

Finally he made up his mind to ask her to go with him to dig for roots around the foot of Pahranagat, and if she consented,—and of course she did, for she was a friendly soul,—he knew in his heart what he would do. They went out by the mesa trail, and it was a soft and blossomy day of spring. Long wands of the creosote with shining fretted foliage were hung with creamy bells of bloom, and doves called softly from the Dripping Spring. They passed rows of owlets sitting by their burrows and saw young rabbits playing in their shallow forms. The Weaving Woman talked gayly as they went, as Indian women talk, with soft mellow voices and laughter breaking in between the words like smooth water flowing over stones. She talked of how the deer had shifted their feeding-grounds and of whether the quail had mated early that year as a sign of a good season, matters of which the Coyote-Spirit knew more than she, only he was not thinking of those things just then. Whenever her back was turned he licked his cruel jaws and whetted his appetite. They passed the level mesa, passed the tumbled fragments of the Black Rock and came to the sharp wall-sided cañons that showed the stars at noon from their deep wells of sombre shade, where no wild creature made its home and no birds ever sang. Then the Weaving Woman grew still at last because of the great stillness, and the Coyote-Spirit said in a hungry, whining voice,—

"Do you know why I brought you here?"

"To show me how still and beautiful the world is here," said the Weaving Woman, and even then she did not seem afraid.

"To eat you up," said the Coyote. With that he looked to see her fall quaking at his feet, and he had it in mind to tell her it was no fault but her own for coming so far astray with one of his kind, but the woman only looked at him and laughed. The sound of her laughter was like water in a bubbling spring.

"Why do you laugh?" said the Coyote, and he was so astonished that his jaws remained open when he had done speaking.

"How could you eat me?" said she. "Only wild beasts could do that."

"What am I, then?"

"Oh, you are only a man."

"I am a coyote," said he.

"Do you think I have no eyes?" said the woman. "Come!" For she did not understand that her eyes were different from other people's, what she really thought was that other people's were different from hers, which is quite another matter, so she pulled the Coyote-Spirit over to a rain-fed pool. In that country the rains collect in basins of the solid rock that grow polished with a thousand years of storm and give back from their shining side a reflection like a mirror. One such lay in the bottom of the black cañon, and the Weaving Woman stood beside it.

Now it is true of Coyote-Spirits that they are so only because of their behavior; not only have they power to turn themselves to men if they wish—but they do not wish, or they would not have become coyotes in the first place—but other people in their company, according as they think man-thoughts or beast-thoughts, can throw over them such a change that they have only to choose which they will be. So the basket-weaver contrived to throw the veil of her mind over the Coyote-Spirit, so that when he looked at himself in the pool he could not tell for the life of him whether he was most coyote or most man, which so frightened him that he ran away and left the Weaving Woman to hunt for roots alone. He ran for three days and nights, being afraid of himself, which is the worst possible fear, and then ran back to see if the basket-maker had not changed her mind. He put his head in at the door of her wickiup.

"Tell me, now, am I a coyote or a man?"

"Oh, a man," said she, and he went off to Pahranagat to think it over. In a day or two he came back.

"And what now?" he said.

"Oh, a man, and I think you grow handsomer every day."

That was really true, for what with her insisting upon it and his thinking about it, the beast began to go out of him and the man to come back. That night he went down to the campoodie to try and steal a kid from the corral, but it occurred to him just in time that a man would not do that, so he went back to Pahranagat and ate roots and berries instead, which was a true sign that he had grown into a man again. Then there came a day when the Weaving Woman asked him to stop at her hearth and eat. There was a savory smell going up from the cooking-pots, cakes of mesquite meal baking in the ashes, and sugary white buds of the yucca palm roasting on the coals. The man who had been a coyote lay on a blanket of rabbit skin and heard the cheerful snapping of the fire. It was all so comfortable and bright that somehow it made him think of the Goat-Girl.

"That is the right sort of a girl," he said to himself. "She has always stayed in the safe open places and gone home early. She should be able to tell me what I am," for he was not quite sure, and since he had begun to walk with men a little, he had heard about the Weaving Woman's eyes.

Next day he went out where the flock fed, not far from the corn lands, and Goat-Girl did not seem in the least afraid of him. So he went again, and the third day he said,—

"Tell me what I seem to you."

"A very handsome man," said she.

"Then will you marry me?" said he; and when the Goat-Girl had taken time to think about it she said yes, she thought she would.

Now, when the man who had been a coyote lay on the blanket of the Weaving Woman's wickiup, he had taken notice how it was made of willows driven into the ground around a pit dug in the earth, and the poles drawn together at the top, and thatched with brush, and he had tried at the foot of Pahranagat until he had built another like it; so when he had married the Goat-Girl, after the fashion of her tribe, he took her there to live. He was not now afraid of anything except that his wife might get to know that he had once been a coyote. It was during the first month of their marriage that he said to her, "Do you know the basket-maker who lives under the bank of the stony wash? They call her the Weaving Woman."

"I have heard something of her and I have bought her baskets. Why do you ask?"

"It is nothing," said the man, "but I hear strange stories of her, that she associates with Coyote-Spirits and such creatures," for he wanted to see what his wife would say to that.

"If that is the case," said she, "the less we see of her the better. One cannot be too careful in such matters."

After that, when the man who had been a coyote and his wife visited the campoodie, they turned out of the stony wash before they reached the wickiup, and came in to the camp by another trail. But I have not heard whether the Weaving Woman noticed it.

1910

■ PAPAGO WEDDING

There was a Papago woman out of Panták who had a marriage paper from a white man after she had borne him five children, and the man himself was in love with another woman. This Shuler was the first to raise cotton for selling in the Gila Valley—but the Pimas and Papagos had raised it long before that—and the girl went with him willingly. As to the writing of marriage, it was not then understood that the white man is not master of his heart, but is mastered by it, so that if it is not fixed in writing it becomes unstable like water and is puddled in the lowest place. The Sisters of San Xavier del Bac had taught her to clean and cook. Shuler called her Susie, which was nearest to her Papago name, and was fond of the children. He sent them to school as they came along, and had carpets in the house.

In all things Susie was a good wife to him, though she had no writing of marriage and she never wore a hat. This was a mistake which she learned from the Sisters. They, being holy women, had no notion of the *brujería* which is worked in the heart of the white man by a hat. Into the presence of their God also, without that which passes for a hat they do not go. Even after her children were old enough to notice it, Susie went about the country with a handkerchief tied over her hair, which was long and smooth on either side of her face, like the shut wings of a raven.

By the time Susie's children were as tall as their mother, there were many white ranchers in the Gila country, with their white wives, who are like Papago women in this, that, if they see a man upstanding and prosperous, they think only that he might make some woman happy, and if they have a cousin or a friend, that she should be the woman. Also the white ones think it so shameful for a man to take a woman to his house without a writing that they have no scruple to take him away from her. At Rinconada there was a woman with large breasts, surpassing well-looking, and with many hats. She had no husband, and was new to the country, and when Shuler drove her about to look at it, she wore each time a different hat.

This the Papagos observed, and, not having visited Susie when she was happy with her man, they went now in numbers, and by this Susie understood that it was in their hearts that she might have need of them. For it was well known that the white woman had told Shuler that it was a shame for him to have his children going about with a Papago woman who had only a handkerchief to cover her head. She said it was keeping Shuler back from being the principal man among the cotton-growers of Gila Valley, to have in his house a woman who would come there without a writing. And when the other white women heard that she had said that, they said the same thing. Shuler said, "My God, this is the truth, I know it," and the woman said that she would go to Susie and tell her that she ought to go back to her own people and not be a shame to her children and Shuler. There was a man of Panták on the road, who saw them go, and turned in his tracks and went back in case Susie should need him, for the Papagos, when it is their kin against whom there is *brujería* made, have in-knowing hearts. Susie sat in the best room with the woman and was polite. "If you want Shuler," she said, "you can have him, but I stay with my children." The white woman grew red in the face and went out to Shuler in the field where he was pretending to look after something, and they went away together.

After that Shuler would not go to the ranch except of necessity. He went around talking to his white friends. "My God," he kept saying, "what can I do, with my children in the hands of that Papago?" Then he sent a lawyer to Susie to say that if she would go away and not shame his children with a mother who had no marriage writing and no hat, he would give her money, so much every month. But the children all came in the room and stood by her, and Susie said, "What I want with money when I got my children and this good ranch?" Then Shuler said, "My God!" again, and, "What can I do?"

The lawyer said he could tell the Judge that Susie was not a proper person to have care of his children, and the Judge would take them away from Susie and give them to Shuler. But when the day came for Susie to come into court, it was seen that, though she had a handkerchief on her hair, her dress was good, and the fringe of her shawl was long and fine. All the five children came also, with new clothes, well-looking. "My God!" said Shuler, "I must get those kids away from that Papago and into the hands of a white woman." But the white people who had come to see the children taken away saw that, although the five looked like Shuler, they had their mouths shut like Papagos; so they waited to see how things turned out.

Shuler's lawyer makes a long speech about how Shuler loves his children, and how sorry he is in his heart to see them growing up like Papagos, and water is coming out of Shuler's eyes. Then the Judge asks Susie if she has anything to say why her children shall not be taken away.

"You want to take thees children away and giff them to Shuler?" Susie asked him. "What for you giff them to Shuler?" says Susie, and the white people listening. She says, "Shuler's not the father of them. Thees children all got different fathers," says Susie. "Shuler—"

Then she makes a sign with her hand. I tell you if a woman makes that sign to a Papago he could laugh himself dead, but he would not laugh off that. Some of the white people who have been in the country a long time know that sign and they begin to laugh.

Shuler's lawyer jumps up . . . "Your Honor, I object—"

The Judge waves his hand. "I warn you the court cannot go behind the testimony of the mother in such a case."

By this time everybody is laughing, so that they do not hear what the lawyer says. Shuler is trying to get out of the side door, and the Judge is shaking hands with Susie.

"You tell Shuler," she says, "if he wants people to think hees the father of thees children he better giff me a writing. Then maybe I think so myself."

"I *will,*" said the Judge, and maybe two–three days after that he takes Shuler out to the ranch and makes the marriage writing.

Then all the children come around Susie and say, "Now, Mother, you will have to wear a hat."

Susie, she says, "Go, children, and ask your father."

But it is not known to the Papagos what happened after that.

1925

WILLA CATHER
(1873–1947)

Although Willa Cather is best known for novels such as O Pioneers! and My Ántonia, her short fiction has been read with increasing interest in recent years. One of the most prominent writers associated with the West and Midwest, Cather often focused on the struggles of European immigrants, the hardships of pioneer life, and the unsettling changes that occurred in American society after World War I. Her work has been praised for its graceful prose style and lyrical voice; feminist scholarship in recent years has explored the complexities underlying the simple beauty of her prose.

Willa Cather was born in Back Creek, Virginia, to a family that traced its ancestors to the earliest Virginia colonists. In 1883, when Cather was ten, her family moved west to Nebraska to take advantage of the cheap land for sale. In the prairie town of Red Cloud, young Willa Cather met the European immigrants who would populate much of her fiction. Although she did not begin school until she was eleven, Cather studied Latin, Greek, European literature, and music with adult friends, and she attended the Latin School in Lincoln before entering the University of Nebraska at seventeen.

During college, Cather contributed a weekly column and reviews to the Nebraska State Journal and then wrote for a weekly newspaper, the Courier. She also began writing fiction at this time. Although this early fiction was not published, it furnished ideas for characters and themes that she later used in both her novels and short stories.

Cather continued contributing to Nebraska publications after she graduated from college. However, when she was invited to join the staff of Pittsburgh's Home Monthly magazine in 1886, she moved to Pennsylvania. In Pittsburgh, she published fiction and wrote columns for the Home Monthly and the Leader. Although Cather's short fiction began appearing in a number of publications, she tried several other short-lived careers—a stint in Washington, D.C., as a translator and several jobs in Pittsburgh as a high-school Latin and English teacher.

In 1903, S. S. McClure, publisher of McClure's, one of the country's most popular magazines, invited her to work for his magazine in New York. In that city's dynamic literary environment, Cather's writing career flourished. When McClure sent her to Boston to research the Christian Science movement, she met the famous Annie Fields and Sarah Orne Jewett, both of whom influenced her greatly. Jewett, in fact, eventually helped persuade Cather to leave McClure's and focus entirely on writing fiction. In one letter, Jewett told Cather that she must leave office life: "Find your own quiet centre of life, and write from that to the world." While

Jewett helped Cather develop her focus and self-confidence as a writer, Cather's relationship with Edith Lewis, begun also during her years at McClure's, *provided a stable personal tie that lasted until Cather's death at age seventy-three.*

In 1911, Cather left McClure's. *Almost immediately, she began publishing novels:* Alexander's Bridge *in 1912,* O Pioneers! *in 1913, and* The Song of the Lark *in 1915. In 1918, she published* My Ántonia, *the story of a girl from Bohemia who triumphs over the hardships of life as an indentured servant in a Nebraska town.* My Ántonia *conveys the spirit and humor of its main character as well as the diverse experiences of immigrant life. Like "The Old Beauty" and much of Cather's fiction,* My Ántonia *views the inner life and independent nature of a female character through the eyes of a male narrator.*

In the 1920s, Cather attained international prominence, publishing One of Ours, My Mortal Enemy, *and* Death Comes for the Archbishop, *along with other novels, short stories, and literary criticism. Throughout the 1920s and 1930s, she received numerous awards, including a Pulitzer Prize in fiction and a William Dean Howells Medal for Fiction, awarded by the Academy of the National Institute of Arts and Letters.*

"The Old Beauty" (published posthumously in 1948) shows the poetic quality of Cather's work, as well as her ability to take us into the mysteries of human character. The time shifts in this story are characteristic of many of Cather's short stories. Set in Europe rather than in the American Midwest, "The Old Beauty" juxtaposes youth and old age, life before and after World War I, and the relationships of three very different people who need and care about each other in very different ways.

THE OLD BEAUTY

I.

One brilliant September morning in 1922 a slender, fair-skinned man with white moustaches, waxed and turned up at the ends, stepped hurriedly out of the Hôtel Splendide at Aix-les-Bains and stood uncertainly at the edge of the driveway. He stood there for some moments, holding, or rather clutching, his gloves in one hand, a light cane in the other. The pavement was wet, glassy with water. The boys were still sprinkling the walk farther down the hill, and the fuchsias and dahlias in the beds sparkled with water drops. The clear air had the freshness of early morning and the smell of autumn foliage.

Two closed litters, carried by porters, came out of a side door and went joggling down the hill toward the baths. The gentleman standing on the kerb followed these eagerly with his eyes, as if about to dash after them; indeed, his mind seemed to accompany them to the turn in the walk where they disappeared, then to come back to him where he stood and at once to dart off in still another direction.

The gentleman was Mr. Henry Seabury, aged fifty-five, American-born, educated in England, and lately returned from a long business career in China. His evident nervousness was due to a shock: an old acquaintance, who had been one of the brilliant figures in the world of the 1890's, had died a few hours ago in this hotel.

As he stood there he was thinking that he ought to send telegrams . . . but to whom? The lady had no immediate family, and the distinguished men of her time who had cherished the slightest attention from her were all dead. No, there was one (perhaps the most variously gifted of that group) who was still living: living in seclusion down on the Riviera, in a great white mansion set in miles of park and garden. A cloud had come over this man in the midst of a triumphant public life. His opponents had ruined his career by a whispering campaign. They had set going a rumour which would have killed any public man in England at that time. Mr. Seabury began composing his telegram to Lord H—. Lord H— would recognize that this death was more than the death of an individual. To him her name would recall a society whose manners, dress, conventions, loyalties, codes of honour, were different from anything existing in the world today.

And there were certainly old acquaintances like himself, men not of her intimate circle, scattered about over the world; in the States, in China, India. But how to reach them?

Three young men came up the hill to resolve his perplexity; three newspaper correspondents, English, French, American. The American spoke to his companions. "There's the man I've seen about with her so much. He's the one we want."

The three approached Mr. Seabury, and the American addressed him. "Mr. Seabury, I believe? Excuse my stopping you, but we have just learned through the British Consulate that the former Lady Longstreet died in this hotel last night. We are newspaper men, and must send dispatches to our papers." He paused to introduce his companions by their names and the names of their journals. "We thought you might be good enough to tell us something about Lady Longstreet, Madame de Couçy, as she was known here."

"Nothing but what all the world knows." This intrusion had steadied Mr. Seabury, brought his scattered faculties to a focus.

"But we must jog the world's memory a little. A great many things have happened since Lady Longstreet was known everywhere."

"Certainly. You have only to cable your papers that Madame de Couçy, formerly Lady Longstreet, died here last night. They have in their files more than I could tell you if I stood here all morning."

"But the circumstances of her death?"

"You can get that from the management. Her life was interesting, but she died like anyone else—just as you will, some day."

Her old friends, everywhere, would of course like to learn something about her life here this summer. No one knew her except as Madame de Couçy, so no one observed her very closely. You were with her a great deal, and the simple story of her life here would be—"

"I understand, but it is quite impossible. Good morning, gentlemen." Mr. Seabury went to his room to write his telegram to Lord H—.

II.

Two months ago Henry Seabury had come here almost directly from China. His hurried trip across America and his few weeks in London scarcely counted. He was hunting for something, some spot that was still more or less as it used to be. Here, at Aix-les-Bains, he found the place unchanged,—and in the hotels many people very like those who used to come there.

The first night after he had settled himself at the Splendide he became interested in two old English ladies who dined at a table not far from his own. They had been coming here for many years, he felt sure. They had the old manner. They were at ease and reserved. Their dress was conservative. They were neither painted nor plucked, their nails were neither red nor green. One was plump, distinctly plump, indeed, but as she entered the dining-room he had noticed that she was quick in her movements and light on her feet. She was radiantly cheerful and talkative. But it was the other lady who interested him. She had an air of distinction, that unmistakable thing, which told him she had been a personage. She was tall, had a fine figure and carriage, but either she was much older than her friend, or life had used her more harshly. Something about her eyes and brow teased his memory. Had he once known her, or did she merely recall a type of woman he used to know? No, he felt that he must have met her, at least, long ago, when she was not a stern, gaunt-cheeked old woman with a yellowing complexion. The hotel management informed him that the lady was Madame de Couçy. He had never known anyone of that name.

The next afternoon when he was sitting under the plane trees in the *Place,* he saw the two ladies coming down the hill; the tall one moving with a peculiar drifting ease, looking into the distance as if the unlevel walk beneath her would naturally accommodate itself to her footing. She kept a white fur well up about her cheeks, though the day was hot. The short one tripped along beside her. They crossed the Square, sat down under the trees, and had tea brought out from the confectioner's. Then the muffled lady let her fur fall back a little and glanced about her. He was careful not to stare, but once, when he suddenly lifted his eyes, she was looking directly at him. He thought he saw a spark of curiosity, perhaps recognition.

The two ladies had tea in the *Place* every afternoon unless it rained; when they did not come Seabury felt disappointed. Sometimes the taller one would pause before she sat down and suggest going farther, to the Casino. Once he was near enough to hear the rosy one exclaiming: "Oh, no! It's much nicer here, really. You are always dissatisfied when we go to the Casino. There are more of the kind you hate there."

The older one with a shrug and a mournful smile sat down resignedly in front of the pastry shop. When she had finished her tea she drew her wrap up about her chin as if about to leave, but her companion began to coax: "Let us wait for the newspaper woman. It's almost time for her, and I do like to get the home papers."

The other reminded her that there would be plenty of papers at the hotel.

"Yes, yes, I know. But I like to get them from her. I'm sure she's glad of our pennies."

When they left their table they usually walked about the Square for a time, keeping to the less frequented end toward the Park. They bought roses at the flower booths, and cyclamen from an old country woman who tramped about with a basketful of them. Then they went slowly up the hill toward the hotel.

III.

Seabury's first enlightenment about these solitary women came from a most unlikely source.

Going up to the summit of Mont Revard in the little railway train one morning, he made the acquaintance of an English family (father, mother, and two grown daughters) whom he liked very much. He spent the day on the mountain in their company, and after that he saw a great deal of them. They were from Devonshire, home-staying people, not tourists. (The daughters had never been on the Continent before.) They had come over to visit the son's grave in one of the war cemeteries in the north of France. The father brought them down to Aix to cheer them up a little. (He and his wife had come there on their honeymoon, long ago.) As the Thompsons were stopping at a cramped, rather mean little hotel down in the town, they spent most of the day out of doors. Usually the mother and one of the daughters sat the whole morning in the *Place,* while the other girl went off tramping with the father. The mother knitted, and the girl read aloud to her. Whichever daughter it happened to be kept watchful eye on Mrs. Thompson. If her face grew too pensive, the girl would close the book and say:

"Now, Mother, do let us have some chocolate and croissants. The breakfast at that hotel is horrid, and I'm famished."

Mr. Seabury often joined them in the morning. He found it very pleasant to be near that kind of family feeling. They felt his friendliness, the mother especially, and were pleased to have him join them at their chocolate, or to go with him to afternoon concerts at the Grand-Cercle.

One afternoon when the mother and both daughters were having tea with him near the Roman Arch, the two English ladies from his hotel crossed the Square and sat down at a table not far away. He noticed that Mrs. Thompson glanced often in their direction. Seabury kept his guests a long while at tea,—the afternoon was hot, and he knew their hotel was stuffy. He was telling the girls something about China, when the two unknown English ladies left their table and got into a taxi. Mrs. Thompson turned to Seabury and said in a low, agitated voice:

"Do you know, I believe the tall one of those two was Lady Longstreet."

Mr. Seabury started. "Oh, no! Could it be possible?"

"I am afraid it is. Yes, she is greatly changed. It's very sad. Six years ago she stayed at a country place near us, in Devonshire, and I used often to see her out on her horse. She still rode then. I don't think I can be mistaken."

In a flash everything came back to Seabury. "You're right, I'm sure of it, Mrs. Thompson. The lady lives at my hotel, and I've been puzzling about her. I knew Lady Longstreet slightly many years ago. Now that you tell me, I can see it. But . . . as you say, she is greatly changed. At the hotel she is known as Madame de Couçy."

"Yes, she married during the war; a Frenchman. But it must have been after she had lost her beauty. I had never heard of the marriage until he was killed,—in '17, I think. Then some of the English papers mentioned that he was the husband of Gabrielle Longstreet. It's very sad when those beautiful ones have to grow old, isn't it? We never have too many of them, at best."

The younger daughter threw her arms about Mrs. Thompson. "Oh, Mother, I wish you hadn't told us! I'm afraid Mr. Seabury does, too. It's such a shock."

He protested. "Yes, it is a shock, certainly. But I'm grateful to Mrs. Thompson. I must be very stupid not to have seen it. I'm glad to know. The two ladies seem very much alone, and the older one looks ill. I might be of some service, if she remembers me. It's all very strange: but one might be useful, perhaps, Mrs. Thompson?"

"That's the way to look at it, Mr. Seabury." Mrs. Thompson spoke gently. "I think she does remember you. When you were talking to Dorothy, turned away from them, she glanced at you often. The lady with her is a friend, don't you think, not a paid companion?"

He said he was sure of it, and she gave him a warm, grateful glance as if he and she could understand how much that meant, then turned to her daughters: "Why, there is Father, come to look for us!" She made a little signal to the stout, flushed man who was tramping across the Square in climbing boots.

IV.

Mr. Seabury did not go back to his hotel for dinner. He dined at a little place with tables in the garden, and returned late to the Splendide. He felt rather knocked up by what Mrs. Thompson had told him,—felt that in this world people have to pay an extortionate price for any exceptional gift whatever. Once in his own room, he lay for a long while in a chaise longue before an open window, watching the stars and the fireflies, recalling the whole romantic story,—all he had ever known of Lady Longstreet. And in this hotel, full of people, she was unknown—she!

Gabrielle Longstreet was a name known all over the globe,—even in China, when he went there twenty-seven years ago. Yet she was not an actress or an adventuress. She had come into the European world in a perfectly regular, if somewhat unusual, way.

Sir Wilfred Longstreet, a lover of yachting and adventure on the high seas, had been driven into Martinique by a tropical hurricane. Strolling about the harbour town, he saw a young girl coming out of a church with her mother; the girl was nineteen, the mother perhaps forty. They were the two most beautiful women he had ever seen. The hurricane passed and was forgotten, but Sir Wilfred Longstreet's yacht still lay in the harbour of Fort de France. He sought out the girl's father, an English colonial from Barbados, who was easily convinced. The mother not so easily: she was a person of character as well as severe beauty. Longstreet had sworn that he would never take his yacht out to sea unless he carried Gabrielle aboard her. The *Sea Nymph* might lie and rot there.

In time the mother was reassured by letters and documents from England. She wished to do well for her daughter, and what very brilliant opportunities were there in Martinique? As for the girl, she wanted to see the world; she had never been off the island. Longstreet made a settlement upon Madame the mother, and submitted to the two services, civil and religious. He took his bride directly back to England. He had not advised his friends of his marriage; he was a young man who kept his affairs to himself.

He kept his wife in the country for some months. When he opened his town house and took her to London, things went as he could not possibly have foreseen. In six weeks she was the fashion of the town; the object of admiration among his friends, and his father's friends. Gabrielle was not socially ambitious, made no effort to please. She was not witty or especially clever,—had no accomplishments beyond speaking French as naturally as English. She said nothing memorable in either language. She was beautiful, that was all. And she was fresh. She came into that society of old London like a quiet country dawn.

She showed no great zest for this life so different from anything she had ever known; a quiet wonderment rather, faintly tinged with pleasure. There was no glitter about her, no sparkle. She never dressed in the mode: refused to wear crinoline in a world that billowed and swelled with it. Into drawing-rooms full of ladies enriched by marvels of hairdressing (switches, ringlets, puffs, pompadours, waves starred with gems), she came with her brown hair parted in the middle and coiled in a small knot at the back of her head. Hairdressers protested, as one client after another adopted the 'mode Gabrielle.' (The knot at the nape of the neck! Charwomen had always worn it; it was as old as mops and pails.)

The English liked high colour, but Lady Longstreet had no red roses in her cheeks. Her skin had the soft glow of orient pearls,—the jewel to which she was most often compared. She was not spirited, she was not witty, but no one ever heard her say a stupid thing. She was often called cold. She seemed unawakened, as if she were still an island girl with reserved island good manners. No woman had been so much discussed and argued about for a long stretch of years. It was to the older men that she was (unconsciously, as it seemed) more gracious. She liked them to tell her about events and personages already in the past; things she had come too late to see.

Longstreet, her husband, was none too pleased by the flutter she caused. It was no great credit to him to have discovered a rare creature; since everyone else discovered her the moment they had a glimpse of her. Men much his superiors in rank and importance looked over his head at his wife, passed him with a nod on their way to her. He began to feel annoyance, and waited for this flurry to pass over. But pass it did not. With her second and third seasons in town her circle grew. Statesmen and officers twenty years Longstreet's senior seemed to find in Gabrielle an escape from long boredom. He was jealous without having the common pretexts for jealousy. He began to spend more and more time on his yacht in distant waters. He left his wife in his town house with his spinster cousin as chaperone. Gabrielle's mother came on from Martinique for a season, and was almost as much admired as her daughter. Sir Wilfred found that the Martiniquaises had considerably overshadowed him. He was no longer the interesting "original" he had once been. His unexpected appearances and disappearances were mere incidents in the house and the life which his wife and his cousin had so well organized. He bore this for six years and then, unexpectedly, demanded divorce. He established the statutory grounds, she petitioning for the decree. He made her a generous settlement.

This brought about a great change in Gabrielle Longstreet's life. She remained in London, and bought a small house near St. James's Park. Longstreet's old cousin, to his great annoyance, stayed on with Gabrielle,—the only one of his family who had not treated her like a poor relation. The loyalty of this spinster, a woman of spirit, Scotch on the father's side, did a good deal to ease Gabrielle's fall in the world. For fall it was, of course. She had her circle, but it was smaller and more intimate. Fewer women invited her now, fewer of the women she used to know. She did not go afield for those who affected art and advanced ideas; they would gladly have championed her cause. She replied to their overtures that she no longer went into society. Her men friends never flinched in their loyalty. Those unembarrassed by wives, the bachelors and widowers, were more assiduous than ever. At that dinner table where Gabrielle and "the Honourable MacPhairson," as the old cousin was called, were sometimes the only women, one met promising young men, not yet settled in their careers, and much older men, so solidly and successfully settled that their presence in a company established its propriety.

Nobody could ever say exactly why Gabrielle's house was so attractive. The men who had the entrée there were not skilful at defining such a thing as "charm" in words: that was not at all their line. And they would have been reluctant to admit that a negligible thing like temperature had anything to do with the pleasant relaxation they enjoyed there. The chill of London houses had been one of the cruellest trials the young Martiniquaise had to bear. When she took a house of her own, she (secretly, as if it were a disgraceful thing to do) had a hot-air furnace put in her cellar, and she kept coal fires burning in the grates at either end of the drawing-room. In colour, however, the rooms were not warm, but rather cool and spring-like. Always flowers, and not too many. There was something more flower-like than the flowers,—something in Gabrielle herself (now more herself than ever she had been as Lady Longstreet); the soft pleasure that came into her face when she put out her hand to greet a hero of perhaps seventy years, the look of admiration in her calm grey eyes. A century earlier her French grandmothers may have greeted the dignitaries of the Church with such a look,—deep feeling, without eagerness of any kind. To a badgered Minister, who came in out of committee meetings and dirty weather, the warm house, the charming companionship which had no request lurking behind it, must have been grateful. The lingering touch of a white hand on his black sleeve can do a great deal for an elderly man who has left a busy and fruitless day behind him and who is worn down by the unreasonable demands of his own party. Nothing said in that room got out into the world. Gabrielle never repeated one man to another,—and as for the Honourable MacPhairson, she never gave anything away, not even a good story!

In time there came about a succession of Great Protectors, and Gabrielle Longstreet was more talked about than in the days of her sensational debut. Whether any of them were ever her lovers, no one could say. They were all men much older than she, and only one of them was known for light behaviour with women. Young men were sometimes asked to her house, but they were made to feel it was by special kindness. Henry Seabury himself had been taken there by young Hardwick, when he was still an undergraduate. Seabury had not known her well, however, until she leased a house in New York and spent two winters there. A jealous woman, and a very clever one, had made things unpleasant for her in London, and Gabrielle had quitted England for a time.

. . .

Sitting alone that night, recalling all he had heard of Lady Longstreet, Seabury tried to remember her face just as it was in the days when he used to know her; the beautiful contour of the cheeks, the low, straight brow, the lovely line from the chin to the base of the throat. Perhaps it was her eyes he remembered best; no glint in them, no sparkle, no drive. When she was moved by admiration, they did not glow, but became more soft, more grave; a kind of twilight shadow deepened in them. That look, with her calm white shoulders, her unconsciousness of her body and whatever clothed it, gave her the air of having come from afar off.

And now it was all gone. There was something tense, a little defiant in the shoulders now. The hands that used to lie on her dress forgotten, as a bunch of white violets might lie there . . . Well, it was all gone.

Plain women, he reflected, when they grow old are—simply plain women. Often they improve. But a beautiful woman may become a ruin. The more delicate her beauty, the more it owes to some exquisite harmony in modelling and line, the more completely it is destroyed. Gabrielle Longstreet's face was now unrecognizable. She gave it no assistance, certainly. She was the only woman in the dining-room who used no make-up. She met the winter barefaced. Cheap counterfeits meant nothing to a woman who had had the real thing for so long. She must have been close upon forty when he knew her in New York,—and where was there such a creature in the world today? Certainly in his hurried trip across America and England he had not been gladdened by the sight of one. He had seen only cinema stars, and women curled and plucked and painted to look like them. Perhaps the few very beautiful women he remembered in the past had been illusions, had benefited by a romantic tradition which played upon them like a kindly light . . . and by an attitude in men which no longer existed.

V.

When Mr. Seabury awoke the next day it was clear to him that any approach to Madame de Couçy must be made through the amiable-seeming friend, Madame Allison as she was called at the hotel, who always accompanied her. He had noticed that this lady usually went down into the town alone in the morning. After breakfasting he walked down the hill and loitered about the little streets. Presently he saw Madame Allison come out of the English bank, with several small parcels tucked under her arm. He stepped beside her.

"Pardon me, Madame, but I am stopping at your hotel, and I have noticed that you are a friend of Madame de Couçy, whom I think I used to know as Gabrielle Longstreet. It was many years ago, and naturally she does not recognize me. Would it displease her if I sent up my name, do you think?"

Mrs. Allison answered brightly. "Oh, she did recognize you, if you are Mr. Seabury. Shall we sit down in the shade for a moment? I find it very warm here, even for August."

When they were seated under the plane trees she turned to him with a friendly smile and frank curiosity. "She is here for a complete rest and isn't seeing people, but I think she would be glad to see an old friend. She remembers you very well. At first she was not sure about your name, but I asked the porter. She recalled it at once and said she met you with Hardwick, General Hardwick, who was killed in the war. Yes, I'm sure she would be glad to see an old friend."

He explained that he was scarcely an old friend, merely one of many admirers; but he used to go to her house when she lived in New York.

"She said you did. She thought you did not recognize her. But we have all changed, haven't we?"

"And have you and I met before, Madame Allison?"

"Oh, drop the Madame, please! We both speak English, and I am Mrs. Allison. No, we never met. You may have seen me, if you went to the Alhambra. I was Cherry Beamish in those days."

"Then I last saw you in an Eton jacket, with your hair cropped. I never had the pleasure of seeing you out of your character parts, which accounts for my not recognizing—"

She cut him short with a jolly laugh. "Oh, thirty years and two stone would account, would account perfectly! I always did boy parts, you remember. They wouldn't have me in skirts. So I had to keep my weight down. Such a comfort not to fuss about it now. One has a right to a little of one's life, don't you think?"

He agreed. "But I saw you in America also. You had great success there."

She nodded. "Yes, three seasons, grand engagements. I laid by a pretty penny. I was married over there, and divorced over there, quite in the American style! He was a Scotch boy, stranded in Philadelphia. We parted with no hard feelings, but he was too expensive to keep." Seeing the hotel bus, Mrs. Allison hailed it. "I *shall* be glad if Gabrielle feels up to seeing you. She is frightfully dull here and not very well."

VI.

The following evening, as Seabury went into the dining-room and bowed to Mrs. Allison, she beckoned him to Madame de Couçy's table. That lady put out her jewelled hand and spoke abruptly.

"Chetty tells me we are old acquaintances, Mr. Seabury. Will you come up to us for coffee after dinner? This is the number of our apartment." As she gave him her card he saw that her hand trembled slightly. Her voice was much deeper than it used to be, and cold. It had always been cool, but soft, like a cool fragrance,—like her eyes and her white arms.

When he rang at Madame de Couçy's suite an hour later, her maid admitted him. The two ladies were seated before an open window, the coffee table near them and the percolator bubbling. Mrs. Allison was the first to greet him. In a moment she retired, leaving him alone with Madame de Couçy.

"It is very pleasant to meet you again, after so many years, Seabury. How did you happen to come?"

Because he had liked the place long ago, he told her.

"And I, for the same reason. I live in Paris now. Mrs. Allison tells me you have been out in China all this while. And how are things there?"

"Not so good now, Lady Longstreet, may I still call you? China is rather falling to pieces."

"Just as here, eh? No, call me as I am known in this hotel, please. When we are alone, you may use my first name; that has survived time and change. As to change, we have got used to it. But you, coming back upon it, this Europe, suddenly . . . it must give you rather a shock."

It was she herself who had given him the greatest shock of all, and in one quick, penetrating glance she seemed to read that fact. She shrugged: there was nothing to be done about it. "Chetty, where are you?" she called.

Mrs. Allison came quickly from another room and poured the coffee. Her presence warmed the atmosphere considerably. She seemed unperturbed by the grimness of her friend's manner; and she herself was a most comfortable little person. Even her too evident plumpness was comfortable, since she didn't seem to mind it. She didn't like living in Paris very well, she said; something rather stiff and chilly about it. But she often ran away and went home to see her nieces and nephews, and they were a jolly lot. Yes, she found it very pleasant here at Aix. And now that an old friend of Gabrielle's had obligingly turned up, they would have someone to talk to, and that would be a blessing.

Madame de Couçy gave a low, mirthless laugh. "She seems to take a good deal for granted, doesn't she?"

"Not where I am concerned, if you mean that. I shall be deeply grateful for someone to talk to. Between the three of us we may find a great deal."

"Be sure we shall," said Mrs. Allison. "We have the past, and the present—which is really very interesting, if only you will let yourself think so. Some of the people here are very novel and amusing, and others are quite like people we used to know. Don't you find it so, Mr. Seabury?"

He agreed with her and turned to Madame de Couçy. "May I smoke?"

"What a question to ask in these days! Yes, you and Chetty may smoke. I will take a liqueur."

Mrs. Allison rose. "Gabrielle has a cognac so old and precious that we keep it locked in a cabinet behind the piano." In opening the cabinet she overturned a framed photograph which fell to the floor. "There goes the General again! No, he didn't break, dear. We carry so many photographs about with us, Mr. Seabury."

Madame de Couçy turned to Seabury. "Do you recognize some of my old friends? There are some of yours, too, perhaps. I think I was never sentimental when I was young, but now I travel with my photographs. My friends mean more to me now than when they were alive. I was too ignorant then to realize what remarkable men they were. I supposed the world was always full of great men."

She left her chair and walked with him about the salon and the long entrance hall, stopping before one and another; uniforms, military and naval, caps and gowns; photographs, drawings, engravings. As she spoke of them the character of her voice changed altogether,—became, indeed, the voice Seabury remembered. The hard, dry tone was a form of disguise, he conjectured; a protection behind which she addressed people from whom she expected neither recognition nor consideration.

"What an astonishing lot they are, seeing them together like this," he exclaimed with feeling. "How can a world manage to get on without them?"

"It hasn't managed very well, has it? You may remember that I was a rather ungrateful young woman. I took what came. A great man's time, his consideration, his affection, were mine in the natural course of things, I supposed. But it's not so now. I bow down to them in admiration . . . gratitude. They are dearer to me than when they were my living friends,—because I understand them better."

Seabury remarked that the men whose pictures looked down at them were too wise to expect youth and deep discernment in the same person.

"I'm not speaking of discernment; that I had, in a way. I mean ignorance. I simply didn't know all that lay behind them. I am better informed now. I read everything they wrote, and everything that has been written about them. That is my chief pleasure."

Seabury smiled indulgently and shook his head. "It wasn't for what you knew about them that they loved you."

She put her hand quickly on his arm. "Ah, you said that before you had time to think! You believe, then, that I did mean something to them?" For the first time she fixed on him the low, level, wondering look that he remembered of old: the woman he used to know seemed breathing beside him. When she turned away from him suddenly, he knew it was to hide the tears in her eyes. He had seen her cry once, a long time ago. He had not forgotten.

He took up a photograph and talked, to bridge over a silence in which she could not trust her voice. "What a fine likeness of X—! He was my hero, among the whole group. Perhaps his contradictions fascinated me. I could never see how one side of him managed to live with the other. Yet I know that both sides were perfectly genuine. He was a mystery. And his end was mysterious. No one will ever know where or how. A secret departure on a critical mission, and never an arrival anywhere. It was like him."

Madame de Couçy turned, with a glow in her eyes such as he had never see there in her youth. "The evening his disappearance was announced . . . Shall I ever forget it! I was in London. The newsboys were crying it in the street. I did not go to bed that night. I sat up in the drawing-room until daylight; hoping, saying the old prayers I used to say with my mother. It was all one could do. . . . Young Harney was with him, you remember. I have always been glad of that. Whatever fate was in store for his chief, Harney would have chosen to share it."

Seabury stayed much longer with Madame de Couçy than he had intended. The ice once broken, he felt he might never find her so much herself again. They sat talking about people who were no longer in this world. She knew much more about them than he. Knew so much that her talk brought back not only the men, but their period; its security, the solid exterior, the exotic contradictions behind the screen; the deep, claret-coloured closing years of Victoria's reign. Nobody ever recognizes a period until it has gone by, he reflected: until it lies behind one it is merely everyday life.

VII.

The next evening the Thompsons, all four of them, were to dine with Mr. Seabury at the Maison des Fleurs. Their holiday was over, and they would be leaving on the following afternoon. They would stop once more at that spot in the north, to place fresh wreaths, before they took the Channel boat.

When Seabury and his guests were seated and the dinner had been ordered, he was aware that the mother was looking at him rather wistfully. He felt he owed her some confidence, since it was she, really, who had enlightened him. He told her that he had called upon Gabrielle Longstreet last evening.

"And how is she, dear Mr. Seabury? Is she less—less forbidding than when we see her in the Square?"

"She was on her guard at first, but that soon passed. I stayed later than I should have done, but I had a delightful evening. I gather that she is a little antagonistic to the present order,—indifferent, at least. But when she talks about her old friends she is quite herself."

Mrs. Thompson listened eagerly. She hesitated and then asked: "Does she find life pleasant at all, do you think?"

Seabury told her how the lady was surrounded by the photographs and memoirs of her old friends; how she never travelled without them. It had struck him that she was living her life over again,—more understandingly than she lived it the first time.

Mrs. Thompson breathed a little sigh. "Then I know that all is well with her. You have done so much to make our stay here pleasant, Mr. Seabury, but your telling us this is the best of all. Even Father will be interested to know that."

The stout man, who wore an ancient tail coat made for him when he was much thinner, came out indignantly. "Even Father! I like that! One of the great beauties of our time, and very popular before the divorce."

His daughter laughed and patted his sleeve. Seabury went on to tell Mrs. Thompson that she had been quite right in surmising the companion to be a friend, not a paid attendant. "And a very charming person, too. She was one of your cleverest music-hall stars. Cherry Beamish."

Here Father dropped his spoon into his soup. "What's that? Cherry Beamish? But we haven't had such another since! Remember her in that coster song, Mother? It went round the world, that did. We were all crazy about her, the boys called her Cherish Beamy. No monkeyshines for her, never got herself mixed up in anything shady."

"Such a womanly woman in private life," Mrs. Thompson murmured. "My Dorothy went to school with two of her nieces. An excellent school, and quite dear. Their Aunt Chetty does everything for them. And now she is with Lady Longstreet! One wouldn't have supposed they'd ever meet, those two. But then things *are* strange now."

There was no lull in conversation at that dinner. After the father had enjoyed several glasses of champagne he delighted his daughters with an account of how Cherry Beamish used to do the tipsy schoolboy coming in at four in the morning and meeting his tutor in the garden.

VIII.

Mr. Seabury sat waiting before the hotel in a comfortable car which he now hired by the week. Gabrielle and Chetty drove out with him every day. This afternoon they were to go to Annecy by the wild road along the Echelles. Presently Mrs. Allison came down alone. Gabrielle was staying in bed, she said. Last night Seabury had dined with them in their apartment, and Gabrielle had talked too much, she was afraid. "She didn't sleep afterward, but I think she will make it up today if she is quite alone."

Seabury handed her into the car. In a few minutes they were running past the lake of Bourget.

"This gives me an opportunity, Mrs. Allison, to ask you how it came about that you've become Lady Longstreet's protector. It's a beautiful friendship."

She laughed. "And an amazing one? But I think you must call me Chetty, as she does, if we are to be confidential. Yes, I suppose it must seem to you the queerest partnership that war and desolation have made. But you see, she was so strangely left. When I first began to look after her a little, two years ago, she was ill in an hotel in Paris (we have taken a flat since), and there was no one, positively no one but the hotel people, the French doctor, and an English nurse who had chanced to be within call. It was the nurse, really, who gave me my cue. I had sent flowers, with no name, of course. (What would a bygone music-hall name mean to Gabrielle Longstreet?) And I called often to inquire. One morning I met Nurse Ames just as she was going out into the Champs-Élysées for her exercise, and she asked me to accompany her. She was an experienced woman, not young. She remembered when Gabrielle Longstreet's name and photographs were known all over the Continent, and when people at home were keen enough upon meeting her. And here she was, dangerously ill in a foreign hotel, and there was no one, simply no one. To be sure, she was registered under the name of her second husband."

Seabury interrupted. "And who was he, this de Couçy? I have heard nothing about him."

"I know very little myself, I never met him. They had been friends a long while, I believe. He was killed in action—less than a year after they were married. His name was a disguise for her, even then. She came from Martinique, you remember, and she had no relatives in England. Longstreet's people had never liked her. So, you see, she was quite alone."

Seabury took her plump little hand. "And that was where you came in, Chetty?"

She gave his fingers a squeeze. "Thank you! That's nice. It was Nurse Ames who did it. The war made a lot of wise nurses. After Gabrielle was well enough to see people, there was no one for her to see! The same thing that had happened to her friends in England had happened over here. The old men had paid the debt of nature, and the young ones were killed or disabled or had lost touch with her. She once had many friends in Paris. Nurse Ames told me that an old French officer, blinded in the war, sometimes came to see her, guided by his little granddaughter. She said her patient had expressed curiosity about the English woman who had sent so many flowers. I wrote a note, asking whether I could be of any service, and signed my professional name. She might recognize it, she might not. We had been on a committee together during the war. She told the nurse to admit me, and that's how it began."

Seabury took her hand again. "Now I want you to be frank with me. Had she then, or has she now, money worries at all?"

Cherry Beamish chuckled. "Not she, you may believe! But I have had a few for her. On the whole, she's behaved very well. She sold her place in Devonshire to advantage, before the war. Her capital is in British bonds. She seems to you harassed?"

"Sometimes."

Mrs. Allison looked grave and was silent for a little. "Yes," with a sigh, "she gets very low at times. She suffers from strange regrets. She broods on the things she might have done for her friends and didn't—thinks she was cold to them. Was she, in those days, so indifferent as she makes herself believe?"

Seabury reflected. "Not exactly indifferent. She wouldn't have been so attractive if she'd been that. She didn't take things very hard, perhaps. She used to strike me as . . . well, we might call it unawakened."

"But wasn't she the most beautiful creature then! I used to see her at the races, and at charity bazaars, in my early professional days. After the war broke out and everybody was all mixed up, I was put on an entertainment committee with her. She wasn't quite the Lady Longstreet of my youth, but she still had that grand style. It was the illness in Paris that broke her. She's changed very fast ever since. You see she thought, once the war was over, the world would be just as it used to be. Of course it isn't."

By this time the car had reached Annecy, and they stopped for tea. The shore of the lake was crowded with young people taking their last dip for the day; sunbrowned backs and shoulders, naked arms and legs. As Mrs. Allison was having her tea on the terrace, she watched the bathers. Presently she twinkled a sly smile at her host. "Do you know, I'm rather glad we didn't bring Gabrielle! It puts her out terribly to see young people bathing naked. She makes comments that are indecent, really! If only she had a swarm of young nieces and nephews, as I have, she'd see things quite differently, and she'd be much happier. Legs were never wicked to us stage people, and now all the young things know they are not wicked."

IX.

When Madame de Couçy went out with Seabury alone, he missed the companionship of Cherry Beamish. With Cherry the old beauty always softened a little; seemed amused by the other's interest in whatever the day produced: the countryside, the weather, the number of cakes she permitted herself for tea. The imagination which made this strange friendship possible was certainly on the side of Cherry Beamish. For her, he could see, there was something in it; to be the anchor, the refuge, indeed, of one so out of her natural orbit,—selected by her long ago as an object of special admiration.

One afternoon when he called, the maid, answering his ring, said that Madame would not go out this afternoon, but hoped he would stay and have tea with her in her salon. He told the lift boy to dismiss the car and went in to Madame de Couçy. She received him with unusual warmth.

"Chetty is out for the afternoon, with some friends from home. Oh, she still has a great many! She is much younger than I, in every sense. Today I particularly wanted to see you alone. It's curious how the world runs away from one, slips by without one's realizing it."

He reminded her that the circumstances had been unusual. "We have lived through a storm to which the French Revolution, which used to be our standard of horrors, was merely a breeze. A rather gentlemanly affair, as one looks back on it. . . . As for me, I am grateful to be alive, sitting here with you in a comfortable hotel (I might be in a prison full of rats), in a France still undestroyed."

The old lady looked into his eyes with the calm, level gaze so rare with her now. "Are you grateful? I am not. I think one should go out with one's time. I particularly wished to see you alone this afternoon. I want to thank you for your tact and gentleness with me one hideous evening long ago; in my house in New York. You were a darling boy to me that night. If you hadn't come along, I don't know how I would have got over it—out of it, even. One can't call the servants."

"But, Gabrielle, why recall a disagreeable incident when you have so many agreeable ones to remember?"

She seemed not to hear him, but went on, speaking deliberately, as if she were reflecting aloud. "It was strange, your coming in just when you did: that night it seemed to me like a miracle. Afterward, I remembered you had been expected at eight. But I had forgotten all that, forgotten everything. Never before or since have I been so frightened. It was something worse than fear."

There was a knock at the door. Madame de Couçy called: "*Entrez!*" without turning round. While the tea was brought she sat looking out of the window, frowning. When the waiter had gone she turned abruptly to Seabury:

"After that night I never saw you again until you walked into the dining-room of this hotel a few weeks ago. I had gone into the country somewhere, hiding with friends, and when I came back to New York, you were already on your way to China. I never had a chance to explain."

"There was certainly no need for that."

"Not for you, perhaps. But for me. You may have thought such scenes were frequent in my life. Hear me out, please," as he protested. "That man had come to my house at seven o'clock that evening and sent up a message begging me to see him about some business matters. (I had been stupid enough to let him make investments for me.) I finished dressing and hurried down to the drawing-room." Here she stopped and slowly drank a cup of tea. "Do you know, after you came in I did not see you at all, not for some time, I think. I was mired down in something . . . *the power of the dog,* the English Prayer Book calls it. But the moment I heard your voice, I knew that I was safe . . . I felt the leech drop off. I have never forgot the sound of your voice that night; so calm, with all a man's strength behind it,—and you were only a boy. You merely asked if you had come too early. I felt the leech drop off. After that I remember nothing. I didn't see you, with my eyes, until you gave me your handkerchief. You stayed with me and looked after me all evening.

"You see, I had let the beast come to my house, oh, a number of times! I had asked his advice and allowed him to make investments for me. I had done the same thing at home with men who knew about such matters; they were men like yourself and Hardwick. In a strange country one goes astray in one's reckonings. I had met that man again and again at the houses of my friends,—your friends! Of course his personality was repulsive to me. One knew at once that under his smoothness he was a vulgar person. I supposed that was not unusual in great bankers in the States."

"You simply chose the wrong banker, Gabrielle. The man's accent must have told you that he belonged to a country you did not admire."

"But I tell you I met him at the houses of decent people."

Seabury shook his head. "Yes, I am afraid you must blame us for that. Americans, even those whom you call the decent ones, do ask people to their houses who shouldn't be there. They are often asked *because* they are outrageous,—and therefore considered amusing. Besides, that fellow had a very clever way of pushing himself. If a man is generous in his contributions to good causes, and is useful on committees and commissions, he is asked to the houses of the people who have these good causes at heart."

"And perhaps I, too, was asked because I was considered notorious? A divorcée, known to have more friends among men than among women at home? I think I see what you mean. There are not many shades in your society. I left the States soon after you sailed for China. I gave up my New York house at a loss to be rid of it. The instant I recognized you in the dining-room downstairs, that miserable evening came back to me. In so far as our acquaintance was concerned, all that had happened only the night before."

"Then I am reaping a reward I didn't deserve, some thirty years afterward! If I had not happened to call that evening when you were so—so unpleasantly surprised, you would never have remembered me at all! We shouldn't be sitting together at this moment. Now may I ring for some fresh tea, dear? Let us be comfortable. This afternoon has brought us closer together. And this little spot in Savoie is a nice place to renew old friendships, don't you think?"

X.

Some hours later, when Mr. Seabury was dressing for dinner, he was thinking of that strange evening in Gabrielle Longstreet's house on Fifty-third Street, New York.

He was then twenty-four years old. She had been very gracious to him all the winter.

On that particular evening he was to take her to dine at Delmonico's. Her cook and butler were excused to attend a wedding. The maid who answered his ring asked him to go up to the drawing-room on the second floor, where Madame was awaiting him. She followed him as far as the turn of the stairway, then, hearing another ring at the door, she excused herself.

He went on alone. As he approached the wide doorway leading into the drawing-room, he was conscious of something unusual; a sound, or perhaps an unnatural stillness. From the doorway he beheld something quite terrible. At the far end of the room Gabrielle Longstreet was seated on a little French sofa—not seated, but silently struggling. Behind the sofa stood a stout, dark man leaning over her. His left arm, about her waist, pinioned her against the flowered silk upholstery. His right hand was thrust deep into the low-cut bodice of her dinner gown. In her struggle she had turned a little on her side; her right arm was in the grip of his left hand, and she was trying to free the other, which was held down by the pressure of his elbow. Neither of those two made a sound. Her face was averted, half hidden against the blue silk back of the sofa. Young Seabury stood still just long enough to see what the situation really was. Then he stepped across the threshold and said with such coolness as he could command: "Am I too early, Madame Longstreet?"

The man behind her started from his crouching position, darted away from the sofa, and disappeared down the stairway. To reach the stairs he passed Seabury, without lifting his eyes, but his face was glistening wet.

The lady lay without stirring, her face now completely hidden. She looked so crushed and helpless, he thought she must be hurt physically. He spoke to her softly: "Madame Longstreet, shall I call—"

"Oh, don't call! Don't call anyone." She began shuddering violently, her face still turned away. "Some brandy, please. Downstairs, in the dining-room."

He ran down the stairs, had to tell the solicitous maid that Madame wished to be alone for the present. When he came back Gabrielle had caught up the shoulder straps of her gown. Her right arm bore red finger marks. She was shivering and sobbing. He slipped his handkerchief into her hand, and she held it over her mouth. She took a little brandy. Then another fit of weeping came on. He begged her to come nearer to the fire. She put her hand on his arm, but seemed unable to rise. He lifted her from that seat of humiliation and took her, wavering between his supporting hands, to a low chair beside the coal grate. She sank into it, and he put a cushion under her feet. He persuaded her to drink the rest of the brandy. She stopped crying and leaned back, her eyes closed, her hands lying nerveless on the arms of the chair. Seabury thought he had never seen her when she was more beautiful . . . probably that was because she was helpless and he was young.

"Perhaps you would like me to go now?" he asked her.

She opened her eyes. "Oh, no! Don't leave me, please. I am so much safer with you here." She put her hand, still cold, on his for a moment, then closed her eyes and went back into that languor of exhaustion.

Perhaps half an hour went by. She did not stir, but he knew she was not asleep: an occasional trembling of the eyelids, tears stealing out from under her black lashes and glistening unregarded on her cheeks; like pearls he thought they were, transparent shimmers on velvet cheeks gone very white.

When suddenly she sat up, she spoke in her natural voice.

"But, my dear boy, you have gone dinnerless all this while! Won't you stay with me and have just a bit of something up here? Do ring for Hopkins, please."

The young man caught at the suggestion. If once he could get her mind on the duties of caring for a guest, that might lead to something. He must try to be very hungry.

The kitchen maid was in and, under Hopkins's direction, got together a creditable supper and brought it up to the drawing-room. Gabrielle took nothing but the hot soup and a little sherry. Young Seabury, once he tasted food, found he had no difficulty in doing away with cold pheasant and salad.

Gabrielle had quite recovered her self-control. She talked very little, but that was not unusual with her. He told her about Hardwick's approaching marriage. For him, the evening went by very pleasantly. He felt with her a closer intimacy than ever before.

When at midnight he rose to take his leave, she detained him beside her chair, holding his hand. "At some other time I shall explain what you saw here tonight. How could such a thing happen in one's own house, in an English-speaking city . . . ?"

"But that was not an English-speaking man who went out from here. He is an immigrant who had made a lot of money. He does not belong."

"Yes, that is true. I wish you weren't going out to China. Not for long, I hope. It's a bad thing to be away from one's own people." Her voice broke, and tears came again. He kissed her hand softly, devotedly, and went downstairs.

He had not seen her again until his arrival at this hotel some weeks ago, when he did not recognize her.

XI.

One evening when Mrs. Allison and Madame de Couçy had been dining with Seabury at the Maison des Fleurs, they went into the tea room to have their coffee and watch the dancing. It was now September, and almost everyone would be leaving next week. The floor was full of young people, English, American, French, moving monotonously to monotonous rhythms,—some of them scarcely moving at all. Gabrielle watched them through her lorgnette, with a look of resigned boredom.

Mrs. Allison frowned at her playfully. "Of course it's all very different," she observed, "but then, so is everything." She turned to Seabury: "You know we used to have to put so much drive into a dance act, or it didn't go at all. Lottie Collins was the only lazy dancer who could get anything over. But the truth was, the dear thing couldn't dance at all; got on by swinging her foot! There must be something in all this new manner, if only one could get it. That couple down by the bar now, the girl with the *very* low back: they are doing it beautifully; she dips and rises like a bird in the air . . . a tired bird, though. That's the disconcerting thing. It all seems so tired."

Seabury agreed with her cheerfully that it was charming, though tired. He felt a gathering chill in the lady on his right. Presently she said impatiently: "Haven't you had enough of this, Chetty?"

Mrs. Allison sighed. "You never see anything in it, do you, dear?"

"I see wriggling. They look to me like lizards dancing—or reptiles coupling."

"Oh, no, dear! No! They are such sweet young things. But they are dancing in a dream. I want to go and wake them up. They are missing so much fun. Dancing ought to be open and free, with the lungs full; not mysterious and breathless. I wish I could see a *spirited* waltz again."

Gabrielle shrugged and gave a dry laugh. "I wish I could dance one! I think I should try, if by any chance I should ever hear a waltz played again."

Seabury rose from his chair. "May I take you up on that? Will you?"

She seemed amused and incredulous, but nodded.

"Excuse me for a moment." He strolled toward the orchestra. When the tango was over he spoke to the conductor, handing him something from his vest pocket. The conductor smiled and bowed, then spoke to his men, who smiled in turn. The saxophone put down his instrument and grinned. The strings sat up in their chairs, pulled themselves up, as it were, tuned for a moment, and sat at attention. At the lift of the leader's hand they began the "Blue Danube."

Gabrielle took Mr. Seabury's arm. They passed a dozen couples who were making a sleepy effort and swung into the open square where the line of tables stopped. Seabury had never danced with Gabrielle Longstreet, and he was astonished. She had attack and style, the grand style, slightly military, quite right for her tall, straight figure. He held her hand very high, accordingly. The conductor caught the idea; smartened the tempo slightly, made the accents sharper. One by one the young couples dropped out and sat down to smoke. The two old waltzers were left alone on the floor. There was a stir of curiosity about the room; who were those two, and why were they doing it? Cherry Beamish heard remarks from the adjoining tables.

"She's rather stunning, the old dear!"

"Aren't they funny?"

"It's so quaint and theatrical. Quite effective in its way."

Seabury had not danced for some time. He thought the musicians drew the middle part out interminably; rather suspected they were playing a joke on him. But his partner lost none of her brilliance and verve. He tried to live up to her. He was grateful when those fiddlers snapped out the last phrase. As he took Gabrielle to her seat, a little breeze of applause broke out from the girls about the room.

"Dear young things!" murmured Chetty, who was flushed with pleasure and excitement. A group of older men who had come in from the dining-room were applauding.

"Let us go now, Seabury. I am afraid we have been making rather an exhibition," murmured Madame de Couçy. As they got into the car awaiting them outside, she laughed good-humouredly. "Do you know, Chetty, I quite enjoyed it!"

XII.

The next morning Mrs. Allison telephoned Seabury that Gabrielle had slept well after an amusing evening: felt so fit that she thought they might seize upon this glorious morning for a drive to the Grande-Chartreuse. The drive, by the route they preferred, was a long one, and hitherto she had not felt quite equal to it. Accordingly, the three left the hotel at eleven o'clock with Seabury's trusty young Savoyard driver, and were soon in the mountains.

It was one of those high-heavenly days that often come among the mountains of Savoie in autumn. In the valleys the hillsides were pink with autumn crocuses thrusting up out of the short sunburned grass. The beech trees still held their satiny green. As the road wound higher and higher toward the heights, Seabury and his companions grew more and more silent. The lightness and purity of the air gave one a sense of detachment from everything one had left behind "down there, back yonder." Mere breathing was a delicate physical pleasure. One had the feeling that life would go on thus forever in high places, among naked peaks cut sharp against a stainless sky.

Ever afterward Seabury remembered that drive as strangely impersonal. He and the two ladies were each lost in a companionship much closer than any they could share with one another. The clean-cut mountain boy who drove them seemed lost in thoughts of his own. His eyes were on the road: he never spoke. Once, when the gold tones of an alpine horn floated down from some hidden pasture far overhead, he stopped the car of his own accord and shut off the engine. He threw a smiling glance back at Seabury and then sat still, while the simple, melancholy song floated down through the blue air. When it ceased, he waited a little, looking up. As the horn did not sing again, he drove on without comment.

At last, beyond a sharp turn in the road, the monastery came into view; acres of slate roof, of many heights and pitches, turrets and steep slopes. The terrifying white mountain crags overhung it from behind, and the green beech wood lay all about its walls. The sunlight blazing down upon that mothering roof showed ruined patches: the Government could not afford to keep such a wilderness of leading in repair.

The monastery, superb and solitary among the lonely mountains, was after all a destination: brought Seabury's party down into man's world again, though it was the world of the past. They began to chatter foolishly, after hours of silent reflection. Mrs. Allison wished to see the kitchen of the Carthusians, and the chapel, but she thought Gabrielle should stay in the car. Madame de Couçy insisted that she was not tired: she would walk about the stone courtyard while the other two went into the monastery.

Except for a one-armed guard in uniform, the great court was empty. Herbs and little creeping plants grew between the cobblestones. The three walked toward the great open well and leaned against the stone wall that encircled it, looking down into its wide mouth. The hewn blocks of the coping were moss-grown, and there was water at the bottom. Madame de Couçy slipped a little mirror from her handbag and threw a sunbeam down into the stone-lined well. That yellow ray seemed to waken the black water at the bottom: little ripples stirred over the surface. She said nothing, but she smiled as she threw the gold plaque over the water and the wet moss of the lower coping. Chetty and Seabury left her there. When he glanced back, just before they disappeared into the labyrinth of buildings, she was still looking down into the well and playing with her little reflector, a faintly contemptuous smile on her lips.

After nearly two hours at the monastery the party started homeward. Seabury told the driver to regulate his speed so that they would see the last light on the mountains before they reached the hotel.

The return trip was ill-starred: they narrowly escaped a serious accident. As they rounded one of those sharp curves, with a steep wall on their right and an open gulf on the left, the chauffeur was confronted by a small car with two women, crossing the road just in front of him. To avoid throwing them over the precipice he ran sharply to the right, grazing the rock wall until he could bring his car to a stop. His passengers were thrown violently forward over the driver's seat. The light car had been on the wrong side of the road, and had attempted to cross on hearing the Savoyard's horn. His nerve and quickness had brought every one off alive, at least.

Immediately the two women from the other car sprang out and ran up to Seabury with shrill protestations; they were very careful drivers, had run this car twelve thousand miles and never had an accident, etc. They were Americans; bobbed, hatless, clad in dirty white knickers and sweaters. They addressed each other as "Marge" and "Jim." Seabury's forehead was bleeding: they repeatedly offered to plaster it up for him.

The Savoyard was in the road, working with his mudguard and his front wheel. Madame de Couçy was lying back in her seat, pale, her eyes closed, something very wrong with her breathing. Mrs. Allison was fanning her with Seabury's hat. The two girls who had caused all the trouble had lit cigarettes and were swaggering about with their hands in their trousers pockets, giving advice to the driver about his wheel. The Savoyard never lifted his eyes. He had not spoken since he ran his car into the wall. The sharp voices, knowingly ordering him to "*regardez, attendez,*" did not pierce his silence or his contempt. Seabury paid no attention to them because he was alarmed about Madame de Couçy, who looked desperately ill. She ought to lie down, he felt sure, but there was no place to put her—the road was cut along the face of a cliff for a long way back. Chetty had aromatic ammonia in her handbag; she persuaded Gabrielle to take it from the bottle, as they had no cup. While Seabury was leaning over her she opened her eyes and said distinctly:

"I think I am not hurt . . . faintness, a little palpitation. If you could get those creatures away . . ."

He sprang off the running-board and drew the two intruders aside. He addressed them; first politely, then forcibly. Their reply was impertinent, but they got into their dirty little car and went. The Savoyard was left in peace; the situation was simplified. Three elderly people had been badly shaken up and bruised, but the brief submersion in frightfulness was over. At last the driver said he could get his car home safely.

During the rest of the drive Madame de Couçy seemed quite restored. Her colour was not good, but her self-control was admirable.

"You must let me give that boy something on my own account, Seabury. Oh, I know you will be generous with him! But I feel a personal interest. He took a risk, and he took the right one. He couldn't run the chance of knocking two women over a precipice. They happened to be worth nobody's consideration, but that doesn't alter the code."

"Such an afternoon to put you through!" Seabury groaned.

"It was natural, wasn't it, after such a morning? After one has been *exaltée,* there usually comes a shock. Oh, I don't mean the bruises we got! I mean the white breeches." Gabrielle laughed, her good laugh, with no malice in it. She put her hand on his shoulder. "How ever did you manage to dispose of them so quickly?"

When the car stopped before the hotel, Madame de Couçy put a tiny card case into the driver's hand with a smile and a word. But when she tried to rise from the seat, she sank back. Seabury and the Savoyard lifted her out, carried her into the hotel and up the lift, into her own chamber. As they placed her on the bed, Seabury said he would call a doctor. Madame de Couçy opened her eyes and spoke firmly:

"That is not necessary. Chetty knows what to do for me. I shall be myself tomorrow. Thank you both, thank you."

Outside the chamber door Seabury asked Mrs. Allison whether he should telephone for Doctor Françon.

"I think not. A new person would only disturb her. I have all the remedies her own doctor gave me for these attacks. Quiet is the most important thing, really."

. . .

The next morning Seabury was awakened very early, something before six o'clock, by the buzz of his telephone. Mrs. Allison spoke, asking in a low voice if he would come to their apartment as soon as possible. He dressed rapidly. The lift was not yet running, so he went up two flights of stairs and rang at their door. Cherry Beamish, in her dressing-gown, admitted him. From her face he knew, at once,—though her smile was almost radiant as she took his hand.

"Yes, it is over for her, poor dear," she said softly. "It must have happened in her sleep. I was with her until after midnight. When I went in again, a little after five, I found her just as I want you to see her now; before her maid comes, before anyone has been informed."

She led him on tiptoe into Gabrielle's chamber. The first shafts of the morning sunlight slanted through the Venetian blinds. A blue dressing-gown hung on a tall chair beside the bed, blue slippers beneath it. Gabrielle lay on her back, her eyes closed. The face that had outfaced so many changes of fortune had no longer need to muffle itself in furs, to shrink away from curious eyes, or harden itself into scorn. It lay on the pillow regal, calm, victorious,—like an open confession.

Seabury stood for a moment looking down at her. Then he went to the window and peered out through the open slats at the sun, come at last over the mountains into a sky that had long been blue: the same mountains they were driving among yesterday.

Presently Cherry Beamish spoke to him. She pointed to the hand that lay on the turned-back sheet. "See how changed her hands are; like those of a young woman. She forgot to take off her rings last night, or she was too tired. Yes, dear, you needed a long rest. And now you are with your own kind."

"I feel that, too, Chetty. She is with them. All is well. Thank you for letting me come." He stooped for a moment over the hand that had been gracious to his youth. They went out into the salon, carefully closing the door behind them.

"Now, my dear, stay here, with her. I will go to the management, and I will arrange all that must be done."

Some hours later, after he had gone through the formalities required by French law, Seabury encountered the three journalists in front of the hotel.

. . .

Next morning the great man from the Riviera to whom Seabury had telegraphed came in person, his car laden with flowers from his conservatories. He stood on the platform at the railway station, his white head uncovered, all the while that the box containing Gabrielle Longstreet's coffin was being carried across and put on the express. Then he shook Seabury's hand in farewell, and bent gallantly over Chetty's. Seabury and Chetty were going to Paris on that same express.

After her illness two years ago Gabrielle de Couçy had bought a lot *à perpétuité* in Père-Lachaise. That was rather a fashion then: Adelina Patti, Sarah Bernhardt, and other ladies who had once held a place in the world made the same choice.

1948

ELLEN GLASGOW
(1873–1945)

A prolific novelist, Ellen Glasgow is known particularly for her depictions of Virginia society after the Civil War. Glasgow did not take active stands on feminist issues other than the suffrage movement, but her novels and short stories frequently depict women's struggles to attain equality or independence in relationships with men.

Even though she was born into a family of ten children, Glasgow experienced a lonely childhood in Richmond, Virginia. Devoted to her mother, she disliked her father and found most of her family unsympathetic. Partial loss of hearing when she was a teenager enhanced her sense of separateness from her family and other people her age. The unhappiness of her early years affected the themes and tone of much of her writing.

As a writer, Glasgow experienced significant success during her lifetime. Her first novel, The Descendant, *was published anonymously in 1897, when she was twenty-four, and* Phases of an Inferior Planet *was published in 1898. It was not until her third novel,* Voice of the People *(1900), that she turned to the Virginia settings and characters that would characterize much of her work. She received a doctor of letters degree from the University of North Carolina in 1930 and was elected to the National Institute of Arts and Letters in 1932. She also received honorary degrees from the University of Richmond, Duke University, and the College of William and Mary.*

Through much of her life, Glasgow traveled extensively. She visited and corresponded with many prominent literary figures of her time, including Thomas Hardy and Hugh Walpole. Although she was engaged to be married several times, each relationship was broken off before the wedding. Glasgow apparently preferred her independence as a single woman and delighted in being able to support herself with her writing. She died at age seventy-two in the house where she had lived for fifty-seven years.

Like many of the women whose works appear in this anthology, Glasgow wrote fiction in order to earn a living; however, she also wanted to convey through her work a "social history" of the South. She was a moralist, interested in dramatizing the problems that women face in a society dominated by men. A number of her stories show the inequities of married life and the sufferings of women married to insensitive men who look upon their wives as possessions.

Complaining that she did not like to work on the small canvas of short fiction, Glasgow published only a dozen short stories. However, her stories were often the seeds from which her longer works grew. "The Difference," while it does not appear as radical now as it did when it appeared in Harper's Magazine *in 1923, reflects the author's ability to convey character, as well as a strong sense of irony, in a few pages. Like many of Glasgow's female characters, the women in "The Difference" are more capable of strong emotion and have a surer sense of moral values than do the men in their lives.*

THE DIFFERENCE

Outside, in the autumn rain, the leaves were falling.

For twenty years, every autumn since her marriage, Margaret Fleming had watched the leaves from this window; and always it had seemed to her that they were a part of her life which she held precious. As they fell she had known that they carried away something she could never recover—youth, beauty, pleasure, or only memories that she wanted to keep. Something gracious, desirable and fleeting; but never until this afternoon had she felt that the wind was sweeping away the illusion of happiness by which she lived. Beyond the panes, against which the rain was beating in gray sheets, she looked out on the naked outlines of the city: bleak houses, drenched grass in squares, and boughs of trees where a few brown or yellow leaves were clinging.

On the hearth rug the letter lay where it had fallen a few minutes—or was it a few hours ago? The flames from the wood fire cast a glow on the white pages; and she imagined that the ugly words leaped out to sting her like scorpions as she moved by them. Not for worlds, she told herself, would she stoop and touch them again. Yet what need had she to touch them when each slanting black line was etched in her memory with acid? Never, though she lived a hundred years, could she forget the way the letters fell on the white paper!

Once, twice, three times, she walked from window to door and back again from door to window. The wood fire burned cheerfully with a whispering sound. As the lights and shadows stirred over the familiar objects she had once loved, her gaze followed them hungrily. She had called this upstairs library George's room, and she realized now that every piece of furniture, every book it contained, had been chosen to please him. He liked the golden brown of the walls, the warm colours in the Persian rugs, the soft depth of the cushioned chairs. He liked, too, the flamboyant red lilies beneath the little Chippendale mirror.

After twenty years of happiness, of comradeship, of mutual dependence, after all that marriage could mean to two equal spirits, was there nothing left except ashes? Could twenty years of happiness be destroyed in an afternoon, in an hour? Stopping abruptly, with a jerk which ran like a spasm through her slender figure, she gazed with hard searching eyes over the red lilies into the mirror. The grave beauty of her face, a beauty less of flesh than of spirit, floated there in the shadows like a flower in a pond.

"I am younger than he is by a year," she thought, "and yet he can begin over again to love, while a new love for me would be desecration."

There was the sound of his step on the stair. An instant later his hand fell on the door, and he entered the room.

Stooping swiftly, she picked up the letter from the rug and hid it in her bosom. Then turning toward him, she received his kiss with a smile. "I didn't wait lunch for you," she said.

"I got it at the club." After kissing her cheek, he moved to the fire and stood warming his hands. "Beastly day. No chance of golf, so I've arranged to see that man from Washington. You won't get out, I suppose?"

She shook her head. "No, I sha'n't get out."

Did he know, she wondered, that this woman had written to her? Did he suspect that the letter lay now in her bosom? He had brought the smell of rain, the taste of dampness, with him into the room; and this air of the outer world enveloped him while he stood there, genial, robust, superbly vital, clothed in his sanguine temperament as in the healthy red and white of his flesh. Still boyish at forty-five, he had that look of perennial innocence which some men carry untarnished through the most enlightening experiences. Even his moustache and his sharply jutting chin could not disguise the softness that hovered always about his mouth, where she noticed now, with her piercing scrutiny, the muscles were growing lax. Strange that she had never seen this until she discovered that George loved another woman! The thought flashed into her mind that she knew him in reality no better than if she had lived with a stranger for twenty years. Yet, until a few hours ago, she would have said, had any one asked her, that their marriage was as perfect as any mating between a man and a woman could be in this imperfect world.

"You're wise. The wind's still in the east, and there is no chance, I'm afraid, of a change." He hesitated an instant, stared approvingly at the red lilies, and remarked abruptly, "Nice colour."

"You always liked red." Her mouth lost its softness. "And I was pale even as a girl."

His genial gaze swept her face. "Oh, well, there's red and red, you know. Some cheeks look best pale."

Without replying to his words, she sat looking up at him while her thoughts, escaping her control, flew from the warm room out into the rough autumn weather. It was as if she felt the beating of the rain in her soul, as if she were torn from her security and whirled downward and onward in the violence of the storm. On the surface of her life nothing had changed. The fire still burned; the lights and shadows still flickered over the Persian rugs; her husband still stood there, looking down on her through the cloudless blue of his eyes. But the real Margaret, the vital part of her, was hidden far away in that deep place where the seeds of mysterious impulses and formless desires lie buried. She knew that there were secrets within herself which she had never acknowledged in her own thoughts; that there were unexpressed longings which had never taken shape even in her imagination. Somewhere beneath the civilization of the ages there was the skeleton of the savage.

The letter in her bosom scorched her as if it were fire. "That was why you used to call me magnolia blossom," she said in a colourless voice, and knew it was only the superficial self that was speaking.

His face softened; yet so perfectly had the note of sentiment come to be understood rather than expressed in their lives that she could feel his embarrassment. The glow lingered in his eyes, but he answered only, "Yes, you were always like that."

An irrepressible laugh broke from her. Oh, the irony, the bitterness! "Perhaps you like them pale!" she tossed back mockingly, and wondered if this Rose Morrison who had written to her was coloured like her name?

He looked puzzled but solicitous. "I'm afraid I must be off. If you are not tired, could you manage to go over these galleys this afternoon? I'd like to read the last chapter aloud to you after the corrections are made." He had written a book on the history of law; and while he drew the roll of proof sheets from his pocket, she remembered, with a pang as sharp as the stab of a knife, all the work of last summer when they had gathered material together. He needed her for his work, she realized, if not for his pleasure. She stood, as she had always done, for the serious things of his life. This book could not have been written without her. Even his success in his profession had been the result of her efforts as well as his own.

"I'm never too tired for that," she responded, and though she smiled up at him, it was a smile that hurt her with its irony.

"Well, my time's up," he said. "By the way, I'll need my heavier golf things if it is fine to-morrow." To-morrow was Sunday, and he played golf with a group of men at the Country Club every Sunday morning.

"They are in the cedar closet. I'll get them out."

"The medium ones, you know. That English tweed."

"Yes, I know. I'll have them ready." Did Rose Morrison play golf? she wondered.

"I'll try to get back early to dinner. There was a button loose on the waistcoat I wore last evening. I forgot to mention it this morning."

"Oh, I'm sorry. I left it to the servants, but I'll look after it myself." Again this perverse humour seized her. Had he ever asked Rose Morrison to sew on a button?

At the door he turned back. "And I forgot to ask you this morning to order flowers for Morton's funeral. It is to be Monday."

The expression on her face felt as stiff as a wax mask, and though she struggled to relax her muscles, they persisted in that smile of inane cheerfulness. "I'll order them at once, before I begin the galleys," she answered.

Rising from the couch on which she had thrown herself at his entrance, she began again her restless pacing from door to window. The library was quiet except for the whispering flames. Outside in the rain the leaves were falling thickly, driven hither and thither by the wind which rocked the dappled boughs of the sycamores. In the gloom of the room the red lilies blazed.

The terror, which had clutched her like a living thing, had its fangs in her heart. Terror of loss, of futility. Terror of the past because it tortured her. Terror of the future because it might be empty even of torture. "He is mine, and I will never give him up," she thought wildly. "I will fight to the end for what is mine."

There was a sound at the door and Winters, the butler, entered. "Mrs. Chambers, Madam. She was quite sure you would be at home."

"Yes, I am at home." She was always at home, even in illness, to Dorothy Chambers. Though they were so different in temperament, they had been friends from girlhood; and much of the gaiety of Margaret's life had been supplied by Dorothy. Now, as her friend entered, she held out her arms. "You come whenever it rains, dear," she said. "It is so good of you." Yet her welcome was hollow, and at the very instant when she returned her friend's kiss she was wishing that she could send her away. That was one of the worst things about suffering; it made one indifferent and insincere.

Dorothy drew off her gloves, unfastened her furs, and after raising her veil over the tip of her small inquisitive nose, held out her hand with a beseeching gesture.

"I've come straight from a committee luncheon. Give me a cigarette."

Reaching for the Florentine box on the desk, Margaret handed it to her. A minute later, while the thin blue flame shot up between them, she asked herself if Dorothy could look into her face and not see the difference?

Small, plain, vivacious, with hair of ashen gold, thin intelligent features, and a smile of mocking brilliance, Dorothy was the kind of woman whom men admire without loving and women love without admiring. As a girl she had been a social success without possessing a single one of the qualities upon which social success is supposed to depend.

Sinking back in her chair, she blew several rings of smoke from her lips and watched them float slowly upward.

"We have decided to give a bridge party. There's simply no other way to raise money. Will you take a table?"

Margaret nodded. "Of course." Suffering outside of herself made no difference to her. Her throbbing wound was the only reality.

"Janet is going to lend us her house." A new note had come into Dorothy's voice. "I haven't seen her since last spring. She had on a new hat, and was looking awfully well. You know Herbert has come back."

Margaret started. At last her wandering attention was fixed on her visitor. "Herbert? And she let him?" There was deep disgust in her tone.

Dorothy paused to inhale placidly before she answered. "Well, what else could she do? He tried to make her get a divorce, and she wouldn't."

A flush stained Margaret's delicate features. "I never understood why she didn't. He made no secret of what he wanted. He showed her plainly that he loved the other woman."

Dorothy's only reply was a shrug; but after a moment, in which she smoked with a luxurious air, she commented briefly, "But man's love isn't one of the eternal verities."

"Well, indifference is, and he proved that he was indifferent to Janet. Yet she has let him come back to her. I can't see what she is to get out of it."

Dorothy laughed cynically. "Oh, she enjoys immensely the attitude of forgiveness, and at last he has permitted her to forgive him. There is a spiritual vanity as well as a physical one, you know, and Janet's weakness is spiritual."

"But to live with a man who doesn't love her? To remember every minute of the day and night that it is another woman he loves?"

"And every time that she remembers it she has the luxury of forgiving again." Keenness flickered like a blade in Dorothy's gray eyes. "You are very lovely, Margaret," she said abruptly. "The years seem only to leave you rarer and finer, but you know nothing about life."

A smile quivered and died on Margaret's lips. "I might retort that you know nothing about love."

With an impatient birdlike gesture Dorothy tossed her burned-out cigarette into the fire. "Whose love?" she inquired as she opened the Florentine box, "Herbert's or yours?"

"It's all the same, isn't it?"

By the flame of the match she had struck Dorothy's expression appeared almost malign. "There, my dear, is where you are wrong," she replied. "When a man and a woman talk of love they speak two different languages. They can never understand each other because women love with their imagination and men with their senses. To you love is a thing in itself, a kind of abstract power like religion; to Herbert it is simply the way he feels."

"But if he loves the other woman, he doesn't love Janet; and yet he wants to return to her."

Leaning back in her chair, Dorothy surveyed her with a look which was at once sympathetic and mocking. Her gaze swept the pure grave features; the shining dusk of the hair; the narrow nose with its slight arch in the middle; the straight red lips with their resolute pressure; the skin so like a fading roseleaf. Yes, there was beauty in Margaret's face if one were only artist or saint enough to perceive it.

"There is so much more in marriage than either love or indifference," she remarked casually. "There is, for instance, comfort."

"Comfort?" repeated Margaret scornfully. She rose, in her clinging draperies of chiffon, to place a fresh log on the fire. "If he really loves the other woman, Janet ought to give him up," she said.

At this Dorothy turned on her. "Would you, if it were George?" she demanded.

For an instant, while she stood there in front of the fire, it seemed to

Margaret that the room whirled before her gaze like the changing colours in a kaleidoscope. Then a gray cloud fell over the brightness, and out of this cloud there emerged only the blaze of the red lilies. A pain struck her in the breast, and she remembered the letter she had hidden there.

"Yes," she answered presently. "I should do it if it were George."

A minute afterward she became conscious that while she spoke, a miracle occurred within her soul.

The tumult of sorrow, of anger, of bitterness, of despair, was drifting farther and farther away. Even the terror, which was worse than any tumult, had vanished. In that instant of renunciation she had reached some spiritual haven. What she had found, she understood presently, was the knowledge that there is no support so strong as the strength that enables one to stand alone.

"I should do it if it were George," she said again very slowly.

"Well, I think you would be very foolish." Dorothy had risen and was lowering her veil. "For when George ceases to be desirable for sentimental reasons, he will still have his value as a good provider." Her mocking laugh grated on Margaret's ears. "Now, I must run away. I only looked in for an instant. I've a tea on hand, and I must go home and dress."

When she had gone, Margaret stood for a minute, thinking deeply. For a minute only, but in that space of time her decision was made. Crossing to the desk, she telephoned for the flowers. Then she left the library and went into the cedar closet at the end of the hall. When she had found the golf clothes George wanted, she looked over them carefully and hung them in his dressing room. Her next task was to lay out his dinner clothes and to sew the loose button on the waistcoat he had worn last evening. She did these things deliberately, automatically, repeating as if it were a formula, "I must forget nothing"; and when at last she had finished, she stood upright, with a sigh of relief, as if a burden had rolled from her shoulders. Now that she had attended to the details of existence, she would have time for the problem of living.

Slipping out of her gray dress, she changed into a walking suit of blue homespun. Then, searching among the shoes in her closet, she selected a pair of heavy boots she had worn in Maine last summer. As she put on a close little hat and tied a veil of blue chiffon over her face, she reflected, with bitter mirth, that only in novels could one hide one's identity behind a veil.

In the hall downstairs she met Winters, who stared at her discreetly but disapprovingly.

"Shall I order the car, madam?"

She shook her head, reading his thoughts as plainly as if he had uttered them, "No, it has stopped raining. I want to walk."

The door closed sharply on her life of happiness, and she passed out into the rain-soaked world where the mist caught her like damp smoke. So this was what it meant to be deserted, to be alone on the earth! The smell of rain, the smell that George had brought with him into the warm room upstairs, oppressed her as if it were the odour of melancholy.

As the chill pierced her coat, she drew her furs closely about her neck, and walked briskly in the direction of the street car. The address on the letter she carried was burned into her memory not in numbers, but in the thought that it was a villa George owned in an unfashionable suburb named Locust Park. Though she had never been there, she knew that, with the uncertain trolley service she must expect, it would take at least two hours to make the trip and return. Half an hour for Rose Morrison; and even then it would be night, and Winters at least would be anxious, before she reached home. Well, that was the best she could do.

The street car came, and she got in and found a seat behind a man who had been shooting and carried a string of partridges. All the other seats were filled with the usual afternoon crowd for the suburbs—women holding bundles or baskets and workmen returning from the factories. A sense of isolation like spiritual darkness descended upon her; and she closed her eyes and tried to bring back the serenity she had felt in the thought of relinquishment. But she could remember only a phrase of Dorothy's which floated like a wisp of thistledown through her thoughts, "Spiritual vanity. With some women it is stronger than physical vanity." Was that her weakness, vanity, not of the body, but of the spirit?

Thoughts blew in and out of her mind like dead leaves, now whirling, now drifting, now stirring faintly in her consciousness with a moaning sound. Twenty years. Nothing but that. Love and nothing else in her whole life . . . The summer of their engagement. A rose garden in bloom. The way he looked. The smell of roses. Or was it only the smell of dead leaves rotting to earth? . . . All the long, long years of their marriage. Little things that one never forgot. The way he laughed. The way he smiled. The look of his hair when it was damp on his forehead. The smell of cigars in his clothes. The three lumps of sugar in his coffee. The sleepy look in his face when he stood ready to put out the lights while she went up the stairs. Oh, the little things that tore at one's heart!

The street car stopped with a jerk, and she got out and walked through the drenched grass in the direction one of the women had pointed out to her.

"The Laurels? That low yellow house at the end of this lane, farther on where the piles of dead leaves are. You can't see the house now, the lane turns, but it's just a stone's throw farther on."

Thanking her, Margaret walked on steadily toward the turn in the lane. Outside of the city the wind blew stronger, and the coloured leaves, bronze, yellow, crimson, lay in a thick carpet over the muddy road. In the west a thin line of gold shone beneath a range of heavy, smoke-coloured clouds. From the trees rain still dripped slowly; and between the road and the line of gold in the west there stretched the desolate autumn landscape.

"Oh, the little things!" her heart cried in despair. "The little things that make happiness!"

Entering the sagging gate of The Laurels, she passed among mounds of sodden leaves which reminded her of graves, and followed the neglected walk between rows of leafless shrubs which must have looked gay in summer. The house was one of many cheap suburban villas (George had bought it, she remembered, at an auction) and she surmised that, until this newest tenant came, it must have stood long unoccupied. The whole place wore, she reflected as she rang the loosened bell, a furtive and insecure appearance.

After the third ring the door was hurriedly opened by a dishevelled maid, who replied that her mistress was not at home.

"Then I shall wait," said Margaret firmly. "Tell your mistress, when she comes in, that Mrs. Fleming is waiting to see her." With a step as resolute as her words, she entered the house and crossed the hall to the living room where a bright coal fire was burning.

The room was empty, but a canary in a gilded cage at the window broke into song as she entered. On a table stood a tray containing the remains of tea; and beside it there was a half-burned cigarette in a bronze Turkish bowl. A book—she saw instantly that it was a volume of the newest plays—lay face downward beneath a pair of eyeglasses, and a rug, which had fallen from the couch, was in a crumpled pile on the floor.

"So she isn't out," Margaret reflected; and turning at a sound, she confronted Rose Morrison.

For an instant it seemed to the older woman that beauty like a lamp blinded her eyes. Then, as the cloud passed, she realized that it was only a blaze, that it was the loveliness of dead leaves when they are burning.

"So you came?" said Rose Morrison, while she gazed at her with the clear and competent eyes of youth. Her voice, though it was low and clear, had no softness; it rang like a bell. Yes, she had youth, she had her flamboyant loveliness; but stronger than youth and loveliness, it seemed to Margaret, surveying her over the reserves and discriminations of the centuries, was the security of one who had never doubted her own judgment. Her power lay where power usually lies, in an infallible self-esteem.

"I came to talk it over with you," began Margaret quietly; and though she tried to make her voice insolent, the deep instinct of good manners was greater than her effort. "You tell me that my husband loves you."

The glow, the flame, in Rose Morrison's face made Margaret think again of leaves burning. There was no embarrassment, there was no evasion even, in the girl's look. Candid and unashamed, she appeared to glory in this infatuation, which Margaret regarded as worse than sinful, since it was vulgar.

"Oh, I am so glad that you did," Rose Morrison's sincerity was disarming. "I hated to hurt you. You can never know what it cost me to write that letter; but I felt that I owed it to you to tell you the truth. I believe that we always owe people the truth."

"And did George feel this way also?"

"George?" The flame mounted until it enveloped her. "Oh, he doesn't know. I tried to spare him. He would rather do anything than hurt you, and I thought it would be so much better if we could talk it over and find a solution just between ourselves. I knew if you cared for George, you would feel as I do about sparing him."

About sparing him! As if she had done anything for the last twenty years, Margaret reflected, except think out new and different ways of sparing George!

"I don't know," she answered, as she sat down in obedience to the other's persuasive gesture. "I shall have to think a minute. You see this has been— well, rather— sudden."

"I know, I know." The girl looked as if she did. "May I give you a cup of tea? You must be chilled."

"No, thank you. I am quite comfortable."

"Not even a cigarette? Oh, I wonder what you Victorian women did for a solace when you weren't allowed even a cigarette!"

You Victorian women! In spite of her tragic mood, a smile hovered on Margaret's lips. So that was how this girl classified her. Yet Rose Morrison had fallen in love with a Victorian man.

"Then I may?" said the younger woman with her full-throated laugh. From her bright red hair, which was brushed straight back from her forehead, to her splendid figure, where her hips swung free like a boy's, she was a picture of barbaric beauty. There was a glittering hardness about her, as if she had been washed in some indestructible glaze; but it was the glaze of youth, not of experience. She reminded Margaret of a gilded statue she had seen once in a museum; and the girl's eyes, like the eyes of the statue, were gleaming, remote and impassive—eyes that had never looked on reality. The dress she wore was made of some strange "art cloth," dyed in brilliant hues, fashioned like a kimono, and girdled at the hips with what Margaret mistook for a queer piece of rope. Nothing, not even her crude and confident youth, revealed Rose Morrison to her visitor so completely as this end of rope.

"You are an artist?" she asked, for she was sure of her ground. Only an artist, she decided, could be at once so arrogant with destiny and so ignorant of life.

"How did you know? Has George spoken of me?"

Margaret shook her head. "Oh, I knew without any one's telling me."

"I have a studio in Greenwich Village, but George and I met last summer at Ogunquit. I go there every summer to paint."

"I didn't know." How easily, how possessively, this other woman spoke her husband's name.

"It began at once." To Margaret, with her inherited delicacy and reticence, there was something repellent in this barbaric simplicity of emotion.

"But you must have known that he was married," she observed coldly.

"Yes, I knew, but I could see, of course, that you did not understand him."

"And you think that you do?" If it were not tragic, how amusing it would be to think of her simple George as a problem!

"Oh, I realize that it appears very sudden to you; but in the emotions time counts for so little. Just living with a person for twenty years doesn't enable one to understand him, do you think?"

"I suppose not. But do you really imagine," she asked in what struck her as a singularly impersonal tone for so intimate a question, "that George is complex?"

The flame, which was revealed now as the illumination of some secret happiness, flooded Rose Morrison's features. As she leaned forward, with clasped hands, Margaret noticed that the girl was careless about those feminine details by which George declared so often that he judged a woman. Her hair was carelessly arranged; her finger nails needed attention; and beneath the kimono-like garment, a frayed place showed at the back of her stocking. Even her red morocco slippers were run down at the heels; and it seemed to Margaret that this physical negligence had extended to the girl's habit of thought.

"He is so big, so strong and silent, that it would take an artist to understand him," answered Rose Morrison passionately. Was this really, Margaret wondered, the way George appeared to the romantic vision?

"Yes, he is not a great talker," she admitted. "Perhaps if he talked more, you might find him less difficult." Then before the other could reply, she inquired sharply, "Did George tell you that he was misunderstood?"

"How you misjudge him!" The girl had flown to his defense; and though Margaret had been, as she would have said, "a devoted wife," she felt that all this vehemence was wasted. After all, George, with his easy, prosaic temperament, was only made uncomfortable by vehemence. "He never speaks of you except in the most beautiful way," Rose Morrison was insisting. "He realizes perfectly what you have been to him, and he would rather suffer in silence all his life than make you unhappy."

"Then what is all this about?" Though she felt it was unfair, Margaret could not help putting the question.

Actually there were tears in Rose Morrison's eyes. "I could not bear to see his life ruined," she answered. "I hated to write to you; but how else could I make you realize that you were standing in the way of his happiness? If it were just myself, I could have borne it in silence. I would never have hurt you just for my own sake; but, the subterfuge, the dishonesty, is spoiling his life. He does not say so, but, oh, I see it every day because I love him!" As she bent over, the firelight caught her hair, and it blazed out triumphantly like the red lilies in Margaret's library.

"What is it that you want me to do?" asked Margaret in her dispassionate voice.

"I felt that we owed you the truth," responded the girl, "and I hoped that you would take what I wrote you in the right spirit."

"You are sure that my husband loves you?"

"Shall I show you his letters?" The girl smiled as she answered, and her full red lips reminded Margaret suddenly of raw flesh. Was raw flesh, after all, what men wanted?

"No!" The single word was spoken indignantly.

"I thought perhaps they would make you see what it means," explained Rose Morrison simply. "Oh, I wish I could do this without causing you pain!"

"Pain doesn't matter. I can stand pain."

"Well, I'm glad you aren't resentful. After all, why should we be enemies? George's happiness means more than anything else to us both."

"And you are sure you know best what is for George's happiness?"

"I know that subterfuge and lies and dishonesty cannot bring happiness." Rose Morrison flung out her arms with a superb gesture. "Oh, I realize that it is a big thing, a great thing, I am asking of you. But in your place, if I stood in his way, I should so gladly sacrifice myself for his sake. I should give him his freedom. I should acknowledge his right to happiness, to self-development."

A bitter laugh broke from Margaret's lips. What a jumble of sounds these catchwords of the new freedom made! What was this self-development which could develop only through the sacrifice of others? How would these immature theories survive the compromises and concessions and adjustments which made marriage permanent?

"I cannot feel that our marriage has interfered with his development," she rejoined presently.

"You may be right," Rose Morrison conceded the point. "But to-day he needs new inspiration, new opportunities. He needs the companionship of a modern mind."

"Yes, he has kept young at my cost," thought the older woman. "I have helped by a thousand little sacrifices, by a thousand little cares and worries, to preserve this unnatural youth which is destroying me. I have taken over the burden of details in order that he might be free for the larger interests of life. If he is young to-day, it is at the cost of my youth."

For the second time that day, as she sat there in silence, with her eyes on the blooming face of Rose Morrison, a wave of peace, the peace of one who has been shipwrecked and then swept far off into some serene haven, enveloped her. Something to hold by, that at least she had found. The law of sacrifice, the ideal of self-surrender, which she had learned in the past. For twenty years she had given freely, abundantly, of her best; and to-day she could still prove to him that she was not beggared. She could still give the supreme gift of her happiness. "How he must love you!" she exclaimed. "How he must love you to have hurt me so much for your sake! Nothing but a great love could make him so cruel."

"He does love me," answered Rose Morrison, and her voice was like the song of a bird.

"He must." Margaret's eyes were burning, but no tears came. Her lips felt cracked with the effort she made to keep them from trembling. "I think if he had done this thing with any other motive than a great love, I should hate him until I died." Then she rose and held out her hand. "I shall not stand in your way," she added.

Joy flashed into the girl's eyes. "You are very noble," she answered. "I am sorry if I have hurt you. I am sorry, too, that I called you old-fashioned."

Margaret laughed. "Oh, I am old-fashioned. I am so old-fashioned that I should have died rather than ruin the happiness of another woman."

The joy faded from Rose Morrison's face. "It was not I," she answered. "It was life. We cannot stand in the way of life."

"Life to-day, God yesterday, what does it matter? It is a generation that has grasped everything except personal responsibility." Oh, if one could only keep the humour! A thought struck her, and she asked abruptly, "When your turn comes, if it ever does, will you give way as I do?"

"That will be understood. We shall not hold each other back."

"But you are young. You will tire first. Then must he give way?" Why, in twenty years George would be sixty-five and Rose Morrison still a young woman!

Calm, resolute, uncompromising, Rose Morrison held open the door. "Whatever happens, he would never wish to hold me back."

Then Margaret passed out, the door closed behind her, and she stood breathing deep draughts of the chill, invigorating air. Well, that was over.

The lawn, with its grave-like mounds of leaves, looked as mournful as a cemetery. Beyond the bare shrubs the road glimmered; the wind still blew in gusts, now rising, now dying away with a plaintive sound; in the west the thread of gold had faded to a pale greenish light. Veiled in the monotonous fall of the leaves, it seemed to Margaret that the desolate evening awaited her.

"How he must love her," she thought, not resentfully, but with tragic resignation. "How he must love her to have sacrificed me as he has done."

This idea, she found as she walked on presently in the direction of the street car, had taken complete possession of her point of view. Through its crystal lucidity she was able to attain some sympathy with her husband's suffering. What agony of mind he must have endured in these past months, these months when they had worked so quietly side by side on his book! What days of gnawing remorse! What nights of devastating anguish! How this newer love must have rent his heart asunder before he could stoop to the baseness of such a betrayal! Tears, which had not come for her own pain, stung her eyelids. She knew that he must have fought it hour by hour, day by day, night by night. Conventional as he was, how violent this emotion must have been to have conquered him so completely. "Terrible as an army with banners," she repeated softly, while a pang of jealousy shot through her heart. Was there in George, she asked now, profounder depths of feeling than she had ever reached; was there some secret garden of romance where she had never entered? Was George larger, wilder, more adventurous in imagination, than she had dreamed? Had the perfect lover lain hidden in his nature, awaiting only the call of youth?

The street car returned almost empty; and she found restfulness in the monotonous jolting, as if it were swinging her into some world beyond space and time, where mental pain yielded to the sense of physical discomfort. After the agony of mind, the aching of body was strangely soothing.

Here and there, the lights of a house flashed among the trees, and she thought, with an impersonal interest, of the neglected villa, surrounded by mounds of rotting leaves, where that girl waited alone for happiness. Other standards. This was how the newer generation appeared to Margaret—other standards, other morals. Facing life stripped bare of every safeguard, of every restraining tradition, with only the courage of ignorance, of defiant inexperience, to protect one. That girl was not willfully cruel. She was simply greedy for emotion; she was grasping at the pretense of happiness like all the rest of her undisciplined generation. She was caught by life because she had never learned to give up, to do without, to stand alone.

Her corner had come, and she stepped with a sensation of relief on the wet pavement. The rain was dripping steadily in a monotonous drizzle. While she walked the few blocks to her door, she forced herself by an effort of will to go on, step by step, not to drop down in the street and lose consciousness.

The tinkle of the bell and the sight of Winters's face restored her to her senses.

"Shall I bring you tea, madam?"

"No, it is too late."

Going upstairs to her bedroom, she took off her wet clothes and slipped into her prettiest tea gown, a trailing thing of blue satin and chiffon. While she ran a comb through her damp hair and touched her pale lips with colour, she reflected that even renunciation was easier when one looked desirable. "But it is like painting the cheeks of the dead," she thought, as she turned away from the mirror and walked with a dragging step to the library. Never, she realized suddenly, had she loved George so much as in this hour when she had discovered him only to lose him.

As she entered, George hurried to meet her with an anxious air. "I didn't hear you come in, Margaret. I have been very uneasy. Has anything happened?"

By artificial light he looked younger even than he had seemed in the afternoon; and this boyishness of aspect struck her as strangely pathetic. It was all a part, she told herself, of that fulfilment which had come too late, of that perilous second blooming, not of youth, but of Indian Summer. The longing to spare him, to save him from the suffering she had endured, pervaded her heart.

"Yes, something has happened," she answered gently. "I have been to see Rose Morrison."

As she spoke the name, she turned away from him, and walking with unsteady steps across the room, stood looking down into the fire. The knowledge of all that she must see when she turned, of the humiliation, the anguish, the remorse in his eyes, oppressed her heart with a passion of shame and pity. How could she turn and look on his wounded soul which she had stripped bare?

"Rose Morrison?" he repeated in an expressionless voice. "What do you know of Rose Morrison?"

At his question she turned quickly, and faced not anguish, not humiliation, but emptiness. There was nothing in his look except the blankness of complete surprise. For an instant the shock made her dizzy; and in the midst of the dizziness there flashed through her mind the memory of an evening in her childhood, when she had run bravely into a dark room where they told her an ogre was hiding, and had found that it was empty.

"She wrote to me." Her legs gave way as she replied, and, sinking into the nearest chair, she sat gazing up at him with an immobile face.

A frown gathered his eyebrows, and a purplish flush (he flushed so easily of late) mounted slowly to the smooth line of his hair. She watch the quiver that ran through his under lip (strange that she had not noticed how it had thickened) while his teeth pressed it sharply. Everything about him was acutely vivid to her, as if she were looking at him closely for the first time. She saw the furrow between his eyebrows, the bloodshot stain on one eyeball, the folds of flesh beneath his jutting chin, the crease in his black tie, the place where his shirt gave a little because it had grown too tight—all these insignificant details would exist indelibly in her brain.

"She wrote to you?" His voice sounded strained and husky, and he coughed abruptly as if he were trying to hide his embarrassment. "What the devil! But you don't know her."

"I saw her this afternoon. She told me everything."

"Everything?" Never had she imagined that he could appear so helpless, so lacking in the support of any conventional theory. A hysterical laugh broke from her, a laugh as utterly beyond her control as a spasm, and at the sound he flushed as if she had struck him. While she sat there she realized that she had no part or place in the scene before her. Never could she speak the words that she longed to utter. Never could she make him understand the real self behind the marionette at which he was looking. She longed with all her heart to say: "There were possibilities in me that you never suspected. I also am capable of a great love. In my heart I also am a creature of romance, of adventure. If you had only known it, you might have found in marriage all that you have sought elsewhere. . . ." This was what she longed to cry out, but instead she said merely, "She told me of your love. She asked me to give you up."

"She asked you to give me up?" His mouth fell open as he finished, and while he stared at her he forgot to shut it. It occurred to her that he had lost the power of inventing a phrase, that he could only echo the ones she had spoken. How like a foolish boy he looked as he stood there, in front of the sinking fire, trying to hide behind that hollow echo!

"She said that I stood in your way." The phrase sounded so grotesque as she uttered it that she found herself laughing again. She had not wished to speak these ugly things. Her heart was filled with noble words, with beautiful sentiments, but she could not make her lips pronounce them in spite of all the efforts she made. And she recalled suddenly the princess in the fairy tale who, when she opened her mouth, found that toads and lizards escaped from it instead of pearls and rubies.

At first he did not reply, and it seemed to her that only mechanical force could jerk his jaw back into place and close the eyelids over his vacant blue eyes. When at last he made a sound it was only the empty echo again, "stood in my way!"

"She is desperately in earnest." Justice wrung this admission from her. "She feels that this subterfuge is unfair to us all. Your happiness, she thinks, is what we should consider first, and she is convinced that I should be sacrificed to your future. She was perfectly frank. She suppressed nothing."

For the first time George Fleming uttered an original sound. "O Lord!" he exclaimed devoutly.

"I told her that I did not wish to stand in your way," resumed Margaret, as if the exclamation had not interrupted the flow of her thoughts. "I told her I would give you up."

Suddenly, without warning, he exploded. "What, in the name of heaven, has it got to do with you?" he demanded.

"To do with me?" It was her turn to echo. "But isn't that girl—" she corrected herself painfully—"isn't she living in your house at this minute?"

He cast about helplessly for an argument. When at last he discovered one, he advanced it with a sheepish air, as if he recognized its weakness. "Well, nobody else would take it, would they?"

"She says that you love her."

He shifted his ground nervously. "I can't help what she says, can I?"

"She offered to show me your letters."

"Compliments, nothing more."

"But you must love her, or you couldn't—you wouldn't—" A burning flush scorched Margaret's body.

"I never said that I . . ." Even with her he had always treated the word love as if it were a dangerous explosive, and he avoided touching it now, "that I cared for her in that way."

"Then you do in another way?"

He glanced about like a trapped animal. "I am not a fool, am I? Why, I am old enough to be her father! Besides, I am not the only one anyway. She was living with a man when I met her, and he wasn't the first. She isn't bad, you know. It's a kind of philosophy with her. She calls it self . . ."

"I know." Margaret cut the phrase short. "I have heard what she calls it." So it was all wasted! Nothing that she could do could lift the situation above the level of the commonplace, the merely vulgar. She was defrauded not only of happiness, but even of the opportunity to be generous. Her sacrifice was as futile as that girl's passion. "But she is in love with you now," she said.

"I suppose she is." His tone had grown stubborn. "But how long would it last? In six months she would be leaving me for somebody else. Of course, I won't see her again," he added, with the manner of one who is conceding a reasonable point. Then, after a pause in which she made no response, his stubbornness changed into resentment. "Anybody would think that you are angry because I am not in love with her!" he exclaimed. "Anybody would think—but I don't understand women!"

"Then you will not—you do not mean to leave me?" she asked; and her manner was as impersonal, she was aware, as if Winters had just given her notice.

"Leave you?" He glanced appreciatively round the room. "Where on earth could I go?"

For an instant Margaret looked at him in silence. Then she insisted coldly, "To her, perhaps. She thinks that you are in love with her."

"Well, I suppose I've been a fool," he confessed, after a struggle, "but you are making too much of it."

Yes, she was making too much of it; she realized this more poignantly than he would ever be able to do. She felt like an actress who has endowed a comic part with the gesture of high tragedy. It was not, she saw clearly now, that she had misunderstood George, but that she had overplayed life.

"We met last summer at Ogunquit." She became aware presently that he was still making excuses and explanations about nothing. "You couldn't go about much, you know, and we went swimming and played golf together. I liked her, and I could see that she liked me. When we came away I thought we'd break it off, but somehow we didn't. I saw her several times in New York. Then she came here unexpectedly, and I offered her that old villa nobody would rent. You don't understand such things, Margaret. It hadn't any more to do with you than—than—" He hesitated, fished in the stagnant waters of his mind and flung out abruptly, "than golf has. It was just sort of—well, sort of—recreation."

Recreation! The memory of Rose Morrison's extravagant passion smote her sharply. How glorified the incident had appeared in the girl's imagination, how cheap and tawdry it was in reality. A continual compromise with the second best, an inevitable surrender to the average, was this the history of all romantic emotion? For an instant, such is the perversity of fate, it seemed to the wife that she and this strange girl were united by some secret bond which George could not share—by the bond of woman's immemorial disillusionment.

"I wouldn't have had you hurt for worlds, Margaret," said George, bending over her. The old gentle voice, the old possessive and complacent look in his sleepy blue eyes, recalled her wandering senses. "If I could only make you see that there wasn't anything in it."

She gazed up at him wearily. The excitement of discovery, the exaltation, the anguish, had ebbed away, leaving only gray emptiness. She had lost more than love, more than happiness, for she had lost her belief in life.

"If there had been anything in it, I might be able to understand," she replied.

He surveyed her with gloomy severity. "Hang it all! You act as if you wanted me to be in love with her." Then his face cleared as if by magic. "You're tired out, Margaret, and you're nervous. There's Winters now. You must try to eat a good dinner."

Anxious, caressing, impatient to have the discussion end and dinner begin, he stooped and lifted her in his arms. For an instant she lay there without moving, and in that instant her gaze passed from his face to the red lilies and the uncurtained window beyond.

Outside the leaves were falling.

1923

GERTRUDE STEIN
(1874–1946)

Gertrude Stein is that odd combination, a writer familiar to many yet read by few. Her experiments with language and style are comparable in importance to those of James Joyce and Virginia Woolf, and she influenced many of the most renowned twentieth-century writers who visited her in Paris—Ernest Hemingway, Sherwood Anderson, and F. Scott Fitzgerald, to name a few.

Born in Allegheny, Pennsylvania, Stein was the youngest of five surviving children born to Amelia and Daniel Stein. Soon after her birth, her family moved to Vienna. They remained abroad until 1879, when they moved to California. Her father's business projects prospered, placing the family in comfortable circumstances. Her mother died when Stein was fourteen; when her father died in 1891, her eldest brother, Michael, assumed legal guardianship for her and her brother Leo while also guaranteeing their financial security.

Stein attended Radcliffe College, where she studied psychology under William James. Under James's supervision she conducted studies of automatic writing that were published in the Harvard Psychological Review *in 1896 and 1898. She pursued her interest in psychology at Johns Hopkins Medical School. Although she excelled in her studies, after two years Stein became bored with medicine and failed to pass the degree requirements, a fate that she thought fortuitous. She thanked the obstetrics professor who failed her and ended her medical career.*

In 1903 she settled with her brother Leo in Paris and began writing and collecting contemporary art. Thus she met, influenced, and was influenced by the most important modernist painters: Cézanne, Matisse, and Picasso, among others. Of greater personal significance was her 1907 meeting with Alice Toklas. The two apparently fell in love while walking through the Luxembourg Gardens. In 1910, Toklas moved in; soon afterward, Leo moved out.

Stein's first novel, Q.E.D.*, drew on an early experience in a lesbian triangle. Another lesbian relationship was the subject of* Fernhurst*, her next significant piece of writing. In 1905 she began work on* Three Lives*, portraits of two German working-class women and a young Black woman. Despite the editors' protests about what they deemed grammatical errors, the work appeared in 1909. Stein began working on* The Making of Americans *in 1906, the same year Picasso completed his famous portrait of her. In this work, Stein tells the history of America through descriptions of Americans. Considered her masterpiece by many,* The Making of Americans *appeared in 1925.*

In 1932, Stein composed in six weeks her most accessible work, The Autobiography of Alice B. Toklas*, a history of the post–World War I artistic* *period. The* Atlantic Monthly *published portions of the book, and it became an American best-seller. A year later, Stein and Toklas toured the United States on a memorable trip Stein described in* Everybody's Autobiography *(1937), another popular and financial success.*

During World War I, Toklas and Stein had worked for the American Fund for French Wounded, transporting supplies in their Ford truck. For their efforts they were awarded the Médaille de la Réconnaissance Française*. During World War II, they lived in the French countryside and narrowly missed having their names on a list of Jews to be sent to the concentration camps. Stein wrote of both experiences in* Wars I Have Seen *(1945).*

In addition to her writing, Stein composed librettos for two of Virgil Thomson's operas, one based on the life of Susan B. Anthony and called The Mother of Us All*. Stein died of cancer on July 27, 1946. Toklas lived for another twenty-one years.*

"Ada," one of the two stories included here, has been described as Stein's first love letter to Alice Toklas and her first attempt to write in her own style. "Miss Furr and Miss Skeene," another word portrait from this early period, is based on two painters, Ethel Mars and Maud Hunt Squire, who were frequent visitors in Paris. In both pieces Stein uses slow-moving, repetitive sentences, the trademarks of her linguistic innovations.

■ ADA

Barnes Colhard did not say he would not do it but he did not do it. He did it and then he did not do it, he did not ever think about it. He just thought some time he might do something.

His father Mr. Abram Colhard spoke about it to every one and very many of them spoke to Barnes Colhard about it and he always listened to them.

Then Barnes fell in love with a very nice girl and she would not marry him. He cried then, his father Mr. Abram Colhard comforted him and they took a trip and Barnes promised he would do what his father wanted him to be doing. He did not do the thing, he thought he would do another thing, he did not do the other thing, his father Mr. Colhard did not want him to do the other thing. He really did not do anything then. When he was a good deal older he married a very rich girl. He had thought perhaps he would not propose to her but his sister wrote to him that it would be a good thing. He married the rich girl and she thought he was the most wonderful man and one who knew everything. Barnes never spent more than the income of the fortune he and his wife had then, that is to say they did not spend more than the income and this was a surprise to very many who knew about him and about his marrying the girl who had such a large fortune. He had a happy life while he was living and after he was dead his wife and children remembered him.

He had a sister who also was successful enough in being one being living. His sister was one who came to be happier than most people come to be in living. She came to be a completely happy one. She was twice as old as her brother. She had been a very good daughter to her mother. She and her mother had always told very pretty stories to each other. Many old men loved to hear her tell these stories to her mother. Every one who ever knew her mother liked her mother. Many were sorry later that not every one liked the daughter. Many did like the daughter but not every one as every one had liked the mother. The daughter was charming inside in her, it did not show outside in her to everyone, it certainly did to some. She did sometimes think her mother would be pleased with a story that did not please her mother, when her mother later was sicker the daughter knew that there were some stories she could tell her that would not please her mother. Her mother died and really mostly altogether the mother and the daughter had told each stories very happily together.

The daughter then kept house for her father and took care of her brother. There were many relations who lived with them. The daughter did not like them to live with them and she did not like them to die with them. The daughter, Ada they had called her after her grandmother who had delightful ways of smelling flowers and eating dates and sugar, did not like it at all then as she did not like so much dying and she did not like any of the living she was doing then. Every now and then some old gentleman told delightful stories to her. Mostly then there were not nice stories told by any one then in her living. She told her father Mr. Abram Colhard that she did not like it at all being one being living then. He never said anything. She was afraid then, she was one needing charming stories and happy telling of them and not having that thing she was always trembling. Then every one who could live with them were dead and there were then the father and the son a young man then and the daughter coming to be that one then. Her grandfather had left some money to them each one of them. Ada said she was going to use it to go away from them. The father said nothing then, then he said something and she said nothing then, then they both said nothing and then it was that she went away from them. The father was quite tender then, she was his daughter then. He wrote her tender letters then, she wrote him tender letters then, she never went back to live with him. He wanted her to come and she wrote him tender letters then. He liked the tender letters she wrote to him. He wanted her to live with him. She answered him by writing tender letters to him and telling very nice stories indeed in them. He wrote nothing and then he wrote again and there was some waiting and then he wrote tender letters again and again.

She came to be happier than anybody else who was living then. It is easy to believe this thing. She was telling some one, who was loving every story that was charming. Some one who was living was almost always listening. Some one who was loving was almost always listening. That one who was loving was almost always listening. That one who was loving was telling about being one then listening. That one being loving was then telling stories having a beginning and a middle and an ending. That one was then one always completely listening. Ada was then one and all her living then one completely telling stories that were charming, completely listening to stories having a beginning and a middle and an ending. Trembling was all living, living was all loving, some one was then the other one. Certainly this one was loving this Ada then. And certainly Ada all her living then was happier in living than any one else who ever could, who was, who is, who ever will be living.

1922

MISS FURR AND MISS SKEENE

Helen Furr had quite a pleasant home. Mrs. Furr was quite a pleasant woman. Mr. Furr was quite a pleasant man. Helen Furr had quite a pleasant voice a voice quite worth cultivating. She did not mind working. She worked to cultivate her voice. She did not find it gay living in the same place where she had always been living. She went to a place where some were cultivating something, voices and other things needing cultivating. She met Georgine Skeene there who was cultivating her voice which some thought was quite a pleasant one. Helen Furr and Georgine Skeene lived together then. Georgine Skeene liked travelling. Helen Furr did not care about travelling, she liked to stay in one place and be gay there. They were together then and travelled to another place and stayed there and were gay there.

They stayed there and were gay there, not very gay there, just gay there. They were both gay there, they were regularly working there both of them cultivating their voices there, they were both gay there. Georgine Skeene was gay there and she was regular, regular in being gay, regular in not being gay, regular in being a gay one who was one not being gay longer than was needed to be one being quite a gay one. They were both gay then there and both working there then.

They were in a way both gay there where there were many cultivating something. They were both regular in being gay there. Helen Furr was gay there, she was gayer and gayer there and really she was just gay there, she was gayer and gayer there, that is to say she found ways of being gay there that she was using in being gay there. She was gay there, not gayer and gayer, just gay there, that is to say she was not gayer by using the things she found there that were gay things, she was gay there, always she was gay there.

They were quite regularly gay there, Helen Furr and Georgine Skeene, they were regularly gay there where they were gay. They were very regularly gay.

To be regularly gay was to do every day the gay thing that they did every day. To be regularly gay was to end every day at the same time after they had been regularly gay. They were regularly gay. They were gay every day. They ended every day in the same way, at the same time, and they had been every day regularly gay.

The voice Helen Furr was cultivating was quite a pleasant one. The voice Georgine Skeene was cultivating was, some said, a better one. The voice Helen Furr was cultivating she cultivated and it was quite completely a pleasant enough one then, a cultivated enough one then. The voice Georgine Skeene was cultivating she did not cultivate too much. She cultivated it quite some. She cultivated and she would sometime go on cultivating it and it was not then an unpleasant one, it would not be then an unpleasant one, it would be a quite richly enough cultivated one, it would be quite richly enough to be a pleasant enough one.

They were gay where there were many cultivating something. The two were gay there, were regularly gay there. Georgine Skeene would have liked to do more travelling. They did some travelling, not very much travelling, Georgine Skeene would have liked to do more travelling, Helen Furr did not care about doing travelling, she liked to stay in a place and be gay there.

They stayed in a place and were gay there, both of them stayed there, they stayed together there, they were gay there, they were regularly gay there.

They went quite often, not very often, but they did go back to where Helen Furr had a pleasant enough home and then Georgine Skeene went to a place where her brother had quite some distinction. They both went, every few years, went visiting to where Helen Furr had quite a pleasant home. Certainly Helen Furr would not find it gay to stay, she did not find it gay, she said she would not stay, she said she did not find it gay, she said she would not stay where she did not find it gay, she said she found it gay where she did stay and she did stay there where very many were cultivating something. She did stay there. She always did find it gay there.

She went to see them where she had always been living and where she did not find it gay. She had a pleasant home there, Mrs. Furr was a pleasant enough woman, Mr. Furr was a pleasant enough man, Helen told them and they were not worrying, that she did not find it gay living where she had always been living.

Georgine Skeene and Helen Furr were living where they were both cultivating their voices and they were gay there. They visited where Helen Furr had come from and then they went to where they were living where they were then regularly living.

There were some dark and heavy men there then. There were some who were not so heavy and some who were not so dark. Helen Furr and Georgine Skeene sat regularly with them. They sat regularly with the ones who were dark and heavy. They sat regularly with the ones who were not so dark. They sat regularly with the ones that were not so heavy. They sat with them regularly, sat with some of them. They went with them regularly went with them. They were regular then, they were gay then, they were where they wanted to be then where it was gay to be then, they were regularly gay then. There were men there then who were dark and heavy and they sat with them with Helen Furr and Georgine Skeene and they went with them with Miss Furr and Miss Skeene, and they went with the heavy and dark men Miss Furr and Miss Skeene went with them, and they sat with them, Miss Furr and Miss Skeene sat with them, and there were other men, some were not heavy men and they sat with Miss Furr and Miss Skeene and Miss Furr and Miss Skeene sat with them, and there were other men who were not dark men and they sat with Miss Furr and Miss Skeene and Miss Furr and Miss Skeene sat with them. Miss Furr and Miss Skeene went with them and they went with Miss Furr and Miss Skeene, some who were not heavy men, some who were not dark men. Miss Furr and Miss Skeene sat regularly, they sat with some men. Miss Furr and Miss Skeene went and there were some men with them. There were men and Miss Furr and Miss Skeene went with them, went somewhere with them, went with some of them.

Helen Furr and Georgine Skeene were regularly living where very many were living and cultivating in themselves something. Helen Furr and Georgine Skeene were living very regularly then, being very regular then in being gay then. They did then learn many ways to be gay and they were then being gay being quite regular in being gay, being gay and they were learning little things, little things in ways of being gay, they were very regular then, they were learning very many little things in ways of being gay, they were being gay and using these little things they were learning to have to be gay with regularly gay with then and they were gay the same amount they had been gay. They were quite gay, they were quite regular, they were learning little things, gay little things, they were gay inside them the same amount they had been gay, they were gay the same length of time they had been gay every day.

They were regular in being gay, they learned little things that are things in being gay, they learned many little things that are things in being gay, they were gay every day, they were regular, they were gay, they were gay the same length of time every day, they were gay, they were quite regularly gay.

Georgine Skeene went away to stay two months with her brother. Helen Furr did not go then to stay with her father and her mother. Helen Furr stayed there where they had been regularly living the two of them and she would then certainly not be lonesome, she would go on being gay. She did go on being gay. She was not any more gay but she was gay longer every day than they had been being gay when they were together being gay. She was gay then quite exactly the same way. She learned a few more little ways of being in being gay. She was quite gay and in the same way, the same way she had been gay and she was gay a little longer in the day, more of each day she was gay. She was gay longer every day than when the two of them had been being gay. She was gay quite in the way they had been gay, quite in the same way.

She was not lonesome then, she was not at all feeling any need of having Georgine Skeene. She was not astonished at this thing. She would have been a little astonished by this thing but she knew she was not astonished at anything and so she was not astonished at this thing not astonished at not feeling any need of having Georgine Skeene.

Helen Furr had quite a completely pleasant voice and it was quite well enough cultivated and she could use it and she did use it but then there was not any way of working at cultivating a completely pleasant voice when it has become a quite completely well enough cultivated one, and there was not much use in using it when one was not wanting it to be helping to make one a gay one. Helen Furr was not needing using her voice to be a gay one. She was gay then and sometimes she used her voice and she was not using it very often. It was quite completely enough cultivated and it was quite completely a pleasant one and she did not use it very often. She was then, she was quite exactly as gay as she had been, she was gay a little longer in the day than she had been.

She was gay exactly the same way. She was never tired of being gay that way. She had learned very many little ways to use in being gay. Very many were telling about using other ways in being gay. She was gay enough, she was always gay exactly the same way, she was always learning little things to use in being gay, she was telling about using other ways in being gay, she was telling about learning other ways in being gay, she was learning other ways in being gay, she would be using other ways in being gay, she would always be gay in the same way, when Georgine Skeene was there not so long each day as when Georgine Skeene was away.

She came to using many ways in being gay, she came to use every way in being gay. She went on living where many were cultivating something and she was gay, she had used every way to be gay.

They did not live together then Helen Furr and Georgine Skeene. Helen Furr lived there the longer where they had been living regularly together. Then neither of them were living there any longer. Helen Furr was living somewhere else then and telling some about being gay and she was gay then and she was living quite regularly then. She was regularly gay then. She was quite regular in being gay then. She remembered all the little ways of being gay. She used all the little ways of being gay. She was quite regularly gay. She told many then the way of being gay, she taught very many then little ways they could use in being gay. She was living very well, she was gay then, she went on living then, she was regular in being gay, she always was living very well and was gay very well and was telling about little ways one could be learning to use in being gay, and later was telling them quite often, telling them again and again.

1922

ZITKALA-SĂ
(1876–1938)

An orator, musician, and political activist, Zitkala-Să was a Dakota Sioux author of distinction. She began publishing stories at the turn of the century, and her collection of traditional Native American tales, Old Indian Legends, appeared in 1901. Between 1900 and 1902 she wrote about her youth in a series of essays published in the Atlantic Monthly. She later collected these with other essays and fiction in American Indian Stories (1921). Her political efforts on behalf of Native Americans led to important changes in the Bureau of Indian Affairs and the foundation of an active organization of Native Americans. Her writing inspired other American Indians to record their tribal legends.

Born Gertrude Simmons, Zitkala-Să spent her first eight years living on the Yankton Sioux Reservation in South Dakota with her mother. Since her white father had left before she was born, Zitkala-Să took her last name from her mother's second husband. Later she chose Zitkala-Să, meaning Red Bird, the name under which she published.

At eight she left the reservation to study at White's Manual Institute, a Quaker school in Wabash, Indiana. After three years of separation from her mother and the Sioux way of life, she returned to the reservation, where she lived for the next four years. She completed her formal education at Earlham College in Richmond, Indiana, between 1895 and 1897. At college she distinguished herself as a writer and an award-winning orator.

After college, she taught for a few years at the Carlisle Indian School, where her students inspired her to publish the stories she remembered from her childhood. In 1902, the year after the tales appeared, she married another Sioux, Raymond T. Bonnin, who worked for the Bureau of Indian Affairs. With him she moved to the Uintah and Ouray reservation in Utah, where they lived with their son for the next fourteen years.

In addition to publishing stories and articles in Harper's and Everybody's Magazine, Zitkala-Să was a violinist who studied at the New England Conservatory of Music. She appeared as a soloist and orator with the Carlisle Indian Band, and in 1913 she collaborated on the Indian opera Sun Dance, which premiered that year in Vernal, Utah. In 1937 the New York Light Opera Guild selected it as the American opera for the year, and it was performed in New York City.

In 1916, to fulfill her obligations as the newly elected secretary of the Society of the American Indian, Zitkala-Să and her family moved to Washington, D.C. Her work included lecturing and campaigning for Native American citizenship; she *insisted, for instance, that the Bureau of Indian Affairs hire Native Americans and settle tribal land claims fairly. She edited the society's* American Indian Magazine *from 1918 to 1919. In 1920, when the organization folded, she helped found an Indian Welfare Committee within the General Federation of Women's Clubs. In 1926 she started her own political organization, the National Council of American Indians. The result of her efforts for Indian self-determination was President Hoover's 1928 appointment of two American Indians to the top positions in the Bureau of Indian Affairs. Until her death in 1938, she was president of the National Council of American Indians and its most effective public speaker and mediator.*

"The Great Spirit" was originally published in the Atlantic Monthly *in 1902 as "Why I Am a Pagan." In this short piece, Zitkala-Să illustrates the differences between Native American and Christian spiritual expression. "A Dream of Her Grandfather," also from the* Atlantic Monthly, *celebrates generational connections between grandfather and granddaughter. It also applauds the granddaughter's decision to work, as her grandfather had done, to alleviate the problems of her people.*

□ THE GREAT SPIRIT

When the spirit swells my breast I love to roam leisurely among the green hills; or sometimes, sitting on the brink of the murmuring Missouri, I marvel at the great blue overhead. With half-closed eyes I watch the huge cloud shadows in their noiseless play upon the high bluffs opposite me, while into my ear ripple the sweet, soft cadences of the river's song. Folded hands lie in my lap, for the time forgot. My heart and I lie small upon the earth like a grain of throbbing sand. Drifting clouds and tinkling waters, together with the warmth of a genial summer day, bespeak with eloquence the loving Mystery round about us. During the idle while I sat upon the sunny river brink, I grew somewhat, though my response be not so clearly manifest as in the green grass fringing the edge of the high bluff back of me.

At length retracing the uncertain footpath scaling the precipitous embankment, I seek the level lands where grow the wild prairie flowers. And they, the lovely little folk, soothe my soul with their perfumed breath.

Their quaint round faces of varied hue convince the heart which leaps with glad surprise that they, too, are living symbols of omnipotent thought. With a child's eager eye I drink in the myriad star shapes wrought in luxuriant color upon the green. Beautiful is the spiritual essence they embody.

I leave them nodding in the breeze, but take along with me their impress upon my heart. I pause to rest me upon a rock embedded on the side of a foothill facing the low river bottom. Here the Stone-Boy, of whom the American aborigine tells, frolics about, shooting his baby arrows and shouting aloud with glee at the tiny shafts of lightning that flash from the flying arrow-beaks. What an ideal warrior he became, baffling the siege of the pests of all the land till he triumphed over their united attack. And here he lay,—Inyan our great-great-grandfather, older than the hill he rested on, older than the race of men who love to tell of his wonderful career.

Interwoven with the thread of this Indian legend of the rock, I fain would trace a subtle knowledge of the native folk which enabled them to recognize a kinship to any and all parts of this vast universe. By the leading of an ancient trail I move toward the Indian village.

With the strong, happy sense that both great and small are so surely enfolded in His magnitude that, without a miss, each has his allotted individual ground of opportunities, I am buoyant with good nature.

Yellow Breast, swaying upon the slender stem of a wild sunflower, warbles a sweet assurance of this as I pass near by. Breaking off the clear crystal song, he turns his wee head from side to side eyeing me wisely as slowly I plod with moccasined feet. Then again he yields himself to his song of joy. Flit, flit hither and yon, he fills the summer sky with his swift, sweet melody. And truly does it seem his vigorous freedom lies more in his little spirit than in his wing.

With these thoughts I reach the log cabin whither I am strongly drawn by the tie of a child to an aged mother. Out bounds my four-footed friend to meet me, frisking about my path with unmistakable delight. Chän is a black shaggy dog, "a thoroughbred little mongrel" of whom I am very fond. Chän seems to understand many words in Sioux, and will go to her mat even when I whisper the word, though generally I think she is guided by the tone of the voice. Often she tries to imitate the sliding inflection and long-drawn-out voice to the amusement of our guests, but her articulation is quite beyond my ear. In both my hands I hold her shaggy head and gaze into her large brown eyes. At once the dilated pupils contract into tiny black dots, as if the roguish spirit within would evade my questioning.

Finally resuming the chair at my desk I feel in keen sympathy with my fellow-creatures, for I seem to see clearly again that all are akin. The racial lines, which once were bitterly real, now serve nothing more than marking out a living mosaic of human beings. And even here men of the same color are like the ivory keys of one instrument where each resembles all the rest, yet varies from them in pitch and quality of voice. And those creatures who are for a time mere echoes of another's note are not unlike the fable of the thin sick man whose distorted shadow, dressed like a real creature, came to the old master to make him follow as a shadow. Thus with a compassion for all echoes in human guise, I greet the solemn-faced "native preacher" whom I find awaiting me. I listen with respect for God's creature, though he mouth most strangely the jangling phrases of a bigoted creed.

As our tribe is one large family, where every person is related to all the others, he addressed me:—

"Cousin, I came from the morning church service to talk with you."

"Yes?" I said interrogatively, as he paused for some word from me.

Shifting uneasily about in the straight-backed chair he sat upon, he began: "Every holy day (Sunday) I look about our little God's house, and not seeing you there, I am disappointed. This is why I come today. Cousin, as I watch you from afar, I see no unbecoming behavior and hear only good reports of you, which all the more burns me with the wish that you were a church member. Cousin, I was taught long years ago by kind missionaries to read the holy book. These godly men taught me also the folly of our old beliefs.

"There is one God who gives reward or punishment to the race of dead men. In the upper region the Christian dead are gathered in unceasing song and prayer. In the deep pit below, the sinful ones dance in torturing flames.

"Think upon these things, my cousin, and choose now to avoid the after-doom of hell fire!" Then followed a long silence in which he clasped tighter and unclasped again his interlocked fingers.

Like instantaneous lightning flashes came pictures of my own mother's making, for she, too, is now a follower of the new superstition.

"Knocking out the chinking of our log cabin, some evil hand thrust in a burning taper of braided dry grass, but failed of his intent, for the fire died out and the half-burned brand fell inward to the floor. Directly above it, on a shelf, lay the holy book. This is what we found after our return from a several days' visit. Surely some great power is hid in the sacred book!"

Brushing away from my eyes many like pictures, I offered midday meal to the converted Indian sitting wordless and with downcast face. No sooner had he risen from the table with "Cousin, I have relished it," than the church bell rang.

Thither he hurried forth with his afternoon sermon. I watched him as he hastened along, his eyes bent fast upon the dusty road till he disappeared at the end of a quarter of a mile.

The little incident recalled to mind the copy of a missionary paper brought to my notice a few days ago, in which a "Christian" pugilist commented upon a recent article of mine, grossly perverting the spirit of my pen. Still I would not forget that the pale-faced missionary and the hoodooed aborigine are both God's creatures, though small indeed their own conceptions of Infinite Love. A wee child toddling in a wonder world, I prefer to their dogma my excursions into the natural gardens where the voice of the Great Spirit is heard in the twittering of birds, the rippling of mighty waters, and the sweet breathing of flowers.

Here, in a fleeting quiet, I am awakened by the fluttering robe of the Great Spirit. To my innermost consciousness the phenomenal universe is a royal mantle, vibrating with His divine breath. Caught in its flowing fringes are the spangles and oscillating brilliants of sun, moon, and stars.

1921

A DREAM OF HER GRANDFATHER

Her grandfather was a Dakota "medicine man." Among the Indians of his day he was widely known for his successful healing work. He was one of the leading men of the tribe and came to Washington, D.C., with one of the first delegations relative to affairs concerning the Indian people and the United States government

His was the first band of the Great Sioux Nation to make treaties with the government in the hope of bringing about an amicable arrangement between the red and white Americans. The journey to the nation's capital was made almost entirely on pony-back, there being no railroads, and the Sioux delegation was beset with many hardships on the trail. His visit to Washington, in behalf of peace among men, proved to be his last earthly mission. From a sudden illness, he died and was buried here.

When his small granddaughter grew up she learned the white man's tongue, and followed in the footsteps of her grandfather to the very seat of government to carry on his humanitarian work. Though her days were filled with problems for welfare work among her people, she had a strange dream one night during her stay in Washington. The dream was this: Returning from an afternoon out, she found a large cedar chest had been delivered to her home in her absence. She sniffed the sweet perfume of the red wood, which reminded her of the breath of the forest,—and admired the box so neatly made, without trimmings. It looked so clean, strong and durable in its native genuineness. With elation, she took the tag in her hand and read her name aloud. "Who sent me this cedar chest?" she asked, and was told it came from her grandfather.

Wondering what gift it could be her grandfather wished now to confer upon her, wholly disregarding his death years ago, she was all eagerness to open the mystery chest.

She remembered her childhood days and the stories she loved to hear about the unusual powers of her grandfather,—recalled how she, the wee girl, had coveted the medicine bags, beaded and embroidered in porcupine quills, in symbols designed by the great "medicine man," her grandfather. Well did she remember her merited rebuke that such things were never made for relics. Treasures came in due time to those ready to receive them.

In great expectancy, she lifted the heavy lid of the cedar chest. "Oh!" she exclaimed, with a note of disappointment, seeing no beaded Indian regalia or trinkets. "Why does my grandfather send such a light gift in a heavy, large box?" She was mystified and much perplexed.

The gift was a fantastic thing, of texture far more delicate than a spider's filmy web. It was a vision! A picture of an Indian camp, not painted on canvas nor yet written. It was dream-stuff, suspended in the thin air, filling the inclosure of the cedar wood container. As she looked upon it, the picture grew more and more real, exceeding the proportions of the chest. It was all so illusive a breath might have blown it away; yet there it was, real as life,—a circular camp of white cone-shaped teepees, astir with Indian people. The village crier, with flowing head-dress of eagle plumes, mounted on a prancing white pony, rode within the arena. Indian men, women and children stopped in groups and clusters, while bright painted faces peered out of teepee doors, to listen to the chieftain's crier.

At this point, she, too, heard the full melodious voice. She heard distinctly the Dakota words he proclaimed to the people. "Be glad! Rejoice! Look up, and see the new day dawning! Help is near! Hear me, every one."

She caught the glad tidings and was thrilled with new hope for her people.

1921

ANZIA YEZIERSKA
(1880?–1970)

Anzia Yezierska's life reflects the struggles of a turn-of-the-century feminist to lead an independent life. Her New York Jewish immigrant community provided the context for her writing; at the same time, this community's sexist attitudes condemned her desire to write. Ironically, her success as a writer brought her acclaim as the voice of the community from which she was alienated.

When she was between eight and ten years old, Anzia Yezierska arrived in Castle Garden, New York, from the Russian-Polish village of Plotsk with her parents and six siblings. Her birth certificate, like those of many immigrants, had been lost, and immigration officials changed her name to Hettie Mayer. Though she accepted this name as a child, Yezierska reclaimed her Eastern European name and identity when she became a writer.

Throughout her childhood, Yezierska fought not only poverty, but also the traditions of her father and brothers that stood in the path of education for women. In 1899, despite her family's objections, she moved into a home for working girls and began attending Columbia University.

Yezierska graduated from Columbia University's Teachers College in 1904 and won a scholarship to the American Academy of Dramatic Arts. During the next few years she taught in the New York public schools and developed an interest in socialist and feminist ideas. In her first published story, "The Free Vacation Home" (1915), Yezierska uses sardonic humor and the idiom of the Jewish immigrants to describe a young mother's life. The year this work appeared, she left her husband and moved with her daughter first to Los Angeles and then to San Francisco. Under financial duress, she sent her daughter back to her husband in California and returned to New York and teaching.

With the encouragement of the educator John Dewey, whose course she attended at Columbia University, Yezierska pursued her writing. In 1919 she published a number of stories, one of which, "The Fat of the Land," was chosen by the 1919 editor of The Best Short Stories. *In 1920, her first collection of short stories,* Hungry Hearts, *appeared. The following year she signed a film contract for $10,000—an enormous sum for the period—and went to Hollywood to work on the screenplay for* Hungry Hearts.

Disenchanted with Hollywood, where she turned down further lucrative film offers, Yezierska returned to New York and published her first novel, Salome of the Tenements. *In her second novel,* Bread Givers, *she turned to the theme that had shaped her life: the daughter's struggle against her father's tyranny. This work was a critical success when it appeared in 1925.*

"Writing is only for such as me," Yezierska wrote to her daughter, "who have never found the right place in life. . . ." Incapable of tolerating the male dominance that was traditional in the community she described in her writing, Yezierska was constantly searching for an alternative community among writers. In the early 1920s she received encouragement from Mary Austin. In the mid-1920s, while on a European trip, she met George Bernard Shaw, H. G. Wells, and Gertrude Stein. In the early 1930s she spent a summer at the MacDowell Colony in New Hampshire. She felt alienated, however, by the middle-class lives of these established writers. Not until she joined the New York Writers' Project with Richard Wright, Claude McKay, and other working-class writers in the mid-1930s did she find the community she sought. In her final book, Red Ribbon on a White Horse, *she captured the spirit of the Writers' Project. Introduced by the poet W. H. Auden, this work of American social history appeared when Yezierska was nearly seventy years old.*

Between 1950 and 1960, Yezierska reviewed more than fifty books for The New York Times Book Review. *She based her last story, "Observation," on her efforts to organize a course about aging taught by old people.* Commentary *published the story in 1963. She died seven years later. Recent feminist critics have claimed for Yezierska the place in the literary tradition she obviously deserves.*

The story included here, from Hungry Hearts, *describes a young, impoverished writer and her efforts to create amidst the distractions of a New York tenement.*

□ MY OWN PEOPLE

With the suitcase containing all her worldly possessions under her arm, Sophie Sapinsky elbowed her way through the noisy ghetto crowds. Pushcart peddlers and pullers-in shouted and gesticulated. Women with market-baskets pushed and shoved one another, eyes straining with the one thought—how to get the food a penny cheaper. With the same strained intentness, Sophie scanned each tenement, searching for a room cheap enough for her dwindling means.

In a dingy basement window a crooked sign, in straggling, penciled letters, caught Sophie's eye: "Room to let, a bargain, cheap."

The exuberant phrasing was quite in keeping with the extravagant dilapidation of the surroundings. "This is the very place," thought Sophie. "There could n't be nothing cheaper in all New York."

At the foot of the basement steps she knocked.

"Come in!" a voice answered.

As she opened the door she saw an old man bending over a pot of potatoes on a shoemaker's bench. A group of children in all degrees of rags surrounded him, greedily snatching at the potatoes he handed out.

Sophie paused for an instant, but her absorption in her own problem was too great to halt the question: "Is there a room to let?"

"Hanneh Breineh, in the back, has a room." The old man was so preoccupied filling the hungry hands that he did not even look up.

Sophie groped her way to the rear hall. A gaunt-faced woman answered her inquiry with loquacious enthusiasm. "A grand room for the money. I'll let it down to you only for three dollars a month. In the whole block is no bigger bargain. I should live so."

As she talked, the woman led her through the dark hall into an airshaft room. A narrow window looked out into the bottom of a chimney-like pit, where lay the accumulated refuse from a score of crowded kitchens.

"Oi weh!" gasped Sophie, throwing open the sash. "No air and no light. Outside shines the sun and here it's so dark."

"It ain't so dark. It's only a little shady. Let me only turn up the gas for you and you'll quick see everything like with sunshine."

The claw-fingered flame revealed a rusty, iron cot, an inverted potato barrel that served for a table, and two soap-boxes for chairs.

Sophie felt of the cot. It sagged and flopped under her touch. "The bed has only three feet!" she exclaimed in dismay.

"You can't have Rockefeller's palace for three dollars a month," defended Hanneh Breineh, as she shoved one of the boxes under the legless corner of the cot. "If the bed ain't so steady, so you got good neighbors. Upstairs lives Shprintzeh Gittle, the herring-woman. You can buy by her the biggest bargains in fish, a few days older. . . . What she got left over from the Sabbath, she sells to the neighbors cheap. . . . In the front lives Shmendrik, the shoemaker. I'll tell you the truth, he ain't no real shoemaker. He never yet made a pair of whole shoes in his life. He's a learner from the old country—a tzadik, a saint; but every time he sees in the street a child with torn feet, he calls them in and patches them up. His own eating, the last bite from his mouth, he divides up with them."

"Three dollars," deliberated Sophie, scarcely hearing Hanneh Breineh's chatter. "I will never find anything cheaper. It has a door to lock and I can shut this woman out . . . I'll take it," she said, handing her the money.

Hanneh Breineh kissed the greasy bills gloatingly. "I'll treat you like a mother! You'll have it good by me like in your own home."

"Thanks—but I got no time to shmoos. I got to be alone to get my work done."

The rebuff could not penetrate Hanneh Breineh's joy over the sudden possession of three dollars.

"Long years on you! May we be to good luck to one another!" was Hanneh Breineh's blessing as she closed the door.

Alone in her room—*her* room, securely hers—yet with the flash of triumph, a stab of bitterness. All that was hers—so wretched and so ugly! Had her eager spirit, eager to give and give, no claim to a bit of beauty—a shred of comfort?

Perhaps her family was right in condemning her rashness. Was it worth while to give up the peace of home, the security of a regular job—suffer hunger, loneliness, and want—for what? For something she knew in her heart was beyond her reach. Would her writing ever amount to enough to vindicate the uprooting of her past? Would she ever become articulate enough to express beautifully what she saw and felt? What had she, after all, but a stifling, sweatshop experience, a meager, night-school education, and this wild, blind hunger to release the dumbness that choked her?

Sophie spread her papers on the cot beside her. Resting her elbows on the potato barrel, she clutched her pencil with tense fingers. In the notebook before her were a hundred beginnings, essays, abstractions, outbursts of chaotic moods. She glanced through the titles: "Believe in Yourself," "The Quest of the Ideal."

Meaningless tracings on the paper, her words seemed to her now—a restless spirit pawing at the air. The intensity of experience, the surge of emotion that had been hers when she wrote—where were they? The words had failed to catch the life-beat—had failed to register the passion she had poured into them.

Perhaps she was not a writer, after all. Had the years and years of night-study been in vain? Choked with discouragement, the cry broke from her, "O—God—God help me! I feel—I see, but it all dies in me—dumb!"

. . .

Tedious days passed into weeks. Again Sophie sat staring into her note-book. "There's nothing here that's alive. Not a word yet says what's in me . . .

"But it *is* in me!" With clenched fist she smote her bosom. "It must be in me! I believe in it! I got to get it out—even if it tears my flesh in pieces—even if it kills me! . . .

"But these words—these flat, dead words . . .

"Whether I can write or can't write—I can't stop writing. I can't rest. I can't breathe. There's no peace, no running away for me on earth except in the struggle to give out what's in me. The beat from my heart—the blood from my veins—must flow out into my words."

She returned to her unfinished essay, "Believe in Yourself." Her mind groping—clutching at the misty incoherence that clouded her thoughts—she wrote on.

"These sentences are yet only wood—lead; but I can't help it—I'll push on—on—I'll not eat—I'll not sleep—I'll not move from this spot till I get it to say on the paper what I got in my heart!"

Slowly the dead words seemed to begin to breathe. Her eyes brightened. Her cheeks flushed. Her very pencil trembled with the eager onrush of words.

Then a sharp rap sounded on her door. With a gesture of irritation Sophie put down her pencil and looked into the burning, sunken eyes of her neighbor, Hanneh Breineh.

"I got yourself a glass of tea, good friend. It ain't much I got to give away, but it's warm even if it's nothing."

Sophie scowled. "You must n't bother yourself with me. I'm so busy—thanks."

"Don't thank me yet so quick. I got no sugar." Hanneh Breineh edged herself into the room confidingly. "At home, in Poland, I not only had sugar for tea—but even jelly—a jelly that would lift you up to heaven. I thought in America everything would be so plenty, I could drink the tea out from my sugar-bowl. But ach! Not in Poland did my children starve like in America!"

Hanneh Breineh, in a friendly manner, settled herself on the sound end of the bed, and began her jeremiad.

"Yosef, my man, ain't no bread-giver. Already he got consumption the second year. One week he works and nine weeks he lays sick."

In despair Sophie gathered her papers, wondering how to get the woman out of her room. She glanced through the page she had written, but Hanneh Breineh, unconscious of her indifference, went right on.

"How many times it is tearing the heart out from my body—should I take Yosef's milk to give to the baby, or the baby's milk to give to Yosef? If he was dead the pensions they give to widows would help feed my children. Now I got only the charities to help me. A black year on them! They should only have to feed their own children on what they give me."

Resolved not to listen to the intruder, Sophie debated within herself: "Should I call my essay 'Believe in Yourself,' or would n't it be stronger to say, 'Trust Yourself'? But if I say, 'Trust Yourself,' would n't they think that I got the words from Emerson?"

Hanneh Breineh's voice went on, but it sounded to Sophie like a faint buzzing from afar. "Gotteniu! How much did it cost me my life to go and swear myself that my little Fannie—only skin and bones—that she is already fourteen! How it chokes me the tears every morning when I got to wake her and push her out to the shop when her eyes are yet shutting themselves with sleep!"

Sophie glanced at her wrist-watch as it ticked away the precious minutes. She must get rid of the woman! Had she not left her own sister, sacrificed all comfort, all association, for solitude and its golden possibilities? For the first time in her life she had the chance to be by herself and think. And now, the thoughts which a moment ago had seemed like a flock of fluttering birds had come so close—and this woman with her sordid wailing had scattered them.

"I'm a savage, a beast, but I got to ask her to get out—this very minute," resolved Sophie. But before she could summon the courage to do what she wanted to do, there was a timid knock at the door, and the wizened little Fannie, her face streaked with tears, stumbled in.

"The inspector said it's a lie. I ain't yet fourteen," she whimpered.

Hanneh Breineh paled. "Woe is me! Sent back from the shop? God from the world—is there no end to my troubles? Why did n't you hide yourself when you saw the inspector come?"

"I was running to hide myself under the table, but she caught me and she said she'll take me to the Children's Society and arrest me and my mother for sending me to work too soon."

"Arrest me?" shrieked Hanneh Breineh, beating her breast. "Let them only come and arrest me! I'll show America who I am! Let them only begin themselves with me! . . . Black is for my eyes . . . the groceryman will not give us another bread till we pay him the bill!"

"The inspector said . . ." The child's brow puckered in an effort to recall the words.

"What did the inspector said? Gotteniu!" Hanneh Breineh wrung her hands in passionate entreaty. "Listen only once to my prayer! Send on the inspector only a quick death! I only wish her to have her own house with twenty-four rooms and each of the twenty-four rooms should be twenty-four beds and the chills and the fever should throw her from one bed to another!"

"Hanneh Breineh, still yourself a little," entreated Sophie.

"How can I still myself without Fannie's wages? Bitter is me! Why do I have to live so long?"

"The inspector said . . ."

"What did the inspector said? A thunder should strike the inspector! Ain't I as good a mother as other mothers? Would n't I better send my children to school? But who'll give us to eat? And who'll pay us the rent?"

Hanneh Breineh wiped her red-lidded eyes with the corner of her apron.

"The president from America should only come to my bitter heart. Let him go fighting himself with the pushcarts how to get the eating a penny cheaper. Let him try to feed his children on the money the charities give me and we'd see if he would n't better send his littlest ones to the shop better than to let them starve before his eyes. Woe is me! What for did I come to America? What's my life—nothing but one terrible, never-stopping fight with the grocer and the butcher and the landlord . . ."

Suddenly Sophie's resentment for her lost morning was forgotten. The crying waste of Hanneh Breineh's life lay open before her eyes like pictures in a book. She saw her own life in Hanneh Breineh's life. Her efforts to write were like Hanneh Breineh's efforts to feed her children. Behind her life and Hanneh Breineh's life she saw the massed ghosts of thousands upon thousands beating—beating out their hearts against rock barriers.

"The inspector said . . ." Fannie timidly attempted again to explain.

"The inspector!" shrieked Hanneh Breineh, as she seized hold of Fannie in a rage. "Hellfire should burn the inspector! Tell me again about the inspector and I'll choke the life out from you—"

Sophie sprang forward to protect the child from the mother. "She's only trying to tell you something."

"Why should she yet throw salt on my wounds? If there was enough bread in the house would I need an inspector to tell me to send her to school? If America is so interested in poor people's children, then why don't they give them to eat till they should go to work? What learning can come into a child's head when the stomach is empty?"

A clutter of feet down the creaking cellar steps, a scuffle of broken shoes, and a chorus of shrill voices, as the younger children rushed in from school.

"Mamma—what's to eat?"

"It smells potatoes!"

"Pfui! The pot is empty! It smells over from Cohen's."

"Jake grabbed all the bread!"

"Mamma—he kicked the piece out from my hands!"

"Mamma—it's so empty in my stomach! Ain't there nothing?"

"Gluttons—wolves—thieves!" Hanneh Breineh shrieked. "I should only live to bury you all in one day!"

The children, regardless of Hanneh Breineh's invectives, swarmed around her like hungry bees, tearing at her apron, her skirt. Their voices rose in increased clamor, topped only by their mother's imprecations. "Gotteniu! Tear me away from these leeches on my neck! Send on them only a quick death! . . . Only a minute's peace before I die!"

"Hanneh Breineh—children! What's the matter?" Shmendrik stood at the door. The sweet quiet of the old man stilled the raucous voices as the coming of evening stills the noises of the day.

"There's no end to my troubles! Hear them hollering for bread, and the grocer stopped to give till the bill is paid. Woe is me! Fannie sent home by the inspector and not a crumb in the house!"

"I got something." The old man put his hands over the heads of the children in silent benediction. "All come in by me. I got sent me a box of cake."

"Cake!" The children cried, catching at the kind hands and snuggling about the shabby coat.

"Yes. Cake and nuts and raisins and even a bottle of wine."

The children leaped and danced around him in their wild burst of joy.

"Cake and wine—a box—to you? Have the charities gone crazy?" Hanneh Breineh's eyes sparkled with light and laughter.

"No—no," Shmendrik explained hastily. "Not from the charities—from a friend—for the holidays."

Shmendrik nodded invitingly to Sophie, who was standing in the door of her room. "The roomerkeh will also give a taste with us our party?"

"Sure will she!" Hanneh Breineh took Sophie by the arm. "Who'll say no in this black life to cake and wine?"

Young throats burst into shrill cries: "Cake and wine—wine and cake—raisins and nuts—nuts and raisins!" The words rose in a triumphant chorus. The children leaped and danced in time to their chant, almost carrying the old man bodily into his room in the wildness of their joy.

The contagion of this sudden hilarity erased from Sophie's mind the last thought of work and she found herself seated with the others on the cobbler's bench.

From under his cot the old man drew forth a wooden box. Lifting the cover he held up before wondering eyes a large frosted cake embedded in raisins and nuts.

Amid the shouts of glee Shmendrik now waved aloft a large bottle of grape-juice.

The children could contain themselves no longer and dashed forward.

"Shah—shah! Wait only!" He gently halted their onrush and waved them back to their seats.

"The glasses for the wine!" Hanneh Breineh rushed about hither and thither in happy confusion. From the sink, the shelf, the windowsill, she gathered cracked glasses, cups without handles—anything that would hold even a few drops of the yellow wine.

Sacrificial solemnity filled the basement as the children breathlessly watched Shmendrik cut the precious cake. Mouths—even eyes—watered with the intensity of their emotion.

With almost religious fervor Hanneh Breineh poured the grape-juice into the glasses held in the trembling hands of the children. So overwhelming was the occasion that none dared to taste till the ritual was completed. The suspense was agonizing as one and all waited for Shmendrik's signal.

"Hanneh Breineh—you drink from my Sabbath wine-glass!"

Hanneh Breineh clinked glasses with Schmendrik. "Long years on you—long years on us all!" Then she turned to Sophie, clinked glasses once more. "May you yet marry yourself from our basement to a millionaire!" Then she lifted the glass to her lips.

The spell was broken. With a yell of triumph the children gobbled the cake in huge mouthfuls and sucked the golden liquid. All the traditions of wealth and joy that ever sparkled from the bubbles of champagne smiled at Hanneh Breineh from her glass of California grape-juice.

"Ach!" she sighed. "How good it is to forget your troubles, and only those that's got troubles have the chance to forget them!"

She sipped the grape-juice leisurely, thrilled into ecstasy with each lingering drop. "How it laughs yet in me, the life, the minute I turn my head from my worries!"

With growing wonder in her eyes, Sophie watched Hanneh Breineh. This ragged wreck of a woman—how passionately she clung to every atom of life! Hungrily, she burned through the depths of every experience. How she flared against wrongs—and how every tiny spark of pleasure blazed into joy!

Within a half-hour this woman had touched the whole range of human emotions, from bitterest agony to dancing joy. The terrible despair at the onrush of her starving children when she cried out, "O that I should only bury you all in one day!" And now the leaping light of the words: "How it laughs yet in me, the life, the minute I turn my head from my worries."

"Ach, if I could only write like Hanneh Breineh talks!" thought Sophie. "Her words dance with a thousand colors. Like a rainbow it flows from her lips." Sentences from her own essays marched before her, stiff and wooden.

How clumsy, how unreal, were her most labored phrases compared to Hanneh Breineh's spontaneity. Fascinated, she listened to Hanneh Breineh, drinking her words as a thirst-perishing man drinks water. Every bubbling phrase filled her with a drunken rapture to create.

"Up till now I was only trying to write from my head. It was n't real—it was n't life. Hanneh Breineh is real. Hanneh Breineh is life."

"Ach! What do the rich people got but dried-up dollars? Pfui on them and their money!" Hanneh Breineh held up her glass to be refilled. "Let me only win a fortune on the lotteree and move myself in my own bought house. Let me only have my first hundred dollars in the bank and I'll lift up my head like a person and tell the charities to eat their own cornmeal. I'll get myself an automobile like the kind rich ladies and ride up to their houses on Fifth Avenue and feed them only once on the eating they like so good for me and my children."

With a smile of benediction Shmendrik refilled the glasses and cut for each of his guests another slice of cake. Then came the handful of nuts and raisins.

As the children were scurrying about for hammers and iron lasts with which to crack their nuts, the basement door creaked. Unannounced, a woman entered—the "friendly visitor" of the charities. Her look of awful amazement swept the group of merry-makers.

"Mr. Shmendrik!—Hanneh Breineh!" Indignation seethed in her voice. "What's this? A feast—a birthday?"

Gasps—bewildered glances—a struggle for utterance!

"I came to make my monthly visit—evidently I'm not needed."

Shmendrik faced the accusing eyes of the "friendly visitor." "Holiday eating . . ."

"Oh—I'm glad you're so prosperous."

Before any one had gained presence of mind enough to explain things, the door had clanked. The "friendly visitor" had vanished.

"Pfui!" Hanneh Breineh snatched up her glass and drained its contents. "What will she do now? Will we get no more dry bread from the charities because once we ate cake?"

"What for did she come?" asked Sophie.

"To see that we don't over-eat ourselves!" returned Hanneh Breineh. "She's a 'friendly visitor'! She learns us how to cook cornmeal. By pictures and lectures she shows us how the poor people should live without meat, without milk, without butter, and without eggs. Always it's on the end of my tongue to ask her, 'You learned us to do without so much, why can't you yet learn us how to eat without eating?' "

The children seized the last crumbs of cake that Shmendrik handed them and rushed for the street.

"What a killing look was on her face," said Sophie. "Couldn't she be a little glad for your gladness?"

"Charity ladies—gladness?" The joy of the grape-wine still rippled in Hanneh Breineh's laughter. "For poor people is only cornmeal. Ten cents a day—to feed my children!"

Still in her rollicking mood Hanneh Breineh picked up the baby and tossed it like a Bacchante. "Could you be happy a lot with ten cents in your stomach? Ten cents—half a can of condensed milk—then fill yourself the rest with water! . . . Maybe yet feed you with all water and save the ten-cent pieces to buy you a carriage like the Fifth Avenue babies! . . ."

The soft sound of a limousine purred through the area grating and two well-fed figures in seal-skin coats, led by the "friendly visitor," appeared at the door.

"Mr. Bernstein, you can see for yourself." The "friendly visitor" pointed to the table.

The merry group shrank back. It was as if a gust of icy wind had swept all the joy and laughter from the basement.

"You are charged with intent to deceive and obtain assistance by dishonest means," said Mr. Bernstein.

"Dishonest?" Shmendrik paled.

Sophie's throat strained with passionate protest, but no words came to her release.

"A friend—a friend"—stammered Shmendrik—"sent me the holiday eating."

The superintendent of the Social Betterment Society faced him accusingly. "You told us that you had no friends when you applied to us for assistance."

"My friend—he knew me in my better time." Shmendrik flushed painfully. "I was once a scholar—respected. I wanted by this one friend to hold myself like I was."

Mr. Bernstein had taken from the bookshelf a number of letters, glanced through them rapidly and handed them one by one to the deferential superintendent.

Shmendrik clutched at his heart in an agony of humiliation. Suddenly his bent body straightened. His eyes dilated. "My letters—my life—you dare?"

"Of course we dare!" The superintendent returned Shmendrik's livid gaze, made bold by the confidence that what he was doing was the only scientific method of administering philanthropy. "These dollars, so generously given, must go to those most worthy. . . . I find in these letters references to gifts of fruit and other luxuries you did not report at our office."

"He never kept nothing for himself!" Hanneh Breineh broke in defensively. "He gave it all for the children."

Ignoring the interruption Mr. Bernstein turned to the "friendly visitor." "I'm glad you brought my attention to this case. It's but one of the many impositions on our charity . . . Come . . ."

"Kossacks! Pogromschiks!" Sophie's rage broke at last. "You call yourselves

Americans? You dare call yourselves Jews? You bosses of the poor! This man Shmendrik, whose house you broke into, whom you made to shame like a beggar—he is the one Jew from whom the Jews can be proud! He gives all he is—all he has—as God gives. *He is* charity.

"But you—you are the greed—the shame of the Jews! *All-right-niks*—fat bellies in fur coats! What do you give from yourselves? You may eat and bust eating! Nothing you give till you've stuffed yourselves so full that your hearts are dead!"

The door closed in her face. Her wrath fell on indifferent backs as the visitors mounted the steps to the street.

Shmendrik groped blindly for the Bible. In a low, quavering voice, he began the chant of the oppressed—the wail of the downtrodden. "I am afraid, and a trembling taketh hold of my flesh. Wherefore do the wicked live, become old, yea, mighty in power?"

Hanneh Breineh and the children drew close around the old man. They were weeping—unconscious of their weeping—deep buried memories roused by the music, the age-old music of the Hebrew race.

Through the grating Sophie saw the limousine pass. The chant flowed on: "Their houses are safe from fear; neither is the rod of God upon them."

Silently Sophie stole back to her room. She flung herself on the cot, pressed her fingers to her burning eyeballs. For a long time she lay rigid, clenched—listening to the drumming of her heart like the sea against rock barriers. Presently the barriers burst. Something in her began pouring itself out. She felt for her pencil—paper—and began to write. Whether she reached out to God or man she knew not, but she wrote on and on all through that night.

The gray light entering her grated window told her that beyond was dawn. Sophie looked up: "Ach! At last it writes itself in me!" she whispered triumphantly. "It's not me—it's their cries—my own people—crying in me! Hanneh Breineh, Shmendrik, they will not be stilled in me, till all America stops to listen."

1920

SUSAN GLASPELL
(1882–1948)

Susan Glaspell's writing depicts the speech, character types, and attitudes of the Midwest. Frequently set in the fictional town of Freeport, which was based on Glaspell's birthplace of Davenport, Iowa, her works revere the pioneer tradition and convey nostalgia for the ideals of a rural society that was quickly being lost to industrialization. However, Glaspell's experiences outside the Midwest, especially working in the theater in New York, gave her a broad perspective. In her best work, she conveys the complexity and limitations of the midwestern people, as well as their deeply embedded values and traditions.

Having graduated from Drake University in Des Moines in 1899, Glaspell settled in Davenport to begin her career as a writer. Although she spent some time doing graduate work in English at the University of Chicago and traveled for a year in Europe, Glaspell lived principally in Davenport until 1913. During those years, she published two novels, The Glory of the Conquered *and* The Visioning, *as well as a collection of stories,* Lifted Masks*—all works heavy with sentimentality and romanticism.*

With her marriage to George Cram Cook in 1913 and subsequent moves to Provincetown, Massachusetts, and New York City, Glaspell's life and writing changed radically. She became involved with the Provincetown Players, one of the most influential "little theaters" in the United States. Founded by Cook in 1915, the Provincetown Players attracted a group of writers and other artists, including Edna St. Vincent Millay, Wallace Stevens, Djuna Barnes, and Eugene O'Neill. With O'Neill, Glaspell became an important contributor of plays for the group, writing seven one-act and four full-length dramas. Still produced today, her first one-act, Suppressed Desires, *spoofs life in Greenwich Village. Other plays included* Trifles, Bernice, *and* Inheritors. *Much of the sentimentality evident in her early fiction disappears in the dramas, replaced with a combination of idealism and satire.*

After Cook's death in 1924, Glaspell wrote a biography of him, The Road to the Temple, *and two more plays,* The Comic Artist *and* Alison's House; *the latter, based on the life of Emily Dickinson, received a Pulitzer Prize. In the last eighteen years of her life, Glaspell again wrote novels and short fiction. Her novels, such as* Brook Evans *and* The Morning Is Near Us, *revisit the scenes and characters of the Midwest; however, the strong sense of movement and dialogue in these later works show the benefits that years of working in theater had had on Glaspell's writing.*

Throughout her work, Glaspell returned again and again to the Midwest as a symbol of significant values and steadfast truths. She also continually used her female characters to embody an idealism, sympathy, and emotion lacking in men. In the short story selected here, which is based on Glaspell's most popular one-act play, Trifles, *we see both the importance of personal attachments among the women and their disdain for approaches that the male characters—mistakenly, in this case—consider logical and rational. Glaspell's fine use of dialogue and evocative sense of place in this story are characteristic of her best writing.*

A JURY OF HER PEERS

When Martha Hale opened the storm-door and got a cut of the north wind, she ran back for her big woolen scarf. As she hurriedly wound that round her head her eye made a scandalized sweep of her kitchen. It was no ordinary thing that called her away—it was probably farther from ordinary than anything that had ever happened in Dickson County. But what her eye took in was that her kitchen was in no shape for leaving: her bread all ready for mixing, half the flour sifted and half unsifted.

She hated to see things half done; but she had been at that when the team from town stopped to get Mr. Hale, and then the sheriff came running in to say his wife wished Mrs. Hale would come too—adding, with a grin, that he guessed she was getting scarey and wanted another woman along. So she had dropped everything right where it was.

"Martha!" now came her husband's impatient voice. "Don't keep folks waiting out here in the cold."

She again opened the storm-door, and this time joined the three men and the one woman waiting for her in the big two-seated buggy.

After she had the robes tucked around her she took another look at the woman who sat beside her on the back seat. She had met Mrs. Peters the year before at the county fair, and the thing she remembered about her was that she didn't seem like a sheriff's wife. She was small and thin and didn't have a strong voice. Mrs. Gorman, sheriff's wife before Gorman went out and Peters came in, had a voice that somehow seemed to be backing up the law with every word. But if Mrs. Peters didn't look like a sheriff's wife, Peters made it up in looking like a sheriff. He was to a dot the kind of man who could get himself elected sheriff—a heavy man with a big voice, who was particularly genial with the law-abiding, as if to make it plain that he knew the difference between criminals and non-criminals. And right there it came into Mrs. Hale's mind, with a stab, that this man who was so pleasant and lively with all of them was going to the Wrights' now as a sheriff.

"The country's not very pleasant this time of year," Mrs. Peters at last ventured, as if she felt they ought to be talking as well as the men.

Mrs. Hale scarcely finished her reply, for they had gone up a little hill and could see the Wright place now, and seeing it did not make her feel like talking. It looked very lonesome this cold March morning. It had always been a lonesome-looking place. It was down in a hollow, and the poplar trees around it were lonesome-looking trees. The men were looking at it and talking about what had happened. The county attorney was bending to one side of the buggy, and kept looking steadily at the place as they drew up to it.

"I'm glad you came with me," Mrs. Peters said nervously, as the two women were about to follow the men in through the kitchen door.

Even after she had her foot on the door-step, her hand on the knob, Martha Hale had a moment of feeling she could not cross that threshold. And the reason it seemed she couldn't cross it now was simply because she hadn't crossed it before. Time and time again it had been in her mind, "I ought to go over and see Minnie Foster"—she still thought of her as Minnie Foster, though for twenty years she had been Mrs. Wright. And then there was always something to do and Minnie Foster would go from her mind. But *now* she could come.

. . .

The men went over to the stove. The women stood close together by the door. Young Henderson, the county attorney, turned around and said, "Come up to the fire, ladies."

Mrs. Peters took a step forward, then stopped. "I'm not—cold," she said.

And so the two women stood by the door, at first not even so much as looking around the kitchen.

The men talked for a minute about what a good thing it was the sheriff had sent his deputy out that morning to make a fire for them, and then Sheriff Peters stepped back from the stove, unbuttoned his outer coat, and leaned his hands on the kitchen table in a way that seemed to mark the beginning of official business. "Now, Mr. Hale," he said in a sort of semi-official voice, "before we move things about, you tell Mr. Henderson just what it was you saw when you came here yesterday morning."

The county attorney was looking around the kitchen.

"By the way," he said, "has anything been moved?" He turned to the sheriff. "Are things just as you left them yesterday?"

Peters looked from cupboard to sink; from that to a small worn rocker a little to one side of the kitchen table.

"It's just the same."

"Somebody should have been left here yesterday," said the county attorney.

"Oh—yesterday," returned the sheriff, with a little gesture as of yesterday having been more than he could bear to think of. "When I had to send Frank to Morris Center for that man who went crazy—let me tell you, I had my hands full *yesterday*. I knew you could get back from Omaha by to-day, George, and as long as I went over everything here myself—"

"Well, Mr. Hale," said the county attorney, in a way of letting what was past and gone go, "tell just what happened when you came here yesterday morning."

Mrs. Hale, still leaning against the door, had that sinking feeling of the mother whose child is about to speak a piece. Lewis often wandered along and got things mixed up in a story. She hoped he would tell this straight and plain, and not say unnecessary things that would just make things harder for Minnie Foster. He didn't begin at once, and she noticed that he looked queer—as if standing in that kitchen and having to tell what he had seen there yesterday morning made him almost sick.

"Yes, Mr. Hale?" the county attorney reminded.

"Harry and I had started to town with a load of potatoes," Mrs. Hale's husband began.

Harry was Mrs. Hale's oldest boy. He wasn't with them now, for the very good reason that those potatoes never got to town yesterday and he was taking them this morning, so he hadn't been home when the sheriff stopped to say he wanted Mr. Hale to come over to the Wright place and tell the county attorney his story there, where he could point it all out. With all Mrs. Hale's other emotions came the fear now that maybe Harry wasn't dressed warm enough—they hadn't any of them realized how that north wind did bite.

"We come along this road," Hale was going on, with a motion of his hand to the road over which they had just come, "and as we got in sight of the house I says to Harry, 'I'm goin' to see if I can't get John Wright to take a telephone.' You see," he explained to Henderson, "unless I can get somebody to go in with me they won't come out this branch road except for a price *I* can't pay. I'd spoke to Wright about it once before; but he put me off, saying folks talked too much anyway, and all he asked was peace and quiet—guess you know about how much he talked himself. But I thought maybe if I went to the house and talked about it before his wife, and said all the women-folks liked the telephones, and that in this lonesome stretch of road it would be a good thing—well, I said to Harry that that was what I was going to say—though I said at the same time that I didn't know as what his wife wanted made much difference to John—"

Now, there he was!—saying things he didn't need to say. Mrs. Hale tried to catch her husband's eye, but fortunately the county attorney interrupted with:

"Let's talk about that a little later, Mr. Hale. I do want to talk about that, but I'm anxious now to get along to just what happened when you got here."

When he began this time, it was very deliberately and carefully:

"I didn't see or hear anything. I knocked at the door. And still it was all quiet inside. I knew they must be up—it was past eight o'clock. So I knocked again, louder, and I thought I heard somebody say, 'Come in.' I wasn't sure—I'm not sure yet. But I opened the door—this door," jerking a hand toward the door by which the two women stood, "and there, in that rocker"—pointing to it—"sat Mrs. Wright."

Every one in the kitchen looked at the rocker. It came into Mrs. Hale's mind that that rocker didn't look in the least like Minnie Foster—the Minnie Foster of twenty years before. It was a dingy red, with wooden rungs up the back, and the middle rung was gone, and the chair sagged to one side.

"How did she—look?" the county attorney was inquiring.

"Well," said Hale, "she looked—queer."

"How do you mean—queer?"

As he asked it he took out a note-book and pencil. Mrs. Hale did not like the sight of that pencil. She kept her eye fixed on her husband, as if to keep him from saying unnecessary things that would go into that notebook and make trouble.

Hale did speak guardedly, as if the pencil had affected him too.

"Well, as if she didn't know what she was going to do next. And kind of—done up."

"How did she seem to feel about your coming?"

"Why, I don't think she minded—one way or other. She didn't pay much attention. I said, 'Ho' do, Mrs. Wright? It's cold, ain't it?' And she said, 'Is it?'—and went on pleatin' at her apron.

"Well, I was surprised. She didn't ask me to come up to the stove, or to sit down, but just set there, not even lookin' at me. And so I said: 'I want to see John.'

"And then she—laughed. I guess you would call it a laugh.

"I thought of Harry and the team outside, so I said, a little sharp, 'Can I see John?' 'No,' says she—kind of dull like. 'Ain't he home?' says I. Then she looked at me. 'Yes,' says she, 'he's home.' 'Then why can't I see him?' I asked her, out of patience with her now. ' 'Cause he's dead,' says she, just as quiet and dull—and fell to pleatin' her apron. 'Dead?' says I, like you do when you can't take in what you've heard.

"She just nodded her head, not getting a bit excited, but rockin' back and forth.

" 'Why—where is he?' says I, not knowing *what* to say.

"She just pointed upstairs—like this"—pointing to the room above.

"I got up, with the idea of going up there myself. By this time I—didn't know what to do. I walked from there to here; then I says: 'Why, what did he die of?'

" 'He died of a rope round his neck,' says she; and just went on pleatin' at her apron."

. . .

Hale stopped speaking, and stood staring at the rocker, as if he were still seeing the woman who had sat there the morning before. Nobody spoke; it was as if every one were seeing the woman who had sat there the morning before.

"And what did you do then?" the county attorney at last broke the silence.

"I went out and called Harry. I thought I might—need help. I got Harry in, and we went upstairs." His voice fell almost to a whisper. "There he was—lying over the—"

"I think I'd rather have you go into that upstairs," the county attorney interrupted, "where you can point it all out. Just go on now with the rest of the story."

"Well, my first thought was to get that rope off. It looked—"

He stopped, his face twitching.

"But Harry, he went up to him, and he said, 'No, he's dead all right, and we'd better not touch anything.' So we went downstairs.

"She was still sitting that same way. 'Has anybody been notified?' I asked. 'No,' says she, unconcerned.

" 'Who did this, Mrs. Wright?' said Harry. He said it businesslike, and she stopped pleatin' at her apron. 'I don't know,' she says. 'You don't *know?*' says Harry. 'Weren't you sleepin' in the bed with him?' 'Yes,' says she, 'but I was on the inside.' 'Somebody slipped a rope round his neck and strangled him, and you didn't wake up?' says Harry. 'I didn't wake up,' she said after him.

"We may have looked as if we didn't see how that could be, for after a minute she said, 'I sleep sound.'

"Harry was going to ask her more questions, but I said maybe that weren't our business; maybe we ought to let her tell her story first to the coroner or the sheriff. So Harry went fast as he could over to High Road—the Rivers' place, where there's a telephone."

"And what did she do when she knew you had gone for the coroner?" The attorney got his pencil in his hand all ready for writing.

"She moved from that chair to this one over here"—Hale pointed to a small chair in the corner—"and just sat there with her hands held together and looking down. I got a feeling that I ought to make some conversation, so I said I had come in to see if John wanted to put in a telephone; and at that she started to laugh, and then she stopped and looked at me—scared."

At the sound of a moving pencil the man who was telling the story looked up.

"I dunno—maybe it wasn't scared," he hastened; "I wouldn't like to say it was. Soon Harry got back, and then Dr. Lloyd came, and you, Mr. Peters, and so I guess that's all I know that you don't."

. . .

He said that last with relief, and moved a little, as if relaxing. Every one moved a little. The county attorney walked toward the stair door.

"I guess we'll go upstairs first—then out to the barn and around there."

He paused and looked around the kitchen.

"You're convinced there was nothing important here?" he asked the sheriff. "Nothing that would—point to any motive?"

The sheriff too looked all around, as if to re-convince himself.

"Nothing here but kitchen things," he said, with a little laugh for the insignificance of kitchen things.

The county attorney was looking at the cupboard—a peculiar, ungainly structure, half closet and half cupboard, the upper part of it being built in the wall, and the lower part just the old-fashioned kitchen cupboard. As if its queerness attracted him, he got a chair and opened the upper part and looked in. After a moment he drew his hand away sticky.

"Here's a nice mess," he said resentfully.

The two women had drawn nearer, and now the sheriff's wife spoke.

"Oh—her fruit," she said, looking to Mrs. Hale for sympathetic understanding. She turned back to the county attorney and explained: "She worried about that when it turned so cold last night. She said the fire would go out and her jars might burst."

Mrs. Peters' husband broke into a laugh.

"Well, can you beat the women! Held for murder, and worrying about her preserves!"

The young attorney set his lips.

"I guess before we're through with her she may have something more serious than preserves to worry about."

"Oh, well," said Mrs. Hale's husband, with good-natured superiority, "women are used to worrying over trifles."

The two women moved a little closer together. Neither of them spoke. The county attorney seemed suddenly to remember his manners—and think of his future.

"And yet," said he, with the gallantry of a young politician, "for all their worries, what would we do without the ladies?"

The women did not speak, did not unbend. He went to the sink and began washing his hands. He turned to wipe them on the roller towel—whirled it for a cleaner place.

"Dirty towels! Not much of a housekeeper, would you say, ladies?"

He kicked his foot against some dirty pans under the sink.

"There's a great deal of work to be done on a farm," said Mrs. Hale stiffly.

"To be sure. And yet"—with a little bow to her—"I know there are some Dickson County farm-houses that do not have such roller towels." He gave it a pull to expose its full length again.

"Those towels get dirty awful quick. Men's hands aren't always as clean as they might be."

"Ah, loyal to your sex, I see," he laughed. He stopped and gave her a keen look. "But you and Mrs. Wright were neighbors. I suppose you were friends, too."

Martha Hale shook her head.

"I've seen little enough of her of late years. I've not been in this house—it's more than a year."

"And why was that? You didn't like her?"

"I liked her well enough," she replied with spirit. "Farmers' wives have their hands full, Mr. Henderson. And then—" She looked around the kitchen.

"Yes?" he encouraged.

"It never seemed a very cheerful place," said she, more to herself than to him.

"No," he agreed; "I don't think any one would call it cheerful. I shouldn't say she had the home-making instinct."

"Well, I don't know as Wright had, either," she muttered.

"You mean they didn't get on very well?" he was quick to ask.

"No; I don't mean anything," she answered, with decision. As she turned a little away from him, she added: "But I don't think a place would be any the cheerfuler for John Wright's bein' in it."

"I'd like to talk to you about that a little later, Mrs. Hale," he said. "I'm anxious to get the lay of things upstairs now."

He moved toward the stair door, followed by the two men.

"I suppose anything Mrs. Peters does'll be all right?" the sheriff inquired. "She was to take in some clothes for her, you know—and a few little things. We left in such a hurry yesterday."

The county attorney looked at the two women whom they were leaving alone there among the kitchen things.

"Yes—Mrs. Peters," he said, his glance resting on the woman who was not Mrs. Peters, the big farmer woman who stood behind the sheriff's wife. "Of course Mrs. Peters is one of us," he said, in a manner of entrusting responsibility. "And keep your eye out, Mrs. Peters, for anything that might be of use. No telling; you women might come upon a clue to the motive—and that's the thing we need."

Mr. Hale rubbed his face after the fashion of a show man getting ready for a pleasantry.

"But would the women know a clue if they did come upon it?" he said; and, having delivered himself of this, he followed the others through the stair door.

. . .

The women stood motionless and silent, listening to the footsteps, first upon the stairs, then in the room above them.

Then, as if releasing herself from something strange, Mrs. Hale began to arrange the dirty pans under the sink, which the county attorney's disdainful push of the foot had deranged.

"I'd hate to have men comin' into my kitchen," she said testily—"snoopin' round and criticizin'."

"Of course it's no more than their duty," said the sheriff's wife, in her manner of timid acquiescence.

"Duty's all right," replied Mrs. Hale bluffly; "but I guess that deputy sheriff that come out to make the fire might have got a little of this on." She gave the roller towel a pull. "Wish I'd thought of that sooner! Seems mean to talk about her for not having things slicked up, when she had to come away in such a hurry."

She looked around the kitchen. Certainly it was not "slicked up." Her eye was held by a bucket of sugar on a low shelf. The cover was off the wooden bucket, and beside it was a paper bag—half full.

Mrs. Hale moved toward it.

"She was putting this in there," she said to herself—slowly.

She thought of the flour in her kitchen at home—half sifted, half not sifted. She had been interrupted, and had left things half done. What had interrupted Minnie Foster? Why had that work been left half done? She made a move as if to finish it,—unfinished things always bothered her,—and then she glanced around and saw that Mrs. Peters was watching her—and she didn't want Mrs. Peters to get that feeling she had got of work begun and then—for some reason—not finished.

"It's a shame about her fruit," she said, and walked toward the cupboard that the county attorney had opened, and got on the chair, murmuring: "I wonder if it's all gone."

It was a sorry enough looking sight, but "Here's one that's all right," she said at last. She held it toward the light. "This is cherries, too." She looked again. "I declare I believe that's the only one."

With a sigh, she got down from the chair, went to the sink, and wiped off the bottle.

"She'll feel awful bad, after all her hard work in the hot weather. I remember the afternoon I put up my cherries last summer."

She set the bottle on the table, and, with another sigh, started to sit down in the rocker. But she did not sit down. Something kept her from sitting down in that chair. She straightened—stepped back, and, half turned away, stood looking at it, seeing the woman who had sat there "pleatin' at her apron."

The thin voice of the sheriff's wife broke in upon her: "I must be getting those things from the front room closet." She opened the door into the other room, started in, stepped back. "You coming with me, Mrs. Hale?" she asked nervously. "You—you could help me get them."

They were soon back—the stark coldness of that shut-up room was not a thing to linger in.

"My!" said Mrs. Peters, dropping the things on the table and hurrying to the stove.

Mrs. Hale stood examining the clothes the woman who was being detained in town had said she wanted.

"Wright was close!" she exclaimed, holding up a shabby black skirt that bore the marks of much making over. "I think maybe that's why she kept so much to herself. I s'pose she felt she couldn't do her part; and then, you don't enjoy things when you feel shabby. She used to wear pretty clothes and be lively—when she was Minnie Foster, one of the town girls, singing in the choir. But that—oh, that was twenty years ago."

With a carefulness in which there was something tender, she folded the shabby clothes and piled them at one corner of the table. She looked up at Mrs. Peters, and there was something in the other woman's look that irritated her.

"She don't care," she said to herself. "Much difference it makes to her whether Minnie Foster had pretty clothes when she was a girl."

Then she looked again, and she wasn't so sure; in fact, she hadn't at any time been perfectly sure about Mrs. Peters. She had that shrinking manner, and yet her eyes looked as if they could see a long way into things.

"This all you was to take in?" asked Mrs. Hale.

"No," said the sheriff's wife; "she said she wanted an apron. Funny thing to want," she ventured in her nervous little way, "for there's not much to get you dirty in jail, goodness knows. But I suppose just to make her feel more natural. If you're used to wearing an apron—. She said they were in the bottom drawer of this cupboard. Yes—here they are. And then her little shawl that always hung on the stair door."

She took the small gray shawl from behind the door leading upstairs, and stood a minute looking at it.

Suddenly Mrs. Hale took a quick step toward the other woman.

"Mrs. Peters!"

"Yes, Mrs. Hale?"

"Do you think she—did it?"

A frightened look blurred the other thing in Mrs. Peters' eyes.

"Oh, I don't know," she said, in a voice that seemed to shrink away from the subject.

"Well, I don't think she did," affirmed Mrs. Hale stoutly. "Asking for an apron, and her little shawl. Worryin' about her fruit."

"Mr. Peters says—." Footsteps were heard in the room above; she stopped, looked up, then went on in a lowered voice: "Mr. Peters says—it looks bad for her. Mr. Henderson is awful sarcastic in a speech, and he's going to make fun of her saying she didn't—wake up."

For a moment Mrs. Hale had no answer. Then, "Well, I guess John Wright didn't wake up—when they was slippin' that rope under his neck," she muttered.

"No, it's *strange*," breathed Mrs. Peters. "They think it was such a—funny way to kill a man."

She began to laugh; at sound of the laugh, abruptly stopped.

"That's just what Mr. Hale said," said Mrs. Hale, in a resolutely natural voice. "There was a gun in the house. He says that's what he can't understand."

"Mr. Henderson said, coming out, that what was needed for the case was a motive. Something to show anger—or sudden feeling."

"Well, I don't see any signs of anger around here," said Mrs. Hale. "I don't—"

She stopped. It was as if her mind tripped on something. Her eye was caught by a dish-towel in the middle of the kitchen table. Slowly she moved toward the table. One half of it was wiped clean, the other half messy. Her eyes made a slow, almost unwilling turn to the bucket of sugar and the half empty bag beside it. Things begun—and not finished.

After a moment she stepped back, and said, in that manner of releasing herself:

"Wonder how they're finding things upstairs? I hope she had it a little more red up up there. You know,"—she paused, and feeling gathered,—"it seems kind of *sneaking:* locking her up in town and coming out here to get her own house to turn against her!"

"But, Mrs. Hale," said the sheriff's wife, "the law is the law."

"I s'pose 'tis," answered Mrs. Hale shortly.

She turned to the stove, saying something about that fire not being much to brag of. She worked with it a minute, and when she straightened up she said aggressively:

"The law is the law—and a bad stove is a bad stove. How'd you like to cook on this?"—pointing with the poker to the broken lining. She opened the oven door and started to express her opinion of the oven; but she was swept into her own thoughts, thinking of what it would mean, year after year, to have that stove to wrestle with. The thought of Minnie Foster trying to bake in that oven—and the thought of her never going over to see Minnie Foster—.

She was startled by hearing Mrs. Peters say: "A person gets discouraged—and loses heart."

The sheriff's wife had looked from the stove to the sink—to the pail of water which had been carried in from outside. The two women stood there silent, above them the footsteps of the men who were looking for evidence against the woman who had worked in that kitchen. That look of seeing into things, of seeing through a thing to something else, was in the eyes of the sheriff's wife now. When Mrs. Hale next spoke to her, it was gently:

"Better loosen up your things, Mrs. Peters. We'll not feel them when we go out."

Mrs. Peters went to the back of the room to hang up the fur tippet she was wearing. A moment later she exclaimed, "Why, she was piecing a quilt," and held up a large sewing basket piled high with quilt pieces.

Mrs. Hale spread some of the blocks out on the table.

"It's a log-cabin pattern," she said, putting several of them together. "Pretty, isn't it?"

They were so engaged with the quilt that they did not hear the footsteps on the stairs. Just as the stair door opened Mrs. Hale was saying:

"Do you suppose she was going to quilt it or just knot it?"

The sheriff threw up his hands.

"They wonder whether she was going to quilt it or just knot it!"

There was a laugh for the ways of women, a warming of hands over the stove, and then the county attorney said briskly:

"Well, let's go right out to the barn and get that cleared up."

"I don't see as there's anything so strange," Mrs. Hale said resentfully, after the outside door had closed on the three men—"our taking up our time with little things while we're waiting for them to get the evidence. I don't see as it's anything to laugh about."

"Of course they've got awful important things on their minds," said the sheriff's wife apologetically.

They returned to an inspection of the block for the quilt. Mrs. Hale was looking at the fine, even sewing, and preoccupied with thoughts of the woman who had done that sewing, when she heard the sheriff's wife say, in a queer tone:

"Why, look at this one."

She turned to take the block held out to her.

"The sewing," said Mrs. Peters, in a troubled way. "All the rest of them have been so nice and even—but—this one. Why, it looks as if she didn't know what she was about!"

Their eyes met—something flashed to life, passed between them; then, as if with an effort, they seemed to pull away from each other. A moment Mrs. Hale sat there, her hands folded over that sewing which was so unlike all the rest of the sewing. Then she had pulled a knot and drawn the threads.

"Oh, what are you doing, Mrs. Hale?" asked the sheriff's wife, startled.

"Just pulling out a stitch or two that's not sewed very good," said Mrs. Hale mildly.

"I don't think we ought to touch things," Mrs. Peters said, a little helplessly.

"I'll just finish up this end," answered Mrs. Hale, still in that mild, matter-of-fact fashion.

She threaded a needle and started to replace bad sewing with good. For a little while she sewed in silence. Then, in that thin, timid voice, she heard:

"Mrs. Hale!"

"Yes, Mrs. Peters?"

"What do you suppose she was so—nervous about?"

"Oh, *I* don't know," said Mrs. Hale, as if dismissing a thing not important enough to spend much time on. "I don't know as she was—nervous. I sew awful queer sometimes when I'm just tired."

She cut a thread, and out of the corner of her eye looked up at Mrs. Peters. The small, lean face of the sheriff's wife seemed to have tightened up. Her eyes had that look of peering into something. But next moment she moved, and said in her thin, indecisive way:

"Well, I must get those clothes wrapped. They may be through sooner than we think. I wonder where I could find a piece of paper—and string."

"In that cupboard, maybe," suggested Mrs. Hale, after a glance around.

One piece of the crazy sewing remained unripped. Mrs. Peters' back turned, Martha Hale now scrutinized that piece, compared it with the dainty, accurate sewing of the other blocks. The difference was startling. Holding this block made her feel queer, as if the distracted thoughts of the woman who had perhaps turned to it to try and quiet herself were communicating themselves to her.

Mrs. Peters' voice roused her.

"Here's a bird-cage," she said. "Did she have a bird, Mrs. Hale?"

"Why, I don't know whether she did or not." She turned to look at the cage Mrs. Peters was holding up. "I've not been here in so long." She sighed. "There was a man round last year selling canaries cheap—but I don't know as she took one. Maybe she did. She used to sing real pretty herself."

Mrs. Peters looked around the kitchen.

"Seems kind of funny to think of a bird here." She half laughed—an attempt to put up a barrier. "But she must have had one—or why would she have a cage? I wonder what happened to it."

"I suppose maybe the cat got it," suggested Mrs. Hale, resuming her sewing.

"No; she didn't have a cat. She's got that feeling some people have about cats—being afraid of them. When they brought her to our house yesterday, my cat got in the room, and she was real upset and asked me to take it out."

"My sister Bessie was like that," laughed Mrs. Hale.

The sheriff's wife did not reply. The silence made Mrs. Hale turn round. Mrs. Peters was examining the bird-cage.

"Look at this door," she said slowly. "It's broke. One hinge has been pulled apart."

Mrs. Hale came nearer.

"Looks as if some one must have been—rough with it."

Again their eyes met—startled, questioning, apprehensive. For a moment neither spoke nor stirred. Then Mrs. Hale, turning away, said brusquely:

"If they're going to find any evidence, I wish they'd be about it. I don't like this place."

"But I'm awful glad you came with me, Mrs. Hale." Mrs. Peters put the bird-cage on the table and sat down. "It would be lonesome for me—sitting here alone."

"Yes, it would, wouldn't it?" agreed Mrs. Hale, a certain determined naturalness in her voice. She had picked up the sewing, but now it dropped in her lap, and she murmured in a different voice: "But I tell you what I *do* wish, Mrs. Peters. I wish I had come over sometimes when she was here. I wish—I had."

"But of course you were awful busy, Mrs. Hale. Your house—and your children."

"I could've come," retorted Mrs. Hale shortly. "I stayed away because it weren't cheerful—and that's why I ought to have come. I"—she looked around—"I've never liked this place. Maybe because it's down in a hollow and you don't see the road. I don't know what it is, but it's a lonesome place, and always was. I wish I had come over to see Minnie Foster sometimes. I can see now—" She did not put it into words.

"Well, you mustn't reproach yourself," counseled Mrs. Peters. "Somehow, we just don't see how it is with other folks till—something comes up."

"Not having children makes less work," mused Mrs. Hale, after a silence, "but it makes a quiet house—and Wright out to work all day—and no company when he did come in. Did you know John Wright, Mrs. Peters?"

"Not to know him. I've seen him in town. They say he was a good man."

"Yes—good," conceded John Wright's neighbor grimly. "He didn't drink, and kept his word as well as most, I guess, and paid his debts. But he was a hard man, Mrs. Peters. Just to pass the time of day with him—." She stopped, shivered a little. "Like a raw wind that gets to the bone." Her eye fell upon the cage on the table before her, and she added, almost bitterly: "I should think she would've wanted a bird!"

Suddenly she learned forward, looking intently at the cage. "But what do you s'pose went wrong with it?"

"I don't know," returned Mrs. Peters; "unless it got sick and died."

But after she said it she reached over and swung the broken door. Both women watched it as if somehow held by it.

"You didn't know—her?" Mrs. Hale asked, a gentler note in her voice.

"Not till they brought her yesterday," said the sheriff's wife.

"She—come to think of it, she was kind of like a bird herself. Real sweet and pretty, but kind of timid and—fluttery. How—she—did—change."

That held her for a long time. Finally, as if struck with a happy thought and relieved to get back to everyday things, she exclaimed:

"Tell you what, Mrs. Peters, why don't you take the quilt in with you? It might take up her mind."

"Why, I think that's a real nice idea, Mrs. Hale," agreed the sheriff's wife, as if she too were glad to come into the atmosphere of a simple kindness. "There couldn't possibly be any objection to that, could there? Now, just what will I take? I wonder if her patches are in here—and her things."

They turned to the sewing basket.

"Here's some red," said Mrs. Hale, bringing out a roll of cloth. Underneath that was a box. "Here, maybe her scissors are in here—and her things." She held it up. "What a pretty box! I'll warrant that was something she had a long time ago—when she was a girl."

She held it in her hand a moment; then, with a little sigh, opened it.

Instantly her hand went to her nose.

"Why—!"

Mrs. Peters drew nearer—then turned away.

"There's something wrapped up in this piece of silk," faltered Mrs. Hale.

"This isn't her scissors," said Mrs. Peters, in a shrinking voice.

Her hand not steady, Mrs. Hale raised the piece of silk. "Oh, Mrs. Peters!" she cried. "It's—"

Mrs. Peters bent closer.

"It's the bird," she whispered.

"But, Mrs. Peters!" cried Mrs. Hale. "*Look* at it! Its *neck*—look at its neck! It's all—other side *to.*"

She held the box away from her.

The sheriff's wife again bent closer.

"Somebody wrung its neck," said she, in a voice that was slow and deep.

And then again the eyes of the two women met—this time clung together in a look of dawning comprehension, of growing horror. Mrs. Peters looked from the dead bird to the broken door of the cage. Again their eyes met. And just then there was a sound at the outside door.

Mrs. Hale slipped the box under the quilt pieces in the basket, and sank into the chair before it. Mrs. Peters stood holding to the table. The county attorney and the sheriff came in from outside.

"Well, ladies," said the county attorney, as one turning from serious things to little pleasantries, "have you decided whether she was going to quilt it or knot it?"

"We think," began the sheriff's wife in a flurried voice, "that she was going to—knot it."

He was too preoccupied to notice the change that came in her voice on that last.

"Well, that's very interesting, I'm sure," he said tolerantly. He caught sight of the bird-cage. "Has the bird flown?"

"We think the cat got it," said Mrs. Hale in a voice curiously even.

He was walking up and down, as if thinking something out.

"Is there a cat?" he asked absently.

Mrs. Hale shot a look up at the sheriff's wife.

"Well, not *now,*" said Mrs. Peters. "They're superstitious, you know; they leave."

She sank into her chair.

The county attorney did not heed her. "No sign at all of any one having come in from the outside," he said to Peters, in the manner of continuing an interrupted conversation. "Their own rope. Now let's go upstairs again and go over it, piece by piece. It would have to have been some one who knew just the—"

The stair door closed behind them and their voices were lost.

The two women sat motionless, not looking at each other, but as if peering into something and at the same time holding back. When they spoke now it was as if they were afraid of what they were saying, but as if they could not help saying it.

"She liked the bird," said Martha Hale, low and slowly. "She was going to bury it in that pretty box."

"When I was a girl," said Mrs. Peters, under her breath, "my kitten—there was a boy took a hatchet, and before my eyes—before I could get there—" She covered her face an instant. "If they hadn't held me back I would have"—

she caught herself, looked upstairs where footsteps were heard, and finished weakly—"hurt him."

Then they sat without speaking or moving.

"I wonder how it would seem," Mrs. Hale at last began, as if feeling her way over strange ground—"never to have had any children around?" Her eyes made a slow sweep of the kitchen, as if seeing what that kitchen had meant through all the years. "No, Wright wouldn't like the bird," she said after that—"a thing that sang. She used to sing. He killed that too." Her voice tightened.

Mrs. Peters moved uneasily.

"Of course we don't know who killed the bird."

"I knew John Wright," was Mrs. Hale's answer.

"It was an awful thing was done in this house that night, Mrs. Hale," said the sheriff's wife. "Killing a man while he slept—slipping a thing round his neck that choked the life out of him."

Mrs. Hale's hand went out to the bird-cage.

"His neck. Choked the life out of him."

"We don't *know* who killed him," whispered Mrs. Peters wildly. "We don't *know.*"

Mrs. Hale had not moved. "If there had been years and years of—nothing, then a bird to sing to you, it would be awful—still—after the bird was still."

It was as if something within her not herself had spoken, and it found in Mrs. Peters something she did not know as herself.

"I know what stillness is," she said, in a queer, monotonous voice. "When we homesteaded in Dakota, and my first baby died—after he was two years old—and me with no other then—"

Mrs. Hale stirred.

"How soon do you suppose they'll be through looking for the evidence?"

"I know what stillness is," repeated Mrs. Peters, in just that same way. Then she too pulled back. "The law has got to punish crime, Mrs. Hale," she said in her tight little way.

"I wish you'd seen Minnie Foster," was the answer, "when she wore a white dress with blue ribbons, and stood up there in the choir and sang."

The picture of that girl, the fact that she had lived neighbor to that girl for twenty years, and had let her die for lack of life, was suddenly more than she could bear.

"Oh, I *wish* I'd come over here once in a while!" she cried. "That was a crime! That was a crime! Who's going to punish that?"

"We mustn't take on," said Mrs. Peters, with a frightened look toward the stairs.

"I might 'a' *known* she needed help! I tell you, it's *queer,* Mrs. Peters. We live close together, and we live far apart. We all go through the same things—it's all just a different kind of the same thing! If it weren't—why do you and I *understand?* Why do we *know*—what we know this minute?"

She dashed her hand across her eyes. Then, seeing the jar of fruit on the table, she reached for it and choked out:

"If I was you I wouldn't *tell* her her fruit was gone! Tell her it *ain't*. Tell her it's all right—all of it. Here—take this in to prove it to her! She—she may never know whether it was broke or not."

She turned away.

Mrs. Peters reached out for the bottle of fruit as if she were glad to take it—as if touching a familiar thing, having something to do, could keep her from something else. She got up, looked about for something to wrap the fruit in, took a petticoat from the pile of clothes she had brought from the front room, and nervously started winding that round the bottle.

"My!" she began, in a high, false voice, "it's a good thing the men couldn't hear us! Getting all stirred up over a little thing like a—dead canary." She hurried over that. "As if that could have anything to do with—with— My, wouldn't they *laugh?*"

Footsteps were heard on the stairs.

"Maybe they would," muttered Mrs. Hale—"maybe they wouldn't."

"No, Peters," said the county attorney incisively; "it's all perfectly clear, except the reason for doing it. But you know juries when it comes to women. If there was some definite thing—something to show. Something to make a story about. A thing that would connect up with this clumsy way of doing it."

In a covert way Mrs. Hale looked at Mrs. Peters. Mrs. Peters was looking at her. Quickly they looked away from each other. The outer door opened and Mr. Hale came in.

"I've got the team round now," he said. "Pretty cold out there."

"I'm going to stay here awhile by myself," the county attorney suddenly announced. "You can send Frank out for me, can't you?" he asked the sheriff. "I want to go over everything. I'm not satisfied we can't do better."

Again, for one brief moment, the two women's eyes found one another.

The sheriff came up to the table.

"Did you want to see what Mrs. Peters was going to take in?"

The county attorney picked up the apron. He laughed.

"Oh, I guess they're not very dangerous things the ladies have picked out."

Mrs. Hale's hand was on the sewing basket in which the box was concealed. She felt that she ought to take her hand off the basket. She did not seem able to. He picked up one of the quilt blocks which she had piled on to cover the box. Her eyes felt like fire. She had a feeling that if he took up the basket she would snatch it from him.

But he did not take it up. With another little laugh, he turned away, saying:

"No; Mrs. Peters doesn't need supervising. For that matter, a sheriff's wife is married to the law. Ever think of it that way, Mrs. Peters?"

Mrs. Peters was standing beside the table. Mrs. Hale shot a look up at her; but she could not see her face. Mrs. Peters had turned away. When she spoke, her voice was muffled.

"Not—just that way," she said.

"Married to the law!" chuckled Mrs. Peters' husband. He moved toward the door into the front room, and said to the county attorney:

"I just want you to come in here a minute, George. We ought to take a look at these windows."

"Oh—windows," said the county attorney scoffingly.

"We'll be right out, Mr. Hale," said the sheriff to the farmer, who was still waiting by the door.

Hale went to look after the horses. The sheriff followed the county attorney into the other room. Again—for one final moment—the two women were alone in that kitchen.

Martha Hale sprang up, her hands tight together, looking at that other woman, with whom it rested. At first she could not see her eyes, for the sheriff's wife had not turned back since she turned away at that suggestion of being married to the law. But now Mrs. Hale made her turn back. Her eyes made her turn back. Slowly, unwillingly, Mrs. Peters turned her head until her eyes met the eyes of the other woman. There was a moment when they held each other in a steady, burning look in which there was no evasion nor flinching. Then Martha Hale's eyes pointed the way to the basket in which was hidden the thing that would make certain the conviction of the other woman—that woman who was not there and yet who had been there with them all through that hour.

For a moment Mrs. Peters did not move. And then she did it. With a rush forward, she threw back the quilt pieces, got the box, tried to put it in her handbag. It was too big. Desperately she opened it, started to take the bird out. But there she broke—she could not touch the bird. She stood there helpless, foolish.

There was the sound of a knob turning in the inner door. Martha Hale snatched the box from the sheriff's wife, and got it in the pocket of her big coat just as the sheriff and the county attorney came back into the kitchen.

"Well, Henry," said the county attorney facetiously, "at least we found out that she was not going to quilt it. She was going to—what is it you call it, ladies?"

Mrs. Hale's hand was against the pocket of her coat.

"We call it—knot it, Mr. Henderson."

1917

ZORA NEALE HURSTON
(1891?–1960)

Anthropologist, folklorist, and novelist, Zora Neale Hurston is the most acclaimed woman writer of the Harlem Renaissance. Because of her southern heritage and her attentive, trained ear, she had a unique access to the dialect of her people, which she re-created in dialogue.

Hurston was born in Eatonville, Florida, a self-governed, all-Black town. The exact year of her birth is uncertain; whereas recent scholarship suggests 1891, other sources claim anywhere between 1896 and 1903. Hurston created much of the confusion by changing the date throughout her life.

Her father, John Hurston, was both Eatonville's preacher and its mayor. Her mother, Lucy Hurston, was a schoolteacher who always favored Zora, one of eight children. Hurston remembers in her autobiography her mother's encouraging words: "Jump at the sun."

While attending Howard University between 1919 and 1924, Hurston was encouraged to write by the philosopher Alain Locke and the poet Georgia Douglas Johnson. Though still a student, she had her first stories printed in the New York magazine Opportunity. *In 1925, Hurston moved to New York City and enrolled at Barnard College, where her work with Franz Boas spurred her interest in anthropology as a means of studying and celebrating African American folklore. In 1927 she returned to Eatonville to do formal folklore research under the guidance of Boas. She listened to folk stories and songs, observed the dances of African Americans, and recorded everything she saw and heard. She graduated with a B.A. from Barnard in 1928 and published her folklore findings in* Mules and Men.

In 1933, with the encouragement of a publishing house editor, she began work on a novel she had been thinking about since 1929. Jonah's Gourd Vine *is based in part on her parents' volatile relationship. In March 1936, Hurston used the Guggenheim Fellowship she had won to travel to Jamaica and Haiti, where in seven straight weeks she wrote* Their Eyes Were Watching God. *The novelist and critic Sherley Anne Williams captured the importance of this work for contemporary African American women writers: "In the speech of her characters I heard my own country voice and saw in the heroine something of my own country self."*

Hurston's other major publications were Moses, Man of the Mountain; *her autobiography,* Dust Tracks on a Road; *and a novel about white southerners,* Seraph on the Suwanee.

"Sweat," the story included here, reveals some of Hurston's best literary and thematic qualities: use of dialect, influence of folklore, and feminist subject. In the

essay "How It Feels to Be Colored Me," Hurston uses a completely different voice. Here she is sassy, ironic, and above all comfortable in her Black skin.

SWEAT

It was eleven o'clock of a Spring night in Florida. It was Sunday. Any other night, Delia Jones would have been in bed for two hours by this time. But she was a washwoman, and Monday morning meant a great deal to her. So she collected the soiled clothes on Saturday when she returned the clean things. Sunday night after church, she sorted them and put the white things to soak. It saved her almost a half day's start. A great hamper in the bedroom held the clothes that she brought home. It was so much neater than a number of bundles lying around.

She squatted in the kitchen floor beside the great pile of clothes, sorting them into small heaps according to color, and humming a song in a mournful key, but wondering through it all where Sykes, her husband, had gone with her horse and buckboard.

Just then something long, round, limp and black fell upon her shoulders and slithered to the floor beside her. A great terror took hold of her. It softened her knees and dried her mouth so that it was a full minute before she could cry out or move. Then she saw that it was the big bull whip her husband liked to carry when he drove.

She lifted her eyes to the door and saw him standing there bent over with laughter at her fright. She screamed at him.

"Sykes, what you throw dat whip on me like dat? You know it would skeer me—looks just like a snake, an' you knows how skeered Ah is of snakes."

"Course Ah knowed it! That's how come Ah done it." He slapped his leg with his hand and almost rolled on the ground in his mirth. "If you such a big fool dat you got to have a fit over a earth worm or a string, Ah don't keer how bad Ah skeer you."

"You aint got no business doing it. Gawd knows it's a sin. Some day Ah'm gointuh drop dead from some of yo' foolishness. 'Nother thing, where you been wid mah rig? Ah feeds dat pony. He aint fuh you to be drivin' wid no bull whip."

"You sho is one aggravatin' nigger woman!" he declared and stepped into the room. She resumed her work and did not answer him at once. "Ah done tole you time and again to keep them white folks' clothes outa dis house."

He picked up the whip and glared down at her. Delia went on with her work. She went out into the yard and returned with a galvanized tub and set it on the washbench. She saw that Sykes had kicked all of the clothes together again, and now stood in her way truculently, his whole manner hoping, *praying,* for an argument. But she walked calmly around him and commenced to re-sort the things.

"Next time, Ah'm gointer kick 'em outdoors," he threatened as he struck a match along the leg of his corduroy breeches.

Delia never looked up from her work, and her thin, stooped shoulders sagged further.

"Ah aint for no fuss t'night Sykes. Ah just come from taking sacrament at the church house."

He snorted scornfully. "Yeah, you just come from de church house on a Sunday night, but heah you is gone to work on them clothes. You ain't nothing by a hypocrite. One of them amen-corner Christians—sing, whoop, and shout, then come home and wash white folks clothes on the Sabbath."

He stepped roughly upon the whitest pile of things, kicking them helter-skelter as he crossed the room. His wife gave a little scream of dismay, and quickly gathered them together again.

"Sykes, you quit grindin' dirt into these clothes! How can Ah git through by Sat'day if Ah don't start on Sunday?"

"Ah don't keer if you never git through. Anyhow, Ah done promised Gawd and a couple of other men, Ah aint gointer have it in mah house. Don't gimme no lip neither, else Ah'll throw 'em out and put mah fist up side yo' head to boot."

Delia's habitual meekness seemed to slip from her shoulders like a blown scarf. She was on her feet; her poor little body, her bare knuckly hands bravely defying the strapping hulk before her.

"Looka heah, Sykes, you done gone too fur. Ah been married to you fur fifteen years, and Ah been takin' in washin' fur fifteen years. Sweat, sweat, sweat! Work and sweat, cry and sweat, pray and sweat!"

"What's that got to do with me?" he asked brutally.

"What's it got to do with you, Sykes? Mah tub of suds is filled yo' belly with vittles more times than yo' hands is filled it. Mah sweat is done paid for this house and Ah reckon Ah kin keep on sweatin' in it."

She seized the iron skillet from the stove and struck a defensive pose, which act surprised him greatly, coming from her. It cowed him and he did not strike her as he usually did.

"Naw you won't," she panted, "that ole snaggle-toothed black woman you runnin' with aint comin' heah to pile up on *mah* sweat and blood. You aint paid for nothin' on this place, and Ah'm gointer stay right heah till Ah'm toted out foot foremost."

"Well, you better quit gittin' me riled up, else they'll be totin' you out sooner than you expect. Ah'm so tired of you Ah don't know whut to do. Gawd! how Ah hates skinny wimmen!"

A little awed by this new Delia, he sidled out of the door and slammed the back gate after him. He did not say where he had gone, but she knew too well. She knew very well that he would not return until nearly daybreak also. Her work over, she went on to bed but not to sleep at once. Things had come to a pretty pass!

She lay awake, gazing upon the debris that cluttered their matrimonial trail. Not an image left standing along the way. Anything like flowers had long ago been drowned in the salty stream that had been pressed from her heart. Her tears, her sweat, her blood. She had brought love to the union and he had brought a longing after the flesh. Two months after the wedding, he had given her the first brutal beating. She had the memory of his numerous trips to Orlando with all of his wages when he had returned to her penniless, even before the first year had passed. She was young and soft then, but now she thought of her knotty, muscled limbs, her harsh knuckly hands, and drew herself up into an unhappy little ball in the middle of the big feather bed. Too late now to hope for love, even if it were not Bertha it would be someone else. This case differed from the others only in that she was bolder than the others. Too late for everything except her little home. She had built it for her old days, and planted one by one the trees and flowers there. It was lovely to her, lovely.

Somehow, before sleep came, she found herself saying aloud: "Oh well, whatever goes over the Devil's back, is got to come under his belly. Sometime or ruther, Sykes, like everybody else, is gointer reap his sowing." After that she was able to build a spiritual earthworks against her husband. His shells could no longer reach her. *Amen.* She went to sleep and slept until he announced his presence in bed by kicking her feet and rudely snatching the covers away.

"Gimme some kivah heah, an' git yo' damn foots over on yo' own side! Ah oughter mash you in yo' mouf fuh drawing dat skillet on me."

Delia went clear to the rail without answering him. A triumphant indifference to all that he was or did.

. . .

The week was as full of work for Delia as all other weeks, and Saturday found her behind her little pony, collecting and delivering clothes.

It was a hot, hot day near the end of July. The village men on Joe Clarke's porch even chewed cane listlessly. They did not hurl the caneknots as usual. They let them dribble over the edge of the porch. Even conversation had collapsed under the heat.

"Heah come Delia Jones," Jim Merchant said, as the shaggy pony came 'round the bend of the road toward them. The rusty buckboard was heaped with baskets of crisp, clean laundry.

"Yep," Joe Lindsay agreed. "Hot or col', rain or shine, jes ez reg'lar ez de weeks roll roun' Delia carries 'em an' fetches 'em on Sat'day."

"She better if she wanter eat," said Moss. "Syke Jones aint wuth de shot an' powder hit would tek tuh kill 'em. Not to *huh* he aint."

"He sho' aint," Walter Thomas chimed in. "It's too bad, too, cause she wuz a right pritty lil trick when he got huh. Ah'd uh mah'ied huh mahseff if he hadnter beat me to it."

Delia nodded briefly at the men as she drove past.

"Too much knockin' will ruin *any* 'oman. He done beat huh 'nough tuh kill three women, let 'lone change they looks," said Elijah Moseley. "How Syke kin stommuck dat big black greasy Mogul he's layin' roun' wid, gits me. Ah swear dat eight-rock couldn't kiss a sardine can Ah done thowed out de back do' 'way las' yeah."

"Aw, she's fat, thass how come. He's allus been crazy 'bout fat women," put in Merchant. "He'd a' been tied up wid one long time ago if he could a' found one tuh have him. Did Ah tell yuh 'bout him come sidlin' roun' *mah* wife—bringin' her a basket uh peecans outa his yard fuh a present? Yessir, mah wife! She tol' him tuh take 'em right straight back home, cause Delia works so hard ovah dat washtub she reckon everything on de place taste lak sweat an' soapsuds. Ah jus' wisht Ah'd a' caught 'im 'roun' dere! Ah'd a' made his hips ketch on fiah down dat shell road."

"Ah know he done it, too. Ah sees 'im grinnin' at every 'oman dat passes," Walter Thomas said. "But even so, he useter eat some mighty big hunks uh humble pie tuh git dat lil' 'oman he got. She wuz ez pritty ez a speckled pup! Dat wuz fifteen yeahs ago. He useter be so skeered uh losin' huh, she could make him do some parts of a husband's duty. Dey never wuz de same in de mind."

"There oughter be a law about him," said Lindsay. "He aint fit tuh carry guts tuh a bear."

Clarke spoke for the first time. "Taint no law on earth dat kin make a man be decent if it aint in 'im. There's plenty men dat takes a wife lak dey do a joint uh sugar-cane. It's round, juicy an' sweet when dey gits it. But dey squeeze an' grind, squeeze an' grind an' wring tell dey wring every drop uh pleasure dat's in 'em out. When dey's satisfied dat dey is wrung dry, dey treats 'em jes lak dey do a cane-chew. Dey throws 'em away. Dey knows whut dey is doin' while dey is at it, an' hates theirselves fuh it but they keeps on hangin' after huh tell she's empty. Den dey hates huh fuh bein' a cane-chew an' in de way."

"We oughter take Syke an' dat stray 'oman uh his'n down in Lake Howell swamp an' lay on de rawhide till they cain't say Lawd a' mussy. He allus wuz uh ovahbearin' niggah, but since dat white 'oman from up north done teached 'im how to run a automobile, he done got too biggety to live—an' we oughter kill 'im," Old Man Anderson advised.

A grunt of approval went around the porch. But the heat was melting their civic virtue and Elijah Moseley began to bait Joe Clarke.

"Come on, Joe, git a melon outa dere an' slice it up for yo' customers. We'se all sufferin' wid de heat. De bear's done got *me!*"

"Thass right, Joe, a watermelon is jes' whut Ah needs tuh cure de eppizudicks," Walter Thomas joined forces with Moseley. "Come on dere, Joe. We all is steady customers an' you aint set us up in a long time. Ah chooses dat long, bowlegged Floridy favorite."

"A god, an' be dough. You all gimme twenty cents and slice way," Clarke retorted. "Ah needs a col' slice m'self. Heah, everybody chip in. Ah'll lend y'll mah meat knife."

The money was quickly subscribed and the huge melon brought forth. At that moment, Sykes and Bertha arrived. A determined silence fell on the porch and the melon was put away again.

Merchant snapped down the blade of his jackknife and moved toward the store door.

"Come on in, Joe, an' gimme a slab uh sow belly an' uh pound uh coffee—almost fuhgot 'twas Sat'day. Got to git on home." Most of the men left also.

Just then Delia drove past on her way home, as Sykes was ordering magnificently for Bertha. It pleased him for Delia to see.

"Git whutsoever yo' heart desires, Honey. Wait a minute, Joe. Give huh two bottles uh strawberry soda-water, uh quart uh parched groundpeas, an' a block uh chewin' gum."

With all this they left the store, with Sykes reminding Bertha that this was his town and she could have it if she wanted it.

The men returned soon after they left, and held their watermelon feast.

"Where did Syke Jones git da 'oman from nohow?" Lindsay asked.

"Ovah Apopka. Guess dey musta been cleanin' out de town when she lef'. She don't look lak a thing but a hunk uh liver wid hair on it."

"Well, she sho' kin squall," Dave Carter contributed. "When she gits ready tuh laff, she jes' opens huh mouf an' latches it back tuh de las' notch. No ole grandpa alligator down in Lake Bell ain't got nothin' on huh."

. . .

Bertha had been in town three months now. Sykes was still paying her room rent at Della Lewis'—the only house in town that would have taken her in. Sykes took her frequently to Winter Park to "stomps." He still assured her that he was the swellest man in the state.

"Sho' you kin have dat lil' ole house soon's Ah kin git dat 'oman outa dere. Everything b'longs tuh me an' you sho' kin have it. Ah sho' 'bominates uh skinny 'oman. Lawdy, you sho' is got one portly shape on you! You kin git *anything* you wants. Dis is *mah* town an' you sho' kin have it."

Delia's work-worn knees crawled over the earth in Gethsemane and up the rocks of Calvary many, many times during these months. She avoided the villagers and meeting places in her efforts to be blind and deaf. But Bertha nullified this to a degree, by coming to Delia's house to call Sykes out to her at the gate.

Delia and Sykes fought all the time now with no peaceful interludes. They slept and ate in silence. Two or three times Delia had attempted a timid friendliness, but she was repulsed each time. It was plain that the breaches must remain agape.

The sun had burned July to August. The heat streamed down like a million hot arrows, smiting all things living upon the earth. Grass withered, leaves browned, snakes went blind in shedding and men and dogs went mad. Dog days!

Delia came home one day and found Sykes there before her. She wondered, but started to go on into the house without speaking, even though he was standing in the kitchen door and she must either stoop under his arm or ask him to move. He made no room for her. She noticed a soap box beside the steps, but paid no particular attention to it, knowing that he must have brought it there. As she was stooping to pass under his outstretched arm, he suddenly pushed her backward, laughingly.

"Look in de box dere Delia, Ah done brung yuh somethin'!"

She nearly fell upon the box in her stumbling, and when she saw what it held, she all but fainted outright.

"Syke! Syke, mah Gawd! You take dat rattlesnake 'way from heah! You *gottuh*, Oh, Jesus, have mussy!"

"Ah aint gut tuh do nuthin' uh de kin'—fact is Ah aint got tuh do nothin' but die. Taint no use uh you puttin' on airs makin' out lak you skeered uh dat snake—he's gointer stay right heah tell he die. He wouldn't bite me cause Ah knows how tuh handle 'im. Nohow he wouldn't risk breakin' out his fangs 'gin *yo'* skinny laigs."

"Naw, now Syke, don't keep dat thing 'roun' heah tuh skeer me tuh death. You knows Ah'm even feared uh earth worms. Thass de biggest snake Ah evah did see. Kill 'im Syke, please."

"Doan ast me tuh do nothin' fuh yuh. Goin' 'roun' tryin' tuh be so damn asterperious. Naw, Ah aint gonna kill it. Ah think uh damn sight mo' uh him dan you! Dat's a nice snake an' anybody doan lak 'im kin jes' hit de grit."

The village soon heard that Sykes had the snake, and came to see and ask questions.

"How de hen-fire did you ketch dat six-foot rattler, Syke?" Thomas asked.

"He's full uh frogs so he caint hardly move, thass how Ah eased up on 'm. But Ah'm a snake charmer an' knows how tuh handle 'em. Shux, dat aint nothin'. Ah could ketch one eve'y day if Ah so wanted tuh."

"Whut he needs is a heavy hick'ry club leaned real heavy on his head. Dat's de bes 'way tuh charm a rattlesnake."

"Naw, Walt, y'll jes' don't understand dese diamon' backs lak Ah do," said Sykes in a superior tone of voice.

The village agreed with Walter, but the snake stayed on. His box remained by the kitchen door with its screen wire covering. Two or three days later it had digested its meal of frogs and literally came to life. It rattled at every movement in the kitchen or the yard. One day as Delia came down the kitchen steps she saw his chalky-white fangs curved like scimitars hung in the wire meshes. This time she did not run away with averted eyes as usual. She stood for a long time in the doorway in a red fury that grew bloodier for every second that she regarded the creature that was her torment.

That night she broached the subject as soon as Sykes sat down to the table.

"Syke, Ah wants you tuh take dat snake 'way fum heah. You done starved me an' Ah put up widcher, you done beat me an' Ah took dat, but you done kilt all mah insides bringin' dat varmint heah."

Sykes poured out a saucer full of coffee and drank it deliberately before he answered her.

"A whole lot Ah keer 'bout how you feels inside uh out. Dat snake aint goin' no damn wheah till Ah gits ready fuh 'im tuh go. So fur as beatin' is concerned, yuh aint took near all dat you gointer take ef yuh stay 'roun' *me.*"

Delia pushed back her plate and got up from the table. "Ah hates you, Sykes," she said calmly. "Ah hates you tuh de same degree dat Ah useter love yuh. Ah done took an' took till mah belly is full up tuh mah neck. Dat's de reason Ah got mah letter fum de church an' moved mah membership tuh Woodbridge—so Ah don't haftuh take no sacrament wid yuh. Ah don't wantuh see yuh 'roun' me atall. Lay 'roun' wid dat 'oman all yuh wants tuh, but gwan 'way fum me an' mah house. Ah hates yuh lak uh suck-egg dog."

Sykes almost let the huge wad of corn bread and collard greens he was chewing fall out of his mouth in amazement. He had a hard time whipping himself up to the proper fury to try to answer Delia.

"Well, Ah'm glad you does hate me. Ah'm sho' tiahed uh you hangin' ontuh me. Ah don't want yuh. Look at yuh stringey ole neck! Yo' rawbony laigs an' arms is enough tuh cut uh man tuh death. You looks jes' lak de devvul's doll-baby tuh *me.* You cain't hate me no worse dan Ah hates you. Ah been hatin' *you* fuh years."

"Yo' ole black hide don't look lak nothin' tuh me, but uh passle uh wrinkled up rubber, wid yo' big ole yeahs flappin' on each side lak uh paih uh buzzard wings. Don't think Ah'm gointuh be run 'way fum mah house neither. Ah'm goin' tuh de white folks bout *you,* mah young man, de very nex' time you lay yo' han's on me. Mah cup is done run ovah." Delia said this with no signs of fear and Sykes departed from the house, threatening her, but made not the slightest move to carry out any of them.

That night he did not return at all, and the next day being Sunday, Delia was glad she did not have to quarrel before she hitched up her pony and drove the four miles to Woodbridge.

She stayed to the night service—"love feast"—which was very warm and full of spirit. In the emotional winds her domestic trials were borne far and wide so that she sang as she drove homeward,

"Jurden water, black an' col'
Chills de body, not de soul
An' Ah wantah cross Jurden in uh calm time."

She came from the barn to the kitchen door and stopped.

"Whut's de mattah, ol' satan, you aint kickin' up yo' racket?" She addressed the snake's box. Complete silence. She went on into the house with a new hope in its birth struggles. Perhaps her threat to go to the white folks had frightened Sykes! Perhaps he was sorry! Fifteen years of misery and suppression had brought Delia to the place where she would hope *anything* that looked toward a way over or through her wall of inhibitions.

She felt in the match safe behind the stove at once for a match. There was only one there.

"Dat niggah wouldn't fetch nothin' heah tuh save his rotten neck, but he kin run thew whut Ah brings quick enough. Now he done toted off nigh on tuh haff uh box uh matches. He done had dat 'oman heah in mah house, too."

Nobody but a woman could tell how she knew this even before she struck the match. But she did and it put her into a new fury.

Presently she brought in the tubs to put the white things to soak. This time she decided she need not bring the hamper out of the bedroom; she would go in there and do the sorting. She picked up the pot-bellied lamp and went in. The room was small and the hamper stood hard by the foot of the white iron bed. She could sit and reach through the bedposts—resting as she worked.

"Ah wantah cross Jurden in uh calm time." She was singing again. The mood of the "love feast" had returned. She threw back the lid of the basket almost gaily. Then, moved by both horror and terror, she sprang back toward the door. *There lay the snake in the basket!* He moved sluggishly at first, but even as she turned round and round, jumped up and down in an insanity of fear, he began to stir vigorously. She saw him pouring his awful beauty from the basket upon the bed, then she seized the lamp and ran as fast as she could to the kitchen. The wind from the open door blew out the light and the darkness added to her terror. She sped to the darkness of the yard, slamming the door after her before she thought to set down the lamp. She did not feel safe even on the ground, so she climbed up in the hay barn.

There for an hour or more she lay sprawled upon the hay a gibbering wreck.

Finally she grew quiet, and after that, coherent thought. With this, stalked through her a cold, bloody rage. Hours of this. A period of introspection, a space of retrospection, then a mixture of both. Out of this an awful calm.

"Well, Ah done de bes' Ah could. If things aint right, Gawd knows taint mah fault."

She went to sleep—a twitch sleep—and woke up to a faint gray sky.

There was a loud hollow sound below. She peered out. Sykes was at the wood-pile, demolishing a wire-covered box.

He hurried to the kitchen door, but hung outside there some minutes before he entered, and stood some minutes more inside before he closed it after him.

The gray in the sky was spreading. Delia descended without fear now, and crouched beneath the low bedroom window. The drawn shade shut out the dawn, shut in the night. But the thin walls held back no sound.

"Dat ol' scratch is woke up now!" She mused at the tremendous whirr inside, which every woodsman knows, is one of the sound illusions. The rattler is a ventriloquist. His whirr sounds to the right, to the left, straight ahead, behind, close under foot—everywhere but where it is. Woe to him who guesses wrong unless he is prepared to hold up his end of the argument! Sometimes he strikes without rattling at all.

Inside, Sykes heard nothing until he knocked a pot lid off the stove while trying to reach the match safe in the dark. He had emptied his pockets at Bertha's.

The snake seemed to wake up under the stove and Sykes made a quick leap into the bedroom. In spite of the gin he had had, his head was clearing now.

"Mah Gawd!" he chattered, "ef Ah could on'y strack uh light!"

The rattling ceased for a moment as he stood paralyzed. He waited. It seemed that the snake waited also.

"Oh, fuh de light! Ah thought he'd be too sick"—Sykes was muttering to himself when the whirr began again, closer, right underfoot this time. Long before this, Sykes' ability to think had been flattened down to primitive instinct and he leaped—onto the bed.

Outside Delia heard a cry that might have come from a maddened chimpanzee, a stricken gorilla. All the terror, all the horror, all the rage that man possibly could express, without a recognizable human sound.

A tremendous stir inside there, another series of animal screams, the intermittent whirr of the reptile. The shade torn violently down from the window, letting in the red dawn, a huge brown hand seizing the window stick, great dull blows upon the wooden floor punctuating the gibberish of sound long after the rattle of the snake had abruptly subsided. All this Delia could see and hear from her place beneath the window, and it made her ill. She crept over to the four-o'clocks and stretched herself on the cool earth to recover.

She lay there. "Delia, Delia!" She could hear Sykes calling in a most despairing tone as one who expected no answer. The sun crept on up, and he called. Delia could not move—her legs were gone flabby. She never moved, he called, and the sun kept rising.

"Mah Gawd!" She heard him moan, "Mah Gawd fum Heben!" She heard him stumbling about and got up from her flower-bed. The sun was growing warm. As she approached the door she heard him call out hopefully, "Delia, is dat you Ah heah?"

She saw him on his hands and knees as soon as she reached the door. He crept an inch or two toward her—all that he was able, and she saw his horribly swollen neck and his one open eye shining with hope. A surge of pity too strong to support bore her away from that eye that must, could not, fail to see the tubs. He would see the lamp. Orlando with its doctors was too far. She could scarcely reach the Chinaberry tree, where she waited in the growing heat while inside she knew the cold river was creeping up and up to extinguish that eye which must know by now that she knew.

1926

HOW IT FEELS TO BE COLORED ME

I am colored but I offer nothing in the way of extenuating circumstances except the fact that I am the only Negro in the United States whose grandfather on the mother's side was *not* an Indian chief.

I remember the very day that I became colored. Up to my thirteenth year I lived in the little Negro town of Eatonville, Florida. It is exclusively a colored town. The only white people I knew passed through the town going to or coming from Orlando. The native whites rode dusty horses, the Northern tourists chugged down the sandy village road in automobiles. The town knew the Southerners and never stopped cane chewing when they passed. But the Northerners were something else again. They were peered at cautiously from behind curtains by the timid. The more venturesome would come out on the porch to watch them go past and got just as much pleasure out of the tourists as the tourists got out of the village.

The front porch might seem a daring place for the rest of the town, but it was a gallery seat for me. My favorite place was atop the gate-post. Proscenium box for a born first-nighter. Not only did I enjoy the show, but I didn't mind the actors knowing that I liked it. I usually spoke to them in passing. I'd wave at them and when they returned my salute, I would say something like this: "Howdy-do-well-I-thank-you-where-you-goin'?" Usually automobile or the horse paused at this, and after a queer exchange of compliments, I would probably "go a piece of the way" with them, as we say in farthest Florida. If one of my family happened to come to the front in time to see me, of course negotiations would be rudely broken off. But even so, it is clear that I was the first "welcome-to-our-state" Floridian, and I hope the Miami Chamber of Commerce will please take notice.

During this period, white people differed from colored to me only in that they rode through town and never lived there. They liked to hear me "speak pieces" and sing and wanted to see me dance the parse-me-la, and gave me generously of their small silver for doing these things, which seemed strange to me for I wanted to do them so much that I needed bribing to stop. Only they didn't know it. The colored people gave no dimes. They deplored any joyful tendencies in me, but I was their Zora nevertheless. I belonged to them, to the nearby hotels, to the county—everybody's Zora.

But changes came in the family when I was thirteen, and I was sent to school in Jacksonville. I left Eatonville, the town of the oleanders, as Zora. When I disembarked from the river-boat at Jacksonville, she was no more. It seemed that I had suffered a sea change. I was not Zora of Orange County any more, I was now a little colored girl. I found it out in certain ways. In my heart as well as in the mirror, I became a fast brown—warranted not to rub nor run.

. . .

But I am not tragically colored. There is no great sorrow dammed up in my soul, nor lurking behind my eyes. I do not mind at all. I do not belong to the sobbing school of Negrohood who hold that nature somehow has given them a lowdown dirty deal and whose feelings are all hurt about it. Even in the helter-skelter skirmish that is my life, I have seen that the world is to the strong regardless of a little pigmentation more or less. No, I do not weep at the world—I am too busy sharpening my oyster knife.

Someone is always at my elbow reminding me that I am the granddaughter of slaves. It fails to register depression with me. Slavery is sixty years in the past. The operation was successful and the patient is doing well, thank you. The terrible struggle that made me an American out of a potential slave said "On the line!" The Reconstruction said "Get set!"; and the generation before said "Go!" I am off to a flying start and I must not halt in the stretch to look behind and weep. Slavery is the price I paid for civilization, and the choice was not with me. It is a bully adventure and worth all that I have paid through my ancestors for it. No one on earth ever had a greater chance for glory. The world to be won and nothing to be lost. It is thrilling to think—to know that for any act of mine, I shall get twice as much praise or twice as much blame. It is quite exciting to hold the center of the national stage, with the spectators not knowing whether to laugh or to weep.

The position of my white neighbor is much more difficult. No brown specter pulls up a chair beside me when I sit down to eat. No dark ghost thrusts its leg against mine in bed. The game of keeping what one has is never so exciting as the game of getting.

I do not always feel colored. Even now I often achieve the unconscious

Zora of Eatonville before the Hegira. I feel most colored when I am thrown against a sharp white background.

For instance at Barnard. "Beside the waters of the Hudson" I feel my race. Among the thousand white persons, I am a dark rock surged upon, and overswept, but through it all, I remain myself. When covered by the waters, I am; and the ebb but reveals me again.

. . .

Sometimes it is the other way around. A white person is set down in our midst, but the contrast is just as sharp for me. For instance, when I sit in the drafty basement that is The New World Cabaret with a white person, my color comes. We enter chatting about any little nothing that we have in common and are seated by the jazz waiters. In the abrupt way that jazz orchestras have, this one plunges into a number. It loses no time in circumlocutions, but gets right down to business. It constricts the thorax and splits the heart with its tempo and narcotic harmonies. This orchestra grows rambunctious, rears on its hind legs and attacks the tonal veil with primitive fury, rending it, clawing it until it breaks through to the jungle beyond. I follow those heathen—follow them exultingly: I dance wildly inside myself; I yell within, I whoop; I shake my assegai above my head, I hurl it true to the mark *yeeeeooww!* I am in the jungle and living in the jungle way. My face is painted red and yellow and my body is painted blue. My pulse is throbbing like a war drum. I want to slaughter something—give pain, give death to what, I do not know. But the piece ends. The men of the orchestra wipe their lips and rest their fingers. I creep back slowly to the veneer we call civilization with the last tone and find the white friend sitting motionless in his seat, smoking calmly.

"Good music they have here," he remarks, drumming the table with his fingertips.

Music. The great blobs of purple and red emotion have not touched him. He has only heard what I felt. He is far away and I see him but dimly across the ocean and the continent that have fallen between us. He is so pale with his whiteness then and I am *so* colored.

. . .

At certain times I have no race, I am *me*. When I set my hat at a certain angle and saunter down Seventh Avenue, Harlem City, feeling as snooty as the lions in front of the Forty-Second Street Library, for instance. So far as my feelings are concerned, Peggy Hopkins Joyce on the Boule Mich with her gorgeous raiment, stately carriage, knees knocking together in a most aristocratic manner, has nothing on me. The cosmic Zora emerges. I belong to no race nor time. I am the eternal feminine with its string of beads.

I have no separate feeling about being an American citizen and colored. I am merely a fragment of the Great Soul that surges within the boundaries. My country, right or wrong.

Sometimes, I feel discriminated against, but it does not make me angry.

It merely astonishes me. How *can* any deny themselves the pleasure of my company? It's beyond me.

But in the main, I feel like a brown bag of miscellany propped against a wall. Against a wall in company with other bags, white, red and yellow. Pour out the contents, and there is discovered a jumble of small things priceless and worthless. A first-water diamond, an empty spool, bits of broken glass, lengths of string, a key to a door long since crumbled away, a rusty knife-blade, old shoes saved for a road that never was and never will be, a nail bent under the weight of things too heavy for any nail, a dried flower or two still a little fragrant. In your hand is the brown bag. On the ground before you is the jumble it held—so much like the jumble in the bags, could they be emptied, that all might be dumped in a single heap and the bags refilled without altering the content of any greatly. A bit of colored glass more or less would not matter. Perhaps that is how the Great Stuffer of Bags filled them in the first place—who knows?

1928

AGNES SMEDLEY
(1892–1950)

As a spokesperson for women and the working class, Agnes Smedley was a central figure in left-wing politics during the first half of the twentieth century. An early radical feminist, she analyzed, throughout her writing, gender, race, and class from an international perspective. She decried women's position as "sex slaves" of men; she condemned the genocide of Native Americans; and she compared the conditions of Chinese peasants to the conditions of African American sharecroppers.

The second of five children, Smedley was born in Campground, Missouri. In 1904 the family moved to a Colorado coal-mining town, where her father hauled sand and bricks for three dollars a day. Hard times followed, and at age fifteen Smedley quit school to help her mother.

Watching her father vent his frustrations on her mother, Smedley concluded that marriage and poverty meant humiliation for women. Her sister's arranged marriage at sixteen confirmed these feelings. When this sister died less than a year later during childbirth, Smedley determined her life would not follow a similar path. In her 1923 autobiographical novel, Daughter of Earth, *she conveys through her heroine the spirit of a young independent woman determined to overcome poverty.*

With the encouragement of an aunt, Smedley moved to the Southwest. She attended school in Arizona and California and became active in feminist and socialist movements. As secretary of the San Diego Open Forum, she arranged speaking engagements for Emma Goldman, Eugene Debs, and other radical activists. Fired from a job because of her membership in the Socialist party, she moved to New York City in 1916.

While living in Greenwich Village, Smedley joined Margaret Sanger's birth control movement, opposed the United States's entry into World War I, and supported India's struggle for independence from British rule. These activities led to a lifelong surveillance by the American government. In 1918, Smedley was arrested and imprisoned for disseminating birth control information and associating with Indian nationalists living in New York. Undaunted by these efforts to suppress her, she managed the Birth Control Review *and wrote for the* New York Call, *the Socialist party newspaper, upon her release from prison.*

In the 1920s, Smedley began living as an expatriate in Germany, Russia, and China. By 1930 she was settled and writing in Shanghai. In articles for the New Republic, *the* Manchester Guardian, *and* The Nation, *she described the oppression of women in Chinese culture, the Chinese war with Japan, and the inchoate revolution of Chinese peasants. When traveling with the Red Army in the late 1930s, she reported on the revolution's potential to liberate women. During these years, she formed friendships with famous Chinese women writers such as Ding Ling and Xiao Hong and wrote four books of social commentary on China.*

Toward the end of her life, Smedley described herself as an imposter rather than a writer. "You see," she wrote to a friend in 1947, "I lack the proper approach to writing. Instead of a perfectly balanced sentence with or without commas or periods, I see armies of barefoot peasants in China and other parts of the world reaching for the stars of humanity but being shot to death for their endeavors." Smedley died in 1950 and was buried in Beijing with other Chinese revolutionaries. Her grave reads simply, "A Friend of China."

Included here are four of Smedley's early articles. Between February 15 and March 14, 1920, she published "Cell Mates" in the New York Call. *In these portraits of four fellow prisoners—Nellie, May, Mollie Steimer, and Kitty Marion—Smedley described life in the New York Tombs, an institution notorious for its appalling conditions. She also demonstrated not only her empathy and admiration for these women but also her skill as a writer. To the best of our knowledge, this is the first time these works have been reprinted.*

MY CELL MATE: NO. 1

My first impression of Nellie was gained when I looked up from my luke-warm breakfast coffee to listen to an avalanche of profanity in an Irish brogue. Nellie was swearing at the food, and was showering blessings of wrath upon the wardens and matrons of the Tombs prison, who, she swore, by all the angels and the Blessed Virgin, had built the jail and ran it for their own pleasure and profit.

The matron spoke: "Shut your mouth, Nellie, or I'll lock you in your cell."

Nellie looked up, took up the matron's words, and set them to music. She sang hilariously and, finishing her coffee, two-stepped past the matron and looked her in the eye, still singing. She two-stepped down the corridor and around the iron gate into the "run," in which old offenders are locked during the day.

Nellie was short, blocky, square in build. Fifty-three summers had come and gone without leaving their touches in her hair. She had grown ugly and scarred, twisted and gnarled like an old oak. But her vitality had never waned. Her figure had been permitted to develop, unhampered by corsets—and it had developed, particularly her stomach and hips. The expression on her square, scarred Irish face was good-natured and happy-go-lucky, with a touch of sadness which gripped your heart at times.

From the North of Ireland, Nellie had come to America while still a girl under 20. And, being pretty and very ignorant, with no means of support, she had, in due course of time, become a prostitute. Since that time she had served innumerable short terms in all the jails in Jersey and New York City. Her offenses generally consisted of intoxication, fighting, or "hustling."

In her day, according to her story, she had been much sought after by "gentlemen," and her "clients" included pillars of the law—all the local judges and such. She told me that once she had been brought by a policeman before one of these estimable personages, and after he had rebuked her and sentenced her to pay a nominal fine, she had made some interesting disclosures in the court room and insisted upon his paying the fine for her.

Nellie had never lost her Irish brogue in all these years, and she greeted those whom she liked with "Top o' the mornin' to ye," and those whom she disliked with a "Well, damn ye, ye're able to git up this mornin' and raise hell, ain't ye?"

The girls at the long, bare breakfast table had laughed as Nellie responded to the matron's rebuke. From back of the iron gates Nellie's voice came like a fog-horn from a distance. She was feeling fine this morning, and the girls finished breakfast quickly.

"Come on, give us a jig, Nellie," one called.

Nellie pulled her old dirty blue skirt half way to her knees, exposing dirty white stockings, and started to jig. It was an Irish jig, and her old run-down shoes made a sound like fire-crackers on the cement floor. She sang as she danced—Irish songs and songs indigenous to the soil of America and to Nellie's peculiar mode of life. Some of these were unprintable. One of them began

> "Oh-h-h-!
> Did you ever have a fight
> In the middle of the night
> With the gur-r-rl you love?"

And so throughout the day Nellie kept the girls at attention, vile in talk, always profane, dipping snuff and brow-beating the matrons. When visitors appeared at the gate and gazed back with round eyes at the strange creatures in the cage, Nellie would call "Oh-h-h! Where did you get that hat?" or "Top o' the mornin' to ye, lady; are ye plannin' to break in?"

No one could be depressed for long with Nellie present. One morning I came in from my gray cell into the dull gray corridor. Life seemed quite as dull and gray as my surroundings. Nellie was sitting on a bench near my door, baking her feet against the radiator. She looked up, and her voice scattered the gloom into a thousand fragments.

> "Oh-h-h
> Good mornin', O Missus O'Grady.
> Why are you so blue today?"

I sat down by her.

"Ye're a nice thing," she said; "and why are ye in this place?"

"I don't think you'd understand if I told you, Nellie," I replied.

Nellie fixed her eyes on space for a few minutes. That expression of sadness crept about her mouth.

"I guess ye're right," she said. "I mighta once. I was a purty gir-rl once"—.

I felt that I had inadvertently recalled long-dead summers of a tragic life. But before I had time to rebuke myself, she kicked the radiator and brightly asked:

"And how do ye like this hotel?"

I asked why she was there. She reflected for a moment.

"By the holy mother uv Jesus," she stated, "I'm as innicent as a baby."

"What is the charge?"

"Hittin' a man on the head with a hammer," she replied.

"I didn't do it," she reiterated, to my back.

"Why didn't you," I asked.

She chuckled and took some snuff.

"Jest ye wait till I git out."

Then she told me how it happened. It took a long time, and she went into the family history and her personal relations with all the neighbors. She had been out all night, it seems, and in the early morning had gone home. She stopped at a saloon beneath her flat and reinforced herself with liquor before facing her husband, Mike.

Tim, the bartender, had warned her:

"Nellie," he cautioned, "ye'd better not go home now. Ye'll sure git in a tussel with Mike if ye do."

But Nellie, according to her own statement, was "feelin' like a bur-r-d"; so she "ups and flits up the stairs jist as airy as ye please."

Mike was indignant, as husbands sometimes are. He questioned his erring and reinforced wife. The forewarned struggle ensued. The kitchen suffered somewhat, and Mike retreated down the stairs to the first landing. There a friend opened the door, grasped his predicament, and came to his assistance. Somewhat pressed, Nellie picked up a hammer which was lying on a trunk, and laid low the intruder.

When Mike's would-be assistant came to consciousness he got a bandage and a policeman, the former for himself and the latter for Nellie.

Nellie concluded her tale. "They arristed me—an', would ye believe me, it wuz Holy Thursday!"

She had been in the Tombs for a number of months. Once Mike came to see her, and she had asked him for a dollar to buy a little extra food. What he replied I don't know, but when she returned to us she sat down in a corner and cried piteously.

The next morning she came in as usual, to see if I wished to get up for breakfast. I asked her to order some extra food from the restaurant.

"And, Nellie," I said, "order yourself a good breakfast."

She grinned and thanked me. And about an hour later her breakfast bill was sent in to me. Nellie had done as I had asked, and had ordered a good breakfast! It included, among other things, four or five pieces of pie. It seems she had stocked up for the winter. And I paid the bill gladly.

When I saw Nellie last she came around to the iron gate to tell me goodby. She had on a clean white waist, and her hair was combed. She was being released without going to trial.

"What are you going to do now?" I asked.

Her old face had that peculiar expression of goodness and sadness—and of helplessness. I knew she didn't know, and that it didn't matter much what she did. She was turned loose on the streets again. No one met her; no one was waiting to welcome her. She turned and left us, a little stooped, and I heard her old shoes click as she went down the cement corridor.

1920

MY CELL MATE: NO. 2

May sat near the barred gate smoking a cigarette and resting her fat hands on her fatter knees. If convicted of forgery this time it meant eight finger-prints—one for each year she had been in the business. She was no amateur; one isn't an amateur at 45, after passing from the factory and stage into private business.

May's complaint wasn't so much that she had been caught, but that she had been caught on such a trifle. She had sent cigars to a fictitious son in Camp Upton and given a check to the cigar store, receiving only $10 in change.

Her bail was $500, but her man, Vic, was too cowardly to furnish it. It meant trouble for him if he did. He had managed to keep out of the law's grip for eight years, just as she had managed to keep in it; but as years went by the danger seemed to creep closer. Even when May had been arrested this time he had been with her. But she had explained to the detectives that he was a strange man who had kindly offered to carry her packages. So he had escaped the law again.

Of course, she realized that Vic couldn't risk arrest; but it seemed unfair at times; she had always shouldered the blame, had always served time, often for him. Even now he wrote letters declaring that had it not been for rheumatism he would have been down to leave money for her personal expenses; but it never occurred to him to send money by mail. Yet again she would forgive him, as women often do. She had his picture in her purse; it was dim and worn with much handling, and she looked at it with mingled anger and compassion. When any one agreed with her that Vic was a worthless scoundrel, she launched into a defense which would have wrung tears from any jury who didn't happen to know the facts.

"How you worry about a $500 bail!" I exclaimed. "Mine is $10,000."

"Well," May retorted, "*I* didn't try to swing the world by the tail. All I wanted was a little change."

"Tell me," I asked her, "why did you stop working in a factory?"

"Go work in a factory and find out," was her reply.

"Well, why did you leave the stage?"

"Look at me," she challenged sarcastically, "and look at my figger!" I looked. It *was* rather discouraging; about five feet high and five feet wide, yellow hair and an accordian pleated chin. Eight years ago she had been thirty-seven. One can't be a successful chorus girl at thirty-seven, after your renowned cuteness becomes buried beneath a bed of fat.

"Couldn't you do something else besides—this?" I inquired, hesitatingly.

"Yes," she grimly retorted. "I could scrub floors or take in washin', or 'hustle,' or do a few little things like that."

May warned me that a "stool pigeon" would undoubtedly be put to watch me and try to get information from me; that perhaps one was there already; that maybe she, herself, was one. She was scornful of my "greenness."

"Gawd!" she exclaimed once, "I guess if some bull came in here dressed up like a priest, you'd believe him. Now listen to me, never trust a man dressed like a priest."

May constituted herself my guardian and carefully kept the other girls out of my cell. "Get out, you hussy, you low-down thief," she yelled at them when they wandered into my cell. And if they didn't get out, she would put them out.

"Don't give them any money," she cautioned me time and again. But when she left, she carried some of my money with her. My "greenness" was very profound.

When taken to court, she wore a hat over which flowed a long black veil.

"Some veil," she laughed. "It ought to be a mask!" But even her jokes were told in a tremulous voice, as if she were telling them to keep from thinking of other things.

When the women returned from court, they told me that a very ugly man had appeared against May and that she, when asked if what he said were true, had replied that "any man with a face like that ought to have a check passed on him." She and the other women had been compelled to walk between the long row of masked detectives, veils thrown back; two of the detectives recognized May. She was given the "Indefinite," which means anything from three months to three years in the penitentiary.

1920

MY CELL MATE: NO. 3

For circulating leaflets opposing intervention in Russia, Mollie Steimer, with three men comrades, had been sentenced to 15 years in prison, a $500 fine and deportation to Russia. A good start for a little Russian girl less than five feet in height who had not yet reached the age of 21.

Mollie had come from the Ukraine five years before, and since that time worked in a waist factory for $10 a week. A few months preceding her arrest she had received $15. She was the eldest of five children. A sister, aged 17, and a brother, aged 14, as well as her father, were all factory workers.

Mollie was sitting in her cell writing when I was put into jail. Her greeting was characteristic of her cast of mind.

"I am glad to see you here!" she said. "I wish the prisons to be filled with the workers. They soon will be. Then we will wake up."

Before her, pasted on the wall, were newspaper photographs of Karl Liebknecht, Eugene V. Debs and John Reed, and, printed in red letters high up on the stone wall, were the words, "Long live the Social Revolution!"

Mollie wore a red Russian smock. Her short hair was glossy black and curled up at the ends. Her face belonged to Russia, and the expression of seriousness and silent determination had first been cast in that country many years before. Her carefully chosen words were expressed with a slight foreign accent. Seldom did she speak of anything save Russia, the revolution in Germany and Austria and the future of the workers in America. She was always looking toward that world which she had described on the witness stand to a judge from Alabama:

"*It will be a new social order,*" she had said, "*in which no group of people shall be in the power of any other group. Every person shall have an equal opportunity to develop himself. None shall live by the product of another. Every one shall produce what he can and enjoy what he needs. He shall have time to gain knowledge and culture. At present humanity is divided into groups called nations. We workers of the world will unite in one human brotherhood. To bring about this I have pledged myself to work all my life.*"

"Is there any such place as you tell about?" the prosecuting attorney had sneered. Mollie replied:

"I believe those who represent Russia have been elected by the workers only. The parasites are not represented in the Bolshevik administration."

The girls in prison loved Mollie. She talked with them at great length, disagreeing with them and frankly criticising them if she thought best. At night she would talk gently to some girl who was trying to smother her sobs in the rough prison blankets. After the cell doors clanged behind us in the late afternoon, Mollie would stand grasping the steel bars. In simple, slow words, she would talk to the girls. She used English which the most humble could understand, and as she spoke the three tiers would become silent and only an occasional question would interrupt her talk.

Mollie's philosophy of life had not been gleaned from books. A child of the soil, the finely worded sentiments of the *intelligencia* did not impress her as being sincere. The *intelligencia* had deserted the workers of Russia when the great crisis came, when the workers of that country had challenged. "Peace to the huts, war to the palaces, hail to the Third International!"

With her own hands Mollie had labored for many years, had longed for, but never enjoyed, the beautiful things of life, and had little, save the most sordid bare necessities. Even the possibility of school had been closed to her. About her in the factory she had seen thousands like herself, pouring out their lives for crumbs, suffering, and then dying, poor and wretched. The class struggle to her became a grim reality.

Mollie championed the cause of the prisoners—the one with venereal disease, the mother with diseased babies, the prostitute, the feeble-minded, the burglar, the murderer. To her they were but products of a diseased social system. She did not complain that even the most vicious of them were sentenced to no more than five or seven years, while she herself was facing 15 years in prison. She asked that the girl with venereal disease be taken to a hospital; the prison physician accused her of believing in free love and in Bolshevism. She asked that the vermin be cleaned from the cells of one of the girls; the matron ordered her to attend to her own affairs—that it was not *her* cell. To quiet her they would lock her in her cell. "Lock me in," she replied to the matron. "I have nothing to lose but my chains."

Then the news of the German revolution and of the armistice came. Outside the whistles shrieked and people yelled. In the prison yard outside some of the men prisoners were herded together as a special favor to join in the rejoicing. The keepers moved about among them, waving their arms and telling the men to be glad. The men stood with limp arms and dull faces, looking into the sky and at each other. A few endeavored to show signs of happiness when the warden came their way.

"Peace has come," Mollie said, standing at my side, "but not for us. Our struggle will be all the more bitter now."

The time came when Mollie's old mother, arising from the sick bed, came with a bandaged ear to the prison to tell her of the death of her father and of her 14-year-old brother. Mollie did not cry. She returned to the cell and quietly sat on the bed beside me. But once I felt the convulsive trembling of her body. Her words came slowly at last:

"You should have seen my father," she said; "so thin, so worked out! Since he was 10 years old he had worked 14 and 15 hours each day. He was so worked out, so thin! I knew he did not have the strength to live if he ever became ill."

Then, later: "Our dreams," she said; "how fragile! I have dreamed for years—oh, such dreams! Of my brother and sister in school, of studying, of a new order of society. In one minute my dreams are shattered!"

Through the bars of the cell door, through the dirty windows across the corridor, could be seen the tops of unbeautiful, dingy buildings. Outside the windows the great stone wall surrounding the prison obstructed all view of the street. The roar of the elevated train, the rattle of drays on cobblestone pavement, and the shouts of men, disturbed but slightly the misery of the jail. From the tiers below came the shouts and curses of the old offenders.

"Our dreams—how fragile!" mingled with the curses of the women, and before long it seemed that the women, too, were saying, "Our dreams—how fragile." At times they laughed it, and at times they cursed and sneered as they said it.

Yet the thought: Can that which is so fragile endure so much? And the doors of the past swung back and revealed dreams which have endured for thousands of years, suffering defeat only to rise again; braving prisons, torture, death, and at last wrecking empires.

. . .

Mollie was released under $10,000 bail to await her appeal to the Supreme Court. I watched her pass through the prison yard. A marshal walked beside her, talking out of the corner of his mouth. He did not offer to carry her suitcase, heavy with books. His neck bulged with fat, his chest was high and his shoulders primitive. Mollie did not listen to him. Her eyes were looking straight ahead into the distance.

Weeks passed, and in the world outside I met Mollie once more. She was on a strike with the 40,000 clothing workers, and was among the many pickets arrested. A few weeks afterward she came to see me. Her shoulders had grown sharp and thin and she was cynical. She had been arrested a number of times upon suspicion; secret service men seemed to follow her and arrest her as a matter of principle. At last she was arrested for alleged distribution of radical leaflets and held at Ellis island for deportation. There she went on hunger strike to protest segregation from her fellow political prisoners. A friend holding her thin, cold hand, asked if she thought it worth while. Mollie replied:

"Every protest against the present system is worth while. Someone must start."

Mollie did not protest against deportation—provided it was done at once, and to Soviet Russia, instead of to the region under Czarist generals. The city authorities evidently conferred with Federal agents, and decided to try her in the city courts instead. She was sentenced to serve six months in Blackwells Island jail, a place notorious for its filth and barbarity.

A short time has now elapsed since the Supreme Court upheld the decision of the lower court on the first indictment against Mollie. And she, frail, childlike, with the spirit which made the Russian revolution possible, will be taken after her jail term is finished to Jefferson City prison, where she is sentenced to spend 15 years of her life at hard labor.

Mollie's reasoning is something like this: Under the Czar we knew there was no hope; we did not delude ourselves into believing that he would release those who worked against the system which he represented and upheld. In

America we have been carefully taught that we live in a democracy, and we are still waiting for some one to feed us democracy. While waiting, we starve to death or are sent to prison where we get free food for 15 or 20 years.

1920

MY CELL MATE: NO. 4

Kitty Marion was serving thirty days for giving a pamphlet on birth control to a Mr. Bamberg, who had come to her office and told her with much feeling of his large family, his low salary and the fear of adding more children to his household. Bamberg turned out to be a "stool pigeon" for the notorious Association for the Suppression of Vice. He justified his existence by making people break the law and then having them arrested. Kitty Marion was one of the victims.

Kitty came clattering down the stone corridors every morning with her scrub pail in her hand. "Three cheers for birth control," she greeted the prisoners and the matrons. And, "three cheers for birth control," the prisoners answered back.

Her marked English accent recalled to mind that she had been one of Mrs. Pankhurst's militants in London, had been imprisoned time without number and had had her throat ruined by forcible feeding. She holds the record; she was force fed 233 times in Holloway prison.

"Dirty work," I remarked one morning as she came in to scrub the Tombs corridors.

"Not half so dirty as cleaning up the man-made laws in this country," she replied. Then we continued our discussion of peace and change.

The prison physician came in to examine two infants.

"Three cheers for birth control," Kitty called to him from her kneeling position. She held her mop rag in mid air. He turned, and she, scrubbing away, remarked:

"Some way or other every time I see a man the more I believe in birth control."

When visitors or keepers came into the prison Kitty was always heard cheering for birth control. When peace was declared she expressed the hope, in a voice that those who run might hear, that now America would apply a little freedom to her own people and grant women the right of personal liberty. So taken up by the injustice of her imprisonment was she that when her room was infested with vermin she remarked that they reminded her of a mass-meeting at Bamberg's vice society; and when she had been forced to put on a striped dress of the convicted women, she looked at it and remarked, "Ah!

blue and white stripes! Now, if there were only a few red stripes and some white stars!"

The matrons were glad when her term was finished. When she left she announced that she had come in a spark but was going out a living flame.

1920

KATHERINE ANNE PORTER
(1894–1980)

Although the novel Ship of Fools *made Katherine Anne Porter an internationally known writer, her short stories and novellas have proven even more durable and popular. Her works trace moral dilemmas, fears, disappointments, and alienation, particularly of her women characters. Internal change is usually more important than external events in her work. The stories are finely wrought, often imbued with layers of irony and subtleties of characterization. Porter conveys a precise sense of place and time, but her works center frequently on age-old themes of evil and goodness, human strength and weakness, innocence and experience.*

A descendant of pioneers, Porter grew up in Texas but lived in Mexico, France, and many parts of the United States. She supported herself as a young woman by working as a reporter, translator, hack writer, and ghost writer. Her first volume of short stories, Flowering Judas, *established her literary reputation.*

During a wandering life that included several unsuccessful marriages, Porter taught at a number of colleges, including Stanford, the University of Chicago, the University of Michigan, and Washington and Lee University. For her small but critically acclaimed body of work, she was awarded two Guggenheim Fellowships, Fulbright and Ford Foundation grants, an O. Henry Award, a National Book Award, and a Pulitzer Prize. Porter moved to the Baltimore-Washington area in the 1960s. Her last work before her death was a memoir of the Sacco-Vanzetti case, which she had protested about in the 1920s.

While Porter's stories are frequently set in Texas, she did not want to be thought of as a southern writer. She considered herself, first and foremost, an artist. She told a newspaper reporter in 1958 that she was "one of the few living people not afraid to pronounce that word." She held high standards for her work, publishing only those pieces she felt confident had artistic merit and destroying manuscripts she felt were unworthy.

"Holiday" exemplifies Porter's ability to create memorable female characters. Taking us back to the youth of our unnamed narrator, the story brings to life a family on an East Texas farm. While capturing the precise, realistic details of place and character, the story focuses on bitter, unpalatable truths about human existence and human nature.

HOLIDAY

At that time I was too young for some of the troubles I was having, and I had not yet learned what to do with them. It no longer can matter what kind of troubles they were, or what finally became of them. It seemed to me then there was nothing to do but run away from them, though all my tradition, background, and training had taught me unanswerably that no one except a coward ever runs away from anything. What nonsense! They should have taught me the difference between courage and foolhardiness, instead of leaving me to find it out for myself. I learned finally that if I still had the sense I was born with, I would take off like a deer at the first warning of certain dangers. But this story I am about to tell you happened before this great truth impressed itself upon me—that we do not run from the troubles and dangers that are truly ours, and it is better to learn what they are earlier than later, and if we don't run from the others, we are fools.

I confided to my friend Louise, a former schoolmate about my own age, not my troubles but my little problem: I wanted to go somewhere for a spring holiday, by myself, to the country, and it should be very simple and nice and, of course, not expensive, and she was not to tell anyone where I had gone; but if she liked, I would send her word now and then, if anything interesting was happening. She said she loved getting letters but hated answering them; and she knew the very place for me, and she would not tell anybody anything. Louise had then—she has it still—something near to genius for making improbable persons, places, and situations sound attractive. She told amusing stories that did not turn grim on you until a little while later, when by chance you saw and heard for yourself. So with this story. Everything was just as Louise had said, if you like, and everything was, at the same time, quite different.

"I know the very place," said Louise, "a family of real old-fashioned German peasants, in the deep blackland Texas farm country, a household in real patriarchal style—the kind of thing you'd hate to live with but is very nice to visit. Old father, God Almighty himself, with whiskers and all; Old mother, matriarch in men's shoes; endless daughters and sons and sons-in-law and fat babies falling about the place; and fat puppies—my favourite was a darling little black thing named Kuno—cows, calves, and sheep and lambs and goats and turkeys and guineas roaming up and down the shallow green hills, ducks and geese on the ponds. I was there in the summer when the peaches and watermelons were in——"

"This is the end of March," I said, doubtfully.

"Spring comes early there," said Louise. "I'll write to the Müllers about you, you just get ready to go."

"Just where is this paradise?"

"Not far from the Louisiana line," said Louise. "I'll ask them to give you my attic—oh, that was a sweet place! It's a big room, with the roof sloping to the floor on each side, and the roof leaks a little when it rains, so the shingles are all stained in beautiful streaks, all black and grey and mossy green, and in one corner there used to be a stack of dime novels, *The Duchess*, Ouida, Mrs. E.D.E.N. Southworth, Ella Wheeler Wilcox's poems—one summer they had a lady boarder who was a great reader, and she went off and left her library. I loved it! And everybody was so healthy and good-hearted, and the weather was perfect. . . . How long do you want to stay?"

I hadn't thought of this, so I said at random, "About a month."

A few days later I found myself tossed off like an express package from a dirty little crawling train onto the sodden platform of a country station, where the stationmaster emerged and locked up the waiting room before the train had got round the bend. As he clumped by me he shifted his wad of tobacco to his cheek and asked, "Where you goin'?"

"To the Müller farm," I said, standing beside my small trunk and suitcase with the bitter wind cutting through my thin coat.

"Anybody meet you?" he asked, not pausing.

"They *said* so."

"All right," he said, and got into his little ragged buckboard with a sway-backed horse and drove away.

I turned my trunk on its side and sat on it facing the wind and the desolate mud-colored shapeless scene and began making up my first letter to Louise. First I was going to tell her that unless she was to be a novelist, there was no excuse for her having so much imagination. In daily life, I was going to tell her, there are also such useful things as the plain facts that should be stuck to, through thick and thin. Anything else led to confusion like this. I was beginning to enjoy my letter to Louise when a sturdy boy about twelve years old crossed the platform. As he neared me, he took off his rough cap and bunched it in his thick hand, dirt-stained at the knuckles. His round cheeks, his round nose, his round chin were a cool, healthy red. In the globe of his face, as neatly circular as if drawn in bright crayon, his narrow, long, tip-tilted eyes, clear as pale-blue water, seemed out of place, as if two incompatible strains had collided in making him. They were beautiful eyes, and the rest of the face was not to be taken seriously. A blue woollen blouse buttoned up to his chin ended abruptly at his waist as if he would outgrow it in another half hour, and his blue drill breeches flapped about his ankles. His old clodhopper shoes were several sizes too big for him. Altogether, it was plain he was not the first one to wear his clothes. He was a cheerful, detached, self-possessed apparition against the tumbled brown earth and ragged dark sky, and I smiled at him as well as I could with a face that felt like wet clay.

He smiled back slightly without meeting my eye, motioning for me to take up my suitcase. He swung my trunk to his head and tottered across the uneven platform, down the steps slippery with mud where I expected to see him crushed beneath his burden like an ant under a stone. He heaved the trunk into the back of his wagon with a fine smash, took my suitcase and tossed it after, then climbed up over one front wheel while I scrambled my way up over the other.

The pony, shaggy as a wintering bear, eased himself into a grudging trot, while the boy, bowed over with his cap pulled down over his ears and eyebrows, held the reins slack and fell into a brown study. I studied the harness, a real mystery. It met and clung in all sorts of unexpected places; it parted company in what appeared to be strategic seats of jointure. It was mended sketchily in risky places with bits of hairy rope. Other seemingly unimportant parts were bound together irrevocably with wire. The bridle was too long for the pony's stocky head, so he had shaken the bit out of his mouth at the start, apparently, and went his own way at his own pace.

Our vehicle was an exhausted specimen of something called a spring wagon, who knows why? There were no springs, and the shallow enclosed platform at the back, suitable for carrying various plunder, was worn away until it barely reached midway of the back wheels, one side of it steadily scraping the iron tire. The wheels themselves spun not dully around and around in the way of common wheels, but elliptically, being loosened at the hubs, so that we proceeded with a drunken, hilarious swagger, like the rolling motion of a small boat on a choppy sea.

The soaked brown fields fell away on either side of the lane, all rough with winter-worn stubble ready to sink and become earth again. The scanty leafless woods ran along an edge of the field nearby. There was nothing beautiful in those woods now except the promise of spring, for I detested bleakness, but it gave me pleasure to think that beyond this there might be something else beautiful in its own being, a river shaped and contained by its banks, or a field stripped down to its true meaning, ploughed and ready for the seed. The road turned abruptly and was almost hidden for a moment, and we were going through the woods. Closer sight of the crooked branches assured me that spring was beginning, if sparely, reluctantly: the leaves were budding in tiny cones of watery green besprinkling all the new shoots; a thin sedate rain began again to fall, not so opaque as a fog, but a mist that merely deepened overhead, and lowered, until the clouds became rain in one swathing, delicate grey.

As we emerged from the woods, the boy roused himself and pointed forward, in silence. We were approaching the farm along the skirts of a fine peach orchard, now faintly colored with young bud, but there was nothing to disguise the gaunt and aching ugliness of the farmhouse itself. In this Texas valley, so gently modulated with small crests and shallows, "rolling country" as the farmers say, the house was set on the peak of the barest rise of ground, as if the most infertile spot had been thriftily chosen for building a shelter. It stood there staring and naked, an intruding stranger, strange even beside the barns ranged generously along the back, low-eaved and weathered to the color of stone.

The narrow windows and the steeply sloping roof oppressed me; I wished to turn away and go back. I had come a long way to be so disappointed, I thought, and yet I must go on, for there could be nothing here for me more painful than what I had left. But as we drew near the house, now hardly visible except for the yellow lamplight in the back, perhaps in the kitchen, my feelings changed again toward warmth and tenderness, or perhaps just an apprehension that I could feel so, maybe, again.

The wagon drew up before the porch, and I started climbing down. No sooner had my foot touched ground than an enormous black dog of the detestable German shepherd breed leaped silently at me, and as silently I covered my face with my arms and leaped back. "Kuno, down!" shouted the boy, lunging at him. The front door flew open and a young girl with yellow hair ran down the steps and seized the ugly beast by the scruff. "He does not mean anything," she said seriously in English. "He is only a dog."

Just Louise's darling little puppy Kuno, I thought, a year or so older. Kuno whined, apologized by bowing and scraping one front paw on the ground, and the girl holding his scruff said, shyly and proudly, "I teach him that. He has always such bad manners, but I teach him!"

I had arrived, it seemed, at the moment when the evening chores were about to begin. The entire Müller household streamed out of the door, each man and woman going about the affairs of the moment. The young girl walked with me up the porch and said, "This is my brother Hans," and a young man paused to shake hands and passed by. "This is my brother Fritz," she said, and Fritz took my hand and dropped it as he went. "My sister Annetje," said the young girl, and a quiet young woman with a baby draped loosely like a scarf over her shoulder smiled and held out her hand. Hand after hand went by, their palms variously younger or older, broad or small, male or female, but all thick hard decent peasant hands, warm and strong. And in every face I saw again the pale, tilted eyes, on every head that taffy-colored hair, as though they might all be brothers and sisters, though Annetje's husband and still another daughter's husband had gone by after greeting me. In the wide hall with a door at front and back, full of cloudy light and the smell of soap, the old mother, also on her way out, stopped to offer her hand. She was a tall strong-looking woman wearing a three-cornered black wool shawl on her head, her skirts looped up over a brown flannel petticoat. Not from her did the young ones get those water-clear eyes. Hers were black and shrewd and searching, a band of hair showed black streaked with grey, her seamed dry face was brown as seasoned bark, and she walked in her rubber boots with the stride of a man. She shook my hand briefly and said in German English that I was welcome, smiling and showing her blackened teeth.

"This is my girl Hatsy," she told me, "and she will show you to your room." Hatsy took my hand as if I were a child needing a guide. I followed her up a flight of steps steep as a ladder, and there we were, in Louise's attic room, with the sloping roof. Yes, the shingles were stained all the colors she had said. There were the dime novels heaped in the corner. For once, Louise had got it straight, and it was homely and familiar, as if I had seen it before. "My mother says we could give you a better place on the downstairs," said Hatsy, in her soft blurred English, "but *she* said in her letter you would like it so." I told her indeed I did like it so. She went down the steep stairs then, and her brother came up as if he were climbing a tree, with the trunk on his head and the suitcase in his right hand, and I could not see what kept the trunk from crashing back to the bottom, as he used the left hand to climb with. I wished to offer help but feared to insult him, having noted well the tremendous ease and style with which he had hurled the luggage around before, a strong man doing his turn before a weakling audience. He put his burden down and straightened up, wriggling his shoulders and panting only a little. I thanked him and he pushed his cap back and pulled it forward again, which I took for some sort of polite response, and clattered out hugely. Looking out of my window a few minutes later, I saw him setting off across the fields carrying a lighted lantern and a large steel trap.

I began changing my first letter to Louise. "I'm going to like it here. I don't quite know why, but it's going to be all right. Maybe I can tell you later—"

The sound of the German speech in the household below was part of the pleasantness, for they were not talking to me and did not expect me to answer. All the German I understood then was contained in five small deadly sentimental songs of Heine's, learned by heart; and this was a very different tongue, Low German corrupted by three generations in a foreign country. A dozen miles away, where Texas and Louisiana melted together in a rotting swamp whose sluggish under-tow of decay nourished the roots of pine and cedar, a colony of French emigrants had lived out two hundred years of exile, not wholly incorruptible, but mystically faithful to the marrow of their bones, obstinately speaking their old French by then as strange to the French as it was to the English. I had known many of these families during a certain long summer happily remembered, and here again, listening to another language nobody could understand except those of this small farming community, I knew that I was again in a house of perpetual exile. These were solid, practical, hard-bitten, land-holding German peasants, who struck their mattocks into the earth deep and held fast wherever they were, because to them life and the land were one indivisible thing; but never in any wise did they confuse nationality with habitation.

I liked the thick warm voices, and it was good not to have to understand what they were saying. I loved that silence which means freedom from the constant pressure of other minds and other opinions and other feelings, that freedom to fold up in quiet and go back to my own center, to find out again, for it is always a rediscovery, what kind of creature it is that rules me finally, makes all the decisions no matter who thinks they make them, even I; who little by little takes everything away except the one thing I cannot live without, and who will one day say, "Now I am all you have left—take me." I paused there a good while listening to this muted unknown language which was silence with music in it; I could be moved and touched but not troubled by it, as by the crying of frogs or the wind in the trees.

The catalpa tree at my window would, I noticed, when it came into leaf, shut off my view of the barns and the fields beyond. When in bloom the branches would almost reach through the window. But now they were a thin screen through which the calves, splotchy red and white, moved prettily against the weathered darkness of the sheds. The brown fields would soon be green again; the sheep washed by the rains and become clean grey. All the beauty of the landscape now was in the harmony of the valley rolling fluently away to the wood's edge. It was an inland country, with the forlorn look of all unloved things; winter in this part of the south is a moribund coma, not the northern death sleep with the sure promise of resurrection. But in my south, my loved and never-forgotten country, after her long sickness, with only a slight stirring, an opening of the eyes between one breath and the next, between night and day, the earth revives and bursts into the plenty of spring with fruit and flowers together, spring and summer at once under the hot shimmering blue sky.

The freshening wind promised another light sedate rain to come at evening. The voices below stairs dispersed, rose again, separately calling from the yards and barns. The old woman strode down the path toward the cow sheds, Hatsy running behind her. The woman wore her wooden yoke, with the milking pails covered and closed with iron hasps, slung easily across her shoulders, but her daughter carried two tin milking pails on her arm. When they pushed back the bars of cedar which opened onto the fields, the cows came through lowing and crowding, and the calves scampered each to his own dam with reaching, opened mouths. Then there was the battle of separating the hungry children from their mothers when they had taken their scanty share. The old woman slapped their little haunches with her open palm, Hatsy dragged at their halters, her feet slipping wide in the mud, the cows bellowed and brandished their horns, the calves bawled like rebellious babies. Hatsy's long yellow braids whisked around her shoulders, her laughter was a shrill streak of gaiety above the angry cow voices and the raucous shouting of the old woman.

From the kitchen porch below came the sound of splashing water, the creaking of the pump handle, and the stamping boots of men. I sat in the window watching the darkness come on slowly, while all the lamps were being lighted. My own small lamp had a handle on the oil bowl, like a cup's. There was also a lantern with a frosted chimney hanging by a nail on the wall. A voice called to me from the foot of my stairs and I looked down into the face of a dark-skinned, flaxen-haired young woman, far advanced in pregnancy, and carrying a prosperous year-old boy on her hip, one arm clutching him to her, the other raised above her head so that her lantern shone upon their heads. "The supper is now ready," she said, and waited for me to come down before turning away.

In the large square room the whole family was gathering at a long table covered with a red checkered cotton cloth, with heaped-up platters of steaming food at either end. A crippled and badly deformed servant girl was setting down pitchers of milk. Her face was so bowed over it was almost hidden, and her whole body was maimed in some painful, mysterious way, probably congenital, I supposed, though she seemed wiry and tough. Her knotted hands shook continually, her wagging head kept pace with her restless elbows. She ran unsteadily around the table scattering plates, dodging whoever stood in her way; no one moved aside for her, or spoke to her, or even glanced after her when she vanished into the kitchen.

The men then moved forward to their chairs. Father Müller took his patriarch's place at the head of the table, Mother Müller looming behind him like a dark boulder. The younger men ranged themselves about on one side, the married ones with their wives standing back of their chairs to serve them, for three generations in this country had not made them self-conscious or disturbed their ancient customs. The two sons-in-law and three sons rolled down their shirt sleeves before beginning to eat. Their faces were polished with recent scrubbing and their open collars were damp.

Mother Müller pointed to me, then waved her hand at her household, telling off their names rapidly. I was a stranger and a guest, so was seated on the men's side of the table, and Hatsy, whose real named turned out to be Huldah, the maiden of the family, was seated on the children's side of the board, attending to them and keeping them in order. These infants ranged from two years to ten, five in number—not counting the one still straddling his mother's hip behind his father's chair—divided between the two married daughters. The children ravened and gorged and reached their hands into the sugar bowl to sprinkle sugar on everything they ate, solemnly elated over their food and paying no attention to Hatsy, who struggled with them only a little less energetically than she did with the calves, and ate almost nothing. She was about seventeen years old, pale-lipped and too thin, and her sleek fine butter-yellow hair, streaked light and dark, real German peasant hair, gave her an air of fragility. But she shared the big-boned structure and the enormous energy and animal force that was like a bodily presence itself in the room; and seeing Father Müller's pale-grey deep-set choleric eyes and high cheekbones, it was easy to trace the family resemblance around the table: it was plain that poor Mother Müller had never had a child of her own—black-eyed, black-haired South Germany people. True, she had borne them, but that was all; they belonged to their father. Even the tawny Gretchen, expecting another baby, obviously the pet of the family, with the sly smiling manner of a spoiled child, who wore the contented air of a lazy, healthy young animal, seeming always about to yawn, had hair like pulled taffy and those slanted clear eyes. She stood now easing the weight of her little boy on her husband's chair back, reaching with her left arm over his shoulder to refill his plate from time to time.

Annetje, the eldest daughter, carried her newly born baby over her shoulder, where he drooled comfortably down her back, while she spooned things from platters and bowls for her husband. Whenever their eyes met, they smiled with a gentle, reserved warmth in their eyes, the smile of long and sure friendship.

Father Müller did not in the least believe in his children's marrying and leaving home. Marry, yes, of course; but must that take a son or daughter from him? He always could provide work and a place in the household for his daughters' husbands, and in time he would do the same for his sons' wives. A new room had lately been built on, to the northeast, Annetje explained to me, leaning above her husband's head and talking across the table, for Hatsy to live in when she should be married. Hatsy turned very beautifully pink and ducked her head almost into her plate, then looked up boldly and said, "Jah, jah, I am marrit now soon!" Everybody laughed except Mother Müller, who said in German that girls at home never knew when they were well off—no, they must go bringing in husbands. This remark did not seem to hurt anybody's feelings, and Gretchen said it was nice that I was going to be here for the wedding. This reminded Annetje of something, and she spoke in English to the table at large, saying that the Lutheran pastor had advised her to attend church oftener and put her young ones in Sunday school, so that God would give her a blessing with her fifth child. I counted around again, and sure enough, with Gretchen's unborn, there were eight children at that table under the age of ten; somebody was going to need a blessing in all that crowd, no doubt. Father Müller delivered a short speech to his daughter in German, then turned to me and said, "What I say iss, it iss all craziness to go to church and pay a preacher goot money to talk his nonsense. Say rather that he pay me to come and lissen, then I vill go!" His eyes glared with sudden fierceness above his square speckled grey and yellow beard that sprouted directly out from the high cheekbones. "He thinks, so, that my time maybe costs nothing? That iss goot! Let him pay me!"

Mother Müller snorted and shuffled her feet. "Ach, you talk, you talk. Now you vill make the pastor goot and mad if he hears. Vot ve do, if he vill not chrissen the babies?"

"You give him goot money, he vill chrissen," shouted Father Müller. "You vait und see!"

"Ah sure, dot iss so," agreed Mother Müller. "Only do not let him hear!"

There was a gust of excited talk in German, with much rapping of knife handles on the table. I gave up trying to understand, but watched their faces. It sounded like a pitched battle, but they were agreeing about something. They were united in their tribal scepticisms, as in everything else. I got a powerful impression that they were all, even the sons-in-law, one human being divided into several separate appearances. The crippled servant girl brought in more food and gathered up plates and went away in her limping run, and she seemed to me the only individual in the house. Even I felt divided into many fragments, having left or lost a part of myself in every place I had travelled, in every life mine had touched, above all, in every death of someone near to me that had carried into the grave some part of my living cells. But the servant, she was whole, and belonged nowhere.

. . .

I settled easily enough into the marginal life of the household ways and habits. Day began early at the Müllers', and we ate breakfast by yellow lamplight, with the grey damp winds blowing with spring softness through the open windows. The men swallowed their last cups of steaming coffee standing, with their hats on, and went out to harness the horses to the ploughs at sunrise. Annetje, with her fat baby slung over her shoulder, could sweep a room or make a bed with one hand, all finished before the day was well begun; and she spent the rest of the day outdoors, caring for the chickens and the pigs. Now and then she came in with a shallow boxful of newly hatched chickens, abject dabs of wet fluff, and put them on a table in her bedroom where she might tend them carefully on their first day. Mother Müller strode about hugely, giving orders right and left, while Father Müller, smoothing his whiskers and lighting his pipe, drove away to town with Mother Müller calling out after him final directions and instructions about household needs. He never spoke a word to her and appeared not to be listening, but he always returned in a few hours with every commission and errand performed exactly. After I had made my own bed and set my attic in order, there was nothing at all for me to do, and I walked out of this enthusiastic bustle into the lane, feeling extremely useless. But the repose, the almost mystical inertia of their minds in the midst of this muscular life, communicated itself to me little by little, and I absorbed it gratefully in silence and felt all the hidden knotted painful places in my own mind beginning to loosen. It was easier to breathe, and I might even weep, if I pleased. In a very few days I no longer felt like weeping.

One morning I saw Hatsy spading up the kitchen garden plot, and my offer to help, to spread the seeds and cover them, was accepted. We worked at this for several hours each morning, until the warmth of the sun and the stooping posture induced in me a comfortable vertigo. I forgot to count the days, they were one like the other except as the colors of the air changed, deepening and warming to keep step with the advancing season, and the earth grew firmer underfoot with the swelling tangle of crowding roots.

The children, so hungry and noisy at the table, were peaceable little folk who played silent engrossed games in the front yard. They were always kneading mud into loaves and pies and carrying their battered dolls and cotton rag animals through the operations of domestic life. They fed them, put them to bed; they got them up and fed them again, set them to their chores making more mud loaves; or they would harness themselves to their carts and gallop away to a great shady chestnut tree on the opposite side of the house. Here the tree became the *Turnverein,* and they themselves were again human beings, solemnly ambling about in a dance and going through the motions of drinking beer. Miraculously changed once more into horses, they harnessed themselves and galloped home. They came at call to be fed and put to sleep with the docility of their own toys or animal playmates. Their mothers handled them with instinctive, constant gentleness; they never seemed to be troubled by them. They were as devoted and caretaking as a cat with her kittens.

Sometimes I took Annetje's next to youngest child, a baby of two years, in her little wagon, and we would go down through the orchard, where the branches were beginning to sprout in cones of watery green, and into the lane for a short distance. I would turn again into a smaller lane, smoother because less travelled, and we would go slowly between the aisle of mulberry trees where the fruit was beginning to hang and curl like green furry worms. The baby would sit in a compact mound of flannel and calico, her pale-blue eyes tilted and shining under her cap, her two lower teeth showing in a rapt smile. Sometimes several of the other children would follow along quietly. When I turned, they all turned without question, and we would proceed back to the house as sedately as we had set out.

The narrow lane, I discovered, led to the river, and it became my favorite walk. Almost every day I went along the edge of the naked wood, passionately occupied with looking for signs of spring. The changes there were so subtle and gradual I found one day that branches of willows and sprays of blackberry vine alike were covered with fine points of green; the color had changed overnight, or so it seemed, and I knew that tomorrow the whole valley and wood and edge of the river would be quick and feathery with golden green blowing in the winds.

And it was so. On that day I did not leave the river until after dark and came home through the marsh with the owls and night jars crying over my head, calling in a strange and broken chorus in the woods until the farthest answering cry was a ghostly echo. When I went through the orchard the trees were all abloom with fireflies. I stopped and looked at it for a long time, then walked slowly, amazed, for I had never seen anything that was more beautiful to me. The trees were freshly budded out with pale bloom, the branches were immobile in the thin darkness, but the flower clusters shivered in a soundless dance of delicately woven light, whirling as airily as leaves in a breeze, as rhythmically as water in a fountain. Every tree was budded out with this living, pulsing fire as fragile and cool as bubbles. When I opened the gate their light shone on my hands like fox fire. When I looked back, the shimmer of golden light was there, it was no dream.

Hatsy was on her knees in the dining room, washing the floor with heavy dark rags. She always did this work at night, so the men with their heavy boots would not be tracking it up again and it would be immaculate in the morning. She turned her young face to me in a stupor of fatigue. "Ottilie! Ottilie!" she called, loudly, and before I could speak, she said, "Ottilie will give you supper. It is waiting, all ready." I tried to tell her that I was not hungry, but she wished to reassure me. "Look, we all must eat. Now or then, it's no trouble." She sat back on her heels, and raising her head, looked over the window sill at the orchard. She smiled and paused for a moment and said happily, "Now it is come spring. Every spring we have that." She bent again over the great pail of water with her mops.

The crippled servant came in, stumbling perilously on the slippery floor, and set a dish before me, lentils with sausage and red chopped cabbage. It was hot and savory and I was truly grateful, for I found I was hungry, after all. I looked at her—so her name was Ottilie?—and said, "Thank you." "She can't talk," said Hatsy, simply stating a fact that need not be emphasized. The blurred, dark face was neither young nor old, but crumpled into criss cross wrinkles, irrelevant either to age or suffering; simply wrinkles, patternless blackened seams as if the perishable flesh had been wrung in a hard cruel fist. Yet in that mutilated face I saw high cheekbones, slanted water-blue eyes, the pupils very large and strained with the anxiety of one peering into a darkness full of danger. She jarred heavily against the table as she turned, her bowed back trembling with the perpetual working of her withered arms, and ran away in aimless, driven haste.

Hatsy sat on her heels again for a moment, tossed her braids back over her shoulder and said, "That is Ottilie. She is not sick now. She is only like that since she was sick when she was a baby. But she can work so well as I can. She cooks. But she cannot talk so you can understand." She went up on her knees, bowed over, and began to scrub again, with new energy. She was really a network of thin taut ligaments and long muscles elastic as woven steel. She would always work too hard, and be tired all her life, and never know that this was anything but perfectly natural; everybody worked all the time, because there was always more work waiting when they had finished what they were doing then. I ate my supper and took my plate to the kitchen and set it on the table. Ottilie was sitting in a kitchen chair with her feet in the open oven, her arms folded and her head waggling a little. She did not see or hear me.

. . .

At home, Hatsy wore an old brown corduroy dress and galoshes without stockings. Her skirts were short enough to show her thin legs, slightly crooked below the knees, as if she had walked too early. "Hatsy, she's a good, quick girl," said Mother Müller, to whom praising anybody or anything did not come easily. On Saturdays, Hatsy took a voluminous bath in a big tub in the closet back of the kitchen, where also were stored the extra chamber pots, slop jars, and water jugs. She then unplaited her yellow hair and bound up the crinkled floss with a wreath of pink cotton rosebuds, put on her pale-blue China silk dress, and went to the *Turnverein* to dance and drink a seidel of dark-brown beer with her suitor, who resembled her brothers enough to be her brother, though I think nobody ever noticed this except myself, and I said nothing because it would have been the remark of a stranger and hopeless outsider. On Sundays, the entire family went to the *Turnverein* after copious washings, getting into starched dresses and shirts, and getting the baskets of food stored in the wagons. The servant, Ottilie, would rush out to see them off, standing with both shaking arms folded over her forehead, shading her troubled eyes to watch them to the turn of the lane. Her muteness seemed nearly absolute; she had no coherent language of signs. Yet three times a day she spread that enormous table with solid food, freshly baked bread, huge platters of vegetables, immoderate roasts of meat, extravagant tarts, strudels, pies—enough for twenty people. If neighbors came in for an afternoon on some holiday, Ottilie would stumble into the big north room, the parlor, with its golden oak melodeon, a harsh-green Brussels carpet, Nottingham lace curtains, crocheted lace antimacassars on the chair backs, to serve them coffee with cream and sugar and thick slices of yellow cake.

Mother Müller sat but seldom in her parlor, and always with an air of formal unease, her knotted big fingers cramped in a cluster. But Father Müller often sat there in the evenings, where no one ventured to follow him unless commanded; he sometimes played chess with his elder son-in-law, who had learned a good while ago that Father Müller was a good player who abhorred an easy victory, and he dared not do less than put up the best fight he was able, but even so, if Father Müller felt himself winning too often, he would roar, "No, you are not trying! You are not doing your best. Now we stop this nonsense!" and son-in-law would find himself dismissed in temporary disgrace.

Most evenings, however, Father Müller sat by himself and read *Das Kapital.* He would settle deeply into the red plush base rocker and spread the volume upon a low table before him. It was an early edition in blotty black German type, stained and ragged in its leather cover, the pages falling apart, a very bible. He knew whole chapters almost by heart, and added nothing to, took nothing from, the canonical, once-delivered text. I cannot say at that time of my life I had never heard of *Das Kapital,* but I had certainly never known anyone who had read it, though if anyone mentioned it, it was always with profound disapproval. It was not a book one had to read in order to reject it. And here was this respectable old farmer who accepted its dogma as a religion—that is to say, its legendary inapplicable precepts were just, right, proper, one must believe in them, of course, but life, everyday living, was another and unrelated thing. Father Müller was the richest man in his community; almost every neighboring farmer rented land from him, and some of them worked it on the share system. He explained this to me one evening after he had given up trying to teach me chess. He was not surprised that I could not learn, at least not in one lesson, and he was not surprised either that I knew nothing about *Das Kapital.* He explained his own arrangements to me thus: "These men, they cannot buy their land. The land must be bought, for Kapital owns it, and Kapital will not give back to the worker the land that is his. Well, somehow, I can always buy land. Why? I do not know. I only know that with my first land here I made good crops to buy more land, and so I rent it cheap, more than anybody else I rent it cheap, I lend money so my neighbors do not fall into the hands of the bank, and so I am not Kapital. Someday these workers, they can buy land from me, for less than they can get it anywhere else. Well, that is what I can do, that is all." He turned over a page, and his angry grey eyes looked out at me under his shaggy brows. "I buy my land with my hard work, all my life, and I rent it cheap to my neighbors, and then they say they will not elect my son-in-law, my Annetje's husband, to be sheriff because I am atheist. So then I say, all right, but next year you pay more for your land or more shares of your crops. If I am atheist I will act like one. So, my Annetje's husband is sheriff, that is all."

He had put a stubby forefinger on a line to mark his place, and now he sank himself into his book, and I left quietly without saying good night.

. . .

The *Turnverein* was an octagonal pavilion set in a cleared space in a patch of woods belonging to Father Müller. The German colony came here to sit about in the cool shade, while a small brass band played cloppity country dances. The girls danced with energy and direction, their starched petticoats rustling like dry leaves. The boys were more awkward, but willing; they clutched their partners' waists and left crumpled sweaty spots where they clutched. Here Mother Müller took her ease after a hard week. Her gaunt limbs would relax, her knees spread squarely apart, and she would gossip over her beer with the women of her own generation. They would cast an occasional caretaking glance at the children playing nearby, allowing the younger mothers freedom to dance or sit in peace with their own friends.

On the other side of the pavilion, Father Müller would sit with the sober grandfathers, their long curved pipes wagging on their chests as they discussed local politics with profound gravity, their hard peasant fatalism tempered only a little by a shrewd worldly distrust of all officeholders not personally known to them, all political plans except their own immediate ones. When Father Müller talked, they listened respectfully, with faith in him as a strong man, head of his own house and his community. They nodded slowly whenever he took his pipe from his mouth and gestured, holding it by the bowl as if it were a stone he was getting ready to throw. On our way back from the *Turnverein* one evening, Mother Müller said to me, "Well, now, by the grace of Gott it is all settled between Hatsy and her man. It is next Sunday by this time they will be marrit."

All the folk who usually went to the *Turnverein* on Sundays came instead to the Müller house for the wedding. They brought useful presents, mostly bed linen, pillow covers, a white counter-pane, with a few ornaments for the bridal chamber—a home-braided round rug in many colors, a brass-bottomed lamp with a round pink chimney decorated with red roses, a stone china wash-bowl and pitcher also covered with red roses; and the bridegroom's gift to the bride was a necklace, a double string of red coral twigs. Just before the short ceremony began, he slipped the necklace over her head with trembling hands. She smiled up at him shakily and helped him disentangle her short veil from the coral, then they joined hands and turned their faces to the pastor, not letting go until time for the exchange of rings—the widest, thickest, reddest gold bands to be found, no doubt—and at that moment they both stopped smiling and turned a little pale. The groom recovered first, and bent over—he was considerably taller than she—and kissed her on the forehead. His eyes were a deep blue, and his hair not really Müller taffy color, but a light chestnut; a good-looking, gentle-tempered boy, I decided, and he looked at Hatsy as if he liked what he saw. They knelt and clasped hands again for the final prayer, then stood together and exchanged the bridal kiss, a very chaste reserved one, still not on the lips. Then everybody came to shake hands and the men all kissed the bride and the women all kissed the groom. Some of the women whispered in Hatsy's ear, and all burst out laughing except Hatsy, who turned red from her forehead to her throat. She whispered in turn to her husband, who nodded in agreement. She then tried to slip away quietly, but the watchful young girls were after her, and shortly we saw her running through the blossoming orchard, holding up her white ruffled skirts, with all the girls in pursuit, shrieking and calling like excited hunters, for the first to overtake and touch her would be the next bride. They returned, breathless, dragging the lucky one with them, and held her against her ecstatic resistance, while all the young boys kissed her.

The guests stayed on for a huge supper, and Ottilie came in, wearing a fresh blue apron, sweat beaded in the wrinkles of her forehead and around her formless mouth, and passed the food around the table. The men ate first and then Hatsy came in with the women for the first time, still wearing her square little veil of white cotton net bound on her hair with peach blossoms shattered in the bride's race. After supper, one of the girls played waltzes and polkas on the melodeon, and everyone danced. The bridegroom drew gallons of beer from a keg set up in the hall, and at midnight everybody went away, warmly emotional and happy. I went down to the kitchen for a pitcher of hot water. The servant was still setting things to rights, hobbling between table and cupboard. Her face was a brown smudge of anxiety, her eyes were wide and dazed. Her uncertain hands rattled among the pans, but nothing could make her seem real, or in any way connected with the life around her. Yet when I set my pitcher on the stove, she lifted the heavy kettle and poured the scalding water into it without spilling a drop.

. . .

The clear honey green of the early morning sky was a mirror of the bright earth. At the edge of the woods there had sprung a reticent blooming of small white and pale-colored flowers. The peach trees were now each a separate nosegay of shell rose and white. I left the house, meaning to take the short path across to the lane of mulberries. The women were deep in the house, the men were away to the fields, the animals were turned into the pastures, and only Ottilie was visible, sitting on the steps of the back porch peeling potatoes. She gazed in my direction with eyes that fell short of me, and seemed to focus on a point midway between us, and gave no sign. Then she dropped her knife and rose, her mouth opened and closed several times, she strained toward me, motioning with her right hand. I went to her, her hands came out and clutched my sleeve, and for a moment I feared to hear her voice. There was no sound from her, but she drew me along after her, full of some mysterious purpose of her own. She opened the door of a dingy bitter-smelling room, windowless, which opened off the kitchen, beside the closet where Hatsy took her baths. A lumpy narrow cot and chest of drawers supporting a blistered looking-glass almost filled the space. Ottilie's lips moved, struggling for speech, as she pulled and tumbled over a heap of rubbish in the top drawer. She took out a photograph and put it in my hands. It was in the old style, faded to a dirty yellow, mounted on cardboard elaborately clipped and gilded at the edges.

I saw a girl child about five years old, a pretty smiling German baby, looking curiously like a slightly elder sister of Annetje's two-year-old, wearing a frilled frock and a prodigious curl of blonde hair, called a roach, on the crown of her head. The strong legs, round as sausages, were encased in long white ribbed stockings, and the square firm feet were laced into old-fashioned soft-soled black boots. Ottilie peered over the picture, twisted her neck, and looked up into my face. I saw the slanted water-blue eyes and the high cheekbones of the Müllers again, mutilated, almost destroyed, but unmistakable. This child was what she had been, and she was without doubt the elder sister of Annetje and Gretchen and Hatsy; in urgent pantomime she insisted that this was so—she patted the picture and her own face, and strove terribly to speak. She pointed to the name written carefully on the back, Ottilie, and touched her mouth with her bent knuckles. Her head wagged in her perpetual nod; her shaking hand seemed to flap the photograph at me in a roguish humor. The bit of cardboard connected her at once somehow to the world of human beings I knew; for an instant some filament lighter than cobweb spun itself out between that living center in her and in me, a filament from some center that held us all bound to our unescapable common source, so that her life and mine were kin, even a part of each other, and the painfulness and strangeness of her vanished. She knew well that she had been Ottilie, with those steady legs and watching eyes, and she was Ottilie still within herself. For a moment, being alive, she knew she suffered, for she stood and shook with silent crying, smearing away her tears with the open palm of her hand. Even while her cheeks were wet, her face changed. Her eyes cleared and fixed themselves upon that point in space which seemed for her to contain her unaccountable and terrible troubles. She turned her head as if she had heard a voice and disappeared in her staggering run into the kitchen, leaving the drawer open and the photograph face downward on the chest.

At midday meal she came hurrying and splashing coffee on the white floor, restored to her own secret existence of perpetual amazement, and again I had been a stranger to her like all the rest but she was no stranger to me, and could not be again.

The youngest brother came in, holding up an opossum he had caught in his trap. He swung the furry body from side to side, his eyes fairly narrowed with pride as he showed us the mangled creature. "No, it is cruel, even for the wild animals," said gentle Annetje to me, "but boys love to kill, they love to hurt things. I am always afraid he will trap poor Kuno." I thought privately that Kuno, a wolfish, ungracious beast, might well prove a match for any trap. Annetje was full of silent, tender solicitudes. The kittens, the puppies, the chicks, the lambs and calves were her special care. She was the only one of the women who caressed the weanling calves when she set the pans of milk before them. Her child seemed as much a part of her as if it were not yet born. Still, she seemed to have forgotten that Ottilie was her sister. So had all the others. I remembered how Hatsy had spoken her name but had not said she was her sister. Their silence about her was, I realized, exactly that—simple forgetfulness. She moved among them as invisible to their imaginations as a ghost. Ottilie their sister was something painful that had happened long ago and now was past and done for; they could not live with that memory or its visible reminder—they forgot her in pure self-defense. But I could not forget her. She drifted into my mind like a bit of weed carried in a current and caught there, floating but fixed, refusing to be carried away. I reasoned it out. The Müllers, what else could they have done with Ottilie? By a physical accident in her childhood she had been stripped of everything but her mere existence. It was not a society or a class that pampered its invalids and the unfit. So long as one lived, one did one's share. This was her place, in this family she had been born and must die; did she suffer? No one asked, no one looked to see. Suffering went with life, suffering and labor. While one lived one worked, that was all, and without complaints, for no one had time to listen, and everybody had his own troubles. So, what else could they have done with Ottilie? As for me, I could do nothing but promise myself that I would forget her, too; and to remember her for the rest of my life.

Sitting at the long table, I would watch Ottilie clattering about in her tormented haste, bringing in that endless food that represented all her life's labors. My mind would follow her into the kitchen where I could see her peering into the great simmering kettles, the crowded oven, her whole body a mere machine of torture. Straight up to the surface of my mind the thought would come urgently, clearly, as if driving time toward the desired event: Let it be now, let it be *now.* Not even tomorrow, no, today. Let her sit down quietly in her rickety chair by the stove and fold those arms, and let us find her there like that, with her head fallen forward on her knees. She will rest then. I would wait, hoping she might not come again, ever again, through that door I gazed at with wincing eyes, as if I might see something unendurable enter through it. Then she would come, and it was only Ottilie, after all, in the bosom of her family, and one of its most useful and competent members; and they with a deep right instinct had learned to live with her disaster on its own terms, and hers; they had accepted and then made use of what was for them only one more painful event in a world full of troubles, many of them much worse than this. So, a step at a time, I followed the Müllers as nearly as I could in their acceptance of Ottilie, and the use they made of her life, for in some way that I could not quite explain to myself, I found great virtue and courage in their steadiness and refusal to feel sorry for anybody, least of all for themselves.

. . .

Gretchen bore her child, a son, conveniently between the hours of supper and bedtime, one evening of friendly and domestic-sounding rain. The next day brought neighboring women from miles around, and the child was bandied about among them as if he were a new kind of medicine ball. Sedate and shy at dances, emotional at weddings, they were ribald and jocose at births. Over coffee and beer the talk grew broad, the hearty gutturals were swallowed in the belly of laughter; those honest hard-working wives and mothers saw life for a few hours as a hearty low joke, and it did them good. The baby bawled and suckled like a young calf, and the men of the family came in for a look and added their joyful improprieties.

Cloudy weather drove them home earlier than they had meant to go. The whole sky was lined with smoky black and grey vapor hanging in ragged wisps like soot in a chimney. The edges of the woods turned dull purple as the horizon reddened slowly, then faded, and all across the sky ran a deep shuddering mumble of thunder. All the Müllers hurried about getting into rubber boots and oilcloth overalls, shouting to each other, making their plan of action. The youngest boy came over the ridge of the hill with Kuno helping him to drive the sheep down into the fold. Kuno was barking, the sheep were baaing and bleating, the horses freed from the ploughs were excited; they whinnied and trotted at the lengths of their halters, their ears laid back. The cows were bawling in distress and the calves cried back to them. All the men went out among the animals to round them up and quiet them and get them enclosed safely. Even as Mother Müller, her half-dozen petticoats looped about her thighs and tucked into her boots, was striding to join them in the barns, the cloud rack was split end to end by a shattering blow of lightning, and the cloudburst struck the house with the impact of a wave against a ship. The wind broke the windowpanes and the floods poured through. The roof beams strained and the walls bent inward, but the house stood to its foundations. The children were huddled into the inner bedroom with Gretchen. "Come and sit on the bed with me now," she told them calmly, "and be still." She sat up with a shawl around her, suckling the baby. Annetje came then and left her baby with Gretchen, too; and standing at the doorsteps with one arm caught over the porch rail, reached down into the furious waters which were rising to the very threshold and dragged in a half-drowned lamb. I followed her. We could not make ourselves heard above the cannonade of thunder, but together we carried the creature into the hall under the stairs, where we rubbed the drowned fleece with rags and pressed his stomach to free him from the water and finally got him sitting up with his feet tucked under him. Annetje was merry with triumph and kept saying in delight, "Alive, alive! look!"

We left him there when we heard the men shouting and beating at the kitchen door and ran to open it for them. They came in, Mother Müller among them, wearing her yoke and milk pails. She stood there with the water pouring from her skirts, the three-cornered piece of black oilcloth on her head dripping, her rubber boots wrinkled down with the weight of her petticoats stuffed into them. She and Father Müller stood near each other, looking like two gnarled lightning-struck old trees, his beard and oilcloth garments streaming, both their faces suddenly dark and old and tired, tired once for all; they would never be rested again in their lives. Father Müller suddenly roared at her, "Go get yourself dry clothes. Do you want to make yourself sick?"

"Ho," she said, taking off her milk yoke and setting the pails on the floor. "Go change yourself. I bring you dry socks." One of the boys told me she had carried a day-old calf on her back up a ladder against the inside wall of the barn and had put it safely in the hayloft behind a barricade of bales. Then she had lined up the cows in the stable, and, sitting on her milking stool in the rising water, she had milked them all. She seemed to think nothing of it.

"Hatsy!" she called, "come help with this milk!" Little pale Hatsy came flying barefoot because she had been called in the midst of taking off her wet shoes, her thick yellow and silver braids thumping on her shoulders as she ran. Her new husband followed her, rather shy of his mother-in-law.

"Let me," he said, wishing to spare his dear bride such heavy work, and started to lift the great pails. "No!" shouted Mother Müller, so the poor young man nearly jumped out of his shirt, "not you. The milk is not business for a man." He fell back and stood there with dark rivulets of mud seeping from his boots, watching Hatsy pour the milk into pans. Mother Müller started to follow her husband to attend him, but said at the door, turning back, "Where is Ottilie?", and no one knew, no one had seen her. "Find her," said Mother Müller, going. "Tell her we want supper now."

Hatsy motioned to her husband, and together they tiptoed to the door of Ottilie's room and opened it silently. The light from the kitchen showed them Ottilie, sitting by herself, folded up on the edge of the bed. Hatsy threw the door wide open for more light and called in a high penetrating voice as if to a deaf person or one at a great distance, "Ottilie! Suppertime. We are hungry!", and the young pair left the kitchen to look under the stairway to see how Annetje's lamb was getting on. Then Annetje, Hatsy, and I got brooms and began sweeping the dirty water and broken glass from the floors of the hall and dining room.

The storm lightened gradually, but the flooding rain continued. At supper there was talk about the loss of animals and their replacement. All the crops must be replanted, the season's labor was for nothing. They were all tired and wet, but they ate heartily and calmly, to strengthen themselves against all the labor of repairing and restoring which must begin early tomorrow morning.

By morning the drumming on the roof had almost ceased; from my window I looked upon a sepia-colored plain of water moving slowly to the valley. The roofs of the barns sagged like the ridge poles of a tent, and a number of drowned animals floated or were caught against the fences. At breakfast Mother Müller sat groaning over her coffee cup. "Ach," she said, "what it is to have such a pain in the head. Here too," she thumped her chest. "All over. Ach, Gott, I'm sick." She got up sighing hoarsely, her cheeks flushed, calling Hatsy and Annetje to help her in the barn.

They all came back very soon, their skirts draggled to the knees, and the two sisters were supporting their mother, who was speechless and could hardly stand. They put her to bed, where she lay without moving, her face scarlet. Everybody was confused, no one knew what to do. They tucked the quilts about her, and she threw them off. They offered her coffee, cold water, beer, but she turned her head away. The sons came in and stood beside her, and joined the cry: "*Mutterchen, Mutti, Mutti,* what can we do? Tell us, what do you need?" But she could not tell them. It was impossible to ride the twelve miles to town for a doctor; fences and bridges were down, the roads were washed out. The family crowded into the room, unnerved in panic, lost unless the sick woman should come to herself and tell them what to do for her. Father Müller came in and, kneeling beside her, he took hold of her hands and spoke to her most lovingly, and when she did not answer him he broke out crying openly in a loud voice, the great tears rolling, "Ach, Gott, Gott. A hundert tousand tollars in the bank"—he glared around at his family and spoke broken English to them, as if he were a stranger to himself and had forgotten his own language—"and tell me, tell, what goot does it do?"

This frightened them, and all at once, together, they screamed and called and implored her in a tumult utterly beyond control. The noise of their grief and terror filled the place. In the midst of this, Mother Müller died.

. . .

In the midafternoon the rain passed, and the sun was a disc of brass in a cruelly bright sky. The waters flowed thickly down to the river, leaving the hill bald and brown, with the fences lying in a flattened tangle, the young peach trees stripped of bloom and sagging at the roots. In the woods had occurred a violent eruption of ripe foliage of a jungle thickness, glossy and burning, a massing of hot peacock green with cobalt shadows.

The household was in such silence, I had to listen carefully to know that anyone lived there. Everyone, even the younger children, moved on tiptoe and spoke in whispers. All afternoon the thud of hammers and the whine of a saw went on monotonously in the barn loft. At dark, the men brought in a shiny coffin of new yellow pine with rope handles and set it in the hall. It lay there on the floor for an hour or so, where anyone passing had to step over it. Then Annetje and Hatsy, who had been washing and dressing the body, appeared in the doorway and motioned: "You may bring it in now."

Mother Müller lay in state in the parlor throughout the night, in her black silk dress with a scrap of white lace at the collar and a small lace cap on her hair. Her husband sat in the plush chair near her, looking at her face, which was very contemplative, gentle, and remote. He wept at intervals, silently, wiping his face and head with a big handkerchief. His daughters brought him coffee from time to time. He fell asleep there toward morning.

The light burned in the kitchen nearly all night, too, and the sound of Ottilie's heavy boots thumping about unsteadily was accompanied by the locust whirring of the coffee mill and the smell of baking bread. Hatsy came to my room. "There's coffee and cake," she said, "you'd better have some," and turned away crying, crumbling her slice in her hand. We stood about and ate in silence. Ottilie brought in a fresh pot of coffee, her eyes bleared and fixed, her gait as aimless-looking and hurried as ever, and when she spilled some on her own hand, she did not seem to feel it.

For a day longer they waited; then the youngest boy went to fetch the Lutheran pastor, and a few neighbors came back with them. By noon many more had arrived, spattered with mud, the horses heaving and sweating. At every greeting the family gave way and wept afresh, as naturally and openly as children. Their faces were drenched and soft with their tears; there was a comfortable relaxed look in the muscles of their faces. It was good to let go, to have something to weep for that nobody need excuse or explain. Their tears were at once a luxury and a cure of souls. They wept away the hard core of secret trouble that is in the heart of each separate man, secure in a communal grief; in sharing it, they consoled each other. For a while they would visit the grave and remember, and then life would arrange itself again in another order, yet it would be the same. Already the thoughts of the living were turning to tomorrow, when they would be at the work of rebuilding and replanting and repairing—even now, today, they would hurry back from the burial to milk the cows and feed the chickens, and they might weep again and again for several days, until their tears could heal them at last.

On that day I realized, for the first time, not death, but the terror of dying. When they took the coffin out to the little country hearse and I saw that the procession was about to form, I went to my room and lay down. Staring at the ceiling, I heard and felt the ominous order and purpose in the movements and sounds below—the creaking harness and hoofbeats and grating wheels, the muted grave voices—and it was as if my blood fainted and receded with fright, while my mind stayed wide awake to receive the awful impress. Yet when I knew they were leaving the yard, the terror began to leave me. As the sounds receded, I lay there not thinking, not feeling, in a mere drowse of relief and weariness.

Through my half-sleep I heard the howling of a dog. It seemed to be a dream, and I was troubled to awaken. I dreamed that Kuno was caught in the trap; then I thought he was really caught, it was no dream and I must wake, because there was no one but me to let him out. I came broad awake, the cry rushed upon me like a wind, and it was not the howl of a dog. I ran downstairs and looked into Gretchen's room. She was curled up around her baby, and they were both asleep. I ran to the kitchen.

Ottilie was sitting in her broken chair with her feet on the edge of the open oven, where the heat had died away. Her hands hung at her sides, the fingers crooked into the palm; her head lay back on her shoulders, and she howled with a great wrench of her body, an upward reach of the neck, without tears. At sight of me she got up and came over to me and laid her head on my breast, and her hands dangled forward a moment. Shuddering, she babbled and howled and waved her arms in a frenzy through the open window over the stripped branches of the orchard toward the lane where the procession had straightened out into formal order. I took hold of her arms where the unnaturally corded muscles clenched and strained under her coarse sleeves; I led her out to the steps and left her sitting there, her head wagging.

In the barnyard there remained only the broken-down spring wagon and the shaggy pony that had brought me to the farm on the first day. The harness was still a mystery, but somehow I managed to join pony, harness, and wagon not too insecurely, or so I could only hope; and I pushed and hauled and tugged at Ottilie and lifted her until she was in the seat and I had the reins in hand. We careened down the road at a grudging trot, the pony jolting like a churn, the wheels spinning elliptically in a truly broad comedy swagger. I watched the jovial antics of those wheels with attention, hoping for the best. We slithered into round pits of green mud, and jogged perilously into culverts where small bridges had been. Once, in what was left of the main road, I stood up to see if I might overtake the funeral train; yes, there it was, going inch-meal up the road over the little hill, a bumbling train of black beetles crawling helter-skelter over clods.

Ottilie, now silent, was doubled upon herself, slipping loosely on the edge of the seat. I caught hold of her stout belt with my free hand, and my fingers slipped between her clothes and bare flesh, ribbed and gaunt and dry against my knuckles. My sense of her realness, her humanity, this shattered being that was a woman, was so shocking to me that a howl as doglike and despairing as her own rose in me unuttered and died again, to be a perpetual ghost. Ottilie slanted her eyes and peered at me, and I gazed back. The knotted wrinkles of her face were grotesquely changed, she gave a choked little whimper, and suddenly she laughed out, a kind of yelp but unmistakably laughter, and clapped her hands for joy, the grinning mouth and suffering eyes turned to the sky. Her head nodded and wagged with the clownish humor of our trundling lurching progress. The feel of the hot sun on her back, the bright air, the jolly senseless staggering of the wheels, the peacock green of the heavens: something of these had reached her. She was happy and gay, and she gurgled and rocked in her seat, leaning upon me and waving loosely around her as if to show me what wonders she saw.

Drawing the pony to a standstill, I studied her face for a while and pondered my ironical mistake. There was nothing I could do for Ottilie, selfishly as I wished to ease my heart of her; she was beyond my reach as well as any other human reach, and yet, had I not come nearer to her than I had to anyone else in my attempt to deny and bridge the distance between us, or rather, her distance from me? Well, we were both equally the fools of life, equally fellow fugitives from death. We had escaped for one day more at least. We would celebrate our good luck, we would have a little stolen holiday, a breath of spring air and freedom on this lovely, festive afternoon.

Ottilie fidgeted, uneasy at our stopping. I flapped the reins, the pony moved on, we turned across the shallow ditch where the small road divided from the main travelled one. I measured the sun westering gently; there would be time enough to drive to the river down the lane of mulberries and to get back to the house before the mourners returned. There would be plenty of time for Ottilie to have a fine supper ready for them. They need not even know she had been gone.

1960

MARITA BONNER
(1899–1971)

An influential contributor to the Harlem Renaissance, Marita Bonner wrote essays, plays, and short fiction that capture the problems of the Black working class, the tensions of urban life, and the complexities of a multiracial society.

Bonner was educated in the Boston area at Brookline High School, where she studied music and German, and at Radcliffe College, where she concentrated on English and comparative literature. Although she had begun to write while at Radcliffe, she did not publish her first pieces until she moved to Washington, D.C., in the mid-1920s. In Washington, she became a member of Georgia Douglas Johnson's "S" Street salon, which included writers such as Langston Hughes, Countee Cullen, Jean Toomer, Alain Locke, and Jessie Fauset. Bonner's first pieces, "The Hands: A Story" and the essay "On Being Young—a Woman—and Colored" were published in 1925 in The Crisis, *a Black journal. In Washington, Bonner also published three experimental dramas that explore the experience of African Americans through the structure of morality plays.*

Upon marrying and moving to Chicago in 1930, Bonner began working on fiction with the multiracial, multiclass Chicago society as a background. Her two-part story "Tin Can" won the literary prize for fiction awarded by Opportunity *magazine in 1933. Like a number of her other stories, "Tin Can" explores the effect of poverty and discrimination on people's characters. In "A Possible Triad on Black Notes," also published in* Opportunity, *Bonner introduces Frye Street, the fictional Chicago setting that brings together people of varying colors and classes, immigrants from Asia, Europe, and the American South. Frye Street is a microcosm of American society.*

As Joyce Flynn has written in an introduction to Bonner's works, the author offers "the perspective of an educated black female consciousness on a rapidly changing America between the two wars." There is little anger in her work; many of her essays and stories are almost meditative, examining the complexities that arise when different races and ethnic groups attempt to coexist.

The essay "On Being Young—a Woman—and Colored" muses on the sad disillusionment that a sensitive, intelligent Black woman experiences growing up. "Light in Dark Places," one of Bonner's last stories, traces the problems of a Black woman whose dreams are defeated by prejudice and the terrors of being a Black woman in a dangerous city.

ON BEING YOUNG—A WOMAN—AND COLORED

You start out after you have gone from kindergarten to sheepskin covered with sundry Latin phrases.

At least you know what you want life to give you. A career as fixed and as calmly brilliant as the North Star. The one real thing that money buys. Time. Time to do things. A house that can be as delectably out of order and as easily put in order as the doll-house of "playing-house" days. And of course, a husband you can look up to without looking down on yourself.

Somehow you feel like a kitten in a sunny catnip field that sees sleek, plump brown field mice and yellow baby chicks sitting coyly, side by side, under each leaf. A desire to dash three or four ways seizes you.

That's Youth.

But you know that things learned need testing—acid testing—to see if they are really after all, an interwoven part of you. All your life you have heard of the debt you owe "Your People" because you have managed to have the things they have not largely had.

So you find a spot where there are hordes of them—of course below the Line—to be your catnip field while you close your eyes to mice and chickens alike.

If you have never lived among your own, you feel prodigal. Some warm untouched current flows through them—through you—and drags you out into the deep waters of a new sea of human foibles and mannerisms; of a peculiar psychology and prejudices. And one day you find yourself entangled—enmeshed—pinioned in the seaweed of a Black Ghetto.

Not a Ghetto, placid like the Strasse that flows, outwardly unperturbed and calm in a stream of religious belief, but a peculiar group. Cut off, flung together, shoved aside in a bundle because of color and with no more in common.

Unless color is, after all, the real bond.

Milling around like live fish in a basket. Those at the bottom crushed into a sort of stupid apathy by the weight of those on top. Those on top leaping, leaping; leaping to scale the sides; to get out.

There are two "colored" movies, innumerable parties—and cards. Cards played so intensely that it fascinates and repulses at once.

Movies.

Movies worthy and worthless—but not even a low-caste spoken stage.

Parties, plentiful. Music and dancing and much that is wit and color and gaiety. But they are like the richest chocolate; stuffed costly chocolates that make the taste go stale if you have too many of them. That make plain whole bread taste like ashes.

There are all the earmarks of a group within a group. Cut off all around from ingress from or egress to other groups. A sameness of type. The smug self-satisfaction of an inner measurement; a measurement by standards known within a limited group and not those of an unlimited, seeing, world. . . . Like the blind, blind mice. Mice whose eyes have been blinded.

Strange longing seizes hold of you. You wish yourself back where you can lay your dollar down and sit in a dollar seat to hear voices, strings, reeds that have lifted the World out, up, beyond things that have bodies and walls. Where you can marvel at new marbles and bronzes and flat colors that will make men forget that things exist in a flesh more often than in spirit. Where you can sink your body in a cushioned seat and sink your soul at the same time into a section of life set before you on the boards for a few hours.

You hear that up at New York this is to be seen; that, to be heard.

You decide the next train will take you there.

You decide the next second that that train will not take you, nor the next—nor the next for some time to come.

For you know that—being a woman—you cannot twice a month or twice a year, for that matter, break away to see or hear anything in a city that is supposed to see and hear too much.

That's being a woman. A woman of any color.

You decide that something is wrong with a world that stifles and chokes; that cuts off and stunts; hedging in, pressing down on eyes, ears and throat. Somehow all wrong.

You wonder how it happens there that—say five hundred miles from the Bay State—Anglo Saxon intelligence is so warped and stunted.

How judgment and discernment are bred out of the race. And what has become of discrimination? Discrimination of the right sort. Discrimination that the best minds have told you weighs shadows and nuances and spiritual differences before it catalogues. The kind they have taught you all of your life was best: that looks clearly past generalization and past appearance to dissect, to dig down to the real heart of matters. That casts aside rapid summary conclusions, drawn from primary inference, as Daniel did the spiced meats.

Why can't they then perceive that there is a difference in the glance from a pair of eyes that look, mildly docile, at "white ladies" and those that, impersonally and perceptively—aware of distinctions—see only women who happen to be white?

Why do they see a colored woman only as a gross collection of desires, all uncontrolled, reaching out for their Apollos and the Quasimodos with avid indiscrimination?

Why unless you talk in staccato squawks—brittle as seashells—unless you "champ" gum—unless you cover two yards square when you laugh—unless your taste runs to violent colors—impossible perfumes and more impossible clothes—are you a feminine Caliban craving to pass for Ariel?

An empty imitation of an empty invitation. A mime; a sham; a copy-cat. A hollow re-echo. A froth, a foam. A fleck of the ashes of superficiality?

Everything you touch or taste now is like the flesh of an unripe persimmon.

. . . Do you need to be told what that is being . . . ?

Old ideas, old fundamentals seem worm-eaten, out-grown, worthless, bitter; fit for the scrap-heap of Wisdom.

What you had thought tangible and practical has turned out to be a collection of "blue-flower" theories.

If they have not discovered how to use their accumulation of facts, they are useless to you in Their world.

Every part of you becomes bitter.

But—"In Heaven's name, do not grow bitter. Be bigger than they are"—exhort white friends who have never had to draw breath in a Jim-Crow train. Who have never had petty putrid insult dragged over them—drawing blood—like pebbled sand on your body where the skin is tenderest. On your body where the skin is thinnest and tenderest.

You long to explode and hurt everything white; friendly; unfriendly. But you know that you cannot live with a chip on your shoulder even if you can manage a smile around your eyes—without getting steely and brittle and losing the softness that makes you a woman.

For chips make you bend your body to balance them. And once you bend, you lose your poise, your balance, and the chip gets into you. The real you. You get hard.

. . . And many things in you can ossify . . .

And you know, being a woman, you have to go about it gently and quietly, to find out and to discover just what is wrong. Just what can be done.

You see clearly that they have acquired things.

Money; money. Money to build with, money to destroy. Money to swim in. Money to drown in. Money.

An ascendancy of wisdom. An incalculable hoard of wisdom in all fields, in all things collected from all quarters of humanity.

A stupendous mass of things.

Things.

So, too, the Greeks . . . Things.

And the Romans. . . .

And you wonder and wonder why they have not discovered how to handle deftly and skillfully, Wisdom, stored up for them—like the honey for the Gods on Olympus—since time unknown.

You wonder and you wonder until you wander out into Infinity, where—if it is to be found anywhere—Truth really exists.

The Greeks had possessions, culture. They were lost because they did not understand.

The Romans owned more than anyone else. Trampled under the heel of Vandals and Civilization, because they would not understand.

Greeks. Did not understand.

Romans. Would not understand.

"They." Will not understand.

So you find they have shut Wisdom up and have forgotten to find the key that will let her out. They have trapped, trammeled, lashed her to themselves with thews and thongs and theories. They have ransacked sea and earth and air to bring every treasure to her. But she sulks and will not work for a world with a whitish hue because it has snubbed her twin sister, Understanding.

You see clearly—off there is Infinity—Understanding. Standing alone, waiting for someone to really want her.

But she is so far out there is no way to snatch at her and really drag her in.

So—being a woman—you can wait.

You must sit quietly without a chip. Not sodden—and weighted as if your feet were cast in the iron of your soul. Not wasting strength in enervating gestures as if two hundred years of bonds and whips had really tricked you into nervous uncertainty.

But quiet; quiet. Like Buddha—who brown like I am—sat entirely at ease, entirely sure of himself; motionless and knowing, a thousand years before the white man knew there was so very much difference between feet and hands.

Motionless on the outside. But on the inside?

Silent.

Still . . . "Perhaps Buddha is a woman."

So you too. Still; quiet; with a smile, ever so slight, at the eyes so that Life will flow into and not by you. And you can gather, as it passes, the essences, the overtones, the tints, the shadows; draw understanding to yourself.

And then you can, when Time is ripe, swoop to your feet—at your full height—at a single gesture.

Ready to go where?

Why . . . Wherever God motions.

1925

LIGHT IN DARK PLACES

Footsteps sounded in the outer hall.

That was the boy!

That was the boy—stepping sporty—tapping hard on his heels and dragging each foot.

That was the boy coming to see Tina.

"What'd he say his name was!" Tina worried.

She would have to speak his name when she opened the door!

Aunt Susie was the only one at home but she would tell Ma when she came home from work, "Some fellow came to see Tina and she ain't knowed his right name! Had to ask him at the door," she'd say.

Ma would get real mad.

And when Ma got real mad, she would beat you with the razor strap.

Aunt Susie was eighty and blind and she sat in the old morris chair by the front room window day and night. Her heart would not let her lie down at night very often.

But Aunt Susie heard every sound that flicked through the three-room flat where she lived with Ma—her niece—and Tina, Ma's youngest daughter.

"She even hear a cat walk by on the back fence, I believe," Ma joked sometimes.

Ma did not joke often. Ma had buried Pa when Tina was six months old and had brought up four children alone in the big city. She went to work at six-thirty in the morning and never got home until eight at night. To work as long as that at the distance from the colored section that Ma had to go each day, left little time for jokes.

Ma was edgy most of the time.

It was not eight yet. Ma was not home. Only Aunt Susie and Tina were there. Now Tina was before the mirror in her cerise rayon taffeta trying to get a frantic peek at her self—trying wildly to remember the name of the boy who was coming.

She really should not have spoken to him last Saturday night when Ma had sent her to the Five and Ten.

But it had been so easy. And besides—all the girls picked up fellows when they felt like it.

You saw a nice guy. You just went over and talked to him. Sometimes it turned out swell. That was how Bessie Jones had met Charlie, her husband. Sometimes it turned out rotten. The police had found Sadie Brown knifed to death in an empty flat over on Hoy Avenue. Folks said she had picked up a guy at a dance and gone out with him instead of going home to the room she shared with her mother.

Anyhow—with Tina it had been easy.

They had both put their feet up on a penny scale at the same time.

They had grinned at each other—bantered a bit—then he had sauntered part of the way home with Tina.

"Be seeing you, baby!" he said as he left. "Maybe next Tuesday!"

Tuesday.

Maybe.

She had remembered that all day in school on Monday and earned a flat failure in every class she was in.

High school was too hard anyhow.

Most of the girls left in their first year to work or to marry. Anything was better than messing with the *Odyssey* and parallelograms and quadratic equations and gym.

Tina meant to get married.

Ma had said she would take Tina out of school if she failed and Tina had been failing consistently and persistently since she had been there.

"I'm going to get married," Tina would say to comfort herself. "Some wise guy—nice looking—look good in his clothes—lots of money!"

The boy in the Five and Ten had worn his clothes with an air that Tina thought was swell.

She would have to have time to uncover the rest.

But now—he was coming along the hall.

His name was—

Tina made one last desperate dive into her mind to find his name.

His knock rattled the door.

"Whatcha sayin', baby," he grinned as Tina opened the door.

He swaggered in, throwing his hat down on the table by the door as he came.

"O.K. Whatcha saying yourself?" Tina responded.

For an answer, the boy pulled up his trousers at the knee and sat down on the sofa. He was chewing gum with a steady click.

Neither he nor Tina spoke for a moment.

His eyes were darting quickly back and forth around the room. He could see that no one was in the kitchen. The bedroom was dark. It would not take long to find out if anyone was in there.

The front room, where he and Tina sat was half dark. He had not seen Aunt Susie's morris chair yet.

He meant to be as bad as he could in the time he was there and he meant to waste no time about it.

"Anything gives Luke a good time!" he always boasted of himself.

It is hard to explain what has produced so many Lukes in the colored race. The teeter-totter on the edge of the decencies of living has filled the colored race with so many Lukes.

There has to be too many young people: too few houses: too many things to long for and too little money to spend freely: too many women: too few men: too many men weak enough to make profit of the fact that they happen to be men: too few women with something in them to make them strong enough to walk over weak men: too much liquor: too many dives: too much street life: too few lovely homes: life from the start—too many people—too few houses.

Too many peasants lured out of cotton and corn fields and jammed down into roach-filled bed-buggy rattle-trap shim-shams of [———] street after street after street of houses fading [———].

Too many neon signs winking promises of an excitement that never was—promising a good time that will never be.

All this slaps a woman—loose.

All this slaps a man loose from every decent bit of manliness.

Walk through an area like the one that Tina and Luke lived in and all the lost thoughts—the lost decencies of living—grasp you at the throat and choke you long after you have passed by.

Are these the things that made Luke what he was?

Luke sat down, hitched his trousers up further at the knee and—satisfied that he and Tina were alone, produced a box of candy.

"Here's something for you, baby!"

"Gee! Yeah! I will! Thanks!" Tina crowed and held out her hands.

"Come and get it!" Luke bantered.

Tina was fifteen in age only. She fluffed out her hair and her skirts and rose.

She reached for the candy.

Luke reached for her.

The box fell to the floor.

"What's that?" Aunt Susie demanded suddenly from her corner by the window. She had been dozing and the noise startled her awake.

Surprise knocked Luke to his feet.

"Aw it's a fellow, Aunt Susie!" Tina's voice was full of scorn and disgust. "She can't see nuthin'!" she whispered to Luke.

"Can *hear* plenty! Who you whispering to!"

"It's—it's—" Tina began weakly.

"It's Luke Jones." The boy became smart again. "Just stop by to see Tina 'bout some—some school lessons."

"You go to the high school too, young man?" Aunt Susie was fully awake and eager to talk now. "Ain't that nice!"

"Yeah!" Luke smothered his impatience in a bored yawn.

"Well—Tina." He rose to his feet. "Be seein' yah!"

Tina was dismayed. "You going? Just got here!"

If old Aunt Susie would go into the bedroom just this once!

"Sure! I gotta run along!" Luke said loudly.

With his head he pantomimed—beckoning Tina to go into the bedroom herself. He kept talking: "Sure! I got right smart studying to do." He walked to the outer door, opened it slightly, reached down quickly and pushed off his oxfords. "So long!" he called aloud and slammed the outside door.

The bedroom door, only a few steps away, Luke gained in one single leap. His feet in their socks made no sound.

Tina gaped amazement at his performance. She had not moved.

Seeing her so stupefied, Luke swaggered a little.

He was a smart guy! He'd show this dumb kid and her blind old lady!

He beckoned again for Tina to enter the room with him indicating that they could close the door that led to the living room.

And Tina was afraid. She was so afraid she even wished Ma would walk in right that minute. What Ma would have done about a man standing in the bedroom door with his shoes off, nobody knows.

Luke was growing angry. This stuff was wasting too much of his time. He could go other places and have a better time.

Who did this fool girl think she was?

He made a fierce gesture—sweeping in toward the room behind him with his hat.

The hat slipped from his fingers and fell with a soft thud to the floor.

Aunt Susie cleared her throat. "Well! Too bad your company had to leave so sudden like, Tina! You, Tina?" she called sharply. "Where you at, gal?"

Tina had to try twice before she could speak. "I'm here, Aunt Susie," she finally managed in a half-croak.

The old lady began a chirruping chatty conversation. "Do look like young men now-days would set a-while and talk with a girl's folks like they used to when I was back home. These uns ain't got no manners in the city, seems to me. What was that fell when y'all were talking?"

"A box of candy." Tina was still frozen afraid.

"Candy! Ain't that nice! I want some but I'll wait a while till after your Ma comes. Candy! I thought it was something else! Funny, I get to feelin' sometimes that anything is liable to happen here in this city! That's why I keep my cane right handy all the time. Somebody might break in here."

"What could you do with any old cane, Aunt Susie?" Tina's voice was full of scorn once more. "You couldn't see nohow to hit nobody!"

"I can't see but I sure can hear!" the old woman countered fiercely. "And look here!" she snatched up her cane, she twisted it, and it came apart.

In the handle of the cane gleamed the three-sided blade of an old-fashioned dagger.

"Lawd! Aunt Susie! Put that thing up! Where you git it," Tina gasped. "I never knew you had nothing like that."

"I ain't meant for you to know it," Aunt Susie told her. "Y'all so foolish you liable to go foolin' with it! I keeps it when I'm settin' here in the dark when y'all are sleepin'! And ef anybody's to make any noise around here what they shouldn't I'd just git up and—"

Aunt Susie sprang to her feet and began to march around the room, thrusting her dagger before her.

She thrust straight at the couch where Luke had been sitting.

"Ooh! Don't, Aunt Susie," Tina whimpered. "You liable to hurt somebody."

"Hurt who! Hurt who! Ain't nobody here is they? That young fellar's gone! I just showing you how I can jab this here thing—all over this place and hit anybody what ain't got no business here!"

She continued her march forward, jabbing and slashing all around her.

Luke, gray-faced, stooped automatically to pick up his hat—snatched it—eeled long the door jamb—across the corner of the living room to the outer door.

One wrench, and Luke was racing down the hall to the street—without the shoes.

"Who's at comin' in? That you Mary?" Aunt Susie paused to ask.

"Now it ain't Ma—it's—it's the wind, Aunt Susie!" Tina lied as glibly as she could.

"The wind! How come the wind gone unlocking doors with safety catches?" Aunt Susie began jabbing and stabbing and moved across the room as she spoke.

Tina saw Luke's oxfords. They were strewn directly in Aunt Susie's path. She would stumble over them in another second.

Tina made a quick grab—took up the shoes and ran to the window. "This here window ain't tight as it might be!" she told Aunt Susie.

Tina pushed up the window quickly and threw Luke's shoes out as far as she could.

Hope he gets 'em, she thought to herself. "Old fool!" she said, suddenly fierce. "I locked the window, Aunt Susie."

Sudden panic gnawed at her: suppose Ma was coming in right now and the shoes had fallen on her?

"I'm going to bed!" Tina became frantic; Ma might be coming even now.

"S'matter? Ain't you going to set up till your Ma comes?"

"No I ain't! I'm going to bed and get out of this old place! Some of these days I'm going to get married and stay away from this old place all the time."

"You going to get married! *To* what—*for* what—*with* what, I'd like to know? You talks the foolishest! And shut that outside door! I heard it open and it ain't never shut yet. Cat or snake must a gone in or out! I ain't heard nothing but I felt something whisk by fast!"

"I tole you it was the wind, Aunt Susie!"

"And I say it somethin 'sides the wind! Anyhow—*shut* it."

Tina banged the outside door and banged the bedroom door behind her.

Aunt Susie stood still a second, then she crossed the room swiftly and went straight to the bedroom door.

She laid her head against the side of the door and listened.

She could hear Tina moving and rustling around the room.

"Tina crying! She mad! That nigger really gone then! Thanks to the Lord!"

She crept back to her seat, and lifted up her cane. She fitted the parts together once again. Then she stuck it behind her in her morris chair.

She sighed and rubbed her hands against her face: "Oh I wish—I wish—" she said to herself and rubbed her eyes fiercely.

Then she sat back in her corner—waiting again.

1941

MERIDEL LESUEUR
(1900–)

Meridel LeSueur's writing focuses on the plight of working-class women in American cities and pioneer women in the Midwest. A radical member of the political left, LeSueur has written fiction, poetry, newspaper articles, history, and autobiographical pieces focusing on the economic, social, and political realities of European immigrants, Native Americans, and working people around the country.

Born in Iowa, LeSueur came from a family dedicated to reform movements. Leaving school at sixteen, LeSueur moved to New York, where she lived in an anarchist commune with activists such as Emma Goldman and Alexander Berkman, and worked as an actress with David Belasco. She also worked as a stuntwoman in Hollywood before turning seriously to writing. She published articles in the Worker, *the* Masses, *and the* San Francisco Call, *and began writing fiction. Her writing after World War I was influenced by the political repressiveness of the times; many of her friends, including Goldman and Berkman, were tried and deported as agitators, and her mother and stepfather were persecuted for being pacifists and socialists. In the late 1920s, LeSueur herself was jailed for participating in a protest against the execution of Sacco and Vanzetti.*

In 1929, after LeSueur had given birth to two daughters, her writing began to focus on themes of mothers and daughters and of women's sexual awakening. Her articles appeared in Vogue, Harper's, Scribner's, *the* Yale Review, *and* Kenyon Review. *Her novel* The Girl *is based on oral and written accounts of women she met during the Depression. In 1940,* Salute to Spring, *a collection of journalism pieces and short stories written during the previous decade, earned her high praise. In 1943 she received a Rockefeller Historical Research Fellowship that enabled her to write* North Star Country, *an impressionistic history of the Midwest.*

In the late 1940s and the 1950s, LeSueur was blacklisted and forced out of jobs. Creative writing students were dissuaded from taking her classes, and most magazines and newspapers would not consider her work. Alfred A. Knopf did accept her children's books on historical figures; however, even these were banned from some libraries and were attacked by red-baiting reviewers. In recent years, LeSueur has been publishing again, and her earlier work is being reprinted. She has returned to poetry as well as novels. Her most recent work emphasizes both the unhappy and the joyful aspects of women's lives and uses mythic themes to show the ties between women and the land.

"Women Are Hungry" is characteristic of LeSueur's passionate writing about the disenfranchised and often forgotten segments of society. The piece also illustrates

the journalistic and fictional techniques she frequently combined to create powerful emotional effects in her work.

WOMEN ARE HUNGRY

Let others sing of the hungry pain of Life,
Let others sing of the hungry pain of love,
I will sing of the hungry pain of hunger.

When you look at the unemployed women and girls you think instantly that there must be some kind of war. The men are gone away from the family; the family is disintegrating; the women try to hold it together, because women have most to do with the vivid life of procreation, food, and shelter. Deprived of their participation in that, they are beggars.

For this reason also they feel want and show it first: poverty is more personal to them than to men. The women looking for jobs or bumming on the road, or that you see waiting for a hand-out from the charities, are already mental cases as well as physical ones. A man can always get drunk, or talk to other men, no matter how broken he is in body and spirit; but a woman, ten to one, will starve alone in a hall bedroom until she is thrown out, and then she will sleep alone in some alley until she is picked up.

When the social fabric begins to give way it gives way from the bottom first. You can look at the bottom and see what is happening and what will continue to happen. The working-class family is going fast. The lower-middle-class family is also going, though not so fast. It is like a landslide. It is like a great chasm opening beneath the feet and swallowing the bottom classes first. The worker who lives from hand to mouth goes first, and then his family goes. The family rots, decays and goes to pieces with the woman standing last, trying to hold it together, and then going too. The man loses his job, cannot find another, then leaves. The older children try to get money, fail, and leave or are taken to the community farms. The mother stays with the little children helped by charity, until they too are sucked under by the diminishing dole and the growing terror.

Where are the women? There is the old woman who has raised her children, and they have all left her now, under the lash of hunger. There is the unattached woman, and the professional one, and the domestic servant. The latter went down two years ago. The professional woman began going down only recently. There are the young school girls—more than a million of them—who were graduated into unemployment two or three years ago. Many of them, particularly those coming from the industrial centers, who never went beyond grammar school, are now hoboes riding on the freights. Their ages run from eight to eighteen. They are the lost children.

You don't see women in bread lines. Statistics make unemployment abstract and not too uncomfortable. The human being is different. To be hungry is different than to count the hungry. There is a whole generation of young girls now who don't remember any boom days and don't believe in any Eldorado, or success, or prosperity. Their thin bones bear witness to a different thing. The women have learned something. Something is seeping into them that is going to make a difference for several generations. Something is happening to them.

II
Old and Young Mothers

We went up three flights of stairs and down a crooked corridor flanked by shut doors. There was not a sound. It was early afternoon. In that house there were about twenty families, and often four lived in one or two rooms, but now everything was pretty quiet. Everybody was taking a nap; the children had not yet come in from school. In the whole building only about five are employed regularly, and about two now and then in the Munsingwear just down the street; the rest are on charity. Six of these families are without men, just holding together like bees, in this huge desolate hive.

Anna, who lives on the top floor, is a cook and supports four people, her mother, sister, and two sons, on her $45 a month. Her man left three years ago to find a job in another city, and at first wrote now and then, and then didn't write at all, and now is lost. Anna comes home every Thursday to see her family, and the rest of the time she does not see them. This is Thursday, and she is home reading out of a Swedish Bible to her mother, who broke her leg last spring.

We listened at the door and then we knocked. The reading stopped. Anna opened the door. Leaning over a round table sat her old mother, her sister, her two blonde sons, and Mrs. Rose. Mrs. Rose is an elderly woman who has raised six tubercular children whose whereabouts she has not known for four years, since they were out of jobs. One was in a foundry in Pittsburgh, another on a wheat ranch in Montana. The other four were on the bum for a while and sometimes wrote her, but now they do not write. Mrs. Rose tries to support herself getting jobs as a housekeeper but has a hard time. Either she doesn't get paid at all or the man tries to sleep with her. She has hair that was hennaed a long time ago. She is lean and bitter and has a great deal of hate in her. She has nothing to do now, so she comes to talk to Anna and her mother in the afternoon and stays to eat there.

Many men have been killed making America. Many were killed laying the railroad, making docks, coal mines, felling the lumber, blasting the land. There were a lot of widows in the last century left to support their children with their physical labor. Everyone remembers many such women even in one small town. They were the women who took in washing, who scrubbed office buildings at nights, or made the party dresses for the merchants' wives and daughters. Everyone remembers many such women and there are many who live in nobody's memory at all.

Anna's mother is such a woman. She had seven children, and her man was killed on the docks in Duluth while she was raising her children on the sand bar. After that she supported them herself, scrubbing office buildings every night until five-thirty. She sent them all through high-school, because in America education would lift them out of the physical labor of her class. Two of her sons were killed riding back and forth from coast to coast on the freight cars. Only one has a little property, a farm, but it is mortgaged and he is likely to lose it at any time now.

They all live in two attic rooms. You can see over the roofs of the town.

They begin to talk, as everyone does, of how to live. It is all nip and tuck. They are used to it, but you never get quite used to being trapped. At any time you may look up with amazement and see that you are trapped. "I've worked all my life," Anna's mother says, "with these arms and hands and sent seven children through high-school and now I can't get enough to eat."

The women all look at one another. The youngest boy, about four, is playing on the floor. The other boy is reading. They all look at the little boy, who looks like his father who was swallowed up, just as if some big crack had opened and swallowed him, or as if a war had devoured him whole. Mrs. Rose has lost all her children like that now. They all seem to be looking at something. Anna gets up to make supper of a sort.

"A person can't get paid nowadays for what a person does," Mrs. Rose says, and she begins telling about the last place she was working in, and the man was a widower with four children, and she worked like a dog for three months without any pay, and bacon rinds cooked with potato peelings most of the time because the garden had burnt up in the sun; and then she couldn't get a cent, not a red cent, and so now she is without work at all, and the cancer growing inside her, and nothing to show for her life and she might as well die.

Anna's mother sits with her broad arms over her stomach. She is full of words about it and pounding the Bible and saying she will write a letter to the President. "It's all in the Bible," she shouts, the tears going down her wrinkled face. "You cannot live by bread alone." She looks at the little boy again. "Anna, we left some milk for him. There will be a glass left. What are you going to feed him?" she cries. "He has got to have milk. You can't make bones with just bread. Everybody knows he has got to have milk."

The women all look at the child. Anna stops by the stove looking at the child. You can't feed a child cream tomorrow to make up for his not having milk today. They know that. Anna goes over and picks him up. It's really to feel his ribs and his legs.

It's hot in the room, all the heat goes up to the attic, and it's turned a bit warm out so they have left the door open, and women keep going by slowly in the hall to the lavatory. They have been going by heavily in the dark hall with swollen faces.

"There are four pregnant women in this attic," Anna's mother says bitterly. "If they knew . . . if they knew . . . they would cut their children out with a butcher knife. . . ."

"Mother!" Anna says. "Sh! they will hear. . . ."

"Better to hear it now than later, and only one has a man working now and then only for the city, and there hasn't been any snow yet this winter to speak of and besides the city is going broke and can't hire so many men."

"What do they do then?"

"Well, when you are going to have a baby you have got to have it. You go ahead and have it, whether a war is going on or not you go right ahead. They got so many women now having babies at the city hospital they only keep them eight days now. The better ones they turn out sooner. They got to have room. It's got so a woman can't have a baby. It's got so a woman is crazy to have a baby."

The other women look at her in fright. The child keeps on playing. Another pregnant woman goes slowly looming in the dark. Anna looks wildly at her two blonde boys. She gives her mother a cup of hot water with milk in it and sugar. The old lady cries pounding the Bible. "It says it all here. Under your own tree . . . it says. Every laborer is worthy of his hire. Every man should be under his own tree and should be paid at sundown. . . ."

Nobody knows what the poor suffer just for bread and burial. Nobody knows about it. Nobody has told about it. Nobody can know about how it feels unless you have been in it, the work there is, just for bread and burial.

The women look at one another. The child plays on the floor, never showing his bright face, his yellow hair shining. The snow keeps falling very softly outside the window.

We all seem to be sitting within some condition that we cannot get out of. Everyone is bright and ready for living and then cannot live.

Pretty soon it gets darker and people begin to come in, doors slam below and the smell of food comes up, and it smells terribly good when you know how hard it is to get, how it takes a whole life and all the energy of a man or a woman to get it for the born and the unborn and the dying, and how it takes some kind of splendid courage to still have children to keep alive when it is the way it is.

The winter evening settles slowly and the snow falls sadly.

The two bitter women tell about their lives in a loud voice and we listen, and something keeps going on and on, something that is killing us all and that nobody seems to stop.

You keep feeling how rich everything is except the thing of making a living. You feel how rich these women are in their necessity to have rich experience and then how they are crippled in their bright living, having too hard a world in which to get bread for the living and burial for the dead.

"I might have been a great singer," Anna's mother suddenly says softly. "Everyone said I might have been a great singer when I sang at Christmas in Sweden and everyone in Stockholm stopped on their way to listen. . . ."

"Is this all the milk?" Anna says pouring out half a glass.

"All the milk," the old woman screams. "My God, everybody knows you can't make bones out of water, doesn't everybody know that you can't make bones out of water? I took that woman next door a little milk. You can't make bones in her without something to eat, can you? Doesn't everybody in the world know that, you can't make bones, a woman can't make bones without the stuff to make it in her? . . ."

"Mama, mama, sit down," Anna cries. "Sit down, mama. Drink your pink tea, mama."

The woman next door, far gone in pregnancy, comes in. "Look, Anna, it is snowing. There will be some shoveling to do."

All the women turn to look at the feathery flakes drifting down. It will have to snow like this a long time before it makes any shoveling.

Milk went up two cents today. Milk is dearer.

III
Farm Girl

Bernice lives in an old block building that was condemned by the city long ago, but is now full to the brim with people because you can get a room for two and three dollars a month. Everyone in the building is on charity. Bernice has been on charity for two years now. She no longer looks for a job. She looked steadily for a job until about six months ago and then she stopped looking. She has been all her life working in other people's kitchens. She is pretty deaf now from hanging out wet clothes in the cold. She doesn't care about that kind of work any more even if she could get it. For the first time in her life since the depression she has had leisure to enjoy herself and find out about things, and have a bit of pleasure. She runs around the streets now with other girls, sometimes with a man, having a good time, talking, laughing, going to picture shows, dancing sometimes when she can pick up a guy.

Bernice is quite moral, because she is afraid of the hazard of being unmoral. She is afraid of what men do, she knows how men are, that you can't trust them a moment and they get you into trouble. Her friend Grace makes that plain. Grace is always in trouble with men, always trying to get out of trouble. Bernice wants to get along and keep out of trouble. Her life has narrowed itself down, like a wary animal's, keeping herself out of trouble and having the best time she can.

The police are pretty hard on a lone girl. When the police see you wandering they always think you are bad if you are a girl. Bernice and her kind are simply hungry. But the police wouldn't think you were wandering out of many kinds of hunger.

No, if you are a girl you are either good or bad and that is all there is to it.

Next to Bernice lives her girl friend Mabel, who has to keep pretty clever, too, to keep the charities from running her into Faribault. They want to have her sterilized and put into the home for girls at Faribault. Mabel is from a farm in Minnesota; she likes men pretty well and isn't clever keeping herself out of trouble. Last year she had a baby, so of course all the charities are down on her, and if any of the workers or the police see her talking to a fellow they are right after her. She is pretty and likes fellows so it is kind of hard on her. A girl has to live, she only has one life.

Mabel has worked in the five-and-ten since she was fourteen and lied about her age. When she had her baby they gave her an intelligence test when she was scared stiff anyway, and it was about forests and she has never seen more than one tree at a time in her life, just growing between the sidewalk and the curb.

Of course, she failed pretty thoroughly, because she was shaking like a leaf all the time because of fright about having a baby. If they had asked her how a girl wolf gets by in a city, where to get the best hand-outs, how to catch a guy that will take you to a show maybe, and a feed after, and how to get away without giving him anything, she would have passed one hundred percent. They asked her about the wrong kind of jungle.

Mabel hasn't worked for three years. She doesn't look for work any more either, and they all refuse to work in women's kitchens in this new arrangement of working for room and board that lets rich women save a lot on their help so they can go to Miami during the winter. They are all on to that. This old block is honeycombed with lone girls like this, wolf girls who get along. There are girls in the building who have been machine operators, trimmers, pressers, button sewers. They all get five dollars' worth of groceries a month from the charities. Sometimes they get an order of Pillsbury's best flour and practice making fancy cakes that are advertised in the ladies' journals, and then they eat cake for a week and have nothing the next three weeks, but it is worth it.

This is incomprehensible to the charity virgins. They can't understand either why the girls leave those stinking holes where they live and go to a picture show whenever they can. They try to go to as many shows as they can. The rooms are heated only by stoves. The charities give them a little wood or coal. The rooms are always cold and infested by the odors of all the foul humanity that has lived in them since 1850, and, besides, cockroaches, bed bugs and lice and enough rats to keep all the cats they can get very fat.

The girls live a great deal on hand-outs from restaurants. Sometimes they beg clear to the other side of town until they get some dish that touches their fancy. Before Mabel's baby was born she had a hankering for spice cakes, and they used to walk from restaurant to restaurant turning down chicken dinners and asking for spice cakes.

Sometimes a man gets sweet on them for a while and if he has a job gives them money now and then. They always manage somehow or other to have a good hat and a bright scarf. They rummage around at the Salvation Army store and fix themselves up for about a quarter. It is pretty marvelous how vivid life stays in a woman, how she always washes out her socks, and looks pretty clean and has some powder for her nose, no matter how pinched she is and how miserable. Women sometimes have a kind of indestructible lust for living in them that is pretty hard to douse.

But they are now seeing something pretty clearly. Keep alone as much as you can, look out for yourself. Keep away from men and marriage, because there isn't anything in it for a girl but a horde of children to be left with. Lie low, get along, beg, borrow or steal, go a lone wolf's way.

It is a philosophy of war and famine. They stay strong and alive and terrible with it. They are like wolves in a jungle, not even traveling in a pack. They sit for hours in wash-rooms, looking, waiting.

Their families are gone. They are alone now. Let the State take care of them. The State is their only family now and they look to it. They have transferred even the quarrels with their families to the charities and the State. They complain lovingly and bitterly about the food they get, the coal, the care at the clinics. They adore going to the clinics; they enjoy the sensation of importance that they have, as if for a moment the State cared passionately for their health.

The boys may still think they are going to be successful, that they are going to step into the big guys' shoes, but there is something funny about the girls. They are thrown up, lost from all the folkways for women, derelict from the family, from every human hunger except the one for bread.

They talk and they say only one thing, "I ain't going to have nothing to do with any of it. I ain't going to have nothing to do with guys. I'll have a time. I want what I want. I'll drink when I like it and have a time but no guys for me. I ain't going to work for nothing either. I ain't going to slave for nothing. I ain't going to do nothing."

So there it is, a strike. They understand something that is going to make a difference for a generation or two. They are on strike. They aren't going to have anything to do with it. They don't like the terms, so they aren't having any of it, and it will make a difference to all our living for a long time.

IV
Teacher

To get any relief work, if you are a teacher, and haven't had any work for a couple of years and have spent all your savings and let your insurance go and pawned everything you own, you have to go to the Board that is handling the relief work for teachers and *prove* to them that you are destitute. You not only have to be destitute but you have to prove it. They are both hard but the last is harder.

Nancy Sanderson's father had been a skilled glass blower. He had made pretty good money in his time before they invented a machine to take the place of the man. They lived pretty well and they always thought they were going to find some splendid new opportunity and go into business for themselves and be smart merchants and have the best house in town and servants. He educated all his six children because he knew that education was a thing that could get you on in America and anyone who had it could get what he wanted. So his four girls were school teachers and his two sons he educated to be engineers, and now they are all out of jobs. Old Sanderson fortunately is dead, but his daughters and his sons are not dead, except one daughter who is now dead because she chose it.

To prove you are destitute you have to go to the State House after having sent your application in before so it would be there ahead of you and everybody would know thoroughly about your being destitute, and then you have to put on your best things and go up there and see if they will give you one of those night classes for the unemployed, to teach. They are going to have classes for the unemployed, for adults, to keep up their ambition in this trying time; besides, it will employ a few teachers who, if they work steadily, will make as much as fifty dollars a month. Anyway, each State has appropriated so much money for this relief work. Some say it is a plan that comes from the educators who are afraid that they are not going to be supported so bountifully in the future, and are trying to make themselves important in the crisis. Some people wonder who is going to pay for it all anyway, whether the teachers will spend enough to put it back where it is taken out. Well, there is a lot of speculation, but probably there is a great deal too in the mind of a girl like Nancy Sanderson going up toward the State House on a frosty morning in a light spring suit to prove she is destitute.

She is alone, and it is hard for a lone woman to get much attention from the charities. She spent the last of her money last spring, all but about fifty dollars, and she does not know how she has been living. She has some friends who do not dream how destitute she has been. They ask her for dinner now and then but she eats so much, as you do when you are hungry, that it generally makes her sick afterwards. Well, there are ways of doing when you are destitute, and you get by some way and you don't know how you do it. A person can see you stand there and you look all right, but of course you have on quite a bit of rouge, but still you don't look starving or anything out of the usual and at the same time you may feel your knees dropping down and the greatest terror in the pit of your stomach. Lack of food is the best thing to give you terror. And, of course, Nancy's family always expected to get ahead, to better themselves. Never for a moment did they expect this.

So you feel very terrible going up to the capitol office building. You've gone up there a lot of times to get a position but that is different. Then you had your Ph.D. and your fur coat and the knowledge that you were going to get on in the world, and you didn't have to watch to see that your elbows did not come through and that your last pair of silk stockings did not spring into a run. The great building with the chariot of horses high above looks terrifying and you feel guilty, as if you had failed somehow and it must be your own fault.

You walk around a long time before you go in and then you go in and up the elevator without thinking and down the long hallway where women who have jobs are working, and you know who they are, like yourself nice girls who work very hard and save for a fur coat and to put some linen by in case of a wedding. And they are always looking to better themselves, too, in some mystical and obscure way that seldom comes about. A pang goes through you for what has happened to women.

There is a bench outside the door where people wait. The bench is full of rather thin but rouged women, waiting. You stand against the wall. Someone is in the office talking to the man who is in charge and there is a stenographer who goes to the huge file and hands him the application he wants.

You stand there. Perhaps there will be too many applications before yours. When you get in a big machine like this office building, then you don't think. You are in the machine. It can do what it likes. How many human lives are filed in a building like that! The woman in the office says desperately, "Twelve hundred new applications for work relief today . . ."

"Good Lord," the man says. He goes on talking in a loud desperate voice to the applicant who is a man and stands doggedly, twisting his cap and trying to answer. You can tell from the voices of both men that they are both caught in something, strained to the breaking point. The man who is asking the questions is part of a machine, too. He has to answer to someone higher up. "Well, you see," he shouts too loud, "you've got to answer these questions. You've got to answer them. You see, we'll give some of this work to someone who has a car, or a bank account, or owns a house, and then we'll be in dutch. . . ." The other man tries to answer in a low voice so no one will hear. He has had dreams, too. He has thought to have some power of his own, like any other man. . . . Then another and another, all squirming, answering in low voices and going away and the man talking more shrilly.

Nancy Sanderson sat down, biting her teeth together, holding her wet hands tight in her lap. She looked all right. To look at her you would have thought she was all right. But hunger tears through you like a locomotive. You can hear your own heart like a trip hammer. You can hear your own blood in your ears like a cataract and you can't hear anything else. You are separated by your tremendous hunger from the ordinary world as if by a tragedy. You can't see what is happening. You can't hear what is being said.

The man was going over her application, trying to make it more definite. He was trying to be patient.

"You see, to get this, you have to prove absolute destitution."

"Yes," she said, wetting her tongue. When you don't eat the saliva begins to dry up in your mouth.

"Do you understand that?"

"Yes, I understand," she said again.

"Well, look here, you say you had fifty dollars left from your savings in the spring. Have you still got that?"

Where was that gone, fifty dollars? Why, fifty dollars doesn't last long.

"No, then what have you been living on? You must have been living on something. How have you been living?"

"I don't know," she cried in agony, and she felt all the starved blood rise and push against her throat like a million crying voices, but she did not cry out and she knew she must not cry because everyone would be embarrassed and they were all embarrassed already, as if they could not help something that was happening and they all felt ashamed and embarrassed.

"What have you been living on since?" the man suddenly shouted.

Everyone looked up, faces looking up from all around.

"I don't know," she barely said, and knowing all of them there squirming like worms when you uncover them.

"You've got to prove it, don't you understand that, you've got to prove it. . . ." The man seemed to be wild and shouting. "You've got to prove it."

She stood up amidst the eyes and saw the long corridor stretching out. She got up and started to walk as if she stepped among fetid and rotting bones and empty eye sockets. A silence followed her, and the people spoke to her in the common silence of hunger.

The manager got up and took a few steps after her, his pencil held out. "Wait," he said. "Perhaps something can be arranged. . . ." It sounded like a speech in a dream.

She went on down the white corridor so clean and white and warm, down into the rich lobby, out into the rich country with the fall light like gold upon the faces of the hungry people, and the horses of state gleaming and roaring into the sky, and she walked down past the nigger shanties and the Jewish tenements and people saw her walking and she looked all right so they paid no attention until she was dead.

When she came to the high bridge she let herself ease off into the air that was so sweet, as if you might skip winter.

They found her and took her to the morgue and of course they knew it was suicide.

V
Moon Bums

The winter moon was hanging down over the stacks of the city. We were to meet down by the fish hatchery where the freights slowed down at the switches to be shunted with the empties. The two girl bums, Fran and Ethel, were taking off for the South. This country is no place to spend the winter, so they were hopping off. I went down past the jungle, down into the thicket, across the tracks to the cliff side where they are hollowed out below into small caves. I saw a tiny fire low down in the cliff and somebody hallooed, "Hey!"

I stooped down and crawled in. They were leaning over a small fire of smoking twigs. They both had on overalls and a lot of sweaters but they were blue from the cold and Ethel's scar on her cheek looked bad. She had come in from Seattle with that cut festering. She had let go of the grab irons and tried to alight running, but her knees had buckled and her face ploughed through the gravel along the tracks. It left a pretty bad cut. It was hard getting some hospital to fix it. You have to be pretty sick if you are a bum before they'll take you in. They shunt you on some place else for repairs. These kids aren't allowed more than twenty-four hours in each place if anybody knows it.

I met up with them just after they landed here from Seattle. I heard a lot of tales from them. They had been traveling and mooching around the country for a year and a half. They were old hands. They knew their onions. They might have been anywhere from sixteen to eighteen. They look like a thousand girls, they have a thousand names. Workers' kids, they have graduated from poverty, sweat shops, machines, diets of pigs' feet, stale hamburger and old bread.

Fran worked in a shirt factory since she was twelve at $1.97 for a fifty-five-hour week. Ethel is younger, and she went to eight grades in school and then worked as a learner in Connecticut where they have young girls work for a dime a week learning, and then most of them are fired when they learn and others are hired. Her family strung safety pins on a wire at night for awhile and then set out in an old car to make the canneries, but they soon separated; the father and mother stayed in a town in Carolina with the three younger children, and the older ones set out on their own. When Ethel made the town last summer the family were gone and nobody had heard of them for six months, so that's out now. She's on her own now for sure.

The South-bound refrigerator empties aren't due for half an hour. We all squat down and hold out our hands. It is bitter cold. I can see the new moon hanging just outside the cave.

"Boy, well we're off again," Fran says. Fran is a thin eerie-looking girl. Kind of a Botticelli-looking girl, with the stone cave behind her and her delicate face on the thin drooping body. But she's wiry, and she told me their life was better than the life in a factory, that they were healthier really.

"Yeah, we're off," Ethel says. She can't talk very well because of the long gash on her cheek. It will make a scar.

"Where are you bound?"

"Boy, I don't know where, I don't know where this car goes. I only know it's headed South and that's enough for me." She swore like a sailor about the cold.

We sat listening to the trains coming up the grade and the wind tearing around the rock like a sea. We looked at one another. We probably never would see one another again. It was like it is in a war.

They had told me a lot of tales, wonderful and terrible. Last winter they had lived in dry goods boxes outside of Chicago with two fellows who were carpenters and made the shacks, and the girls did the cooking and the fellows did the foraging. They didn't live with the men because they didn't want to. The men were awfully homely, so they didn't want to. They just took care of the house and the men did the mooching, because a man isn't picked up in the city like a girl is. A girl is always considered a moral culprit when she begs in the city, and she is sterilized or sent away to a farm or a home which she hates.

You have to look out for this. In the summer this causes a curious return to an old matriarchy. The girls gang up and live in the jungles and the boys do the mooching and the foraging, and the girls keep the jungles clean and cook the mulligan and make the boys wash, and sometimes they sleep together. They warm each other. But there is principally one kind of hunger, the hunger for bread. There isn't much prostitution because there is no money. The girls want to keep away from pregnancy and disease.

"It ain't honey and pie," Fran told me. "You get slapped and kicked around plenty and it's root, hog, or die. A girl don't have it any worse than a boy, not as bad maybe, because there is some terrible homos on the road, but it's bad. You got to roost anywhere and be ready to high tail it any old time."

Now they were high tailing it again. The long, long hoot of the train coming up the grade came right into the low cave. "There she is," Ethel said, her eyes dilating, and she reached nervously for her bundle. "I get kind of nervous when I hear that. I never get used to it. My stomach gives right away."

"With that feed in you," Fran said. "We got all the leavings at the fort. Tasted all right but you never can tell about garbage. We ate garbage in Spokane and our stomachs have been yelling."

We listened to the long long hoot. "She takes her time coming up the grade," Fran said.

How did she know? Had she been in Minneapolis before?

"Sure I been here," she said looking at me. "I don't know when. I been so many places, but I remember these caves and the long grade with the bullengine hooting like that for about ten minutes. We might as well stay inside out of that wind."

I felt queer. I wanted to make them stay. But the statistics kept going through my head . . . one million vagrant children. . . . The long wail of the engine came nearer. The two girls got up. Fran stepped on the fire. The young moon hung brighter.

Ethel had told me, "No more jobs for me. There's nothing to it, working your guts out. My family did it and look at them, no better than if they'd been on the bum."

Fran said, "No marrying for me and our kind. A fellow can't get a job now the way I see it. No kids for me when I see what happens to them. I should stand around like my mother and see my kids thin as rails and going up in a puff of smoke every winter, all that blood and work going up. There's nothing in it. . . ."

The ground began to shake as if it were about to crack open and swallow us. We ran out into the cold wind. The ground shook more. The blackness before us seemed to gather and mount. Number 29 was coming up the hard grade along the Mississippi. Fran and Ethel stood with their bundles. They looked like twigs as the light from the engine swathed over them. They looked like nothing.

"Fran . . . Ethel . . .," I screamed. The black engine came in a blast and forced us back against the cliff for a moment, then passed, and we all ran forward together as if released. Fran and Ethel were shouting something at me. I could see their mouths and their ghastly grins, trying to smile at me. Ethel went ahead waving her bundle, the gash showing livid down her cheek. I shouted at them but they could not have heard. They were shouting back at me, but I could only feel the ground shake and the ghostly force of the wind. I ran after them as if some ghastly suction were taking me in too.

The train stopped banging back upon itself . . . the engine let out a great hiss. The two girls scuttled like mice through the couplings between the cars and I ran down looking through every space, but I couldn't see them any more. I read the lettering . . . Golden California . . . Seedless . . . Chicago . . . Omaha.

I didn't see them any more. I shall never see them any more.

1940

KAY BOYLE
(1903–)

Kay Boyle's novels, poems, and, particularly, short stories have received literary awards over the course of five decades. A well-known figure in the expatriate American community in Paris during the 1920s and 1930s, Boyle excelled as a complex crafter of words. She has always used her writing to fight injustice. Her works have ranged in subject matter from the spread of fascism in Europe in the 1930s to the civil rights and antiwar movements in the United States of the 1960s and 1970s.

Born to a wealthy family in Minnesota, Boyle traveled extensively in her youth and was introduced by her mother and grandmother to the radical thought and writing of figures such as Gertrude Stein and James Joyce. Although she never attained a college degree, Boyle attended the Conservatory of Music in Cincinnati and the Ohio Mechanics Institute before working her way through secretarial school. Moving to New York, Boyle worked first at Vogue *magazine and then at* Broom, *where she met many of the well-known writers of her day. Her first poems were published in* Broom *and* Contact, *and her first book of short stories appeared in 1929.*

Much of Boyle's most important work appeared in the 1930s in publications such as Harper's, Scribner's, *and* The New Yorker. *After World War II, Boyle wrote for* The Nation *and as a foreign correspondent for* The New Yorker. *However, during the McCarthy era, her work was rejected by many prominent publications, and her husband was dismissed from the State Department.*

In the early 1960s, her name cleared, she received her second Guggenheim Fellowship and accepted a teaching position at San Francisco State University and then at Eastern Washington State University. In 1968, she published her edition of Robert McAlmon's memoirs, Being Geniuses Together, *with additional chapters of her own, recapturing the stories of the "lost generation" of expatriate Americans in Paris. Her 1975 novel* The Underground Woman *focuses on her arrests for demonstrating against U.S. involvement in the Vietnam War. In 1980 she received a Senior Fellowship for Literature from the National Endowment for the Arts. She is a member of the American Academy of Arts and Letters.*

In 1949, Boyle wrote: "I feel guilt for every act of oppression that has been committed in my time, and the older I grow the more I want to write about those commonplace things that we all accept which lead to acts and eventually to states of official oppression." For Boyle, being a writer is being a crusader. When asked by the San Francisco Chronicle *to submit a sketch of how she saw herself, Boyle sketched herself as a winged angel—carrying a bomb in each hand.*

Many of Kay Boyle's stories focus on the discovery and loss of love. In "Winter Night," we meet a girl and an old woman whose very different experiences have led to similar pain and help create a friendship between them.

WINTER NIGHT

There is a time of apprehension which begins with the beginning of darkness, and to which only the speech of love can lend security. It is there, in abeyance, at the end of every day, not urgent enough to be given the name of fear but rather of concern for how the hours are to be reprieved from fear, and those who have forgotten how it was when they were children can remember nothing of this. It may begin around five o'clock on a winter afternoon when the light outside is dying in the windows. At that hour the New York apartment in which Felicia lived was filled with shadows, and the little girl would wait alone in the living room, looking out at the winter-stripped trees that stood black in the park against the isolated ovals of unclean snow. Now it was January, and the day had been a cold one; the water of the artificial lake was frozen fast, but because of the cold and the coming darkness, the skaters had ceased to move across its surface. The street that lay between the park and the apartment house was wide, and the two-way streams of cars and busses, some with their headlamps already shining, advanced and halted, halted and poured swiftly on to the tempo of the traffic signals' altering lights. The time of apprehension had set in, and Felicia, who was seven, stood at the window in the evening and waited before she asked the question. When the signals below would change from red to green again, or when the double-decker bus would turn the corner below, she would ask it. The words of it were already there, tentative in her mouth, when the answer came from the far end of the hall.

"Your mother," said the voice among the sound of kitchen things, "she telephoned up before you came in from nursery school. She won't be back in time for supper. I was to tell you a sitter was coming in from the sitting parents' place."

Felicia turned back from the window into the obscurity of the living room, and she looked toward the open door, and into the hall beyond it where the light from the kitchen fell in a clear yellow angle across the wall and onto the strip of carpet. Her hands were cold, and she put them in her jacket pockets as she walked carefully across the living-room rug and stopped at the edge of light.

"Will she be home late?" she said.

For a moment there was the sound of water running in the kitchen, a long way away, and then the sound of the water ceased, and the high, Southern voice went on:

"She'll come home when she gets ready to come home. That's all I have to say. If she wants to spend two dollars and fifty cents and ten cents' carfare on top of that three or four nights out of the week for a sitting parent to come in here and sit, it's her own business. It certainly ain't nothing to do with you or me. She makes her money, just like the rest of us does. She works all day down there in the office, or whatever it is, just like the rest of us works, and she's entitled to spend her money like she wants to spend it. There's no law in the world against buying your own freedom. Your mother and me, we're just buying our own freedom, that's all we're doing. And we're not doing nobody no harm."

"Do you know who she's having supper with?" said Felicia from the edge of dark. There was one more step to take, and then she would be standing in the light that fell on the strip of carpet, but she did not take the step.

"Do I know who she's having supper with?" the voice cried out in what might have been derision, and there was the sound of dishes striking the metal ribs of the drainboard by the sink. "Maybe it's Mr. Van Johnson, or Mr. Frank Sinatra, or maybe it's just the Duke of Wincers for the evening. All I know is you're having soft-boiled egg and spinach and applesauce for supper, and you're going to have it quick now because the time is getting away."

The voice from the kitchen had no name. It was as variable as the faces and figures of the women who came and sat in the evenings. Month by month the voice in the kitchen altered to another voice, and the sitting parents were no more than lonely aunts of an evening or two who sometimes returned and sometimes did not to this apartment in which they had sat before. Nobody stayed anywhere very long any more, Felicia's mother told her. It was part of the time in which you lived, and part of the life of the city, but when the fathers came back, all this would be miraculously changed. Perhaps you would live in a house again, a small one, with fir trees on either side of the short brick walk, and Father would drive up every night from the station just after darkness set in. When Felicia thought of this, she stepped quickly into the clear angle of light, and she left the dark of the living room behind her and ran softly down the hall.

The drop-leaf table stood in the kitchen between the refrigerator and the sink, and Felicia sat down at the place that was set. The voice at the sink was speaking still, and while Felicia ate it did not cease to speak until the bell of the front door rang abruptly. The girl walked around the table and went down the hall, wiping her dark palms in her apron, and, from the drop-leaf table, Felicia watched her step from the angle of light into darkness and open the door.

"You put in an early appearance," the girl said, and the woman who had rung the bell came into the hall. The door closed behind her, and the girl showed her into the living room, and lit the lamp on the bookcase, and the shadows were suddenly bleached away. But when the girl turned, the woman turned from the living room too and followed her, humbly and in silence, to the threshold of the kitchen. "Sometimes they keep me standing around waiting after it's time for me to be getting on home, the sitting parents do," the girl said, and she picked up the last two dishes from the table and put them in the sink. The woman who stood in the doorway was a small woman, and when she undid the white silk scarf from around her head, Felicia saw that her hair was black. She wore it parted in the middle, and it had not been cut, but was drawn back loosely into a knot behind her head. She had very clean white gloves on, and her face was pale, and there was a look of sorrow in her soft black eyes. "Sometimes I have to stand out there in the hall with my hat and coat on, waiting for the sitting parents to turn up," the girl said, and, as she turned on the water in the sink, the contempt she had for them hung on the kitchen air. "But you're ahead of time," she said, and she held the dishes, first one and then the other, under the flow of steaming water.

The woman in the doorway wore a neat black coat, not a new-looking coat, and it had no fur on it, but it had a smooth velvet collar and velvet lapels. She did not move, or smile, and she gave no sign that she had heard the girl speaking above the sound of water at the sink. She simply stood looking at Felicia, who sat at the table with the milk in her glass not finished yet.

"Are you the child?" she said at last, and her voice was low, and the pronunciation of the words a little strange.

"Yes, this here's Felicia," the girl said, and the dark hands dried the dishes and put them away. "You drink up your milk quick now, Felicia, so's I can rinse your glass."

"I will wash the glass," said the woman. "I would like to wash the glass for her," and Felicia sat looking across the table at the face in the doorway that was filled with such unspoken grief. "I will wash the glass for her and clean off the table," the woman was saying quietly. "When the child is finished, she will show me where her night things are."

"The others, they wouldn't do anything like that," the girl said, and she hung the dishcloth over the rack. "They wouldn't put their hand to housework, the sitting parents. That's where they got the name for them," she said.

Whenever the front door closed behind the girl in the evening, it would usually be that the sitting parent who was there would take up a book of fairy stories and read aloud for a while to Felicia; or else would settle herself in the big chair in the living room and begin to tell the words of a story in drowsiness to her, while Felicia took off her clothes in the bedroom, and folded them, and put her pajamas on, and brushed her teeth, and did her hair. But this time, that was not the way it happened. Instead, the woman sat down on the other chair at the kitchen table, and she began at once to speak, not of good fairies or bad, or of animals endowed with human speech, but to speak quietly, in spite of the eagerness behind her words, of a thing that seemed of singular importance to her.

"It is strange that I should have been sent here tonight," she said, her eyes moving slowly from feature to feature of Felicia's face, "for you look like a child that I knew once, and this is the anniversary of that child."

"Did she have hair like mine?" Felicia asked quickly, and she did not keep her eyes fixed on the unfinished glass of milk in shyness any more.

"Yes, she did. She had hair like yours," said the woman, and her glance paused for a moment on the locks which fell straight and thick on the shoulders of Felicia's dress. It may have been that she thought to stretch out her hand and touch the ends of Felicia's hair, for her fingers stirred as they lay clasped together on the table, and then they relapsed into passivity again. "But it is not the hair alone, it is the delicacy of your face, too, and your eyes the same, filled with the same spring lilac color," the woman said, pronouncing the words carefully. "She had little coats of golden fur on her arms and legs," she said, "and when we were closed up there, the lot of us in the cold, I used to make her laugh when I told her that the fur that was so pretty, like a little fawn's skin on her arms, would always help to keep her warm."

"And did it keep her warm?" asked Felicia, and she gave a little jerk of laughter as she looked down at her own legs hanging under the table, with the bare calves thin and covered with a down of hair.

"It did not keep her warm enough," the woman said, and now the mask of grief had come back upon her face. "So we used to take everything we could spare from ourselves, and we would sew them into cloaks and other kinds of garments for her and for the other children. . . ."

"Was it a school?" said Felicia when the woman's voice had ceased to speak.

"No," said the woman softly, "it was not a school, but still there were a lot of children there. It was a camp—that was the name the place had; it was a camp. It was a place where they put people until they could decide what was to be done with them." She sat with her hands clasped, silent a moment, looking at Felicia. "That little dress you have on," she said, not saying the words to anybody, scarcely saying them aloud. "Oh, she would have liked that little dress, the little buttons shaped like hearts, and the white collar—"

"I have four school dresses," Felicia said. "I'll show them to you. How many dresses did she have?"

"Well, there, you see, there in the camp," said the woman, "she did not have any dresses except the little skirt and the pullover. That was all she had. She had brought just a handkerchief of her belongings with her, like everybody else—just enough for three days away from home was what they told us, so she did not have enough to last the winter. But she had her ballet slippers," the woman said, and her clasped fingers did not move. "She had brought them because she thought during her three days away from home she would have the time to practice her ballet."

"I've been to the ballet," Felicia said suddenly, and she said it so eagerly that she stuttered a little as the words came out of her mouth. She slipped quickly down from the chair and went around the table to where the woman sat. Then she took one of the woman's hands away from the other that held it fast, and she pulled her toward the door. "Come into the living room and

I'll do a pirouette for you," she said, and then she stopped speaking, her eyes halted on the woman's face. "Did she—did the little girl—could she do a pirouette very well?" she said.

"Yes, she could. At first she could," said the woman, and Felicia felt uneasy now at the sound of sorrow in her words. "But after that she was hungry. She was hungry all winter," she said in a low voice. "We were all hungry, but the children were the hungriest. Even now," she said, and her voice went suddenly savage, "when I see milk like that, clean, fresh milk standing in a glass, I want to cry out loud, I want to beat my hands on the table, because it did not have to be . . ." She had drawn her fingers abruptly away from Felicia now, and Felicia stood before her, cast off, forlorn, alone again in the time of apprehension. "That was three years ago," the woman was saying, and one hand was lifted, as in weariness, to shade her face. "It was somewhere else, it was in another country," she said, and behind her hand her eyes were turned upon the substance of a world in which Felicia had played no part.

"Did—did the little girl cry when she was hungry?" Felicia asked, and the woman shook her head.

"Sometimes she cried," she said, "but not very much. She was very quiet. One night when she heard the other children crying, she said to me, 'You know, they are not crying because they want something to eat. They are crying because their mothers have gone away.'"

"Did the mothers have to go out to supper?" Felicia asked, and she watched the woman's face for the answer.

"No," said the woman. She stood up from her chair, and now that she put her hand on the little girl's shoulder, Felicia was taken into the sphere of love and intimacy again. "Shall we go into the other room, and you will do your pirouette for me?" the woman said, and they went from the kitchen and down the strip of carpet on which the clear light fell. In the front room, they paused hand in hand in the glow of the shaded lamp, and the woman looked about her, at the books, the low tables with the magazines and ash trays on them, the vase of roses on the piano, looking with dark, scarcely seeing eyes at these things that had no reality at all. It was only when she saw the little white clock on the mantelpiece that she gave any sign, and then she said quickly: "What time does your mother put you to bed?"

Felicia waited a moment, and in the interval of waiting the woman lifted one hand and, as if in reverence, touched Felicia's hair.

"What time did the little girl you knew in the other place go to bed?" Felicia asked.

"Ah, God, I do not know, I do not remember," the woman said.

"Was she your little girl?" said Felicia softly, stubbornly.

"No," said the woman. "She was not mine. At least, at first she was not mine. She had a mother, a real mother, but the mother had to go away."

"Did she come back late?" asked Felicia.

"No, ah, no, she could not come back, she never came back," the woman said, and now she turned, her arm around Felicia's shoulders, and she sat down in the low soft chair. "Why am I saying all this to you, why am I doing it?" she cried out in grief, and she held Felicia close against her. "I had thought to speak of the anniversary to you, and that was all, and now I am saying these other things to you. Three years ago today, exactly, the little girl became my little girl because her mother went away. That is all there is to it. There is nothing more."

Felicia waited another moment, held close against the woman, and listening to the swift, strong heartbeats in the woman's breast.

"But the mother," she said then in the small, persistent voice, "did she take a taxi when she went?"

"This is the way it used to happen," said the woman, speaking in hopelessness and bitterness in the softly lighted room. "Every week they used to come into the place where we were and they would read a list of names out. Sometimes it would be the names of children they would read out, and then a little later they would have to go away. And sometimes it would be the grown people's names, the names of the mothers or big sisters, or other women's names. The men were not with us. The fathers were somewhere else, in another place."

"Yes," Felicia said. "I know."

"We had been there only a little while, maybe ten days or maybe not so long," the woman went on, holding Felicia against her still, "when they read the name of the little girl's mother out, and that afternoon they took her away."

"What did the little girl do?" Felicia said.

"She wanted to think up the best way of getting out so that she could go find her mother," said the woman, "but she could not think of anything good enough until the third or fourth day. And then she tied her ballet slippers up in the handkerchief again, and she went up to the guard standing at the door." The woman's voice was gentle, controlled now. "She asked the guard please to open the door so that she could go out. 'This is Thursday,' she said, 'and every Tuesday and Thursday I have my ballet lessons. If I miss a ballet lesson, they do not count the money off, so my mother would be just paying for nothing, and she cannot afford to pay for nothing. I missed my ballet lesson on Tuesday,' she said to the guard, 'and I must not miss it again today.'"

Felicia lifted her head from the woman's shoulder, and she shook her hair back and looked in question and wonder at the woman's face.

"And did the man let her go?" she said.

"No, he did not. He could not do that," said the woman. "He was a soldier and he had to do what he was told. So every evening after her mother went, I used to brush the little girl's hair for her," the woman went on saying. "And while I brushed it, I used to tell her the stories of the ballets. Sometimes

I would begin with *Narcissus,*" the woman said, and she parted Felicia's locks with her fingers, "so if you will go and get your brush now, I will tell it while I brush your hair."

"Oh, yes," said Felicia, and she made two whirls as she went quickly to the bedroom. On the way back, she stopped and held on to the piano with the fingers of one hand while she went up on her toes. "Did you see me? Did you see me standing on my toes?" she called to the woman, and the woman sat smiling in love and contentment at her.

"Yes, wonderful, really wonderful," she said. "I am sure I have never seen anyone do it so well." Felicia came spinning toward her, whirling in pirouette after pirouette, and she flung herself down in the chair close to her, with her thin bones pressed against the woman's soft, wide hip. The woman took the silver-backed, monogrammed brush and the tortoise-shell comb in her hands, and now she began to brush Felicia's hair. "We did not have any soap at all and not very much water to wash in, so I never could fix her as nicely and prettily as I wanted to," she said, and the brush stroked regularly, carefully down, caressing the shape of Felicia's head.

"If there wasn't very much water, then how did she do her teeth?" Felicia said.

"She did not do her teeth," said the woman, and she drew the comb through Felicia's hair. "There were not any toothbrushes or tooth paste, or anything like that."

Felicia waited a moment, constructing the unfamiliar scene of it in silence, and then she asked the tentative question.

"Do I have to do my teeth tonight?" she said.

"No," said the woman, and she was thinking of something else, "you do not have to do your teeth."

"If I am your little girl tonight, can I pretend there isn't enough water to wash?" said Felicia.

"Yes," said the woman, "you can pretend that if you like. You do not have to wash," she said, and the comb passed lightly through Felicia's hair.

"Will you tell me the story of the ballet?" said Felicia, and the rhythm of the brushing was like the soft, slow rocking of sleep.

"Yes," said the woman. "In the first one, the place is a forest glade with little pale birches growing in it, and they have green veils over their faces and green veils drifting from their fingers, because it is the springtime. There is the music of a flute," said the woman's voice softly, softly, "and creatures of the wood are dancing—"

"But the mother," Felicia said as suddenly as if she had been awakened from sleep. "What did the little girl's mother say when she didn't do her teeth and didn't wash at night?"

"The mother was not there, you remember," said the woman, and the brush moved steadily in her hand. "But she did send one little letter back. Sometimes the people who went away were able to do that. The mother wrote it in a train, standing up in a car that had no seats," she said, and she might have been telling the story of the ballet still, for her voice was gentle and the brush did not falter on Felicia's hair. "There were perhaps a great many other people standing up in the train with her, perhaps all trying to write their little letters on the bits of paper they had managed to hide on them, or that they had found in forgotten corners as they traveled. When they had written their letters, then they must try to slip them out through the boards of the car in which they journeyed, standing up," said the woman, "and these letters fell down on the tracks under the train, or they were blown into the fields or onto the country roads, and if it was a kind person who picked them up, he would seal them in envelopes and send them to where they were addressed to go. So a letter came back like this from the little girl's mother," the woman said, and the brush followed the comb, the comb the brush in steady pursuit through Felicia's hair. "It said good-by to the little girl, and it said please to take care of her. It said: 'Whoever reads this letter in the camp, please take good care of my little girl for me, and please have her tonsils looked at by a doctor if this is possible to do.'"

"And then," said Felicia softly, persistently, "what happened to the little girl?"

"I do not know. I cannot say," the woman said. But now the brush and comb had ceased to move, and in the silence Felicia turned her thin, small body on the chair, and she and the woman suddenly put their arms around each other. "They must all be asleep now, all of them," the woman said, and in the silence that fell on them again, they held each other closer. "They must be quietly asleep somewhere, and not crying all night because they are hungry and because they are cold. For three years I have been saying 'They must all be asleep, and the cold and the hunger and the seasons or night or day or nothing matters to them—'"

. . .

It was after midnight when Felicia's mother put her key in the lock of the front door, and pushed it open, and stepped into the hallway. She walked quickly to the living room, and just across the threshold she slipped the three blue foxskins from her shoulders and dropped them, with her little velvet bag, upon the chair. The room was quiet, so quiet that she could hear the sound of breathing in it, and no one spoke to her in greeting as she crossed toward the bedroom door. And then, as startling as a slap across her delicately tinted face, she saw the woman lying sleeping on the divan, and Felicia, in her school dress still, asleep within the woman's arms.

1946

ANN LANE PETRY
(1908–   )

In her 1946 novel The Street, *Ann Lane Petry describes the struggles of a young woman raising a son in post-Depression Harlem. The popular success of this masterpiece made her the first Black woman to sell over one million copies of a book. Still, although Petry earned critical acclaim for all three of her novels when they appeared, she never received the sustained attention that male contemporaries, such as Richard Wright, were accorded. Recent feminist critics, however, have argued that Petry stretched the boundaries of Black writers by portraying a world complicated by gender as well as by race and economics.*

Petry grew up in the only African American family in a predominantly white, middle-class New England town. Her father, Peter Clarke, and her mother, Bertha Lane, owned and ran two local drugstores near their home in Old Saybrook, Connecticut.

Like her father, Petry received a pharmacy degree from the University of Connecticut and then worked in the family pharmacies. After marrying George Petry in 1938, she moved with him and their daughter to New York, where she pursued a writing career. She began as a saleswoman and writer for Harlem's Amsterdam News *and eventually became a reporter and woman's page editor for Harlem's* People's Voice. *As a journalist, Petry observed a Harlem dramatically different from that of the Harlem Renaissance. In her writing she described the racism and sexism that thrived in these impoverished neighborhoods of the city. As a student at Columbia University in 1943–1944, she studied psychology and psychiatry to enhance her ability to develop fictional characters.*

Petry's street and classroom training led to the publication of several short stories in The Crisis *and* Phylon. *She received a Houghton Mifflin Literary Fellowship in 1945 to help her complete* The Street. *The honors continued the following year when her story "Like a Winding Sheet" appeared in* Best American Stories of 1946.

A year after publishing her second novel, Country Place *(1947), Petry returned to Connecticut to raise her family and continue her writing. Her third novel,* The Narrows, *appeared in 1953. She has also written several children's books.*

In 1971, Miss Muriel and Other Stories *appeared. From this collection, "Has Anybody Seen Miss Dora Dean?" has been selected to appear here. At the heart of this story of small-town life is suicide, recalled by the narrator from her childhood. It is a story about storytelling, about how people invent to explain and understand the incomprehensible. The story also describes one woman's reaching across a generation and a family for the comfort and understanding of another.*

HAS ANYBODY SEEN MISS DORA DEAN?

One afternoon last winter, when the telephone rang in my house in Wheeling, New York, I started not to answer it; it was snowing, I was reading a book I had been waiting for weeks to get hold of, and I did not want to be disturbed. But it seemed to me that the peals of the bell were longer, more insistent than usual, so I picked up the phone and said, "Hello."

It was Peter Forbes—and neither that name nor any other is the actual one—and he was calling from Bridgeport. He said abruptly, and wheezily, for he is an asthmatic, "Ma is terribly ill. Really awfully sick."

He paused, and I said I was very sorry. His mother, Sarah Forbes, and my mother had grown up together in a black section of Bridgeport.

Peter said, "She's got some dishes she wants you to have. So will you come as soon as you can? Because she is really very sick."

I had heard that Sarah, who was in her seventies, was not well, but I was startled to learn that she was "terribly ill," "really very sick." I said, "I'll come tomorrow. Will that be all right?"

"No, no," he said. "Please come today. Ma keeps worrying about these dishes. So will you please come—well, right away? She is really terribly, terribly ill."

Knowing Sarah as well as I did, I could understand his insistence. Sarah had an unpleasant voice; it was a querulous, peevish voice. When she was angry or irritated, or wanted you to do something that you did not want to do, she talked and talked and talked, until finally her voice seemed to be pursuing you. It was like a physical pursuit from which there was no escape.

I said, "I'll leave right away," and hung up.

It took me three hours to drive from Wheeling to Bridgeport, though the distance is only forty-five miles. But it is forty-five miles of winding road—all hills and sharp curves. The slush in the road was beginning to freeze, and the windshield wiper kept getting stuck; at frequent intervals I had to stop the car and get out and push the snow away so that the wiper could function again.

During that long, tedious drive, I kept thinking about Sarah and remembering things about her. It was at least two years since I had seen her. But before that, over a period of twenty years, I had seen her almost every summer, because Peter drove over to Wheeling to go fishing, and his mother came too. She usually accompanied him whenever he went out for a ride. He would leave her at my house, so that she could visit with me while he and his two boys went fishing.

I thoroughly enjoyed these visits, for Sarah could be utterly charming when she was so minded. She was a tall woman with rather bushy black hair that had a streak of gray near the front. Her skin was a wonderful reddish brown color and quite unwrinkled, in spite of her age. She would have been extremely attractive if she hadn't grown so fat. All this fat was deposited on her abdomen and behind. Her legs had stayed thin, and her feet were long and thin, and her head, neck, and shoulders were small, but she was huge from waist to knee. In silhouette, she looked rather like a pouter pigeon in reverse. Her legs were not sturdy enough to support so much weight, and she was always leaning against doors, or against people for support. This gave her an air of helplessness, which was completely spurious. She had a caustic sense of humor, and though she was an old woman, if something struck her as being funny, she would be seized by fits of giggling just as if she were a very young and silly girl.

. . .

I knew a great deal about Sarah Forbes. This knowledge stemmed from a long-distance telephone call that she made to my mother thirty-three years ago, when I was nine years old. I overheard my mother's side of the conversation. I can still repeat what she said, word for word, even imitating the intonation, the inflection of her voice.

In those days we lived in the building that housed my father's drugstore, in Wheeling. Our kitchen was on the ground floor, behind the store, and the bedrooms were upstairs, above it. Just as other children sat in the family living room, I sat in the drugstore—right near the front window on a bench when the weather was cold, outside on the wooden steps that extended across the front of the building when the weather was warm. Sitting outside on those splintery steps, I could hear everything that went on inside. In summer, the big front door of the store stayed wide open all day, and there was a screen door with fancy scrollwork on all the wooden parts. There were windows on either side of the door. On each window my father had painted his name in white letters with the most wonderful curlicues and flourishes, and under it the word "Druggist." On one window it said "Cold Soda," and on the other window "Ice Cream" and over the door it said "Drug Store."

Whether I sat inside the store or outside it, I had a long, sweeping view of the church, the church green, and the street. The street was as carefully composed as a painting: tall elm trees, white fences, Federal houses.

If I was sitting outside on the steps, listening to what went on in the store, no one paid any attention to me, but if I was sitting inside on the bench near the window, my mother or my father would shoo me out whenever a customer reached the really interesting part of the story he was telling. I was always being shooed out until I discovered that if I sat motionless on the bench, with a book held open in front of me, and did not glance up, everyone forgot about me. Occasionally, someone would stop right in the middle of a hair-raising story, and then my father would say, "Oh, she's got her nose in a book. She's just like she's deaf when she's got her nose in a book. You can say anything you want to and she won't hear a word." It was like having a permanent season ticket in a theater where there was a continuous performance and the same play was never given twice.

My special interest in Sarah dates from a rainy afternoon when I was sitting inside the store. It was a dull afternoon—no customers, nothing, just the busy sound of rain dripping from the eaves, hitting the wooden steps. The wall telephone rang, and my mother, wiping her hands on her apron, came to answer it from the kitchen, which was just behind the prescription room of the store. Before she picked up the receiver, she said, "That's a long-distance call. I can tell by the way the operator is ringing. That's a long-distance call."

I sat up straight. I picked up my book and I heard the tinkling sound of money being dropped in at the other end. Then I heard my mother saying, "Why, Sarah, how are you? . . . What? What did you say? . . . found him? Found him where?" She listened. "Oh, *no!*" She listened again. "Oh, my dear! Why, how dreadful! Surely an accident. You think—!" A longer period of listening. "Oh, no. Why that's impossible. Nobody would deliberately—" She didn't finish what she was going to say, and listened again. "A letter? Forbes left a letter? Tear it up! You mustn't let anyone know that—" There was a long pause. "But you must think of Peter. These things have an effect on—Excuse me."

She turned and looked at me. I had put the book down on the bench, and I was staring straight at her, breathing quite fast and listening so intently that my mouth was open.

She said, "Go out and play."

I kept staring at her, not moving, because I was trying to figure out what in the world she and Sarah Forbes had been discussing. What had happened that no one must know about?

She said again, her voice rising slightly, "Go out and play."

So I went the long way, through the back of the store and the prescription room and the kitchen, and I slammed the back door, and then I edged inside the prescription room again, very quietly, and I heard my mother say, "He must have had a heart attack and fallen right across the railroad tracks just as the train was due. That's the only possible explanation. And, Sarah, burn that letter. Burn it up!" She hung up the phone, and then she said to herself, "How dreadful. How perfectly dreadful!"

. . .

Whether Sarah took my mother's advice and burned Forbes' letter I do not know, but it became common knowledge that he had committed suicide, and his death was so reported in the Bridgeport newspapers. His body had been found on the railroad tracks near Shacktown, an outlying, poverty-stricken section of Bridgeport, where the white riffraff lived and the lowest brothels were to be found. He was the only person that my father and my mother and my aunts had ever known who had killed himself, and they talked about him endlessly—not his suicide but his life as they had known it. His death seemed to have put them on the defensive. They sounded as though he had said to them, "This life all of us black folk lead is valueless; it is disgusting, it is cheap, it is contemptible, and I am throwing it away, so that everyone will know exactly what I think of it." They did not say this, but they sounded perplexed and uneasy whenever they spoke of Forbes, and they seemed to feel that if they could pool their knowledge of him they might be able to reach some acceptable explanation of why he had killed himself. I heard Forbes and Sarah discussed, off and on, all during the period of my growing up.

I never saw Forbes. The Wingates, an enormously wealthy white family for whom he worked, had stopped coming to Wheeling before I was born, and he had stopped coming there too. But I heard him described so often that I knew exactly what he looked like, how he sounded when he talked, what kind of clothes he wore. He was a tall, slender black man. He was butler, social secretary, gentleman's gentleman. When Mr. Wingate become ill, he played the role of male nurse. Then, after Mr. Wingate's death, he ran the house for Mrs. Wingate. He could cook, he could sew, he could act as coachman if necessary; he did all the buying and all the hiring.

The Wingates were summer residents of Wheeling. Their winter home was in Bridgeport. In Wheeling, they owned what they called a cottage; it was an exact replica of an old Southern mansion—white columns, long graveled driveways, carefully maintained lawns, brick stables, and all within six hundred feet of Long Island Sound.

During the summer, Forbes rode a bicycle over to my father's drugstore every pleasant afternoon. He said he needed the exercise. Whenever I heard my family describing Forbes, I always thought how dull and uninteresting he must have been. There would never be anything unexpected about him, never anything unexplained. He would always move exactly as he was supposed to when someone pulled the proper strings. He was serious, economical, extremely conservative—a tall, elegant figure in carefully pressed black clothes and polished shoes. His voice was slightly effeminate, his speech very precise. Mrs. Wingate was an Episcopalian and so was Forbes.

But one day when my father was talking about Forbes, some six months after his death, he suddenly threw his head back and laughed. He said, "I can see him now, bicycling down the street, with those long legs of his pinched up in those straight tight pants he wore, pumping his legs up and down, and whistling 'Has Anybody Seen Miss Dora Dean?' with his coattails flying in the wind. I can see him now." And he laughed again.

At that time, I could not understand why my father should have found this funny. Years later, I learned that the tune Forbes whistled was one that Bert Williams and George Walker, a memorable team of black comedians, had made famous along with their cakewalk. They were singing "Dora Dean" in New York in about 1896. Dora Dean, the girl of the song, played the lead in a hit show called "The Creole Show," which was notable for a chorus of sixteen beautiful brown girls. I suppose it amused my father to think that Forbes, who seemed to have silver polish in his veins instead of good red blood, should be whistling a tune that suggested cakewalks, beautiful brown girls, and ragtime.

Mrs. Wingate's name entered into the discussions of Forbes because he worked for her. It was usually my mother who spoke of Mrs. Wingate, and she said the same thing so often that I can quote her: "Mrs. Wingate always said she simply couldn't live without Forbes. She said he planned the menus, he checked the guest lists, he supervised the wine cellar—he did everything. Remember how she used to come into the store and say he was her mind, her heart, her hands? That was a funny thing to say, wasn't it?" There would be a pause, and then she would say, "Wasn't it too bad that she let herself get so fat?"

It was from my mother that I learned what Mrs. Wingate looked like. She was short and blond, and her face looked like the face of a fat china doll—pink and white and round. She used rice powder and rouge to achieve this effect. She bought these items in our drugstore. The powder came wrapped in thin white paper with a self stripe, and the rouge came in little round cardboard boxes, and inside there was a round, hard cake of reddish powder and a tiny powder puff to apply it with. She must have used a great deal of rouge, because at least once during the summer she would send Forbes up to the drugstore with a carton filled with these little empty rouge boxes. He would put them on the counter, saying, in his careful, precise, high-pitched voice, "Mrs. Wingate thought you might be able to use these." My father said he dumped them on the pile of rubbish in back of the store, to be burned, wondering what in the world she thought he would or could use them for. They smelled of perfume, and the reddish powder had discolored them, even on the outside.

Mrs. Wingate grew fatter and fatter, until, finally, getting her in and out of carriages, and then, during a later period, in and out of cars—even cars that were specially built—was impossible unless Forbes was on hand.

Forbes was lean, but he was wiry and tremendously strong. He could get Mrs. Wingate in and out of a carriage or a car without effort; at least he gave the illusion of effortlessness. My father said it was Mrs. Wingate who panted, who frowned, whose flesh quivered, whose forehead was dampened with sweat.

My father always ended his description of this performance by saying, "Remember how he used to have that white woman practically on his back? Yes, sir, practically on his back."

After I heard my father say that, I retained a curious mental picture of Forbes—a lean, wiry black man carrying an enormously fat pink and white woman piggyback. He did not lean over or bend over under the woman's weight; he stood straight, back unbent, so that she kept sliding down, down, down, and as he carried this quivering, soft-fleshed Mrs. Wingate, he was whistling "Has Anybody Seen Miss Dora Dean?"

. . .

I don't know that Forbes was actually looking for a reasonable facsimile of Dora Dean, but he found one, and he fell in love with her when he was forty years old. That was in 1900. He was so completely the perfect servant, with no emotional ties of his own and no life of his own, that my family seemed to think it was almost shocking that his attention should have been diverted from his job long enough to let him fall in love.

But it must have been inevitable from the first moment he saw Sarah Trumbull. I have a full-length photograph of her taken before she was married. She might well have been one of those beautiful girls in "The Creole Show." In the photograph, she has a young, innocent face—lovely eyes, and a pointed chin, and a very pretty mouth with a quirk at the corner that suggests a sense of humor. Her hair is slightly frizzy, and it is worn in a high, puffed-out pompadour, which serves as a frame for the small, exquisite face. She is wearing a shirtwaist with big, stiff sleeves, and a tight choker of lace around her throat. This costume makes her waist look tiny and her neck long and graceful.

My mother had been born in Bridgeport, and though she was older than Sarah, she had known her quite well. Sarah was the only child of a Baptist minister, and, according to my mother's rather severe standards, she was a silly, giggling girl with a reputation for being fast. She was frivolous, flirtatious. She liked to play cards, and played pinochle for money. She played the violin very well, and she used to wear a ring with a diamond in it on her little finger, and just before she started to play, she would polish it on her skirt, so that it would catch the light and wink at the audience. She had scandalized the people in her father's church because she played ragtime on the piano at dances, parties, and cakewalks. (I overheard my father say that he had always heard this called "whorehouse music"; he couldn't understand how it got to be "ragtime.")

Anyway, one night in 1900 Forbes had a night off and went to a dance in New Haven, and there was Sarah Trumbull in a white muslin dress with violet ribbons, playing ragtime on the piano. And there was a cakewalk that night, and Forbes and Sarah were the winners. I found a yellowed clipping about it in one of my mother's scrapbooks—that's how I know what Sarah was wearing.

I have never seen a cakewalk but I have heard it described. About fourteen couples took part, and they walked in time to music—not in a circle but in a square, with the men on the inside. The participants were always beautifully dressed, and they walked with grace and style. It was a strutting kind of walk. The test of their skill lay in the way they pivoted when they turned the corners. The judges stopped the music at intervals and eliminated possibly three couples at a time. The most graceful couple was awarded a beautifully decorated cake, so that they had literally walked to win a cake.

In those days, Sarah Trumbull was tall, slender, and graceful, and John Forbes was equally tall, slender, and graceful. He was probably very solemn and she was probably giggling as they turned the corners in a cakewalk.

A year later, they were married in the Episcopal Church (colored) in

Bridgeport. Sarah was a Baptist and her father was a Baptist minister, but she was married in an Episcopal church. If this had been a prize fight, I would say that Mrs. Wingate won the first round on points.

. . .

When my family discussed Forbes, they skipped the years after his marriage and went straight from his wedding to Sarah Trumbull in an Episcopal church (colored) to his death, twenty-four years later. Because I knew so little of the intervening years, I pictured him as being as ageless as a highly stylized figure in a marionette show—black, erect, elegantly dressed, effeminate, temperamental as a cat. I had never been able to explain why our cats did the things they did, and since there did not seem to be any reasonable explanation for Forbes' suicide, I attributed to him the unreasonableness of a cat.

The conversations in which my parents conjectured why Forbes killed himself were inconclusive and repetitive. My mother would sigh and say that she really believed Forbes killed himself because Sarah was such a slovenly housekeeper—that he just couldn't bear the dirt and the confusion in which he had to live, because, after all, he was accustomed to the elegance of the Wingate mansion.

My father never quite agreed. He said, "Well, yes, except that he'd been married to Sarah for twenty years or so. Why should he suddenly get upset about dirt after all that time?"

Once, my mother pressed him for his point of view, and he said, "Maybe he was the type that never should have married."

"What do you mean by that?"

"Well, he'd worked for that Mrs. Wingate, and he waited too long to get married, and then he married a young girl. How old was Sarah—twenty, wasn't she? And he as forty at the time, and—"

"Yes, yes," my mother said impatiently. "But what did you mean when you said he was a type that never should have married?"

"Well, if he'd been another type of man, I would have said there was more than met the eye between him and Mrs. Wingate. But he was so ladylike there couldn't have been. Mrs. Wingate thought a lot of him, and he thought a lot of Mrs. Wingate. That's all there was to it—it was just like one of those lifetime friendships between two ladies."

" 'Between two ladies'!" my mother said indignantly. "Why, what a wicked thing to say! Forbes was— Well, I've never seen another man, white or black, with manners like his. He was a perfect gentleman."

"Too perfect," my father said dryly. "That type don't make good husbands."

"But something must have *happened* to make him kill himself. He was thrifty and hard-working and intelligent and honest. Why should he kill himself?"

My father tried to end the conversation. "It isn't good to keep talking about the dead like this, figuring and figuring about why they did something—

it's like you were pulling at them, trying to pull them back. After all, how do you know but you might succeed in bringing them back? It's best to let them alone. Let Forbes alone. It isn't for nothing that they have that saying about let them rest in peace."

There was silence for a while. Then my mother said softly, "But I do wish I knew why he killed himself."

My father said, "Sarah told you he said in the letter he was tired of living. I don't believe that. But I guess we have to accept it. There's just one thing I'd like to know."

"What's that?"

"I keep wondering what he was doing in Shacktown. That seems a strange place for a respectable married man like Forbes. That's where all those barefooted foreign women live, and practically every one of those orange-crate houses they live in has a red light in the window. It seems like a strange part of the city for a respectable married man like Forbes to have been visiting."

. . .

By the time I was ten, Forbes' death had for me a kind of reality of its own—a theatrical reality. I used to sit on the steps in front of the drugstore, and half close my eyes so that I could block out the church green and the picket fences and the elm trees and the big old houses, and I would pretend that I was looking at a play instead. I set it up in my mind's eye. The play takes place on the wrong side of the railroad tracks, where the land is all cinders, in a section where voluptuous, big-hipped foreign women go barefooted, wrap their heads and shoulders in brilliant red and green shawls, and carry bundles on their heads—that is, those who work. Those who do not work wear hats with so many feathers on them they look as if they had whole turkeys on their heads. The houses in this area are built entirely of packing cases and orange crates. There is the sound of a train in the distance, and a thin, carefully dressed black man, in a neat black suit and polished shoes, walks swiftly onstage and up the slight incline toward the railroad tracks—no path there, no road. It is a winter's night and cold. This is Forbes and he is not wearing an overcoat.

As narrator for an imaginary audience, I used to say, "What is he doing in this part of town in his neat black suit and his starched white shirt? He could not possibly know anyone here in Shacktown, a place built of cinders and packing cases. Bleak. Treeless. No road here. What is he doing here? Where is he going?"

The train whistles, and Forbes walks up the embankment and lies down across the tracks. The train comes roaring into sight and it slices him in two—quickly, neatly. And the curtain comes down as a telephone rings in a drugstore miles away.

This picture of Forbes remained with me, unchanged; I still see him like that. But in the intervening years Sarah changed. My first distinct recollection of her was of a stout middle-aged woman with a querulous voice, which was always lifted in complaint. Her complaint centered on money—the lack of it, the importance of it. But even in middle age there were vestigial remains of the girl who scandalized the religious black folk of Bridgeport by pounding out whorehouse music on the piano, and who looked as though she had just stepped out of the chorus line of "The Creole Show": the wonderful smooth reddish brown skin, the giggle over which she seemed to have no control, and the flirtatious manner of a Gay Nineties beauty. The coyness and the fits of giggling she had as an old woman were relics of these mannerisms.

. . .

I got to Bridgeport just at dusk. As I rang the bell of the two-story frame house where Sarah lived, I remembered something. This was the house that Mrs. Wingate had given to Forbes and Sarah as a wedding present. They had lived in it together exactly three weeks, and then Forbes went back to live at the Wingate mansion. Mrs. Wingate had asked him to come back because she might want to go out at night, and how could she get in and out of a car without him? It would be very inconvenient to have to wait for him to come all the way from the other side of town. (The Wingate mansion was at the south end of the city, and the dark brown, two-story taxpayer was at the north end of the city.) Mrs. Wingate had said that Sarah would, of course, stay where she was. She increased Forbes' wages and promised to remember him most generously in her will.

"It was a funny thing," my mother once said. "You know, Sarah used to call Forbes by his first name, John, when he was courting her, and when they were first married. After he went back to live at Mrs. Wingate's, she called him Forbes. All the rest of his life, she called him by his last name, just as though she was talking to Mrs. Wingate's butler."

One of Peter Forbes' gangling boys—Sarah's younger grandson—opened the door, and I stopped thinking about the past. He was a nice-mannered, gentle-looking boy, tall and thin, his face shaped rather like Sarah's in the old photograph—a small-boned face. His skin was the same wonderful reddish brown color. I wondered why he wasn't in school, and immediately asked him.

"I've finished," he said. "I finished last June. I'm eighteen and I'm going in the Army."

I said what most people say when confronted by evidence of the passage of time. "It doesn't seem possible."

He said, "Yeah, that's right," took a deep breath, and said, "Nana's in the bedroom. You'd better come right in."

He seemed to be affected by the same need for haste that had made his father urge me to come see Sarah right away. I did not pause even long enough to take my coat off; I followed him down a dark hall, trying to remember what his real name was. Sarah had brought Peter's children up. Peter had been married to a very nice girl, and they had two boys. The very nice girl left Peter after the second baby was born and never came back. Sarah had given nicknames to the boys; the older was called Boodie, and the younger was Lud. It was Lud who had answered the door. I could not remember anything but the nickname—Lud.

We entered a bedroom at the back of the house. The moment I saw Sarah, I knew that she was dying. She was sitting slumped over in a wheelchair. In the two years since I had seen her, she had become a gaunt old woman with terrible bruised shadows under her eyes and she was so thin that she looked like a skeleton. Her skin, which had been that rich reddish brown, was now overlaid with gray.

Lud said, "Nana, she's here. She's come, Nana."

Sarah opened her eyes and nodded. The eyes that I had remembered as black and penetrating were dull and their color had changed; they were light brown. I bent over and kissed her.

"I'm not so bright today," she said, and the words came out slowly, as though she had to think about using the muscles of her throat, her tongue, her lips—had to think, even, before she breathed. After she finished speaking, she closed her eyes and she looked as though she were already dead.

"She isn't asleep," Lud said. "You just say something to her. She'll answer—won't you, Nana?"

Sarah did not answer. I took off my coat, for the heat in the room was unbearable, and I looked around for a place to put it and laid it on a chair, thinking that the room had not changed. It was exactly as I remembered it, and I had not been in it for twenty years. There was too much furniture, the windows were heavily curtained, there were was a figured carpet on the floor, and a brass bed, a very beautiful brass bed; one of the walls was covered with framed photographs.

A white cat darted through the room, and I jumped, startled, remembering another white cat that used to dart through these same rooms—but that was twenty years ago. "That's surely not the same cat, Lud? The one you've always had?"

"We've had this one about three years."

"Oh. But the other cat was white, too, wasn't it? It was deaf and it had never been outside the house—isn't that right? And it had blue eyes."

"So's this one. He doesn't go outside. He's deaf and he's got blue eyes." Lud grinned and his face was suddenly lively and very young. "And he's white," he said, and then laughed out loud. "Nana calls him our white folks."

"What's the cat's name?"

"Willie."

That was the name of the other cat, the one I had known. And Willie, so Sarah Forbes had said (boasted, perhaps?)—Willie did not like men. I wondered if this cat did.

"Is he friendly?"

"No," Lud said.

"Doesn't like men," Sarah Forbes said. Her voice was strong and clear, and it had its old familiar querulousness. The boy and I looked at her in surprise. She seemed about to say something more, and I wondered what it was going to be, for there was a kind of malevolence in her expression.

But Peter Forbes came into the room and she did not say anything. We shook hands and talked about the weather, and I thought how little he had changed during the years I had known him. He is a tall, slender man, middle-aged now, with a shaggy head and a petulant mouth that has deeply etched lines at the corners.

At the sight of Peter, Sarah seemed to grow stronger. She sat up straight. "Wheel me out to the dining room," she ordered.

"Yes, Ma," he said obediently. The wheelchair made no sound. "You come, too," he said to me.

"There's some china . . ." Sarah's voice trailed off, and she was slumping again, almost onto one arm of the wheelchair, her arms, head, and neck absolutely limp. She looked like a discarded rag doll.

We stood in the dining room and looked at her, all three of us. I said, "I'd better go. She's not well enough to be doing this. She hasn't the strength."

"You can't go," Peter said, with a firmness that surprised me. "Ma has some dishes she wants you to have. She's been talking about them for days now. She won't give us a minute's peace until you have them. You've got to stay until she gives them to you." Then he added, very politely and quite winningly, "Please don't go."

So I stayed. The dining room was just as hot as the bedroom. It, too, was filled with furniture—a dining room set, three cabinets filled with china and glassware, a studio couch, and in a bay window, a big aquarium with fish in it.

Willie, the white cat, ran into the room from the hall, clawed his way up the draperies at the bay window and sat crouched on the cornice, staring into the fish tank. His round blue eyes kept following the movements of the fish, back and forth, back and forth.

"Doesn't he try to catch the fish?" I asked.

Lud said, "That's what he wants to do. But he can't get at them. So he just watches them."

"Why, that's terrible," I said. "Can't you—"

Sarah had straightened up again. "Open those doors," she said.

"Yes, Ma." Peter opened one of the china cabinets.

"Get my cane."

"Yes, Ma." He went into the bedroom and came back with a slender Malacca cane. She took it from him in a swift snatching movement, and, holding it and pointing with it, was transformed. She was no longer a hideous old woman dying slowly but an arrogant, commanding figure.

"That," she said, "and that," pointing imperiously to a shelf in the china cabinet where a tall chocolate pot stood, with matching cups and saucers, covered thick with dust.

"Get a carton and some newspapers." She pointed at Lud, and she jabbed him viciously in the stomach with the cane. He jumped, and said, "Oh, oo-ooh!" pain and outrage in his voice.

"Go get the carton," Peter said matter-of-factly.

While we waited for Lud to come back, Sarah seemed to doze. Finally, Peter sat down and motioned for me to sit down. He picked up a newspaper and began to read.

Something about the way Sarah had ordered him around set me to wondering what kind of childhood Peter had had. He must have been about twelve years old when Mrs. Wingate died and left thirty-five thousand dollars to Forbes.

With this money, Forbes took what he called a flyer in real estate; he acquired an equity in six tenement houses. My mother had disapproved. She distrusted the whole idea of mortgages and loans, and she felt that Forbes was gambling with his inheritance; if his tenants were unable to pay the rent, he would be unable to meet the interest on his notes and would lose everything.

During this period, Mother went to see Sarah fairly often and she always came away from these visits quite disturbed. She said that Sarah, who had at one time cared too much about her looks, now did not seem to care at all. The house was dreadful—confused and dusty. She said that Forbes had changed. He was still immaculate, but he was now too thin—bony—and his movements were jerky. He seemed to have a dreadful, almost maniacal urge to keep moving, and he would sit down, stand up, walk about the room, sit down again, get up, walk about again. At first she used to say that he was nervous, and then she amended this and enlarged it by saying he was distraught.

Mrs. Wingate had been dead exactly two years when Forbes committed suicide. Immediately, all of Sarah's friends predicted financial disaster for her. Forbes' money was tied up in heavily mortgaged real estate, and shortly after his death the depression came along, with its eviction notices and foreclosures.

I glanced at Sarah, dozing in the wheelchair, her chin resting on her chest. At twenty, she had been a silly, giggling girl. And yet somewhere under the surface there must have been the makings of a cold, shrewd property owner, a badgering, browbeating fishwife of a woman who could intimidate drunks, evict widows and orphans—a woman capable of using an umbrella or a hatpin as a weapon. She had made regular weekly collections of rent, because she soon learned that if she went around only once a month, the rent money would have gone for food or for liquor or for playing the numbers. Peter went with her when she made her collections. He was tall, thin, and asthmatic, and wore tweed knee pants and long stockings—a ridiculous costume for a boy in his teens.

It was during those years that Sarah perfected her technique of leaning against people, and began to develop a whining voice. She began to get fat. Her behind seemed to swell up, but her legs stayed thin, like pipestems, so that she walked carefully. She was what my father called spindle-shanked.

I suppose she had to whine, to threaten, to cajole, perhaps cry, in order to screw the rent money out of her tenants; at any rate, she succeeded. Years later, she told Mother that she had not lost a single piece of property. She finally sold all of it except the two-story taxpayer where they lived. She said that the bank that held the mortgages and notes had congratulated her; they told her that no real estate operator in Bridgeport had been able to do what she had done—bring all his property through the depression intact.

Sarah straightened up in the wheelchair and pointed with her cane. "That," she said. Peter hesitated. "That" seemed to be some white cups and saucers with no adornment of any kind. Sarah threatened Peter with the cane, and he took them out of the cabinet and put them on the table.

"Perfect," she said to me. "Six of them. All perfect. Belonged to my grandmother. Handed down. They're yours now. You hand them down."

I shook my head. "Wait a minute," I said, slowly and distinctly, in order to be sure she understood. "What about your grandsons? What about Lud and Boodie? These cups should belong to Lud and Boodie."

"They will run with whores," she said coldly. "Just like Peter does. Just like Forbes kept trying to do, only he couldn't. That's what he was after in Shacktown that time, and when he found he couldn't—just wasn't able to—he laid himself down on the railroad track." She paused for a moment. "I cried for three days afterward. For three whole days." She paused again. "I wasn't crying because of what happened to him. I was crying because of what had happened to me. To my whole life. My whole life."

I could not look at Peter. I heard him take a deep breath.

Sarah said, "Those cups are yours. I'm giving them to you so that I'll know where they are. I'll know who owns them. If they should stay here . . ." She shrugged.

Lud came back with the carton and a pile of newspapers and Sarah did not even glance in his direction. She said, "The chocolate cups belonged to a French king. Mrs. Wingate gave them to me for a wedding present when I married her Forbes. I want you to have them so that I'll know who owns them."

We wrapped the pieces of china separately, and put wads of crumpled newspaper in between as we packed the carton. Sarah watched us. Sometimes she half closed her eyes, but she kept looking until we had finished. After that, her head slumped and her breathing changed. It was light, shallow, with pauses in between. I could hear the thumping of her heart way across the room.

I said, "Good-bye, Sarah," and kissed the back of her neck, but she did not answer or move.

It was still snowing when Lud carried the carton out to the car for me, held the door open, and closed it after I got in. I thought he did it with a kind of gracefulness that he couldn't possibly have acquired from Peter; perhaps it was something inherited from Forbes, his grandfather.

Lud said, "Did those cups really belong to one of the kings of France?"

"Maybe. I really don't know. I wish you'd put them back in the house.

This whole carton of china is more yours than it is mine. These things belonged to your grandmother and they should stay in your family."

"Oh, no," he said hastily, and he stepped away from the car. "I don't want them. What would I do with them? Besides, Nana's ghost would come back and bug me." He laughed uneasily. "And if Nana's ghost bugged anybody, they'd flip for sure."

When I got home, I washed the chocolate set, and having got rid of the accumulated dust of fifty years, I decided that it could easily have belonged to one of the kings of France. It was of the very old, soft-paste type of porcelain. It had been made in the Sèvres factory and it was exquisitely decorated in the lovely color known as rose pompadour.

I was admiring the shape of the cups when the telephone rang. It was Peter Forbes. He said, "Ma died in her sleep just a few minutes after you left."

1958

EUDORA WELTY
(1909–)

One of the most respected American fiction writers associated with the South, Eudora Welty has written novels, autobiographical pieces, reviews, and essays. She is best known for her short stories, many of which have been collected and anthologized, and for her cycle of stories, The Golden Apples. *Much of her fiction captures the sense of place, the rhythms of speech, and the community life that characterize Mississippi. Her stories frequently use elements of fairy tales and myths to reveal conflicting forces of order and chaos, light and dark, passivity and rebellion.*

Born in Jackson, Mississippi, Welty grew up reading voraciously and writing stories. She attended Mississippi State College for Women and then received her B.A. in English from the University of Wisconsin in 1929. Although she attended Columbia University's School of Business, she found it hard to find work during the Depression: she worked in advertising, wrote radio scripts, and traveled extensively as junior publicity agent for the Works Progress Administration. In her late twenties, Welty began publishing stories she had been working on. Several stories appeared in the respected Southern Review *and, with the acquisition of an influential agent, she began to sell to national magazines.*

For the last fifty years, Welty has published beautifully crafted stories that appeal to a wide range of readers. She has received every major literary award, including O. Henry Awards, a Guggenheim Fellowship, and a Pulitzer Prize. She has received numerous honorary degrees and has taught as a writer-in-residence at many colleges and universities, including Oxford and Cambridge. Her fiction has been collected in A Curtain of Green, The Wide Net, The Bride of Innisfallen, *and* Collected Stories.

One Writer's Beginnings *(1983) provides many insights into Welty's perceptions of herself as a writer. She has said that as an artist she has always exposed herself to risk—experimentation with form, themes, and subjects. She compares herself to the character of the piano teacher Miss Eckhart in her story "June Recital": like Miss Eckhart, Welty is driven by love for her art and the desire to share it with others. There is, also, a musical quality to Welty's writing, as well as many musical allusions in her works that strengthen their similarity to the work of her fictional creation, Miss Eckhart the musician.*

"Livvie" illustrates some of Welty's experimentation with narrative techniques and subject matter. As the central character shakes off the dominion of her ordered domestic life to take up with someone who offers youth and sexual ardor, we see that her actions have moral complexities that she does not realize. The narrative

thread of the story is seemingly simple, but it enables the reader to see several facets of a moral and emotional issue. In Welty's work, nothing is quite as simple as it might seem.

LIVVIE

Solomon carried Livvie twenty-one miles away from her home when he married her. He carried her away up on the Old Natchez Trace into the deep country to live in his house. She was sixteen—only a girl, then. Once people said he thought nobody would ever come along there. He told her himself that it had been a long time, and a day she did not know about, since that road was a traveled road with *people* coming and going. He was good to her, but he kept her in the house. She had not thought that she could not get back. Where she came from, people said an old man did not want anybody in the world to ever find his wife, for fear they would steal her back from him. Solomon asked her before he took her, would she be happy?—very dignified, for he was a colored man that owned his land and had it written down in the courthouse; and she said, "Yes, sir," since he was an old man and she was young and just listened and answered. He asked her, if she was choosing winter, would she pine for spring, and she said, "No indeed." Whatever she said, always, was because he was an old man . . . while nine years went by. All the time, he got older, and he got so old he gave out. At last he slept the whole day in bed, and she was young still.

It was a nice house, inside and outside both. In the first place, it had three rooms. The front room was papered in holly paper, with green palmettos from the swamp spaced at careful intervals over the walls. There was fresh newspaper cut with fancy borders on the mantel-shelf, on which were propped photographs of old or very young men printed in faint yellow—Solomon's people. Solomon had a houseful of furniture. There was a double settee, a tall scrolled rocker and an organ in the front room, all around a three-legged table with a pink marble top, on which was set a lamp with three gold feet, besides a jelly glass with pretty hen feathers in it. Behind the front room, the other room had the bright iron bed with the polished knobs like a throne, in which Solomon slept all day. There were snow-white curtains of wiry lace at the window, and a lace bedspread belonged on the bed. But what old Solomon slept so sound under was a big feather-stitched piece-quilt in the pattern "Trip Around the World," which had twenty-one different colors, four hundred and forty pieces, and a thousand yards of thread, and that was what Solomon's mother made in her life and old age. There was a table holding the Bible, and a trunk with a key. On the wall were two calendars, and a diploma from somewhere in Solomon's family, and under that, Livvie's one possession was nailed, a picture of the little white baby of the family she worked for, back in Natchez before she was married. Going through that room and on to the kitchen, there was a big wood stove and a big round table always with a wet top and with the knives and forks in one jelly glass and the spoons in another, and a cut-glass vinegar bottle between, and going out from those, many shallow dishes of pickled peaches, fig preserves, watermelon pickles and blackberry jam always sitting there. The churn sat in the sun, the doors of the safe were always both shut, and there were four baited mousetraps in the kitchen, one in every corner.

The outside of Solomon's house looked nice. It was not painted, but across the porch was an even balance. On each side there was one easy chair with high springs, looking out, and a fern basket hanging over it from the ceiling, and a dishpan of zinnia seedlings growing at its foot on the floor. By the door was a plow-wheel, just a pretty iron circle, nailed up on one wall, and a square mirror on the other, a turquoise-blue comb stuck up in the frame, with the wash stand beneath it. On the door was a wooden knob with a pearl in the end, and Solomon's black hat hung on that, if he was in the house.

Out front was a clean dirt yard with every vestige of grass patiently uprooted and the ground scarred in deep whorls from the strike of Livvie's broom. Rose bushes with tiny blood-red roses blooming every month grew in threes on either side of the steps. On one side was a peach tree, on the other a pomegranate. Then coming around up the path from the deep cut of the Natchez Trace below was a line of bare crape-myrtle trees with every branch of them ending in a colored bottle, green or blue. There was no word that fell from Solomon's lips to say what they were for, but Livvie knew that there could be a spell put in trees, and she was familiar from the time she was born with the way bottle trees kept evil spirits from coming into the house—by luring them inside the colored bottles, where they cannot get out again. Solomon had made the bottle trees with his own hands over the nine years, in labor amounting to about a tree a year, and without a sign that he had any uneasiness in his heart, for he took as much pride in his precautions against spirits coming in the house as he took in the house, and sometimes in the sun the bottle trees looked prettier than the house did.

It was a nice house. It was in a place where the days would go by and surprise anyone that they were over. The lamplight and the firelight would shine out the door after dark, over the still and breathing country, lighting the roses and the bottle trees, and all was quiet there.

But there was nobody, nobody at all, not even a white person. And if there had been anybody, Solomon would not have let Livvie look at them, just as he would not let her look at a field hand, or a field hand look at her. There was no house near, except for the cabins of the tenants that were forbidden to her, and there was no house as far as she had been, stealing away down the still, deep Trace. She felt as if she waded a river when she went, for the dead leaves on the ground reached as high as her knees, and when she was all scratched and bleeding she said it was not like a road that went anywhere. One day, climbing up the high bank, she had found a graveyard without a church, with ribbon-grass growing about the foot of an angel (she had climbed up because she thought she saw angel wings), and in the sun, trees shining like burning flames through the great caterpillar nets which enclosed them. Scarey thistles stood looking like the prophets in the Bible in Solomon's house. Indian paint brushes grew over her head, and the mourning dove made the only sound in the world. Oh, for a stirring of the leaves, and a breaking of the nets! But not by a ghost, prayed Livvie, jumping down the bank. After Solomon took to his bed, she never went out, except one more time.

Livvie knew she made a nice girl to wait on anybody. She fixed things to eat on a tray like a surprise. She could keep from singing when she ironed, and to sit by a bed and fan away the flies, she could be so still she could not hear herself breathe. She could clean up the house and never drop a thing, and wash the dishes without a sound, and she would step outside to churn, for churning sounded too sad to her, like sobbing, and if it made her homesick and not Solomon, she did not think of that.

But Solomon scarcely opened his eyes to see her, and scarcely tasted his food. He was not sick or paralyzed or in any pain that he mentioned, but he was surely wearing out in the body, and no matter what nice hot thing Livvie would bring him to taste, he would only look at it now, as if he were past seeing how he could add anything more to himself. Before she could beg him, he would go fast asleep. She could not surprise him any more, if he would not taste, and she was afraid that he was never in the world going to taste another thing she brought him—and so how could he last?

. . .

But one morning it was breakfast time and she cooked his eggs and grits, carried them in on a tray, and called his name. He was sound asleep. He lay in a dignified way with his watch beside him, on his back in the middle of the bed. One hand drew the quilt up high, though it was the first day of spring. Through the white lace curtains a little puffy wind was blowing as if it came from round cheeks. All night the frogs had sung out in the swamp, like a commotion in the room, and he had not stirred, though she lay wide awake and saying "Shh, frogs!" for fear he would mind them.

He looked as if he would like to sleep a little longer, and so she put back the tray and waited. When she tiptoed and stayed so quiet, she surrounded herself with a little reverie, and sometimes it seemed to her when she was so stealthy that the quiet she kept was for a sleeping baby, and that she had a baby and was its mother. When she stood at Solomon's bed and looked down at him, she would be thinking, "He sleeps so well," and she would hate to wake him up. And in some other way, too, she was afraid to wake him up because even in his sleep he seemed to be such a strict man.

Of course, nailed to the wall over the bed—only she would forget who it was—there was a picture of him when he was young. Then he had a fan of hair over his forehead like a king's crown. Now his hair lay down on his head, the spring had gone out of it. Solomon had a lightish face, with eyebrows scattered but rugged, the way privet grows, strong eyes, with second sight, a strict mouth, and a little gold smile. This was the way he looked in his clothes, but in bed in the daytime he looked a different and smaller man, even when he was wide awake, and holding the Bible. He looked like somebody kin to himself. And then sometimes when he lay in sleep and she stood fanning the flies away, and the light came in, his face was like new, so smooth and clear that it was like a glass of jelly held to the window, and she could almost look through his forehead and see what he thought.

She fanned him and at length he opened his eyes and spoke her name, but he would not taste the nice eggs she had kept warm under a pan.

Back in the kitchen she ate heartily, his breakfast and hers, and looked out the open door at what went on. The whole day, and the whole night before, she had felt the stir of spring close to her. It was as present in the house as a young man would be. The moon was in the last quarter and outside they were turning the sod and planting peas and beans. Up and down the red fields, over which smoke from the brush-burning hung showing like a little skirt of sky, a white horse and a white mule pulled the plow. At intervals hoarse shouts came through the air and roused her as if she dozed neglectfully in the shade, and they were telling her, "Jump up!" She could see how over each ribbon of field were moving men and girls, on foot and mounted on mules, with hats set on their heads and bright with tall hoes and forks as if they carried streamers on them and were going to some place on a journey—and how as if at a signal now and then they would all start at once shouting, hollering, cajoling, calling and answering back, running, being leaped on and breaking away, flinging to earth with a shout and lying motionless in the trance of twelve o'clock. The old women came out of the cabins and brought them the food they had ready for them, and then all worked together, spread evenly out. The little children came too, like a bouncing stream overflowing the fields, and set upon the men, the women, the dogs, the rushing birds, and the wave-like rows of earth, their little voices almost too high to be heard. In the middle distance like some white and gold towers were the haystacks, with black cows coming around to eat their edges. High above everything, the wheel of fields, house, and cabins, and the deep road surrounding like a moat to keep them in, was the turning sky, blue with long, far-flung white mare's-tail clouds, serene and still as high flames. And sound asleep while all this went around him that was his, Solomon was like a little still spot in the middle.

Even in the house the earth was sweet to breathe. Solomon had never let Livvie go any farther than the chicken house and the well. But what if she would walk now into the heart of the fields and take a hoe and work until she fell stretched out and drenched with her efforts, like other girls, and laid her cheek against the laid-open earth, and shamed the old man with her humbleness and delight? To shame him! A cruel wish could come in uninvited and so fast while she looked out the back door. She washed the dishes and scrubbed the table. She could hear the cries of the little lambs. Her mother, that she had not seen since her wedding day, had said one time, "I rather a man be anything, than a woman be mean."

So all morning she kept tasting the chicken broth on the stove, and when it was right she poured off a nice cupful. She carried it in to Solomon, and there he lay having a dream. Now what did he dream about? For she saw him sigh gently as if not to disturb some whole thing he held round in his mind, like a fresh egg. So even an old man dreamed about something pretty. Did he dream of her, while his eyes were shut and sunken, and his small hand with the wedding ring curled close in sleep around the quilt? He might be dreaming of what time it was, for even through his sleep he kept track of it like a clock, and knew how much of it went by, and waked up knowing where the hands were even before he consulted the silver watch that he never let go. He would sleep with the watch in his palm, and even holding it to his cheek like a child that loves a plaything. Or he might dream of journeys and travels on a steamboat to Natchez. Yet she thought he dreamed of her; but even while she scrutinized him, the rods of the foot of the bed seemed to rise up like a rail fence between them, and she could see that people never could be sure of anything as long as one of them was asleep and the other awake. To look at him dreaming of her when he might be going to die frightened her a little, as if he might carry her with him that way, and she wanted to run out of the room. She took hold of the bed and held on, and Solomon opened his eyes and called her name, but he did not want anything. He would not taste the good broth.

. . .

Just a little after that, as she was taking up the ashes in the front room for the last time in the year, she heard a sound. It was somebody coming. She pulled the curtains together and looked through the slit.

Coming up the path under the bottle trees was a white lady. At first she looked young, but then she looked old. Marvelous to see, a little car stood steaming like a kettle out in the field-track—it had come without a road.

Livvie stood listening to the long, repeated knockings at the door, and after a while she opened it just a little. The lady came in through the crack, though she was more than middle-sized and wore a big hat.

"My name is Miss Baby Marie," she said.

Livvie gazed respectfully at the lady and at the little suitcase she was holding close to her by the handle until the proper moment. The lady's eyes were running over the room, from palmetto to palmetto, but she was saying, "I live at home . . . out from Natchez . . . and get out and show these pretty cosmetic things to the white people and the colored people both . . . all around . . . years and years . . . Both shades of powder and rouge . . . It's the kind of work a girl can do and not go clear 'way from home. . . ." And the harder she looked, the more she talked. Suddenly she turned up her nose and said, "It is not Christian or sanitary to put feathers in a vase," and then she took a gold key out of the front of her dress and began unlocking the locks on her suitcase. Her face drew the light, the way it was covered with intense white and red, with a little patty-cake of white between the wrinkles by her upper lip. Little red tassels of hair bobbed under the rusty wires of her picture-hat, as with an air of triumph and secrecy she now drew open her little suitcase and brought out bottle after bottle and jar after jar, which she put down on the table, the mantel-piece, the settee, and the organ.

"Did you ever see so many cosmetics in your life?" cried Miss Baby Marie.

"No'm," Livvie tried to say, but the cat had her tongue.

"Have you ever applied cosmetics?" asked Miss Baby Marie next.

"No'm," Livvie tried to say.

"Then look!" she said, and pulling out the last thing of all, "Try this!" she said. And in her hand was unclenched a golden lipstick which popped open like magic. A fragrance came out of it like incense, and Livvie cried out suddenly, "Chinaberry flowers!"

Her hand took the lipstick, and in an instant she was carried away in the air through the spring, and looking down with a half-drowsy smile from a purple cloud she saw from above a chinaberry tree, dark and smooth and neatly leaved, neat as a guinea hen in the dooryard, and there was her home that she had left. On one side of the tree was her mama holding up her heavy apron, and she could see it was loaded with ripe figs, and on the other side was her papa holding a fish-pole over the pond, and she could see it transparently, the little clear fishes swimming up to the brim.

"Oh, no, not chinaberry flowers—secret ingredients," said Miss Baby Marie. "My cosmetics have secret ingredients—not chinaberry flowers."

"It's purple," Livvie breathed, and Miss Baby Marie said, "Use it freely. Rub it on."

Livvie tiptoed out to the wash stand on the front porch and before the mirror put the paint on her mouth. In the wavery surface her face danced before her like a flame. Miss Baby Marie followed her out, took a look at what she had done, and said, "That's it."

Livvie tried to say "Thank you" without moving her parted lips where the paint lay so new.

By now Miss Baby Marie stood behind Livvie and looked in the mirror over her shoulder, twisting up the tassels of her hair. "The lipstick I can let you have for only two dollars," she said, close to her neck.

"Lady, but I don't have no money, never did have," said Livvie.

"Oh, but you don't pay the first time. I make another trip, that's the way I do. I come back again—later."

"Oh," said Livvie, pretending she understood everything so as to please the lady.

"But if you don't take it now, this may be the last time I'll call at your house," said Miss Baby Marie sharply. "It's far away from anywhere, I'll tell you that. You don't live close to anywhere."

"Yes'm. My husband, he keep the *money,*" said Livvie, trembling. "He is strict as he can be. He don't know *you* walk in here—Miss Baby Marie!"

"Where is he?"

"Right now, he in yonder sound asleep, an old man. I wouldn't ever ask him for anything."

Miss Baby Marie took back the lipstick and packed it up. She gathered up the jars for both black and white and got them all inside the suitcase, with the same little fuss of triumph with which she had brought them out. She started away.

"Good-bye," she said, making herself look grand from the back, but at the last minute she turned around in the door. Her old hat wobbled as she whispered, "Let me see your husband."

Livvie obediently went on tiptoe and opened the door to the other room. Miss Baby Marie came behind her and rose on her toes and looked in.

"My, what a little tiny old, old man!" she whispered, clasping her hands and shaking her head over them. "What a beautiful quilt! What a tiny old, old man!"

"He can sleep like that all day," whispered Livvie proudly.

They looked at him awhile so fast asleep, and then all at once they looked at each other. Somehow that was as if they had a secret, for he had never stirred. Livvie then politely, but all at once, closed the door.

"Well! I'd certainly like to leave you with a lipstick!" said Miss Baby Marie vivaciously. She smiled in the door.

"Lady, but I told you I don't have no money, and never did have."

"And never will?" In the air and all around, like a bright halo around the white lady's nodding head, it was a true spring day.

"Would you take eggs, lady?" asked Livvie softly.

"No, I have plenty of eggs—plenty," said Miss Baby Marie.

"I still don't have no money," said Livvie, and Miss Baby Marie took her suitcase and went on somewhere else.

Livvie stood watching her go, and all the time she felt her heart beating in her left side. She touched the place with her hand. It seemed as if her heart beat and her whole face flamed from the pulsing color of her lips. She went to sit by Solomon and when he opened his eyes he could not see a change in her. "He's fixin' to die," she said inside. That was the secret. That was when she went out of the house for a little breath of air.

She went down the path and down the Natchez Trace a way, and she did not know how far she had gone, but it was not far, when she saw a sight. It was a man, looking like a vision—she standing on one side of the Old Natchez Trace and he standing on the other.

As soon as this man caught sight of her, he began to look himself over.

Starting at the bottom with his pointed shoes, he began to look up, lifting his peg-top pants the higher to see fully his bright socks. His coat long and wide and leaf-green he opened like doors to see his high-up tawny pants and his pants he smoothed downward from the points of his collar, and he wore a luminous baby-pink satin shirt. At the end, he reached gently above his wide platter-shaped round hat, the color of a plum, and one finger touched at the feather, emerald green, blowing in the spring winds.

No matter how she looked, she could never look so fine as he did, and she was not sorry for that, she was pleased.

He took three jumps, one down and two up, and was by her side.

"My name is Cash," he said.

He had a guinea pig in his pocket. They began to walk along. She stared on and on at him, as if he were doing some daring spectacular thing, instead of just walking beside her. It was not simply the city way he was dressed that made her look at him and see hope in its insolence looking back. It was not only the way he moved along kicking the flowers as if he could break through everything in the way and destroy anything in the world, that made her eyes grow bright. It might be, if he had not appeared *that day* she would never have looked so closely at him, but the time people come makes a difference.

They walked through the still leaves of the Natchez Trace, the light and the shade falling through trees about them, the white irises shining like candles on the banks and the new ferns shining like green stars up in the oak branches. They came out at Solomon's house, bottle trees and all. Livvie stopped and hung her head.

Cash began whistling a little tune. She did not know what it was, but she had heard it before from a distance, and she had a revelation. Cash was a field hand. He was a transformed field hand. Cash belonged to Solomon. But he had stepped out of his overalls into this. There in front of Solomon's house he laughed. He had a round head, a round face, all of him was young, and he flung his head up, rolled it against the mare's-tail sky in his round hat, and he could laugh just to see Solomon's house sitting there. Livvie looked at it, and there was Solomon's black hat hanging on the peg on the front door, the blackest thing in the world.

"I been to Natchez," Cash said, wagging his head around against the sky. "I taken a trip, I ready for Easter!"

How was it possible to look so fine before the harvest? Cash must have stolen the money, stolen it from Solomon. He stood in the path and lifted his spread hand high and brought it down again and again in his laughter. He kicked up his heels. A little chill went through her. It was as if Cash was bringing that strong hand down to beat a drum or to rain blows upon a man, such an abandon and menace were in his laugh. Frowning, she went closer to him and his swinging arm drew her in at once and the fright was crushed from her body, as a little match-flame might be smothered out by what it lighted.

She gathered the folds of his coat behind him and fastened her red lips to his mouth, and she was dazzled at herself then, the way he had been dazzled at himself to begin with.

In that instant she felt something that could not be told—that Solomon's death was at hand, that he was the same to her as if he were dead now. She cried out, and uttering little cries turned and ran for the house.

At once Cash was coming, following after, he was running behind her. He came close, and half-way up the path he laughed and passed her. He even picked up a stone and sailed it into the bottle trees. She put her hands over her head, and sound clattered through the bottle trees like cries of outrage. Cash stamped and plunged zigzag up the front steps and in at the door.

When she got there, he had stuck his hands in his pockets and was turning slowly about in the front room. The little guinea pig peeped out. Around Cash, the pinned-up palmettos looked as if a lazy green monkey had walked up and down and around the walls leaving green prints of his hands and feet.

She got through the room and his hands were still in his pockets, and she fell upon the closed door to the other room and pushed it open. She ran to Solomon's bed, calling "Solomon! Solomon!" The little shape of the old man never moved at all, wrapped under the quilt as if it were winter still.

"Solomon!" She pulled the quilt away, but there was another one under that, and she fell on her knees beside him. He made no sound except a sigh, and then she could hear in the silence the light springy steps of Cash walking and walking in the front room, and the ticking of Solomon's silver watch, which came from the bed. Old Solomon was far away in his sleep, his face looked small, relentless, and devout, as if he were walking somewhere where she could imagine the snow falling.

. . .

Then there was a noise like a hoof pawing the floor, and the door gave a creak, and Cash appeared beside her. When she looked up, Cash's face was so black it was bright, and so bright and bare of pity that it looked sweet to her. She stood up and held up her head. Cash was so powerful that his presence gave her strength even when she did not need any.

Under their eyes Solomon slept. People's faces tell of things and places not known to the one who looks at them while they sleep, and while Solomon slept under the eyes of Livvie and Cash his face told them like a mythical story that all his life he had built, little scrap by little scrap, respect. A beetle could not have been more laborious or more ingenious in the task of its destiny. When Solomon was young, as he was in his picture overhead, it was the infinite thing with him, and he could see no end to the respect he would contrive and keep in a house. He had built a lonely house, the way he would make a cage, but it grew to be the same with him as a great monumental pyramid and sometimes in his absorption of getting it erected he was like the builder-slaves of Egypt who forgot or never knew the origin and meaning of the thing to which they gave all the strength of their bodies and used up all their days. Livvie and Cash could see that as a man might rest from a life-labor he lay in his bed, and they could hear how, wrapped in his quilt, he sighed to himself comfortably in sleep, while in his dreams he might have been an ant, a beetle, a bird, an Egyptian, assembling and carrying on his back and building with his hands, or he might have been an old man of India or a swaddled baby, about to smile and brush all away.

Then without warning old Solomon's eyes flew wide open under the hedge-like brows. He was wide awake.

And instantly Cash raised his quick arm. A radiant sweat stood on his temples. But he did not bring his arm down—it stayed in the air, as if something might have taken hold.

It was not Livvie—she did not move. As if something said "Wait," she stood waiting. Even while her eyes burned under motionless lids, her lips parted in a stiff grimace, and with her arms stiff at her sides she stood above the prone old man and the panting young one, erect and apart.

Movement when it came came in Solomon's face. It was an old and strict face, a frail face, but behind it, like a covered light, came an animation that could play hide and seek, that would dart and escape, had always escaped. The mystery flickered in him, and invited from his eyes. It was that very mystery that Cash with his quick arm would have to strike, and that Livvie could not weep for. But Cash only stood holding his arm in the air, when the gentlest flick of his great strength, almost a puff of his breath, would have been enough, if he had known how to give it, to send the old man over the obstruction that kept him away from death.

"Young ones can't wait," said Solomon.

Livvie shuddered violently, and then in a gush of tears she stooped for a glass of water and handed it to him, but he did not see her.

"So here come the young man Livvie wait for. Was no prevention. No prevention. Now I lay eyes on young man and it come to be somebody I know all the time, and been knowing since he were born in a cotton patch, and watched grow up year to year, Cash McCord, growed to size, growed up to come in my house in the end—ragged and barefoot."

Solomon gave a cough of distaste. Then he shut his eyes vigorously, and his lips began to move like a chanter's.

"When Livvie married, her husband were already somebody. He had paid great cost for his land. He spread sycamore leaves over the ground from wagon to door, day he brought her home, so her foot would not have to touch ground. He carried her through his door. Then he growed old and could not lift her, and she were still young."

Livvie's sobs followed his words like a soft melody repeating each thing as he stated it. His lips moved for a little without sound, or she cried too fervently, and unheard he might have been telling his whole life, and then he said, "God forgive Solomon for sins great and small. God forgive Solomon for carrying away too young girl for wife and keeping her away from her people and from all the young people would clamor for her back."

Then he lifted up his right hand toward Livvie where she stood by the bed and offered her his silver watch. He dangled it before her eyes, and she hushed crying; her tears stopped. For a moment the watch could be heard ticking as it always did, precisely in his proud hand. She lifted it away. Then he took hold of the quilt; then he was dead.

. . .

Livvie left Solomon dead and went out of the room. Stealthily, nearly without noise, Cash went beside her. He was like a shadow, but his shiny shoes moved over the floor in spangles, and the green downy feather shone like a light in his hat. As they reached the front room, he seized her deftly as a long black cat and dragged her hanging by the waist round and round him, while he turned in a circle, his face bent down to hers. The first moment, she kept one arm and its hand stiff and still, the one that held Solomon's watch. Then the fingers softly let go, all of her was limp, and the watch fell somewhere on the floor. It ticked away in the still room, and all at once there began outside the full song of a bird.

They moved around and around the room and into the brightness of the open door, then he stopped and shook her once. She rested in silence in his trembling arms, unprotesting as a bird on a nest. Outside the redbirds were flying and criss-crossing, the sun was in all the bottles on the prisoned trees, and the young peach was shining in the middle of them with the bursting light of spring.

1943

HORTENSE CALISHER
(1911–)

Born to a Jewish father from Virginia and a Jewish mother from Germany, Hortense Calisher has always fought against being typed as a certain type of artist—European, American, Southern, Jewish, or even woman writer. Her writings have continually stirred up controversy: her stories about anti-Semitism and racism among Jews, for instance, were turned down by magazine editors fearful of making readers angry. "You will never write truthfully about any ethnic group and please it," Calisher has said.

Much of Calisher's fiction is highly autobiographical, yet as she herself points out, "in all quasi-autobiography, as one exorcises the family world the mere facts begin to disappear, in favor of the mere truth." Calisher's stories are often sensitive, evocative tales that describe small but significant moments of insight and pain. Although she has taken part in antiwar protests and other sorts of political activism, she believes her real activism takes place in her writing: "There I will dare anything."

Born into an upper-middle-class family in New York City, Calisher received her B.A. in 1932 from Barnard College despite the financial struggles of the Depression. One of her first jobs was as a social worker with the Department of Public Welfare, where she encountered firsthand the grim poverty of the 1930s. Married to an engineer, Calisher traveled with him to numerous industrial cities and stayed home raising their child. Writing poems but not trying to publish them, Calisher led an existence similar to ones portrayed in her stories in which women are frustrated because housewifely duties must take precedence over artistic concerns. She began publishing fiction in 1948 and from then on faced the problems of being an artist as well as wife and mother.

Having published short stories in prestigious magazines such as The New Yorker, *Calisher also worked as a journalist in the early 1950s, writing articles for* The Reporter. *In the 1960s, while going through a divorce, she taught writing at Barnard College and then at the Writers' Workshop at the University of Iowa. She has also been a writer-in-residence at Columbia, Brandeis, and the University of Pennsylvania.*

Calisher's short-story collections In the Absence of Angels *and* Tales of the Mirror *include some of her best stories, including semiautobiographical tales centered on Hester Elkins.* Herself *is an autobiographical examination of Calisher's life as a writer. Her novels include* Queenie *and* Eagle Eye. *The novel* On Keeping Women *discusses in part whether the breakup of family life is a type of liberation.*

"The Rabbi's Daughter," which was published in the collection Extreme Magic, *is autobiographical in part, concerning as it does the unhappiness of a woman whose present life will not let her satisfy her yearnings to be an artist. Like Calisher, Eleanor has married an engineer with whom she cannot share her inner life. Calisher writes of Eleanor: "She, whose feminism scarcely has a name, doesn't know that she will revolt." The story exemplifies Calisher's ability to portray vividly even minor characters, like Dr. Ruth Brinn, while swiftly bringing us into the complex consciousness of the central figure. The story also reflects Calisher's use of Jewish characters to convey problems and situations common to women and artists of all cultures.*

THE RABBI'S DAUGHTER

They all came along with Eleanor and her baby in the cab to Grand Central, her father and mother on either side of her, her father holding the wicker bassinet on his carefully creased trousers. Rosalie and Helene, her cousins, smart in their fall ensembles, just right for the tingling October dusk, sat in the two little seats opposite them. Aunt Ruth, Dr. Ruth Brinn, her father's sister and no kin to the elegant distaff cousins, had insisted on sitting in front with the cabman. Eleanor could see her now, through the glass, in animated talk, her hat tilted piratically on her iron-gray braids.

Leaning forward, Eleanor studied the dim, above-eye-level picture of the driver. A sullen-faced young man, with a lock of black hair belligerent over his familiar nondescript face: "Manny Kaufman." What did Manny Kaufman think of Dr. Brinn? In ten minutes she would drag his life history from him, answering his unwilling statements with the snapping glance, the terse nods which showed that she got it all, at once, understood him down to the bone. At the end of her cross-questioning she would be quite capable of saying, "Young man, you are too pale! Get another job!"

"I certainly don't know why you wanted to wear that get-up," said Eleanor's mother, as the cab turned off the Drive toward Broadway. "On a train. And with the baby to handle, all alone." She brushed imaginary dust from her lap, scattering disapproval with it. She had never had to handle her babies alone.

Eleanor bent over the basket before she answered. She was a thin fair girl whom motherhood had hollowed, rather than enhanced. Tucking the bottle-bag further in, feeling the wad of diapers at the bottom, she envied the baby blinking solemnly up at her, safe in its surely serviced world.

"Oh, I don't know," she said. "It just felt gala. New Yorkish. Some people dress down for a trip. Others dress up—like me." Staring at her own lap, though, at the bronze velveteen which had been her wedding dress, sensing the fur blob of hat insecure on her unprofessionally waved hair, shifting the shoes, faintly scuffed, which had been serving her for best for two years, she felt the sickening qualm, the frightful inner blush of the inappropriately dressed.

In front of her, half-turned toward her, the two cousins swayed neatly in unison, two high-nostriled gazelles, one in black, one in brown, both in pearls, wearing their propriety, their utter rightness, like skin. She had known her own excess when she had dressed for the trip yesterday morning, in the bare rooms, after the van had left, but her suits were worn, stretched with wearing during pregnancy, and nothing went with anything any more. Tired of house dresses, of the spotted habiliments of maternity, depressed with her three months' solitude in the country waiting out the lease after Dan went on to the new job, she had reached for the wedding clothes, seeing herself cleansed and queenly once more, mysterious traveler whose appearance might signify anything, approaching the pyrrhic towers of New York, its effervescent terminals, with her old brilliance, her old style.

Her father sighed. "Wish that boy could find a job nearer New York."

"You know an engineer has to go where the plants are," she said, weary of the old argument. "It's not like you—with your own business and everything. Don't you think I'd like . . . ?" She stopped, under Rosalie's bright, tallying stare.

"I know, I know." He leaned over the baby, doting.

"What's your new house like?" said Rosalie.

"You know," she said gaily, "after all Dan's letters, I'm not just sure, except that it's part of a two-family. They divide houses every which way in those towns. He's written about 'Bostons,' and 'flats,' and 'duplexes.' All I really know is it has automatic heat, thank goodness, and room for the piano." She clamped her lips suddenly on the hectic, chattering voice. Why had she had to mention the piano, especially since they were just passing Fifty-seventh Street, past Carnegie with all its clustering satellites—the Pharmacy, the Playhouse, the Russian restaurant—and in the distance, the brindled windows of the galleries, the little chiffoned store fronts, spitting garnet and saffron light? All her old life smoked out toward her from these buildings, from this parrot-gay, music-scored street.

"Have you been able to keep up with your piano?" Helene's head cocked, her eyes screened.

"Not—not recently. But I'm planning a schedule. After we're settled." In the baby's nap time, she thought. When I'm not boiling formulas or wash. In the evenings, while Dan reads, if I'm only—just not too tired. With a constriction, almost of fear, she realized that she and Dan had not even discussed whether the family on the other side of the house would mind the practicing. That's how far I've come away from it, she thought, sickened.

"All that time spent." Her father stroked his chin with a scraping sound and shook his head, then moved his hand down to brace the basket as the cab swung forward on the green light.

My time, she thought, my life—your money, knowing her unfairness in the same moment, knowing it was only his devotion, wanting the best for her, which deplored. Or, like her mother, did he mourn too the preening pride in the accomplished daughter, the long build-up, Juilliard, the feverish, relative-ridden Sunday afternoon recitals in Stengel's studio, the program at Town Hall, finally, with her name, no longer Eleanor Goldman, but Elly Gold, truncated hopefully, euphoniously for the professional life to come, that had already begun to be, thereafter, in the first small jobs, warm notices?

As the cab rounded the corner of Fifth, she saw two ballerinas walking together, unmistakable with their dark Psyche knots over their fichus, their sandaled feet angled outwards, the peculiar compensating tilt of their little strutting behinds. In that moment it was as if she had taken them all in at once, seen deep into their lives. There was a studio of them around the hall from Stengel's, and under the superficial differences the atmosphere in the two studios had been much the same: two tight, concentric worlds whose *aficionados* bickered and endlessly discussed in their separate argots, whose students, glowing with the serious work of creation, were like trajectories meeting at the burning curve of interest.

She looked at the cousins with a dislike close to envy, because they neither burned nor were consumed. They would never throw down the fixed cards. Conformity would protect them. They would marry for love if they could; if not, they would pick, prudently, a candidate who would never remove them from the life to which they were accustomed. Mentally they would never even leave Eighty-sixth Street, and their homes would be like their mothers', like her mother's, *bibelots* suave on the coffee tables, bonbon dishes full, but babies postponed until they could afford to have them born at Doctors Hospital. "After all the money Uncle Harry spent on her, too," they would say later in mutually confirming gossip. For to them she would simply have missed out on the putative glory of the prima donna; that it was the work she missed would be out of their ken.

. . .

The cab swung into the line of cars at the side entrance to Grand Central. Eleanor bent over the basket and took out the baby. "You take the basket, Dad." Then, as if forced by the motion of the cab, she reached over and thrust the bundle of baby onto Helene's narrow brown crepe lap, and held it there until Helene grasped it diffidently with her suede gloves.

"She isn't—she won't wet, will she?" said Helene.

A porter opened the door. Eleanor followed her mother and father out and then reached back into the cab. "I'll take her now." She stood there hugging the bundle, feeling it close, a round comforting cyst of love and possession.

Making her way through the snarled mess of traffic on the curb, Aunt Ruth came and stood beside her. "Remember what I told you!" she called to the departing driver, wagging her finger at him.

"What did you tell him?" said Eleanor.

"Huh! What I told him!" Her aunt shrugged, the blunt Russian shrug of inevitability; her shrewd eyes ruminant over the outthrust chin, the spread hands. "Can I fix life? Life in Brooklyn on sixty dollars a week? I'm only a medical doctor!" She pushed her hat forward on her braids. "Here! Give me that baby!" She whipped the baby from Eleanor's grasp and held it with authority, looking speculatively at Eleanor. "Go on! Walk ahead with them!" She grinned. "Don't I make a fine nurse? Expensive, too!"

Down at the train, Eleanor stood at the door of the roomette while the other women, jammed inside, divided their ardor for the miniature between the baby and the telescoped comforts of the cubicle. At the end of the corridor, money and a pantomime of cordiality passed between her father and the car porter. Her father came back down the aisle, solid gray man, refuge of childhood, grown shorter than she. She stared down at his shoulder, rigid, her eyes unfocused, restraining herself from laying her head upon it.

"All taken care of," he said. "He's got the formula in the icebox and he'll take care of getting you off in the morning. Wish you could have stayed longer, darling." He pressed an envelope into her hand. "Buy yourself something. Or the baby." He patted her shoulder. "No . . . now never mind now. This is between you and me."

"Guess we better say good-bye, dear," said her mother, emerging from the roomette with the others. Doors slammed, passengers swirled around them. They kissed in a circle, nibbling and diffident.

Aunt Ruth did not kiss her, but took Eleanor's hands and looked at her, holding on to them. She felt her aunt's hands moving softly on her own. The cousins watched brightly.

"What's this, what's this?" said her aunt. She raised Eleanor's hands, first one, then the other, as if weighing them in a scale, rubbed her own strong, diagnostic thumb back and forth over Eleanor's right hand, looking down at it. They all looked down at it. It was noticeably more spatulate, coarser-skinned than the left, and the middle knuckles were thickened.

"So . . . ," said her aunt. "So-o . . . ," and her enveloping stare had in it that warmth, tinged with resignation, which she offered indiscriminately to cabmen, to nieces, to life. "So . . . , the 'rabbi's daughter' is washing dishes!" And she nodded, in requiem.

"Prescription?" said Eleanor, smiling wryly back.

"No prescription!" said her aunt. "In my office I see hundreds of girls like you. And there is no little pink pill to fit." She shrugged, and then whirled on the others. "Come. Come on." They were gone, in a last-minute flurry of ejaculations. As the train began to wheel past the platform, Eleanor caught a blurred glimpse of their faces, her parents and aunt in anxious trio, the two cousins neatly together.

People were still passing by the door of the roomette, and a woman in one group paused to admire the baby, frilly in the delicately lined basket, "Ah, look!" she cooed. "Sweet! How old is she?"

"Three months."

"It *is* a she?"

Eleanor nodded.

"Sweet!" the woman said again, shaking her head admiringly, and went on down the aisle. Now the picture was madonna-perfect, Eleanor knew—the harsh, tintype lighting centraled down on her and the child, glowing in the viscous paneling that was grained to look like wood, highlighted in the absurd plush-cum-metal fixtures of this sedulously planned manger. She shut the door.

The baby began to whimper. She made it comfortable for the night, diapering it quickly, clipping the pins in the square folds, raising the joined ankles in a routine that was like a jigging ballet of the fingers. Only after she had made herself ready for the night, hanging the dress quickly behind a curtain, after she had slipped the last prewarmed bottle out of its case and was holding the baby close as it fed, watching the three-cornered pulse of the soft spot winking in and out on the downy head—only then did she let herself look closely at her two hands.

The difference between them was not enough to attract casual notice, but enough, when once pointed out, for anyone to see. She remembered Stengel's strictures on practicing with the less able left one. "Don't think you can gloss over, Miss. It shows!" But that the scrubbing hand, the working hand, would really "show" was her first intimation that the daily makeshift could become cumulative, could leave its imprint on the flesh with a crude symbolism as dully real, as conventionally laughable, as the first wrinkle, the first gray hair.

She turned out the light and stared into the rushing dark. The physical change was nothing, she told herself, was easily repaired; what she feared almost to phrase was the death by postponement, the slow uneventful death of impulse. "Hundreds of girls like you," she thought, fearing for the first time the compromises that could arrive upon one unaware, not in the heroic renunciations, but erosive, gradual, in the slow chip-chipping of circumstance. Outside the window the hills of the Hudson Valley loomed and receded, rose up, piled, and slunk again into foothills. For a long time before she fell asleep she probed the dark for their withdrawing shapes, as if drama and purpose receded with them.

In the morning the porter roused her at six, returning an iced bottle of formula, and one warmed and made ready. She rose with a granular sense of return to the real, which lightened as she attended to the baby and dressed. Energized, she saw herself conquering whatever niche Dan had found for them, revitalizing the unknown house as she had other houses, with all the artifices of her New York chic, squeezing ragouts from the tiny salary spent cagily at the A & P, enjoying the baby instead of seeing her in the groggy focus of a thousand tasks. She saw herself caught up at odd hours in the old exaltation of practice, even if they had to hire a mute piano, line a room with cork. Nothing was impossible to the young, bogey-dispersing morning.

. . .

The station ran past the window, such a long one, sliding through the greasy lemon-colored lights, that she was almost afraid they were not going to stop, or that it was the wrong one, until she saw Dan's instantly known contour, jointed, thin, and his face, raised anxiously to the train windows with the vulnerability of people who do not know they are observed. She saw him for a minute as other passengers, brushing their teeth hastily in the washrooms, might look out and see him, a young man, interesting because he was alone on the platform, a nice young man in a thick jacket and heavy work pants, with a face full of willingness and anticipation. Who would get off for him?

As she waited in the jumble of baggage at the car's end, she warned herself that emotion was forever contriving toward moments which, when achieved, were not single and high as they ought to have been, but often splintered slowly—just walked away on the little centrifugal feet of detail. She remembered how she had mulled before their wedding night, how she had been unable to see beyond the single devouring picture of their two figures turning, turning toward one another. It had all happened, it had all been there, but memory could not recall it so, retaining instead, with the pedantic fidelity of some poet whose interminable listings recorded obliquely the face of the beloved but never invoked it, a whole rosary of irrelevancies, in the telling of which the two figures merged and were lost. Again she had the sense of life pushing her on by minute, imperceptible steps whose trend would not be discerned until it was too late, as the tide might encroach upon the late swimmer, making a sea of the sand he left behind.

"Dan!" she called. "Dan!"

He ran toward her. She wanted to run too, to leap out of the hemming baggage and fall against him, rejoined. Instead, she and the bags and the basket were jockeyed off the platform by the obsequious porter, and she found herself on the gray boards of the station, her feet still rocking with the leftover rhythm of the train, holding the basket clumsily between her and Dan, while the train washed off hoarsely behind them. He took the basket from her, set it down, and they clung and kissed, but in all that ragged movement, the moment subdivided and dispersed.

"Good Lord, how big she is!" he said, poking at the baby with a shy, awkward hand.

"Mmm. Tremendous!" They laughed together, looking down.

"Your shoes—what on earth?" she said. They were huge, laced to the ankle, the square tips inches high, like blocks of wood on the narrow clerkly feet she remembered.

"Safety shoes. You have to wear them around a foundry. Pretty handy if a casting drops on your toe."

"Very swagger." She smiled up at him, her throat full of all there was to tell—how, in the country, she had spoken to no one but the groceryman for so long that she had begun to monologue to the baby; how she had built up the first furnace fire piece by piece, crouching before it in awe and a sort of pride, hoping, as she shifted the damper chains, that she was pulling the right one; how the boy who was to mow the lawn had never come, and how at last she had taken a scythe to the knee-deep, insistent grass and then grimly, jaggedly, had mown. But now, seeing his face dented with fatigue, she saw too his grilling neophyte's day at the foundry, the evenings when he must have dragged hopefully through ads and houses, subjecting his worn wallet and male ingenuousness to the soiled witcheries of how many landlords, of how many narrow-faced householders tipping back in their porch chairs, patting tenderly at their bellies, who would suck at their teeth and look him over. "You permanent here, mister?" Ashamed of her city-bred heroisms, she said nothing.

"You look wonderful," he said. "Wonderful."

"Oh." She looked down. "A far cry from."

"I borrowed a car from one of the men, so we can go over in style." He swung the basket gaily under one arm. "Let's have breakfast first, though."

"Yes, let's." She was not eager to get to the house.

They breakfasted in a quick-lunch place on the pallid, smudged street where the car was parked, and she waited, drinking a second cup of coffee from a grainy white mug while Dan went back to the station to get the trunk. The mug had an indistinct blue V on it in the middle of a faded blue line running around the rim; it had probably come secondhand from somewhere else. The fork she had used had a faint brassiness showing through its nickel-colored tines and was marked "Hotel Ten Eyck, Albany," although this was not Albany. Even the restaurant, on whose white, baked look the people made gray transient blurs which slid and departed, had the familiar melancholy which pervaded such places because they were composed everywhere, in a hundred towns, of the same elements, but were never lingered in or personally known. This town would be like that too; one would be able to stand in the whirling center of the five-and-dime and fancy oneself in a score of other places where the streets had angled perhaps a little differently and the bank had been not opposite the post office, but a block down. There would not even be a need for fancy because, irretrievably here, one was still in all the resembling towns, and going along these streets one would catch oneself nodding to faces known surely, plumbed at a glance, since these were overtones of faces in all the other towns that had been and were to be.

They drove through the streets, which raised an expectation she knew to be doomed, but cherished until it should be dampened by knowledge. Small houses succeeded one another, gray, coffee-colored, a few white ones, many with two doors and two sets of steps.

"Marlborough Road," she said. "My God."

"Ours is Ravenswood Avenue."

"No!"

"Slicker!" he said. "Ah, darling, I can't believe you're here." His free arm tightened and she slid down on his shoulder. The car made a few more turns, stopped in the middle of a block, and was still.

. . .

The house, one of the white ones, had two close-set doors, but the two flights of steps were set at opposite ends of the ledge of porch, as if some craving for a privacy but doubtfully maintained within had leaked outside. Hereabouts, in houses with the cramped deadness of diagrams, was the special ugliness created by people who would keep themselves a toehold above the slums by the exercise of a terrible, ardent neatness which had erupted into the foolish or the grotesque—the two niggling paths in the common driveway, the large trellis arching pompously over nothing. On Sundays they would emerge, the fathers and mothers, dressed soberly, even threadbare, but dragging children outfitted like angelic visitants from the country of the rich, in poke bonnets and suitees of pink and mauve, larded triumphantly with fur.

As Dan bent over the lock of one of the doors, he seemed to her like a man warding off a blow.

"Is the gas on?" she said hurriedly. "I've got one more bottle."

He nodded. "It heats with gas, you know. That's why I took it. They have cheap natural gas up here." He pushed the door open, and the alien, anti-people smell of an empty house came out toward them.

"I know. You said. Wait till I tell you about me and the furnace in the other place." Her voice died away as, finally, they were inside.

He put the basket on the floor beside him. "Well," he said, "this am it."

"Why, there's the sofa!" she said. "It's so funny to see everything—just two days ago in Erie, and now here." Her hand delayed on the familiar pillows, as if on the shoulder of a friend. Then, although a glance had told her that no festoonings of the imagination were going to change this place, there was nothing to do but look.

The door-cluttered box in which they stood predicated a three-piece "suite" and no more. In the center of its mustard woodwork and a wallpaper like cold cereal, two contorted pedestals supported less the ceiling than the status of the room. Wedged in without hope of rearrangment, her own furniture had an air of outrage, like social workers who had come to rescue a hovel and had been confronted, instead, with the proud glare of mediocrity.

She returned the room's stare with an enmity of her own. Soon I will get to know you the way a woman gets to know a house—where the baseboards are roughest, and in which corners the dust drifts—the way a person knows the blemishes of his own skin. But just now I am still free of you—still a visitor.

"Best I could do." The heavy shoes clumped, shifting.

"It'll be all right," she said. "You wait and see." She put her palms on his shoulders. "It just looked queer for a minute, with windows only on one side." She heard her own failing voice with dislike, quirked it up for him. "Half chick. That's what it is. Half-chick house!"

"Crazy!" But some of the strain left his face.

"Uh-huh, *Das Ewig Weibliche,* that's me!" She half pirouetted. "Dan!" she said. "Dan, where's the piano?"

"Back of you. We had to put it in the dinette. I thought we could eat in the living room anyway."

She opened the door. There it was, filling the box room, one corner jutting into the entry to the kitchenette. Tinny light, whitening down from a meager casement, was recorded feebly on its lustrous flanks. Morning and evening she would edge past it, with the gummy dishes and the clean. Immobile, in its cage, it faced her, a great dark harp lying on its side.

"Play something, for luck." Dan came up behind her, the baby bobbing on his shoulder.

She shook her head.

"Ah, come on." His free arm cinched the three of them in a circle, so that the baby participated in their kiss. The baby began to cry.

"See," she said. "We better feed her."

"I'll warm the bottle. Have to brush up on being a father." He nudged his way through the opening. She heard him rummaging in a carton, then the clinking of a pot.

She opened the lid of the piano and struck the A, waiting until the tone had died away inside her, then struck a few more notes. The middle register had flattened first, as it always did. Sitting down on the stool, she looked into her lap as if it belonged to someone else. What was the piano doing here, this opulent shape of sound, five hundred miles from where it was the day before yesterday; what was she doing here, sitting in the lopped-off house, in the dress that had been her wedding dress, listening to the tinkle of a bottle against a pan? What was the mystery of distance—that it was not only geographical but clove through the map, into the heart?

She began to play, barely flexing her fingers, hearing the nails she had let grow slip and click on the keys. Then, thinking of the entities on the other side of the wall, she began to play softly, placating, as if she would woo them, the town, providence. She played a Beethoven andante with variations, then an adagio, seeing the Von Bülow footnotes before her: ". . . the ascending diminished fifth may be phrased, as it were, like a question, to which the succeeding bass figure may be regarded as the answer."

. . .

The movement finished but she did not go on to the scherzo. Closing the lid, she put her head down on her crossed arms. Often, on the fringes of concerts, there were little haunting crones of women who ran up afterward to horn in on the congratulatory shop-talk of the players. She could see one of them now, batting her stiff claws together among her fluttering draperies, nodding eagerly for notice: "I studied . . . I played too, you know . . . years ago . . . with De Pachmann!"

So many variants of the same theme, she thought, so many of them—

the shriveled, talented women. Distance has nothing to do with it; be honest—they are everywhere. Fifty-seventh Street is full of them. The women who were once "at the League," who cannot keep themselves from hanging the paintings, the promising *juvenilia,* on their walls, but who flinch, deprecating, when one notices. The quondam writers, chary of ridicule, who sometimes, over wine, let themselves be persuaded into bringing out a faded typescript, and to whom there is never anything to say, because it is so surprisingly good, so fragmentary, and was written—how long ago? She could still hear the light insistent note of the A, thrumming unresolved, for herself, and for all the other girls. A man, she thought jealously, can be reasonably certain it was his talent which failed him, but the women, for whom there are still so many excuses, can never be so sure.

"You're tired." Dan returned, stood behind her.

She shook her head, staring into the shining case of the piano, wishing that she could retreat into it somehow and stay there huddled over its strings, like those recalcitrant nymphs whom legend immured in their native wood or water, but saved.

"I have to be back at the plant at eleven." He was smiling uncertainly, balancing the baby and the bottle.

She put a finger against his cheek, traced the hollows under his eyes. "I'll soon fatten you up," she murmured, and held out her arms to receive the baby and the long, coping day.

"Won't you crush your dress? I can wait till you change."

"No." She heard her own voice, sugared viciously with wistfulness. "Once I change I'll be settled. As long as I keep it on . . . I'm still a visitor."

Silenced, he passed her the baby and the bottle.

This will have to stop, she thought. Or will the denied half of me persist, venomously arranging for the ruin of the other? She wanted to warn him standing there, trusting, in the devious shadow of her resentment.

The baby began to pedal its feet and cry, a long nagging ululation. She sprinkled a few warm drops of milk from the bottle on the back of her own hand. It was just right, the milk, but she sat on, holding the baby in her lap, while the drops cooled. Flexing the hand, she suddenly held it out gracefully, airily, regarding it.

"This one is still 'the rabbi's daughter,'" she said. Dan looked down at her, puzzled. She shook her head, smiling back at him, quizzical and false, and bending, pushed the nipple in the baby's mouth. At once it began to suck greedily, gazing back at her with the intent, agate eyes of satisfaction.

1964

TILLIE OLSEN
(1913–   )

As a writer, political activist, and feminist critic, Tillie Olsen links the radical politics of the first half of this century to the feminism of the second half. In the 1930s, she described in poetry, essays, and fiction the lives of working people throughout the country. In her collection of essays from the 1970s, Silences, she inspired two decades of feminist scholarship with her eloquent exhortations: "You who teach, read writers who are women. There is a whole literature to be reestimated, revalued. Some works will prove to be, like the lives of their authors, mortal—speaking only to their time. Others now forgotten, obscured, ignored, will live again for us."

Olsen's parents, Samuel and Ida Lerner, immigrated to the United States following the failed 1905 Russian revolution. They settled in Nebraska, where Samuel became state chair of the Nebraska Socialist party. Born around 1913, Olsen was the second oldest of six children in this working-class family. She began keeping a journal at sixteen and wrote a humor column called "Squeaks" for her high-school paper. After the eleventh grade, she dropped out of school to help support her family.

Olsen continued her education in the Omaha public library, where she read most of the literature collection. She counted Walt Whitman, Katherine Mansfield, Langston Hughes, Willa Cather, and Ellen Glasgow as early favorites. More important, however, was her discovery of Rebecca Harding Davis's "Life in the Iron Mills" in a water-stained copy of the Atlantic Monthly she had purchased for a dime. Davis's novella told the young Olsen that "literature can be made out of the lives of despised people. . . . You, too, must write."

At seventeen, Olsen joined the youth organization of the Communist party and wrote for the Young People's Socialist League. The party assigned her to Kansas City, where she went to jail for handing out fliers to workers outside a packinghouse. In 1932 she began writing her working-class novel, Yonnondio. When she became a single parent at nineteen, she set aside the novel. She moved to California and started a family with Jack Olsen, a fellow socialist.

In 1934 she published two poems, the opening chapter of Yonnondio, and two essays. "The Strike" was based on her knowledge of the San Francisco maritime strike of 1934, and "Thousand-dollar Vagrant" described her arrest for strike-related activities. She also reported for socialist magazines such as the New York Partisan Review and the San Francisco Partisan.

For the next twenty years she worked, raised her four children, and felt "the simplest circumstances for creation did not exist." Not until the mid-1950s did she *write again. Her first story, "I Stand Here Ironing," describes her experiences as a working-class mother. In the 1960s and 1970s she published three major books:* Tell Me a Riddle, *a collection of stories;* Yonnondio: From the Thirties, *the polished novel; and* Silences, *a collection of her feminist essays.*

The story that has been selected, "O Yes," first appeared in the Prairie Schooner *under the title "Baptism." Written in 1956 and included in* Tell Me a Riddle, *the story reflects Olsen's abiding interest in how gender, race, and class affect human relationships.*

O YES

1

They are the only white people there, sitting in the dimness of the Negro church that had once been a corner store, and all through the bubbling, swelling, seething of before the services, twelve-year-old Carol clenches tight her mother's hand, the other resting lightly on her friend, Parialee Phillips, for whose baptism she has come.

The white-gloved ushers hurry up and down the aisle, beckoning people to their seats. A jostle of people. To the chairs angled to the left for the youth choir, to the chairs angled to the right for the ladies' choir, even up to the platform, where behind the place for the dignitaries and the mixed choir, the new baptismal tank gleams—and as if pouring into it from the ceiling, the blue-painted River of Jordan, God standing in the waters, embracing a brown man in a leopard skin and pointing to the letters of gold:

REJOICE

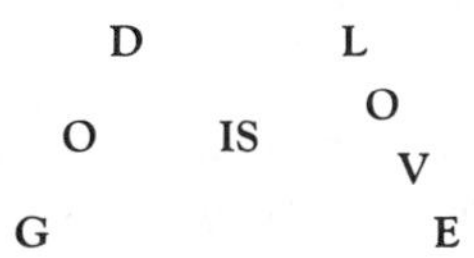

I AM THE WAY   THE TRUTH   THE LIFE

At the clear window, the crucified Christ embroidered on the starched white curtain leaps in the wind of the sudden singing. And the choirs march in. Robes of wine, of blue, of red.

"We stands and sings too," says Parialee's mother, Alva, to Helen; though already Parialee has pulled Carol up. Singing, little Lucinda Phillips fluffs out her many petticoats; singing, little Bubbie bounces up and down on his heels.

Any day now I'll reach that land of freedom,

Yes, o yes

Any day now, know that promised land

The youth choir claps and taps to accent the swing of it. Beginning to tap, Carol stiffens. "Parry, look. Somebody from school."

"Once more once," says Parialee, in the new way she likes to talk now.

"Eddie Garlin's up there. He's in my math."

"Couple cats from Franklin Jr. chirps in the choir. No harm or alarm."

Anxiously Carol scans the faces to see who else she might know, who else might know her, but looks quickly down to Lucinda's wide skirts, for it seems Eddie looks back at her, sullen or troubled, though it is hard to tell, faced as she is into the window of curtained sunblaze.

I know my robe will fit me well
I tried it on at the gates of hell

If it were a record she would play it over and over, Carol thought, to untwine the intertwined voices, to search how the many rhythms rock apart and yet are one glad rhythm.

When I get to heaven gonna sing and shout
Nobody be able to turn me out

"That's Mr. Chairback Evans going to invocate," Lucinda leans across Parry to explain. "He don't invoke good like Momma."

"Shhhh."

"Momma's the only lady in the church that invocates. She made the prayer last week. (Last month, Lucy.) I made the children's 'nouncement last time. (That was way back Thanksgiving.) And Bubbie's 'nounced too. Lots of times."

"Lucy-inda. SIT!"

Bible study announcements and mixed-choir practice announcements and Teen Age Hearts meeting announcements.

If Eddie said something to her about being there, worried Carol, if he talked to her right in front of somebody at school.

Messengers of Faith announcements and Mamboettes announcement and Committee for the Musical Tea.

Parry's arm so warm. Not realizing, starting up the old game from grade school, drumming a rhythm on the other's arm to see if the song could be guessed. "Parry, guess."

But Parry is pondering the platform.

The baptismal tank? "Parry, are you scared . . . the baptizing?"

"This cat? No." Shaking her head so slow and scornful, the barrette in her hair, sun fired, strikes a long rail of light. And still ponders the platform.

New Strangers Baptist Church invites you and Canaan Fair Singers announcements and Battle of Song and Cosmopolites meet. "O Lord, I couldn't find no ease," a solo. The ladies' choir:

O what you say seekers, o what you say seekers,
Will you never turn back no more?

The mixed choir sings:

Ezekiel saw that wheel of time
Every spoke was of humankind . . .

And the slim worn man in the pin-stripe suit starts his sermon On the Nature of God. How God is long-suffering. Oh, how long he has suffered. Calling the roll of the mighty nations, that rose and fell and now are dust for grinding the face of Man.

O voice of drowsiness and dream to which Carol does not need to listen. As long ago. Parry warm beside her too, as it used to be, there in the classroom at Mann Elementary, and the feel of drenched in sun and dimness and dream. Smell and sound of the chalk wearing itself away to nothing, rustle of books, drumming tattoo of Parry's fingers on her arm: *Guess.*

And as the preacher's voice spins happy and free, it is the used-to-be play-yard. Tag. Thump of the volley ball. Ecstasy of the jump rope. Parry, do pepper. Carol, do pepper. Parry's bettern Carol, Carol's bettern Parry. . . .

Did someone scream?

It seemed someone screamed—but all were sitting as before, though the sun no longer blared through the windows. She tried to see up where Eddie was, but the ushers were standing at the head of the aisle now, the ladies in white dresses like nurses or waitresses wear, the men holding their white-gloved hands up so one could see their palms.

"And God is Powerful," the preacher was chanting. "Nothing for him to scoop out the oceans and pat up the mountains. Nothing for him to scoop up the miry clay and create man. Man, I said, create Man."

The lady in front of her moaned "O *yes*" and others were moaning "O *yes.*"

"And when the earth mourned the Lord said, Weep not, for all will be returned to you, every dust, every atom. And the tired dust settles back, goes back. Until that Judgment Day. That great day."

"O *yes.*"

The ushers were giving out fans. Carol reached for one and Parry said: "What *you* need one for?" but she took it anyway.

"You think Satchmo can blow; you think Muggsy can blow; you think Dizzy can blow?" He was straining to an imaginary trumpet now, his head far back and his voice coming out like a trumpet.

"Oh Parry, he's so good."

"Well. Jelly jelly."

"Nothing to Gabriel on that great getting-up morning. And the horn wakes up Adam, and Adam runs to wake up Eve, and Eve moans; Just one more minute, let me sleep, and Adam yells, Great Day, woman, don't you know it's the Great Day?"

"*Great Day, Great Day,*" the mixed choir behind the preacher rejoices:

> *When our cares are past*
> *when we're home at last. . . .*

"And Eve runs to wake up Cain." Running round the platform, stooping and shaking imaginary sleepers, "and Cain runs to wake up Abel." Looping, scalloping his voice—"Grea-aaa-aat Daaaay." All the choirs thundering:

> *Great Day*
> *When the battle's fought*
> *And the victory's won*

Exultant spirals of sound. And Carol caught into it (Eddie forgotten, the game forgotten) chanting with Lucy and Bubbie: "*Great Day.*"

"Ohhhhhhhhhh," his voice like a trumpet again, "the re-unioning. Ohhhhhhhhh, the rejoicing. After the ages immemorial of longing."

Someone *was* screaming. And an awful thrumming sound with it, like feet and hands thrashing around, like a giant jumping of a rope.

"*Great Day.*" And no one stirred or stared as the ushers brought a little woman out into the aisle, screaming and shaking, just a little shrunk-up woman, not much taller than Carol, the biggest thing about her her swollen hands and the cascades of tears wearing her face.

The shaking inside Carol too. Turning and trembling to ask: "What . . . that lady?" But Parry still ponders the platform; little Lucy loops the chain of her bracelet round and round; and Bubbie sits placidly, dreamily. Alva Phillips is up fanning a lady in front of her; two lady ushers are fanning other people Carol cannot see. And her mother, her mother looks in a sleep.

Yes. He raised up the dead from the grave. He made old death behave.

Yes. Yes. From all over, hushed. ***O Yes***

He was your mother's rock. Your father's mighty tower. And he gave us a little baby. A little baby to love.

I am so glad

Yes, your friend, when you're friendless. Your father when you're fatherless. Way maker. Door opener.

Yes

When it seems you can't go on any longer, he's there. You can, he says, you can.

Yes

And that burden you have been carrying—ohhhhh that burden—not for always will it be. No, not for always.

Stay with me, Lord

I will put my Word in you and it is power. I will put my Truth in you and it is power.

O Yes

Out of your suffering I will make you to stand as a stone. A tried stone. Hewn out of the mountains of ages eternal.

Ohhhhhhhhhhh. Out of the mire I will lift your feet. Your tired feet from so much wandering. From so much work and wear and hard times.

Yes

From so much journeying—and never the promised land. And I'll wash them in the well your tears made. And I'll shod them in the gospel of peace, and of feeling good. Ohhhhhhhhh.

O Yes.

Behind Carol, a trembling wavering scream. Then the thrashing. Up above, the singing:

They taken my blessed Jesus and flogged him to the woods
And they made him hew out his cross and they dragged him to
Calvary
Shout brother, Shout shout shout. He never cried a word.

Powerful throbbing voices. Calling and answering to each other.

They taken my blessed Jesus and whipped him up the hill
With a knotty whip and a raggedy thorn he never cried a word
Shout, sister. Shout shout shout. He never cried a word.

Go tell the people the Saviour has risen
Has risen from the dead and will live forevermore
And won't have to die no more.

Halleloo.

Shout, brother, shout
We won't have to die no more!

A single exultant lunge of shriek. Then the thrashing. All around a clapping. Shouts with it. The piano whipping, whipping air to a froth. Singing now.

I once was lost who now am found
Was blind who now can see

On Carol's fan, a little Jesus walked on wondrously blue waters to where bearded disciples spread nets out of a fishing boat. If she studied the fan—became it—it might make a wall around her. If she could make what was happening (*what* was happening?) into a record small and round to listen to far and far as if into a seashell—the stamp and rills and spirals all tiny (but never any screaming).

wade wade in the water

Jordan's water is chilly and wild
I've got to get home to the other side
God's going to trouble the waters

The music leaps and prowls. Ladders of screamings. Drumming feet of ushers running. And still little Lucy fluffs her skirts, loops the chain on her bracelet; still Bubbie sits and rocks dreamily; and only eyes turn for an instant to the aisle as if nothing were happening. "Mother, let's go home," Carol begs, but her mother holds her so tight. Alva Phillips, strong Alva, rocking too and chanting, O *Yes.* No, do not look.

Wade,
Sea of trouble all mingled with fire
Come on my brethren it's time to go higher
Wade wade

The voices in great humming waves, slow, slow (when did it become the humming?), everyone swaying with it too, moving like in slow waves and singing, and up where Eddie is, a new cry, wild and open, "O help me, Jesus," and when Carol opens her eyes she closes them again, quick, but still can see the new known face from school (not Eddie), the thrashing, writhing body struggling against the ushers with the look of grave and loving support on their faces, and hear the torn, tearing cry: "Don't take me away, life everlasting don't take me away."

And now the rhinestones in Parry's hair glitter wicked; the white hands of the ushers, fanning, foam in the air; the blue-painted waters of Jordan swell and thunder; Christ spirals on his cross in the window—and she is drowned under the sluice of the slow singing and the sway.

. . .

So high up and forgotten the waves and the world, so stirless the deep cool green and the wrecks of what had been. Here now Hostess Foods, where Alva Phillips works her nights—but different from that time Alva had taken them through before work, for it is all sunken under water, the creaking loading platform where they had left the night behind; the closet room where Alva's swaddles of sweaters, boots, and cap hung, the long hall lined with pickle barrels, the sharp freezer door swinging open.

Bubbles of breath that swell. A gulp of numbing air. She swims into the chill room where the huge wheels of cheese stand, and Alva swims too, deftly oiling each machine: slicers and wedgers and the convey, that at her touch start to roll and grind. The light of day blazes up and Alva is holding a cup, saying: Drink this, baby.

"DRINK IT." Her mother's voice and the numbing air demanding her to pay attention. Up through the waters and into the car.

"That's right, lambie, now lie back." Her mother's lap.

"Mother."

"Shhhhh. You almost fainted, lambie."

Alva's voice. "You gonna be all right, Carol. . . . Lucy, I'm telling you for the last time, you and Buford get back into that church. Carol is *fine.*"

"Lucyinda, if I had all your petticoats I could float." Crying. "Why didn't you let me wear my full skirt with the petticoats, Mother."

"Shhhhh, lamb." Smoothing her cheek. "Just breathe, take long deep breaths."

". . . How you doing now, you little ol' consolation prize?" It is Parry, but she does not come in the car or reach to Carol through the open window: "No need to cuss and fuss. You going to be sharp as a tack, Jack."

Answering automatically: "And cool as a fool."

Quick, they look at each other.

"Parry, we have to go home now, don't we, Mother? I almost fainted, didn't I, Mother? . . . Parry, I'm sorry I got sick and have to miss your baptism."

"Don't feel sorry. I'll feel better you not there to watch. It was our mommas wanted you to be there, not me."

"Parry!" Three voices.

"Maybe I'll come over to play kickball after. If you feeling better. Maybe. Or bring the pogo." Old shared joys in her voice. "Or any little thing."

In just a whisper: "Or any little thing. Parry. Good-bye, Parry."

. . .

And why does Alva have to talk now?

"You all right? You breathin' deep like your momma said? Was it too close 'n hot in there? Did something scare you, Carrie?"

Shaking her head to lie, "No."

"I blames myself for not paying attention. You not used to people letting go that way. Lucy and Bubbie, Parialee, they used to it. They been coming since they lap babies."

"Alva, that's all right. Alva. Mrs. Phillips."

"You *was* scared. Carol, it's something to study about. You'll feel better if you understand."

Trying not to listen.

"You not used to hearing what people keeps inside, Carol. You know how music can make you feel things? Glad or sad or like you can't sit still? That was religion music, Carol."

"I have to breathe deep, Mother said."

"Not everybody feels religion the same way. Some it's in their mouth, but some it's like a hope in their blood, their bones. And they singing songs every word that's real to them, Carol, every word out of they own life. And the preaching finding lodgment in their hearts."

The screaming was tuning up in her ears again, high above Alva's patient voice and the waves lapping and fretting.

"Maybe somebody's had a hard week, Carol, and they locked up with it. Maybe a lot of hard weeks bearing down."

"Mother, my head hurts."

"And they're home, Carol, church is home. Maybe the only place they can feel how they feel and maybe let it come out. So they can go on. And it's all right."

"Please, Alva. Mother, tell Alva my head hurts."

"Get Happy, we call it, and most it's a good feeling, Carol. When you got all that locked up inside you."

"Tell her we have to go home. It's all right, Alva. Please, Mother. Say good-bye. Good-bye."

. . .

When I was carrying Parry and her father left me, and I fifteen years old, one thousand miles away from home, sin-sick and never really believing, as still I don't believe all, scorning, for what have it done to help, waiting there in the clinic and maybe sleeping, a voice called: Alva, Alva. So mournful and so sweet: Alva. Fear not, I have loved you from the foundation of the universe. And a little small child tugged on my dress. He was carrying a parade stick, on the end of it a star that outshined the sun. Follow me, he said. And the real sun went down and he hidden his stick. How dark it was, how dark. I could feel the darkness with my hands. And when I could see, I screamed. Dump trucks run, dumping bodies in hell, and a convey line run, never ceasing with souls, weary ones having to stamp and shove them along, and the air like fire. Oh I never want to hear such screaming. Then the little child jumped on a motorbike making a path no bigger than my little finger. But first he greased my feet with the hands of my momma when I was a knee baby. They shined like the sun was on them. Eyes he placed all around my head, and as I journeyed upward after him, it seemed I heard a mourning: "Mama Mama you must help carry the world." The rise and fall of nations I saw. And the voice called again Alva Alva, and I flew into a world of light, multitudes singing, Free, free, I am so glad.

2

Helen began to cry, telling her husband about it.

"You and Alva ought to have your heads examined, taking her there cold like that," Len said. "All right, wreck my best handkerchief. Anyway, now that she's had a bath, her Sunday dinner. . . ."

"And been fussed over," seventeen-year-old Jeannie put in.

"She seems good as new. Now *you* forget it, Helen."

I can't. Something . . . deep happened. If only I or Alva had told her what it would be like. . . . But I didn't realize."

You don't realize a lot of things, Mother, Jeannie said, but not aloud.

"So Alva talked about it after instead of before. Maybe it meant more that way."

"Oh Len, she didn't listen."

"You don't know if she did or not. Or what there was in the experience for her. . . ."

Enough to pull that kid apart two ways even more, Jeannie said, but still not aloud.

"I was so glad she and Parry were going someplace together again. Now that'll be between them too. Len, they really need, miss each other. What happened in a few months? When I think of how close they were, the hours of makebelieve and dressup and playing ball and collecting. . . ."

"Grow up, Mother." Jeannie's voice was harsh. "Parialee's collecting something else now. Like her own crowd. Like jivetalk and rhythmandblues. Like teachers who treat her like a dummy and white kids who treat her like dirt; boys who think she's really something and chicks who. . . ."

"Jeannie, I know. It hurts."

"Well, maybe it hurts Parry too. Maybe. At least she's got a crowd. Just don't let it hurt Carol though, 'cause there's nothing she can do about it. That's all through, her and Parialee Phillips, put away with their paper dolls."

"No, Jeannie, no."

"It's like Ginger and me. Remember Ginger, my best friend in Horace Mann. But you hardly noticed when it happened to us, did you . . . because she was white? Yes, Ginger, who's got two kids now, who quit school year before last. Parry's never going to finish either. What's she got to do with Carrie any more? They're going different places. Different places, different crowds. And they're sorting. . . ."

"Now wait, Jeannie. Parry's just as bright, just as capable."

"They're in junior high, Mother. Don't you know about junior high? How they sort? And it's all where you're going. Yes and Parry's colored and Carrie's white. And you have to watch everything, what you wear and how you wear it and who you eat lunch with and how much homework you do and how you act to the teacher and what you laugh at. . . . And run with your crowd."

"It's that final?" asked Len. "Don't you think kids like Carol and Parry can show it doesn't *have* to be that way."

"They can't. They can't. They don't let you."

"No need to shout," he said mildly. "And who do you mean by 'they' and what do you mean by 'sorting'?"

How they sort. A foreboding of comprehension whirled within Helen. What was it Carol had told her of the Welcome Assembly the first day in junior high? The models showing How to Dress and How Not to Dress and half the girls in their loved new clothes watching their counterparts up on the stage—*their* straight skirt, their sweater, their earrings, lipstick, hairdo—"How Not to Dress," "a bad reputation for your school." It was nowhere in Carol's description, yet picturing it now, it seemed to Helen that a mute cry of violated dignity hung in the air. Later there had been a story of going to another Low 7 homeroom on an errand and seeing a teacher trying to wipe the forbidden lipstick off a girl who was fighting back and cursing. Helen could hear Carol's frightened, self-righteous tones: ". . . and I hope they expel her; she's the kind that gives Franklin Jr. a bad rep; she doesn't care about anything and always gets into fights." Yet there was nothing in these incidents to touch the heavy comprehension that waited. . . . Homework, the wonderings those times Jeannie and Carol needed help: "What if there's no one at home to give the help, and the teachers with their two hundred and forty kids a day can't or don't or the kids don't ask and they fall hopelessly behind, what then?"—but this too was unrelated. And what had it been that time about Parry? "Mother, Melanie and Sharon won't go if they know Parry's coming." Then of course you'll go with Parry, she's been your friend longer, she had answered, but where was it they were going and what had finally happened? Len, my head hurts, she felt like saying, in Carol's voice in the car, but Len's eyes were grave on Jeannie who was saying passionately:

"If you think its so goddam important why do we have to live here where it's for real; why don't we move to Ivy like Betsy (yes, I know, money), where it's the deal to be buddies, in school anyway, three coloured kids and their father's a doctor or judge or something big wheel and one always gets elected President or head song girl or something to prove oh how we're democratic. . . . What do you want of that poor kid anyway? Make up your mind. Stay friends with Parry—but be one of the kids. Sure. Be a brain—but not a square. Rise on up, college prep, but don't get separated. Yes, stay one of the kids but. . . ."

"Jeannie. You're not talking about Carol at all, are you, Jeannie? Say it again. I wasn't listening. I was trying to think."

"She will not say it again," Len said firmly, "you look about ready to pull a Carol. One a day's our quota. And you, Jeannie, we'd better cool it. Too much to talk about for one session. . . . Here, come to the window and watch the Carol and Parry you're both all worked up about."

In the wind and the shimmering sunset light, half the children of the block are playing down the street. Leaping, bouncing, hallooing, tugging the kites of spring. In the old synchronized understanding, Carol and Parry kick, catch, kick, catch. And now Parry jumps on her pogo stick (the last time), Carol shadowing her, and Bubbie, arching his body in a semicircle of joy, bounding after them, high, higher, higher.

. . .

And the months go by and supposedly it is forgotten, except for the now and then when, self-important, Carol will say: I really truly did nearly faint, didn't I, Mother, that time I went to church with Parry?

And now seldom Parry and Carol walk the hill together. Melanie's mother drives by to pick up Carol, and the several times Helen has suggested Parry, too, Carol is quick to explain: "She's already left" or "She isn't ready; she'll make us late."

And after school? Carol is off to club or skating or library or someone's house, and Parry can stay for kickball only on the rare afternoons when she does not have to hurry home where Lucy, Bubbie, and the cousins wait to be cared for, now Alva works the four to twelve-thirty shift.

No more the bending together over the homework. All semester the teachers have been different, and rarely Parry brings her books home, for where is there space or time and what is the sense? And the phone never rings with: what you going to wear tomorrow, are you bringing your lunch, or come on over, let's design some clothes for the Katy Keane comic-book contest. And Parry never drops by with Alva for Saturday snack to or from grocery shopping.

And the months go by and the sorting goes on and seemingly it is over until that morning when Helen must stay home from work, so swollen and feverish is Carol with mumps.

> The afternoon before, Parry had come by, skimming up the stairs, spilling books and binders on the bed: Hey frail, lookahere and wail, your momma askin for homework, what she got against YOU? . . . looking quickly once then not looking again and talking fast. . . . Hey, you bloomed. You gonna be your own pumpkin, hallowe'en? Your momma know yet it's mu-umps? And lumps. Momma says: no distress, she'll be by tomorrow morning see do you need anything while your momma's to work. . . . (Singing: *whole lotta*

shakin goin on.) All your 'signments is inside; Miss Rockface says the teachers to write 'em cause I mightn't get it right all right.

> *But did not tell:* Does your mother work for Carol's mother? Oh, you're neighbors! Very well, I'll send along a monitor to open Carol's locker but you're only to take these things I'm writing down, nothing else. Now say after me: Miss Campbell is trusting me to be a good responsible girl. And go right to Carol's house. After school. Not stop anywhere on the way. Not lose anything. And only take. What's written on the list.

You really gonna mess with that book stuff? Sign on *mine* says do-not-open-until-eX-mas. . . . That Mrs. Fernandez doll she didn't send nothin, she was the only, says feel better and read a book to report if you feel like and I'm the most for takin care for you; she's my most, wish I could get her but she only teaches 'celerated. . . . Flicking the old read books on the shelf but not opening to mock-declaim as once she used to . . . Vicky, Eddie's g.f. in Rockface office, she's on suspended for sure, yellin to Rockface: you bitchkitty don't you give me no more bad shit. That Vicky she can sure sling-ating-ring it. Staring out the window as if the tree not there in which they had hid out and rocked so often. . . . For sure. (*Keep mo-o-vin.*) Got me a new pink top and lilac skirt. Look sharp with this purple? Cinching in the wide belt as if delighted with what newly swelled above and swelled below. Wear it Saturday night to Sweet's, Modernaires Sounds of Joy, Leroy and Ginny and me goin if Momma'll stay home. IF. (*Shake my baby shake*). How come old folks still likes to party? Huh? Asking of Rembrandt's weary old face looking from the wall. How come (softly) you long-gone you. Touching her face to his quickly, lightly. NEXT mumps is your buddybud Melanie's turn to tote your stuff. *I'm* gettin the hoovus goovus. Hey you so unneat, don't care what you bed with. Removing the books and binders, ranging them on the dresser one by one, marking lipstick faces—bemused or mocking or amazed—on each paper jacket. Better. Fluffing out smoothing the quilt with exaggerated energy. Any little thing I can get, cause I gotta blow. Tossing up and catching their year-ago, arm-in-arm graduation picture, replacing it deftly, upside down, into its mirror crevice. Joe. Bring you joy juice or fizz water or kickapoo? Adding a frown line to one bookface. Twanging the paper fishkite, the Japanese windbell overhead, setting the mobile they had once made of painted eggshells and decorated straws to twirling and rocking. And is gone.

She talked to the lipstick faces after, in her fever, tried to stand on her head to match the picture, twirled and twanged with the violent overhead.

Sleeping at last after the disordered night. Having surrounded herself with the furnishings of that world of childhood she no sooner learned to live in comfortably, then had to leave.

The dollhouse stands there to arrange and rearrange; the shell and picture card collections to re-sort and remember; the population of dolls given away to little sister, borrowed back, propped all around to dress and undress and caress.

She has thrown off her nightgown because of the fever, and her just budding breast is exposed where she reaches to hold the floppy plush dog that had been her childhood pillow.

Not for anything would Helen have disturbed her. Except that in the unaccustomedness of a morning at home, in the bruised restlessness after the sleepless night, she clicks on the radio—and the storm of singing whirls into the room:

. . . of trouble all mingled with fire
Come on my brethren we've got to go higher
Wade, wade. . . .

And Carol runs down the stairs, shrieking and shrieking. "Turn it off, Mother, turn it off." Hurling herself at the dial and wrenching it so it comes off in her hand.

"Ohhhhh," choked and convulsive, while Helen tries to hold her, to quiet.

"Mother, why did they sing and scream like that?"

"At Parry's church?"

"Yes." Rocking and strangling the cries. "I hear it all the time." Clinging and beseeching. ". . . What was it, Mother? Why?"

Emotion, Helen thought of explaining, *a characteristic of the religion of all oppressed peoples, yes your very own great-grandparents*—thought of saying. And discarded.

Aren't you now, haven't you had feelings in yourself so strong they had to come out some way? ("what howls restrained by decorum")—thought of saying. And discarded.

Repeat Alva: *hope . . . every word out of their own life. A place to let go. And church is home.* And discarded.

The special history of the Negro people—history?—just you try living what must be lived every day—thought of saying. And discarded.

And said nothing.

And said nothing

And soothed and held.

"Mother, a lot of the teachers and kids don't like Parry when they don't even know what she's like. Just because. . . ." Rocking again, convulsive and shamed. "And I'm not really her friend any more."

No news. Betrayal and shame. Who betrayed? Whose shame? Brought herself to say aloud: "But may be friends again. As Alva and I are."

The sobbing a whisper. "That girl Vicky who got that way when I fainted, she's in school. She's the one keeps wearing the lipstick and they wipe it off and she's always in trouble and now maybe she's expelled. Mother."

"Yes, lambie."

"She acts so awful outside but I remember how she was in church and whenever I see her now I have to wonder. And hear . . . like I'm her, Mother, like I'm her." Clinging and trembling. "Oh why do I have to feel it's happening to me too?

"Mother, I want to forget about it all, and not care—like Melanie. Why can't I forget? Oh why is it like it is and why do I have to care?"

Caressing, quieting.

Thinking: *caring asks doing. It is a long baptism into the seas of humankind, my daughter. Better immersion than to live untouched. . . . Yet how will you sustain?*

Why is it like it is?

Sheltering her daughter close, mourning the illusion of the embrace.

And why do I have to care?

While in her, her own need leapt and plunged for the place of strength that was not—where one could scream or sorrow while all knew and accepted, and gloved and loving hands waited to support and understand.

For Margaret Heaton, who always taught

1956

JEAN STAFFORD
(1915–1979)

Jean Stafford's work echoes that of many of her American forebears. She deftly combines elements of Hawthorne's gothic, Wharton's realism, and Twain's comedy to convey her unique observations as a modern woman writer. The cynical tone that characterizes her work seems the inevitable heritage of a writer born during World War I who began publishing during World War II.

Born the youngest of four children in Covina, California, Stafford moved with her family to Boulder, Colorado, when she was ten. Writing a thesis on thirteenth-century English poetry, she earned a B.A. and an M.A. from the University of Colorado in four years. The summer following graduation, she attended the Colorado University Writers' Conference, where she heard Robert Frost, Robert Penn Warren, and Thomas Wolfe read and discuss their work.

After a year of studying in Europe, she attended the 1937 writers' conference at Colorado University and met Ford Madox Ford, John Crowe Ransom, Sherwood Anderson, and the young poet Robert Lowell. The following year she taught English literature at Stephens College in Missouri. Disappointed with teaching, she spent the next year in Iowa University's writing program. When friends persuaded her to leave Iowa, she accepted a job with the Basic English Institute in Cambridge, Massachusetts. In Cambridge, she renewed her acquaintance with Lowell. The two writers were married in 1940 and divorced in 1948.

Stafford began writing as a young girl; she won a statewide competition for a story at age fifteen. Her first novel, Boston Adventure, *published when she was twenty-eight, became a best-seller. Critics compared her favorably to Truman Capote and Gore Vidal.* The Mountain Lion, *published three years later, was widely praised, and Stafford became a regular, respected contributor to* The New Yorker.

After publishing The Catherine Wheel, *her third novel, in 1952, Stafford turned exclusively to short fiction, publishing forty-six stories in all. Her stories of the 1930s and 1940s frequently appeared in anthologies. During the 1950s she won seven O. Henry awards for short fiction.* The Collected Stories *earned her a Pulitzer Prize in 1970.*

In the 1970s, Stafford wrote primarily nonfiction. Her profiles of Martha Mitchell, Anne Morrow Lindbergh, and Lee Harvey Oswald's mother are incisive commentaries not only on her subjects, but also on contemporary culture. For the last two years of her life, she suffered from aphasia and was unable to speak or to write. She died after a long illness on March 26, 1979.

Although Stafford wrote "The Philosophy Lesson" in 1948, it first appeared twenty years later in The New Yorker. *Like its heroine, Stafford, as a university student, posed for life-drawing classes for seventy-five cents an hour. Its subject, suicide, had haunted Stafford ever since Lucy McKee Cooke, a brilliant roommate, killed herself in November 1935.*

THE PHILOSOPHY LESSON

Cora Savage watched the first real snowfall of the year through the long, trefoiled windows of the studio where the Life Class met. It was a high, somber room in one of the two square towers of the auditorium, which, because of some personal proclivity of the donor, were exorbitantly Gothic and had nothing to do with the other buildings on the campus, which were serene and low and Italian Renaissance. Here, in this chilly room, three mornings a week from nine until twelve, twenty-seven students met in smocks to render Cora, naked, on canvases in oil, and on sheets of coarse-grained paper in charcoal, seriously applying those principles of drawing they had learned, in slide talks, in their lecture classes. But just as Cora had predicted to her anxious United Presbyterian mother, the students took no more account of Cora than if she had been a plaster cast or an assemblage of apples and lemons for a still-life study. At first, the class had been disquieted by her inhuman ability to remain motionless so long, and they chattered about it among themselves as if she had no ears to hear. Their instructor, Mr. Steele, a fat and comfort-loving man who spent a good part of the three hours seated on a padded bench, reading and, from time to time, brewing coffee for himself on a hot plate behind a screen, told them bluffly that since this talent of hers could not possibly last, they should take advantage of it while it did. Thereafter, they ceased to speak of her except in the argot of their craft. Mr. Steele, deep in Trollope, was polite if they sought him out for help, and, once an hour, he made a tour of the room, going from easel to easel commenting kindly but perfunctorily.

Cora rested only twice in the three hours. After she struck the pose at nine, she waited, in heavy pain, for the deep bell to ring in the chapel tower, signaling the passage of fifty minutes. When she stepped off the dais with the first peal and came to recognizable life again by putting on her blue flannel wrapper, a tide of comfort immediately and completely washed away the cramps and tingles in her arms and legs. For ten minutes, then, she sat on the edge of her platform, smoking cigarettes, which, because of her fatigue, made her agreeably dizzy and affected her eyes so that the light altered, shifting, like the light on the prairies, from sage-green to a submarine violet, to saffron, to the color of a Seckel pear. When the bell rang again, on the hour, she turned herself to stone. She did not talk to the students, unless they spoke first to her, nor did she look at their drawings and paintings until afterward, when everyone was gone and she stepped out from behind her screen, fully dressed. Then she wandered about through the thicket of easels and saw the travesties of herself, grown fat, grown shriveled, grown horsefaced, turned into Clara Bow. The representations of her face were, nearly invariably, the faces of the authors of the work. Her complete anonymity to them at once enraged and fascinated her.

As she posed, she stared through those high, romantic windows at the sky and the top of a cottonwood tree. Usually, because the tension of her muscles would not allow her to think or to pursue a fantasy to its happy ending, she counted slowly by ones, to a hundred, and she had become so precise in her timing that five minutes passed in each counting: ten hundreds, a thousand, and then the bell commenced to ring. Often she felt she must now surely faint or cry out against the pain that began midway through the first hour, began as an itching and a stinging in the part of her body that bore the most weight and then gradually overran her like a disease until the whole configuration of bone and muscle dilated and all her pulses throbbed. Nerves jerked in her neck and a random shudder seized her shoulder blades and sometimes, although it was cold in the studio, all her skin was hot and her blood roared; her heart deafened her. If she had closed her eyes, she would have fallen down—nothing held her to her position except the scene through the windows, an abridgment of the branches of the cottonwood tree whose every twig and half-dead leaf she knew by heart so that she still saw it, if her mind's eye wandered. She knew the differences of the sheen on its bark in rain and in sun and how the dancing of the branches varied with the winds; she waited for birds and squirrels, and if they came, she lost track of her numbers and the time went quickly. She had grown fond of the tree through knowledge of it and at noon, when she left the building—this beautiful release was like the first day after an illness and all the world was fresh—she greeted it as if it were her possession, and she thought how pleasant it would look when its leaves came back to it in April.

Thus, while she recognized the chills and fevers and the pins and needles that bedeviled her, she remained detached from them as if their connection with her was adventitious and the real business at hand was the thorough study of her prospect of bits of wood and bits of cloud, and counting to tell the hours.

On the day of the first snowfall, though, she did not deny her discomfort, she simply and truly did not feel it and, although she was pinioned, she drifted in a charming ease, a floating, as if she hovered, slowly winding, like the flakes themselves. The snow began in the second hour, just as she resumed her pose, one in which she held a pole upright like a soldier with a spear. It was the most unmerciful attitude she had yet held, for all her weight lay on her right heel, which seemed to seek a grafting with the dais, and the arm that held the pole swelled until she imagined in time it would be so bellied out that her vaccination scar would appear as an umbilical indentation. For the first time she had felt put upon, and during her first rest she had been angry with the students and with Mr. Steele, who took it for granted that she was made of a substance different from theirs. And, when a girl in Oxford glasses and a spotless green linen smock, radiating good will, came to sit for a moment on the dais and said admiringly, "That would *kill* me! Are you going to do this professionally?" she was the more affronted; the servant whose ambitions go beyond his present status does not wish to be complimented on the way he polishes the silver.

When the snow came, the studio was dematerialized. The storm began so suddenly, with so little warning from the skies, that for a moment Cora doubted its existence, whirling there in the cottonwood, and thought that her eyes had invented it out of a need to vary their view. She loved the snow. When she had first heard of heaven, she had thought it would be a place where snow was forever falling and forever concealing the harshness of the world. And she had never remembered, when she was a child, from one year to the next how cold snow was; always, when the first flakes flew, she had run out in her bare feet, expecting the miraculous purity to be as soft as a cat, and then she ran back into the house to lie on the floor in the front hall, giggling with surprise.

In Missouri, by the river, the snow was as hard as a floor, but now and then a soft place would take her unawares and she would go in up to the top of her galoshes, and then she was a mess, her astrakhan coat covered with snow, her tasseled yellow mittens soaking wet. They went, she and her father and her brother Randall, for the Christmas greens each year, for holly and ground hemlock and partridge berry to put in the long, cold summer parlor where a green carpet spread like a lawn. The purple light of early Christmas morning came through the scrim curtains as the Savage children, Cora and Randall, Abigail and Evangeline, opened their presents. Often snow fell on Christmas day, shutting them in, protecting them, putting a spell on them. The little girls, wearing new tam-o'-shanters, wearing the bracelets and rings and fake wrist watches sent by cousins, surrounded by double-jointed dolls and sets of colored pencils, pig banks, patent-leather pocketbooks, jackstones, changeable taffeta hair ribbons, teased their poor brother with his ungainly boy's things—tool chests, fishing gear, the year he was eight, a .22.

The snow had been best, perhaps, most elegant there in Missouri. There had been times when Grandmother Savage had driven over from Kavanagh to call; she had an old-fashioned sleigh with rakish curled runners. In the little parlor, what Mr. Savage derisively called "the pastor's parlor," they drank hot cocoa from fat, hand-painted cups, bordered with a frieze of asters. And all the while the snow was coming down.

More elegant in Missouri, but it had been more keenly exciting here in Adams. Randall and Cora (by now Cora was a tomboy and disdained her older sisters) often took their sleds over the practice ski jumps in the foothills behind the college. The wind was knocked out of them as they hit the ground and once Cora lost control and went hurtling into a barbed-wire fence. It seemed to her, on reflection, that she had slowly revolved on her head, like a top, for a long time before the impact. Then, too frightened to move lest she find she could not, she had lain there waiting for her brother. Blood, in niggardly drops, from the wounds in her forehead stained the snow. Afterward, she had been afraid of the ski jumps and had only coasted down a steep hill that terminated in a cemetery; but this was dangerous enough, and reckless children sometimes crashed into the spiked palings of the iron fence and broke their heads wide open. There were so many of these accidents and the injuries were often so nearly serious that a city ordinance was passed, forbidding anyone to slide down that street. Then, added to the danger, there was the additional thrill of possibly being caught by the police and put into jail. One hid oneself and one's sled behind the spooky little stone house at the graveyard's edge, where the caretaker kept his lawn mower and gardening tools, and waited for the Black Maria. But it never came.

Cora was pleased today that probably she alone in the studio had seen what was happening outside. The students were intent on their work, applying to each other for criticism or for pallette knives, measuring parts of Cora with pencils held at arm's length as they squinted and grimaced; sometimes, to her mistrust, they came quite close to examine the shape of a muscle or the color of a shadow on her skin. For the time being, the snow was a private experience; perhaps everything at this moment proceeded from her own mind, even this grubby room with its forest of apparatus and its smell of banana oil, even all these people. She thought of Bishop Berkeley, whom Dr. Bosch had assigned to the class in Introduction to Philosophy; she thought of the way Berkeley had dismantled the world of its own reality and had made each idiom of it into an idea in the mind of God. "Or in his own mind," said Dr. Bosch dryly, for he had no use for the Bishop. This morning, Cora had much use for him, and she concluded that she would be at peace forever if she could believe that she existed only for herself and possibly for a superior intelligence and that no one existed for her save when he was tangibly present.

As she pondered this quieting phenomenon (it just might work, she just might tutor herself to believe in such sublimity), the door to the studio opened and she turned away from the window. A latecomer entered, a boy in a sheep-lined mackinaw and a freshman beanie; his ashen corduroy trousers, freckled with oil paint, were tucked into the tops of his yellow field boots. His name was Ernie Wharton and he had been in high school with Cora; in the beginning, she had resented him and had disliked hearing that familiar voice she had heard the year before in Spanish II. Once she had even been in a play with him and on several evenings after rehearsal he had walked her home and they had talked at length at the foot of the steps on Benedict Street, where the smell of lilacs nearly led her to infatuation. But they had only gone on talking learnedly of *The Ode on Intimations of Immortality,* which both of them admired.

On the first day of the Life Class, he, too, had been embarrassed, and had looked only at the model's feet and at her face, but in time he merged into the general background and was no more specific to her than any of the others.

Panting, as if he had been running, red from the cold, his canine face (the face of an amiable dog, a border collie) wore a look of befuddlement and at first Cora thought it stemmed from worry over his being so late, but she knew this could not be true, for Mr. Steele paid no heed at all to the arrival and departure of his students. Indeed, he did not so much as look up from *Framley Parsonage* when the outside air came rushing through the door, up the spiral staircase. No one gave Ernie's entrance more than passing recognition, no one but Cora, at whom he looked directly and whom he seemed to address, as if he had come to bring this news exclusively to her. "Somebody just committed suicide on the Base Line," he said.

In their incredulity, the class fell over itself, dropped pencils, splashed turpentine, tore paper, catapulted against their easels, said, "Oh, damn it." Then they surrounded Ernie, who stood against the door as if he did not mean to stay but was only a courier stopping at one of the many stations on his route. Although no one was looking at her, Cora continued to hold her pose and to look at the snow in her tree, but she listened and, now and then, stole a glance at the narrator's face, awry with dismay and with a sort of excruciated pleasure in the violent finality of the act he described. A second-year pre-medical student, two hours before, had been run over by the morning mail train coming from Denver. He had driven his car to the outskirts of town and there it had been found at a crossing, its motor still running. The engineer had seen the body on the tracks but he had had no time to stop the train, and the man had been broken to pieces. Wharton had gone out there (they were fraternity brothers; the president had called him just as he was leaving for class) and had seen the butchered mess, the head cut loose, the legs shivered, one hand, perched like a bird, on a scrub oak. His name was Bernard Allen, said Ernie, and he had been one prince of a fellow.

Bernard Allen!

The girl in Oxford glasses went pale and said, "My godfather, I knew *him!* I went to the Phi Gam tea dance with him Friday."

(Friday? thought Cora. But that was the night he and Maisie Perrine went horseback riding. That was the night I saw his white hair shining like this snow as I looked out my bedroom window toward the boarding house where Maisie lives next door to us. I, spying at all hours of the day and night, spying and tortured at what I saw, saw Bernard Allen's blue Cord town car draw up to Mrs. Mullen's house at midnight last Friday. Bernard and Maisie must have been to a dance, for Maisie was wearing a long dress of gold lamé and her sable coat. "I'll be waiting on the porch. Don't be long," said Maisie. They kissed connubially. "I hate to have you take off that gorgeous dress," said Bernard, and she replied, "I'd look good riding a horse in this, wouldn't I?" He let her out of the car and took her to the door and then he drove away. Half an hour later he was back and Maisie, in riding clothes, ran down the sagging steps of Mrs. Mullen's front porch. Where would they find a stable open at this time of night? They could. They would. For they had claimed the pot of gold and were spending it all on everything their hearts desired, on clothes and cars and bootleg whiskey. Probably one of them kept a string of blooded horses somewhere with a stableman so highly paid that he did not mind being waked up in the middle of the night. "Why didn't you bring Luster?" asked Maisie. "Because he doesn't like the moon." Luster was his dog, a golden retriever. They drove away then in the direction of Left Hand Canyon. I suppose eventually I went to sleep.)

Forgetting now that Ernie Wharton's facts were immediate and that, because he had been united with the dead boy in a secret order, his was the right to tell the tale and to lead the speculation—forgetting this, the art students shrilly turned to the girl in Oxford glasses. Had he been strange, they asked her, had he seemed cracked?

"He was like everybody else," she said, "like all pre-meds. You know, a little high-hat the way they all are because they know those six-dollar words."

She did not like to speak ill of the dead, she said, but, frankly, Bernard had been the world's worst dancer and, as she looked back on it, she thought he had probably been tight. Not that that made any difference, she quickly added, because she was broad-minded, but it might throw some light on his suicide. Maybe he was drunk this morning. It was unlikely, she supposed, that he would have been drinking at eight-thirty in the morning. Still, you never could tell. She could not think of anything else about him. Except that he had this pure white hair—not blond, not towheaded; he had had a grandfather's white hair. It had been a blind date and a very short one, for they'd only gone to the dance and that was over at six and then she had gone right home to dress for the SAE formal. It had been just one of those dates that fills an afternoon and comes to nothing, when you get along all right, but you aren't much interested. Christmas, though, it gave her the creeps.

All the time the girl talked, Ernie stared at her, dumbstruck with rage. How *dare* she be so flip, said his frosty eyes. Presently, because her facts were thin, the students returned to him and they interrogated him closely as if he were a witness in a court of law. What had they done with the car? How long was it before the police arrived? Where did the guy come from? Had his family been told? At first, Ernie answered factually but abstractedly and then, hectored by a repetition of the same questions, he grew impatient and, turning wrathfully on the girl in the green smock, he shouted, "I'm not sure you knew him at all. He was engaged. He was engaged to be married to Maisie Perrine, and they announced it at the Chi Psi dance about three hours after you claim to have been at a tea dance with him."

The girl laughed lightly. "Keep your shirt on, sonny. That doesn't cut any ice. Can't you be engaged to somebody and take somebody else to a tea dance?"

Ernie said, "Not if you're so deep you end up by killing yourself."

"Oh, bushwa," said the girl and went back to her easel, but she was the only one who did, and among the others a moral debate began: whether suicide *did* demonstrate depth, whether suicide was an act of cowardice or of bravery.

Cora no longer listened. She was thinking of Maisie Perrine and wondering whether her yellow Cadillac roadster was there now at the crossing, its top whitened with snow, the windshield wipers going. Maybe she did not know yet and was still in class, still undisheveled in her orderly, expensive clothes, her sumptuous red hair shining, her fine hand taking down notes on Middle English marketplace romances. What would happen when she heard? And where was Luster, where was Bernard Allen's fond golden dog?

And what was the misery that had brought the boy to suicide? Rich, privileged, in love, he and his girl had seemed the very paradigm of joy. Why had he done it? And yet, why not? Why did not she, who was seldom happy, do it herself? A darkness beat her like the wings of an enormous bird and frantic terror of the ultimate hopelessness shook her until the staff she held slipped and her heart seemed for a moment to fail. She began to sweat and could feel the drops creeping down her legs. The bell rang and her pole went clattering to the floor, knocking over a portrait on an easel nearby, and all the students, still talking of the death that morning, looked up with exclamations of shock, but she could tell by their faces that none of them had been thinking her thoughts, that she alone, silent and stationary there on the dais, had shared Bernard Allen's experience and had plunged with him into sightlessness. No. No, wait a minute. Each mortal in the room must, momentarily, have died. But just as the fledgling artists put their own faces on their canvases, so they had perished in their own particular ways.

The snow was a benison. It forgave them all.

1968

SHIRLEY JACKSON
(1916–1965)

Though she is best known for her short story "The Lottery," Shirley Jackson was a prolific writer who experimented with diverse prose styles. Life among the Savages *(1953), for example, is a comical view of family life that paved the way for writers such as Erma Bombeck.* The Haunting of Hill House *(1959), on the other hand, is a horror story that Stephen King has called the best of all time. Another novel,* The Bird's Nest *(1954), is a psychological exploration of a woman with multiple personalities.*

Born in San Francisco, the first child of Geraldine and Leslie Jackson, Shirley Jackson grew up in Burlingame, California. In 1933, her family moved to Rochester, New York, where Jackson attended the University of Rochester for two years. In the fall of 1937, she enrolled at Syracuse University, where she studied journalism and creative writing. After earning her degree, she married Stanley Hyman, a fellow student, and with him moved to New York City. In 1942, Hyman became a staff writer for The New Yorker, *and the couple remained in New York, raising their first child. When Hyman was offered a position in the English Department of Bennington College three years later, they moved to North Bennington, Vermont. Except for a two-year sojourn in Connecticut, Jackson lived in Vermont until the end of her life.*

Jackson began writing as a young child. At age thirteen she kept a regular diary, and as a teen she would frequently get up in the middle of the night to write a story. Throughout college she wrote daily, publishing fifteen pieces in campus magazines while at Syracuse University. The New Republic *published her first story in 1941. Four stories appeared in* The New Yorker *in 1943 and another four in 1944. From that point on, her writing was critically and financially successful.*

Jackson, a self-described witch, chose a career that complemented her own eccentricity. "The very nicest thing about being a writer," she once said, "is that you can afford to indulge yourself endlessly with oddness, and nobody can really do anything about it." On another occasion she described writing as "a way of making daily life into a wonderfully unusual thing instead of a grind." Her work illustrates this point: she based her first published story on her experiences as a salesclerk at Macy's department store. At the same time, she pragmatically used the income from her writing. The proceeds from her first novel, for example, were spent to fix her teeth. "The Tooth," the story selected here, begins with an ordinary trip to the dentist. In typical Jackson style, however, the ordinary soon becomes extraordinary.

THE TOOTH

The bus was waiting, panting heavily at the curb in front of the small bus station, its great blue-and-silver bulk glittering in the moonlight. There were only a few people interested in the bus, and at that time of night no one passing on the sidewalk: the one movie theatre in town had finished its show and closed its doors an hour before, and all the movie patrons had been to the drugstore for ice cream and gone on home; now the drugstore was closed and dark, another silent doorway in the long midnight street. The only town lights were the street lights, the lights in the all-night lunchstand across the street, and the one remaining counter lamp in the bus station where the girl sat in the ticket office with her hat and coat on, only waiting for the New York bus to leave before she went home to bed.

Standing on the sidewalk next to the open door of the bus, Clara Spencer held her husband's arm nervously. "I feel so funny," she said.

"Are you all right?" he asked. "Do you think I ought to go with you?"

"No, of course not," she said, "I'll be all right." It was hard for her to talk because of her swollen jaw; she kept a handkerchief pressed to her face and held hard to her husband. "Are you sure *you'll* be all right?" she asked. "I'll be back tomorrow night at the latest. Or else I'll call."

"Everything will be fine," he said heartily. "By tomorrow noon it'll be all gone. Tell the dentist if there's anything wrong I can come right down."

"I feel so funny," she said. "Light-headed, and sort of dizzy."

"That's because of the dope," he said. "All that codeine, and the whisky, and nothing to eat all day."

She giggled nervously. "I couldn't comb my hair, my hand shook so. I'm glad it's dark."

"Try to sleep in the bus," he said. "Did you take a sleeping pill?"

"Yes," she said. They were waiting for the bus driver to finish his cup of coffee in the lunchstand; they could see him through the glass window, sitting at the counter, taking his time. "I feel so *funny,*" she said.

"You know, Clara," he made his voice very weighty, as though if he spoke more seriously his words would carry more conviction and be therefore more comforting, "you know, I'm glad you're going down to New York to have Zimmerman take care of this. I'd never forgive myself if it turned out to be something serious and I let you go to this butcher up here."

"It's just a *toothache,*" Clara said uneasily, "nothing very serious about a *toothache.*"

"You can't tell," he said. "It might be abscessed or something; I'm sure he'll have to pull it."

"Don't even talk like that," she said, and shivered.

"Well, it looks pretty bad," he said soberly, as before. "Your face so swollen, and all. Don't you worry."

"I'm not worrying," she said. "I just feel as if I were all tooth. Nothing else."

The bus driver got up from the stool and walked over to pay his check. Clara moved toward the bus, and her husband said, "Take your time, you've got plenty of time."

"I just feel funny," Clara said.

"Listen," her husband said, "that tooth's been bothering you off and on for years; at least six or seven times since I've known you you've had trouble with that tooth. It's about time something was done. You had a toothache on our honeymoon," he finished accusingly.

"Did I?" Clara said. "You know," she went on, and laughed, "I was in such a hurry I didn't dress properly. I have on old stockings and I just dumped everything into my good pocketbook."

"Are you sure you have enough money?" he said.

"Almost twenty-five dollars," Clara said. "I'll be home tomorrow."

"Wire if you need more," he said. The bus driver appeared in the doorway of the lunchroom. "Don't worry," he said.

"Listen," Clara said suddenly, "are you *sure* you'll be all right? Mrs. Lang will be over in the morning in time to make breakfast, and Johnny doesn't need to go to school if things are too mixed up."

"I know," he said.

"Mrs. Lang," she said, checking on her fingers. "I called Mrs. Lang, I left the grocery order on the kitchen table, you can have the cold tongue for lunch and in case I don't get back Mrs. Lang will give you dinner. The cleaner ought to come about four o'clock, I won't be back so give him your brown suit and it doesn't matter if you forget but be sure to empty the pockets."

"Wire if you need more money," he said. "Or call. I'll stay home tomorrow so you can call at home."

"Mrs. Lang will take care of the baby," she said.

"Or you can wire," he said.

The bus driver came across the street and stood by the entrance to the bus.

"Okay?" the bus driver said.

"Good-bye," Clara said to her husband.

"You'll feel all right tomorrow," her husband said. "It's only a toothache."

"I'm fine," Clara said. "Don't you worry." She got on the bus and then stopped, with the bus driver waiting behind her. "Milkman," she said to her husband. "Leave a note telling him we want eggs."

"I will," her husband said. "Good-bye."

"Good-bye," Clara said. She moved on into the bus and behind her the driver swung into his seat. The bus was nearly empty and she went far back and sat down at the window outside which her husband waited. "Good-bye," she said to him through the glass, "take care of yourself."

"Good-bye," he said, waving violently.

The bus stirred, groaned, and pulled itself forward. Clara turned her head to wave good-bye once more and then lay back against the heavy soft seat. Good Lord, she thought, what a thing to do! Outside, the familiar street slipped past, strange and dark and seen, unexpectedly, from the unique station of a person leaving town, going away on a bus. It isn't as though it's the first time I've ever been to New York, Clara thought indignantly, it's the whisky and the codeine and the sleeping pill and the toothache. She checked hastily to see if her codeine tablets were in her pocketbook; they had been standing, along with the aspirin and a glass of water, on the dining-room sideboard, but somewhere in the lunatic flight from her home she must have picked them up, because they were in her pocketbook now, along with the twenty-odd dollars and her compact and comb and lipstick. She could tell from the feel of the lipstick that she had brought the old, nearly finished one, not the new one that was a darker shade and had cost two-fifty. There was a run in her stocking and a hole in the toe that she never noticed at home wearing her old comfortable shoes, but which was now suddenly and disagreeably apparent inside her best walking shoes. Well, she thought, I can buy new stockings in New York tomorrow, after the tooth is fixed, after everything's all right. She put her tongue cautiously on the tooth and was rewarded with a split-second crash of pain.

The bus stopped at a red light and the driver got out of his seat and came back toward her. "Forgot to get your ticket before," he said.

"I guess I was a little rushed at the last minute," she said. She found the ticket in her coat pocket and gave it to him. "When do we get to New York?" she asked.

"Five-fifteen," he said. "Plenty of time for breakfast. One-way ticket?"

"I'm coming back by train," she said, without seeing why she had to tell him, except that it was late at night and people isolated together in some strange prison like a bus had to be more friendly and communicative than at other times.

"Me, I'm coming back by bus," he said, and they both laughed, she painfully because of her swollen face. When he went back to his seat far away at the front of the bus she lay back peacefully against the seat. She could feel the sleeping pill pulling at her; the throb of the toothache was distant now, and mingled with the movement of the bus, a steady beat like her heartbeat which she could hear louder and louder, going on through the night. She put her head back and her feet up, discreetly covered with her skirt, and fell asleep without saying good-bye to the town.

She opened her eyes once and they were moving almost silently through the darkness. Her tooth was pulsing steadily and she turned her cheek against the cool back of the seat in weary resignation. There was a thin line of lights along the ceiling of the bus and no other light. Far ahead of her in the bus she could see the other people sitting; the driver, so far away as to be only a tiny figure at the end of a telescope, was straight at the wheel, seemingly awake. She fell back into her fantastic sleep.

She woke up later because the bus had stopped, the end of that silent motion through the darkness so positive a shock that it woke her stunned, and it was a minute before the ache began again. People were moving along the aisle of the bus and the driver, turning around, said, "Fifteen minutes." She got up and followed everyone else out, all but her eyes still asleep, her feet moving without awareness. They were stopped beside an all-night restaurant, lonely and lighted on the vacant road. Inside, it was warm and busy and full of people. She saw a seat at the end of the counter and sat down, not aware that she had fallen asleep again when someone sat down next to her and touched her arm. When she looked around foggily he said, "Traveling far?"

"Yes," she said.

He was wearing a blue suit and he looked tall; she could not focus her eyes to see any more.

"You want coffee?" he asked.

She nodded and he pointed to the counter in front of her where a cup of coffee sat steaming.

"Drink it quickly," he said.

She sipped at it delicately; she may have put her face down and tasted it without lifting the cup. The strange man was talking.

"Even farther than Samarkand," he was saying, "and the waves ringing on the shore like bells."

"Okay, folks," the bus driver said, and she gulped quickly at the coffee, drank enough to get her back into the bus.

When she sat down in her seat again the strange man sat down beside her. It was so dark in the bus that the lights from the restaurant were unbearably glaring and she closed her eyes. When her eyes were shut, before she fell asleep, she was closed in alone with the toothache.

"The flutes play all night," the strange man said, "and the stars are as big as the moon and the moon is as big as a lake."

As the bus started up again they slipped back into the darkness and only the thin thread of lights along the ceiling of the bus held them together, brought the back of the bus where she sat along with the front of the bus where the driver sat and the people sitting there so far away from her. The lights tied them together and the strange man next to her was saying, "Nothing to do all day but lie under the trees."

Inside the bus, traveling on, she was nothing; she was passing the trees and the occasional sleeping houses, and she was in the bus but she was between here and there, joined tenuously to the bus driver by a thread of lights, being carried along without effort of her own.

"My name is Jim," the strange man said.

She was so deeply asleep that she stirred uneasily without knowledge, her forehead against the window, the darkness moving along beside her.

Then again that numbing shock, and, driven awake, she said, frightened, "What's happened?"

"It's all right," the strange man—Jim—said immediately. "Come along."

She followed him out of the bus, into the same restaurant, seemingly, but when she started to sit down at the same seat at the end of the counter he took her hand and led her to a table. "Go and wash your face," he said. "Come back here afterward."

She went into the ladies' room and there was a girl standing there powdering her nose. Without turning around the girl said, "Costs a nickel. Leave the door fixed so's the next one won't have to pay."

The door was wedged so it would not close, with half a match folder in the lock. She left it the same way and went back to the table where Jim was sitting.

"What do you want?" she said, and he pointed to another cup of coffee and a sandwich. "Go ahead," he said.

While she was eating her sandwich she heard his voice, musical and soft, "And while we were sailing past the island we heard a voice calling us. . . ."

Back in the bus Jim said, "Put your head on my shoulder now, and go to sleep."

"I'm all right," she said.

"No," Jim said. "Before, your head was rattling against the window."

Once more she slept, and once more the bus stopped and she woke frightened, and Jim brought her again to a restaurant and more coffee. Her tooth came alive then, and with one hand pressing her cheek she searched through the pockets of her coat and then through her pocketbook until she found the little bottle of codeine pills and she took two while Jim watched her.

She was finishing her coffee when she heard the sound of the bus motor and she started up suddenly, hurrying, and with Jim holding her arm she fled back into the dark shelter of her seat. The bus was moving forward when she realized that she had left her bottle of codeine pills sitting on the table in the restaurant and now she was at the mercy of her tooth. For a minute she stared back at the lights of the restaurant through the bus window and then she put her head on Jim's shoulder and he was saying as she fell asleep, "The sand is so white it looks like snow, but it's hot, even at night it's hot under your feet."

Then they stopped for the last time, and Jim brought her out of the bus and they stood for a minute in New York together. A woman passing them in the station said to the man following her with suitcases, "We're just on time, it's five-fifteen."

"I'm going to the dentist," she said to Jim.

"I know," he said, "I'll watch out for you."

He went away, although she did not see him go. She thought to watch for his blue suit going through the door, but there was nothing.

I ought to have thanked him, she thought stupidly, and went slowly into the station restaurant, where she ordered coffee again. The counter man looked at her with the worn sympathy of one who has spent a long night watching people get off and on buses. "Sleepy?" he asked.

"Yes," she said.

She discovered after a while that the bus station joined Pennsylvania Terminal and she was able to get into the main waiting-room and find a seat on one of the benches by the time she fell asleep again.

Then someone shook her rudely by the shoulder and said, "What train you taking, lady, it's nearly seven." She sat up and saw her pocketbook on her lap, her feet neatly crossed, a clock glaring into her face. She said, "Thank you," and got up and walked blindly past the benches and got on to the escalator. Someone got on immediately behind her and touched her arm; she turned and it was Jim. "The grass is so green and so soft," he said, smiling, "and the water of the river is so cool."

She stared at him tiredly. When the escalator reached the top she stepped off and started to walk to the street she saw ahead. Jim came along beside her and his voice went on, "The sky is bluer than anything you've ever seen, and the songs. . . ."

She stepped quickly away from him and thought that people were looking at her as they passed. She stood on the corner waiting for the light to change and Jim came swiftly up to her and then away. "Look," he said as he passed, as he held out a handful of pearls.

. . .

Across the street there was a restaurant, just opening. She went in and sat down at a table, and a waitress was standing beside her frowning. "You was asleep," the waitress said accusingly.

"I'm very sorry," she said. It was morning. "Poached eggs and coffee, please."

It was a quarter to eight when she left the restaurant, and she thought, if I take a bus, and go straight downtown now, I can sit in the drugstore across the street from the dentist's office and have more coffee until about eight-thirty and then go into the dentist's when it opens and he can take me first.

The buses were beginning to fill up; she got into the first bus that came along and could not find a seat. She wanted to go to Twenty-third Street, and got a seat just as they were passing Twenty-sixth Street; when she woke she was so far downtown that it took her nearly half-an-hour to find a bus and get back to Twenty-third.

At the corner of Twenty-third Street, while she was waiting for the light to change, she was caught up in a crowd of people, and when they crossed the street and separated to go different directions someone fell into step beside her. For a minute she walked on without looking up, staring resentfully at the sidewalk, her tooth burning her, and then she looked up, but there was no blue suit among the people pressing by on either side.

When she turned into the office building where her dentist was, it was still very early morning. The doorman in the office building was freshly shaven and his hair was combed; he held the door open briskly, as at five o'clock he would be sluggish, his hair faintly out of place. She went in through the door with a feeling of achievement; she had come successfully from one place to another, and this was the end of her journey and her objective.

The clean white nurse sat at the desk in the office; her eyes took in the swollen cheek, the tired shoulders, and she said, "You poor thing, you look worn out."

"I have a toothache." The nurse half-smiled, as though she were still waiting for the day when someone would come in and say, "My feet hurt." She stood up into the professional sunlight. "Come right in," she said. "We won't make you wait."

There was sunlight on the headrest of the dentist's chair, on the round white table, on the drill bending its smooth chromium head. The dentist smiled with the same tolerance as the nurse; perhaps all human ailments were contained in the teeth, and he could fix them if people would only come to him in time. The nurse said smoothly, "I'll get her file, doctor. We thought we'd better bring her right in."

She felt, while they were taking an X-ray, that there was nothing in her head to stop the malicious eye of the camera, as though the camera would look through her and photograph the nails in the wall next to her, or the dentist's cuff buttons, or the small thin bones of the dentist's instruments; the dentist said, "Extraction," regretfully to the nurse, and the nurse said, "Yes, doctor, I'll call them right away."

Her tooth, which had brought her here unerringly, seemed now the only part of her to have any identity. It seemed to have had its picture taken without her; it was the important creature which must be recorded and examined and gratified; she was only its unwilling vehicle, and only as such was she of interest to the dentist and the nurse, only as the bearer of her tooth was she worth their immediate and practised attention. The dentist handed her a slip of paper with the picture of a full set of teeth drawn on it; her living tooth was checked with a black mark, and across the top of the paper was written "Lower molar; extraction."

"Take this slip," the dentist said, "and go right up to the address on this card; it's a surgeon dentist. They'll take care of you there."

"What will they do?" she said. Not the question she wanted to ask, not: What about me? or, How far down do the roots go?

"They'll take that tooth out," the dentist said testily, turning away. "Should have been done years ago."

I've stayed too long, she thought, he's tired of my tooth. She got up out of the dentist chair and said, "Thank you. Good-bye."

"Good-bye," the dentist said. At the last minute he smiled at her, showing her his full white teeth, all in perfect control.

"Are you all right? Does it bother you too much?" the nurse asked.

"I'm all right."

"I can give you some codeine tablets," the nurse said. "We'd rather you didn't take anything right now, of course, but I think I could let you have them if the tooth is really bad."

"No," she said, remembering her little bottle of codeine pills on the table of a restaurant between here and there. "No, it doesn't bother me too much."

"Well," the nurse said, "good luck."

She went down the stairs and out past the doorman; in the fifteen minutes she had been upstairs he had lost a little of his pristine morningness, and his bow was just a fraction smaller than before.

"Taxi?" he asked, and, remembering the bus down to Twenty-third Street, she said, "Yes."

Just as the doorman came back from the curb, bowing to the taxi he seemed to believe he had invented, she thought a hand waved to her from the crowd across the street.

She read the address on the card the dentist had given her and repeated it carefully to the taxi driver. With the card and the little slip of paper with "Lower molar" written on it and her tooth identified so clearly, she sat without moving, her hands still around the papers, her eyes almost closed. She thought she must have been asleep again when the taxi stopped suddenly, and the driver, reaching around to open the door, said, "Here we are, lady." He looked at her curiously.

"I'm going to have a tooth pulled," she said.

"Jesus," the taxi driver said. She paid him and he said, "Good luck," as he slammed the door.

This was a strange building, the entrance flanked by medical signs carved in stone; the doorman here was faintly professional, as though he were competent to prescribe if she did not care to go any farther. She went past him, going straight ahead until an elevator opened its door to her. In the elevator she showed the elevator man the card and he said, "Seventh floor."

She had to back up in the elevator for a nurse to wheel in an old lady in a wheel chair. The old lady was calm and restful, sitting there in the elevator with a rug over her knees; she said, "Nice day" to the elevator operator and he said, "Good to see the sun," and then the old lady lay back in her chair and the nurse straightened the rug around her knees and said, "Now we're not going to worry," and the old lady said irritably, "Who's worrying?"

They got out at the fourth floor. The elevator went on up and then the operator said, "Seven," and the elevator stopped and the door opened.

"Straight down the hall and to your left," the operator said.

There were closed doors on either side of the hall. Some of them said "DDS," some of them said "Clinic," some of them said "X-Ray." One of them, looking wholesome and friendly and somehow most comprehensible, said "Ladies." Then she turned to the left and found a door with the name on the card and she opened it and went in. There was a nurse sitting behind a glass window, almost as in a bank, and potted palms in tubs in the corners of the waiting room, and new magazines and comfortable chairs. The nurse behind the glass window said, "Yes?" as though you had overdrawn your account with the dentist and were two teeth in arrears.

She handed her slip of paper through the glass window and the nurse looked at it and said, "Lower molar, yes. They called about you. Will you come right in, please? Through the door to your left."

Into the vault? she almost said, and then silently opened the door and went in. Another nurse was waiting, and she smiled and turned, expecting to be followed, with no visible doubt about her right to lead.

There was another X-ray, and the nurse told another nurse: "Lower molar," and the other nurse said, "Come this way, please."

There were labyrinths and passages, seeming to lead into the heart of the office building, and she was put, finally, in a cubicle where there was a couch with a pillow and a washbasin and a chair.

"Wait here," the nurse said. "Relax if you can."

"I'll probably go to sleep," she said.

"Fine," the nurse said. "You won't have to wait long."

She waited probably for over an hour, although she spent the time half-sleeping, waking only when someone passed the door; occasionally the nurse looked in and smiled, once she said, "Won't have to wait much longer." Then, suddenly, the nurse was back, no longer smiling, no longer the good hostess, but efficient and hurried. "Come along," she said, and moved purposefully out of the little room into the hallways again.

Then, quickly, more quickly than she was able to see, she was sitting in the chair and there was a towel around her head and a towel under her chin and the nurse was leaning a hand on her shoulder.

"Will it hurt?" she asked.

"No," the nurse said, smiling. "You know it won't hurt, don't you?"

"Yes," she said.

The dentist came in and smiled down on her from over her head. "Well," he said.

"Will it hurt?" she said.

"Now," he said cheerfully, "we couldn't stay in business if we hurt people." All the time he talked he was busying himself with metal hidden under a towel, and great machinery being wheeled in almost silently behind her. "We couldn't stay in business at all," he said. "All you've got to worry about is telling us all your secrets while you're asleep. Want to watch out for that, you know. Lower molar?" he said to the nurse.

"Lower molar, doctor," she said.

Then they put the metal-tasting rubber mask over her face and the dentist said, "You know," two or three times absent-mindedly while she could still see him over the mask. The nurse said "Relax your hands, dear," and after a long time she felt her fingers relaxing.

First of all things get so far away, she thought, remember this. And remember the metallic sound and taste of all of it. And the outrage.

And then the whirling music, the ringing confusedly loud music that went on and on, around and around, and she was running as fast as she could down a long horribly clear hallway with doors on both sides and at the end of the hallway was Jim, holding out his hands and laughing, and calling something she could never hear because of the loud music, and she was running and then she said, "I'm not afraid," and someone from the door next to her took her arm and pulled her through and the world widened alarmingly until it would never stop and then it stopped with the head of the dentist looking down at her and the window dropped into place in front of her and the nurse was holding her arm.

"Why did you pull me back?" she said, and her mouth was full of blood. "I wanted to go on."

"I didn't pull you," the nurse said, but the dentist said, "She's not out of it yet."

She began to cry without moving and felt the tears rolling down her face and the nurse wiped them off with a towel. There was no blood anywhere around except in her mouth; everything was as clean as before. The dentist was gone, suddenly, and the nurse put out her arm and helped her out of the chair. "Did I talk?" she asked suddenly, anxiously. "Did I say anything?"

"You said, 'I'm not afraid,' " the nurse said soothingly. "Just as you were coming out of it."

"No," she said, stopping to pull at the arm around her. "Did I *say* anything? Did I say where he is?"

"You didn't say *anything,*" the nurse said. "The doctor was only teasing you."

"Where's my tooth?" she asked suddenly, and the nurse laughed and said, "All gone. Never bother you again."

She was back in the cubicle, and she lay down on the couch and cried, and the nurse brought her whisky in a paper cup and set it on the edge of the wash-basin.

"God has given me blood to drink," she said to the nurse, and the nurse said, "Don't rinse your mouth or it won't clot."

. . .

After a long time the nurse came back and said to her from the doorway, smiling, "I see you're awake again."

"Why?" she said.

"You've been asleep," the nurse said. "I didn't want to wake you."

She sat up; she was dizzy and it seemed that she had been in the cubicle all her life.

"Do you want to come along now?" the nurse said, all kindness again. She held out the same arm, strong enough to guide any wavering footstep; this time they went back through the long corridor to where the nurse sat behind the bank window.

"All through?" this nurse said brightly. "Sit down a minute, then." She indicated a chair next to the glass window, and turned away to write busily. "Do not rinse your mouth for two hours," she said, without turning around. "Take a laxative tonight, take two aspirin if there is any pain. If there is much pain or excessive bleeding, notify this office at once. All right?" she said, and smiled brightly again.

There was a new little slip of paper; this one said, "Extraction," and underneath, "Do not rinse mouth. Take mild laxative. Two aspirin for pain. If pain is excessive or any hemorrhage occurs, notify office."

"Good-bye," the nurse said pleasantly.

"Good-bye," she said.

With the little slip of paper in her hand, she went out through the glass door and, still almost asleep, turned the corner and started down the hall. When she opened her eyes a little and saw that it was a long hall with doorways on either side, she stopped and then saw the door marked "Ladies" and went in. Inside there was a vast room with windows and wicker chairs and glaring white tiles and glittering silver faucets; there were four or five women around the wash-basins, combing their hair, putting on lipstick. She went directly to the nearest of the three wash-basins, took a paper towel, dropped her pocket-book and the little slip of paper on the floor next to her, and fumbled with the faucets, soaking the towel until it was dripping. Then she slapped it against her face violently. Her eyes cleared and she felt fresher, so she soaked the paper again and rubbed her face with it. She felt out blindly for another paper towel, and the woman next to her handed her one, with a laugh she could hear, although she could not see for the water in her eyes. She heard one of the women say, "Where we going for lunch?" and another one say, "Just downstairs, prob'ly. Old fool says I gotta be back in half-an-hour."

Then she realized that at the wash-basin she was in the way of the women in a hurry so she dried her face quickly. It was when she stepped a little aside to let someone else get to the basin and stood up and glanced into the mirror that she realized with a slight stinging shock that she had no idea which face was hers.

She looked into the mirror as though into a group of strangers, all staring at her or around her; no one was familiar in the group, no one smiled at her or looked at her with recognition; you'd think my own face would know me, she thought, with a queer numbness in her throat. There was a creamy chinless face with bright blond hair, and a sharp-looking face under a red veiled hat, and a colorless anxious face with brown hair pulled straight back, and a square rosy face under a square haircut, and two or three more faces pushing close to the mirror, moving, regarding themselves. Perhaps it's not a mirror, she thought, maybe it's a window and I'm looking straight through at women washing on the other side. But there were women combing their hair and consulting the mirror; the group was on her side, and she thought, I hope I'm not the blonde, and lifted her hand and put it on her cheek.

She was the pale anxious one with the hair pulled back and when she realized it she was indignant and moved hurriedly back through the crowd of women, thinking, It isn't fair, why don't I have any color in my face? There were some pretty faces there, why didn't I take one of those? I didn't have time, she told herself sullenly, they didn't give me time to think, I could have had one of the nice faces, even the blonde would be better.

She backed up and sat down in one of the wicker chairs. It's mean, she was thinking. She put her hand up and felt her hair; it was loosened after her sleep but that was definitely the way she wore it, pulled straight back all around and fastened at the back of her neck with a wide tight barrette. Like a schoolgirl, she thought, only—remembering the pale face in the mirror—only I'm older than that. She unfastened the barrette with difficulty and brought it around where she could look at it. Her hair fell softly around her face; it was warm and reached to her shoulders. The barrette was silver; engraved on it was the name, "Clara."

"Clara," she said aloud. "*Clara?*" Two of the women leaving the room smiled back at her over their shoulders; almost all the women were leaving now, correctly combed and lipsticked, hurrying out talking together. In the space of a second, like birds leaving a tree, they all were gone and she sat alone in the room. She dropped the barrette into the ashstand next to her chair; the ashstand was deep and metal, and the barrette made a satisfactory clang falling down. Her hair down on her shoulders, she opened her pocketbook, and began to take things out, setting them on her lap as she did so. Handkerchief, plain, white, uninitialled. Compact, square and brown tortoiseshell plastic, with a powder compartment and a rouge compartment; the rouge compartment had obviously never been used, although the powder cake was half-gone. That's why I'm so pale, she thought, and set the compact down. Lipstick, a rose shade, almost finished. A comb, an opened package of cigarettes and a package of matches, a change purse, and a wallet. The change purse was red imitation leather with a zipper across the top; she opened it and dumped the money out into her hand. Nickels, dimes, pennies, a quarter. Ninety-seven cents. Can't go far on that, she thought, and opened the brown leather wallet; there was money in it but she looked first for papers and found nothing. The only thing in the wallet was money. She counted it; there were nineteen dollars. I can go a little farther on *that,* she thought.

There was nothing else in the pocketbook. No keys—shouldn't I have keys? she wondered—no papers, no address book, no identification. The pocketbook itself was imitation leather, light grey, and she looked down and discovered that she was wearing a dark grey flannel suit and a salmon pink blouse with a ruffle around the neck. Her shoes were black and stout with moderate heels and they had laces, one of which was untied. She was wearing beige stockings and there was a ragged tear in the right knee and a great ragged run going down her leg and ending in a hole in the toe which she could feel inside her shoe. She was wearing a pin on the lapel of her suit which, when she turned it around to look at it, was a blue plastic letter C. She took the pin off and dropped it into the ashstand, and it made a sort of clatter at the bottom, with a metallic clang when it landed on the barrette. Her hands were small, with stubby fingers and no nail polish; she wore a thin gold wedding ring on her left hand and no other jewelry.

Sitting alone in the ladies' room in the wicker chair, she thought, The least I can do is get rid of these stockings. Since no one was around she took off her shoes and stripped away the stockings with a feeling of relief when her toe was released from the hole. Hide them, she thought: the paper towel wastebasket. When she stood up she got a better sight of herself in the mirror; it was worse than she had thought: the grey suit bagged in the seat, her legs were bony, and her shoulders sagged. I look fifty, she thought; and then, consulting the face, but I can't be more than thirty. Her hair hung down untidily around the pale face and with sudden anger she fumbled in the pocketbook and found the lipstick; she drew an emphatic rosy mouth on the pale face, realizing as she did so that she was not very expert at it, and with the red mouth the face looking at her seemed somehow better to her, so she opened the compact and put on pink cheeks with the rouge. The cheeks were uneven and patent, and the red mouth glaring, but at least the face was no longer pale and anxious.

She put the stockings into the wastebasket and went barelegged out into the hall again, and purposefully to the elevator. The elevator operator said, "Down?" when he saw her and she stepped in and the elevator carried her silently downstairs. She went back past the grave professional doorman and out into the street where people were passing, and she stood in front of the building and waited. After a few minutes Jim came out of a crowd of people passing and came over to her and took her hand.

Somewhere between here and there was her bottle of codeine pills, upstairs on the floor of the ladies' room she had left a little slip of paper headed "Extraction"; seven floors below, oblivious of the people who stepped sharply along the sidewalk, not noticing their occasional curious glances, her hand in Jim's and her hair down on her shoulders, she ran barefoot through hot sand.

1949

CARSON McCULLERS
(1917–1967)

Author of The Heart Is a Lonely Hunter, *Carson McCullers is often associated with Southern Gothic, a school of writing whose prominent members include William Faulkner, Tennessee Williams, and Flannery O'Connor. Many critics have read her five novels as reflecting her interest in "Southern grotesqueries," a term used to describe characters with physical manifestations of their emotional and psychological deficiencies. Feminist critics, however, have expanded our appreciation of McCullers's fiction by reading these characters as social and political outsiders.*

Born Lula Carson Smith in Columbus, Georgia, McCullers was the eldest child of three in a middle-class family. Though her academic achievements were far from memorable, her mother nurtured her daughter's precocious love of music. McCullers practiced the piano faithfully for at least three hours a day. But when her music teacher moved, she abandoned music to become a writer. At the age of seventeen she headed for New York City—she raised the money by selling some family heirlooms—where she studied writing at Columbia University and New York University. She published her first short story, "Wunderkind," when she was nineteen. Her first novel, The Heart Is a Lonely Hunter, *published when she was twenty-three, became a best-seller.*

McCullers lived much of her life surrounded by some of the most talented artists of her generation. During the summer of 1940, she met Eudora Welty, Katherine Anne Porter, and W. H. Auden at Bread Loaf, a writers' colony in Middlebury, Vermont. For a number of years, she lived in a Brooklyn townhouse where artists such as Gypsy Rose Lee, Paul and Jane Bowles, Richard Wright, and Salvador Dali resided or frequently visited. After their meeting in 1946, she and Tennessee Williams maintained a lifelong friendship.

Her friendships with other artists helped McCullers sustain her early success. In 1943 she published a memorable collection of stories, The Ballad of the Sad Cafe. *In 1950 her novel-turned-play,* The Member of the Wedding, *opened on Broadway to rave reviews, and in the late 1960s the director John Huston adapted her novel* Reflections in a Golden Eye *into a film with Marlon Brando and Elizabeth Taylor.*

Her successful professional life, however, was plagued by illnesses. Her childhood was marred by rheumatic fever. In 1947, while traveling in Europe, she suffered two strokes, the second of which paralyzed her left side. She developed pleurisy and double pneumonia in the early 1940s and cancer in the 1960s. McCullers died in 1967.

McCullers first published "Madame Zilensky and the King of Finland," the story that has been selected, in the December 20, 1941, issue of The New Yorker. *It reflects McCullers's knowledge of music and illustrates her interest in counterpoint, which serves as both the story's symbol and its design.*

MADAME ZILENSKY AND THE KING OF FINLAND

To Mr. Brook, the head of the music department at Ryder College, was due all the credit for getting Madame Zilensky on the faculty. The college considered itself fortunate; her reputation was impressive, both as a composer and as a pedagogue. Mr. Brook took on himself the responsibility of finding a house for Madame Zilensky, a comfortable place with a garden, which was convenient to the college and next to the apartment house where he himself lived.

No one in Westbridge had known Madame Zilensky before she came. Mr. Brook had seen her pictures in musical journals, and once he had written to her about the authenticity of a certain Buxtehude manuscript. Also, when it was being settled that she was to join the faculty, they had exchanged a few cables and letters on practical affairs. She wrote in a clear, square hand, and the only thing out of the ordinary in these letters was the fact that they contained an occasional reference to objects and persons altogether unknown to Mr. Brook, such as "the yellow cat in Lisbon" or "poor Heinrich." These lapses Mr. Brook put down to the confusion of getting herself and her family out of Europe.

Mr. Brook was a somewhat pastel person; years of Mozart minuets, of explanations about diminished sevenths and minor triads, had given him a watchful vocational patience. For the most part, he kept to himself. He loathed academic fiddle-faddle and committees. Years before, when the music department had decided to gang together and spend the summer in Salzburg, Mr. Brook sneaked out of the arrangement at the last moment and took a solitary trip to Peru. He had a few eccentricities himself and was tolerant of the peculiarities of others; indeed, he rather relished the ridiculous. Often, when confronted with some grave and incongruous situation, he would feel a little inside tickle, which stiffened his long, mild face and sharpened the light in his gray eyes.

Mr. Brook met Madame Zilensky at the Westbridge station a week before the beginning of the fall semester. He recognized her instantly. She was a tall, straight woman with a pale and haggard face. Her eyes were deeply shadowed and she wore her dark, ragged hair pushed back from her forehead. She had large, delicate hands, which were very grubby. About her person as a whole there was something noble and abstract that made Mr. Brook draw back for a moment and stand nervously undoing his cuff links. In spite of her clothes—a long, black skirt and a broken-down old leather jacket—she made an impression of vague elegance. With Madame Zilensky were three children, boys between the ages of ten and six, all blond, blank-eyed, and beautiful. There was one other person, an old woman who turned out later to be the Finnish servant.

This was the group he found at the station. The only luggage they had with them was two immense boxes of manuscripts, the rest of their paraphernalia having been forgotten in the station at Springfield when they changed trains. That is the sort of thing that can happen to anyone. When Mr. Brook got them all into a taxi, he thought the worst difficulties were over, but Madame Zilensky suddenly tried to scramble over his knees and get out of the door.

"My God!" she said. "I left my—how do you say?—my tick-tick-tick—"

"Your watch?" asked Mr. Brook.

"Oh no!" she said vehemently. "You know, my tick-tick-tick," and she waved her forefinger from side to side, pendulum fashion.

"Tick-tick," said Mr. Brook, putting his hands to his forehead and closing his eyes. "Could you possibly mean a metronome?"

"Yes! Yes! I think I must have lost it there where we changed trains."

Mr. Brook managed to quiet her. He even said, with a kind of dazed gallantry, that he would get her another one the next day. But at the time he was bound to admit to himself that there was something curious about this panic over a metronome when there was all the rest of the lost luggage to consider.

. . .

The Zilensky ménage moved into the house next door, and on the surface everything was all right. The boys were quiet children. Their names were Sigmund, Boris, and Sammy. They were always together and they followed each other around Indian file, Sigmund usually the first. Among themselves they spoke a desperate-sounding family Esperanto made up of Russian, French, Finnish, German, and English; when other people were around, they were strangely silent. It was not any one thing that the Zilenskys did or said that made Mr. Brook uneasy. There were just little incidents. For example, something about the Zilensky children subconsciously bothered him when they were in a house, and finally he realized that what troubled him was the fact that the Zilensky boys never walked on a rug; they skirted it single file on the bare floor, and if a room was carpeted, they stood in the doorway and did not go inside. Another thing was this: Weeks passed and Madame Zilensky seemed to make no effort to get settled or to furnish the house with anything more than a table and some beds. The front door was left open day and night, and soon the house began to take on a queer, bleak look like that of a place abandoned for years.

The college had every reason to be satisfied with Madame Zilensky. She taught with a fierce insistence. She could become deeply indignant if some Mary Owens or Bernadine Smith would not clean up her Scarlatti trills. She got hold of four pianos for her college studio and set four dazed students to playing Bach fugues together. The racket that came from her end of the department was extraordinary, but Madame Zilensky did not seem to have a nerve in her, and if pure will and effort can get over a musical idea, then Ryder College could not have done better. At night Madame Zilensky worked on her twelfth symphony. She seemed never to sleep; no matter what time of night Mr. Brook happened to look out of his sitting-room window, the light in her studio was always on. No, it was not because of any professional consideration that Mr. Brook became so dubious.

It was in late October when he felt for the first time that something was unmistakably wrong. He had lunched with Madame Zilensky and had enjoyed himself, as she had given him a very detailed account of an African safari she had made in 1928. Later in the afternoon she stopped in at his office and stood rather abstractly in the doorway.

Mr. Brook looked up from his desk and asked, "Is there anything you want?"

"No, thank you," said Madame Zilensky. She had a low, beautiful, sombre voice. "I was only just wondering. You recall the metronome. Do you think perhaps that I might have left it with that French?"

"Who?" asked Mr. Brook.

"Why, that French I was married to," she answered.

"Frenchman," Mr. Brook said mildly. He tried to imagine the husband of Madame Zilensky, but his mind refused. He muttered half to himself, "The father of the children."

"But no," said Madame Zilensky with decision. "The father of Sammy."

Mr. Brook had a swift prescience. His deepest instincts warned him to say nothing further. Still, his respect for order, his conscience, demanded that he ask, "And the father of the other two?"

Madame Zilensky put her hand to the back of her head and ruffled up her short, cropped hair. Her face was dreamy, and for several moments she did not answer. Then she said gently, "Boris is of a Pole who played the piccolo."

"And Sigmund?" he asked. Mr. Brook looked over his orderly desk, with the stack of corrected papers, the three sharpened pencils, the ivory-elephant paperweight. When he glanced up at Madame Zilensky, she was obviously thinking hard. She gazed around at the corners of the room, her brows lowered and her jaw moving from side to side. At last she said, "We were discussing the father of Sigmund?"

"Why, no," said Mr. Brook. "There is no need to do that."

Madame Zilensky answered in a voice both dignified and final. "He was a fellow-countryman."

Mr. Brook really did not care one way or the other. He had no prejudices; people could marry seventeen times and have Chinese children so far as he was concerned. But there was something about this conversation with Madame Zilensky that bothered him. Suddenly he understood. The children didn't look at all like Madame Zilensky, but they looked exactly like each other, and as they all had different fathers, Mr. Brook thought the resemblance astonishing.

But Madame Zilensky had finished with the subject. She zipped up her leather jacket and turned away.

"That is exactly where I left it," she said, with a quick nod. "*Chez* that French."

. . .

Affairs in the music department were running smoothly. Mr. Brook did not have any serious embarrassments to deal with, such as the harp teacher last year who had finally eloped with a garage mechanic. There was only this nagging apprehension about Madame Zilensky. He could not make out what was wrong in his relations with her or why his feelings were so mixed. To begin with, she was a great globe-trotter, and her conversations were incongruously seasoned with references to far-fetched places. She would go along for days without opening her mouth, prowling through the corridor with her hands in the pockets of her jacket and her face locked in meditation. Then suddenly she would buttonhole Mr. Brook and launch out on a long, volatile monologue, her eyes reckless and bright and her voice warm with eagerness. She would talk about anything or nothing at all. Yet, without exception, there was something queer, in a slanted sort of way, about every episode she ever mentioned. If she spoke of taking Sammy to the barbershop, the impression she created was just as foreign as if she were telling of an afternoon in Bagdad. Mr. Brook could not make it out.

The truth came to him very suddenly, and the truth made everything perfectly clear, or at least clarified the situation. Mr. Brook had come home early and lighted a fire in the little grate in his sitting room. He felt comfortable and at peace that evening. He sat before the fire in his stocking feet, with a volume of William Blake on the table by his side, and he had poured himself a half-glass of apricot brandy. At ten o'clock he was drowsing cozily before the fire, his mind full of cloudy phrases of Mahler and floating half-thoughts. Then all at once, out of this delicate stupor, four words came to his mind: "The King of Finland." The words seemed familiar, but for the first moment he could not place them. Then all at once he tracked them down. He had been walking across the campus that afternoon when Madame Zilensky stopped him and began some preposterous rigmarole, to which he had only half listened; he was thinking about the stack of canons turned in by his counterpoint class. Now the words, the inflections of her voice, came back to him with insidious exactitude. Madame Zilensky had started off with the following remark: "One day, when I was standing in front of a *pâtisserie,* the King of Finland came by in a sled."

Mr. Brook jerked himself up straight in his chair and put down his glass of brandy. The woman was a pathological liar. Almost every word she uttered outside of class was an untruth. If she worked all night, she would go out of her way to tell you she spent the evening at the cinema. If she ate lunch at the Old Tavern, she would be sure to mention that she had lunched with her children at home. The woman was simply a pathological liar, and that accounted for everything.

Mr. Brook cracked his knuckles and got up from his chair. His first reaction was one of exasperation. That day after day Madame Zilensky would have the gall to sit there in his office and deluge him with her outrageous falsehoods! Mr. Brook was intensely provoked. He walked up and down the room, then he went into his kitchenette and made himself a sardine sandwich.

An hour later, as he sat before the fire, his irritation had changed to a scholarly and thoughtful wonder. What he must do, he told himself, was to regard the whole situation impersonally and look on Madame Zilensky as a doctor looks on a sick patient. Her lies were of the guileless sort. She did not dissimulate with any intention to deceive, and the untruths she told were never used to any possible advantage. That was the maddening thing; there was simply no motive behind it all.

Mr. Brook finished off the rest of the brandy. And slowly, when it was almost midnight, a further understanding came to him. The reason for the lies of Madame Zilensky was painful and plain. All her life long Madame Zilensky had worked—at the piano, teaching, and writing those beautiful and immense twelve symphonies. Day and night she had drudged and struggled and thrown her soul into her work, and there was not much of her left over for anything else. Being human, she suffered from this lack and did what she could to make up for it. If she passed the evening bent over a table in the library and later declared that she had spent that time playing cards, it was as though she had managed to do both those things. Through the lies, she lived vicariously. The lie doubled the little of her existence that was left over from work and augmented the little rag end of her personal life.

Mr. Brook looked into the fire, and the face of Madame Zilensky was in his mind—a severe face, with dark, weary eyes and delicately disciplined mouth. He was conscious of a warmth in his chest, and a feeling of pity, protectiveness, and dreadful understanding. For a while he was in a state of lovely confusion.

Later on he brushed his teeth and got into his pajamas. He must be practical. What did this clear up? That French, the Pole with the piccolo, Bagdad? And the children, Sigmund, Boris, and Sammy—who were they? Were they really her children after all, or had she simply rounded them up from somewhere? Mr. Brook polished his spectacles and put them on the table by his bed. He must come to an immediate understanding with her. Otherwise, there would exist in the department a situation which could become most problematical. It was two o'clock. He glanced out of his window and saw that the light in Madame Zilensky's workroom was still on. Mr. Brook got into bed, made terrible faces in the dark, and tried to plan what he would say next day.

Mr. Brook was in his office by eight o'clock. He sat hunched up behind his desk, ready to trap Madame Zilensky as she passed down the corridor. He did not have to wait long, and as soon as he heard her footsteps he called out her name.

Madame Zilensky stood in the doorway. She looked vague and jaded. "How are you? I had such a fine night's rest," she said.

"Pray be seated, if you please," said Mr. Brook. "I would like a word with you."

Madame Zilensky put aside her portfolio and leaned back wearily in the armchair across from him. "Yes?" she asked.

"Yesterday you spoke to me as I was walking across the campus," he said slowly. "And if I am not mistaken, I believe you said something about a pastry shop and the King of Finland. Is that correct?"

Madame Zilensky turned her head to one side and stared retrospectively at a corner of the window sill.

"Something about a pastry shop," he repeated.

Her tired face brightened. "But of course," she said eagerly. "I told you about the time I was standing in front of this shop and the King of Finland—"

"Madame Zilensky!" Mr. Brook cried. "There *is* no King of Finland."

Madame Zilensky looked absolutely blank. Then, after an instant, she started off again. "I was standing in front of Bjarne's *pâtisserie* when I turned away from the cakes and suddenly saw the King of Finland—"

"Madame Zilensky, I just told you that there is no King of Finland."

"In Helsingfors," she started off again desperately, and again he let her get as far as the King, and then no further.

"Finland is a democracy," he said. "You could not possibly have seen the King of Finland. Therefore, what you have just said is an untruth. A pure untruth."

Never afterward could Mr. Brook forget the face of Madame Zilensky at that moment. In her eyes there was astonishment, dismay, and a sort of cornered horror. She had the look of one who watches his whole interior world split open and disintegrate.

"It is a pity," said Mr. Brook with real sympathy.

But Madame Zilensky pulled herself together. She raised her chin and said coldly, "I am a Finn."

"That I do not question," answered Mr. Brook. On second thought, he did question it a little.

"I was born in Finland and I am a Finnish citizen."

"That may very well be," said Mr. Brook in a rising voice.

"In the war," she continued passionately, "I rode a motorcycle and was a messenger."

"Your patriotism does not enter into it."

"Just because I am getting out the first papers—"

"Madame Zilensky!" said Mr. Brook. His hands grasped the edge of the desk. "That is only an irrelevant issue. The point is that you maintained and testified that you saw—that you saw—" But he could not finish. Her face stopped him. She was deadly pale and there were shadows around her mouth. Her eyes were wide open, doomed, and proud. And Mr. Brook felt suddenly like a murderer. A great commotion of feelings—understanding, remorse, and unreasonable love—made him cover his face with his hands. He could not speak until this agitation in his insides quieted down, and then he said very faintly, "Yes. Of course. The King of Finland. And was he nice?"

. . .

An hour later, Mr. Brook sat looking out of the window of his office. The trees along the quiet Westbridge street were almost bare, and the gray buildings of the college had a calm, sad look. As he idly took in the familiar scene, he noticed the Drakes' old Airedale waddling along down the street. It was a thing he had watched a hundred times before, so what was it that struck him as strange? Then he realized with a kind of cold surprise that the old dog was running along backward. Mr. Brook watched the Airedale until he was out of sight, then resumed his work on the canons which had been turned in by the class in counterpoint.

1941

HISAYE YAMAMOTO
(1921–)

Hisaye Yamamoto's precise, seemingly simple style, muted ironies, and restrained characters spring from both Japanese and American literary traditions. Her stories, while focusing primarily on Japanese American characters, explore the complexities of cross-cultural experiences and family relationships. Some of her most powerful stories draw on her firsthand knowledge of Japanese American (Nisei) children and native Japanese (Issei) parents and on the contradictions and dilemmas faced by Japanese American women.

Born in Redondo Beach, California, Yamamoto began writing when she was a teenager. She majored in French, Spanish, German, and Latin at Compton Junior College. During World War II, while her family was confined in an Arizona concentration camp, she wrote for the camp newspaper. Yamamoto continued working as a journalist for the Los Angeles Tribune *for three years after the war. After serving as a volunteer on a Catholic Worker rehabilitation farm on Staten Island, New York, she married and returned to California, where she continues her active life as a fiction writer.*

Despite the prejudice suffered by Japanese Americans after World War II, Yamamoto began to receive recognition as a writer in the early 1950s. Four short stories, "Seventeen," "The Brown House," "Yoneko's Earthquake," and "Epithalamium," appeared in Martha Foley's "Distinctive Short Stories" lists. "Yoneko's Earthquake" also appeared in Best American Short Stories: 1952. *Yamamoto received a John Hay Whitney Foundation Opportunity Fellowship in 1950. Her stories have appeared in publications such as* Partisan Review, Kenyon Review, Harper's Bazaar, Asian American Journal, Amerasia Journal, *and* Hokubei Mainichi, *as well as in numerous anthologies. In 1986 she received the Before Columbus Foundation's American Book Award for Lifetime Achievement.*

In "The Legend of Miss Sasagawara," Yamamoto builds a portrait of a character through the eyes of an onlooker. The principal setting, a Japanese detention camp described matter-of-factly by the narrator, forms an integral part of the story's theme. The story reveals Yamamoto's understated style and subtle use of details leading, in this case, to a surprise ending.

THE LEGEND OF MISS SASAGAWARA

Even in that unlikely place of wind, sand, and heat, it was easy to imagine Miss Sasagawara a decorative ingredient of some ballet. Her daily costume, brief and fitting closely to her trifling waist, generously billowing below, and bringing together arrestingly rich colors like mustard yellow and forest green, appeared to have been cut from a coarse-textured homespun; her shining hair was so long it wound twice about her head to form a coronet; her face was delicate and pale, with a fine nose, pouting bright mouth, and glittering eyes; and her measured walk said, "Look, I'm *walking!*" as though walking were not a common but a rather special thing to be doing. I first saw her so one evening after mess, as she was coming out of the women's latrine going toward her barracks, and after I thought she was out of hearing, I imitated the young men of the Block (No. 33), and gasped, "Wow! How much does *she* weigh?"

"Oh, haven't you heard?" said my friend Elsie Kubo, knowing very well I had not. "That's Miss Sasagawara."

It turned out Elsie knew all about Miss Sasagawara, who with her father was new to Block 33. Where had she accumulated all her items? Probably a morsel here and a morsel there, and, anyway, I forgot to ask her sources, because the picture she painted was so distracting: Miss Sasagawara's father was a Buddhist minister, and the two had gotten permission to come to this Japanese evacuation camp in Arizona from one further north, after the death there of Mrs. Sasagawara. They had come here to join the Rev. Sasagawara's brother's family, who lived in a neighboring Block, but there had been some trouble between them, and just this week the immigrant pair had gotten leave to move over to Block 33. They were occupying one end of the Block's lone empty barracks, which had not been chopped up yet into the customary four apartments. The other end had been taken over by a young couple, also newcomers to the Block, who had moved in the same day.

"And do you know what, Kiku?" Elsie continued. "Oooh, that gal is really temperamental. I guess it's because she was a ballet dancer before she got stuck in camp, I hear people like that are temperamental. Anyway, the Sasakis, the new couple at the other end of the barracks, think she's crazy. The day they all moved in, the barracks was really dirty, all covered with dust from the dust storms and everything, so Mr. Sasaki was going to wash the whole barracks down with a hose, and he thought he'd be nice and do the Sasagawaras' side first. You know, do them a favor. But do you know what? Mr. Sasaki got the hose attached to the faucet outside and started to go in the door, and he said all the Sasagawaras' suitcases and things were on top of the Army cots and Miss Sasagawara was trying to clean the place out with a pail of water and a broom. He said, 'Here let me flush the place out with a hose for you; it'll be faster.' And she turned right around and screamed at him, 'What are you trying to do? Spy on me? Get out of here or I'll throw this water on you!' He said he was so surprised he couldn't move for a minute, and before he knew it, Miss Sasagawara just up and threw that water at him, pail and all. Oh, he said he got out of that place fast, but fast. Madwoman, he called her."

But Elsie had already met Miss Sasagawara, too, over at the apartment of the Murakamis, where Miss Sasagawara was borrowing Mrs. Murakami's Singer, and had found her quite amiable. "She said she was thirty-nine years old—imagine, thirty–nine, she looks so young, more like twenty-five; but she said she wasn't sorry she never got married, because she's had her fun. She said she got to go all over the country a couple of times, dancing in the ballet."

And after we emerged from the latrine, Elsie and I, slapping mosquitoes in the warm, gathering dusk, sat on the stoop of her apartment and talked awhile, jealously of the scintillating life Miss Sasagawara had led until now and nostalgically of the few ballets we had seen in the world outside. (How faraway Los Angeles seemed!) But we ended up as we always did, agreeing that our mission in life, pushing twenty as we were, was first to finish college somewhere when and if the war ever ended and we were free again, and then to find good jobs and two nice, clean young men, preferably handsome, preferably rich, who would cherish us forever and a day.

My introduction, less spectacular, to the Rev. Sasagawara came later, as I noticed him, a slight and fragile-looking old man, in the Block mess hall (where I worked as a waitress, and Elsie, too) or in the laundry room or going to and from the latrine. Sometimes he would be farther out, perhaps going to the post office or canteen or to visit friends in another Block or on some business to the Administration buildings, but wherever he was headed, however doubtless his destination, he always seemed to be wandering lostly. This may have been because he walked so slowly, with such negligible steps, or because he wore perpetually an air of bemusement, never talking directly to a person, as though, being what he was, he could not stop for an instant his meditation on the higher life.

I noticed, too, that Miss Sasagawara never came to the mess hall herself. Her father ate at the tables reserved for the occupants, mostly elderly, of the end barracks known as the bachelors' dormitory. After each meal, he came up to the counter and carried away a plate of food, protected with one of the pinkish apple wrappers we waitresses made as wrinkleless as possible and put out for napkins, and a mug of tea or coffee. Sometimes Miss Sasagawara could be seen rinsing out her empties at the one double-tub in the laundry that was reserved for private dishwashing.

If any one in the Block or in the entire camp of 15,000 or so people had talked at any length with Miss Sasagawara (everyone happening to speak of her called her that, although her first name, Mari, was simple enough and rather pretty) after her first and only visit to use Mrs. Murakami's sewing machine, I never heard of it. Nor did she ever willingly use the shower room, just off the latrine, when anyone else was there. Once, when I was up past midnight writing letters and went for my shower, I came upon her under the full needling force of a steamy spray, but she turned her back to me and did not answer my surprised hello. I hoped my body would be as smooth and spare and well-turned when I was thirty-nine. Another time Elsie and I passed in front of the Sasagawara apartment, which was really only a cubicle because the once-empty barracks had soon been partitioned off into six units for families of two, and we saw her there on the wooden steps, sitting with her wide, wide skirt spread splendidly about her. She was intent on peeling a grapefruit, which her father had probably brought to her from the mess hall that morning, and Elsie called, "Hello there!" Miss Sasagawara looked up and stared, without recognition. We were almost out of earshot when I heard her call, "Do I know you?" and I could have almost sworn that she sounded hopeful, if not downright wistful, but Elsie, already miffed at having expended friendliness so unprofitably, seemed not to have heard, and that was that.

Well, if Miss Sasagawara was not one to speak to, she was certainly one to speak of, and she came up quite often as topic for the endless conversations which helped along the monotonous days. My mother said she had met the late Mrs. Sasagawara once, many years before the war, and to hear her tell it, a sweeter, kindlier woman there never was. "I suppose," said my mother, "that I'll never meet anyone like her again; she was a lady in every sense of the word." Then she reminded me that I had seen the Rev. Sasagawara before. Didn't I remember him as one of the three bhikshus who had read the sutras at Grandfather's funeral?

I could not say that I did. I barely remembered Grandfather, my mother's father. The only thing that came back with clarity was my nausea at the wake and the funeral, the first and only ones I had ever had occasion to attend, because it had been reproduced several times since—each time, in fact, that I had crossed again the actual scent or suspicion of burning incense. Dimly I recalled the inside of the Buddhist temple in Los Angeles, an immense, murky auditorium whose high and huge platform had held, centered in the background, a great golden shrine touched with black and white. Below this platform, Grandfather, veiled by gauze, had slept in a long grey box which just fitted him. There had been flowers, oh, such flowers, everywhere. And right in front of Grandfather's box had been the incense stand, upon which squatted two small bowls, one with a cluster of straw-thin sticks sending up white tendrils of smoke, the other containing a heap of coarse, grey powder. Each mourner in turn had gone up to the stand, bowing once, his palms touching in prayer before he reached it; had bent in prayer over the stand; had taken then a pinch of incense from the bowl of crumbs and, bowing over it reverently, cast it into the other, the active bowl; had bowed, the hands praying again; had retreated a few steps and bowed one last time, the hands still joined, before returning to his seat. (I knew the ceremony well from having been severely coached in it on the evening of the wake.) There had been tears and tears and here and there a sudden sob.

And all this while, three men in black robes had been on the platform, one standing in front of the shining altar, the others sitting on either side, and the entire trio incessantly chanting a strange, mellifluous language in unison. From time to time there had reverberated through the enormous room, above the singsong, above the weeping, above the fragrance, the sharp, startling whang of the gong.

So, one of those men had been Miss Sasagawara's father. . . . This information brought him closer to me, and I listened with interest later when it was told that he kept here in his apartment a small shrine, much more intricately constructed than that kept by the usual Buddhist household, before which, at regular hours of the day, he offered incense and chanted, tinkling (in lieu of the gong) a small bell. What did Miss Sasagawara do at these prayer periods, I wondered; did she participate, did she let it go in one ear and out the other, or did she abruptly go out on the steps, perhaps to eat a grapefruit?

. . .

Elsie and I tired one day of working in the mess hall. And this desire for greener fields came almost together with the Administration announcement that henceforth the wages of residents doing truly vital labor, such as in the hospital or on the garbage trucks that went from mess hall to mess hall, would be upped to nineteen dollars a month instead of the common sixteen.

"Oh, I've always wanted to be a nurse!" Elsie confided, as the Block manager sat down to his breakfast after reading out the day's bulletin in English and Japanese.

"What's stopped you?" I asked.

"Mom," Elsie said. "She thinks it's dirty work. And she's afraid I'll catch something. But I'll remind her of the extra three dollars."

"It's never appealed to me much, either," I confessed. "Why don't we go over to garbage? It's the same pay."

Elsie would not even consider it. "Very funny. Well, you don't have to be a nurse's aide, Kiku. The hospital's short all kinds of help. Dental assistants, receptionists. . . . Let's go apply after we finish this here."

So, willy-nilly, while Elsie plunged gleefully into the pleasure of wearing a trim blue-and-white striped seersucker, into the duties of taking temperatures and carrying bedpans, and into the fringe of medical jargon (she spoke very casually now of catheters, enemas, primiparas, multiparas), I became a relief receptionist at the hospital's front desk, taking my hours as they were assigned. And it was on one of my midnight-to-morning shifts that I spoke to Miss Sasagawara for the first time.

The cooler in the corridor window was still whirring away (for that desert heat in summer had a way of lingering intact through the night to merge with the warmth of the morning sun), but she entered bundled in an extraordinarily long black coat, her face made petulant, not unprettily, by lines of pain.

"I think I've got appendicitis," she said breathlessly, without preliminary.

"May I have your name and address?" I asked, unscrewing my pen.

Annoyance seemed to outbalance agony for a moment, but she answered soon enough, in a cold rush, "Mari Sasagawara, Thirty-three-seven C."

It was necessary also to learn her symptoms, and I wrote down that she had chills and a dull aching at the back of her head, as well as these excruciating flashes in her lower right abdomen.

"I'll have to go wake up the doctor. Here's a blanket, why don't you lie down over there on the bench until he comes?" I suggested.

She did not answer, so I tossed the Army blanket on the bench, and when I returned from the doctors' dormitory, after having tapped and tapped on the door of young Dr. Moritomo, who was on night duty, she was still standing where I had left her, immobile and holding onto the wooden railing shielding the desk.

"Dr. Moritomo's coming right away," I said. "Why don't you sit down at least?"

Miss Sasagawara said, "Yes," but did not move.

"Did you walk all the way?" I asked incredulously, for Block 33 was a good mile off, across the canal.

She nodded, as if that were not important, also as if to thank me kindly to mind my own business.

Dr. Moritomo (technically, the title was premature; evacuation had caught him with a few months to go on his degree), wearing a maroon bathrobe, shuffled in sleepily and asked her to come into the emergency room for an examination. A short while later, he guided her past my desk into the laboratory, saying he was going to take her blood count.

When they came out, she went over to the electric fountain for a drink of water, and Dr. Moritomo said reflectively, "Her count's all right. Not appendicitis. We should keep her for observation, but the general ward is pretty full, isn't it? Hm, well, I'll give her something to take. Will you tell one of the boys to take her home?"

This I did, but when I came back from arousing George, one of the ambulance boys, Miss Sasagawara was gone, and Dr. Moritomo was coming out of the laboratory where he had gone to push out the lights. "Here's George, but that girl must have walked home," I reported helplessly.

"She's in no condition to do that. George, better catch up with her and take her home," Dr. Moritomo ordered.

Shrugging, George strode down the hall; the doctor shuffled back to bed; and soon there was the shattering sound of one of the old Army ambulances backing out of the hospital drive.

George returned in no time at all to say that Miss Sasagawara had refused to get on the ambulance.

"She wouldn't even listen to me. She just kept walking and I drove alongside and told her it was Dr. Moritomo's orders, but she wouldn't even listen to me."

"She wouldn't?"

"I hope Doc didn't expect me to drag her into the ambulance."

"Oh, well," I said. "I guess she'll get home all right. She walked all the way up here."

"Cripes, what a dame!" George complained, shaking his head as he started back to the ambulance room. "I never heard of such a thing. She wouldn't even listen to me."

. . .

Miss Sasagawara came back to the hospital about a month later. Elsie was the one who rushed up to the desk where I was on day duty to whisper, "Miss Sasagawara just tried to escape from the hospital!"

"Escape? What do you mean, escape?" I said.

"Well, she came in last night, and they didn't know what was wrong with her, so they kept her for observation. And this morning, just now, she ran out of the ward in just a hospital nightgown and the orderlies chased after her and caught her and brought her back. Oh, she was just fighting them. But once they got her back to bed, she calmed down right away, and Miss Morris asked her what was the big idea, you know, and do you know what she said? She said she didn't want any more of those doctors pawing her. *Pawing* her, imagine!"

After an instant's struggle with self-mockery, my curiosity led me down the entrance corridor after Elsie into the longer, wider corridor admitting to the general ward. The whole hospital staff appeared to have gathered in the room to get a look at Miss Sasagawara, and the other patients, or those of them that could, were sitting up attentively in their high, white, and narrow beds. Miss Sasagawara had the corner bed to the left as we entered and, covered only by a brief hospital apron, she was sitting on the edge with her legs dangling over the side. With her head slightly bent, she was staring at a certain place on the floor, and I knew she must be aware of that concentrated gaze, of trembling old Dr. Kawamoto (he had retired several years before the war, but he had been drafted here), of Miss Morris, the head nurse, of Miss Bowman, the nurse in charge of the general ward during the day, of the other patients, of the nurse's aides, of the orderlies, and of everyone else who tripped in and out abashedly on some pretext or other in order to pass by her bed. I knew this by her smile, for as she continued to look at that same piece of the floor, she continued, unexpectedly, to seem wryly amused with the entire proceedings. I peered at her wonderingly through the triangular peephole created by someone's hand on hip, while Dr. Kawamoto, Miss Morris, and Miss Bowman tried to persuade her to lie down and relax. She was as smilingly immune to tactful suggestions as she was to tactless gawking.

There was no future to watching such a war of nerves as this; and besides,

I was supposed to be at the front desk, so I hurried back in time to greet a frantic young mother and father, the latter carrying their small son who had had a hemorrhage this morning after a tonsillectomy yesterday in the outpatient clinic.

A couple of weeks later on the late shift I found George, the ambulance driver, in high spirits. This time he had been the one selected to drive a patient to Phoenix, where special cases were occasionally sent under escort, and he was looking forward to the moment when, for a few hours, the escort would permit him to go shopping around the city and perhaps take in a new movie. He showed me the list of things his friends had asked him to bring back for them, and we laughed together over the request of one plumpish nurse's aide for the biggest, richest chocolate cake he could find.

"You ought to have seen Mabel's eyes while she was describing the kind of cake she wanted," he said. "Man, she looked like she was eating it already!"

Just then one of the other drivers, Bobo Kunitomi, came up and nudged George, and they withdrew a few steps from my desk.

"Oh, I ain't particularly interested in that," I heard George saying.

There was some murmuring from Bobo, of which I caught the words, "Well, hell, you might as well, just as long as you're getting to go out there."

George shrugged, then nodded, and Bobo came over to the desk and asked for pencil and paper. "This is a good place. . . ." he said, handing George what he had written.

Was it my imagination, or did George emerge from his chat with Bobo a little ruddier than usual? "Well, I guess I better go get ready," he said, taking leave. "Oh, anything you want, Kiku? Just say the word."

"Thanks, not this time," I said. "Well, enjoy yourself."

"Don't worry," he said. "I will!"

He had started down the hall when I remembered to ask, "Who are you taking, anyway?"

George turned around. "Miss Sa-sa-ga-wa-ra," he said, accenting every syllable. "Remember that dame? The one who wouldn't let me take her home?"

"Yes," I said. "What's the matter with her?"

George, saying not a word, pointed at his head and made several circles in the air with his first finger.

"Really?" I asked.

Still mum, George nodded in emphasis and pity before he turned to go.

. . .

How long was she away? It must have been several months, and when, towards late autumn, she returned at last from the sanitarium in Phoenix, everyone in Block 33 was amazed at the change. She said hello and how are you as often and easily as the next person, although many of those she greeted were surprised and suspicious, remembering the earlier rebuffs. There were some who never did get used to Miss Sasagawara as a friendly being.

One evening when I was going toward the latrine for my shower, my youngest sister, ten-year-old Michi, almost collided with me and said excitedly, "You going for your shower now, Kiku?"

"You want to fight about it?" I said, making fists.

"Don't go now, don't go now! Miss Sasagawara's in there," she whispered wickedly.

"Well," I demanded. "What's wrong with that, honey?"

"She's scary. Us kids were in there and she came in and we finished, so we got out, and she said, 'Don't be afraid of me. I won't hurt you.' Gee, we weren't even afraid of her, but when she said that, gee!"

"Oh, go home and go to bed," I said.

Miss Sasagawara was indeed in the shower and she welcomed me with a smile. "Aren't you the girl who plays the violin?"

I giggled and explained. Elsie and I, after hearing Menuhin on the radio, had in a fit of madness sent to Sears and Roebuck for beginners' violins that cost five dollars each. We had received free instruction booklets, too, but unable to make heads or tails from them, we contented ourselves with occasionally taking the violins out of their paper bags and sawing every which way away.

Miss Sasagawara laughed aloud—a lovely sound. "Well, you're just about as good as I am. I sent for a Spanish guitar. I studied it about a year once, but that was so long ago I don't remember the first thing and I'm having to start all over again. We'd make a fine orchestra."

That was the only time we really exchanged words and some weeks later I understood she had organized a dancing class from among the younger girls in the Block. My sister Michi, becoming one of her pupils, got very attached to her and spoke of her frequently at home. So I knew that Miss Sasagawara and her father had decorated their apartment to look oh, so pretty, that Miss Sasagawara had a whole big suitcase full of dancing costumes, and that Miss Sasagawara had just lots and lots of books to read.

The fruits of Miss Sasagawara's patient labor were put on show at the Block Christmas party, the second such observance in camp. Again, it was a gay, if odd, celebration. The mess hall was hung with red and green crepe paper streamers and the greyish mistletoe that grew abundantly on the ancient mesquite surrounding the camp. There were even electric decorations on the token Christmas tree. The oldest occupant of the bachelor's dormitory gave a tremulous monologue in an exaggerated Hiroshima dialect; one of the young boys wore a bow-tie and whispered a popular song while the girls shrieked and pretended to be growing faint; my mother sang an old Japanese song; four of the girls wore similar blue dresses and harmonized on a sweet tune; a little girl in a grass skirt and superfluous brassiere did a hula; and the chief cook came out with an ample saucepan and, assisted by the waitresses, performed the familiar *dojosukui,* the comic dance about a man who is merely trying to scoop up a few loaches from an uncooperative lake. Then Miss Sasagawara shooed her eight little girls, including Michi, in front, and while they formed a stiff pattern and waited, self-conscious in the rustly crepe paper dresses they had made themselves, she set up a portable phonograph on the floor and vigorously turned the crank.

Something was past its prime, either the machine or the record or the needle, for what came out was a feeble rasp but distantly related to the Mozart minuet it was supposed to be. After a bit I recognized the melody; I had learned it as a child to the words,

> When dames wore hoops and powdered hair,
> And very strict was e-ti-quette,
> When men were brave and ladies fair,
> They danced the min-u-et. . . .

And the little girls, who might have curtsied and stepped gracefully about under Miss Sasagawara's eyes alone, were all elbows and knees as they felt the Block's one-hundred-fifty or more pairs of eyes on them. Although there was sustained applause after their number, what we were benevolently approving was the great effort, for the achievement had been undeniably small. Then Santa came with a pillow for a stomach, his hands each dragging a bulging burlap bag. Church people outside had kindly sent these gifts, Santa announced, and every recipient must write and thank the person whose name he would find on an enclosed slip. So saying, he called by name each Block child under twelve and ceremoniously presented each eleemosynary package, and a couple of the youngest children screamed in fright at this new experience of a red and white man with a booming voice.

At the last, Santa called, "Miss Mari Sasagawara!" and when she came forward in surprise, he explained to the gathering that she was being rewarded for her help with the Block's younger generation. Everyone clapped and Miss Sasagawara, smiling graciously, opened her package then and there. She held up her gift, a peach-colored bath towel, so that it could be fully seen, and everyone clapped again.

. . .

Suddenly I put this desert scene behind me. The notice I had long awaited, of permission to relocate to Philadelphia to attend college, finally came, and there was a prodigious amount of packing to do, leave papers to sign, and goodbyes to say. And once the wearying, sooty train trip was over, I found myself in an intoxicating new world of daily classes, afternoon teas, and evening concerts, from which I dutifully emerged now and then to answer the letters from home. When the beautiful semester was over, I returned to Arizona, to that glowing heat, to the camp, to the family; for although the war was still on, it had been decided to close down the camps, and I had been asked to go back and spread the good word about higher education among the young people who might be dispersed in this way.

Elsie was still working in the hospital, although she had applied for entrance into the cadet nurse corps and was expecting acceptance any day, and the long conversations we held were mostly about the good old days, the good old days when we had worked in the mess hall together, the good old days when we had worked in the hospital together.

"What ever became of Miss Sasagawara?" I asked one day, seeing the Rev. Sasagawara go abstractedly by. "Did she relocate somewhere?"

"I didn't write you about her, did I?" Elsie said meaningfully. "Yes, she's relocated all right. Haven't seen her around, have you?"

"Where did she go?"

Elsie answered offhandedly. "California."

"California?" I exclaimed. "We can't go back to California. What's she doing in California?"

So Elsie told me: Miss Sasagawara had been sent back there to a state institution, oh, not so very long after I had left for school. She had begun slipping back into her aloof ways almost immediately after Christmas, giving up the dancing class and not speaking to people. Then Elsie had heard a couple of very strange, yes, very strange things about her. One thing had been told by young Mrs. Sasaki, that next-door neighbor of the Sasagawaras.

Mrs. Sasaki said she had once come upon Miss Sasagawara sitting, as was her habit, on the porch. Mrs. Sasaki had been shocked to the core to see that the face of this thirty-nine-year-old woman (or was she forty now?) wore a beatific expression as she watched the activity going on in the doorway of her neighbors across the way, the Yoshinagas. This activity had been the joking and loud laughter of Joe and Frank, the young Yoshinaga boys, and three or four of their friends. Mrs. Sasaki would have let the matter go, were it not for the fact that Miss Sasagawara was so absorbed a spectator of this horseplay that her head was bent to one side and she actually had one finger in her mouth as she gazed, in the manner of a shy child confronted with a marvel. "What's the matter with you, watching the boys like that?" Mrs. Sasaki had cried. "You're old enough to be their mother!" Startled, Miss Sasagawara had jumped up and dashed back into her apartment. And when Mrs. Sasaki had gone into hers, adjoining the Sasagawaras', she had been terrified to hear Miss Sasagawara begin to bang on the wooden walls with something heavy like a hammer. The banging, which sounded as though Miss Sasagawara were using all her strength on each blow, had continued wildly for at least five minutes. Then all had been still.

The other thing had been told by Joe Yoshinaga who lived across the way from Miss Sasagawara. Joe and his brother slept on two Army cots pushed together on one side of the room, while their parents had a similar arrangement on the other side. Joe had standing by his bed an apple crate for a shelf, and he was in the habit of reading his sports and western magazines in bed and throwing them on top of the crate before he went to sleep. But one morning he had noticed his magazines all neatly stacked inside the crate, when he was sure he had carelessly thrown some on top the night before, as usual. This happened several times, and he finally asked his family whether one of them had been putting his magazines away after he fell asleep. They had said no and laughed, telling him he must be getting absent-minded. But the mystery had been solved late one night, when Joe gradually awoke in his cot with the feeling that he was being watched. Warily he had opened one eye slightly and had been thoroughly awakened and chilled in the bargain by what he saw. For what he saw was Miss Sasagawara sitting there on his apple crate, her long hair all undone and flowing about her. She was dressed in a white nightgown and her hands were clasped on her lap. And all she was doing was sitting there watching him, Joe Yoshinaga. He could not help it, he had sat up and screamed. His mother, a light sleeper, came running to see what had happened, just as Miss Sasagawara was running out the door, the door they had always left unlatched or even wide open in summer. In the morning Mrs. Yoshinaga had gone straight to the Rev. Sasagawara and asked him to do something about his daughter. The Rev. Sasagawara, sympathizing with her indignation in his benign but vague manner, had said he would have a talk with Mari.

And, concluded Elsie, Miss Sasagawara had gone away not long after. I was impressed, although Elsie's sources were not what I would ordinarily pay much attention to, Mrs. Sasaki, that plump and giggling young woman who always felt called upon to explain that she was childless by choice, and Joe Yoshinaga, who had a knack of blowing up, in his drawling voice, any incident in which he personally played even a small part (I could imagine the field day he had had with this one). Elsie puzzled aloud over the cause of Miss Sasagawara's derangement and I, who had so newly had some contact with the recorded explorations into the virgin territory of the human mind, sagely explained that Miss Sasagawara had no doubt looked upon Joe Yoshinaga as the image of either the lost lover or the lost son. But my words made me uneasy by their glibness, and I began to wonder seriously about Miss Sasagawara for the first time.

Then there was this last word from Miss Sasagawara herself, making her strange legend as complete as I, at any rate, would probably ever know it. This came some time after I had gone back to Philadelphia and the family had joined me there, when I was neck deep in research for my final paper. I happened one day to be looking through the last issue of a small poetry magazine that had suspended publication midway through the war. I felt a thrill of recognition at the name, Mari Sasagawara, signed to a long poem, introduced as ". . . the first published poem of a Japanese-American woman who is, at present, an evacuee from the West Coast making her home in a War Relocation center in Arizona."

It was a *tour de force,* erratically brilliant and, through the first readings, tantalizingly obscure. It appeared to be about a man whose lifelong aim had been to achieve Nirvana, that saintly state of moral purity and universal wisdom. This man had in his way certain handicaps, all stemming from his having acquired, when young and unaware, a family for which he must provide.

The day came at last, however, when his wife died and other circumstances made it unnecessary for him to earn a competitive living. These circumstances were considered by those about him as sheer imprisonment, but he had felt free for the first time in his long life. It became possible for him to extinguish within himself all unworthy desire and consequently all evil, to concentrate on that serene, eight-fold path of highest understanding, highest mindedness, highest speech, highest action, highest livelihood, highest recollectedness, highest endeavor, and highest meditation.

This man was certainly noble, the poet wrote, this man was beyond censure. The world was doubtless enriched by his presence. But say that someone else, someone sensitive, someone admiring, someone who had not achieved this sublime condition and who did not wish to, were somehow called to companion such a man. Was it not likely that the saint, blissfully bent on cleansing from his already radiant soul the last imperceptible blemishes (for, being perfect, would he not humbly suspect his own flawlessness?) would be deaf and blind to the human passions rising, subsiding, and again rising, perhaps in anguished silence, within the selfsame room? The poet could not speak for others; of course; she could only speak for herself. But she would describe this man's devotion as a sort of madness, the monstrous sort which, pure of itself, might possibly bring troublous, scented scenes to recur in the other's sleep.

1950

GRACE PALEY
(1922–)

With only a small yet impressive body of work, Grace Paley has established herself as one of the important short-story writers of our time. Her brief, sometimes misleadingly simple tales give us insights into complex relationships and into life's comedies and tragedies. Her accurate ear for dialect and her eye for the telling detail help bring her characters to life; she has created a number of memorably powerful women characters and has captured the tensions between lovers as well as between husbands and wives and children and parents. While her stories are modern in tone and subject matter, often reflecting her social and political concerns, they also frequently draw on the traditions of old Yiddish tales.

Born into a Jewish family in the Bronx, Paley has spent much of her life in and near New York City. She studied at Hunter College and New York University but never received a college degree and turned to writing only after being a housewife and mother for many years. Her works have appeared in magazines such as Atlantic *and* Esquire. *Her collections of stories include* The Little Disturbances of Man, Enormous Changes, *and* Later the Same Day. *Paley collaborated with the artist Vera B. Williams on* Long Walks and Intimate Talks, *a collection of stories, poems, and paintings.*

Paley has combined her domestic and authorial careers with an ongoing political involvement. In the 1950s, she agitated against the conditions in one of New York's worst prisons, the Women's House of Detention. A founder of the Greenwich Village Peace center in 1961, she was an antiwar activist throughout the 1960s. In the 1970s she spoke out to condemn Soviet repression; in 1971 she attended the World Peace Conference in Moscow. She has been arrested on several occasions for civil disobedience while participating in political protests.

Paley is as committed to teaching as she is to writing and social activism; like a number of the writers in this anthology, her writing is just one part of her commitment to others. She spends much of her time with students and with writers just learning their craft. She has taught at a number of schools, including Columbia University, Syracuse University, and Sarah Lawrence College, and has participated in numerous writers' workshops and symposia. She has always avoided, however, what she terms "literary life." In an interview summarized by Neil Isaacs in his study of her short fiction, Paley says, "There are people on my block who are writers I'm very fond of, and I'm very close to, friends like [Donald] Barthelme. . . . But I didn't want my everyday life to have anything to do with writers unless they *were willing to have everyday lives."*

"The Long-Distance Runner," which first appeared in Esquire, *is included in*

the collection Enormous Changes at the Last Minute. *This story reflects Paley's wry, offbeat humor and shows her mastery of the dialects spoken by both white and black characters. It also takes us into the consciousness of Faith, a middle-aged woman who breaks away from her present existence to look into her past and, at the same time, to see "what in the world is coming next."*

THE LONG-DISTANCE RUNNER

One day, before or after forty-two, I became a long-distance runner. Though I was stout and in many ways inadequate to this desire, I wanted to go far and fast, not as fast as bicycles and trains, not as far as Taipei, Hingwen, places like that, islands of the slant-eyed cunt, as sailors in bus stations say when speaking of travel, but round and round the country from the sea side to the bridges, along the old neighborhood streets a couple of times, before old age and urban renewal ended them and me.

I tried the country first, Connecticut, which being wooded is always full of buds in spring. All creation is secret, isn't that true? So I trained in the wide-zoned suburban hills where I wasn't known. I ran all spring in and out of dogwood bloom, then laurel.

People sometimes stopped and asked me why I ran, a lady in silk shorts halfway down over her fat thighs. In training, I replied and rested only to answer if closely questioned. I wore a white sleeveless undershirt as well, with excellent support, not to attract the attention of old men and prudish children.

Then summer came, my legs seemed strong. I kissed the kids goodbye. They were quite old by then. It was near the time for parting anyway. I told Mrs. Raftery to look in now and then and give them some of that rotten Celtic supper she makes.

I told them they could take off any time they wanted to. Go lead your private life, I said. Only leave me out of it.

A word to the wise . . . said Richard.

You're depressed Faith, Mrs. Raftery said. Your boy friend Jack, the one you think's so hotsy-totsy, hasn't called and you're as gloomy as a tick on Sunday.

Cut the folkshit with me, Raftery, I muttered. Her eyes filled with tears because that's who she is: folkshit from bunion to topknot. That's how she got liked by me, loved, invented and endured.

When I walked out the door they were all reclining before the television set, Richard, Tonto and Mrs. Raftery, gazing at the news. Which proved with moving pictures that there *had* been a voyage to the moon and Africa and South America hid in a furious whorl of clouds.

I said, Goodbye. They said, Yeah, O.K., sure.

If that's how it is, forget it, I hollered and took the Independent subway to Brighton Beach.

At Brighton Beach I stopped at the Salty Breezes Locker Room to change my clothes. Twenty-five years ago my father invested $500 in its future. In fact he still clears about $3.50 a year, which goes directly (by law) to the Children of Judea to cover their deficit.

No one paid too much attention when I started to run, easy and light on my feet. I ran on the boardwalk first, past my mother's leafleting station—between a soft-ice-cream stand and a degenerated dune. There she had been assigned by her comrades to halt the tides of cruel American enterprise with simple socialist sense.

I wanted to stop and admire the long beach. I wanted to stop in order to think admiringly about New York. There aren't many rotting cities so tan and sandy and speckled with citizens at their salty edges. But I had already spent a lot of life lying down or standing and staring. I had decided to run.

. . .

After about a mile and a half I left the boardwalk and began to trot into the old neighborhood. I was running well. My breath was long and deep. I was thinking pridefully about my form.

Suddenly I was surrounded by about three hundred blacks.

Who you?

Who that?

Look at her! Just look! When you seen a fatter ass?

Poor thing. She ain't right. Leave her, you boys, you bad boys.

I used to live here, I said.

Oh yes, they said, in the white old days. That time too bad to last.

But we loved it here. We never went to Flatbush Avenue or Times Square. We loved our block.

Tough black titty.

I like your speech, I said. Metaphor and all.

Right on. We get that from talking.

Yes my people also had a way of speech. And don't forget the Irish. The gift of gab.

Who they? said a small boy.

Cops.

Nowadays, I suggested, there's more than Irish on the police force.

You right, said two ladies. More more, much much more. They's French Chinamen Russkies Congoleans. Oh missee, you too right.

I lived in that house, I said. That apartment house. All my life. Till I got married.

Now that *is* nice. Live in one place. My mother live that way in South Carolina. One place. Her daddy farmed. She said. They ate. No matter winter war bad times. Roosevelt. Something! Ain't that wonderful! And it weren't cold! Big trees!

That apartment. I looked up and pointed. There. The third floor.

They all looked up. So what! You blubrous devil! said a dark young man. He wore horn-rimmed glasses and had that intelligent look that City College boys used to have when I was eighteen and first looked at them.

He seemed to lead them in contempt and anger, even the littlest ones who moved toward me with dramatic stealth singing, Devil, Oh Devil. I don't think the little kids had bad feeling because they poked a finger into me, then laughed.

Still I thought it might be wise to keep my head. So I jumped right in with some facts. I said, How many flowers' names do you know? Wild flowers, I mean. My people only knew two. That's what they say now anyway. Rich or poor, they only had two flowers' names. Rose and violet.

Daisy, said one boy immediately.

Weed, said another. That *is* a flower, I thought. But everyone else got the joke.

Saxifrage, lupine, said a lady. Viper's bugloss, said a small Girl Scout in medium green with a dark green sash. She held up a *Handbook of Wild Flowers.*

How many you know, fat mama? a boy asked warmly. He wasn't against my being a mother or fat. I turned all my attention to him.

Oh sonny, I said, I'm way ahead of my people. I know in yellows alone: common cinquefoil, trout lily, yellow adder's-tongue, swamp buttercup and common buttercup, golden sorrel, yellow or hop clover, devil's-paintbrush, evening primrose, black-eyed Susan, golden aster, also the yellow pickerelweed growing down by the water if not in the water, and dandelions of course. I've seen all these myself. Seen them.

You could see China from the boardwalk, a boy said. When it's nice.

I know more flowers than countries. Mostly young people these days have traveled in many countries.

Not me. I ain't been nowhere.

Not me either, said about seventeen boys.

I'm not allowed, said a little girl. There's drunken junkies.

But *I! I!* cried out a tall black youth, very handsome and well dressed. I am an African. My father came from the high stolen plains. *I* have been everywhere. I was in Moscow six months, learning machinery. I was in France, learning French. I was in Italy, observing the peculiar Renaissance and the people's sweetness. I was in England, where I studied the common law and the urban blight. I was at the Conference of Dark Youth in Cuba to understand our passion. I am now here. Here am I to become an engineer and return to my people, around the Cape of Good Hope in a Norwegian sailing vessel. In this way I will learn the fine old art of sailing in case the engines of the new society of my old inland country should fail.

We had an extraordinary amount of silence after that. Then one old lady in a black dress and high white lace collar said to another old lady dressed exactly the same way, Glad tidings when someone got brains in the head not fish juice. Amen, said a few.

Whyn't you go up to Mrs. Luddy living in your house, you lady, huh? The Girl Scout asked this.

Why she just groove to see you, said some sarcastic snickerer.

She got palpitations. Her man, he give it to her.

That ain't all, he be a natural gift-giver.

I'll take you, said the Girl Scout. My name is Cynthia. I'm in Troop 355, Brooklyn.

I'm not dressed, I said, looking at my lumpy knees.

You shouldn't wear no undershirt like that without no runnin number or no team writ on it. It look like a undershirt.

Cynthia! Don't take her up there, said an important boy. Her head strange. Don't you take her. Hear?

Lawrence, she said softly, you tell me once more what to do I'll wrap you round that lamppost.

Git! she said, powerfully addressing *me.*

In this way I was led into the hallway of the whole house of my childhood.

. . .

The first door I saw was still marked in flaky gold, 1A. That's where the janitor lived, I said. He was a Negro.

How come like that? Cynthia made an astonished face. How come the janitor was a black man?

Oh Cynthia, I said. Then I turned to the opposite door, first floor front, 1B. I remembered. Now, here, this was Mrs. Goreditsky, very very fat lady. All her children died at birth. Born, then one, two, three. Dead. Five children, then Mr. Goreditsky said, I'm bad luck on you Tessie and he went away. He sent $15 a week for seven years. Then no one heard.

I know her, poor thing, said Cynthia. The city come for her summer before last. The way they knew, it smelled. They wropped her up in a canvas. They couldn't get through the front door. It scraped off a piece of her. My uncle Ronald had to help them, but he got disgusted.

Only two years ago. She was still here! Wasn't she scared?

So we all, said Cynthia. White ain't everything.

Who lived up here, she asked, 2B? Right now, my best friend Nancy Rosalind lives here. She got two brothers, and her sister married and got a baby. She very light-skinned. Not her mother. We got all colors amongst us.

Your best friend? That's funny. Because it was *my* best friend. Right in that apartment. Joanna Rosen.

What become of her? Cynthia asked. She got a running shirt too?

Come on Cynthia, if you really want to know, I'll tell you. She married this man, Marvin Steirs.

Who's he?

I recollected his achievements. Well, he's the president of a big corporation, JoMar Plastics. This corporation owns a steel company, a radio station, a new Xerox-type machine that lets you do twenty-five different pages at once. This corporation has a foundation, The JoMar Fund for Research in Conservation. Capitalism is like that, I added, in order to be politically useful.

How come you know? You go over to their house a lot?

No. I happened to read all about them on the financial page, just last week. It made me think: a different life. That's all.

Different spokes for different folks, said Cynthia.

I sat down on the cool marble steps and remembered Joanna's cousin Ziggie. He was older than we were. He wrote a poem which told us we were lovely flowers and our legs were petals, which nature would force open no matter how many times we said no.

Then I had several other interior thoughts that I couldn't share with a child, the kind that give your face a blank or melancholy look.

Now you're not interested, said Cynthia. Now you're not gonna say a thing. Who lived here, 2A? Who? Two men lives here now. Women coming and women going. My mother says, Danger sign: Stay away, my darling, stay away.

I don't remember, Cynthia. I really don't.

You got to. What'd you come for, anyways?

Then I tried. 2A. 2A. Was it the twins? I felt a strong obligation as though remembering was in charge of the *existence* of the past. This is not so.

Cynthia, I said, I don't want to go any further. I don't even want to remember.

Come on, she said, tugging at my shorts, don't you want to see Mrs. Luddy, the one lives in your old house? That be fun, no?

No. No, I don't want to see Mrs. Luddy.

Now you shouldn't pay no attention to those boys downstairs. She will like you. I mean, she is kind. She don't like most white people, but she might like you.

No Cynthia, it's not that, but I don't want to see my father and mother's house now.

I didn't know what to say. I said, Because my mother's dead. This was a lie, because my mother lives in her own room with my father in the Children of Judea. With her hand over her socialist heart, she reads the paper every morning after breakfast. Then she says sadly to my father, Every day the same. Dying . . . dying, dying from killing.

My mother's dead Cynthia. I can't go in there.

Oh . . . oh, the poor thing, she said, looking into my eyes. Oh, if my mother died, I don't know what I'd do. Even if I was old as you. I could kill myself. Tears filled her eyes and started down her cheeks. If my mother died, what would I do? She is my protector, she won't let the pushers get me. She hold me tight. She gonna hide me in the cedar box if my Uncle Rudford comes try to get me back. She *can't* die, my mother.

Cynthia—honey—she won't die. She's young. I put my arm out to comfort her. You could come live with me, I said. I got two boys, they're nearly grown up. I missed it, not having a girl.

What? What you mean now, live with you and boys. She pulled away and ran for the stairs. Stay way from me, honky lady. I know them white boys. They just gonna try and jostle my black womanhood. My mother told me about that, keep you white honky devil boys to your devil self, you just leave me be you old bitch you. Somebody help me, she started to scream, you hear. Somebody help. She gonna take me away.

She flattened herself to the wall, trembling. I was too frightened by her fear of me to say, honey, I wouldn't hurt you, it's me. I heard her helpers, the voices of large boys crying, We coming, we coming, hold your head up, we coming. I ran past her fear to the stairs and up them two at a time. I came to my old own door. I knocked like the landlord, loud and terrible.

Mama not home, a child's voice said. No, no, I said. It's me! a lady! Someone's chasing me, let me in. Mama not home, I ain't allowed to open up for nobody.

It's me! I cried out in terror. Mama! Mama! let me in!

The door opened. A slim woman whose age I couldn't invent looked at me. She said, Get in and shut that door tight. She took a hard pinching hold on my upper arm. Then she bolted the door herself. Them hustlers after you. They make me pink. Hide this white lady now, Donald. Stick her under your bed, you got a high bed.

Oh that's O.K. I'm fine now, I said. I felt safe and at home.

You in my house, she said. You do as I say. For two cents, I throw you out.

I squatted under a small kid's pissy mattress. Then I heard the knock. It was tentative and respectful. My mama don't allow me to open. Donald! someone called. Donald!

Oh no, he said. Can't do it. She gonna wear me out. You know her. She already tore up my ass this morning once. Ain't *gonna* open up.

. . .

I lived there for about three weeks with Mrs. Luddy and Donald and three little baby girls nearly the same age. I told her a joke about Irish twins. Ain't Irish, she said.

Nearly every morning the babies woke us at about 6:45. We gave them all a bottle and went back to sleep till 8:00. I made coffee and she changed diapers. Then it really stank for a while. At this time I usually said, Well listen, thanks really, but I've got to go I guess. I guess I'm going. She'd usually say, Well, guess again. *I* guess you ain't. Or if she was feeling disgusted she'd say, Go on now! Get! You wanna go, I guess by now I have snorted enough white lady stink to choke a horse. Go on!

I'd get to the door and then I'd hear voices. I'm ashamed to say I'd become fearful. Despite my wide geographical love of mankind, I would be attacked by fears.

There was a sentimental truth that lay beside all that going and not going. It *was* my house where I'd lived long ago my family life. There was a tile on the bathroom floor that I myself had broken, dropping a hammer on the toe of my brother Charles as he stood dreamily shaving, his prick halfway up his undershorts. Astonishment and knowledge first seized me right there. The kitchen was the same. The table was the enameled table common to our class, easy to clean, with wooden undercorners for indigent and old cockroaches that couldn't make it to the kitchen sink. (However, it was not the same table, because I have inherited that one, chips and all.)

The living room was something like ours, only we had less plastic. There may have been less plastic in the world at that time. Also, my mother had set beautiful cushions everywhere, on beds and chairs. It was the way she expressed herself, artistically, to embroider at night or take strips of flowered cotton and sew them across ordinary white or blue muslin in the most delicate designs, the way women have always used materials that live and die in hunks and tatters to say: This is my place.

Mrs. Luddy said, Uh huh!

Of course, I said, men don't have that outlet. That's how come they run around so much.

Till they drunk enough to lay down, she said.

Yes, I said, on a large scale you can see it in the world. First they make something, then they murder it. Then they write a book about how interesting it is.

You got something there, she said. Sometimes she said, Girl, you don't know *nothing*.

We often sat at the window looking out and down. Little tufts of breeze grew on that windowsill. The blazing afternoon was around the corner and up the block.

You say men, she said. Is that men? she asked. What you call—a Man?

Four flights below us, leaning on the stoop, were about a dozen people and around them devastation. Just a minute, I said. I had seen devastation on my way, running, gotten some of the pebbles of it in my running shoe and the dust of it in my eyes. I had thought with the indignant courtesy of a citizen, This is a disgrace to the City of New York which I love and am running through.

But now, from the commanding heights of home, I saw it clearly. The tenement in which Jack my old and present friend had come to gloomy manhood had been destroyed, first by fire, then by demolition (which is a swinging ball of steel that cracks bedrooms and kitchens). Because of this work, we could see several blocks wide and a block and a half long. Crazy Eddy's house still stood, famous 1510 gutted, with black window frames, no glass, open laths.

The stubbornness of the supporting beams! Some persons or families still lived on the lowest floors. In the lots between, a couple of old sofas lay on their fat faces, their springs sticking up into the air. Just as in wartime a half-dozen ailanthus trees had already found their first quarter inch of earth and begun a living attack on the dead yards. At night, I knew animals roamed the place, squalling and howling, furious New York dogs and street cats and mighty rats. You would think you were in Bear Mountain Park, the terror of venturing forth.

Someone ought to clean that up, I said.

Mrs. Luddy said, Who you got in mind? Mrs. Kennedy?—

Donald made a stern face. He said, That just what I gonna do when I get big. Gonna get the Sanitary Man in and show it to him. You see that, you big guinea you, you clean it up right now! Then he stamped his feet and fierced his eyes.

Mrs. Luddy said, Come here, you little nigger. She kissed the top of his head and gave him a whack on the backside all at one time.

Well, said Donald, encouraged, look out there now you all! Go on I say, look! Though we had already seen, to please him we looked. On the stoop men and boys lounged, leaned, hopped about, stood on one leg, then another, took their socks off, and scratched their toes, talked, sat on their haunches, heads down, dozing.

Donald said, Look at them. They ain't got self-respect. They got Afros *on* their heads, but they don't know they black *in* their heads.

I thought he ought to learn to be more sympathetic. I said, There are reasons that people are that way.

Yes, ma'am, said Donald.

Anyway, how come you never go down and play with the other kids, how come you're up here so much?

My mama don't like me do that. Some of them is bad. Bad. I might become a dope addict. I got to stay clear.

You just a dope, that's a fact, said Mrs. Luddy.

He ought to be with kids his age more, I think.

He see them in school, miss. Don't trouble your head about it if you don't mind.

Actually, Mrs. Luddy didn't go down into the street either. Donald did all the shopping. She let the welfare investigator in, the meterman came into the kitchen to read the meter. I saw him from the back room, where I hid. She did pick up her check. She cashed it. She returned to wash the babies, change their diapers, wash clothes, iron, feed people, and then in free half hours she sat by that window. She was waiting.

I believed she was watching and waiting for a particular man. I wanted to discuss this with her, talk lovingly like sisters. But before I could freely say, Forget about that son of a bitch, he's a pig, I did have to offer a few solid facts about myself, my kids, about fathers, husbands, passers-by, evening companions, and the life of my father and mother in this room by this exact afternoon window.

I told her for instance, that in my worst times I had given myself one extremely simply physical pleasure. This was cream cheese for breakfast. In fact, I insisted on it, sometimes depriving the children of very important articles and foods.

Girl, you don't know nothing, she said.

Then for a little while she talked gently as one does to a person who is innocent and insane and incorruptible because of stupidity. She had had two such special pleasures for hard times she said. The first, men, but they turned rotten, white women had ruined the best, give them the idea their dicks made of solid gold. The second pleasure she had tried was wine. She said, I do like wine. You *has* to have something just for yourself by yourself. Then she said, But you can't raise a decent boy when you liquor-dazed every night.

White or black, I said, returning to men, they did think they were bringing a rare gift, whereas it was just sex, which is common like bread, though essential.

Oh, you can do without, she said. There's folks does without.

I told her Donald deserved the best. I loved him. If he had flaws, I hardly noticed them. It's one of my beliefs that children do not have flaws, even the worst do not.

Donald was brilliant—like my boys except that he had an easier disposition. For this reason I decided, almost the second moment of my residence in that household, to bring him up to reading level at once. I told him we would work with books and newspapers. He went immediately to his neighborhood library and brought some hard books to amuse me. *Black Folktales* by Julius Lester and *The Pushcart War,* which is about another neighborhood but relevant.

Donald always agreed with me when we talked about reading and writing. In fact, when I mentioned poetry, he told me he knew all about it, that David Henderson, a known black poet, had visited his second-grade class. So Donald was, as it turned out, well ahead of my nosy tongue. He was usually very busy shopping. He also had to spend a lot of time making faces to force the little serious baby girls into laughter. But if the subject came up, he could take *the* poem right out of the air into which language and event had just gone.

An example: That morning, his mother had said, Whew, I just got too much piss and diapers and wash. I wanna just sit down by that window and rest myself. He wrote a poem:

Just got too much pissy diapers
and wash and wash
just wanna sit down by that window
and look out
ain't nothing there.

Donald, I said, you are plain brilliant. I'm never going to forget you. For God's sakes don't you forget me.

You fool with him too much, said Mrs. Luddy. He already don't even remember his grandma, you never gonna meet someone like her, a curse never came past her lips.

I do remember, Mama, I remember. She lying in bed, right there. A man standing in the door. She say, Esdras, I put a curse on you head. You worsen tomorrow. How come she said like that?

Gomorrah, I believe Gomorrah, she said. She know the Bible inside out.

Did she live with you?

No. No, she visiting. She come up to see us all, her children, how we doing. She come up to see sights. Then she lay down and died. She was old.

I remained quiet because of the death of mothers. Mrs. Luddy looked at me thoughtfully, then she said:

My mama had stories to tell, she raised me on. *Her* mama was a little thing, no sense. Stand in the door of the cabin all day, sucking her thumb. It was slave times. One day a young field boy come storming along. He knock on the door of the first cabin hollering, Sister, come out, it's freedom. She come out. She say, Yeah? When? He say, Now! It's freedom now! Then he knock at the next door and say, Sister! It's freedom! Now! From one cabin he run to the next cabin, crying out, Sister, it's freedom now!

Oh I remember that story, said Donald. Freedom now! Freedom now! He jumped up and down.

You don't remember nothing boy. Go on, get Eloise, she want to get into the good times.

Eloise was two but undersized. We got her like that, said Donald. Mrs. Luddy let me buy her ice cream and green vegetables. She was waiting for kale and chard, but it was too early. The kale liked cold. You not about to be here November, she said. No, no. I turned away, lonesomeness touching me and sang our Eloise song:

Eloise loves the bees
the bees they buzz
like Eloise does

Then Eloise crawled all over the splintery floor, buzzing wildly.

Oh you crazy baby, said Donald, buzz buzz buzz.

Mrs. Luddy sat down by the window.

You all make a lot of noise, she said sadly. You just right on noisy.

The next morning Mrs. Luddy woke me up.

Time to go, she said.

What?

Home.

What? I said.

Well, don't you think your little spoiled boys crying for you? Where's Mama? They standing in the window. Time to go lady. This ain't Free Vacation Farm. Time we was by ourself a little.

Oh Ma, said Donald, she ain't a lot of trouble. Go on, get Eloise, she hollering. And button up your lip.

She didn't offer me coffee. She looked at me strictly all the time. I tried to look strictly back, but I failed because I loved the sight of her.

Donald was teary, but I didn't dare turn my face to him, until the parting minute at the door. Even then, I kissed the top of his head a little too forcefully and said, Well, I'll see you.

On the front stoop there were about half a dozen mid-morning family people and kids arguing about who had dumped garbage out of which window. They were very disgusted with one another.

Two young men in handsome dashikis stood in counsel and agreement at the street corner. They divided a comment. How come white womens got rotten teeth? And look so old? A young woman waiting at the light said, Hush . . .

I walked past them and didn't begin my run till the road opened up somewhere along Ocean Parkway. I was a little stiff because my way of life had used only small movements, an occasional stretch to put a knife or teapot out of reach of the babies. I ran about ten, fifteen blocks. Then my second wind came, which is classical, famous among runners, it's the beginning of flying.

In the three weeks I'd been off the street, jogging had become popular. It seemed that I was only one person doing her thing, which happened like most American eccentric acts to be the most "in" thing I could have done. In fact, two young men ran alongside of me for nearly a mile. They ran silently beside me and turned off at Avenue H. A gentleman with a mustache, running poorly in the opposite direction, waved. He called out, Hi, senora.

Near home I ran through our park, where I had aired my children on weekends and late-summer afternoons. I stopped at the northeast playground, where I met a dozen young mothers intelligently handling their little ones. In order to prepare them, meaning no harm, I said, In fifteen years, you girls will be like me, wrong in everything.

. . .

At home it was Saturday morning. Jack had returned looking as grim as ever, but he'd brought cash and a vacuum cleaner. While the coffee perked, he showed Richard how to use it. They were playing tick tack toe on the dusty wall.

Richard said, Well! Look who's here! Hi!

Any news? I asked.

Letter from Daddy, he said. From the lake and water country in Chile. He says it's like Minnesota.

He's never been to Minnesota, I said. Where's Anthony?

Here I am, said Tonto, appearing. But I'm leaving.

Oh yes, I said. Of course. Every Saturday he hurries through breakfast or misses it. He goes to visit his friends in institutions. These are well-known places like Bellevue, Hillside, Rockland State, Central Islip, Manhattan. These visits take him all day and sometimes half the night.

I found some chocolate-chip cookies in the pantry. Take them, Tonto, I said. I remember nearly all his friends as little boys and girls always hopping, skipping, jumping and cookie-eating. He was annoyed. He said, No! Chocolate cookies is what the commissaries are full of. How about money?

Jack dropped the vacuum cleaner. He said, No! They have parents for that.

I said, Here, five dollars for cigarettes, one dollar each.

Cigarettes! said Jack. Goddamnit! Black lungs and death! Cancer! Emphysema! He stomped out of the kitchen, breathing. He took the bike from the back room and started for Central Park, which has been closed to cars but opened to bicycle riders. When he'd been gone about ten minutes, Anthony said, It's really open only on Sundays.

Why didn't you say so? Why can't you be decent to him? I asked. It's important to me.

Oh Faith, he said, patting me on the head because he'd grown so tall, all that air. It's good for his lungs. And his muscles! He'll be back soon.

You should ride too, I said. You don't want to get mushy in your legs. You should go swimming once a week.

I'm too busy, he said. I have to see my friends.

Then Richard, who had been vacuuming under his bed, came into the kitchen. You still here, Tonto?

Going going gone, said Anthony, don't bat your eye.

Now listen, Richard said, here's a note. It's for Judy, if you get as far as Rockland. Don't forget it. Don't open it. Don't read it. I know he'll read it.

Anthony smiled and slammed the door.

Did I lose weight? I asked. Yes, said Richard. You look O.K. You never look too bad. But where were you? I got sick of Raftery's boiled potatoes. Where were you, Faith?

Well! I said. Well! I stayed a few weeks in my old apartment, where Grandpa and Grandma and me and Hope and Charlie lived, when we were little. I took you there long ago. Not so far from the ocean where Grandma made us very healthy with sun and air.

What are you talking about? said Richard. Cut the baby talk.

Anthony came home earlier than expected that evening because some people were in shock therapy and someone else had run away. He listened to me for a while. Then he said, I don't know what she's talking about either.

Neither did Jack, despite the understanding often produced by love after absence. He said, Tell me again. He was in a good mood. He said, You can even tell it to me twice.

I repeated the story. They all said, What?

Because it isn't usually so simple. Have you known it to happen much nowadays? A woman inside the steamy energy of middle age runs and runs. She finds the houses and streets where her childhood happened. She lives in them. She learns as though she was still a child what in the world is coming next.

1974

FLANNERY O'CONNOR
(1925–1964)

Traditional in basic narrative form, Flannery O'Connor's fiction combines a dark, ironic humor with disturbing, bizarre characters, violent actions, and serious moral themes. Most of her work is set in Georgia or Tennessee, often in backwoods areas, and focuses on the characters, language, and attitudes of the rural South. O'Connor's Catholicism pervades her writing; themes of grace and prophecy as well as delicate moral issues are woven into her stories. Her characters have been termed "grotesque"; they are oddities, eccentrics, sometimes fanatics, often struggling, absurdly or tragically, for redemption.

Born in Savannah, Georgia, O'Connor traveled very infrequently. After attending Georgia State College for Women and receiving her Master of Fine Arts degree in creative writing at the University of Iowa, she spent much of her adult life in her Georgia home. She began publishing short stories and articles while in her early twenties. Some stories appeared in well-known national magazines such as Mademoiselle, Esquire, and Harper's Bazaar; however, most of her work was published in prestigious journals with smaller readerships, such as the Sewanee Review, Kenyon Review, and Partisan Review. In 1950 she was struck by disseminated lupus, a disease that gradually disabled her until her death fourteen years later.

During her short lifetime, Flannery O'Connor wrote two novels, Wise Blood and The Violent Bear It Away, and thirty-one short stories. The majority of her stories were collected in two volumes, A Good Man Is Hard to Find and Everything That Rises Must Converge. This small body of work established her as one of the most important writers of the American South.

O'Connor was an artist whose creations came slowly. She wrote and rewrote, even when her illness made it difficult for her to move at all. In a letter to her former teacher, Paul Engle, she wrote, "I work all the time, but I cannot work fast. No one can convince me that I shouldn't rewrite as much as I do." Her painstaking labors resulted in perfectly crafted stories that stand curiously apart from the work of her contemporaries. "I am not writing a conventional novel," she told her publisher in a letter about Wise Blood, "and I think that the quality of the novel I write will derive precisely from the peculiarity or aloneness, if you will, of the experience I write from."

"A View of the Woods" is an example of what Joyce Carol Oates has termed O'Connor's "enigmatic, troubling, and highly idiosyncratic fiction." O'Connor takes us into the consciousness of an old man and his possessive relationship with one granddaughter. Like many of O'Connor's tales, this story turns on a *chilling act of violence that leads to a powerful but ambiguous moment of revelation.*

A VIEW OF THE WOODS

The week before, Mary Fortune and the old man had spent every morning watching the machine that lifted out dirt and threw it in a pile. The construction was going on by the new lakeside on one of the lots that the old man had sold to somebody who was going to put up a fishing club. He and Mary Fortune drove down there every morning about ten o'clock and he parked his car, a battered mulberry-colored Cadillac, on the embankment that overlooked the spot where the work was going on. The red corrugated lake eased up to within fifty feet of the construction and was bordered on the other side by a black line of woods which appeared at both ends of the view to walk across the water and continue along the edge of the fields.

He sat on the bumper and Mary Fortune straddled the hood and they watched, sometimes for hours, while the machine systematically ate a square red hole in what had once been a cow pasture. It happened to be the only pasture that Pitts had succeeded in getting the bitterweed off and when the old man had sold it, Pitts had nearly had a stroke; and as far as Mr. Fortune was concerned, he could have gone on and had it.

"Any fool that would let a cow pasture interfere with progress is not on my books," he had said to Mary Fortune several times from his seat on the bumper, but the child did not have eyes for anything but the machine. She sat on the hood, looking down into the red pit, watching the big disembodied gullet gorge itself on the clay, then, with the sound of a deep sustained nausea and a slow mechanical revulsion, turn and spit it up. Her pale eyes behind her spectacles followed the repeated motion of it again and again and her face—a small replica of the old man's—never lost its look of complete absorption.

No one was particularly glad that Mary Fortune looked like her grandfather except the old man himself. He thought it added greatly to her attractiveness. He thought she was the smartest and the prettiest child he had ever seen and he let the rest of them know that if, IF that was, he left anything to anybody, it would be Mary Fortune he left it to. She was now nine, short and broad like himself, with his very light blue eyes, his wide prominent forehead, his steady penetrating scowl and his rich florid complexion; but she was like him on the inside too. She had, to a singular degree, his intelligence, his strong will, and his push and drive. Though there was seventy years' difference in their ages, the spiritual distance between them was slight. She was the only member of the family he had any respect for.

He didn't have any use for her mother, his third or fourth daughter (he could never remember which), though she considered that she took care of him. She considered—being careful not to say it, only to look it—that she was the one putting up with him in his old age and that she was the one he should leave the place to. She had married an idiot named Pitts and had had seven children, all likewise idiots except the youngest, Mary Fortune, who was a throwback to him. Pitts was the kind who couldn't keep his hands on a nickel and Mr. Fortune had allowed them, ten years ago, to move onto his place and farm it. What Pitts made went to Pitts but the land belonged to Fortune and he was careful to keep the fact before them. When the well had gone dry, he had not allowed Pitts to have a deep well drilled but had insisted that they pipe their water from the spring. He did not intend to pay for a drilled well himself and he knew that if he let Pitts pay for it, whenever he had occasion to say to Pitts, "It's my land you're sitting on," Pitts would be able to say to him, "Well, its my pump that's pumping the water you're drinking."

Being there ten years, the Pittses had got to feel as if they owned the place. The daughter had been born and raised on it but the old man considered that when she married Pitts she showed that she preferred Pitts to home; and when she came back, she came back like any other tenant, though he would not allow them to pay rent for the same reason he would not allow them to drill a well. Anyone over sixty years of age is in an uneasy position unless he controls the greater interest and every now and then he gave the Pittses a practical lesson by selling off a lot. Nothing infuriated Pitts more than to see him sell off a piece of the property to an outsider, because Pitts wanted to buy it himself.

Pitts was a thin, long-jawed, irascible, sullen, sulking individual and his wife was the duty-proud kind: It's my duty to stay here and take care of Papa. Who would do it if I didn't? I do it knowing full well I'll get no reward for it. I do it because it's my duty.

The old man was not taken in by this for a minute. He knew they were waiting impatiently for the day when they could put him in a hole eight feet deep and cover him up with dirt. Then, even if he did not leave the place to them, they figured they would be able to buy it. Secretly he had made his will and left everything in trust to Mary Fortune, naming his lawyer and not Pitts as executor. When he died Mary Fortune could make the rest of them jump; and he didn't doubt for a minute that she would be able to do it.

Ten years ago they had announced that they were going to name the new baby Mark Fortune Pitts, after him, if it were a boy, and he had not delayed in telling them that if they coupled his name with the name Pitts he would put them off the place. When the baby came, a girl, and he had seen that even at the age of one day she bore his unmistakable likeness, he had relented and suggested himself that they name her Mary Fortune, after his beloved mother, who had died seventy years ago, bringing him into the world.

The Fortune place was in the country on a clay road that left the paved road fifteen miles away and he would never have been able to sell off any lots if it had not been for progress, which had always been his ally. He was not one of these old people who fight improvement, who object to everything new and cringe at every change. He wanted to see a paved highway in front of his house with plenty of new-model cars on it, he wanted to see a supermarket store across the road from him, he wanted to see a gas station, a motel, a drive-in picture-show within easy distance. Progress had suddenly set all this in motion. The electric power company had built a dam on the river and flooded great areas of the surrounding country and the lake that resulted touched his land along a half-mile stretch. Every Tom, Dick and Harry, every dog and his brother, wanted a lot on the lake. There was talk of their getting a telephone line. There was talk of paving the road that ran in front of the Fortune place. There was talk of an eventual town. He thought this should be called Fortune, Georgia. He was a man of advanced vision, even if he was seventy-nine years old.

The machine that drew up the dirt had stopped the day before and today they were watching the hole being smoothed out by two huge yellow bulldozers. His property had amounted to eight hundred acres before he began selling lots. He had sold five twenty-acre lots on the back of the place and every time he sold one, Pitts's blood pressure had gone up twenty points. "The Pittses are the kind that would let a cow pasture interfere with the future," he said to Mary Fortune, "but not you and me." The fact that Mary Fortune was a Pitts too was something he ignored, in a gentlemanly fashion, as if it were an affliction the child was not responsible for. He liked to think of her as being thoroughly of his clay. He sat on the bumper and she sat on the hood with her bare feet on his shoulders. One of the bulldozers had moved under them to shave the side of the embankment they were parked on. If he had moved his feet a few inches out, the old man could have dangled them over the edge.

"If you don't watch him," Mary Fortune shouted above the noise of the machine, "he'll cut off some of your dirt!"

"Yonder's the stob," the old man yelled. "He hasn't gone beyond the stob."

"Not YET he hasn't," she roared.

The bulldozer passed beneath them and went on to the far side. "Well you watch," he said. "Keep your eyes open and if he knocks that stob, I'll stop him. The Pittses are the kind that would let a cow pasture or a mule lot or a row of beans interfere with progress," he continued. "The people like you and me with heads on their shoulders know you can't stop the marcher time for a cow. . . ."

"He's shaking the stob on the other side!" she screamed and before he could stop her, she had jumped down from the hood and was running along the edge of the embankment, her little yellow dress billowing out behind.

"Don't run so near the edge," he yelled but she had already reached the stob and was squatting down by it to see how much it had been shaken. She leaned over the embankment and shook her fist at the man on the bulldozer. He waved at her and went on about his business. More sense in her little finger than all the rest of that tribe in their heads put together, the old man said to himself, and watched with pride as she started back to him.

She had a head of thick, very fine, sand-colored hair—the exact kind he had had when he had had any—that grew straight and was cut just above her eyes and down the sides of her cheeks to the tips of her ears so that it formed a kind of door opening onto the central part of her face. Her glasses were silver-rimmed like his and she even walked the way he did, stomach forward, with a careful abrupt gait, something between a rock and a shuffle. She was walking so close to the edge of the embankment that the outside of her right foot was flush with it.

"I said don't walk so close to the edge," he called; "you fall off there and you won't live to see the day this place gets built up." He was always very careful to see that she avoided dangers. He would not allow her to sit in snakey places or put her hands on bushes that might hide hornets.

She didn't move an inch. She had a habit of his of not hearing what she didn't want to hear and since this was a little trick he had taught her himself, he had to admire the way she practiced it. He foresaw that in her own old age it would serve her well. She reached the car and climbed back onto the hood without a word and put her feet back on his shoulders where she had had them before, as if he were no more than a part of the automobile. Her attention returned to the far bulldozer.

"Remember what you won't get if you don't mind," her grandfather remarked.

He was a strict disciplinarian but he had never whipped her. There were some children, like the first six Pittses, whom he thought should be whipped once a week on principle, but there were other ways to control intelligent children and he had never laid a rough hand on Mary Fortune. Furthermore, he had never allowed her mother or her brothers and sisters so much as to slap her. The elder Pitts was a different matter.

He was a man of a nasty temper and of ugly unreasonable resentments. Time and again, Mr. Fortune's heart had pounded to see him rise slowly from his place at the table—not the head, Mr. Fortune sat there, but from his place at the side—and abruptly, for no reason, with no explanation, jerk his head at Mary Fortune and say, "Come with me," and leave the room, unfastening his belt as he went. A look that was completely foreign to the child's face would appear on it. The old man could not define the look but it infuriated him. It was a look that was part terror and part respect and part something else, something very like cooperation. This look would appear on her face and she would get up and follow Pitts out. They would get in his truck and drive down the road out of earshot, where he would beat her.

Mr. Fortune knew for a fact that he beat her because he had followed them in his car and had seen it happen. He had watched from behind a boulder about a hundred feet away while the child clung to a pine tree and Pitts, as methodically as if he were whacking a bush with a sling blade, beat her around the ankles with his belt. All she had done was jump up and down as if she were standing on a hot stove and make a whimpering noise like a dog that was being peppered. Pitts had kept at it for about three minutes and then he had turned, without a word, and got back in his truck and left her there, and she had slid down under the tree and taken both feet in her hands and rocked back and forth. The old man had crept forward to catch her. Her face was contorted into a puzzle of small red lumps and her nose and eyes were running. He sprang on her and sputtered, "Why didn't you hit him back? Where's your spirit? Do you think I'd a let him beat me?"

She had jumped up and started backing away from him with her jaw stuck out. "Nobody beat me," she said.

"Didn't I see it with my own eyes?" he exploded.

"Nobody is here and nobody beat me," she said. "Nobody's ever beat me in my life and if anybody did, I'd kill him. You can see for yourself nobody is here."

"Do you call me a liar or a blindman!" he shouted. "I saw him with my own two eyes and you never did a thing but let him do it, you never did a thing but hang onto that tree and dance up and down a little and blubber and if it had been me, I'd a swung my fist in his face and . . ."

"Nobody was here and nobody beat me and if anybody did I'd kill him!" she yelled and then turned and dashed off through the woods.

"And I'm a Poland china pig and black is white!" he had roared after her and he had sat down on a small rock under the tree, disgusted and furious. This was Pitts's revenge on him. It was as if it were *he* that Pitts was driving down the road to beat and it was as if *he* were the one submitting to it. He had thought at first that he could stop him by saying that if he beat her, he would put them off the place but when he had tried that, Pitts had said, "Put me off and you put her off too. Go right ahead. She's mine to whip and I'll whip her every day of the year if it suits me."

Anytime he could make Pitts feel his hand he was determined to do it and at present he had a little scheme up his sleeve that was going to be a considerable blow to Pitts. He was thinking of it with relish when he told Mary Fortune to remember what she wouldn't get if she didn't mind, and he added, without waiting for an answer, that he might be selling another lot soon and that if he did, he might give her a bonus but not if she gave him any sass. He had frequent little verbal tilts with her but this was a sport like putting a mirror up in front of a rooster and watching him fight his reflection.

"I don't want no bonus," Mary Fortune said.

"I ain't ever seen you refuse one."

"You ain't ever seen me ask for one neither," she said.

"How much have you laid by?" he asked.

"Noner yer bidnis," she said and stamped his shoulders with her feet. "Don't be buttin into my bidnis."

"I bet you got it sewed up in your mattress," he said, "just like an old nigger woman. You ought to put it in the bank. I'm going to start you an account just as soon as I complete this deal. Won't anybody be able to check on it but me and you."

The bulldozer moved under them again and drowned out the rest of what he wanted to say. He waited and when the noise had passed, he could hold it in no longer. "I'm going to sell the lot right in front of the house for a gas station," he said. "Then we won't have to go down the road to get the car filled up, just step out the front door."

The Fortune house was set back about two hundred feet from the road and it was this two hundred feet that he intended to sell. It was the part that his daughter airily called "the lawn" though it was nothing but a field of weeds.

"You mean," Mary Fortune said after a minute, "the lawn?"

"Yes mam!" he said. "I mean the lawn," and he slapped his knee.

She did not say anything and he turned and looked up at her. There in the little rectangular opening of hair was his face looking back at him, but it was a reflection not of his present expression but of the darker one that indicated his displeasure. "That's where we play," she muttered.

"Well there's plenty of other places you can play," he said, irked by this lack of enthusiasm.

"We won't be able to see the woods across the road," she said.

The old man stared at her. "The woods across the road?" he repeated.

"We won't be able to see the view," she said.

"The view?" he repeated.

"The woods," she said; "we won't be able to see the woods from the porch."

"The woods from the porch?" he repeated.

Then she said, "My daddy grazes his calves on that lot."

The old man's wrath was delayed an instant by shock. Then it exploded in a roar. He jumped up and turned and slammed his fist on the hood of the car. "He can graze them somewheres else!"

"You fall off that embankment and you'll wish you hadn't," she said.

He moved from in front of the car around to the side, keeping his eye on her all the time. "Do you think I care where he grazes his calves! Do you think I'll let a calf interfere with my bidnis? Do you think I give a damn hoot where that fool grazes his calves?"

She sat, her red face darker than her hair, exactly reflecting his expression now. "He who calls his brother a fool is subject to hell fire," she said.

"Jedge not," he shouted, "lest ye be not jedged!" The tinge of his face was a shade more purple than hers. "You!" he said. "You let him beat you any time he wants to and don't do a thing but blubber a little and jump up and down!"

"He nor nobody else has ever touched me," she said, measuring off each word in a deadly flat tone. "Nobody's ever put a hand on me and if anybody did, I'd kill him."

"And black is white," the old man piped, "and night is day!"

The bulldozer passed below them. With their faces about a foot apart, each held the same expression until the noise had receded. Then the old man said, "Walk home by yourself. I refuse to ride with a Jezebel!"

"And I refuse to ride with the Whore of Babylon," she said and slid off the other side of the car and started off through the pasture.

"A whore is a woman!" he roared. "That's how much you know!" But she did not deign to turn around and answer him back, and as he watched the small robust figure stalk across the yellow-dotted field toward the woods, his pride in her, as if it couldn't help itself, returned like the gentle little tide on the new lake—all except that part of it that had to do with her refusal to stand up to Pitts; that pulled back like an undertow. If he could have taught her to stand up to Pitts the way she stood up to him, she would have been a perfect child, as fearless and sturdy-minded as anyone could want; but it was her one failure of character. It was the one point on which she did not resemble him. He turned and looked away over the lake to the woods across it and told himself that in five years, instead of woods, there would be houses and stores and parking places, and that the credit for it could go largely to him.

He meant to teach the child spirit by example and since he had definitely made up his mind, he announced that noon at the dinner table that he was negotiating with a man named Tilman to sell the lot in front of the house for a gas station.

His daughter, sitting with her worn-out air at the foot of the table, let out a moan as if a dull knife were being turned slowly in her chest. "You mean the lawn!" she moaned and fell back in her chair and repeated in an almost inaudible voice, "He means the lawn."

The other six Pitts children began to bawl and pipe, "Where we play!" "Don't let him do that, Pa!" "We won't be able to see the road!" and similar idiocies. Mary Fortune did not say anything. She had a mulish reserved look as if she were planning some business of her own. Pitts had stopped eating and was staring in front of him. His plate was full but his fists sat motionless like two dark quartz stones on either side of it. His eyes began to move from child to child around the table as if he were hunting for one particular one of them. Finally they stopped on Mary Fortune sitting next to her grandfather. "You done this to us," he muttered.

"I didn't," she said but there was no assurance in her voice. It was only a quaver, the voice of a frightened child.

Pitts got up and said, "Come with me," and turned and walked out, loosening his belt as he went, and to the old man's complete despair, she slid away from the table and followed him, almost ran after him, out the door and into the truck behind him, and they drove off.

This cowardice affected Mr. Fortune as if it were his own. It made him physically sick. "He beats an innocent child," he said to his daughter, who was apparently still prostrate at the end of the table, "and not one of you lifts a hand to stop him."

"You ain't lifted yours neither," one of the boys said in an undertone and there was a general mutter from that chorus of frogs.

"I'm an old man with a heart condition," he said. "I can't stop an ox."

"She put you up to it," his daughter murmured in a languid listless tone, her head rolling back and forth on the rim of her chair. "She puts you up to everything."

"No child never put me up to nothing!" he yelled. "You're no kind of a mother! You're a disgrace! That child is an angel! A saint!" he shouted in a voice so high that it broke and he had to scurry out of the room.

The rest of the afternoon he had to lie on his bed. His heart, whenever he knew the child had been beaten, felt as if it were slightly too large for the space that was supposed to hold it. But now he was more determined than ever to see the filling station go up in front of the house, and if it gave Pitts a stroke, so much the better. If it gave him a stroke and paralyzed him, he would be served right and he would never be able to beat her again.

Mary Fortune was never angry with him for long, or seriously, and though he did not see her the rest of that day, when he woke up the next morning, she was sitting astride his chest ordering him to make haste so that they would not miss the concrete mixer.

The workmen were laying the foundation for the fishing club when they arrived and the concrete mixer was already in operation. It was about the size and color of a circus elephant; they stood and watched it churn for a half-hour or so. At eleven-thirty, the old man had an appointment with Tilman to discuss his transaction and they had to leave. He did not tell Mary Fortune where they were going but only that he had to see a man.

Tilman operated a combination country store, filling station, scrap-metal dump, used-car lot and dance hall five miles down the highway that connected with the dirt road that passed in front of the Fortune place. Since the dirt road would soon be paved, he wanted a good location on it for another such enterprise. He was an up-and-coming man—the kind, Mr. Fortune thought, who was never just in line with progress but always a little ahead of it so that he could be there to meet it when it arrived. Signs up and down the highway announced that Tilman's was only five miles away, only four, only three, only two, only one; "Watch out for Tilman's, Around this bend!" and finally, "Here it is, Friends, TILMAN's!" in dazzling red letters.

Tilman's was bordered on either side by a field of old used-car bodies, a kind of ward for incurable automobiles. He also sold outdoor ornaments, such as stone cranes and chickens, urns, jardinieres, whirligigs, and farther back from the road, so as not to depress his dance-hall customers, a line of tombstones and monuments. Most of his businesses went on out-of-doors, so that his store building itself had not involved excessive expense. It was a one-room wooden structure onto which he had added, behind, a long tin hall equipped for dancing. This was divided into two sections, Colored and White, each with its private nickelodeon. He had a barbecue pit and sold barbecued sandwiches and soft drinks.

As they drove up under the shed of Tilman's place, the old man glanced at the child sitting with her feet drawn up on the seat and her chin resting on her knees. He didn't know if she would remember that it was Tilman he was going to sell the lot to or not.

"What you going in here for?" she asked suddenly, with a sniffing look as if she scented an enemy.

"Noner yer bidnis," he said. "You just sit in the car and when I come out, I'll bring you something."

"Don'tcher bring me nothing," she said darkly, "because I won't be here."

"Haw!" he said. "Now you're here, it's nothing for you to do but wait," and he got out and without paying her any further attention, he entered the dark store where Tilman was waiting for him.

When he came out in half an hour, she was not in the car. Hiding, he decided. He started walking around the store to see if she was in the back. He looked in the doors of the two sections of the dance hall and walked on around by the tombstones. Then his eye roved over the field of sinking automobiles and he realized that she could be in or behind any one of two hundred of them. He came back out in front of the store. A Negro boy, drinking a purple drink, was sitting on the ground with his back against the sweating ice cooler.

"Where did that little girl go to, boy?" he asked.

"I ain't seen nair little girl," the boy said.

The old man irritably fished in his pocket and handed him a nickel and said, "A pretty little girl in a yeller cotton dress."

"If you speakin about a stout chile look lak you," the boy said, "she gone off in a truck with a white man."

"What kind of a truck, what kind of a white man?" he yelled.

"It were a green pick-up truck," the boy said smacking his lips, "and a white man she call 'daddy.' They gone thataway some time ago."

The old man, trembling, got in his car and started home. His feelings raced back and forth between fury and mortification. She had never left him before and certainly never for Pitts. Pitts had ordered her to get in the truck and she was afraid not to. But when he reached this conclusion he was more furious than ever. What was the matter with her that she couldn't stand up to Pitts? Why was there this one flaw in her character when he had trained her so well in everything else? It was an ugly mystery.

When he reached the house and climbed the front steps, there she was sitting in the swing, looking glum-faced in front of her across the field he was going to sell. Her eyes were puffy and pink-rimmed but he didn't see any red marks on her legs. He sat down in the swing beside her. He meant to make his voice severe but instead it came out crushed, as if it belonged to a suitor trying to reinstate himself.

"What did you leave me for? You ain't ever left me before," he said.

"Because I wanted to," she said, looking straight ahead.

"You never wanted to," he said. "He made you."

"I toljer I was going and I went," she said in a slow emphatic voice, not looking at him, "and now you can go on and lemme alone." There was something very final, in the sound of this, a tone that had not come up before in their disputes. She stared across the lot where there was nothing but a profusion of pink and yellow and purple weeds, and on across the red road, to the sullen line of black pine woods fringed on top with green. Behind that line was a narrow gray-blue line of more distant woods and beyond that nothing but the sky, entirely blank except for one or two threadbare clouds. She looked into this scene as if it were a person that she preferred to him.

"It's my lot, ain't it?" he asked. "Why are you so up-in-the-air about me selling my own lot?"

"Because it's the lawn," she said. Her nose and eyes began to run horribly but she held her face rigid and licked the water off as soon as it was in reach of her tongue. "We won't be able to see across the road," she said.

The old man looked across the road to assure himself again that there was nothing over there to see. "I never have seen you act in such a way before," he said in an incredulous voice. "There's not a thing over there but the woods."

"We won't be able to see 'um," she said, "and that's the *lawn* and my daddy grazes his calves on it."

At that the old man stood up. "You act more like a Pitts than a Fortune," he said. He had never made such an ugly remark to her before and he was sorry the instant he had said it. It hurt him more than it did her. He turned and went in the house and upstairs to his room.

Several times during the afternoon, he got up from his bed and looked out the window across the "lawn" to the line of woods she said they wouldn't be able to see any more. Every time he saw the same thing: woods—not a mountain, not a waterfall, not any kind of planted bush or flower, just woods. The sunlight was woven through them at that particular time of the afternoon so that every thin pine trunk stood out in all its nakedness. A pine trunk is a pine trunk, he said to himself, and anybody that wants to see one don't have to go far in this neighborhood. Every time he got up and looked out, he was reconvinced of his wisdom in selling the lot. The dissatisfaction it caused Pitts would be permanent, but he could make it up to Mary Fortune by buying her something. With grown people, a road led either to heaven or hell, but with children there were always stops along the way where their attention could be turned with a trifle.

The third time he got up to look at the woods, it was almost six o'clock and the gaunt trunks appeared to be raised in a pool of red light that gushed from the almost hidden sun setting behind them. The old man stared for some time, as if for a prolonged instant he were caught up out of the rattle of everything that led to the future and were held there in the midst of an uncomfortable mystery that he had not apprehended before. He saw it, in his hallucination, as if someone were wounded behind the woods and the trees were bathed in blood. After a few minutes this unpleasant vision was broken by the presence of Pitts's pick-up truck grinding to a halt below the window. He returned to his bed and shut his eyes and against the closed lids hellish red trunks rose up in a black wood.

At the supper table nobody addressed a word to him, including Mary Fortune. He ate quickly and returned again to his room and spent the evening pointing out to himself the advantages for the future of having an establishment like Tilman's so near. They would not have to go any distance for gas. Anytime they needed a loaf of bread, all they would have to do would be step out their front door into Tilman's back door. They could sell milk to Tilman. Tilman was a likable fellow. Tilman would draw other business. The road would soon be paved. Travelers from all over the country would stop at Tilman's. If his daughter thought she was better than Tilman, it would be well to take her down a little. All men were created free and equal. When this phrase sounded in his head, his patriotic sense triumphed and he realized that it was his duty to sell the lot, that he must insure the future. He looked out the window at the moon shining over the woods across the road and listened for a while to the hum of crickets and treefrogs, and beneath their racket, he could hear the throb of the future town of Fortune.

He went to bed certain that just as usual, he would wake up in the morning looking into a little red mirror framed in a door of fine hair. She would have forgotten all about the sale and after breakfast they would drive into town and get the legal papers from the courthouse. On the way back he would stop at Tilman's and close the deal.

When he opened his eyes in the morning, he opened them on the empty ceiling. He pulled himself up and looked around the room but she was not there. He hung over the edge of the bed and looked beneath it but she was not there either. He got up and dressed and went outside. She was sitting in the swing on the front porch, exactly the way she had been yesterday, looking across the lawn into the woods. The old man was very much irritated. Every morning since she had been able to climb, he had waked up to find her either on his bed or underneath it. It was apparent that this morning she preferred the sight of the woods. He decided to ignore her behavior for the present and then bring it up later when she was over her pique. He sat down in the swing beside her but she continued to look at the woods. "I thought you and me'd go into town and have us a look at the boats in the new boat store," he said.

She didn't turn her head but she asked suspiciously, in a loud voice, "What else are you going for?"

"Nothing else," he said.

After a pause she said, "If that's all, I'll go," but she did not bother to look at him.

"Well put on your shoes," he said. "I ain't going to the city with a barefoot woman." She did not bother to laugh at this joke.

The weather was as indifferent as her disposition. The sky did not look as if it were going to rain or as if it were not going to rain. It was an unpleasant gray and the sun had not troubled to come out. All the way into town, she sat looking at her feet, which stuck out in front of her, encased in heavy brown school shoes. The old man had often sneaked up on her and found her alone in conversation with her feet and he thought she was speaking with them silently now. Every now and then her lips moved but she said nothing to him and let all his remarks pass as if she had not heard them. He decided it was going to cost him considerable to buy her good humor again and that he had better do it with a boat, since he wanted one too. She had been talking boats ever since the water backed up onto his place. They went first to the boat store. "Show us the yachts for po' folks!" he shouted jovially to the clerk as they entered.

"They're all for po' folks!" the clerk said. "You'll be po' when you finish buying one!" He was a stout youth in a yellow shirt and blue pants and he had a ready wit. They exchanged several clever remarks in a rapid-fire succession. Mr. Fortune looked at Mary Fortune to see if her face had brightened. She stood staring absently over the side of an outboard motor boat at the opposite wall.

"Ain't the lady interested in boats?" the clerk asked.

She turned and wandered back out onto the sidewalk and got in the car again. The old man looked after her with amazement. He could not believe that a child of her intelligence could be acting this way over the mere sale of a field. "I think she must be coming down with something," he said. "We'll come back again," and he returned to the car.

"Let's go get us an ice-cream cone," he suggested, looking at her with concern.

"I don't want no ice-cream cone," she said.

His actual destination was the courthouse but he did not want to make this apparent. "How'd you like to visit the ten-cent store while I tend to a little bidnis of mine?" he asked. "You can buy yourself something with a quarter I brought along."

"I ain't got nothing to do in no ten-cent store," she said. "I don't want no quarter of yours."

If a boat was of no interest, he should not have thought a quarter would be and reproved himself for that stupidity. "Well what's the matter, sister?" he asked kindly. "Don't you feel good?"

She turned and looked him straight in the face and said with a slow concentrated ferocity, "It's the lawn. My daddy grazes his calves there. We won't be able to see the woods any more."

The old man had held his fury in as long as he could. "He beats you!" he shouted. "And you worry about where he's going to graze his calves!"

"Nobody's ever beat me in my life," she said, "and if anybody did, I'd kill him."

A man seventy-nine years of age cannot let himself be run over by a child of nine. His face set in a look that was just as determined as hers. "Are you a Fortune," he said, "or are you a Pitts? Make up your mind."

Her voice was loud and positive and belligerent. "I'm Mary—Fortune—Pitts," she said.

"Well I," he shouted, "am PURE Fortune!"

There was nothing she could say to this and she showed it. For an instant she looked completely defeated, and the old man saw with a disturbing clearness that this was the Pitts look. What he saw was the Pitts look, pure and simple, and he felt personally stained by it, as if it had been found on his own face. He turned in disgust and backed the car out and drove straight to the courthouse.

The courthouse was a red and white blaze-faced building set in the center of a square from which most of the grass had been worn off. He parked in front of it and said, "Stay here," in an imperious tone and got out and slammed the car door.

It took him a half-hour to get the deed and have the sale paper drawn up and when he returned to the car, she was sitting on the back seat in the corner. The expression on that part of her face that he could see was foreboding and withdrawn. The sky had darkened also and there was a hot sluggish tide in the air, the kind felt when a tornado is possible.

"We better get on before we get caught in a storm," he said and emphatically, "because I got one more place to stop at on the way home," but he might have been chauffeuring a small dead body for all the answer he got.

. . .

On the way to Tilman's he reviewed once more the many just reasons that were leading him to his present action and he could not locate a flaw in any of them. He decided that while this attitude of hers would not be permanent, he was permanently disappointed in her and that when she came around she would have to apologize; and that there would be no boat. He was coming to realize slowly that his trouble with her had always been that he had not shown enough firmness. He had been too generous. He was so occupied with these thoughts that he did not notice the signs that said how many miles to Tilman's until the last one exploded joyfully in his face: "Here it is, Friends, TILMAN'S!" He pulled in under the shed.

He got out without so much as looking at Mary Fortune and entered the dark store where Tilman, leaning on the counter in front of a triple shelf of canned goods, was waiting for him.

Tilman was a man of quick action and few words. He sat habitually with his arms folded on the counter and his insignificant head weaving snake-fashion above them. He had a triangular-shaped face with the point at the bottom and the top of his skull was covered with a cap of freckles. His eyes were green and very narrow and his tongue was always exposed in his partly opened mouth. He had his checkbook handy and they got down to business at once. It did not take him long to look at the deed and sign the bill of sale. Then Mr. Fortune signed it and they grasped hands over the counter.

Mr. Fortune's sense of relief as he grasped Tilman's hand was extreme. What was done, he felt, was done and there could be no more argument, with her or with himself. He felt that he had acted on principle and that the future was assured.

Just as their hands loosened, an instant's change came over Tilman's face and he disappeared completely under the counter as if he had been snatched by the feet from below. A bottle crashed against the line of tinned goods behind where he had been. The old man whirled around. Mary Fortune was in the door, red-faced and wild-looking, with another bottle lifted to hurl. As he ducked, it broke behind him on the counter and she grabbed another from the crate. He sprang at her but she tore to the other side of the store, screaming something unintelligible and throwing everything within her reach. The old man pounced again and this time he caught her by the tail of her dress and pulled her backward out of the store. Then he got a better grip and lifted her, wheezing and whimpering but suddenly limp in his arms, the few feet to the car. He managed to get the door open and dump her inside. Then he ran around to the other side and got in himself and drove away as fast as he could.

His heart felt as if it were the size of the car and was racing forward, carrying him to some inevitable destination faster than he had ever been carried before. For the first five minutes he did not think but only sped forward as if he were being driven inside his own fury. Gradually the power of thought returned to him. Mary Fortune, rolled into a ball in the corner of the seat, was snuffling and heaving.

He had never seen a child behave in such a way in his life. Neither his own children nor anyone else's had ever displayed such temper in his presence, and he had never for an instant imagined that the child he had trained himself, the child who had been his constant companion for nine years, would embarrass him like this. The child he had never lifted a hand to!

Then he saw, with the sudden vision that sometimes comes with delayed recognition, that that had been his mistake.

She respected Pitts because, even with no just cause, he beat her; and if he—with his just cause—did not beat her now, he would have nobody to blame but himself if she turned out a hellion. He saw that the time had come, that he could no longer avoid whipping her, and as he turned off the highway onto the dirt road leading to home, he told himself that when he finished with her, she would never throw another bottle again.

He raced along the clay road until he came to the line where his own property began and then he turned off onto a side path, just wide enough for the automobile and bounced for a half a mile through the woods. He stopped the car at the exact spot where he had seen Pitts take his belt to her. It was a place where the road widened so that two cars could pass or one could turn around, an ugly red bald spot surrounded by long thin pines that appeared to be gathered there to witness anything that would take place in such a clearing. A few stones protruded from the clay.

"Get out," he said and reached across her and opened the door.

She got out without looking at him or asking what they were going to do and he got out on his side and came around the front of the car.

"Now I'm going to whip you!" he said and his voice was extra loud and hollow and had a vibrating quality that appeared to be taken up and passed through the tops of the pines. He did not want to get caught in a downpour while he was whipping her and he said, "Hurry up and get ready against that tree," and began to take off his belt.

What he had in mind to do appeared to come very slowly as if it had to penetrate a fog in her head. She did not move but gradually her confused expression began to clear. Where a few seconds before her face had been red and distorted and unorganized, it drained now of every vague line until nothing was left on it but positiveness, a look that went slowly past determination and reached certainty. "Nobody has ever beat me," she said, "and if anybody tries it, I'll kill him."

"I don't want no sass," he said and started toward her. His knees felt very unsteady, as if they might turn either backward or forward.

She moved exactly one step back, and keeping her eye on him steadily, removed her glasses and dropped them behind a small rock near the tree he had told her to get ready against. "Take off your glasses," she said.

"Don't give me orders!" he said in a high voice and slapped awkwardly at her ankles with his belt.

She was on him so quickly that he could not have recalled which blow he felt first, whether the weight of her whole solid body or the jabs of her feet or the pummeling of her fist on his chest. He flailed the belt in the air, not knowing where to hit but trying to get her off him until he could decide where to get a grip on her.

"Leggo!" he shouted. "Leggo I tell you!" But she seemed to be everywhere, coming at him from all directions at once. It was as if he were being attacked not by one child but by a pack of small demons all with stout brown school shoes and small rocklike fists. His glasses flew to the side.

"I toljer to take them off," she growled without pausing.

He caught his knee and danced on one foot and a rain of blows fell on his stomach. He felt five claws in the flesh of his upper arm where she was hanging from while her feet mechanically battered his knees and her free fist pounded him again and again in the chest. Then with horror he saw her face rise up in front of his, teeth exposed, and he roared like a bull as she bit the side of his jaw. He seemed to see his own face coming to bite him from several sides at once but he could not attend to it for he was being kicked indiscriminately, in the stomach and then in the crotch. Suddenly he threw himself on the ground and began to roll like a man on fire. She was on top of him at once, rolling with him and still kicking, and now with both fists free to batter his chest.

"I'm an old man!" he piped. "Leave me alone!" But she did not stop. She began a fresh assault on his jaw.

"Stop stop!" he wheezed. "I'm your grandfather!"

She paused, her face exactly on top of his. Pale identical eye looked into pale identical eye. "Have you had enough?" she asked.

The old man looked up into his own image. It was triumphant and hostile. "You been whipped," it said, "by me," and then it added, bearing down on each word, "and I'm PURE Pitts."

In the pause she loosened her grip and he got hold of her throat. With a sudden surge of strength, he managed to roll over and reverse their positions so that he was looking down into the face that was his own but had dared to call itself Pitts. With his hands still tight around her neck, he lifted her head and brought it down once hard against the rock that happened to be under it. Then he brought it down twice more. Then looking into the face in which the eyes, slowly rolling back, appeared to pay him not the slightest attention, he said, "There's not an ounce of Pitts in me."

He continued to stare at his conquered image until he perceived that though it was absolutely silent, there was no look of remorse on it. The eyes had rolled back down and were set in a fixed glare that did not take him in. "This ought to teach you a good lesson," he said in a voice that was edged with doubt.

He managed painfully to get up on his unsteady kicked legs and to take two steps, but the enlargement of his heart which had begun in the car was still going on. He turned his head and looked behind him for a long time at the little motionless figure with its head on the rock.

Then he fell on his back and looked up helplessly along the bare trunks into the tops of the pines and his heart expanded once more with a convulsive motion. It expanded so fast that the old man felt as if he were being pulled after it through the woods, felt as if he were running as fast as he could with the ugly pines toward the lake. He perceived that there would be a little opening there, a little place where he could escape and leave the woods behind him. He could see it in the distance already, a little opening where the white sky was reflected in the water. It grew as he ran toward it until suddenly the whole lake opened up before him, riding majestically in little corrugated folds toward his feet. He realized suddenly that he could not swim and that he had not bought the boat. On both sides of him he saw that the gaunt trees had thickened into mysterious dark files that were marching across the water and away into the distance. He looked around desperately for someone to help him but the place was deserted except for one huge yellow monster which sat to the side, as stationary as he was, gorging itself on clay.

1957

MAYA ANGELOU
(1928–   )

As an actress, musician, and writer, Maya Angelou is one of the most gifted and versatile artists of her generation. She has toured throughout Europe and Africa with Porgy and Bess, *composed scores for two screenplays and written lyrics for Roberta Flack. She received Tony Award nominations in 1973 for her Broadway debut and in 1977 for her performance in* Roots. *Her poetry book* Just Give Me a Cool Drink of Water 'fore I Diiie *was nominated in 1972 for a Pulitzer Prize. She is the recent recipient of a prestigious MacArthur Foundation award.*

Born Marguerita Johnson in St. Louis on April 4, 1928, Angelou was raised by her grandmother in the small southern town of Stamps, Arkansas. As a young girl, she read widely, memorizing the work of writers from Shakespeare to the Harlem Renaissance poet Georgia Douglas Johnson. The melody and rhythm of her prose echo not only this literary heritage but also the blues and spirituals she has heard throughout her life. A disciplined writer who works daily from six in the morning to noon, Angelou has traced her life and her times through five volumes of autobiography.

One of the few writers who have chosen autobiography as the vehicle for their most serious work, Angelou sees this genre as "stemming from the slave narrative and developing into a new American literary form." Her goal is to make autobiography literature. The task is enormous, as she has confessed: "I'm learning the form. I am molding the form and the form is molding me." Nonetheless, her volumes reflect the qualities she attributes to the best of this genre: "A good autobiographer seems to write about herself and is in fact writing about the temper of the times."

The selections we have chosen are from I Know Why the Caged Bird Sings. *"Preach It" humorously depicts the southern Black church community of Stamps, Arkansas. The second selection conveys Angelou's early, determined fight against racist and sexist discrimination in San Francisco. Together, these pieces reflect Angelou's pride in her identity. As she has said, "I am feminist, I am black, I am a human being. The three are inseparable."*

from I KNOW WHY THE CAGED BIRD SINGS

Preach It

Reverend Howard Thomas was the presiding elder over a district in Arkansas that included Stamps. Every three months he visited our church, stayed at Momma's over the Saturday night and preached a loud passionate sermon on Sunday. He collected the money that had been taken in over the preceding months, heard reports from all the church groups and shook hands with the adults and kissed all small children. Then he want away. (I used to think that he went west to heaven, but Momma straightened me out. He just went to Texarkana.)

Bailey and I hated him unreservedly. He was ugly, fat, and he laughed like a hog with the colic. We were able to make each other burst with giggling when we did imitations of the thick-skinned preacher. Bailey was especially good at it. He could imitate Reverend Thomas right in front of Uncle Willie and never get caught because he did it soundlessly. He puffed out his cheeks until they looked like wet brown stones, and wobbled his head from side to side. Only he and I knew it, but that was old Reverend Thomas to a tee.

His obesity, while disgusting, was not enough to incur the intense hate that we felt for him. The fact that he never bothered to remember our names was insulting, but neither was that slight, alone, enough to make us despise him. But the crime that tipped the scale and made our hate not only just but imperative was his actions at the dinner table. He ate the biggest, brownest and best parts of the chicken at every Sunday meal.

The only good thing about his visits was the fact that he always arrived late on Saturday nights, after we had had dinner. I often wondered if he tried to catch us at the table. I believe so, for when he reached the front porch his little eyes would glitter toward the empty dining room and his face would fall with disappointment. Then immediately, a thin curtain would fall over his features and he'd laugh a few barks, "Uh, huh, uh, huh, Sister Henderson, just like a penny with a hole in it, I always turns up."

Right on cue every time, Momma would answer, "That's right, Elder Thomas, thank the blessed Jesus, come right in."

He'd step in the front door and put down his Gladstone (that's what he called it) and look around for Bailey and me. Then he opened his awful arms and groaned, "Suffer little children to come unto me, for such is the Kingdom of Heaven."

Bailey went to him each time with his hand stretched out, ready for a manly handshake, but Reverend Thomas would push away the hand and encircle my brother for a few seconds. "You still a boy, buddy. Remember that. They tell me the Good Book say, 'When I was a child I spake as a child, I thought as a child, but when I became a man, I put away childish things.' " Only then would he open his arms and release Bailey.

I never had the nerve to go up to him. I was quite afraid that if I tried to say, "Hello, Reverend Thomas," I would choke on the sin of mocking him. After all, the Bible did say, "God is not mocked," and the man was God's representative. He used to say to me, "Come on, little sister. Come and get this blessing." But I was so afraid and I also hated him so much that my emotions mixed themselves up and it was enough to start me crying. Momma told him time after time, "Don't pay her no mind, Elder Thomas, you know how tender-hearted she is."

He ate the leftovers from our dinner and he and Uncle Willie discussed the developments of the church programs. They talked about how the present minister was attending to his flock, who got married, who died and how many children had been born since his last visit.

Bailey and I stood like shadows in the rear of the Store near the coal-oil tank, waiting for the juicy parts. But when they were ready to talk about the latest scandal, Momma sent us to her bedroom with warnings to have our Sunday School lesson perfectly memorized or we knew what we could expect.

We had a system that never failed. I would sit in the big rocking chair by the stove and rock occasionally and stamp my feet. I changed voices, now soft and girlish, then a little deeper like Bailey's. Meanwhile, he would creep back into the Store. Many times he came flying back to sit on the bed and to hold the open lesson book just before Momma suddenly filled the doorway.

"You children get your lesson good, now. You know all the other children looks up to you all." Then, as she turned back into the Store Bailey followed right on her footsteps to crouch in the shadows and listen for the forbidden gossip.

Once, he heard how Mr. Coley Washington had a girl from Lewisville staying in his house. I didn't think that was so bad, but Bailey explained that Mr. Washington was probably "doing it" to her. He said that although "it" was bad just about everybody in the world did it to somebody, but no one else was supposed to know that. And once, we found out about a man who had been killed by whitefolks and thrown into the pond. Bailey said the man's things had been cut off and put in his pocket and he had been shot in the head, all because the whitefolks said he did "it" to a white woman.

Because of the kinds of news we filched from those hushed conversations, I was convinced that whenever Reverend Thomas came and Momma sent us to the back room they were going to discuss whitefolks and "doing it." Two subjects about which I was very dim.

On Sunday mornings Momma served a breakfast that was geared to hold us quiet from 9:30 A.M. to 3 P.M. She fried thick pink slabs of home-cured ham and poured the grease over sliced red tomatoes. Eggs over easy, fried potatoes and onions, yellow hominy and crisp perch fried so hard we would pop them in our mouths and chew bones, fins and all. Her cathead biscuits were at least three inches in diameter and two inches thick. The trick to eating catheads was to get the butter on them before they got cold—then they were delicious. When, unluckily, they were allowed to get cold, they tended to a gooeyness, not unlike a wad of tired gum.

We were able to reaffirm our findings on the catheads each Sunday that Reverend Thomas spent with us. Naturally enough, he was asked to bless the table. We would all stand; my uncle, leaning his walking stick against the wall, would lean his weight on the table. Then Reverend Thomas would begin. "Blessed Father, we thank you this morning . . ." and on and on and on. I'd stop listening after a while until Bailey kicked me and then I cracked my lids to see what had promised to be a meal that would make any Sunday proud. But as the Reverend droned on and on and on to a God who I thought must be bored to hear the same things over and over again, I saw that the ham grease had turned white on the tomatoes. The eggs had withdrawn from the edge of the platter to bunch in the center like children left out in the cold. And the catheads had sat down on themselves with the conclusiveness of a fat woman sitting in an easy chair. And still he talked on. When he finally stopped, our appetites were gone, but he feasted on the cold food with a non-talking but still noisy relish.

In the Christian Methodist Episcopal Church the children's section was on the right, cater-cornered from the pew that held those ominous women called the Mothers of the Church. In the young people's section the benches were placed close together, and when a child's legs no longer comfortably fitted in the narrow space, it was an indication to the elders that that person could now move into the intermediate area (center church). Bailey and I were allowed to sit with the other children only when there were informal meetings, church socials or the like. But on the Sundays when Reverend Thomas preached, it was ordained that we occupy the first row, called the mourners' bench. I thought we were placed in front because Momma was proud of us, but Bailey assured me that she just wanted to keep her grandchildren under her thumb and eye.

Reverend Thomas took his text from Deuteronomy. And I was stretched between loathing his voice and wanting to listen to the sermon. Deuteronomy was my favorite book in the Bible. The laws were so absolute, so clearly set down, that I knew if a person truly wanted to avoid hell and brimstone, and being roasted forever in the devil's fire, all she had to do was memorize Deuteronomy and follow its teaching, word for word. I also liked the way the word rolled off the tongue.

Bailey and I sat alone on the front bench, the wooden slats pressing hard on our behinds and the backs of our thighs. I would have wriggled just a bit, but each time I looked over at Momma, she seemed to threaten, "Move and I'll tear you up," so, obedient to the unvoiced command, I sat still. The church ladies were warming up behind me with a few hallelujahs and Praise the Lords and Amens, and the preacher hadn't really moved into the meat of the sermon.

It was going to be a hot service.

On my way into church, I saw Sister Monroe, her open-faced gold crown glinting when she opened her mouth to return a neighborly greeting. She lived in the country and couldn't get to church every Sunday, so she made up for her absences by shouting so hard when she did make it that she shook the whole church. As soon as she took her seat, all the ushers would move to her side of the church because it took three women and sometimes a man or two to hold her.

Once when she hadn't been to church for a few months (she had taken off to have a child), she got the spirit and started shouting, throwing her arms around and jerking her body, so that the ushers went over to hold her down, but she tore herself away from them and ran up to the pulpit. She stood in front of the altar, shaking like a freshly caught trout. She screamed at Reverend Taylor. "Preach it. I say, preach it." Naturally he kept on preaching as if she wasn't standing there telling him what to do. Then she screamed an extremely fierce "I said, preach it" and stepped up on the altar. The Reverend kept on throwing out phrases like home-run balls and Sister Monroe made a quick break and grasped for him. For just a second, everything and everyone in the church except Reverend Taylor and Sister Monroe hung loose like stockings on a washline. Then she caught the minister by the sleeve of his jacket and his coattail, and she rocked him from side to side.

I have to say this for our minister, he never stopped giving us the lesson. The usher board made its way to the pulpit, going up both aisles with a little more haste than is customarily seen in church. Truth to tell, they fairly ran to the minister's aid. Then two of the deacons, in their shiny Sunday suits, joined the ladies in white on the pulpit, and each time they pried Sister Monroe loose from the preacher he took another deep breath and kept on preaching, and Sister Monroe grabbed him in another place, and more firmly. Reverend Taylor was helping his rescuers as much as possible by jumping around when he got a chance. His voice at one point got so low it sounded like a roll of thunder, then Sister Monroe's "Preach it" cut through the roar, and we all wondered (I did, in any case) if it would ever end. Would they go on forever, or get tired out at last like a game of blindman's bluff that lasted too long, with nobody caring who was "it"?

I'll never know what might have happened, because magically the pandemonium spread. The spirit infused Deacon Jackson and Sister Willson, the chairman of the usher board, at the same time. Deacon Jackson, a tall, thin, quiet man, who was also a part-time Sunday school teacher, gave a scream like a falling tree, leaned back on thin air and punched Reverend Taylor on the arm. It must have hurt as much as it caught the Reverend unawares. There was a moment's break in the rolling sounds and Reverend Taylor jerked around surprised, and hauled off and punched Deacon Jackson. In the same second Sister Willson caught his tie, looped it over her fist a few times, and pressed down on him. There wasn't time to laugh or cry before all three of them were down on the floor behind the altar. Their legs spiked out like kindling wood.

Sister Monroe, who had been the cause of all the excitement, walked off the dais, cool and spent, and raised her flinty voice in the hymn, "I came to Jesus, as I was, worried, wound, and sad, I found in Him a resting place and He has made me glad."

The minister took advantage of already being on the floor and asked in a choky little voice if the church would kneel with him to offer a prayer of thanksgiving. He said we had been visited with a mighty spirit, and let the whole church say Amen.

On the next Sunday, he took his text from the eighteenth chapter of the Gospel according to St. Luke, and talked quietly but seriously about the Pharisees, who prayed in the streets so that the public would be impressed with their religious devotion. I doubt that anyone got the message—certainly not those to whom it was directed. The deacon board, however, did appropriate funds for him to buy a new suit. The other was a total loss.

Our presiding elder had heard the story of Reverend Taylor and Sister Monroe, but I was sure he didn't know her by sight. So my interest in the service's potential and my aversion to Reverend Thomas caused me to turn him off. Turning off or tuning out people was my highly developed art. The custom of letting obedient children be seen but not heard was so agreeable to me that I went one step further: Obedient children should not see or hear if they chose not to do so. I laid a handful of attention on my face and tuned up the sounds in the church.

Sister Monroe's fuse was already lit, and she sizzled somewhere to the right behind me. Elder Thomas jumped into the sermon, determined, I suppose, to give the members what they came for. I saw the ushers from the left side of the church near the big windows begin to move discreetly, like pallbearers, toward Sister Monroe's bench. Bailey jogged my knee. When the incident with Sister Monroe, which we always called simply "the incident," had taken place, we had been too astounded to laugh. But for weeks after, all we needed to send us into violent outbursts of laughter was a whispered "Preach it." Anyway, he pushed my knee, covered his mouth and whispered, "I say, preach it."

I looked toward Momma, across that square of stained boards, over the collection table, hoping that a look from her would root me safely to my sanity. But for the first time in memory Momma was staring behind me at Sister Monroe. I supposed that she was counting on bringing that emotional lady up short with a severe look or two. But Sister Monroe's voice had already reached the danger point. "Preach it!"

There were a few smothered giggles from the children's section, and Bailey nudged me again. "I say, preach it"—in a whisper. Sister Monroe echoed him loudly, "I say, preach it!"

Two deacons wedged themselves around Brother Jackson as a preventive measure and two large determined-looking men walked down the aisle toward Sister Monroe.

While the sounds in the church were increasing, Elder Thomas made the regrettable mistake of increasing his volume too. Then suddenly, like a summer rain, Sister Monroe broke through the cloud of people trying to hem her in, and flooded up to the pulpit. She didn't stop this time but continued immediately to the altar, bound for Elder Thomas, crying, "I say, preach it."

Bailey said out loud, "Hot dog" and "Damn" and "She's going to beat his butt."

But Reverend Thomas didn't intend to wait for that eventuality, so as Sister Monroe approached the pulpit from the right he started descending from the left. He was not intimidated by his change of venue. He continued preaching and moving. He finally stopped right in front of the collection table, which put him almost in our laps, and Sister Monroe rounded the altar on his heels, followed by the deacons, ushers, some unofficial members and a few of the bigger children.

Just as the elder opened his mouth, pink tongue waving, and said, "Great God of Mount Nebo," Sister Monroe hit him on the back of his head with her purse. Twice. Before he could bring his lips together, his teeth fell, no, actually his teeth jumped, out of his mouth.

The grinning uppers and lowers lay by my right shoe, looking empty and at the same time appearing to contain all the emptiness in the world. I could have stretched out a foot and kicked them under the bench or behind the collection table.

Sister Monroe was struggling with his coat, and the men had all but picked her up to remove her from the building. Bailey pinched me and said without moving his lips, "I'd like to see him eat dinner now."

I looked at Reverend Thomas desperately. If he appeared just a little sad or embarrassed, I could feel sorry for him and wouldn't be able to laugh. My sympathy for him would keep me from laughing. I dreaded laughing in church. If I lost control, two things were certain to happen. I would surely pee, and just as surely get a whipping. And this time I would probably die because everything was funny—Sister Monroe, and Momma trying to keep her quiet with those threatening looks, and Bailey whispering "Preach it" and Elder Thomas with his lips flapping loose like tired elastic.

But Reverend Thomas shrugged off Sister Monroe's weakening clutch, pulled out an extra-large white handkerchief and spread it over his nasty little teeth. Putting them in his pocket, he gummed, "Naked I came into the world, and naked I shall go out."

Bailey's laugh had worked its way up through his body and was escaping through his nose in short hoarse snorts. I didn't try any longer to hold back the laugh, I just opened my mouth and released sound. I heard the first titter jump up in the air over my head, over the pulpit and out the window. Momma said out loud, "Sister!" but the bench was greasy and I slid off onto the floor. There was more laughter in me trying to get out. I didn't know there was that much in the whole world. It pressed at all my body openings, forcing everything in its path. I cried and hollered, passed gas and urine. I didn't see Bailey descend to the floor, but I rolled over once and he was kicking and screaming too. Each time we looked at each other we howled louder than before, and though he tried to say something, the laughter attacked him and he was only able to get out "I say, preach." And then I rolled over onto Uncle Willie's rubber-tipped cane. My eyes followed the cane up to his good brown hand on the curve and up the long, long white sleeve to his face. The one side pulled down as it usually did when he cried (it also pulled down when he laughed). He stuttered, "I'm gonna whip you this time myself."

I have no memory of how we got out of church and into the parsonage next door, but in that overstuffed parlor, Bailey and I received the whipping of our lives. Uncle Willie ordered us between licks to stop crying. I tried to, but Bailey refused to cooperate. Later he explained that when a person is beating you you should scream as loud as possible; maybe the whipper will become embarrassed or else some sympathetic soul might come to your rescue. Our savior came for neither of these reasons, but because Bailey yelled so loud and disturbed what was left of the service, the minister's wife came out and asked Uncle Willie to quiet us down.

Laughter so easily turns to hysteria for imaginative children. I felt for weeks after that I had been very, very sick, and until I completely recovered my strength I stood on laughter's cliff and any funny thing could hurl me off to my death far below.

Each time Bailey said "Preach it" to me, I hit him as hard as I could and cried.

A Job on the Streetcars

Later, my room had all the cheeriness of a dungeon and the appeal of a tomb. It was going to be impossible to stay there, but leaving held no attraction for me, either. Running away from home would be anticlimactic after Mexico, and a dull story after my month in the car lot. But the need for change bulldozed a road down the center of my mind.

I had it. The answer came to me with the suddenness of a collision. I would go to work. Mother wouldn't be difficult to convince; after all, in school I was a year ahead of my grade and Mother was a firm believer in self-sufficiency. In fact, she'd be pleased to think that I had that much gumption, that much of her in my character. (She liked to speak of herself as the original "do-it-yourself girl.")

Once I had settled on getting a job, all that remained was to decide which kind of job I was most fitted for. My intellectual pride had kept me from selecting typing, shorthand or filing as subjects in school, so office work was ruled out. War plants and shipyards demanded birth certificates, and mine would reveal me to be fifteen, and ineligible for work. So the well-paying defense jobs were also out. Women had replaced men on the streetcars as conductors and motormen, and the thought of sailing up and down the hills of San Francisco in a dark-blue uniform, with a money changer at my belt, caught my fancy.

Mother was as easy as I had anticipated. The world was moving so fast, so much money was being made, so many people were dying in Guam, and Germany, that hordes of strangers became good friends overnight. Life was cheap and death entirely free. How could she have the time to think about my academic career?

To her question of what I planned to do, I replied that I would get a job on the streetcars. She rejected the proposal with: "They don't accept colored people on the streetcars."

I would like to claim an immediate fury which was followed by the noble determination to break the restricting tradition. But the truth is, my first reaction was one of disappointment. I'd pictured myself, dressed in a neat blue serge suit, my money changer swinging jauntily at my waist, and a cheery smile for the passengers which would make their own work day brighter.

From disappointment, I gradually ascended the emotional ladder to haughty indignation, and finally to that state of stubbornness where the mind is locked like the jaws of an enraged bulldog.

I would go to work on the streetcars and wear a blue serge suit. Mother gave me her support with one of her usual terse asides, "That's what you want to do? Then nothing beats a trial but a failure. Give it everything you've got. I've told you many times, 'Can't do is like Don't Care.' Neither of them have a home."

Translated, that meant there was nothing a person can't do, and there should be nothing a human being didn't care about. It was the most positive encouragement I could have hoped for.

. . .

In the offices of the Market Street Railway Company the receptionist seemed as surprised to see me there as I was surprised to find the interior dingy and the décor drab. Somehow I had expected waxed surfaces and carpeted floors. If I had met no resistance, I might have decided against working for such a poor-mouth-looking concern. As it was, I explained that I had come to see about a job. She asked, was I sent by an agency, and when I replied that I was not, she told me they were only accepting applicants from agencies.

The classified pages of the morning papers had listed advertisements for motorettes and conductorettes and I reminded her of that. She gave me a face full of astonishment that my suspicious nature would not accept.

"I am applying for the job listed in this morning's *Chronicle* and I'd like to be presented to your personnel manager." While I spoke in supercilious accents, and looked at the room as if I had an oil well in my own backyard, my armpits were being pricked by millions of hot pointed needles. She saw her escape and dived into it.

"He's out. He's out for the day. You might call tomorrow and if he's in,

I'm sure you can see him." Then she swiveled her chair around on its rusty screws and with that I was supposed to be dismissed.

"May I ask his name?"

She half turned, acting surprised to find me still there.

"His name? Whose name?"

"Your personnel manager."

We were firmly joined in the hypocrisy to play out the scene.

"The personnel manager? Oh, he's Mr. Cooper, but I'm not sure you'll find him here tomorrow. He's . . . Oh, but you can try."

"Thank you."

"You're welcome."

And I was out of the musty room and into the even mustier lobby. In the street I saw the receptionist and myself going faithfully through paces that were stale with familiarity, although I had never encountered that kind of situation before and, probably, neither had she. We were like actors who, knowing the play by heart, were still able to cry afresh over the old tragedies and laugh spontaneously at the comic situations.

The miserable little encounter had nothing to do with me, the me of me, any more than it had to do with that silly clerk. The incident was a recurring dream, concocted years before by stupid whites and it eternally came back to haunt us all. The secretary and I were like Hamlet and Laertes in the final scene, where, because of harm done by one ancestor to another, we were bound to duel to the death. Also because the play must end somewhere.

I went further than forgiving the clerk, I accepted her as a fellow victim of the same puppeteer.

On the streetcar, I put my fare into the box and the conductorette looked at me with the usual hard eyes of white contempt. "Move into the car, please move on in the car." She patted her money changer.

Her Southern nasal accent sliced my meditation and I looked deep into my thoughts. All lies, all comfortable lies. The receptionist was not innocent and neither was I. The whole charade we had played out in that crummy waiting room had directly to do with me, Black, and her, white.

I wouldn't move into the streetcar but stood on the ledge over the conductor, glaring. My mind shouted so energetically that the announcement made my veins stand out, and my mouth tighten into a prune.

I WOULD HAVE THE JOB. I WOULD BE A CONDUCTORETTE AND SLING A FULL MONEY CHANGER FROM MY BELT. I WOULD.

The next three weeks were a honeycomb of determination with apertures for the days to go in and out. The Negro organizations to whom I appealed for support bounced me back and forth like a shuttlecock on a badminton court. Why did I insist on that particular job? Openings were going begging that paid nearly twice the money. The minor officials with whom I was able to win an audience thought me mad. Possibly I was.

Downtown San Francisco became alien and cold, and the streets I had loved in a personal familiarity were unknown lanes that twisted with malicious intent. Old buildings, whose gray rococo façades housed my memories of the Forty-Niners, and Diamond Lil, Robert Service, Sutter and Jack London, were then imposing structures viciously joined to keep me out. My trips to the streetcar office were of the frequency of a person on salary. The struggle expanded. I was no longer in conflict only with the Market Street Railway but with the marble lobby of the building which housed its offices, and elevators and their operators.

During this period of strain Mother and I began our first steps on the long path toward mutual adult admiration. She never asked for reports and I didn't offer any details. But every morning she made breakfast, gave me carfare and lunch money, as if I were going to work. She comprehended the perversity of life, that in the struggle lies the joy. That I was no glory seeker was obvious to her, and that I had to exhaust every possibility before giving in was also clear.

On my way out of the house one morning she said, "Life is going to give you just what you put in it. Put your whole heart in everything you do, and pray, then you can wait." Another time she reminded me that "God helps those who help themselves." She had a store of aphorisms which she dished out as the occasion demanded. Strangely, as bored as I was with clichés, her inflection gave them something new, and set me thinking for a little while at least. Later when asked how I got my job, I was never able to say exactly. I only knew that one day, which was tiresomely like all the others before it, I sat in the Railway office, ostensibly waiting to be interviewed. The receptionist called me to her desk and shuffled a bundle of papers to me. They were job application forms. She said they had to be filled in triplicate. I had little time to wonder if I had won or not, for the standard questions reminded me of the necessity for dexterous lying. How old was I? List my previous jobs, starting from the last held and go backward to the first. How much money did I earn, and why did I leave the position? Give two references (not relatives).

Sitting at a side table my mind and I wove a cat's ladder of near truths and total lies. I kept my face blank (an old art) and wrote quickly the fable of Marguerite Johnson, aged nineteen, former companion and driver for Mrs. Annie Henderson (a White Lady) in Stamps, Arkansas.

I was given blood tests, aptitude tests, physical coordination tests, and Rorschachs, then on a blissful day I was hired as the first Negro on the San Francisco streetcars.

Mother gave me the money to have my blue serge suit tailored, and I learned to fill out work cards, operate the money changer and punch transfers. The time crowded together and at an End of Days I was swinging on the back of the rackety trolley, smiling sweetly and persuading my charges to "step forward in the car, please."

For one whole semester the street cars and I shimmied up and scooted down the sheer hills of San Francisco. I lost some of my need for the Black ghetto's shielding-sponge quality, as I clanged and cleared my way down Market Street, with its honky-tonk homes for homeless sailors, past the quiet retreat of Golden Gate Park and along closed undwelled-in-looking dwellings of the Sunset District.

My work shifts were split so haphazardly that it was easy to believe that my superiors had chosen them maliciously. Upon mentioning my suspicions to Mother, she said, "Don't worry about it. You ask for what you want, and you pay for what you get. And I'm going to show you that it ain't no trouble when you pack double."

She stayed awake to drive me out to the car barn at four thirty in the mornings, or to pick me up when I was relieved just before dawn. Her awareness of life's perils convinced her that while I would be safe on the public conveyances, she "wasn't about to trust a taxi driver with her baby."

When the spring classes began, I resumed my commitment with formal education. I was so much wiser and older, so much more independent, with a bank account and clothes that I had bought for myself, that I was sure that I had learned and earned the magic formula which would make me a part of the gay life my contemporaries led.

Not a bit of it. Within weeks, I realized that my schoolmates and I were on paths moving diametrically away from each other. They were concerned and excited over the approaching football games, but I had in my immediate past raced a car down a dark and foreign Mexican mountain. They concentrated great interest on who was worthy of being student body president, and when the metal bands would be removed from their teeth, while I remembered sleeping for a month in a wrecked automobile and conducting a streetcar in the uneven hours of the morning.

Without willing it, I had gone from being ignorant of being ignorant to being aware of being aware. And the worst part of my awareness was that I didn't know what I was aware of. I knew I knew very little, but I was certain that the things I had yet to learn wouldn't be taught to me at George Washington High School.

I began to cut classes, to walk in Golden Gate Park or wander along the shiny counter of the Emporium Department Store. When Mother discovered that I was playing truant, she told me that if I didn't want to go to school one day, if there were no tests being held, and if my school work was up to standard, all I had to do was tell her and I could stay home. She said that she didn't want some white woman calling her up to tell her something about her child that she didn't know. And she didn't want to be put in the position of lying to a white woman because I wasn't woman enough to speak up. That put an end to my truancy, but nothing appeared to lighten the long gloomy day that going to school became.

To be left alone on the tightrope of youthful unknowing is to experience the excruciating beauty of full freedom and the threat of eternal indecision.

Few, if any, survive their teens. Most surrender to the vague but murderous pressure of adult conformity. It becomes easier to die and avoid conflicts than to maintain a constant battle with the superior forces of maturity.

Until recently each generation found it more expedient to plead guilty to the charge of being young and ignorant, easier to take the punishment meted out by the older generation (which had itself confessed to the same crime short years before). The command to grow up at once was more bearable than the faceless horror of wavering purpose, which was youth.

The bright hours when the young rebelled against the descending sun had to give way to twenty-four-hour periods called "days" that were named as well as numbered.

The Black female is assaulted in her tender years by all those common forces of nature at the same time that she is caught in the tripartite crossfire of masculine prejudice, white illogical hate and Black lack of power.

The fact that the adult American Negro female emerges a formidable character is often met with amazement, distaste and even belligerence. It is seldom accepted as an inevitable outcome of the struggle won by survivors and deserves respect if not enthusiastic acceptance.

1969

CYNTHIA OZICK
(1928–   )

Best known for her short stories, Cynthia Ozick writes with elusive, rich imagery and carefully crafted sentences and paragraphs. Much of her work reflects the importance of Jewish history, especially the Holocaust, as well as the Bible and Jewish literature, to the consciousness of both Jews and Christians.

Born in New York City, Ozick attended public school and Hunter College High School. Two powerful early influences affected the course of her future work: the anti-Semitism directed at her as a child and the inspiration of her uncle, Abraham Regelson, a well-known Hebrew poet who helped her to find her way as a writer.

Ozick graduated *cum laude* with a B.A. in English from New York University and then received her M.A. in English literature from Ohio State University. After her marriage in 1952, Ozick worked as a copywriter for Filene's department store and taught briefly at NYU. She worked for many years on two long novels, one of which, *Trust*, was published by the New American Library in 1966. While working on these long books, Ozick also spent time reading Jewish texts and Jewish philosophers. In 1966, she published "The Pagan Rabbi," one of her best-known short stories, in the *Hudson Review*.

The 1970s and 1980s brought Ozick international acclaim. Five of her short stories were chosen for the Best American Short Stories, and she received numerous awards and honorary degrees. Her works have been translated into eleven languages.

Ozick's works include poetry, translations of Yiddish poetry, fiction, and essays that often focus on feminist, political, and religious themes. Her first collection of short stories, *The Pagan Rabbi and Other Stories*, won the Jewish Book Council Award and B'nai B'rith Jewish Heritage Award in 1971. Many of her short stories, including "The Shawl," were first published in *The New Yorker*.

In an article in *Ms.*, Ozick writes: "I am, as a writer, whatever I wish to become. I can think myself into a male, or a female, or a stone, or a raindrop, or a Tibetan, or the spine of a cactus." She has made it clear she does not want to be termed a "woman writer." She believes the term is antifeminist, since it sets women apart; she does not want a world in which there are writers and then there are women writers. She is, however, very much a feminist writer. She is also a Jewish writer who believes that Judaism encompasses a humanistic view affirming the importance of both sexes.

"The Shawl" takes us into a German concentration camp. In a few brief but powerful pages, Ozick portrays the very different natures of her two main *characters and captures in one tragic moment some of the horrors of the Holocaust that haunt Jewish consciousness.*

THE SHAWL

Stella, cold, cold, the coldness of hell. How they walked on the roads together, Rosa with Magda curled up between sore breasts, Magda wound up in the shawl. Sometimes Stella carried Magda. But she was jealous of Magda. A thin girl of fourteen, too small, with thin breasts of her own, Stella wanted to be wrapped in a shawl, hidden away, asleep, rocked by the march, a baby, a round infant in arms. Magda took Rosa's nipple, and Rosa never stopped walking, a walking cradle. There was not enough milk; sometimes Magda sucked air; then she screamed. Stella was ravenous. Her knees were tumors on sticks, her elbows chicken bones.

Rosa did not feel hunger; she felt light, not like someone walking but like someone in a faint, in trance, arrested in a fit, someone who is already a floating angel, alert and seeing everything, but in the air, not there, not touching the road. As if teetering on the tips of her fingernails. She looked into Magda's face through a gap in the shawl: a squirrel in a nest, safe, no one could reach her inside the little house of the shawl's windings. The face, very round, a pocket mirror of a face: but it was not Rosa's bleak complexion, dark like cholera, it was another kind of face altogether, eyes blue as air, smooth feathers of hair nearly as yellow as the Star sewn into Rosa's coat. You could think she was one of *their* babies.

Rosa, floating, dreamed of giving Magda away in one of the villages. She could leave the line for a minute and push Magda into the hands of any woman on the side of the road. But if she moved out of line they might shoot. And even if she fled the line for half a second and pushed the shawl-bundle at a stranger, would the woman take it? She might be surprised, or afraid; she might drop the shawl, and Magda would fall out and strike her head and die. The little round head. Such a good child, she gave up screaming, and sucked now only for the taste of the drying nipple itself. The neat grip of the tiny gums. One mite of a tooth tip sticking up in the bottom gum, how shining, an elfin tombstone of white marble gleaming there. Without complaining, Magda relinquished Rosa's teats, first the left, then the right; both were cracked, not a sniff of milk. The duct-crevice extinct, a dead volcano, blind eye, chill hole, so Magda took the corner of the shawl and milked it instead. She sucked and sucked, flooding the threads with wetness. The shawl's good flavor, milk of linen.

It was a magic shawl, it could nourish an infant for three days and three nights. Magda did not die, she stayed alive, although very quiet. A peculiar smell, of cinnamon and almonds, lifted out of her mouth. She held her eyes open every moment, forgetting how to blink or nap, and Rosa and sometimes Stella studied their blueness. On the road they raised one burden of a leg after another and studied Magda's face. "Aryan," Stella said, in a voice grown as thin as a string; and Rosa thought how Stella gazed at Magda like a young cannibal. And the time that Stella said "Aryan," it sounded to Rosa as if Stella had really said "Let us devour her."

But Magda lived to walk. She lived that long, but she did not walk very well, partly because she was only fifteen months old, and partly because the spindles of her legs could not hold up her fat belly. It was fat with air, full and round. Rosa gave almost all her food to Magda, Stella gave nothing; Stella was ravenous, a growing child herself, but not growing much. Stella did not menstruate. Rosa did not menstruate. Rosa was ravenous, but also not; she learned from Magda how to drink the taste of a finger in one's mouth. They were in a place without pity, all pity was annihilated in Rosa, she looked at Stella's bones without pity. She was sure that Stella was waiting for Magda to die so she could put her teeth into the little thighs.

Rosa knew Magda was going to die very soon; she should have been dead already, but she had been buried away deep inside the magic shawl, mistaken there for the shivering mound of Rosa's breasts; Rosa clung to the shawl as if it covered only herself. No one took it away from her. Magda was mute. She never cried. Rosa hid her in the barracks, under the shawl, but she knew that one day someone would inform; or one day someone, not even Stella, would steal Magda to eat her. When Magda began to walk Rosa knew that Magda was going to die very soon, something would happen. She was afraid to fall asleep; she slept with the weight of her thigh on Magda's body; she was afraid she would smother Magda under her thigh. The weight of Rosa was becoming less and less; Rosa and Stella were slowly turning into air.

Magda was quiet, but her eyes were horribly alive, like blue tigers. She watched. Sometimes she laughed—it seemed a laugh, but how could it be? Magda had never seen anyone laugh. Still, Magda laughed at her shawl when the wind blew its corners, the bad wind with pieces of black in it, that made Stella's and Rosa's eyes tear. Magda's eyes were always clear and tearless. She watched like a tiger. She guarded her shawl. No one could touch it; only Rosa could touch it. Stella was not allowed. The shawl was Magda's own baby, her pet, her little sister. She tangled herself up in it and sucked on one of the corners when she wanted to be very still.

Then Stella took the shawl away and made Magda die.

Afterward Stella said: "I was cold."

And afterward she was always cold, always. The cold went into her heart: Rosa saw that Stella's heart was cold. Magda flopped onward with her little pencil legs scribbling this way and that, in search of the shawl; the pencils faltered at the barracks opening, where the light began. Rosa saw and pursued.

But already Magda was in the square outside the barracks, in the jolly light. It was the roll-call arena. Every morning Rosa had to conceal Magda under the shawl against a wall of the barracks and go out and stand in the arena with Stella and hundreds of others, sometimes for hours, and Magda, deserted, was quiet under the shawl, sucking on her corner. Every day Magda was silent, and so she did not die. Rosa saw that today Magda was going to die, and at the same time a fearful joy ran in Rosa's two palms, her fingers were on fire, she was astonished, febrile: Magda, in the sunlight, swaying on her pencil legs, was howling. Ever since the drying up of Rosa's nipples, ever since Magda's last scream on the road, Magda had been devoid of any syllable; Magda was a mute. Rosa believed that something had gone wrong with her vocal cords, with her windpipe, with the cave of her larynx; Magda was defective, without a voice; perhaps she was deaf; there might be something amiss with her intelligence; Magda was dumb. Even the laugh that came when the ash-stippled wind made a clown out of Magda's shawl was only the air-blown showing of her teeth. Even when the lice, head lice and body lice, crazed her so that she became as wild as one of the big rats that plundered the barracks at daybreak looking for carrion, she rubbed and scratched and kicked and bit and rolled without a whimper. But now Magda's mouth was spilling a long viscous rope of clamor.

"Maaaa—"

It was the first noise Magda had ever sent out from her throat since the drying up of Rosa's nipples.

"Maaaa . . . aaa!"

Again! Magda was wavering in the perilous sunlight of the arena, scribbling on such pitiful little bent shins. Rosa saw. She saw that Magda was grieving for the loss of her shawl, she saw that Magda was going to die. A tide of commands hammered in Rosa's nipples: Fetch, get, bring! But she did not know which to go after first, Magda or the shawl. If she jumped out into the arena to snatch Magda up, the howling would not stop, because Magda would still not have the shawl; but if she ran back into the barracks to find the shawl, and if she found it, and if she came after Magda holding it and shaking it, then she would get Magda back, Magda would put the shawl in her mouth and turn dumb again.

Rosa entered the dark. It was easy to discover the shawl. Stella was heaped under it, asleep in her thin bones. Rosa tore the shawl free and flew—she could fly, she was only air—into the arena. The sunheat murmured of another life, of butterflies in summer. The light was placid, mellow. On the other side of the steel fence, far away, there were green meadows speckled with dandelions and deep-colored violets; beyond them, even farther, innocent tiger lilies, tall, lifting their orange bonnets. In the barracks they spoke of "flowers," of "rain": excrement, thick turd-braids, and the slow stinking maroon waterfall that slunk down from the upper bunks, the stink mixed with a bitter fatty floating smoke that greased Rosa's skin. She stood for an instant at the margin of the arena. Sometimes the electricity inside the fence would seem to hum;

even Stella said it was only an imagining, but Rosa heard real sounds in the wire: grainy sad voices. The farther she was from the fence, the more clearly the voices crowded at her. The lamenting voices strummed so convincingly, so passionately, it was impossible to suspect them of being phantoms. The voices told her to hold up the shawl, high; the voices told her to shake it, to whip with it, to unfurl it like a flag. Rosa lifted, shook, whipped, unfurled. Far off, very far, Magda leaned across her air-fed belly, reaching out with the rods of her arms. She was high up, elevated, riding someone's shoulder. But the shoulder that carried Magda was not coming toward Rosa and the shawl, it was drifting away, the speck of Magda was moving more and more into the smoky distance. Above the shoulder a helmet glinted. The light tapped the helmet and sparkled it into a goblet. Below the helmet a black body like a domino and a pair of black boots hurled themselves in the direction of the electrified fence. The electric voices began to chatter wildly. "Maamaa, maaa-maaa," they all hummed together. How far Magda was from Rosa now, across the whole square, past a dozen barracks, all the way on the other side! She was no bigger than a moth.

All at once Magda was swimming through the air. The whole of Magda traveled through loftiness. She looked like a butterfly touching a silver vine. And the moment Magda's feathered round head and her pencil legs and balloonish belly and zigzag arms splashed against the fence, the steel voices went mad in their growling, urging Rosa to run and run to the spot where Magda had fallen from her flight against the electrified fence; but of course Rosa did not obey them. She only stood, because if she ran they would shoot, and if she tried to pick up the sticks of Magda's body they would shoot, and if she let the wolf's screech ascending now through the ladder of her skeleton break out, they would shoot; so she took Magda's shawl and filled her own mouth with it, stuffed it in and stuffed it in, until she was swallowing up the wolf's screech and tasting the cinnamon and almond depth of Magda's saliva; and Rosa drank Magda's shawl until it dried.

1980

PAULE MARSHALL
(1929–   )

Paule Marshall is both a forerunner of and a participant in the current renaissance in Black women's writing. Her books serve as links between Harlem Renaissance writers such as Zora Neale Hurston and Nella Larson and contemporary writers such as Alice Walker and Audre Lorde.

Marshall was raised in a Brooklyn brownstone by her West Indian parents, who had emigrated from Barbados during World War I. Her earliest memories are of doing homework with her sister at the kitchen table while her mother, aunts, and neighbors gossiped and discussed politics.

Marshall graduated Phi Beta Kappa from Brooklyn College (now City University of New York) in 1953 and attended Hunter College in 1955. She worked as a librarian in the New York public libraries and was a researcher and staff writer for Our World, *a Black magazine, in the mid-1950s. During this period she married, traveled throughout the Caribbean, and worked nights on a novel about her girlhood in Brooklyn's West Indian community.*

Critics praised this first novel, Brown Girl, Brownstones, *when it appeared in 1959. Marshall wrote her next book shortly after her son's birth, on the days when she could manage to pay a babysitter.* Soul Clap Hands and Sing, *a collection of novellas whose shared theme is aging, earned Marshall a Rosenthal Award from the National Institute of Arts and Letters. She followed this work with her second novel,* The Chosen Place, the Timeless People. *The chosen place of its title is a Caribbean island modeled after Barbados; the novel's heroine plays a major role in the island's social, political, and cultural issues.* Praisesong for the Widow *(1983), her third novel, received the Before Columbus Foundation American Book Award in 1984. In her fourth novel,* Daughters *(1991), Marshall continues her fictional exploration of women's lives.*

Although she prefers to devote her time to her writing, Marshall has taught and lectured on creative writing at numerous universities, including Yale, Oxford, Michigan State, Lake Forrest, Iowa, Columbia, and Cornell. She and her second husband divide their time between New York City and the West Indies.

Marshall received early storytelling lessons from her mother and her West Indian friends, who, Marshall has written, made language "an art form that—in keeping with the African tradition in which art and life are one—was an integral part of their lives." Marshall named these women "poets in the kitchen" and described their influence: "They taught me my first lessons in the narrative art. They trained my ear. They set a standard of excellence. This is why the best of my work must be attributed to them; it stands as testimony to the rich legacy of language and culture they so freely passed on to me in the wordshop of the kitchen."

The story we have chosen first appeared in Soul Clap Hands and Sing. *Marshall wrote "Brooklyn" to rid herself of the anger she felt after receiving a "B" in a class in which she deserved an "A." The story's source is its author's experience with sexual harassment, although, as Marshall has commented, there was no term for the experience during the 1950s when she was in college.*

BROOKLYN

A summer wind, soaring just before it died, blew the dusk and the first scattered lights of downtown Brooklyn against the shut windows of the classroom, but Professor Max Berman—B.A., 1919, M.A., 1921, New York; Docteur de l'Université, 1930, Paris—alone in the room, did not bother to open the windows to the cooling wind. The heat and airlessness of the room, the perspiration inching its way like an ant around his starched collar were discomforts he enjoyed, they obscured his larger discomfort: the anxiety which chafed his heart and tugged his left eyelid so that he seemed to be winking, roguishly, behind his glasses.

To steady his eye and ease his heart, to fill the time until his students arrived and his first class in years began, he reached for his cigarettes. As always he delayed lighting the cigarette so that his need for it would be greater and, thus, the relief and pleasure it would bring, fuller. For some time he fondled it, his fingers shaping soft, voluptuous gestures, his warped old man's hands looking strangely abandoned on the bare desk and limp as if the bones had been crushed, and so white—except for the tobacco burn on the index and third fingers—it seemed his blood no longer traveled that far.

He lit the cigarette finally and as the smoke swelled his lungs, his eyelid stilled and his lined face lifted, the plume of white hair wafting above his narrow brow; his body—short, blunt, the shoulders slightly bent as if in deference to his sixty-three years—settled back in the chair. Delicately Max Berman crossed his legs and, looking down, examined his shoes for dust. (The shoes were of a very soft, fawn-colored leather and somewhat foppishly pointed at the toe. They had been custom made in France and were his one last indulgence. He wore them in memory of his first wife, a French Jewess from Alsace-Lorraine whom he had met in Paris while lingering over his doctorate and married to avoid returning home. She had been gay, mindless and very excitable—but at night, she had also been capable of a profound stillness as she lay in bed waiting for him to turn to her, and this had always awed and delighted him. She had been a gift—and her death in a car accident had been a judgment on him for never having loved her, for never, indeed, having even allowed her to matter.) Fastidiously Max Berman unbuttoned his jacket and straightened his vest, which had a stain two decades old on the pocket. Through the smoke his veined eyes contemplated other, more pleasurable scenes. With his neatly shod foot swinging and his cigarette at a rakish tilt, he might have been an old *boulevardier* taking the sun and an absinthe before the afternoon's assignation.

A young face, the forehead shiny with earnestness, hung at the half-opened door. "Is this French Lit, fifty-four? Camus and Sartre?"

Max Berman winced at the rawness of the voice and the flat "a" in Sartre and said formally, "This is Modern French Literature, number fifty-four, yes, but there is some question as to whether we will take up Messieurs Camus and Sartre this session. They might prove hot work for a summer evening course. We will probably do Gide and Mauriac, who are considerably more temperate. But come in nonetheless. . . ."

He was the gallant, half rising to bow her to a seat. He knew that she would select the one in the front row directly opposite his desk. At the bell her pen would quiver above her blank notebook, ready to commit his first word—indeed, the clearing of his throat—to paper, and her thin buttocks would begin sidling toward the edge of her chair.

His eyelid twitched with solicitude. He wished that he could have drawn the lids over her fitful eyes and pressed a cool hand to her forehead. She reminded him of what he had been several lifetimes ago: a boy with a pale, plump face and harried eyes, running from the occasional taunts at his yarmulke along the shrill streets of Brownsville in Brooklyn, impeded by the heavy satchel of books which he always carried as proof of his scholarship. He had been proud of his brilliance at school and the Yeshiva, but at the same time he had been secretly troubled by it and resentful, for he could never believe that he had come by it naturally or that it belonged to him alone. Rather, it was like a heavy medal his father had hung around his neck—the chain bruising his flesh—and constantly exhorted him to wear proudly and use well.

The girl gave him an eager and ingratiating smile and he looked away. During his thirty years of teaching, a face similar to hers had crowded his vision whenever he had looked up from a desk. Perhaps it was fitting, he thought, and lighted another cigarette from the first, that she should be present as he tried again at life, unaware that behind his rimless glasses and within his ancient suit, he had been gutted.

He thought of those who had taken the last of his substance and smiled tolerantly. "The boys of summer," he called them, his inquisitors, who had flailed him with a single question: "Are you now or have you ever been a member of the Communist party?" Max Berman had never taken their question seriously—perhaps because he had never taken his membership in the party seriously—and he had refused to answer. What had disturbed him, though, even when the investigation was over, was the feeling that he had really been under investigation for some other offense which did matter and of which he was guilty; that behind their accusations and charges had lurked another which had not been political but personal. For had he been disloyal to the government? His denial was a short, hawking laugh. Simply, he had never ceased being religious. When his father's God had become useless and even a little embarrassing, he had sought others: his work for a time, then the party. But he had been middle-aged when he joined and his faith, which had been so full as a boy, had grown thin. He had come, by then, to distrust all pieties, so that when the purges in Russia during the thirties confirmed his distrust, he had withdrawn into a modest cynicism.

But he had been made to answer for that error. Ten years later his inquisitors had flushed him out from the small community college in upstate New York where he had taught his classes from the same neat pack of notes each semester and had led him bound by subpoena to New York and bandied his name at the hearings until he had been dismissed from his job.

He remembered looking back at the pyres of burning autumn leaves on the campus his last day and feeling that another lifetime had ended—for he had always thought of his life as divided into many small lives, each with its own beginning and end. Like a hired mute, he had been present at each dying and kept the wake and wept professionally as the bier was lowered into the ground. Because of this feeling, he told himself that his final death would be anticlimactic.

After his dismissal he had continued living in the small house he had built near the college, alone except for an occasional visit from a colleague, idle but for some tutoring in French, content with the income he received from the property his parents had left him in Brooklyn—until the visits and tutoring had tapered off and a silence had begun to choke the house, like weeds springing up around a deserted place. He had begun to wonder then if he were still alive. He would wake at night from the recurrent dream of the hearings, where he was being accused of an unstated crime, to listen for his heart, his hand fumbling among the bedclothes to press the place. During the day he would pass repeatedly in front of the mirror with the pretext that he might have forgotten to shave that morning or that something had blown into his eye. Above all, he had begun to think of his inquisitors with affection and to long for the sound of their voices. They, at least, had assured him of being alive.

As if seeking them out, he had returned to Brooklyn and to the house in Brownsville where he had lived as a boy and had boldly applied for a teaching post without mentioning the investigation. He had finally been offered the class which would begin in five minutes. It wasn't much: a six-week course in the summer evening session of a college without a rating, where classes were held in a converted factory building, a college whose campus took in the bargain department stores, the five-and-dime emporiums and neon-spangled movie houses of downtown Brooklyn.

Through the smoke from his cigarette, Max Berman's eyes—a waning blue that never seemed to focus on any one thing—drifted over the students who had gathered meanwhile. Imbuing them with his own disinterest, he believed that even before the class began, most of them were longing for its end and already anticipating the soft drinks at the soda fountain downstairs and the synthetic dramas at the nearby movie.

They made him sad. He would have liked to lead them like a Pied Piper back to the safety of their childhoods—all of them: the loud girl with the formidable calves of an athlete who reminded him, uncomfortably, of his second wife (a party member who was always shouting political heresy from some picket line and who had promptly divorced him upon discovering his irreverence); the two sallow-faced young men leaning out the window as if searching for the wind that had died; the slender young woman with crimped black hair who sat very still and apart from the others, her face turned toward the night sky as if to a friend.

Her loneliness interested him. He sensed its depth and his eye paused. He saw then that she was a Negro, a very pale mulatto with skin the color of clear, polished amber and a thin, mild face. She was somewhat older than the others in the room—a schoolteacher from the South, probably, who came north each summer to take courses toward a graduate degree. He felt a fleeting discomfort and irritation: discomfort at the thought that although he had been sinned against as a Jew he still shared in the sin against her and suffered from the same vague guilt, irritation that she recalled his own humiliations: the large ones, such as the fact that despite his brilliance he had been unable to get into a medical school as a young man because of the quota on Jews (not that he had wanted to be a doctor; that had been his father's wish) and had changed his studies from medicine to French; the small ones which had worn him thin: an eye widening imperceptibly as he gave his name, the savage glance which sought the Jewishness in his nose, his chin, in the set of his shoulders, the jokes snuffed into silence at his appearance. . . .

Tired suddenly, his eyelid pulsing, he turned and stared out the window at the gaudy constellation of neon lights. He longed for a drink, a quiet place and then sleep. And to bear him gently into sleep, to stay the terror which bound his heart then reminding him of those oleographs of Christ with the thorns binding his exposed heart—fat drops of blood from one so bloodless—to usher him into sleep, some pleasantly erotic image: a nude in a boudoir scattered with her frilly garments and warmed by her frivolous laugh, with the sun like a voyeur at the half-closed shutters. But this time instead of the usual Rubens nude with thighs like twin portals and a belly like a huge alabaster bowl into which he poured himself, he chose Gauguin's Aita Parari, her languorous form in the straight back chair, her dark, sloping breasts, her eyes like the sun under shadow.

With the image still on his inner eye, he turned to the Negro girl and appraised her through a blind of cigarette smoke. She was still gazing out at the night sky and something about her fixed stare, her hands stiffly arranged in her lap, the nerve fluttering within the curve of her throat, betrayed a vein of tension within the rock of her calm. It was as if she had fled long ago to a remote region within herself, taking with her all that was most valuable and most vulnerable about herself.

She stirred finally, her slight breasts lifting beneath her flowered summer dress as she breathed deeply—and Max Berman thought again of Gauguin's girl with the dark, sloping breasts. What would this girl with the amber-colored skin be like on a couch in a sunlit room, nude in a straight-back chair? And as the question echoed along each nerve and stilled his breathing, it seemed suddenly that life, which had scorned him for so long, held out her hand again—but still a little beyond his reach. Only the girl, he sensed, could bring him close enough to touch it. She alone was the bridge. So that even while he repeated to himself that he was being presumptuous (for she would surely refuse him) and ridiculous (for even if she did not, what could he do—his performance would be a mere scramble and twitch), he vowed at the same time to have her. The challenge eased the tightness around his heart suddenly; it soothed the damaged muscle of his eye and as the bell rang he rose and said briskly, "Ladies and gentlemen, may I have your attention, please. My name is Max Berman. The course is Modern French Literature, number fifty-four. May I suggest that you check your program cards to see whether you are in the right place at the right time."

. . .

Her essay on Gide's *The Immoralist* lay on his desk and the note from the administration informing him, first, that his past political activities had been brought to their attention and then dismissing him at the end of the session weighed the inside pocket of his jacket. The two, her paper and the note, were linked in his mind. Her paper reminded him that the vow he had taken was still an empty one, for the term was half over and he had never once spoken to her (as if she understood his intention she was always late and disappeared as soon as the closing bell rang, leaving him trapped in a clamorous circle of students around his desk), while the note which wrecked his small attempt to start anew suddenly made that vow more urgent. It gave him the edge of desperation he needed to act finally. So that as soon as the bell rang, he returned all the papers but hers, announced that all questions would have to wait until their next meeting and, waving off the students from his desk, called above their protests, "Miss Williams, if you have a moment, I'd like to speak with you briefly about your paper."

She approached his desk like a child who had been cautioned not to talk to strangers, her fingers touching the backs of the chair as if for support, her gaze following the departing students as though she longed to accompany them.

Her slight apprehensiveness pleased him. It suggested a submissiveness which gave him, as he rose uncertainly, a feeling of certainty and command. Her hesitancy was somehow in keeping with the color of her skin. She seemed to bring not only herself but the host of black women whose bodies had been despoiled to make her. He would not only possess her but them also, he thought (not really thought, for he scarcely allowed these thoughts to form before he snuffed them out). Through their collective suffering, which she contained, his own personal suffering would be eased; he would be pardoned for whatever sin it was he had committed against life.

"I hope you weren't unduly alarmed when I didn't return your paper along with the others," he said, and had to look up as she reached the desk. She was taller close up and her eyes, which he had thought were black, were a strong, flecked brown with very small pupils which seemed to shrink now from the sight of him. "But I found it so interesting I wanted to give it to you privately."

"I didn't know what to think," she said, and her voice—he heard it for the first time for she never recited or answered in class—was low, cautious, Southern.

"It was, to say the least, refreshing. It not only showed some original and mature thinking on your part, but it also proved that you've been listening in class—and after twenty-five years and more of teaching it's encouraging to find that some students do listen. If you have a little time I'd like to tell you, more specifically, what I liked about it. . . ."

Talking easily, reassuring her with his professional tone and a deft gesture with his cigarette, he led her from the room as the next class filed in, his hand cupped at her elbow but not touching it, his manner urbane, courtly, kind. They paused on the landing at the end of the long corridor with the stairs piled in steel tiers above and plunging below them. An intimate silence swept up the stairwell in a warm gust and Max Berman said, "I'm curious. Why did you choose *The Immoralist?*"

She started suspiciously, afraid, it seemed, that her answer might expose and endanger the self she guarded so closely within.

"Well," she said finally, her glance reaching down the stairs to the door marked EXIT at the bottom, "when you said we could use anything by Gide I decided on *The Immoralist,* since it was the first book I read in the original French when I was in undergraduate school. I didn't understand it then because my French was so weak, I guess, but I always thought about it afterward for some odd reason. I was shocked by what I did understand, of course, but something else about it appealed to me, so when you made the assignment I thought I'd try reading it again. I understood it a little better this time. At least I think so. . . ."

"Your paper proves you did."

She smiled absently, intent on some other thought. Then she said cautiously, but with unexpected force, "You see, to me, the book seems to say that the only way you begin to know what you are and how much you are capable of is by daring to try something, by doing something which tests you. . . ."

"Something bold," he said.

"Yes."

"Even sinful."

She paused, questioning this, and then said reluctantly, "Yes, perhaps even sinful."

"The salutary effects of sin, you might say." He gave the little bow.

But she had not heard this; her mind had already leaped ahead. "The only trouble, at least with the character in Gide's book, is that what he finds out about himself is so terrible. He is so unhappy. . . ."

"But at least he knows, poor sinner." And his playful tone went unnoticed.

"Yes," she said with the same startling forcefulness. "And another thing, in finding out what he is, he destroys his wife. It was as if she had to die in order for a person to live and know himself. Perhaps in order for a person to live and know himself somebody else must die. Maybe there's always a balancing out. . . . In a way"—and he had to lean close now to hear her—"I believe this."

Max Berman edged back as he glimpsed something move within her abstracted gaze. It was like a strong and restless seed that had taken root in the darkness there and was straining now toward the light. He had not expected so subtle and complex a force beneath her mild exterior and he found it disturbing and dangerous, but fascinating.

"Well, it's a most interesting interpretation," he said. "I don't know if M. Gide would have agreed, but then he's not around to give his opinion. Tell me, where did you do your undergraduate work?"

"At Howard University."

"And you majored in French?"

"Yes."

"Why, if I may ask?" he said gently.

"Well, my mother was from New Orleans and could still speak a little Creole and I got interested in learning how to speak French through her, I guess. I teach it now at a junior high school in Richmond. Only the beginner courses because I don't have my master's. You know, *je vais, tu vas, il va* and *Frere Jacques*. It's not very inspiring."

"You should do something about that then, my dear Miss Williams. Perhaps it's time for you, like our friend in Gide, to try something new and bold."

"I know," she said, and her pale hand sketched a vague, despairing gesture. "I thought maybe if I got my master's . . . that's why I decided to come north this summer and start taking some courses. . . ."

Max Berman quickly lighted a cigarette to still the flurry inside him, for the moment he had been awaiting had come. He flicked her paper, which he still held. "Well, you've got the makings of a master's thesis right here. If you like I will suggest some ways for you to expand it sometime. A few pointers from an old pro might help."

He had to turn from her astonished and grateful smile—it was like a child's. He said carefully, "The only problem will be to find a place where we can talk quietly. Regrettably, I don't rate an office. . . ."

"Perhaps we could use one of the empty classrooms," she said.

"That would be much too dismal a setting for a pleasant discussion."

He watched the disappointment wilt her smile and when he spoke he made certain that the same disappointment weighed his voice. "Another difficulty is that the term's half over, which gives us little or no time. But let's not give up. Perhaps we can arrange to meet and talk over a weekend. The only hitch there is that I spend weekends at my place in the country. Of course you're perfectly welcome to come up there. It's only about seventy miles from New York, in the heart of what's very appropriately called the Borsch Circuit, even though, thank God, my place is a good distance from the borsch. That is, it's very quiet and there's never anybody around except with my permission."

She did not move, yet she seemed to start; she made no sound, yet he thought he heard a bewildered cry. And then she did a strange thing, standing there with the breath sucked into the hollow of her throat and her smile, that had opened to him with such trust, dying—her eyes, her hands faltering up begged him to declare himself.

"There's a lake near the house," he said, "so that when you get tired of talking—or better, listening to me talk—you can take a swim, if you like. I would very much enjoy that sight." And as the nerve tugged at his eyelid, he seemed to wink behind his rimless glasses.

Her sudden, blind step back was like a man groping his way through a strange room in the dark, and instinctively Max Berman reached out to break her fall. Her arms, bare to the shoulder because of the heat (he knew the feel of her skin without even touching it—it would be like a rich, fine-textured cloth which would soothe and hide him in its amber warmth), struck out once to drive him off and then fell limp at her side, and her eyes became vivid and convulsive in her numbed face. She strained toward the stairs and the exit door at the bottom, but she could not move. Nor could she speak. She did not even cry. Her eyes remained dry and dull with disbelief. Only her shoulders trembled as though she was silently weeping inside.

It was as though she had never learned the forms and expressions of anger. The outrage of a lifetime, of her history, was trapped inside her. And she stared at Max Berman with this mute, paralyzing rage. Not really at him but to his side, as if she caught sight of others behind him. And remembering how he had imagined a column of dark women trailing her to his desk, he sensed that she glimpsed a legion of old men with sere flesh and lonely eyes flanking him: "old lechers with a love on every wind. . . ."

"I'm sorry, Miss Williams," he said, and would have welcomed her insults, for he would have been able, at least, to distill from them some passion and a kind of intimacy. It would have been, in a way, like touching her. "It was only that you are a very attractive young woman and although I'm no longer young"—and he gave the tragic little laugh which sought to dismiss that fact—"I can still appreciate and even desire an attractive woman. But I was wrong. . . ." His self disgust, overwhelming him finally, choked off his voice.

"And so very crude. Forgive me. I can offer no excuse for my behavior other than my approaching senility."

He could not even manage the little marionette bow this time. Quickly he shoved the paper on Gide into her lifeless hand, but it fell, the pages separating, and as he hurried past her downstairs and out the door, he heard the pages scattering like dead leaves on the steps.

. . .

She remained away until the night of the final examination, which was also the last meeting of the class. By that time Max Berman, believing that she would not return, had almost succeeded in forgetting her. He was no longer even certain of how she looked, for her face had been absorbed into the single, blurred, featureless face of all the women who had ever refused him. So that she startled him as much as a stranger would have when he entered the room that night and found her alone amid a maze of empty chairs, her face turned toward the window as on the first night and her hands serene in her lap. She turned at his footstep and it was as if she had also forgotten all that had passed between them. She waited until he said, "I'm glad you decided to take the examination. I'm sure you won't have any difficulty with it"; then she gave him a nod that was somehow reminiscent of his little bow and turned again to the window.

He was relieved yet puzzled by her composure. It was as if during her three-week absence she had waged and won a decisive contest with herself and was ready now to act. He was wary suddenly and all during the examination he tried to discover what lay behind her strange calm, studying her bent head amid the shifting heads of the other students, her slim hand guiding the pen across the page, her legs—the long bone visible, it seemed, beneath the flesh. Desire flared and quickly died.

"Excuse me, Professor Berman, will you take up Camus and Sartre next semester, maybe?" The girl who sat in front of his desk was standing over him with her earnest smile and finished examination folder.

"That might prove somewhat difficult, since I won't be here."

"No more?"

"No."

"I mean, not even next summer?"

"I doubt it."

"Gee, I'm sorry. I mean, I enjoyed the course and everything."

He bowed his thanks and held his head down until she left. Her compliment, so piteous somehow, brought on the despair he had forced to the dim rear of his mind. He could no longer flee the thought of the exile awaiting him when the class tonight ended. He could either remain in the house in Brooklyn, where the memory of his father's face above the radiance of the Sabbath candles haunted him from the shadows, reminding him of the certainty he had lost and never found again, where the mirrors in his father's room were still shrouded with sheets, as on the day he lay dying and moaning into his beard that his only son was a bad Jew; or he could return to the house in the country, to the silence shrill with loneliness.

The cigarette he was smoking burned his fingers, rousing him, and he saw over the pile of examination folders on his desk that the room was empty except for the Negro girl. She had finished—her pen lay aslant the closed folder on her desk—but she had remained in her seat and she was smiling across the room at him—a set, artificial smile that was both cold and threatening. It utterly denuded him and he was wildly angry suddenly that she had seen him give way to despair; he wanted to remind her (he could not stay the thought; it attacked him like an assailant from a dark turn in his mind) that she was only black after all. . . . His head dropped and he almost wept with shame.

The girl stiffened as if she had seen the thought and then the tiny muscles around her mouth quickly arranged the bland smile. She came up to his desk, placed her folder on top of the others and said pleasantly, her eyes like dark, shattered glass that spared Max Berman his reflection, "I've changed my mind. I think I'd like to spend a day at your place in the country if your invitation still holds."

He thought of refusing her, for her voice held neither promise nor passion, but he could not. Her presence, even if it was only for a day, would make his return easier. And there was still the possibility of passion despite her cold manner and the deliberate smile. He thought of how long it had been since he had had someone, of how badly he needed the sleep which followed love and of awakening certain, for the first time in years, of his existence.

"Of course the invitation still holds. I'm driving up tonight."

"I won't be able to come until Sunday," she said firmly. "Is there a train then?"

"Yes, in the morning," he said, and gave her the schedule.

"You'll meet me at the station?"

"Of course. You can't miss my car. It's a very shabby but venerable Chevy."

She smiled stiffy and left, her heels awakening the silence of the empty corridor, the sound reaching back to tap like a warning finger on Max Berman's temple.

. . .

The pale sunlight slanting through the windshield lay like a cat on his knees, and the motor of his old Chevy, turning softly under him, could have been the humming of its heart. A little distance from the car a log-cabin station house—the logs blackened by the seasons—stood alone against the hills, and the hills, in turn, lifted softly, still green although the summer was ending, into the vague autumn sky.

The morning mist and pale sun, the green that was still somehow new, made it seem that the season was stirring into life even as it died, and this contradiction pained Max Berman at the same time that it pleased him. For it was his own contradiction after all: his desires which remained those of a young man even as he was dying.

He had been parked for some time in the deserted station, yet his hands were still tensed on the steering wheel and his foot hovered near the accelerator. As soon as he had arrived in the station he had wanted to leave. But like the girl that night on the landing, he was too stiff with tension to move. He could only wait, his eyelid twitching with foreboding, regret, curiosity and hope.

Finally and with no warning the train charged through the fiery green, setting off a tremor underground. Max Berman imagined the girl seated at a window in the train, her hands arranged quietly in her lap and her gaze scanning the hills that were so familiar to him, and yet he could not believe that she was really there. Perhaps her plan had been to disappoint him. She might be in New York or on her way back to Richmond now, laughing at the trick she had played on him. He was convinced of this suddenly, so that even when he saw her walking toward him through the blown steam from under the train, he told himself that she was a mirage created by the steam. Only when she sat beside him in the car, bringing with her, it seemed, an essence she had distilled from the morning air and rubbed into her skin, was he certain of her reality.

"I brought my bathing suit but it's much too cold to swim," she said and gave him the deliberate smile.

He did not see it; he only heard her voice, its warm Southern lilt in the chill, its intimacy in the closed car—and an excitement swept him, cold first and then hot, as if the sun had burst in his blood.

"It's the morning air," he said. "By noon it should be like summer again."

"Is that a promise?"

"Yes."

By noon the cold morning mist had lifted above the hills and below, in the lake valley, the sunlight was a sheer gold net spread out on the grass as if to dry, draped on the trees and flung, glinting, over the lake. Max Berman felt it brush his shoulders gently as he sat by the lake waiting for the girl, who had gone up to the house to change into her swimsuit.

He had spent the morning showing her the fields and small wood near his house. During the long walk he had been careful to keep a little apart from her. He would extend a hand as they climbed a rise or when she stepped uncertainly over a rock, but he would not really touch her. He was afraid that at his touch, no matter how slight and casual, her scream would spiral into the morning calm, or worse, his touch would unleash the threatening thing he sensed behind her even smile.

He had talked of her paper and she had listened politely and occasionally even asked a question or made a comment. But all the while detached, distant, drawn within herself as she had been that first night in the classroom. And then halfway down a slope she had paused and, pointing to the canvas tops of her white sneakers, which had become wet and dark from the dew secreted in the grass, she had laughed. The sound, coming so abruptly in the midst of her tense quiet, joined her, it seemed, to the wood and wide fields, to the hills; she shared their simplicity and held within her the same strong current of life. Max Berman had felt privileged suddenly, and humble. He had stopped questioning her smile. He had told himself then that it would not matter even if she stopped and picking up a rock bludgeoned him from behind.

"There's a lake near my home, but it's not like this," the girl said, coming up behind him. "Yours is so dark and serious-looking."

He nodded and followed her gaze out to the lake, where the ripples were long, smooth welts raised by the wind, and across to the other bank, where a group of birches stepped delicately down to the lake and bending over touched the water with their branches as if testing it before they plunged.

The girl came and stood beside him now—and she was like a pale gold naiad, the spirit of the lake, her eyes reflecting its somber autumnal tone and her body as supple as the birches. She walked slowly into the water, unaware, it seemed, of the sudden passion in his gaze, or perhaps uncaring; and as she walked she held out her arms in what seemed a gesture of invocation (and Max Berman remembered his father with the fringed shawl draped on his outstretched arms as he invoked their God each Sabbath with the same gesture); her head was bent as if she listened for a voice beneath the water's murmurous surface. When the ground gave way she still seemed to be walking and listening, her arms outstretched. The water reached her waist, her small breasts, her shoulders. She lifted her head once, breathed deeply and disappeared.

She stayed down for a long time and when her white cap finally broke the water some distance out, Max Berman felt strangely stranded and deprived. He understood suddenly the profound cleavage between them and the absurdity of his hope. The water between them became the years which separated them. Her white cap was the sign of her purity, while the silt darkening the lake was the flotsam of his failures. Above all, their color—her arms a pale, flashing gold in the sunlit water and his bled white and flaccid with the veins like angry blue penciling—marked the final barrier.

He was sad as they climbed toward the house late that afternoon and troubled. A crow cawed derisively in the bracken, heralding the dusk which would not only end their strange day but would also, he felt, unveil her smile, so that he would learn the reason for her coming. And because he was sad, he said wryly, "I think I should tell you that you've been spending the day with something of an outcast."

"Oh," she said and waited.

He told her of the dismissal, punctuating his words with the little hoarse, deprecating laugh and waving aside the pain with his cigarette. She listened, polite but neutral, and because she remained unmoved, he wanted to confess all the more. So that during dinner and afterward when they sat outside on the porch, he told her of the investigation.

"It was very funny once you saw it from the proper perspective, which I did, of course," he said. "I mean here they were accusing me of crimes I couldn't remember committing and asking me for the names of people with whom I had never associated. It was pure farce. But I made a mistake. I should have done something dramatic or something just as farcical. Bared my breast in the public market place or written a tome on my apostasy, naming names. It would have been a far different story then. Instead of my present ignominy I would have been offered a chairmanship at Yale. . . . No? Well, Brandeis then. I would have been draped in honorary degrees. . . ."

"Well, why didn't you confess?" she said impatiently.

"I've often asked myself the same interesting question, but I haven't come up with a satisfactory answer yet. I suspect, though, that I said nothing because none of it really mattered that much."

"What did matter?" she asked sharply.

He sat back, waiting for the witty answer, but none came, because just then the frame upon which his organs were strung seemed to snap and he felt his heart, his lungs, his vital parts fall in a heap within him. Her question had dealt the severing blow, for it was the same question he understood suddenly that the vague forms in his dream asked repeatedly. It had been the plaintive undercurrent to his father's dying moan, the real accusation behind the charges of his inquisitors at the hearing.

For what had mattered? He gazed through his sudden shock at the night squatting on the porch steps, at the hills asleep like gentle beasts in the darkness, at the black screen of the sky where the events of his life passed in a mute, accusing review—and he saw nothing there to which he had given himself or in which he had truly believed since the belief and dedication of his boyhood.

"Did you hear my question?" she asked, and he was glad that he sat within the shadows clinging to the porch screen and could not be seen.

"Yes, I did," he said faintly, and his eyelid twitched. "But I'm afraid it's another one of those I can't answer satisfactorily." And then he struggled for the old flippancy. "You make an excellent examiner, you know. Far better than my inquisitors."

"What will you do now?" Her voice and cold smile did not spare him.

He shrugged and the motion, a slow, eloquent lifting of the shoulders, brought with it suddenly the weight and memory of his boyhood. It was the familiar gesture of the women hawkers in Belmont Market, of the men standing outside the temple on Saturday mornings, each of them reflecting his image of God in their forbidding black coats and with the black, tumbling beards in which he had always imagined he could hide as in a forest. All this had mattered, he called loudly to himself, and said aloud to the girl, "Let me see if I can answer this last one at least. What *will* I do?" He paused and swung his leg so that his foot in the fastidious French shoe caught the light from the house. "Grow flowers and write my memoirs. How's that? That would be the proper way for a gentleman and scholar to retire. Or hire one of those hefty housekeepers who will bully me and when I die in my sleep draw the sheet over my face and call my lawyer. That's somewhat European, but how's that?"

When she said nothing for a long time, he added more soberly, "But that's not a fair question for me any more. I leave all such considerations to the young. To you, for that matter. What will you do, my dear Miss Williams?"

It was as if she had been expecting the question and had been readying her answer all the time that he had been talking. She leaned forward eagerly and with her face and part of her body fully in the light, she said, "I will do something. I don't know what yet, but something."

Max Berman started back a little. The answer was so unlike her vague, resigned "I know" on the landing that night when he had admonished her to try something new.

He edged back into the darkness and she leaned further into the light, her eyes overwhelming her face and her mouth set in a thin, determined line. "I will do something," she said, bearing down on each word, "because for the first time in my life I feel almost brave."

He glimpsed this new bravery behind her hard gaze and sensed something vital and purposeful, precious, which she had found and guarded like a prize within her center. He wanted it. He would have liked to snatch it and run like a thief. He no longer desired her but it, and starting forward with a sudden envious cry, he caught her arm and drew her close, seeking it.

But he could not get to it. Although she did not pull away her arm, although she made no protest as his face wavered close to hers, he did not really touch her. She held herself and her prize out of his desperate reach and her smile was a knife she pressed to his throat. He saw himself for what he was in her clear, cold gaze: an old man with skin the color and texture of dough that had been kneaded by the years into tragic folds, with faded eyes adrift behind a pair of rimless glasses and the roughened flesh at his throat like a bird's wattles. And as the disgust which he read in her eyes swept him, his hand dropped from her arm. He started to murmur, "Forgive me . . ." when suddenly she caught hold of his wrist, pulling him close again, and he felt the strength which had borne her swiftly through the water earlier hold him now as she said quietly and without passion, "And do you know why, Dr. Berman, I feel almost brave today? Because ever since I can remember my parents were always telling me, 'Stay away from white folks. Just leave them alone. You mind your business and they'll mind theirs. Don't go near them.' And they made sure I didn't. My father, who was the principal of a colored grade school in Richmond, used to drive me to and from school every day. When I needed something from downtown my mother would take me and if the white saleslady asked me anything she would answer. . . .

"And my parents were also always telling me, 'Stay away from niggers,' and that meant anybody darker than we were." She held out her arm in the light and Max Berman saw the skin almost as white as his but for the subtle amber shading. Staring at the arm she said tragically, "I was so confused I never really went near anybody. Even when I went away to college I kept to myself. I didn't marry the man I wanted to because he was dark and I knew my parents would disapprove. . . ." She paused, her wistful gaze searching the darkness for the face of the man she had refused, it seemed, and not finding it she went on sadly. "So after graduation I returned home and started teaching and I was just as confused and frightened and ashamed as always. When my parents died I went on the same way. And I would have gone on like that the rest of my life if it hadn't been for you, Dr. Berman"—and the sarcasm leaped behind her cold smile. "In a way you did me a favor. You let me know how you and most of the people like you—see me."

"My dear Miss Williams, I assure you I was not attracted to you because you were colored. . . ." And he broke off, remembering just how acutely aware of her color he had been.

"I'm not interested in your reasons!" she said brutally. "What matters is what it meant to me. I thought about this these last three weeks and about my parents, how wrong they had been, how frightened, and the terrible thing they had done to me . . . and I wasn't confused any longer." Her head lifted, tremulous with her new assurance. "I can do something now! I can begin," she said with her head poised. "Look how I came all the way up here to tell you this to your face. Because how could you harm me? You're so old you're like a cup I could break in my hand." And her hand tightened on his wrist, wrenching the last of his frail life from him, it seemed. Through the quick pain he remembered her saying on the landing that night: "Maybe in order for a person to live someone else must die" and her quiet "I believe this" then. Now her sudden laugh, an infinitely cruel sound in the warm night, confirmed her belief.

Suddenly she was the one who seemed old, indeed ageless. Her touch became mortal and Max Berman saw the darkness that would end his life gathered in her eyes. But even as he sprang back, jerking his arm away, a part of him rushed forward to embrace that darkness, and his cry, wounding the night, held both ecstasy and terror.

"That's all I came for," she said, rising. "You can drive me to the station now."

They drove to the station in silence. Then, just as the girl started from the car, she turned with an ironic, pitiless smile and said, "You know, it's been a nice day, all things considered. It really turned summer again as you said it would. And even though your lake isn't anything like the one near my home, it's almost as nice."

Max Berman bowed to her for the last time, accepting with that gesture his responsibility for her rage, which went deeper than his, and for her anger, which would spur her finally to live. And not only for her, but for all those at last whom he had wronged through his indifference: his father lying in the room of shrouded mirrors, the wives he had never loved, his work which he had never believed in enough and lastly (even though he knew it was too late and he would not be spared), himself.

Too weary to move, he watched the girl cross to the train which would bear her south, her head lifted as though she carried life as lightly there as if it were a hat made of tulle. When the train departed his numbed eyes followed it until its rear light was like a single firefly in the immense night or the last flickering of his life. Then he drove back through the darkness.

1961

ADRIENNE RICH
(1929–   )

Born to Jewish parents in Baltimore, Adrienne Rich graduated Phi Beta Kappa from Radcliffe College in 1951. She published her first book of poems, A Change of World, *that same year and received the Yale Younger Poets Award for her work. With her second volume of poetry,* The Diamond Cutters, *she established herself as a powerful poet, with an elegant style and precise control of language.*

From her marriage, which lasted from 1953 to 1970, Rich concluded that marriage and motherhood force middle-class women into painfully restrictive roles established by a patriarchal society. She described these experiences later in Snapshots of a Daughter-in-Law *and* Of Woman Born: Motherhood as Experience and Institution.

In the 1960s, Rich began to write forcibly about political and feminist issues. Her essays and speeches often focus on the waste of women's lives and the need for women to acquire power and to effect real changes in society. She also writes about the relation of the individual to society and about themes such as war, violence, and pacifism.

In 1970, Rich gave up her professorship at Rutgers University and moved to Massachusetts, where she began writing about what she terms in "Compulsory Heterosexuality and Lesbian Experience" the lesbian continuum*—the full range of "woman-identified experience." Rich believes this experience to be a source of creativity, energy, and power.*

Rich is a prolific writer. Among her collections of poetry are Necessities of Life, Diving into the Wreck, The Dream of a Common Language, *and* A Wild Patience. *Her prose collections, which include* On Lies, Secrets, and Silence: Selected Prose *and* Blood, Bread and Poetry: Selected Prose, *contain articles on feminism, gay and lesbian rights, racism, and the role of the artist. Rich has taught at Columbia University, Brandeis University, Swarthmore College, and a number of other colleges and universities. Currently she lives with the novelist Michelle Cliff and teaches at Stanford University.*

In "Compulsory Heterosexuality and Lesbian Existence," Rich examines how and why lesbian relationships have often been invalidated, even by feminists, and why even feminist scholarship frequently neglects lesbian texts. Male power, she insists, has forced women into heterosexual existence through a variety of methods, all of which curtail the energy that comes from identification between women.

COMPULSORY HETEROSEXUALITY AND LESBIAN EXISTENCE

FOREWORD

I want to say a little about the way "Compulsory Heterosexuality" was originally conceived and the context in which we are now living. It was written in part to challenge the erasure of lesbian existence from so much of scholarly feminist literature, an erasure which I felt (and feel) to be not just anti-lesbian, but anti-feminist in its consequences, and to distort the experience of heterosexual women as well. It was not written to widen divisions but to encourage heterosexual feminists to examine heterosexuality as a political institution which disempowers women—and to change it. I also hoped that other lesbians would feel the depth and breadth of woman identification and woman bonding that has run like a continuous though stifled theme through the heterosexual experience, and that this would become increasingly a politically activating impulse, not simply a validation of personal lives. I wanted the essay to suggest new kinds of criticism, to incite new questions in classrooms and academic journals, and to sketch, at least, some bridge over the gap between *lesbian* and *feminist*. I wanted, at the very least, for feminists to find it less possible to read, write, or teach from a perspective of unexamined heterocentricity.

Within the three years since I wrote "Compulsory Heterosexuality"—with this energy of hope and desire—the pressures to conform in a society increasingly conservative in mood have become more intense. The New Right's messages to women have been, precisely, that we are the emotional and sexual property of men, and that the autonomy and equality of women threaten family, religion, and state. The institutions by which women have traditionally been controlled—patriarchal motherhood, economic exploitation, the nuclear family, compulsory heterosexuality—are being strengthened by legislation, religious fiat, media imagery, and efforts at censorship. In a worsening economy, the single mother trying to support her children confronts the feminization of poverty which Joyce Miller of the National Coalition of Labor Union Women has named one of the major issues of the 1980s. The lesbian, unless in disguise, faces discrimination in hiring and harassment and violence in the street. Even within feminist-inspired institutions such as battered-women's shelters and Women's Studies programs, open lesbians are fired and others warned to stay in the closet. The retreat into sameness—assimilation for those who can manage it—is the most passive and debilitating of responses to political repression, economic insecurity, and a renewed open season on difference.

Originally written in 1978 for the "Sexuality" issue of *Signs*, this essay was published there in 1980. In 1982 Antelope Publications reprinted it as part of a feminist pamphlet series. The foreword was written for the pamphlet.

I want to note that documentation of male violence against women—within the home especially—has been accumulating rapidly in this period. . . . At the same time, in the realm of literature which depicts woman bonding and woman identification as essential for female survival, a steady stream of writing and criticism has been coming from women of color in general and lesbians of color in particular—the latter group being even more profoundly erased in academic feminist scholarship by the double bias of racism and homophobia.[1]

There has recently been an intensified debate on female sexuality among feminists and lesbians, with lines often furiously and bitterly drawn, with *sadomasochism* and *pornography* as key words which are variously defined according to who is talking. The depth of women's rage and fear regarding sexuality and its relation to power and pain is real, even when the dialogue sounds simplistic, self-righteous, or like parallel monologues.

Because of all these developments, there are parts of this essay that I would word differently, qualify, or expand if I were writing it today. But I continue to think that heterosexual feminists will draw political strength for change from taking a critical stance toward the ideology which *demands* heterosexuality, and that lesbians cannot assume that we are untouched by that ideology and the institutions founded upon it. There is nothing about such a critique that requires us to think of ourselves as victims, as having been brainwashed or totally powerless. Coercion and compulsion are among the conditions in which women have learned to recognize our strength. Resistance is a major theme in this essay and in the study of women's lives, if we know what we are looking for.

---

[1] See, for example, Paula Gunn Allen, *The Sacred Hoop: Recovering the Feminine in American Indian Traditions* (Boston: Beacon, 1986); Beth Brant, ed., *A Gathering of Spirit: Writing and Art by North American Indian Women* (Montpelier, Vt.: Sinister Wisdom Books, 1984); Gloria Anzaldúa and Cherríe Moraga, eds., *This Bridge Called My Back: Writings by Radical Women of Color* (Watertown, Mass.: Persephone, 1981; distributed by Kitchen Table/Women of Color Press, Albany, N.Y.); J.R. Roberts, *Black Lesbians: An Annotated Bibliography* (Tallahassee, Fla.: Naiad, 1981); Barbara Smith, ed., *Home Girls: A Black Feminist Anthology* (Albany, N.Y.: Kitchen Table/Women of Color Press, 1984). As Lorraine Bethel and Barbara Smith pointed out in *Conditions 5: The Black Women's Issue* (1980), a great deal of fiction by Black women depicts primary relationships between women. I would like to cite here the work of Ama Ata Aidoo, Toni Cade Bambara, Buchi Emecheta, Bessie Head, Zora Neale Hurston, Alice Walker. Donna Allegra, Red Jordan Arobateau, Audre Lorde, Ann Allen Shockley, among others, write directly as Black lesbians. For fiction by other lesbians of color, see Elly Bulkin, ed., *Lesbian Fiction: An Anthology* (Watertown, Mass.: Persephone, 1981).

See also, for accounts of contemporary Jewish-lesbian existence, Evelyn Torton Beck, ed., *Nice Jewish Girls: A Lesbian Anthology* (Watertown, Mass.: Persephone, 1982; distributed by Crossing Press, Trumansburg, N.Y. 14886); Alice Bloch, *Lifetime Guarantee* (Watertown, Mass.: Persephone, 1982); and Melanie Kaye-Kantrowitz and Irena Klepfisz, eds., *The Tribe of Dina: A Jewish Women's Anthology* (Montpelier, Vt.: Sinister Wisdom Books, 1986).

The earliest formulation that I know of heterosexuality as an institution was in the lesbian-feminist paper *The Furies*, founded in 1971. For a collection of articles from that paper, see Nancy Myron and Charlotte Bunch, eds., *Lesbianism and the Women's Movement* (Oakland, Calif.: Diana Press, 1975; distributed by Crossing Press, Trumansburg, N.Y. 14886).

I

> Biologically men have only one innate orientation—a sexual one that draws them to women,—while women have two innate orientations, sexual toward men and reproductive toward their young.[2]

> I was a woman terribly vulnerable, critical, using femaleness as a sort of standard or yardstick to measure and discard men. Yes—something like that. I was an Anna who invited defeat from men without ever being conscious of it. (But I am conscious of it. And being conscious of it means I shall leave it all behind me and become—but what?) I was stuck fast in an emotion common to women of our time, that can turn them bitter, or Lesbian, or solitary. Yes, that Anna during that time was . . .
>
> [Another blank line across the page:][3]

The bias of compulsory heterosexuality, through which lesbian experience is perceived on a scale ranging from deviant to abhorrent or simply rendered invisible, could be illustrated from many texts other than the two just preceding. The assumption made by Rossi, that women are "innately" sexually oriented only toward men, and that made by Lessing, that the lesbian is simply acting out of her bitterness toward men, are by no means theirs alone; these assumptions are widely current in literature and in the social sciences.

I am concerned here with two other matters as well: first, how and why women's choice of women as passionate comrades, life partners, co-workers, lovers, community has been crushed, invalidated, forced into hiding and disguise; and second, the virtual or total neglect of lesbian existence in a wide range of writings, including feminist scholarship. Obviously there is a connection here. I believe that much feminist theory and criticism is stranded on this shoal.

My organizing impulse is the belief that it is not enough for feminist thought that specifically lesbian texts exist. Any theory or cultural/political creation that treats lesbian existence as a marginal or less "natural" phenomenon, as mere "sexual preference," or as the mirror image of either heterosexual or male homosexual relations is profoundly weakened thereby, whatever its other contributions. Feminist theory can no longer afford merely to voice a toleration of "lesbianism" as an "alternative life style" or make token allusion to lesbians. A feminist critique of compulsory heterosexual orientation for women is long overdue. In this exploratory paper, I shall try to show why.

I will begin by way of examples, briefly discussing four books that have appeared in the last few years, written from different viewpoints and political

[2] Alice Rossi, "Children and Work in the Lives of Women," paper delivered at the University of Arizona, Tuscon, February 1976.

[3] Doris Lessing, *The Golden Notebook,* 1962 (New York: Bantam, 1977), p. 480.

orientations, but all presenting themselves, and favorably reviewed, as feminist.[4] All take as a basic assumption that the social relations of the sexes are disordered and extremely problematic, if not disabling, for women; all seek paths toward change. I have learned more from some of these books than from others, but on this I am clear: each one might have been more accurate, more powerful, more truly a force for change had the author dealt with lesbian existence as a reality and as a source of knowledge and power available to women, or with the institution of heterosexuality itself as a beachhead of male dominance.[5] In none of them is the question ever raised as to whether, in a different context or other things being equal, women would *choose* heterosexual coupling and marriage; heterosexuality is presumed the "sexual preference" of "most women," either implicitly or explicitly. In none of these books, which concern themselves with mothering, sex roles, relationships, and societal prescriptions for women, is compulsory heterosexuality ever examined as an institution powerfully affecting all these, or the idea of "preference" or "innate orientation" even indirectly questioned.

In *For Her Own Good: 150 Years of the Experts' Advice to Women* by Barbara Ehrenreich and Deirdre English, the authors' superb pamphlets *Witches, Midwives and Nurses: A History of Women Healers* and *Complaints and Disorders: The Sexual Politics of Sickness* are developed into a provocative and complex

---

[4] Nancy Chodorow, *The Reproduction of Mothering* (Berkeley: University of California Press, 1978); Dorothy Dinnerstein, *The Mermaid and the Minotaur: Sexual Arrangements and the Human Malaise* (New York: Harper & Row, 1976); Barbara Ehrenreich and Deirdre English, *For Her Own Good: 150 Years of the Experts' Advice to Women* (Garden City, N.Y.: Doubleday, Anchor, 1978); Jean Baker Miller, *Toward a New Psychology of Women* (Boston: Beacon, 1976).

[5] I could have chosen many other serious and influential recent books, including anthologies, which would illustrate the same point: e.g., *Our Bodies, Ourselves,* the Boston Women's Health Book Collective's best seller (New York: Simon and Schuster, 1976), which devotes a separate (and inadequate) chapter to lesbians, but whose message is that heterosexuality is most women's life preference; Berenice Carroll, ed., *Liberating Women's History: Theoretical and Critical Essays* (Urbana: University of Illinois Press, 1976), which does not include even a token essay on the lesbian presence in history, though an essay by Linda Gordon, Persis Hunt, et al. notes the use by male historians of "sexual deviance" as a category to discredit and dismiss Anna Howard Shaw, Jane Addams, and other feminists ("Historical Phallacies: Sexism in American Historical Writing"); and Renate Bridenthal and Claudia Koonz, eds., *Becoming Visible: Women in European History* (Boston: Houghton Mifflin, 1977), which contains three mentions of male homosexuality but no materials that I have been able to locate on lesbians. Gerda Lerner, ed., *The Female Experience: An American Documentary* (Indianapolis: Bobbs-Merrill, 1977), contains an abridgement of two lesbian-feminist–position papers from the contemporary movement but no other documentation of lesbian existence. Lerner does note in her preface, however, how the charge of deviance has been used to fragment women and discourage women's resistance. Linda Gordon, in *Woman's Body, Woman's Right: A Social History of Birth Control in America* (New York: Viking, Grossman, 1976), notes accurately that "it is not that feminism has produced more lesbians. There have always been many lesbians, despite the high levels of repression; and most lesbians experience their sexual preference as innate" (p. 410).

[A.R., 1986: I am glad to update the first annotation in this footnote. "*The New*" *Our Bodies, Ourselves* (New York: Simon and Schuster, 1984) contains an expanded chapter on "Loving Women: Lesbian Life and Relationships" and furthermore emphasizes *choices* for women throughout—in terms of sexuality, health care, family, politics, etc.]

study. Their thesis in this book is that the advice given to American women by male health professionals, particularly in the areas of marital sex, maternity, and child care, has echoed the dictates of the economic marketplace and the role capitalism has needed women to play in production and/or reproduction. Women have become the consumer victims of various cures, therapies, and normative judgments in different periods (including the prescription to middle-class women to embody and preserve the sacredness of the home—the "scientific" romanticization of the home itself). None of the "experts" advice has been either particularly scientific or women-oriented; it has reflected male needs, male fantasies about women, and male interest in controlling women—particularly in the realms of sexuality and motherhood—fused with the requirements of industrial capitalism. So much of this book is so devastatingly informative and is written with such lucid feminist wit, that I kept waiting as I read for the basic proscription against lesbianism to be examined. It never was.

This can hardly be for lack of information. Jonathan Katz's *Gay American History*[6] tells us that as early as 1656 the New Haven Colony prescribed the death penalty for lesbians. Katz provides many suggestive and informative documents on the "treatment" (or torture) of lesbians by the medical profession in the nineteenth and twentieth centuries. Recent work by the historian Nancy Sahli documents the crackdown on intense female friendships among college women at the turn of the present century.[7] The ironic title *For Her Own Good* might have referred first and foremost to the economic imperative to heterosexuality and marriage and to the sanctions imposed against single women and widows—both of whom have been and still are viewed as deviant. Yet, in this often enlightening Marxist-feminist overview of male prescriptions for female sanity and health, the economics of prescriptive heterosexuality go unexamined.[8]

Of the three psychoanalytically based books, one, Jean Baker Miller's *Toward a New Psychology of Women,* is written as if lesbians simply do not exist, even as marginal beings. Given Miller's title, I find this astonishing. However, the favorable reviews the book has received in feminist journals, including *Signs* and *Spokeswoman,* suggest that Miller's heterocentric assumptions are widely shared. In *The Mermaid and the Minotaur: Sexual Arrangements and the Human Malaise,* Dorothy Dinnerstein makes an impassioned argument for the sharing of parenting between women and men and for an end to what she perceives as the male/female symbiosis of "gender arrangements," which she feels are leading the species further and further into violence and self-

[6] Jonathan Katz, ed., *Gay American History: Lesbians and Gay Men in the U.S.A.* (New York: Thomas Y. Crowell, 1976).
[7] Nancy Sahli, "Smashing Women's Relationships before the Fall," *Chrysalis: A Magazine of Women's Culture* 8 (1979): 17–27.
[8] This is a book which I have publicly endorsed. I would still do so, though with the above caveat. It is only since beginning to write this article that I fully appreciated how enormous is the unasked question in Ehrenreich and English's book.

extinction. Apart from other problems that I have with this book (including her silence on the institutional and random terrorism men have practiced on women—and children—throughout history,[9] and her obsession with psychology to the neglect of economic and other material realities that help to create psychological reality), I find Dinnerstein's view of the relations between women and men as "a collaboration to keep history mad" utterly ahistorical. She means by this a collaboration to perpetuate social relations which are hostile, exploitative, and destructive to life itself. She sees women and men as equal partners in the making of "sexual arrangements," seemingly unaware of the repeated struggles of women to resist oppression (their own and that of others) and to change their condition. She ignores, specifically, the history of women who—as witches, *femmes seules,* marriage resisters, spinsters, autonomous widows, and/or lesbians—have managed on varying levels *not* to collaborate. It is this history, precisely, from which feminists have so much to learn and on which there is overall such blanketing silence. Dinnerstein acknowledges at the end of her book that "female separatism," though "on a large scale and in the long run wildly impractical," has something to teach us: "Separate, women could in principle set out to learn from scratch—undeflected by the opportunities to evade this task that men's presence has so far offered—what intact self-creative humanness is."[10] Phrases like "intact self-creative humanness" obscure the question of what the many forms of female separatism have actually been addressing. The fact is that women in every culture and throughout history *have* undertaken the task of independent, nonheterosexual, woman-connected existence, to the extent made possible by their context, often in the belief that they were the "only ones" ever to have done so. They have undertaken it even though few women have been in an economic position to resist marriage altogether, and even though attacks against unmarried women have ranged from aspersion and mockery to deliberate gynocide, including the burning and torturing of millions

---

[9] See, for example, Kathleen Barry, *Female Sexual Slavery* (Englewood Cliffs, N.J.: Prentice-Hall, 1979); Mary Daly, *Gyn/Ecology: The Metaethics of Radical Feminism* (Boston: Beacon, 1978); Susan Griffin, *Woman and Nature: The Roaring inside Her* (New York: Harper & Row, 1978); Diana Russell and Nicole van de Ven, eds., *Proceedings of the International Tribunal of Crimes against Women* (Millbrae, Calif.: Les Femmes, 1976); and Susan Brownmiller, *Against Our Will: Men, Women and Rape* (New York: Simon and Schuster, 1975); *Aegis: Magazine on Ending Violence against Women* (Feminist Alliance against Rape, P.O. Box 21033, Washington, D.C. 20009).

[A.R., 1986: Work on both incest and on woman battering has appeared in the 1980s which I did not cite in the essay. See Florence Rush, *The Best-kept Secret* (New York: McGraw-Hill, 1980); Louise Armstrong, *Kiss Daddy Goodnight: A Speakout on Incest* (New York: Pocket Books, 1979); Sandra Butler, *Conspiracy of Silence: The Trauma of Incest* (San Francisco: New Glide, 1978); F. Delacoste and F. Newman, eds., *Fight Back!: Feminist Resistance to Male Violence* (Minneapolis: Cleis Press, 1981); Judy Freespirit, *Daddy's Girl: An Incest Survivor's Story* (Langlois, Ore.: Diaspora Distribution, 1982); Judith Herman, *Father-Daughter Incest* (Cambridge, Mass.: Harvard University Press, 1981); Toni McNaron and Yarrow Morgan, eds., *Voices in the Night: Women Speaking about Incest* (Minneapolis: Cleis Press, 1982); and Betsy Warrior's richly informative, multipurpose compilation of essays, statistics, listings, and facts, the *Battered Women's Directory* (formerly entitled *Working on Wife Abuse*), 8th ed. (Cambridge, Mass.: 1982).]

[10] Dinnerstein, p. 272.

of widows and spinsters during the witch persecutions of the fifteenth, sixteenth, and seventeenth centuries in Europe.

Nancy Chodorow does come close to the edge of an acknowledgment of lesbian existence. Like Dinnerstein, Chodorow believes that the fact that women, and women only, are responsible for child care in the sexual division of labor has led to an entire social organization of gender inequality, and that men as well as women must become primary carers for children if that inequality is to change. In the process of examining, from a psychoanalytic perspective, how mothering by women affects the psychological development of girl and boy children, she offers documentation that men are "emotionally secondary" in women's lives, that "women have a richer, ongoing inner world to fall back on . . . men do not become as emotionally important to women as women do to men."[11] This would carry into the late twentieth century Smith-Rosenberg's findings about eighteenth- and nineteenth-century women's emotional focus on women. "Emotionally important" can, of course, refer to anger as well as to love, or to that intense mixture of the two often found in women's relationships with women—one aspect of what I have come to call the "double life of women" (see below). Chodorow concludes that because women have women as mothers, "the mother remains a primary internal object [*sic*] to the girl, so that heterosexual relationships are on the model of nonexclusive, second relationship for her, whereas for the boy they re-create an exclusive, primary relationship." According to Chodorow, women "have learned to deny the limitations of masculine lovers for both psychological and practical reasons."[12]

But the practical reasons (like witch burnings, male control of law, theology, and science, or economic nonviability within the sexual division of labor) are glossed over. Chodorow's account barely glances at the constraints and sanctions which historically have enforced or ensured the coupling of women with men and obstructed or penalized women's coupling or allying in independent groups with other women. She dismisses lesbian existence with the comment that "lesbian relationships do tend to re-create mother-daughter emotions and connections, but most women are heterosexual" (implied: more mature, having developed beyond the mother-daughter connection?). She then adds: "This heterosexual preference and taboos on homosexuality, in addition to objective economic dependence on men, make the option of primary sexual bonds with other women unlikely—though more prevalent in recent years."[13] The significance of that qualification seems irresistible, but Chodorow does not explore it further. Is she saying that lesbian existence has become more *visible* in recent years (in certain groups), that economic and other pressures have changed (under capitalism, socialism, or both), and that consequently more women are rejecting the heterosexual "choice"? She argues that women want children because their heterosexual relationships lack richness and intensity,

---

[11] Chodorow, pp. 197–198.
[12] *Ibid.*, pp. 198–199.
[13] *Ibid.*, p. 200.

that in having a child a woman seeks to re-create her own intense relationship with her mother. It seems to me that on the basis of her own findings, Chodorow leads us implicitly to conclude that heterosexuality is *not* a "preference" for women, that, for one thing, it fragments the erotic from the emotional in a way that women find impoverishing and painful. Yet her book participates in mandating it. Neglecting the covert socializations and the overt forces which have channeled women into marriage and heterosexual romance, pressures ranging from the selling of daughters to postindustrial economics to the silences of literature to the images of the television screen, she, like Dinnerstein, is stuck with trying to reform a man-made institution—compulsory heterosexuality—as if, despite profound emotional impulses and complementarities drawing women toward women, there is a mystical/biological heterosexual inclination, a "preference" or "choice" which draws women toward men.

Moreover, it is understood that this "preference" does not need to be explained unless through the tortuous theory of the female Oedipus complex or the necessity for species reproduction. It is lesbian sexuality which (usually, and incorrectly, "included" under male homosexuality) is seen as requiring explanation. This assumption of female heterosexuality seems to me in itself remarkable: it is an enormous assumption to have glided so silently into the foundations of our thought.

The extension of this assumption is the frequently heard assertion that in a world of genuine equality, where men are nonoppressive and nurturing, everyone would be bisexual. Such a notion blurs and sentimentalizes the actualities within which women have experienced sexuality; it is a liberal leap across the tasks and struggles of here and now, the continuing process of sexual definition which will generate its own possibilities and choices. (It also assumes that women who have chosen women have done so simply because men are oppressive and emotionally unavailable, which still fails to account for women who continue to pursue relationships with oppressive and/or emotionally unsatisfying men.) I am suggesting that heterosexuality, like motherhood, needs to be recognized and studied as a *political institution*—even, or especially, by those individuals who feel they are, in their personal experience, the precursors of a new social relation between the sexes.

II

If women are the earliest sources of emotional caring and physical nurture for both female and male children, it would seem logical, from a feminist perspective at least, to pose the following questions: whether the search for love and tenderness in both sexes does not originally lead toward women; *why in fact women would ever redirect that search;* why species survival, the means of impregnation, and emotional/erotic relationships should ever have become so rigidly identified with each other; and why such violent structures should be found necessary to enforce women's total emotional, erotic loyalty and subservience to men. I doubt that enough feminist scholars and theorists have taken the pains to acknowledge the societal forces which wrench women's emotional and erotic energies away from themselves and other women and from woman-identified values. These forces, as I shall try to show, range from literal physical enslavement to the disguising and distorting of possible options.

I do not, myself, assume that mothering by women is a "sufficient cause" of lesbian existence. But the issue of mothering by women has been much in the air of late, usually accompanied by the view that increased parenting by men would minimize antagonism between the sexes and equalize the sexual imbalance of power of males over females. These discussions are carried on without reference to compulsory heterosexuality as a phenomenon, let alone as an ideology. I do not wish to psychologize here, but rather to identify sources of male power. I believe large numbers of men could, in fact, undertake child care on a large scale without radically altering the balance of male power in a male-identified society.

In her essay "The Origin of the Family," Kathleen Gough lists eight characteristics of male power in archaic and contemporary societies which I would like to use as a framework: "men's ability to deny women sexuality or to force it upon them; to command or exploit their labor to control their produce; to control or rob them of their children; to confine them physically and prevent their movement; to use them as objects in male transactions; to cramp their creativeness; or to withhold from them large areas of the society's knowledge and cultural attainments."[14] (Gough does not perceive these power characteristics as specifically enforcing heterosexuality, only as producing sexual inequality.) Below, Gough's words appear in italics; the elaboration of each of her categories, in brackets, is my own.

Characteristics of male power include *the power of men*

1. *to deny women* [their own] *sexuality*—[by means of clitoridectomy and infibulation; chastity belts; punishment, including death, for female adultery; punishment, including death, for lesbian sexuality; psychoanalytic denial of the clitoris; strictures against masturbation; denial of maternal and postmenopausal sensuality; unnecessary hysterectomy; pseudolesbian images in the media and literature; closing of archives and destruction of documents relating to lesbian existence]
2. *or to force it* [male sexuality] *upon them*—[by means of rape (including marital rape) and wife beating; father-daughter, brother-sister incest; the socialization of women to feel that male sexual "drive" amounts to a right;[15] idealization of heterosexual romance in art, literature, the media, advertising, etc.; child marriage; arranged marriage; prostitution; the harem; psychoanalytic doctrines of frigidity and vaginal orgasm; pornographic depictions of women responding pleasurably to

---

[14] Kathleen Gough, "The Origin of the Family," in *Toward an Anthropology of Women*, ed. Rayna [Rapp] Reiter (New York: Monthly Review Press, 1975), pp. 69–70.
[15] Barry, pp. 216–219.

sexual violence and humiliation (a subliminal message being that sadistic heterosexuality is more "normal" than sensuality between women)]

3. *to command or exploit their labor to control their produce*—[by means of the institution of marriage and motherhood as unpaid production; the horizontal segregation of women in paid employment; the decoy of the upwardly mobile token woman; male control of abortion, contraception, sterilization, and childbirth; pimping; female infanticide, which robs mothers of daughters and contributes to generalized devaluation of women]
4. *to control or rob them of their children*—[by means of father right and "legal kidnapping";[16] enforced sterilization; systematized infanticide; seizure of children from lesbian mothers by the courts; the malpractice of male obstetrics; use of the mother as "token torturer"[17] in genital mutilation or in binding the daughter's feet (or mind) to fit her for marriage]
5. *to confine them physically and prevent their movement*—[by means of rape as terrorism, keeping women off the streets; purdah; foot binding; atrophying of women's athletic capabilities; high heels and "feminine" dress codes in fashion; the veil; sexual harassment on the streets; horizontal segregation of women in employment; prescriptions for "full-time" mothering at home; enforced economic dependence of wives]
6. *to use them as objects in male transactions*—[use of women as "gifts"; bride price; pimping; arranged marriage; use of women as entertainers to facilitate male deals—e.g., wife-hostess, cocktail waitress required to dress for male sexual titillation, call girls, "bunnies," geisha, *kisaeng* prostitutes, secretaries]
7. *to cramp their creativeness*—[witch persecutions as campaigns against midwives and female healers, and as pogrom against independent, "unassimilated" women;[18] definition of male pursuits as more valuable than female within any culture, so that cultural values become the embodiment of male subjectivity; restriction of female self-fulfillment to marriage and motherhood; sexual exploitation of women by male artists and teachers; the social and economic disruption of women's creative aspirations;[19] erasure of female tradition][20]

---

[16] Anna Demeter, *Legal Kidnapping* (Boston: Beacon, 1977), pp. xx, 126–128.

[17] Daly, pp. 139–141, 163–165.

[18] Barbara Ehrenreich and Deirdre English, *Witches, Midwives and Nurses: A History of Women Healers* (Old Westbury, N.Y.: Feminist Press, 1973); Andrea Dworkin, *Woman Hating* (New York: Dutton, 1974), pp. 118–154; Daly, pp. 178–222.

[19] See Virginia Woolf, *A Room of One's Own* (London: Hogarth, 1929), and *id.*, *Three Guineas* (New York: Harcourt Brace, [1938] 1966); Tillie Olsen, *Silences* (Boston: Delacorte, 1978); Michelle Cliff, "The Resonance of Interruption," *Chrysalis: A Magazine of Women's Culture* 8 (1979): 29–37.

[20] Mary Daly, *Beyond God the Father* (Boston: Beacon, 1973), pp. 347–351; Olsen, pp. 22–46.

8. *to withhold from them large areas of the society's knowledge and cultural attainments*—[by means of noneducation of females; the "Great Silence" regarding women and particularly lesbian existence in history and culture;[21] sex-role tracking which deflects women from science, technology, and other "masculine" pursuits; male social/professional bonding which excludes women; discrimination against women in the professions]

These are some of the methods by which male power is manifested and maintained. Looking at the schema, what surely impresses itself is the fact that we are confronting not a simple maintenance of inequality and property possession, but a pervasive cluster of forces, ranging from physical brutality to control of consciousness, which suggests that an enormous potential counterforce is having to be restrained.

Some of the forms by which male power manifests itself are more easily recognizable as enforcing heterosexuality on women than are others. Yet each one I have listed adds to the cluster of forces within which women have been convinced that marriage and sexual orientation toward men are inevitable—even if unsatisfying or oppressive—components of their lives. The chastity belt; child marriage; erasure of lesbian existence (except as exotic and perverse) in art, literature, film; idealization of heterosexual romance and marriage—these are some fairly obvious forms of compulsion, the first two exemplifying physical force, the second two control of consciousness. While clitoridectomy has been assailed by feminists as a form of woman torture,[22] Kathleen Barry first pointed out that it is not simply a way of turning the young girl into a "marriageable" woman through brutal surgery. It intends that women in the intimate proximity of polygynous marriage will not form sexual relationships with each other, that—from a male, genital-fetishist perspective—female erotic connections, even in a sex-segregated situation, will be literally excised.[23]

The function of pornography as an influence on consciousness is a major public issue of our time, when a multibillion-dollar industry has the power to disseminate increasingly sadistic, women-degrading visual images. But even so-called soft-core pornography and advertising depict women as objects of sexual appetite devoid of emotional context, without individual meaning or personality—essentially as a sexual commodity to be consumed by males. (So-called lesbian pornography, created for the male voyeuristic eye, is equally devoid of emotional context or individual personality.) The most pernicious message

---

[21] Daly, *Beyond God the Father,* p. 93.

[22] Fran P. Hosken, "The Violence of Power: Genital Mutilation of Females," *Heresies: A Feminist Journal of Art and Politics* 6 (1979): 28–35; Russell and van de Ven, pp. 194–195.

[A.R., 1986: See especially "Circumcision of Girls," In Nawal El Saadawi, *The Hidden Face of Eve: Women in the Arab World* (Boston: Beacon, 1982), pp. 33–43.]

[23] Barry, pp. 163–164.

relayed by pornography is that women are natural sexual prey to men and love it, that sexuality and violence are congruent, and that for women sex is essentially masochistic, humiliation pleasurable, physical abuse erotic. But along with this message comes another, not always recognized: that enforced submission and the use of cruelty, if played out in heterosexual pairing, is sexually "normal," while sensuality between women, including erotic mutuality and respect, is "queer," "sick," and either pornographic in itself or not very exciting compared with the sexuality of whips and bondage.[24] Pornography does not simply create a climate in which sex and violence are interchangeable; *it widens the range of behavior considered acceptable from men in heterosexual intercourse*—behavior which reiteratively strips women of their autonomy, dignity, and sexual potential, including the potential of loving and being loved by women in mutuality and integrity.

In her brilliant study *Sexual Harassment of Working Women: A Case of Sex Discrimination,* Catherine A. MacKinnon delineates the intersection of compulsory heterosexuality and economics. Under capitalism, women are horizontally segregated by gender and occupy a structurally inferior position in the workplace. This is hardly news, but MacKinnon raises the question why, even if capitalism "requires some collection of individuals to occupy low-status, low-paying positions . . . such persons must be biologically female," and goes on to point out that "the fact that male employers often do not hire qualified women, *even when they could pay them less than men* suggests that more than the profit motive is implicated" [emphasis added].[25] She cites a wealth of material documenting the fact that women are not only segregated in low-paying service jobs (as secretaries, domestics, nurses, typists, telephone operators, child-care workers, waitresses), but that "sexualization of the woman" is part of the job. Central and intrinsic to the economic realities of women's lives is the requirement that women will "market sexual attractiveness to men, who tend to hold the economic power and position to enforce their predilections." And MacKinnon documents that "sexual harassment perpetuates the interlocked structure by which women have been kept sexually in thrall to men at the bottom of the labor market. Two forces of American society converge: men's control over women's sexuality and capital's control over employees' work lives."[26] Thus, women in the workplace are at the mercy of sex as power in a vicious circle. Economically disadvantaged, women—whether waitresses or professors—endure sexual harassment to keep their jobs and learn to behave in a complaisantly and ingratiatingly heterosexual manner because they discover

[24] The issue of "lesbian sadomasochism" needs to be examined in terms of dominant cultures' teachings about the relation of sex and violence. I believe this to be another example of the "double-life" of women.
[25] Catharine A. MacKinnon, *Sexual Harassment of Working Women: A Case of Sex Discrimination* (New Haven, Conn.: Yale University Press, 1979), pp. 15–16.
[26] *Ibid.*, p. 174.

this is their true qualification for employment, whatever the job description. And, MacKinnon notes, the woman who too decisively resists sexual overtures in the workplace is accused of being "dried up" and sexless, or lesbian. This raises a specific difference between the experiences of lesbians and homosexual men. A lesbian, closeted on her job because of heterosexist prejudice, is not simply forced into denying the truth of her outside relationships or private life. Her job depends on her pretending to be not merely heterosexual, but a heterosexual *woman* in terms of dressing and playing the feminine, deferential role required of "real" women.

MacKinnon raises radical questions as to the qualitative differences between sexual harassment, rape, and ordinary heterosexual intercourse. ("As one accused rapist put it, he hadn't used 'any more force than is usual for males during the preliminaries.' ") She criticizes Susan Brownmiller[27] for separating rape from the mainstream of daily life and for her unexamined premise that "rape is violence, intercourse is sexuality," removing rape from the sexual sphere altogether. Most crucially she argues that "taking rape from the realm of 'the sexual,' placing it in the realm of 'the violent,' allows one to be against it without raising any questions about the extent to which the institution of heterosexuality has defined force as a normal part of 'the preliminaries.' "[28] "Never is it asked whether, under conditions of male supremacy, the notion of 'consent' has any meaning."[29]

The fact is that the workplace, among other social institutions, is a place where women have learned to accept male violation of their psychic and physical boundaries as the price of survival; where women have been educated—no less than by romantic literature or by pornography—to perceive themselves as sexual prey. A woman seeking to escape such casual violations along with economic disadvantage may well turn to marriage as a form of hoped-for protection, while bringing into marriage neither social nor economic power, thus entering that institution also from a disadvantaged position. MacKinnon finally asks:

> What if inequality is built into the social conceptions of male and female sexuality, of masculinity and femininity, of sexiness and heterosexual attractiveness? Incidents of sexual harassment suggest that male sexual desire itself may be aroused by female vulnerability. . . . Men feel they can take advantage, so they want to, so they do. Examination of sexual harassment, precisely because the episodes appear commonplace, forces one to confront the fact

---

[27] Brownmiller, *op. cit.*

[28] MacKinnon, p. 219. Susan Schecter writes: "The push for heterosexual union at whatever cost is so intense that . . . it has become a cultural force of its own that creates battering. The ideology of romantic love and its jealous possession of the partner as property provide the masquerade for what can become severe abuse" (*Aegis: Magazine on Ending Violence against Women* [July–August 1979]: 50–51).

[29] MacKinnon, p. 298.

> that sexual intercourse normally occurs between economic (as well as physical) unequals . . . the apparent legal requirement that violations of women's sexuality appear out of the ordinary before they will be punished helps prevent women from defining the ordinary conditions of their own consent.[30]

Given the nature and extent of heterosexual pressures—the daily "eroticization of women's subordination," as MacKinnon phrases it[31]—I question the more or less psychoanalytic perspective (suggested by such writers as Karen Horney, H. R. Hayes, Wolfgang Lederer, and, most recently, Dorothy Dinnerstein) that the male need to control women sexually results from some primal male "fear of women" and of women's sexual insatiability. It seems more probable that men really fear not that they will have women's sexual appetites forced on them or that women want to smother and devour them, but that women could be indifferent to them altogether, that men could be allowed sexual and emotional—therefore economic—access to women *only* on women's terms, otherwise being left on the periphery of the matrix.

The means of assuring male sexual access to women have recently received searching investigation by Kathleen Barry.[32] She documents extensive and appalling evidence for the existence, on a very large scale, of international female slavery, the institution once known as "white slavery" but which in fact has involved, and at this very moment involves, women of every race and class. In the theoretical analysis derived from her research, Barry makes the connection between all enforced conditions under which women live subject to men: prostitution, marital rape, father-daughter and brother-sister incest, wife beating, pornography, bride price, the selling of daughters, purdah, and genital mutilation. She sees the rape paradigm—where the victim of sexual assault is held responsible for her own victimization—as leading to the rationalization and acceptance of other forms of enslavement where the woman is presumed to have "chosen" her fate, to embrace it passively, or to have courted it perversely through rash or unchaste behavior. On the contrary, Barry maintains, "female sexual slavery is present in ALL situations where women or girls cannot change the conditions of their existence; where regardless of how they got into those conditions, e.g., social pressure, economic hardship, misplaced trust or the longing for affection, they cannot get out; and where they are subject to sexual violence and exploitation."[33] She provides a spectrum of concrete examples, not only as to the existence of a widespread international traffic in women, but also as to how this operates—whether in the form of a

---

[30] *Ibid.*, p. 220.
[31] *Ibid.*, p. 221.
[32] Barry, *op.cit.*
[A.R., 1986: See also Kathleen Barry, Charlotte Bunch, and Shirley Castley, eds., *International Feminism: Networking against Female Sexual Slavery* (New York: International Women's Tribune Center, 1984).]
[33] Barry, p. 33.

"Minnesota pipeline" funneling blonde, blue-eyed midwestern runaways to Times Square, or the purchasing of young women out of rural poverty in Latin America or Southeast Asia, or the providing of *maisons d'abattage* for migrant workers in the eighteenth arrondissement of Paris. Instead of "blaming the victim" or trying to diagnose her presumed pathology, Barry turns her floodlight on the pathology of sex colonization itself, the ideology of "cultural sadism" represented by the pornography industry and by the overall identification of women primarily as "sexual beings whose responsibility is the sexual service of men."[34]

Barry delineates what she names a "sexual domination perspective" through whose lens sexual abuse and terrorism of women by men has been rendered almost invisible by treating it as natural and inevitable. From its point of view, women are expendable as long as the sexual and emotional needs of the male can be satisfied. To replace this perspective of domination with a universal standard of basic freedom for women from gender-specific violence, from constraints on movement, and from male right of sexual and emotional access is the political purpose of her book. Like Mary Daly in *Gyn/Ecology,* Barry rejects structuralist and other cultural-relativist rationalizations for sexual torture and anti-woman violence. In her opening chapter, she asks of her readers that they refuse all handy escapes into ignorance and denial. "The only way we can come out of hiding, break through our paralyzing defenses, is to know it all—the full extent of sexual violence and domination of women. . . . In *knowing,* in facing directly, we can learn to chart our course out of this oppression, by envisioning and creating a world which will preclude sexual slavery."[35]

"Until we name the practice, give conceptual definition and form to it, illustrate its life over time and in space, those who are its most obvious victims will also not be able to name it or define their experience."

But women are all, in different ways and to different degrees, its victims; and part of the problem with naming and conceptualizing female sexual slavery is, as Barry clearly sees, compulsory heterosexuality.[36] Compulsory heterosexuality simplifies the task of the procurer and pimp in world-wide prostitution rings and "eros centers," while, in the privacy of the home, it leads the daughter to "accept" incest/rape by her father, the mother to deny that it is happening, the battered wife to stay on with an abusive husband. "Befriending or love" is a major tactic of the procurer, whose job it is to turn the runaway or the confused young girl over to the pimp for seasoning. The ideology of heterosexual

---

[34] *Ibid.*, p. 103.
[35] *Ibid.*, p. 5.
[36] *Ibid.*, p. 100.

[A.R., 1986: This statement has been taken as claiming that "all women are victims" purely and simply, or that "all heterosexuality equals sexual slavery." I would say, rather, that all women are affected, though differently, by dehumanizing attitudes and practices directed at women as a group.]

romance, beamed at her from childhood out of fairy tales, television, films, advertising, popular songs, wedding pageantry, is a tool ready to the procurer's hand and one which he does not hesitate to use, as Barry documents. Early female indoctrination in "love" as an emotion may be largely a Western concept; but a more universal ideology concerns the primacy and uncontrollability of the male sexual drive. This is one of many insights offered by Barry's work:

> As sexual power is learned by adolescent boys through the social experience of their sex drive, so do girls learn that the locus of sexual power is male. Given the importance placed on the male sex drive in the socialization of girls as well as boys, early adolescence is probably the first significant phase of male identification in a girl's life and development. . . . As a young girl becomes aware of her own increasing sexual feelings . . . she turns away from her heretofore primary relationships with girlfriends. As they become secondary to her, recede in importance in her life, her own identity also assumes a secondary role and she grows into male identification.[37]

We still need to ask why some women never, even temporarily, turn away from "heretofore primary relationships" with other females. And why does male identification—the casting of one's social, political, and intellectual allegiances with men—exist among lifelong sexual lesbians? Barry's hypothesis throws us among new questions, but it clarifies the diversity of forms in which compulsory heterosexuality presents itself. In the mystique of the overpowering, all-conquering male sex drive, the penis-with-a-life-of-its own, is rooted the law of male sex right to women, which justifies prostitution as a universal cultural assumption on the one hand, while defending sexual slavery within the family on the basis of "family privacy and cultural uniqueness" on the other.[38] The adolescent male sex drive, which, as both young women and men are taught, once triggered cannot take responsibility for itself or take no for an answer, becomes, according to Barry, the norm and rationale for adult male sexual behavior: a condition of *arrested sexual development.* Women learn to accept as natural the inevitability of this "drive" because they receive it as dogma. Hence, marital rape; hence, the Japanese wife resignedly packing her husband's suitcase for a weekend in the *kisaeng* brothels of Taiwan; hence, the psychological as well as economic imbalance of power between husband and wife, male employer and female worker, father and daughter, male professor and female student.

The effect of male identification means

> internalizing the values of the colonizer and actively participating in carrying out the colonization of one's self and one's sex. . . . Male identification is the act whereby women place men above women, including themselves, in

[37] *Ibid.*, p. 218.
[38] *Ibid.*, p. 140.

> credibility, status, and importance in most situations, regardless of the comparative quality the women may bring to the situation. . . . Interaction with women is seen as a lesser form of relating on every level.[39]

What deserves further exploration is the doublethink many women engage in and from which no woman is permanently and utterly free: However woman-to-woman relationships, female support networks, a female and feminist value system are relied on and cherished, indoctrination in male credibility and status can still create synapses in thought, denials of feeling, wishful thinking, a profound sexual and intellectual confusion.[40] I quote here from a letter I received the day I was writing this passage: "I have had very bad relationships with men—I am now in the midst of a very painful separation. I am trying to find my strength through women—without my friends, I could not survive." How many times a day do women speak words like these or think them or write them, and how often does the synapse reassert itself?

Barry summarizes her findings:

> Considering the arrested sexual development that is understood to be normal in the male population, and considering the numbers of men who are pimps, procurers, members of slavery gangs, corrupt officials participating in this traffic, owners, operators, employees of brothels and lodging and entertainment facilities, pornography purveyors, associated with prostitution, wife beaters, child molesters, incest perpetrators, johns (tricks) and rapists, one cannot but be momentarily stunned by the enormous male population engaging in female sexual slavery. The huge number of men engaged in these practices should be cause for declaration of an international emergency, a crisis in sexual violence. But what should be cause for alarm is instead accepted as normal sexual intercourse.[41]

Susan Cavin, in a rich and provocative, if highly speculative, dissertation, suggests that patriarchy becomes possible when the original female band, which includes children but ejects adolescent males, becomes invaded and outnumbered by males; that not patriarchal marriage, but the rape of the mother by the son, becomes the first act of male domination. The entering wedge, or leverage, which allows this to happen is not just a simple change in sex ratios; it is also the mother-child bond, manipulated by adolescent males in order to remain within the matrix past the age of exclusion. Maternal affection is used

---

[39] *Ibid.*, p. 172.

[40] Elsewhere I have suggested that male identification has been a powerful source of white women's racism and that it has often been women already seen as "disloyal" to male codes and systems who have actively battled against it (Adrienne Rich, "Disloyal to Civilization: Feminism, Racism, Gynephobia," in *On Lies, Secrets, and Silence: Selected Prose, 1966–1978* [New York: W. W. Norton, 1979]).

[41] Barry, p. 220.

to establish male right of sexual access, which, however, must ever after be held by force (or through control of consciousness) since the original deep adult bonding is that of woman for woman.[42] I find this hypothesis extremely suggestive, since one form of false consciousness which serves compulsory heterosexuality is the maintenance of a mother-son relationship between women and men, including the demand that women provide maternal solace, nonjudgmental nurturing, and compassion for their harassers, rapists, and batterers (as well as for men who passively vampirize them).

But whatever its origins, when we look hard and clearly at the extent and elaboration of measures designed to keep women within a male sexual purlieu, it becomes an inescapable question whether the issue feminists have to address is not simple "gender inequality" nor the domination of culture by males nor mere "taboos against homosexuality," but the enforcement of heterosexuality for women as a means of assuring male right of physical, economic, and emotional access.[43] One of many means of enforcement is, of course, the rendering invisible of the lesbian possibility, an engulfed continent which rises fragmentedly into view from time to time only to become submerged again. Feminist research and theory that contribute to lesbian invisibility or marginality are actually working against the liberation and empowerment of women as a group.[44]

The assumption that "most women are innately heterosexual" stands as a theoretical and political stumbling block for feminism. It remains a tenable assumption partly because lesbian existence has been written out of history or catalogued under disease, partly because it has been treated as exceptional rather than intrinsic, partly because to acknowledge that for women heterosexuality may not be a "preference" at all but something that has had to be imposed, managed, organized, propagandized, and maintained by force is an immense step to take if you consider yourself freely and "innately" heterosexual.

---

[42] Susan Cavin, "Lesbian Origins" (Ph.D. diss., Rutgers University, 1978), unpublished, ch. 6.
[A.R., 1986: This dissertation was recently published as *Lesbian Origins* (San Francisco: Ism Press, 1986).]

[43] For my perception of heterosexuality as an economic institution I am indebted to Lisa Leghorn and Katherine Parker, who allowed me to read the unpublished manuscript of their book *Woman's Worth: Sexual Economics and the World of Women* (London and Boston: Routledge & Kegan Paul, 1981).

[44] I would suggest that lesbian existence has been most recognized and tolerated where it has resembled a "deviant" version of heterosexuality—e.g., where lesbians have, like Stein and Toklas, played heterosexual roles (or seemed to in public) and have been chiefly identified with male culture. See also Claude E. Schaeffer, "The Kuterai Female Berdache: Courier, Guide, Prophetess and Warrior," *Ethnohistory* 12, no. 3 (Summer 1965): 193–236. (Berdache: "an individual of a definite physiological sex [m. or f.] who assumes the role and status of the opposite sex and who is viewed by the community as being of one sex physiologically but as having assumed the role and status of the opposite sex" [Schaeffer, p. 231].) Lesbian existence has also been relegated to an upper-class phenomenon, an elite decadence (as in the fascination with Paris salon lesbians such as Renée Vivien and Natalie Clifford Barney), to the obscuring of such "common women" as Judy Grahn depicts in her *The Work of a Common Woman* (Oakland, Calif.: Diana Press, 1978) and *True to Life Adventure Stories* (Oakland, Calif.: Diana Press, 1978).

Yet the failure to examine heterosexuality as an institution is like failing to admit that the economic system called capitalism or the caste system of racism is maintained by a variety of forces, including both physical violence and false consciousness. To take the step of questioning heterosexuality as a "preference" or "choice" for women—and to do the intellectual and emotional work that follows—will call for a special quality of courage in heterosexually identified feminists, but I think the rewards will be great: a freeing-up of thinking, the exploring of new paths, the shattering of another great silence, new clarity in personal relationships.

III

I have chosen to use the terms *lesbian existence* and *lesbian continuum* because the word *lesbianism* has a clinical and limiting ring. *Lesbian existence* suggests both the fact of the historical presence of lesbians and our continuing creation of the meaning of that existence. I mean the term *lesbian continuum* to include a range—through each woman's life and throughout history—of woman-identified experience, not simply the fact that a woman has had or consciously desired genital sexual experience with another woman. If we expand it to embrace many more forms of primary intensity between and among women, including the sharing of a rich inner life, the bonding against male tyranny, the giving and receiving of practical and political support, if we can also hear it in such associations as *marriage resistance* and the "haggard" behavior identified by Mary Daly (obsolete meanings: "intractable," "willful," "wanton," and "unchaste," "a woman reluctant to yield to wooing"),[45] we begin to grasp breadths of female history and psychology which have lain out of reach as a consequence of limited, mostly clinical, definitions of *lesbianism*.

Lesbian existence comprises both the breaking of a taboo and the rejection of a compulsory way of life. It is also a direct or indirect attack on male right of access to women. But it is more than these, although we may first begin to perceive it as a form of naysaying to patriarchy, an act of resistance. It has, of course, included isolation, self-hatred, breakdown, alcoholism, suicide, and intrawoman violence; we romanticize at our peril what it means to love and act against the grain, and under heavy penalties; and lesbian existence has been lived (unlike, say, Jewish or Catholic existence) without access to any knowledge of a tradition, a continuity, a social underpinning. The destruction of records and memorabilia and letters documenting the realities of lesbian existence must be taken very seriously as a means of keeping heterosexuality compulsory for women, since what has been kept from our knowledge is joy, sensuality, courage, and community, as well as guilt, self-betrayal, and pain.[46]

---

[45] Daly, *Gyn/Ecology*, p. 15.

[46] "In a hostile world in which women are not supposed to survive except in relation with and in service to men, entire communities of women were simply erased. History tends to bury what it

Lesbians have historically been deprived of a political existence through "inclusion" as female versions of male homosexuality. To equate lesbian existence with male homosexuality because each is stigmatized is to erase female reality once again. Part of the history of lesbian existence is, obviously, to be found where lesbians, lacking a coherent female community, have shared a kind of social life and common cause with homosexual men. But there are differences: women's lack of economic and cultural privilege relative to men; qualitative differences in female and male relationships—for example, the patterns of anonymous sex among male homosexuals, and the pronounced ageism in male homosexual standards of sexual attractiveness. I perceive the lesbian experience as being, like motherhood, a profoundly *female* experience, with particular oppressions, meanings, and potentialities we cannot comprehend as long as we simply bracket it with other sexually stigmatized existences. Just as the term *parenting* serves to conceal the particular and significant reality of being a parent who is actually a mother, the term *gay* may serve the purpose of blurring the very outlines we need to discern, which are of crucial value for feminism and for the freedom of women as a group.[47]

As the term *lesbian* has been held to limiting, clinical associations in its patriarchal definition, female friendship and comradeship have been set apart from the erotic, thus limiting the erotic itself. But as we deepen and broaden the range of what we define as lesbian existence, as we delineate a lesbian continuum, we begin to discover the erotic in female terms: as that which is unconfined to any single part of the body or solely to the body itself; as an energy not only diffuse but, as Audre Lorde has described it, omnipresent in "the sharing of joy, whether physical, emotional, psychic," and in the sharing of work; as the empowering joy which "makes us less willing to accept powerlessness, or those other supplied states of being which are not native to me, such as resignation, despair, self-effacement, depression, self-denial."[48] In another context, writing of women and work, I quoted the autobiographical passage in which the poet H.D. described how her friend Bryher supported her in persisting with the visionary experience which was to shape her mature work:

---

seeks to reject" (Blanche W. Cook, " 'Women Alone Stir My Imagination': Lesbianism and the Cultural Tradition," *Signs: Journal of Women in Culture and Society* 4, no. 4 [Summer 1979]: 719–720). The Lesbian Herstory Archives in New York City is one attempt to preserve contemporary documents on lesbian existence—a project of enormous value and meaning, working against the continuing censorship and obliteration of relationships, networks, communities in other archives and elsewhere in the culture.

[47] [A.R., 1986: The shared historical and spiritual "crossover" functions of lesbians and gay men in cultures past and present are traced by Judy Grahn in *Another Mother Tongue: Gay Words, Gay Worlds* (Boston: Beacon, 1984). I now think we have much to learn both from the uniquely female aspects of lesbian existence and from the complex "gay" identity we share with gay men.]

[48] Audre Lorde, "Uses of the Erotic: The Erotic as Power," in *Sister Outsider* (Trumansburg, N.Y.: Crossing Press, 1984).

> I knew that this experience, this writing-on-the-wall before me, could not be shared with anyone except the girl who stood so bravely there beside me. This girl said without hesitation, "Go on." It was she really who had the detachment and integrity of the Pythoness of Delphi. But it was I, battered and dissociated . . . who was seeing the pictures, and who was reading the writing or granted the inner vision. Or perhaps, in some sense, we were "seeing" it together, for without her, admittedly, I could not have gone on.[49]

If we consider the possibility that all women—from the infant suckling at her mother's breast, to the grown woman experiencing orgasmic sensations while suckling her own child, perhaps recalling her mother's milk smell in her own, to two women, like Virginia Woolf's Chloe and Olivia, who share a laboratory,[50] to the woman dying at ninety, touched and handled by women—exist on a lesbian continuum, we can see ourselves as moving in and out of this continuum, whether we identify ourselves as lesbian or not.

We can then connect aspects of woman identification as diverse as the impudent, intimate girl friendships of eight or nine year olds and the banding together of those women of the twelfth and fifteenth centuries known as Beguines who "shared houses, rented to one another, bequeathed houses to their room-mates . . . in cheap subdivided houses in the artisans' area of town," who "practiced Christian virtue on their own, dressing and living simply and not associating with men," who earned their livings as spinsters, bakers, nurses, or ran schools for young girls, and who managed—until the Church forced them to disperse—to live independent both of marriage and of conventual restrictions.[51] It allows us to connect these women with the more celebrated "Lesbians" of the women's school around Sappho of the seventh century B.C., with the secret sororities and economic networks reported among African women, and with the Chinese marriage-resistance sisterhoods—communities of women who refused marriage or who, if married, often refused to consummate their marriages and soon left their husbands, the only women in China who were not footbound and who, Agnes Smedley tells us, welcomed the births of daughters and organized successful women's strikes in the silk mills.[52] It allows

[49] Adrienne Rich, "Conditions for Work: The Common World of Women," in *On Lies, Secrets, and Silence,* p. 209; H.D., *Tribute to Freud* (Oxford: Carcanet, 1971), pp. 50–54.
[50] Woolf, *A Room of One's Own,* p. 126.
[51] Gracia Clark, "The Beguines: A Mediaeval Women's Community," *Quest: A Feminist Quarterly* 1, no. 4 (1975): 73–80.
[52] See Denise Paulmé, ed., *Women of Tropical Africa* (Berkeley: University of California Press, 1963), pp. 7, 266–267. Some of these sororities are described as "a kind of defensive syndicate against the male element," their aims being "to offer concerted resistance to an oppressive patriarchate," "independence in relation to one's husband and with regard to motherhood, mutual aid, satisfaction of personal revenge." See also Audre Lorde, "Scratching the Surface: Some Notes on Barriers to Women and Loving," in *Sister Outsider,* pp. 45–52; Marjorie Topley, "Marriage Resistance in Rural Kwangtung," in *Women in Chinese Society,* ed. M. Wolf and R. Witke (Stanford, Calif.: Stanford University Press, 1978), pp. 67–89; Agnes Smedley, *Portraits of Chinese Women in*

us to connect and compare disparate individual instances of marriage resistance: for example, the strategies available to Emily Dickinson, a nineteenth-century white woman genius, with the strategies available to Zora Neale Hurston, a twentieth-century Black woman genius. Dickinson never married, had tenuous intellectual friendships with men, lived self-convented in her genteel father's house in Amherst, and wrote a lifetime of passionate letters to her sister-in-law Sue Gilbert and a smaller group of such letters to her friend Kate Scott Anthon. Hurston married twice but soon left each husband, scrambled her way from Florida to Harlem to Columbia University to Haiti and finally back to Florida, moved in and out of white patronage and poverty, professional success, and failure; her survival relationships were all with women, beginning with her mother. Both of these women in their vastly different circumstances were marriage resisters, committed to their own work and selfhood, and were later characterized as "apolitical." Both were drawn to men of intellectual quality; for both of them women provided the ongoing fascination and sustenance of life.

If we think of heterosexuality as *the* natural emotional and sensual inclination for women, lives such as these are seen as deviant, as pathological, or as emotionally and sensually deprived. Or, in more recent and permissive jargon, they are banalized as "life styles." And the work of such women, whether merely the daily work of individual or collective survival and resistance or the work of the writer, the activist, the reformer, the anthropologist, or the artist—the work of self-creation—is undervalued, or seen as the bitter fruit of "penis envy" or the sublimation of repressed eroticism or the meaningless rant of a "man-hater." But when we turn the lens of vision and consider the degree to which and the methods whereby heterosexual "preference" has actually been imposed on women, not only can we understand differently the meaning of individual lives and work, but we can begin to recognize a central fact of women's history: that women have always resisted male tyranny. A feminism of action, often though not always without a theory, has constantly re-emerged in every culture and in every period. We can then begin to study women's struggle against powerlessness, women's radical rebellion, not just in male-defined "concrete revolutionary situations"[53] but in all the situations male ideologies have not perceived as revolutionary—for example, the refusal of some women to produce children, aided at great risk by other women;[54] the refusal to produce a higher standard of living and leisure for men (Leghorn and

---

Revolution, ed. J. MacKinnon and S. MacKinnon (Old Wesbury, N.Y.: Feminist Press, 1976), pp. 103–110.

[53] See Rosalind Petchesky, "Dissolving the Hyphen: A Report on Marxist-Feminist Groups 1–5," in *Capitalist Patriarchy and the Case for Socialist Feminism,* ed. Zillah Eisenstein (New York: Monthly Review Press, 1979), p. 387.

[54] [A.R., 1986: See Angela Davis, *Women, Race and Class* (New York: Random House, 1981), p. 102; Orlando Patterson, *Slavery and Social Death: A Comparative Study* (Cambridge: Harvard University Press, 1982), p. 133.]

Parker show how both are part of women's unacknowledged, unpaid, and ununionized economic contribution). We can no longer have patience with Dinnerstein's view that women have simply collaborated with men in the "sexual arrangements" of history. We begin to observe behavior, both in history and in individual biography, that has hitherto been invisible or misnamed, behavior which often constitutes, given the limits of the counterforce exerted in a given time and place, radical rebellion. And we can connect these rebellions and the necessity for them with the physical passion of woman for woman which is central to lesbian existence: the erotic sensuality which has been, precisely, the most violently erased fact of female experience.

Heterosexuality has been both forcibly and subliminally imposed on women. Yet everywhere women have resisted it, often at the cost of physical torture, imprisonment, psychosurgery, social ostracism, and extreme poverty. "Compulsory heterosexuality" was named as one of the "crimes against women" by the Brussels International Tribunal on Crimes against Women in 1976. Two pieces of testimony from two very different cultures reflect the degree to which persecution of lesbians is a global practice here and now. A report from Norway relates:

> A lesbian in Oslo was in a heterosexual marriage that didn't work, so she started taking tranquillizers and ended up at the health sanatorium for treatment and rehabilitation. . . . The moment she said in family group therapy that she believed she was a lesbian, the doctor told her she was not. He knew from "looking into her eyes," he said. She had the eyes of a woman who wanted sexual intercourse with her husband. So she was subjected to so-called "couch therapy." She was put into a comfortably heated room, naked, on a bed, and for an hour her husband was to . . . try to excite her sexually. . . . The idea was that the touching was always to end with sexual intercourse. She felt stronger and stronger aversion. She threw up and sometimes ran out of the room to avoid this "treatment." The more strongly she asserted that she was a lesbian, the more violent the forced heterosexual intercourse became. This treatment went on for about six months. She escaped from the hospital, but she was brought back. Again she escaped. She has not been there since. In the end she realized that she had been subjected to forcible rape for six months.

And from Mozambique:

> I am condemned to a life of exile because I will not deny that I am a lesbian, that my primary commitments are, and will always be to other women. In the new Mozambique, lesbianism is considered a left-over from colonialism and decadent Western civilization. Lesbians are sent to rehabilitation camps to learn through self-criticism the correct line about themselves. . . . If I am forced to denounce my own love for women, if I therefore denounce myself,

> I could go back to Mozambique and join forces in the exciting and hard struggle of rebuilding a nation, including the struggle for the emancipation of Mozambiquan women. As it is, I either risk the rehabilitation camps, or remain in exile.[55]

Nor can it be assumed that women like those in Carroll Smith-Rosenberg's study, who married, stayed married, yet dwelt in a profoundly female emotional and passional world, "preferred" or "chose" heterosexuality. Women have married because it was necessary, in order to survive economically, in order to have children who would not suffer economic deprivation or social ostracism, in order to remain respectable, in order to do what was expected of women, because coming out of "abnormal" childhoods they wanted to feel "normal", and because heterosexual romance has been represented as the great female adventure, duty, and fulfillment. We may faithfully or ambivalently have obeyed the institution, but our feelings—and our sensuality—have not been tamed or contained within it. There is no statistical documentation of the numbers of lesbians who have remained in heterosexual marriages for most of their lives. But in a letter to the early lesbian publication *The Ladder,* the playwright Lorraine Hansberry had this to say:

> I suspect that the problem of the married woman who would prefer emotional-physical relationships with other women is proportionally much higher than a similar statistic for men. (A statistic surely no one will ever really have.) This is because the estate of woman being what it is, how could we ever begin to guess the numbers of women who are not prepared to risk a life alien to what they have been taught all their lives to believe was their "natural" destiny—AND—their only expectation for ECONOMIC security. It seems to be that this is why the question has an immensity that it does not have for male homosexuals. . . . A woman of strength and honesty may, if she chooses, sever her marriage and marry a new male mate and society will be upset that the divorce rate is rising so—but there are few places in the United States, in any event, where she will be anything remotely akin to an "outcast." Obviously this is not true for a woman who would end her marriage to take up life with another woman.[56]

This *double-life*—this apparent acquiescence to an institution founded on male interest and prerogative—has been characteristic of female experience: in motherhood and in many kinds of heterosexual behavior, including the rituals

[55] Russell and van de Ven, pp. 42–43, 56–57.

[56] I am indebted to Jonathan Katz's *Gay American History (op. cit.)* for bringing to my attention Hansberry's letters to *The Ladder* and to Barbara Grier for supplying me with copies of relevant pages from *The Ladder,* quoted here by permission of Barbara Grier. See also the reprinted series of *The Ladder,* ed. Jonathan Katz *et al.* (New York: Arno, 1975), and Deirdre Carmody, "Letters by Eleanor Roosevelt Detail Friendship with Lorena Hickok," *New York Times* (October 21, 1979).

of courtship; the pretense of asexuality by the nineteenth-century wife; the simulation of orgasm by the prostitute, the courtesan, the twentieth-century "sexually liberated" woman.

Meridel LeSueur's documentary novel of the depression, *The Girl,* is arresting as a study of female double-life. The protagonist, a waitress in a St. Paul working-class speakeasy, feels herself passionately attracted to the young man Butch, but her survival relationships are with Clara, an older waitress and prostitute, with Belle, whose husband owns the bar, and with Amelia, a union activist. For Clara and Belle and the unnamed protagonist, sex with men is in one sense an escape from the bedrock misery of daily life, a flare of intensity in the gray, relentless, often brutal web of day-to-day existence:

> It was like he was a magnet pulling me. It was exciting and powerful and frightening. He was after me too and when he found me I would run, or be petrified, just standing in front of him like a zany. And he told me not to be wandering with Clara to the Marigold where we danced with strangers. He said he would knock the shit out of me. Which made me shake and tremble, but it was better than being a husk full of suffering and not knowing why.[57]

Throughout the novel the theme of the double-life emerges; Belle reminisces about her marriage to the bootlegger Hoinck:

> You know, when I had that black eye and said I hit it on the cupboard, well he did it the bastard, and then he says don't tell anybody. . . . He's nuts, that's what he is, nuts, and I don't see why I live with him, why I put up with him a minute on this earth. But listen kid, she said, I'm telling you something. She looked at me and her face was wonderful. She said, Jesus Christ, Goddam him I love him that's why I'm hooked like this all my life, Goddam him I love him.[58]

After the protagonist has her first sex with Butch, her women friends care for her bleeding, give her whiskey, and compare notes.

> My luck, the first time and I got into trouble. He gave me a little money and I come to St. Paul where for ten bucks they'd stick a huge vet's needle into you and you start it and then you were on your own. . . . I never had no child. I've just had Hoinck to mother, and a hell of a child he is.[59]

> Later they made me go back to Clara's room to lie down. . . . Clara lay down beside me and put her arms around me and wanted me to tell her about it

[57] Meridel LeSueur, *The Girl* (Cambridge, Mass.: West End Press, 1978), pp. 10–11. LeSueur describes, in an afterword, how this book was drawn from the writings and oral narrations of women in the Workers Alliance who met as a writers' group during the depression.
[58] *Ibid.*, p. 20.
[59] *Ibid.*, pp. 53–54.

> but she wanted to tell about herself. She said she started it when she was twelve with a bunch of boys in an old shed. She said nobody had paid any attention to her before and she became very popular. . . . They like it so much, she said, why shouldn't you give it to them and get presents and attention? I never cared anything for it and neither did my mama. But it's the only thing you got that's valuable.[60]

Sex is thus equated with attention from the male, who is charismatic though brutal, infantile, or unreliable. Yet it is the women who make life endurable for each other, give physical affection without causing pain, share, advise, and stick by each other. (*I am trying to find my strength through women—without my friends, I could not survive.*) LeSueur's *The Girl* parallels Toni Morrison's remarkable *Sula,* another revelation of female double life:

> Nel was the one person who had wanted nothing from her, who had accepted all aspects of her. . . . Nel was one of the reasons Sula had drifted back to Medallion. . . . The men . . . had merged into one large personality: the same language of love, the same entertainments of love, the same cooling of love. Whenever she introduced her private thoughts into their rubbings and goings, they hooded their eyes. They taught her nothing but love tricks, shared nothing but worry, gave nothing but money. She had been looking all along for a friend, and it took her a while to discover that a lover was not a comrade and could never be—for a woman.

But Sula's last thought at the second of her death is "Wait'll I tell Nel." And after Sula's death, Nel looks back on her own life:

> "All that time, all that time, I thought I was missing Jude." And the loss pressed down on her chest and came up into her throat. "We was girls together," she said as though explaining something. "O Lord, Sula," she cried, "Girl, girl, girlgirlgirl!" It was a fine cry—loud and long—but it had no bottom and it had no top, just circles and circles of sorrow.[61]

The Girl and *Sula* are both novels which examine what I am calling the lesbian continuum, in contrast to the shallow or sensational "lesbian scenes" in recent commercial fiction.[62] Each shows us woman identification untarnished (till the end of LeSueur's novel) by romanticism; each depicts the competition of heterosexual compulsion for women's attention, the diffusion and frustration

[60] *Ibid.*, p. 55.

[61] Toni Morrison, *Sula* (New York: Bantam, 1973), pp. 103–104, 149. I am indebted to Lorraine Bethel's essay " 'This Infinity of Conscious Pain': Zora Neale Hurston and the Black Female Literary Tradition," in *All the Women Are White, All the Blacks are Men, but Some of Us Are Brave: Black Women's Studies,* ed. Gloria T. Hull, Patricia Bell Scott, and Barbara Smith (Old Westbury, N.Y.: Feminist Press, 1982).

[62] See Maureen Brady and Judith McDaniel, "Lesbians in the Mainstream: The Image of Lesbians in Recent Commercial Fiction," *Conditions* 6 (1979): 82–105.

of female bonding that might, in a more conscious form, reintegrate love and power.

IV

Woman identification is a source of energy, a potential springhead of female power, curtailed and contained under the institution of heterosexuality. The denial of reality and visibility to women's passion for women, women's choice of women as allies, life companions, and community, the forcing of such relationships into dissimulation and their disintegration under intense pressure have meant an incalculable loss to the power of all women *to change the social relations of the sexes, to liberate ourselves and each other.* The lie of compulsory female heterosexuality today afflicts not just feminist scholarship, but every profession, every reference work, every curriculum, every organizing attempt, every relationship or conversation over which it hovers. It creates, specifically, a profound falseness, hypocrisy, and hysteria in the heterosexual dialogue, for every heterosexual relationship is lived in the queasy strobe light of that lie. However we choose to identify ourselves, however we find ourselves labeled, it flickers across and distorts our lives.[63]

The lie keeps numberless women psychologically trapped, trying to fit mind, spirit, and sexuality into a prescribed script because they cannot look beyond the parameters of the acceptable. It pulls on the energy of such women even as it drains the energy of "closeted" lesbians—the energy exhausted in the double life. The lesbian trapped in the "closet," the woman imprisoned in prescriptive ideas of the "normal" share the pain of blocked options, broken connections, lost access to self-definition freely and powerfully assumed.

The lie is many-layered. In Western tradition, one layer—the romantic—asserts that women are inevitably, even if rashly and tragically, drawn to men; that even when that attraction is suicidal (e.g., *Tristan and Isolde,* Kate Chopin's *The Awakening*), it is still an organic imperative. In the tradition of the social sciences it asserts that primary love between the sexes is "normal"; that women *need* men as social and economic protectors, for adult sexuality, and for psychological completion; that the heterosexually constituted family is the basic social unit; that women who do not attach their primary intensity to men must be, in functional terms, condemned to an even more devastating outsiderhood than their outsiderhood as women. Small wonder that lesbians are reported to be a more hidden population than male homosexuals. The Black lesbian-feminist critic Lorraine Bethel, writing on Zora Neale Hurston, remarks that for a Black woman—already twice an outsider—to choose to assume still an-

[63] See Russell and van de Ven, p. 40: "Few heterosexual women realize their lack of free choice about their sexuality, and few realize how and why compulsory heterosexuality is also a crime against them."

other "hated identity" is problematic indeed. Yet the lesbian continuum has been a life line for Black women both in Africa and the United States.

> Black women have a long tradition of bonding together . . . in a Black/women's community that has been a source of vital survival information, psychic and emotional support for us. We have a distinct Black woman-identified folk culture based on our experiences as Black women in this society; symbols, language and modes of expression that are specific to the realities of our lives. . . . Because Black women were rarely among those Blacks and females who gained access to literary and other acknowledged forms of artistic expression, this Black female bonding and Black woman-identification has often been hidden and unrecorded except in the individual lives of Black women through our own memories of our particular Black female tradition.[64]

Another layer of the lie is the frequently encountered implication that women turn to women out of hatred for men. Profound skepticism, caution, and righteous paranoia about men may indeed be part of any healthy woman's response to the misogyny of male-dominated culture, to the forms assumed by "normal" male sexuality, and to *the failure even of "sensitive" or "political" men to perceive or find these troubling.* Lesbian existence is also represented as mere refuge from male abuses, rather than as an electric and empowering charge between women. One of the most frequently quoted literary passages on lesbian relationship is that in which Colette's Renée, in *The Vagabond,* describes "the melancholy and touching image of two weak creatures who have perhaps found shelter in each other's arms, there to sleep and weep, safe from man who is often cruel, and there to taste *better than any pleasure, the bitter happiness of feeling themselves akin, frail and forgotten* [emphasis added]."[65] Colette is often considered a lesbian writer. Her popular reputation has, I think, much to do with the fact that she writes about lesbian existence as if for a male audience; her earliest "lesbian" novels, the Claudine series, were written under compulsion for her husband and published under both their names. At all events, except for her writings on her mother, Colette is a less reliable source on the lesbian continuum than, I would think, Charlotte Brontë, who understood that while women may, indeed must, be one another's allies, mentors, and comforters in the female struggle for survival, there is quite extraneous delight in each other's company and attraction to each other's minds and character, which attend a recognition of each others' strengths.

---

[64] Bethel, " 'This Infinity of Conscious Pain,' " *op. cit.*

[65] Dinnerstein, the most recent writer to quote this passage, adds ominously: "But what has to be added to her account is that these 'women enlaced' are sheltering each other not just from what men want to do to them, but also from what they want to do to each other" (Dinnerstein, p. 103). The fact is, however, that woman-to-woman violence is a minute grain in the universe of male-against-female violence perpetuated and rationalized in every social institution.

By the same token, we can say that there is a *nascent* feminist political content in the act of choosing a woman lover or life partner in the face of institutionalized heterosexuality.[66] But for lesbian existence to realize this political content in an ultimately liberating form, the erotic choice must deepen and expand into conscious woman identification—into lesbian feminism.

The work that lies ahead, of unearthing and describing what I call here "lesbian existence," is potentially liberating for all women. It is work that must assuredly move beyond the limits of white and middle-class Western Women's Studies to examine women's lives, work, and groupings within every racial, ethnic, and political structure. There are differences, moreover, between "lesbian existence" and the "lesbian continuum," differences we can discern even in the movement of our own lives. The lesbian continuum, I suggest, needs delineation in light of the "double-life" of women, not only women self-described as heterosexual but also of self-described lesbians. We need a far more exhaustive account of the forms the double life has assumed. Historians need to ask at every point how heterosexuality as institution has been organized and maintained through the female wage scale, the enforcement of middle-class women's "leisure," the glamorization of so-called sexual liberation, the withholding of education from women, the imagery of "high art" and popular culture, the mystification of the "personal" sphere, and much else. We need an economics which comprehends the institution of heterosexuality, with its doubled workload for women and its sexual divisions of labor, as the most idealized of economic relations.

The question inevitably will arise: Are we then to condemn all heterosexual relationships, including those which are least oppressive? I believe this question, though often heartfelt, is the wrong question here. We have been stalled in a maze of false dichotomies which prevents our apprehending the institution as a whole: "good" versus "bad" marriages; "marriage for love" versus arranged marriage; "liberated" sex versus prostitution; heterosexual intercourse versus rape; *Liebeschmerz* versus humiliation and dependency. Within the institution exist, of course, qualitative differences of experience; but the absence of choice remains the great unacknowledged reality, and in the absence of choice, women will remain dependent upon the chance or luck of particular relationships and will have no collective power to determine the meaning and place of sexuality in their lives. As we address the institution itself, moreover, we begin to perceive a history of female resistance which has never fully understood itself because it has been so fragmented, miscalled, erased. It will require a courageous grasp of the politics and economics, as well as the cultural propaganda, of heterosexuality to carry us beyond individual cases or diversified group situations into the complex kind of overview needed to undo the power

---

[66] Conversation with Blanche W. Cook, New York City, March 1979.

men everywhere wield over women, power which has become a model for every other form of exploitation and illegitimate control.

1978

AFTERWORD

In 1980, Ann Snitow, Christine Stansell, and Sharon Thompson, three Marxist-feminist activists and scholars, sent out a call for papers for an anthology on the politics of sexuality. Having just finished writing "Compulsory Heterosexuality" for *Signs,* I sent them that manuscript and asked them to consider it. Their anthology, *Powers of Desire,* was published by the Monthly Review Press New Feminist Library in 1983 and included my paper. During the intervening period, the four of us were in correspondence, but I was able to take only limited advantage of this dialogue due to ill health and resulting surgery. With their permission, I reprint here excerpts from that correspondence as a way of indicating that my essay should be read as one contribution to a long exploration in progress, not as my own "last word" on sexual politics. I also refer interested readers to *Powers of Desire* itself.

Dear Adrienne,

. . . In one of our first letters, we told you that we were finding parameters of left-wing/feminist sexual discourse to be far broader than we imagined. Since then, we have perceived what we believe to be a crisis in the feminist movement about sex, an intensifying debate (although not always an explicit one), and a questioning of assumptions once taken for granted. While we fear the link between sex and violence, as do Women Against Pornography, we wish we better understood its sources in ourselves as well as in men. In the Reagan era, we can hardly afford to romanticize any old norm of a virtuous and moral sexuality.

In your piece, you are asking the question, what would women choose in a world where patriarchy and capitalism did *not* rule? We agree with you that heterosexuality is an institution created between these grind stones, but we don't conclude, therefore, that it is entirely a male creation. You only allow for female historical agency insofar as women exist on the lesbian continuum while we would argue that women's history, like men's history, is created out of a dialectic of necessity and choice.

All three of us (hence one lesbian, two heterosexual women) had questions about your use of the term "false consciousness" for women's heterosexuality. In general, we think the false-consciousness model can blind us to the necessities and desires that comprise the lives of the oppressed. It can also lead to the too easy denial of others' experience when that experience is different from our own. We posit, rather, a complex social model in which all erotic life is a continuum, one which therefore includes relations with men.

Which brings us to this metaphor of the continuum. We know you are a poet, not an historian, and we look forward to reading your metaphors all our lives—and standing straighter as feminists, as women, for having read them. But the metaphor of the lesbian continuum is open to all kinds of misunderstandings, and these sometimes have odd political effects. For example, Sharon reports that at a recent meeting around the abortion-rights struggle, the notions of continuum arose in the discussion several times and underwent divisive transformation. Overall, the notion that two ways of being existed on the same continuum was interpreted to mean that those two ways were the *same*. The sense of range and gradation that your description evokes disappeared. Lesbianism and female friendship became exactly the same thing. Similarly, heterosexuality and rape became the same. In one of several versions of the continuum that evolved, a slope was added, like so:

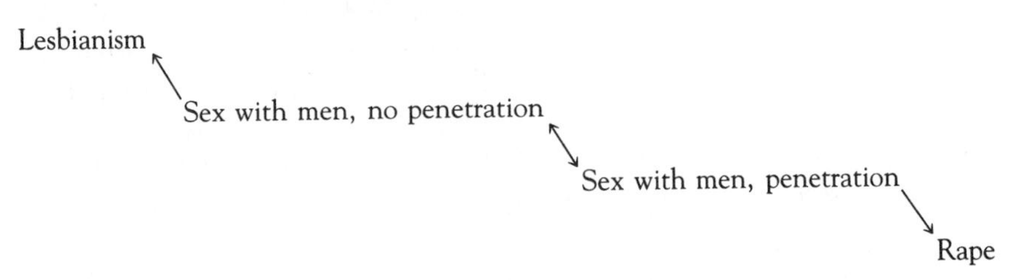

This sloped continuum brought its proponents to the following conclusion: An appropriate, workable abortion-rights strategy is to inform all women that heterosexual penetration is rape, whatever their subjective experience to the contrary. All women will immediately recognize the truth of this and opt for the alternative of nonpenetration. The abortion-rights struggle will thus be simplified into a struggle against coercive sex and its consequences (since no enlightened woman would voluntarily undergo penetration unless her object was procreation—a peculiarly Catholic-sounding view).

The proponents of this strategy were young women who have worked hard in the abortion-rights movement for the past two or more years. They are inexperienced but they are dedicated. For this reason, we take their reading of your work seriously. We don't think, however, that it comes solely, or even at all, from the work itself. As likely a source is the tendency to dichotomize that has plagued the women's movement. The source of that tendency is harder to trace.

In that regard, the hints in "Compulsory" about the double life of women intrigue us. You define the double life as "the apparent acquiescence to an institution founded on male interest and prerogative." But that definition doesn't really explain your other references—to, for instance, the "intense mixture" of love and anger in lesbian relationships and to the peril of romanticizing what it means "to love and act against the grain." We think these comments raise extremely important issues for feminists right now; the problem of division and anger among us needs airing and analysis. Is this, by any chance, the theme of a piece you have in the works?

. . . We would still love it if we could have a meeting with you in the next few months. Any chance? . . . Greetings and support from us—in all your undertakings.

We send love,
Sharon, Chris, and Ann

New York City
April 19, 1981

Dear Ann, Chris, and Sharon,
. . . It's good to be back in touch with you, you who have been so unfailingly patient, generous, and persistent. Above all, it's important to me that you know that ill health, not a withdrawal because of political differences, delayed my writing back to you. . . .

"False consciousness" can, I agree, be used as a term of dismissal for any thinking we don't like or adhere to. But, as I tried to illustrate in some detail, there is a real, identifiable system of heterosexual propaganda, of defining women as existing for the sexual use of men, which goes beyond "sex role" or "gender" stereotyping or "sexist imagery" to include a vast number of verbal and nonverbal messages. And this I call "control of consciousness." The possibility of a woman who does not exist sexually for men—the lesbian possibility—is buried, erased, occluded, distorted, misnamed, and driven underground. The feminist books—Chodorow, Dinnerstein, Ehrenreich and English, and others—which I discuss at the beginning of my essay contribute to this invalidation and erasure, and as such are part of the problem.

My essay is founded on the belief that we all think from within the limits of certain solipsisms—usually linked with privilege, racial, cultural, and economic as well as sexual—which present themselves as "the universal," "the way things are," "all women," etc., etc. I wrote it equally out of the belief that in becoming conscious of our solipsisms we have certain kinds of choices, that we can and must re-educate ourselves. I never have maintained that heterosexual feminists are walking about in a state of "brainwashed" false consciousness. Nor have such phrases as "sleeping with the enemy" seemed to me either profound or useful. *Homophobia* is too diffuse a term and does not go very far in helping us identify and talk about the sexual solipsism of heterosexual feminism. In this paper I was trying to ask heterosexual feminists to examine their experience of heterosexuality critically and antagonistically, to critique the institution of which they are a part, to struggle with the norm and its implications for women's freedom, to become more open to the considerable resources offered by the lesbian-feminist perspective, to refuse to settle for the personal privilege and solution of the individual "good relationship" within the institution of heterosexuality.

As regards "female historical agency," I wanted, precisely, to suggest that the victim model is insufficient; that there *is* a history of female agency and choice which has actually challenged aspects of male supremacy; that, like male supremacy, these can be found in many different cultures. . . . It's not that I think all female agency has been solely and avowedly lesbian. But by erasing lesbian existence from female history, from theory, from literary criticism . . . from feminist approaches to economic structure, ideas about "the family," etc., an enormous amount of female agency is kept unavailable, hence unusable. I wanted to demonstrate that that kind of obliteration continues to be acceptable in seriously regarded feminist texts. What surprised me in the responses to my essay, including your notes, is how almost every aspect of it has been considered, except this—to me—central one. I was taking a position which was neither lesbian/separatist in the sense of dismissing heterosexual women nor a "gay civil rights" plea for . . . openness to lesbianism as an "option" or an "alternate life style." I was urging that lesbian *existence* has been an unrecognized and unaffirmed claiming by women of their sexuality, thus a pattern of resistance, thus also a kind of borderline position from which to analyze and challenge the relationship of heterosexuality to male supremacy. And that lesbian existence, when recognized, demands a conscious restructuring of feminist analysis and criticism, not just a token reference or two.

I certainly agree with you that the term *lesbian continuum* can be misused. It was, in the example you report of the abortion-rights meeting, though I would think anyone who had read my work from *Of Woman Born* onward would know that my position on abortion and sterilization abuse is more complicated than that. My own problem with the phrase is that it can be, is, used by women who have not yet begun to examine the privileges and solipsisms of heterosexuality, as a safe way to describe their felt connections with women, without having to share in the risks and threats of lesbian existence. What I had thought to delineate rather complexly as a continuum has begun to sound more like "life-style shopping." *Lesbian continuum*—the phrase—came from a desire to allow for the greatest possible variation of female-identified experience, while paying a different kind of respect to *lesbian existence*—the traces and knowledge of women who have made their primary erotic and emotional choices for women. If I were writing the paper today, I would still want to make this distinction, but would put more caveats around *lesbian continuum.* I fully agree with you that Smith-Rosenberg's "female world" is not a social ideal, enclosed as it is within prescriptive middle-class heterosexuality and marriage.

My own essay could have been stronger had it drawn on more of the literature by Black women toward which Toni Morrison's *Sula* inevitably pointed me. In reading a great deal more of Black women's fiction I began to perceive a different set of valences from those found in white women's fiction for the most part: a different quest for the woman hero, a different relationship both to sexuality with men and to female loyalty and bonding. . . .

You comment briefly on your reactions to some of the radical-feminist works I cited in my first footnote.[67] I am myself critical of some of them even as I found them vitally useful. What most of them share is a taking seriously of misogyny—of organized, institutionalized, normalized hostility and violence against women. I feel no "hierarchy of oppressions" is needed in order for us to take misogyny as seriously as we take racism, anti-Semitism, imperialism. To take misogyny seriously needn't mean that we perceive women merely as victims, without responsibilities or choices; it does mean recognizing the "necessity" in that "dialectic of necessity and choice"—identifying, describing, refusing to turn aside our eyes. I think that some of the apparent reductiveness, or even obsessiveness, of some white radical-feminist theory derives from racial and/or class solipsism, but also from the immense effort of trying to render woman hating visible amid so much denial. . . .

Finally, as to poetry and history: I want both in my life; I need to see through both. If metaphor can be misconstrued, history can also lead to misconstrual when it obliterates acts of resistance or rebellion, wipes out transformational models, or sentimentalizes power relationships. I know you know this. I believe we are all trying to think and write out of our best consciences, our most open consciousness. I expect that quality in this book which you are editing, and look forward with anticipation to the thinking—and the actions—toward which it may take us.

In sisterhood,
Adrienne

Montague, Massachusetts
November 1981

[67] See footnote 9, p. 591.

TONI MORRISON
(1931–)

Toni Morrison is best known for her novels, which include The Bluest Eye, Sula, Song of Solomon, Tar Baby, and Beloved. Sula, nominated for the National Book Award in Fiction for 1973, brought national recognition to Morrison. Song of Solomon won the fiction award of the National Book Critics' Circle for 1977, Tar Baby remained on the New York Times best-seller lists for four months in 1981, and Beloved won the Pulitzer Prize for fiction in 1988.

Morrison's books are often about self-knowledge as well as about connections across generations and between women as sisters, mothers, and friends. The importance of one's ancestors to a sense of self, especially for African Americans, is a theme that pervades her work, as does the importance of spiritual elements to everyday life. In her work, Morrison has said, she attempts to "blend the acceptance of the supernatural and a profound rootedness in the real world . . . with neither taking precedence over the other."

Born in Ohio as Chloe Anthony Wofford, Morrison graduated from high school with honors, attended Howard University, and received her M.A. from Cornell in 1955. She has taught at Texas Southern University, Howard University, SUNY/Purchase, Bard College, Yale University, and Princeton University. As a senior editor at Random House for a number of years, she helped to bring into print the work of Toni Cade Bambara and other African American writers. Her articles have appeared in a wide range of publications, including the New York Times Book Review, the New Republic, Essence, The Nation, and Vogue.

Morrison has said that, in her writing, she is "simply trying to recreate something out of an old art form . . . the something that defines what makes a book 'black.' " She wants to capture the way Black people talk, the rhythms and metaphors they employ. She uses the African-American folk traditions and aesthetic as integral parts of her fiction.

For Morrison, writing, teaching, and social activism are essential activities. Like Toni Cade Bambara, Alice Walker, and others, Morrison writes both to teach and to inspire the African American community and readers from all cultures. In much of her work, Morrison shows the varying ways in which a person can be Black, female—and human. Although her works often show the oppression and humiliation of African Americans by whites, Morrison also shows her readers how they can find themselves through their history, their ancestors, and their sense of community.

In "A Slow Walk of Trees," first published in the New York Times Magazine in 1976, Morrison examines racism and the history of African

Americans in the United States through the perspectives of her grandparents and parents as well as through her own experience.

A SLOW WALK OF TREES

His name was John Solomon Willis, and when at age 5 he heard from the old folks that "the Emancipation Proclamation was coming," he crawled under the bed. It was his earliest recollection of what was to be his habitual response to the promise of white people: horror and an instinctive yearning for safety. He was my grandfather, a musician who managed to hold on to his violin but not his land. He lost all 88 acres of his Indian mother's inheritance to legal predators who built their fortunes on the likes of him. He was an unreconstructed black pessimist who, in spite of or because of emancipation, was convinced for 85 years that there was no hope whatever for black people in this country. His rancor was legitimate, for he, John Solomon, was not only an artist but a first-rate carpenter and farmer, reduced to sending home to his family money he made playing the violin because he was not able to find work. And this during the years when almost half the black male population were skilled craftsmen who lost their jobs to white ex-convicts and immigrant farmers.

His wife, however, was of a quite different frame of mind and believed that all things could be improved by faith in Jesus and an effort of the will. So it was she, Ardelia Willis, who sneaked her seven children out of the back window into the darkness, rather than permit the patron of their sharecropper's existence to become their executioner as well, and headed north in 1912, when 99.2 percent of all black people in the U.S. were native-born and only 60 percent of white Americans were. And it was Ardelia who told her husband that they could not stay in the Kentucky town they ended up in because the teacher didn't know long division.

They have been dead now for 30 years and more and I still don't know which of them came closer to the truth about the possibilities of life for black people in this country. One of their grandchildren is a tenured professor at Princeton. Another, who suffered from what the Peruvian poet called "anger that breaks a man into children," was picked up just as he entered his teens and emotionally lobotomized by the reformatories and mental institutions specifically designed to serve him. Neither John Solomon nor Ardelia lived long enough to despair over one or swell with pride over the other. But if they were alive today each would have selected and collected enough evidence to support the accuracy of the other's original point of view. And it would be difficult to convince either one that the other was right.

Some of the monstrous events that took place in John Solomon's America have been duplicated in alarming detail in my own America. There was the public murder of a President in a theater in 1865 and the public murder of another President on television in 1963. The Civil War of 1861 had its encore as the civil-rights movement of 1960. The torture and mutilation of a black West Point Cadet (Cadet Johnson Whittaker) in 1880 had its rerun with the 1970's murders of students at Jackson State College, Texas Southern and Southern University in Baton Rouge. And in 1976 we watch for what must be the thousandth time a pitched battle between the children of slaves and the children of immigrants—only this time, it is not the New York draft riots of 1863, but the busing turmoil in Paul Revere's home town, Boston.

Hopeless, he'd said. Hopeless. For he was certain that white people of every political, religious, geographical and economic background would band together against black people everywhere when they felt the threat of our progress. And a hundred years after he sought safety from the white man's "promise," somebody put a bullet in Martin Luther King's brain. And not long before that some excellent samples of the master race demonstrated their courage and virility by dynamiting some little black girls to death. If he were here now, my grandfather, he would shake his head, close his eyes and pull out his violin—too polite to say, "I told you so." And his wife would pay attention to the music but not to the sadness in her husband's eyes, for she would see what she expected to see—not the occasional historical repetition, but, *like the slow walk of certain species of trees from the flatlands up into the mountains,* she would see the signs of irrevocable and permanent change. She, who pulled her girls out of an inadequate school in the Cumberland Mountains, knew all along that the gentlemen from Alabama who had killed the little girls would be rounded up. And it wouldn't surprise her in the least to know that the number of black college graduates jumped 12 percent in the last three years: 47 percent in 20 years. That there are 140 black mayors in this country; 14 black judges in the District Circuit, 4 in the Courts of Appeals and one on the Supreme Court. That there are 17 blacks in Congress, one in the Senate; 276 in state legislatures—223 in state houses, 53 in state senates. That there are 112 elected black police chiefs and sheriffs, 1 Pulitzer prize winner; 1 winner of the Prix de Rome; a dozen or so winners of the Guggenheim; 4 deans of predominantly white colleges. . . . Oh, her list would go on and on. But so would John Solomon's sweet sad music.

While my grandparents held opposite views on whether the fortunes of black people were improving, my own parents struck similarly opposed postures, but from another slant. They differed about whether the moral fiber of white people would ever improve. Quite a different argument. The old folks argued about how and if black people could improve themselves, who could be counted on to help us, who would hinder us and so on. My parents took issue over the question of whether it was possible for white people to improve. They assumed that black people were the humans of the globe, but had serious doubts about the quality and existence of white humanity. Thus my father, distrusting every word and every gesture of every white man on earth, assumed that the white man who crept up the stairs one afternoon had come to molest his daughters and threw him down the stairs and then our tricycle after him. (I think my father was wrong, but considering what I have seen since, it may have been very healthy for me to have witnessed that as my first black-white encounter.) My mother, however, *believed* in them—their possibilities. So when the meal we got on relief was bug-ridden, she wrote a long letter to Franklin Delano Roosevelt. And when white bill collectors came to our door, it was she who received them civilly and explained in a sweet voice that we were people of honor and that the debt would be taken care of. Her message to Roosevelt got through—our meal improved. Her message to the bill collectors did not always get through and there was occasional violence when my father (self-exiled to the bedroom for fear he could not hold his temper) would hear that her reasonableness had failed. My mother was always wounded by these scenes, for she thought the bill collector knew that she loved good credit more than life and that being in arrears on payment horrified her probably more than it did him. So she thought he was rude because he was white. For years she walked to utility companies and department stores to pay bills in person and even now she does not seem convinced that checks are legal tender. My father loved excellence, worked hard (he held three jobs at once for 17 years) and was so outraged by the suggestion of personal slackness that he could explain it to himself only in terms of racism. He was a fastidious worker who was frightened of one thing: unemployment. I can remember now the doomsday-cum-graveyard sound of "laid off" and how the minute school was out he asked us, "Where you workin'?" Both my parents believed that all succor and aid came from themselves and their neighborhood, since "they"—white people in charge and those not in charge but in obstructionist positions—were in some way fundamentally, genetically corrupt.

So I grew up in a basically racist household with more than a child's share of contempt for white people. And for each white friend I acquired who made a small crack in that contempt, there was another who repaired it. For each one who related to me as a person, there was one who in my presence at least, became actively "white." And like most black people of my generation, I suffer from racial vertigo that can be cured only by taking what one needs from one's ancestors. John Solomon's cynicism and his deployment of his art as both weapon and solace, Ardelia's faith in the magic that can be wrought by sheer effort of the will; my mother's openmindedness in each new encounter and her habit of trying reasonableness first; my father's temper, his impatience and his efforts to keep "them" (throw them) out of his life. And it is out of these learned and selected attitudes that I look at the quality of life for my people in this country now. These widely disparate and sometimes conflicting views, I suspect, were held not only by me, but by most black people. Some I know are clearer in their positions, have not sullied their anger with optimism or dirtied their hope with despair. But most of us are plagued by a sense of being worn shell-thin by constant repression and hostility as well as the impression of being buoyed by visible testimony of tremendous strides. There *is* repetition of the grotesque in our history. And there *is* the miraculous walk of trees. The question is whether our walk is progress or merely movement. O.J. Simpson leaning on a Hertz car *is* better than the Gold Dust Twins on the back of a soap box. But is "Good Times" better than Stepin Fetchit? Has the first order of business been taken care of? Does the law of the land work for us?

Are white people who murder black people punished with at least the same dispatch that sends black teen-age truants to Coxsackie? Can we relax now and discuss "The Jeffersons" instead of genocide? Or is the difference between the two only the difference between a greedy pointless white life-style and a messy pointless black death? Now that Mr. Poitier and Mr. Belafonte have shot up all the racists in "Buck and the Preacher," have they all gone away? Can we really move into better neighborhoods and not be set on fire? Is there anybody who will lay me a $5 bet on it?

The past decade is a fairly good index of the odds at which you lay your money down.

Ten years ago in Queens, as black people like me moved into a neighborhood 20 minutes away from the Triborough Bridge, "for sale" signs shot up in front of white folks' houses like dandelions after a hot spring rain. And the black people smiled. "Goody, goody," said my neighbor. "Maybe we can push them on out to sea. You think?"

Now I live in another neighborhood, 20 minutes away from the George Washington Bridge, and again the "for sale" signs are pushing up out of the ground. Fewer, perhaps, and for different reasons, perhaps. Still the Haitian lady and I smile at each other. "My, my," she says "they goin' on up to the hills? Seem like they just come from there." "The woods," I say. "They like to live in the woods." She nods with infinite understanding, then shrugs. The Haitians have already arranged for one mass in the church to be said in French, already have their own newspaper, stores, community center. That's not movement. That's progress.

But the decade has other revelations. Ten years ago, young, bright, energetic blacks were sought out, pursued and hired into major corporations, major networks, and onto the staffs of newspapers and national magazines. *Many survived that courtship, some even with their souls intact.* Newscasters, corporate lawyers, marketing specialists, journalists, production managers, plant foremen, college deans. But many more spend a lot of time on the telephone these days, or at the typewriter preparing résumés, which they send out (mostly to friends now) with little notes attached: "Is there anything you know of?" Or they think there is a good book in the story of what happened to them, the great hoax that was played on them. They are right, of course, about the hoax, for many of them were given elegant executive jobs with the work drained out. Work minus power. Work minus decision-making. Work minus dominion. Affirmative Action Make Believe that a lot of black people *did* believe because they also believed that the white people in those nice offices were not like the ones in the general store or in the plumbers' union—that they were fundamentally kind, or fair, or something. Anything but the desperate prisoners of economics they turned out to be, holding on to their dominion with a tenacity and sang-froid that can only be described as Nixonian. So the bright and the black (architects, reporters, vice-presidents in charge of public relations) walk the streets right along with that astounding 38 percent of the black teen-aged female work force that does not have and never has had a job. So the black female college graduate earns two-thirds of what a white male high-school dropout earns. So the black people who put everything into community-action programs supported by Government funds have found themselves bereft of action, bereft of funds and all but bereft of community.

This decade has been rife with disappointment in practically every place where we thought we saw permanent change: Hostos, CUNY, and the black-studies departments that erupted like minivolcanoes on campuses all over the nation; easy integrations of public-school systems; acceleration of promotion in factories and businesses. But now when we describe what has happened we cannot do it without using the verbs of upheaval and destruction: Open admission *closes;* minority-student quotas *fall* or *discontinue;* salary gaps between blacks and whites *widen;* black-studies departments *merge.* And the only growth black people can count on is in the prison population and the unemployment line. Even busing, which used to be a plain, if emotional, term at best, has now taken on an adjective normally reserved for rape and burglary—it is now called "forced" busing.

All of that counts, but I'm not sure that in the long haul it matters. Maybe Ardelia Willis had the best idea. One sees signs of her vision and the fruits of her prophecy in spite of the dread-lock statistics. The trees *are* walking, albeit slowly and quietly and without the fanfare of a cross-country run. It seems that at last black people have abandoned our foolish dependency on the Government to do the work that we once thought all of its citizenry would be delighted to do. Our love affair with the Federal Government is over. We misjudged the ardor of its attention. We thought its majority constituency would *prefer* having their children grow up among happy, progressive, industrious, contented black children rather than among angry, disenchanted and dangerous ones. That the profit motive of industry alone would keep us employed and therefore spending, and that our poverty was bad for business. We thought landlords wanted us to have a share in our neighborhoods and therefore love and care for them. That city governments wanted us to control our schools and therefore preserve them.

We were wrong. And now, having been eliminated from the lists of urgent national priorities, from TV documentaries and the platitudes of editorials, black people have chosen, or been forced to seek safety from the white man's promise, but happily not under a bed. More and more, there is the return to Ardelia's ways: the exercise of the will, the recognition of obstacles as only that—obstacles, not fixed stars. Black judges are fixing appropriate rather than punitive bail for black "offenders" and letting the rest of the community of jurisprudence scream. Young black women are leaving plush Northern jobs to sit in their living rooms and teach black children, work among factory women and spend months finding money to finance the college education of young blacks. Groups of blacks are buying huge tracts of land in the South and cutting off entirely the dependency of whole communities on grocery chains. For the first time, significant numbers of black people are returning or migrating to the South to focus on the acquisition of land, the transferral of crafts and skills, and the sharing of resources, the rebuilding of neighborhoods.

In the shambles of closing admissions, falling quotas, widening salary gaps and merging black-studies departments, builders and healers are working quietly among us. They are not like the heroes of old, the leaders we followed blindly and upon whom we depended for everything, or the blacks who had accumulated wealth for its own sake, fame, medals or some public acknowledgment of success. These are the people whose work is real and pointed and clear in its application to the race. Some are old and have been at work for a long time in and out of the public eye. Some are new and just finding out what their work is. But they are unmistakably the natural aristocrats of the race. The ones who refuse to imitate, to compromise, and who are indifferent to public accolade. Whose work is free or priceless. They take huge risks economically and personally. They are not always popular, even among black people, but they are the ones whose work black people respect. They are the healers. Some are nowhere near the public eye: Ben Chavis, preacher and political activist languishing now in North Carolina prisons; Robert Moses, a pioneering activist; Sterling Brown, poet and teacher; Father Al McKnight, land reformer; Rudy Lombard, urban sociologist; Lerone Bennett, historian; C. L. R. James, scholar; Alyce Gullattee, psychologist and organizer. Others are public legends: Judge Crockett, Judge Bruce Wright, Stevie Wonder, Ishmael Reed, Miles Davis, Richard Pryor, Muhammad Ali, Fannie Lou Hamer, Eubie Blake, Angela Davis, Bill Russell. . . .

But a complete roll-call is neither fitting nor necessary. They know who they are and so do we. They clarify our past, make livable our present and are certain to shape our future. And since the future is where our immortality as a race lies, no overview of the state of black people at this time can ignore some speculation on the only ones certain to live it—the children.

They are both exhilarating and frightening, those black children, and a source of wonderment to me. Although statistics about black teen-age crime and the "failure" of the courts to gut them are regularly printed and regularly received with outrage and fear, the children I know and see, those born after 1960, do not make such great copy. They are those who have grown up with nothing to prove to white people, whose perceptions of themselves are so new, so different, so focused they appear to me to be either magnificent hybrids or throwbacks to the time when our ancestors were called "royal." They are the baby sisters of the sit-in generation, the sons of the neighborhood blockbusters, the nephews of jailed revolutionaries, and a huge number who have had college graduates in their families for three and four generations. I thought we had left them nothing to love and nothing to want to know. I thought that those who exhibited some excitement about their future had long ago looked into the eyes of their teachers and were either saddened or outraged by the death of possibility they found there. I thought that those who were interested in the past had looked into the faces of their parents and seen betrayal. I thought the state had deprived them of a land and the landlords and banks had deprived them of a turf. So how is it that, with nothing to love, nothing they need to know, landless, turfless, minus a future and a past, these black children look us dead in the eye? They seem not to know how to apologize. And even when they are wrong they do not ask for forgiveness. It is as though they are waiting for us to apologize to them, to beg their pardon, to seek their approval. What species of black is this that not only does not choose to grovel, but doesn't know how? How will they keep jobs? How will they live? Won't they be killed before they reproduce? But they are unafraid. Is it because they refuse to see the world as we did? Is it because they have rejected both land and turf to seek instead a world? Maybe they finally got the message that we had been shouting into their faces; that they *live* here, *belong* here on this planet earth and that it is *theirs.* So they watch us with the eyes of poets and carpenters and musicians and scholars and other people who know who they are because they have invented themselves and know where they are going because they have envisioned it. All of which would please Ardelia—and John Solomon, too, I think. After all, he did hold on to his violin.

1976

AUDRE LORDE
(1934–)

Accomplished poet and essayist, Audre Lorde speaks for thousands of Black, lesbian, and feminist women whose experiences have been excluded from literature. Throughout seven books of poetry and five books of prose she gives a voice to the silent. "Primarily," she points out, "I write for those women who do not speak."

In 1924, ten years before she was born, Audre Lorde's parents came to the United States from Grenada. They moved to Harlem, where her father opened a real estate office; when business improved, the Lordes and their three daughters moved to Washington Heights, a wealthier New York City neighborhood.

Lorde's writing career began at Hunter High School, where she was literary editor of the arts magazine. Despite a teacher's lack of encouragement, she sent a poem to Seventeen *magazine; the poem was accepted and published when she was fifteen. During high school, she said, "writing poetry became an ordinary effort, not a secret and rebellious vice." Lorde received a B.A. in literature and philosophy from Hunter College in 1959 and a Master of Library Science from Columbia University in 1961.*

Radical politics always have been part of Audre Lorde's life. She worked to prevent the execution of the Rosenbergs in the 1950s and helped organize the Black Studies Department of John Jay College in the 1960s. She has worked for Welfare Mothers' Rights and against forced sterilization.

Lorde's prose reflects the inextricable connections between the personal and the political. Her autobiographical Zami: A New Spelling of My Name, *for example, describes how the New York Black literary circles of the 1940s and 1950s ostracized her because of her lesbianism. In a recent essay, "Turning the Beat Around: Lesbian Parenting 1986," she calls for a new definition of family. Finally, Lorde combines the personal and the political with poignant courage in her chronicle of living with breast cancer, the* Cancer Journals.

Lorde has received critical recognition from the literary establishment. In 1968 she was awarded a National Endowment for the Arts residency grant, and in 1972 she received a Creative Arts Public Service Award grant. Her third book of poetry, From a Land Where Other People Live, *was nominated for the 1974 National Book Award, and in 1980 she was elected to the Hunter College Hall of Fame. At the same time, the women's community celebrates Lorde's work through such tributes as the 1990 "I Am Your Sister Conference," named after Lorde's 1986 collection.*

We have chosen two essays from Lorde's collection Sister Outsider: *"The Transformation of Silence into Language and Action" and "Uses of the Erotic: The*

Erotic as Power." In the first, she describes her battle against "the tyrannies of silence"; in the second, she calls for a feminist transformation of female passion.

THE TRANSFORMATION OF SILENCE INTO LANGUAGE AND ACTION

I have come to believe over and over again that what is most important to me must be spoken, made verbal and shared, even at the risk of having it bruised or misunderstood. That the speaking profits me, beyond any other effect. I am standing here as a Black lesbian poet, and the meaning of all that waits upon the fact that I am still alive, and might not have been. Less than two months ago I was told by two doctors, one female and one male, that I would have to have breast surgery, and that there was a 60 to 80 percent chance that the tumor was malignant. Between that telling and the actual surgery, there was a three-week period of the agony of an involuntary reorganization of my entire life. The surgery was completed, and the growth was benign.

But within those three weeks, I was forced to look upon myself and my living with a harsh and urgent clarity that has left me still shaken but much stronger. This is a situation faced by many women, by some of you here today. Some of what I experienced during that time has helped elucidate for me much of what I feel concerning the transformation of silence into language and action.

In becoming forcibly and essentially aware of my mortality, and of what I wished and wanted for my life, however short it might be, priorities and omissions became strongly etched in a merciless light, and what I most regretted were my silences. Of what had I *ever* been afraid? To question or to speak as I believed could have meant pain, or death. But we all hurt in so many different ways, all the time, and pain will either change or end. Death, on the other hand, is the final silence. And that might be coming quickly, now, without regard for whether I had ever spoken what needed to be said, or had only betrayed myself into small silences, while I planned someday to speak, or waited for someone else's words. And I began to recognize a source of power within myself that comes from the knowledge that while it is most desirable not to be afraid, learning to put fear into perspective gave me great strength.

I was going to die, if not sooner then later, whether or not I had ever spoken myself. My silences had not protected me. Your silence will not protect you. But for every real word spoken, for every attempt I had ever made to speak those truths for which I am still seeking, I had made contact with other women while we examined the words to fit a world in which we all believed, bridging our differences. And it was the concern and caring of all those women which gave me strength and enabled me to scrutinize the essentials of my living.

The women who sustained me through that period were Black and white, old and young, lesbian, bisexual, and heterosexual, and we all shared a war against the tyrannies of silence. They all gave me a strength and concern without which I could not have survived intact. Within those weeks of acute fear came the knowledge—within the war we are all waging with the forces of death, subtle and otherwise, conscious or not—I am not only a casualty, I am also a warrior.

What are the words you do not yet have? What do you need to say? What are the tyrannies you swallow day by day and attempt to make your own, until you will sicken and die of them, still in silence? Perhaps for some of you here today, I am the face of one of your fears. Because I am woman, because I am Black, because I am lesbian, because I am myself—a Black woman warrior poet doing my work—come to ask you, are you doing yours?

. . .

And of course I am afraid, because the transformation of silence into language and action is an act of self-revelation, and that always seems fraught with danger. But my daughter, when I told her of our topic and my difficulty with it, said, "Tell them about how you're never really a whole person if you remain silent, because there's always that one little piece inside you that wants to be spoken out, and if you keep ignoring it, it gets madder and madder and hotter and hotter, and if you don't speak it out one day it will just up and punch you in the mouth from the inside."

In the cause of silence, each of us draws the face of her own fear—fear of contempt, of censure, or some judgment, or recognition, of challenge, of annihilation. But most of all, I think, we fear the visibility without which we cannot truly live. Within this country where racial difference creates a constant, if unspoken, distortion of vision, Black women have on one hand always been highly visible, and so, on the other hand, have been rendered invisible through the depersonalization of racism. Even within the women's movement, we have had to fight, and still do, for that very visibility which also renders us most vulnerable, our Blackness. For to survive in the mouth of this dragon we call america, we have had to learn this first and most vital lesson—that we were never meant to survive. Not as human beings. And neither were most of you here today, Black or not. And that visibility which makes us most vulnerable is that which also is the source of our greatest strength. Because the machine will try to grind you into dust anyway, whether or not we speak. We can sit in our corners mute forever while our sisters and our selves are wasted, while our children are distorted and destroyed, while our earth is poisoned; we can sit in our safe corners mute as bottles, and we will still be no less afraid.

In my house this year we are celebrating the feast of Kwanza, the African-American festival of harvest which begins the day after Christmas and lasts for seven days. There are seven principles of Kwanza, one for each day. The first principle is Umoja, which means unity, the decision to strive for and maintain unity in self and community. The principle for yesterday, the second day, was Kujichagulia—self-determination—the decision to define ourselves, name ourselves, and speak for ourselves, instead of being defined and spoken for by others. Today is the third day of Kwanza, and the principle for today is Ujima—collective work and responsibility—the decision to build and maintain ourselves and our communities together and to recognize and solve our problems together.

Each of us is here now because in one way or another we share a commitment to language and to the power of language, and to the reclaiming of that language which has been made to work against us. In the transformation of silence into language and action, it is vitally necessary for each one of us to establish or examine her function in that transformation and to recognize her role as vital within that transformation.

For those of us who write, it is necessary to scrutinize not only the truth of what we speak, but the truth of that language by which we speak it. For others, it is to share and spread also those words that are meaningful to us. But primarily for us all, it is necessary to teach by living and speaking those truths which we believe and know beyond understanding. Because in this way alone we can survive, by taking part in a process of life that is creative and continuing, that is growth.

And it is never without fear—of visibility, of the harsh light of scrutiny and perhaps judgment, of pain, of death. But we have lived through all of those already, in silence, except death. And I remind myself all the time now that if I were to have been born mute, or had maintained an oath of silence my whole life long for safety, I would still have suffered, and I would still die. It is very good for establishing perspective.

And where the words of women are crying to be heard, we must each of us recognize our responsibility to seek those words out, to read them and share them and examine them in their pertinence to our lives. That we not hide behind the mockeries of separations that have been imposed upon us and which so often we accept as our own. For instance, "I can't possibly teach Black women's writing—their experience is so different from mine." Yet how many years have you spent teaching Plato and Shakespeare and Proust? Or another, "She's a white woman and what could she possibly have to say to me?" Or, "She's a lesbian, what would my husband say, or my chairman?" Or again, "This woman writes of her sons and I have no children." And all the other endless ways in which we rob ourselves of ourselves and each other.

We can learn to work and speak when we are afraid in the same way we have learned to work and speak when we are tired. For we have been socialized to respect fear more than our own needs for language and definition, and while we wait in silence for that final luxury of fearlessness, the weight of that silence will choke us.

The fact that we are here and that I speak these words is an attempt to break that silence and bridge some of those differences between us, for it is not difference which immobilizes us, but silence. And there are so many silences to be broken.

1978

USES OF THE EROTIC: THE EROTIC AS POWER

There are many kinds of power, used and unused, acknowledged or otherwise. The erotic is a resource within each of us that lies in a deeply female and spiritual plane, firmly rooted in the power of our unexpressed or unrecognized feeling. In order to perpetuate itself, every oppression must corrupt or distort those various sources of power within the culture of the oppressed that can provide energy for change. For women, this has meant a suppression of the erotic as a considered source of power and information in our lives.

We have been taught to suspect this resource, vilified, abused, and devalued within western society. On the one hand, the superficially erotic has been encouraged as a sign of female inferiority; on the other hand, women have been made to suffer and to feel both contemptible and suspect by virtue of its existence.

It is a short step from there to the false belief that only by the suppression of the erotic within our lives and consciousness can women be truly strong. But that strength is illusory, for it is fashioned within the context of male models of power.

As women, we have come to distrust that power which rises from our deepest and nonrational knowledge. We have been warned against it all our lives by the male world, which values this depth of feeling enough to keep women around in order to exercise it in the service of men, but which fears this same depth too much to examine the possibilities of it within themselves. So women are maintained at a distant/inferior position to be psychically milked, much the same way ants maintain colonies of aphids to provide a life-giving substance for their masters.

But the erotic offers a well of replenishing and provocative force to the woman who does not fear its revelation, nor succumb to the belief that sensation is enough.

The erotic has often been misnamed by men and used against women. It has been made into the confused, the trivial, the psychotic, the plasticized sensation. For this reason, we have often turned away from the exploration and consideration of the erotic as a source of power and information, confusing it with its opposite, the pornographic. But pornography is a direct denial of the power of the erotic, for it represents the suppression of true feeling. Pornography emphasizes sensation without feeling.

The erotic is a measure between the beginnings of our sense of self and the chaos of our strongest feelings. It is an internal sense of satisfaction to which, once we have experienced it, we know we can aspire. For having experienced the fullness of this depth of feeling and recognizing its power, in honor and self-respect we can require no less of ourselves.

It is never easy to demand the most from ourselves, from our lives, from our work. To encourage excellence is to go beyond the encouraged mediocrity of our society is to encourage excellence. But giving in to the fear of feeling and working to capacity is a luxury only the unintentional can afford, and the unintentional are those who do not wish to guide their own destinies.

This internal requirement toward excellence which we learn from the erotic must not be misconstrued as demanding the impossible from ourselves nor from others. Such a demand incapacitates everyone in the process. For the erotic is not a question only of what we do; it is a question of how acutely and fully we can feel in the doing. Once we know the extent to which we are capable of feeling that sense of satisfaction and completion, we can then observe which of our various life endeavors bring us closest to that fullness.

The aim of each thing which we do is to make our lives and the lives of our children richer and more possible. Within the celebration of the erotic in all our endeavors, my work becomes a conscious decision—a longed-for bed which I enter gratefully and from which I rise up empowered.

. . .

Of course, women so empowered are dangerous. So we are taught to separate the erotic demand from most vital areas of our lives other than sex. And the lack of concern for the erotic root and satisfactions of our work is felt in our disaffection from so much of what we do. For instance, how often do we truly love our work even at its most difficult?

The principal horror of any system which defines the good in terms of profit rather than in terms of human need, or which defines human need to the exclusion of the psychic and emotional components of that need—the principal horror of such a system is that it robs our work of its erotic value, its erotic power and life appeal and fulfillment. Such a system reduces work to a travesty of necessities, a duty by which we earn bread or oblivion for ourselves and those we love. But this is tantamount to blinding a painter and then telling her to improve her work, and to enjoy the act of painting. It is not only next to impossible, it is also profoundly cruel.

As women, we need to examine the ways in which our world can be truly different. I am speaking here of the necessity for reassessing the quality of all the aspects of our lives and of our work, and of how we move toward and through them.

The very word *erotic* comes from the Greek word *eros,* the personification of love in all its aspects—born of Chaos, and personifying creative power and harmony. When I speak of the erotic, then, I speak of it as an assertion of the lifeforce of women; of that creative energy empowered, the knowledge and use of which we are now reclaiming in our language, our history, our dancing, our loving, our work, our lives.

There are frequent attempts to equate pornography and eroticism, two diametrically opposed uses of the sexual. Because of these attempts, it has become fashionable to separate the spiritual (psychic and emotional) from the political, to see them as contradictory or antithetical. "What do you mean, a poetic revolutionary, a meditating gunrunner?" In the same way, we have attempted to separate the spiritual and the erotic, thereby reducing the spiritual to a world of flattened affect, a world of the ascetic who aspires to feel nothing. But nothing is farther from the truth. For the ascetic position is one of the highest fear, the gravest immobility. The severe abstinence of the ascetic becomes the ruling obsession. And it is one not of self-discipline but of self-abnegation.

The dichotomy between the spiritual and the political is also false, resulting from an incomplete attention to our erotic knowledge. For the bridge which connects them is formed by the erotic—the sensual—those physical, emotional, and psychic expressions of what is deepest and strongest and richest within each of us, being shared: the passions of love, in its deepest meanings.

Beyond the superficial, the considered phrase, "It feels right to me," acknowledges the strength of the erotic into a true knowledge, for what that means is the first and most powerful guiding light toward any understanding. And understanding is a handmaiden which can only wait upon, or clarify, that knowledge, deeply born. The erotic is the nurturer or nursemaid of all our deepest knowledge.

. . .

The erotic functions for me in several ways, and the first is in providing the power which comes from sharing deeply any pursuit with another person. The sharing of joy, whether physical, emotional, psychic, or intellectual, forms a bridge between the sharers which can be the basis for understanding much of what is not shared between them, and lessens the threat of their difference.

Another important way in which the erotic connection functions is the open and fearless underlining of my capacity for joy. In the way my body stretches to music and opens into response, hearkening to its deepest rhythms, so every level upon which I sense also opens to the erotically satisfying experience, whether it is dancing, building a bookcase, writing a poem, examining an idea.

That self-connection shared is a measure of the joy which I know myself to be capable of feeling, a reminder of my capacity for feeling. And that deep and irreplaceable knowledge of my capacity for joy comes to demand from all of my life that it be lived within the knowledge that such satisfaction is possible, and does not have to be called *marriage,* nor *god,* nor *an afterlife.*

This is one reason why the erotic is so feared, and so often relegated to the bedroom alone, when it is recognized at all. For once we begin to feel deeply all the aspects of our lives, we begin to demand from ourselves and from our life-pursuits that they feel in accordance with that joy which we know ourselves to be capable of. Our erotic knowledge empowers us, becomes a lens through which we scrutinize all aspects of our existence, forcing us to evaluate those aspects honestly in terms of their relative meaning within our lives. And this is a grave responsibility, projected from within each of us, not to settle for the convenient, the shoddy, the conventionally expected, nor the merely safe.

During World War II, we bought sealed plastic packets of white, uncolored margarine, with a tiny, intense pellet of yellow coloring perched like a topaz just inside the clear skin of the bag. We would leave the margarine out for a while to soften, and then we would pinch the little pellet to break it inside the bag, releasing the rich yellowness into the soft pale mass of margarine. Then taking it carefully between our fingers, we would knead it gently back and forth, over and over, until the color had spread throughout the whole pound bag of margarine, thoroughly coloring it.

I find the erotic such a kernel within myself. When released from its intense and constrained pellet, it flows through and colors my life with a kind of energy that heightens and sensitizes and strengthens all my experience.

. . .

We have been raised to fear the *yes* within ourselves, our deepest cravings. But, once recognized, those which do not enhance our future lose their power and can be altered. The fear of our desires keeps them suspect and indiscriminately powerful, for to suppress any truth is to give it strength beyond endurance. The fear that we cannot grow beyond whatever distortions we may find within ourselves keeps us docile and loyal and obedient, externally defined, and leads us to accept many facets of our oppression as women.

When we live outside ourselves, and by that I mean on external directives only rather than from our internal knowledge and needs, when we live away from those erotic guides from within ourselves, then our lives are limited by external and alien forms, and we conform to the needs of a structure that is not based on human need, let alone an individual's. But when we begin to live from within outward, in touch with the power of the erotic within ourselves, and allowing that power to inform and illuminate our actions upon the world around us, then we begin to be responsible to ourselves in the deepest sense. For as we begin to recognize our deepest feelings, we begin to give up, of necessity, being satisfied with suffering and self-negation, and with the numbness which so often seems like their only alternative in our society. Our acts against oppression become integral with self, motivated and empowered from within.

In touch with the erotic, I become less willing to accept powerlessness, or those other supplied states of being which are not native to me, such as resignation, despair, self-effacement, depression, self-denial.

And yes, there is a hierarchy. There is a difference between painting a black fence and writing a poem, but only one of quantity. And there is, for me, no difference between writing a good poem and moving into sunlight against the body of a woman I love.

This brings me to the last consideration of the erotic. To share the power of each other's feelings is different from using another's feelings as we would use a kleenex. When we look the other way from our experience, erotic or otherwise, we use rather than share the feelings of those others who participate in the experience with us. And use without consent of the used is abuse.

In order to be utilized, our erotic feelings must be recognized. The need for sharing deep feeling is a human need. But within the European-American tradition, this need is satisfied by certain proscribed erotic comings-together. These occasions are almost always characterized by a simultaneous looking away, a pretense of calling them something else, whether a religion, a fit, mob violence, or even playing doctor. And this misnaming of the need and the deed give rise to that distortion which results in pornography and obscenity—the abuse of feeling.

When we look away from the importance of the erotic in the development and sustenance of our power, or when we look away from ourselves as we satisfy our erotic needs in concert with others, we use each other as objects of satisfaction rather than share our joy in the satisfying, rather than make connection with our similarities and our differences. To refuse to be conscious of what we are feeling at any time, however comfortable that might seem, is to deny a large part of the experience, and to allow ourselves to be reduced to the pornographic, the abused, and the absurd.

The erotic cannot be felt secondhand. As a Black lesbian feminist, I have a particular feeling, knowledge, and understanding for those sisters with whom I have danced hard, played, or even fought. This deep participation has often been the forerunner for joint concerted actions not possible before.

But this erotic charge is not easily shared by women who continue to operate under an exclusively European-American male tradition. I know it was not available to me when I was trying to adapt my consciousness to this mode of living and sensation.

Only now, I find more and more women-identified women brave enough to risk sharing the erotic's electrical charge without having to look away, and without distorting the enormously powerful and creative nature of that exchange. Recognizing the power of the erotic within our lives can give us the energy to pursue genuine change within our world, rather than merely settling for a shift of characters in the same weary drama.

For not only do we touch our most profoundly creative source, but we do that which is female and self-affirming in the face of a racist, patriarchal, and anti-erotic society.

1978

ESTELA PORTILLO TRAMBLEY (1936–)

Estela Portillo Trambley's belief that there are no limits to Chicana literary expression motivates her writing. She counts among her influences writers from Balzac to T. S. Eliot, Chekhov to Ezra Pound, in addition to the major contemporary Latino writers Octavio Paz, Alfonso Reyes, and Pablo Neruda. A blend of intellectual history and human experience characterizes Portillo Trambley's writing. Her work inspires a younger generation of Chicana writers to expand their artistic visions.

Portillo Trambley was born to a working-class family in El Paso, Texas. She received her B.A. in 1957 from the University of Texas in El Paso and an M.A. from the same institution in 1977. She taught high school English between 1957 and 1964 in El Paso and then became the chair of the English department, a post she held for six years—all while raising five children. She currently teaches at El Paso Community College, where she is the director of Theater Arts.

Her frequently anthologized play "The Day of the Swallows" appeared in 1972. In 1973 she edited Mujeres en Arte y Literatura. *A collection of stories,* Rain of Scorpions and Other Writings, *appeared in 1976;* Sor Juana and Other Plays, *a collection of her plays, followed in 1983.*

Two of her musicals and three of her dramas were produced at Chamizal National Theater in El Paso between 1974 and 1977. The play Puente Negro *won the Second Annual Women's Play competition at St. Edward's University in Austin, Texas, in January 1984. Jorge Huerta directed the Spanish translation of this play in a production by La Compania de Teatro de Alburquerque. She published her novel* Trini *in 1986. Her radio drama "The Burning," based on the story we have included, was produced at the Western Public Radio Workshop in 1983.*

As a playwright and a novelist, Portillo Trambley is acutely aware of the differences these genres pose for a writer. "The writing of the novel," she has written, "is . . . lonely, retrospective, and inward . . . Drama involves the players, the audience outside of myself . . . But the 'power of myself,' the lonely and creative elation of novel-writing is winning over. The energy is from within." At the same time, her desire in all her writing is to "gather the essences, the organic of the pure Chicano . . . to perceive outlooks on life and the magnificent tenacity in struggle."

In "The Burning" Portillo Trambley describes differences among women of a barrio. Indeed, fear of difference leads the women of Spanish, Christian heritage to commit violence against the Mexican Indian woman. Yet a paradox at the heart of the story allows for the triumph of Lela, the woman they have ostracized and condemned.

THE BURNING

The women of the barrio, the ones pock-marked by life, sat in council. Existence in dark cubicles of wounds had withered the spirit. Now, all as one, had found a heath. One tired soul stood up to speak. "Many times I see the light she makes of darkness, and that light is a greater blackness, still."

There was some skepticism from the timid. "Are you sure?"

"In those caves outside the town, she lives for days away from everybody. At night, when she is in the caves, small blinking lights appear, like fireflies. Where do they come from? I say, the blackness of her drowns the life in me."

Another woman with a strange wildness in her eyes nodded her head in affirmation. "Yes, she drinks the bitterness of good and swallows, like the devil-wolf, the red honey milk of evil."

A cadaverous one looked up into a darkened sky. "I hear thunder; lightning is not far." In unison they agreed, "We could use some rain."

The oldest one among them, one with dirty claws, stood up with arms outstretched and stood menacingly against the first lightning bolt that cleaved the darkness. Her voice was harsh and came from ages past. "She must burn!"

The finality was a cloud, black and tortured. Each looked into another's eyes to find assent or protest. There was only frenzy, tight and straining. The thunder was riding the lightning now, directly over their heads. It was a blazing canopy that urged them on to deeds of fear. There was still no rain. They found blistering words to justify the deed to come. One woman, heavy with anger, crouched to pour out further accusations. "She is the devil's pawn. On nights like this, when the air is heavy like thick blood, she sings among the dead, preferring them to the living. You know why she does it . . . eh? I'll tell you! She chases the dead back to their graves."

"Yes, yes. She stays and stays when death comes. Never a whimper, nor a tear, but I sense she feels the death as life like one possessed. They say she catches the flitting souls of the dead and turns them into flies. That way the soul never finds heaven."

"Flies! Flies! She is a plague!"

A clap of thunder reaffirmed. The old one with nervous, clutching claws made the most grievous charge, the cause for this meeting of the judgment. She shaped with bony gestures the anger of the heart. "She is the enemy of God! She put obscenities on our doorsteps to make us her accomplices. Sacrilege against the holy church!"

There was a fervor now, rising like a tide. They were for her burning now. All the council howled that Lela must burn that night. The sentence belonged to night alone. The hurricane could feed in darkness. Fear could be disguised as outrage at night. There were currents now that wanted sacrifice. Sacrifice is the umbilical cord of superstition. It would devastate before finding a calm. Lela was the eye of the storm, the artery that must flow to make them whole when the earth turned to light. To catch an evil when it bounced as shadow in their lives, to find it trapped in human body, this was an effective stimulant to some; to others it was a natural depressant to cut the fear, the dam of frustration. This would be their method of revelation. The doubt of themselves would dissolve.

But women know mercy! Mercy? It was swallowed whole by chasms of desire and fear of the unknown. Tempests grow in narrow margins that want a freedom they don't understand. Slaves always punish the free.

But who was Lela? She had come across the mountain to their pueblo many years before. She had crossed la Barranca del Cobre alone. She had walked into the pueblo one day, a bloody, ragged, half-starved young girl. In an apron she carried some shining sand. She stood there, like a frightened fawn, at the edge of the village. As the people of the pueblo gathered around her strangeness, she smiled, putting out her hand for touch. They drew back and she fell to the ground in exhaustion.

They took her in, but she remained a stranger the rest of her life in the pueblo upon which she had stumbled. At the beginning, she seemed but a harmless child. But, as time passed and she resisted their pattern of life, she was left alone. The people knew she was a Tarahumara from Batopilas. Part of her strangeness was the rooted depth of her own religion. She did not convert to Christianity. People grew hostile and suspicious of her.

But she had also brought with her the miracle sand. It had strange curative powers. In no time, she began to cure those in the pueblo who suffered from skin disease, from sores, or open wounds.

"Is it the magic of her devil gods?" the people asked themselves. Still, they came for the miracle cure that was swift and clean. She became their *curandera* outside their Christian faith.

The people in her new home needed her, and she loved them in silence and from a distance. She forgave them for not accepting her strangeness and learned to find adventure in the Oneness of herself.

Many times she wanted to go back to Batopilas, but too many people needed her here. She learned the use of medicinal herbs and learned to set broken bones. This was what she was meant to do in life. This purpose would not let her return to Batopilas. Still, she did not convert to Christianity. The people, begrudgingly, believed in her curative powers, but did not believe in her. Many years had passed and Lela was now an old woman, and the council of women this night of impending storm had decided her fate.

Lela lay dying in her one room hut. There was a fire with teeth that consumed her body. She only knew that her time was near an end as she lay in her small cot. Above the bed was a long shelf she had built herself that held rows of clay figurines. These were painted in gay colors and the expression on the tiny faces measured the seasons of the heart. They were live little faces showing the full circle of human joy and pain, doubt and fear, humor and sobriety. In all expressions there was a fierceness for life.

Lela had molded them through the years, and now they stood over her head like guardians over their maker. . . . Clay figurines, an act of love learned early in her childhood of long ago. In Batopilas, each home had its own rural god. He was a friend and a comforter. The little rural gods were like any other people. They did not rule or demand allegiance. The little rural gods of river, sky, fire, seed, birds, all were chosen members of each family. Because they sanctified all human acts, they were the actions of the living, like an aura. They were a shrine to creation.

Lela's mother had taught the little girl to mold the clay figures that represented the rural gods. This was her work and that of Lela's in the village, to provide clay little gods for each home and for festive occasions. This is why Lela never gave them up in her new home. She had molded them with her hands, but they dwelled boundless in the center of her being. The little gods had always been very real, very important, in her reverence for life.

There had been in Batopilas a stone image of the greater god, Tecuat. He was an impressive god of power that commanded silence and obedience. People did not get close to Tecuat except in ritual. As a girl, Lela would tiptoe respectfully around the figure of Tecuat, then she would breathe a sigh of relief and run off to find the little gods.

This was her game, god-hunting. One day, she had walked too far towards the pines, too far towards a roar that spoke of rushing life. She followed a yellow butterfly that also heard a command of dreams. She followed the butterfly that flitted towards a lake. As she followed, she looked for little gods in the glint of the sun, and in the open branches that pierced the absoluteness of the sky. The soft breath of wind was the breath of little gods, and the crystal shine of rocks close to the lake was a winking language that spoke of peace and the wildness of all joy.

When she had reached the lake, she stepped into the water without hesitation. She felt the cool wet mud against her open toes. She walked into the water, touching the ripple of its broken surface with her finger tips. After a while, there was no more bottom. She began to cut the water with smooth, clean strokes, swimming out towards the pearl-green rocks that hid the roar. She floated for a while looking up at the light filtering through eternal trees. The silence spoke of something other than itself. It spoke in colors born of water and sun. She began to swim more rapidly towards the turn that led to the cradle of the roar, the waterfall. . . .

This is what Lela, the old Lela dying on her bed, was remembering . . .

the waterfall. It helped to ease the pain that came in waves that broke against her soul and blackened the world. Then, there was the calm, the calm into which the experience machine brought back the yesterdays that were now soft, kind memories. She opened her eyes and looked up at the row of clay figures. She was not alone. "The waterfall . . ." she whispered to herself. She remembered the grotto behind the waterfall. It had been her hermitage of dreams, of wonder. Here her Oneness had knitted all the little gods unto herself until she felt the whole of earth—things within her being. Suddenly, the pain cut her body in two. She gripped the edge of the cot. There were blurs of throbbing white that whirled into black, and all her body trembled until another interval of peace returned for a little while.

There was no thought; there was no dream in the quiet body. She was a simple calm that would not last. The calm was a gift from the little gods. She slept. It was a fitful, brief sleep that ended with the next crash of pain. The pain found gradual absorption. She could feel the bed sheet clinging to her body, wet with perspiration. She asked herself in a half-moan, "When will the body give way?" Give way . . . give way, for so long, Lela had given way and had found ways to open herself and the world she understood. It had been a vital force in her. She could have been content in Batopilas. The simple truths of Nature might have fulfilled her to the end of her days if she had remained in Batopilas. But there was always that reach in her for a larger self. Nature was a greatness, but she felt a different hunger and a different thirst.

There was a world beyond Batopilas; there were people beyond Batopilas. She was no longer a child. It was easy to find little gods in Nature, but as she grew older, it became a child's game. There was time to be a child, but there was now time for something more. That is why, one day, she had walked away from Batopilas.

Beyond the desert, she would find another pueblo. She knew there were many pueblos and many deserts. There was nothing to fear because her little gods were with her. On the first day of her journey, she walked all day. The piercing sun beat down on her and the world, as she scanned the horizon for signs of a way. Something at a distance would be a hope, would be a way to something new, a way to the larger self. At dusk, she felt great hunger and great thirst. Her body ached and her skin felt parched and dry. The night wind felt cold, so she looked for a shelter against the wind. She found a clump of mesquite behind some giant sahuaros. This was not the greenness she knew so well, but a garden of stars in the night sky comforted her until she fell asleep.

At first light she awakened refreshed and quickly resumed her journey. She knew she must make the best out of the early hours before the sun rose. By late morning, the desert yielded a mountain at a distance. She reached the mountain in time to rest from the sun and the physical effort of her journey. When the sun began to fall, she started up a path made narrow by a blanket of desert brush. It tore the flesh of her feet and legs as she made her way up the path. In a little while, it was hard to find sure footing. The path had lost itself in a cleavage of rocks. Night had fallen. She was not afraid, for the night sky, again, was full of blinking little gods.

Then it happened. She lost her footing and fell down, down over a crevice between two huge boulders. As she fell, her lungs filled with air. Her body hit soft sand, but the edge of her foot felt the sharpness of a stone. She lay there stunned for a few minutes until she felt a sharp pain at the side of her foot. Somewhat dizzy, she sat up and noticed that the side of her foot was bleeding profusely. She sat there and watched the blood-flow that found its way into the soft sand. She looked up at the boulders that silently rebuked her helplessness; then she began to cry softly. She had to stanch the blood. She wiped away her tears with the side of her sleeve and tore off a piece of skirt to use as a bandage. As she looked down at the wound again, she noticed that the sand where she had fallen was extremely crystalline and loose. It shone against a rising moon. She scooped up a handful and looked at it with fascination. "The sand of little gods," she whispered to herself. She took some sand and rubbed it on the wound before she applied the bandage. By now, she felt a burning fever. She wrapped the strip of skirt around the wound now covered with the fine, shining sand. Then she slept. But it was a fitful sleep, for her body burned with fever. Half awake and half in a dream, she saw the sands take the shapes of happy, little gods. Then, at other times, the pain told her she was going to die. After a long time, her exhausted body slept until the dawn passed over her head.

When she finally awakened, she felt extremely well. Her body was rested and her temperature, to her great surprise, was normal. She looked down at the wound. The blood was caked on the bandage. She took it off to look at the wound. She could hardly believe her eyes. There was no longer any open wound. There was a healthy scab, and the area around the wound had no infection. It was a healing that normally would have taken weeks. She stood on her foot and felt no pain. "My little gods!" she thought. She fell down on her knees and kissed the shining sand. After a while, she removed her apron and filled it with the shining sand. She secured it carefully before she set off on her climb. As she made her way out of the crevice, she marked the path leading to the shining sand to find her way to it again. It was hard making marks with a sharp stone, and it seemed to take forever. At last, she reached the top of the crevice and noticed, to her great joy, that it led down to a pueblo at a distance. She made her way to strangers that day. Now, at the end of a lifetime, Lela felt the pain roll, roll, roll, roll itself into a blindness. She struggled through the blackness until she gasped back the beginning of the calm. With the new calm came a ringing memory from her childhood. She saw the kindly face of the goddess, Ta Te. She who was born of the union of clean rock, she who was eternal. Yes, Ta Te understood all the verdant things . . . the verdant things.

. . .

And who were these women who sat in council? They were one full sweep of hate; they were one full wave of fear. Now these village women were outlined against a greyish sky where a storm refused to break. Spiderlike, apelike, toadlike was the ferocity of their deadness. These were creatures of the earth who mingled with mankind. But they were minions to torture because the twist of littleness bound them to condemn all things unknown, all things untried. The infernal army could not be stopped now. The scurrying creatures began to gather firewood in the gloom. With antlike obedience they hurried back and forth carrying wood to Lela's hut. They piled it in a circle around her little house. The rhythm of their feet sang, "We'll do! We'll do!"

"The circle of fire will drain her powers!" claimed the old one with claws.

"Show me! Show me! Show me!" Voices lost as one.

As the old one with claws ordered more wood, the parish priest came running from his church. With raised arms he shouted as he ran, "Stop! Do you hear? Stop this madness!"

It can be argued that evil is not the reversal of good, but the vacuum of good. Thus, the emptiness is a standing still, a being dead, an infinite pain . . . like dead wood. No one listened to him.

"Burn! Burn! Burn!"

Life? The wood? The emptiness? The labor pains were that of something already lost, something left to the indefinite in life. The priest went from one woman to another begging, pleading, taking the wood from their hands.

"Burn! Burn! Burn!"

The old priest reasoned. "All is forgiven, my children. She only made some figurines of clay!"

There was a hush. The one woman with the claws approached the priest and spit out the condemnation, "She took our holy saints, Mary, Joseph, and many others and made them obscene. How can you defend the right hand of the devil? Drinking saints! Winking saints! Who can forgive the hideous suggestions of her clay devils? Who?"

The priest said simply, "You."

But if there is only darkness in a narrow belief, who can believe beyond the belief, or even understand the belief itself? The women could not forgive because they did not believe beyond a belief that did not go beyond symbol and law. Somehow, symbol and law, without love, leaves no opening. The clay figures in the church with sweet, painted faces lifted to heaven were much more than figures of clay to these women. Their still postures with praying hands were a security. Now, the priest who had blessed them with holy water said they were not a sanctuary of God. Why did he contradict himself?

The old one with the claws felt triumphant. "She has made our saints into pagan gods!"

The priest shook his head sadly. "It is not a sin, what she did!"

No one listened. The piling of wood continued until the match was lit. Happy . . . Happy fire . . . it would burn the sin and the sinner.

. . .

Something in Lela told her this was the last struggle now. She looked up at her clay figurines one last time. Her eyes had lost their focus. The little gods had melted into one another; all colors were mixed. They grew into silver strands of light that crossed and mingled and found new forms that pulled away from one center. In half consciousness, she whispered, "Yes, yes, pull away. Find other ways, other selves, grow. . . ."

She smiled; the last calm had taken her back to the caves outside the pueblo. The caves were not like the grotto behind the waterfall, but they were a place for Oneness, where one could look for the larger self. Here the solitude of the heart was a bird in space. Here, in the silence of aloneness, she had looked for the little gods in the townspeople. In her mind, she had molded their smiles, their tears, their embraces, their seeking, their *just being.* Her larger self told her that the miracle of the living act was supreme, the giving, the receiving, the stumbling, and the getting up.

In the caves she had sadly thought of how she had failed to reach them as a friend. Her silences and her strangeness had kept them apart. But, she would find a way of communicating, a way of letting them know that she loved them. "If I give shape and form to their beauty," she thought. "If I cannot tell them I love them with words. . . ."

The light of the moving, mixing little gods was becoming a darkness. Her body would give in now. Yet, she still wished for Batopilas and the old ways with her last breath, "If only . . . if only I could be buried in the tradition of my fathers . . . a clean burning for new life . . . but here, here, there is a dark hole for the dead body. . . . Oh, little gods, take me back to my fathers. . . ."

The little gods were racing to the waterfall.

1975

TONI CADE BAMBARA
(1939–   )

Toni Cade Bambara combines a deep involvement in urban communities and African American cultural life with her work as a writer of fiction and nonfiction. Her beliefs as an educator, organizer, and activist are reflected in her writing, as is her commitment to civil rights and the women's movement. Two important models, she says, have been Ida B. Wells and Harriet Tubman: "I am drawn temperamentally toward 'pistol-packing mamas,' so from a very early age right up until this moment, they have always been models for me. Their courage, their absolute unwillingness to engage in the politics of silence and the politics of invisibility and amnesia has always inspired me."

Born in New York City, Bambara received her B.A. from Queens College in 1959, attended the University of Florence and Ecole de Mime Etienne Decroux in Paris, and received her M.A. from City University of New York in 1964. She has worked as a social worker, recreational and occupational therapist, scriptwriter, and reviewer of films, plays, and books and has taught at a number of schools, including Rutgers University, Livingston College, Spelman College, and Duke University. Always involved in community work, she was director of Colony House in Brooklyn and worked with programs such as the Tutorial Project of the Houston Street Public Library. She is a founding member of the Southern Collective of African-American Writers.

Bambara began publishing her writing while still in college. Her first published short story, "Sweet Town," appeared in Vendome *magazine in 1959. In the early 1970s, as editor of two anthologies,* The Black Woman *and* Tales and Stories for Black Folks, *Bambara used the medium of books to convey some of the messages she was communicating as an educator and social activist. The first anthology, which focused on black women's attitudes toward and participation in the civil rights and women's movements, included works by Audre Lorde, Alice Walker, and Paule Marshall.* Tales and Stories for Black Folks *emphasizes the cultural importance of storytelling, especially among young people, in the African American community. Bambara's focus on youth appears again in her collection of short stories,* Gorilla, My Love, *that shows the importance of self-knowledge and a supportive community for young people.*

Travels to Cuba and Vietnam in the 1970s both increased Bambara's belief that a writer can be a powerful force for change and helped her to write about a broad range of cultures. The collection of stories The Sea Birds Are Still Alive *and her novel* The Salt Eaters *reflect connections between different ethnic communities while emphasizing the importance of personal faith and social activism.*

In "Witchbird," which appeared in The Sea Birds Are Still Alive, *Bambara explores the sustaining and liberating powers of art—in this case, music—while taking us into the consciousness of a blues singer. Although beset by daily irritations and disappointments, the singer realizes that when she re-creates the works of the great blues artists, she gives new life both to the women who sang them and to the women they sang about: "So many women in them songs, waiting to be released into the air again, freed to roam."*

WITCHBIRD

I

Curtains blew in and wrecked my whole dressing-table arrangement. Then in he came, eight kinds of darkness round his shoulders, this nutty bird screechin on his arm, on a nine-speed model, hand brakes and all. Said, "Come on, we goin ride right out of here just like you been wantin to for long time now." Patting the blanket lassoed to the carrier, leaning way back to do it, straddling the bike and thrusting his johnson out in front, patting, thrusting, insinuating. Bird doing a two-step on the handle bars.

Damn if I'm riding nowhere on some bike. I like trains. Am partial to fresh-smelling club cars with clear windows and cushy seats with white linen at the top for my cheek to snooze against. Not like the hulking, oil-leaking, smoke-belching monstrosity I came home on when the play closed. Leaning my cheek against the rattling windowpane, like to shook my teeth loose. Cigar stench, orange peels curling on the window sills, balls of wax paper greasy underfoot, the linen rank from umpteen different hair pomades. Want the trains like before, when I was little and the porter hauled me up by my wrists and joked with me about my new hat, earning the five my mama slipped him, leisurely. Watching out for my person, saving a sunny seat in the dining car, clearing the aisle of perverts from round my berth, making sure I was in the no-drama section of the train once we crossed the Potomac.

"Well, we can cross over to the other side," he saying, "you in a rut, girl, let's go." Leaning over the edge of the boat, trailing a hand in the blue-green Caribbean. No way. I like trains. Then uncorking the champagne, the bottle lodged between his thighs. Then the pop of the cork, froth cascading all over his lap. I tell you I'm partial to trains. "Well, all right," he sayin, stepping out his pants. "We go the way you want, any way you want. Cause you need a change," he saying, chuggin over my carpet in this bubble-top train he suddenly got. Bird shouting at me from the perch of eye-stinging white linen. And I know something gotta be wrong. Cause whenever I've asked for what I want in life, I never get it. So he got to be the devil or some kind of other ugly no-good thing.

"Get on out my room," I'm trying to say, jaws stuck. Whole right side and left paralyzed like I'm jammed in a cage. "You tromping on my house shoes and I don't play that. Them's the house shoes Heywood gave me for Mother's Day." Some joke. Heywood come up empty-handed every rent day, but that don't stop him from boarding all his ex ole ladies with me freebee. But yellow satin Hollywood slippers with pompoms on Mother's Day, figuring that's what I'm here for. Shit, I ain't nobody's mother. I'm a singer. I'm an actress. I'm a landlady look like. Hear me. Applaud me. Pay me.

"But look here," he saying, holding up a pair of house shoes even finer than mine. Holding em up around his ears like whatshisname, not the Sambo kid, the other little fellah. "Come on and take this ride with me."

All this talk about crossing over somewhere in dem golden slippers doing something to my arms. They jiggling loose from me like they through the bars of the cage, cept I know I'm under the covers in a bed, not a box. Just a jiggling. You'd think I was holding a hazel switch or a willow rod out in the woods witching for water. Peach twig better actually for locating subterranean springs. And I try to keep my mind on water, cause water is always a good thing. Creeks, falls, foundations, artesian wells. Baptism, candlelight ablutions, skinny-dipping in the lake, C&C with water on the side. The root of all worthy civilizations, water. Can heal you. Scrunched up under the quilts, the sick tray pushed to the side, the heal of rain washing against the window can heal you or make you pee the bed one, which'll wake you from fever, from sleep, will save you. Save me. Cause damn if this character ain't trying to climb into my berth. And if there's one thing I can do without, it's phantom fucking.

. . .

"Honey? You told me to wake you at dark. It's dark." Gayle, the brown-skin college girl my sometime piano player–sometime manager–mosttime friend Heywood dumped on me last time through here, jiggling my arms. Looking sorrowful about waking me up, she knows how sacred sleep can be, though not how scary.

"Here," she says, sliding my house shoes closer to the bed. "You know Heywood was all set to get you some tired old navy-blue numbers. I kept telling him you ain't nobody's grandma," she says, backing up to give me room to stretch, looking me over like she always does, comparing us I guess to flatter her own vanity, or wondering maybe if it's possible Heywood sees beyond friend, colleague, to maybe woman. All the time trying to pry me open and check out is there some long ago Heywood-me history. The truth is there's nothing to tell. Heywood spot him a large, singing, easygoing type woman, so he dumps his girl friends on me is all. I slide into the cold slippers. They're too soft now and give no support. Cheap-ass shoes. Here it is only Halloween, and they falling apart already. I'm sucking my teeth but can't even hear myself good for the caterwauling that damn bird's already set up in the woods, tearing up the bushes, splitting twigs with the high notes. Bird make me think some singer locked up inside, hostage. Cept that bird ain't enchanting, just annoying.

"Laney's fixing a plate of supper for Miz Mary," Gayle is saying, sliding a hand across my dressing-table scarf like she dying to set her buns down and mess in my stuff. My make-up kit ain't even unpacked, I'm noticing, and the play been closed for over a month. I ain't even taken the time to review what that role's done to my sense of balance, my sense of self. But who's got time, what with all of Heywood's women cluttering up my house, my life? Prancing around in shorty nightgowns so I don't dare have company in. A prisoner in my own house.

"Laney say come on, she'll walk to the shop with you, Honey. Me too. I think my number hit today. Maybe I can help out with the bills."

Right. I'd settle for some privacy. Had such other plans for my time right in through here. Bunch of books my nephew sent untouched. Stacks of *Variety* unread under the kitchen table. The new sheet music gathering dust on the piano. Been wanting to go over the old songs, the ole Bessie numbers, Ma Rainey, Trixie Smith, early Lena. So many women in them songs waiting to be released into the air again, freed to roam. Good time to be getting my new repertoire together too instead of rushing into my clothes and slapping my face together just because Laney can't bear walking the streets alone after dark, and Gayle too scared to stay in the place by herself. Not that Heywood puts a gun to my head, but it's hard to say no to a sister with no place to go. So they wind up here, expecting me to absorb their blues and transform them maybe into songs. Been over a year since I've written any new songs. Absorbing, absorbing, bout to turn to mush rather than crystallize, sparkling.

II

Magazine lady on the phone this morning asked if I was boarding any new up-and-coming stars. Very funny. Vera, an early Heywood ex, had left here once her demo record was cut, went to New York and made the big time. Got me a part in the play, according to the phone voice contracted to do a four-page spread on Vera Willis, Star. But that ain't how the deal went down at all.

"I understand you used to room together" was how the phone interview started off. Me arranging the bottles and jars on my table, untangling the junk in my jewelry boxes. Remembering how Vera considered herself more guest than roommate, no problem whatsoever about leaving all the work to me, was saving herself for Broadway or Hollywood one. Like nothing I could be about was all that important so hey, Honey, pick up the mop. Me sitting on the piano bench waiting for Heywood to bring in a batch of cheat sheets, watching Vera in the yard with my nieces turning double dudge. Then Vera gets it in her mind to snatch away the rope and sing into the wooden handle, strolling, sassy, slinky between the dogwoods, taking poses, kicking at the tail of the rope and making teethy faces like Heywood taught her. The little girls stunned by this performance so like their own, only this one done brazenly, dead serious, and by a grown-up lady slithering about the yard.

Staring out the window, I felt bad. I thought it was because Vera was just not pretty. Not pretty and not nice. Obnoxious in fact, selfish, vain, lazy. But yeah she could put a song over, though she didn't have what you'd call musicianship. Like she'd glide into a song, it all sounding quite dull normal at first. Then a leg would shoot out as though from a split in some juicy material kicking the mike cord out the way, then the song would move somewhere. As though the spirit of music had hovered cautious around her chin thinking it over, looking her over, then liking that leg, swept into her mouth and took hold of her throat and the song possessed her, electrified the leg, sparked her into pretty. Later realizing I was staring at her, feeling bad because of course she'd make it, have what she wanted, go everywhere, meet everybody, be everything but self-deserving.

First-class bitch was my two cents with the producers, just to make it crystal clear I didn't intend riding in on her dress tails but wanted to be judged by my own work, my reputation, my audition. Don't nobody do me no favors, please, cause I'm the baddest singer out here and one of the best character actresses around. And just keeping warmed up till a Black script comes my way.

Wasn't much of a part, but a good bit at the end. My daddy used to instruct, if you can't be the star of the show, aim for a good bit at the end. People remember that one good line or that one striking piece of business by the bit player in the third act. Well, just before the end, I come on for my longest bit in the play. I'm carrying this veil, Vera's mama's veil. The woman's so grief-stricken and whatnot, she ain't even buttoned up right and forgot to put on her veil. So here I come with the veil, and the mourners part the waves to give me a path right to the grave site. But once I see the coffin, my brown-sugar honey chile darlin dead and boxed, I forget all about the blood mama waiting for her veil. Forget all about maintaining my servant place in the bourgy household. I snatch off my apron and slowly lift that veil, for I am her true mother who cared for her and carried her through. I raise the hell outta that veil, transforming myself into Mother with a capital M. I let it drape slowly, slowly round my corn rolls, slowly lower it around my brow, my nose, mouth opening and the song bursting my jaws asunder as the curtain—well, not curtain, but the lights, cause we played it in the round, dim. Tore the play up with the song.

Course we did have a set-to about the costume. The designer saw my point—her talents were being squandered copying the pancake box. Playwright saw my point too, why distort a perfectly fine character just cause the director has mammy fantasies. An African patchwork apron was the only concession I'd make. Got to be firm about shit like that, cause if you ain't some bronze Barbie doll type or the big fro murder-mouth militant sister, you Aunt Jemima. Not this lady. No way. Got to fight hard and all the time with the scripts and the people. Cause they'll trap you in a fiction. Breath drained, heart stopped, vibrancy fixed, under arrest. Whole being entrapped, all possibility impaled, locked in some stereotype. And how you look trying to call from the box and be heard much less be understood long enough to get out and mean something useful and for real?

Sometimes I think I do a better job of it with the bogus scripts than with the life script. Fight harder with directors than with friends who trap me in their scenarios, put a drama on my ass. That's the problem with friends sometimes, they invest in who you were or seem to have been, capture you and you're through. Forget what you had in mind about changing, growing, developing. Got you typecasted. That's why I want some time off to think, to work up a new repertoire of songs, of life. So many women in them songs, in them streets, in me, waiting to be freed up.

Dozing, drifting into sleep sometime, the script sliding off the quilts into a heap, I hear folks calling to me. Calling from the box. Mammy Pleasant, was it? Tubman, slave women bundlers, voodoo queens, maroon guerrillas, combatant ladies in the Seminole nation, calls from the swamps, the tunnels, the classrooms, the studios, the factories, the roofs, from the doorway hushed or brassy in a dress way too short but it don't mean nuthin heavy enough to have to explain, just like Bad Bitch in the Sanchez play was saying. But then the wagon comes and they all rounded up and caged in the Bitch-Whore-Mouth mannequin with the dead eyes and the mothball breath, never to be heard from again. But want to sing a Harriet song and play a Pleasant role and bring them all center stage.

Wives weeping from the pillow not waking him cause he got his own weight to tote, wife in the empty road with one slipper on and the train not stopping, mother anxious with the needle and thread or clothespin as the children grow either much too fast to escape the attention of the posse or not fast enough to take hold. Women calling from the lock-up of the Matriarch cage. I want to put some of these new mother poems in those books the nephew sends to music. They got to be sung, hummed, shouted, chanted, swung.

Too many damn ransom notes fluttering in the window, or pitched in through the glass. Too much bail to post. Too many tunnels to dig and too much dynamite to set. I read the crazy scripts just to keep my hand in, cause I knew these newbreed Bloods going to do it, do it, do it. But meanwhile, I gotta work . . . and hell. Then read one of them books my nephew always sending and hearing the voices speaking free not calling from these new Black poems. Speaking free. So I know I ain't crazy. But fast as we bust one, two loose, here come some crazy cracker throwing a croaker sack over Nat Turner's head, or white folks taking Malcolm hostage. And one time in Florida, dreaming in the hotel room about the Mary McLeod Bethune exhibit, I heard the woman calling from some diary entry they had under glass, a voice calling, muffled under the gas mask they clamped on hard and turned her on till she didn't know what was what. But calling for Black pages.

Then waking and trying to resume the reading, cept I can't remember just whom I'm supposed to try to animate in those dead, white pages I got to deal with till a Blood writes me my own. And catch myself calling to the white pages as I ripple them fast, listening to the pages for the entrapped voices calling, calling as the pages flutter.

Shit. It's enough to make you crazy. Where is my play, I wanna ask these new Bloods at the very next conference I hear about. Where the hell is my script? When I get to work my show?

. . .

"A number of scandalous rumors followed the run of the play, taking up an inordinate amount of space in the reviews," the lady on the phone was saying, me caught up in my own dialogue. "I understand most of the men connected with the play and Vera Willis had occasion to . . ."

There was Heywood, of course. Hadn't realized they'd gotten back together till that weekend we were packing the play off to New York. Me packing ahead of schedule and anxious to get out of D.C. fast, cause Bradwell, who used to manage the club where I been working for years, had invited me to his home for the weekend. For old times' sake, he'd said. Right. He'd married somebody else, a singer we used to crack on as I recall, not a true note in her, her tits getting her over. And now she'd left him rolling around lonely in the brownstone on Edgecombe Avenue she'd once thought she just had to have. I went out and bought two hussy nightgowns. I was gonna break out in a whole new number. But never did work up the nerve. Never did have the occasion, ole Bradwell crying the blues about his wife. So what am I there for—to absorb, absorb, and transform if you can, ole girl. Absorb, absorb and try to convert it all to something other than fat.

Heywood calling to ask me to trade my suite near the theater for his room clear cross town.

"You can have both," I said, chuckling. "I'm off for the weekend."

"How come? Where you going?"

"Rendezvous. Remember the guy that used to own—"

"Cut the comedy. Where you going?"

"I'm telling you. I got a rendezvous with this gorgeous man I—"

"Look here," he cut in, "I'd invited Laney up to spend the weekend. That was before me and Vera got together again. I was wondering if you'd bail me out, maybe hang out with Laney till I can—"

"Heywood, you deaf? I just now told you I'm off to spend the—"

"Seriously?"

Made me so mad, I just hung up. Hung up and called me a fast cab.

III

Laney, Gayle, and me turn into Austin and run smack into a bunch of ghosts. Skeletons, pirates, and little devils with great flapping shopping bags set up a whirlwind around us. Laney spins around like in a speeded-up movie, holding Mary's dinner plate away from her dress and moaning, comically. Comically at first. But then our bird friend in the woods starts shrieking and Laney moaning for real. Gayle empties her bag into one of the opened sacks, then leans in to retrieve her wallet, though I can't see why. All I got for the kids is a short roll of crumbly Lifesavers, hair with tobacco and lint from my trench coat lining. Screaming and wooo-wooooing, they jack-rabbit on down Austin. Then we heading past the fish truck, my mind on some gumbo, when suddenly Gayle stops. She heard it soon's I did. Laney still walking on till I guess some remark didn't get a uh-hunh and she turns around to see us way behind, Gayle's head cocked to the side.

"What it is?" Laney looking up and down the street for a clue. Other than the brother dumping the last of the ice from the fish truck and a few cats hysterical at the curb, too self-absorbed to launch a concerted attack on the truck, there ain't much to keep the eyes alive. "What?" Laney whispers.

From back of the houses we hear some mother calling her son, the voice edgy on the last syllable, getting frantic. Probably Miz Baker, whose six-foot twelve-year-old got a way of scooting up and down that resembles too much the actions of a runaway bandit to the pigs around here. Mainly, he got the outlaw hue, and running too? Shit, Miz Baker stay frantic. The boy answers from the woods, which starts the bird up again, screeching, ripping through the trees, like she trying to find a way out of them woods and heaven help us if she do, cause she dangerous with rage.

"That him?" Gayle asks, knowing I'm on silence this time of night.

"Who?" Laney don't even bother looking at me, cause she knows I got a whole night of singing and running off at the mouth to get through once Mary lets me out from under the dryer and I get to the club. "Witchbird?" Laney takes a couple steps closer to us. "Yawl better tell me what's up," she says, "cause this here gettin spoooo-keeee!"

It's mostly getting dark and Laney don't wanna have to take the shortcut through the woods. Witchbird gotta way of screaming on you sudden, scare the shit outta you. Laney trying to balance that plate of dinner and not lose the juice. She is worried you can tell, and not just about Mary's mouth over cold supper. Laney's face easy to read, everything surfaces to the skin. Dug that the day Heywood brought her by. She knew she was being cut loose, steered safely to cove, the boat shoving off and bye, baby, bye. Sad crinkling round the eyes, purples under the chin, throat pulsating. Gayle harder to read, a Scorpio, she plays it close to the chest unless she can play it for drama.

"Tell me, Gayle. What it is?"

"Heywood back in town."

"Ohhh, girl, don't tell me that." Laney takes a coupla sideways steps, juggling the plate onto one hand so she can tug down the jersey she barmaids in. "You better come on."

"You know one thing," Gayle crooning it, composing a monologue, sound like. "There was a time when that laugh could turn me clear around in the street and make me forget just where I thought I was going." On cue, Heywood laughs one of his laughs and Gayle's head tips, locating his whereabouts. She hands me her suede bag heavy with the pic comb and the schoolbooks. It's clear she fixin to take off. "I really loved that dude," she saying, theatrics gone. Laney moves on, cause she don't want to hear nuthin about Heywood and especially from Gayle. "He gets his thing off," Laney had said to Gayle the night she was dumped, "behind the idea of his harem sprawled all over Honey's house gassing about him. I refuse," she had said and stuck to it.

"I really, really did," Gayle saying, something leaking in her voice.

Laney hears it and steps back. It's spilling on her shoes, her dress, soaking into her skin. She moves back again cause Gayle's zone is spreading. Gayle so filling up and brimming over, she gotta take over more and more room to accommodate the swell. Her leaking splashes up against me too—Heywood taking a solo, teeth biting out a rhythm on the back of his lower lip, Heywood at the wheel leaning over for a kiss fore he cranks up, Heywood wound up in rumpled sheets with his cap pulled down, sweat beading on his nose, waiting on breakfast, Heywood doing the dance of the hot hands and Gayle scrambling for a potholder to catch the coffeepot he'd reached for with his fool self, Heywood falling off the porch and Gayle's daddy right on him. Gayle's waves wash right up on me and I don't want no parts of it. Let it all wash right through me, can't use it, am to the brim with my own stuff waiting to be transformed. Washes through me so fast the pictures blur and all I feel is heat and sparks. And then I hear the laugh again.

"Oh, shit," Laney says, watching the hem of Gayle's dress turning into the alley. "That girl is craaaaa-zeee, ya heah?" Her legs jiggling to put her in the alley in more ways than one, but that plate leaking pot likker and demanding its due.

Bright's strung up lights in the alley and you can make him out clear, hunched over the bathtub swishing barbeque sauce with a sheet-wrapped broom. Cora visible too, doing a shonuff flower arrangement on the crushed ice with the watermelon slices. And there's Heywood, ole lanky Heywood in his cap he says Babs Gonzales stole from Kenny Clarke and he in turn swiped from Babs. One arm lazy draped around Gayle's shoulders, the other crooked in the fence he lounges against, sipping some of Bright's bad brandy brew, speakeasy style. Other folks around the card table sipping from jelly jars or tin cups. But Heywood would have one of Cora's fine china numbers. He's looking good.

"What's goin on?" Laney asks in spite of herself, but refuses to move where she can see into the yard. All she got to do is listen, cause Heywood is the baritone lead of the eight-part card game opus.

"Ho!"

"Nigger, just play the card."

"Gonna. Gonna do that direckly. Right on yawl's ass."

"Do it to em, Porter."

"Don't tell him nuthin. He don't wanna know nuthin. He ain't never been nuthin but a fool."

Porter spits on the card and slaps it on his forehead.

"Got the bitch right here"—he's pointing—"the bitch that's gonna set ya."

"Nigger, you nasty, you know that? You a nasty-ass nigger and that's why don't nobody never wanna play with yo nasty-ass self."

"Just play the card, Porter."

"Ho!" He bangs the card down with a pop and the table too.

"Iz you crazy?"

"If Porter had any sense, he'd be dangerous."

"Sense enough to send these blowhards right out the back door. Ho!"

"You broke the table and the ashtray, fool."

"And that was my last cigarette too. Gimme a dollar."

"Dollar! I look like a fool? If you paying Bright a dollar for cigarettes, you the fool."

"I want the dollar for some barbeque."

"What! What!" Porter sputtering and dancing round the yard. "How come I gotta replace one cigarette with a meal?"

"Okay then, buy some watermelon and some of the fire juice."

"You don't logic, man. You sheer don't logic. All I owe you is a cigarette."

"What about the table?"

"It ain't your table, nigger."

Laney is click-clicking up the street, giving wide berth to the path that leads through the woods. "Why Gayle want to put herself through them changes all over again," she is mumbling, grinding her heels in the broken pavement, squashing the dandelions. "I wouldn't put myself through none of that mess again for all the money." She picking up speed and I gotta trot to catch up. "I don't know how you can stay friends with a man like that, Honey."

"He don't do me no harm," I say, then mad to break my silence.

"Oh, no?" She trying to provoke me into debating it, so she says it again, "Oh, no?"

I don't want to get into this, all I want is to get into Mary's shampoo chair, to laze under Mary's hands and have her massage all the hurt up out of my body, tension emulsified in the coconut-oil suds, all fight sprayed away. My body been so long on chronic red alert messin with them theater folks, messing with stock types, real types, messing with me, I need release, not hassles.

"You think it's no harm the way he uses you, Honey? What are you, his mother, his dumping grounds? Why you put up with it? Why you put up with us, with me? Oh, Honey, I—"

I walk right along, just like she ain't talking to me. I can't take in another thing.

IV

"Well, all right! Here she come, Broadway star," someone bellows at me as the bell over the door jangles.

"Come on out from under that death, Honey," Mary says soon's we get halfway in the door. "Look like you sportin a whole new look in cosmetics.

Clown white, ain't it? Or is it Griffin All White applied with a putty knife?" Mary leaves her customer in the chair to come rip the wig off my head. "And got some dead white woman on your head too. Why you wanna do this to yourself, Honey? You auditioning for some zombie movie?"

"Protective covering," Bertha says, slinging the magazine she'd been reading onto the pile. "You know how Honey likes to put herself out of circulation, Mary. Honey, you look like one of them creatures Nanna Mae raised from the dead. What they do to you in New York, girl? We thought you'd come back tired, but not embalmed."

"Heard tell a duppy busted up some posh do on the hill last Saturday," Mary's customer saying. "Lotta zombies round here."

"Some say it was the ghost of Willie Best come back to kill him somebody."

"Long's it's some white somebody, okay by me."

"Well, you know colored folks weren't exactly kind to the man when he was alive. Could be—"

"Heard Heywood's back on the scene," Bertha comes over to say to me. She lifts my hand off the armrest and checks my manicure and pats my hand to make up for, I guess, her not-so-warm greeting. "Be interesting to see just what kinda bundle he gonna deposit on your doorstep this time." Laney cuts her eye at Bertha, surrenders up the juiceless meal and splits. "Like you ain't got nuthin better to do with ya tits but wet-nurse his girls."

I shove Bertha's hand off mine and stretch out in my favorite chair. Mary's got a young sister now to do the scratchin and hot oil. She parts hair with her fingers, real gentle-like. Feels good. I'm whipped. I think on all I want to do with the new music and I'm feelin crowded, full up, rushed.

"No use you trying to ig me, Honey," Bertha says real loud. "Cause I'm Mary's last customer. We got all night."

"Saw Frieda coming out the drugstore," somebody is saying. "Package looked mighty interesting."

Everybody cracking up, Bertha too. I ease my head back and close my eyes under the comb scratching up dandruff.

"Obviously Ted is going on the road again and Frieda gonna pack one of her famous box snacks."

"Got the recipe for the oatmeal cookies richeah," someone saying. "One part rolled oats, one long drip of sorghum, fistful of raisins, and a laaaarge dose of saltpeter."

"Salt pete–er salt pete–er," somebody singing through the nose, outdoing Dizzy.

"Whatchu say!"

"Betcha there'll be plenty straaange mashed potatoes on the table tonight."

The young girl's rubbin is too hard in the part and the oil too hot. But she so busy cracking up, she don't notice my ouchin.

"Saltpetertaters, what better dish to serve a man going on the road for three days. Beats calling him every hour on the half-hour telling him to take a cold shower."

"Best serve him with a summons for being so downright ugly. Can't no woman be really serious about messin with Ted, he too ugly."

"Some that looks ugly . . ." Couldn't catch the rest of it, but followed the giggling well enough after what sounded like a second of silence.

"Mary"—someone was breathless with laughter—"when you and the sisters gonna give another one of them balls?"

"Giiirl," howls Bertha, "Wasn't that ball a natural ball?"

V

Bertha and Mary and me organized this Aquarian Ball. We so busy making out the lists, hooking people up, calling in some new dudes from the Islands just to jazz it up, hiring musicians and all, we clean forgot to get me an escort. I'd just made Marshall the trumpet player give me back my key cause all he ever wanted to do was bring by a passle of fish that needed cleaning and frying, and I was sick of being cook and confidante. I bet if I lost weight, people'd view me different. Other than Marshall, wasn't no man on the horizon, much less the scene. Mary, me and Bertha playing bid whist and I feel a Boston in my bones, so ain't paying too much attention to the fact that this no escort status of mine is serious business as far as Bertha's concerned.

"What about Heywood?" she says, scooping up the kitty.

Right on cue as always, in comes ole lanky Heywood with his cap yanked down around his brow and umpteen scarves around his mouth looking like Jesse James. He's got a folio of arrangements to deliver to me, but likes to make a big production first of saying hello to sisters. So while he's doing his rhyming couplets and waxing lyric and whatnot, I'm looking him over, trying to unravel my feelings about this man I've known, worked with, befriended for so long. Good manager, never booked me in no dumps. Always sees to it that the money ain't funny. A good looker and all, but always makes me feel more mother or older sister, though he four months to the day older than me. Naaw, I conclude, Heywood just my buddy. But I'm thinking too that I need a new buddy, cause he's got me bagged somehow. Put me in a bag when I wasn't looking. Folks be sneaky with their scenarios and secret casting.

"Say, handsome," Bertha say, jumping right on it, "ain't you taking Honey here to the ball?"

"Why somebody got to take her? I thought yawl was giving it."

"That ain't no answer. Can't have Honey waltzin in without—"

"Hold on," he saying, unwrapping the scarves cause we got the oven up high doing the meat patties.

"Never mind all that," says Mary. "Who you know can do it? Someone nice now."

"Well, I'll tell you," he says, stretching his arm around me. "I don't know no men good enough for the queen here."

"You a drag and a half," says Bertha.

"And I don't want to block traffic either," he says. "I mean if Honey comes in with my fine self on her arm, no man there is—"

"Never mind that," says Mary, slapping down an ace. "What about your friends, I'm askin you?"

"Like I said, I don't know anybody suitable."

"What you mean is, you only knows the ladies," says Bertha, disgusted. "You the type dude that would probably come up with a basket case for escort anyway. Club foot, hunchback, palsied moron or something. Just to make sure Honey is still available for you to mammify."

"Now wait a minute," he says, rising from the chair and pushing palms against the air like he fending us off. "How I get involved in yawl's arrangements?"

"You a friend, ain't ya? You a drag, that's for sure." Bertha lays down her hand, we thought to hit Heywood, come to find she trump tight.

Heywood puts the folio in my lap and rewraps the scarves for take-off, and we spend the afternoon being sullen, and damn near burnt up the meat patties.

"I'm getting tired of men like that," grumbles Bertha after while. "Either it's 'Hey, Mama, hold my head,' or 'Hey, Sister,' at three in the morning. When it get to be 'Sugar Darling'? I'm tired of it. And you, Honey, should be the tiredest of all."

. . .

"So I just took my buns right to her house, cause she my friend and what else a friend for?" one of the women is saying. Mary's easing my head back on the shampoo tray, so I can't see who's talking.

"So did you tell her?"

"I surely did. I held her by the shoulders and said, 'Helen, you do know that Amos is on the dope now, don't you?' And she kinda went limp in my arms like she was gonna just crumble and not deal with it."

"A myth all that stuff about our strength and strength and then some," Bertha saying.

" 'If Amos blow his mind now, who gonna take care of you in old age, Helen?' I try to tell her."

"So what she say?"

"She don't say nuthin. She just cry."

"It's a hellafyin thing. No jobs, nary a fit house in sight, famine on the way, but the dope just keep comin and comin."

I don't know Helen or Amos. Can't tell whether Amos is the son or the husband. Ain't that a bitch. But I feel bad inside. I crumple up too hearing it. Picturing a Helen seeing her Amos in a heap by the bathtub, gagging, shivering, defeated, not like he should be. Getting the blankets to wrap him up, holding him round, hugging him tight, rocking, rocking, rocking.

"You need a towel?" Mary whispers, bending under the dryer. No amount of towel's gonna stop the flood, I'm thinking. I don't even try to stop. Let it pour, let it get on out so I can travel light. I'm thinking maybe I'll do Billie's number tonight. Biting my lip and trying to think on the order of songs I'm going to get through this evening and where I can slip Billie in.

"What's with you, Honey?"

"Mary got this damn dryer on KILL," I say, and know I am about to talk myself hoarse and won't be fit for singing.

1974

MAXINE HONG KINGSTON
1940–   )

With the publication of her novel, Tripmaster Monkey: His Fake Book *(1989), Maxine Hong Kingston established herself as a major American writer. Blending the influence of American poets such as Walt Whitman and William Carlos Williams with Chinese myths and fables and the jargon of the 1960s, Kingston's latest work reflects her dazzling gift for language.*

Kingston is the eldest of Tom and Brave Orchid (Ying Lan) Hong's six surviving children. Her parents met, married, and had two children in Canton, China. A scholar and teacher, her father immigrated to the United States in the 1920s. Left in China to fend for herself, Kingston's mother suffered the deaths of both her children, attended To Keung School of Midwifery, and began a medical practice. She left this career in 1940 to be reunited with her husband in New York. The couple moved to Stockton, California, where Kingston was born.

Kingston describes her childhood in her two memoirs, The Woman Warrior: Memoirs of a Girlhood among Ghosts *and* China Men. *In the first, she weaves fact, fiction, and fantasy, both imitating her mother's Chinese dialect and re-creating her art of talking-story. In the second, Kingston relies on social history, family tales, and her imagination to tell her taciturn father's story.*

Kingston began writing as a young girl. She had an early article on the Chinese New Year published in the Stockton newspaper, and she won a journalism scholarship to the University of California, Berkeley. She received her B.A. in 1962 and married a fellow student, Earll Kingston, in 1963. After earning a teaching credential, she taught high school in northern California while participating in the free speech movement at Berkeley in the 1960s.

In 1967 the couple and their young son moved to Hawaii, where Kingston continued to teach high school and college English. She also began to write seriously. The result, The Woman Warrior, *appeared to much acclaim in 1976, winning the National Book Critics Circle Award for nonfiction.* China Men, *similarly well received, won the 1980 National Book Award in nonfiction.* Tripmaster Monkey: His Fake Book *is her first novel. Kingston currently lives in Oakland and teaches creative writing at the University of California, Berkeley.*

"At the Western Palace," taken from The Woman Warrior, *is based on Kingston's recollections of her aunt, Moon Orchid. Kingston conveys the insurmountable difficulties this aunt encountered in the 1960s when she immigrated to the United States from Hong Kong.*

from THE WOMAN WARRIOR

At the Western Palace

When she was about sixty-eight years old, Brave Orchid took a day off to wait at San Francisco International Airport for the plane that was bringing her sister to the United States. She had not seen Moon Orchid for thirty years. She had begun this waiting at home, getting up a half-hour before Moon Orchid's plane took off in Hong Kong. Brave Orchid would add her will power to the forces that keep an airplane up. Her head hurt with the concentration. The plane had to be light, so no matter how tired she felt, she dared not rest her spirit on a wing but continuously and gently pushed up on the plane's belly. She had already been waiting at the airport for nine hours. She was wakeful.

Next to Brave Orchid sat Moon Orchid's only daughter, who was helping her aunt wait. Brave Orchid had made two of her own children come too because they could drive, but they had been lured away by the magazine racks and the gift shops and coffee shops. Her American children could not sit for very long. They did not understand sitting; they had wandering feet. She hoped they would get back from the pay t.v.'s or the pay toilets or wherever they were spending their money before the plane arrived. If they did not come back soon, she would go look for them. If her son thought he could hide in the men's room, he was wrong.

"Are you all right, Aunt?" asked her niece.

"No, this chair hurts me. Help me pull some chairs together so I can put my feet up."

She unbundled a blanket and spread it out to make a bed for herself. On the floor she had two shopping bags full of canned peaches, real peaches, beans wrapped in taro leaves, cookies, Thermos bottles, enough food for everybody, though only her niece would eat with her. Her bad boy and bad girl were probably sneaking hamburgers, wasting their money. She would scold them.

Many soldiers and sailors sat about, oddly calm, like little boys in cowboy uniforms. (She thought "cowboy" was what you would call a Boy Scout.) They should have been crying hysterically on their way to Vietnam. "If I see one that looks Chinese," she thought, "I'll go over and give him some advice." She sat up suddenly; she had forgotten about her own son, who was even now in Vietnam. Carefully she split her attention, beaming half of it to the ocean, into the water to keep him afloat. He was on a ship. He was in Vietnamese waters. She was sure of it. He and the other children were lying to her. They had said he was in Japan, and then they said he was in the Philippines. But when she sent him her help, she could feel that he was on a ship in Da Nang. Also she had seen the children hide the envelopes that his letters came in.

"Do you think my son is in Vietnam?" she asked her niece, who was dutifully eating.

"No. Didn't your children say he was in the Philippines?"

"Have you ever seen any of his letters with Philippine stamps on them?"

"Oh, yes. Your children showed me one."

"I wouldn't put it past them to send the letters to some Filipino they know. He puts Manila postmarks on them to fool me."

"Yes, I can imagine them doing that. But don't worry. Your son can take care of himself. All your children can take care of themselves."

"Not him. He's not like other people. Not normal at all. He sticks erasers in his ears, and the erasers are still attached to the pencil stubs. The captain will say, 'Abandon ship,' or 'Watch out for bombs,' and he won't hear. He doesn't listen to orders. I told him to flee to Canada, but he wouldn't go."

She closed her eyes. After a short while, plane and ship under control, she looked again at the children in uniforms. Some of the blond ones looked like baby chicks, their crew cuts like the downy yellow on baby chicks. You had to feel sorry for them even though they were Army and Navy Ghosts.

Suddenly her son and daughter came running. "Come, Mother. The plane's landed early. She's here already." They hurried, folding up their mother's encampment. She was glad her children were not useless. They must have known what this trip to San Francisco was about then. "It's a good thing I made you come early," she said.

Brave Orchid pushed to the front of the crowd. She had to be in front. The passengers were separated from the people waiting for them by glass doors and walls. Immigration Ghosts were stamping papers. The travellers crowded along some conveyor belts to have their luggage searched. Brave Orchid did not see her sister anywhere. She stood watching for four hours. Her children left and came back. "Why don't you sit down?" they asked.

"The chairs are too far away," she said.

"Why don't you sit on the floor then?"

No, she would stand, as her sister was probably standing in a line she could not see from here. Her American children had no feelings and no memory.

To while away time, she and her niece talked about the Chinese passengers. These new immigrants had it easy. On Ellis Island the people were thin after forty days at sea and had no fancy luggage.

"That one looks like her," Brave Orchid would say.

"No, that's not her."

Ellis Island had been made out of wood and iron. Here everything was new plastic, a ghost trick to lure immigrants into feeling safe and spilling their secrets. Then the Alien Office could send them right back. Otherwise, why did they lock her out, not letting her help her sister answer questions and spell her name? At Ellis Island when the ghost asked Brave Orchid what year her husband had cut off his pigtail, a Chinese who was crouching on the floor motioned her not to talk. "I don't know," she had said. If it weren't for that Chinese man, she might not be here today, or her husband either. She hoped some Chinese, a janitor or a clerk, would look out for Moon Orchid. Luggage conveyors fooled immigrants into thinking the Gold Mountain was going to be easy.

Brave Orchid felt her heart jump—Moon Orchid. "There she is," she shouted. But her niece saw it was not her mother at all. And it shocked her to discover the woman her aunt was pointing out. This was a young woman, younger than herself, no older than Moon Orchid the day the sisters parted. "Moon Orchid will have changed a little, of course," Brave Orchid was saying. "She will have learned to wear western clothes." The woman wore a navy blue suit with a bunch of dark cherries at the shoulder.

"No, Aunt," said the niece. "That's not my mother."

"Perhaps not. It's been so many years. Yes, it is your mother. It must be. Let her come closer, and we can tell. Do you think she's too far away for me to tell, or is it my eyes getting bad?"

"It's too many years gone by," said the niece.

Brave Orchid turned suddenly—another Moon Orchid, this one a neat little woman with a bun. She was laughing at something the person ahead of her in line said. Moon Orchid was just like that, laughing at nothing. "I would be able to tell the difference if one of them would only come closer," Brave Orchid said with tears, which she did not wipe. Two children met the woman with the cherries, and she shook their hands. The other woman was met by a young man. They looked at each other gladly, then walked away side by side.

Up close neither one of those women looked like Moon Orchid at all. "Don't worry, Aunt," said the niece. "I'll know her."

"I'll know her too. I knew her before you did."

The niece said nothing, although she had seen her mother only five years ago. Her aunt liked having the last word.

Finally Brave Orchid's children quit wandering and drooped on a railing. Who knew what they were thinking? At last the niece called out, "I see her! I see her! Mother! Mother!" Whenever the doors parted, she shouted, probably embarrassing the American cousins, but she didn't care. She called out, "Mama! Mama!" until the crack in the sliding doors became too small to let in her voice. "Mama!" What a strange word in an adult voice. Many people turned to see what adult was calling, "Mama!" like a child. Brave Orchid saw an old, old woman jerk her head up, her little eyes blinking confusedly, a woman whose nerves leapt toward the sound anytime she heard "Mama!" Then she relaxed to her own business again. She was a tiny, tiny lady, very thin, with little fluttering hands, and her hair was in a gray knot. She was dressed in a gray wool suit; she wore pearls around her neck and in her earlobes. Moon Orchid *would* travel with her jewels showing. Brave Orchid momentarily saw, like a larger, younger outline around this old woman, the sister she had been waiting for. The familiar dim halo faded, leaving the woman so old, so gray. So old. Brave Orchid pressed against the glass. *That* old lady? Yes, that old lady facing the ghost who stamped her papers without questioning her was her sister. Then, without noticing her family, Moon Orchid walked smiling over to the Suitcase Inspector Ghost, who took her boxes apart, pulling out puffs of tissue. From where she was, Brave Orchid could not see what her sister had chosen to carry across the ocean. She wished her sister would look her way. Brave Orchid thought that if *she* were entering a new country, she would be at the windows. Instead Moon Orchid hovered over the unwrapping, surprised at each reappearance as if she were opening presents after a birthday party.

"Mama!" Moon Orchid's daughter kept calling. Brave Orchid said to her children, "Why don't you call your aunt too? Maybe she'll hear us if all of you call out together." But her children slunk away. Maybe that shame-face they so often wore was American politeness.

"Mama!" Moon Orchid's daughter called again, and this time her mother looked right at her. She left her bundles in a heap and came running. "Hey!" the Customs Ghost yelled at her. She went back to clear up her mess, talking inaudibly to her daughter all the while. Her daughter pointed toward Brave Orchid. And at last Moon Orchid looked at her—two old women with faces like mirrors.

Their hands reached out as if to touch the other's face, then returned to their own, the fingers checking the grooves in the forehead and along the sides of the mouth. Moon Orchid, who never understood the gravity of things, started smiling and laughing, pointing at Brave Orchid. Finally Moon Orchid gathered up her stuff, strings hanging and papers loose, and met her sister at the door, where they shook hands, oblivious to blocking the way.

"You're an old woman," said Brave Orchid.

"Aiaa. *You're* an old woman."

"But you are really old. Surely, you can't say that about me. I'm not old the way you're old."

"But *you* really are old. You're one year older than I am."

"Your hair is white and your face all wrinkled."

"You're so skinny."

"You're so fat."

"Fat women are more beautiful than skinny women."

The children pulled them out of the doorway. One of Brave Orchid's children brought the car from the parking lot, and the other heaved the luggage into the trunk. They put the two old ladies and the niece in the back seat. All the way home—across the Bay Bridge, over the Diablo hills, across the San Joaquin River to the valley, the valley moon so white at dusk—all the way home, the two sisters exclaimed every time they turned to look at each other, "Aiaa! How old!"

Brave Orchid forgot that she got sick in cars, that all vehicles but palanquins made her dizzy. "You're so old," she kept saying. "How did you get so old?"

Brave Orchid had tears in her eyes. But Moon Orchid said, "You look older than I. You *are* older than I," and again she'd laugh. "You're wearing an old mask to tease me." It surprised Brave Orchid that after thirty years she could still get annoyed at her sister's silliness.

. . .

Brave Orchid's husband was waiting under the tangerine tree. Moon Orchid recognized him as the brother-in-law in photographs, not as the young man who left on a ship. Her sister had married the ideal in masculine beauty, the thin scholar with the hollow cheeks and the long fingers. And here he was, an old man, opening the gate he had built with his own hands, his hair blowing silver in twilight. "Hello," he said like an Englishman in Hong Kong. "Hello," she said like an English telephone operator. He went to help his children unload the car, gripping the suitcase handles in his bony fingers, his bony wrists locked.

Brave Orchid's husband and children brought everything into the dining room, provisions for a lifetime move heaped all over the floor and furniture. Brave Orchid wanted to have a luck ceremony and then to put things away where they belonged, but Moon Orchid said, "I've got presents for everybody. Let me get them." She opened her boxes again. Her suitcase lids gaped like mouths; Brave Orchid had better hurry with the luck.

"First I've got shoes for all of you from Lovely Orchid," Moon Orchid said, handing them out to her nieces and nephews, who grimaced at one another. Lovely Orchid, the youngest aunt, owned either a shoe store or a shoe factory in Hong Kong. That was why every Christmas she sent a dozen pairs, glittering with yellow and pink plastic beads, sequins, and turquoise blue flowers. "She must give us the leftovers," Brave Orchid's children were saying in English. As Brave Orchid ran back and forth turning on all the lights, every lamp and bulb, she glared sideways at her children. They would be sorry when they had to walk barefoot through snow and rocks because they didn't take what shoes they could, even if the wrong size. She would put the slippers next to the bathtub on the linoleum floors in winter and trick her lazy children into wearing them.

"May I have some scissors? Oh, where are my scissors?" said Moon Orchid. She slit the heel of a black embroidered slipper and pulled out the cotton—which was entangled with jewels. "You'll have to let me pierce your ears," she told her nieces, rubbing their earlobes. "Then you can wear these." There were earrings with skewers like gold krisses. There was a jade heart and an opal. Brave Orchid interrupted her dashing about to rub the stones against her skin.

Moon Orchid laughed softly in delight. "And look here. Look here," she said. She was holding up a paper warrior-saint, and he was all intricacies and light. A Communist had cut a wisp of black paper into a hero with sleeves like butterflies' wings and with tassels and flags, which fluttered when you breathed on him. "Did someone really cut this out by hand?" the children kept asking. "Really?" The eyebrows and mustache, the fierce wrinkles between the eyes, the face, all were the merest black webs. His open hand had been cut out finger by finger. Through the spaces you could see light and the room and each other. "Oh, there's more. There's more," said Moon Orchid happily. She picked up another paper cutout and blew on it. It was the scholar who always carries a fan; her breath shook its blue feathers. His brush and quill and scrolls tied with ribbon jutted out of lace vases. "And more"—an orange warrior-poet with sword and scroll; a purple knight with doily armor, holes for scales; a wonderful archer on a red horse with a mane like fire; a modern Communist worker with a proud gold hammer; a girl Communist soldier with pink pigtails and pink rifle. "And this is Fa Mu Lan," she said. "She was a woman warrior, and really existed." Fa Mu Lan was green and beautiful, and her robes whirled out as she drew her sword.

"Paper dolls," said Brave Orchid to her children. "I'd have thought you were too old to be playing with dolls." How greedy to play with presents in front of the giver. How impolite ("untraditional" in Chinese) her children were. With a slam of her cleaver, she cracked rock candy into jagged pieces. "Take some," she urged. "Take more." She brought the yellow crystals on a red paper plate to her family, one by one. It was very important that the beginning be sweet. Her children acted as if this eating were a bother. "Oh, all right," they said, and took the smallest slivers. Who would think that children could dislike candy? It was abnormal, not in the nature of children, not human. "Take a big piece," she scolded. She'd make them eat it like medicine if necessary. They were so stupid, surely they weren't adults yet. They'd put the bad mouth on their aunt's first American day; you had to sweeten their noisy barbarous mouths. She opened the front door and mumbled something. She opened the back door and mumbled something.

"What do you say when you open the door like that?" her children used to ask when they were younger.

"Nothing. Nothing," she would answer.

"Is it spirits, Mother? Do you talk to spirits? Are you asking them in or asking them out?"

"It's nothing," she said. She never explained anything that was really important. They no longer asked.

When she came back from talking to the invisibilities, Brave Orchid saw that her sister was strewing the room. The paper people clung flat against the lampshades, the chairs, the tablecloths. Moon Orchid left fans unfolded and dragons with accordion bodies dangling from doorknobs. She was unrolling white silk. "Men are good at stitching roosters," she was pointing out bird embroidery. It was amazing how a person could grow old without learning to put things away.

"Let's put these things away," Brave Orchid said.

"Oh, Sister," said Moon Orchid. "Look what I have for you," and she held up a pale green silk dress lined in wool. "In winter you can look like summer and be warm like summer." She unbuttoned the frogs to show the lining, thick and plaid like a blanket.

"Now where would I wear such a fancy dress?" said Brave Orchid. "Give it to one of the children."

"I have bracelets and earrings for them."

"They're too young for jewelry. They'll lose it."

"They seem very big for children."

"The girls broke six jade bracelets playing baseball. And they can't endure pain. They scream when I squeeze their hands into the jade. Then that very day, they'll break it. We'll put the jewelry in the bank, and we'll buy glass and black wood frames for the silk scrolls." She bundled up the sticks that opened into flowers. "What were you doing carrying these scraps across the ocean?"

Brave Orchid took what was useful and solid into the back bedroom, where Moon Orchid would stay until they decided what she would do permanently. Moon Orchid picked up pieces of string, but bright colors and movements distracted her. "Oh, look at this," she'd say. "Just look at this. You have carp." She was turning the light off and on in the goldfish tank, which sat in the rolltop desk that Brave Orchid's husband had taken from the gambling house when it shut down during World War II. Moon Orchid looked up at the grandparents' photographs that hung on the wall above the desk. Then she turned around and looked at the opposite wall; there, equally large, were pictures of Brave Orchid and her husband. They had put up their own pictures because later the children would not have the sense to do it.

"Oh, look," said Moon Orchid. "Your pictures are up too. Why is that?"

"No reason. Nothing," said Brave Orchid. "In America you can put up anybody's picture you like."

On the shelf of the rolltop desk, like a mantel under the grandparents' photos, there were bowls of plastic tangerines and oranges, crepe-paper flowers, plastic vases, porcelain vases filled with sand and incense sticks. A clock sat on a white runner crocheted with red phoenixes and red words about how lucky and bright life is. Moon Orchid lifted the ruffles to look inside the pigeon holes. There were also pen trays and little drawers, enough so that the children could each have one or two for their very own. The fish tank took up half the desk space, and there was still room for writing. The rolltop was gone; the children had broken it slat by slat when they hid inside the desk, pulling the top over themselves. The knee hole had boxes of toys that the married children's children played with now. Brave Orchid's husband had padlocked one large bottom cabinet and one drawer.

"Why do you keep it locked?" Moon Orchid asked. "What's in here?"

"Nothing," he said. "Nothing."

"If you want to poke around," said Brave Orchid, "why don't you find out what's in the kitchen drawers so you can help me cook?"

They cooked enough food to cover the dining room and kitchen tables.

"Eat!" Brave Orchid ordered. "Eat!" She would not allow anybody to talk while eating. In some families the children worked out a sign language, but here the children spoke English, which their parents didn't seem to hear.

After they ate and cleaned up, Brave Orchid said, "Now! We have to get down to business."

"What do you mean?" said her sister. She and her daughter held one another's hands.

"Oh, no. I don't want to listen to this," said Brave Orchid's husband, and left to read in bed.

The three women sat in the enormous kitchen with the butcher's block and two refrigerators. Brave Orchid had an inside stove in the kitchen and a stove outside on the back porch. All day long the outside stove cooked peelings and gristle into chicken feed. It horrified the children when they caught her throwing scraps of chicken into the chicken feed. Both stoves had been turned off for the night now, and the air was cooling.

"Wait until morning, Aunt," said Moon Orchid's daughter. "Let her get some sleep."

"Yes, I do need rest after travelling all the way from China," she said. "I'm here. You've done it and brought me here." Moon Orchid meant that they should be satisfied with what they had already accomplished. Indeed, she stretched happily and appeared quite satisfied to be sitting in that kitchen at that moment. "I want to go to sleep early because of jet lag," she said, but Brave Orchid, who had never been on an airplane, did not let her.

"What are we going to do about your husband?" Brave Orchid asked quickly. That ought to wake her up.

"I don't know. Do we have to do something?"

"He does not know you're here."

Moon Orchid did not say anything. For thirty years she had been receiving money from him from America. But she had never told him that she wanted to come to the United States. She waited for him to suggest it, but he never did. Nor did she tell him that her sister had been working for years to transport her here. First Brave Orchid had found a Chinese-American husband for her daughter. Then the daughter had come and had been able to sign the papers to bring Moon Orchid over.

"We have to tell him you've arrived," said Brave Orchid.

Moon Orchid's eyes got big like a child's. "I shouldn't be here," she said.

"Nonsense. I want you here, and your daughter wants you here."

"But that's all."

"Your husband is going to have to see you. We'll make him recognize you. Ha. Won't it be fun to see his face? You'll go to his house. And when his second wife answers the door, you say, 'I want to speak to my husband,' and you name his personal name. 'Tell him I'll be sitting in the family room.' Walk past her as if she were a servant. She'll scold him when he comes home from work, and it'll serve him right. You yell at him too."

"I'm scared," said Moon Orchid. "I want to go back to Hong Kong."

"You can't. It's too late. You've sold your apartment. See here. We know his address. He's living in Los Angeles with his second wife, and they have three children. Claim your rights. Those are *your* children. He's got two sons. *You* have two sons. You take them away from her. You become their mother."

"Do you really think I can be a mother of sons? Don't you think they'll be loyal to her, since she gave birth to them?"

"The children will go to their true mother—you," said Brave Orchid. "That's the way it is with mothers and children."

"Do you think he'll get angry at me because I came without telling him?"

"He deserves your getting angry with him. For abandoning you and for abandoning your daughter."

"He didn't abandon me. He's given me so much money. I've had all the food and clothes and servants I've ever wanted. And he's supported our daughter too, even though she's only a girl. He sent her to college. I can't bother him. I mustn't bother him."

"How can you let him get away with this? Bother him. He deserves to be bothered. How dare he marry somebody else when he has you? How can you sit there so calmly? He would've let you stay in China forever. *I* had to send for your daughter, and *I* had to send for you. Urge her," she turned to her niece. "Urge her to go look for him."

"I think you should go look for my father," she said. "I'd like to meet him. I'd like to see what my father looks like."

"What does it matter what he's like?" said her mother. "You're a grown woman with a husband and children of your own. You don't need a father—or a mother either. You're only curious."

"In this country," said Brave Orchid, "many people make their daughters their heirs. If you don't go see him, he'll give everything to the second wife's children."

"But he gives us everything anyway. What more do I have to ask for? If I see him face to face, what is there to say?"

"I can think of hundreds of things," said Brave Orchid. "Oh, how I'd love to be in your place. I could tell him so many things. What scenes I could make. You're so wishy-washy."

"Yes, I am."

"You have to ask him why he didn't come home. Why he turned into a barbarian. Make him feel bad about leaving his mother and father. Scare him. Walk right into his house with your suitcases and boxes. Move right into the bedroom. Throw her stuff out of the drawers and put yours in. Say, 'I am the first wife, and she is our servant.' "

"Oh, no, I can't do that. I can't do that at all. That's terrible."

"Of course you can. I'll teach you. 'I am the first wife, and she is our servant.' And you teach the little boys to call you Mother."

"I don't think I'd be very good with little boys. Little American boys. Our brother is the only boy I've known. Aren't they very rough and unfeeling?"

"Yes, but they're yours. Another thing I'd do if I were you, I'd get a job and help him out. Show him I could make his life easier; how I didn't need his money."

"He has a great deal of money, doesn't he?"

"Yes, he can do some job the barbarians value greatly."

"Could I find a job like that? I've never had a job."

"You could be a maid in a hotel," Brave Orchid advised. "A lot of immigrants start that way nowadays. And the maids get to bring home all the leftover soap and the clothes people leave behind."

"I would clean up after people, then?"

Brave Orchid looked at this delicate sister. She was such a little old lady. She had long fingers and thin, soft hands. And she had a high-class city accent from living in Hong Kong. Not a trace of village accent remained; she had been away from the village for that long. But Brave Orchid would not relent; her dainty sister would just have to toughen up. "Immigrants also work in the canneries, where it's so noisy it doesn't matter if they speak Chinese or what. The easiest way to find a job, though, is to work in Chinatown. You get twenty-five cents an hour and all your meals if you're working in a restaurant."

If she were in her sister's place, Brave Orchid would have been on the phone immediately, demanding one of those Chinatown jobs. She would make the boss agree that she start work as soon as he opened his doors the next morning. Immigrants nowadays were bandits, beating up store owners and stealing from them rather than working. It must've been the Communists who taught them those habits.

Moon Orchid rubbed her forehead. The kitchen light shined warmly on the gold and jade rings that gave her hands a completeness. One of the rings was a wedding ring. Brave Orchid, who had been married for almost fifty years, did not wear any rings. They got in the way of all the work. She did not want the gold to wash away in the dishwater and the laundry water and the field water. She looked at her younger sister whose very wrinkles were fine. "Forget about a job," she said, which was very lenient of her. "You won't have to work. You just go to your husband's house and demand your rights as First Wife. When you see him, you can say, 'Do you remember me?' "

"What if he doesn't?"

"Then start telling him details about your life together in China. Act like a fortuneteller. He'll be so impressed."

"Do you think he'll be glad to see me?"

"He better be glad to see you."

As midnight came, twenty-two hours after she left Hong Kong, Moon Orchid began to tell her sister that she really was going to face her husband. "He won't like me," she said.

"Maybe you should dye your hair black, so he won't think you're old. Or I have a wig you can borrow. On the other hand, he should see how you've suffered. Yes, let him see how he's made your hair turn white."

These many hours, her daughter held Moon Orchid's hand. The two of them had been separated for five years. Brave Orchid had mailed the daughter's young photograph to a rich and angry man with citizenship papers. He was a tyrant. Mother and daughter were sorry for one another. "Let's not talk about this anymore," said Moon Orchid. "We can plan tomorrow. I want to hear about my grandchildren. Tell me about them. I have three grandchildren, don't I?" she asked her daughter.

Brave Orchid thought that her niece was like her mother, the lovely, useless type. She had spent so much time trying to toughen up these two. "The children are very smart, Mother," her niece was saying. "The teachers say they are brilliant. They can speak Chinese and English. They'll be able to talk to you."

"My children can talk to you too," said Brave Orchid. "Come. Talk to your aunt," she ordered.

Her sons and daughters mumbled and disappeared—into the bathroom, the basement, the various hiding places they had dug throughout the house. One of them locked herself in the pantry-storeroom, where she had cleared off a shelf for a desk among the food. Brave Orchid's children were antisocial and secretive. Ever since they were babies, they had burrowed little nests for themselves in closets and underneath stairs; they made tents under tables and behind doors. "My children are also very bright," she said. "Let me show you before you go to sleep." She took her sister to the living room where she had a glass case, a large upside-down fish tank, and inside were her children's athletic trophies and scholarship trophies. There was even a beauty contest trophy. She had decorated them with runners about luck.

"Oh my, isn't that wonderful?" said the aunt. "You must be so proud of them. Your children must be so smart." The children who were in the living room groaned and left. Brave Orchid did not understand why they were ashamed of the things they could do. It was hard to believe that they could do the things the trophies said they did. Maybe they had stolen them from the real winners. Maybe they had bought cups and medallions and pretended they'd won them. She'd have to accuse them and see how they reacted. Perhaps they fooled the Ghost Teachers and Ghost Coaches, who couldn't tell smart Chinese from dumb Chinese. Her children certainly didn't seem like much.

She made some of the children sleep on the floor and put Moon Orchid and her daughter in their room. "Will my mother be living at your house or my house?" her niece asked Brave Orchid.

"She's going to live with her own husband." Brave Orchid was firm. She would not forget about this subject in the morning.

The next day, immediately after breakfast, Brave Orchid talked about driving to Los Angeles. They would not take the coast route along mountainsides that dropped into the sea—the way her children, who liked carnival rides, would want to go. She would make them take the inland route, flat and direct.

"The first thing you've got to ask your husband," she said, "is why he never came back to China when he got rich."

"All right," said Moon Orchid. She was poking about the house, holding cans up to her ear, trailing after the children.

"He probably has a car," Brave Orchid persisted. "He can drive you places. Should he tell you to go away, turn around at the door and say, 'May I come and watch your television now and then?' Oh, wouldn't that be pathetic? But he won't kick you out. No, he won't. You walk right into the bedroom, and you open the second wife's closet. Take whatever clothes you like. That will give you an American wardrobe."

"Oh, I can't do that."

"You can! You can! Take First Sister-in-Law as your example." Their only brother had had a first wife in the village, but he took a second wife in Singapore, where he had gone to make his gold. Big Wife suffered during the Revolution. "The Communists will kill me," she wrote to her husband, "and you're having fun in Singapore." Little Wife felt so sorry for her, she reminded her husband that he owed it to Big Wife to get her out of China before it was too late. Little Wife saved the passage fare and did the paper work. But when Big Wife came, she chased Little Wife out of the house. There was nothing for their husband to do but build a second house, one for each wife and the children of each wife. They did get together, however, for yearly family portraits. Their sons' first and second wives were also in the pictures, first wives next to the husbands and second wives standing among the children. "Copy our sister-in-law," Brave Orchid instructed. "Make life unbearable for the second wife, and she'll leave. He'll have to build her a second house."

"I wouldn't mind if she stays," said Moon Orchid. "She can comb my hair and keep house. She can wash the dishes and serve our meals. And she can take care of the little boys." Moon Orchid laughed. Again it occurred to Brave Orchid that her sister wasn't very bright, and she had not gotten any smarter in the last thirty years.

"You must make it plain to your husband right at the start what you expect of him. That is what a wife is for—to scold her husband into becoming a good man. Tell him there will be no third wife. Tell him you may go visiting anytime you please. And I, the big sister, may visit your house for as long as I please. Let him know exactly how much money you expect for allowance."

"Should I ask for more or less money now that I'm here?"

"More, of course. Food costs more here. Tell him that your daughter, who is the oldest, must inherit his property. You have to establish these things at the start. Don't begin meek."

Sometimes Moon Orchid seemed to listen too readily—as if her sister were only talking-story. "Have you seen him in all these years?" she asked Brave Orchid.

"No. The last time I saw him was in China—with you. What a terrible, ugly man he must be not to send for you. I'll bet he's hoping you'd be satisfied with his money. How evil he is. You've had to live like a widow for thirty years. You're lucky he didn't have his second wife write you telling you he's dead."

"Oh, no, he wouldn't do that."

"Of course not. He would be afraid of cursing himself."

"But if he is so ugly and mean, maybe I shouldn't bother with him."

"I remember him," said her daughter. "He wrote me a nice letter."

"You can't remember him," said her mother. "You were an infant when he left. He never writes letters; he only sends money orders."

Moon Orchid hoped that the summer would wear away while her sister talked, that Brave Orchid would then find autumn too cold for travel. Brave Orchid did not enjoy travelling. She found it so nauseating that she was still recovering from the trip to San Francisco. Many of the children were home for the summer, and Moon Orchid tried to figure out which one was which. Brave Orchid had written about them in her letters, and Moon Orchid tried to match them up with the descriptions. There was indeed an oldest girl who was absent-minded and messy. She had an American name that sounded like "Ink" in Chinese. "Ink!" Moon Orchid called out; sure enough, a girl smeared with ink said, "Yes?" Then Brave Orchid worried over a daughter who had the mark of an unlucky woman; yes, there was certainly a girl with an upper lip as curled as Brigitte Bardot's. Moon Orchid rubbed this niece's hands and cold feet. There was a boy Brave Orchid said was thick headed. She had written that when he crawled as a baby his head was so heavy he kept dropping it on the floor. Moon Orchid did indeed see a boy whose head was big, his curls enlarging it, his eyebrows thick and slanted like an opera warrior's. Moon Orchid could not tell whether he was any less quick than the others. None of them were articulate or friendly. Brave Orchid had written about a boy whose oddity it was to stick pencil stubs in his ears. Moon Orchid sneaked up on the boys and lifted their hair to look for pencil stubs. "He hangs upside down from the furniture like a bat," his mother wrote. "And he doesn't obey." Moon Orchid didn't find a boy who looked like a bat, and no stubs, so decided that that boy must be the one in Vietnam. And the nephew with the round face and round eyes was the "inaccessible cliff." She immediately recognized the youngest girl, "the raging billows." "Stop following me around!" she shouted at her aunt. "Quit hanging over my neck!"

"What are you doing?" Moon Orchid would ask. "What are you reading?"

"Nothing!" this girl would yell. "You're breathing on me. Don't breathe on me."

It took Moon Orchid several weeks to figure out just how many children there were because some only visited and did not live at home. Some seemed to be married and had children of their own. The babies that spoke no Chinese at all, she decided, were the grandchildren.

None of Brave Orchid's children was happy like the two real Chinese babies who died. Maybe what was wrong was that they had no Oldest Son and no Oldest Daughter to guide them. "I don't see how any of them could support themselves," Brave Orchid said. "I don't see how anybody could want to marry them." Yet, Moon Orchid noticed, some of them seemed to have a husband or a wife who found them bearable.

"They'll never learn how to work," Brave Orchid complained.

"Maybe they're still playing," said Moon Orchid, although they didn't act playful.

"Say good morning to your aunt," Brave Orchid would order, although some of them were adults. "Say good morning to your aunt," she commanded every morning.

"Good morning, Aunt," they said, turning to face her, staring directly into her face. Even the girls stared at her—like cat-headed birds. Moon Orchid jumped and squirmed when they did that. They looked directly into her eyes as if they were looking for lies. Rude. Accusing. They never lowered their gaze; they hardly blinked.

"Why didn't you teach your girls to be demure?" she ventured.

"Demure!" Brave Orchid yelled. "They *are* demure. They're so demure, they barely talk."

It was true that the children made no conversation. Moon Orchid would try to draw them out. They must have many interesting savage things to say, raised as they'd been in the wilderness. They made rough movements, and their accents were not American exactly, but peasant like their mother's, as if they had come from a village deep inside China. She never saw the girls wear the gowns she had given them. The young, raging one, growled in her sleep, "Leave me alone." Sometimes when the girls were reading or watching television, she crept up behind them with a comb and tried to smooth their hair, but they shook their heads, and they turned and fixed her with those eyes. She wondered what they thought and what they saw when they looked at her like that. She liked coming upon them from the back to avoid being looked at. They were like animals the way they stared.

She hovered over a child who was reading, and she pointed at certain words. "What's that?" she tapped at a section that somebody had underlined or annotated. If the child was being patient, he said, "That's an important part."

"Why is it important?"

"Because it tells the main idea here."

"What's the main idea?"

"I don't know the Chinese words for it."

"They're so clever," Moon Orchid would exclaim. "They're so smart. Isn't it wonderful they know things that can't be said in Chinese?"

"Thank you," the child said. When she complimented them, they agreed with her! Not once did she hear a child deny a compliment.

"You're pretty," she said.

"Thank you, Aunt," they answered. How vain. She marveled at their vanity.

"You play the radio beautifully," she teased, and sure enough, they gave one another puzzled looks. She tried all kinds of compliments, and they never said, "Oh, no, you're too kind. I can't play it at all. I'm stupid. I'm ugly." They were capable children; they could do servants' work. But they were not modest.

"What time is it?" she asked, testing what kinds of minds they had, raised away from civilization. She discovered they could tell time very well. And they knew the Chinese words for "thermometer" and "library."

She saw them eat undercooked meat, and they smelled like cow's milk. At first she thought they were so clumsy, they spilled it on their clothes. But soon she decided they themselves smelled of milk. They were big and smelled of milk; they were young and had white hair.

When Brave Orchid screamed at them to dress better, Moon Orchid defended them, sweet wild animals that they were. "But they enjoy looking like furry animals. That's it, isn't it? You enjoy looking like wild animals, don't you?"

"I don't look like a wild animal!" the child would yell like its mother.

"Like an Indian, then. Right?"

"No!"

Moon Orchid stroked their poor white hair. She tugged at their sleeves and poked their shoulders and stomachs. It was as if she were seeing how much it took to provoke a savage.

"Stop poking me!" they would roar, except for the girl with the cold hands and feet.

"Mm," she mused. "Now the child is saying, 'Stop poking me.' "

Brave Orchid put her sister to work cleaning and sewing and cooking. Moon Orchid was eager to work, roughing it in the wilderness. But Brave Orchid scolded her, "Can't you go any faster than that?" It infuriated Brave Orchid that her sister held up each dish between thumb and forefinger, squirted detergent on the back and front, and ran water without plugging up the drain. Moon Orchid only laughed when Brave Orchid scolded, "Oh, stop that with the dishes. Here. Take this dress and hem it." But Moon Orchid immediately got the thread tangled and laughed about that.

In the mornings Brave Orchid and her husband arose at 6 a.m. He drank a cup of coffee and walked downtown to open up the laundry. Brave Orchid made breakfast for the children who would take the first laundry shift; the ones going to summer school would take the afternoon and night shifts. She put her husband's breakfast into the food container that she had bought in Chinatown, one dish in each tier of the stack. Some mornings Brave Orchid brought the food to the laundry, and other days she sent it with one of the children, but the children let the soup slosh out when they rode over bumps on their bikes. They dangled the tiers from one handlebar and the rice kettle from the other.

They were too lazy to walk. Now that her sister and niece were visiting, Brave Orchid went to the laundry later. "Be sure you heat everything up before serving it to your father," she yelled after her son. "And make him coffee after breakfast. And wash the dishes." He would eat with his father and start work.

She walked her sister and niece to the laundry by way of Chinatown. Brave Orchid pointed out the red, green, and gold Chinese school. From the street they could hear children's voices singing the lesson "I Am a Person of the Middle Nation." In front of one of the benevolent associations, a literate man was chanting the *Gold Mountain News,* which was taped to the window. The listening crowd looked at the pictures and said, "Aiaa."

"So this is the United States," Moon Orchid said. "It certainly looks different from China. I'm glad to see the Americans talk like us."

Brave Orchid was again startled at her sister's denseness. "These aren't the Americans. These are the overseas Chinese."

By the time they got to the laundry, the boiler was screaming hot and the machines were ready. "Don't touch or lean against any machine," Brave Orchid warned her sister. "Your skin would fry and peel off." In the midst of the presses stood the sleeve machine, looking like twin silver spaceships. Brave Orchid's husband fitted the shirt sleeves over it with a karate chop between the shoulder blades. "You mustn't back into that," said Brave Orchid.

"You should start off with an easy job," she said. But all the jobs seemed hard for Moon Orchid, who was wearing stockings and dress shoes and a suit. The buttons on the presses seemed too complicated for her to push—and what if she caught her hands or her head inside a press? She was already playing with the water jets dancing on springs from the ceiling. She could fold towels, Brave Orchid decided, and handkerchiefs, but there would be no clean dry clothes until afternoon. Already the temperature was going up.

"Can you iron?" Brave Orchid asked. Perhaps her sister could do the hand-finishing on the shirts when they came off the machines. This was usually Brave Orchid's husband's job. He had such graceful fingers, so good for folding shirts to fit the cardboard patterns that he had cut from campaign posters and fight and wrestling posters. He finished the shirts with a blue band around each.

"Oh, I'd love to try that," Moon Orchid said. Brave Orchid gave her sister her husband's shirts to practice on. She showed her how family clothes were marked with the ideograph "middle," which is a box with a line through its center. Moon Orchid tugged at the first shirt for half an hour, and she folded it crooked, the buttonholes not lined up with the buttons at all. When a customer came in, her ironing table next to the little stand with the tickets, she did not say "hello" but giggled, leaving the iron on the shirt until it turned yellow and had to be whitened with peroxide. Then she said it was so hot she couldn't breathe.

"Go take a walk," Brave Orchid said, exasperated. Even the children could work. Both girls and boys could sew. "Free Mending and Buttons," said the lettering on the window. The children could work all of the machines, even when they were little and had to stand on apple crates to reach them.

"Oh, I can't go out into Gold Mountain myself," Moon Orchid said.

"Walk back toward Chinatown," suggested Brave Orchid.

"Oh, come with me, please," Moon Orchid said.

"I have to work," said her sister. Brave Orchid placed an apple crate on the sidewalk in front of the laundry. "You sit out here in the cool air until I have a little time." She hooked the steel pole to the screw that unrolled the awning. "Just keep turning until the shadow covers the crate." It took Moon Orchid another half-hour to do this. She rested after every turn and left the pole hanging.

At noon, when the temperature inside reached one hundred and eleven degrees, Brave Orchid went out to the sidewalk and said, "Let's eat." She had heated the leftovers from breakfast on the little stove at the back of the laundry. In back there was also a bedroom for the nights when they finished packaging too tired to walk home. Then five or six people would crowd into the bed together. Some slept on the ironing tables, and the small children slept on the shelves. The shades would be pulled over the display windows and the door. The laundry would become a cozy new home, almost safe from the night footsteps, the traffic, the city outside. The boiler would rest, and no ghost would know there were Chinese asleep in their laundry. When the children were sick and had to stay home from school, they slept in that bedroom so that Brave Orchid could doctor them. The children said that the boiler, jumping up and down, bursting steam, flames shooting out the bottom, matched their dreams when they had a fever.

After lunch, Brave Orchid asked her husband if he and the children could handle the laundry by themselves. She wanted to take Moon Orchid out for some fun. He said that the load was unusually light today.

The sisters walked back to Chinatown. "We're going to get some more to eat," said Brave Orchid. Moon Orchid accompanied her to a gray building with a large storefront room, overhead fans turning coolly and cement floor cool underfoot. Women at round tables were eating black seaweed gelatin and talking. They poured Karo syrup on top of the black quivering mass. Brave Orchid seated Moon Orchid and dramatically introduced her, "This is my sister who has come to Gold Mountain to reclaim her husband." Many of the women were fellow villagers; others might as well have been villagers, together so long in California.

"Marvelous. You could blackmail him," the women advised. "Have him arrested if he doesn't take you back."

"Disguise yourself as a mysterious lady and find out how bad he is."

"You've got to do some husband beating, that's what you've got to do."

They were joking about her. Moon Orchid smiled and tried to think of a joke too. The large proprietress in a butcher's apron came out of the kitchen lugging tubs full of more black gelatin. Standing over the tables and smoking a cigarette, she watched her customers eat. It was so cool here, black and light-yellow and brown, and the gelatin was so cool. The door was open to the street, no passers-by but Chinese, though at the windows the venetian blinds slitted the sunlight as if everyone were hiding. Between helpings the women sat back, waving fans made out of silk, paper, sandalwood, and pandanus fronds. They were like rich women in China with nothing to do.

"Game time," said the proprietress, clearing the tables. The women had only been taking a break from their gambling. They spread ringed hands and mixed the ivory tiles click-clack for the next hemp-bird game. "It's time to go," said Brave Orchid, leading her sister outside. "When you come to America, it's a chance to forget some of the bad Chinese habits. A person could get up one day from the gambling table and find her life over." The gambling women were already caught up in their game, calling out good-byes to the sisters.

They walked past the vegetable, fish, and meat markets—not as abundant as in Canton, the carp not as red, the turtles not as old—and entered the cigar and seed shop. Brave Orchid filled her sister's thin hands with carrot candy, melon candy, and sheets of beef jerky. Business was carried out at one end of the shop, which was long and had benches against two walls. Rows of men sat smoking. Some of them stopped gurgling on their silver or bamboo water pipes to greet the sisters. Moon Orchid remembered many of them from the village; the cigar store owner, who looked like a camel, welcomed her. When Brave Orchid's children were young, they thought he was the Old Man of the North, Santa Claus.

As they walked back to the laundry, Brave Orchid showed her sister where to buy the various groceries and how to avoid Skid Row. "On days when you are not feeling safe, walk around it. But you can walk through it unharmed on your strong days." On weak days you notice bodies on the sidewalk, and you are visible to Panhandler Ghosts and Mugger Ghosts.

Brave Orchid and her husband and children worked hardest in the afternoon when the heat was the worst, all the machines hissing and thumping. Brave Orchid did teach her sister to fold the towels. She placed her at the table where the fan blew most. But finally she sent one of the children to walk her home.

From then on Moon Orchid only visited the laundry late in the day when the towels came out of the dryers. Brave Orchid's husband had to cut a pattern from cardboard so Moon Orchid could fold handkerchiefs uniformly. He gave her a shirt cardboard to measure the towels. She never could work any faster than she did on the first day.

The summer days passed while they talked about going to find Moon Orchid's husband. She felt she accomplished a great deal by folding towels. She spent the evening observing the children. She liked to figure them out. She described them aloud. "Now they're studying again. They read so much. Is it because they have enormous quantities to learn, and they're trying not to be savages? He is picking up his pencil and tapping it on the desk. Then he opens his book to page 168. His eyes begin to read. His eyes go back and forth. They go from left to right, from left to right." This makes her laugh. "How wondrous—eyes reading back and forth. Now he's writing his thoughts down. What's *that* thought?" she asked, pointing.

She followed her nieces and nephews about. She bent over them. "Now she is taking a machine off the shelf. She attaches two metal spiders to it. She plugs in the cord. She cracks an egg against the rim and pours the yolk and white out of the shell into the bowl. She presses a button, and the spiders spin the eggs. What are you making?"

"Aunt, please take your finger out of the batter."

"She says, 'Aunt, please take your finger out of the batter,' " Moon Orchid repeated as she turned to follow another niece walking through the kitchen. "Now what's this one doing? Why, she's sewing a dress. She's going to try it on." Moon Orchid would walk right into the children's rooms while they were dressing. "Now she must be looking over her costumes to see which one to wear." Moon Orchid pulled out a dress. "This is nice," she suggested. "Look at all the colors."

"No, Aunt. That's the kind of dress for a party. I'm going to school now."

"Oh, she's going to school now. She's choosing a plain blue dress. She's picking up her comb and brush and shoes, and she's going to lock herself up in the bathroom. They dress in bathrooms here." She pressed her ear against the door. "She's brushing her teeth. Now she's coming out of the bathroom. She's wearing the blue dress and a white sweater. She's combed her hair and washed her face. She looks in the refrigerator and is arranging things between slices of bread. She's putting an orange and cookies in a bag. Today she's taking her green book and her blue book. And tablets and pencils. Do you take a dictionary?" Moon Orchid asked.

"No," said the child, rolling her eyeballs up and exhaling loudly. "We have dictionaries at school," she added before going out the door.

"They have dictionaries at school," said Moon Orchid, thinking this over. "She knows 'dictionary.' " Moon Orchid stood at the window peeping. "Now she's shutting the gate. She strides along like an Englishman."

The child married to a husband who did not speak Chinese translated for him, "Now she's saying that I'm taking a machine off the shelf and that I'm attaching two metal spiders to it. And she's saying the spiders are spinning with legs intertwined and beating the eggs electrically. Now she says I'm hunting for something in the refrigerator and—ha!—I've found it. I'm taking out butter—'cow oil.' 'They eat a lot of cow oil,' she's saying."

"She's driving me nuts!" the children told each other in English.

At the laundry Moon Orchid hovered so close that there was barely room between her and the hot presses. "Now the index fingers of both hands press the buttons, and—ka-lump—the press comes down. But one finger on a button will release it—ssssss—the steam lets loose. Sssst—the water squirts." She could describe it so well, you would think she could do it. She wasn't as hard to take at the laundry as at home, though. She could not endure the heat, and after a while she had to go out on the sidewalk and sit on her apple crate. When they were younger the children used to sit out there too during their breaks. They played house and store and library, their orange and apple crates in a row. Passers-by and customers gave them money. But now they were older, they stayed inside or went for walks. They were ashamed of sitting on the sidewalk, people mistaking them for beggars. "Dance for me," the ghosts would say before handing them a nickel. "Sing a Chinese song." And before they got old enough to know better, they'd dance and they'd sing. Moon Orchid sat out there by herself.

Whenever Brave Orchid thought of it, which was everyday, she said, "Are you ready to go see your husband and claim what is yours?"

"Not today, but soon," Moon Orchid would reply.

But one day in the middle of summer, Moon Orchid's daughter said, "I have to return to my family. I promised my husband and children I'd only be gone a few weeks. I should return this week." Moon Orchid's daughter lived in Los Angeles.

"Good!" Brave Orchid exclaimed. "We'll all go to Los Angeles. You return to your husband, and your mother returns to hers. We only have to make one trip."

"You ought to leave the poor man alone," said Brave Orchid's husband. "Leave him out of women's business."

"When your father lived in China," Brave Orchid told the children, "he refused to eat pastries because he didn't want to eat the dirt the women kneaded from between their fingers."

"But I'm happy here with you and all your children," Moon Orchid said. "I want to see how this girl's sewing turns out. I want to see your son come back from Vietnam. I want to see if this one gets good grades. There's so much to do."

"We're leaving on Friday," said Brave Orchid. "I'm going to escort you, and you will arrive safely."

On Friday Brave Orchid put on her dress-up clothes, which she wore only a few times during the year. Moon Orchid wore the same kind of clothes she wore every day and was dressed up. Brave Orchid told her oldest son he had to drive. He drove, and the two old ladies and the niece sat in the back seat.

They set out at gray dawn, driving between the grape trees, which hunched like dwarfs in the fields. Gnomes in serrated outfits that blew in the morning wind came out of the earth, came up in rows and columns. Everybody was only half awake. "A long time ago," began Brave Orchid, "the emperors had four wives, one at each point of the compass, and they lived in four palaces. The Empress of the West would connive for power, but the Empress of the East was good and kind and full of light. You are the Empress of the East, and the

Empress of the West has imprisoned the Earth's Emperor in the Western Palace. And you, the good Empress of the East, come out of the dawn to invade her land and free the Emperor. You must break the strong spell she has cast on him that has lost him the East."

Brave Orchid gave her sister last-minute advice for five hundred miles. All her possessions had been packed into the trunk.

"Shall we go into your house together," asked Brave Orchid, "or do you want to go by yourself?"

"You've got to come with me. I don't know what I would say."

"I think it would be dramatic for you to go by yourself. He opens the door. And there you are—alive and standing on the porch with all your luggage. 'Remember me?' you say. Call him by his own name. He'll faint with shock. Maybe he'll say, 'No. Go away.' But you march right in. You push him aside and go in. Then you sit down in the most important chair, and you take off your shoes because you belong."

"Don't you think he'll welcome me?"

"She certainly wasn't very imaginative," thought Brave Orchid.

"It's against the law to have two wives in this country," said Moon Orchid. "I read that in the newspaper."

"But it's probably against the law in Singapore too. Yet our brother has two, and his sons have two each. The law doesn't matter."

"I'm scared. Oh, let's turn back. I don't want to see him. Suppose he throws me out? Oh, he will. He'll throw me out. And he'll have a right to throw me out, coming here, disturbing him, not waiting for him to invite me. Don't leave me by myself. You can talk louder than I can."

"Yes, coming with you would be exciting. I can charge through the door and say, 'Where is your wife?' And he'll answer, 'Why, she's right here.' And I'll say, 'This isn't your wife. Where is Moon Orchid? I've come to see her. I'm her first sister, and I've come to see that she is being well taken care of.' Then I accuse him of murderous things; I'd have him arrested—and you pop up to his rescue. Or I can take a look at his wife, and I say, 'Moon Orchid, how young you've gotten.' And he'll say, 'This isn't Moon Orchid.' And you come in and say, 'No. I am.' If nobody's home, we'll climb in a window. When they get back we'll be at home; you the hostess, and I your guest. You'll be serving me cookies and coffee. And when he comes in I'll say, 'Well, I see your husband is home. Thank you so much for the visit.' And you say, 'Come again anytime.' Don't make violence. Be routine."

Sometimes Moon Orchid got into the mood. "Maybe I could be folding towels when he comes in. He'll think I'm so clever. I'll get to them before his wife does." But the further they came down the great central valley—green fields changing to fields of cotton on dry, brown stalks, first a stray bush here and there, then thick—the more Moon Orchid wanted to turn back. "No. I can't go through with this." She tapped her nephew on the shoulder. "Please turn back. Oh, you must turn the car around. I should be returning to China. I shouldn't be here at all. Let's go back. Do you understand me?"

"Don't go back," Brave Orchid ordered her son. "Keep going. She can't back out now."

"What do you want me to do? Make up your minds," said the son, who was getting impatient.

"Keep going," said Brave Orchid. "She's come this far, and we can't waste all this driving. Besides, we have to take your cousin back to her house in Los Angeles. We have to drive to Los Angeles anyway."

"Can I go inside and meet my grandchildren?"

"Yes," said her daughter.

"We'll see them after you straighten out things with your husband," said Brave Orchid.

"What if he hits me?"

"I'll hit *him.* I'll protect you. I'll hit him back. The two of us will knock him down and make him listen." Brave Orchid chuckled as if she were looking forward to a fight. But when she saw how terrified Moon Orchid was, she said, "It won't come to a fight. You mustn't start imagining things. We'll simply walk up to the door. If he answers, you'll say, 'I have decided to come live with you in the Beautiful Nation.' If *she* answers the door, you'll say, 'You must be Little Wife. I am Big Wife.' Why, you could even be generous. 'I'd like to see our husband, please,' you say. I brought my wig," said Brave Orchid. "Why don't you disguise yourself as a beautiful lady? I brought lipstick and powder too. And at some dramatic point, you pull off the wig and say, 'I am Moon Orchid.' "

"That is a terrible thing to do. I'd be so scared. I am so scared."

"I want to be dropped off at my house first," said the niece. "I told my family I'd be home to make lunch."

"All right," said Brave Orchid, who had tried to talk her niece into confronting her father five years ago, but all she had done was write him a letter telling him she was in Los Angeles. He could visit her, or she could visit him if he wanted to see her, she had suggested. But he had not wanted to see her.

When the car stopped in front of her daughter's house, Moon Orchid asked, "May I get out to meet my grandchildren?"

"I told you no," said Brave Orchid. "If you do that you'll stay here, and it'll take us weeks to get up our courage again. Let's save your grandchildren as a reward. You take care of this other business, and you can play with your grandchildren without worry. Besides, you have some children to meet."

"Grandchildren are more wonderful than children."

After they left the niece's suburb, the son drove them to the address his mother had given him, which turned out to be a skyscraper in downtown Los Angeles.

"Don't park in front," said his mother. "Find a side street. We've got to take him by surprise. We mustn't let him spot us ahead of time. We have to catch the first look on his face."

"Yes, I think I would like to see the look on his face."

Brave Orchid's son drove up and down the side streets until he found a parking space that could not be seen from the office building.

"You have to compose yourself," said Brave Orchid to her sister. "You must be calm as you walk in. Oh, this is most dramatic—in broad daylight and in the middle of the city. We'll sit here for a while and look at his building."

"Does he own that whole building?"

"I don't know. Maybe so."

"Oh, I can't move. My knees are shaking so much I won't be able to walk. He must have servants and workers in there, and they'll stare at me. I can't bear it."

Brave Orchid felt a tiredness drag her down. She had to baby everyone. The traffic was rushing, Los Angeles noon-hot, and she suddenly felt carsick. No trees. No birds. Only city. "It must be the long drive," she thought. They had not eaten lunch, and the sitting had tired her out. Movement would strengthen her; she needed movement. "I want you to stay here with your aunt while I scout that building," she instructed her son. "When I come back, we'll work out a plan." She walked around the block. Indeed, she felt that her feet stepping on the earth, even when the earth was covered with concrete, gained strength from it. She breathed health from the air, though it was full of gasoline fumes. The bottom floor of the building housed several stores. She looked at the clothes and jewelry on display, picking out some for Moon Orchid to have when she came into her rightful place.

Brave Orchid rushed along beside her reflection in the glass. She used to be young and fast; she was still fast and felt young. It was mirrors, not aches and pains, that turned a person old, everywhere white hairs and wrinkles. Young people felt pain.

The building was a fine one; the lobby was chrome and glass, with ashtray stands and plastic couches arranged in semicircles. She waited for the elevator to fill before she got in, not wanting to operate a new machine by herself. Once on the sixth floor she searched alertly for the number in her address book.

How clean his building was. The rest rooms were locked, and there were square overhead lights. No windows, though. She did not like the quiet corridors with carpets but no windows. They felt like tunnels. He must be very wealthy. Good. It would serve a rich man right to be humbled. She found the door with his number on it; there was also American lettering on the glass. Apparently this was his business office. She hadn't thought of the possibility of catching him at his job. Good thing she had decided to scout. If they had arrived at his house, they would not have found him. Then they would have had to deal with *her.* And she would have phoned him, spoiled the surprise, and gotten him on her side. Brave Orchid knew how the little wives maneuvered; her father had had two little wives.

She entered the office, glad that it was a public place and she needn't knock. A roomful of men and women looked up from their magazines. She could tell by their eagerness for change that this was a waiting room. Behind a sliding glass partition sat a young woman in a modern nurse's uniform, not a white one, but a light blue pantsuit with white trim. She sat before an elegant telephone and an electric typewriter. The wallpaper in her cubicle was like aluminum foil, a metallic background for a tall black frame around white paint with dashes of red. The wall of the waiting room was covered with burlap, and there were plants in wooden tubs. It was an expensive waiting room. Brave Orchid approved. The patients looked well dressed, not sickly and poor.

"Hello. May I help you?" said the receptionist, parting the glass. Brave Orchid hesitated, and the receptionist took this to mean that she could not speak English. "Just a moment," she said, and went into an inner room. She brought back another woman, who wore a similar uniform except that it was pink trimmed in white. This woman's hair was gathered up into a bunch of curls at the back of her head; some of the curls were fake. She wore round glasses and false eyelashes, which gave her an American look. "Have you an appointment?" she asked in poor Chinese; she spoke less like a Chinese than Brave Orchid's children. "My husband, the doctor, usually does not take drop-in patients," she said. "We're booked up for about a month." Brave Orchid stared at her pink-painted fingernails gesticulating, and thought she probably would not have given out so much information if she weren't so clumsy with language.

"I have the flu," Brave Orchid said.

"Perhaps we can give you the name of another doctor," said this woman, who was her sister-in-law. "This doctor is a brain surgeon and doesn't work with flu." Actually she said, "This doctor cuts brains," a child making up the words as she went along. She wore pink lipstick and had blue eyelids like the ghosts.

Brave Orchid, who had been a surgeon too, thought that her brother-in-law must be a clever man. She herself could not practice openly in the United States because the training here was so different and because she could never learn English. He was smart enough to learn ghost ways. She would have to be clever to outwit him. She needed to retreat and plan some more. "Oh, well, I'll go to another doctor, then," she said, and left.

She needed a new plan to get her sister and brother-in-law together. This nurse-wife was so young, and the office was so rich with wood, paintings, and fancy telephones, that Brave Orchid knew it wasn't because he couldn't get the fare together that he hadn't sent for his old wife. He had abandoned her for this modern, heartless girl. Brave Orchid wondered if the girl knew that her husband had a Chinese wife. Perhaps she should ask her.

But no, she mustn't spoil the surprise by giving any hints. She had to get away before he came out into the corridor, perhaps to go to one of the locked rest rooms. As she walked back to her sister, she noted corners and passageways, broom closets, other offices—ambush spots. Her sister could crouch behind a drinking fountain and wait for him to get thirsty. Waylay him.

"I met his second wife," she said, opening the car door.

"What's she like?" asked Moon Orchid. "Is she pretty?"

"She's very pretty and very young; just a girl. She's his nurse. He's a doctor like me. What a terrible, faithless man. You'll have to scold him for years, but first you need to sit up straight. Use my powder. Be as pretty as you can. Otherwise you won't be able to compete. You do have one advantage, however. Notice he has her be his worker. She is like a servant, so you have room to be the wife. She works at the office; you work at the house. That's almost as good as having two houses. On the other hand, a man's real partner is the hardest worker. You couldn't learn nursing, could you? No, I guess not. It's almost as difficult as doing laundry. What a petty man he turned out to be, giving up responsibility for a pretty face." Brave Orchid reached for the door handle. "Are you ready?"

"For what?"

"To go up there, of course. We're at his office, and I think we ought to be very direct. There aren't any trees to hide you, no grass to soften your steps. So, you walk right into his office. You make an announcement to the patients and the fancy nurses. You say, 'I am the doctor's wife. I'm going to see my husband.' Then you step to the inner door and enter. Don't knock on any doors. Don't listen if the minor wife talks to you. You walk past her without changing pace. When you see him, you say, 'Surprise!' You say, 'Who is that woman out there? She claims to be your wife.' That will give him a chance to deny her on the spot."

"Oh, I'm so scared. I can't move. I can't do that in front of all those people—like a stage show. I won't be able to talk." And sure enough, her voice was fading into a whisper. She was shivering and small in the corner of the seat.

"So. A new plan, then," said Brave Orchid, looking at her son, who had his forehead on the steering wheel. "You," she said. "I want you to go up to his office and tell your uncle that there has been an accident out in the street. A woman's leg has been broken, and she's crying in pain. He'll have to come. You bring him to the car."

"Mother."

"Mm," mused Brave Orchid. "Maybe we ought to put your aunt in the middle of the street, and she can lie down with her leg bent under her." But Moon Orchid kept shaking her head in trembling no's.

"Why don't you push her down in the intersection and pour ketchup on her? I'll run over her a little bit," said her son.

"Stop being silly," she said. "You Americans don't take life seriously."

"Mother, this is ridiculous. This whole thing is ridiculous."

"Go. Do what I tell you," she said.

"I think your schemes will be useless, Mother."

"What do you know about Chinese business?" she said. "Do as I say."

"Don't let him bring the nurse," said Moon Orchid.

"Don't you want to see what she looks like?" asked Brave Orchid. "Then you'll know what he's giving up for you."

"No. No. She's none of my business. She's unimportant."

"Speak in English," Brave Orchid told her son. "Then he'll feel he has to come with you."

She pushed her son out of the car. "I don't want to do this," he said.

"You'll ruin your aunt's life if you don't. You can't understand business begun in China. Just do what I say. Go."

Slamming the car door behind him, he left.

Moon Orchid was groaning now and holding her stomach. "Straighten up," said Brave Orchid. "He'll be here any moment." But this only made Moon Orchid groan louder, and tears seeped out behind her closed eyelids.

"You want a husband, don't you?" said Brave Orchid. "If you don't claim him now, you'll never have a husband. Stop crying," she ordered. "Do you want him to see you with your eyes and nose swollen when that young so-called wife wears lipstick and nail polish like a movie star?"

Moon Orchid managed to sit upright, but she seemed stiff and frozen.

"You're just tired from the ride. Put some blood into your cheeks," Brave Orchid said, and pinched her sister's withered face. She held her sister's elbow and slapped the inside of her arm. If she had had time, she would have hit until the black and red dots broke out on the skin; that was the tiredness coming out. As she hit, she kept an eye on the rearview mirror. She saw her son come running, his uncle after him with a black bag in his hand. "Faster. Faster," her son was saying. He opened the car door. "Here she is," he said to his uncle. "I'll see you later." And he ran on down the street.

The two old ladies saw a man, authoritative in his dark western suit, start to fill the front of the car. He had black hair and no wrinkles. He looked and smelled like an American. Suddenly the two women remembered that in China families married young boys to older girls, who baby-sat their husbands their whole lives. Either that or, in this ghost country, a man could somehow keep his youth.

"Where's the accident?" he said in Chinese. "What is this? You don't have a broken leg."

Neither woman spoke. Brave Orchid held her words back. She would not let herself interfere with this meeting after long absence.

"What is it?" he asked. "What's wrong?" These women had such awful faces. "What is it, Grandmothers?"

"Grandmother?" Brave Orchid shouted. "This is your wife. I am your sister-in-law."

Moon Orchid started to whimper. Her husband looked at her. And recognized her. "You," he said. "What are you doing here?"

But all she did was open and shut her mouth without any words coming out.

"Why are you here?" he asked, eyes wide. Moon Orchid covered her face with one hand and motioned no with the other.

Brave Orchid could not keep silent. Obviously he was not glad to see his wife. "I sent for her," she burst out. "I got her name on the Red Cross list, and I sent her the plane ticket. I wrote her every day and gave her the heart to come. I told her how welcome she would be, how her family would welcome her, how her husband would welcome her. I did what you, the husband, had time to do in these last thirty years."

He looked directly at Moon Orchid the way the savages looked, looking for lies. "What do you want?" he asked. She shrank from his stare; it silenced her crying.

"You weren't supposed to come here," he said, the front seat a barrier against the two women over whom a spell of old age had been cast. "It's a mistake for you to be here. You can't belong. You don't have the hardness for this country. I have a new life."

"What about me?" whispered Moon Orchid.

"Good," thought Brave Orchid. "Well said. Said with no guile."

"I have a new wife," said the man.

"She's only your second wife," said Brave Orchid. "This is your real wife."

"In this country a man may have just one wife."

"So you'll get rid of that creature in your office?" asked Brave Orchid.

He looked at Moon Orchid. Again the rude American eyes. "You go live with your daughter. I'll mail you the money I've always sent you. I could get arrested if the Americans knew about you. I'm living like an American." He talked like a child born here.

"How could you ruin her old age?" said Brave Orchid.

"She has had food. She has had servants. Her daughter went to college. There wasn't anything she thought of that she couldn't buy. I have been a good husband."

"You made her live like a widow."

"That's not true. Obviously the villagers haven't stoned her. She's not wearing mourning. The family didn't send her away to work. Look at her. She'd never fit into an American household. I have important American guests who come inside my house to eat." He turned to Moon Orchid. "You can't talk to them. You can barely talk to me."

Moon Orchid was so ashamed, she held her hands over her face. She wished she could also hide her dappled hands. Her husband looked like one of the ghosts passing the car windows, and she must look like a ghost from China. They had indeed entered the land of ghosts, and they had become ghosts.

"Do you want her to go back to China then?" Brave Orchid was asking.

"I wouldn't wish that on anyone. She may stay, but I do not want her in my house. She has to live with you or with her daughter, and I don't want either of you coming here anymore."

Suddenly his nurse was tapping on the glass. So quickly that they might have missed it, he gestured to the old women, holding a finger to his mouth for just a moment: he had never told his American wife that he had a wife in China, and they mustn't tell her either.

"What's happening?" she asked. "Do you need help? The appointments are piling up."

"No. No," he said. "This woman fainted in the street. I'll be up soon."

They spoke to each other in English.

The two old women did not call out to the young woman. Soon she left. "I'm leaving too now," said the husband.

"Why didn't you write to tell her once and for all you weren't coming back and you weren't sending for her?" Brave Orchid asked.

"I don't know," he said. "It's as if I had turned into a different person. The new life around me was so complete; it pulled me away. You became people in a book I had read a long time ago."

"The least you can do," said Brave Orchid, "is invite us to lunch. Aren't you inviting us to lunch? Don't you owe us a lunch? At a good restaurant?" She would not let him off easily.

So he bought them lunch, and when Brave Orchid's son came back to the car, he had to wait for them.

Moon Orchid was driven back to her daughter's house, but though she lived in Los Angeles, she never saw her husband again. "Oh, well," said Brave Orchid. "We're all under the same sky and walk the same earth; we're alive together during the same moment." Brave Orchid and her son drove back north, Brave Orchid sitting in the back seat the whole way.

Several months went by with no letter from Moon Orchid. When she had lived in China and in Hong Kong, she had written every other week. At last Brave Orchid telephoned long distance to find out what was happening. "I can't talk now," Moon Orchid whispered. "They're listening. Hang up quickly before they trace you." Moon Orchid hung up on Brave Orchid before the minutes she had paid for expired.

That week a letter came from the niece saying that Moon Orchid had become afraid. Moon Orchid said that she had overheard Mexican ghosts plotting on her life. She had been creeping along the baseboards and peeping out windows. Then she had asked her daughter to help her find an apartment at the other end of Los Angeles, where she was now hiding. Her daughter visited her every day, but Moon Orchid kept telling her, "Don't come see me because the Mexican ghosts will follow you to my new hiding place. They're watching your house."

Brave Orchid phoned her niece and told her to send her mother north immediately, where there were no Mexicans, she said. "This fear is an illness," she told her niece. "I will cure her." ("Long ago," she explained to her children, "when the emperors had four wives, the wife who lost in battle was sent to the Northern Palace. Her feet would sink little prints into the snow.")

Brave Orchid sat on a bench at the Greyhound station to wait for her sister. Her children had not come with her because the bus station was only a five-block walk from the house. Her brown paper shopping bag against her, she dozed under the fluorescent lights until her sister's bus pulled into the terminal. Moon Orchid stood blinking on the stairs, hanging tightly to the railing for old people. Brave Orchid felt the tears break inside her chest for the old feet that stepped one at a time onto the cold Greyhound cement. Her sister's skin hung loose, like a hollowed frog's, as if she had shrunken inside it. Her clothes bagged, not fitting sharply anymore. "I'm in disguise," she said. Brave Orchid put her arms around her sister to give her body warmth. She held her hand along the walk home, just as they had held hands when they were girls.

The house was more crowded than ever, though some of the children had gone away to school; the jade trees were inside for the winter. Along walls and on top of tables, jade trees, whose trunks were as thick as ankles, stood stoutly, green now and without the pink skin the sun gave them in the spring.

"I am so afraid," said Moon Orchid.

"There is no one after you," said Brave Orchid. "No Mexicans."

"I saw some in the Greyhound station," said Moon Orchid.

"No. No, those were Filipinos." She held her sister's earlobes and began the healing chant for being unafraid. "There are no Mexicans after you," she said.

"I know. I got away from them by escaping on the bus."

"Yes, you escaped on the bus with the mark of the dog on it."

In the evening, when Moon Orchid seemed quieter, her sister probed into the cause of this trouble.

"What made you think anyone was after you?"

"I heard them talking about me. I snuck up on them and heard them."

"But you don't understand Mexican words."

"They were speaking English."

"You don't understand English words."

"This time, miraculously, I understood. I decoded their speech. I penetrated the words and understood what was happening inside."

Brave Orchid tweaked her sister's ears for hours, chanting her new address to her, telling her how much she loved her and how much her daughter and nephews and nieces loved her, and her brother-in-law loved her. "I won't let anything happen to you. I won't let you travel again. You're home. Stay home. Don't be afraid." Tears fell from Brave Orchid's eyes. She had whisked her sister across the ocean by jet and then made her scurry up and down the Pacific coast, back and forth across Los Angeles. Moon Orchid had misplaced herself, her spirit (her "attention," Brave Orchid called it) scattered all over the world. Brave Orchid held her sister's head as she pulled on her earlobe. She would make it up to her. For moments an attentiveness would return to Moon Orchid's face. Brave Orchid rubbed the slender hands, blew on the fingers, tried to stoke up the flickerings. She stayed home from the laundry day after day. She threw out the Thorazine and vitamin B that a doctor in Los Angeles had prescribed. She made Moon Orchid sit in the kitchen sun while she picked over the herbs in cupboards and basement and the fresh plants that grew in the winter garden. Brave Orchid chose the gentlest plants and made medicines and foods like those they had eaten in their village.

At night she moved from her own bedroom and slept beside Moon Orchid. "Don't be afraid to sleep," she said. "Rest. I'll be here beside you. I'll help your spirit find the place to come back to. I'll call it for you; you go to sleep." Brave Orchid stayed awake watching until dawn.

Moon Orchid still described aloud her nieces' and nephews' doings, but now in a monotone, and she no longer interrupted herself to ask questions. She would not go outside, even into the yard. "Why, she's mad," Brave Orchid's husband said when she was asleep.

Brave Orchid held her hand when she appeared vague. "Don't go away, Little Sister. Don't go any further. Come back to us." If Moon Orchid fell asleep on the sofa, Brave Orchid sat up through the night, sometimes dozing in a chair. When Moon Orchid fell asleep in the middle of the bed, Brave Orchid made a place for herself at the foot. She would anchor her sister to this earth.

But each day Moon Orchid slipped further away. She said that the Mexicans had traced her to this house. That was the day she shut the drapes and blinds and locked the doors. She sidled along the walls to peep outside. Brave Orchid told her husband that he must humor his sister-in-law. It was right to shut the windows; it kept her spirit from leaking away. Then Moon Orchid went about the house turning off the lights like during air raids. The house became gloomy; no air, no light. This was very tricky, the darkness a wide way for going as well as coming back. Sometimes Brave Orchid would switch on the lights, calling her sister's name all the while. Brave Orchid's husband installed an air conditioner.

The children locked themselves up in their bedrooms, in the storeroom and basement, where they turned on the lights. Their aunt would come knocking on the doors and say, "Are you all right in there?"

"Yes, Aunt, we're all right."

"Beware," she'd warn. "Beware. Turn off your lights so you won't be found. Turn off the lights before they come for us."

The children hung blankets over the cracks in the doorjambs; they stuffed clothes along the bottoms of doors. "Chinese people are very weird," they told one another.

Next Moon Orchid removed all the photographs, except for those of the grandmother and grandfather, from the shelves, dressers, and walls. She gathered up the family albums. "Hide these," she whispered to Brave Orchid. "Hide these. When they find me, I don't want them to trace the rest of the family. They use photographs to trace you." Brave Orchid wrapped the pictures and the albums in flannel. "I'll carry these far away where no one will find us," she said. When Moon Orchid wasn't looking, she put them at the bottom of a storage box in the basement. She piled old clothes and old shoes on top. "If they come for me," Moon Orchid said, "everyone will be safe."

"We're all safe," said Brave Orchid.

The next odd thing Moon Orchid did was to cry whenever anyone left the house. She held on to them, pulled at their clothes, begged them not to go. The children and Brave Orchid's husband had to sneak out. "Don't let them go," pleaded Moon Orchid. "They will never come back."

"They will come back. Wait and see. I promise you. Watch for them. Don't watch for Mexicans. This one will be home at 3:30. This one at 5:00. Remember who left now. You'll see."

"We'll never see that one again," Moon Orchid wept.

At 3:30 Brave Orchid would remind her, "See? It's 3:30; sure enough, here he comes." ("You children come home right after school. Don't you dare stop for a moment. No candy store. No comic book store. Do you hear?")

But Moon Orchid did not remember. "Who is this?" she'd ask. "Are you going to stay with us? Don't go out tonight. Don't leave in the morning."

She whispered to Brave Orchid that the reason the family must not go out was that "they" would take us in airplanes and fly us to Washington, D.C., where they'd turn us into ashes. Then they'd drop the ashes in the wind, leaving no evidence.

Brave Orchid saw that all variety had gone from her sister. She was indeed mad. "The difference between mad people and sane people," Brave Orchid explained to the children, "is that sane people have variety when they talk-story. Mad people have only one story that they talk over and over."

Every morning Moon Orchid stood by the front door whispering, whispering. "Don't go. The planes. Ashes. Washington, D.C. Ashes." Then, when a child managed to leave, she said, "That's the last time we'll see him again. They'll get him. They'll turn him into ashes."

And so Brave Orchid gave up. She was housing a mad sister who cursed the mornings for her children, the one in Vietnam too. Their aunt was saying terrible things when they needed blessing. Perhaps Moon Orchid had already left this mad old body, and it was a ghost bad-mouthing her children. Brave Orchid finally called her niece, who put Moon Orchid in a California state mental asylum. Then Brave Orchid opened up the windows and let the air and light come into the house again. She moved back into the bedroom with her husband. The children took the blankets and sheets down from the doorjambs and came back into the living room.

Brave Orchid visited her sister twice. Moon Orchid was thinner each time, shrunken to bone. But, surprisingly, she was happy and had made up a new story. She pranced like a child. "Oh, Sister, I am so happy here. No one ever leaves. Isn't that wonderful? We are all women here. Come. I want you to meet my daughters." She introduced Brave Orchid to each inmate in the ward—her daughters. She was especially proud of the pregnant ones. "My dear pregnant daughters." She touched the women on the head, straightened collars, tucked blankets. "How are you today, dear daughter?" "And, you know," she said to Brave Orchid, "we understand one another here. We speak the same language, the very same. They understand me, and I understand them." Sure enough, the women smiled back at her and reached out to touch her as she went by. She had a new story, and yet she slipped entirely away, not waking up one morning.

Brave Orchid told her children they must help her keep their father from marrying another woman because she didn't think she could take it any better than her sister had. If he brought another woman into the house, they were to gang up on her and play tricks on her, hit her, and trip her when she was carrying hot oil until she ran away. "I am almost seventy years old," said the father, "and haven't taken a second wife, and don't plan to now." Brave Orchid's daughters decided fiercely that they would never let men be unfaithful to them. All her children made up their minds to major in science or mathematics.

1976

ALICE WALKER
1944–   )

As the author of The Color Purple and The Temple of My Familiar, Alice Walker has become one of the most widely read writers in the United States. Her works focus on the freedom and creativity of Black women as well as on the importance of the history of Black people. Walker looks unflinchingly at the relationships between men and women and between parents and children; she has chronicled the racism and sexism that affect Black women, insisting that sexism is not an issue for white women alone. While her writing tells of injustice and suffering, it is also positive: Walker affirms the innate artistry and spirituality in women as well as the potential for change in human nature.

Born in Georgia, the eighth child in a family of sharecroppers, Walker attended Spelman College and then received her B.A. from Sarah Lawrence College in 1965. In the 1960s, she immersed herself in the civil rights movement, working with voter registration in Georgia as well as with welfare rights and Head Start in Mississippi. Her marriage to a white civil rights lawyer caused controversy among both whites and Blacks, although, as she pointed out, many of the prominent Black male activists who criticized her had themselves been involved with white women. Thus she saw ever more clearly that Black women suffered from sexism within their own families and communities. Walker began talking to Black women, collecting their tales and experiences, recording details of their everyday existence.

In 1968, Walker published her first collection of poems, Once, focusing in part on her experiences as a civil rights worker. Her first novel, The Third Life of Grange Copeland, which depicts three generations, established the focus of much of her later work: the importance of African American history and traditions. The Third Life of Grange Copeland also examines the cruelty that can exist between family members and the causes for that cruelty. Meridian, Walker's second novel, deals with the experiences of civil rights workers in the 1960s.

In 1982, Walker won the Pulitzer Prize for The Color Purple. Since then Walker has published a fourth novel, The Temple of My Familiar; short stories; biographical and critical works on writers such as Langston Hughes; and essays, lectures, and poems. Her research on the writer and anthropologist Zora Neale Hurston led to the re-publication of her work. Walker has been awarded both Guggenheim and National Endowment for the Arts fellowships. She has taught at Wellesley, Yale, and the University of California at Berkeley. With her companion, Robert Allen, she founded Wild Tree Press, which publishes works by contemporary writers of color.

A key to Alice Walker's work as a writer may be found in "In Search of

Our Mothers' Gardens." This pivotal essay celebrates the "anonymous" Black women, revealing the artistry in their lives. It also conveys Walker's mission as a writer: to retell these women's experiences and to find ourselves in the tales of our mothers and grandmothers. In "Roselily," a story about a woman on the brink of marrying a man she does not love, Walker takes the reader into the consciousness of the main character while also conveying the limitations of her experience and her choices.

■ ROSELILY

Dearly Beloved,

She dreams; dragging herself across the world. A small girl in her mother's white robe and veil, knee raised waist high through a bowl of quicksand soup. The man who stands beside her is against this standing on the front porch of her house, being married to the sound of cars whizzing by on highway 61.

we are gathered here

Like cotton to be weighed. Her fingers at the last minute busily removing dry leaves and twigs. Aware it is a superficial sweep. She knows he blames Mississippi for the respectful way the men turn their heads up in the yard, the women stand waiting and knowledgeable, their children held from mischief by teachings from the wrong God. He glares beyond them to the occupants of the cars, white faces glued to promises beyond a country wedding, noses thrust forward like dogs on a track. For him they usurp the wedding.

in the sight of God

Yes, open house. That is what country black folks like. She dreams she does not already have three children. A squeeze around the flowers in her hands chokes off three and four and five years of breath. Instantly she is ashamed and frightened in her superstition. She looks for the first time at the preacher, forces humility into her eyes, as if she believes he is, in fact, a man of God. She can imagine God, a small black boy, timidly pulling the preacher's coattail.

to join this man and this woman

She thinks of ropes, chains, handcuffs, his religion. His place of worship. Where she will be required to sit apart with covered head. In Chicago, a word she hears when thinking of smoke, from his description of what a cinder was, which they never had in Panther Burn. She sees hovering over the heads of the clean neighbors in her front yard black specks falling, clinging, from the sky. But in Chicago. Respect, a chance to build. Her children at last from underneath the detrimental wheel. A chance to be on top. What a relief, she thinks. What a vision, a view, from up so high.

in holy matrimony.

Her fourth child she gave away to the child's father who had some money. Certainly a good job. Had gone to Harvard. Was a good man but weak because good language meant so much to him he could not live with Roselily. Could not abide TV in the living room, five beds in three rooms, no Bach except from four to six on Sunday afternoons. No chess at all. She does not forget to worry about her son among his father's people. She wonders if the New England climate will agree with him. If he will ever come down to Mississippi, as his father did, to try to right the country's wrongs. She wonders if he will be stronger than his father. His father cried off and on throughout her pregnancy. Went to skin and bones. Suffered nightmares, retching and falling out of bed. Tried to kill himself. Later told his wife he found the right baby through friends. Vouched for, the sterling qualities that would make up his character.

It is not her nature to blame. Still, she is not entirely thankful. She supposes New England, the North, to be quite different from what she knows. It seems right somehow to her that people who move there to live return home completely changed. She thinks of the air, the smoke, the cinders. Imagines cinders big as hailstones; heavy, weighing on the people. Wonders how this pressure finds its way into the veins, roping the springs of laughter.

If there's anybody here that knows a reason why

But of course they know no reason why beyond what they daily have come to know. She thinks of the man who will be her husband, feels shut away from him because of the stiff severity of his plain black suit. His religion. A lifetime of black and white. Of veils. Covered head. It is as if her children are already gone from her. Not dead, but exalted on a pedestal, a stalk that has no roots. She wonders how to make new roots. It is beyond her. She wonders what one does with memories in a brand-new life. This had seemed easy, until she thought of it. "The reasons why . . . the people who" . . . she thinks, and does not wonder where the thought is from.

these two should not be joined

She thinks of her mother, who is dead. Dead, but still her mother. Joined. This is confusing. Of her father. A gray old man who sold wild mink, rabbit, fox skins to Sears, Roebuck. He stands in the yard, like a man waiting for a train. Her young sisters stand behind her in smooth green dresses, with flowers in their hands and hair. They giggle, she feels, at the absurdity of the wedding. They are ready for something new. She thinks the man beside her should marry one of them. She feels old. Yoked. An arm seems to reach out from behind her and snatch her backward. She thinks of cemeteries and the long sleep of grandparents mingling in the dirt. She believes that she believes in ghosts. In the soil giving back what it takes.

together,

In the city. He sees her in a new way. This she knows, and is grateful. But is it new enough? She cannot always be a bride and virgin, wearing robes and veil. Even now her body itches to be free of satin and voile, organdy and lily of the valley. Memories crash against her. Memories of being bare to the sun. She wonders what it will be like. Not to have to go to a job. Not to work in a sewing plant. Not to worry about learning to sew straight seams in workingmen's overalls, jeans, and dress pants. Her place will be in the home, he has said, repeatedly, promising her rest she had prayed for. But now she wonders. When she is rested, what will she do? They will make babies—she thinks practically about her fine brown body, his strong black one. They will be inevitable. Her hands will be full. Full of what? Babies. She is not comforted.

let him speak

She wishes she had asked him to explain more of what he meant. But she was impatient. Impatient to be done with sewing. With doing everything for three children, alone. Impatient to leave the girls she had known since childhood, their children growing up, their husbands hanging around her, already old, seedy. Nothing about them that she wanted, or needed. The fathers of her children driving by, waving, not waving; reminders of times she would just as soon forget. Impatient to see the South Side, where they would live and build and be respectable and respected and free. Her husband would free her. A romantic hush. Proposal. Promises. A new life! Respectable, reclaimed, renewed. Free! In robe and veil.

or forever hold

She does not even know if she loves him. She loves his sobriety. His refusal to sing just because he knows the tune. She loves his pride. His blackness and his gray car. She loves his understanding of her *condition.* She thinks she loves the effort he will make to redo her into what he truly wants. His love of her makes her completely conscious of how unloved she was before. This is something; though it makes her unbearably sad. Melancholy. She blinks her eyes.

Remembers she is finally being married, like other girls. Like other girls, women? Something strains upward behind her eyes. She thinks of the something as a rat trapped, cornered, scurrying to and fro in her head, peering through the windows of her eyes. She wants to live for once. But doesn't know quite what that means. Wonders if she has ever done it. If she ever will. The preacher is odious to her. She wants to strike him out of the way, out of her light, with the back of her hand. It seems to her he has always been standing in front of her, barring her way.

his peace.

The rest she does not hear. She feels a kiss, passionate, rousing, within the general pandemonium. Cars drive up blowing their horns. Firecrackers go off. Dogs come from under the house and begin to yelp and bark. Her husband's hand is like the clasp of an iron gate. People congratulate. Her children press against her. They look with awe and distaste mixed with hope at their new father. He stands curiously apart, in spite of the people crowding about to grasp his free hand. He smiles at them all but his eyes are as if turned inward. He knows they cannot understand that he is not a Christian. He will not explain himself. He feels different, he looks it. The old women thought he was like one of their sons except that he had somehow got away from them. Still a son, not a son. Changed.

She thinks how it will be later in the night in the silvery gray car. How they will spin through the darkness of Mississippi and in the morning be in Chicago, Illinois. She thinks of Lincoln, the president. That is all she knows about the place. She feels ignorant, *wrong,* backward. She presses her worried fingers into his palm. He is standing in front of her. In the crush of well-wishing people, he does not look back.

1973

IN SEARCH OF OUR MOTHERS' GARDENS

I described her own nature and temperament. Told how they needed a larger life for their expression. . . . I pointed out that in lieu of proper channels, her emotions had overflowed into paths that dissipated them. I talked, beautifully I thought, about an art that would be born, an art that would open the way for women the likes of her. I asked her to hope, and build

> up an inner life against the coming of that day. . . . I sang, with a strange quiver in my voice, a promise song.
>
> —*Jean Toomer, "Avey,"* CANE

The poet speaking to a prostitute who falls asleep while he's talking—

When the poet Jean Toomer walked through the South in the early twenties, he discovered a curious thing: black women whose spirituality was so intense, so deep, *so unconscious,* that they were themselves unaware of the richness they held. They stumbled blindly through their lives: creatures so abused and mutilated in body, so dimmed and confused by pain, that they considered themselves unworthy even of hope. In the selfless abstractions their bodies became to the men who used them, they became more than "sexual objects," more even than mere women: they became "Saints." Instead of being perceived as whole persons, their bodies became shrines: what was thought to be their minds became temples suitable for worship. These crazy Saints stared out at the world, wildly, like lunatics—or quietly, like suicides; and the "God" that was in their gaze was as mute as a great stone.

Who were these Saints? These crazy, loony, pitiful women?

Some of them, without a doubt, were our mothers and grandmothers.

In the still heat of the post-Reconstruction South, this is how they seemed to Jean Toomer: exquisite butterflies trapped in an evil honey, toiling away their lives in an era, a century, that did not acknowledge them, except as "the *mule* of the world." They dreamed dreams that no one knew—not even themselves, in any coherent fashion—and saw visions no one could understand. They wandered or sat about the countryside crooning lullabies to ghosts, and drawing the mother of Christ in charcoal on courthouse walls.

They forced their minds to desert their bodies and their striving spirits sought to rise, like frail whirlwinds from the hard red clay. And when those frail whirlwinds fell, in scattered particles, upon the ground, no one mourned. Instead, men lit candles to celebrate the emptiness that remained, as people do who enter a beautiful but vacant space to resurrect a God.

Our mothers and grandmothers, some of them: moving to music not yet written. And they waited.

They waited for a day when the unknown thing that was in them would be made known; but guessed, somehow in their darkness, that on the day of their revelation they would be long dead. Therefore to Toomer they walked, and even ran, in slow motion. For they were going nowhere immediate, and the future was not yet within their grasp. And men took our mothers and grandmothers, "but got no pleasure from it." So complex was their passion and their calm.

To Toomer, they lay vacant and fallow as autumn fields, with harvest time never in sight: and he saw them enter loveless marriages, without joy;

and become prostitutes, without resistance; and become mothers of children, without fulfillment.

For these grandmothers and mothers of ours were not Saints, but Artists; driven to a numb and bleeding madness by the springs of creativity in them for which there was no release. They were Creators, who lived lives of spiritual waste, because they were so rich in spirituality—which is the basis of Art—that the strain of enduring their unused and unwanted talent drove them insane. Throwing away this spirituality was their pathetic attempt to lighten the soul to a weight their work-worn, sexually abused bodies could bear.

What did it mean for a black woman to be an artist in our grandmothers' time? In our great-grandmothers' day? It is a question with an answer cruel enough to stop the blood.

Did you have a genius of a great-great-grandmother who died under some ignorant and depraved white overseer's lash? Or was she required to bake biscuits for a lazy backwater tramp, when she cried out in her soul to paint watercolors of sunsets, or the rain falling on the green and peaceful pasturelands? Or was her body broken and forced to bear children (who were more often than not sold away from her)—eight, ten, fifteen, twenty children—when her one joy was the thought of modeling heroic figures of rebellion, in stone or clay?

How was the creativity of the black woman kept alive, year after year and century after century, when for most of the years black people have been in America, it was a punishable crime for a black person to read or write? And the freedom to paint, to sculpt, to expand the mind with action did not exist. Consider, if you can bear to imagine it, what might have been the result if singing, too, had been forbidden by law. Listen to the voices of Bessie Smith, Billie Holiday, Nina Simone, Roberta Flack, and Aretha Franklin, among others, and imagine those voices muzzled for life. Then you may begin to comprehend the lives of our "crazy," "Sainted" mothers and grandmothers. The agony of the lives of women who might have been Poets, Novelists, Essayists, and Short-Story Writers (over a period of centuries), who died with their real gifts stifled within them.

And, if this were the end of the story, we would have cause to cry out in my paraphrase of Okot p'Bitek's great poem:

> O, my clanswomen
> Let us all cry together!
> Come,
> Let us mourn the death of our mother,
> The death of a Queen
> The ash that was produced
> By a great fire!
> O, this homestead is utterly dead
> Close the gates
> With *lacari* thorns,

For our mother,
The creator of the Stool is lost!
And all the young women
Have perished in the wilderness!

But this is not the end of the story, for all the young women—our mothers and grandmothers, *ourselves*—have not perished in the wilderness. And if we ask ourselves why, and search for and find the answer, we will know beyond all efforts to erase it from our minds, just exactly who, and of what, we black American women are.

One example, perhaps the most pathetic, most misunderstood one, can provide a backdrop for our mothers' work: Phillis Wheatley, a slave in the 1700s.

Virginia Woolf, in her book *A Room of One's Own*, wrote that in order for a woman to write fiction she must have two things, certainly: a room of her own (with key and lock) and enough money to support herself.

What then are we to make of Phillis Wheatley, a slave, who owned not even herself? This sickly, frail black girl who required a servant of her own at times—her health was so precarious—and who, had she been white, would have been easily considered the intellectual superior of all the women and most of the men in the society of her day.

Virginia Woolf wrote further, speaking of course not of our Phillis, that "any woman born with a great gift in the sixteenth century [insert "eighteenth century," insert "black woman," insert "born or made a slave"] would certainly have gone crazed, shot herself, or ended her days in some lonely cottage outside the village, half witch, half wizard [insert "Saint"], feared and mocked at. For it needs little skill and psychology to be sure that a highly gifted girl who had tried to use her gift for poetry would have been so thwarted and hindered by contrary instincts [add "chains, guns, the lash, the ownership of one's body by someone else, submission to an alien religion"], that she must have lost her health and sanity to a certainty."

The key words, as they relate to Phillis, are "contrary instincts." For when we read the poetry of Phillis Wheatley—as when we read the novels of Nella Larsen or the oddly false-sounding autobiography of that freest of all black women writers, Zora Hurston—evidence of "contrary instincts" is everywhere. Her loyalties were completely divided, as was, without question, her mind.

But how could this be otherwise? Captured at seven, a slave of wealthy, doting whites who instilled in her the "savagery" of the Africa they "rescued" her from . . . one wonders if she was even able to remember her homeland as she had known it, or as it really was.

Yet, because she did try to use her gift for poetry in a world that made her a slave, she was "so thwarted and hindered by . . . contrary instincts, that she . . . lost her health. . . ." In the last years of her brief life, burdened not only with the need to express her gift but also with a penniless, friendless "freedom" and several small children for whom she was forced to do strenuous work to feed, she lost her health, certainly. Suffering from malnutrition and neglect and who knows what mental agonies, Phillis Wheatley died.

So torn by "contrary instincts" was black, kidnapped, enslaved Phillis that her description of "the Goddess"—as she poetically called the Liberty she did not have—is ironically, cruelly humorous. And, in fact, has held Phillis up to ridicule for more than a century. It is usually read prior to hanging Phillis's memory as that of a fool. She wrote:

> The Goddess comes, she moves divinely fair,
> Olive and laurel binds her *golden* hair.
> Wherever shines this native of the skies,
> Unnumber'd charms and recent graces rise. [My italics]

It is obvious that Phillis, the slave, combed the "Goddess's" hair every morning; prior, perhaps, to bringing in the milk, or fixing her mistress's lunch. She took her imagery from the one thing she saw elevated above all others.

With the benefit of hindsight we ask, "How could she?"

But at last, Phillis, we understand. No more snickering when your stiff, struggling, ambivalent lines are forced on us. We know now that you were not an idiot or a traitor, only a sickly little black girl, snatched from your home and country and made a slave; a woman who still struggled to sing the song that was your gift, although in a land of barbarians who praised you for your bewildered tongue. It is not so much what you sang, as that you kept alive, in so many of our ancestors, *the notion of song.*

. . .

Black women are called, in the folklore that so aptly identifies one's status in society, "the *mule* of the world," because we have been handed the burdens that everyone else—*everyone else*—refused to carry. We have also been called "Matriarchs," "Superwomen," and "Mean and Evil Bitches." Not to mention "Castraters" and "Sapphire's Mama." When we have pleaded for understanding, our character has been distorted; when we have asked for simple caring, we have been handed empty inspirational appellations, then stuck in the farthest corner. When we have asked for love, we have been given children. In short, even our plainer gifts, our labors of fidelity and love, have been knocked down our throats. To be an artist and a black woman, even today, lowers our status in many respects, rather than raises it: and yet, artists we will be.

Therefore we must fearlessly pull out of ourselves and look at and identify with our lives the living creativity some of our great-grandmothers were not allowed to know. I stress *some* of them because it is well known that the majority of our great-grandmothers knew, even without "knowing" it, the reality of their spirituality, even if they didn't recognize it beyond what happened in the singing at church—and they never had any intention of giving it up.

. . .

How they did it—those millions of black women who were not Phillis Wheatley, or Lucy Terry or Frances Harper or Zora Hurston or Nella Larsen or Bessie Smith; or Elizabeth Catlett, or Katherine Dunham, either—brings me to the title of this essay, "In Search of Our Mothers' Gardens," which is a personal account that is yet shared, in its theme and its meaning, by all of us. I found, while thinking about the far-reaching world of the creative black woman, that often the truest answer to a question that really matters can be found very close.

. . .

In the late 1920s my mother ran away from home to marry my father. Marriage, if not running away, was expected of seventeen-year-old girls. By the time she was twenty, she had two children and was pregnant with a third. Five children later, I was born. And this is how I came to know my mother: she seemed a large, soft, loving-eyed woman who was rarely impatient in our home. Her quick, violent temper was on view only a few times a year, when she battled with the white landlord who had the misfortune to suggest to her that her children did not need to go to school.

She made all the clothes we wore, even my brothers' overalls. She made all the towels and sheets we used. She spent the summers canning vegetables and fruits. She spent the winter evenings making quilts enough to cover all our beds.

During the "working" day, she labored beside—not behind—my father in the fields. Her day began before sunup, and did not end until late at night. There was never a moment for her to sit down, undisturbed, to unravel her own private thoughts; never a time free from interruption—by work or the noisy inquiries of her many children. And yet, it is to my mother—and all our mothers who were not famous—that I went in search of the secret of what has fed that muzzled and often mutilated, but vibrant, creative spirit that the black woman has inherited, and that pops out in wild and unlikely places to this day.

But when, you will ask, did my overworked mother have time to know or care about feeding the creative spirit?

The answer is so simple that many of us have spent years discovering it. We have constantly looked high, when we should have looked high—and low.

For example: in the Smithsonian Institution in Washington, D.C., there hangs a quilt unlike any other in the world. In fanciful, inspired, and yet simple and identifiable figures, it portrays the story of the Crucifixion. It is considered rare, beyond price. Though it follows no known pattern of quilt-making, and though it is made of bits and pieces of worthless rags, it is obviously the work of a person of powerful imagination and deep spiritual feeling. Below this quilt I saw a note that says it was made by "an anonymous Black woman in Alabama, a hundred years ago."

If we could locate this "anonymous" black woman from Alabama, she would turn out to be one of our grandmothers—an artist who left her mark in the only materials she could afford, and in the only medium her position in society allowed her to use.

As Virginia Woolf wrote further, in *A Room of One's Own*:

> Yet genius of a sort must have existed among women as it must have existed among the working class. [Change this to "slaves" and "the wives and daughters of sharecroppers."] Now and again an Emily Brontë or a Robert Burns [change this to "a Zora Hurston or a Richard Wright"] blazes out and proves its presence. But certainly it never got itself on to paper. When, however, one reads of a witch being ducked, of a woman possessed by devils [or "Sainthood"], of a wise woman selling herbs [our root workers], or even a very remarkable man who had a mother, then I think we are on the track of a lost novelist, a suppressed poet, of some mute and inglorious Jane Austen. . . . Indeed, I would venture to guess that Anon, who wrote so many poems without signing them, was often a woman. . . .

And so our mothers and grandmothers have, more often than not anonymously, handed on the creative spark, the seed of the flower they themselves never hoped to see: or like a sealed letter they could not plainly read.

And so it is, certainly, with my own mother. Unlike "Ma" Rainey's songs, which retained their creator's name even while blasting forth from Bessie Smith's mouth, no song or poem will bear my mother's name. Yet so many of the stories that I write, that we all write, are my mother's stories. Only recently did I fully realize this: that through years of listening to my mother's stories of her life, I have absorbed not only the stories themselves, but something of the manner in which she spoke, something of the urgency that involves the knowledge that her stories—like her life—must be recorded. It is probably for this reason that so much of what I have written is about characters whose counterparts in real life are so much older than I am.

But the telling of these stories, which came from my mother's lips as naturally as breathing, was not the only way my mother showed herself as an artist. For stories, too, were subject to being distracted, to dying without conclusion. Dinners must be started, and cotton must be gathered before the big rains. The artist that was and is my mother showed itself to me only after many years. This is what I finally noticed:

Like Mem, a character in *The Third Life of Grange Copeland,* my mother adorned with flowers whatever shabby house we were forced to live in. And not just your typical straggly country stand of zinnias, either. She planted ambitious gardens—and still does—with over fifty different varieties of plants that bloom profusely from early March until late November. Before she left home for the fields, she watered her flowers, chopped up the grass, and laid out new beds. When she returned from the fields she might divide clumps of bulbs, dig a cold pit, uproot and replant roses, or prune branches from her taller bushes or trees—until night came and it was too dark to see.

Whatever she planted grew as if by magic, and her fame as a grower of flowers spread over three counties. Because of her creativity with her flowers, even my memories of poverty are seen through a screen of blooms—sunflowers, petunias, roses, dahlias, forsythia, spirea, delphiniums, verbena . . . and on and on.

And I remember people coming to my mother's yard to be given cuttings from her flowers; I hear again the praise showered on her because whatever rocky soil she landed on, she turned into a garden. A garden so brilliant with colors, so original in its design, so magnificent with life and creativity, that to this day people drive by our house in Georgia—perfect strangers and imperfect strangers—and ask to stand or walk among my mother's art.

I notice that it is only when my mother is working in her flowers that she is radiant, almost to the point of being invisible—except as Creator: hand and eye. She is involved in work her soul must have. Ordering the universe in the image of her personal conception of Beauty.

Her face, as she prepares the Art that is her gift, is a legacy of respect she leaves to me, for all that illuminates and cherishes life. She has handed down respect for the possibilities—and the will to grasp them.

For her, so hindered and intruded upon in so many ways, being an artist has still been a daily part of her life. This ability to hold on, even in very simple ways, is work black women have done for a very long time.

This poem is not enough, but it is something, for the woman who literally covered the holes in our walls with sunflowers.

They were women then
My mama's generation
Husky of voice—Stout of
Step
With fists as well as
Hands
How they battered down
Doors
And ironed
Starched white
Shirts
How they led
Armies
Headragged Generals
Across mined
Fields
Booby-trapped
Kitchens
To discover books
Desks

A place for us
How they knew what we
Must know
Without knowing a page
Of it
Themselves

Guided by my heritage of a love of beauty and a respect for strength—in search of my mother's garden, I found my own.

And perhaps in Africa over two hundred years ago, there was just such a mother; perhaps she painted vivid and daring decorations in oranges and yellows and greens on the walls of her hut; perhaps she sang—in a voice like Roberta Flack's—*sweetly* over the compounds of her village; perhaps she wove the most stunning mats or told the most ingenious stories of all the village storytellers. Perhaps she was herself a poet—though only her daughter's name is signed to the poems that we know.

Perhaps Phillis Wheatley's mother was also an artist.

Perhaps in more than Phillis Wheatley's biological life is her mother's signature made clear.

1974

LESLIE MARMON SILKO (1948–)

Poet, novelist, and short-story writer, Leslie Marmon Silko is one of the most celebrated Native American writers of her generation. She brings to literature a singular voice that blends her Laguna, Mexican, and white heritages.

Silko grew up on the Laguna Pueblo Reservation in New Mexico, about one hundred miles from Albuquerque, which is where she was born. In 1969, she graduated from the University of New Mexico with a major in English literature. She attended three semesters in the American Indian Law Program at the University of New Mexico but left to pursue a writing career.

Silko's first publication, the story "The Man to Send Rain Clouds," earned her a National Endowment for the Humanities Discovery Grant when it appeared in 1969. In 1974, she published her first book, a collection of poems titled Laguna Woman, *and seven of her stories were anthologized. Her stories have been included in* Best Stories of 1975 *and* Two Hundred Years of Great American Short Stories.

An avid reader who developed an early love for Milton and Shakespeare, Silko emphasizes that the primary influence on her writing has been the constant stream of stories she heard growing up at Laguna. Silko celebrates one such storyteller, her Aunt Susie, who, like many of her community, "passed down an entire culture by word of mouth, an entire history, an entire vision of the world which depended upon memory and retelling by subsequent generations."

Silko began writing stories in the fifth grade and discovered in a creative writing class her storehouse of stories to tell. She feels an urgency about writing, sensing that "there are these stories that just have to be told in the same way the wind goes blowing across the mesa." Her advice to other writers is to "make whatever language you have really speak for you."

Silko wrote her first novel while living in Ketchikan, Alaska. Ceremony *was highly praised when it appeared in 1977.* Storyteller, *a collection of poetry, short stories, photography, and memoirs, followed in 1981. Her achievements have earned her a National Endowment for the Arts Fellowship and a MacArthur Foundation grant. Currently, she is completing her second novel,* Almanac of the Dead.

In 1977, Silko claimed that "Storyteller" is her favorite story. Set in the tundra of Bethel, Alaska, it describes how racial and sexual violence shape a young woman's life.

STORYTELLER

Every day the sun came up a little lower on the horizon, moving more slowly until one day she got excited and started calling the jailer. She realized she had been sitting there for many hours, yet the sun had not moved from the center of the sky. The color of the sky had not been good lately; it had been pale blue, almost white, even when there were no clouds. She told herself it wasn't a good sign for the sky to be indistinguishable from the river ice, frozen solid and white against the earth. The tundra rose up behind the river but all the boundaries between the river and hills and sky were lost in the density of the pale ice.

She yelled again, this time some English words which came randomly into her mouth, probably swear words she'd heard from the oil drilling crews last winter. The jailer was an Eskimo, but he would not speak Yupik to her. She had watched people in other cells, when they spoke to him in Yupik he ignored them until they spoke English.

He came and stared at her. She didn't know if he understood what she was telling him until he glanced behind her at the small high window. He looked at the sun, and turned and walked away. She could hear the buckles on his heavy snowmobile boots jingle as he walked to the front of the building.

It was like the other buildings that white people, the Gussucks, brought with them: BIA and school buildings, portable buildings that arrived sliced in halves, on barges coming up the river. Squares of metal panelling bulged out with the layers of insulation stuffed inside. She had asked once what it was and someone told her it was to keep out the cold. She had not laughed then, but she did now. She walked over to the small double-pane window and she laughed out loud. They thought they could keep out the cold with stringy yellow wadding. Look at the sun. It wasn't moving; it was frozen, caught in the middle of the sky. Look at the sky, solid as the river with ice which had trapped the sun. It had not moved for a long time; in a few more hours it would be weak, and heavy frost would begin to appear on the edges and spread across the face of the sun like a mask. Its light was pale yellow, worn thin by the winter.

She could see people walking down the snow-packed roads, their breath steaming out from their parka hoods, faces hidden and protected by deep ruffs of fur. There were no cars or snowmobiles that day; the cold had silenced their machines. The metal froze; it split and shattered. Oil hardened and moving parts jammed solidly. She had seen it happen to their big yellow machines and the giant drill last winter when they came to drill their test holes. The cold stopped them, and they were helpless against it.

Her village was many miles upriver from this town, but in her mind she could see it clearly. Their house was not near the village houses. It stood alone on the bank upriver from the village. Snow had drifted to the eaves of the roof on the north side, but on the west side, by the door, the path was almost clear. She had nailed scraps of red tin over the logs last summer. She had done it for the bright red color, not for added warmth the way the village people had done. This final winter had been coming even then; there had been signs of its approach for many years.

. . .

She went because she was curious about the big school where the Government sent all the other girls and boys. She had not played much with the village children while she was growing up because they were afraid of the old man, and they ran when her grandmother came. She went because she was tired of being alone with the old woman whose body had been stiffening for as long as the girl could remember. Her knees and knuckles were swollen grotesquely, and the pain had squeezed the brown skin of her face tight against the bones; it left her eyes hard like river stone. The girl asked once what it was that did this to her body, and the old woman had raised up from sewing a sealskin boot, and stared at her.

"The joints," the old woman said in a low voice, whispering like wind across the roof, "the joints are swollen with anger."

Sometimes she did not answer and only stared at the girl. Each year she spoke less and less, but the old man talked more—all night sometimes, not to anyone but himself; in a soft deliberate voice, he told stories, moving his smooth brown hands above the blankets. He had not fished or hunted with the other men for many years, although he was not crippled or sick. He stayed in his bed, smelling like dry fish and urine, telling stories all winter; and when warm weather came, he went to his place on the river bank. He sat with a long willow stick, poking at the smoldering moss he burned against the insects while he continued with the stories.

The trouble was that she had not recognized the warnings in time. She did not see what the Gussuck school would do to her until she walked into the dormitory and realized that the old man had not been lying about the place. She thought he had been trying to scare her as he used to when she was very small and her grandmother was outside cutting up fish. She hadn't believed what he told her about the school because she knew he wanted to keep her there in the log house with him. She knew what he wanted.

The dormitory matron pulled down her underpants and whipped her with a leather belt because she refused to speak English.

"Those backwards village people," the matron said, because she was an Eskimo who had worked for the BIA for a long time, "they kept this one until she was too big to learn." The other girls whispered in English. They knew how to work the showers, and they washed and curled their hair at night. They ate Gussuck food. She lay on her bed and imagined what her grandmother might be sewing, and what the old man was eating in his bed. When summer came, they sent her home.

The way her grandmother had hugged her before she left for school had been a warning too, because the old woman had not hugged or touched her for many years. Not like the old man, whose hands were always hunting, like ravens circling lazily in the sky, ready to touch her. She was not surprised when the priest and the old man met her at the landing strip, to say that the old lady was gone. The priest asked her where she would like to stay. He referred to the old man as her grandfather, but she did not bother to correct him. She had already been thinking about it; if she went with the priest, he would send her away to a school. But the old man was different. She knew he wouldn't send her back to school. She knew he wanted to keep her.

. . .

He told her one time, that she would get too old for him faster than he got too old for her; but again she had not believed him because sometimes he lied. He had lied about what he would do with her if she came into his bed. But as the years passed, she realized what he said was true. She was restless and strong. She had no patience with the old man who had never changed his slow smooth motions under the blankets.

The old man was in his bed for the winter; he did not leave it except to use the slop bucket in the corner. He was dozing with his mouth open slightly; his lips quivered and sometimes they moved like he was telling a story even while he dreamed. She pulled on the sealskin boots, the mukluks with the bright red flannel linings her grandmother had sewn for her, and she tied the braided red yarn tassels around her ankles over the gray wool pants. She zipped the wolfskin parka. Her grandmother had worn it for many years, but the old man said that before she died, she instructed him to bury her in an old black sweater, and to give the parka to the girl. The wolf pelts were creamy colored and silver, almost white in some places, and when the old lady had walked across the tundra in the winter, she was invisible in the snow.

She walked toward the village, breaking her own path through the deep snow. A team of sled dogs tied outside a house at the edge of the village leaped against their chains to bark at her. She kept walking, watching the dusky sky for the first evening stars. It was warm and the dogs were alert. When it got cold again, the dogs would lie curled and still, too drowsy from the cold to bark or pull at the chains. She laughed loudly because it made them howl and snarl. Once the old man had seen her tease the dogs and he shook his head. "So that's the kind of woman you are," he said, "in the wintertime the two of us are no different from those dogs. We wait in the cold for someone to bring us a few dry fish."

She laughed out loud again, and kept walking. She was thinking about the Gussuck oil drillers. They were strange; they watched her when she walked near their machines. She wondered what they looked like underneath their quilted goosedown trousers; she wanted to know how they moved. They would be something different from the old man.

. . .

The old man screamed at her. He shook her shoulders so violently that her head bumped against the log wall. "I smelled it!" he yelled, "as soon as I woke up! I am sure of it now. You can't fool me!" His thin legs were shaking inside the baggy wool trousers; he stumbled over her boots in his bare feet. His toenails were long and yellow like bird claws; she had seen a gray crane last summer fighting another in the shallow water on the edge of the river. She laughed out loud and pulled her shoulder out of his grip. He stood in front of her. He was breathing hard and shaking; he looked weak. He would probably die next winter.

"I'm warning you," he said, "I'm warning you." He crawled back into his bunk then, and reached under the old soiled feather pillow for a piece of dry fish. He lay back on the pillow, staring at the ceiling and chewed dry strips of salmon. "I don't know what the old woman told you," he said, "but there will be trouble." He looked over to see if she was listening. His face suddenly relaxed into a smile, his dark slanty eyes were lost in wrinkles of brown skin. "I could tell you, but you are too good for warnings now. I can smell what you did all night with the Gussucks."

. . .

She did not understand why they came there, because the village was small and so far upriver that even some Eskimos who had been away to school did not want to come back. They stayed downriver in the town. They said the village was too quiet. They were used to the town where the boarding school was located, with electric lights and running water. After all those years away at school, they had forgotten how to set nets in the river and where to hunt seals in the fall. When she asked the old man why the Gussucks bothered to come to the village, his narrow eyes got bright with excitement.

"They only come when there is something to steal. The fur animals are too difficult for them to get now, and the seals and fish are hard to find. Now they come for oil deep in the earth. But this is the last time for them." His breathing was wheezy and fast; his hands gestured at the sky. "It is approaching. As it comes, ice will push across the sky." His eyes were open wide and he stared at the low ceiling rafters for hours without blinking. She remembered all this clearly because he began the story that day, the story he told from that time on. It began with a giant bear which he described muscle by muscle, from the curve of the ivory claws to the whorls of hair at the top of the massive skull. And for eight days he did not sleep, but talked continuously of the giant bear whose color was pale blue glacier ice.

. . .

The snow was dirty and worn down in a path to the door. On either side of the path, the snow was higher than her head. In front of the door there were jagged yellow stains melted into the snow where men had urinated. She stopped in the entry way and kicked the snow off her boots. The room was dim; a kerosene lantern by the cash register was burning low. The long wooden shelves were jammed with cans of beans and potted meats. On the bottom shelf a jar of mayonnaise was broken open, leaking oily white clots on the floor. There was no one in the room except the yellowish dog sleeping in the front of the long glass display case. A reflection made it appear to be lying on the knives and ammunition inside the case. Gussucks kept dogs inside their houses with them; they did not seem to mind the odors which seeped out of the dogs. "They tell us we are dirty for the food we eat—raw fish and fermented meat. But we do not live with dogs," the old man once said. She heard voices in the back room, and the sound of bottles set down hard on tables.

They were always confident. The first year they waited for the ice to break up on the river, and then they brought their big yellow machines up river on barges. They planned to drill their test holes during the summer to avoid the freezing. But the imprints and graves of their machines were still there, on the edge of the tundra above the river, where the summer mud had swallowed them before they ever left sight of the river. The village people had gathered to watch the white men, and to laugh as they drove the giant machines, one by one, off the steel ramp into the bogs; as if sheer numbers of vehicles would somehow make the tundra solid. But the old man said they behaved like desperate people, and they would come back again. When the tundra was frozen solid, they returned.

Village women did not even look through the door to the back room. The priest had warned them. The storeman was watching her because he didn't let Eskimos or Indians sit down at the tables in the back room. But she knew he couldn't throw her out if one of his Gussuck customers invited her to sit with him. She walked across the room. They stared at her, but she had the feeling she was walking for someone else, not herself, so their eyes did not matter. The red-haired man pulled out a chair and motioned for her to sit down. She looked back at the storeman while the red-haired man poured her a glass of red sweet wine. She wanted to laugh at the storeman the way she laughed at the dogs, straining against the chains, howling at her.

The red-haired man kept talking to the other Gussucks sitting around the table, but he slid one hand off the top of the table to her thigh. She looked over at the storeman to see if he was still watching her. She laughed out loud at him and the red-haired man stopped talking and turned to her. He asked if she wanted to go. She nodded and stood up.

Someone in the village had been telling him things about her, he said as they walked down the road to his trailer. She understood that much of what he was saying, but the rest she did not hear. The whine of the big generators at the construction camp sucked away the sound of his words. But English was of no concern to her anymore, and neither was anything the Christians in the village might say about her or the old man. She smiled at the effect of the subzero air on the electric lights around the trailers; they did not shine. They left only flat yellow holes in the darkness.

It took him a long time to get ready, even after she had undressed for him. She waited in the bed with the blankets pulled close, watching him. He adjusted the thermostat and lit candles in the room, turning out the electric lights. He searched through a stack of record albums until he found the right one. She was not sure about the last thing he did; he taped something on the wall behind the bed where he could see it while he lay on top of her. He was shriveled and white from the cold; he pushed against her body for warmth. He guided her hands to his thighs; he was shivering.

She had returned a last time because she wanted to know what it was he stuck on the wall above the bed. After he finished each time, he reached up and pulled it loose, folding it carefully so that she could not see it. But this time she was ready; she waited for his fast breathing and sudden collapse on top of her. She slid out from under him and stood up beside the bed. She looked at the picture while she got dressed. He did not raise his face from the pillow, and she thought she heard teeth rattling together as she left the room.

. . .

She heard the old man move when she came in. After the Gussuck's trailer, the log house felt cool. It smelled like dry fish and cured meat. The room was dark except for the blinking yellow flame in the mica window of the oil stove. She squatted in front of the stove and watched the flames for a long time before she walked to the bed where her grandmother had slept. The bed was covered with a mound of rags and fur scraps the old woman had saved. She reached into the mound until she felt something cold and solid wrapped in a wool blanket. She pushed her fingers around it until she felt smooth stone. Long ago, before the Gussucks came, they had burned the whale oil in the big stone lamp which made light and heat as well. The old woman had saved everything they would need when the time came.

In the morning, the old man pulled a piece of dry caribou meat from under the blankets and offered it to her. While she was gone, men from the village had brought a bundle of dry meat. She chewed it slowly, thinking about the way they still came from the village to take care of the old man and his stories. But she had a story now, about the red-haired Gussuck. The old man knew what she was thinking, and his smile made his face seem more round than it was.

"Well," he said, "what was it?"

"A woman with a big dog on top of her."

He laughed softly to himself and walked over to the water barrel. He dipped the tin cup into the water.

"It doesn't surprise me," he said.

. . .

"Grandma," she said, "there was something red in the grass that morning. I remember." She had not asked about her parents before. The old woman stopped splitting the fish bellies open for the willow drying racks. Her jaw muscles pulled so tightly against her skull, the girl thought the old woman would not be able to speak.

"They bought a tin can full of it from the storeman. Late at night. He told them it was alcohol safe to drink. They traded a rifle for it." The old woman's voice sounded like each word stole strength from her. "It made no difference about the rifle. That year the Gussuck boats had come, firing big guns at the walrus and seals. There was nothing left to hunt after that anyway. So," the old lady said, in a low soft voice the girl had not heard for a long time, "I didn't say anything to them when they left that night."

"Right over there," she said, pointing at the fallen poles, half buried in the river sand and tall grass, "in the summer shelter. The sun was high half the night then. Early in the morning when it was still low, the policeman came around. I told the interpreter to tell him that the storeman had poisoned them." She made outlines in the air in front of her, showing how their bodies lay twisted on the sand; telling the story was like laboring to walk through deep snow; sweat shone in the white hair around her forehead. "I told the priest too, after he came. I told him the storeman lied." She turned away from the girl. She held her mouth even tighter, set solidly, not in sorrow or anger, but against the pain, which was all that remained. "I never believed," she said, "not much anyway. I wasn't surprised when the priest did nothing."

The wind came off the river and folded the tall grass into itself like river waves. She could feel the silence the story left, and she wanted to have the old woman go on.

"I heard sounds that night, grandma. Sounds like someone was singing. It was light outside. I could see something red on the ground." The old woman did not answer her; she moved to the tub full of fish on the ground beside the workbench. She stabbed her knife into the belly of a whitefish and lifted it onto the bench. "The Gussuck storeman left the village right after that," the old woman said as she pulled the entrails from the fish, "otherwise, I could tell you more." The old woman's voice flowed with the wind blowing off the river; they never spoke of it again.

When the willows got their leaves and the grass grew tall along the river banks and around the sloughs, she walked early in the morning. While the sun was still low on the horizon, she listened to the wind off the river; its sound was like the voice that day long ago. In the distance, she could hear the engines of the machinery the oil drillers had left the winter before, but she did not go near the village or the store. The sun never left the sky and the summer became the same long day, with only the winds to fan the sun into brightness or allow it to slip into twilight.

She sat beside the old man at his place on the river bank. She poked the smoky fire for him, and felt herself growing wide and thin in the sun as if she had been split from belly to throat and strung on the willow pole in preparation for the winter to come. The old man did not speak anymore. When men from the village brought him fresh fish he hid them deep in the river grass where it was cool. After he went inside, she split the fish open and spread them to dry on the willow frame the way the old woman had done. Inside, he dozed and talked to himself. He had talked all winter, softly and incessantly, about the giant polar bear stalking a lone hunter across Bering Sea ice. After all the months the old man had been telling the story, the bear was within a hundred feet of the man; but the ice fog had closed in on them now and the man could only smell the sharp ammonia odor of the bear, and hear the edge of the snow crust crack under the giant paws.

One night she listened to the old man tell the story all night in his sleep, describing each crystal of ice and the slightly different sounds they made under each paw; first the left and then the right paw, then the hind feet. Her grandmother was there suddenly, a shadow around the stove. She spoke in her low wind voice and the girl was afraid to sit up to hear more clearly. Maybe what she said had been to the old man because he stopped telling the story and began to snore softly the way he had long ago when the old woman had scolded him for telling his stories while others in the house were trying to sleep. But the last words she heard clearly: "It will take a long time, but the story must be told. There must not be any lies." She pulled the blankets up around her chin, slowly, so that her movements would not be seen. She thought her grandmother was talking about the old man's bear story; she did not know about the other story then.

She left the old man wheezing and snoring in his bed. She walked through river grass glistening with frost; the bright green summer color was already fading. She watched the sun move across the sky, already lower on the horizon, already moving away from the village. She stopped by the fallen poles of the summer shelter where her parents had died. Frost glittered on the river sand too; in a few more weeks there would be snow. The predawn light would be the color of an old woman. An old woman sky full of snow. There had been something red lying on the ground the morning they died. She looked for it again, pushing aside the grass with her foot. She knelt in the sand and looked under the fallen structure for some trace of it. When she found it, she would know what the old woman had never told her. She squatted down close to the gray poles and leaned her back against them. The wind made her shiver.

The summer rain had washed the mud from between the logs; the sod blocks stacked as high as her belly next to the log walls had lost their square-cut shape and had grown into soft mounds of tundra moss and stiff-bladed grass bending with clusters of seed bristles. She looked at the northwest, in the direction of the Bering Sea. The cold would come down from there to find narrow slits in the mud, rainwater holes in the outer layer of sod which protected the log house. The dark green tundra stretched away flat and continuous. Somewhere the sea and the land met; she knew by their dark green colors there were no boundaries between them. That was how the cold would come: when the boundaries were gone the polar ice would range across the land into the sky. She watched the horizon for a long time. She would stand in that place on the north side of the house and she would keep watch on the northwest horizon, and eventually she would see it come. She would watch for its approach in the stars, and hear it come with the wind. These preparations were unfamiliar, but gradually she recognized them as she did her own footprints in the snow.

. . .

She emptied the slop jar beside his bed twice a day and kept the barrel full of water melted from river ice. He did not recognize her anymore, and when he spoke to her, he called her by her grandmother's name and talked about people and events from long ago, before he went back to telling the story. The giant bear was creeping across the new snow on its belly, close enough now that the man could hear the rasp of its breathing. On and on in a soft singing voice, the old man caressed the story, repeating the words again and again like gentle strokes.

The sky was gray like a river crane's egg; its density curved into the thin crust of frost already covering the land. She looked at the bright red color of the tin against the ground and the sky and she told the village men to bring the pieces for the old man and her. To drill the test holes in the tundra, the Gussucks had used hundreds of barrels of fuel. The village people split open the empty barrels that were abandoned on the river bank, and pounded the red tin into flat sheets. The village people were using the strips of tin to mend walls and roofs for winter. But she nailed it on the log walls for its color. When she finished, she walked away with the hammer in her hand, not turning around until she was far away, on the ridge above the river banks, and then she looked back. She felt a chill when she saw how the sky and the land were already losing their boundaries, already becoming lost in each other. But the red tin penetrated the thick white color of earth and sky; it defined the boundaries like a wound revealing the ribs and heart of a great caribou about to bolt and be lost to the hunter forever. That night the wind howled and when she scratched a hole through the heavy frost on the inside of the window, she could see nothing but the impenetrable white; whether it was blowing snow or snow that had drifted as high as the house, she did not know.

It had come down suddenly, and she stood with her back to the wind looking at the river, its smoky water clotted with ice. The wind had blown the snow over the frozen river, hiding thin blue streaks where fast water ran under ice translucent and fragile as memory. But she could see shadows of boundaries, outlines of paths which were slender branches of solidity reaching out from the earth. She spent days walking on the river, watching the colors of ice that would safely hold her, kicking the heel of her boot into the snow crust, listening for a solid sound. When she could feel the paths through the soles of her feet, she went to the middle of the river where the fast gray water churned under a thin pane of ice. She looked back. On the river bank in the distance she could see the red tin nailed to the log house, something not swallowed up by the heavy white belly of the sky or caught in the folds of the frozen earth. It was time.

. . .

The wolverine fur around the hood of her parka was white with the frost from her breathing. The warmth inside the store melted it, and she felt tiny drops of water on her face. The storeman came in from the back room. She unzipped the parka and stood by the oil stove. She didn't look at him, but stared instead at the yellowish dog, covered with scabs of matted hair, sleeping in front of the stove. She thought of the Gussuck's picture, taped on the wall above the bed and she laughed out loud. The sound of her laughter was piercing; the yellow dog jumped to its feet and the hair bristled down its back. The storeman was watching her. She wanted to laugh again because he didn't know about the ice. He did not know that it was prowling the earth, or that it had already pushed its way into the sky to seize the sun. She sat down in the chair by the stove and shook her long hair loose. He was like a dog tied up all winter, watching while the others got fed. He remembered how she had gone with the oil drillers, and his blue eyes moved like flies crawling over her body. He held his thin pale lips like he wanted to spit on her. He hated the people because they had something of value, the old man said, something which the Gussucks could never have. They thought they could take it, suck it out of the earth or cut it from the mountains; but they were fools.

There was a matted hunk of dog hair on the floor by her foot. She thought of the yellow insulation coming unstuffed: their defense against the freezing going to pieces as it advanced on them. The ice was crouching on the northwest horizon like the old man's bear. She laughed out loud again. The sun would be down now; it was time.

The first time he spoke to her, she did not hear what he said, so she did not answer or even look up at him. He spoke to her again but his words were only noises coming from his pale mouth, trembling now as his anger began to unravel. He jerked her up and the chair fell over behind her. His arms were shaking and she could feel his hands tense up, pulling the edges of the parka tighter. He raised his fist to hit her, his thin body quivering with rage; but the fist collapsed with the desire he had for the valuable things, which, the old man had rightly said, was the only reason they came. She could hear his heart pounding as he held her close and arched his hips against her, groaning and breathing in spasms. She twisted away from him and ducked under his arms.

She ran with a mitten over her mouth, breathing through the fur to protect her lungs from the freezing air. She could hear him running behind her, his heavy breathing, the occasional sound of metal jingling against metal. But he ran without his parka or mittens, breathing the frozen air; its fire squeezed the lungs against the ribs and it was enough that he could not catch her near his store. On the river bank he realized how far he was from his stove, and the wads of yellow stuffing that held off the cold. But the girl was not able to run very fast through the deep drifts at the edge of the river. The twilight was luminous and he could still see clearly for a long distance; he knew he could catch her so he kept running.

When she neared the middle of the river she looked over her shoulder. He was not following her tracks; he went straight across the ice, running the shortest distance to reach her. He was close then; his face was twisted and scarlet from the exertion and the cold. There was satisfaction in his eyes; he was sure he could outrun her.

She was familiar with the river, down to the instant ice flexed into hairline fractures, and the cracking bone-sliver sounds gathered momentum with the opening ice until the churning gray water was set free. She stopped and turned to the sound of the river and the rattle of swirling ice fragments where he fell through. She pulled off a mitten and zipped the parka to her throat. She was conscious then of her own rapid breathing.

She moved slowly, kicking the ice ahead with the heel of her boot, feeling for sinews of ice to hold her. She looked ahead and all around herself; in the twilight, the dense white sky had merged into the flat snow-covered tundra. In the frantic running she had lost her place on the river. She stood still. The east bank of the river was lost in the sky; the boundaries had been swallowed by the freezing white. But then, in the distance, she saw something red, and suddenly it was as she had remembered it all those years.

. . .

She sat on her bed and while she waited, she listened to the old man. The hunter had found a small jagged knoll on the ice. He pulled his beaver fur cap off his head; the fur inside it steamed with his body heat and sweat. He left it upside down on the ice for the great bear to stalk, and he waited downwind on top of the ice knoll; he was holding the jade knife.

She thought she could see the end of his story in the way he wheezed out the words; but still he reached into his cache of dry fish and dribbled water into his mouth from the tin cup. All night she listened to him describe each breath the man took, each motion of the bear's head as it tried to catch the sound of the man's breathing, and tested the wind for his scent.

. . .

The state trooper asked her questions, and the woman who cleaned house for the priest translated them into Yupik. They wanted to know what happened to the storeman, the Gussuck who had been seen running after her down the road onto the river late last evening. He had not come back, and the Gussuck boss in Anchorage was concerned about him. She did not answer for a long time because the old man suddenly sat up in his bed and began to talk excitedly, looking at all of them—the trooper in his dark glasses and the housekeeper in her corduroy parka. He kept saying, "The story! The story! Eh-ya! The great bear! The hunter!"

They asked her again, what happened to the man from the Northern Commercial store. "He lied to them. He told them it was safe to drink. But I will not lie." She stood up and put on the gray wolfskin parka. "I killed him," she said, "but I don't lie."

. . .

The attorney came back again, and the jailer slid open the steel doors and opened the cell to let him in. He motioned for the jailer to stay to translate for him. She laughed when she saw how the jailer would be forced by this Gussuck to speak Yupik to her. She liked the Gussuck attorney for that, and for the thinning hair on his head. He was very tall, and she liked to think about the exposure of his head to the freezing; she wondered if he would feel the ice descending from the sky before the others did. He wanted to know why she told the state trooper she had killed the storeman. Some village children had seen it happen, he said, and it was an accident. "That's all you have to say to the judge: it was an accident." He kept repeating it over and over again to her, slowly in a loud but gentle voice: "It was an accident. He was running after you and he fell through the ice. That's all you have to say in court. That's all. And they will let you go home. Back to your village." The jailer translated the words sullenly, staring down at the floor. She shook her head. "I will not change the story, not even to escape this place and go home. I intended that he die. The story must be told as it is." The attorney exhaled loudly; his eyes looked tired. "Tell her that she could not have killed him that way. He was a white man. He ran after her without a parka or mittens. She could not have planned that." He paused and turned toward the cell door. "Tell her I will do all I can for her. I will explain to the judge that her mind is confused." She laughed out loud when the jailer translated what the attorney had said. The Gussucks did not understand the story; they could not see the way it must be told, year after year as the old man had done, without lapse or silence.

She looked out the window at the frozen white sky. The sun had finally broken loose from the ice but it moved like a wounded caribou running on strength which only dying animals find, leaping and running on bullet-shattered lungs. Its light was weak and pale; it pushed dimly through the clouds. She turned and faced the Gussuck attorney.

"It began a long time ago," she intoned steadily, "in the summertime. Early in the morning, I remember, something red in the tall river grass. . . ."

. . .

The day after the old man died, men from the village came. She was sitting on the edge of her bed, across from the woman the trooper hired to watch her. They came into the room slowly and listened to her. At the foot of her bed they left a king salmon that had been slit open wide and dried last summer. But she did not pause or hesitate; she went on with the story, and she never stopped, not even when the woman got up to close the door behind the village men.

. . .

The old man would not change the story even when he knew the end was approaching. Lies could not stop what was coming. He thrashed around on the bed, pulling the blankets loose, knocking bundles of dried fish and meat on the floor. The hunter had been on the ice for many hours. The freezing winds on the ice knoll had numbed his hands in the mittens, and the cold had exhausted him. He felt a single muscle tremor in his hand that he could not stop, and the jade knife fell; it shattered on the ice, and the blue glacier bear turned slowly to face him.

1975

CHERRÍE MORAGA
(1952–)

Cherríe Moraga emerged in the 1980s as an important feminist voice and a force behind the publication of writings by Chicanas. A founder of Kitchen Table: Women of Color Press, she is the co-editor of This Bridge Called My Back: Writings by Radical Women of Color *and* Cuentos: Stories by Latinas.

Born in Whittier, California, in 1952 to a Chicana mother and an Anglo father, Moraga describes her childhood in poems, essays, and short fiction that she has collected in Loving in the War Years: Lo Que Nunca Paso Por Sus Labios *and* Giving Up the Ghost. *Her play* Shadow of a Man *was acclaimed when it opened in San Francisco in 1990. One of the first in her family to earn a college degree, Moraga also received an M.A. from San Francisco State University. She has lived and taught in Boston and New York. Currently she teaches Chicano studies at the University of California, Berkeley.*

Much of her work deals with the tension between her two worlds: her Mexican American family and her lesbian-feminist community. "It is difficult for me to separate in my mind whether it is my writing or my lesbianism which has made me an outsider to my family," she has written. "The obvious answer is both. For my lesbianism first brought me into writing." On the other hand, throughout her writing, Moraga challenges white, middle-class assumptions in the feminist community. She weaves back and forth between Spanish and English, while at the same time rejecting "double-talk": "I refuse to let anybody's *movement determine for me what is safe and fair to say."*

The legend of the Aztec princess Malinche serves as a mythic underpinning in Moraga's work. As a translator, adviser, and mistress to the Spanish conqueror Cortez, Malinche is blamed by scholars for the destruction of the Indian culture and people of Mexico. Called "La Vendida," Malinche embodies Moraga's fear that she too might be seen as "a traitor to her race." As she has written, "I must, like other Chicanas before me, examine the effects this myth has on my/our racial/sexual identity and my relationship with other Chicanas."

"Pesadilla" is taken from Loving in the War Years. *Characteristic of Moraga's style, the story shifts between English and Spanish in its blending of analysis and fiction. The nightmare the title refers to is the potential for poverty, racism, and misogyny to infect the lesbian relationship between two women of color.*

PESADILLA

There came the day when Cecilia began to think about color.

. . .

Not the color of trees or painted billboards or the magnificent spreads of color laid down upon the hundreds of Victorians that lined the streets of her hometown city. She began to think about skin color. And the thought took hold of her and would not give; would not let loose. So that every person—man, woman, and child—had its particular grade of shade. And that fact meant all the difference in the world.

Soon her body began to change with this way of seeing. She felt her skin, like a casing, a beige bag into which the guts of her life were poured. And inside it, she swam through her day. Upstream. Downtown. Underground. Always, the shell of this skin, leading her around.

So that nothing seemed fair to her anymore: the war, the rent, the prices, the weather. And it spoiled her time.

Then one day, color moved in with her. Or, at least, that was how she thought of it when the going was the roughest between her and her love. That was how she thought of it after the animal had come and left. Splattered himself all around their new apartment or really the old apartment they had broken their backs to make liveable.

. . .

After brushing their way out the front door, leaving the last coat of varnish on the hard-wood floor to dry, Cecilia and Deborah had for the first time in weeks given themselves the afternoon off. They returned in the early evening, exhausted from the heat, and the crowds, and the noise of the subways and slowly began the long trek up to their sixth-floor apartment. *Why couldn't we have found an apartment with an elevator in the building,* Cecilia thought each time she found herself at the bottom of the stairs, arms full of packages, staring up at the long journey ahead of her. But no, *this* was the apartment they had wanted—the one they believed their love could rescue from its previous incarnation.

The woman who lived there before them was said to have had five dogs and five children, crowded into the one bedroom apartment. Each time Juanito came by from across the hall to spy on them at work, he had a different version to tell of "La Loca" who had lived there before them. "She was evicted," he would announce, almost proudly, with all the authority an eight-year-old can muster, puffing out his bare brown chest. "She was so dirty, you could smell it down to the basement!"

The signs of filth, yes, still remained. But *that* Cecilia and Deborah believed they could remove—under coats of paint and plaster. The parts of broken toys found in the corners of cupboards, children's crayola markings on the wall, torn pieces of teenage magazines stuck up with dust-covered strips of scotch tape—all indicated too many people in too small a space. *¿Quién sabe la pena que sufría esa mujer?* Cecilia thought.

It was the woman's rage, however, that could not be washed out of the apartment walls. There was no obliterating from Cecilia's mind the smell and sight of the dogfood she had found stuffed into the mouth of the bathroom sink—red and raw in its anger. As Cecilia scraped it out—"¡La Mierda del-mundo que coma mierda!"—she tried not to believe that all this was the bad omen she suddenly felt rising hot and thick in her throat.

Finally, making it up to the sixth floor landing, the two women dropped their bags, exhausted, and Cecilia drew her keys out from her purse. But before she could turn the key in the lock, the door easily gave way. She quickly tried to convince herself that yes, she had been negligent. The last to leave. The first to forget in her fatigue to secure the lock.

But she knew different. Entering the apartment, her heart pounding, Cecilia led the way down the long hallway—a dark labyrinth to the pesadilla that awaited them. At the end of it, she could see their bedroom, the light burning. A tornado had hit it!

No, this was not the result of some faceless natural disaster. This was a live and breathing thing. An animal. An animal had broken in.

And the women broke down. *What kind of beast* they cried *would do this?* His parts drawn all over their freshly painted walls for them to see and suck and that's what he told them there on the wall

SUCK MY DICK YOU HOLE

He had wanted money and finding no such thing, but a picture of a woman who could have been a sister or a lover or a momma and no sign of man around, he wrote:

I'M BLACK YOU MOTHERFUCKER BITCH
YOU BUTCH

And Cecilia knew if he had had the time and sense enough he would have even written her lover's name out there upon the bedroom wall.

He wanted Dee, too. Even in his hatred, he wanted Cecilia's lover. Everybody, it seemed, had *something* to say about Deborah's place on the planet.

Seeing his scratches on the wall, both women knew they were very close to giving it up altogether. Cecilia closing up the thought just as it broke open inside her. Closing in on Deborah, she brought the woman into her arms and they fell against the wall, crying. The animal's scrawl disappearing behind them.

It was the first time in their life together that Cecilia wondered if she were up to the task of such loving.

It had scarcely been a week since they had carried down their five flights of stairs the last torn-up suitcase of the animal's debris. They needed the rest, the relief from the city and found it in the home of friends by the Hudson, drinking iced seltzer with lime in the bake of the sun. The violation, a million miles away from the one hour's drive out of town.

Dee grew blacker as she slept on the deck. And when Cecilia rose to refill her glass it took the greatest rigidity of spine *not* to bend down and kiss the wet and shining neck of the woman stretched out before her, sound asleep.

Cecilia wanted her. She was afraid to want her.

Closing the sliding glass door behind her, the house hit Cecilia with a cool that she had nearly forgotten in the heavy humidity of the city. Even the city park could not provide this quality of coolness—cement blocks hovering around it on all fours. This was the kind of coolness that only grew from a ground now hollowed out by tunnels and steaming underground trains.

Berkeley. It reminded her of the hills of Berkeley. The blend of drying jasmine and eucalyptus hot-whipped into a cloudless sky, the scent carrying itself into the bay.

In Brooklyn, she still found it hard to believe she lived by the water. The tops of neighboring ships were to her merely another line of differently shaped structures rising up from the stiff water-floor. The real mother ocean was three thousand miles behind her.

The kitchen was flooded with sunlight and houseplants—those that hung and those that seemed to grow right out from under the linoleum floor. Cecilia found herself breathing more deeply than she had in months. She felt calmer somehow. A feeling she had left somewhere, she thought, *back in california.*

But what? . . . What exactly *was it?*

The smell?

The light? She held the bottle to pour. *Yes, both these things, but . . .* "Salud." She mimed a toast in the air, pushing back the thought coming at her, her heart speeding up.

It was . . . white.

It was whiteness and . . . safety.

Old lovers that carried their whiteness like freedom/and breath/and light. Their shoulders, always straight-backed and sweetly oiled for color. In their faces, the luxury of trust.

It was whiteness and money.

In this way, she had learned to be a lesbian. Not that any of her friends actually had cash on hand. In fact, she was the one among them who came from the least, but who always seemed to have the most—the one that always managed to find something "steady." But there was the ambience of money: the trips cross-country, the constant career changes, the pure cotton clothing, and yes, the sunshine. In her memory, it was never dark, except at night when it was always quiet and nearly suburban.

But the feeling she remembered most, the feeling that she could not shake, was of some other presence living amongst them. Some white man somewhere—their names always mono-syllabled: Tom, Dick, Jack. Like boys, flat-topped and tough—cropping up in a photograph, a telephone call, a letter, who in the crunch, would be their ticket.

Nobody would have said that then (or even thought of it that way). Cecilia certainly wouldn't have. But she could see it now, now that they were gone—the man's threatening and benevolent presence living with them all. They were his daughters after all, as long as they remained without a man.

Blood is blood.

It was that night that Deborah had her attack (or "fit" as Deborah used to describe them, mimicking some 1930 sci-fi version of epileptics or schizophrenics). It was the first time Cecilia had ever witnessed one in Dee, although for years Dee had spoken of them, sometimes beneath a rush of tears.

Standing on her knees in bed, she would go through the motions once again of the man coming down on her with the back of his hand. The hand enlarging as it advanced—broad and blacker than she's ever seen it. "That's when my fits began," she'd say, then suddenly, "Blahblahblah-blahblah-blahblah! Po' lil cullud girl, me!"

He was the second and last man her mother kicked out.

("My babies come first." Both their mommas could have been found saying the same thing, wrists bent back into hipbones. That's what had brought them together—the dark, definite women of their childhood.)

But that night, there was no joking. Waking to Deborah's absence in the bed, Cecilia quickly got up and, entering the bathroom, found her lover thrown back against the tank of the toilet, mouth open, unconscious.

It was not how Cecilia had imagined it. No tongue-gagging. No gutteral sounds, no jerking movements. No joke.

Gathering the dead weight into her arms, Cecilia brought the heavy head to her chest, holding it there. The weight like a hot rock against her breastbone—the same shape of the fear now forming inside her heart.

And then, as if she had rehearsed the role, she began to rock the body. And the more she rocked, the more the motion slowly began to dissolve the stone inside her chest and allowed, finally for her tears to come. She rocked. She cried. "Oh Deborah, baby, wake up!" She cried, "¡Por Favor, despiértate! ¡Chula, por favor!" She rocked. Until at last, she felt the head stiffen and pull away.

"Get my pills," Deborah moaned.

Cecilia rushed back into the bedroom and began rumaging around in Deborah's bag, trying frantically to find the pills, finally dumping the entire contents onto the floor. There on her knees she felt something turn in her. She felt her heart like a steel clamp inside her chest, twisting what was only moments ago a living beating fear into a slow cool numbing between her breasts.

Her loving couldn't change a thing.

Cecilia remembered the first time she had ever felt this same sensation of "coldness." Her memory rushing back in flashes to the picture of a woman, her mother, elbows dug into the kitchen table, yellow, the photograph curled into her hand, yellow too, tears streaming down her cheeks.

Again. A river return.

A river whose pull always before that moment had swept Cecilia off her chair and into her mother's arms.

But on that particular day, Cecilia stepped outside the circle of pain her mother drew like hot liquid into the little girl's body. The mother's tears comingling with her own, like communion.

Cecilia didn't understand why her feelings were changing, only that they had to change. *Change or die,* she thought. And suddenly she grew stiff and fixed in her chair, hands pressed between her knees, riveted against the tide of rage and regret she knew her mother memories would call forth. Old wounds still oozing with the blood of sinners in wartime.

"I forgive," her mother would announce. "But I never forget."

And mustering up what courage she could, the girl first whispered to herself, then shouted outloud, "You gotta change, Mama! You gotta let it go!"

When she didn't change. When Cecilia had prayed and pleaded, practiced and preached every form of childish support she could think of, she left the woman. It was years later, but she took a walk right out of that kitchen and family-way of passing on daughter-to-daughter misery. Her momma cursing after her, "You're just like the rest of 'em. You don't know how to love."

"Honey? Are you coming?"

"Yeah, right away, baby." Cecilia grabbed the pills and came back into the bathroom to find Deborah now with eyes open and blinking alive. But Cecilia couldn't rid herself of the feeling in her chest. It was as if a different woman had stepped back into the room and Cecilia now stood somewhere else, outside the room, watching this other one nurse her lover back to health. In silence, giving Deborah the pills. In silence, moving her back to bed. In silence, watching her fall into a deep and exhausted sleep.

Lying awake in bed, the sunlight cracking through the window, Cecilia thought of the times as a child when she always lived her nights like days while the rest of the house slept. Never soundly sleeping like the woman now curled under her arm.

Getting up six and seven times a night, locking and re-locking the doors. Praying in whispers the same prayers over and over and over again, nodding into sleep, resisting. Resisting the pictures the dreams would bring. The women, wanting. The men, like flaming devils, swollen with desire.

Locking and re-locking the doors. Keeping the fearful out, while it wrestled inside her without restraint. During those hours before dawn, *anything* was possible—the darkness giving permission for the spirit to shake itself loose in Deborah.

Cecilia wanted Dee. She was afraid to want her. Afraid to feel another woman's body. Like family.

When she discovered the first woman wouldn't change, it had sort of wrapped things up for the rest of them. Still she'd go through the changes of asking for changes como su abuelita during the english mass mouthing spanish a million miles an hour, kissing the crucifix of the rosary wrapped 'round her neck at each and every "amen."

Nothing to disturb her order of things. No matter what was said or done in english, she knew the spanish by heart. In her heart, which long ago forgot the clear young reason for the kissings, the vicious beatings of the breast, the bending to someone else's will.

What frightened Cecilia so was to feel this gradual reawakening in her bones. For weeks her hands had merely skimmed her lover's flesh, never reaching in.

Cecilia pressed her nose into Dee's hair. The sun, almost full now in the window, had warmed the fibers into a cushion of heat which promised rest, continuance. In the intake of breath, there was more familiarity, more loss of resistance, more sense of landing *somewhere* than any naming she had tried to do with words inside her head.

Words were nothing to the smell.

Pesadilla.

There is a man on the fire escape. He is crouched just below the window sill. I could barely catch the curve of his back descending, but I have seen the movement. I know it is the animal, returned.

The figure suddenly rises to attack!

D E B O R A H ! !

The dark woman looking in through the glass is as frightened as I am. She is weeping. I will not let her in.

1979

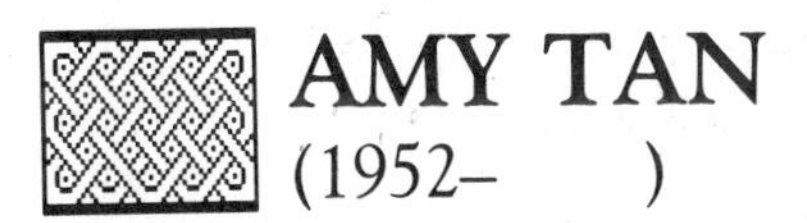

AMY TAN
(1952–)

With her novels The Joy Luck Club and The Kitchen God's Wife, Amy Tan joins a growing group of writers who are expressing what it means to be an American woman with Chinese ancestors. Although in some ways their experiences are similar to those of all immigrant Americans, Asian American women often encounter particularly painful conflicts of language and culture, many of which are dramatized in Tan's work.

Tan was born in Oakland, California, soon after her parents arrived from China. Her mother, who was born into a wealthy Shanghai family, left China after surviving a brutal first marriage. Her experiences in war-torn China are the subject of The Kitchen God's Wife. Tan's father, an electrical engineer and a Baptist minister, died when Tan was fifteen; however, during her childhood he introduced her to a wide range of Western and Chinese tales that became part of her development as a writer.

While growing up in the United States, Tan says she despised her Asian features and heritage. She was unable to accept her cultural identity until her teens, when she lived for a few years in Europe. However, even into her thirties, she has said, "there was shame and self-hate." Her mother, like some of the ambitious mothers in Tan's fiction, had a brilliant career in mind for her daughter: in an interview, Tan recounts with a smile that her mother wanted her to become a neurosurgeon while being a concert pianist on the side. Now, whenever Tan receives an award for her writing, she says, "I give it to my mother."

Tan won a writing contest when she was eight years old, and earned a B.A. in English and an M.A. in linguistics from San Francisco State University. She turned her writing skills toward technical and business writing as an adult. However, upon reading Louise Erdrich's Love Medicine, featuring stories told by different generations of Native Americans, Tan became captivated with the idea of depicting the tragedies and comedies of her own divided culture. As a result of the critical and financial success of The Joy Luck Club and The Kitchen God's Wife—both best-sellers—she now writes fiction full-time.

The Joy Luck Club is a series of stories focusing on four Chinese-born women, the "club" members who meet to play mah-jongg, and their American-born daughters. The stories dramatize conflicts between cultures and between mothers and daughters while providing intimate looks into the lives of Asian American families. Formed initially to ward off the horrors of war in China, the Joy Luck Club now acts to help preserve the memories and the culture being eroded by life in America.

The selection included here, originally published as a short story, became a chapter in The Joy Luck Club. *In "Rules of the Game," the reader sees into the life of a Chinese American girl—her relationships with her siblings and adults and the success that brings her into painful conflict with her mother.*

from THE JOY LUCK CLUB

Rules of the Game

I was six when my mother taught me the art of invisible strength. It was a strategy for winning arguments, respect from others, and eventually, though neither of us knew it at the time, chess games.

"Bite back your tongue," scolded my mother when I cried loudly, yanking her hand toward the store that sold bags of salted plums. At home, she said, "Wise guy, he not go against wind. In Chinese we say, Come from South, blow with wind—poom!—North will follow. Strongest wind cannot be seen."

The next week I bit back my tongue as we entered the store with the forbidden candies. When my mother finished her shopping, she quietly plucked a small bag of plums from the rack and put it on the counter with the rest of the items.

. . .

My mother imparted her daily truths so she could help my older brothers and me rise above our circumstances. We lived in San Francisco's Chinatown. Like most of the other Chinese children who played in the back alleys of restaurants and curio shops, I didn't think we were poor. My bowl was always full, three five-course meals every day, beginning with a soup full of mysterious things I didn't want to know the names of.

We lived on Waverly Place, in a warm, clean, two-bedroom flat that sat above a small Chinese bakery specializing in steamed pastries and dim sum. In the early morning, when the alley was still quiet, I could smell fragrant red beans as they were cooked down to a pasty sweetness. By daybreak, our flat was heavy with the odor of fried sesame balls and sweet curried chicken crescents. From my bed, I would listen as my father got ready for work, then locked the door behind him, one-two-three clicks.

At the end of our two-block alley was a small sandlot playground with swings and slides well-shined down the middle with use. The play area was bordered by wood-slat benches where old-country people sat cracking roasted watermelon seeds with their golden teeth and scattering the husks to an impatient gathering of gurgling pigeons. The best playground, however, was the dark alley itself. It was crammed with daily mysteries and adventures. My brothers and I would peer into the medicinal herb shop, watching old Li dole out onto a stiff sheet of white paper the right amount of insect shells, saffron-colored seeds, and pungent leaves for his ailing customers. It was said that he once cured a woman dying of an ancestral curse that had eluded the best of American doctors. Next to the pharmacy was a printer who specialized in gold-embossed wedding invitations and festive red banners.

Farther down the street was Ping Yuen Fish Market. The front window displayed a tank crowded with doomed fish and turtles struggling to gain footing on the slimy green-tiled sides. A hand-written sign informed tourists, "Within this store, is all for food, not for pet." Inside, the butchers with their blood-stained white smocks deftly gutted the fish while customers cried out their orders and shouted, "Give me your freshest," to which the butchers always protested, "All are freshest." On less crowded market days, we would inspect the crates of live frogs and crabs which we were warned not to poke, boxes of dried cuttlefish, and row upon row of iced prawns, squid, and slippery fish. The sanddabs made me shiver each time; their eyes lay on one flattened side and reminded me of my mother's story of a careless girl who ran into a crowded street and was crushed by a cab. "Was smash flat," reported my mother.

At the corner of the alley was Hong Sing's, a four-table café with a recessed stairwell in front that led to a door marked "Tradesmen." My brothers and I believed the bad people emerged from this door at night. Tourists never went to Hong Sing's, since the menu was printed only in Chinese. A Caucasian man with a big camera once posed me and my playmates in front of the restaurant. He had us move to the side of the picture window so the photo would capture the roasted duck with its head dangling from a juice-covered rope. After he took the picture, I told him he should go into Hong Sing's and eat dinner. When he smiled and asked me what they served, I shouted, "Guts and duck's feet and octopus gizzards!" Then I ran off with my friends, shrieking with laughter as we scampered across the alley and hid in the entryway grotto of the China Gem Company, my heart pounding with hope that he would chase us.

My mother named me after the street that we lived on: Waverly Place Jong, my official name for important American documents. But my family called me Meimei, "Little Sister." I was the youngest, the only daughter. Each morning before school, my mother would twist and yank on my thick black hair until she had formed two tightly wound pigtails. One day, as she struggled to weave a hard-toothed comb through my disobedient hair, I had a sly thought.

I asked her, "Ma, what is Chinese torture?" My mother shook her head. A bobby pin was wedged between her lips. She wetted her palm and smoothed the hair above my ear, then pushed the pin in so that it nicked sharply against my scalp.

"Who say this word?" she asked without a trace of knowing how wicked I was being. I shrugged my shoulders and said, "Some boy in my class said Chinese people do Chinese torture."

"Chinese people do many things," she said simply. "Chinese people do business, do medicine, do painting. Not lazy like American people. We do torture. Best torture."

. . .

My older brother Vincent was the one who actually got the chess set. We had gone to the annual Christmas party held at the Finest Chinese Baptist Church at the end of the alley. The missionary ladies had put together a Santa bag of gifts donated by members of another church. None of the gifts had names on them. There were separate sacks for boys and girls of different ages.

One of the Chinese parishioners had donned a Santa Claus costume and a stiff paper beard with cotton balls glued to it. I think the only children who thought he was the real thing were too young to know that Santa Claus was not Chinese. When my turn came up, the Santa man asked me how old I was. I though it was a trick question; I was seven according to the American formula and eight by the Chinese calendar. I said I was born on March 17, 1951. That seemed to satisfy him. He then solemnly asked if I had been a very, very good girl this year and did I believe in Jesus Christ and obey my parents. I knew the only answer to that. I nodded back with equal solemnity.

Having watched the other children opening their gifts, I already knew that the big gifts were not necessarily the nicest ones. One girl my age got a large coloring book of biblical characters, while a less greedy girl who selected a smaller box received a glass vial of lavender toilet water. The sound of the box was also important. A ten-year-old boy had chosen a box that jangled when he shook it. It was a tin globe of the world with a slit for inserting money. He must have thought it was full of dimes and nickels, because when he saw that it had just ten pennies, his face fell with such undisguised disappointment that his mother slapped the side of his head and led him out of the church hall, apologizing to the crowd for her son who had such bad manners he couldn't appreciate such a fine gift.

As I peered into the sack, I quickly fingered the remaining presents, testing their weight, imagining what they contained. I chose a heavy, compact one that was wrapped in shiny silver foil and a red satin ribbon. It was a twelve-pack of Life Savers and I spent the rest of the party arranging and rearranging the candy tubes in the order of my favorites. My brother Winston chose wisely as well. His present turned out to be a box of intricate plastic parts; the instructions on the box proclaimed that when they were properly assembled he would have an authentic miniature replica of a World War II submarine.

Vincent got the chess set, which would have been a very decent present to get at a church Christmas party, except it was obviously used and, as we discovered later, it was missing a black pawn and a white knight. My mother graciously thanked the unknown benefactor, saying, "Too good. Cost too much." At which point, an old lady with fine white, wispy hair nodded toward our family and said with a whistling whisper, "Merry, merry Christmas."

When we got home, my mother told Vincent to throw the chess set away. "She not want it. We not want it," she said, tossing her head stiffly to the side with a tight, proud smile. My brothers had deaf ears. They were already lining up the chess pieces and reading from the dog-eared instruction book.

. . .

I watched Vincent and Winston play during Christmas week. The chess board seemed to hold elaborate secrets waiting to be untangled. The chessmen were more powerful than Old Li's magic herbs that cured ancestral curses. And my brothers wore such serious faces that I was sure something was at stake that was greater than avoiding the tradesmen's door to Hong Sing's.

"Let me! Let me!" I begged between games when one brother or the other would sit back with a deep sigh of relief and victory, the other annoyed, unable to let go of the outcome. Vincent at first refused to let me play, but when I offered my Life Savers as replacements for the buttons that filled in for the missing pieces, he relented. He chose the flavors: wild cherry for the black pawn and peppermint for the white knight. Winner could eat both.

As our mother sprinkled flour and rolled out small doughy circles for the steamed dumplings that would be our dinner that night, Vincent explained the rules, pointing to each piece. "You have sixteen pieces and so do I. One king and queen, two bishops, two knights, two castles, and eight pawns. The pawns can only move forward one step, except on the first move. Then they can move two. But they can only take men by moving crossways like this, except in the beginning, when you can move ahead and take another pawn."

"Why?" I asked as I moved my pawn. "Why can't they move more steps?"

"Because they're pawns," he said.

"But why do they go crossways to take other men? Why aren't there any women and children?"

"Why is the sky blue? Why must you always ask stupid questions?" asked Vincent. "This is a game. These are the rules. I didn't make them up. See. Here. In the book." He jabbed a page with a pawn in his hand. "Pawn. P-A-W-N. Pawn. Read it yourself."

My mother patted the flour off her hands. "Let me see book," she said quietly. She scanned the pages quickly, not reading the foreign English symbols, seeming to search deliberately for nothing in particular.

"This American rules," she concluded at last. "Every time people come out from foreign country, must know rules. You not know, judge say, Too bad, go back. They not telling you why so you can use their way go forward. They say, Don't know why, you find out yourself. But they knowing all the time. Better you take it, find out why yourself." She tossed her head back with a satisfied smile.

I found out about all the whys later. I read the rules and looked up all the big words in a dictionary. I borrowed books from the Chinatown library. I studied each chess piece, trying to absorb the power each contained.

I learned about opening moves and why it's important to control the center early on; the shortest distance between two points is straight down the middle. I learned about the middle game and why tactics between two adversaries are like clashing ideas; the one who plays better has the clearest plans for both attacking and getting out of traps. I learned why it is essential in the endgame to have foresight, a mathematical understanding of all possible moves, and patience; all weaknesses and advantages become evident to a strong adversary and are obscured to a tiring opponent. I discovered that for the whole game one must gather invisible strengths and see the endgame before the game begins.

I also found out why I should never reveal "why" to others. A little knowledge withheld is a great advantage one should store for future use. That is the power of chess. It is a game of secrets in which one must show and never tell.

I loved the secrets I found within the sixty-four black and white squares. I carefully drew a handmade chessboard and pinned it to the wall next to my bed, where at night I would stare for hours at imaginary battles. Soon I no longer lost any games or Life Savers, but I lost my adversaries. Winston and Vincent decided they were more interested in roaming the streets after school in their Hopalong Cassidy cowboy hats.

. . .

On a cold spring afternoon, while walking home from school, I detoured through the playground at the end of our alley. I saw a group of old men, two seated across a folding table playing a game of chess, others smoking pipes, eating peanuts, and watching. I ran home and grabbed Vincent's chess set, which was bound in a cardboard box with rubber bands. I also carefully selected two prized rolls of Life Savers. I came back to the park and approached a man who was observing the game.

"Want to play?" I asked him. His face widened with surprise and he grinned as he looked at the box under my arm.

"Little sister, been a long time since I play with dolls," he said, smiling benevolently. I quickly put the box down next to him on the bench and displayed my retort.

Lau Po, as he allowed me to call him, turned out to be a much better player than my brothers. I lost many games and many Life Savers. But over the weeks, with each diminishing roll of candies, I added new secrets. Lau Po gave me the names. The Double Attack from the East and West Shores. Throwing Stones on the Drowning Man. The Sudden Meeting of the Clan. The Surprise from the Sleeping Guard. The Humble Servant Who Kills the King. Sand in the Eyes of Advancing Forces. A Double Killing Without Blood.

There were also the fine points of chess etiquette. Keep captured men in neat rows, as well-tended prisoners. Never announce "Check" with vanity, lest someone with an unseen sword slit your throat. Never hurl pieces into the sandbox after you have lost a game, because then you must find them again, by yourself, after apologizing to all around you. By the end of the summer, Lau Po had taught me all he knew, and I had become a better chess player.

A small weekend crowd of Chinese people and tourists would gather as I played and defeated my opponents one by one. My mother would join the crowds during these outdoor exhibition games. She sat proudly on the bench, telling my admirers with proper Chinese humility, "Is luck."

A man who watched me play in the park suggested that my mother allow me to play in local chess tournaments. My mother smiled graciously, an answer that meant nothing. I desperately wanted to go, but I bit back my tongue. I knew she would not let me play among strangers. So as we walked home I said in a small voice that I didn't want to play in the local tournament. They would have American rules. If I lost, I would bring shame on my family.

"Is shame you fall down nobody push you," said my mother.

During my first tournament, my mother sat with me in the front row as I waited for my turn. I frequently bounced my legs to unstick them from the cold metal seat of the folding chair. When my name was called, I leapt up. My mother unwrapped something in her lap. It was her *chang,* a small tablet of red jade which held the sun's fire. "Is luck," she whispered, and tucked it into my dress pocket. I turned to my opponent, a fifteen-year-old boy from Oakland. He looked at me, wrinkling his nose.

As I began to play, the boy disappeared, the color ran out of the room, and I saw only my white pieces and his black ones waiting on the other side. A light wind began blowing past my ears. It whispered secrets only I could hear.

"Blow from the South," it murmured. "The wind leaves no trail." I saw a clear path, the traps to avoid. The crowd rustled. "Shhh! Shhh!" said the corners of the room. The wind blew stronger. "Throw sand from the East to distract him." The knight came forward ready for the sacrifice. The wind hissed, louder and louder. "Blow, blow, blow. He cannot see. He is blind now. Make him lean away from the wind so he is easier to knock down."

"Check," I said, as the wind roared with laughter. The wind died down to little puffs, my own breath.

. . .

My mother placed my first trophy next to a new plastic chess set that the neighborhood Tao society had given to me. As she wiped each piece with a soft cloth, she said, "Next time win more, lose less."

"Ma, it's not how many pieces you lose," I said. "Sometimes you need to lose pieces to get ahead."

"Better to lose less, see if you really need."

At the next tournament, I won again, but it was my mother who wore the triumphant grin.

"Lost eight piece this time. Last time was eleven. What I tell you? Better off lose less!" I was annoyed, but I couldn't say anything.

I attended more tournaments, each one farther away from home. I won all games, in all divisions. The Chinese bakery downstairs from our flat displayed my growing collection of trophies in its window, amidst the dust-covered cakes that were never picked up. The day after I won an important regional tournament, the window encased a fresh sheet cake with whipped-cream frosting and red script saying, "Congratulations, Waverly Jong, Chinatown Chess Champion." Soon after that, a flower shop, headstone engraver, and funeral parlor offered to sponsor me in national tournaments. That's when my mother decided I no longer had to do the dishes. Winston and Vincent had to do my chores.

"Why does she get to play and we do all the work," complained Vincent.

"Is new American rules," said my mother. "Meimei play, squeeze all her brains out for win chess. You play, worth squeeze towel."

By my ninth birthday, I was a national chess champion. I was still some 429 points away from grand-master status, but I was touted as the Great American Hope, a child prodigy and a girl to boot. They ran a photo of me in *Life* magazine next to a quote in which Bobby Fischer said, "There will never be a woman grand master." "Your move, Bobby," said the caption.

The day they took the magazine picture I wore neatly plaited braids clipped with plastic barrettes trimmed with rhinestones. I was playing in a large high school auditorium that echoed with phlegmy coughs and the squeaky rubber knobs of chair legs sliding across freshly waxed wooden floors. Seated across from me was an American man, about the same age as Lau Po, maybe fifty. I remember that his sweaty brow seemed to weep at my every move. He wore a dark, malodorous suit. One of his pockets was stuffed with a great white kerchief on which he wiped his palm before sweeping his hand over the chosen chess piece with great flourish.

In my crisp pink-and-white dress with scratchy lace at the neck, one of two my mother had sewn for these special occasions, I would clasp my hands under my chin, the delicate points of my elbows poised lightly on the table in the manner my mother had shown me for posing for the press. I would swing my patent leather shoes back and forth like an impatient child riding on a school bus. Then I would pause, suck in my lips, twirl my chosen piece in midair as if undecided, and then firmly plant it in its new threatening place, with a triumphant smile thrown back at my opponent for good measure.

. . .

I no longer played in the alley of Waverly Place. I never visited the playground where the pigeons and old men gathered. I went to school, then directly home to learn new chess secrets, cleverly concealed advantages, more escape routes.

But I found it difficult to concentrate at home. My mother had a habit of standing over me while I plotted out my games. I think she thought of herself as my protective ally. Her lips would be sealed tight, and after each move I made, a soft "Hmmmmph" would escape from her nose.

"Ma, I can't practice when you stand there like that," I said one day. She retreated to the kitchen and made loud noises with the pots and pans.

When the crashing stopped, I could see out of the corner of my eye that she was standing in the doorway. "Hmmmph!" Only this one came out of her tight throat.

My parents made many concessions to allow me to practice. One time I complained that the bedroom I shared was so noisy that I couldn't think. Thereafter, my brothers slept in a bed in the living room facing the street. I said I couldn't finish my rice; my head didn't work right when my stomach was too full. I left the table with half-finished bowls and nobody complained. But there was one duty I couldn't avoid. I had to accompany my mother on Saturday market days when I had no tournament to play. My mother would proudly walk with me, visiting many shops, buying very little. "This my daughter Wave-ly Jong," she said to whoever looked her way.

One day, after we left a shop I said under my breath, "I wish you wouldn't do that, telling everybody I'm your daughter." My mother stopped walking. Crowds of people with heavy bags pushed past us on the sidewalk, bumping into first one shoulder, then another.

"Aiii-ya. So shame be with mother?" She grasped my hand even tighter as she glared at me.

I looked down. "It's not that, it's just so obvious. It's just so embarrassing."

"Embarrass you be my daughter?" Her voice was cracking with anger.

"That's not what I meant. That's not what I said."

"What you say?"

I knew it was a mistake to say anything more, but I heard my voice speaking. "Why do you have to use me to show off? If you want to show off, then why don't you learn to play chess?"

My mother's eyes turned into dangerous black slits. She had no words for me, just sharp silence.

I felt the wind rushing around my hot ears. I jerked my hand out of my mother's tight grasp and spun around, knocking into an old woman. Her bag of groceries spilled to the ground.

"Aii-ya! Stupid girl!" my mother and the woman cried. Oranges and tin cans careened down the sidewalk. As my mother stooped to help the old woman pick up the escaping food, I took off.

I raced down the street, dashing between people, not looking back as my mother screamed shrilly, "Meimei! Meimei!" I fled down an alley, past dark curtained shops and merchants washing the grime off their windows. I sped into the sunlight, into a large street crowded with tourists examining trinkets and souvenirs. I ducked into another dark alley, down another street, up another alley. I ran until it hurt and I realized I had nowhere to go, that I was not running from anything. The alleys contained no escape routes.

My breath came out like angry smoke. It was cold. I sat down on an upturned plastic pail next to a stack of empty boxes, cupping my chin with my hands, thinking hard. I imagined my mother, first walking briskly down one street or another looking for me, then giving up and returning home to await my arrival. After two hours, I stood up on creaking legs and slowly walked home.

The alley was quiet and I could see the yellow lights shining from our flat like two tiger's eyes in the night. I climbed the sixteen steps to the door, advancing quietly up each so as not to make any warning sounds. I turned the knob; the door was locked. I heard the chair moving, quick steps, the locks turning—click! click! click!—and then the door opened.

"About time you got home," said Vincent. "Boy, are you in trouble."

He slid back to the dinner table. On a platter were the remains of a large fish, its fleshy head still connected to bones swimming upstream in vain escape. Standing there waiting for my punishment, I heard my mother speak in a dry voice.

"We not concerning this girl. This girl not have concerning for us."

Nobody looked at me. Bone chopsticks clinked against the insides of bowls being emptied into hungry mouths.

I walked into my room, closed the door, and lay down on my bed. The room was dark, the ceiling filled with shadows from the dinnertime lights of neighboring flats.

In my head, I saw a chessboard with sixty-four black and white squares. Opposite me was my opponent, two angry black slits. She wore a triumphant smile. "Strongest wind cannot be seen," she said.

Her black men advanced across the plane, slowly marching to each successive level as a single unit. My white pieces screamed as they scurried and fell off the board one by one. As her men drew closer to my edge, I felt myself growing light. I rose up into the air and flew out the window. Higher and higher, above the alley, over the tops of tiled roofs, where I was gathered up by the wind and pushed up toward the sky until everything below me disappeared and I was alone.

I closed my eyes and pondered my next move.

1986

LOUISE ERDRICH
(1954–   )

Louise Erdrich's first novel, Love Medicine, *established her in the forefront of a new generation of Native American writers. Like the writing of N. Scott Momaday and Leslie Marmon Silko, her fiction looks squarely at Native American life in a postindustrial world. Her first three novels tell the generational story of a mixed-race family.* American Horse, *her fourth novel, traces this family of characters from 1972 to the present. Although she is the author of two volumes of poetry,* Jacklight *and* Baptism of Desire, *Erdrich prefers fiction, which allows her a wider canvas.*

Born in Little Falls, Minnesota, Erdrich grew up around Wahpeton, North Dakota, where both parents worked for the Bureau of Indian Affairs. Her ancestors were German, French, and Turtle Mountain Chippewa. Raised as a Catholic, she spent a great deal of her childhood on the Turtle Mountain Reservation. She majored in English and creative writing at Dartmouth College, where she earned a B.A. in 1976. She went on to earn an M.A. in creative writing at Johns Hopkins University in 1977. After completing her formal education, she became editor of the Boston Indian Council newspaper, The Circle.

Erdrich points to her parents as important early supporters. Her father gave her a nickel for every story she wrote, and her mother sewed the stories into books. Thus encouraged, she felt like a published writer at a young age and developed a lasting interest in reading and writing. She also recalls family storytelling feeding her imagination. "Everybody in my whole family is a storyteller," she has said, "whether a liar or a storyteller—whatever. When I think what's a story, I can hear somebody in my family, my dad or my mom or my grandma, telling it." Indeed, the characters who populate her fiction spring from her own community; her strong female characters, she has pointed out, reflect strong women she has known: "We are taught to present a demure face to the world and yet there is a kind of energy behind it in many women that is transformational energy, and not only transforming to them but to other people."

Erdrich lives in Cornish, New Hampshire, with writer Michael Dorris—with whom she collaborates "in all aspects of writing and life"—and their children. The Crown of Columbus *is the first novel to appear with both their names.*

The selection included here first appeared in a slightly different version as "The Manifestation at Argus." It has been taken from Erdrich's second novel, The Beet Queen.

from THE BEET QUEEN
CHAPTER TWO *1932*

Sita Kozka

My cousin Mary came in on the early freight train one morning, with nothing but an old keepsake box full of worthless pins and buttons. My father picked her up in his arms and carried her down the hallway into the kitchen. I was too old to be carried. He sat her down, then my mother said, "Go clean the counters, Sita." So I don't know what lies she told them after that.

Later on that morning, my parents put her to sleep in my bed. When I objected to this, saying that she could sleep on the trundle, my mother said, "Cry sakes, you can sleep there too, you know." And this is how I ended up that night, crammed in the trundle, which is too short for me. I slept with my legs dangling out in the cold air. I didn't feel welcoming toward Mary the next morning, and who can blame me?

Besides, on her first waking day in Argus, there were the clothes.

It is a good thing she opened the blue keepsake box at breakfast and found little bits of trash, like I said, because if I had not felt sorry for my cousin that day, I would not have stood for Mary and my mother ripping through my closet and bureau. "This fits perfectly," my mother said, holding up one of my favorite blouses, "try it on!" And Mary did. Then she put it in her drawer, which was another thing. I had to clear out two of my bureau drawers for her.

"Mother," I said, after this had gone on for some time and I was beginning to think I would have to wear the same three outfits all the next school year, "Mother, this has really gone far enough."

"Crap," said my mother, who talks that way. "Your cousin hasn't got a stitch."

Yet she had half of mine by then, quite a wardrobe, and all the time it was increasing as my mother got more excited about dressing the poor orphan. But Mary wasn't really an orphan, although she played on that for sympathy. Her mother was still alive, even if she had left my cousin, which I doubted. I really thought that Mary just ran away from her mother because she could not appreciate Adelaide's style. It's not everyone who understands how to use their good looks to the best advantage. My Aunt Adelaide did. She was always my favorite, and I just died for her to visit. But she didn't come often because my mother couldn't understand style either.

"Who are you trying to impress?" she'd hoot when Adelaide came out to dinner in a dress with a fur collar. My father would blush red and cut his meat. He didn't say much, but I knew he did not approve of Adelaide any more than her older sister did. My mother said she'd always spoiled Adelaide because she was the baby of the family. She said the same of me. But I don't think that I was ever spoiled, not one iota, because I had to work the same as anyone cleaning gizzards.

I hated Wednesdays because that was the day we killed chickens. The farmer brought them stacked in cages made of thin wooden slats. One by one, Canute, who did most of the slaughtering, killed them by sticking their necks with the blade of his long knife. After the chickens were killed, plucked, and cut open, I got the gizzards. Coffee can after coffee can full of gizzards. I still have dreams. I had to turn each gizzard inside out and wash it in a pan of water. All the gravel and hard seed fell out into the bottom. Sometimes I found bits of metal and broken glass. Once I found a brilliant. "Mother!" I yelled, holding it out in my palm. "I found a diamond!" Everyone was so excited that they clustered around me. And then my mother took the little sparkling stone to the window. It didn't scratch the glass at all, of course, and I had to clean the rest of the gizzards. But for one brief moment I was sure the diamond had made us rich, which brings me to another diamond. A cow's diamond, my inheritance.

It was a joke, really, about the inheritance, at least it was a joke to my papa. A cow's diamond is the hard rounded lens inside a cow's eye that shines when you look through it at the light, almost like an opal. You could never make a ring of it or use it for any kind of jewelry, since it might shatter, and of course it had no worth. My father mainly carried it as a lucky piece. He'd flip it in the air between customers, and sometimes in a game of cribbage I'd see him rub it. I wanted it. One day I asked if he would give it to me.

"I can't," he said. "It's my butcher's luck. It can be your inheritance, how about that?"

I suppose my mouth dropped open in surprise because my father always gave me anything I asked for. For instance, we had a small glass candy case out front, over the sausages, and I could eat candy anytime I wanted. I used to bring root-beer barrels into class for the girls I liked. I never chewed gum balls though, because I heard Auntie Adelaide tell mother once, in anger, that only tramps chewed gum. This was when my mother was trying to quit smoking and she kept a sack of gum balls in the pocket of her apron. I was in the kitchen with them when they had this argument. "Tramps!" my mother said, "That's the pot calling the kettle black!" Then she took the gum from her mouth and rubbed it into Adelaide's long wavy hair. "I'll kill you!" my Auntie raged. It was something to see grown-ups behaving this way, but I don't blame Auntie Adelaide. I'd feel the same if I had to cut out a big knot of gum like she did and have a shorter patch of hair. I never chewed gum. But anything else in the store I wanted, I just took. Or I asked and it was handed right over. So you can see why my father's refusal was a surprise.

I had my pride even as a child, and I never mentioned it again. But here is what happened two days after Mary Adare came.

We were waiting to be tucked in that night. I was in my own bed, and she was in the trundle. She was short enough to fit there without hanging off the edge. The last thing she did before going to sleep was to put Adelaide's old keepsake box up on my bureau. I didn't say anything, but really it was sad. I guess my papa thought so, too. I guess he took pity on her. That night he came in the room, tucked the blankets around me, kissed me on the forehead, and said, "Sleep tight." Then he bent over Mary and kissed her too. But to Mary he said, "Here is a jewel."

It was the cow's diamond that I wanted, the butcher's luck. When I looked over the edge of my bed and saw the pale lens glowing in her hand, I could have spit. I pretended to be asleep when she asked me what it was. Find out for yourself, I thought, and said nothing. A few weeks later, when she knew her way around town, she got some jeweler to drill a hole through one end of the lucky piece. Then she hung the cow's diamond around her neck on a piece of string, as if it were something valuable. Later on she got a gold link chain.

First my room, then my clothing, then the cow's diamond. But the worst was yet to come when she stole Celestine.

My best friend, Celestine, lived three miles out of town with her half brother and much older half sister, who were Chippewas. There weren't all that many who came down from the reservation, but Celestine's mother had been one. Her name was Regina I-don't-know-what, and she worked for Dutch James, keeping his house when he was a bachelor and after, once they married. I overheard how Celestine came just a month past the wedding, and how Regina brought down the three other children Dutch James hadn't known about. Somehow it worked out. They all lived together up until the time of Dutch James's peculiar death. He froze solid in our very meat locker. But that is an event no one in this house will discuss.

Anyway, those others were never court adopted and went by the last name Kashpaw. Celestine was a James. Because her parents died when Celestine was young, it was the influence of her big sister that was more important to Celestine. She knew the French language, and sometimes Celestine spoke French to lord it over us in school, but more often she got teased for her size and the odd flimsy clothes that her sister Isabel picked out of the dime store in Argus.

Celestine was tall, but not clumsy. More what my mother called statuesque. No one told Celestine what to do. We came and went and played anywhere we felt like. My mother would never have let me play in a graveyard, for example, but when visiting Celestine, that's what we did. There was a cemetery right on the land of Dutch James's homestead, a place filled with the graves of children who died in some plague of cough or influenza. They'd been forgotten, except by us. Their little crosses of wood or bent iron were tilted. We straightened them, even recarved the names on the wooden ones with a kitchen knife. We dug up violets from the oxbow and planted them. The graveyard was our place, because of what we did. We liked to sit there on hot afternoons. It was so pleasant. Wind ruffled the long grass, worms sifted the earth below us, swallows from the mudbanks dove through the sky in pairs. It was a nice place, really, not even very sad. But of course Mary had to ruin it.

I underestimated Mary Adare. Or perhaps I was too trusting, since it was I who suggested we go visit Celestine one day in early summer. I started out by giving Mary a ride on the handlebars of my bicycle, but she was so heavy I could hardly steer.

"You pedal," I said, stopping in the road. She fell off, then jumped up and stood the bicycle upright. I suppose I was heavy, too. But her legs were tireless. Celestine's Indian half brother, Russell Kashpaw, approached us on the way to Celestine's. "Who's your slave today?" he said. "She's cuter than you'll ever be!" I knew he said things like that because he meant the opposite, but Mary didn't. I felt her swell proudly in my old sundress. She made it all the way to Celestine's, and when we got there I jumped off and ran straight in the door.

Celestine was baking, just like a grown-up. Her big sister let her make anything she wanted, no matter how sweet. Celestine and Mary mixed up a batch of cookie dough. Mary liked cooking too. I didn't. So they measured and stirred, timed the stove and put out the cooling racks while I sat at the table with a piece of waxed paper, rolled out the dough, and cut it into fancy shapes.

"Where did you come from?" Celestine asked Mary as we worked.

"She came from Hollywood," I said. Celestine laughed at that, but then she saw it wasn't funny to Mary, and she stopped.

"Truly," said Celestine.

"Minnesota," said Mary.

"Are your mother and father still there?" asked Celestine. "Are they still alive?"

"They're dead," said Mary promptly. My mouth fell open, but before I could get a word of the real truth in, Celestine said, "Mine are dead too."

And then I knew why Celestine had been asking these questions, when she already knew the whole story and its details from me. Mary and Celestine smiled into each other's eyes. I could see that it was like two people meeting in a crowd, who knew each other from a long time before. And what was also odd, they looked suddenly alike. It was only when they were together. You'd never notice it when they weren't. Celestine's hair was a tarnished red brown. Her skin was olive, her eyes burning black. Mary's eyes were light brown and her hair was dark and lank. Together, like I said, they looked similar. It wasn't even their build. Mary was short and stocky, while Celestine was tall. It was something else, either in the way they acted or the way they talked. Maybe it was a common sort of fierceness.

After they went back to their mixing and measuring, I could see that they were friendlier too. They stood close together, touched shoulders, laughed and admired everything the other one did until it made me sick.

"Mary's going to Saint Catherine's next fall," I interrupted. "She'll be downstairs with the little girls."

Celestine and I were in the seventh grade, which meant our room was on the top floor now, and also that we would wear special blue wool berets in choir. I was trying to remind Celestine that Mary was too young for our serious attention, but I made the mistake of not knowing what had happened last week, when Mary went into the school to take tests from Sister Leopolda.

"I'll be in your class," said Mary.

"What do you mean?" I said. "You're only eleven!"

"Sister put me ahead one grade," said Mary, "into yours."

The shock of it made me bend to my cookie cutting, speechless. She was smart. I already knew she was good at getting her way through pity. But smartness I did not expect, or going ahead a grade. I pressed the little tin cutters of hearts, stars, boys, and girls into the cookie dough. The girl shape reminded me of Mary, square and thick.

"Mary," I said, "aren't you going to tell Celestine what was in the little blue box you stole out of your mother's closet?"

Mary looked right at me. "Not a thing," she said.

Celestine stared at me like I was crazy.

"The jewels," I said to Mary, "the rubies and the diamonds."

We looked at each other in the eye, and then Mary seemed to decide something. She blinked at me and reached into the front of the dress. She pulled out the cow's diamond on a string.

"What's that?" Celestine showed her interest at once.

Mary displayed the wonder of how the light glanced through her treasure and fell, fractured and glowing, on the skin of her palm. The two of them stood by the window taking turns with the cow's lens, ignoring me. I sat at the table eating cookies. I ate the feet. I nibbled up the legs. I took the arms off in two snaps and then bit off the head. What was left was a shapeless body. I ate that up too. All the while I was watching Celestine. She wasn't pretty, but her hair was thick and full of red lights. Her dress hung too long behind her knees, but her legs were strong. I liked her tough hands. I liked the way she could stand up to boys. But more than anything else, I liked Celestine because she was mine. She belonged to me, not Mary, who had taken so much already.

"We're going out now," I told Celestine. She always did what I said. She came, although reluctantly, leaving Mary at the window.

"Let's go to our graveyard," I whispered, "I have to show you something."

I was afraid she wouldn't go with me, that she would choose right there to be with Mary. But the habit of following me was too strong to break. She came out the door, leaving Mary to take the last batch of cookies from the oven.

We left the back way and walked out to the graveyard.

"What do you want?" said Celestine when we stepped into the long secret grass. Wild plum shaded us from the house. We were alone.

We stood in the hot silence, breathing air thick with dust and the odor of white violets. She pulled a strand of grass and put the tender end between her lips, then stared at me from under her eyebrows.

Maybe if Celestine had quit staring, I wouldn't have done what I did. But she stood there in her too-long dress, chewing a stem of grass, and let the sun beat down on us until I thought of what to show her. My breasts were tender. They always hurt. But they were something that Mary didn't have.

One by one, I undid the buttons of my blouse. I took it off. My shoulders felt pale and fragile, stiff as wings. I took off my undervest and cupped my breasts in my hands.

My lips were dry. Everything went still.

Celestine broke the stillness by chewing grass, loud, like a rabbit. She hesitated just a moment and then turned on her heel. She left me there, breasts out, never even looking back. I watched her vanish through the bushes, and then a breeze flowed down on me, passing like a light hand. What the breeze made me do next was almost frightening. Something happened, I turned in a slow circle. I tossed my hands out and waved them. I swayed as if I heard music from below. Quicker, and then wilder, I lifted my feet. I began to tap them down, and then I was dancing on their graves.

Mary Adare

How long was Sita going to shimmy there, I wondered, with her shirt off and thunderclouds lowering? I heard Celestine walk into the kitchen below and bang the oven door open, so I came down. I stood in the kitchen door watching her lift each cookie off the sheet with a spatula. She never broke one. She never looked up. But she knew I was there, and she knew that I'd been up on the second floor, watching Sita. I know that she knew because she hardly glanced up when I spoke.

"It's dark all of a sudden," I said; "there's a storm."

"Sita's mother'll be mad," said Celestine, dusting flour off her hands.

We went out to get Sita, but before we were halfway across the yard Sita came, walked right past us, jumped on her bicycle, and rode away. That is how I got caught in the rain that afternoon. It swept down in sheets while I still had a mile left to walk. I slogged in the back door of the house and stood dripping on the hemp mat.

Fritzie rushed at me with a thick towel and practically took my head off rubbing it dry.

"Sita! Get out here and apologize to your cousin," she hollered. She had to call Sita twice before she came.

. . .

On the first day of school that next fall, we walked out of the door together, both carrying fat creamy tablets and new pencils in identical wooden pencil boxes, both wearing blue. Sita's dress was new with sizing, mine was soft from many washings. It didn't bother me to wear Sita's hand-me-downs because I knew it bothered her so much to see those outgrown dresses, faded and unevenly hemmed by Fritzie, diminished by me and worn to tatters, not enshrined as Sita probably wished.

We walked down the dirt road together and then, hidden from Fritzie's view by the short pines, we separated. Or rather, Sita ran long legged, brightly calling, toward a group of girls also dressed in stiff new material, white stockings, unscuffed shoes. Colored ribbons, plumped in bows, hung down their backs. I lagged far behind. It didn't bother me to walk alone.

And yet, once we stood in the gravel school yard, milling about in clumps, and once we were herded into rows, and once Celestine began to talk to me and once Sita meanly said I'd come in on the freight train, I suddenly became an object of fascination. Popular. I was new in Argus. Everybody wanted to be my friend. But I had eyes only for Celestine. I found her and took her hand. Her flat black eyes were shaded by thick lashes, soft as paint-brushes. Her hair had grown out into a tail. She was strong. Her arms were thick from wrestling with her brother Russell, and she seemed to have grown even taller than a month ago. She was bigger than the eighth-grade boys, almost as tall as Sister Leopolda, the tallest of all the nuns.

We walked up the pressed-rock stairs following our teacher, a round-faced young Dominican named Sister Hugo. And then, assigned our seats in alphabetical order, I was satisfied to find myself in the first desk, ahead of Sita.

Sita's position soon changed, of course. Sita always got moved up front because she volunteered to smack erasers together, wash blackboards, and copy out poems in colored chalk with her perfect handwriting. Much to her relief, I soon became old hat. The girls no longer clustered around me at recess but sat by her on the merry-go-round and listened while she gossiped, stroked her long braid and rolled her blue eyes to attract the attention of the boys in the upper grade.

Halfway through the school year, however, I recaptured my classmates' awe. I didn't plan it or even try to cause the miracle, it simply happened, on a cold frozen day late in winter.

Overnight that March, the rain had gone solid as it fell. Frozen runnels paved the ground and thick cakes of ice formed beneath the eaves where the dripping water solidified midair. We slid down the glossy streets on the way to school, but later that morning, before we got our boots and coats from the closet for the recess hour, Sister Hugo cautioned us that sliding was forbidden. It was dangerous. But once we stood beneath the tall steel slide outdoors, this seemed unfair, for the slide was more a slide than ever, frozen black in one clear sheet. The railings and steps were coated with invisible glare. At the bottom of the slide a pure glass fan opened, inviting the slider to hit it feet first and swoop down the center of the school yard, which was iced to the curbs.

I was the first and only slider.

I climbed the stairs with Celestine behind me, several boys behind her, and Sita hanging toward the rear with her girl friends, who all wore dainty black gum boots and gloves, which were supposed to be more adult, instead of mittens. The railings made a graceful loop on top, and the boys and bolder girls used it to gain extra momentum or even somersault before they slid down. But that day it was treacherous, so slick that I did not dare hoist myself up. Instead, I grabbed the edges of the slide. And then I realized that if I went down at all, it would have to be head first.

From where I crouched the ride looked steeper, slicker, more dangerous than I'd imagined. But I did have on the product of my mother's stolen spoons, the winter coat of such heavy material I imagined I would slide across the school yard on it as if it were a piece of cardboard.

I let go. I went down with terrifying speed. But instead of landing on my padded stomach I hit the ice full force, with my face.

I blacked out for a moment, then sat up, stunned. I saw forms run toward me through a haze of red and glittering spots. Sister Hugo got to me first, grabbed my shoulders, removed my wool scarf, probed the bones of my face with her strong, short fingers. She lifted my eyelids, wacked my knee to see if I was paralyzed, waggled my wrists.

"Can you hear me?" she cried, mopping at my face with her big manly handkerchief, which turned bright red. "If you hear me, blink your eyes!"

I only stared. My own blood was on the cloth. The whole playground was frighteningly silent. Then I understood my head was whole and that no one was even looking at me. They were all crowded at the end of the slide. Even Sister Hugo was standing there now, her back turned. When several of the more pious students sank to their knees, I could not contain myself. I lurched to my feet and tottered over. Somehow I managed to squeeze through their cluster, and then I saw.

The pure gray fan of ice below the slide had splintered, on impact with my face, into a shadowy white likeness of my brother Karl.

He stared straight at me. His cheeks were hollowed out, his eyes dark pits. His mouth was held in a firm line of pain and the hair on his forehead had formed wet spikes, the way it always did when he slept or had a fever.

Gradually, the bodies around me parted and then, very gently, Sister Hugo led me away. She took me up the stairs and helped me onto a cot in the school infirmary.

She looked down at me. Her cheeks were red from the cold, like polished apples, and her brown eyes were sharp with passion.

"Father is coming," she said, then popped quickly out.

As soon as she was gone, I jumped off the cot and went straight to the window. An even larger crowd had collected at the base of the slide, and now Sister Leopolda was setting up a tripod and other photographic equipment. It seemed incredible that Karl's picture should warrant such a stir. But he was always like that. People noticed him. Strangers gave him money while I was ignored, just like now, abandoned with my wounds. I heard the priest's measured creak on the stairs, then Sister Hugo's quick skip, and I jumped back.

Father opened the back door and allowed his magnificence to be framed in it for a moment while he fixed me with his most penetrating stare. Priests were only called in on special cases of discipline or death, and I didn't know which one this was.

He motioned to Sister Hugo, and she ducked from the room.

He drew a chair up beneath his bulk and sat down. I lay flat, as if for his inspection, and there was a long and uncomfortable silence.

"Do you pray to see God?" he asked finally.

"Yes!" I said.

"Your prayers were answered," Father stated. He folded his fingers into the shape of a church and bit harshly on the steeple, increasing the power of his stare.

"Christ's Dying Passion," he said. "Christ's face formed in the ice as surely as on Veronica's veil."

I knew what he meant at last, and so kept silent about Karl. The others at Saint Catherine's did not know about my brother, of course. To them the image on the ice was that of the Son of God.

As long as the ice on the playground lasted, I was special in the class again, sought out by Sita's friends, teachers, even boys who were drawn to the glory of my black eyes and bruises. But I stuck with Celestine. After the sliding, we were even better friends than before. One day the newspaper photographer came to school and I made a great commotion about not having my picture taken unless it was with her. We stood together in the cold wind, at the foot of the slide.

GIRL'S MISHAP SHAPES MIRACLE was the headline in the *Argus Sentinel.*

For two weeks the face was cordoned off and farmers drove for miles to kneel by the cyclone fence outside of Saint Catherine's school. Rosaries were draped on the red slats, paper flowers, little ribbons and even a dollar or two.

And then one day, the sun came out and suddenly warmed the earth. The face of Karl, or Christ, dispersed into little rivulets that ran all through the town. Echoing in gutters, disappearing, swelling through culverts and collecting in basements, he made himself impossibly everywhere and nowhere all at once so that all spring before the town baked hard, before the drought began, I felt his presence in the whispering and sighing of the streams.

Celestine James

I have a back view of Mary when she shoots down the slide to earth. Her heavy gray wool coat stands out like a bell around the white clapper of her drawers, but the wind never ruffles her blue scarf. She is motionless in her speed, until she hits. Then suddenly things move fast, everywhere, all at once.

Mary rolls over twice. Blood drenches her face. Sister Hugo runs toward her and then there are screams. Sita draws attention to herself by staggering to the merry-go-round, dizzy at the sight of her cousin's blood. A tortured saint, maybe even Catherine herself, she drapes her body among the iron spokes at the center of the wheel, and calls out, in a feeble but piercing tone, for help.

Sita is five times as strong as she looks, and can beat me in a fight, so I do not go to her. Sister Hugo is now leading Mary up the stairs with her handkerchief and the blue scarf pressed on Mary's forehead. I have backed down the iced-over slide steps like magic, and now I run after the two of them. But Sister Hugo bars me from the door once they reach the infirmary.

"Go back down," she says in a shaking voice. Her eyes blaze strangely underneath her starched linen brow. "It may not last," she says. "Run to the convent! Tell Leopolda to haul herself right over with the camera!"

I am confused.

"The ice, the face," said Sister Hugo frantically. "Now *get!*"

And so I run, so amazed and excited at how she has expressed herself, not like a teacher but just like a farmer, that I do not ring the convent bell but leap straight into the entryway and scream up the echoing stairs. By then I know, because it is in the air of the school yard, that some kind of miracle had resulted from Mary's fall.

So I shout, "A MIRACLE" at the top of my lungs. To do that in a convent is like shouting fire in a crowded movie. They all rush down suddenly, an avalanche of black wool. Leopolda springs down last of all, with a fearsome eagerness. A tripod is strapped on one shoulder. Drapes, lights, and a box camera are crammed in her arms. It is like she has been right behind her door, armed with equipment, praying year in and year out for this moment to arrive.

Back on the school ground, all is chaos. A crowd has formed around the end of the slide. Later on, the face they stare at is included in the catechism textbooks throughout the Midwest as The Manifestation At Argus, with one of Sister Leopolda's photographs to illustrate. In the article, Mary is described as "a local foundling," and the iced slide becomes "an innocent trajectory of divine glory." The one thing they never write about is how Sister Leopolda is found several nights after Mary's accident. She is kneeling at the foot of the slide with her arms bare, scourging herself past the elbows with dried thistles, drawing blood. After that she is sent somewhere to recuperate.

But that day, in all of the confusion, I sneak back into the school building. As I walk down the hall Father comes out of the infirmary door. He is lost in a serious thought and never lifts his head, so he does not see me. As soon as he is down the hall I slip straight in, alarmed because a priest near a sick person spells doom.

But Mary is recovered from the blow, I think at first, because she's sitting up.

"Did you see him!" she says immediately, clutching my arm. She looks deranged, either with her sudden importance or with the wound. Her head is taped in gauze now, which would give her a nun-like air except that the pits of her eyes are beginning to show disreputable black and purple bruises.

"They say it's a miracle," I tell her. I expect her to laugh but she grips my hand hard. Her eyes take on a glitter that I start to suspect.

"It was a sign," she says, "but not what they think."

"How do you mean?"

"It was Karl."

She has never mentioned Karl before, but from Sita I know he is her brother who has run off on a boxcar heading west.

"Lay back," I tell Mary. "Your head got knocked."

"He's got to bother me," she says loudly. "He can't leave me alone."

Her face screws up. She is thinking deeply like the priest and has lost all track of me or even of herself. Her eyes glare into the distance, light and still, and I see that she is very annoyed.

. . .

After Sister Hugo sends me out of the infirmary, I walk down the stairs, out into the cold overcast weather, and join the throng clustered around the miraculous face. Only to me, it is not so miraculous. I stare hard at the patterns of frozen mud, the cracked ice, the gravel that shows through the ice, the gray snow. Other people looking from the same angle see it. I do not, although I kneel until my knees grow numb.

That night the face is all that Russell and my big sister Isabel can talk about.

"Your girl friend's going to put us on the map," declares Isabel. She's all we have, and she takes care of us by holding down jobs with farmers, cooking, and sometimes even threshing right along with the men. "Girls have been canonized for less," she now says. Isabel carries the banner in Saint Catherine's Procession every year, looking huge and sorrowful, but pure. My mother was big too. It seems like I got all of my father's coloring, but am growing very quickly into my mother's size.

"I bet Sita's about ready to kill that little Mary," Russell says with a sharp laugh. Sita has made fun of him for being an Indian, and he is always glad to see her taken down a notch.

"They are taking a picture of Mary for the papers," I tell him. Isabel is impressed, but not Russell, because he plays football and has been in the papers many times for making touchdowns. People say he is one Indian who won't go downhill in life but have success, and he does, later, depending on how you look at it.

The next morning, before school starts, he comes with me to inspect the ice. During the night, someone has put up a low slat and wire fence around the sacred patch. Russell kneels by the fence and blesses himself. He says some sort of prayer, and then walks his bicycle down the icy road to the high school. He has seen it too. I am left at the bottom of the slide again, kneeling and squinting, even crossing my eyes to try and make the face appear. All the while the nuns are setting up the altar, right there in the school yard, for a special mass. I begin to wish that I had asked Russell to point out the features for me exactly, so that I can see Christ, too. Even now, I consider questioning the nuns, but in the end I don't have the courage, and all through the mass, standing with the seventh grade, watching Mary, Sita, Fritzie and Pete take communion first, I pretend that I am moved by the smashed spot, which is all I can see.

1986

HELENA MARÍA VIRAMONTES (1954–   )

Along with Gloria Anzaldúa, Denise Chavez, Sandra Cisneros, and Cherríe Moraga, Helena Viramontes is part of a young generation of talented Latina writers committed to fiction that accurately reflects their experiences between two languages and two cultures.

Viramontes was born and raised in East Los Angeles, in a Spanish-speaking family that included six sisters, three brothers, countless relatives and friends. Her father was a construction worker; her mother ran the household. Viramontes began writing fiction in 1975. Her early models included Jorge Luis Borges, Gabriel Garcia Marquez, and Juan Rulfo, from whom she learned to experiment with form and voice. Her discovery of Gwendolyn Brooks, Ntozake Shange, Alice Walker, and Toni Morrison helped her develop the confidence to make the lives of women her subject matter.

Her work consistently has been well received. Statement Magazine *awarded first prize in fiction to two of her short stories, "Requiem for the Poor" and "Broken Web." Her story "Birthday" received first prize in the Irvine Chicano Literary contest. She has been coordinator of the L.A. Latino Writers Association, Literary Editor of* Xhisme Arte Magazine, *and organizer of university and community poetry and fiction readings. She coedited* Chicana Creativity and Criticism: Charting New Frontiers in American Literature *and is the literary editor of* 201: Homenaje a la Ciudad de Los Angeles. The Moths and Other Stories *is her first collection.*

In her essay " 'Nopalitos': The Making of Fiction," Viramontes describes the power of writing to transform experience: "[I]t is a great consolation," she writes, "to know that whatever miserable things happen in my lifetime, goodness will inevitably result because I will write about it." Like Alice Walker, Paule Marshall, and Maxine Hong Kingston, she inherited her capacity for invention from her mother, declaring that from her childhood she held on to two things, "love of stories and love of my mother." The courage of women who live under oppressive conditions is the subject in much of her writing, "[b]ecause," as she puts it, "I want to do justice to their voices. To tell these women, in my own gentle way, that I will fight for them, that they provide me with my own source of humanity."

"Miss Clairol," the story that is included, first appeared in 1980. Viramontes uses crisp imagery and dialogue to convey the relationship between a mother and daughter caught in the snares of poverty and white middle-class dreams.

MISS CLAIROL

Arlene and Champ walk to K-Mart. The store is full of bins mounted with bargain buys from T-shirts to rubber sandals. They go to aisle 23, Cosmetics. Arlene, wearing bell bottom jeans two sizes too small, can't bend down to the Miss Clairol boxes, asks Champ.

–Which one mamá–asks Champ, chewing her thumb nail.

–Shit, mija, I dunno.–Arlene smacks her gum, contemplating the decision.–Maybe I need a change, tú sabes. What do you think?–She holds up a few blond strands with black roots. Arlene has burned the softness of her hair with peroxide; her hair is stiff, breaks at the ends and she needs plenty of Aqua Net hairspray to tease and tame her ratted hair, then folds it back into a high lump behind her head. For the last few months she has been a platinum "Light Ash" blond, before that a Miss Clairol "Flame" redhead, before that Champ couldn't even identify the color—somewhere between orange and brown, a "Sun Bronze." The only way Champ knows her mother's true hair color is by her roots which, like death, inevitably rise to the truth.

–I hate it, tú sabes, when I can't decide.–Arlene is wearing a pink, strapless tube top. Her stomach spills over the hip hugger jeans. Spits the gum onto the floor.–Fuck it.–And Champ follows her to the rows of nailpolish, next to the Maybelline rack of make-up, across the false eyelashes that look like insects on display in clear, plastic boxes. Arlene pulls out a particular color of nailpolish, looks at the bottom of the bottle for the price, puts it back, gets another. She has a tattoo of purple XXX's on her left finger like a ring. She finally settles for a purple-blackish color, Ripe Plum, that Champ thinks looks like the color of Frankenstein's nails. She looks at her own stubby nails, chewed and gnawed.

Walking over to the eyeshadows, Arlene slowly slinks out another stick of gum from her back pocket, unwraps and crumbles the wrapper into a little ball, lets it drop on the floor. Smacks the gum.

–Grandpa Ham used to make chains with these gum wrappers–she says, toeing the wrapper on the floor with her rubber sandals, her toes dotted with old nailpolish.–He started one, tú sabes, that went from room to room. That was before he went nuts–she says, looking at the price of magenta eyeshadow.–Sabes que? What do you think?–lifting the eye shadow to Champ.

–I dunno know–responds Champ, shrugging her shoulders the way she always does when she is listening to something else, her own heartbeat, what Gregorio said on the phone yesterday, shrugs her shoulders when Miss Smith says OFELIA, answer my question. She is too busy thinking of things people otherwise dismiss like parentheses, but sticks to her like gum, like a hole on a shirt, like a tattoo, and sometimes she wishes she weren't born with such adhesiveness. The chain went from room to room, round and round like a web, she remembers. That was before he went nuts.

–Champ. You listening? Or in lala land again?–Arlene has her arms akimbo on a fold of flesh, pissed.

–I said, I dunno know.–Champ whines back, still looking at the wrapper on the floor.

–Well you better learn, tú sabes, and fast too. Now think, will this color go good with Pancha's blue dress?–Pancha is Arlene's comadre. Since Arlene has a special date tonight, she lent Arlene her royal blue dress that she keeps in a plastic bag at the end of her closet. The dress is made of chiffon, with satin-like material underlining, so that when Arlene first tried it on and strutted about, it crinkled sounds of elegance. The dress fits too tight. Her plump arms squeeze through, her hips breathe in and hold their breath, the seams do all they can to keep the body contained. But Arlene doesn't care as long as it sounds right.

–I think it will–Champ says, and Arlene is very pleased.

–Think so? So do I mija.–

They walk out the double doors and Champ never remembers her mother paying.

. . .

It is four in the afternoon, but already Arlene is preparing for the date. She scrubs the tub, Art Labo on the radio, drops crystals of Jean Nate into the running water, lemon scent rises with the steam. The bathroom door ajar, she removes her top and her breasts flop and sag, pushes her jeans down with some difficulty, kicks them off, and steps in the tub.

–Mija. MIJA–she yells.–Mija, give me a few bobby pins.–She is worried about her hair frizzing and so wants to pin it up.

Her mother's voice is faint because Champ is in the closet. There are piles of clothes on the floor, hangers thrown askew and tangled, shoes all piled up or thrown on the top shelf. Champ is looking for her mother's special dress. Pancha says every girl has one at the end of her closet.

–Goddamn it Champ.–

Amidst the dirty laundry, the black hole of the closet, she finds nothing.

–NOW–

–Alright, ALRIGHT. Cheeze amá, stop yelling–says Champ, and goes in the steamy bathroom, checks the drawers, hairbrushes jump out, rollers, strands of hair, rummages through bars of soap, combs, eyeshadows, finds nothing; pulls open another drawer, powder, empty bottles of oil, manicure scissors, kotex, dye instructions crinkled and botched, finally, a few bobby pins.

After Arlene pins up her hair, she asks Champ,–Sabes que? Should I wear my hair up? Do I look good with it up?–Champ is sitting on the toilet.

–Yea, amá, you look real pretty.–

–Thanks mija–says Arlene, Sabes que? When you get older I'll show you how you can look just as pretty–and she puts her head back, relaxes, like the Calgon commercials.

. . .

Champ lays on her stomach, T.V. on to some variety show with pogo stick dancers dressed in outfits of stretchy material and glitter. She is wearing one of Gregorio's white T-shirts, the ones he washes and bleaches himself so that the whiteness is impeccable. It drapes over her deflated ten year old body like a dress. She is busy cutting out Miss Breck models from the stacks of old magazines Pancha found in the back of her mother's garage. Champ collects the array of honey colored haired women, puts them in a shoe box with all her other special things.

Arlene is in the bathroom, wrapped in a towel. She has painted her eyebrows so that the two are arched and even, penciled thin and high. The magenta shades her eyelids. The towel slips, reveals one nipple blind from a cigarette burn, a date to forget. She rewraps the towel, likes her reflection, turns to her profile for additional inspection. She feels good, turns up the radio to . . . your love. For your loveeeee, I will do anything, I will do anything, forrr your love. For your kiss . . .

Champ looks on. From the open bathroom door, she can see Arlene, anticipation burning like a cigarette from her lips, sliding her shoulders to the ahhhh ahhhhh, and pouting her lips until the song ends. And Champ likes her mother that way.

Arlene carefully stretches black eyeliner, like a fallen question mark, outlines each eye. The work is delicate, her hand trembles cautiously, stops the process to review the face with each line. Arlene the mirror is not Arlene the face who has worn too many relationships, gotten too little sleep. The last touch is the chalky, beige lipstick.

By the time she is finished, her ashtray is full of cigarette butts, Champ's variety show is over, and Jackie Gleason's dancing girls come on to make kaleidoscope patterns with their long legs and arms. Gregorio is still not home, and Champ goes over to the window, checks the houses, the streets, corners, roams the sky with her eyes.

Arlene sits on the toilet, stretches up her nylons, clips them to her girdle. She feels good thinking about the way he will unsnap her nylons, and she will unroll them slowly, point her toes when she does.

Champ opens a can of Campbell soup, finds a perfect pot in the middle of a stack of dishes, pulls it out to the threatening rumble of the tower. She washes it out, pours the contents of the red can, turns the knob. After it boils, she puts the pot on the sink for it to cool down. She searches for a spoon.

Arlene is romantic. When Champ begins her period, she will tell her things that only women can know. She will tell her about the first time she made love with a boy, her awkwardness and shyness forcing them to go under the house, where the cool, refined soil made a soft mattress. How she closed her eyes and wondered what to expect, or how the penis was the softest skin she had ever felt against her, how it tickled her, searched for a place to connect. She was eleven and his name was Harry.

She will not not tell Champ that her first fuck was a guy named Puppet who ejaculated prematurely, at the sight of her apricot vagina, so plump and fuzzy.–Pendejo–she said–you got it all over me.–She rubbed the gooey substance off her legs, her belly in disgust. Ran home to tell Rat and Pancha, her mouth open with laughter.

Arlene powder puffs under her arms, between her breasts, tilts a bottle of *Love Cries* perfume and dabs behind her ears, neck and breasts for those tight caressing songs which permit them to grind their bodies together until she can feel a bulge in his pants and she knows she's in for the night.

Jackie Gleason is a bartender in a saloon. He wears a black bow tie, a white apron, and is polishing a glass. Champ is watching him, sitting in the radius of the gray light, eating her soup from the pot.

Arlene is a romantic. She will dance until Pancha's dress turns a different color, dance until her hair becomes undone, her hips jiggering and quaking beneath a new pair of hosiery, her mascara shadowing under her eyes from the perspiration of the ritual, dance spinning herself into Miss Clairol, and stopping only when it is time to return to the sewing factory, time to wait out the next date, time to change hair color. Time to remember or to forget.

Champ sees Arlene from the window. She can almost hear Arlene's nylons rubbing against one another, hear the crinkling sound of satin when she gets in the blue and white shark-finned Dodge. Champ yells goodbye. It all sounds so right to Arlene who is too busy cranking up the window to hear her daughter.

1988

THEMATIC TABLE OF CONTENTS

This supplemental table of contents has been designed to aid instructors and students interested in examining similar themes and perspectives in the speeches, essays, and stories included in *American Women Writers.* These categories enhance our understanding of the parallels between selections by women of diverse backgrounds and historical periods.

In choosing the categories, we recognize the feminist premise that the personal is political: no personal choice is without political implication; no political choice is without personal ramification. Although we have included category titles such as "Making Personal Choices" and "Affirming Ethnicity and Culture," the works in these categories highlight concerns evident throughout the book. Similarly, we encourage readers to recognize that the essays, articles, and speeches in "Making Political Points" reinforce issues underlying many of the selections in other categories.

It is our hope that readers will use this thematic table of contents as a springboard for discussing issues and themes that have recurred in women's writing over the past two centuries.

The pieces arranged under the heading "Growing Up" show the world from a child's perspective. Here we encounter the young Louisa May Alcott learning the unpleasantness of working as a housemaid and watch Maya Angelou laugh at the antics of her fellow churchgoers. Tillie Olsen shows how ethnicity shapes identity, whereas Louise Erdrich examines the significance of friendship. Through the young girls created by Helena Maria Viramontes and Alice Cary, we learn of the pain of poverty and the mystery of the mundane.

"Affirming Ethnicity and Culture" includes selections that explore and celebrate the writers' ethnic and cultural backgrounds, as well as their struggle for political freedom. Excerpts from Harriet Jacobs's *Incidents in the Life of a Slave Girl* fall naturally into this section, as does Sui Sin Far's story revealing the contradictions and complexities of Chinese American culture. Similarly, the piece included by Sarah Winnemucca Hopkins immerses us in the traditions and society of Native Americans.

"Creating Rooms of One's Own" focuses on aspirations to creativity. In Constance Fenimore Woolson's "Miss Grief," for instance, we meet a talented but impoverished woman writer seen through the eyes of a well-to-do man of inferior talent. The selection from Harriet Jacobs's slave narrative, "The Loophole of Retreat," describes the creative impulse that enables this slave woman to turn her cramped hiding place into a room of her own. Anzia Yezierska depicts a writer's efforts to describe the anguish of impoverished immigrants in the 1920s. Jean Stafford captures a female student's feelings of alienation within a university in "The Philosophy Lesson." Paule Marshall, also using a university setting, shows how a professor's sexual harassment interferes with a young woman's ambitions in "Brooklyn."

Under "Making Personal Choices" we have grouped selections about marriage and celibacy and heterosexual and lesbian relationships. Kate Chopin's "The Falling in Love of Fedora" and Gertrude Stein's stories introduce lesbian possibilities; Cherríe Moraga describes the difficulties women have maintaining lesbian relationships in a predominantly heterosexual culture. Eudora Welty's "Livvie" and Alice Walker's "Roselily" depict the limitations for women in marriage. Mary Freeman's "The Revolt of 'Mother' " and Susan Glaspell's "A Jury of Her Peers" show women responding to those limitations. Shirley Jackson's "The Tooth" and Grace Paley's "The Long Distance Runner," on the other hand, develop the theme of flight from marriage.

The section "Making Political Points" brings together significant speeches and essays of nineteenth- and twentieth-century American women. Readers can compare the voices of Sojourner Truth and Elizabeth Cady Stanton; the educational concerns of Margaret Fuller, Charlotte Perkins Gilman, and Anna Cooper; the analyses of being Black and female by Marita Bonner, Zora Neale Hurston, and Audre Lorde. The inclusion of contemporary essayists helps answer questions about how social, political, and personal dilemmas change women's lives and shape the way writers tell their stories.

In "Growing Old," we encounter the power and the insights of old age. Alice Brown tells the story of a woman who flowers in her old age. Willa Cather's "Old Beauty" and Maxine Hong Kingston's "At the Western Palace" reflect cultural attitudes toward women and aging. Elizabeth Cady Stanton's personal essay conveys the dignity and integrity of a commanding woman in her eighties.

GROWING UP

AFFIRMING ETHNICITY AND CULTURE

CREATING ROOMS OF ONE'S OWN

MAKING PERSONAL CHOICES

MAKING POLITICAL POINTS

GROWING OLD

BIBLIOGRAPHY

GENERAL WORKS

Allen, Paula Gunn. *The Sacred Hoop: Recovering the Feminine in American Indian Tradition.* Boston: Beacon Press, 1986.

———. *Studies in American Indian Literature: Critical Essays and Course Designs.* New York: The Modern Language Association of America, 1983.

Anzaldúa, Gloria, ed. *Making Face, Making Soul/Haciendo Cara: Creative and Critical Perspectives by Feminists of Color.* San Francisco: An Aunt Lute Foundation Book, 1990.

Asian Women United of California, eds. *Making Waves: An Anthology of Writing by and about Asian American Women.* Boston: Beacon Press, 1989.

Auerbach, Nina. *Communities of Women: An Idea in Fiction.* Cambridge: Harvard University Press, 1978.

Bataille, Gretchen M., and Kathleen Mullen Sands. *American Indian Women, Telling Their Lives.* Lincoln and London: University of Nebraska Press, 1984.

Baym, Nina. *Woman's Fiction: A Guide to Novels by and about Women in America, 1820–1870.* Ithaca and London: Cornell University Press, 1978.

Benstock, Shari, ed. *Women of the Left Bank: Paris, 1900–1940.* Austin: University of Texas Press, 1986.

Benstock, Shari, ed. *Feminist Issues in Literary Scholarship.* Bloomington and Indianapolis: Indiana University Press, 1987.

Braxton, Joanne M., and Andree Nicola McLaughlin, eds. *Wild Women in the Whirlwind: Afra-American Culture and the Contemporary Literary Renaissance.* New Brunswick, N.J.: Rutgers University Press, 1990.

Brodzki, Bella, and Celeste Schenck, eds. *Life/Lines: Theorizing Women's Autobiography.* Ithaca and London: Cornell University Press, 1988.

Butler-Evans, Elliott. *Race, Gender, and Desire: Narrative Strategies in the Fiction of Toni Cade Bambara, Toni Morrison, and Alice Walker.* Philadelphia: Temple University Press, 1989.

Carby, Hazel. *Reconstructing Womanhood: The Emergence of the Afro-American Woman Novelist.* London: Oxford University Press, 1987.

Christian, Barbara. *Black Feminist Criticism: Perspectives on Black Women Writers.* New York: Pergamon Press, 1985.

———. *Black Women Novelists: The Development of a Tradition, 1892–1976.* Westport, Conn.: Greenwood Press, 1980.

De Lauretis, Teresa, ed. *Feminist Studies/Critical Studies.* Bloomington: Indiana University Press, 1986.

Douglas, Ann. *The Feminization of American Culture.* New York: Knopf, 1977.

DuBois, Ellen Carol, Gail Paradise Kelly, Elizabeth Lapovsky Kennedy, Carolyn W. Korsmeyer, and Lillian S. Robinson, eds. *Feminist Scholarship: Kindling in the Groves of Academe.* Urbana and Chicago: University of Illinois Press, 1987.

DuBois, Ellen Carol, and Vicki L. Ruiz. *Unequal Sister: A Multicultural Reader in U.S. Women's History.* New York and London: Routledge, 1990.

Ellmann, Mary. *Thinking about Women.* New York: Harcourt Brace Jovanovich, 1968.

Evans, Mari, ed. *Black Women Writers (1950–1980): A Critical Evaluation.* Garden City, N.Y.: Doubleday, 1984.

Fadermann, Lillian. *Surpassing the Love of Men: Romantic Friendship and Love between Women from the Renaissance to the Present.* New York: Morrow, 1981.

Fetterly, Judith. *The Resisting Reader: A Feminist Approach to American Fiction.* Bloomington: Indiana University Press, 1978.

Flynn, Elizabeth A., and Patrocinio P. Schweickart. *Gender and Reading: Essays on Readers, Texts, and Contexts.* Baltimore and London: The Johns Hopkins Press, 1986.

Gates, Henry Louis, Jr., ed. *Reading Black, Reading Feminist: A Critical Anthology.* New York: Meridian, 1990.

Gelfant, Blanche H. *Women Writing in America: Voices in Collage.* Hanover, N.H., and London: University Press of New England, 1984.

Gilbert, Sandra M., and Susan Gubar. *The Madwoman in the Attic: The Woman Writer and the Nineteenth-Century Literary Imagination.* New Haven and London: Yale University Press, 1979.

———. *No Man's Land: The Place of the Woman Writer in the Twentieth Century.* Vol. 1, *The War of the Words.* Vol. 2, *Sexchanges.* New Haven and London: Yale University Press, 1988 and 1989.

Greene, Gayle, and Coppelia Kahn. *Making a Difference: Feminist Literary Criticism.* London and New York: Routledge, 1988.

Herrera-Sobek, María. *Beyond Stereotypes: The Critical Analysis of Chicana Literature.* Binghamton, N.Y.: Bilingual Press/Editorial Bilingue, 1985.

Herrera-Sobek, María, and Helena María Viramontes, eds. *Chicana Creativity and Criticism: Charting New Frontiers in American Literature.* Houston: Arte Publico Press, 1988.

Horno-Delgado, Asunción, Eliana Ortega, Nancy M. Scott, and Nancy Saporta Sternbach, eds. *Breaking Boundaries: Latina Writing and Critical Readings.* Amherst: The University of Massachusetts Press, 1989.

Hsu, Kai-yu, and Helen Palubinskas, eds. *Asian-American Authors.* Boston: Houghton Mifflin, 1972.

Hull, Gloria T., Patricia Bell Scott, and Barbara Smith, eds. *All the Women Are White, All the Blacks Are Men, But Some of Us Are Brave: Black Women's Studies.* Old Westbury, N.Y.: The Feminist Press, 1981.

Jay, Karla, and Joanne Glasgow. *Lesbian Texts and Contexts: Radical Revisions.* New York and London: New York University Press, 1990.

Kaplan, Carey, and Ellen Cronan Rose. *The Canon and the Common Reader.* Knoxville: The University of Tennessee Press, 1990.

Kelley, Mary. *Private Woman, Public Stage: Literary Domesticity in Nineteenth-Century America.* New York: Oxford University Press, 1984.

Kim, Elaine H. *Asian-American Literature: An Introduction to the Writings and Their Social Context.* Philadelphia: Temple University Press, 1982.

Kolodny, Annette. *The Lay of the Land: Metaphor as Experience and History in American Life and Letters.* Chapel Hill: The University of North Carolina Press, 1975.

Lauter, Paul. "Race and Gender in the Shaping of the American Literary Canon: A Case from the Twenties." In *Feminist Criticism and Social Change: Sex, Class and Race in Literature and Culture.* Eds. Judith Newton and Deborah Rosenfelt. New York and London: Methuen, 1985.

Lerner, Gerda, ed. *Black Women in White America: A Documentary History.* New York: Vintage Books, 1973.
Millett, Kate. *Sexual Politics.* Garden City, N.Y.: Doubleday & Company, 1970.
Olsen, Tillie. *Silences.* New York: Delacorte Press/Seymour Lawrence, 1978.
Pryse, Marjorie, and Hortense J. Spillers, eds. *Conjuring: Black Women, Fiction, and Literary Tradition.* Bloomington: Indiana University Press, 1985.
Robinson, Lillian S. "Treason Our Text: Feminist Challenges to the Literary Canon." In *Tulsa Studies in Women's Literature.* Vol. 2 (1983): 83–98.
Showalter, Elaine. *The New Feminist Criticism.* New York: Pantheon, 1985.
Sterling, Dorothy, ed. *We Are Your Sisters: Black Women in the Nineteenth Century.* New York and London: W. W. Norton, 1984.
Tate, Claudia, ed. *Black Women Writers at Work.* New York: Continuum, 1983.
Toth, Emily, ed. *Regionalism and the Female Imagination.* New York: Human Sciences Press, 1985.
Willis, Susan. *Specifying: Black Women Writing the American Experience.* Madison: The University of Wisconsin Press, 1987.
Woolf, Virginia. *A Room of One's Own.* New York and London: Harcourt Brace, 1929.

WORKS ON INDIVIDUAL WRITERS INCLUDED IN THIS ANTHOLOGY

Louisa May Alcott

Langland, Elizabeth. "Female Stories of Experience: Alcott's *Little Women* in Light of *Work.* In *The Voyage In: Fictions of Female Development.* Eds. Elizabeth Abel, Marianne Hirsch, and Elizabeth Langland. Hanover, N.H.: University Press of New England, 1983.
Marsella, Joy. *The Promise of Joy: Children and Women in the Short Stories of Louisa May Alcott.* Westport, Conn.: Greenwood Press, 1983.
Saxton, Martha. *Louisa May Alcott: A Modern Biography.* New York: Avon, 1978.

Maya Angelou

Cudjoe, Selwyn. "Maya Angelou and the Autobiographical Statement." In *Black Women Writers (1950–1980): A Critical Evaluation.* Ed. Mari Evans. Garden City, N.Y.: Doubleday, 1984.
Elliot, Jeffrey M. *Conversations with Maya Angelou.* Jackson and London: University Press of Mississippi, 1989.
O'Neale, Sondra. "Reconstruction of the Composite Self: New Images of Black Women in Maya Angelou's Continuing Autobiography." *Black Women Writers (1950–1980): A Critical Evaluation.* Ed. Mari Evans. Garden City, N.Y.: Doubleday, 1984.

Mary Hunter Austin

Austin, Mary. *Earth Horizon: Autobiography.* Boston and New York: Houghton Mifflin, 1932.
Jaycox, Faith. "Regeneration through Liberation: Mary Austin's "The Walking Woman" and Western Narrative Formula." *Legacy* No. 1 (1989): 5–12.

Stineman, Esther Lanigan. *Mary Austin: Song of a Maverick.* New Haven and London: Yale University Press, 1989.

Toni Cade Bambara

Chandler, Zala. "Voices beyond the Veil: An Interview with Toni Cade Bambara and Sonia Sanchez." *Wild Women in the Whirlwind.* Eds. Joanne M. Braxton and Andree Nicola McLaughlin. New Brunswick, N.J.: Rutgers University Press, 1990.

Traylor, Eleanor W. "Music as Theme: The Jazz Mode in the Works of Toni Cade Bambara." *Black Women Writers (1950–1980): A Critical Evaluation.* Ed. Mari Evans. Garden City, N.Y.: Doubleday, 1984.

Vertreace, Martha M. "Toni Cade Bambara: The Dance of Character and Community." *American Women Writing Fiction: Memory, Identity, Family, Space.* Ed. Mickey Pearlman. Lexington: University Press of Kentucky, 1989.

Marita Bonner

Flynn, Joyce and Joyce Occomy Stricklin, eds. "Introduction." In *Frye Street and Environs: The Collected Works of Marita Bonner.* Boston: Beacon Press, 1987.

Flynn, Joyce. "Marita Bonner Occomy (1899–1971)." In *Afro-American Writers from the Harlem Renaissance to 1940. Dictionary of Literary Biography 51.* Detroit: Gale Research, 1987.

Roses, Lorraine, and Ruth Elizabeth Randolph. "Marita Bonner: In Search of Other Mothers' Gardens." *Black American Literature Forum* 21 (Spring–Summer 1987): 165–183.

Kay Boyle

Grumbach, Doris. "Kay Boyle: A Tribute." *Twentieth Century Literature* 34 (Fall 1988): 280–282.

Spanier, Sarah Whipple. *Kay Boyle.* Carbondale: Southern Illinois University Press, 1986.

———. "Kay Boyle: In a Woman's Voice." In *Faith of a (Woman) Writer.* Eds. Alice Kessler-Harris and William McBrien. Westport, Conn.: Greenwood Press, 1988.

Alice Brown

Fisken, Beth Wynne. "Profile: Alice Brown (1857–1948)." *Legacy* 6, No. 2 (1989): 51–57.

———. "Within the Limits of Alice Brown's 'Dooryards': Introspective Powers in *Tiverton Tales.*" *Legacy* 5, No. 1 (1988): 15–25.

Toth, Susan Allen. "A Forgotten View from Beacon Hill: Alice Brown's New England Short Stories." *Colby Library Quarterly* 10 (March 1973): 1–16.

Hortense Calisher

Calisher, Hortense. *Herself.* New York: Arbor House, 1972.

Hahn, Emily. "In Appreciation of Hortense Calisher." *Wisconsin Studies in Contemporary Literature* 6 (Summer 1965): 243–249.

Shinn, Thelma J. *Radiant Daughters: Fictional American Women.* Westport, Conn.: Greenwood Press, 1986.

Alice Cary

Fetterley, Judith. "Introduction." In *Clovernook Sketches and Other Stories.* Ed. Judith Fetterley. New Brunswick, N.J.: Rutgers University Press, 1987.

Pattee, Fred L. *The Feminine Fifties.* Port Washington: N.Y.: Kennikat Press, 1966.

Willa Cather

O'Brien, Sharon. *Willa Cather: The Emerging Voice.* New York: Oxford University Press, 1987.

Wagner-Martin, Linda. "Willa Cather: Reassessment and Discovery." *Contemporary Literature* 30 (Fall 1989): 444–447.

Wasserman, Loretta. "Willa Cather's 'The Old Beauty' Reconsidered." *Studies in American Fiction* 16, No. 2 (1988): 217–227.

Kate Chopin

Koloski, Bernard. *Approaches to Teaching Chopin's* The Awakening. New York: Modern Language Association of America, 1988.

Seyersted, Per. *Kate Chopin: A Critical Biography.* Baton Rouge: Louisiana State University Press, 1969.

Toth, Emily. *Kate Chopin: A Life of the Author of* The Awakening. New York: Morrow, 1990.

Anna Julia Cooper

Gabel, Leona C. *From Slavery to the Sorbonne and Beyond: The Life and Writings of Anna Julia Cooper.* Northampton, Mass.: Department of History of Smith College, 1982.

Shockley, Ann Allen. *Afro-American Women Writers: 1746–1933.* Boston: G. K. Hall, 1988.

Washington, Mary Helen. "Anna Julia Cooper: The Black Feminist Voice of the 1890's." *Legacy* 4, No. 2 (1987): 3–15.

Rebecca Harding Davis

Langford, Gerald. *The Richard Harding Davis Years: A Biography of a Mother and Son.* New York: Holt, Rinehart and Winston, 1961.

Olsen, Tillie. "Biographical Interpretation." In Rebecca Harding Davis, *Life in the Iron Mills.* New York: The Feminist Press at the City University of New York, 1985.

Yellin, Jean Fagan. "The Feminization of Rebecca Harding Davis." *American Literary History* 2 (1990): 203–219.

Louise Erdrich

Erdrich, Louise. Interview. "Whatever Is Really Yours." In Joseph Bruchac, *Survival This Way: Interviews with American Indian Poets.* Tucson: Sun Tracks and The University of Arizona Press, 1987.

———. Interview. "Louise Erdrich and Michael Dorris." In Laura Coltelli, *Winged Words: American Indian Writers Speak.* Lincoln and London: University of Nebraska Press, 1990.

Magalaner, Marvin. "Louise Erdrich: Of Cars, Time, and the River." *American Women*

Writing Fiction: Memory, Identity, Family, Space. Ed. Mickey Pearlman. Lexington: University Press of Kentucky, 1989.

Sui Sin Far

Ling, Amy. "Edith Eaton: Pioneer Chinamerican Writer and Feminist," *American Literary Realism* 16 (Autumn 1983): 287–298.

———. "Pioneers and Paradigms: The Eaton Sister." In *Between Worlds: Women Writers of Chinese Ancestry.* New York: Pergamon Press, 1990.

White-Parks, Annette. "Introduction to 'The Wisdom of the New.' " *Legacy* 6, No. 1 (1989): 34–37.

Mary Wilkins Freeman

DeEulis, Marilyn Davis. "Her Box of a House: Spatial Restriction as Psychic Signpost in Mary Wilkins Freeman's 'Revolt of Mother.' " *Markham Review* 8 (Spring 1979): 51–52.

Glasser, Leah Blatt. "*Legacy* Profile: Mary Wilkins Freeman (1852–1930). *Legacy* 4, No. 1 (1987): 37–45.

Reichardt, Mary R. "Mary Wilkins Freeman: One Hundred Years of Criticism." *Legacy* 4, No. 1 (1987): 31–44.

Margaret Fuller

Blanchard, Paula. *Margaret Fuller: From Transcendentalism to Revolution.* New York: Delacorte Press, 1978.

Chevigny, Bell Gale. *The Woman and the Myth: Margaret Fuller's Life and Writings.* Old Westbury, N.Y.: The Feminist Press, 1976.

Urbanski, Marie O. "Margaret Fuller's *Woman in the Nineteenth Century:* A Literary Study." In *Contributions in Women's Studies 13.* Westport, Conn.: Greenwood Press, 1980.

Charlotte Perkins Gilman

Gilman, Charlotte Perkins. *The Living of Charlotte Perkins Gilman.* New York: Harper & Row, 1975.

Meyerling, Sheryl L., ed. *Charlotte Perkins Gilman: The Woman and Her Work.* Ann Arbor, Mich.: UMI Research Press, 1989.

Treichler, Paula. "Escaping the Sentence: Diagnosis and Discourse in 'The Yellow Wallpaper.' " *Tulsa Studies in Women's Literature* 3 (1984): 61–77.

Ellen Glasgow

Donovan, Josephine. *After the Fall: The Demeter-Persephone Myth in Wharton, Cather, and Glasgow.* University Park: Pennsylvania State University Press, 1989.

Raper, Julius Rowan. *From the Sunken Garden: The Fiction of Ellen Glasgow, 1916–1945.* Baton Rouge: Louisiana State University Press, 1980.

Saunders, Catherine E. *Writing the Margins: Edith Wharton, Ellen Glasgow, and the Literary Tradition of the Ruined Women.* Cambridge: Department of English and American Literature and Language, Harvard University, 1987.

Susan Glaspell

Ben-Zvi, Linda. "Susan Glaspell's Contributions to Contemporary Women Playwrights." In *Feminine Focus: The New Women Playwrights.* Ed. Brater, Enoch. Oxford: Oxford University Press, 1989.

Fetterley, Judith. "Reading about Reading: 'A Jury of Her Peers,' 'The Murders in the Rue Morgue,' and 'The Yellow Wallpaper.' " In *Gender and Reading: Essays on Readers, Texts, and Contexts.* Eds. Elizabeth A. Flynn and Patrocinio P. Schweickart. Baltimore and London: The Johns Hopkins University Press, 1986.

Mael, Phyllis. "*Trifles*: The Path to Sisterhood." *Literature/Film Quarterly* 17 (1989): 281–284.

Frances Ellen Watkins Harper

Christian Barbara. "Shadows Uplifted." *Black Women Novelists: The Development of a Tradition, 1892–1976.* Westport, Conn.: Greenwood Press, 1980.

Foster, Frances Smith. "Introduction." In Frances E. W. Harper, *Iola Leroy, or Shadows Uplifted.* New York and Oxford: Oxford University Press, 1988.

Graham, Maryemma. "Introduction." In *The Complete Poems of Frances E. W. Harper,* ed. Maryemma Graham. New York and Oxford: Oxford University Press, 1988.

Sara Winnemucca Hopkins

Canfield, Gale Whitney. *Sara Winnemucca of the Northern Paiutes.* Norman and London: University of Oklahoma Press, 1983.

Carr, Helen. "In Other Words: Native American Women's Autobiography." In *Life/Lines: Theorizing Women's Autobiography.* Eds. Bella Brodzki and Celeste Schenck. Ithaca, N.Y.: Cornell University Press, 1988.

Hopkins, Sarah Winnemucca. *Life among the Piutes: Their Wrongs and Claims.* Ed. Mary Mann. Bishop, Cal.: Sierra Media, 1969.

Zora Neale Hurston

Hemenway, Robert E. *Zora Neale Hurston: A Literary Biography.* Urbana and Chicago: University of Illinois Press, 1977.

Holloway, Karla. *The Character of the Word: The Texts of Zora Neale Hurston.* Westport, Conn.: Greenwood Press, 1987.

Walker, Alice. *In Search of Our Mothers' Gardens.* New York: Harcourt Brace Jovanovich, 1983.

Shirley Jackson

Carpenter, Lynette. "Domestic Comedy, Black Comedy, and Real Life: Shirley Jackson, a Woman Writer." In *Faith of a (Woman) Writer.* Eds. Alice Kessler-Harris and William McBrien. Westport, Conn.: Greenwood Press, 1988.

———. "The Establishment and Preservation of Female Power in Shirley Jackson's *We Have Always Lived in the Castle.*" *Frontiers* 8, No. 1 (1984): 32–38.

Oppenheimer, Judy. *Private Demons: The Life of Shirley Jackson.* New York: G. P. Putnam, 1988.

Harriet Jacobs

Smith, Valerie. " 'Loopholes of Retreat': Architecture and Ideology in Harriet Jacobs's *Incidents in the Life of a Slave Girl.*" In *Reading Black, Reading Feminist: A Critical Anthology.* Ed. Henry Louis Gates, Jr. New York: Meridian, 1990.

Yellin, Jean Fagan. "Introduction." In Harriet Jacobs, *Incidents in the Life of a Slave Girl, Written by Herself.* Cambridge: Harvard University Press, 1987.

Washington, Mary Helen. "Meditations on History: The Slave Woman's Voice." *Invented Lives: Narratives of Black Women, 1860–1960.* Ed. Mary Helen Washington. Garden City, N.Y.: Doubleday Anchor, 1987.

Sara Orne Jewett

Fryer, Judith. "What Goes on in the Ladies Room? Sarah Orne Jewett, Annie Fields, and Their Community of Women." *Massachusetts Review* 30 (Winter 1989): 610–628.

Nagel, Gwen, ed. *Critical Essays on Sarah Orne Jewett.* Boston: G. K. Hall, 1984.

Sherman, Sarah Way. *Sarah Orne Jewett: An American Persephone.* Hanover, N.H.: University Press of New England, 1989.

Maxine Hong Kingston

Cheung, King-Kok. " 'Don't Tell': Imposed Silences in *The Color Purple* and *The Woman Warrior.*" *PMLA* 103 (March 1988): 162–174.

Sidonie Smith, "Maxine Hong Kingston's Woman Warrior." *A Poetics of Women's Autobiography: Marginality and the Fictions of Self-Representation.* Bloomington: Indiana University Press, 1987.

Talbot, Stephen. "Talking Story." *San Francisco Examiner Image,* June 24, 1990: 6–17.

Meridel LeSueur

Hedges, Elaine. "Introduction." In Meridel LeSueur, *Ripening.* Old Westbury, N.Y.: The Feminist Press, 1982.

Pratt, Linda Ray. "Woman Writer in the CP: The Case of Meridel LeSueur." *Women's Studies* 14 (1988): 247–264.

Yount, Neala Schleuning. " 'America: Song We Sang Without Knowing'—Meridel LeSueur's America." Ph.D. dissertation, University of Minnesota, 1978.

Audre Lorde

Lorde, Audre. "My Words Will Be There." *Black Women Writers (1950–1980): A Critical Evaluation.* Ed. Mari Evans. Garden City, N.Y.: Doubleday, 1984.

Martin, Joan. "The Unicorn Is Black: Audre Lorde in Retrospect." *Black Women Writers (1950–1980): A Critical Evaluation.* Ed. Mari Evans. Garden City, N.Y.: Doubleday, 1984.

Raynaud, Claudine. " 'A Nutmeg Nestled Inside Its Covering of Mace': Audre Lorde's *Zami.*" In *Life/Lines: Theorizing Women's Autobiography.* Eds. Bella Brodzki and Celeste Schenck. Ithaca, N.Y.: Cornell University Press, 1988.

Paule Marshall

Christian, Barbara. "Paule Marshall: A Literary Biography." *Black Feminist Criticism: Perspectives on Black Women Writers.* New York: Pergamon Press, 1985.
Collier, Eugenia. "The Closing of the Circle: Movement from Division to Wholeness in Paule Marshall's Fiction." In *Black Women Writers (1950–1980): A Critical Evaluation.* Ed. Mari Evans. Garden City, N.Y.: Doubleday, 1984.
Marshall, Paule. "The Making of a Writer: From the Poets in the Kitchen." *The New York Times Book Review,* January 9, 1983.

Carson McCullers

Boyle, Kay. " 'I Wish I Had Written *The Ballad of the Sad Cafe* by Carson McCullers.' " In *I Wish I'd Written That—Selections Chosen by Favorite American Authors.* Ed. Eugene J. Woods. New York: McGraw-Hill, 1946.
Carr, Virginia Spencer. *The Lonely Hunter: A Biography of Carson McCullers.* Garden City, N.Y.: Doubleday, 1975.
Gossett, Louise Y. "Dispossessed Love: Carson McCullers." *Violence in Recent Southern Fiction.* Durham, N.C.: Duke University Press, 1965.

Cherríe Moraga

Martin, Biddy. "Lesbian Identity and Autobiographical Difference[s]." In *Life/Lines: Theorizing Women's Autobiography.* Eds. Bella Brodzki and Celeste Schenck. Ithaca, N.Y.: Cornell University Press, 1988.
Moraga, Cherríe. "A Long Line of Vendidas." *Loving in the War Years.* Boston: South End Press, 1983.
Sternbach, Nancy Saporta. " 'A Deep Racial Memory of Love': the Chicana Feminism of Cherríe Moraga." In *Breaking Boundaries: Latina Writing and Critical Readings.* Eds. Asunción Horno-Delgado, et al. Amherst: The University of Massachusetts Press, 1989.

Toni Morrison

Bloom, Harold, ed. *Toni Morrison.* New York and Philadelphia: Chelsea House Publishers, 1990.
Darling, Marsha. "In the Realm of Responsibility: A Conversation with Toni Morrison." *Women's Review of Books* 5 (March 1988): 5–6.
Samuels, Wilfred D. and Clenora Hudson-Weems. *Toni Morrison.* Boston: Twayne Publishers, 1990.

Flannery O'Connor

Brinkmeyer, Robert H., Jr. *The Art and Vision of Flannery O'Connor.* Baton Rouge: Louisiana State University Press, 1987.
Friedman, Melvin J., and Beverly Lyon Clark, eds. *Critical Essays on Flannery O'Connor.* Boston: G. K. Hall, 1985.
Paulson, Suzanne Morrow. *Flannery O'Connor: A Study of the Short Fiction.* Boston: Twayne, 1988.

Tillie Olsen

Burkom, Selma and Margaret Williams. "De-riddling Tillie Olsen's Writings." *San Jose Studies* 2 (1976): 65–83.

Orr, Elaine Neil. *Tillie Olsen and a Feminist Spiritual Vision.* Jackson and London: University Press of Mississippi, 1987.

Rosenfelt, Deborah. "From the Thirties: Tillie Olsen and the Radical Tradition." In *Feminist Criticism and Social Change: Sex, Class and Race in Literature and Culture.* Eds. Judith Newton and Deborah Rosenfelt. New York and London: Methuen, 1985.

Cynthia Ozick

Bloom, Harold, ed. *Cynthia Ozick: Critical Views.* New York: Chelsea House, 1986.

Criswell, Jeanne Sallade. "Cynthia Ozick and Grace Paley: Diverse Vision in Jewish and Women's Literature." In *Since Flannery O'Connor: Essays on the Contemporary American Short Story.* Eds. Loren Logsdon and Charles W. Mayer. Macomb: Western Illinois University, 1987.

Scrafford, Barbara. "Nature's Silent Scream: A Commentary on Cynthia Ozick's 'The Shawl.' " *Critique* 31 (Fall 1989): 11–15.

Grace Paley

Baba, Minako. "Faith Darwin as Writer-Heroine: A Study of Grace Paley's Short Stories." *Studies in American Jewish Literature* 7 (Spring 1988): 40–54.

Isaacs, Neil D. *Grace Paley: A Study of the Short Fiction.* Boston: Twayne Publishers, 1990.

Taylor, Jacqueline. *Grace Paley: Illuminating the Dark Lives.* Austin: University of Texas Press, 1990.

Ann Lane Petry

Bell, Bernard W. "Ann Petry's Demythologizing of American Culture and Afro-American Character." In *Conjuring: Black Women, Fiction, and Literary Tradition.* Eds. Marjorie Pryse and Hortense J. Spillers. Bloomington: Indiana University Press, 1985.

McKay, Nellie Y. "Introduction." In Ann Petry, *The Narrows.* Boston: Beacon Press, 1988.

Washington, Gladys J. "A World Made Cunningly: A Closer Look at Ann Petry's Short Fiction." *College Language Association Journal* 30 (September 1986): 14–29.

Katherine Anne Porter

Bloom, Harold, ed. *Modern Critical Views: Katherine Anne Porter.* New York: Chelsea, 1986.

DeMouy, Jane Krause. *Katherine Porter's Women: The Eye of Her Fiction.* Austin: University of Texas Press, 1983.

Welty, Eudora. "The Eye of the Story." In *Katherine Anne Porter: A Collection of Critical Essays*. Ed. Robert Penn Warren. Englewood Cliffs, N.J.: Prentice-Hall, 1979.

Estela Portillo Trambley

Dewey, Janice. "Dona Josefa: Bloodpulse of Transition and Change." *Breaking Boundaries: Latina Writing and Critical Readings*. Eds. Asunción Horno-Delgado, et al. Amherst: The University of Massachusetts Press, 1989.

Martinez, Eliud. "Personal Vision in the Short Stories of Estela Portillo Trambley." In *Beyond Stereotypes: The Critical Analysis of Chicana Literature*. Ed. Maria Herrera-Sobek. Binghamton, N.Y.: Bilingual Press, 1985.

Vowell, Faye Nell. "A *Melus* Interview: Estela Portillo Trambley." *Melus* 9 (Winter 1982): 59–66.

Adrienne Rich

Farwell, Marilyn. "Toward a Definition of the Lesbian Literary Imagination." *Signs*, Vol. 14, No. 1 (Autumn 1988): 100–118.

Lorde, Audre. "An Interview: Audre Lorde and Adrienne Rich." In *Sister Outsider: Essays and Speeches by Audre Lorde*. Trumansburg, N.Y.: Crossing Press, 1984.

McDaniel, Judith. *Reconstituting the World: The Poetry and Vision of Adrienne Rich*. Argyle, N.Y.: Spinsters Ink, 1979.

Leslie Marmon Silko

Silko, Leslie Marmon. "Stories and Their Tellers—A Conversation with Leslie Marmon Silko." In *The Third Woman: Minority Women Writers of the United States*. Ed. Dexter Fisher. Boston: Houghton Mifflin, 1980.

———. "Leslie Marmon Silko." *Winged Words: American Indian Writers Speak*. Ed. Laura Coltelli. Lincoln and London: University of Nebraska Press, 1990.

Seyersted, Per. *Leslie Marmon Silko*. Meridian, Idaho: J & D Printing, 1980.

Agnes Smedley

Hoffman, Nancy. "Afterword." In Agnes Smedley, *Daughter of Earth*. New York: The Feminist Press at The City University of New York, 1987.

MacKinnon, Janice R., and Stephen R. MacKinnon. *Agnes Smedley: The Life and Times of an American Radical*. Berkeley: University of California Press, 1988.

Scheffler, Judith A. "Agnes Smedley's 'Cell Mates': A Writer's Discovery of Voice, Form, and Subject in Prison." *Faith of a (Woman) Writer*. Eds. Alice Kessler-Harris and William McBrien. Westport, Conn.: Greenwood Press, 1988.

Jean Stafford

Roberts, David. *Jean Stafford: A Biography*. Boston and Toronto: Little, Brown, 1988.

Goodman, Charlotte Margolis. *Jean Stafford: The Savage Heart*. Austin: University of Texas Press, 1990.

Ryan, Maureen. *Innocence and Estrangement in the Fiction of Jean Stafford*. Baton Rouge and London: Louisiana State University Press, 1987.

Elizabeth Cady Stanton

Banner, Lois W. *Elizabeth Cady Stanton: A Radical for Woman's Rights.* Boston and Toronto: Little, Brown, 1980.

Griffith, Elisabeth. *In Her Own Right: The Life of Elizabeth Cady Stanton.* New York and Oxford: Oxford University Press, 1984.

Stanton, Elizabeth Cady. *Eighty Years and More.* London: T. Fisher Unwin, 1898.

Gertrude Stein

Mellow, James R. *Charmed Circle: Gertrude Stein and Company.* New York and Washington: Praeger, 1974.

Neuman, Shirley, and Ira B. Nadel, eds. *Gertrude Stein and the Making of Literature.* Boston: Northeastern University Press, 1988.

Stein, Gertrude. *The Autobiography of Alice B. Toklas.* New York: Vintage, 1933.

Amy Tan

Feldman, Gayle. "The Joy Luck Club: Chinese Magic, American Blessings and a Publishing Fairy Tale." *Publishers Weekly,* July 7, 1989: 24.

Lipson, Eden Ross. "The Wicked English-Speaking Daughter." *The New York Times Book Review,* March 19, 1989: 3.

Rothstein, Mervyn. "Amy Tan: A Novelist Still Trying to Adapt to Success." *The New York Times,* June 11, 1991: C13.

Sojourner Truth

Bernard, Jacqueline. *Journey Toward Freedom: The Story of Sojourner Truth.* New York: The Feminist Press at the City University of New York, 1990.

Gilbert, Olive, compiler. *Narrative of Sojourner Truth, A Northern Slave.* New York: Arno, 1968.

Joseph, Gloria I. "Sojourner Truth: Archetypal Black Feminist." In *Wild Women in the Whirlwind: Afra-American Culture and the Contemporary Literary Renaissance.* Eds. Joanne M. Braxton and Andree Nicola McLaughlin. New Brunswick, N.J.: Rutgers University Press, 1990.

Helena María Viramontes

Alarcon, Norma. "Making 'Familia' From Scratch: Split Subjectivities in the Work of Helena María Viramontes and Cherríe Moraga." *Chicana Creativity and Criticism: Charting New Frontiers in American Literature.* Eds. Maria Herrera-Sobek and Helena María Viramontes. Houston: Arte Publico Press, 1988.

Viramontes, Helena María. " 'Nopalitos': The Making of Fiction (testimonio)." In *Breaking Boundaries: Latina Writing and Critical Readings.* Eds. Asunción Horno-Delgados, et al. Amherst: The University of Massachusetts Press, 1989.

Yarbo-Bejarana. "Introduction." In Helena María Viramontes, *The Moths and Other Stories.* Houston: Arte Publico Press, 1988.

Alice Walker

Bloom, Harold, ed. *Alice Walker.* New York: Chelsea, 1989.

Pryse, Marjorie. "Zora Neale Hurston, Alice Walker and the 'Ancient Power' of Black Women." Introduction to *Conjuring: Black Women, Fiction, and Literary Tradition.* Eds. Marjorie Pryse and Hortense J. Spillers. Bloomington: Indiana University Press, 1985.

Washington, Mary Helen. "I Sign My Mother's Name: Alice Walker, Dorothy West, Paule Marshall." In *Mothering the Mind: Twelve Studies of Writers and Their Silent Partners.* Eds. Ruth Perry and Martine Watson Brownley. New York: Holmes and Meier, 1984.

Eudora Welty

Devlin, Albert J., ed. *Welty: A Life in Literature.* Jackson: University Press of Mississippi, 1987.

Manning, Carol Sue. *Ears Opening Like Morning Glories: Eudora Welty and the Love of Story Telling.* Westport, Conn.: Greenwood Press, 1985.

Welty, Eudora. *One Writer's Beginnings.* New York: Warner Books, 1985.

Edith Wharton

Goodman, Susan. *Edith Wharton's Women: Friends and Rivals.* Hanover, N.H., and London: University of New England Press, 1990.

Olin-Ammentorp, Julie. "Edith Wharton's Challenge to Feminist Criticism." *Studies in American Fiction* 16, No. 2 (1988): 237–244.

Wolff, Cynthia Griffin. *A Feast of Words: The Triumph of Edith Wharton.* New York: Oxford University Press, 1977.

Harriet E. Wilson

Curtis, David Ames, and Henry Louis Gates, Jr. "Establishing the Identity of *Our Nig.*" In *Wild Women in the Whirlwind: Afra-American Culture and the Contemporary Literary Renaissance.* Eds. Joanne M. Braxton and Andree Nicola McLaughlin. New Brunswick, N.J.: Rutgers University Press, 1990.

Gates, Jr., Henry Louis. "Introduction." In Harriet E. Wilson, *Our Nig.* New York: Vintage Books, 1983.

Tate, Claudia. "Allegories of Female Desire: Or, Rereading Nineteenth-Century Sentimental Novels of Black Female Authority." In *Changing Our Own Words: Essays on Criticism, Theory, and Writing by Black Women.* Ed. Cheryl A. Wall. New Brunswick, N.J.: Rutgers University Press, 1989.

Constance Fenimore Woolson

Dean, Sharon. "Constance Fenimore Woolson and Henry James: The Literary Relationship." *Massachusetts Studies in English* 7 (1980): 1–9.

Torsney, Cheryl B. "Introduction to 'Miss Grief' by Constance Fenimore Woolson." *Legacy* 4, No. 1 (1987): 11–25.

Weimer, Joan Myers. "Women Artists as Exiles in the Fiction of Constance Fenimore Woolson." *Legacy* 3, No. 1 (1986): 3–15.

Hisaye Yamamoto

Cheung, King-Kok. "Introduction." In Hisaye Yamamoto, *Seventeen Syllables and Other Stories*. New York: Kitchen Table/Women of Color Press, 1988.

Crow, Charles L. "A *Melus* Interview: Hisaye Yamamoto." *Melus* 14 (Spring 1987): 73–84.

Yogi, Stan. "Legacies Revealed: Uncovering Buried Plots in the Stories of Hisaye Yamamoto." *Studies in American Fiction* 17 (Autumn 1989): 169–181.

Anzia Yezierska

Henriksen, Louise Levitas. *Anzia Yezierska: A Writer's Life*. New Brunswick, N.J.: Rutgers University Press, 1988.

Kamel, Rose. " 'Anzia Yezierska, Get Out of Your Own Way': Selfhood and Otherness in the Autobiographical Fiction of Anzia Yezierska." *Studies in American Jewish Literature* 3 (1983): 40–50.

Yezierska, Anzia. *Red Ribbon on a White Horse*. New York: Persea Books. 1979.

Zitkala-Să

Fisher, Dexter. "Foreword." In Zitkala-Să, *American Indian Stories*. Lincoln and London: University of Nebraska Press, 1985.

Picotte, Agnes M. "Foreword." In Zitkala-Să, *Old Indian Legends*. Lincoln and London: University of Nebraska Press, 1985.

Stout, Mary. "Zitkala-Să: The Literature of Politics." In *Coyote Was Here: Essays on Contemporary Native American Literary and Political Mobilization*. Ed. Bo Scholer. Aarhus, Denmark: Seklos, Department of English, University of Aarhus, 1984.

Acknowledgments (continued from copyright page)

Mary Hunter Austin, "Papago Wedding" from *One Smoke Stories.* Copyright © 1934 by Mary Austin. Copyright renewed 1961 by Kenneth M. Chapman and Mary C. Wheelwright. Reprinted by permission of Houghton Mifflin Company.

Toni Cade Bambara, "Witchbird" from *The Sea Birds are Still Alive.* Copyright © 1974, 1976, 1977 by Toni Cade Bambara. Reprinted by permission of Random House, Inc.

Marita Bonner, "On Being Young—a Woman—and Colored" and "Light in Dark Places" from *Frye Street and Environs.* Copyright © 1987 by Joyce Flynn and Joyce Occomy Stricklin. Reprinted by permission of Beacon Press.

Kay Boyle, "Winter Night" from *Fifty Stories.* Copyright © 1945, 1950, 1955, 1964, 1966, 1980 by Kay Boyle. Reprinted by permission of Watkins/Loomis Agency, Inc.

Hortense Calisher, "The Rabbi's Daughter" from *The Collected Stories of Hortense Calisher.* Copyright © 1975 by William Morrow & Company, Inc. Reprinted by permission of the publisher.

Willa Cather, "The Old Beauty" from *The Old Beauty and Others.* Copyright © 1948 by Alfred A. Knopf, Inc. Reprinted by permission of the publisher.

Louise Erdrich, Chapter II, from *The Beet Queen.* Copyright © 1986 by Louise Erdrich. Reprinted by permission of Henry Holt and Company, Inc.

Ellen Glasgow, "The Difference" from *The Shadowy Third and Other Stories.* Copyright © 1923 by Doubleday, Page and Co. Copyright © renewed 1951 by First and Merchants National Bank of Richmond, VA. Reprinted by permission of Harcourt Brace Jovanovich, Inc.

Susan Glaspell, "A Jury of Her Peers." Copyright © 1946 by Susan Glaspell. Reprinted by permission of Curtis Brown, Ltd.

Zora Neale Hurston, "Sweat" and "How it Feels to Be Colored Me." Reprinted by permission of Lucy Hurston.

Shirley Jackson, "The Tooth" from *The Lottery.* Copyright © 1948, by Shirley Jackson. Copyright © renewed 1976, 1977 by Laurence Hyman, Barry Hyman, Mrs. Sarah Webster, and Mrs. Joanne Schnurer. Reprinted by permission of Farrar, Straus, and Giroux, Inc.

Maxine Hong Kingston, "At the Western Palace" from *The Woman Warrior: Memories of a Childhood Among Ghosts.* Copyright © 1975, 1976 by Maxine Hong Kingston. Reprinted by permission of Alfred A. Knopf, Inc.

Meridel LeSueur, "Women Are Hungry" from *Ripening.* Published in 1982 by the Feminist Press.

Audre Lorde, "The Transformation of Silence into Language and Action" and "Uses of the Erotic: The Erotic as Power." Copyright © 1984 by Audre Lorde. Reprinted by permission of The Crossing Press.

Carson McCullers, "Madame Zilensky and the King of Finland" from *The Ballad of the Sad Cafe and Collected Short Stories.* Copyright © 1936, 1941, 1942, 1950. (c) 1955 by Carson McCullers. Copyright © renewed 1979 by Floria V. Lasky. Reprinted by permission of Houghton Mifflin Company.

Paule Marshall, "Brooklyn." Copyright © 1961 by Paule Marshall. From the book *Reena and Other Stories* by Paule Marshall. Published 1983 by the Feminist Press at the City University of New York. All rights reserved.

Cherríe Moraga, "Pesadilla" from *Loving in the War Years.* Reprinted by permission of the author and the publisher, South End Press, 116 Saint Botolph Street, Boston, MA 02115.

Toni Morrison, "A Slow Walk of Trees." Copyright © 1976 by The New York Times Company. Reprinted by permission.

Flannery O'Connor, "A View of the Woods" from *The Complete Stories.* Copyright © 1957, 1965, 1971 by the Estate of Mary Flannery O'Connor. Reprinted by permission of Farrar, Straus, and Giroux, Inc.

Tillie Olsen, "O Yes" from *Tell Me a Riddle.* Copyright © 1956, 1957, 1960, 1961 by Tillie Olsen. Reprinted by permission of Delacorte Press/Seymour Lawrence, a division of Bantam Doubleday Dell Publishing Group, Inc.

Cynthia Ozick, "The Shawl" from *The Shawl.* Copyright © 1980, 1983 by Cynthia Ozick. Originally appeared in *The New Yorker.* Reprinted by permission of Alfred A. Knopf, Inc.

Grace Paley, "The Long Distance Runner" from *Enormous Changes at the Last Minute.* Copyright © 1974 by Grace Paley. Reprinted by permission of Farrar, Straus, and Giroux, Inc.

Ann Lane Petry, "Has Anybody Seen Miss Dora Dean?" Copyright © 1947, 1975 by Ann Petry. Reprinted by permission of Russell and Volkening as agents for the author.

Katherine Anne Porter, "Holiday" from *The Leaning Tower and Other Stories.* Copyright © 1960 by Katherine Anne Porter, renewed 1988 by Isabel Bayley. Reprinted by permission of Harcourt Brace Jovanovich, Inc.

Adrienne Rich, "Compulsory Heterosexuality and Lesbian Existence." Copyright © 1986 by Adrienne Rich. Reprinted by permission of *Blood, Bread, and Poetry: Selected Prose 1979–1985* by Adrienne Rich, by permission of the author and W. W. Norton & Company, Inc.

Leslie Marmon Silko, "Storyteller" from *Storyteller.* Copyright © 1981 by Leslie Marmon Silko. Reprinted by permission of the publisher, Seaver Books, New York.

Jean Stafford, "The Philosophy Lesson" from *The Collected Stories.* Copyright © 1955, 1969 by Jean Stafford. Reprinted by permission of Farrar, Straus, and Giroux, Inc.

Gertrude Stein, "Ada" and "Miss Furr and Miss Skeene" from *Selected Writings of Gertrude Stein.* Copyright © 1946 by Random House, Inc. Reprinted by permission of the publisher.

Amy Tan, "Waverly Jong: Rules of the Game" from *The Joy Luck Club.* Copyright © 1989 by Amy Tan. Reprinted by permission of the Putnam Publishing Group.

Estela Portillo Trambley, "The Burning." Reprinted by permission of the author.

Helena Maria Viramontes, "Miss Clairol." First published in *Chicana Creativity and Criticism: Charting New Frontiers in American Literature,* eds. Maria Herrera Sobek and Helena Maria Viramontes (Houston: Arte Publico Press of the University of Houston, 1988). Reprinted by permission of the publisher.

Alice Walker, "Roselily" from *In Love & Trouble: Stories of Black Women.* Copyright © 1972 by Alice Walker. "In Search of Our Mothers' Gardens" from *In Search of Our Mothers' Gardens.* Copyright © 1974 by Alice Walker. Reprinted by permission of Harcourt Brace Jovanovich, Inc.

Eudora Welty, "Livvie" from *The Wide Net.* Copyright © 1942, renewed 1970 by Eudora Welty. Reprinted by permission of Harcourt Brace Jovanovich, Inc.

Edith Wharton, "Autres Temps . . ." from *The Collected Stories of Edith Wharton.* New York: Macmillan, 1968.

Hisaye Yamamoto, "The Legend of Miss Sasagawara." Copyright © 1950 by Kenyon Review, renewed 1977 by Hisaye Yamamoto DeSoto. Reprinted by permission of the author and Kitchen Table: Women of Color Press.

Anzia Yezierska, "My Own People" from *Hungry Hearts and Other Stories.* Copyright 1985 by Louise Levitas Henriksen. Reprinted by permission of Louise Levitas Henriksen.

Zitkala-Să, "A Dream of Her Grandfather" and "The Great Spirit." Reprinted from *American Indian Stories,* published by The University of Nebraska Press.